The Cambridge Handbook of Research Methods and Statistics for the Social and Behavioral Sciences

Volume 2

In a time where new research methods are constantly being developed and science is evolving, researchers must continually educate themselves on cutting-edge methods and best practices related to their field. The second of three volumes, this Handbook provides comprehensive and up-to-date coverage of a variety of issues important in developing, designing, and collecting data to produce high-quality research efforts. First, leading scholars from around the world provide an in-depth explanation of various advanced methodological techniques. In Part II, chapters cover general important methodological considerations across all types of data collection. In Part III, the chapters cover self-report measures. Part IV covers behavioral measures and their considerations for use. In Part V, various physiological measures are covered. The final part of the handbook covers issues that directly concern qualitative data collection approaches. Throughout the book, examples and real-world research efforts from dozens of different disciplines are discussed.

JOHN E. EDLUND is Professor of Psychology at the Rochester Institute of Technology, USA. He has won numerous teaching awards and is passionate about the improvement of research methods and the dissemination of psychological knowledge.

AUSTIN LEE NICHOLS is Associate Professor of Organizational Psychology at Central European University in Vienna, Austria. He has worked in various faculty and research positions around the world in both psychology and management, published in a variety of research disciplines, and won awards for his teaching, research, and service.

Cambridge Handbooks in Psychology

The Cambridge Handbook of Research Methods and Statistics for the Social and Behavioral Sciences

Volume 2: Performing Research

Edited by
John E. Edlund
Rochester Institute of Technology

Austin Lee Nichols
Central European University

Shaftesbury Road, Cambridge CB2 8EA, United Kingdom

One Liberty Plaza, 20th Floor, New York, NY 10006, USA

477 Williamstown Road, Port Melbourne, VIC 3207, Australia

314–321, 3rd Floor, Plot 3, Splendor Forum, Jasola District Centre, New Delhi – 110025, India

103 Penang Road, #05–06/07, Visioncrest Commercial, Singapore 238467

Cambridge University Press is part of Cambridge University Press & Assessment, a department of the University of Cambridge.

We share the University's mission to contribute to society through the pursuit of education, learning and research at the highest international levels of excellence.

www.cambridge.org
Information on this title: www.cambridge.org/9781316518557

DOI: 10.1017/9781009000796

© Cambridge University Press & Assessment 2024

This publication is in copyright. Subject to statutory exception and to the provisions of relevant collective licensing agreements, no reproduction of any part may take place without the written permission of Cambridge University Press & Assessment.

When citing this work, please include a reference to the DOI 10.1017/9781009000796

First published 2024

A catalogue record for this publication is available from the British Library.

A Cataloging-in-Publication data record for this book is available from the Library of Congress

ISBN 978-1-316-51855-7 Hardback
ISBN 978-1-009-00971-3 Paperback

Cambridge University Press & Assessment has no responsibility for the persistence or accuracy of URLs for external or third-party internet websites referred to in this publication and does not guarantee that any content on such websites is, or will remain, accurate or appropriate.

I dedicate this volume of the handbook to my family. Clark and Addison – you are both so amazing at everything you do and bring such joy into this world. I am glad to be raising such great humans. Adrianne – you are my everything. It is just that simple. You are AWESOME. I love the three of you with all of my heart!

John E. Edlund

I dedicate this book to all of our amazing authors without whom this would not have been possible. I also want to deeply thank my wife for continuing to support our efforts to better equip scientists to contribute to society through their research. Finally, I thank the earth for only rotating approximately every 24 hours because anything less just wouldn't provide enough time in the day.

Austin Lee Nichols

Contents

List of Figures	*page* x
List of Tables	xiv
List of Contributors	xvi
Preface	xix

Part I. Quantitative Data Collection Sources   1

1 Student Samples in Research   3
   MICHAEL BASIL

2 Mechanical Turk: A Versatile Tool in the Behavioral Scientist's Toolkit   24
   AARON J. MOSS, DAVID HAUSER, CHESKIE ROSENZWEIG, JONATHAN ROBINSON, AND LEIB LITMAN

3 Social Media Research   48
   ROSANNA E. GUADAGNO AND ALBERTO F. OLIVIERI

4 Prolific: Crowdsourcing Academic Online Research   72
   EYAL PEER

5 Field Research   93
   SHERRY JUEYU WU

6 Organizational Research   116
   VICTOR E. SOJO AND MELISSA A. WHEELER

7 Integrating Culture in Research   140
   BRIEN K. ASHDOWN AND ANGELA T. MAITNER

8 Mixed Methods and Multimethod Research   163
   JUDITH SCHOONENBOOM

Part II. Important Methodological Considerations   187

9 Reliability   189
   TENKO RAYKOV

10	Measurement Validity in the Social and Behavioral Sciences: Some "Whys" and "Hows" JOHN J. SKOWRONSKI	211
11	Statistical Power: How Not to Miss What's Right in Front of You ERIN M. BUCHANAN	232
12	Interdisciplinary and Integrative Research RICK SZOSTAK	261
13	The Importance of Replication JON E. GRAHE AND KELLY M. CUCCOLO	283
14	The Inner Workings of Registered Reports ZOLTAN DIENES	305

Part III. Self-Report Measures — 327

15	Self-Report Measures TING YAN	329
16	Question and Questionnaire Design SIERRA DAVIS THOMANDER AND JON A. KROSNICK	352

Part IV. Behavioral Measures — 371

17	Reaction Time Measures JEREMY D. HEIDER	373
18	Eyetracking Research ANJALI K. JOGESHWAR AND JEFF B. PELZ	398

Part V. Physiological Measures — 425

19	Measuring Hormones: Considerations for Biospecimen Collection, Assay, and Analysis SHANNIN N. MOODY, AMALI I. STEPHENS, JENNY MAI PHAN, OLGA MIOCEVIC, AMITA KAPOOR, WEN WANG, ALLISSA L. VAN STEENIS, SCOTT LE, LOTTE VAN DAMMEN, AND ELIZABETH A. SHIRTCLIFF	427
20	Cardiovascular Measures for Social and Behavioral Research MARY G. CAREY	455
21	Electrodermal Activity: Applications and Challenges MD-BILLAL HOSSAIN, YOUNGSUN KONG, HUGO F. POSADA-QUINTERO, AND KI H. CHON	475
22	Surface Electromyography JOSEPH S. BASCHNAGEL, MOET AITA, AND MICHAEL MCTIGHE	497

| 23 | EEG and ERP | 519 |

CHRISTIAN PANITZ, RICHARD T. WARD, JOURDAN POULIOT, AND ANDREAS KEIL

Part VI: Qualitative Data Collection Sources — 545

| 24 | Open-Ended Survey Questions | 547 |

GLORIA FRASER

| 25 | Qualitative Archival Data: A Call to Creativity | 571 |

CONSTANCE JONES AND ANDREA WIEMANN

| 26 | Interviews: Processes, Strategies, and Reflections | 591 |

ZOË B. CORWIN AND JORDAN HARPER

| 27 | Case Studies: A Personal Account of Choices and Dilemmas | 616 |

CHRISTINE MEYER

| 28 | Focus Groups | 640 |

NOA AMIR, CHANDANA GUHA, SIMON CARTER, AND ALLISON JAURÉ

| 29 | Observational Data | 665 |

LESLEY BAILLIE AND SHANLEE HIGGINS

Index — 686

Figures

2.1	The worker dashboard on MTurk. Each row represents a HIT that can be completed for pay.	page 26
2.2	The MTurk graphical user interface. This point-and-click system can be used to create several basic HITs.	27
2.3	Example code that can be sent to MTurk via API to execute actions like launching a HIT.	27
2.4	MTurk participant activity as a share of worker experience.	34
3.1	Retweets of messages related to the Black Lives Matter social movement. Light gray indicates IRA bots and trolls, dark gray the other retweets.	58
4.1	Number of participants and researchers on Prolific according to the year they joined.	74
4.2	Number of participants on Prolific by territory and year.	74
4.3a	Number of participants on Prolific by year and ethnicity.	75
4.3b	Number of participants on Prolific by year and gender.	75
4.3c	Percent of participants on Prolific by personal income level and year.	76
4.3d	Percent of participants on Prolific by age group and year.	76
4.4	Screenshots of the filtering dialog on Prolific before (left) and after (right) restricting to participants with approval rate of 98% or above.	78
4.5	Mean overall data quality score between sites and type of device used.	87
4.6	Replication (Cohen's d) of three effects among the different samples and conditions.	88
8.1	Visualizing an emergent design: the sexual health education example.	173
11.1	Decision errors, power, and correct rejections for null hypothesis testing.	233
11.2	Study 1 illustrates two separate statistics classrooms each learning a different software to determine the influence of computer programs on final grades.	235
11.3	Study 2 illustrates a survey design where students' data literacy is assessed to understand its relationship with future employment in data analytics.	235

11.4	A depiction of Study 3 that examines the implementation of gamification in a statistics classroom to improve data literacy.	236
11.5	The relationship between planned sample size and power in the correlation study measuring data literacy skills and future income.	238
11.6	The relationship between sample size planned, power, and effect size (the lines) for our correlation study measuring data literacy and income using $\alpha = .05$.	239
11.7	The relationship between sample size planned, power, and the α criterion for our data literacy correlation study where $r \sim .25$.	240
11.8	The relationship between sample size planned, power, and the type of research design if we could measure our study on statistics classrooms in both a between and repeated measures design.	241
11.9	A screen capture of G*Power for estimating the required sample size for the first study on statistics classrooms.	244
11.10	An estimation of prospective power (i.e., calculated before the study is conducted) for our first study on statistics classrooms using the same criterion as the previous power estimation but a specific sample size we know we can collect in the left-hand panel.	245
11.11	An estimation of sensitivity for our first study on statistics classrooms using the same criterion as the previous power estimation but a specific sample size we know we can collect in the left-hand panel.	246
11.12	Sample size estimation for Study 2 examining the correlation between data literacy and income.	247
11.13	The code used from the *pwr* library in *R* to estimate the sample size for the classroom comparison study.	248
11.14	The code used from the *pwr* library to estimate the sample size needed for the correlation study on data literacy and job income.	249
11.15	The code for simulating the data and estimating power for our repeated measures study on data literacy and gamification.	250
11.16	AIPE estimation code and sample size output from MBESS used to estimate the number of participants needed to find a *d* value between 0.10 and 0.50 (0.30 ± 0.20 width).	252
11.17	AIPE estimation code and sample size output for the correlation study.	253
11.18	The code for 95% power using the *pwr* package in *R* for our statistics classroom example.	253
11.19	The code for 95% power for the data literacy and job income correlation example.	254
11.20	The relationship between post hoc power and *p*-values for $r = .30$.	256
12.1	Influences on economic growth.	267
13.1	Replications of "Willow Sitting in Front of Piano."	288
14.1	Biases that may arise from seeing data first.	307
14.2	How evidence counts against a theory	308

14.3	Picking a point in the multiverse.	313
17.1	Sample stimuli for the Stroop Color and Word Test (SCWT).	380
17.2	Sample stimuli for the Eriksen flanker task.	382
17.3	Sample procedure for the race-based evaluative priming task.	383
17.4	Visual example of the race-based Implicit Association Test.	384
18.1	Extraocular muscles.	400
18.2	Directions of eye movements.	401
18.3	Horizontal and vertical eye position as a function of time.	402
18.4	Smooth pursuit eye movement with "catch-up" saccades.	403
18.5	Vestibular-ocular response (VOR) eye movements.	403
18.6	Gaze orientation record for over one minute.	404
18.7	Tobii Pro Spectrum – Remote eyetracker mounted below computer monitor.	405
18.8	EyeGaze Edge – Remote eyetracker mounted below computer display.	406
18.9	Tower eyetracker (EyeLink 1000 Tower).	407
18.10	Positive Science – wearable eyetracker.	408
18.11	Tobii Pro Glasses 3 – wearable eyetracker.	408
18.12	Pupil Labs Invisible – wearable eyetracker.	409
18.13	Frame of output video from wearable eyetracker (Positive Science).	409
18.14	HTC Vive with integrated eyetracker (Pupil Labs).	410
18.15	Virtual environment.	410
18.16	Gaze on calibration board.	411
18.17	Average gaze location with 0.05° average precision and 0° (top) and 1° (bottom) inaccuracy.	412
18.18	Gaze locations with 0° average inaccuracy and high (top) and low (bottom) precision.	413
18.19	Accuracy and precision in eyetracker data.	413
18.20	Raw plots for drift and noise in gaze.	414
18.21	Plots showing fixations throughout a reading task.	416
19.1	Tasso device on upper arm.	430
19.2	Tasso collection and processing kit.	431
19.3	Hair sample processing.	432
19.4	Hair types.	433
19.5	Feces collection and processing.	435
19.6	ELISA assay process.	439
19.7	Liquid-chromatography mass spectrometry.	441
20.1	Heart rate variability.	459
20.2	An electrocardiogram.	460
20.3	ECG lead Mason-Likert configuration.	461
20.4	A novel 12-lead ECG patch with recorder, "QT ECG."	468
21.1a	EDA data collection setup for laboratory environment.	477
21.1b	Examples of wearable EDA devices.	477
21.2	Morphology of typical skin conductance response (SCR).	478

21.3	Decomposition of EDA into tonic and phasic components.	480
21.4	Motion artifact detection in EDA using machine learning method.	482
21.5	DCAE reconstruction of EDA signal B&W from MA-corrupted data (black).	483
22.1	Skeletal muscle anatomy.	499
22.2	Facial EMG electrode placement.	502
22.3	EMG signal measured from the orbicularis oculi muscle: (a) Raw EMG signal and (b) EMG signal after band pass filtering (28–500 Hz), rectification, and RMS integration.	505
23.1	Generation of the EEG signal.	520
23.2	EEG electrodes.	525
23.3	Examples of common artifacts in EEG data.	528
23.4	Event-related potential (ERP).	531
23.5	Spectrum and spectrogram.	535
24.1	Examples of the three most common types of OESQs.	548
24.2	Defining key survey terms.	558
24.3	Example debriefing sheet.	559
24.4	Example research recruitment posts.	561
24.5	Recruitment materials for the Rainbow Mental Health Support Experiences study.	561
24.6	Addition of an open-ended response to list of researcher-derived responses.	565
24.7	Example of an "any others comments" question.	566
26.1	Key steps in preparing for the interview.	594
27.1	Media articles covering the change processes in Statistics Norway in 2017.	631
27.2	Illustration of the Gioia data structure template.	633
27.3	Temporal bracketing in reform case.	636
28.1	Eight different research questions which can be addressed by focus group studies.	643
28.2	The four constructs: strategies to ensure trustworthiness in focus group research.	659

Tables

2.1	Basic demographics	page 32
2.2	Annual household income for Mechanical Turk and the US population	33
3.1	A non-exhaustive list of social media companies offering academic APIs	56
3.2	A non-exhaustive list of pre-existing social media data sets	57
5.1	Example research designs with low vs. high degrees of naturalism	94
5.2	Random assignment in within-subjects, between-subjects, and waitlist design	102
11.1	A traditional power table outlining effect size, power, and planned sample size for independent t-tests	242
11.2	Where to find common statistical tests in G*Power menus	243
11.3	Simulation estimation of power for several potential sample sizes and number of measurement days for the gamification of data literacy study	251
13.1	Possible planning and tracking project completion	296
17.1	Comparison of product features across DirectRT, E-Prime, and SuperLab	387
19.1	Sample specimen pros and cons	436
19.2	Cost and ease of collection, transport, and storage	437
19.3	General pros and cons to each approach	442
19.4	Comparisons of pros and cons	445
20.1	12-lead ECG measures for research: both resting and 24-hour Holter	458
22.1	A summary of steps for implementing EMG measurement	500
22.2	Manufacturers of commonly used bioamplifiers used in research settings	503
23.1	Properties of different brain imaging methods relative to EEG	522
23.2	List of common EEG artifacts and strategies to avoid them	527
23.3	Common ERP components	532
24.1	Advantages and disadvantages of using OESQs	551
24.2	Survey design decisions when using open-ended questions	555
24.3	Dummy and nominal codes for gender and sexual orientation	564
25.1	Major texts demonstrating secondary data analysis of Intergenerational Studies data	577

26.1	Examples of interview questions highlighting varying structures and types	598
27.1	Two templates for qualitative case studies	619
27.2	Five interview genres: purposes and practices	629
27.3	Steps of an analysis	632
27.4	Analyzing data for excessive change	634
28.1	The five different questions that guide focus group discussion	648
28.2	Analyzing group interaction	655

Contributors

MOET AITA, Rochester Institute of Technology

NOA AMIR, University of Sydney

BRIEN K. ASHDOWN, American University of Sharjah

LESLEY BAILLIE, London South Bank University

JOSEPH S. BASCHNAGEL, Rochester Institute of Technology

MICHAEL BASIL, University of Lethbridge

ERIN M. BUCHANAN, Harrisburg University of Science and Technology

MARY G. CAREY, University of Rochester

SIMON CARTER, University of Sydney

KI H. CHON, University of Connecticut

ZOË B. CORWIN, University of Southern California

KELLY M. CUCCOLO, Michigan Virtual

ZOLTAN DIENES, University of Sussex

GLORIA FRASER, Victoria University of Wellington

JON E. GRAHE, Pacific Lutheran University

ROSANNA E. GUADAGNO, University of Oulu

CHANDANA GUHA, University of Sydney

JORDAN HARPER, Morgan State University

DAVID HAUSER, Queen's University

JEREMY D. HEIDER, Southeastern Missouri State University

SHANLEE HIGGINS, Anglia Ruskin University

MD-BILLAL HOSSAIN, University of Connecticut

ALLISON JAURÉ, University of Sydney

ANJALI K. JOGESHWAR, Rochester Institute of Technology

CONSTANCE JONES, California State University, Fresno

AMITA KAPOOR, University of Wisconsin–Madison

ANDREAS KEIL, University of Florida

YOUNGSUN KONG, University of Connecticut

JON A. KROSNICK, Stanford University

SCOTT LE, Iowa State University

LEIB LITMAN, CloudResearch and Lander College

ANGELA T. MAITNER, American University of Sharjah

MICHAEL MCTIGHE, Rochester Institute of Technology

CHRISTINE MEYER, Norwegian School of Economics

OLGA MIOCEVIC, Northland College

SHANNIN N. MOODY, Louisiana State University

AARON J. MOSS, CloudResearch and Siena College

ALBERTO F. OLIVIERI, University of Oulu

CHRISTIAN PANITZ, University of Florida and University of Bremen

EYAL PEER, Hebrew University of Jerusalem

JEFF B. PELZ, Rochester Institute of Technology

JENNY MAI PHAN, Children's National Hospital

HUGO F. POSADA-QUINTERO, University of Connecticut

JOURDAN POULIOT, University of Florida

TENKO RAYKOV, Michigan State University

JONATHAN ROBINSON, CloudResearch and Lander College

CHESKIE ROSENZWEIG, CloudResearch and Columbia University

JUDITH SCHOONENBOOM, University of Vienna

ELIZABETH A. SHIRTCLIFF, University of Oregon

JOHN J. SKOWRONSKI, Northern Illinois University

VICTOR E. SOJO, University of Melbourne

AMALI I. STEPHENS, Iowa State University

RICK SZOSTAK, University of Alberta

SIERRA DAVIS THOMANDER, Stanford University

LOTTE VAN DAMMEN, Association of Dutch Burn Centres

ALLISSA L. VAN STEENIS, University of Oregon

WEN WANG, University of Oregon

RICHARD T. WARD, University of Florida

MELISSA A. WHEELER, RMIT University

ANDREA WIEMANN, California State University, Fresno

SHERRY JUEYU WU, University of California, Los Angeles

TING YAN, Westat

Preface

The Cambridge Handbook of Research Methods and Statistics for the Social and Behavioral Sciences is meant to be the most comprehensive and contemporary collection of topics related to research methods and statistics spanning these related yet extremely diverse fields of research. This second volume, *Performing Research*, provides researchers a vast array of tools to consider using in their research paradigms. Although each chapter has a separate focus, the chapters build upon one another to provide experienced and novice researchers alike the tools to engage in the highest-quality research possible.

Throughout these chapters, the leading researchers in a variety of disciplines seek to share their knowledge and experience in a way that is both accessible and useful. They do so by writing in a way that is both understandable to novice researchers but also deeply discusses the challenges related to each topic and provides new information to even the most highly experienced scientists. This volume begins with a discussion of the various ways researchers can access participants for quantitative research and the various strengths and weaknesses to each approach. This first part includes a modern discussion of participant pools, organizational-based research, and international research (and everything in-between).

The second part of this volume considers important methodological considerations in the design of the research. This section features in-depth discussions of reliability, validity, power, replication, and doing quality interdisciplinary research (among other topics). The third part pivots to topics that other volumes often presume a familiarity with in all researchers – the proper use of self-report measures. This section covers important considerations in the design of any self-report measure along with the concerns uniquely associated with questionnaire design.

The fourth part of the volume turns the focus to various behavioral measure approaches used by social and behavioral scientists. This section covers eyetracking, implicit, and reaction time-based measures that are incredibly useful for understanding human behavior. The fifth part changes the focus to physiological measures. This section features chapters looking at diverse topics such as EMG, hormones, and fMRI measures with a goal to familiarize the reader with the proper interpretation of these kinds of measures.

The final Part of Volume 2 turns to an explicit focus on qualitative measures. This expansive section considers all manner of qualitative data, from the analysis of open-ended survey items, to case studies, to pure observational data.

In all, these authors span over a dozen disciplines, many more countries, and have led groundbreaking world-class research paradigms. It is for this reason that we are confident in their ability to teach you and to help you progress in your career as a scientist.

PART I

Quantitative Data Collection Sources

1 Student Samples in Research

Michael Basil

Abstract

This chapter provides an overview on the use and validity of student samples in the behavioral and social sciences. In some instances, data collected from students can be of limited value or even inappropriate; however, in other cases, this approach provides useful data. I offer three general ways to evaluate the use of student samples. First, consider the research design. Descriptive studies that rely on students to draw inferences about the overall population are likely problematic. Second, statistical controls such as multivariate analyses that adjust for other factors may reduce some of the biases that may be introduced through sampling. Third, consider the theorized mechanism – a clear theoretical mechanism that does not vary based on the demographics of the sample allows us to put more faith in constrained samples. Despite these approaches, and regardless of our methods, statistics, and theoretical mechanism, we should be cautious with generalizability claims.

Keywords: Sampling Students, Generalizability, Validity, Surveys, Experiments

Although some research relies on a census of an entire population, for the last 200 years there has been an increased reliance on examining a limited portion of a population (i.e., a sample) to try to understand the overall population (Fienberg & Tanur, 1996; Kruskal & Mosteller, 1980). This concept is not completely novel; as an example, Stephan (1948) points to the long history of the simple act of tasting or testing a small portion of a liquid. Over these past 200 years, the use of sampling a portion of a population has been applied in a wide variety of fields and in a wide variety of situations by researchers throughout the social and behavioral sciences. The primary reasons scientists use samples are the convenience, accessibility, and lower costs of research (Espinosa & Ortinau, 2016).

This chapter will focus on the use of student samples in research, specifically the validity of sampling college or university students. As mentioned earlier, reliance on samples to make inferences about the overall population can be traced to efforts in the late nineteenth and early twentieth century, involving Nicolai Kiaer, Jerzy Neyman, and R. A. Fisher (Fienberg & Tanur, 1996; Kruskal & Mosteller, 1980). The notion of sampling was likely originally conceptualized to examine the effects of agricultural experiments, but as the social and behavioral sciences evolved, the use of statistics has been applied to allow researchers to take the results from samples of people and draw inferences about the general population. The field of inferential statistics developed so that we can derive probability-based confidence intervals for the likelihood of the results holding for the overall population. Statistically speaking, however, confidence intervals are predicated on the notion that the population was sampled at random, with no systematic biases (Kish, 1957; Tabachnick & Fidell, 2018). When samples are not simple random samples, these confidence intervals are often biased.

In this chapter, I propose three critical questions to consider about the use of student samples and some broad guidelines on interpreting the validity of data collected from homogeneous samples in general, with a special focus on college or university students. To evaluate the use of student samples, three questions should be posed. First, what is the research method? Descriptive surveys must be representative of the overall population they wish to represent. If the sample is composed entirely of students, then extrapolating to other student groups may or may not be reasonable, depending on the student body we are talking about, and drawing inferences to the general public may be even more problematic. For example, results of a study on sexual attitudes and behaviors based on a sample from a small religious college consisting of younger unmarried people likely will not bear much resemblance to a commuter college with an older, married population, and drawing inferences about the general public is likely even more problematic. In the case of most experiments, because a manipulation is randomly assigned to a group and the effect is measured, representativeness is often believed to be less important (Falk et al., 2013). Specifically, experimental research demonstrates whether the manipulation affects the sample. Inferential statistics provide confidence intervals showing the likelihood that the observed difference would hold to the population from which the sample was drawn (Edgington, 1966). Although we cannot say definitively whether the same effect would hold for a different population, we can largely rule out self-selection bias and third variables as possible sources of bias.

A second question to ask when using student samples is whether there are any statistical controls over other factors. Simple descriptive analyses are most susceptible to bias through sampling. Increasingly, however, due to common practice and because of increased computing power, more research relies on bivariate or multivariate statistical analyses with multiple independent variables on the outcome measures. This reduces some of the potential biases involved or allows them to be detected. For example, including students' religious orientation, age, and whether they are married would likely reveal insights into the differences in students' sexual attitudes and behaviors between religious and commuter colleges. If there is a difference in sexual attitudes that can be explained by religion, age, or marital status, this can be discovered through statistical analyses and would help when interpreting the findings. This approach is not as powerful as random assignment but does provide a means of assessing whether other factors may be biasing our findings (see Chapter 10 in this volume).

The third question to ask about sampling is whether the nature of the sample itself is likely to affect the theoretical mechanism in some identifiable way. When studying a particular phenomenon, is there reason to believe that the underlying process or mechanism behind the phenomenon would be different for different groups of the population? If there is, then we should probably not be using a student sample, or at least should not seek to generalize the results beyond the sampled population. To generalize such a study, it would be necessary to replicate the findings with a different sample. This question is largely a matter of logic and theory but can be guided by previous research in that area. Further, making specific a priori predictions about the underlying process and measuring that helps us better understand the process and reduce the likelihood of Type I errors.

Different Forms of Sampling

In several natural science fields, including medicine, research is often conducted on non-human animals, including rats and monkeys. For example, chemicals that may be possible carcinogens or experimental drugs are often tested on animals for ethical or even practical reasons. The research is valuable if the underlying process is believed to be similar across species. Demonstrating that a chemical is a carcinogen in animals will often be enough to result in a ban on the chemical for human use. In other cases, research on animals is simply one piece of a program of research in which a variety of theoretical and practical concerns are examined. For example, testing drug efficacy, tolerance, and toxicity with animals is often seen as a necessary step before testing it on humans, although ethical concerns are becoming more prevalent with this practice (Goyal, 2015).

In the social and behavioral sciences, tests on non-human animals are less common. However, some research examining phenomena across different species suggests evidence of the universality of some mechanisms. For example, research may discover that memory problems in humans are associated with lower levels of a particular neurotransmitter. After this finding, researchers may prefer to test the effects of increasing levels of that neurotransmitter on animals. If these results are promising, the study may be replicated with humans. The human replication may be consistent with what was found with animals, or perhaps the results will be different, yet either result is informative.

When examining human behavior, a great deal of scientific research draws on student samples for its investigations. Within some fields in the social and behavioral sciences, such as psychology, student samples are common practice, while in others such as anthropology they are very unusual. In anthropology, and in fields which apply anthropological or ethnographic methods, the issue of generalizability tends to be less important than in many other social and behavioral sciences, often because they focus on unique populations and do not seek to generalize the findings to other populations (Gold, 1997; Honigmann, 2003). There are also some fields such as business that make frequent use of both student and non-student samples (Espinosa & Ortinau, 2016; Peterson, 2001; Simonson et al., 2001).

Importantly, for some fields, especially those in the qualitative and ethnographic tradition, research is often less about understanding the breadth of the overall population, but instead about developing a deeper understanding about a narrower population. This is because in these cases the population of interest is not people in general, but instead only a particular group such as Kaska Indians or Samoan girls (Honigmann, 2003). This approach has even developed its own term – "sociological sampling" (Gold, 1997). Instead of breadth, the aim is increasing the validity of those data by avoiding observer bias and documenting the findings (Gold, 1997, p. 399). As a result, one basic question to ask is who you want your research to generalize to. That is, before deciding on a sample, it is important to think about what population we want to generalize to, and then think about ways to generate a sample of that population. While we focus on "generalization" to population to which the results can apply, it can also apply to the external validity of the situation and the generalized knowledge that results (Shapiro, 2002).

If we examine current practice, student samples are a common source of data in the social and behavioral sciences. Instead of dismissing this research out of hand, we should consider two questions: first, is the sample appropriate to the question being posed and, second, does the sample used raise a concern about the validity and generalizability of those findings? When making simple population estimates, a non-representative sample is indeed a problem. In theoretical investigations, would the sample that is chosen alter the underlying relationships? When looking at a hypothesized relationship between two variables, or when no inferences about the general population need to be drawn, then a student sample can be appropriate. If we are interested in understanding older adults or even all adults, then a student sample does not make sense. The mechanism underlying the process and the theory should suggest whether we can draw inferences about the general population.

Background on Student Samples

Just as the simple act of stirring a chemical solution before sampling will usually lead to a more accurate measurement (Stephan, 1948), this concept can also be applied to our understanding of sampling – we are likely to find greater reliability in a more homogeneous sample. The question of generalizability, or validity, however, is different. The issue of generalizability leads us to the critical question of whether we want to draw conclusions about people in general, and if we do, whether college students will allow us to do that. In an historical retrospective, a debate on the generalizability of student samples occurred in the field of psychology as early as the 1940s (McNemar, 1946). In 1986, David Sears suggested that reliance on college sophomores constricts our understanding of human behavior and the mind. Importantly, Sears was not suggesting that student samples were useless, but that they were limiting. In his thesis, Sears (1986) identified specific characteristics of student samples that raise concerns. The three characteristics that he identified are that students (a) may have a less strongly formulated sense of self (and a stronger need for peer approval), (b) may have higher than average cognitive skills, and (c) may have a higher level of compliance to authority. Importantly, Sears considered and evaluated the possible influence of each of these factors. His concern that students may be problematic did not result in his dismissal of student samples out of hand, or a rejection of all findings to date; instead, he examined the potential biases themselves.

Consider the potential effects of these three characteristics if our sample were limited to students. First, if students have a weaker sense of self, students' opinions may be more volatile than those of older adults, so studies on topics such as attitude change may be biased. This does not mean that research using students cannot contribute to knowledge about attitude change; if students' opinions are more volatile, the process of opinion formation and change may not be qualitatively different but may change more readily. As a result, drawing inferences about *how* attitudes change may be correct, but the *likelihood* or *rate* of attitude change based on studies of students may be biased. Importantly, comparing persuasion results from a college student sample with those of adults is necessary to gain insights into that question.

Sears's second concern was that students have higher than average cognitive skills. It is possible that these increased skills change the nature of the mental processes that are performed. Research investigating decision-making, for example, might be biased. However, higher cognitive abilities could also work in our favor, resulting in more accurate questionnaire responses and reports of their mental activity. Interestingly, however, most studies of students show that these cognitively skilled students are mostly unsystematic in their decisions (Kahneman et al., 1982). If cognitively skilled students are unsystematic, then the public may be even more unsystematic. Findings from this line of research, therefore, might be biased in overestimating the rate of systematic thinking by the general population, but likely not our understanding of the underlying process. If the goal of the research is to look at the likelihood that this occurs, then the results are problematic; if the goal is to measure the effects of unsystematic thinking on the decisions that are made, then the results are most likely valid (for a discussion of validity, see Volume 1 of this Handbook).

The third concern Sears raised about students is that they may be more compliant to authority. Although there is some evidence of that students may be more influenced by demand effects, such as the willingness to complete a study, their compliance with our predictions is not always present (Nichols & Maner, 2008). So, let's examine the potential effect on research findings. At its most fundamental, increased demand effects may work in favor of science, making students more likely to complete the studies and complete them accurately. There are, however, two ways we typically avoid potential compliance effects in our research. First, the research subject is often "blind" to the hypothesis so the notion of artificially supporting the hypothesis should be reduced. Second, quantitative research often relies on objective measurements when possible, and also tries to separate these measurements from one another to reduce the "carryover" effects which might either color the results or allow participants to guess the hypothesis.

The points so far should not suggest that student samples are never a problem. A representative sample is usually better than a non-representative one. But not all studies need to make use of representative samples of the population, for a variety of reasons. Researchers and critics need to examine their research question and methods to ask whether there is any reason to suspect that the findings from a student or non-representative sample may bias the results from the question being examined or the population one is trying to understand. It would be wrong to simply reject all student samples out of hand; instead, we should question whether there is any logic or evidence to believe that the results of a study using students would be different if they were obtained from a broader sample (Greenberg, 1987). This should be done with any sample.

Some critics seem to suggest that there is no way of knowing in which instances student samples may not be generalizable to the overall population. This position is then extended to propose that all studies should avoid using students altogether (James & Sonner, 2001). I believe this reflects a fundamental misunderstanding about the importance of the sample and the overall research process. These misunderstandings also ignore many generally accepted forms of scientific practice where student and other non-representative samples are used regularly in scientific research and ignore some practical reasons why student and non-representative samples provide value to the research. The assumption that a more representative sample is inherently superior is problematic, because other sampling biases may more directly affect the conclusions. For example, imagine trying to understand investment strategies and drawing a representative sample only from investment advisors – this would not represent everyday self-directed investors.

Several new ways of gathering data online can make convenience samples one of the most cost-efficient ways to gather data (Bello et al., 2009; this volume, Chapters 2 and 4). Online samples, as well as those of college students, may provide a very convenient and cost-efficient opportunity to understand human behavior. Thoughtful use of both types of non-random samples can provide better value for our research budgets and sponsors. This may also result in novel and unique research ideas and insights, especially from exploratory research. By making a distinction between descriptive research and pilot tests, versus those that test theories using surveys and experiments, we can know in advance whether the use of a student sample is potentially problematic. Toward this end I will categorize research in four basic types – descriptive, pilot, correlational, and experimental. Later I will examine the importance of the statistical analysis and the underlying theory.

Research Design

Descriptive Studies

Descriptive studies are "concerned with and designed only to describe the existing distribution of variables, without regard to causal or other hypotheses" (Aggarwal & Ranganathan, 2019, p. 34). Frequently reported by the news media, these studies draw a sample to understand the overall population. Importantly, a biased sample will not reflect the demographics, beliefs, or behaviors of the overall population. That is, these findings are inherently subject to sampling bias. A classic example of sampling bias is the 1936 *Literary Digest* presidential election poll in the United States which showed that Langdon would defeat Roosevelt, which was different from the actual election result (Babbie, 1992, pp. 192–194; Traugott, 2011). Evidence suggests that the findings were biased by sampling people who owned either a telephone or an automobile, and in 1936, this included too many affluent and, therefore, Republican respondents. Although the poll might be interpreted to demonstrate that most of the telephone and car owners preferred Langdon to Roosevelt, it did not accurately reflect what percentage of voters preferred Langdon to Roosevelt. Extrapolating to the overall population was wrong, as the results of the election clearly indicated. In the example of the Langdon-Roosevelt poll, the results were reported as a simple univariate analysis of the percentage of the population favoring Langdon or Roosevelt. Because there were no statistical controls or measures of affluence, a variable frequently related to political preferences, nor of its relationship with whom they favored, we should be wary of the findings. No comparison of the sample to the population, or investigation of other potentially biasing factors was done. As this example illustrates, descriptive research which relies on a non-random sample is potentially problematic if one wants to draw inferences about the general population (Smith, 1983). When we apply the 1936 election estimates to the issue of student samples, this suggests that developing population estimates based on a student sample is likely problematic. This is the reason that many critics have raised concerns about the use of student samples for research purposes (Potter et al., 1993). However, the same concerns would be true of studying only Fox News or CNBC viewers.

Several studies have shown that students can vary from the public on a variety of dimensions (Barr & Hitt, 1986; Espinosa & Ortinau, 2016; Hanel & Vione, 2016; Lamb & Stem, 1980). For example, Espinosa and Ortinau (2016) demonstrated that students' ratings of restaurants differed from those of the public. As a result, these researchers and others have asserted that students should not be used in research to represent the overall population (James & Sonner, 2001). If the study is simply descriptive, this is a reasonable conclusion. However, although many studies have demonstrated an inconsistency between student and other samples, it is important to observe that many others have not (e.g., Clara et al., 2003). Further, Greenberg (1987) explains that finding some between-subjects differences does not demonstrate that the relationships would be different for other participants, nor negate the value of college student samples.

It is also important to observe that in descriptive research, even attempts to generate a random sample from an entire population can result in a non-representative sample (e.g., Jennings & Wlezien, 2018). Lower response rates will increase the likelihood of this occurring (Babbie, 1992, pp. 266–267). Non-representativeness can also occur via the sample itself, how it was obtained, how participants were recruited, as well as attrition through the course of research (Caspaldi & Patterson, 1987; Crabbe & Pinkerton, 1992; Dura & Kiecolt-Glaser, 1990; Edlund & Swann, 1989; Frame & Strauss, 1987; Lynch et al., 1993; Mishra et al., 1993; Norden et al., 1995; Walsch et al., 1992; Wesiner et al., 1995). The fundamental conclusion on sampling is that when we are relying on a sample it is hard to know whether we have achieved a truly "representative" view of the entire population, and this is true of student and non-student samples alike. One typical test is to compare the demographics of the sample with the underlying population; to the extent that the sample demographics reflect the overall population, this supports the argument of having drawn a representative sample. A high response rate of above 50% is helpful but does not guarantee the results are any more representative than a lower response rate (Lesser & Kalsbeek 1992; Rindfuss et al., 2015). However, it is important to consider that even as the percentage of the public that has attended college increases and grows more diverse, a representative sample from a single country may not be representative of humans (James & Sonner, 2001).

Back to the case of the *Literary Digest* Langdon-Roosevelt poll: if the nature of the sample's possible effect on political leanings had been considered, we should have concluded that drawing a sample of people who were more affluent could bias the results. We might have even rejected the conclusion. Using a more current approach, the sample could have been "reconstituted" to correct for the oversampling of the affluent (Bowen, 1994). That is to say that the result was not necessarily "wrong" for the sample from which it was drawn; it was the interpretation of the findings to the voting population that was problematic.

Although we hope that student samples would at least provide an understanding of the student-age population, evidence suggests that even specific samples of students may not provide a good picture of other types of students, or of students in general as older students may be a more reasonable surrogate for working adults than for students (James & Sonner, 2001). So, not only is it problematic to extrapolate from students to the general public, but it is also even problematic to generalize from one sample of students to other students.

Pilot and Exploratory Research

Some research using student samples defends the use of samples as simply exploratory. The use of convenience samples for exploratory research has a long history. Stephan (1948) points out that the field of astronomy began with a focus on the most visible astronomical bodies, including the moon and the larger planets, before examining less prominent bodies. In the same way, student samples can serve a useful function for pilot studies and other exploratory research. Akin to how studies with animals can provide preliminary tests of carcinogens, research with students can be a basis for pilot and exploratory research. Even those cynical about student samples generally acknowledge the value of student samples for exploratory research (Bello et al., 2009; Potter et al., 1993). This argument acknowledges that although students may have a variety of differences from the general population, they also share many similarities.

Evidence suggests that pilot or exploratory studies that rely on student samples are useful. In the field of medicine, Casadevall and Fang (2008, p. 3836) defend the value of descriptive research, yet qualify the validity of findings with a limited sample:

> Descriptive observations play a vital role in scientific progress, particularly during the initial explorations made possible by technological breakthroughs. At its best, descriptive research can illuminate novel phenomena or give rise to novel hypotheses that can in turn be examined by hypothesis-driven research. However,

descriptive research by itself is seldom conclusive. Thus, descriptive and hypothesis-driven research should be seen as complementary and iterative.

Bello et al. (2009, p. 363) in an editorial in the *Journal of International Business Studies* propose that "results based on students are likely to be ecologically valid if they are replicated or corroborated by results based on employees or managers." The notion that results from student samples should only be considered as preliminary until replicated with a broader or more appropriate sample are common in the literature (e.g., Ferber, 1977; James & Sonner, 2001; Potter et al., 1993; Wells, 1993). Ferber (1977), for example, suggests "One justifiable use of a convenience sample is for exploratory purposes, that is, to get different views on the dimensions of a problem, to probe for possible explanations or hypotheses, and to explore constructs for dealing with particular problems or issues." Considering those admonitions, although more than 80% of US social psychology studies use student samples, only about 5% raise generalizability as a possible limitation (Banyard & Hunt, 2000; Compeau et al., 2012). As the field of psychology has been more outspoken on this issue, the use of students is generally of less concern in other fields. For example, in the field of marketing, Ashraf and Merunka (2017) found only about 20% of studies relied on student-only samples. In the field of political science, evidence suggests that student samples are used frequently in experimental research (Krupnikov et al., 2021). Concerns about the use of student samples have been raised in criminology (Payne & Chappell, 2008) and logistics (Thomas, 2011). Although there are few studies examining the prevalence of student samples in the other behavioral sciences, there are many instances of research in these fields which compares a student sample with another type of sample, suggesting at least awareness of this concern.

Several studies have compared the results of a student sample with those of a different sample or population (e.g., Hallingberg et al., 2018). Although there are differences between students and non-students, Greenberg (1987) argues that this does not mean that any observed effects are invalid. Many studies use small-scale tests of interventions before they are attempted on a larger population and are used frequently to test new education curricula. As a preliminary test, these pilot studies may help identify issues related to a variety of interventions before they are launched on a larger scale (Beebe, 2007). Student samples have also been shown to be useful in scale construction (Pernice et al., 2008). Therefore, student samples can be useful for pilot and exploratory research because of their availability and lower costs (Henry, 2008), and may be especially useful for general exploration or as a basis for arguing for funding for a broader sample (Van Teijlingen & Hundley, 2010). Some research has provided suggestions for improving the translation from pilot to full-scale efforts (Beets et al., 2020; Hallingberg et al., 2018; Wolfe, 2013).

Correlational Studies Examining Relationships

Much research tests relationships between factors, often using surveys. The best of these studies examine predicted relationships between variables (Kardes, 1996; Lucas, 2003). In defense of this approach, many theorists propose that student samples provide valuable insights and validity, even if tested with a constrained sample. Bello et al. (2009, p. 363) propose that, "if a study is guided by a well-defined theory with sophisticated predictions, and if the results based on student participants confirm the predictions, it is likely that these results can generalize to a target population." That is, this approach proposes that research focused on examining a relationship which depends on some underlying process, especially if it predicts a specific if-then relationship, can be tested with a convenience sample such as students. The validity of such an approach is more defensible if the underlying process or intervening variables are assessed to demonstrate its viability.

One approach to generalization argues that if the relationship holds with one population, the burden of proof may be on subsequent researchers to demonstrate the relationship does not hold for other populations; in the absence of such a demonstration, it is reasonable to accept that relationship. In support of this assertion, Heggestad et al. (2015) demonstrate that low response rates did not significantly bias their estimates of correlations between variables. Another study demonstrating consistency of underlying theoretical relationships across different samples is illustrated by Basil et al. (2002). This study examined reactions to the death of Princess Diana and compared three different samples – college students, a web-based sample, and a random-digit telephone sample. The results demonstrated significant demographic differences in the age and gender of respondents, as well as the overall level of identification with Princess Diana; however, the *relationship* between level of identification and the attitudinal and behavioral outcomes were statistically consistent. That is, the greater the identification, the greater their desire to watch her funeral, and this held across all three samples. As the authors suggest, and consistent with Bello et al.'s (2009) assertion, these findings support the notion that theoretical if-then relationships may not be as affected by sample differences as simple descriptive comparisons. Similar results exist elsewhere (e.g., Harrison, 1995).

There are other theorists who propose that constrained samples such as students often not only fail in their external validity, but also fail to demonstrate the internal validity that theory testing demands (Peterson & Merunka, 2014). To test this proposition, Peterson and Merunka (2014) analyzed studies of ethics across four dozen samples and demonstrated more variability than the Basil et al. (2002) and Heggestad et al. (2015) studies, finding significant differences not only in means, but also in variances, intercorrelations, and path parameters. Similarly, Cappelen et al. (2015), in a study comparing a game playing the role of a dictator versus one involving trust found that the student sample differed from the representative sample in the importance of moral motives, the level of selfish behavior, and the gender effects observed. These findings raise concerns about the use of student samples to test theory, which will be discussed as a third concern.

Experimental Research

A long tradition suggests that experiments are less prone to sampling issues, compared to other forms of research. This is because experiments randomly assign participants to a condition while they directly manipulate an independent variable and measure its effect on an outcome. These two factors avoid self-selection bias. Further, participants are randomly assigned to conditions, so there is no possibility of self-selection into specific groups. For example, half are given treatment A and half treatment B. Every other factor remains the same. As a result, the only difference between participants in condition A and condition B should be the variable being manipulated (Thomas, 2011). Babbie observed that "probability sampling is seldom used in experiments to select participants from a larger population. The logic of random selection is ... [r]andomization" (Babbie, 1992, p. 242). Because participants are randomly assigned to conditions and the researcher is manipulating the variable in question, experiments using students can provide important insights into causality and examination of underlying mechanism. In addition, because a narrower sample can reduce other sources of variation, non-representativeness may even provide a benefit (Lynch, 1982).

For these reasons, when a manipulation is randomly assigned to a group and the effect is measured, representativeness is believed to be less important (Berkowitz & Donnerstein, 1982). This approach has allowed us to demonstrate rather conclusively that the manipulation affected our sample. At the most basic, this can be referred to as within-subject differences (Greenberg, 1987). Inferential statistics then provide confidence intervals that partially reflect the likely difference in the population from which the sample was drawn. Although we cannot say definitively whether the same effect would hold for a different population, we can at least rule out self-selection bias and third variables as a possible explanation.

Lucas (2003) has a thorough discussion of the often misplaced concerns about the lack of external validity in experiments. He argues that claims that student samples reduce the external validity of experiments is wrong for four reasons. First, experiments are focused on predicted theoretical relationships. Second, few theories specify the population to which these relationships apply. Third, sampling is simply a matter of procedure, not inherent in the method. Fourth, findings always depend on the whole variety of circumstances in which they were gathered, and generalization is more related to the operationalizations, measures, and, most importantly, the accuracy of the theory. Lynch (1982) and Thomas (2011) have both argued that homogeneity in experimental research is beneficial as it will increase the likelihood of falsely rejecting the null hypothesis and therefore, he argues that homogeneous samples may have some advantages over representative samples if only a theory is false.

As one example of the lower importance of samples in experimental research, Falk et al. (2013) examined whether students were more likely to participate in a study of donations or to trust others – the self-selection problem; they found no difference in participation rates. Further, they also demonstrated similar levels of trust, thus suggesting that student samples were likely a valid means to test theories of prosocial behavior. Finding that college-age students differ on unrelated factors, such as different hobbies, interests, personality characteristics, or levels of depression, from older adults, does not mean that the effects of an appeal for donations may not work on a different population. What is most important is the underlying nature of that response.

Analysis Method: Statistical Controls

In addition to the research design, another important factor that may influence the results of a study is the analysis method. One tool that may be applied is a more robust statistical analysis (Amaya & Presser, 2016; Krackardt, 1987). That is, as we move from a univariate to a bivariate or multivariate analysis that controls for other factors, we are potentially adjusting for other important factors. Simple univariate analysis that reports the means or percentages from the overall sample has a higher potential for bias (Amaya & Presser, 2016). Specifically, univariate statistics do not allow the researcher to control for other possible factors. Analyzing a biased sample with univariate analysis will allow whatever biases that exist in the sample to bias the results. As demonstrated in the Langdon-Roosevelt poll, simple percentages using descriptive statistics are very susceptible to bias through sampling. When considerations of income are measured, statistical analyses can appropriately adjust for these differences, and the results can be interpreted more accurately. In addition, is it possible to weight the sample by any important factors found and come up with a less biased result.

Over the past several decades, an increase in computing power has resulted in the use of more sophisticated statistical tools (Efron & Tibshirani, 1991). As a result, it is more common for researchers to make use of bivariate or multivariate statistical analyses to examine the effects of multiple independent variables – not only the ones predicted, but other third variables that can bias the results. As a result of these more sophisticated analyses, research can reveal what other factors may be biasing the outcome measures (Guttman, 1973; Meyer et al., 2019). This reduces some of the potential biases involved. For example, in the Langdon-Roosevelt poll, asking people their income or party affiliation and comparing this to the national data would have likely revealed an oversampling of rich and Republican voters. Weighting the sample accordingly, as more recent approaches to polling have done, likely would have produced a less biased result, but still can sometimes fail to accurately predict the overall outcome. Similarly, including information on students that could affect your outcome measures would allow bivariate or multivariate statistical analysis to adjust for these factors – similar to when Lynch (1982) suggests "blocking variables." Blocking variables examine other possible factors. Importantly, finding an interaction with one of your demographic factors is an indication that your results may depend on the sample and may suggest potential boundary conditions (Greenberg, 1987). Of course, this requires a broad enough sample to have a range in those demographic factors – something that may not occur with a sample of college sophomores from a traditional college or university. Statistically adjusting for sample differences is not a foolproof solution, but it does allow us to control for some of the possible contributing factors that may affect research findings.

The Importance of Theory

Previous theorists have proposed that student samples are less problematic when the research involves a test of theory. For example, "if a study is guided by a well-defined theory with sophisticated predictions, and if the results based on student participants confirm the predictions, it is likely that these results can generalize to a target population" (Bello et al., 2009, p. 363). The rationale is that evaluating specific a priori predictions reduces the likelihood of Type I errors (Coleman, 2007). Applying this reasoning, when studying a particular phenomenon with a student sample, there are two things we should do. First, we should consider whether there is reason to believe the underlying phenomenon may be different for different groups of the population. Second, we should measure any potentially relevant factors that might also affect the underlying process and outcomes.

First, the researcher should consider whether there is any reason to believe that the underlying process may be different in the sample. A researcher should consider whether the results may be affected by the sample and examine any research or theories that would shed light on any bias. Imagine that we are measuring students' response to a scary movie. Four hundred students watch a movie. Half view the scary movie; the other half watch a comedy. Not only are students compared to students, but the individuals in one condition are compared to people's reactions in another condition. Imagine that all students show higher levels of arousal response to the scary movie than the comedy. Next, this difference is shown statistically to occur by chance less than 1 time in 20. Could the researcher reasonably conclude that scary movies result in more arousal than comedies?

It might be concluded that the findings are valid, at minimum, for students. We have learned something by doing the study. We cannot say, however, whether the findings are valid for individuals beyond the group from which we sampled or the extent to which they are similar. Looking at the literature, we find that younger people generally have more robust physiological responses. However, since it is generally believed that people have similar physiology, we might conclude a similar relationship would exist for other populations. Because the underlying process of fear reactions is believed to be physiologically determined, it is therefore likely to be consistent across people. So, although the results from a younger sample may overestimate the size of the effect, the overall effect would still be expected for other populations. It may however be more difficult to attain the effect, or the effect may be smaller, in the general population, since this physiological response is expected to be larger for younger people.

If there is reason to believe that the sample would fundamentally alter the results, that researcher should broaden the sample. The theory would suggest it. In the case of responses to movies, is it reasonable to conclude that this result would hold for the general population? This is a judgment call, but if the theory is that physiological responses function similarly, it is hard to believe that something that triggers a physiological response in a 20-year-old wouldn't also trigger one in a 50-year-old. Therefore, we would expect a similar underlying process in 20-year-olds as in 50-year-olds. It seems likely, then, that we can say that people are aroused by scary movies. This is an empirical question, but, like all empirical research, we should conclude that any association that we observed is only tentatively supported when tested with a student sample.

The second caveat is that analyses should include all factors that are likely to be relevant as variables. It would be important to measure both intervening variables suggested by the theory as well as potentially relevant demographics. After the research is completed, the researcher should consider the findings to see if the underlying process appears similar and the results varied by the demographics – for example, by examining age or gender effects. If there is evidence that the sample could have affected the results, it is incumbent on the researcher to report this. The ability to avoid possible sampling problems is important. It should make a researcher careful in thinking through which sample to use. Therefore, careful consideration of the possible influence of the sample is strongly advised in all situations. If our scary movie findings replicate, but we find that arousal varies depending on the age of the participant, this may not mean that scary movies do not elicit a similar reaction in people of different ages, but it may indicate that the absolute level of physiological responses may vary. Also, given this replication we may reasonably conclude that people of different races would react similarly, short people similar to tall people, etc. People who doubt the similarity are free to conduct a replication with the requisite sample.

Applying this test to the study of other dependent variables, an important question that would be asked is whether there is any reason to believe that students' reactions are qualitatively different from the rest of the population. As mentioned, some evidence suggests that their physiological responses may be stronger. In some cases, this may make the effects more measurable. Because of the nature of a student sample, this increased response might not bias the nature of the effect but might bias its size. However, let's imagine we are measuring attitude change. Harkening back to Sears's (1986) critique of the use of student samples, in this example it seems possible that students' attitudes are less fixed, and therefore more malleable (although this is only an assertion). In this case our test of attitude change likely would demonstrate greater attitude change than with a sample of the general population. Is there reason to believe that attitudes and the attitude change process are qualitatively different in students than in older adults? It seems unlikely, but if there is reason to suspect this difference, or any indication by looking at the interactions mentioned above, we should entertain that possibility and consider a replication with a different sample. In sum, although research results may be valid, and even reliable, replication with a variety of samples is critical if one wishes to establish the generalizability of these findings to an overall population (Deffner et al., 2022).

Recommendations for the Interpretation of Student Samples

Instead of inherently rejecting all research done with student samples, it is important to consider whether a sample could bias the results, their interpretation, or their generalizability. For example, if a study tries to predict what people think about a current event using only univariate statistics, then a student-only sample would likely pose a threat to the validity of those findings. If, however, the study examines the relationship between political orientation and how people interpret a current event, and therefore is theoretically based, these effects are more likely to apply to the public. While we could not estimate accurately the rate of the public's political orientation from a student sample, there are fewer reasons to believe that the effects of political orientation on interpretations would be different in the overall population. The question, then, should be whether the process being examined is likely to hold for the overall population. Unless the underlying process is likely to be different, it would be wrong to reject it. If there are those who question this relationship, they are free to replicate the study using a broader sample. It is the dialogue between the theoretical advancements and the practical applications that leads to the most valuable insights in social and behavioral science. To paraphrase what is often attributed to Kurt Lewin, the only thing more valuable than a good theory may be a good theory that has been supported through a variety of different tests. Therefore, it is in our best interest to continue to use and value student samples but to be careful in suggesting to which population the results may generalize, especially when the sample could potentially bias the results or increase the possibility of confirming the hypothesis.

In addition to our concerns about the participants sampled, if we take a broader view on the issue of sampling, the question of generalizability also can be seen in the use of stimuli. To what extent would the stimuli used in your study generalize to other situations? In the case of scary movies, to generalize to the population of "scary movies" it is advantageous to rely on a variety of scary movies, something that has been referred to as M>1 research (Jackson, 1992; Jackson & Jacobs, 1983). Sampling messages is a form of replication that increases our confidence in our generalizations and allows better estimates of effect sizes (Monin & Oppenheimer, 2014). Therefore, in the same way that sampling a wider variety of participants adds greater generalizability to our findings, sampling stimuli as well as conceptual replications also add greater generalizability to our findings (Crandall & Sherman, 2016).

Conclusions

Concerns about the generalizability of research results are warranted. Although many theorists believe that students introduce less error into research than a "representative" sample through higher completion rates, greater attention, and higher cognitive ability (Burnett & Dune, 1986; Lynch, 1982), the issue of how generalizable a study's results are should always be considered. Suggestions that studies drawn from a broad sample of the public are inherently better are not always true. In addition to self-selection, non-response and attrition, the context and the stimuli may all affect the representativeness of the conclusions that are drawn (Shapiro, 2002). As a result, studies from a "non-representative" sample of students can be less biased than a broader sample of the population. The guidelines offered here – considering the research method, whether uni-, bi-, or multivariate analyses were involved, and whether we are testing a theory with a priori predictions – should provide a means to evaluate the potential validity of student samples. These questions should provide clues about where and when the breadth of the sample might threaten our findings. If these concerns arise, a replication may be in order.

This review has focused on the potential differences between a student sample and the overall population from which those students are drawn. A more macro question, however, is whether a study based on people in the United States, or North America, Europe, or a clinical population, is representative of people in general (Nielsen et al., 2017). Some of the previously mentioned studies demonstrate that what was learned from a North American sample may not generalize to people in other parts of the world (e.g., Baláž et al., 2013; Kim et al., 2018). As a result, a student sample from a particular country is theoretically no more limiting than even a representative sample from a single country in our ability to generalize to the global population (Nielsen et al., 2017).

Although some would have us eliminate students as a source of information, we should ask whether the practical advantages outweigh the additional costs. Having an easily accessible research population at a lower cost allows us to ask more questions. In addition to the specific issues of student samples that have been the focus of this review, new ways of gathering data online mean the question of limited samples has an even broader relevance. Given limited resources such as declining levels of grant money, there may be more need to rely on limited samples, including students and online samples, especially with initial research. Thoughts on how to best use these samples can provide important insights into their value. This can result in research being able to explore more novel questions and provide unique research insights from a broader research base.

The bottom line here is that the automatic dismissal of research using student samples is not warranted. Although increasing the breadth of a sample is helpful, it does not inherently increase the validity of the findings. As I have proposed earlier (Basil, 1996, p. 439), "the hallmark of science is not the quality of the sample, but the testing of a theory in situations that allow its possible falsification." In sum, student samples are no worse than any other convenience sample and any one sample is only part of the evidence for a theory. However, we should be careful in claiming to what populations our results may generalize. Evaluating our samples with this perspective should help us understand where there might be concerns, or when the conclusions should be tempered. With this insight, researchers can discover which studies are worthy of replication. Such replications could provide answers to these concerns. The additional research should provide work for meta-analyses for years and perhaps even finally answer the questions about when we need to be concerned about the validity of student samples. Returning the discussion to Sears (1986, p. 527): "We have ... learned a great deal from studying college sophomores in the laboratory. But it may be appropriate to be somewhat more tentative about the portrait of human nature we have developed from this database."

References

Amaya, A., & Presser, S. (2016). Nonresponse bias for univariate and multivariate estimates of social activities and roles. *Public Opinion Quarterly, 81*(1), 1–36.

Aggarwal, R., & Ranganathan, P. (2019). Study designs: Part 2 – descriptive studies. *Perspectives in Clinical Research, 10*(1), 34–36.

Ashraf, R., & Merunka, D. (2017). The use and misuse of student samples: An empirical investigation of European marketing research. *Journal of Consumer Behaviour, 16*(4), 295–308.

Babbie, E. (1992). *The Practice of Social Research*, 6th ed. Wadsworth.

Baláž, V., Bačová, V., Drobná, E., Dudeková, K., & Adamík, K. (2013). Testing prospect theory parameters. *Ekonomicky časopis, 61*, 655–671.

Banyard, P., & Hunt, N. (2000). Reporting research: Something missing? *The Psychologist: Bulletin of the British Psychological Society, 13*(2), 68–71.

Barr, S. H., & Hitt, M. A. (1986). A comparison of selection decision models in manager versus student samples. *Personnel Psychology, 39*(3), 599–617.

Basil, M. D. (1996). The use of student samples in communication research. *Journal of Broadcasting and Electronic Media, 40*, 431–440.

Basil, M. D., Brown, W. J., & Bocarnea, M. C. (2002). Differences in univariate values versus multivariate relationships: Findings from a study of Diana, Princess of Wales. *Human Communication Research, 28*, 501–514.

Beebe, L. H. (2007). What can we learn from pilot studies? *Perspectives in Psychiatric Care, 43*(4), 213–218.

Beets, M. W., Weaver, R. G., Ioannidis, J., Geraci, M., Brazendale, K., Decker, L., & Milat, A. J. (2020). Identification and evaluation of risk of generalizability biases in pilot versus efficacy/effectiveness trials: A systematic review and meta-analysis. *International Journal of Behavioral Nutrition and Physical Activity, 17*(1), 1–20.

Bello, D., Leung, K., Radebaugh, L., Tung, R. L., & Van Witteloostuijn, A. (2009). From the editors: Student samples in international business research. *Journal of International Business Studies, 40*(3), 361–364.

Berkowitz, L., & Donnerstein, E. (1982). External validity is more than skin deep: Some answers to criticisms of laboratory experiments. *American Psychologist, 37*(3), 245.

Bowen, G. L. (1994). Estimating the reduction in nonresponse bias from using a mail survey as a backup for nonrespondents to a telephone interview survey. *Research on Social Work Practice, 4*, 115–128.

Burnett, J. J., & Dune, P. M. (1986). An appraisal of the use of student subjects in marketing research. *Journal of Business Research, 14*(4), 329–343.

Cappelen, A. W., Nygaard, K., Sørensen, E. Ø., & Tungodden, B. (2015). Social preferences in the lab: A comparison of students and a representative population. *Scandinavian Journal of Economics, 117*(4), 1306–1326.

Casadevall, A., & Fang, F. C. (2008). Descriptive science. *Infection and Immunity, 76*(9), 3835–3836.

Caspaldi, D., & Patterson, G. R. (1987). An approach to the problem of recruitment and retention rates for longitudinal research. *Behavioral Assessment, 9*, 169–177.

Clara, I. P., Cox, B. J., Enns, M. W., Murray, L. T., & Torgrude, L. J. (2003). Confirmatory factor analysis of the multidimensional scale of perceived social support in clinically distressed and student samples. *Journal of Personality Assessment, 81*(3), 265–270.

Coleman, S. (2007). Testing theories with qualitative and quantitative predictions. *European Political Science, 6*(2), 124–133.

Compeau, D., Marcolin, B., Kelley, H., & Higgins, C. (2012). Research commentary – Generalizability of information systems research using student subjects – A reflection on our practices and recommendations for future research. *Information Systems Research, 23*(4), 1093–1109.

Crabbe, B. D., & Pinkerton, K. A. (1992). Sources of bias in Health Commission and tobacco industry surveys in Australia. *Australian Psychologist, 27*, 103–108.

Crandall, C. S., & Sherman, J. W. (2016). On the scientific superiority of conceptual replications for scientific progress. *Journal of Experimental Social Psychology, 66*, 93–99.

Deffner, D., Rohrer, J. M., & McElreath, R. (2022). A causal framework for cross-cultural generalizability. *Advances in Methods and Practices in Psychological Science, 5*(3), 25152459221106366.

Dura, J. R., & Kiecolt-Glaser, J. K. (1990). Sample bias in caregiving research. *Journals of Gerontology, 45*, P200–P204.

Edgington, E. S. (1966). Statistical inference and nonrandom samples. *Psychological Bulletin, 66*(6), 485–487.

Edlund, M. J., & Swann, A. C. (1989). Continuing in treatment as a form of selection bias. *American Journal of Psychiatry, 146*, 254–256.

Efron, B., & Tibshirani, R. (1991). Statistical data analysis in the computer age. *Science, 253* (5018), 390–395.

Espinosa, J. A., & Ortinau, D. J. (2016). Debunking legendary beliefs about student samples in marketing research. *Journal of Business Research, 69*(8), 3149–3158.

Falk, A., Meier, S., & Zehnder, C. (2013). Do lab experiments misrepresent social preferences? The case of self-selected student samples. *Journal of the European Economic Association, 11*(4), 839–852.

Ferber, R. (1977). Research by convenience. *Journal of Consumer Research, 4*(1), 57–58.

Fienberg, S. E., & Tanur, J. M. (1996). Reconsidering the fundamental contributions of Fisher and Neyman on experimentation and sampling. *International Statistical Review/ Revue Internationale de Statistique, 64*(3), 237–253.

Frame, C. L., & Strauss, C. C. (1987). Parental informed consent and sample bias in grade-school children. *Journal of Social and Clinical Psychology, 5*, 227–236.

Gold, R. L. (1997). The ethnographic method in sociology. *Qualitative Inquiry, 3*(4), 388–402.

Goyal, R. (2015). Animal testing in the history of anesthesia: Now and then, some stories, some facts. *Journal of Anaesthesiology, Clinical Pharmacology, 31*(2), 149–151.

Greenberg, J. (1987). The college sophomore as guinea pig: Setting the record straight. *Academy of Management Review, 12*(1), 157–159.

Guttman, I. (1973). Care and handling of univariate or multivariate outliers in detecting spuriosity – a Bayesian approach. *Technometrics, 15*(4), 723–738.

Hallingberg, B., Turley, R., Segrott, J., et al. (2018). Exploratory studies to decide whether and how to proceed with full-scale evaluations of public health interventions: A systematic review of guidance. *Pilot and feasibility studies, 4*(1), 1–12.

Hanel, P. H., & Vione, K. C. (2016). Do student samples provide an accurate estimate of the general public? *PLOS ONE, 11*(12), e0168354.

Harrison, D. A. (1995). Volunteer motivation and attendance decisions: Competitive theory testing in multiple samples from a homeless shelter. *Journal of Applied Psychology, 80*(3), 371–385.

Heggestad, E. D., Rogelberg, S., Goh, A., & Oswald, F. L. (2015). Considering the effects of nonresponse on correlations between surveyed variables. *Journal of Personnel Psychology*, *14*(2), 91–103.

Henry, P. J. (2008). Student sampling as a theoretical problem. *Psychological Inquiry*, *19*(2), 114–126

Honigmann, J. J. (2003). Sampling in ethnographic fieldwork. In R. G. Burgess (ed.), *Field Research: A Sourcebook and Field Manual* (pp. 134–152). Routledge.

Jackson, S. (1992). *Message Effects Research: Principles of Design and Analysis*. Guilford Press.

Jackson, S., & Jacobs, S. (1983). Generalizing about messages: Suggestions for design and analysis of experiments. *Human Communication Research*, *9*(2), 169–191.

James, W. L., & Sonner, B. S. (2001). Just say no to traditional student samples. *Journal of Advertising Research*, *41*(5), 63–71.

Jennings, W., & Wlezien, C. (2018). Election polling errors across time and space. *Nature Human Behaviour*, *2*(4), 276–283.

Kahneman, D., Slovic, R., & Tversky, A. (1982). *Judgment under Uncertainty: Heuristics and Biases*. Cambridge University Press.

Kardes, F. R. (1996). In defense of experimental consumer psychology. *Journal of Consumer Psychology*, *5*, 279–296.

Kim, H., Schimmack, U., Oishi, S., & Tsutsui, Y. (2018). Extraversion and life satisfaction: A cross-cultural examination of student and nationally representative samples. *Journal of Personality*, *86*(4), 604–618.

Kish, L. (1957). Confidence intervals for clustered samples. *American Sociological Review*, *22*(2), 154–165.

Krackardt, D. (1987). QAP partialling as a test of spuriousness. *Social Networks*, *9*(2), 171–186.

Krupnikov, Y., Nam, H. H., Style, H., Druckman, J. N., & Green, D. P. (2021). Convenience samples in political science experiments. In J. Druckman and D. Green (eds.), *Advances in Experimental Political Science* (pp. 165–183). Cambridge University Press.

Kruskal, W., & Mosteller, F. (1980). Representative sampling, IV: The history of the concept in statistics, 1895–1939. *International Statistical Review/Revue Internationale de Statistique*, *48*(2), pp. 169–195.

Lamb Jr., C. W., & Stem Jr., D. E. (1980). An evaluation of students as surrogates in marketing studies. *Advances in Consumer Research*, *7*(1), 796–799.

Lesser, V. M., & Kalsbeek, W. D. (1999). Nonsampling errors in environmental surveys. *Journal of Agricultural, Biological, and Environmental Statistics*, *4*(4), 473–488.

Lucas, J. W. (2003). Theory-testing, generalization, and the problem of external validity. *Sociological Theory*, *21*, 236–253.

Lynch, D. L., Stern, A. E., Oates, R. K., & O'Toole, B. I. (1993). Who participates in child sexual abuse research? *Journal of Child Psychology and Psychiatry and Allied Disciplines*, *34*, 935–944.

Lynch, J. G. (1982). The role of external validity in theoretical research. *Journal of Consumer Research*, *10*, 109–111.

McNemar, Q. (1946) Opinion attitude methodology. *Psychological Bulletin*, *43*, 289–374.

Meyer, J., Kohn, I., Stahl, K., Hakala, K., Seibert, J., & Cannon, A. J. (2019). Effects of univariate and multivariate bias correction on hydrological impact projections in alpine catchments. *Hydrology and Earth System Sciences*, *23*, 1339–1354.

Mishra, S. I., Dooley, D., Catalano, R., & Serxner, S. (1993). Telephone health surveys: Potential bias from noncompletion. *American Journal of Public Health*, *83*, 94–99.

Monin, B., & Oppenheimer, D. M. (2014). The limits of direct replications and the virtues of stimulus sampling. *Social Psychology*, *45*(4), 299–300.

Nichols, A. L., & Maner, J. K. (2008). The good-subject effect: Investigating participant demand characteristics. *Journal of General Psychology*, *135*(2), 151–166.

Nielsen, M., Haun, D., Kärtner, J., & Legare, C. H. (2017). The persistent sampling bias in developmental psychology: A call to action. *Journal of Experimental Child Psychology*, *162*, 31–38.

Norden, K. A., Klein, D. N., Ferro, T., & Kasch, K. (1995). Who participates in a family study? *Comprehensive Psychiatry*, *36*, 199–206.

Payne, B. K., & Chappell, A. (2008). Using student samples in criminological research. *Journal of Criminal Justice Education*, *19*(2), 175–192.

Pernice, R. E., Ommundsen, R., Van Der Veer, K., & Larsen, K. (2008). On use of student samples for scale construction. *Psychological Reports*, *102*(2), 459–464.

Peterson, R. A. (2001). On the use of college students in social science research: Insights from a second-order meta-analysis. *Journal of Consumer Research*, *28*, 450–461.

Peterson, R. A., & Merunka, D. R. (2014). Convenience samples of college students and research reproducibility. *Journal of Business Research*, *67*(5), 1035–1041.

Potter, W. J., Cooper, R., & Dupagne, M. (1993). The three paradigms of mass media research in mainstream communication journals. *Communication Theory*, *3*, 317–355.

Rindfuss, R. R., Choe, M. K., Tsuya, N. O., Bumpass, L. L., & Tamaki, E. (2015). Do low survey response rates bias results? Evidence from Japan. *Demographic Research*, *32*, 797–828.

Sears, D. O. (1986). College sophomore in the laboratory: Influences of a narrow data base on social psychology's view of human nature. *Journal of Personality and Social Psychology*, *51*, 515–530.

Shapiro, M. A. (2002). Generalizability in communication research. *Human Communication Research*, *28*(4), 491–500.

Simonson, I., Carmon, Z., Dhar, R., Drolet, A., & Nowlis, S. M. (2001). Consumer research: In search of identity. In S. T. Fiske, D. L. Schacter, & C. Zahn-Waxler (eds.), *Annual Review of Psychology* (vol. 52, pp. 249–275). Annual Reviews.

Smith, T. M. F. (1983). On the validity of inferences from non-random samples. *Journal of the Royal Statistical Society: Series A (General)*, *146*(4), 394–403.

Stephan, F. F. (1948). History of the uses of modern sampling procedures. *Journal of the American Statistical Association*, *43*(241), 12–39.

Tabachnick, B. G., & Fidell, L. S. (2018). *Using Multivariate Statistics*. Pearson.

Thomas, R. W. (2011). When student samples make sense in logistics research. *Journal of Business Logistics*, *32*(3), 287–290.

Traugott, M. (2011). The accuracy of opinion polling and its relation to its future. In R. I. Shapiro & L. R. Jacobs (eds.), *The Oxford Handbook of American Public Opinion and the Media* (pp. 316–331). Oxford University Press.

Van Teijlingen, E., & Hundley, V. (2010). The importance of pilot studies. *Social Research Update*, *35*(4), 49–59.

Walsch, J. P., Sproull, L. S., & Hesse, B. W. (1992). Self-selected and randomly selected respondents in a computer network. *Public Opinion Quarterly*, *56*, 241–244.

Wells, W. D. (1993). Discovery-oriented consumer research. *Journal of Consumer Research*, *19*(4), 489–504.

Wesiner, C., Schmidt, L., & Tam, T. (1995). Assessing bias in community-based prevalence estimates: Towards an unduplicated count of problem drinkers and drug users. *Addiction, 90*, 391–405.

Wolfe, B. E. (2013). The value of pilot studies in clinical research: A clinical translation of the research article titled "In search of an adult attachment stress provocation to measure effect on the oxytocin system." *Journal of the American Psychiatric Nurses Association, 19*(4), 192–194.

2 Mechanical Turk: A Versatile Tool in the Behavioral Scientist's Toolkit

Aaron J. Moss, David Hauser, Cheskie Rosenzweig, Jonathan Robinson, and Leib Litman

Abstract

Building a successful research career often requires being adept at the methods and tools of the time. For social and behavioral scientists today, that means navigating online participant platforms and the tools used to create online studies. In this chapter, we describe how Amazon's Mechanical Turk (MTurk) can be leveraged as a source for participant recruitment. We provide a brief history of MTurk's usage by researchers, describe the challenges researchers have faced with the site, and summarize the status of issues like data quality, sample representativeness, and ethics in online research. Along the way, we provide tips for how researchers can use MTurk to collect high-quality data and to start and advance a research career.

Keywords: Online Research, Amazon Mechanical Turk, Data Quality, Research Methods, Online Sampling

In 1949, a man freshly done with his PhD assumed the post of Assistant Professor of Psychology at the University of Minnesota; his name was Stanley Schachter. Over the next 43 years, Schachter made substantial contributions to psychology's understanding of human behavior. Among the topics he studied were emotion, group dynamics, obesity, nicotine addiction, birth order and achievement, and group thinking in cults. Upon his retirement from Columbia University in 1992, Schachter was author or co-author of five books, three chapters, and nine articles. For this output, he received numerous awards – including induction into the National Academy of Sciences – and, by some metrics, became the seventh most eminent psychologist of the twentieth century (Haggbloom et al., 2002).

Schachter was successful for many reasons. He was adept at experimental methods; he studied interesting topics that addressed societal problems; and his research was fun. He often crafted elaborate cover stories that disguised the study's true purpose from participants. A through line in Schachter's success may be the idea of discernment. He appears to have done especially well using the resources at his disposal to design interesting studies that tackled important questions and earned the respect of his contemporaries. Behavioral researchers today face the same challenge even if the tools of the trade have changed. In Schachter's time, laboratory studies with deceptive cover stories were relatively new. Today, it's the tools of online data collection that are relatively new. For most researchers, building a successful career will entail at least some reliance on these data collection tools. Thus, in this chapter, we tell the history of academic research with one of the most popular sources for online data: Amazon's Mechanical Turk (MTurk; Buhrmester et al., 2011). We describe how MTurk operates, highlight its strengths, outline its weaknesses, and offer tips to effectively use MTurk in social and behavioral research.

What Is Mechanical Turk?

MTurk is a platform built on a simple idea: even in a world of increasingly sophisticated technology, there are many things humans do better than computers (Pontin, 2007). MTurk connects people who have tasks that require human thinking (requesters) with others willing to complete those tasks (workers). The tasks requesters post are called human intelligence tasks, or HITs. Requesters decide how much to pay workers for approved tasks and are assessed a fee from Amazon that is sometimes 20% of the worker's compensation but more often 40% (the number depends on how many people complete the assignment).

Most MTurk HITs are not research related. In a typical HIT, workers may transcribe audio to text, identify and record information from images, test a website's functionality, review an app's user experience, or perform some other activity that artificial intelligence is ill-suited to do (see Hitlin, 2016). Many MTurk tasks are posted by computer scientists seeking training data for machine learning – a phenomenon known as human in the loop AI. Other tasks are posted by businesses looking for an affordable way to complete tedious work. Perhaps a third of tasks are from academics conducting human subjects research (Hitlin, 2016). In this case, researchers are "requesters" and participants are the "workers" who complete a study.

After a worker signs up on MTurk, the site looks like an internet forum (see Figure 2.1). Workers can browse or text search for HITs (e.g., search for "survey" to see recent HITs with that keyword). Clicking a HIT displays its instructions and enables workers to "accept" it (i.e., indicate that they wish to complete it). After completing a HIT, workers submit it for the requester's review. Once submitted, the requester can approve or reject the submission; workers are paid for approved tasks and penalized for rejected ones. The penalty for a rejection is not only that workers have payment for the task withheld but also that their reputation suffers – a consequence that can lead to less available HITs in the future.

Workers participate in MTurk tasks for different reasons. Approximately 7% of people view MTurk as a full-time commitment to earn money (Moss et al., 2023; cf. Gray & Suri, 2019). A larger portion of people view MTurk as part-time or gig work, and more than half of people view MTurk as a way to earn extra money during their leisure hours (see Moss et al., 2023). Differences in how people view MTurk lead to

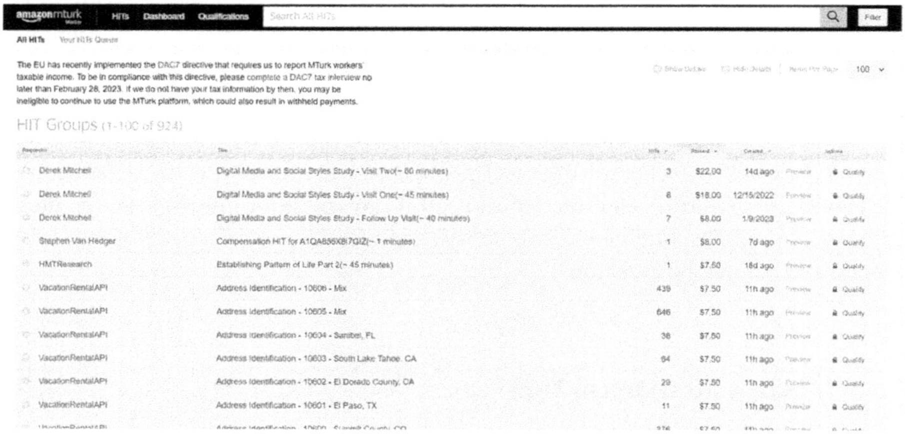

Figure 2.1 *The worker dashboard on MTurk. Each row represents a HIT that can be completed for pay.*

differences in time spent on the site, the share of tasks completed, and earnings (Moss et al., 2023; Robinson, et al., 2019; Kaplan et al., 2018; TurkerView, 2019). The differences among workers are important because they affect the research experience, and in some cases, research output. Beyond these basics, MTurk is a dynamic marketplace where everything – from the type of requester using the site (e.g., business, academic), to the number of active workers and their demographic composition, to the total number of tasks available and the average wage paid – can, and has, changed over time. To show how social and behavioral research fits within the MTurk ecosystem, we begin by describing how researchers interact with MTurk.

How to Use MTurk for Research

Using MTurk for research requires understanding how to navigate the MTurk interface. There are two ways to do this. The first is with MTurk's graphical user interface, or GUI; the second is with MTurk's application programming interface, or API. Both allow requesters to post HITs (for academic researchers, these are often studies or surveys) and manage workers but vary in the functionality and skill required to use them.

MTurk's GUI is a point-and-click system with basic tools (Figure 2.2). A requester can, for example, program a rudimentary survey or insert a URL to an external survey platform (e.g., Qualtrics). The requester can also specify how long the study lasts, how much it pays, how many people can complete it, and whether people need qualifications – the system MTurk uses to make things like demographic targeting possible. Afterward, the requester can post the study and gather data (see Robinson & Litman, 2020 for a guide to posting studies on MTurk).

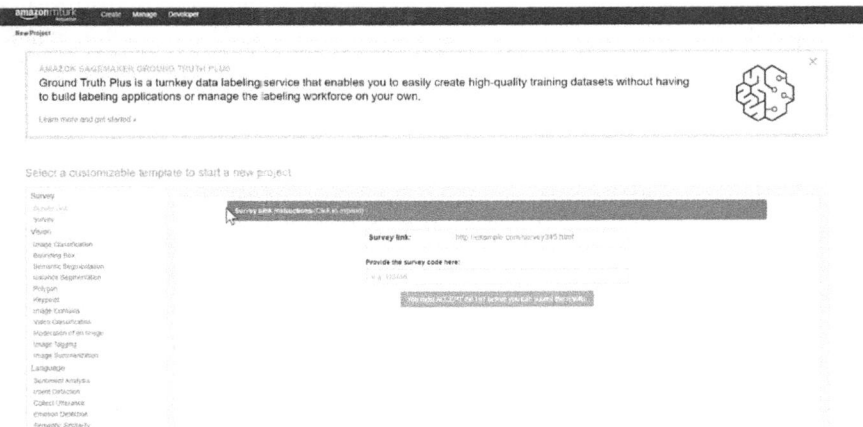

Figure 2.2 *The MTurk graphical user interface. This point-and-click system can be used to create several basic HITs.*

```
# Create the HIT
response = client.create_hit(
    MaxAssignments=3,
    LifetimeInSeconds=600,
    AssignmentDurationInSeconds=600,
    Reward=mturk_environment['reward'],
    Title='Answer a simple question',
    Keywords='question, answer, research',
    Description='Answer a simple question. Created from
    mturk-code-samples.',
    Question=question_sample,
    QualificationRequirements=worker_requirements,
)
```

Figure 2.3 *Example code that can be sent to MTurk via API to execute actions like launching a HIT.*

Using MTurk's API (Figure 2.3) requires the same specifications (i.e., inputting things like the number of participants allowed and how much the study pays), but requesters communicate these details with command line code. In addition, the API gives requesters access to advanced features not available through the GUI. For example, if a requester wants to email participants to let them know a new study is available, the GUI allows sending one email to one participant at a time. Through the API, however, the requester can send thousands of emails to thousands of participants simultaneously. The API also allows requesters to schedule a study launch time, automate participant approvals, easily control study eligibility, and tap several other features that increase MTurk's functionality.

The problem with having so much functionality in an API, however, is that most social and behavioral scientists do not code. Even with increasing numbers of researchers learning to code for data analysis and other applications, most research teams are still comprised of people with advanced knowledge in research methods, statistics, and the theories of human or animal behavior but not computer coding languages. Thus, for most people, MTurk's advanced features are inaccessible.

Third-party services help bridge this gap. Organizations such as psiTurk, CloudResearch, RTurk, Positly, FindingFive, and others have built GUIs that interface with MTurk to facilitate research. Some services are open access, and others are for-profit. In nearly all cases, however, third parties increase MTurk's functionality by presenting researchers with a point-and-click system that communicates with MTurk's API or simplifies API interactions via some other means. Additionally, because many third-party services were created with behavioral scientists in mind, they often address concerns behavioral researchers have in ways MTurk does not (e.g., data quality filters, simple inclusion/exclusion of participants based on completing prior studies, anonymization).

To illustrate the advantages of third-party applications, consider CloudResearch (formerly TurkPrime; Litman et al., 2017). Over the past six years, approximately 10,000 researchers have used CloudResearch to conduct over 300,000 MTurk studies with approximately 500,000 participants and over 50 million completed assignments. CloudResearch enjoys such popularity because it offers a simple user interface along with functionality that makes MTurk more flexible for a fee of 10% of each participant's compensation. CloudResearch also maintains a detailed database of MTurk activity that allows researchers to target studies toward participants based on hundreds of characteristics. Using its database, CloudResearch shares information with researchers about important issues such as sampling, participant demographics, research ethics, data quality, and other topics (e.g., Fordsham et al., 2019; Hauser et al., 2022; Litman et al., 2021; Moss et al., 2023; Robinson et al., 2019).

Finally, CloudResearch can rapidly respond to changes on MTurk. After Amazon increased its service fee to 40% for HITs with more than 10 assignments in 2015 (i.e., studies that recruit at least 10 participants), CloudResearch introduced "batching" tools to ensure researchers paid only 20%. Shortly after concerns with data quality emerged in 2018 (e.g., Bai, 2018), CloudResearch instituted a participant vetting system that provides significantly better data quality than MTurk alone (e.g., Berry et al., 2022; Hauser et al., 2022; Rivera et al., 2022). In these ways and others, third-party applications enable better research on MTurk.

Regardless of how researchers access MTurk, there are many ways to use it. Researchers can, for example, gather survey and experimental data (e.g., Buhrmester et al., 2011; Horton et al., 2011; Mullinix et al., 2015). They can also conduct ethnographic interviews, ask people to participate in user experience tests, recruit panels for longitudinal research, have people annotate text for linguistic analysis, pair people up for interactive tasks or conversations, ask people to code open-ended data, have couples participate in studies together, draw on participants as research assistants, and have people participate in experience sampling or daily diary studies along with many, many other types of tasks (Arechar et al., 2018; Boynton & Richman, 2014; Campbell & Reiman, 2022; Gallo & Gran-Ruaz, 2021; Garbinsky et al., 2020; Hall et al., 2020; Kittur et al., 2008). In fact, if a task can be adapted to the internet and researchers can maintain data quality, then the study can probably be conducted on MTurk.

The control MTurk offers researchers is one reason why it was initially so appealing. With other platforms, such as market research panels, researchers do not control study compensation, cannot communicate with participants, and have fewer options for tailoring data collection (see Chandler et al., 2019). Historically, market research panels also bundled services such as survey programming and project management into the cost of gathering data. MTurk allowed researchers to shed those costs, manage their own projects, recruit hundreds of participants for less than a dollar each initially (e.g., Bohannon, 2011), and elicit unprecedented levels of participant engagement by controlling compensation. A typical project for 350 participants that lasts 10 minutes and pays each person $1.50 can be completed for under $700 (Participant costs ($1.50 * 350 = $525) + Service fees (~30% * $525 = $157.50) = Total $682.50). For these reasons, the platform was widely adopted and remains popular today (e.g., Aguinis et al., 2021). Even so, there are some concerns researchers need to be aware of to use MTurk effectively.

Challenges with MTurk

Data Quality

The first question researchers sought to answer about MTurk was whether participants would provide high-quality data. Because online participants are anonymous and researchers cannot control the study environment, there was initially concern that the noise to signal ratio of MTurk studies would be too great. Therefore, several early papers examined data quality (e.g., Buhrmester et al., 2011; Paolacci et al., 2010; Horton et al., 2011).

What these papers demonstrated was that data quality on MTurk was similar to other populations often used by social and behavioral scientists (e.g., college students and community samples). Across many contexts, MTurk participants provided reliable answers to established measures, passed attention-check questions, and replicated psychological effects such as cognitive biases, logical fallacies, and behavior in economic games (e.g., Bohannon, 2011; Buhrmester et al., 2011; Horton et al., 2011; Litman et al., 2015). Perhaps more impressively, researchers were able to collect high-quality reaction time data (e.g., Crump et al., 2013), and when MTurk participants were compared to other samples, MTurkers typically produced higher-quality data (e.g., Clifford & Jerit, 2014; Hauser & Schwarz, 2016; Kees et al., 2017). Thus, despite many researchers' reservations, the data from MTurk appeared to be high-quality.

But, that does not mean there were no issues. Researchers occasionally found participants who appeared to respond randomly (Downs et al., 2010) or who lied to qualify for studies (e.g., Chandler & Paolacci, 2017; Nichols & Edlund, 2020;

Wessling et al., 2017). These issues were usually explained with the idea that no sample source is perfect, and because data-quality problems appeared less common on MTurk than from traditional sample sources, the use of MTurk soared.

Then came a turning point. In the summer of 2018, problems with MTurk data quality increased dramatically (e.g., Ahler et al., 2021; Bai, 2018; Chmielewski & Kucker, 2020; Ryan, 2018). Large percentages of participants began providing nonsense answers to open-ended text box prompts, straightlining through matrix-style questions, and showing evidence of originating from identical geolocations (e.g., the exact same web address). This was (prematurely) dubbed the "bot crisis" and lowered many researchers' confidence in the quality of MTurk data. Even though understanding what changed in 2018 took time, evidence eventually emerged that participants from outside of the US were using technology like virtual private networks to hide their location and access studies meant for people within the US (Dennis et al., 2020; Dennis et al., 2020; Litman et al., 2021; Kennedy et al., 2018). The motive for doing this is presumably financial as a few dollars from MTurk may go a long way in the local economy of people in India, Venezuela, or a host of other countries. Either way, managing the threat of survey fraud – a threat that is not unique to MTurk but affects all online platforms – is something researchers must confront to use MTurk effectively. We return to this topic in the best practices section.

Sample Representativeness

Population Size. Finding out how many participants are active on MTurk has been difficult. Shortly after its launch, Amazon advertised over 500,000 participants. But, as research later revealed, this number may have been more marketing hype than a description of engaged users.

The first attempts to estimate the size of the MTurk participant pool cleverly adapted capture-recapture analysis from fields like ecology and epidemiology. One paper estimated that the average laboratory reaches about 7,500 participants over three months (Stewart et al., 2015). Another paper estimated that 2,000 participants were active at any given moment and roughly 100,000 were active over 28 months (Difallah et al., 2018). Neither of these estimates was close to 500,000. Data from CloudResearch, which maintains a large database of MTurk activity (see Moss et al., 2023 and Robinson et al., 2019), indicate that from 2016 to 2022 there were over 500,000 participants who completed at least one study; in recent years, around 100,000 people have completed HITs annually.

More meaningful than the number of people who complete studies annually, however, is the number of people researchers can sample at any given time. CloudResearch data show that approximately 30,000 participants complete a study on MTurk each month (Moss, 2021; Robinson et al., 2019). From 2016 to 2020, an average of 6,000 new people joined MTurk each month. These numbers indicate that there is a large pool of people on MTurk to draw from and many new people joining the platform each month. But the question remains: who are these people?

Demographic Representation. The broadest question to ask about MTurk demographics concerns the nationality of participants. Even though Amazon allows participants to sign up from anywhere, to be useful for research there needs to be enough people within a country to make sampling several hundred participants possible at any time. The only two countries that reliably meet this criterion are the US and India (see Difallah et al., 2018). Data gathered in English with participants from India have always been of suspect quality (Litman et al., 2015), meaning most research on MTurk samples US participants.

Among US MTurk participants, there is more diversity than is common in either student or community samples (e.g., Berinsky et al., 2012; Buhrmester et al., 2011). Whereas undergraduate samples tend to be 70% female, for instance, the percentage on MTurk is 57% (Robinson et al., 2020). Participants on MTurk are older than undergraduates (Berinsky et al., 2012; Moss et al., 2023; Robinson et al., 2019), more racially and ethnically diverse (e.g., Chandler et al., 2019; Levay et al., 2016), roughly matched to the US population in terms of political party affiliation (a recent improvement over MTurk's early years, see Litman et al., 2021, p. 141), and well dispersed among US states and urban and rural environments (Robinson et al., 2020). Perhaps surprising to some, people on MTurk are slightly more likely to be employed than the population overall, and the distribution of household income is reasonably well matched to the general population except for people making below $20,000 per year (25% of participants on MTurk compared to 21% in the US population) and those making more than $100,000 per year (17% on MTurk versus 30% in the US population).

One important way people on MTurk differ from the general population is age. Only 17% of MTurkers are over 40 compared to 53% in the general population. Younger people are often more educated, more liberal, and less religious than older people in the US, and this is also true when comparing MTurk to the US population (Casey et al., 2017; Hitlin, 2016; Huff & Tingley, 2015; Levay et al., 2016; Robinson et al., 2020; see Tables 2.1 and 2.2). Some differences between MTurk and the US population disappear when age is controlled for (e.g., rates of marriage, see Robinson et al., 2020), but age does not account for all differences (Robinson et al., 2020).

Although continued caution is warranted, the identified demographic differences between MTurk and the US population do not appear to bias most studies. Multiple large-scale investigations have shown that most experimental effects obtained in nationally representative samples replicate on MTurk (Mullinix et al., 2015; Coppock, 2019). In addition, when there are theoretical reasons to believe an effect may be influenced by the demographic composition of people on MTurk, researchers can take steps to address the issue – something we return to in the best practices section.

A final note on participant composition concerns recent inquiries into the psychological characteristics of people on MTurk. Some research suggests people on MTurk may be more conscientious, less agreeable, more neurotic, and more socially anxious than people in the general population (McCredie & Morey, 2019; Miller et al., 2017; Paolacci & Chandler, 2014). Other research indicates that people on

Table 2.1 *Basic demographics*

Age	MTurk	US Population
18–29	32.45	-
30–39	34.05	-
40–49	16.17	-
50–59	10.72	-
60–69	5.11	-
70+	1.50	-
Gender		
Male	43.27	49.5
Female	56.44	50.5
Other	0.30	-
Race		
White	75.01	75.8
Black	12.67	13.6
American Indian or Alaska Native	0.89	1.3
Asian	7.10	6.1
Native Hawaiian or Pacific Islander	0.50	0.3
Other	3.83	2.9
Hispanic		
Yes	11.08	18.9
Highest degree		
No college degree	37.62	51.7
Associate degree	12.92	10.5
Bachelor's degree	34.50	23.5
Graduate degree	14.96	14.4
Marital status		
Married	45.51	47.80
Never married	42.39	33.85
Widowed	1.69	5.65
Separated	1.24	1.9
Divorced	9.17	10.8
Children		
Yes	46.10	40.0
Political party		
Republican	22.35	27
Democrat	38.68	27
Independent	28.77	43
Other	1.64	-
No preference	8.56	-
Political views		
Extremely liberal	9.44	4.2
Liberal	19.04	13
Slightly liberal	14.26	10

Table 2.1 (*cont.*)

Age	MTurk	US Population
Moderate	22.86	22.4
Slightly conservative	12.18	10
Conservative	12.03	18
Extremely conservative	3.88	5.2
I haven't thought about this	6.31	17.2

Note: The MTurk data are from Moss et al. (2023), the only study to gather a stratified random sample from the MTurk population. US population data are from a variety of sources including the US Census, Gallup, and ANES. Anywhere data are missing are instances where we could not find nationally representative data or data in a format to match our MTurk data. In some instances, there are differences between how the question was asked on MTurk and in comparison sources. US Census data on degree obtainment is only based on adults aged 25 or older; the MTurk data is based on all respondents. Similarly, Census data on households with children is based on children under the age of 18; MTurk data is based on all respondents.

Table 2.2 *Annual household income for Mechanical Turk and the US population*

Annual household income	MTurk	CPS (2018)
< $10 k	6.31	5.93
$10 k–$19,999	6.60	8.77
$20 k–$29,999	11.67	8.66
$30 k–$39,999	10.82	8.73
$40 K–$49,999	11.02	7.80
$50 k–$59,999	11.22	7.56
$60 k–$69,999	7.94	6.69
$70 k–$79,999	7.30	6.02
$80 k–$89,999	5.06	4.98
$90 k–$99,999	5.16	4.42
$100 k–$149 k	11.97	14.95
>$150 k	4.92	15.47

Note: This table is reprinted from Moss et al. (2023); they gathered a stratified random sample from the MTurk population. CPS = Current Population Survey, the primary source of labor force statistics for the US population. CPS data are based on 2018 income.

MTurk may be more prone to depression and negative health behaviors (Ophir et al., 2020; Walters et al., 2018). However, such comparisons are more speculative than demographic comparisons because there is less precise population data about psychological characteristics. For example, some of these characteristics may vary by the time of day and day of the week when a sample is gathered (e.g., Arechar et al.,

2017; Casey et al., 2017; Fordsham et al., 2019). There is still more work to be done to understand if and how these differences affect study results.

Experience and Non-naivete. MTurk presents a special case of what researchers call non-naivete or participant experience. Participants who have been on MTurk since its early days may have completed thousands or even tens of thousands of studies. Although this amount of experience is not typical, it is possible that a participant's repeated exposure to common manipulations and measures may make them "bad" for the purposes of a study (e.g., Chandler et al., 2015; Hauser et al., 2022).

Evidence currently indicates that non-naivete is a problem for research only some of the time (Benndorf et al., 2017; Chandler et al., 2015; Hauser et al., 2019; Rand, 2018; Zwaan et al., 2018). As with external validity, it is worth being cautious about non-naivete (see Hauser et al., 2019), but some research paradigms appear more susceptible than others. For example, evidence suggests that the effects of non-naivete are likely to emerge in measures that rely on ability (e.g., Thomson & Oppenheimer, 2016; cf. Stagnaro et al., 2018), intuition (Rand, 2018), or decision-making, especially when participants are assigned to different between-subjects conditions in the same experiment and the delay between exposures is short (Chandler et al., 2014). In other paradigms, participants may show practice effects such as when people who are asked to answer questions under time pressure get more efficient over time. As with laboratory research, studies that involve deception can probably be conducted only once before people get suspicious. Beyond these documented instances of non-naivete, however, there is ample research suggesting that prior exposure does not matter (e.g., Krupnikov & Levine, 2014; Robinson et al., 2019; Zwaan et al., 2018). Even so, the effect of non-naivete is something researchers must carefully consider with each study (see Hauser et al., 2019).

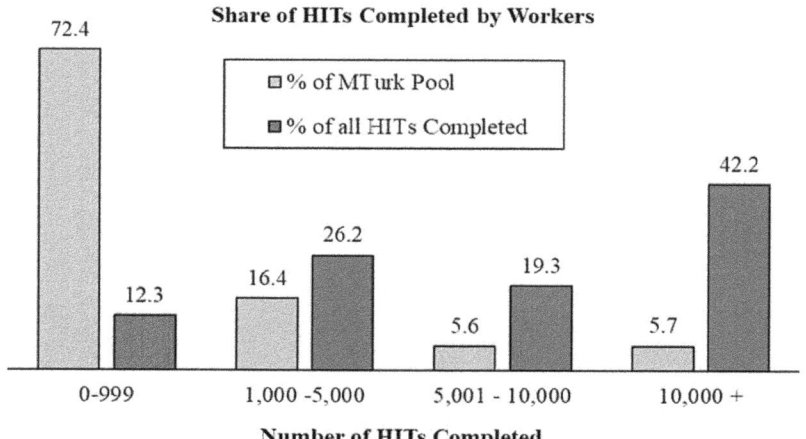

Figure 2.4 *MTurk participant activity as a share of worker experience.*
Note: *This figure is reprinted from Robinson et al. (2019). Data are from CloudResearch.*

These considerations carry extra weight in the context of data about participant activity. Less than 6% of MTurk participants completed approximately 40% of studies through 2018 (Robinson et al., 2019; see Figure 2.4). Meanwhile, the largest group of people on MTurk – those with less than 1,000 previous HITs – completed only about 12% of studies. Participants who complete many studies are not only accumulating experience but also likely learning how MTurk operates, finding ways to be more efficient (e.g., Kaplan et al., 2018), and possibly engaging in conversation with other participants (an issue called study crosstalk, see Edlund et al., 2017). Crosstalk can be especially damaging if participants share study critical information, but researchers may reduce crosstalk by asking participants not to discuss the study and providing a debriefing about the importance of avoiding crosstalk (Edlund et al., 2017; Edlund et al., 2014).

Although participant non-naivete looks severe on MTurk, the situation may be exacerbated by decisions researchers make when sampling. Specifically, in Robinson et al.'s (2019) analysis, 35% of MTurk participants had less than 100 HITs completed. Because researchers often require MTurk participants to have at least 100 previous HITs and at least a 95% approval rating (see Peer et al., 2014), a large percentage of naive participants were *locked out* of studies, not just beaten out by more active participants. Things do not need to be this way. Multiple studies have found that inexperienced MTurk participants (generally defined as those with 100 HITs or less) provide quality data comparable to that from more experienced participants (Meyers et al., 2020; Robinson et al., 2019). Thus, the problem of non-naivete could be less severe if researchers changed sampling practices by dropping reputation qualifications or instituting quotas based on participant experience.

Ethics

Perhaps the central ethical issue raised about MTurk has been that participants are vulnerable to exploitation. Most concerns about exploitation have centered on financial precarity (Fort et al., 2011; Paolacci et al., 2010; Williamson, 2016), but some have included physical disability and mental health (e.g., Mehrotra, 2020). Despite years of discussion, debate, and investigation among academics, the picture many people hold of MTurk is shaped by what is presented in the news (e.g., Newman, 2019; Semuels, 2018). For instance, a prominent article in *The Atlantic* characterized MTurk as a poorly paid hell that forces people with no other options for earning money into digital piece work (Semuels, 2018).

A problem with these depictions is that the methods used to understand MTurk are susceptible to biases that can yield an unrepresentative picture. For example, participants who agree to be interviewed are a self-selected sample. Interviews, by nature, preclude talking with a large swath of participants – something necessary for representation. Surveys can reach participants at scale, but the way MTurk operates – leaving studies open on a first-come-first-served basis – means that, without a representative sampling strategy, researchers will have results biased toward the most active participants who select into the survey.

In contrast to popular portrayals of MTurk, a probability-based survey with representative results found that few MTurkers experience exploitation or financial precarity (Moss et al., 2023). Using CloudResearch as a sampling frame, Moss et al. (2023) gathered a stratified random sample of MTurk workers and asked about a wide range of issues, including financial precarity, reasons for spending time on MTurk, wages, and other topics. The results revealed that people on MTurk were largely in similar financial conditions as people in the general population. Furthermore, people on MTurk were not disproportionately likely to report a physical or mental disability. Thus, these findings suggest that popular characterizations of MTurk may be disproportionate to reality.

A second ethical issue involving MTurk concerns wages. Discussions about wages are often buttressed with assumptions about who participants are, why they are on MTurk, and their financial circumstances. Nevertheless, the wages paid to participants are often a flashpoint in debates about MTurk (e.g., Newman, 2019), and because many tasks are known to pay a small amount of money (e.g., Paolacci et al., 2010), most people assumed that participants made little – maybe a dollar or two per hour. However, when Pew investigated MTurk in 2016, around half of US-based participants said they made less than $5 per hour, while nearly 40% reported earning between $5 and $7.99 per hour, and 8% of people said they earned more than $8 per hour (Hitlin, 2016). Additionally, a large analysis of real wages based on API data from a worker-run group showed that its members earned more than $20 per hour (TurkerView, 2019). The representative sample from Moss et al. (2023) reported that, across all levels of worker experience, it is possible for MTurkers to earn *at least* $8.97 per hour, with more experienced participants reporting wages in the range of $25 per hour. Finally, the Fair Crowd Work organization – a group that collects data about online platforms and supports crowd work unionization – also places MTurk wages near $11 per hour for experienced participants (Fair Crowd Work, n.d.).

Not all research agrees with these estimates, however. A notable exception is Hara et al. (2018) who developed a browser plug-in that tracked participants' time on MTurk and HIT activity. From this data, they calculated median hourly earnings of less than $2 per hour. Even though their data have been widely cited, there are several reasons to question how well the data represent the MTurk population. First, Hara et al.'s findings are significantly lower than all other sources, raising the possibility that they may be an outlier. Second, they report *no* demographic information about participants or how they were recruited – extraordinary omissions for a paper many people assume *represents* wages on MTurk. Finally, the analysis includes a potential outlier among requesters (one requester posted more than 10% of all tasks). For all these reasons, it is worth questioning how well the Hara data represent MTurkers overall while also acknowledging the value of the approach and the difficulty of calculating hourly wages on a microtask platform (see Moss et al., 2023).

A final ethical criticism often made of MTurk concerns how participants are treated by requesters. Similar to the narrative about financial precarity, various reports from academic and popular press pieces have described MTurk as an unfair and possibly even abusive environment. Many accounts of worker mistreatment stem from disagreements with requesters (e.g., disagreement over a rejection) or negligence on the part of requesters that wind up costing participants time or money. More concerning, some reports suggest that participants are subjected to abusive conditions, especially within content moderation tasks (e.g., YouTube may have asked participants to view potentially disturbing content; see Matsakis, 2018) or some academic studies. There are also frequent complaints about indifference from Amazon when requesters or workers misuse the platform.

What is often missing from popular press pieces is an analysis of how often participants have negative experiences. According to data from Moss et al. (2020), people's positive experiences on MTurk far outnumber negative ones. Participants reported that they seldom have HITs rejected, encounter disturbing content, or have negative interactions with requesters. In fact, participants rated requesters on MTurk as fairer and more honest than employers outside of MTurk. Thus, like other ethical issues, it appears that criticisms of MTurk are disproportionate to the reality of people's experiences.

Of course, a lack of widespread mistreatment does not alleviate researchers from the obligation to ensure participants are treated with respect and that studies adhere to the principles of ethical research. Several aspects of the online environment make conducting research difficult and communication with participants challenging. Online platforms often have norms for payment, study setup, and participant expectations. Researchers should ensure they are aware of these norms and strive to treat participants with the same respect that participants in other settings receive. Several publications discuss how to ensure the ethical treatment of online research participants (e.g., Litman & Robinson, 2020b).

Best Practices for MTurk Research

Managing Data Quality

If data quality on MTurk is a challenge, how can researchers reliably use MTurk for research? Luckily, there are a few strategies to implement. Perhaps the easiest solution is to use a vetted pool of participants. Since 2020, CloudResearch has conducted a meticulous vetting of nearly all worker accounts on MTurk. This vetting consists of running participants through various data-quality measures and examining researcher-generated data about which participants have provided suspect data in the past (see Litman et al., 2020; Hauser et al., 2022). Together, these measures allow CloudResearch to remove the most problematic participants on MTurk and significantly improve the quality of data researchers can gather (see Hauser et al., 2022; Rivera et al., 2022). Moreover, because the measures were carefully validated before being put into practice, they do not harm demographic diversity or result in a pool of overly experienced participants (e.g., Hauser et al., 2022).

A second way to manage data quality is to selectively recruit proficient participants. For several years this was recommended practice on MTurk (see Hauser et al.,

2019) because of research indicating that participants with at least a 95% approval rating and at least 100 HITs completed provided better data quality than those who had not met these reputation criteria (see Peer et al., 2014). However, recent research has shown that the relationship between MTurk reputation and data quality is more complicated, and the "95% approval rating and 100 completed HITs" restriction is insufficient for maintaining data quality today (for a more detailed explanation why this is the case, see Hauser et al., 2022). Higher reputation qualifications can still lead to quality data, but as requirements increase, researchers draw from a smaller and smaller pool of participants (see Robinson et al., 2019).

Finally, the most time-consuming and effortful option is for researchers to institute defensive measures to maintain data quality. Often these measures are intended to prevent low-quality participants from entering the survey (e.g., block them) or identify the data of low-quality participants to exclude from data analyses. These measures include scanning IP addresses, implementing attention-check questions, using open-ended items, examining synonym-antonym pairs, examining checks of cultural knowledge, and using checks of language proficiency (see Burleigh et al., 2018; Hauser et al., 2019; Litman et al., 2021). Most researchers who take this approach elect to identify and exclude low-quality data. This requires that, after the data are collected, researchers sift through the responses and decide whom to approve and whom to reject. Anyone who provides unusable data or shows clear evidence of not taking the survey seriously by straightlining, providing gibberish open-ended responses, or submitting the survey with no data at all is a candidate for rejection.

Although this approach may sound like standard practice for many researchers, the hardest part of this strategy is often selecting data quality measures and setting criteria for what warrants exclusion *before* the study is conducted. As pointed out elsewhere, there is little consensus or empirical evidence about which measures do the best job of detecting participants who provide low-quality data (Hauser et al., 2019; Hauser et al., 2022). Once a useful measure is introduced, researchers tend to recycle it to the point that participants learn which response will allow them to pass the check without necessarily providing effort or attention throughout the entire survey (Hauser & Schwarz, 2016). Interrogating data quality for a whole sample is also time-consuming, even if valuable. Researchers must compute several statistics, examine various reports, and then decide how many participants to exclude from the analyses. If enough participants are discarded, more data may need to be gathered, consuming more time. For this reason, most researchers will find using a combination of the three strategies outlined here – relying on a vetted sample, using some reputation qualifications, and measuring data within the survey – most effective.

Demographics and Sampling

As outlined above, a lot is known about how participants on MTurk compare to the US population. Whenever researchers are concerned about some variable's potential to skew research findings, there are two courses of action. First, by measuring characteristics where MTurk is known to deviate from the general population, researchers can control for the biasing effects of an unrepresentative sample after the data are collected using survey weighting (e.g., Levay et al., 2016). Second, when possible, researchers may choose to stratify their sample during data collection. Doing so can bring samples from MTurk more in line with the US population along critical dimensions.

For example, one experimental effect that has notably failed to replicate on MTurk is the "God on Our Side" manipulation (Converse & Epley, 2007; Mullinix et al., 2015). In this paradigm, participants are asked about their support for abortion and are randomly assigned to express their opinion either before or after contemplating God's opinion about abortion. People assigned to think about God's view first generally support abortion less than those assigned to express their personal view first. This effect presumably fails on MTurk because people are substantially less religious on MTurk than in the general population. However, when participants are sampled from MTurk so that the overall level of religious affiliation matches the general population (i.e., when the sample is stratified), the effect replicates (Litman, 2019). Similar sampling strategies can be employed when researchers have theoretical reasons to believe participants from MTurk are different than the population of interest.

Ethics

Conducting ethical research on MTurk is much like conducting ethical research in the lab. The important differences are that researchers need to pay within platform norms (currently about $7.50/hour on MTurk), promptly respond to communications from participants, explain the reason for rejections or exclusions, and work to ensure survey links and tasks are working properly before launching. Given the lack of contact between researchers and participants, researchers should understand how even honest mistakes can degrade the participant experience. Despite the challenges, it is possible to conduct research that respects participants, protects their data and privacy, and adheres to the ethical standards that most behavioral organizations expect (see Litman & Robinson, 2020a).

Final Thoughts

We believe MTurk has great potential for researchers across the social and behavioral sciences. As in its early days, MTurk remains a useful platform for quick data that provide insight into how people think about a topic, respond to experimental manipulations, or behave in various situations. MTurk gives researchers access to a sizable pool of people, tools for controlling studies, and the ability to engender unprecedented levels of participant engagement. Moreover, MTurk is affordable for most researchers. Getting the most out of MTurk entails understanding its strengths and weaknesses and launching studies that maximize those strengths while eliminating or minimizing the weaknesses.

MTurk's strengths lie in its flexibility and ability to elicit participant engagement. Especially when compared to market research panels, MTurk participants are more willing to engage in long, demanding, or unusual activities. This engagement allows researchers to push the boundaries of online data collection. For instance, in the last few years, researchers have paired participants with strangers and asked them to discuss contentious political issues, studied face touching and eye tracking via video interview (Keller et al., 2021), and completed intensive longitudinal studies that are simply unfeasible without a site such as MTurk (see Moss, 2022). When studies draw on MTurk's strengths, they allow researchers to gather meaningful data with fewer barriers than offline data collection. In some cases (particularly for researchers at smaller institutions or for early career researchers with smaller budgets), MTurk can make research projects possible that would be completely infeasible in the laboratory. This is where MTurk is at its best.

The challenges with MTurk include studies that rely on complex demographic targeting or try to make descriptive statements about the general population. As a site with roughly 30,000 participants per month, MTurk does not have enough people to make niche sampling possible (Chandler et al., 2019). Even though researchers can employ quotas to control sample composition, people on MTurk deviate from the general population in ways that make generalizing descriptive results a dubious endeavor. Thus, when researchers need to gather niche samples or are interested in making broad statements about the population, they may be better off conducting their study with platforms better suited to those purposes (see Chandler et al., 2019, for alternatives).

Conclusion

Several things contribute to a successful research career, but an often overlooked factor is discernment. Researchers must constantly decide which projects to pursue and which to prioritize, which ideas are likely to have an impact and which are passing fancies, which collaborations are worthwhile and which are not. After deciding what is worth doing, researchers are confronted with *how* to do it. Given the limits on time, resources, and energy, most researchers turn to online sources for data collection because it is fast and relatively affordable. MTurk has been an especially common choice of participants over the last decade. Moving forward, MTurk can continue to play an important role in the social and behavioral sciences, but it will be most effective when researchers exercise the discernment to match MTurk's strengths with the aims of their study. When researchers exercise such judgment, MTurk can serve as a versatile tool that contributes to a successful research career.

References

Aguinis, H., Villamor, I., & Ramani, R. S. (2021). MTurk research: Review and recommendations. *Journal of Management, 47*(4), 823–837. https://doi.org/10.1177/0149206320969787

Ahler, D. J., Roush, C. E., & Sood, G. (2021). The micro-task market for lemons: Data quality on Amazon's Mechanical Turk. *Political Science Research and Methods*, 1–20. https://doi.org/10.1017/psrm.2021.57

American National Election Studies. (2020). *The ANES Guide to Public Opinion and Electoral Behavior.* https://electionstudies.org/data-tools/anes-guide/anes-guide.html?chart=lib_con_identification_7_pt

Arechar, A. A., Gächter, S., & Molleman, L. (2018). Conducting interactive experiments online. *Experimental Economics*, *21*(1), 99–131. https://doi.org/10.1007/s10683-017-9527-2

Arechar, A. A., Kraft-Todd, G. T., & Rand, D. G. (2017). Turking overtime: How participant characteristics and behavior vary over time and day on Amazon Mechanical Turk. *Journal of the Economic Science Association*, *3*(1), 1–11. https://doi.org/10.1007/s40881-017-0035-0

Bai, H. (2018, August 8). Evidence that a large amount of low quality responses on MTurk can be detected with repeated GPS coordinates. *MaxHuiBai.com*. www.maxhuibai.com/blog/evidence-that-responses-from-repeating-gps-are-random

Barr, J. (2011, June 23). Get better results with Amazon Mechanical Turk Masters. *Amazon Web Services.* https://aws.amazon.com/blogs/aws/amazon-mechanical-turk-master-workers

Benndorf, V., Moellers, C., & Normann, H.-T. (2017). Experienced vs. inexperienced participants in the lab: Do they behave differently? *Journal of the Economic Science Association*, *3*(1), 12–25. https://doi.org/10.1007/s40881-017-0036-z

Berinsky, A. J., Huber, G. A., & Lenz, G. S. (2012). Evaluating online labor markets for experimental research: Amazon.com's Mechanical Turk. *Political Analysis*, *20*(3), 351–368. https://doi.org/10.1093/pan/mpr057

Berry, C., Kees, J., & Burton, S. (2022). Drivers of data quality in advertising research: Differences across MTurk and professional panel samples. *Journal of Advertising*, *51*(4), 1–15. https://doi.org/10.1080/00913367.2022.2079026

Bohannon, J. (2011). Social science for pennies. *Science*, *334*(6054), 307. https://doi.org/10.1126/science.334.6054.307

Boynton, M. H., & Richman, L. S. (2014). An online daily diary study of alcohol use using Amazon's Mechanical Turk. *Drug and Alcohol Review*, *33*(4), 456–461. https://doi.org/10.1111/dar.12163

Buchanan, E. A., & Hvizdak, E. E. (2009). Online survey tools: Ethical and methodological concerns of human research ethics committees. *Journal of Empirical Research on Human Research Ethics*, *4*(2), 37–48. https://doi.org/10.1525/jer.2009.4.2.37

Buhrmester, M. D., Kwang, T., & Gosling, S. D. (2011). Amazon's Mechanical Turk: A new source of inexpensive, yet high-quality, data? *Perspectives on Psychological Science*, *6*(1), 3–5. https://doi.org/10.1177/1745691610393980

Buhrmester, M. D., Talaifar, S., & Gosling, S. D. (2018). An evaluation of Amazon's Mechanical Turk, its rapid rise, and its effective use. *Perspectives on Psychological Science*, *13*(2), 149–154. https://doi.org/10.1177/1745691617706516

Burleigh, T., Kennedy, R., & Clifford, S. (2018). How to screen out VPS and international respondents using qualtrics: A protocol. *SSRN*, 3265459. https://papers.ssrn.com/abstract=3265459

Campbell, D. S., & Reiman, A.-K. (2022). Has social psychology lost touch with reality? Exploring public perceptions of the realism and consequentiality of social psychological research. *Journal of Experimental Social Psychology*, *98*, 104255. https://doi.org/10.1016/j.jesp.2021.104255

Casey, L. S., Chandler, J., Levine, A. S., Proctor, A., & Strolovitch, D. Z. (2017). Intertemporal differences among MTurk workers: Time-based sample variations and implications for online data collection. *SAGE Open*, *7*(2), 215824401771277. https://doi.org/10.1177/2158244017712774

Chandler, J. J., & Paolacci, G. (2017). Lie for a dime: When most prescreening responses are honest but most study participants are impostors. *Social Psychological and Personality Science*, *8*(5), 500–508. https://doi.org/10.1177/1948550617698203

Chandler, J. J., Paolacci, G., Peer, E., Mueller, P., & Ratliff, K. A. (2015). Using nonnaive participants can reduce effect sizes. *Psychological Science*, *26*(7), 1131–1139. https://doi.org/10.1177/0956797615585115

Chandler, J. J., Rosenzweig, C., Moss, A. J., Robinson, J., & Litman, L. (2019). Online panels in social science research: Expanding sampling methods beyond Mechanical Turk. *Behavior Research Methods*, *51*(5), 2022–2038. https://doi.org/10.3758/s13428-019-01273-7

Chandler, J., Sisso, I., & Shapiro, D. (2020). Participant carelessness and fraud: Consequences for clinical research and potential solutions. *Journal of Abnormal Psychology*, *129*(1), 49–55. https://doi.org/10.1037/abn0000479

Chmielewski, M., & Kucker, S. C. (2020). An MTurk crisis? Shifts in data quality and the impact on study results. *Social Psychological and Personality Science*, *11*(4), 464–473. https://doi.org/10.1177/1948550619875149

Clifford, S., & Jerit, J. (2014). Is there a cost to convenience? An experimental comparison of data quality in laboratory and online studies. *Journal of Experimental Political Science*, *1*(2), 120–131. https://doi.org/10.1017/xps.2014.5

Converse, B. A., & Epley, N. (2007). With God on our side. *TESS: Time-Sharing Experiments for the Social Sciences*. www.tessexperiments.org/study/converse561

Coppock, A. (2019). Generalizing from survey experiments conducted on Mechanical Turk: A replication approach. *Political Science Research and Methods*, *7*(3), 613–628. https://doi.org/10.1017/psrm.2018.10

Crump, M. J. C., McDonnell, J. V., & Gureckis, T. M. (2013). Evaluating Amazon's Mechanical Turk as a tool for experimental behavioral research. *PLOS ONE*, *8*(3), e57410. https://doi.org/10.1371/journal.pone.0057410

Dennis, J. M. (2001). Are internet panels creating professional respondents? *Marketing Research*, *13*(2), 34–38.

Dennis, S. A., Goodson, B. M., & Pearson, C. (2020). Online worker fraud and evolving threats to the integrity of MTurk data: A discussion of virtual private servers and the limitations of IP-based screening procedures. *Behavioral Research in Accounting*, *32*(1), 119–134.

Difallah, D., Filatova, E., & Ipeirotis, P. (2018). Demographics and dynamics of Mechanical Turk workers. In Y. Chang (ed.) *Proceedings of the Eleventh ACM International Conference on Web Search and Data Mining* (pp. 135–143). ACM. https://doi.org/10.1145/3159652.3159661

Downs, J. S., Holbrook, M. B., Sheng, S., & Cranor, L. F. (2010, April). Are your participants gaming the system? Screening Mechanical Turk workers. In J. Kaye (ed.), *Proceedings of the 2016 CHI Conference on Human Factors in Computing Systems* (pp. 2399–2402). ACM.

Edlund, J. E., Lange, K. M., Sevene, A. M., Umansky, J., Beck, C. D., & Bell, D. J. (2017). Participant crosstalk: Issues when using the Mechanical Turk. *Tutorials in Quantitative Methods for Psychology, 13*(3), 174–182. http://dx.doi.org/10.20982/tqmp.13.3.p174

Edlund, J. E., Nichols, A. L., Okdie, B. M., Guadagno, R. E., Eno, C. A., Heider, J. D., et al. (2014). The prevalence and prevention of crosstalk: A multi-institutional study. *Journal of Social Psychology, 154*(3), 181–185. https://doi.org/10.1080/00224545.2013.872596

Enyon, R., Fry, J., & Schroeder, R. (2016). The ethics of online research. In N. G. Fielding, R. M. Lee, & G. Blank (eds.), *The SAGE Handbook of Online Research Methods* (pp. 19–37). SAGE Publications.

Fair Crowd Work. (n.d.). Amazon Mechanical Turk. http://faircrowd.work/platform/amazon-mechanical-turk (retrieved June 9, 2022).

Fordsham, N., Moss, A. J., Krumholtz, S., Roggina, T., Robinson, J., & Litman, L. (2019). Variation among Mechanical Turk Workers across time of day presents an opportunity and a challenge for research [preprint]. *PsyArXiv*. https://doi.org/10.31234/osf.io/p8bns

Fort, K., Adda, G., & Bretonnel Cohen, K. (2011). Amazon Mechanical Turk: Gold mine or coal mine? *Computational Linguistics, 37*(2), 413–420. https://doi.org/10.1162/COLI_a_00057

Gallo, J., & Gran-Ruaz, S. (2021, October 1). Racial *trauma scale*: Creative interview strategies employed in the development of a new clinical tool for measuring race-based stress and trauma. CloudResearch Innovations in Online Research Conference (virtual). www.youtube.com/watch?v=hKCK_dWfUfI&t=1568s

Gallup News. (2007, September 20). Party affiliation. https://news.gallup.com/poll/15370/Party-Affiliation.aspx

Garbinsky, E. N., Gladstone, J. J., Nikolova, H., & Olson, J. G. (2020). Love, lies, and money: Financial infidelity in romantic relationships. *Journal of Consumer Research, 47*(1), 1–24. https://doi.org/10.1093/jcr/ucz052

Gray, M. L., & Suri, S. (2019). *Ghost Work: How to Stop Silicon Valley from Building a New Global Underclass*. Houghton Mifflin Harcourt.

Haggbloom, S. J., Warnick, R., Warnick, J. E., Jones, V. K., Yarbrough, G. L., Russell, T. M., et al. (2002). The 100 most eminent psychologists of the 20th century. *Review of General Psychology, 6*(2), 139–152. https://doi.org/10.1037/1089-2680.6.2.139

Hall, M. P., Lewis Jr., N. A., Chandler, J., & Litman, L. (2020). Conducting longitudinal research on Amazon Mechanical Turk. In L. Litman & J. Robinson (eds.), *Conducting Online Research on Amazon Mechanical Turk and Beyond* (pp. 198–216). SAGE Publications.

Hara, K., Adams, A., Milland, K., Savage, S., Callison-Burch, C., & Bigham, J. P. (2018). A data-driven analysis of workers' earnings on Amazon Mechanical Turk. In *Proceedings of the 2018 CHI Conference on Human Factors in Computing Systems* (pp. 1–14). ACM. https://doi.org/10.1145/3173574.3174023

Hauser, D. J., Moss, A. J., Rosenzweig, C., Jaffe, S., & Robinson, J. (2022). Evaluating CloudResearch's approved group as a solution for problematic data quality on MTurk. *Behavioral Research Methods, 55*(8), 3953–3964. https://doi.org/10.31234/osf.io/48yxj

Hauser, D. J., Paolacci, G., & Chandler, J. (2019). Common concerns with MTurk as a participant pool: Evidence and solutions. In F. R. Kardes, P. M. Herr, &

N. Schwarz (eds.), *Handbook of Research Methods in Consumer Psychology* (pp. 319–337). Routledge.

Hauser, D. J., & Schwarz, N. (2016). Attentive Turkers: MTurk participants perform better on online attention checks than do subject pool participants. *Behavior Research Methods*, *48*(1), 400–407. https://doi.org/10.3758/s13428-015-0578-z

Hillyguys, D. S., Jackson, N., & Young, M. (2014). Professional respondents in non-probability online panels. In M. Callegaro et al. (eds.), *Online Panel Research: A Data Quality Perspective*, 1st ed. (pp. 219–237). Wiley.

Hitlin, P. (2016). Research in the crowdsourcing age, a case study. *Pew Research Center*. www.pewresearch.org/internet/2016/07/11/what-is-mechanical-turk

Horton, J. J., Rand, D. G., & Zeckhauser, R. J. (2011). The online laboratory: Conducting experiments in a real labor market. *Experimental Economics*, *14*(3), 399–425. https://doi.org/10.1007/s10683-011-9273-9

Huff, C., & Tingley, D. (2015). "Who are these people?" Evaluating the demographic characteristics and political preferences of MTurk survey respondents. *Research & Politics*, *2*(3), 205316801560464. https://doi.org/10.1177/2053168015604648

Kaplan, T., Saito, S., Hara, K., & Bigham, J. P. (2018, June 15). Striving to earn more: A survey of work strategies and tool use among crowd workers. *Proceedings of the AAAI Conference on Human Computation and Crowdsourcing*, *6*, 70–78. https://doi.org/10.1609/hcomp.v6i1.13327

Kees, J., Berry, C., Burton, S., & Sheehan, K. (2017). An analysis of data quality: Professional panels, student subject pools, and Amazon's Mechanical Turk. *Journal of Advertising*, *46*(1), 141–155. https://doi.org/10.1080/00913367.2016.1269304

Keller, L., Kabengele, M.-C., & Gollwitzer, P. M. (2021). The self-regulation of face touching – a preregistered experiment testing if-then plans as a means to promote COVID-19 prevention. *Psychology & Health*, *38*(8), 1–19. https://doi.org/10.1080/08870446.2021.2005793

Kennedy, R., Clifford, S., Burleigh, T., Waggoner, P., & Jewell, R. (2018). How Venezuela's economic crisis is undermining social science research – about everything. *Washington Post*, November 7, www.washingtonpost.com/news/monkey-cage/wp/2018/11/07/how-the-venezuelan-economic-crisis-is-undermining-social-science-research-about-everything-not-just-venezuela (retrieved May 27, 2022).

Kittur, A., Chi, E. H., & Suh, B. (2008). Crowdsourcing user studies with Mechanical Turk. *CHI '08: Proceedings of the Twenty-Sixth Annual CHI Conference on Human Factors in Computing Systems* (pp. 453–456). ACM. https://doi.org/10.1145/1357054.1357127

Krupnikov, Y., & Levine, A. S. (2014). Cross-sample comparisons and external validity. *Journal of Experimental Political Science*, *1*(1), 59–80. https://doi.org/10.1017/xps.2014.7

Levay, K. E., Freese, J., & Druckman, J. N. (2016). The demographic and political composition of Mechanical Turk samples. *SAGE Open*, *6*(1), 215824401663643. https://doi.org/10.1177/2158244016636433

Litman, L. (2019, May). *Composition of Online Participant Pools Moderates Effect Sizes of Experimental Manipulations*. Association for Psychological Science.

Litman, L., & Robinson, J. (2020a). Conducting ethical online research: A data-driven approach. In L. Litman & J. Robinson (eds.), *Conducting Online Research on Amazon Mechanical Turk and Beyond* (pp. 234–263). SAGE Publications.

Litman, L., & Robinson, J. (2020b). Introduction. In L. Litman & J. Robinson (eds.), *Conducting Online Research on Amazon Mechanical Turk and Beyond* (pp. 1–26). SAGE Publications.

Litman, L., Robinson, J., & Abberbock, T. (2017). TurkPrime.com: A versatile crowdsourcing data acquisition platform for the behavioral sciences. *Behavior Research Methods*, *49*(2), 433–442. https://doi.org/10.3758/s13428-016-0727-z

Litman, L., Robinson, J., & Rosenzweig, C. (2015). The relationship between motivation, monetary compensation, and data quality among US- and India-based workers on Mechanical Turk. *Behavior Research Methods*, *47*(2), 519–528. https://doi.org/10.3758/s13428-014-0483-x

Litman, L., Rosenzweig, C., Jaffe, S. N., Gautam, R., Robinson, J., & Moss, A. J. (2021). Bots or inattentive humans? Identifying sources of low-quality data in online platforms [preprint]. *PsyArXiv*. https://doi.org/10.31234/osf.io/wr8ds

Litman, L., Rosenzweig, C., & Moss, A. J. (2020, July 15). New solutions dramatically improve research data quality on MTurk. *CloudResearch* [blog]. www.cloudresearch.com/resources/blog/new-tools-improve-research-data-quality-mturk

Loepp, E., & Kelly, J. T. (2020). Distinction without a difference? An assessment of MTurk worker types. *Research & Politics*, *7*(1), 2053168019901185. https://doi.org/10.1177/2053168019901185

Matsakis, L. (2018, March 22). A window into how YouTube trains AI to moderate videos. *Wired*. www.wired.com/story/youtube-mechanical-turk-content-moderation-ai

Matthijsse, S. M., de Leeuw, E. D., & Hox, J. J. (2015). Internet panels, professional respondents, and data quality. *Methodology*, *11*(3), 81–88.

McCredie, M. N., & Morey, L. C. (2019). Who are the Turkers? A characterization of MTurk workers using the Personality Assessment Inventory. *Assessment*, *26*(5), 759–766. https://doi.org/10.1177/1073191118760709

Mehrotra, D. (2020). Horror Stories From Inside Amazon's Mechanical Turk. *Gizmodo*, January 28. https://gizmodo.com/horror-stories-from-inside-amazons-mechanical-turk-1840878041

Meyers, E. A., Walker, A. C., Fugelsang, J. A., & Koehler, D. J. (2020). Reducing the number of non-naïve participants in Mechanical Turk samples. *Methods in Psychology*, *3*, 100032. https://doi.org/10.1016/j.metip.2020.100032

Miller, J. D., Crowe, M., Weiss, B., Maples-Keller, J. L., & Lynam, D. R. (2017). Using online, crowdsourcing platforms for data collection in personality disorder research: The example of Amazon's Mechanical Turk. *Personality Disorders: Theory, Research, and Treatment*, *8*(1), 26–34. https://doi.org/10.1037/per0000191

Moss, A. J. (2021, December 1). Five years of Mechanical Turk data in five figures. *CloudResearch* [blog]. www.cloudresearch.com/resources/blog/mechanical-turk-data-five-years-in-five-figures

(2022, March 4). How CloudResearch and IARPA completed the largest longitudinal online research project ever. *CloudResearch* [blog]. www.cloudresearch.com/resources/blog/the-largest-longitudinal-online-research-project

Moss, A. J., Rosenzweig, C., Robinson, J., Jaffe, S. N., & Litman, L. (2023). Is it ethical to use Mechanical Turk for behavioral research? Relevant data from a representative survey of MTurk participants and wages. *Behavior Research Methods*, *55*(8), 4048–4067.

Mullinix, K. J., Leeper, T. J., Druckman, J. N., & Freese, J. (2015). The generalizability of survey experiments. *Journal of Experimental Political Science*, *2*(2), 109–138. https://doi.org/10.1017/XPS.2015.19

Newman, A. (2019, November 15). I found work on an Amazon Website. I made 97 cents an hour. *New York Times*. www.nytimes.com/interactive/2019/11/15/nyregion/amazon-mechanical-turk.html

Nichols, A. L., & Edlund, J. E. (2020). Why don't we care more about carelessness? Understanding the causes and consequences of careless participants. *International Journal of Social Research Methodology*, *23*(6), 625–638. https://doi.org/10.1080/13645579.2020.1719618

Ogletree, A. M., & Katz, B. (2021). How do older adults recruited using MTurk differ from those in a national probability sample? *International Journal of Aging and Human Development*, *93*(2), 700–721. https://doi.org/10.1177/0091415020940197

Ophir, Y., Sisso, I., Asterhan, C. S. C., Tikochinski, R., & Reichart, R. (2020). The Turker blues: Hidden factors behind increased depression rates among Amazon's Mechanical Turkers. *Clinical Psychological Science*, *8*(1), 65–83. https://doi.org/10.1177/2167702619865973

Paolacci, G., & Chandler, J. (2014). Inside the Turk: Understanding Mechanical Turk as a participant pool. *Current Directions in Psychological Science*, *23*(3), 184–188. https://doi.org/10.1177/0963721414531598

Paolacci, G., Chandler, J., & Ipeirotis, P. G. (2010). Running experiments on Amazon Mechanical Turk. *SSRN*, 1626226. https://papers.ssrn.com/abstract=1626226

Peer, E., Vosgerau, J., & Acquisti, A. (2014). Reputation as a sufficient condition for data quality on Amazon Mechanical Turk. *Behavior Research Methods*, *46*(4), 1023–1031. https://doi.org/10.3758/s13428-013-0434-y

Pontin, J. (2007, March 25). Artificial intelligence, with help from the humans. *New York Times*. www.nytimes.com/2007/03/25/business/yourmoney/25Stream.html

Rand, D. G. (2018). Non-naïvety may reduce the effect of intuition manipulations. *Nature Human Behaviour*, *2*(9), 602. https://doi.org/10.1038/s41562-018-0404-6

Rivera, E. D., Wilkowski, B. M., Moss, A. J., Rosenzweig, C., & Litman, L. (2022). Assessing the efficacy of a participant-vetting procedure to improve data-quality on Amazon's Mechanical Turk. *Methodology*, *18*(2), 126–143. https://doi.org/10.5964/meth.8331

Robinson, J., & Litman, L. (2020). Conducting a study on Mechanical Turk. In L. Litman & J. Robinson (eds.), *Conducting Online Research on Amazon Mechanical Turk and Beyond* (pp. 49–78). SAGE Publications.

Robinson, J., Litman, L., & Rosenzweig, C. (2020). Who are the Mechanical Turk workers? In L. Litman & J. Robinson (eds.), *Conducting Online Research on Amazon Mechanical Turk and Beyond* (pp. 121–147). SAGE Publications.

Robinson, J., Rosenzweig, C., Moss, A. J., & Litman, L. (2019). Tapped out or barely tapped? Recommendations for how to harness the vast and largely unused potential of the Mechanical Turk participant pool. *PLOS ONE*, *14*(12), e0226394. https://doi.org/10.1371/journal.pone.0226394

Rouse, S. V. (2020). Reliability of MTurk data from masters and workers. *Journal of Individual Differences*, *41*(1), 30–36. https://doi.org/10.1027/1614-0001/a000300

Ryan, T. J. (2018, August 12). Data contamination on Mturk [blog]. https://timryan.web.unc.edu/2018/08/12/data-contamination-on-mturk

Semuels, A. (2018, January 23). The internet is enabling a new kind of poorly paid hell. *The Atlantic*. www.theatlantic.com/business/archive/2018/01/amazon-mechanical-turk/551192

Simonton, D. K. (2000). Methodological and theoretical orientation and the long-term disciplinary impact of 54 eminent psychologists. *Review of General Psychology, 4*(1), 13–24. https://doi.org/10.1037/1089-2680.4.1.13

Stagnaro, M., Pennycook, G., & Rand, D. G. (2018). Performance on the cognitive reflection test is stable across time. *SSRN*, 3115809. https://papers.ssrn.com/abstract=3115809

Stewart, N., Ungemach, C., Harris, A. J. L., Bartels, D. M., Newell, B. R., Paolacci, G., & Chandler, J. (2015). The average laboratory samples a population of 7,300 Amazon Mechanical Turk workers. *Judgment and Decision Making, 10*(5), 479–491.

Thomson, K. S., & Oppenheimer, D. M. (2016). Investigating an alternate form of the cognitive reflection test. *Judgment and Decision Making, 11*(1), 99–113.

TurkerView. (2019, November 18). Writer who never learned to drive works for Uber. Makes $0.97/hr. https://blog.turkerview.com/writer-who-never-learned-to-drive-works-for-uber

US Census Bureau. (2020, February 5). Marital status in the United States. www.census.gov/library/visualizations/interactive/marital-status-in-united-states.html

US Census Bureau. (2021, November 29). Census Bureau releases new estimates on America's families and living arrangements. www.census.gov/newsroom/press-releases/2021/families-and-living-arrangements.html

US Census Bureau. (2022, February 24). Census Bureau releases new educational attainment data. www.census.gov/newsroom/press-releases/2022/educational-attainment.html

US Census Bureau. (n.d.). QuickFacts: United States. www.census.gov/quickfacts/fact/table/US/POP010220

Walters, K., Christakis, D. A., & Wright, D. R. (2018). Are Mechanical Turk worker samples representative of health status and health behaviors in the U.S.? *PLOS ONE, 13*(6), e0198835. https://doi.org/10.1371/journal.pone.0198835

Wessling, K., Huber, J., & Netzer, O. (2017). MTurk character misrepresentation: Assessment and solutions. *Journal of Consumer Research, 44*(1), 211–230. https://doi.org/10.1093/jcr/ucx053

Williamson, V. (2016). On the ethics of crowdsourced research. *PS: Political Science & Politics, 49*(01), 77–81. https://doi.org/10.1017/S104909651500116X

Zwaan, R. A., Pecher, D., Paolacci, G., Bouwmeester, S., Verkoeijen, P., Dijkstra, K., & Zeelenberg, R. (2018). Participant nonnaiveté and the reproducibility of cognitive psychology. *Psychonomic Bulletin & Review, 25*(5), 1968–1972. https://doi.org/10.3758/s13423-017-1348-y

3 Social Media Research

Rosanna E. Guadagno and Alberto F. Olivieri

Abstract

The purpose of this chapter is to review the contemporary methods used to collect and examine data on social media and to explore the common pitfalls of internet research. The discussion focuses on the importance of internet research while also reviewing common practices of data retrieval (e.g., crowdsourcing and snowball sampling). We will also explain a commonly used tool to analyze data collected using social media. Specifically, one section is dedicated to the Linguistic Inquiry and Word Count software (LIWC); another section focuses on a brief overview of machine learning (ML) techniques and data visualization. At the end of the chapter, we will also examine some common ethical concerns, focusing mainly on anonymity and privacy, while also giving a general overview on the European General Data Protection Regulation (GDPR). Future directions for social media will then be addressed.

Keywords: Social Media, Social Networking, Research Methods, Internet, Ethics in Research

The amount of data available on social media is vast and potentially overwhelming, especially for newer researchers. Nonetheless, the analysis of this type of data can provide real insights into human behavior. For instance, analyses of digital footprints have shown that gendered behavior persists on social media such that women's posts generally show more emotions associated with feminine gender stereotypes relative to men (Park et al., 2015). For men, their social media posts are also consistently masculine activities and match expectations for independence and agency. Other research has found that people's personality characteristics, sexual orientation, political leaning, and other individual differences can also be predicted by their digital footprints (e.g., Kosinski et al., 2013; Kern et al., 2019). The analysis of the text in people's social media posts can also predict their psychological states (Boyd & Pennebaker, 2017). Data collected from social media can also be used to predict and create models of the viral spread of information. However, social media are just a tool, and as such, can be improperly applied with unethical or malicious intent.

Love it or hate it, social media have become a staple of modern life. While this relatively new type of digital communication has existed in some form since the mid-1990s (Guadagno, in press), empirical work only began to accumulate later. Furthermore, there are still substantial gaps in the literature that need to be filled before scholars can fully understand the effect social media have on people's thoughts, beliefs, behavior, and interpersonal relationships. For researchers, the stories recounted in this chapter serve as a cautionary tale of what not to do for scientists and scholars interested in using social media to conduct research. The present chapter provides a roadmap for ethical research on social media. We examine various methodologies for recruiting participants and collecting data and conclude with a detailed discussion of the ethical considerations for research on social media.

What Are Social Media?

"Social media" refers to a subset of Web 2.0 technologies that shifted people's internet use toward an emphasis on self-generated content (Oinas-Kukkonen & Oinas-Kukkonen, 2013). In the early days, social media largely consisted of *social networking sites* (SNS; e.g., MySpace). These days, "social media" is the more common phrase used to describe all related technology. Renowned internet researchers danah boyd and Nicole Ellison were the first to provide a concise operational definition of social media and their operationalization is still in use today. Specially, boyd and Ellison define social media as follows:

> Web-based services that allow individuals to (1) construct a public or semi-public profile within a bounded system, (2) articulate a list of other users with whom they share a connection, and (3) view and traverse their list of connections and those made by others within the system. (boyd & Ellison, 2007, p. 211)

While specific social media platforms have unique characteristics and purposes (e.g., LinkedIn is primarily used for career networking while Facebook is used primarily to keep in touch with friends and family), there are several features that are shared by social media applications. These are (1) each user has their own profile that they can then personalize and is visible to other users; (2) people connect with others – friends, family, strangers – and communicate with them through the application; (3) users read and interact with content (text, videos, photographs) created by other users they are typically (but not always) connected with. Over the years that social media have been widely used, this new technology has facilitated new friendships and romantic relationships, job opportunities, helped people find old friends, discover new family, and served as a source of news and information.

One other notable aspect of social media pertains to its global research. People all over the world use social media, although the different applications may vary by country. For instance, social media applications created by countries in the Western world are banned in China (Guadagno, in press). As a result, although people in China may use social media similarly to people elsewhere, the specific applications they use are different. Everything we do while using social media, whether it be simply browsing or actively posting photos or messages in public or private, is logged by the social media application. This information is used by social media companies for many purposes – some benign (e.g., improving the user experience and suggesting new connections and groups) and others potentially unethical (microtargeting ads, performing experiments on users without their explicit consent). This information is often used to create and refine algorithms – computer programs that perform a specific pre-set task – that predict the type of social media content people are likely to engage with and subsequently present users with that content.

Just as social media applications record people's actions, so can researchers – either directly via webscraping digital footprints or indirectly by assessing people's perceptions of their social media use through experiments and surveys. In the sections below, we review the different options for finding and recruiting participants and conducting research on their social media use. The literature on social media is extremely broad both in terms of topic studied and methodology used. In light of this, the present chapter reviews the different options and considerations and also provides resources for further information.

Collecting Social Media Data

Social media have some unique affordances that make them a rich and almost endless resource for researchers (Bayer et al., 2020). One of the most prominent features of the "social" part in social media is the large amount of data on human behaviors and interactions now easily accessible. Researchers who want to focus on understanding social behavior and trends can access vast amounts of information regarding human communications, trending topics, and responses to events or stimuli. Other useful research avenues that could stem from diving deep into social data are sentiment analysis for specific topics or brands – an invaluable approach for fields like marketing, public relations, or political science.

Another crucial aspect to consider is the immediacy or real-time nature of the information gathered from social media. This enhances research on crisis and disaster management, and it holds potential for educational research. Moreover, controversial topics, events, and virality, in a continuously shifting landscape, must be constantly kept under scrutiny to properly track and study dis- and misinformation. Finally, a fundamental dimension of social media is the network structure itself. Techniques such as community detection can lead to the discovery of online groups and their interactions, while digital ethnography can offer novel views on the life cycle of these communities.

There are a variety of ways to recruit participants and collect data, and these are somewhat dependent on the population of interest, the specific research question(s) a scholar wishes to answer, and the type of data best suited to answer the question. In the sections below, we first explore the different ways in which researchers select samples and recruit participants, then transition to a discussion of the ways in which data on social media can be collected, and finish with an overview of data analyses that are well-suited for this type of data.

Finding Participants

In this section, we review options for recruiting participants, including recruiting participants straight from social media and recruiting crowdsourced samples. We will explore the specific characteristics of each approach in subsequent sections, briefly explaining only the more superficial differences. Social media platform selection must also keep in mind the structure and focus of the platform and how those characteristics can influence the demographics and the types of interaction of its userbase.

Snowball Sampling

While this form of sampling is widely used for a variety of research projects (see Chandler, 2023 for an overview of the technique), the technique works especially well on social media. As the phrase suggests, snowball sampling refers to the selection of a small number of participants, then asking for their assistance in identifying and recruiting other potential participants. Researcher(s) can start the sampling by sharing a link to their study on their social media pages and ask their connections to share the link as well. If the research calls for a specialized sample, there are myriad specialty groups in many forms of social media, and the researcher(s) can post a request for participants in these groups. Once a participant has completed the study, researcher(s) can also ask participants themselves to share the link to the study with any additional contacts that may fit the recruitment criteria.

This technique is well-suited to sampling from atypical (e.g., people who enjoy ice swimming) or difficult to access samples (e.g., mothers of children with rare diseases). It is also very easy to implement. However, this technique does not provide a randomly sampled group of participants, so the results of any studies using snowball sampling have limited generalizability (Parker et al., 2019). Snowball sampling on social media has been shown to recruit such difficult to reach samples as mothers of children with developmental disabilities (Lee & Spratling, 2019) and nurses (Chambers et al., 2020). Researchers have also developed snowball sampling methods to obtain digital footprints such as tweets from difficult to identify online communities (Wang et al., 2017).

Crowdsourced Data Collection

The term "crowdsourcing" was coined in 2006 and describes "the practice of obtaining needed services, ideas, or content by soliciting contributions from a large group of people and especially from the online community rather than from traditional employees or suppliers" (Merriam-Webster, n.d.). While non-scholarly crowdsourced data appear all over social media, especially as reviews of films, television, video games, businesses, consumer goods, and software applications, crowdsourced data collection refers to the use of specific software services that provide a researcher with their sample of participants for a nominal fee (e.g., Amazon's Mechanical Turk, Prolific, Survey Monkey, YouGov). While some services offer the option to recruit directly from people who meet the recruitment criteria (e.g., Mechanical Turk), others offer access to pre-selected samples (e.g., Prolific Academic). Furthermore, some services are coupled with data collection software (e.g., Survey Monkey). See Guadagno (2019) or Chapter 2 (this volume) for a detailed description of how Mechanical Turk works).

Recent empirical work has established the rising dominance of crowdsourced samples for social and behavioral research. For instance, Anderson et al. (2019) sampled studies published in the top-tier social psychology journals and found that for the year 2015, approximately half the articles published in these journals used such samples. Other research has demonstrated similar increases in the use of crowdsourced samples more broadly (Chandler & Shapiro, 2016; Zhou & Fishbach, 2016). Numerous disciplines in the social and behavioral sciences have largely benefited specifically from the use of MTurk. For instance, some disciplines (e.g., public administration and management research) found that using MTurk has proven useful to their fields (Wright & Goodman, 2019). Other disciplines such as market research provide another prime example where MTurk has successfully replaced traditional surveys. MTurk is often able to give results within hours and within an acceptable error rate compared to traditional approaches, making scientific investigations with it extremely cost-effective (Bentley et al., 2017). Thus, while this method is used more broadly than just research on social media, it represents a means of recruiting participants that is convenient, relatively inexpensive, and broadens the diversity of samples relative to undergraduate psychology samples (Casler et al., 2013; Berinsky et al., 2012). Furthermore, research suggests that data collected with a crowdsourced sample yield results that replicate studies conducted in a traditional laboratory setting. This has been demonstrated across a variety of disciplines, including psychology (Buhrmester et al., 2011) political science (Clifford et al., 2015), and market research (Bentley et al., 2017).

While this method of participant recruitment may seem like a panacea, crowdsourcing research in this manner is not without its drawbacks. First, the vast majority of potential participants are often from a limited number of geographic locations (e.g., MTurk research participants primarily hail from the United States and India), making it difficult to recruit representative samples outside of those nations (Antoun et al. 2016; Paolacci & Chandler, 2014; Ross et al., 2009). Furthermore, it is important for researchers to always keep in mind that they have limited control over the extent to which participants are completing anonymous online experiments. This characteristic of crowdsourcing platforms could potentially skew the results. Therefore, in the analysis phase, researchers should proceed carefully. It is fundamental to add quality controls to crowdsourced studies to ensure reliable data.

Attention checks that ask participants to select a certain response option have been shown to resolve this issue (Nichols & Edlund, 2020; Rouse, 2015). There also seems to be a relationship between rate of pay, length of study, and quality of data collected such that shorter, higher-paying studies tend to attract more attentive participants (Buhrmester et al., 2011). Other issues include differential attrition, with participants often dropping out of some experimental conditions at much higher rates than participants randomly assigned to other conditions (Zhou & Fishbach, 2016), and participant crosstalk, in which participants share the details of an experiment with other potential participants (Edlund et al., 2017). With respect to this latter issue, there are websites (e.g., https://turkopticon.net) created to allow crowdsourced subjects to compare their experiences across the studies they participate in. On these websites, subjects compare details of the study, the length of time to complete the study, and assessments of the quality of pay. Fortunately, the problem of participant crosstalk on these third-party websites can be attenuated by asking participants in the study to refrain from sharing key details at the conclusion of debriefing (Edlund et al., 2017; see also Clark & Blackhart, 2023).

Obtaining Data

While the prior section addressed different ways to recruit participants into an experiment or survey on social media, this section reviews the different types of data that can be collected on people and the psychological properties surrounding their social media use. These include surveys, social media simulators, and web-scraping of digital footprints.

Surveys

Surveys are a series of questions in which researchers ask people about their thoughts, beliefs, feelings, and behaviors. This is also the method used to assess personality inventories (Burger, 2014). Some survey methods are intended to gather information about a target population; other times, surveys are used to assess the dependent variable(s) in an experiment. Surveys are inexpensive to administer and are often used to study psychological processes that are not easily observable because they are rare or occur as part of internal, cognitive processes. The generalizability of surveys is often limited, as it is difficult to recruit truly representative samples of a population. Furthermore, survey data is often prone to social desirability bias (Grimm, 2010) – the phenomenon in which people report thoughts, beliefs, feelings, or behaviors that are considered normative, appropriate, or socially acceptable. There are a wide variety of digital services that provide the tools to create and post a survey designed by members of the research team (e.g., Qualtrics, Google Forms, Survey Monkey), and most universities typically have a license for such software.

The utility of surveys goes beyond experimental research, as they are frequently used also for correlational and quasi-experimental research. For instance, a study where the authors evaluated how gender and personality traits influence the usage among undergraduate students of social networking sites, such as Facebook and MySpace, used surveys to assess this research question. Their findings revealed that men typically use these platforms with the goal of forming new relationships while women use them more for maintaining existing relationships. Additionally, it was observed that women low in agreeableness used instant messaging more often, and men low in openness played more games on these sites. These findings highlight the significance of individual differences in online behavior (Muscanell & Guadagno, 2012).

Another survey study compared the use of social network sites (SNS) between two age-matched groups of young adults. The first group was comprised of college students from a large introductory psychology subject pool; the second group was homeless young adults from metropolitan shelters. The findings indicated a similar use of technology across the two groups, regardless of socio-economic status and ethnicity. The results cast doubts on the concept of "digital divide" as still relevant, showing minimal differences between the subsamples and suggesting the need for a paradigm shift (Guadagno, Muscanell, & Pollio, 2013). See Chapters 16 and 17 in this volume for more details on these issues.

Social Media Simulations

While the researchers working for social media companies perform experiments on people regularly, scholars outside of these companies have more limited options. One option is to create a simulated version of social media for participants to use during an experiment. This is typically done by either running a simulation designed by other researchers (e.g., the many dis/mis-information games; Roozenbeek & Van der Linden, 2019) or programming your own content and pre-selecting responses to participants (Prevency, n.d.; Jagayat, 2022).

In the early days of social media research, we would create social media simulations (e.g., Guadagno, Muscanell, Rice, & Roberts, 2013) using a now defunct online survey and experiment creation tool that the first author helped create called RiddleMeThis (RiddleMeThis.net). Specifically, this software was created in 2003 for use in the first author's dissertation and then later commercialized. It was the first customizable web-based data collection tool with menu-based survey creation options. A user could create a randomized experiment and assess dependent variables all in one form posted on the internet. The software would also time participants' responses and had a menu for easy viewing and exporting of data once a study was completed. Unfortunately, this product was eventually made obsolete by Qualtrics and other, similar products.

Collecting Digital Footprints

Every time a person posts on social media, is tagged in a photo, sends a direct message, leaves a review, or purchases a product from an online store, they create a digital trace of their activity called a digital footprint. Digital footprints such as these get aggregated into a digital dossier – a file containing detailed records about a person. Generally, people inadvertently create such records with their internet use. Between our social media profiles, our mobile phone use (i.e., texting, emails, apps, GPS), our online shopping, banking, and other online activities, quite a bit of information about us is available for others to find online.

Social media companies use this information to sell to advertisers, to predict what content will keep people engaged on their site, and what products, services, and entertainment will be most appealing to individual users. The more digital footprints we accumulate, the more accurate these predictive models and algorithms are.

Although this may sound unethical, it is generally legal for social media companies to do this (although some parts of the world, such as the European Union, are changing their laws to provide people with more control over their digital dossiers), and consent to participate in social media companies' research is also currently embedded in the end user agreements that people are supposed to read as part of the account creation process.

Researchers working outside of social media companies generally do not have the same access to people's digital dossiers owing to corporate privacy policies, but there are methods to obtain them. An early solution to this issue was a process called webscraping in which researchers would download social media data and participant profile information to use in their studies. In some instances, participants consented to have their data collected in this manner; in others, the data was simply collected without the consent of the content creators. Zimmer (2018) detailed some of the more notable instances of these practices becoming public.

One example is the 2016 case of researchers from Denmark who released a data set from the online dating service OkCupid. The data included identifying information about the participants, including their user ids, age, gender, geographic location, type of relationship sought, and personality characteristics. Thus, it is important that, when using this technique, participants provide consent for their data to be used in a study and any publicly released data set does not include identifying information. In my own work, my research team created a Facebook web scraper, but it was only used on participants who consented and allowed us to briefly friend them to collect the data (Guadagno, Loewald, et al., 2013).

It is important to note that this type of webscraping is typically prohibited by social media companies today. Twitter/X policy regarding webscraping is clearly expressed in their TOS: "crawling the Services is permissible if done in accordance with the provisions of the robots.txt file, however, scraping the Services without our prior consent is expressly prohibited." Similarly, TikTok states in their TOS the prohibition that scraping can "not access any data or TikTok content other than through the TikTok Research API (including without limitation, no use of scraping or other technical or manual techniques for extraction of content)." Facebook takes a more aggressive approach as they actively combat scraping, as stated in an article from 2021: "We devote substantial resources to combating unauthorized scraping on Facebook products. We have a dedicated External Data Misuse (EDM) team made up of more than 100 people, including data scientists, analysts and engineers focused on our efforts to detect, block and deter scraping." This is common practice for most social media platforms. They restrict data access through the use of their official API to control more tightly any data retrieval process. This is just one of multiple layers of a more general user data protection system that should be integral to any social media platform that prioritizes the safekeeping of its userbase sensitive data.

In the past, social media companies collaborated directly with academic researchers, but this practice has become markedly less common as scandal after scandal (e.g., Cambridge Analytica's illicit accessing of Facebook data and the emotional contagion study described below) was revealed by the news media. Nonetheless, there are options for researchers interested in collecting digital footprints from social media. For instance, many social media companies provide licenses for academic researchers to obtain an Application Programming Interface (API) to view the social media application from the perspective of software developers and access and download any publicly shared information on users such as their posts, likes, shares, the prevalence of search terms, URL (uniform resource locator, a clickable link to a specific website) archives, and performance data in either real time or historically. See Table 3.1 for a non-exhaustive list of social media companies currently offering this option. Furthermore, there are myriad published guides to using and analyzing this type of data (e.g., Acker & Kreisberg, 2020; Barrie & Ho, 2022).

In addition to the API option, in which researchers obtain data directly from a social media application, there are various academic and corporate archives that are available to researchers and sometimes to the general public. For instance, Google Trends allows anyone with the URL to view what people are searching for in real time or historically. This site also allows people to view this data globally or specific to a geographic location. This methodology and the fascinating insights that can be gleaned from such data are described in detail by Seth Stephens-Davidowitz (2017). See Table 3.2 for more details as well as a list of other similar options for collecting digital footprints.

Table 3.1 *A non-exhaustive list of social media companies offering academic APIs*

Application	Link	Data description	Restrictions
Facebook/Meta	https://fort.fb.com/researcher-apis	Provides anonymized access to people's posts in real time or historically, keyword search, and data from FB groups	Limited to US researchers and some EU countries
Reddit	www.reddit.com/r/redditdev/comments/1twwz2/new_api_access_for_researchers_academic_students	Access to real-time and historical posts based on keywords, user id, subreddits	University researchers
TikTok	https://developers.tiktok.com/products/research-api	Account information such as profile and activity on the app, keywords, and videos with corresponding meta-data	Access limited to some members of our Content and Safety Advisory Councils and US academic researchers
Twitter/X	https://developer.twitter.com/en	Real-time or historical data	Non-commercial use only

Table 3.2 *A non-exhaustive list of pre-existing social media data sets*

Description	Link	Data Description	Restrictions
Facebook data sets	https://fort.fb.com/researcher-datasets	Offers different data sets for academic researchers (e.g., ad targeting, civic engagement, URL shares)	Researchers must apply for access with a research proposal
Google Ad Trends	https://trends.google.com	Database of Google search terms across time and geographic location	None – tool is free for use
Social Science One	https://socialscience.one/facebook-dataverse	Provides over 57 million URLs shared on Facebook along with aggregated data on the type of user interaction with the content (e.g., liked, shared, flagged as hate speech, fact checked, or commented)	RFPs must be submitted by a researcher with PI status (i.e., can serve as a PI on a grant application)
Twitter/X data sets	https://transparency.twitter.com/en/reports/moderation-research.html	Provides data on information operations and other data sets related to content moderation	The information operation data set is available to anyone, other data sets limited to members of the Twitter Moderation Research Consortium

Analysis Approaches

In the sections below, various techniques are reviewed, regarding the modeling of the spread of viral content and the role of machine learning in assisting with the analysis of digital footprints.

Modeling Viral Spread

One of the ways researchers measure the viral spread of content on social media is through the number of likes and shares a particular message receives. From this approach, it is widely known that the timing of a social media message (Phing & Yazdanifard, 2014), the emotional response evoked by the message (Guadagno, Rempala, Murphy, & Okdie, 2013), and the number of followers predict the likelihood of content going viral (Jenders et al., 2013). More recent approaches use data visualization – a graphical representation of data – to model the viral spread of content. For instance, the work of Professor Kate Starbird and colleagues has used this method to model the viral spread of disinformation. Specifically, this work

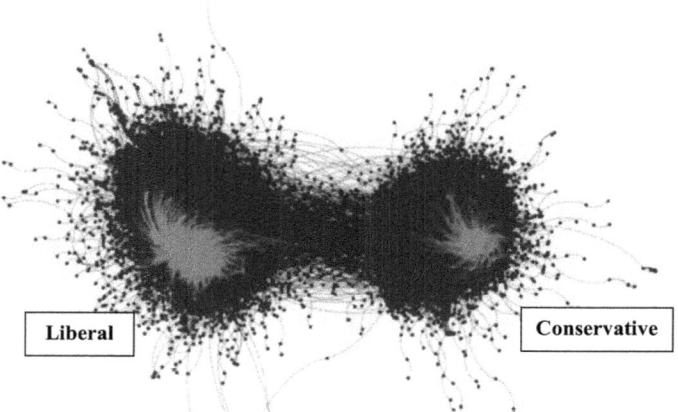

Figure 3.1 *Retweets of messages related to the Black Lives Matter social movement. Light gray indicates IRA bots and trolls, dark gray the other retweets. Reprinted from Arif et al. (2018)*

demonstrated how the Russian Internet Research Agency (IRA) used bots (i.e., computer programs pretending to be social media users) and trolls (i.e., employees of the IRA pretending to be Americans) to spread disinformation about the Black Lives Matter social movement (Arif et al., 2018). This work also illustrated how these messages differed as a function of whether the Russian bots and trolls were supporting this movement and pretending to be politically liberal Americans.

In the paper, the authors explain how they used a plugin of the Gephi software, Twitter Streaming Importer developed by Matthew Totet (https://github.com/totet matt), to collect real-time data from Twitter, through the Twitter Streaming API. The team selected a series of hashtags as keywords, primarily associated with shootings and the Black Lives Matter movement ("gun shot," "gunman," "shooter," and "shooting," with the further addition of "BlackLivesMatter," "BlueLivesMatter," or "AllLivesMatter" – "*LM") to query Twitter and retrieved 58.8 million tweets of raw unfiltered data. After cleaning the initial data set, and applying filters to reduce interference from noise, the authors, using the community detection algorithms present in Gephi, were able to create a visualization of the retweet network among the accounts. This resulted in a clear grouping of the accounts into two, almost completely separated, communities. These communities remained consistently distinct even after tweaks and changes of the algorithm parameters.

The researchers, through this approach, were able to classify these two communities as divided by political lines (right and left leaning), basing their evaluation on the prevalent hashtags and most-followed accounts within each group. Moreover, they also discovered the most influential accounts in the two clusters. In the network, they were able to pinpoint the known RU-IRA accounts, giving a thorough description and visualization of this part of the online discourse revolving around #BLM and violent events involving shooting. Figure 3.1 reproduces a visual representation of their findings, showcasing the descriptive power of a network visualization, and the value of tools like Gephi and the Twitter Streaming Importer.

Sentiment Analysis

Sentiment analysis refers to the analysis of text-based communications to infer psychological states (e.g., mood, opinions, motivations). Although there are myriad software products available to perform this task, the predominant software used in psychology and other social science disciplines is called the Language Inquiry Word Count (LIWC, pronounced "Luke"; Boyd et al., 2022) and has been used in over 20,000 studies. Sentiment analysis is also referred to as *opinion mining*, although the emphasis in this case is on extraction of psychological states.

The LIWC can analyze text written in many languages and, in addition to data on a person's psychological state, provides useful summary statistics such as the total number of words, mean words per sentence, and overall level of analytic thinking (Boyd et al., 2022). It also provides analyses of the focus of the text (e.g., social, perceptual, personal, and biological processes) and analyzes the cognitive processes (e.g., certainty, causation) expressed in the text. In addition, the software allows for the creation of custom dictionaries to focus on a particular topic. For instance, we once created a custom dictionary to assess prosocial behaviors in a study about helping in video games (Lee et al., 2017). Other studies have examined online civility (Ksiazek, 2015), task focus during a negotiation (Ireland & Henderson, 2014), and concerns about privacy (Vasalou et al., 2011) by creating custom dictionaries using the LIWC.

The LIWC currently is able to categorize any kind of text into more than 80 different language dimensions. It is also capable of providing a summary of some of the data dimensions of the text provided (e.g., the total number of words in a passage, the average number of words per sentence, the percent of words in the passages that were identified by the dictionary, and the percent of long words; Boyd & Pennebaker, 2015). Moreover, LIWC has integrated functionalities that can be used to classify text and then map it with psychological states, personal concerns, and punctuation. It is noteworthy to mention that the LIWC text analysis tools are able to uncover the various relationships between the linguistic characteristics of people's writing and their health, personalities, and thought processes (Boyd & Pennebaker, 2015). An interesting feature of this system is the ability to create ad hoc dictionaries. This ability paves the way for more focused research avenues; some examples of such ability is researching using terms related to privacy concerns (Vasalou et al., 2011), civility in online discussions (Ksiazek, 2015), and task engagement in negotiations (Ireland & Henderson, 2014).

One study that utilized the LIWC tools explored how people modified their online post habits, comparing a two-month period before the New York September 11 attacks and two months after them (Cohn et al., 2004). The author's approach focused on the analysis of more than 1,000 posts and discovered a sizable shift in the participants' psychology after the terrorist attacks. In the fortnight following these attacks, a spike in negative emotions was registered, and the participants showed a heightened social and cognitive engagement. On the other hand, the social distance measured from their writing also showed signs of growth. The same group had all these changes reverted back to their original pre-attack levels after six weeks from the attack. The study clearly supports the efficacy of the LIWC. The tool also made it possible for the authors to delve deep into how people cope with and recover from traumatic events.

Another study, conducted by Ashokkumar and Pennebaker (2021), involved the analysis of Reddit language and large-scale survey data and also employed the LIWC tool to track the psychological effects of the COVID-19 pandemic. The authors found three distinct emotional phases: a "warning phase," an "isolation phase," and a "normalization phase." The LIWC scores were used to examine changes in a wide array of emotions such as anxiety, sadness, anger, and positive emotions. This revealed a surge in anxiety during the warning and isolation phases and a continued increase in sadness and decrease in positive emotions. LIWC analysis also highlighted a drop in analytic thinking during the isolation and normalization phases. This suggested a shift in the responses toward becoming more immediate, with a waning analytical thinking approach in response to the pandemic. The magnitude of these changes was seemingly directly correlated with the areas where COVID-19 was more virulent. The study showcases the utility of LIWC as a tool for understanding large-scale psychological responses to major societal events.

Further research has shown that the LIWC can be useful in predicting depression (De Choudhury et al., 2013), discovering people's personality characteristics (Park et al., 2015), and, presaging the #MeToo movement, detecting improvement in women's psychological well-being after tweeting about sexual harassment (Foster, 2015). Application software such as the LIWC has multiple times revealed its utility when properly employed by the researchers.

Machine Learning

It is recognized that machine learning (ML) techniques have had a huge influence in multiple research fields, but their reception in other traditional disciplines was somewhat colder. Jacobucci and Grimm (2020) propose that this difference might be explained by the unreliability of results, in turn exacerbated by measurement errors that can negatively influence the outcome. They demonstrated how measurement quality was the primary factor for electing to use ML or not, regardless of the sample size. This experiment validates a well-known but informal principle in computer science and information and communications technology known as "Garbage in, Garbage out" and highlights the fundamental importance of using the best practices in both data cleaning and wrangling. The general principle that the article proved still stands, but it is fundamental to acknowledge that the development of ML or deep learning (DL) tools is proceeding at breakneck pace. At the time of this writing (2023), results and error tolerance of newly developed algorithms could significantly differ from the ones presented in the article. Objects in pictures, text, and even context can now be recognized by new models and tools with more accuracy and speed than in the past. As an example, projects like ChatGPT,

Midjourney, and others from companies all over the world are creating new challenges and opportunities for researchers.

A brief analysis of the advantages and disadvantages of using ML techniques with internet research will follow. The huge amount of data that can be retrieved with internet research techniques is well suited for creating new ML models, as they need huge data sets to be able to generalize well and not overfit the data sample, as well as be effective as a predictive model (Zhou et al., 2017).

On the other hand, the researchers should be extremely aware of how biased data could create models that reinforce pre-existing biases. The need to correct unwanted bias unfortunately invites the possible introduction of personal biases in the attempt to clean the data set. The researcher should strike a difficult balance between the two issues – to remove as much bias as possible without falling into data manipulation to achieve the desired outcome. The situation is further complicated by the various definitions and interpretations of the word "bias" across different disciplines (Hellström et al., 2020). It is worth noting that the issue of bias is present both in ML approaches and in internet research, but the subject is particularly debated in the field of ML. This entire subject is vast and complex, and integrating ML techniques in an internet research project will come with its strengths and weaknesses that should always be kept in mind.

Ethical Concerns

"We spent $1 m harvesting millions of Facebook profiles"

Accounts vary on who came up with the idea of using social media for political microtargeting. Nonetheless, the role of Cambridge Analytica (CA) in using this methodology to influence political beliefs is incontrovertible. In the months leading up to the 2016 US presidential election, Cambridge Analytica was the primary proponent of a new form of internet advertising targeting people based on their personal characteristics. This approach is known as political microtargeting – "monitoring people's online behavior, and using the collected data, sometimes enriched with other data," with the final scope of influencing its targets, deploying "individually targeted political advertisements" (Dobber et al., 2019). CA was more than a data science and data analytics firm; it marketed itself as a "full-service propaganda machine" (Cadwalladr et al., 2021) and was led by Alexander Nix. CA set up a fake office in Cambridge to create an impression that they were based out of the University of Cambridge and sold their services to political candidates in the United States and elsewhere.

Their research methods were ethically and legally questionable. Specifically, in 2014, CA collected Facebook profile data, without consent, from millions of Facebook users. The operation involved the use of *thisisyourdigitallife* – an app where users knowingly and voluntarily shared their data as subjects of a personality test for a monetary reward. Unbeknownst to them, the app also collected data from their social media connections, leading to the creation of an enormous database with tens of millions of datapoints from completely unaware users (Graham-Harrison & Cadwalladr, 2021). This data was used to create a system to microtarget voters with political advertisements tailored to them based on information such as their geographic location and personality profile.

While a smaller subsample of participants were paid to provide access to their Facebook profiles, CA collected more than participant data. CA's application collected profile data on everyone each participant was connected to on Facebook. These data were then used to create a microtargeting algorithm that would predict how to influence each person's political opinions by predicting the kind of advertising content that each person would find persuasive and the number of times these ads needed to be shown to their targets. As a result, every voter whose information had been collected was targeted by CA's algorithm and sent different advertisements leading them to different internet content.

It is worth noting that CA managed to retrieve data from millions of users without the consent of the majority of them. The scale of this endeavor would not have been possible without the consent and prolonged lack of concern regarding the data leak from Facebook itself. At least 87 million Facebook users had their data taken in this manner (Solon, 2018). Eventually, a data scientist within Cambridge Analytica, Christopher Wylie, went to the press and blew the whistle on the company's unethical conduct (Graham-Harrison & Cadwalladr, 2021; Cadwalladr et al., 2021). Once people knew what CA was doing, the company folded as governments and law enforcement started investigating the legality of their practices. CA's actions became one of the biggest scandals of the social media era. Not only did CA interfere in the 2016 US presidential election, and attempt to influence voters in favor of the Republican candidate, but it also has been widely accused of influencing the Brexit vote.

Another high-profile example comes from academia. A study on the virality of emotions online made headlines and stirred discussions both outside and inside various academic circles. During the summer of 2014, news regarding the manipulation of users' Facebook feeds and nonconsensual data collection by Facebook started to emerge. The headlines conveyed a sense of outrage, shock, resignation, and helplessness that properly reflected the emotional impact of the experiment Facebook conducted. In this experiment, data from 700,000 users was collected without their knowledge or consent.

This experiment took place in 2012 and lasted a week. For the duration of the experiment, Facebook collected data from several hundred randomly selected participants from their userbase. Their research question focused on whether positive and negative emotions were "contagious" and spread on social media. Moreover, the experiment comprised two different studies with a test and a control group for each. The user news feed of the first test group was altered with a reduced number of positive terms (e.g., love, nice, sweet; Pennebaker et al., 2007). The second test group was similarly manipulated but with negative terms instead (e.g., hurt, ugly, nasty). Both of the control groups had random posts removed from their news feed, in similar numbers to their paired test group.

The authors analyzed more than 3 million posts with a text analysis tool – the LIWC – described in detail earlier in this chapter. The objective was to determine whether strong positive or negative emotions could be viral and spread through the user's Facebook social network. The two dependent variables were the quantity of either positive or negative emotions expressed by the test subjects. The researchers found that their initial prediction that emotions would spread through social media was supported, such that users with a negatively manipulated news feed shared more negative emotions than the control group. Similar results emerged for the group where positive emotions were artificially enhanced; there was a major increase in positive emotions spread.

When the public was made aware of this experiment, the reactions were mostly negative, focusing especially on the lack of proper ethical considerations. The only reference to them was a statement where previous consent was mentioned: "consistent with Facebook's Data Use Policy, to which all users agree prior to creating an account on Facebook, constituting informed consent for this research" (Kramer et al., 2014, p. 8789). In the academic community, this lackluster approach produced discussions regarding the procedures employed with human subjects on social media and the ethical treatment of these participants.

The social and personality psychology community and related social sciences were especially involved, as the paper directly connected to those disciplines. Even the editor of the journal that published the paper, Dr. Inder Verma, expressed editorial concerns regarding the lack of informed consent – both a standard practice in any research involving human test subjects and a requirement for any research using federally funded institutions (corporations such as Facebook are not currently held accountable to the same rules; Verma, 2014).

While conducting internet research, there are four primary pitfalls to always keep in mind, so as to avoid unethical behaviors. The first consideration is the anonymity and confidentiality of the participants. The second one focuses on privacy concerns. The third involves validating the veracity of the responses and the non-naivete of the participants. Finally, the fourth one addresses fair compensation. Academics have tackled these questions already, leading to the development of a comprehensive set of recommendations and guidelines to guide others in producing ethically conscious experiments. An example of a guideline comes from the Association of Internet Researchers (AoIR). In their publication they address ethics in internet research (Markham & Buchanan, 2012) in which examples and insights are given to readers approaching the field. Some interesting questions that are put forward are: Is an avatar a person? What are the long-term ethical considerations of directly quoting someone's online posts? and What are the risks for participants when a technology prevents the removal of identifying information (e.g., facial recognition data)?

Another perspective on ethical issues in internet research is provided by members of university IRBs. In one study by Buchanan and Hvizdak (2009), these IRB members raised attention on topics such as security of data, participant anonymity, data deletion/loss and recovery, access to electronic data, validity of data collected online, the impact of anonymity on participants' responses, age verification, consent, and perception of the university. In the sections below, we discuss the first two issues, as they are relevant to all types of research on social media reviewed in this chapter.

Participant Anonymity, Confidentiality, and Consent

We outlined above four main ethical concerns regarding internet research. The first of these is related to obtaining informed consent from the participants while also being able to shield their identities and other sensitive information. Gosling and Mason (2015) highlighted some issues related to the anonymity of internet research. They wrote that "researchers have less control over and knowledge of the research environment and cannot monitor the experience of participants, or indeed their true identities" (Buchanan & Williams, 2010, p. 894). In contrast to a traditionally offline lab experiment, where the researchers have the possibility to debrief participants who decided to withdraw, in an internet-based experiment, where the participants have been recruited with the methods previously discussed in the chapter, they cannot be properly debriefed after an early dropout. Moreover, the researcher can't be sure that each and every participant has fully read and understood the debriefing (Miller et al., 2017). It is also worth noting how research conducted with anonymous participants is a double-edged sword. On the one hand it protects the identity of the participants; on the other hand, the researchers have new concerns regarding proper consent and debrief, double participation, and difficulties in case of needed direct intervention to help a distressed participant.

Furthermore, true anonymity is also difficult to achieve. In one experiment, Dawson (2014) was able to retrieve the source of the text from 10 out of 112 target articles. From the 10 papers he had source material from, only one paper reported receiving IRB approval to publish identifiable data. Of the remaining nine studies, five neither anonymized the text nor discussed ethical considerations, and one tried but failed to anonymize the data. The author summarized how it is possible, with the right expertise, motivation, or data, to deanonymize experiment participants. We, as researchers, should realize that, although it is important to safeguard the participants' anonymity and confidentiality, the anonymity itself can also limit certain research avenues in which it would be informative or useful to know the identities of the research participants. The advice of these authors is to use digital data with consent of the people providing the content if possible. If this is not possible, the data must be truly anonymized by a thorough check of the data to ensure that individual participants cannot be identified.

Privacy Concerns

Most people have an interest in knowing their past and their roots, and one of the most interesting startups that exploits this curiosity is the tech startup 23andme.com. The company extracts and analyzes DNA samples from saliva provided by their customers and sent to the company via mail. After the analysis, 23andme.com reaches out to the customer and gives them a variety of information about their genetic predispositions (e.g., likelihood of flushing after consuming alcohol, lactose intolerance, being under- or overweight), DNA ancestry, and informs consumers if they are carriers for congenital diseases (e.g., Tay Sachs, Alzheimer's). This means that information regarding genetic makeup and other sensitive information is stored on the servers of this company. The implications of a data leak could be severe, potentially leading to violations of customer privacy and unexpected negative consequences such as discrimination based on genetic predispositions.

This small example should demonstrate how privacy is one of the main ethical concerns for internet research, and the more data-rich the internet becomes, the more prominent this issue will become. Researchers should also be mindful of how privacy standards can be vastly different from jurisdiction to jurisdiction. Some of the most well-known privacy laws are the European General Data Protection Regulation (GDPR), the Canadian Personal Information Protection and Electronic Documents Act (PIPEDA), and the United States California Consumer Privacy Act (CCPA). Even with this variability between jurisdictions, it is worth remembering the preeminent position of the GDPR on the world stage. This piece of legislation is seen as a benchmark for any other privacy legislation, and it has influenced global discourse on topics including personal data processing and storage. Article 5 – "Principles relating to processing of personal data" – explicitly states that personal data shall be treated lawfully, fairly, and transparently; they should be collected in line with the stated purpose and not processed outside the original scope. Data also must be accurate and up to date, their storage should not exceed the necessary time based on the purpose of collection, and the data should remain integral and confidential. For all of those processes, the entity who controls the data is accountable for the proper handling and storing and must demonstrate compliance with the GDPR legislation.

This fundamental point about privacy had already been noticed by Gosling and Mason (2015). They argued how the many ethical concerns found in internet research are born from outdated guidelines and rules that were defined before the widespread diffusion of internet research itself. In addition to normal procedures about informed consent and debriefing, they argued how the definition of "public behavior" should be a factor in determining whether the data collected is to be considered public or private. This is especially true when researchers are planning to use webscraping techniques or APIs collecting data from social media, forums, message boards, and other online discussions.

Most internet users, or "netizens," do not realize how their continuous presence on the internet will inevitably lead to the creation of a digital footprint. The more time they spend online in almost any capacity, the more data about their personal life, thoughts, and activities will seep through from the offline to the online world. Though almost all online activities leave traces, social media applications, such as Facebook, LinkedIn, and Google, often contribute the most to this digital footprint. To make the situation worse, these companies provide the option for people to log in to third-party websites, allowing an easier than ever tracking of online activities of specific users.

Ease of access and use is always a trade-off with people's privacy, and companies are not always able to strike the correct balance between confidentiality, integrity, and availability of data. Switching to a researcher's perspective, these online breadcrumb trails are invaluable, as they provide easy means for tracking people's online activities on different websites, and they give insights on technology use and perception. On the other hand, the privacy of the people under investigation will be in danger, both offline and online. This is still an open issue, as there is still no academic consensus among internet researchers. However, there are interesting considerations about determining whether a specific internet behavior is public behavior or not and whether it can be observed and/or recorded without consent (Buchanan and Williams, 2010).

Conclusion

Topics, narratives, and modes of interaction are always shifting in new, unique, and interesting ways. In this chapter, we tried to give an extensive review of contemporary research methods while also talking about common pitfalls and malpractices. Gosling and Mason (2015) make clear that internet research is giving scientists both more new avenues of study but also new challenges and ethical issues. Despite those challenges, the positives that these new technologies put forward by far outweigh any drawbacks. In their work, they also stress the point that researchers must be careful while studying events and people on the internet, as the targets of our research are constantly moving, and it is difficult to follow the continuous new iterations and developments. As the field of internet research continues to evolve, it is essential that researchers remain informed about new tools, techniques, and ethical considerations. Looking ahead, the field will undoubtedly present new challenges and opportunities, and it is our responsibility as researchers to navigate these with integrity and a commitment to ethical research practices.

References

Acker, A., & Kreisberg, A. (2020). Social media data archives in an API-driven world. *Archival Science*, *20*, 105–123.

Albertson, B., & Gadarian, S. (2014, July 1). Was the Facebook emotion experiment unethical? *Washington Post*. www.washingtonpost.com/news/monkey-cage/wp/2014/07/01/was-the-facebook-emotion-experiment-unethical/?utm_term=.15088275b53c

Anderson, C. A., Allen, J. J., Plante, C., Quigley-McBride, A., Lovett, A., & Rokkum, J. N. (2019). The MTurkification of social and personality psychology. *Personality and Social Psychology Bulletin*, *45*(6), 842–850.

Antoun, C., Zhang, C., Conrad, F. G., & Schober, M. F. (2016). Comparisons of online recruitment strategies for convenience samples: Craigslist, Google AdWords, Facebook, and Amazon Mechanical Turk. *Field methods*, *28*(3), 231–246.

Arif, A., Stewart, L. G., & Starbird, K. (2018). Acting the part: Examining information operations within #BlackLivesMatter discourse. *Proceedings of the ACM on Human-Computer Interaction*, *2*(CSCW), 1–27.

Ashokkumar, A., & Pennebaker, J. W. (2021). Social media conversations reveal large psychological shifts caused by COVID-19's onset across US cities. *Science Advances*, *7*(39), eabg7843.

Barrie, C., & Ho, J. C. (2022). *Using the Twitter Academic API with R for Social Science Research*. SAGE Publications. https://dx.doi.org/10.4135/9781529609233

Bayer, J. B., Triệu, P., & Ellison, N. B. (2020). Social media elements, ecologies, and effects. *Annual Review of Psychology*, *71*, 471–497.

Bentley, F. R., Daskalova, N., & White, B. (2017, May). Comparing the reliability of Amazon Mechanical Turk and Survey Monkey to traditional market research surveys. In *Proceedings of the 2017 CHI conference extended abstracts on human factors in computing systems* (pp. 1092–1099). ACM.

Berinsky, A. J., Huber, G. A., & Lenz, G. S. (2012). Evaluating online labor markets for experimental research: Amazon.com's Mechanical Turk. *Political analysis*, *20*(3), 351–368.

Boyd, R. L., Ashokkumar, A., Seraj, S., & Pennebaker, J. W. (2022). *The Development and Psychometric Properties of LIWC-22*. University of Texas at Austin.

Boyd, R. L., & Pennebaker, J. W. (2015). A way with words: Using language for psychological science in the modern era. In C. V. Dimofte, C. P. Haugtvedt, & R. F. Yalch (eds.), *Consumer Psychology in a Social Media World* (pp. 222–236). Routledge.

Boyd, R. L., & Pennebaker, J. W. (2017). Language-based personality: A new approach to personality in a digital world. *Current Opinion in Behavioral Sciences*, *18*, 63–68.

Buchanan, E. A., & Hvizdak, E. E. (2009). Online survey tools: Ethical and methodological concerns of human research ethics committees. *Journal of Empirical Research on Human Research Ethics*, *4*(2), 37–48.

Buchanan, T., & Williams, J. E. (2010). Ethical issues in psychological research on the internet. In S. D. Gosling & J. A. Johnson (eds.), *Advanced Methods for Conducting Online Behavioral Research* (pp. 255–271). American Psychological Association.

Buhrmester, M., Kwang, T., & Gosling, S. D. (2011). Amazon's Mechanical Turk: A new source of inexpensive, yet high-quality, data? *Perspectives on Psychological Science*, *6*(1), 3–5.

Burger, J. M. (2014). *Personality*. Cengage Learning.

Butler, L., Lamont, P., Wan, D. L. Y., Prike, T., Nasim, M., Walker, B., et al. (2022). The (mis) information game: A social media simulator. *Behavior Research Methods*. https://doi.org/10.3758/s13428-023-02153-x

boyd, D. M., & Ellison, N. B. (2007). Social network sites: Definition, history, and scholarship. *Journal of Computer-Mediated Communication*, *13*(1), 210–230. https://doi.org/10.1111/j.1083-6101.2007.00393.x

Cadwalladr, C., Khalili, M., Phillips, C., Silver, M., Jenkins, A., Search, J., et al. (2021). Cambridge Analytica whistleblower: "We spent $1m harvesting millions of Facebook profiles" [video]. *Guardian*, March 17. www.theguardian.com/uk-news/video/2018/mar/17/cambridge-analytica-whistleblower-we-spent-1m-harvesting-millions-of-facebook-profiles-video

Casler, K., Bickel, L., & Hackett, E. (2013). Separate but equal? A comparison of participants and data gathered via Amazon's MTurk, social media, and face-to-face behavioral testing. *Computers in Human Behavior*, *29*(6), 2156–2160.

Chambers, C. (2014). Facebook fiasco: Was Cornell's study of "emotional contagion" an ethics breach? *Guardian*, July 1. www.theguardian.com/science/head-quarters/2014/jul/01/facebook-cornell-study-emotional-contagion-ethics-breach

Chambers, M., Bliss, K., & Rambur, B. (2020). Recruiting research participants via traditional snowball vs Facebook advertisements and a website. *Western Journal of Nursing Research*, *42*(10), 846–851.

Chandler, J. (2023). Participant recruitment. In A. Nichols & J. E. Edlund (eds.), *Cambridge Handbook of Research Methods and Statistics for the Social and Behavioral Sciences* (vol. 1, pp. 179–201). Cambridge University Press.

Chandler, J., & Shapiro, D. (2016). Conducting clinical research using crowdsourced convenience samples. *Annual Review of Clinical Psychology*, 12, 53–81.

Clark, T., & Blackhart, G. (2023). Debriefing and post-experimental procedures. In A. Nichols & J. E. Edlund (eds.), *Cambridge Handbook of Research Methods and Statistics for the Social and Behavioral Sciences* (vol. 1, pp. 244–265). Cambridge University Press.

Clifford, S., Jewell, R. M., & Waggoner, P. D. (2015). Are samples drawn from Mechanical Turk valid for research on political ideology? *Research & Politics*, *2*(4), 2053168015622072.

Cohn, M. A., Mehl, M. R., & Pennebaker, J. W. (2004). Linguistic markers of psychological change surrounding September 11, 2001. *Psychological Science*, *15*(10), 687–693.

Dawson, P. (2014). Our anonymous online research participants are not always anonymous: Is this a problem? *British Journal of Educational Technology*, *45*(3), 428–437.

De Choudhury, M., Gamon, M., Counts, S., & Horvitz, E. (2013). Predicting depression via social media. *ICWSM*, *13*, 1–10.

Dobber, T., Ó Fathaigh, R., & Zuiderveen Borgesius, F. J. (2019). The regulation of online political micro-targeting in Europe. *Internet Policy Review*, *8*(4). https://policyreview.info/articles/analysis/regulation-online-political-micro-targeting-europe

Edlund, J. E., Lange, K. M., Sevene, A. M., Umansky, J., Beck, C. D., & Bell, D. J. (2017). Participant crosstalk: Issues when using the Mechanical Turk. *Tutorials in Quantitative Methods for Psychology*, *13*(3), 174–182.

Foster, M. D. (2015). Tweeting about sexism: The well-being benefits of a social media collective action. *British Journal of Social Psychology*, *54*(4), 629–647.

Gosling, S. D., & Mason, W. (2015). Internet research in psychology. *Annual Review of Psychology*, 66, 877–902.

Graham-Harrison, E., & Cadwalladr, C. (2021). Revealed: 50 million Facebook profiles harvested for Cambridge Analytica in major data breach. *Guardian*, September 29. www.theguardian.com/news/2018/mar/17/cambridge-analytica-facebook-influence-us-election

Grimm, P. (2010). Social desirability bias. In C. L. Cooper (ed.), *Wiley International Encyclopedia of Marketing*. Wiley.

Guadagno, R. E. (2019). Using the internet for research. In J. E. Edlund & A. L. Nichols (eds.), *Advanced Research Methods for the Social and Behavioral Sciences* (pp. 68–82). Cambridge University Press.

Guadagno, R. E. (in press). *Psychological Processes in Social Media: Why We Click*. Academic Press.

Guadagno, R. E., Loewald, T. A., Muscanell, N. L., Barth, J. M., Goodwin, M. K., & Yang, Y. (2013). Facebook history collector: A new method for directly collecting data from Facebook. *International Journal of Interactive Communication Systems and Technologies (IJICST)*, *3*(1), 57–67.

Guadagno, R. E., Muscanell, N. L., & Pollio, D. E. (2013). The homeless use Facebook?! Similarities of social network use between college students and homeless young adults. *Computers in Human Behavior*, *29*(1), 86–89. https://doi.org/10.1016/j.chb.2012.07.019

Guadagno, R. E., Muscanell, N. L., Rice, L. M., & Roberts, N. (2013). Social influence online: The impact of social validation and likability on compliance. *Psychology of Popular Media Culture*, *2*(1), 51–60.

Guadagno, R. E., Rempala, D. M., Murphy, S., & Okdie, B. M. (2013). What makes a video go viral? An analysis of emotional contagion and internet memes. *Computers in Human Behavior*, *29*(6), 2312–2319.

Hellström, T., Dignum, V., & Bensch, S. (2020). Bias in machine learning: What is it good for? [preprint]. *Arxiv*. https://doi.org/10.48550/arXiv.2004.00686

Hill, K. (2014). Facebook manipulated 689,003 users' emotions for science. *Forbes*, June 28. www.forbes.com/sites/kashmirhill/2014/06/28/facebook-manipulated-689003-users-emotions-for-science/#593f5cbf197c

Ireland, M. E., & Henderson, M. D. (2014). Language style matching, engagement, and impasse in negotiations. *Negotiation and Conflict Management Research*, *7*(1), 1–16.

Jacobucci, R., & Grimm, K. J. (2020). Machine learning and psychological research: The unexplored effect of measurement. *Perspectives on Psychological Science*, *15*(3), 809–816. https://doi.org/10.1177/1745691620902467

Jagayat, A. (2022, October 4). Mock social media website tool. *OSF*. https://osf.io/m2xd8

Jenders, M., Kasneci, G., & Naumann, F. (2013, May). Analyzing and predicting viral tweets. In Daniel Schwabe (ed.), *Proceedings of the 22nd International Conference on World Wide Web* (pp. 657–664). ACM.

Kendall, C., Kerr, L. R., Gondim, R. C., Werneck, G. L., Macena, R. H. M., Pontes, M. K., et al. (2008). An empirical comparison of respondent-driven sampling, time location sampling, and snowball sampling for behavioral surveillance in men who have sex with men, Fortaleza, Brazil. *AIDS and Behavior*, *12*, 97–104.

Kern, M. L., McCarthy, P. X., Chakrabarty, D., & Rizoiu, M. A. (2019). Social media-predicted personality traits and values can help match people to their ideal jobs. *Proceedings of the National Academy of Sciences*, *116*(52), 26459–26464.

Kosinski, M., Stillwell, D., & Graepel, T. (2013). Private traits and attributes are predictable from digital records of human behavior. *Proceedings of the National Academy of Sciences*, *110*(15), 5802–5805.

Kramer, A. D., Guillory, J. E., & Hancock, J. T. (2014). Experimental evidence of massive-scale emotional contagion through social networks. *Proceedings of the National Academy of Sciences*, *111*(24), 8788–8790.

Ksiazek, T. B. (2015). Civil interactivity: How news organizations' commenting policies explain civility and hostility in user comments. *Journal of Broadcasting & Electronic Media*, *59*(4), 556–573.

Lee, J., Gillath, O., Kimbrough, A. M., & Guadagno, R. E. (2017, January). Development and validation of helping in gaming scales. Poster presented at the Media Psychology Preconference, San Antonio, TX.

Lee, J., & Spratling, R. (2019). Recruiting mothers of children with developmental disabilities: Adaptations of the snowball sampling technique using social media. *Journal of Pediatric Health Care*, *33*(1), 107–110.

Markham, A., & Buchanan, E. (2012). *Recommendations from the AoIR Ethics Working Committee* (Version 2.0).

Merriam-Webster. (n.d.). Crowdsourcing. In Merriam-Webster.com [dictionary]. www.merriam-webster.com/dictionary/crowdsourcing (retrieved March 6, 2024).

Miller, J. D., Crowe, M., Weiss, B., Maples-Keller, J. L., & Lynam, D. R. (2017). Using online, crowdsourcing platforms for data collection in personality disorder research: The example of Amazon's Mechanical Turk. *Personality Disorders: Theory, Research, and Treatment*, *8*(1), 26–34.

Murray, M. (2014). Users angered at Facebook emotion-manipulation study. *Today*, June 30. www.today.com/health/users-angered-facebook-emotion-manipulation-study-1D79863049

Muscanell, N. L., & Guadagno, R. E. (2012). Make new friends or keep the old: Gender and personality differences in social networking use. *Computers in Human Behavior*, *28*(1), 107–112. https://doi.org/10.1016/j.chb.2011.08.016

Nichols, A., & Edlund, J. E. (2020). Why don't we care more about carelessness? Understanding the causes and consequences of careless participants. *International Journal of Social Research Methodology*, *23*(6), 625–638. https://doi.org/10.1080/13645579.2020.1719618

Oinas-Kukkonen, H., & Oinas-Kukkonen, H. (2013). *Humanizing the Web: Change and Social Innovation*. Palgrave Macmillan.

Paolacci, G., & Chandler, J. (2014). Inside the Turk: Understanding Mechanical Turk as a participant pool. *Current Directions in Psychological Science*, *23*(3), 184–188.

Park, G., Schwartz, H. A., Eichstaedt, J. C., Kern, M. L., Kosinski, M., Stillwell, D. J., et al. (2015). Automatic personality assessment through social media language. *Journal of Personality and Social Psychology*, *108*(6), 934–952.

Parker, C., Scott, S., & Geddes, A. (2019). *Snowball Sampling*. SAGE Publications. https://dx.doi.org/10.4135/9781526421036831710

Pennebaker, J. W., Chung, C. K., Ireland, M., Gonzales, A., & Booth, R. J. (2007). The development and psychometric properties of LIWC2007. LIWC. www.liwc.net/LIWC2007LanguageManual.pdf

Pennebaker, J. W., Francis, M. E., & Booth, R. J. (2001). Linguistic inquiry and word count: LIWC 2001. LIWC. www.researchgate.net/publication/246699633_Linguistic_inquiry_and_word_count_LIWC

Phing, A. N. M., & Yazdanifard, R. (2014). How does ALS ice bucket challenge achieve its viral outcome through marketing via social media? *Global Journal of Management and Business Research*, *14*(E7), 57–64.

Roozenbeek, J., & van der Linden, S. (2019). Fake news game confers psychological resistance against online misinformation. *Palgrave Communications*, *5*(12). https://doi.org/10.1057/s41599-019-0279-9

Ross, J., Zaldivar, A., Irani, L., & Tomlinson, B. (2009). Who are the Turkers? Worker demographics in Amazon Mechanical Turk. In *CHI '10 Extended Abstracts on Human Factors in Computing Systems* (pp. 2863–2872). ACM.

Rouse, S. V. (2015). A reliability analysis of Mechanical Turk data. *Computers in Human Behavior*, *43*, 304–307.

Prevency. (n.d.). The solution for a realistic social media simulation. https://socialmediasimulator.com

Solon, O. (2018). Facebook says Cambridge Analytica may have gained 37m more users' data. *Guardian*, April 4. www.theguardian.com/technology/2018/apr/04/facebook-cambridge-analytica-user-data-latest-more-than-thought

Stephens-Davidowitz, S. (2017). *Everybody Lies: Big Data, New Data, and What the Internet Can Tell Us about Who We Really Are*. HarperLuxe.

Vasalou, A., Gill, A. J., Mazanderani, F., Papoutsi, C., & Joinson, A. (2011). Privacy dictionary: A new resource for the automated content analysis of privacy. *Journal of the Association for Information Science and Technology*, *62*(11), 2095–2105.

Vaughn-Nichols, S. J. (2014). We're all just lab rats in Facebook's laboratory. *ZDNet*, June 30. www.zdnet.com/article/were-all-just-lab-rats-in-facebooks-laboratory/

Verma, I. M. (2014). Editorial expression of concern: Experimental evidence of massive-scale emotional contagion through social networks. *Proceedings of the National Academy of Sciences*, *111*(29), 10779–10779.

Wang, T., Brede, M., Ianni, A., & Mentzakis, E. (2017, February). Detecting and characterizing eating-disorder communities on social media. In M. de Rijke (ed.), *Proceedings of the Tenth ACM International Conference on Web Search and Data Mining* (pp. 91–100). ACM.

Wright, S. A., & Goodman, J. K. (2019). Mechanical Turk in consumer research: Perceptions and usage in marketing academia. In F. R. Kardes, P. M. Herr, & N. Schwarz (eds.), *Handbook of Research Methods in Consumer Psychology* (pp. 338–357). Routledge.

Zhou, H., & Fishbach, A. (2016). The pitfall of experimenting on the web: How unattended selective attrition leads to surprising (yet false) research conclusions. *Journal of Personality and Social Psychology*, *111*(4), 493–504.

Zhou, L., Pan, S., Wang, J., & Vasilakos, A. V. (2017). Machine learning on big data: Opportunities and challenges. *Neurocomputing*, *237*, 350–361.

Zimmer, M. (2018). Addressing conceptual gaps in big data research ethics: An application of contextual integrity. *Social Media + Society*, *4*(2), 2056305118768300.

4 Prolific: Crowdsourcing Academic Online Research

Eyal Peer

Abstract

Prolific is a website that offers researchers the ability to recruit and sample participants for online research. In contrast to earlier crowdsourcing platforms, such as Amazon Mechanical Turk (MTurk), it focuses primarily on academic and marketing research – typically done through online surveys and experiments. In this chapter, I aim to introduce this platform to researchers conducting online studies and to provide knowledge and practical advice on how to best use the platform for online research. The review includes explanations of how the site works, the composition of its pool of participants, the options available to researchers for sampling and recruiting participants online, how to achieve advanced abilities by connecting Prolific to research software (e.g., Qualtrics, Gorilla), and how to ensure high data quality when using Prolific. I then review the evidence on the current state of data quality on Prolific, suggesting that it can provide higher data quality than MTurk and also better than some commercial panels. I conclude with a summary of the advantages and disadvantages of using Prolific for online research and potential future developments in the platform that could promote more credible online research.

Keywords: Prolific, Online Research, Crowdsourcing, Data Quality, Online Sampling

Overview

Prolific (originally called "Prolific Academic") is a UK-based company that founded and maintains the website prolific.co. The site offers researchers a platform to post invitations to online studies and recruit participants to take part in studies, for a monetary reward. The platform connects researchers to participants in an anonymous manner and acts as a mediator that distributes the researchers' studies to participants and provides participants the ability to take part in the study and get paid for their completion. Prolific then profits from the commission (currently 30%) researchers pay for every participant who successfully completed the study.

In this chapter, I first review how the Prolific platform works to connect participants and researchers for completing online studies and then describe the current participant pool available for researchers. I next turn to explain several key aspects of using the site from a researcher's point of view. These include the options for sampling on Prolific, advanced options that Prolific (combined with Qualtrics) offers researchers, how to ensure high data quality on Prolific, and the current state of data quality on Prolific. I conclude with a summary of the advantages Prolific offers researchers (also in relation to other platforms), the current shortcomings of the site, and how researchers should take them into account when conducting online studies. This chapter aims to provide researchers with comprehensive information that can assist them in their decision on whether, when, and how to use Prolific and how to best utilize its advantages to yield the optimal results for them. The chapter does not, however, provide specific tutorials or instructions on how to use specific features. That is mostly because Prolific is still a new and growing platform, and the user interface is likely to change and improve over time. Additionally, there are many online tutorials on Prolific's site, and elsewhere, that promise to be more updated than this chapter could be.

How It Works

Researchers sign up for the site using an email account and can immediately post invitations for studies. The researcher first enters the details of the study (title, description, sample size, payment details) and the link to the online questionnaire (e.g., on Qualtrics), and is then asked to add money to the account (in GBP) to publish the study to participants. Participants sign up for the site and, after they complete a sign-up process (that includes verifying their identity, providing a bank account, and completing a preliminary questionnaire), participants can select which studies to complete. Participants first "accept" a study to get the link to the survey, and submit it when they complete the study. Participants can also "return" the study without completing it, at any stage, without getting paid. Researchers can monitor the incoming submissions and, when the study is complete, review the submissions and approve or reject them. Only when a submission is approved by the researcher (or automatically approved after a pre-set time), the participant receives their payment. Participants may also send messages to researchers through the site in case of questions, problems, or any disputes. Researchers can also grant bonuses to participants who completed their study.

The Users

As of January 2021, there were approximately 1.39 million participants registered on the site and more than 100,000 researchers, according to Prolific's data.[1] Figure 4.1 shows how the rates of participants and researchers have increased from 2014, and that the highest increase in participants was in 2020 and 2021, during the COVID-19 global pandemic. More important is the size of the *active* participants pool – the participants who have taken a study in the last 90 days. According to Prolific's data,

---

[1] All the data reported here was provided courtesy of Prolific. I thank Andrew Gordon from Prolific for that.

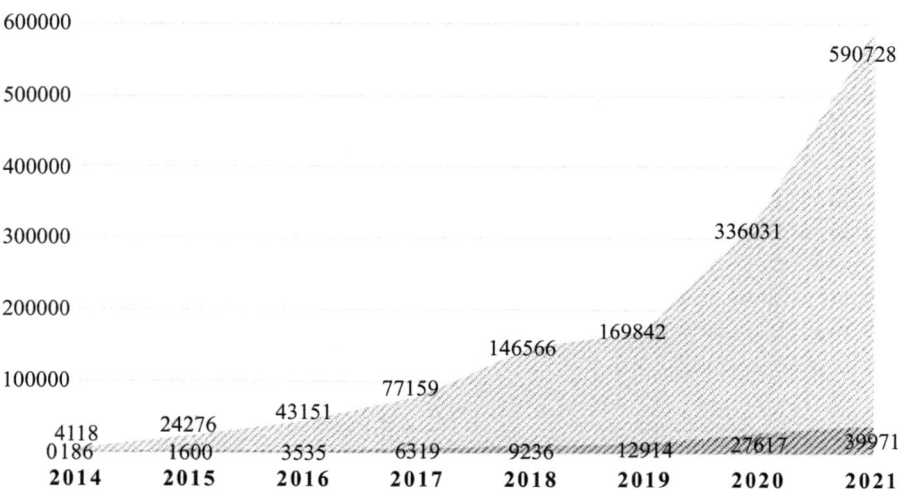

Figure 4.1 Number of participants and researchers on Prolific according to the year they joined.

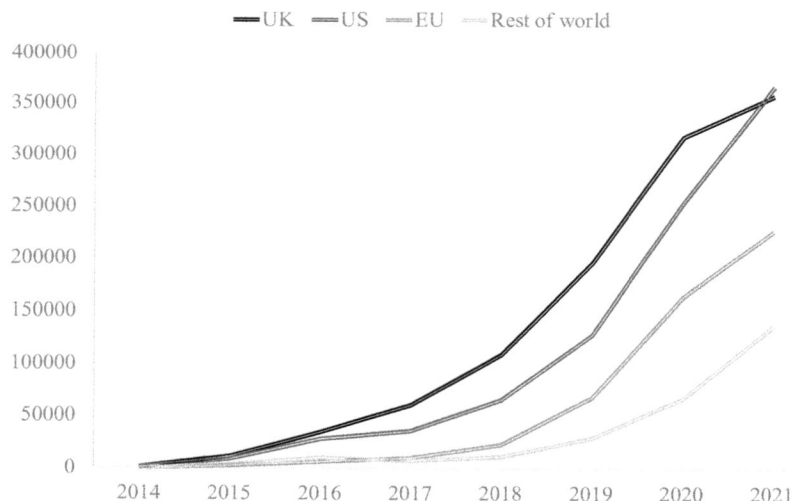

Figure 4.2 Number of participants on Prolific by territory and year.

in June 2022 the active users pool included around 123,000 users. Most participants were from either the US or UK: in 2021 42% were from the US and 42% were from the UK, while only 16% were from other countries. As Figure 4.2 shows, while in the past years there were more participants from the UK, the number of US participants has risen. These participants serve approximately 12,000 researchers, 33% of them from the US, 25% from Europe, 22% from the UK, and 19% from other countries.

Demographics of the Participant Pool

Figures 4.3a to 4.3d show the distribution of registered participants in Prolific's pool over the years by their ethnicity, gender, personal income, and age groups. Notably, over the years, the sample has become predominately white and female. Most participants are now of low to medium income, and the share of younger participants, which decreased in the early years, has risen again in recent years. However, these data are based on the total registered participant pool and not the pool of active users. When researchers set up their study on Prolific, they may choose various options on

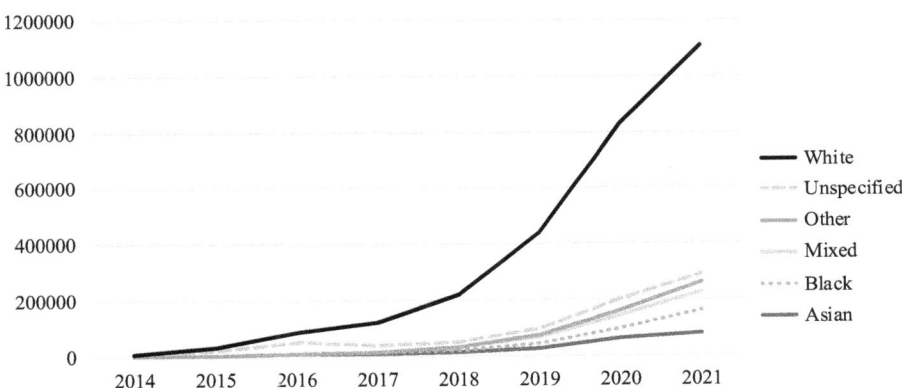

Figure 4.3a *Number of participants on Prolific by year and ethnicity.*

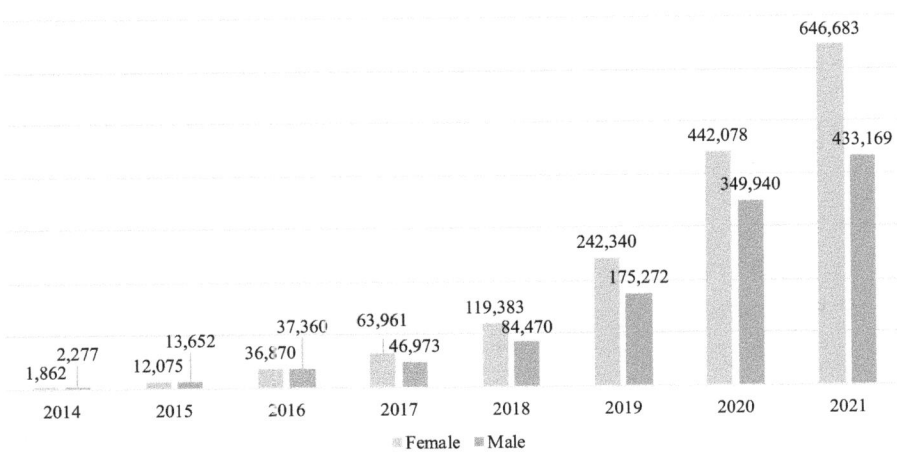

Figure 4.3b *Number of participants on Prolific by year and gender.*

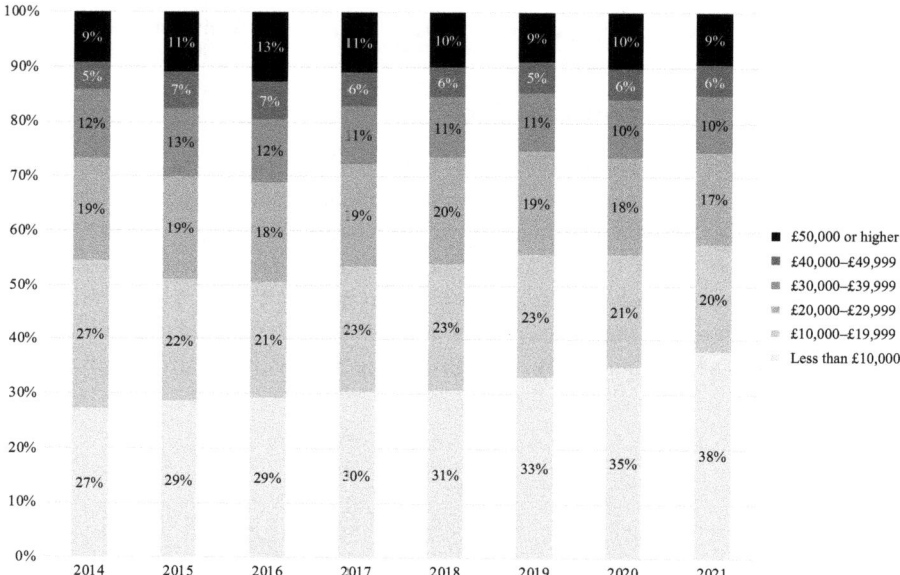

Figure 4.3c *Percent of participants on Prolific by personal income level and year.*

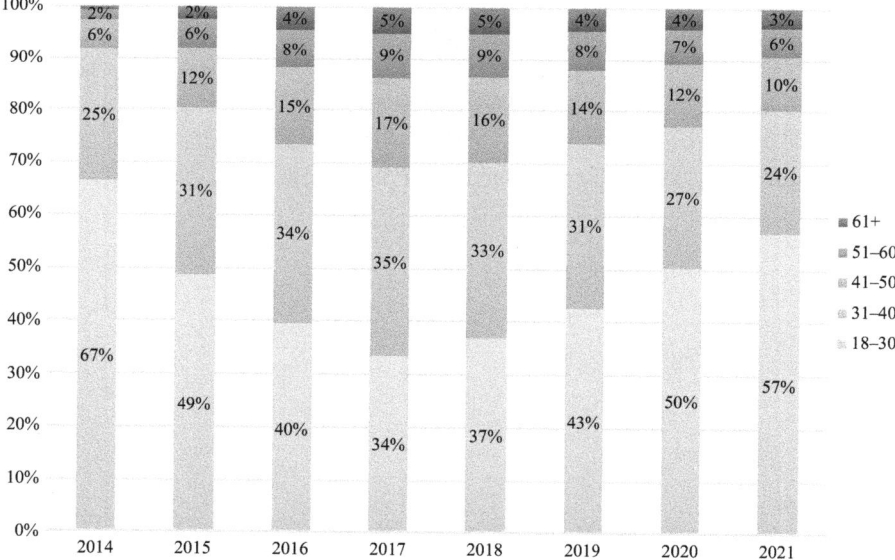

Figure 4.3d *Percent of participants on Prolific by age group and year.*

how to sample from the active participants pool and can use several methods to ensure the representativeness of their sample; or, to ensure that it will not be biased or skewed toward some groups, as is explained in the next section.

Sampling on Prolific

When researchers set up their study on Prolific, they can choose from several options to determine which types and groups of participants would be eligible to be sampled for their study. The default option on Prolific is that a study is published to all registered participants, and it is filled on a "first-come-first-served" basis. Once the target sample is reached, the study is no longer available to other participants. While this is the general approach, I have learned from officials at Prolific that the site also uses an algorithm to distribute new studies among the active participants. This serves to make sure that researchers don't get the same participants in different studies and to keep the participants engaged and active. However, this does not ensure a representative or balanced sample, thus Prolific offers additional predefined options for sampling.

Representative Sampling

Outside of the default option, researchers may choose to request a representative sample, based on either US or UK current census data. In this option, Prolific manages quotas of participants, on variables of gender and age, and presents the study to participants according to the quotas. This option may slow down the rate of responses to some degree, but it ensures a more diverse and representative sample than the default option. As of 2023, Prolific does not charge any extra fee for this option.

Another option researchers may choose is to request a "balanced" sample – this will include similar numbers of males and females. This feature was added to Prolific following a surge of female TikTok users who joined the site after a viral video[2] by a teen influencer that encouraged her (mostly female) followers to sign up for Prolific to get the opportunity to earn money by using the site. The increase of female participants in the sample was detected by some researchers who complained about it, and Prolific responded by presenting fewer studies to this demographic group (young female) and offering researchers the option of the balanced sample. Once this option is selected, Prolific ensures that participants will be close to 50% of each gender. This incident highlights how important it is for researchers to actively monitor the demographic composition of their sample when using online platforms such as Prolific.

Prescreened Sampling

In addition to these three general options of sampling (default, representative, balanced), researchers may also prescreen participants ex-ante using a list of more than 250 filters available on the site. These include geographic filters (e.g., country/ state of birth or residence), primary demographics (e.g., age, gender, ethnicity, marital status), family attributes, employment type, employment status or

---

[2] www.prolific.co/blog/we-recently-went-viral-on-tiktok-heres-what-we-learned

experience, education level and type, financial status, health-related aspects (including COVID-19), political and societal beliefs, interests and habits, what kind of technology they have (e.g., if they have a webcam or use a specific operating system), and more. These variables are collected from participants during their "onboarding" process when they register for the site. However, not all users provide all data, so some filters include many missing values. Additionally, variables and filters are often added to the onboarding questionnaire, so some users were not asked about some of the variables in their questionnaire, resulting in missing values. To prevent cases where applying too many filters, or applying filters that have many missing values, would detrimentally reduce the available pool, Prolific presents to researchers the estimated pool after the filter is applied. When a filter is selected, Prolific calculates the estimated number of participants in their active pool (users that completed a study in the last 90 days) that would be eligible for the study with the selected filters. This gives researchers the information needed to make important decisions about which filters to apply and what to expect, in terms of response time and sampling frame, if they apply those filters.

Researchers can also filter based on previous participation on Prolific, including participants' number of previous submissions, their approval rate, and whether they completed your previous studies. The approval rate is determined by the percent of completed submissions that were approved by the researchers out of all submissions completed. However, I have learned from officials at Prolific that, because some participants don't have enough submissions for this percent to be meaningful, the system actually computes a 95% confidence interval around the approval rate of each participant and uses the upper bound of the interval as the effective approval rate. As a result, the approval rate is highly skewed. For instance, as can be seen in Figure 4.4, which shows screenshots of the screening dialog on Prolific, when filtering to users with 98% approval rate or higher, the number of eligible participants is reduced by only 3,000 participants (out of 120,000). That is, nearly 97% of the eligible participants have an approval rating above 98%. This effectively makes the approval rate metric of little use to researchers, as I discuss further in the following section about data quality.

Another potentially useful filter is the language participants report understanding. According to Prolific's data of June 2022, 71% of participants state that their first language is English, 6% Spanish, 4% Portuguese, 4% Polish, 3% Italian, 2%

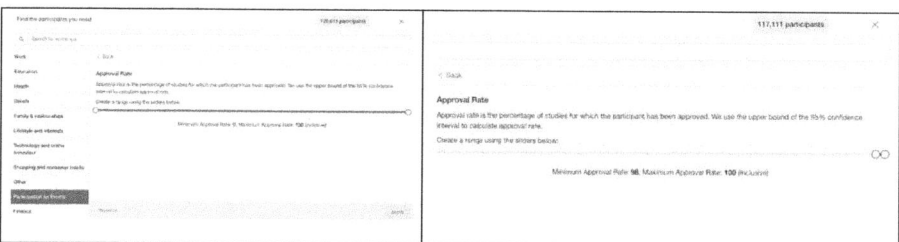

Figure 4.4 *Screenshots of the filtering dialog on Prolific before (left) and after (right) restricting to participants with approval rate of 98% or above.*

German, and 1% of participants each report French, Dutch, Greek, Hungarian, or Chinese as their first language. Alternatively, you may choose participants based on the language they indicated they are fluent in (participants can indicate fluency in more than one language). In June 2022, more than half a million registered users said they are fluent in English, approximately 60,000 in Spanish, 27,000 in French, and 20,000 in Polish, German, or Portuguese. Additionally, researchers can also create custom screeners – lists of participants' IDs they can use to define whom they want to invite ("allowlist") or whom they want to ban from their studies ("blocklist").

Using these pre-filters can be highly advantageous to a study, as it can help prevent responses from participants who are irrelevant to the research (e.g., not from the age range the study is exploring), might not understand the instructions (e.g., not fluent in the survey's language), or are not naive to the research (e.g., has taken a similar study before in which they were exposed to similar research materials). However, using pre-filters should be done with caution. First, multiple pre-filters can seriously reduce the size of the participants pool, can increase the time needed to collect the sample, and might also introduce a selection bias that can impair the ability to generalize the findings of the research. Additionally, a reduced sampling frame may mean the study will attract the more active participants, whom may be less naive to experimental materials; this has been found to reduce estimations of known effect sizes (Chandler et al., 2015). Nevertheless, pre-filters can be useful to many researchers who are interested in sampling from specific populations for their studies, and the range of available filters on Prolific is diverse and comprehensive. I elaborate on how pre-filters can be effectively used to enhance data quality later in this chapter.

Connecting Prolific to Survey Software

One of Prolific's key advantages lies in its easy connectivity to research software, such as Qualtrics, Gorilla, or others. This streamlines the process of submission approvals and provides several advanced options for online research. Researchers who use Qualtrics or Gorilla for their study can direct the participant to the study from Prolific, and then, when the participant reaches the end of the study, the participant can be automatically redirected to Prolific with a code signaling to Prolific that the participant indeed finished the study. This makes it both easier and safer for researchers because they do not have to check each individual submission or rely on participants' reports that they indeed completed the study. This can also be better than the often used approach of providing participants with completion codes that force researchers to check each code (if they provide unique codes for each participant) or to take the risk that participants will share the code with others, who will make a submission without actually completing the study.

Autocompletion Codes

To use the option of automatic completion codes, researchers need to take several steps when configuring their study. First, when setting up the study on Prolific, researchers need to enter the URL of the study on Qualtrics and choose the option that appends to that URL parameters that include the participant ID on Prolific. Next, researchers need to set an "embedded data" element on their Qualtrics survey flow that stores the participants' IDs in the study's data, allowing the tracking and monitoring of the participant. Lastly, the researcher needs to copy the completion code URL from the Prolific study, insert it in the end of the survey on Qualtrics, and enter it as a redirect URL. This automatically enters a completion code only for participants who did get to the end of the study. When participants complete the study, they are automatically redirected back to Prolific with the proper completion code. Prolific identifies the code and marks the submission for that participant as approved. This means that the researcher can focus their time on the other submissions that did not include the code and, if needed, reject them for not completing the study.

Having the participants' ID stored within the data file also enables researchers to easily decide which participants to approve (if they completed the study), reject (e.g., if they failed to follow instructions), or even block (if they behaved inappropriately). Importantly, Prolific participants' personal information is still kept confidential from researchers, and there is no way by which researchers can identify a person by their Prolific participant ID, because that data is only available to Prolific and not to the researchers. Thus, from an ethical perspective, retaining Prolific participants' IDs does not constitute personally identifying information. This is in contrast to Amazon MTurk workers' IDs that can be linked to people's Amazon accounts and may lead to identifying information. However, it is still best practice to remove participants' IDs from a data file when, for example, posting the data file in a public repository.

Additional Options

Connecting a study on Prolific to Qualtrics or Gorilla can provide researchers with additional features, including paying bonuses based on performance, inviting participants to complete another study (e.g., for longitudinal research), and also pre-allocation of participants to research conditions or treatments. For bonuses, researchers can create a list of participants' IDs and the amount to pay each participant, based, for example, on how many questions or tasks they got correct in the study. Then, the researchers need to upload that list to Prolific and pay all the bonuses in bulk (Prolific charges a commission per bonus).

To invite participants to another study, researchers can send them a message through Prolific to take part in a new study they created in which they set a pre-filter that the study is only available for participants who completed the previous study or for specific participants based on an "allowlist" they want to include. This allows researchers to plan and conduct longitudinal studies that require participants to report their behaviors multiple times, or to conduct a follow-up study on participants who completed a study. For example, researchers may want to conduct a first wave of a study that includes the experimental manipulation or treatments they're exploring and then resample those participants several days later to measure some individual trait or scale (e.g., that researchers could not have measured in the same study to avoid affecting the other parts of the study or because the study would be too long). Similarly, researchers can design a longitudinal study in which participants are asked to report every week or month (or other period). However, if the longitudinal study involves multiple instances over time, it could become somewhat cumbersome to design and manage on the system as it is currently. This is because each instance needs to be defined as a study on its own, and a custom "allowlist" must be created and maintained across the instances. Alternatively, Prolific screeners include the option to include (or exclude) participants from previous studies that were done on the researcher's account.

Lastly, researchers can use participants' IDs to pre-allocate participants to a specific group or treatment based on their individual traits or demographics. For example, a researcher may want to show one treatment to participants who are of high income and a different treatment to those who are of lower income. If the researcher asks participants for their income at the beginning of the study, it might prime them to this concept and bias their subsequent behavior. To disguise the purpose of your study, without using deception, researchers can assign a condition to each group of participants, based on their IDs, on Qualtrics or Gorilla, and then test different treatments on different groups of participants.

Additionally, the Gorilla experiment builder (https://gorilla.sc) also offers researchers two more features for advanced online research. The first is that Gorilla has built-in features for longitudinal studies that can make it easier to invite Prolific participants for studies that require multiple instances. The second is that Gorilla offers *multiplayer* studies: these are studies in which several participants (two or more) interact with each other remotely through the survey software. This is required in studies that examine, for example, negotiation, cooperation, competition, and other social interactions. Gorilla has a unique interface with Prolific for this type of study. Through their interface, they allow researchers to set up a "lobby" to which participants from Prolific first enter, and are held in waiting there, until a sufficient number of additional participants is recruited to start the multiplayer session (see more information at https://gorilla.sc/gorilla-for-multiplayer-studies). This allows researchers who use Gorilla to set up multiplayer studies and recruit groups of participants who complete the study together in the interactive environment that Gorilla provides.

Lastly, it is important to note that although Qualtrics and Gorilla offer, as detailed above, various advanced options for research, some of the above abilities can be achieved in practically any survey software the researcher uses. First, a researcher can ask participants for their Prolific ID (ideally at the end of the study) to award them bonuses or to invite them to (or exclude them from) future studies. This, however, relies on participants typing their ID correctly. Secondly, researchers can run longitudinal studies using Prolific even if they're not storing the ID with the help of Qualtrics by, for example, providing participants with a unique code at the end of the first stage that they will be asked to enter in the subsequent stages. This relies on participants not losing their unique code and could lead to some misses. Thus, researchers who don't use Qualtrics or Gorilla can still use Prolific for the main objectives of recruiting participants online in a fast and trustworthy manner, that will hopefully result in high-quality data for their research.

How to Ensure High Data Quality on Prolific

Data quality is critical to online research for several reasons. First, unlike the campus laboratory, researchers cannot confirm the identity of the participant and make sure they (a) are taking the study themselves, (b) meet the study's eligibility criteria (e.g., that they are not minor), and (c) do not take the study more than once. Second, the online environment is open to various kinds of misconduct by participants that can harm data quality. Because participants are not proctored or supervised, they may skip important instructions, not pay enough attention, take the study while doing something else, or misrepresent themselves and provide false responses (e.g., Nichols & Edlund, 2020).

Aspects of Data Quality

Extensive research has focused on issues of online data quality to examine different attributes of quality among different types of audiences (for a comprehensive review see Thomas & Clifford, 2017). Aspects of data quality can be measured on the individual (participant) level or the aggregate (group or sample) level. Individual-level data-quality measures include whether participants pay enough *attention* to instructions and research material, show *comprehension* of the messages delivered to them in the study, respond in an *honest* and truthful manner, and are *naive* to the research material (and respond to it candidly). These individual-level data-quality measures can also be regarded as *process* measures, as they usually are not the end goal of a given study and are used to verify that the participants indeed engage in the procedure of the study as designed by the researcher. Low levels of attention or comprehension would surely lead to noisy and unreliable findings, and dishonest or non-naive responses could invalidate research findings.

At the aggregate or group level, there are additional data-quality measures that should be considered. These include *reliability* of responses (e.g., to scales or trait measures), whether the sample shows high *replicability* of known and validated effects, and the degree of *representativeness* of the sample that the platform yields (e.g., that it is not biased or skewed toward some demographics). In the following, I expand on each of these measures, and then I discuss how researchers can use Prolific to ensure high data quality.

Attention refers to the extent to which participants actually read questions before answering them. Typically, this has been measured using attention-check questions (ACQs, also known as instructional manipulation checks, or IMCs; see Oppenheimer et al., 2009) in which the respondent is asked a seemingly benign question (e.g., "Which sport do you like the most?") but the preface to the question includes instructions to answer in a specific manner (e.g., choose "other" and then type "check"). Another form of ACQ is to embed a nonsensical item within a long scale or questionnaire, to which only one response in the scale's option can be justified (e.g., "When watching TV, I had a fatal heart attack"; here, attentive participants must answer "Never"; see Paolacci et al., 2010).

Comprehension refers to the degree to which participants understand a task's instructions (Berinsky et al., 2014; Rand et al., 2012). Although this may seem related to attention, it both refers to whether participants read the full instructions and captures whether they are able to convey instructions clearly back to researchers. For example, this may include whether participants can correctly summarize instructions for an experimental task that asks them to make some judgment, perform some task, or consider different alternatives for a certain goal. Previous research has indeed shown that excluding participants who fail to pay attention is not the same as excluding those who miscomprehend instructions (Berinsky et al., 2014).

Honesty refers to the extent to which participants provide truthful responses (e.g., to demographic questions) or provide accurate responses when asked to self-report their performance. Extant research on unethical behavior has repeatedly shown that, when given the opportunity, many people will choose to over-report their performance on experimental tasks to earn a higher pay (Gerlach et al., 2019). While such dishonesty is prevalent, it can sometimes be detrimental to behavioral research. For example, it has been shown that MTurk participants will sometimes lie about their demographic characteristics in order to falsely claim eligibility for a study (Chandler & Paolacci, 2017).

Naivete primarily refers to whether participants are familiar with the research material that is used in the study (Chandler & Paolacci, 2017) but can also refer to how active participants are in completing surveys online. Non-naive participants, who are already familiar with some research material, could compromise a study's finding because they might answer a given question based on their previous experience and not based on the specific instructions of the study. For example, if a researcher aims to examine how participants would respond to a novel variation of the known Trolley problem, non-naive participants might ignore the variation and respond to it like they did in a previous study. Research has indeed shown that non-naive participants can reduce effect sizes of known and replicable effects (Chandler et al., 2015).

As mentioned above, these aspects of data quality are measured on the individual level. This means that researchers can monitor how participants are doing on any of these measures and choose to exclude individual participants from their studies to ensure high data quality. The other aspects of data quality mentioned above – reliability, replicability, and representativeness – are measured on the group or aggregate level and thus cannot be used to exclude specific individual participants from the study.

Reliability relates to the extent to which participants' responses (mainly to scale items) are internally consistent (e.g., as measured by Cronbach's alpha) and can be used to measure people's traits, individual tendencies, or preferences. Reliability is considered a prerequisite to validity of measures and thus can be highly important for behavioral research that aims at understanding people's attitudes, behavioral intentions, or individual differences in responding to behavioral interventions. **Replicability** concerns whether known and previously validated effects are significantly replicated in the given sample. For example, researchers have examined whether samples from different platforms replicate known effects such as the Asian Disease problem (Tversky & Kahneman, 1981) in which a positive frame leads more people to choose a risk-averse option while a complementary negative frame leads more people to choose a risk-seeking option. Lastly, **representativeness** can refer to how similar or dissimilar the sample obtained from the platform is to a predefined distribution on demographic variables such as age, gender, income, and education. In its simplest form, representativeness can indicate whether the sample is significantly skewed or biased toward one demographic (e.g., including too many males or too few elderly).

To ensure high data quality, researchers can take either (or both) of two general approaches: screen ex-ante or exclude ex-post. The ex-ante approach is to apply pre-filters to try to screen out participants who would perform poorly on the study. This approach is thus applied on the platform itself, before participants enter the study. The ex-post approach involves detecting responses, or participants, that provided low-quality data and should be excluded from the analysis. This approach is thus applied to the data that resulted from the study, after it has been completed. In the next sections, I review these approaches separately and then also present a potential combination of the two approaches to ensure high data quality.

Ex-ante Steps to Ensure Data Quality

To make sure only participants who can potentially provide high data quality are included in the study, researchers can filter the sample on Prolific to include only participants who have high approval ratings in their past submissions. Previous research on MTurk showed that approval ratings (or "reputation") can predict high data quality – participants who had 95% or above approval ratings failed attention-check questions less frequently than those who had lower approval ratings and provided better data quality overall (Peer et al., 2014). However, for that approach to be effective, there must be adequate variance and range in participants' approval ratings. According to Prolific data, as of June 2022, 72% of active participants (N=123,481) had an approval rating of 100%, 12.5% had an approval rating of 99%, and another 12.5% had approval ratings between 95% and 98%. That is, almost 85% of participants had an approval rating of 99% or 100%. As explained earlier, this is partly because Prolific calculates approval rating only for participants who have a minimal number of submissions, and the approval rating is not the simple average rate of approved submissions. While this might be justified on the grounds that this approach makes sure that "novice" participants, who have made only a few submissions, don't get an artificially high score, in practice it does not lead to a desirable outcome. In reality, the current scores of approval ratings cannot be used to prescreen participants in any worthwhile manner and can even be counterproductive. For example, limiting the sample to those with 95% approval rating or above would only leave out 3.1% of participants. Moreover, recent research that examined data quality on Prolific with or without pre-filters (in two studies), found that while approval ratings improved the data quality on MTurk and CloudResearch, they did not show any effect on the Prolific samples (Peer et al., 2022).

Still, researchers can try to ensure high data quality by prescreening participants based on other parameters. First, it's always wise to exclude participants who completed previous related studies such as a pilot you ran or an earlier version of your study. Second, one can choose individual-level filters that can ensure participants are in the best position to be able to understand the instructions. That may include selecting only participants whose first language is English (or the language of the survey) or choosing a more restrictive age range, if the study is about behaviors that mostly relate to specific age groups (e.g., more young participants for a study about TikTok or more older participants for a study about retirement). However, as mentioned earlier, such prescreeners may introduce some generalizability issues. It's also important to check how applying such pre-filters reduces the sampling frame by observing the number of eligible participants Prolific can provide after applying each filter (see above).

Ex-post Steps to Improve Data Quality

A different, and likely more common, approach to ensuring higher data quality is excluding participants ex-post if they show some signs of poor data quality. This can be done by including attention-check questions (ACQs) in the survey and then excluding participants who fail them. There are various types of ACQs that have been cleverly designed to detect inattentive responses accurately and reliably, such as the ones described earlier. The common usage of such ACQs is to ex-post filter the inattentive responses from the data file, and researchers can decide to either remove the participant from the data entirely or only exclude the participant's responses to a particular part of the survey following the ACQ. Another use of ACQs is to place them in the beginning of the study and to design the survey flow such that it will prevent participants who fail the ACQ from completing the study.

The application of ACQs is done on the survey level and, in some cases, can be done without any effects on the Prolific side of managing the study. That is the case if the researcher chooses to simply exclude failed responses from the analysis and not report that on Prolific. However, if the researcher approves the submissions of such failed responses, and pays the participants, they would be contributing to the inflation and inefficacy of approval ratings of participants on Prolific (see above). That would mean researchers would spend some of their research funds (potentially taxpayers' money) on bad responses that do not contribute to the scientific goal of the study. Thus, many researchers may choose to also report the failed responses on Prolific, by, for example, rejecting submissions made by participants who failed the ACQ. When a submission is rejected, Prolific asks researchers to specify the reason and provides that reason for rejection back to the participant; the participant can contest it by messaging back to the researcher.

If the researcher rejects submissions that failed ACQs, they might encounter objections from participants. For example, if a participant did complete the study but only failed an ACQ at the end, they might feel they should still get paid for their efforts in the other parts of the study and contest the rejection to the researcher or ask Prolific to get involved. Currently, Prolific guides researchers to reject submissions of participants who failed at least two ACQs in the study, and in such cases the objection of the contesting participant would not be accepted. However, this approach is still problematic because (a) IRBs might not approve not paying participants who did complete the study, and (b) researchers would also probably not want to waste too much time dealing with participants contesting rejection. These are probably the reasons why approval ratings have become inflated – even when participants provide bad responses, researchers may refrain from rejecting their submission, preferring to absorb the (typically small) costs of paying for bad responses, and thus avoid the hassle of dealing with objections.

To summarize, researchers can ensure high data quality by either ex-ante screening for participants with high approval ratings, based on other relevant filters that exist on Prolific, or they can improve data quality ex-post by excluding participants who failed ACQs. Findings from a recent study (Peer et al., 2023) suggest that the former approach of ex-ante screening of participants is more effective than the ex-post approach of relying on ACQs. I expand on these findings in the next section, which reviews the current state of data quality of studies obtained from Prolific.

The State of Data Quality on Prolific

Several studies have recently surveyed and examined the data quality of Prolific compared to other sources or audiences. Peer et al. (2017) compared Prolific to Amazon Mechanical Turk (MTurk), CrowdFlower (now called "Figure Eight"), and a university sample and found that Prolific exhibited a low dropout rate (about 7% only) and a high level of data quality. Prolific participants failed ACQs less than other platforms, showed high reliability in the measured scales, and were less familiar with the experimental tasks – this also led to high replicability of the effects examined. Additionally, when given the option to "cheat" and gain a bonus by over-reporting the results of a die roll, Prolific participants were less likely to provide dishonest responses, compared to MTurk. That paper concluded that Prolific "seems to be the most viable alternative to MTurk" (Peer et al., 2017, p. 160).

Several years later, Peer et al. (2022) examined, in two studies including almost 4,000 participants, several aspects of data quality in Prolific, MTurk, and CloudResearch. Among all the platforms, Prolific provided data with the highest quality on almost all measures. Prolific participants devoted more attention to the questions of the study, conveyed better comprehension of instructions, answered questionnaire items more carefully, and behaved more honestly when given the opportunity to cheat to increase their gains. Figure 4.5 shows the differences in a composite data quality score that sums the scores of attention (0–2), comprehension (0–2), and honesty (0–1), as measured in Study 1 of Peer et al. (2022). As can be

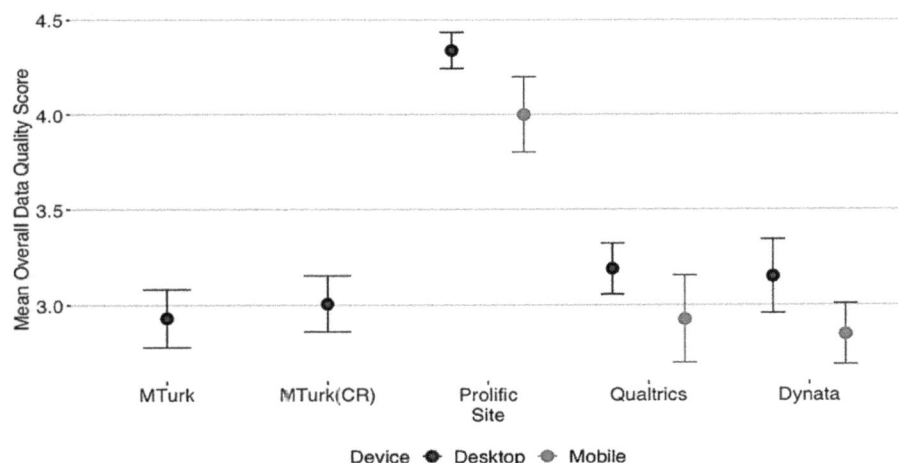

Figure 4.5 *Mean overall data quality score between sites and type of device used. Note: MTurk samples had less than 5% of mobile users, and these groups are not shown on the graph.*

seen, the highest data quality observed in that study was among the Prolific sample – first among desktop users, but also among mobile users. It's important to note that the two MTurk samples compared in that study (one from the native MTurk site and one through the CloudResearch interface) both did not include any pre-filters; these were also not applied to the Prolific sample or the samples from the other two panels (Qualtrics Panel and Dynata). The second study in that article did apply pre-filters to all samples and showed, as was found in another study (Hauser et al., 2022), that CloudResearch's "pre-approved" pool of participants (a subsample managed by the site out of the MTurk pool), can also provide data quality that is as high as that of Prolific.

Another interesting finding in Peer et al. (2022) was that Prolific participants reported fewer hours per week using the site, compared to MTurk, and that lower rates of activeness were associated with higher scores on the data quality aspects. This coincides with the finding that only 4% of participants on Prolific (compared to 30% on MTurk) report using the site as their main source of income. It appears that Prolific participants engage in online studies less frequently than MTurk workers, and that may explain why they are more attentive, more naive, and less dishonest. Of course, this is not a causal explanation, but from a researcher's perspective aiming to choose the best platform to spend their research budget, it is important and helpful to know that participants from Prolific will probably be more "fresh" and more attentive to the survey.

Another recent study (Douglas, Ewell, & Brauer, 2023) replicated and confirmed the findings above, showing that Prolific and CloudResearch provided higher data quality than MTurk, and also resulted in better quality than participants from a Qualtrics panel or student participants from a campus recruitment system

(SONA). Based on a binary distinction between high- vs. low-quality participants (based on failing attention-check questions or other filters), the authors estimated that the cost of a high-quality participant on Prolific and CloudResearch is, on average, much lower ($1.9 or $2.0, respectively) than the cost of a high-quality participant from MTurk ($4.36) or Qualtrics ($8.17). While these estimations should not be taken at face value, because actual costs depend on the length of the survey, type of sampling, etc., it can be inferred from this study that researchers should use Prolific (or CloudResearch) more often than the other platforms or panels to ensure the most efficient spending of their valuable research budgets (sometimes funded by taxpayers' money). As it is paramount for any research to rely on the best data quality it can get, it seems that the basic step toward higher data quality is to first choose to use a platform that provides the best data quality ex-ante.

Effects of Filters and Attention-Check Questions on Data Quality

As explained earlier, researchers can try to ensure or improve high data quality by applying filters ex-ante (e.g., based on approval ratings) or exclude those who fail ACQs ex-post. Most recently, in another study (Peer et al., 2023), we compared the data quality of Prolific to MTurk and CloudResearch when applying each or both of these measures. We sampled from these platforms with filters either on or off and included an ACQ either at the beginning of the study (where it might affect subsequent responses) or the end (where it can only identify inattentive respondents). We examined the data quality of these samples on different measures; Figure 4.6 shows the differences in replicability of three known and validated behavioral effects

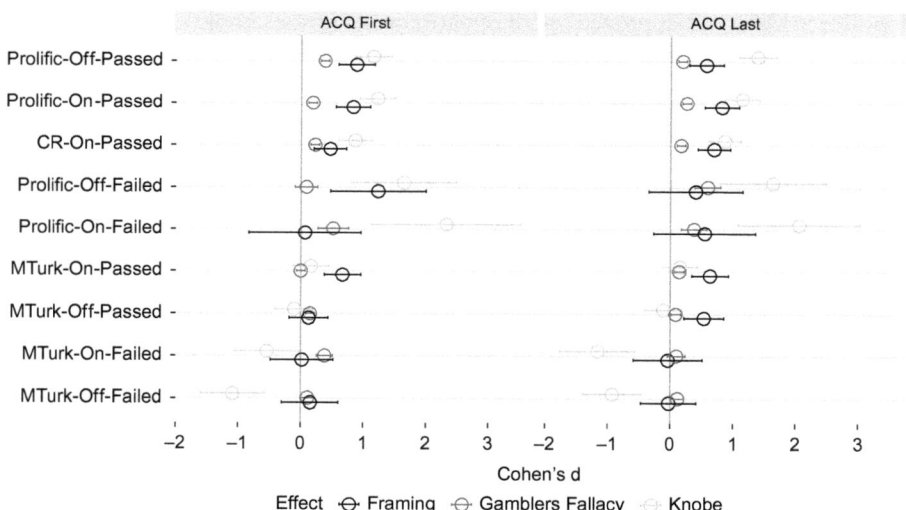

Figure 4.6 *Replication (Cohen's d) of three effects among the different samples and conditions. From Peer et al. (2023). Note: Figure shows only conditions with more than 50 participants; CR = CloudResearch*

between the samples in the different conditions. In Prolific, all effects replicated significantly among participants who passed the ACQ, whether filters were on or off and whether the ACQ was first or last. On CloudResearch, all effects replicated among those who passed the ACQ (given first or last). On MTurk, only the framing effect replicated under specific conditions – when filters were on and the ACQ was passed (first or last) or when filters were off and the ACQ was passed and last. The other effects did not replicate in any of the MTurk samples and conditions. This again confirms the high data quality of Prolific that is evident even when no filters are applied.

Summary: Pros and Cons of Prolific

To summarize, Prolific can offer considerable advantages to researchers who wish to conduct their studies online. First, similar to all other online platforms (such as MTurk or CloudResearch), it provides researchers with the ability to be independent and self-reliant in conducting research. The researcher can choose when to run their survey, how much and which participants to sample, whether to prescreen any participants ex-ante, how much to pay for the survey (above a set minimum), offer a bonus based on performance or other reason, monitor the progress of data collection, and pause or stop it at any time (or increase places if so desired), etc. These are important advantages compared to campus labs and even compared to employing panel companies (such as Qualtrics Panel or SurveyMonkey Audience) which handle the administration for the study and often take away some of the autonomy from the researcher.

Compared to other platforms (such as MTurk and CloudResearch) that also offer self-service to researchers, Prolific's advantages lie mainly in the fact that it is solely devoted to academic and marketing research and does not involve other "micro-tasks," such as labeling or cataloguing items, that are highly frequent on MTurk and CloudResearch. Micro-tasks can take up most of participants' time because of the higher frequency of such tasks offered on MTurk. In fact, Amazon has reported that less than 1% of the tasks on MTurk are academic research. As a result, participants from MTurk may get to a study after spending many hours working online, and they may be more motivated to complete the study as quickly as possible, rather than as correctly and candidly as they can. In that sense, CloudResearch, which offers many advantages to researchers compared to the native MTurk interface, is not immune to this problem because, in the end, it samples from the same pool of MTurk workers. Prolific, on the other hand, seems to have a different pool of participants (e.g., Peer et al., 2022, found that only 23% of Prolific users said they also use MTurk), who seem to use the platform much less often and for shorter amounts of time. Although the link between that and higher data quality has yet to be empirically supported, it is reasonable to consider it as an advantage for Prolific, compared to MTurk or CloudResearch.

Prolific offers several additional advantages to researchers that have already been mentioned above. These include the option to request a representative sample, or a gender-balanced sample, to easily pay bonuses in bulk to participants, and to automatically manage approval of the study if the survey is hosted on Qualtrics (or other software that can provide a completion code). Although researchers can pay bonuses or auto-approve submissions through CloudResearch, researchers cannot do that using the native MTurk interface, and CloudResearch does not (currently) offer an option for a representative or balanced sample (although one can accomplish that using quotas on Qualtrics).

Disadvantages

In contrast, the disadvantages of using Prolific mostly stem from it still being a relatively young platform that must substantially invest in participant recruitment and retention. First, the pool of participants on Prolific is substantially smaller than other platforms. As mentioned above, the active participant pool, in June 2022, was approximately 120,000 participants. Estimations are that the pool on MTurk is closer to half a million; however, some claim that its effective size is much smaller (e.g., as low as 7,300 according to Stewart et al., 2015). Prolific also does not yet have a sound infrastructure for managing participants' quality, as explained earlier in relation to the low variance in approval ratings. Another shortcoming of Prolific (that other platforms also share) is its overreliance on participants from English-speaking countries such as the US and UK, who comprise almost 90% of their participant pool. Although this can be helpful for Western researchers, and for studies focusing on US or UK cultures, the platform does not help researchers interested in other cultures or who conduct studies that require other languages.

Finally, Prolific minimum rates of payment to participants are higher than on MTurk, and that may deter many researchers from using it. Currently, Prolific mandates paying participants at least 6 GBP per hour (about 7.5 USD) and checks the median duration of a study to calculate the actual rate in each study. If that actual rate falls below 6 GBP/hour, the platform will send a message to the researcher asking them to provide bonus payments to compensate participants for the extra time. Although this is mainly done to ensure a decent payment for participants, it puts the price tag of running an experiment on Prolific generally higher than running the same study on MTurk. Although researchers from affluent countries, with rich research budgets, should not be deterred by this difference, it might steer other researchers to use MTurk instead, even at the cost of lower data quality.

Conclusion

Prolific was founded with the purpose to provide academic and market researchers with a better tool for conducting online research that is easy, fast, and provides high data quality. On their website, they aim to do that by "enabling fast, reliable and large-scale data collection by connecting researchers with participants around the world." Their mission is "to make trustworthy data more accessible to everybody – from individuals to businesses to governments – and facilitate world-changing research." That is a worthy mission with important goals, and it appears that Prolific has managed to attract a large body of researchers and participants with a high and steady rate of growth. Prolific managers were wise to identify several aspects of online data collection that were missing for academic and market research and provide these to its users.

From the participant side, Prolific offers individuals the option to take part in high-quality studies and ensures they receive adequate pay for their time. For researchers, Prolific offers an online interface that is entirely self-service (bypassing the need to interact with project managers when using panel companies), does not require any license or setup fees, and is easy to use and manage. Prolific offers its researchers access to a large pool of participants, although it might be smaller than that of MTurk or of other panel companies. However, the active pool of participants seems large enough (more than 120,000) to facilitate running frequent studies on large samples. Moreover, Prolific offers researchers various options to pre-select their sample of participants, run longitudinal studies, design incentive-compatible studies using bonuses, and much more. Prolific still needs to improve its participant quality mechanism, use better measures than the current approval ratings, and perhaps improve its pricing system to find a way to make it more attractive than Mturk to underprivileged researchers.

Overall, Prolific seems to be one of the best options for academic researchers who wish to conduct their studies online. Studies have shown that the data collection on Prolific is fast, even with large samples, that it is trustworthy for researchers in terms of low dropout rates and built-in mechanisms to prevent bots or multiple submissions, and that it provides high data quality in terms of participants' attention to instructions, comprehension of tasks, reliability of scales, and replicability of known effects. The studies also show lower rates of dishonest responses among participants on Prolific; this may be a result of its fairer compensation scheme. In all, Prolific offers an excellent tool for academic researchers for fast, reliable, and high-quality online research.

References

Berinsky, A. J., Margolis, M. F., & Sances, M. W. (2014). Separating the shirkers from the workers? Making sure respondents pay attention on self-administered surveys. *American Journal of Political Science, 58*(3), 739–753.

Chandler, J. J., Mueller, P., & Paolacci, G. (2014). Nonnaïveté among Amazon Mechanical Turk workers: Consequences and solutions for behavioral researchers. *Behavior Research Methods, 46*(1), 112–130.

Chandler, J. J., & Paolacci, G. (2017). Lie for a dime: When most prescreening responses are honest but most study participants are impostors. *Social Psychological and Personality Science, 8*(5), 500–508.

Chandler, J. J., Paolacci, G., Peer, E., Mueller, P., & Ratliff, K. A. (2015). Using nonnaive participants can reduce effect sizes. *Psychological Science, 26*(7), 1131–1139.

Chandler, J. J., Rosenzweig, C., Moss, A. J., Robinson, J., & Litman, L. (2019). Online panels in social science research: Expanding sampling methods beyond Mechanical Turk. *Behavior Research Methods*, *51*(5), 2022–2038.

Douglas, B. D., Ewell, P. J., & Brauer, M. (2023). Data quality in online human-subjects research: Comparisons between MTurk, Prolific, CloudResearch, Qualtrics, and SONA. *PLOS ONE*, *18*(3), e0279720.

Gerlach, P., Teodorescu, K., & Hertwig, R. (2019). The truth about lies: A meta-analysis on dishonest behavior. *Psychological Bulletin*, *145*(1), 1–44.

Goodman, J. K., Cryder, C. E., & Cheema, A. (2013). Data collection in a flat world: The strengths and weaknesses of Mechanical Turk samples. *Journal of Behavioral Decision Making*, *26*(3), 213–224.

Goodman, J. K., & Paolacci, G. (2017). Crowdsourcing consumer research. *Journal of Consumer Research*, *44*(1), 196–210.

Hauser, D. J., Moss, A. J., Rosenzweig, C., Jaffe, S., & Robinson, J. (2022). Evaluating CloudResearch's approved group as a solution for problematic data quality on MTurk. *Behavioral Research Methods*, *55*(8), 3953–3964. https://doi.org/10.31234/osf.io/48yxj

Nichols, A. L., & Edlund, J. E. (2020). Why don't we care more about carelessness? Understanding the causes and consequences of careless participants. *International Journal of Social Research Methodology*, *23*(6), 625-638.

Oppenheimer, D. M., Meyvis, T., & Davidenko, N. (2009). Instructional manipulation checks: Detecting satisficing to increase statistical power. *Journal of Experimental Social Psychology*, *45*(4), 867–872.

Paolacci, G., Chandler, J., & Ipeirotis, P. G. (2010). Running experiments on Amazon Mechanical Turk. *Judgment and Decision making*, *5*(5), 411–419.

Peer, E., Brandimarte, L., Samat, S., & Acquisti, A. (2017). Beyond the Turk: Alternative platforms for crowdsourcing behavioral research. *Journal of Experimental Social Psychology*, *70*, 153–163.

Peer, E., Rothschild, D., & Gordon, A. (2023). Behavioral Lab 3.0. Towards the next generation of online behavioral research [preprint]. *PsyArXiv*.

Peer, E., Rothschild, D., Gordon, A., Evernden, Z., & Damer, E. (2022). Data quality of platforms and panels for online behavioral research. *Behavior Research Methods*, *54*, 1643–1662. https://doi.org/10.3758/s13428-021-01694-3

Peer, E., Vosgerau, J., & Acquisti, A. (2014). Reputation as a sufficient condition for data quality on Amazon Mechanical Turk. *Behavior Research Methods*, *46*(4), 1023–1031.

Stewart, N., Ungemach, C., Harris, A. J., Bartels, D. M., Newell, B. R., Paolacci, G., & Chandler, J. (2015). The average laboratory samples a population of 7,300 Amazon Mechanical Turk workers. *Judgment and Decision Making*, *10*(5), 479–491.

Thomas, K. A., & Clifford, S. (2017). Validity and Mechanical Turk: An assessment of exclusion methods and interactive experiments. *Computers in Human Behavior*, *77*, 184–197.

Tversky, A., & Kahneman, D. (1981). The framing of decisions and the psychology of choice. *Science*, *211*(4481), 453–458.

5 Field Research

Sherry Jueyu Wu

Abstract
Field research refers to research conducted with high degrees of naturalism. Compared with other research methodologies, field research can preserve the rigor of traditional laboratory research while augmenting the ecological validity and social impact of the research findings. The first part of this chapter provides a definition of field research and discusses its advantages and challenges. The second part of the chapter provides a brief overview of qualitative field methods and an in-depth overview of experimental field methods. It discusses different types of randomization schemes in field experiments, such as cluster randomization, block randomization, and wait-list designs. It further discusses the design and implementation concerns when conducting field experiments, including spillover, attrition, and non-compliance. The third part of the chapter provides an overview of some important considerations for conducting field research, including pilot testing, replicability and generalizability across contexts, and how geographical and technological advances impact field research.

Keywords: Field Research, Field Experiments, Research Methodology, Naturalism, Research Design, Generalizability, Causal Inference, Practical Guidance

What Is Field Research?

One goal of social and behavioral science is to explain and predict people's behavior in the real world. As a means to approximate people's natural behavior, field research is particularly well-positioned to achieve this goal. Field research is defined as research with high degrees of naturalism. Notably, the term "field" is open to different interpretations. Some argue that the field refers to leaving one's home institution for data-gathering purposes (Kapiszewski et al., 2015). Some define the field as research subjects' own settings where personal interaction happens (Wood, 2009), while others do not put an emphasis on the physical locale (Paluck & Cialdini, 2014). After all, very naturalistic and immersive studies can take place in the laboratory, and artificial interventions can be conducted in non-laboratory settings.

Field research is often compared and contrasted with quick research conducted in artificial laboratory or online settings. A key aspect of field research is that the researcher is gathering evidence *in contexts* – within the settings where individual decisions, social interactions, and group dynamics of interest naturally take place.

Researchers can assess the *naturalism* of a study based on four considerations (Gerber & Green, 2012):

(1) Do the **participants** involved in the research resemble the real-world actors who ordinarily encounter the phenomena under study?
(2) Does the **context** within which participants are studied resemble the context of interest?
(3) Does the **treatment** participants undergo resemble the intervention of interest in the world? (Note that this criterion applies specifically to experimental research, as non-experimental studies do not typically have different treatment conditions.)
(4) Do the **outcome measures or the assessed responses** resemble the actual outcomes of theoretical or practical interest?

Regarding a specific research study, if the answers to the abovementioned four questions are all yes, this research is undoubtedly field research; if the answers to these questions are mixed (i.e., some yes and some no), the research may not be strictly field research. Since the degree of naturalism may be gauged along the four dimensions above (authenticity of participants, context, treatments, and outcome measures), a proper classification scheme of field research would encompass at least 16 categories, a taxonomy that far exceeds anyone's interest or patience. It suffices to say that field research takes many forms and exists on a continuum of naturalism.

Let's consider an example research question: What is the effect of participatory goal setting on employees' work productivity? Table 5.1 shows how researchers could attempt to study this question, using low or high degrees of naturalism on each dimension. The combination of the "low naturalism" column in each of these dimensions would constitute a research study that is so low in naturalism, it would not be considered field research. The combination of the "high naturalism" column in each of these dimensions would clearly constitute field research.

A study that has a high degree of naturalism on some dimensions but a low degree of naturalism on others may often still be considered field research. For example, Harrison and List (2004) define experiments that are high in naturalism in participants

Table 5.1 *Example research designs with low vs. high degrees of naturalism*

Research question: What is the effect of participatory goal setting on worker productivity?

	Low degree of naturalism	**High degree of naturalism**
Participants	Convenience sample recruited on Amazon Mechanical Turk	Sample of employees who work virtually for a company
Context	On the participant's computer at home, embedded in an online survey	On the participant's computer, interacting with colleagues through Zoom
Treatment	Written instructions telling the participant to imagine they are discussing their work goals with their colleagues	Weekly morning meetings on Zoom for two months, in which the workers discuss their goals for the day
Outcome measures	Participants' expected productivity	Ratings of worker productivity and performance reviews

as *artefactual field experiments* (also known as *lab-in-the-field*), experiments that are high in naturalism in participants, treatment, and outcome measures as *framed field experiments*, and experiments that are high in naturalism in all the dimensions as *natural field experiments*. This chapter focuses on field research that is relatively high in all naturalism dimensions.

Canvassing the types of field experiments that have been conducted by social and behavioral scientists, we see few limits to the kinds of treatments that can be randomized and the varieties of contexts researchers explore. Social and behavioral scientists have conducted randomized experiments in national parks (Cialdini et al., 2006), factories (Wu & Paluck, 2020; 2022), daycare centers (Gneezy & Rustichini, 2000), schools (Walton & Cohen, 2011), and post-war communities (Paluck, 2009), randomizing over media programs (Blair et al., 2019; Paluck, 2009), morning meetings (Wu & Paluck, 2022), and financial incentives (Haushofer & Shapiro, 2016). These randomized experiments target real-world behaviors and measure a wide range of outcomes such as perceived social norms, group belongingness, attitudes toward generalized authority and justice, among many others.

Advantages of Field Research

According to William James, considered the founder of modern psychology, one ultimate goal for studying human behavior is to provide explanations for why people behave as they do in the world (James, 1907; Gantman et al., 2018). To do this, theories need to have a "close relation to life" (Lewin, 1944/1997, p. 288). Theory-driven research without attention to the real world may lead to less consequential or even misleading conclusions (Cialdini, 1980; Paluck & Cialdini, 2014). Field research has a clear advantage in achieving the ultimate aim set out by James. Conducted in a naturalistic setting, field research often focuses on participants who come from the social group of interest, delivers treatments of interest that are more realistic and impactful, and measures outcomes that may readily occur in that setting. Compared with laboratory research, archival studies, and qualitative research, field research, especially field experiments, has the following advantages.

Ecological Validity

Compared with laboratory experiments, the most obvious advantage of field research is its high degree of naturalism that boosts the ecological validity of research. Ecological validity refers to how well a study's variables and findings can be generalized to a real-world context. Because by definition field research is conducted with high degrees of naturalism, it is more likely to stay true to or at least better approximate the processes that take place in individuals' decision-making, interpersonal interactions, and affective and motivational expressions. Interpretation of results from laboratory experiments might be complicated by the possibility that participants in a laboratory setting may respond differently to researcher-constructed stimuli compared with how an average person would respond to a naturally occurring phenomenon outside of the laboratory. Meanwhile, results from field research are typically more generalizable to the population being studied, and better predict the target population's behaviors in real-world settings, increasing external validity more generally.

Broadness of Research Constructs

While there is a lot to gain from the predominance of standardized laboratory paradigms, such as the precision of manipulation and the ease of execution, there is also a lot to lose, such as the breadth of topics that call for a field setting. Field research enables social and behavioral scientists to study topics and behavioral processes that otherwise cannot be faithfully or ethically abstracted in a constrained laboratory (Ferrero & Pinto, 2023). For example, it is difficult, if not impossible, to recreate mental processes of violence and conflict in laboratory paradigms without breaching ethics. Similarly, researchers cannot recreate prolonged poverty in a constrained laboratory. In general, research constructs that involve sustained behavioral patterns and behavioral changes call for a more dynamic investigation and are thus better suited for the field than the laboratory.

In addition, field research broadens research samples to include populations who are not typically recruited into laboratory research. It also broadens research settings to include communities and world regions where human-subject laboratories are not common (e.g., migrant workers in Chinese factories, Wu & Paluck, 2022; women leaders in Indian village councils, Beaman et al., 2009). Therefore, field research is more inclusive in reaching diverse samples and research settings, which also indirectly increases the broadness of research constructs.

Causal Testing

As we will discuss in the following section, field experiments can be a powerful method for testing causality. Just as laboratory experiments import various elements from a natural setting to stagecraft into an abstracted version of the world, field experiments export experimental control from the laboratory to the field (Paluck & Cialdini, 2014). Field experiments enable researchers to test the causal impact of a treatment in the presence of other moving social environmental factors. They can also help specify the boundary conditions in which an effect may hold across different time periods, populations, treatment variations, and other important contextual factors.

Intervention Program Evaluation

Field experiments sometimes take the form of program evaluation designed to gauge the extent to which resources are deployed effectively (Gerber & Green, 2012). Let's take a messaging intervention as an example. In order to test whether a vaccination advertising campaign can increase community members' vaccination rate, a field experiment might randomize the geographic areas in which the messaging campaign is deployed and measure differences in vaccination rates between treatment and control regions.

From the standpoint of program evaluation, this approach is arguably superior to a laboratory experiment where participants are shown different messages and later asked whether they will get vaccinated (e.g., Cui et al., 2022). While laboratory experiments may be able to detect the direction of an effect – whether certain messages are more effective than others – they are unlikely to capture the full intensity of an intervention. For example, laboratory experiments are less likely to capture the possibility that some participants in targeted areas will miss the message, process it inattentively, or forget the message amid life's other distractions. Field experiments can help researchers gauge both the direction and the size of an intervention program, and assess its outcomes in relation to the resources spent on the program.

Social Impact

From the standpoint of non-academic communities, field research renders social and behavioral research more relevant and scalable. Because field research takes place in people's everyday lives and organizations' regular operations, it can often be seen as more valuable to key stakeholders in non-academic communities, such as governments, non-profits, and private companies. Findings from field research are more likely to be incorporated into policy decision-making compared with laboratory research in social and behavioral sciences (Dolan & Galizzi, 2014; Hansen & Tummers, 2020).

Challenges of Field Research

Field research may have several challenges. The first challenge is practical: field research tends to be more costly and more difficult to implement compared with research conducted in a laboratory or an online setting. Laboratories are often conveniently located in one's home institution, making it easy for university researchers to monitor research progress and supervise research assistants. Field researchers may need to go the extra mile to reach a field site that can be far away from one's home institution or even home country. Field research also tends to take longer because more groundwork must be laid down first to gain the trust and approval of local community stakeholders and participants.

Second, it may require more effort and creativity to ensure internal validity – that treatment and measurement precision is achieved in field research, particularly when randomization and experimental manipulation are involved. An advantage of conducting experiments under controlled laboratory conditions is that researchers can more easily administer multiple variations of a treatment to test fine-grained theoretical propositions, and the decision process for research design is often unilateral. Field interventions are often more complicated: researchers need to work with logistical constraints posed by the field setting and local stakeholders, often with many moving pieces influencing the decision-making of the research design. Some may argue that it is more difficult to obtain evidence for mediation processes in the field, especially when such processes are believed to occur at the level of individual cognition or emotion. However, it is worth noting that exploring mediation is a challenge for laboratory experiments as well (Bullock et al., 2010).

Time and again, researchers have overcome practical hurdles and come up with innovative solutions to tackle what are commonly seen as disadvantages of field research. Researchers have grown increasingly resourceful in designing interventions to understand big questions and in measuring the effects of hard-to-manipulate variables with improved precision, such as the effects of culture, wars, and poverty. In the next part, we will focus on some common randomization schemes for field experiments, to ensure internal validity, and potential design and statistical concerns that are more common in the field.

Non-experimental Methods in Field Research

Scholars can use both non-experimental and experimental methods when conducting field research. Common non-experimental methods include naturalistic observation, qualitative interviews, descriptive surveys, and quasi-experiments. When using naturalistic observation, researchers embed themselves in a particular place or with a particular group of people, and observe how people behave. The goal is to develop an understanding of why people think or behave the way they do in their natural context. Researchers using this method often take detailed field notes, and may record how often a particular behavior occurs. Another increasingly common form of naturalistic observation is scraping content from websites, such as Facebook and Twitter/X, and using natural language processing to develop insights from a large amount of text.

Qualitative interviews and descriptive surveys involve asking participants questions, and recording their answers. When conducting qualitative interviews in field settings, researchers ask participants a series of open-ended questions. Interviews can be conducted one-on-one or in focus groups. Follow-up questions can be adapted dynamically based on the participants' answers. The goal is to get a rich picture of people's life experiences, attitudes, and behaviors. Descriptive surveys involve asking participants a series of primarily close-ended questions. These may be done as one-off oral interviews, or surveys that participants fill in themselves. Researchers may also want to get data from participants at frequent intervals over a specific time period.

Quasi-experiments aim to evaluate causality when randomization is not possible in the field. Quasi-experiments take advantage of naturally occurring events in the world and use analytical methods to proximate causality to some extent. For example, interrupted time series analysis is used to assess the impact of an event that occurs at an observed time point where outcome observations before and after the event are available. A causal relationship is proposed when the level of outcome observations is changed significantly after the event occurs. Note that a key assumption here is that the only exposure that changes is the event. The causal inference is more convincing when the researchers show that the level of other continuously collected observations unrelated to the event are in fact unchanged when the event occurs. One example of this method is the study of perceived social norms supporting gay marriage before, during, and after the June 2015 US Supreme Court ruling in favor of same-sex marriage (Tankard and Paluck, 2017).

Non-experimental and experimental methods are highly synergistic in field research, particularly for theory-building and theory-testing. Non-experimental methods can be used to generate research questions and develop hypotheses that can then be tested using experimental methods. They can also be used to develop a better understanding of a particular context and to suggest what types of interventions may be most effective in that context. In the next section, we take a deep dive into experimental methods in field research.

Experimental Methods in Field Research

There is sometimes a misconception that because field research is rich in context and external validity, it would be difficult to achieve internal validity by ruling out confounders and estimating causality. With proper design, experiments in the field can be just as rigorous as experiments in a laboratory setting (Duflo & Banerjee, 2017; Eden, 2017; Gerber & Green, 2012). Causal inference in field settings has greatly improved over the years, thanks to innovations in empirical methodologies in field experimentation that address challenges particular to the field setting (Gerber & Green, 2012; Paluck & Cialdini, 2014; Rubin, 2005; Shadish et al., 2002; Duflo et al., 2007). In this section, we review common randomization methods for field experiments, and discuss some design and causal estimation issues that are more common in field experimentation.

Simple Randomization

Simple randomization in the field is similar to the typical randomization scheme adopted by laboratory experiments: the randomization unit is individual subjects. Researchers use a random procedure, such as a coin flip, to determine whether a subject is assigned to a treatment or to a control condition. The procedure of assigning treatment and control conditions at random ensures that no systematic differences exist for either treatment or control conditions beyond the experimental manipulation. In other words, when no experimental manipulation or treatment is administered, there is no reason to expect that subjects randomly assigned to a treatment condition would outperform or underperform those in a control condition. Thus any difference observed between conditions after the administration of treatments can be attributed to the specific treatments.

In addition to simple random assignments commonly adopted by laboratory experiments, there are other randomization schemes that may better suit specific research questions or solve practical constraints in the field. Below, we discuss three such classes of randomization designs commonly used in the field: cluster randomization, block randomization, and waitlist designs.

Cluster Randomization

Cluster randomization refers to a procedure where *clusters of subjects*, rather than individual subjects, are randomly assigned into different conditions. There are many topics that require social and behavioral scientists to go beyond using individuals as the experimental unit. Sometimes we are interested in research questions that target groups of individuals. For example, what are the effects of a particular work environment on employee productivity and morale? How does participating in couples therapy affect relationships? How does instructors' teaching style affect academic performance? A common feature in all the above questions is that, in order to get a causal estimate of a particular treatment (e.g., a work environment, couples therapy, teaching style) in a natural context, usually more than one individual is "treated" at the same time. In simple randomization, each of the subjects is *individually* assigned to a treatment or a control condition. However, if one were to randomly assign couples therapy or a teaching style, more likely than not, subjects need to be assigned as a *cluster* to a treatment or a control condition – the experimental units are couples and classrooms in these examples.

To visualize the difference between individual-level and cluster-level random assignment, imagine an experiment on the effect of participatory group structure on worker productivity. Suppose a textile factory has its employees work together in 60 groups of 30, and each group has its own supervisor. Workers are assigned to a particular group once hired by the factory, and they don't rotate. A researcher wants to examine how having the opportunity to speak up freely in group meetings influences group productivity and institutional belongingness. The researcher proposes to randomly assign different group meeting structures to half of the groups, and then measure productivity and belongingness among the 1,800 people in the factory. The N of individuals is 1,800, but there are only 60 clusters.

Since workers only hold meetings in their existing groups, a simple randomization scheme that assigns individual workers to a treatment or a control condition is simply not feasible and would not faithfully capture the group phenomenon. Under cluster random assignment, *groups* of individuals (i.e., the clusters) are assigned to a treatment or a control condition. Statistically, cluster randomization will generate more sampling variability than simple randomization if subjects within the same cluster tend to share common features that are related to the measured outcome (Gerber & Green, 2012). See Wu and Paluck (2022) for a study that uses cluster randomization on the aforementioned topic of worker productivity.

Cluster randomization is sometimes necessary for theoretical, practical, and statistical reasons. Theoretically, cluster randomization allows social and behavioral scientists to estimate the causal impact of group and community phenomena that go beyond individual behavior. Researchers interested in group and community dynamics often need to treat the group or the community, rather than a single individual, as their experimental unit. Practically, certain types of interventions can only be implemented on the cluster level. In the case of academic curricula, in most schools it is not feasible to administer different teaching curricula to specific students within a classroom; instead, an instructor has to deliver the curriculum to the entire classroom. Statistically, cluster randomization is one of the solutions to the spillover problem (see the spillover section below). If researchers are concerned about potential interference between individual subjects (e.g., workers in the same team are able to observe other workers' assigned conditions and change their own behavior accordingly), randomly assigning clusters of associated subjects (e.g., teams of workers) may resolve the spillover problem.

Block Randomization

Block randomization refers to a procedure where participants are first partitioned into subgroups – called blocks or strata, and then complete random assignment occurs within each block. To visualize an example of block randomization, suppose an experimental design aims to examine differential effects of an intervention on urban versus rural residents. Suppose the region where the research sample is drawn is highly urbanized, so its urban residents significantly outnumber its rural residents. To study the differential effects, the design calls for a balanced proportion of urban and rural residents across conditions. If one were to use simple randomization, chances are high that the proportions of urban and rural residents in each condition would be imbalanced, especially when the sample size is small (because assignment imbalance can still occur in random assignment). However, block randomization can be used to ensure that an equal proportion of urban and rural residents will be assigned to each experimental condition.

How do we conduct block randomization? In the above example, the researcher would first partition the sample into two subgroups: urban and rural residents (i.e., the blocks). Among the subgroup of urban residents, the researcher would randomly assign participants to either the treatment condition or the control condition; among the subgroup of rural residents, they would do the same randomization. In effect, block randomization creates a series of simple random assignments, one per block.

Block randomization is used to address two types of design concerns. First, block randomization can address constraints from practical or ethical imperatives. For example, an education program may have requirements about how many participants with particular characteristics must be placed into a treatment condition. Block randomization allows researchers to build a randomized experiment around these constraints.

Second, block randomization addresses important statistical concerns, including reducing sampling variability and ensuring that certain subgroups are available for separate analysis (Gerber & Green, 2012). Block randomization can significantly improve the precision with which the average treatment effect is estimated, especially when the sample size is relatively small. It produces the most gain in the improvement of estimation precision when the variables that are used for blocking strongly predict the outcome variables. However, outcome variables cannot be observed until the study is actually conducted. So researchers can look at the prior literature and field observations to predict which baseline variables, that are not affected by the experimental manipulation, are the strongest predictors of the outcomes that one wants to measure. For example, if a researcher plans to test whether an intervention improves students' test scores, they could look at the prior research on whether students' test scores are correlated with geographic region, race, and ethnicity, and previous test scores, and use block randomization based on these baseline variables.

Block randomization is not always feasible. Sometimes field experiments are conducted under severe time and/or financial constraints, and background information necessary to form blocks is not always available in the experimental design phase. However, for the abovementioned advantages, field experimenters often suggest "Block what you can, and randomize what you cannot" (Gerber & Green, 2012, p. 110).

Waitlist Design

In a waitlist design (also known as a stepped-wedge design or randomized rollout), every experimental unit (e.g., an individual participant or a cluster) will be treated eventually, and random assignment determines the time point at which they receive the treatment. The waitlist design is also known as the stepped-wedge design because as subjects gradually move from control to treatment, the chart of treatment assignments looks like a series of steps (Hussey & Hughes, 2007).

A waitlist design tracks subjects over time as they move from untreated to treated, or from treated to untreated. This design combines elements of within-subjects and between-subjects designs. At a given point in time, some subjects have already been treated while others have not, and comparisons can be made between these two groups. Additionally, over time, individual subjects move from a control condition to a treatment condition or vice versa. For example, suppose a researcher is interested in the effect of a TV advertisement on product sales. The TV advertisements need to be aired to nine independent media markets. A between-subject experimental design requires half of the media markets to be randomly assigned to the treatment condition and the other half to the control condition (see Table 5.2, left panel). But due to

Table 5.2 *Random assignment in within-subjects, between-subjects, and waitlist design*

		Between-subjects Time			Within-subjects Time				Waitlist design Time			
		T1			T1	T2			T1	T2	T3	T4	T5
Subjects	S1	1	Subjects	S1	0	1	Subjects	S1	0	1	1	1	1
	S2	1		S2	0	1		S2	0	0	1	1	1
	S3	0		S3	0	1		S3	0	0	0	1	1
	S4	0		S4	0	1		S4	0	0	0	0	1

Note: 0 refers to a control condition, and 1 refers to a treatment condition. A between-subject design assigns subjects to different conditions in the same time period, whereas a within-subject design and a waitlist design typically involve multiple time periods.

financial or scheduling constraints, only two or three markets can be approached at one time. A strategic field experimentalist could explain to the advertising company that, given an immediate launch of TV advertisements to *all* of the markets is not feasible, a lottery would represent a fair procedure to roll out the new TV advertisements. Three randomly selected markets could receive the TV ads in the first week, another three randomly selected markets could receive the TV ads in the second week, and the rest in the third week. The outcome measures can be accumulated product sales in each TV market per week (see Table 5.2, right panel). See Wu and Paluck (2021) for a field experiment using a more complicated waitlist design.

Waitlist design has two primary advantages. First, because waitlist designs combine elements of both between-subjects and within-subjects designs, they enable researchers to extract statistically meaningful estimates from relatively small numbers of subjects (see Aronow & Samii, 2017; Rubin, 2001; Gerber & Green, 2012 for technical discussions of causal estimation). Second, it helps address practical constraints in the field. Like the example mentioned above, sometimes it is not practically or ethically feasible to withhold a treatment from a subset of participants in the interest of forming a pure control group. Governments, non-profits, and private companies often require all participants to be treated eventually, especially when the treatments are high-impact. In such cases, researchers can use a waitlist design to overcome the constraint of withholding treatment from a control group.

Design and Implementation Concerns in Field Research

Spillover

In an experiment, we implicitly assume that one subject's potential outcomes are not influenced by the treatment administered to other subjects. This refers to the non-interference assumption – potential outcomes are unaffected by how the randomization happens. Non-interference is one of the core assumptions needed to establish unbiased causal estimates. On the contrary, interference (also known as spillover) refers to the situation in which a participant's potential outcomes vary not only according to the experimental condition they receive but also according to the experimental conditions that other participants receive.

Many social phenomena may cause the treatment of one participant or experimental unit to have spillover for other participants or experimental units. For example, the effect of being vaccinated on one's probability of contracting a disease depends on whether the people around them are vaccinated. The causal effect of vaccination is likely to be small if one is surrounded by vaccinated others, and large if one is surrounded by unvaccinated others. Another example is social comparison: an intervention that offers unconditional cash transfer or housing assistance to a treatment group may change the way in which those in the control group evaluate their own financial or housing conditions. Consequently, potential outcomes in the control group might change when the treatment group is treated. In addition, interventions that send messages about commercial products or not-for-profit causes may spread from individuals who receive the treatment to others who are in the control condition and nominally untreated. In this case, the causal estimate of direct treatment would be biased.

The aforementioned spillover examples take place across different participants or experimental units in a field site and are also known as spatial spillover. Spillover can also happen within a participant or experimental unit on the dimension of time. For example, in within-subjects experiments, where outcomes for a participant are tracked over time, participants may experience intertemporal interference if they remember past interventions or respond to future interventions differently.

The above list of examples reminds field researchers to pay special attention to potential spillover when designing an experiment and when estimating the average treatment effect from an intervention. Below, we briefly introduce design principles that accommodate some forms of spillover across experimental units (detailed statistical concerns are beyond the scope of this chapter; see Aronow & Samii, 2012, and Hudgens & Halloran, 2008, for in-depth analyses). First, if spillover happens mostly within clusters, researchers can consider cluster randomization rather than simple randomization. Second, researchers can turn to experimental designs that relax the non-interference assumption (i.e., subject i is unaffected by whether others are treated) by randomly assigning varying degrees of secondhand exposure. Third, researchers can assess the nature of the spillover and use non-experimental units to investigate spillover (see Gerber & Green, 2012). For example, spatial spillovers may decay as they radiate geographically; temporal spillovers may dissipate after a certain amount of time. By understanding the conditions under which that interference occurs, we can use the randomization procedure to simulate the probabilities of exposure to spillovers and to compare weighted means.

Attrition

Attrition is a common source of bias in all forms of social research, but the sting of attrition is perhaps felt most by those conducting field experiments. Attrition occurs when a participant drops out of the research, and their outcome data are missing. When attrition systematically correlates with treatment assignment – meaning that participants in a certain experimental condition are more or less likely to drop out of the research than those in other conditions – the remaining subjects assigned to the treatment or control conditions (after removing the attrited observations from the data set) no longer constitute random samples of the original collection of participants. Therefore, a comparison of group averages will be a biased estimator of the average treatment effect.

The sources of attrition take various forms in field research. For example, participants may be unwilling to fill out a post-treatment questionnaire. Researchers investigating a long-term effect of an intervention may lose track of participants who change addresses or names. Field stakeholders such as firms, organizations, or government agencies may decide to block researchers' access to certain outcomes; this is particularly common when research focuses on sensitive topics such as corruption. Finally, some outcome variables may be unavailable to certain participants due to experimental design: an intervention that aims to test the effect of a job training on worker wages in six months will inherently miss outcomes for the participants who are jobless at that time.

Because attrition may produce biased estimates, we encourage researchers to start a field project by first considering the availability of outcome measures to reduce the probability of attrition ex-ante. In the data collection process, to maximize the chances of obtaining outcome measures of interest, field researchers should aim to maintain good administrative records or good relations with those in charge of releasing information, clearly explain the expectations with participants, and follow up diligently to minimize attrition. For measurement outcomes, researchers can draw data from multiple sources and gather several outcome measures so that missing data on one variable might be imputed from other parallel measures. Of course, many sources of attrition are out of researchers' control. In these cases, researchers can address attrition by making assumptions about the statistical properties of the missing data, including reweighting (e.g., inverse probability weighting) and placing bounds on the average treatment effect (see Dinardo et al., 2006; Gerber & Green, 2012; Graham, 2009).

Non-compliance

Thus far, we have discussed the design and interpretation of field experiments when the treatment and control conditions are assumed to be implemented as planned. However, sometimes the actual experimental conditions that participants experience in the field do not match their assigned experimental conditions. One-sided non-compliance, or failure-to-treat, refers to the situation where some of the participants assigned to the treatment condition do not actually receive the treatment. Two-sided non-compliance refers to the more complicated situation in which some participants in the assigned treatment condition go untreated, and some participants in the assigned control condition end up receiving the treatment.

It is not uncommon for participants randomly assigned to a treatment condition to go untreated. When conducting research in natural settings, researchers sometimes are unable to administer the treatment to all participants assigned to the treatment condition because of logistical issues such as miscommunication, research personnel shortages, or transportation problems. Sometimes participants targeted for treatments are difficult to reach. In certain field experimental designs such as canvassing experiments (e.g., Broockman & Kalla, 2016; Gerber & Green, 2000), canvassers who are sent to visit households door-to-door about an upcoming election or other social causes may find some assigned households are simply not home when they arrive or that some households refuse the treatment. In these cases, an *encouragement design* invites participants in the assigned treatment condition to participate in the treatment offered by the researchers when non-compliance is anticipated to be common.

Whether non-compliance poses a problem to the research depends on the research objective. If one's goal is to evaluate the overall impact of a program with natural variations in its failure to deliver the treatment, then non-compliance is a feature of the program and thus not an inference issue. But when the goal of the field research is to obtain a meaningful average causal effect of *the treatment*, rather than the assigned experimental condition, non-compliance poses a challenge – it narrows the scope of what can be estimated and reduces the precision of the estimates.

There are several design recommendations for field researchers to avoid these problems. First, researchers can conduct a pilot study to gauge whether non-compliance is likely an issue and, if so, whether non-compliance can be overcome by adjusting the treatment or the methods of how the treatment is delivered. Second, if compliance rates are expected to remain low, one can consider the feasibility of an encouragement design and the use of a placebo condition rather than a pure control condition (Gerber et al., 2010). For example, Nickerson (2008) conducted a canvassing experiment where registered voters were randomly assigned either to be encouraged to vote (treatment condition) or to be encouraged to recycle (placebo condition). Comparing those who receive the treatment and those who receive the placebo enables the researchers to draw relatively unbiased inferences about the causal effect of the treatment on the treated. Third, researchers should clearly define the criteria used to classify participants as treated or untreated (or partially treated). They should ensure that these criteria are followed consistently, and that systematic procedures are in place to measure the actual receipt of treatment. When estimating the effect of partial treatment, one will need an augmented experimental design that varies whether participants are encouraged to receive full or partial treatment. Finally, in terms of estimation, adding covariates (e.g., participant demographics) can help assess condition balance and improve the precision of estimates. Randomization inference and instrumental variables can be used when appropriate to improve the estimates (see Gerber & Green, 2012, for more detailed recommendations; Angrist, Imbens, & Rubin, 1996, for a more technical discussion).

Important Considerations in Field Research

Pilot Testing in Field Research

Pilot testing is a useful way to learn about the sample and the field site where researchers are conducting their research, and to minimize the possibility that a research design would bring unintended consequences (Paluck & Shafir, 2017). Piloting typically refers to testing out a research paradigm before the actual research trial. Piloting can also mean taking time to investigate and understand stakeholders' and participants' construal[1] in the field setting – how they understand the behavior in question and how the situation involved in a research paradigm might affect their construal, prior to designing the full intervention. Many social and behavioral

---

[1] Construal is defined as individuals' interpretation of a stimulus, whether the stimulus is a survey question, a choice set, an experimenter, or a study environment (Paluck & Shafir, 2017; Ross & Nisbett, 1991).

scientists use the technique of "cognitive interviewing" (Shafer & Lohse, 2005; Willis, 2004) to test participants' perceptions of certain information to improve the development of research materials. This technique involves asking participants to think aloud and elaborate on their reactions to information of interest, talking through their reactions, and asking why they are providing the responses they provide.

As one example, I was once tasked with a challenge to reduce the littering behavior of factory workers in a large textile factory in China (Wu & Paluck, 2021). One reason for piloting was to see how likely a known intervention will be effective in the current field site. From observation and archival data, I learned that workers were unresponsive to factory rules and monetary incentives to throw waste in trash cans, rather than on the floors. Thus, I viewed this question as a way to test ideas about how to design nudges for new contexts. Another reason for piloting in this field setting was to understand the motivations behind workers' littering behavior. I learned, through field observation and interviews, that the factory workers were extremely motivated, as piece-rate workers, to not take seconds away from their work to throw trash into trash cans. However, although throwing the cloth on the floor sped up workers in the short run, throwing away the trash ultimately boosts productivity in the long term by preventing a pause when cleaners come through. In the end, I proposed to place golden coin decals on the floors because of a specific construal workers hold in this context: golden coins are believed to be an omen for fortune and luck, and should not be touched by waste. Therefore, instead of a nudge that guided workers, I designed a nudge to create a countervailing motivation to avoid throwing waste on the floor by changing the idea of the floor from a waste space to a space where waste was inappropriate. Without piloting, we would have otherwise missed this underlying motivation behind workers' littering behavior.

There are many reasons why construal plays an important role in the design of field research projects and why pilot testing can help refine a field research design. The bottom line is that as social and behavioral scientists, we should practice what we preach: context matters, and the design of an intervention and measurement tools must be particular to a specific context. There are rarely off-the-shelf interventions that would work the same way for different populations in different contexts because people in different settings may not necessarily share the same construal of the research intervention and its measurements. To design field research that is generalizable and reliable, we encourage field researchers to spend time doing activities that will help them understand the people and the contexts of interest better. It is also important for researchers to test their assumptions to achieve shared construal between investigators who are designing the research and participants who are experiencing the research.

Expanding the Field Terrain

Just as variations in human genotypes lead to diverse phenotypic behavioral expressions, environmental variations, in terms of geographic and cultural dynamics, produce rich systems of meanings and local cultural values that impact human behavior. While field research takes place in different institutional and organizational settings such as schools, companies, and local communities, I also want to point out more broadly that the geography in which individual research studies take place matters for a number of reasons: the variability of social issues and research questions that are posed by the world's geographic shift, the accuracy and generalizability of findings, and theory-building.

Geographic dynamics energize field research. The events and evolving phenomena in the world have created new questions and arenas for cutting-edge field research in social and behavioral sciences. For example, the atrocities of the world wars stimulated scholars to re-examine conformity and obedience. World War II motivated scholars to pay more attention to action research, group dynamics, and intergroup relations (Marrow, 1977). Decolonization in Asia and Africa after World War II drew field researchers to the politics and social issues of newly independent nations. Also, the beginning of the Cold War spurred the development of area studies centers in the United States that provided financial and institutional support for field research in certain world regions (Kapiszewski et al., 2015). Continuing geographic shifts, such as globalization and the rising prominence of certain countries, may draw new waves of field research to those areas. All of the events and phenomena that are happening in the vast geography of the world will influence the types of questions scientists pose and where and how we conduct field research to answer them.

One cause for concern is that much of behavioral research is based on findings from societies that are "WEIRD" – Western, Educated, Industrialized, Rich, and Democratic (Henrich et al., 2010; Rozin, 2010). To understand and generate theories about the breadth and depth of human behavior, we need to go beyond the current narrow field database, even if doing so means we need to go extra miles to recruit an inconvenient sample or reach faraway field settings. There are several reasons and ways to overcome this issue. First, field researchers should actively seek to conduct studies in non-WEIRD field settings and to recruit non-WEIRD participants whenever possible. When writing manuscripts, authors should clearly describe the characteristics of the participant sample and the intervention context. This includes (but is not limited to) the distribution of participants' gender, age, race, and ethnicity, and any notable features of the research context that may help others theorize the generalizability of relevant findings.

This recommendation is consistent with the recent call for detailing and justifying the racial demographics of samples to reduce racial inequality in behavioral research (Roberts et al., 2020). In addition, we strongly encourage researchers to explicitly discuss questions of generalizability and representativeness when presenting their research to grant agencies or writing empirical results for academic journals. From an institutional perspective, journal editors and reviewers should give researchers credit for recruiting and comparing diverse and hard-to-reach samples, and press authors to explicitly discuss the generalizability of their findings.

Replicability and Generalizability of Field Research

Since field studies are typically conducted in a specific context, they may lead to highly context-specific interventions and measurement. Thus, while field experiments are high in naturalism and are generalizable to the specific population being studied, it can be difficult to know if and when results from one context will generalize to another, and it can be challenging to compare across studies (Dunning, 2016). An emerging trend in field research to deal with this challenge is called a coordinated study (sometimes called a harmonized study), where multiple studies designed to test the same research question are conducted either sequentially or simultaneously in a range of contexts (Blair & McClendon, 2021; Ferraro & Agrawal, 2021).

A recent initiative led by the Evidence in Governance and Politics (EGAP) network provides a model for how social and behavioral scientists can conduct coordinated field studies: the Metaketa Initiative. The goal of a metaketa (the Basque word for "accumulation") is to compile a team of researchers who will implement coordinated field research studies to provide a reliable answer to a research question. The research question and intervention are developed by a steering group, that then solicits applications from researchers with the expertise to conduct studies in different locations. Researchers are selected to ensure maximum variation in contexts. Once the full team is compiled, the researchers agree on a set of comparable interventions and measures. The steering committee analyzes the results from each site in a meta-analysis and writes up the results in a publication.

For example, a recent meta-keta initiative wanted to test whether community policing increases trust in and cooperation with the police and reduces rates of crime. A steering committee selected proposals to conduct studies on this topic in six countries (Brazil, Colombia, Liberia, Pakistan, Philippines, and Uganda). In each country, the researchers implemented theoretically consistent community policing programs, along with at least one additional complementary intervention of the researchers' choice. Once the studies were completed at each site, the steering committee analyzed all of the data in a meta-analysis. A paper was then published, detailing their findings that community policing does not increase trust in the police or reduce crime (Blair et al., 2021). If one individual study had found null effects of a community policing intervention, it would be impossible to know whether community policing was ineffective in that particular context or if it is ineffective more generally. Additionally, there may be questions about whether the study was properly implemented. However, when there is consistent evidence from six studies with theoretically similar interventions and outcome measurements, scholars can feel more confident that the conclusions are replicable and generalizable.

Technological Advancement and Field Research

The world has witnessed an unprecedented advancement in new technologies that has significant consequences for field research. How does technological advancement, particularly the broad use of the internet, influence field research? First of all, technological advancement introduces new ways of delivering interventions and conducting field research. The internet and smartphones broaden the types of media through which a treatment can be delivered in the field. For example, researchers can now send text messages (Dai et al., 2021), use push notifications on smart phone applications (Carpenter et al., 2020), broadcast radio and audio shows (Blair et al., 2019), expose internet users to different webpage designs, and encourage online voting in rural communities (Wu et al., 2023). The internet also broadens the media through which data can be collected. Instead of paper surveys, field researchers can now use tablets and digital surveys to collect individual responses. The technology landscape in the world, such as the availability of police body camera footage, broadens behavioral measurements that would otherwise be extremely difficult to collect (Voigt et al., 2017).

Not only does technology influence the *form* or medium of research delivery, but also the *focus* of research questions. Similar to the observation that geographic change energizes new research areas, technological advancement brings new topics for field research. Technological advances have opened up new virtual spaces for behaviors, interactions, and inquiries, generating novel questions ripe for research. For example, field researchers today are keen to understand social media such as Facebook and Twitter: What are the effects of social media on the self and on interpersonal relationships? How does misinformation spread across social media and influence behavior? How do gig economies impact the future of work? These are all research questions brought up by the changing role of the internet and technology in people's everyday life. Sometimes, geographical and technological change interact to galvanize new research domains. For example, in the changing geopolitical dynamics in certain world regions, field researchers are examining the role of social media in mobilizing massive protests in Egypt and Lebanon (Radsch, 2009), in the 2021 January 6 Capitol riot in the US, and when, how, and why the Chinese government censors social media posts (King et al., 2013; Pan, 2019).

Advantages. There are many advantages of using the internet as the field site. First, if the interventions can be delivered via the internet, this may drastically reduce the cost involved in training research personnel and implementing the study in a physical field site. In some cases, when both the deployment of an intervention and the data collection can be done online, researchers may not even need to leave their home institutions to conduct field research. Second, the internet also makes certain interventions easier to scale and incentivizes wider adoption across institutions (e.g., Chang et al., 2019; Beshears et al., 2021). Finally, certain research topics that rely on the internet as a communication medium, such as the propagation of misinformation through social media and the effectiveness of virtual learning, can only be tested using the internet as the field site.

Limitations. There are also considerable limitations to using the internet, especially when used exclusively as a research data source or as a field site. First, while the internet broadens the possibilities of research design, delivery, and scalability, it also excludes populations who do not have reliable internet access. Around a third of the world's population has never used the internet, and about half do not own a smartphone (International Telecommunication Union, 2021; Pew Research

Center, 2024). Field research that relies on the internet as a sole data source thus effectively excludes at least a third of the world's population, who are more likely to be from less developed countries and from a marginalized background. Second, while the internet is better equipped to deliver fast and short messages to a large number of subjects at once, online interventions may be less immersive, less likely to grasp sustained attention, and less interactive compared with other types of field research. Relatedly, while online field research facilitates many research domains such as online marketing, messaging campaigns, and human–machine interactions, it precludes the study of face-to-face interacting groups and other intricate social processes that only manifest fully offline.

Conclusion

Field research is important for continuing to develop and refine theories that reflect how people think and behave in their natural environments, and for testing theory-informed interventions. Given the rapid pace of innovation in field research methods, we are confident that field research will continue producing cutting-edge and standard-setting scholarship that provides compelling answers to many significant questions posed by social and behavioral sciences.

References

Angrist, J. D., Imbens, G. W., & Rubin, D. B. (1996). Identification of causal effects using instrumental variables. *Journal of the American Statistical Association*, *91*(434), 444–455.

Aronow, P. M., & Samii, C. (2017). Estimating average causal effects under general interference, with application to a social network experiment. *Annals of Applied Statistics*, *11*, 1912–1947.

Astuti, R., & Bloch, M. (2010). Why a theory of human nature cannot be based on the distinction between universality and variability: Lessons from anthropology. *Behavioral and Brain Sciences*, *33*(2–3), 83–84.

Beaman, L., Chattopadhyay, R., Duflo, E., Pande, R., & Topalova, P. (2009). Powerful women: Does exposure reduce bias? *Quarterly Journal of Economics*, *124*(4), 1497–1540.

Beshears, J., Dai, H., Milkman, K. L., & Benartzi, S. (2021). Using fresh starts to nudge increased retirement savings. *Organizational Behavior and Human Decision Processes*, *167*, 72–87.

Blair, G., Littman, R., & Paluck, E. L. (2019). Motivating the adoption of new community-minded behaviors: An empirical test in Nigeria. *Science Advances*, *5*(3), eaau5175.

Blair, G., & McClendon, G. (2021). Conducting experiments in multiple contexts. In J. Druckman (ed.), *Advances in Experimental Political Science* (pp. 411–428). Cambridge University Press.

Blair, G., Weinstein, J. M., Christia, F., Arias, E., Badran, E., Blair, R. A., et al. (2021). Community policing does not build citizen trust in police or reduce crime in the Global South. *Science, 374*(6571), eabd3446.

Broockman, D., & Kalla, J. (2016). Durably reducing transphobia: A field experiment on door-to-door canvassing. *Science, 352*(6282), 220–224.

Bullock, J., Green, D., & Ha, S. (2010). Yes, but what's the mechanism? (Don't expect an easy answer). *Journal of Personality and Social Psychology, 98*, 550–558.

Carpenter, S. M., Menictas, M., Nahum-Shani, I., Wetter, D. W., & Murphy, S. A. (2020). Developments in mobile health just-in-time adaptive interventions for addiction science. *Current Addiction Reports, 7*(3), 280–290.

Chang, E. H., Milkman, K. L., Gromet, D. M., Rebele, R. W., Massey, C., Duckworth, A. L., & Grant, A. M. (2019). The mixed effects of online diversity training. *Proceedings of the National Academy of Sciences, 116*(16), 7778–7783.

Cialdini, R. B. (1980). Full-cycle social psychology. *Applied Social Psychology Annual, 1*, 21–47.

Cialdini, R. B., Demaine, L. J., Sagarin, B. J., Barrett, D. W., Rhoads, K., & Winter, P. L. (2006). Managing social norms for persuasive impact. *Social Influence, 1*(1), 3–15.

Cui, Z., Liu, L., Li, D., Wu, S. J., & Zhai, X. (2022). Safety messaging boosts parental vaccination intention for children ages 5–11. *Vaccines, 10*, 1205.

Dai, H., Saccardo, S., Han, M. A., Roh, L., Raja, N., Vangala, S., et al. (2021). Behavioural nudges increase COVID-19 vaccinations. *Nature, 597*(7876), 404–409.

DiNardo, J., McCrary, J., & Sanbonmatsu, L. (2006). Constructive proposals for dealing with attrition: An empirical example. Working paper, University of Michigan.

Dolan, P., & Galizzi, M. M. (2014). Getting policy-makers to listen to field experiments. *Oxford Review of Economic Policy, 30*(4), 725–752.

Duflo, E., & Banerjee, A. (2017). *Handbook of Field Experiments*. Elsevier.

Duflo, E., Glennerster, R., & Kremer, M. (2007). Using randomization in development economics research: A toolkit. *Handbook of Development Economics, 4*, 3895–3962.

Dunning, T. (2016). Transparency, replication, and cumulative learning: What experiments alone cannot achieve. *Annual Review of Political Science, 19*, 541–563.

Eden, D. (2017). Field experiments in organizations. *Annual Review of Organizational Psychology and Organizational Behavior, 4*, 91–122.

Ferraro, P. J., & Agrawal, A. (2021). Synthesizing evidence in sustainability science through harmonized experiments: Community monitoring in common pool resources. *Proceedings of the National Academy of Sciences, 118*(29), e2106489118.

Ferrero, M., & Pinto, I. (2023). A regenerative tourism approach for the development of marginalised areas: Insights from two best practices in Southern Italy. *Turistica – Italian Journal of Tourism, 32*(1), 128–149.

Gantman, A., Gomila, R., Martinez, J. E., Matias, J. N., Elizabeth, L. P., Starck, J., et al. (2018). A pragmatist philosophy of psychological science and its implications for replication. *Behavioral and Brain Sciences, 41*.

Gerber, A. S., & Green, D. P. (2000). The effects of canvassing, telephone calls, and direct mail on voter turnout: A field experiment. *American Political Science Review, 94*(3), 653–663.

Gerber, A. S., & Green, D. P. (2012). *Field Experiments: Design, Analysis, and Interpretation*. W. W. Norton.

Gerber, A. S., Huber, G. A., Doherty, D., Dowling, C. M., & Ha, S. E. (2010). Personality and political attitudes: Relationships across issue domains and political contexts. *American Political Science Review*, *104*(1), 111–133.

Gneezy, U., & Rustichini, A. (2000). A fine is a price. *Journal of Legal Studies*, *29*(1), 1–17.

Graham, J. (2009). Missing data analysis: Making it work in the real world. *Annual Review of Psychology*, *60*, 549–576.

Hansen, J. A., & Tummers, L. (2020). A systematic review of field experiments in public administration. *Public Administration Review*, *80*(6), 921–931.

Harrison, G. W., & List, J. A. (2004). Field experiments. *Journal of Economic Literature*, *42*(4), 1009–1055.

Haushofer, J., & Shapiro, J. (2016). The short-term impact of unconditional cash transfers to the poor: Experimental evidence from Kenya. *Quarterly Journal of Economics*, *131*(4), 1973–2042. https://doi.org/10.1093/qje/qjw025

Henrich, J., Heine, S. J., & Norenzayan, A. (2010). The weirdest people in the world? *Behavioral and Brain Sciences*, *33*(2–3), 61–83.

Hudgens, M. G., & Halloran, M. E. (2008). Toward causal inference with interference. *Journal of the American Statistical Association*, *103*(482), 832–842.

Hussey, M. A., & Hughes, J. P. (2007). Design and analysis of stepped wedge cluster randomized trials. *Contemporary Clinical Trials*, *28*(2), 182–191.

International Telecommunication Union. (2021, November). Facts and figures 2021: 2.9 billion people still offline. https://www.itu.int/hub/2021/11/facts-and-figures-2021-2-9-billion-people-still-offline

James, W. (1907). Pragmatism's conception of truth. *Journal of Philosophy, Psychology and Scientific Methods*, *4*(6), 141–155.

Kapiszewski, D., MacLean, L. M., & Read, B. L. (2015). *Field Research in Political Science: Practices and Principles*. Cambridge University Press.

King, G., Pan, J., & Roberts, M. (2013). How censorship in China allows government criticism but silences collective expression. *American Political Science Review*, *107*(2), 326–343.

Lewin, K. (1944/1997). Problems of research in social psychology. In Lewin, *Resolving Social Conflicts; & Field Theory in Social Science*. American Psychological Association.

(1947). Frontiers in group dynamics: II. channels of group life; social planning and action research. *Human Relations*, *1*(2), 143–153.

Marrow, A. J. (1977). *The Practical Theorist: The Life and Work of Kurt Lewin*. Teachers College Press.

Moore-Berg, S. L., Bernstein, K., Gallardo, R. A., Hameiri, B., Littman, R., O'Neil, S., & Pasek, M. H. (2022). Translating social science for peace: Benefits, challenges, and recommendations. *Peace and Conflict: Journal of Peace Psychology*, *28*(3), 274–283.

Nickerson, D. W. (2008). Is voting contagious? Evidence from two field experiments. *American Political Science Review*, *102*(1), 49–57.

Paluck, E. L. (2009). Reducing intergroup prejudice and conflict using the media: A field experiment in Rwanda. *Journal of Personality and Social Psychology*, *96*, 574–587.

Paluck, E. L., & Cialdini, R. B. (2014). Field research methods. In C. M. Judd & H. T. Reis (eds.), *Handbook of Research Methods in Social and Personality Psychology*, 2nd ed. (pp. 81–98) Cambridge University Press.

Paluck, E. L., & Shafir, E. (2017). The psychology of construal in the design of field experiment. In A. V. Banerjee & E. Duflo (eds.), *Handbook of Economic Field Experiments* (vol. 1, pp. 245–268). North-Holland.

Pan, J. (2019). How Chinese officials use the internet to construct their public image. *Political Science Research and Methods, 7*(2), 197–213.

Pew Research Center. (2024, April). *Internet/Broadband Fact Sheet.* www.pewresearch.org/internet/fact-sheet/internet-broadband

Radsch, C. (2009). From cell phones to coffee: Issues of access in Egypt and Lebanon. In C. L. Sriram, J. C. King, J. A. Mertus, O. Martin-Ortega, & J. Herman (eds.), *Surviving Field Research: Working in Violent and Difficult Situations.* Routledge. https://doi.org/10.4324/9780203875278

Read, B. L., Kapiszewski, D., & MacLean, L. M. (2015). Field research in political science: Practices and principles. In Read, Kapiszewski, & MacLean (eds.), *Field Research in Political Science: Practices and Principles* (pp. 1–33). Cambridge University Press.

Roberts, S. O., Bareket-Shavit, C., Dollins, F. A., Goldie, P. D., & Mortenson, E. (2020). Racial inequality in psychological research: Trends of the past and recommendations for the future. *Perspectives on Psychological Science, 15*(6), 1295–1309.

Ross, L., & Nisbett, R. E. (1991). *The Person and the Situation: Perspectives of Social Psychology.* McGraw-Hill.

Rozin, P. (2010). The weirdest people in the world are a harbinger of the future of the world. *Behavioral and Brain Sciences, 33*(2–3), 108–109.

Rubin, D. B. (2001). Using propensity scores to help design observational studies: Application to the tobacco litigation. *Health Services and Outcomes Research Methodology, 2*(3), 169–188.

(2005). Causal inference using potential outcomes. *Journal of the American Statistical Association, 100*(469), 322–331.

Shadish, W. R., Cook, T. D., & Campbell, D. T. (2002). *Experimental and Quasi-Experimental Designs for Generalized Causal Inference.* Houghton Mifflin.

Shafer, K., & Lohse, B. (2005). How to conduct a cognitive interview: A nutrition education example. US Department of Agriculture, National Institute of Food and Agriculture.

Silver, L. (2019, February 5). Smartphone ownership is growing rapidly around the world but not always equally. Pew Research Center. www.pewresearch.org/global/2019/02/05/digital-connectivity-growing-rapidly-in-emerging-economies

Tankard, M. E., & Paluck, E. L. (2017). The effect of a Supreme Court decision regarding gay marriage on social norms and personal attitudes. *Psychological Science, 28*(9), 1334–1344. https://doi.org/10.1177/0956797617709594

Voigt, R., Camp, N. P., Prabhakaran, V., Hamilton, W. L., Hetey, R. C., Griffiths, C. M., et al. (2017). Language from police body camera footage shows racial disparities in officer respect. *Proceedings of the National Academy of Sciences, 114*(25), 6521–6526.

Walton, G. M., & Cohen, G. L. (2011). A brief social-belonging intervention improves academic and health outcomes of minority students. *Science, 331*(6023), 1447–1451.

Willis, G. (2004). *Cognitive Interviewing.* SAGE Publications. https://doi.org/10.4135/9781412983655

Wood, E. J. (2009). Field research. In C. Boix & S. C. Stokes (eds.), *The Oxford Handbook of Comparative Politics* (pp. 123–146). Oxford University Press.

Wu, S. J., Mai, M., Yi, F., Truex, R., & Zhuang, M. (2023). Bootstrapping participation: A field experiment on participatory budgeting and civic engagement in China. Working paper.

Wu, S. J., & Paluck, E. L. (2020). Participatory practices at work change attitudes and behavior toward societal authority and justice. *Nature Communications*, *11*(1), 2633.

Wu, S. J., & Paluck, E. L. (2021). Designing nudges for the context: Golden coin decals nudge workplace behavior in China. *Organizational Behavior and Human Decision Processes*, *163*, 43–50.

Wu, S. J., & Paluck, E. L. (2022). Having a voice in your group: Increasing productivity through group participation. *Behavioural Public Policy*, First View, 1–21.

Wu, S. J., Yuhan Mei, B., & Cervantez, J. (2022). Preferences and perceptions of workplace participation: A cross-cultural study. *Frontiers in Psychology*, *13*, 806481.

6 Organizational Research

Victor E. Sojo and Melissa A. Wheeler

Abstract

This chapter focuses on the study of organizations as complex and dynamic social systems. We start our discussion of quantitative organizational research by outlining what organizations are and why we need to study them. We dive into doing research in organizations with specific focus on using theory to guide research methods and three critical organizational dimensions that should inform research design choices: units and levels of analysis, structures and hierarchies, and time and change. We then present and analyze the potential and limitations of descriptive, correlational, and experimental designs in organizational research, using contemporary examples of research to ground our analysis. We also cover data collection considerations, sampling strategies, and sources of organizational data. We close this chapter with discussions of equity issues, in particular ethics, diversity, and inclusion in organizational research.

Keywords: Organizations, Organizational Research, Research Design, Units of Analysis, Data Collection, Research Ethics

Introduction

Organizations are complex, fascinating beasts, and we must do our best to understand them. Organizations and their processes have been studied by multiple disciplines, including psychology, management, industrial relations, sociology, economics, political science, occupational therapy, ergonomics, architecture, and design, to name a few. Therefore, it is not surprising to find a wide range of definitions of organizations, topics of interest, theories, research designs, data collection and analytical approaches, and applications of knowledge. In this chapter, we will focus on organizational research from a social and behavioral sciences perspective and, as much as possible, we will reference multidisciplinary research.

There are challenges in defining organizations and in describing how they operate. Both lay (Heath & Staudenmayer, 2000) and academic theories vary in their operationalizations of organizations. However, certain commonalities are discernible across definitions. For example, notions of order, cooperation, and interdependence in the actions of people are all common in definitions of organizations (Eldridge & Crombie, 2013). More formally, organizations are types of social systems containing a set of members who more or less share a collective identity, relationships, goals, values, and a program of activities and procedures defined by the members' interactions and roles (Caplow, 1964). Interestingly, teams share all these properties with organizations (Kozlowski & Ilgen, 2006). In organizational research, teams are considered organizational subsystems. Of course, the nature and strength of the collective identity, whether the creation of the system was deliberate, and the clarity and specificity of the roles, activities, goals, and values are all matters of degree rather than absolute demarcation.

For instance, organizations can emerge organically and be later crystallized by more deliberate actions (e.g., from business idea to venture). The activities, goals, and values of organizations can be numerous, vague, and contradictory, and change over time (e.g., organizations with very diversified services). Similarly, organizational membership (e.g., employees, board members, investors), the roles the different members fulfill (e g., team leader, advisor, individual contributor) and the relationships between them (e.g., colleague, supervisor, subordinate) are not always clearly defined and are also subject to change. Therefore, organizations are not consistently coherent and stable entities, but complex and dynamic ones. We must attempt to study organizations and their processes with that in mind.

There are many reasons to research organizations. From a historical and sociological perspective, during the nineteenth and twentieth centuries, large organizations became ubiquitous and started dominating many important aspects of human life. Then, organizations were expected to help humans solve the conflicts between collective and individual interests and needs, by aligning them and helping the world thrive (Reed, 2006). Nevertheless, the impact of organizations on human life goes beyond aligning collective and individual interests and, on many occasions, organizations do not achieve such alignment. Organizations can influence the way we define ourselves (e.g., job involvement), our private lives (e.g., work–family conflict), our relationships with other humans (e.g., our emotions and behaviors toward co-workers), and the physical environment where we live (e.g., the impact of organizational leaders' decisions on communities and the planet). With such a large influence on everything that happens on our planet, organizations are an important topic of study.

Using Theory to Guide Organizational Research

Organizational research designs and data collection are informed by theories and hypotheses. In turn, research designs and data collection help us improve the quality of theories and hypotheses in a complementary and cyclical fashion. Wherever we look in contemporary organizational research, we will find calls for more rigorous research (Cortina & Landis, 2013) that should produce knowledge relevant and useful to individuals, organizations, and communities around the world (Wickert et al., 2021). We continue to see organizational research that is plagued by issues of weak theory, research design, and measurement (Aguinis et al., 2019; Aguinis & Vandenberg, 2014). This oversight restricts the capacity of organizational research to make meaningful contributions to theory development within the discipline or to organizational policy and practice.

A fundamental objective of scientific research is the development and refinement of valid theories. Given the proliferation of new theories and explanations within organizational research, it is possible to argue that we are making progress in theory development (Aguinis & Vandenberg, 2014). However, we might be failing in the process of *theory refinement*. That is, it is crucial to expose theories to rigorous tests and to continuously refine or discard theories and associated hypotheses that fail these tests (Edwards, 2010).

The question about how to improve the quality of existing theories in organizational research has been addressed in different ways. For instance, a reasonable step in the process of organizational research is asking yourself whether the study you are designing is crucial. That is, has the focal theory of your research been placed in a position to be contradicted or expanded by the findings (Aguinis & Vandenberg, 2014; Campbell & Stanley, 1963)? If the design you are using will not allow you and others to evaluate whether the evidence obtained contradicts or expands the theory, it is necessary to consider a different or more complex research design.

At a more concrete level, the development and refinement of organizational theory requires a strong effort to guarantee the validity of the operationalization of variables. This is needed to make sure we are manipulating and measuring meaningful proxies for our constructs of interest (Kerlinger & Lee, 1999). Similarly, if our theories and hypotheses describe dynamic processes that are operating within (e.g., changes across time) and between multiple units of analysis (e.g., individuals, teams, organizations), then the research designs we are using need to account for this multilevel dynamic process (Cortina & Landis, 2013; Vantilborgh et al., 2018).

Of course, these recommendations are not new. Most organizational quantitative methods textbooks provide some concrete strategies to approach research in the way specified above (Brewerton & Millward, 2001; Campbell & Stanley, 1963; Kerlinger & Lee, 1999; Schwab, 2004). Still, contemporary organizational research is found lacking across many of these areas. Limitations in the training of organizational researchers around theory development and advanced designs, difficulties in data collection, pressure to publish quantity over quality research, lack of funding to engage in programmatic research, and limited time to learn new approaches and refine research ideas are only a few of the culprits mentioned in explanations about the limitations in contemporary research (Aguinis & Vandenberg, 2014; Park et al., 2023). In the following section, we outline a series of design considerations that are important to improve the quality of organizational research and their implications for the selection of appropriate research designs.

Research Design Considerations

Designing organizational research requires us to consider some basic properties of organizations to identify the nature of the phenomena at hand. In this section, we will focus on units and levels of analysis, structures and hierarchies, and time and change as central aspects of organizations that should inform research design choices.

Units and Levels of Analysis

There are multiple *units of analysis* in organizational research. A unit of analysis is the central entity you are trying to understand or the focus of your study. We can put our efforts into understanding experiences at different levels: at the individual level (e.g., personality traits that moderate the relationship between workplace stress and intentions to leave the organization), at the team level (e.g., the organic distribution of tasks and social roles among team members over time), or at the organizational level (e.g., the relationship between organizational structures and organizational cultures). Historically, organizational psychology and organizational behavior researchers have prioritized the experiences of individuals and teams within organizations as the focus of their research – typically referred to as micro and meso levels of analysis in organizational research (Heath & Sitkin, 2001; Johns, 2018). Meanwhile, researchers in strategy, industrial relations, employment relations, and sociology of organizations have emphasized organization-level process as their unit of analysis, as well as environmental factors impacting organizations (Harley, 2018; Porter, 1991) – often described as a macro level of analysis.

We can go beyond studying processes within specific entities (e.g., individuals, teams, organizations) and focus on the *relationships between entities* as our unit of analysis. For instance, we can study dyads (e.g., spirals of abuse between pairs of workers; Aquino & Lamertz, 2004), social networks (e.g., positive and negative gossip communication within and between teams; Grosser et al., 2010), or relations between teams or organizations (e.g., changes in the interactions between procurers and vendors; Gulati et al., 2005).

Researching relationships *across levels of analysis* is also important. For instance, we can explore the relationship between individual- and team-level processes (e.g., leadership behaviors and patterns of incivility among team members; Sojo & Roberts, 2019), between organizational processes and stakeholder behaviors (e.g., investors' reactions to the appointment of black CEOs; Jeong et al., 2022) or between organizational processes and industry/national processes (e.g., the impact of government legislation on human resources discriminatory practices; Trzebiatowski et al., 2020). In brief, organizational researchers need to make deliberate decisions about their units and levels of analysis, taking into consideration the nature of the problems or research questions in front of them. This is a path to designing studies that validly capture the nature of organizational life.

Organizational Structures and Hierarchies

Within organizations, there are specific configurations of relationships between individuals and teams, including hierarchies. Organizations of any size can have complex organizational structures. This complexity can emerge because of the different operational needs across organizational divisions, informal structures that are allowed to emerge in different units (often only partially formalized), and many other reasons. Even in organizations that describe themselves as flat and nimble, it is possible to identify situations in which specific individuals become leaders and where teams are nested within larger units, thus establishing dependency relationships (Osis & Donins, 2017). Therefore, it is critical to remember that there might be differences between prescribed, embraced, and actual organizational structures.

These differences are meaningful and should be included as research considerations. Also, there is no good reason to assume that, in an organization with diversified products and services, we will find a single, coherent hierarchical structure encompassing all levels and work units. In fact, the opposite is more likely the case. This degree of variability makes it vital for researchers to first familiarize themselves with the organizations where they are conducting studies and to consider how they will incorporate and account or control (experimentally or statistically) for the attributes of organizational structures in their research designs.

Time and Change

Arguably, one key concern of social and behavioral science research in general, and organizational research in particular, is the need to study processes with full consideration of their dynamic features. That is, organizational processes are called *processes* because they are not static phenomena; they are events or steps, linked in a series with an onset and offset. The series of steps or events leads to change or transformation over time and follows some principles or rules (Roe, 2008; Wang et al., 2016). Even micro-organizational variables once construed as stable, such as personality, are now recognized to vary across contexts (Beckman et al., 2020) and over time (McAdams & Olson, 2010). In short, organizational processes are dynamic in nature because they "emerge, evolve, and dissolve over time" (Vantilborgh et al., 2018, p. 1045).

Despite the dynamic nature of processes, the late twentieth century saw a surge of cross-sectional surveys as the default tool to conduct organizational research (Roe, 2008). While cross-sectional surveys can be useful to identify patterns of experiences across populations and associations between variables, they have severe limitations in helping us understand stages in organizational processes, the changes that might emerge from these processes or, importantly, in establishing causation (Aguinis & Vandenberg, 2014). This lack of fit between process and measurement has prompted innumerable calls for research procedures that better account for the dynamic nature of organizational processes in terms of the validity of measures, research designs (Vantilborgh et al., 2018), and statistical models (Cortina & Landis, 2013). Ultimately, if we are to theorize about organizational processes, our research designs must afford us the possibility of ascertaining the emergence, fluctuations, and changes produced by these processes over time.

Research Design in Organizations

Our research designs establish the procedures we will use to obtain valid and reliable data about the units of analysis we will investigate to answer our research questions (Schwab, 2004). Based on our research questions, we need to make decisions about what units of analysis we will study (e.g., individuals, teams, organizations), whether to focus on the relations, differences or changes over time of these units of analysis, the specific conditions where and when we will conduct our studies, the steps we will follow to collect data about the units of analysis, and the instruments we will use to collect our data. A logical first step in this process involves elucidating the nature of our research questions. What is it exactly we are trying to understand? Do we want to know the *what, when, where, how,* and/or *why* of an organizational process?

At a descriptive level, we can explore the *what* – understanding the ways in which an organizational process manifests, including its different dimensions (e.g., what types of workplace sexual harassment are more prevalent? Charlesworth et al., 2011). We might want to know the *when* and *where* – in other words, we can look at the conditions under which an organizational process is more likely to emerge (e.g., what type of employees, and in what industries and situations, are more likely to experience workplace sexual harassment? Cortina et al., 2002). Finally, we can be interested in the *how* or *why* – we might want to understand the mechanisms through which an organizational phenomenon emerges, how it changes under certain conditions, and how it dissipates (e.g., what processes enable, motivate, and precipitate workplace sexual harassment? Sojo & Roberts, 2019).

Our research questions must inform our decisions on whether we design our research procedures to *observe* or to *manipulate* organizational phenomena. A simple distinction we can make on how to investigate a phenomenon is whether we will observe it as it naturally occurs or attempt to actively manipulate it and test its effects (Hedrick et al., 1993). Here, we are making decisions about what to do with the variables we are measuring in our units of analysis. Research questions about *what, when,* and *where* an organizational process is/emerges often lead us to observe this phenomenon as it is, without active manipulation of independent variables. Here, we have the options of conducting exploratory/descriptive studies or correlational studies (Black, 2002). Research questions about *how* and *why* an organizational process emerges/unfolds can be answered by observing phenomena as they naturally occur. However, these questions are better addressed via research that manipulates conditions to evaluate the impact of such changes. We can use correlational (with some limitations) and experimental research to answer these types of questions (Black, 2002). Below, we discuss the potential and limitations of exploratory/descriptive, correlational, and experimental designs as approaches to investigate organizational processes. After that, we focus on data collection.

Exploratory/Descriptive Studies

Exploratory/descriptive studies allow for an in-depth examination of a particular organizational process, providing new insights, or generating new research questions. While exploratory/descriptive studies should have clear objectives informed by current theories and evidence, they do not require outlining hypotheses to be tested. These studies are typically cross-sectional, concerned with the current state of organizational processes – the information that we have here and now (Brewerton &

Millward, 2001). In organizational research, exploratory/descriptive studies can present an in-depth quantitative exploration of the situation of a particular unit of analysis (e.g., evaluating perceptions of ethicality of dubious practices among workers in the finance sector; Wheeler et al., 2016).

One significant risk of exploratory/descriptive studies is the potential for multiple variables, that have not been experimentally or statistically controlled, to impact the study results without the researchers being aware. This problem can be partially prevented by using previous research and theories to guide the objectives and approach to the exploratory research. While it is rare to see entirely descriptive/exploratory research published in mainstream organizational studies journals, producing this kind of study can help expose contradictions and missing elements in current theories (Aguinis & Vandenberg, 2014); this is both intrinsically valuable and can help generate new hypotheses to be tested.

Correlational Studies

Correlational studies comprise the largest set of studies in contemporary organizational research, and this has been the case for a long time (Mitchell, 1985). When properly designed, correlational studies have the capacity to help us elucidate very complex relationships taking place in different organizational contexts, while preserving external validity. Often, correlational studies use statistical coefficients to estimate the magnitude of the association between the variables of interest by focusing on differences *between* units of analysis. There are three basic properties of the associations between variables in correlational studies: their strength (i.e., how closely two variables are correlated), direction (i.e., whether the correlation is positive or negative), and shape (i.e., what rate of change exists between the correlated variables, which creates linear or non-linear relations; Brewerton & Millward, 2001). Perfect linear correlations are rare in real-world organizations. However, correlations are too often *assumed* to be linear. Researchers should instead evaluate the shape of the relationships they are studying, starting with a basic bivariate scatter plot, and identify which function better describes the nature of the relationship they are investigating, before making decisions about appropriate inferential statistical analyses to conduct or drawing conclusions.

While cross-sectional studies can be used to identify associations and provide insights for future research, they have severe limitations in their capacity to help us ascertain whether changes are occurring in the organizational processes we are studying or whether there are causal relationships between the variables. That is, they have several threats to internal validity (Campbell & Stanley, 1963). Because of these limitations, most high-impact, mainstream journals publishing quantitative organizational research are less likely to accept cross-sectional correlational studies by themselves (e.g., Antonakis et al., 2019; Bono & McNamara, 2011). This practice is not due to an inherent bias against cross-sectional research. The concern here is that there is a mismatch between the nature of the organizational phenomena we are researching (i.e., the fact that they are processes with changes over time) and the selection of a cross-sectional design (Bono & McNamara, 2011), and the well-known *endogeneity problem* – the potential for reverse causation or when a third variable explains the relationship between our variables of interest (Schwerdt & Woessmann, 2020).

Longitudinal correlational studies also evaluate the relationship between organizational variables without manipulating them. However, they go a step further by separating measurements of key variables across time points. In these designs, the predictors are measured at an earlier time relative to the intervening variables (e.g., mediators or moderators) and criteria, to mimic the hypothesized temporal dynamic relations between these variables. The simplest form of longitudinal study preserves the concern with differences *between* units of analysis and temporally separates the measures of predictors and mediators or moderators from the criteria (e.g., evaluating the mediating role of job self-efficacy and job demand in the ethnicity–depression relationship; Adamovic et al., 2022). This type of design is also common in studies dedicated to measurement development and validation to establish criterion-related validity and test-retest reliability (Brewerton & Millward, 2001).

Other organizational longitudinal studies focus on *within-unit* differences. Researchers have recognized that evaluating changes within units of analysis across time, in the short and long term, is critical to understanding dynamic organizational processes. To model a dynamic process, researchers take multiple samples of the same units, such as individuals, teams, organizations, or inter-unit relations across time. These studies can help evaluate how intra-individual changes are systematic and predict other organizational processes (e.g., evaluation of temporary task-contingent personality changes as a predictor of adaptive job performance; Minbashian et al., 2010) or how change over time in our units of analysis can both be predicted by and predict organizational processes (e.g., evaluation of the impact of patterns of growth over the years in female representation within organizations on collective employee turnover; Maurer & Qureshi, 2021), among many other dynamic processes.

Some of the designs used in these longitudinal studies, such as experience sampling methods, have the potential to reduce memory bias when surveys are used. That is, the errors in recollection that occur when participants are asked to report on events that happened a long time ago or to engage in mental aggregation are less likely to occur with multiple measures of contemporary events (Beal, 2015). Similarly, by taking multiple measures of the set of relevant variables, investigators can reduce bias due to responses impacted by events (e.g., momentary negative affect at an individual level, seasonal effects in spending behavior at the firm level) that took place at a specific point in time (Spector, 2006). Finally, by using different sources (e.g., supervisor, subordinates) and types of data (e.g., survey responses, permanent records, biological markers via wearable devices) we can prevent common-method bias in our measurement process and reduce the risk of inflated correlations.

There are many ways to improve the quality, including internal and external validity, of correlational studies. As indicated earlier, using sound theories as the guide for the selection of constructs to measure and the kind of relationships to explore is a necessary first step. Theory should also guide the inclusion of control variables to rule out potential alternative explanations to the associations you might find. However, the way we use control variables can impact Type I and Type II errors. For instance, control variables can increase Type II errors if they partial out true variance from the substantive relationship being studied (e.g., Spector et al., 2000). Also, excluding control variables that are not correlated with the dependent variable is necessary to prevent reductions in statistical power or increased chances of Type I error via a spurious suppressor (Becker, 2005). Finally, researchers need to make sure the measures they are using are valid and reliable and must articulate a clear explanation of why specific variables and measures were selected (Aguinis & Vandenberg, 2014).

Longitudinal correlational studies represent an improvement in the match between the research design and the nature of the phenomena that are typically studied in organizations, relative to cross-sectional research. Yet, the risk of test reactivity due to multiple exposures to the measurement instruments impacting how people might respond to subsequent measures remains. Also, longitudinal organizational studies are hard to execute with time-poor workers who are often volunteering to participate in the research. Similarly, these studies still lack the rigor of experimental research, increasing risk to internal validity. Nevertheless, when properly designed and executed, longitudinal correlational designs can help us understand organizational processes as they occur and achieve better external validity by allowing us to make inferences about the populations, contexts, and measures to which we can generalize our findings (Campbell & Stanley, 1963).

Experimental Studies

Experimental research is still considered the preeminent way to test hypotheses in organizational research and beyond (Eden, 2017; Van Quaquebeke et al., 2022). The push for experimental research in organizations is based on (i) a clear understanding of organizational phenomena as processes emerging from precipitating events, producing changes, and somehow ending, and (ii) the need to develop and refine theories in a way that allow us to establish causal relationships (Eden, 2017; Aguinis & Vandenberg, 2014). Notions (i) and (ii) above underpin the logic of experimental research:

- the active manipulation of independent variables;
- use of randomization in the creation of experimental groups and allocation of their treatments to help ensure pre-experimental equivalence;
- evaluation of how the independent variables impact mediators and dependent variables in a temporal sequence;
- isolation of the potential impact of extraneous variables that can hinder internal validity.

(Campbell & Stanley, 1963; Kerlinger & Lee, 1999)

In organizational research, we see a continuum between laboratory and field experiments. At one end, we find *laboratory experiments* that allow for the manipulation of independent variables, randomization of participants and treatment, and measurement of mediating and dependent variables in a controlled environment, reducing the impact of threats to internal validity (Campbell & Stanley, 1963). Laboratory experiments are particularly useful to test the underlying mechanisms for organizational processes (e.g., manipulating participant affect and perceived power to test their impact on focus and yield during dyadic negotiation simulations; Overbeck et al., 2010). At the other end, we have *field experiments*, where we are still manipulating independent variables, using randomization in the allocation of treatments and creation of treatment groups, to test their effects on dependent variables in otherwise largely unaltered settings (e.g., randomization of nurses to treatment conditions based on the experimental manipulation of type of reward, visibility of the reward, and contact with service beneficiary to test their effect on the number of correct surgical kits assemblage; Bellé, 2015). For an overview of field research, see Chapter 5 in this volume by Sherry Wu.

The distinction between lab and field experiments is one of forms and degrees of control of variables that can impact the internal validity of the study and the creation or use of settings and sampling procedures that help enhance external validity (Eden, 2017). For instance, we can find experiments where interventions are delivered in controlled environments but where there is clear interest in increasing external validity. This can be accomplished by manipulating organizational practices or having organizational operations as dependent variables, with the objective of providing validated practical tools to organizational agents (e.g., a randomized control trial to evaluate the impact of an unconscious bias training program on the self-efficacy of workers to prevent bias in recruitment and selection; Stratemeyer et al., 2018).

Historically, lab experiments in organizational research have had a micro focus, with behavioral disciplines dominating the field. Research focused on individual and team units of analysis affords the possibility of experimental manipulation of variables in artificially created environments, as well as randomizations of participants and experimental treatments, as ways to reduce the impact of potentially confounding variables. However, the processes are different in terms of selecting control conditions (e.g., it might be impractical for organizational purposes), as well as accounting for or eliminating all factors that might impact internal validity. This can be seen when we need to test interventions with large units of analysis, such as organizations. Then, field experiments allow for controls of independent and confounding variables to preserve internal validity, while enhancing our capacity to generalize findings to organizational conditions similar to those where the study was conducted (Eden, 2017).

Cluster randomized controlled trials (CRCT) are a promising approach to field experiments that target large units of analysis such as teams, sites, or organizations. CRCTs are useful in situations where investigators want to preserve the benefits of randomization, yet they are researching real organizational units of analysis where randomization of individuals into treatment groups is not feasible or desirable (Hunter et al., 2013). In these experiments, participants remain in groups they already belong to, and the group is randomized into treatment conditions (Vetter & Chou, 2014). CRCTs allow for some level of pre-experimental equivalence and the potential to statistically control for variables that may moderate the effect of the intervention at the individual and cluster levels of analysis (e.g., a CRCT to evaluate the impact of a mental health intervention among workers using an intervention-waitlist design across multiple hospitals; Mulfinger et al., 2019).

When complete experimental designs are not possible, researchers can use quasi-experimental designs, making the most of naturally occurring interventions to test their effects on dependent variables, in otherwise largely unaltered settings (e.g., testing the impact of government legislation on human resources discriminatory practices across two jurisdictions; Trzebiatowski et al., 2020). While quasi-experiments do not use randomization and restrict our capacity to establish pre-experimental equivalence, in many settings they provide the best approximation to a test of our hypotheses and treatment effects. In summary, organizations are complex systems, with multiple goals, interests, and logics operating at the same time. Those conditions could limit investigators' capacity to execute perfect experimental research designs. Nevertheless, you should not feel discouraged or assume that field experiments are impossible or too hard (for a broader discussion of field experiments in organizations, see Eden, 2017). Instead, use negotiation skills, networking, and plain language to explain to relevant organizational stakeholders the value in achieving research conditions as close to pure experiments as possible, and present a plan with specific requirements to achieve those conditions.

Data Collection

There are several aspects of organizational data collection worth discussing. We start this section with some key considerations. Then, we focus on sampling strategies and sources of data, including getting access to organizations.

Conceptual and Contextual Considerations

The process of data collection in organizations starts with theorizing. One of the most important ways in which theories are meant to guide our research approach is by providing us with clearly defined constructs to explore. This process involves using previous research to both define our concepts and differentiate them from related constructs (MacKenzie, 2003). In organizational measurement, we want to capture all relevant aspects of the construct, while avoiding capturing elements that are not part of it. However, most of the words we use to define the constructs of interest are regularly used by lay people (e.g., groups, culture, negotiation), and in many cases refer to internal cognitive and affect processes (e.g., personality, values, problem-solving). Therefore, we need to make sure we use unambiguous definitions of the concepts we are studying before we select or develop measurement tools (Aguinis & Vandenberg, 2014). Part of this specification process is defining with clarity at what unit of analysis the construct is operating.

For instance, are we interested in understanding *individual experiences* of being a target of workplace sexual harassment or are we researching *perceptions* of sexually predatory *organizational cultures*? These questions do not deal with the same concepts (i.e., personal experiences versus perceptions), and they are not concerned with the same units of analysis (i.e., individual versus organizational; Sojo et al., 2016). We need to define the construct of interest (e.g., workplace sexual harassment) for a unit of analysis (e.g., individuals, teams, organizations, dyads, networks) that is relevant to our research question before proceeding to define our sampling strategy or select measures for it. Once we know what we want to measure, we can focus on selecting or developing data collection protocols that are valid and reliable (for a discussion on these topics, see Chapter 9 on reliability by Tenko Raykov and Chapter 10 on validity by John Skowronski in this volume), as well as decide where we would obtain relevant data.

Sampling Strategies

An important aspect of quantitative scientific research is being able to generalize our findings from the samples we study to the populations they belong to. Effective sampling requires defining the units of analysis that are relevant to our research questions (e.g., individuals, dyads, organizations). The next step is engaging in a process to either include all the relevant units that exist in the population or select a subset of them that matches the most relevant properties of the population (i.e., a representative sample). Therefore, sampling requires a good understanding of the distribution of attributes of the population that are relevant to our research questions (Black, 2002).

There are many ways to conduct sampling in organizational research. Random sampling, where each member of a population of units of analysis has an equal chance of being selected, is considered the gold standard of sampling. There are different forms of this strategy. For instance, some involve stratification by specific attributes (e.g., gender, region, industry) to guarantee similar representation of those attributes in our sample relative to the population. We can also sample clusters of units (e.g., workers nested in hospitals, organizations nested in regions). This process can be staged by first selecting regions, then specific organizations in those regions and then specific workers or clients in those organizations (Black, 2002; Kerlinger & Lee, 1999). In all these cases, we require a complete enough list of potential units of analysis (i.e., the population), and means to contact them, to be able to effectively do random sampling.

Therefore, it is unsurprising that non-random samples are very common, if not the norm, in organizational research (Fisher & Sandell, 2015). Sometimes investigators use purposive sampling, handpicking units they believe are representative of the most study-relevant attributes of the population. Usually, investigators default to convenient samples, by conducting their research on units of analysis that are available to them (Black, 2002; Kerlinger & Lee, 1999). A critical problem with this approach is that organizations can have a variety of specific dynamics that are not found elsewhere, limiting our capacity to generalize findings from non-random samples (Landers & Behrend, 2015). There are different ways to tackle this conundrum. We can use probabilistic sampling, when possible, and provide accurate and systematic descriptions of the context where our studies were conducted, the relevant attributes of their population, and characteristics of the sample obtained. Transparent reporting of sample limitations is required for others to accurately replicate research findings. Similarly, the potential and limitations of the sample must be discussed, and findings should be interpreted in that context.

Sources of Organizational Data

Knowledge about and access to sources of data impact the sampling strategies researchers use. The most basic distinction in types of organizational data we can make is between primary and secondary sources. *Primary data* are collected via direct surveying, evaluation, or observation of organizational stakeholders (e.g., employees, managers, clients) and stages of organizational processes. *Secondary data* include stakeholder and administrative information related to organizational processes that has already been collected, and more or less systematized, by an organization or third party.

Primary Organizational Data

Primary data in organizations can take many forms. If your research question requires collecting data about the internal cognitive and emotional processes, experiences, and behaviors of individuals and teams in organizations, then psychometric questionnaires, surveys, implicit measures, reaction time, physiological instruments (both wearables and in the laboratory), and observation protocols can all be useful tools to gather primary data.

Getting access to organizations may be a necessary step to gather primary data. You will need a level of clarity about your project that makes it possible for you to explain to any organizational stakeholder the *what, why, how, when*, and *where* of your research. Vagueness about what you are trying to achieve can increase the likelihood of being shut down by time-poor, risk-averse stakeholders in the initial stages of getting access to an organization. Ambiguity in your explanation can also allow organizational actors (e.g., executive team) to shape your project in a way that does not help you answer the research questions (Brewerton & Millward, 2001).

Before you can brief organizational stakeholders to secure their buy-in, you need to be invited to do so. There are many ways to get there. A bottom-up approach would include making lists of private sector peak bodies (e.g., chambers of commerce, professional associations), government agencies, and firms that might be interested in your research, either to partner with you and promote the research among their networks or to directly participate in your research. Once those lists are created, you need to decide how you will approach them. You can think of your personal and professional contacts inside and outside academia who can put you in touch with organizations, or you can do a cold call/email. Sometimes talking to junior employees among your personal networks can be the first step in this process.

At this point, your research design might be an important consideration. For instance, if your research question requires the use of a cluster randomized controlled trial, you might need access to several organizations from a sector or region (e.g., all the hospitals in a specific jurisdiction to investigate the longitudinal impact of employee engagement on patient outcomes and insurance costs; Garud et al., 2022). In this situation, it would be too cumbersome to reach out to each individual organization. Putting your efforts into connecting with private sector peak bodies and government agencies that will help you reach out to the target organizations might be a more sensible approach.

Another way to get access to organizations requires playing a longer game. Regular engagement with public and private sector entities can help you develop your own network of organizations. This network can be enhanced by attending and presenting at industry and government conferences and events, publishing popular media articles based on your research, making submissions to government inquiries into issues directly relevant to your research, and when possible, volunteering your time to advise government and not-for-profit organizations. If your research is excellent and has direct relevance to organizational decision-making, creating these networks will allow you to have real-world impact and get access to organizations for future research projects. You might even find yourself in a situation where organizations *come to you* with resources and opportunities to do research.

Once you have a foot in the door, you need to think about how to persuade stakeholders to come on board. In previous research projects we have conducted, we have produced plain-language two-page briefs for senior leaders about our proposed projects. In these briefs, we cover the applied and scientific needs to conduct the research, how we would do it, what we would need from the organization (e.g., access to documents, spaces, employees, funding) and its stakeholders (e.g., attending briefings, answering surveys, wearing devices), and the direct (when they exist) and indirect benefits to the organization. (See Appendix for an example.)

Online Panels. An efficient way to collect data about organizational processes is using online panels. Online panels are electronic databases of individuals who have registered their interest to participate in web-based research studies (Callegaro et al., 2014). Access to these prospective participants is brokered by online panel platforms (e.g., Qualtrics, StudyResponse, MTurk). There are several advantages to using these panels of participants. For instance, researchers can reach participants from across the world, in specific industries or occupations, in a relatively affordable and efficient manner (Porter et al., 2019). Similarly, these platforms can be useful to access minority populations who might be hard to reach (e.g., LGBTIQ+ or low socio-economic status workers; Smith et al., 2015).

However, the use of online panels for organizational research has been called into question (Porter et al., 2019). For instance, these participants might have experience with widely used experimental paradigms that rely on deception, biasing their responses and reducing the strengths of experimental manipulations (Chandler et al., 2014). Also, the representativeness of the samples can be a problem if platforms do not use probability-based methods for sampling, the researchers do not specify relevant attributes to stratify samples on, or you need access to difficult-to-access samples such as leaders or high-paid workers. Finally, online participants' inattentiveness has been presented as a problem. However, the levels of participants' attention and psychometric properties of instruments are comparable across online panels and standard samples of university students and traditional participant pools (Goodman & Paolacci, 2017; Hauser & Schwarz, 2016). Similarly, meta-analytic research has shown, across a range of applied psychology studies, that results based on online panels are not different from results based on samples of university students, workers, and members of the community collected via direct approaches (Walter et al., 2019).

Secondary Organizational Data

Many important research questions require the use of secondary data. For instance, studies about the relationship between macro processes (e.g., organizational strategies, the link between government regulation and firm processes) or cross-level processes (e.g., organizational processes impacting team- and individual-level processes and vice versa) can be conducted relying on secondary data. The richness of these databases cannot be underestimated. You can get access to annual reports, remuneration for company directors and executives, general and financial company announcements, products and services, key personnel, and more for publicly listed companies (e.g., Connect 4, D&B Hoovers, MarketLine, Mint Global). These sources will allow you to conduct longitudinal research about organizational, economic sector, and region variables. Your university might already have access to them. Ask your librarian.

Similarly, national bureaus of statistics around the world often enter partnerships with academics or have protocols to facilitate access to databases of organizational information. For instance, the Australian Bureau of Statistics (2022) grants access to the Business Longitudinal Analysis Data Environment (BLADE), a database system that contains information about business characteristics, trade, investment in research and development, intellectual property, tax, and many other organization-level variables that allows for rich longitudinal analysis of firms and the environment where they operate. These data sets can be objective and reliable when institutions have safeguarding mechanisms in data collection and storage; they also facilitate multisource research. Finally, linking individual-level survey responses and independently collected administrative data about organizations can allow for the testing of multilevel hypotheses, yet not without addressing methodological and ethical complexities (for a review, see Calderwood & Lessof, 2009).

Ethical Considerations

Researchers should operate with integrity and follow the ethical guidelines of the discipline and jurisdiction where they are conducting research. Ethical guidelines, more broadly, are described in detail in Chapter 2 within Volume 1 of this Handbook. Below, we focus on three ethical risks that are specifically relevant to organizational research.

Reputational Risks

Companies can be exposed to reputational risks if participants from de-identified organizations share facts that others may be able to recognize, and thus detect the identity of the unnamed organization. There is also a risk to employees, even when their names and identities have been masked. For instance, certain circumstances may be too particular to one individual so that a colleague or supervisor might be able to pinpoint the de-identified participant, who in turn may suffer reputational damage and other consequences, such as loss of employment. This risk often results in an unwillingness from employees to participate in organizational research. Aggregated, quantitative research in organizations minimizes the risks of the disclosure of such information, but this reputational risk is important to keep in mind for mixed-methods research that contains open-ended responses.

Privacy Risks

The use of secondary sources can also lead to privacy risks. For example, when matching administrative data on organizations to supplement your primary organizational data, it is vital to ensure that consent to match data has been secured (Calderwood & Lessof, 2009) and that *de-identified* organizations cannot be recognized and identified via the secondary organizational data you have incorporated. Having these discussions with partner organizations before commencing the research is an important step for ensuring transparency and facilitating a relationship based on trust.

In longitudinal designs, where employees are sampled at multiple points in time, researchers must decide how to guarantee participants' privacy, as some identifying feature is needed to match anonymized responses across assessments. Instead of requesting a name or an email address from participants at each time point, allocate to each participant a unique identifier that they must include in surveys they submit. If email addresses must be included due to the logistics of your study design, storing identified data securely and separately from participants' responses is required. Participants also need to be informed of confidentiality, privacy, and data storage procedures.

Risk of Coercion

Dependent relationships can lead to risk of coercion when recruiting participants in organizational research. Using personal contacts comes with the risk of dependent relationships, where there can be an unequal distribution of power and influence (Clark & McCann, 2005). If the researcher is in a position (or a perceived position) of higher power or seniority, or if organizational leaders agree to take part in a study, employees may feel coerced to participate (Brewerton & Millward, 2001); this is a violation of people's rights to autonomy and to their option to withdraw at any time (or within a specified time). Existing relationships need to be disclosed and risks associated with dependent and unequal relationships mitigated by, for example, having an independent researcher or recruitment service send out invitations to participants and explaining with clarity that participation is completely voluntary, to reduce the risk of coercion.

Diversity, Equity, and Inclusion in Organizational Research

As scholars of organizational research, it is important to observe and challenge the lack of diversity in the theories, methods, researchers, and participants within the discipline. To provoke a discussion on this topic, Cunliffe (2022) argues that not only is theory generation in organization and management studies done by men, but there is also a requirement for all contributors to theorize and write more like men. That is, there are norms for the academic writing of "good theories" to be based on a *masculinized rationality* that is devoid of people's rich experiences of how they engage with work, life, and self. Interestingly enough, it does not stop at theorizing. Bibliometric research indicates that journal articles about research methods are predominantly written by male academics (Aguinis et al., 2019) from wealthy developed economies. While Cunliffe's critique comes from a qualitative research methodology, the ethical considerations of the lack of inclusion, or the mandate to assimilate to successfully publish, are also applicable to quantitative research and the foundational theories that support organizational research.

To illustrate a practical way to address the lack of diversity in the authors of organizational research and theory, we all have the power to decide whom we cite in academic publications (Holman, 2022). We should critically reflect on the authors we cite in our manuscripts and consider replacing antiquated citations with high-quality studies by contemporary and, both disciplinarily and demographically, diverse authors who may be otherwise overlooked. Reviewers also have a role to play as gatekeepers of which papers successfully make it through the peer review process and are published in academic journals. Researchers and reviewers can acknowledge Cunliffe's (2022) and Cortina and Landis' (2013) perspectives by genuinely being more open to novel and innovative ways of theorizing and designing organizational research.

PhD programs have a big responsibility too. They can both improve the quality of teaching in organizational theory and methods, and actively recruit PhD candidates who are more diverse across several demographic characteristics, paying particular attention to protected attributes in their jurisdiction. It is easier to address calls for more diverse participants in organizational research when we collaborate with researchers who are also more diverse. For instance, the authors of this chapter do not conduct research about gender, sexuality, ethnicity, or disability without having diverse collaborators across those demographic dimensions. This approach does not guarantee eliminating all our *blind spots*, but it is a useful strategy to consider lived experiences and learn from different academics. Similarly, when studying industries or roles that are male- or female-dominated, such as mining or nursing, researchers must decide if it is more appropriate to recruit a sample that represents the current demographics of the role, or one that aims for a more balanced representation of men and women. In the first instance, we would capture the attitudes and behaviors of those who predominantly make up the role. Yet, a more balanced sample can help to ensure that minority voices are heard, and traditional views of gendered roles are challenged, giving researchers a better understanding of all individuals in a workplace or industry – not just of those who comprise the majority.

Another practical solution of relevance to the field of organizational research is avoiding (both in planning and attending) academic panels on research methods that are made up of only men, or in some cases, only white men, colloquially referred to as "manels." You can simply start by asking the organizers whether they have considered the diversity of the panelists. Finally, you can join other minority voices in online communities for support, amplification, and the sharing of opportunities, such as social media groups that bring together underrepresented groups who are passionate about research methods.

Conclusions

Given the ubiquity of organizations, organizational research has the potential to contribute significantly to understanding and positively impacting human life. Improving the quality of our approaches, including diversifying our collaborators, theories, questions, designs, and samples, has the potential to provide a more comprehensive look at what is happening in and around organizations worldwide. Doing organizational research is a privilege, and we can give back to organizations and the community by making sure we conduct our research and peer review with a developmental mindset (e.g., no gatekeeping), ethically, rigorously, and prioritizing the welfare of all our stakeholders.

Appendix

Briefs for Organizational Leaders

[Project title – make it descriptive and in plain language]
[Researchers' titles, full names, and academic/industry affiliations]

Research background:

[Explain why the research matters using scientific evidence of the existence of an organizational problem.]
[Provide relevant industry data to support your claims.]
[Explain why you need to do the research in order to help the stakeholders solve an organizational problem.]
[Describe a process model of the problem you are investigating – *500 to 800 words.*]

[Insert a figure with a diagram depicting the process model you described above – *1/3 of a page.*]

1. **Project objectives**: [Explain in plain language the objectives of the project; no more than three to keep it simple – *100 words.*]
2. **Research strategy**:

    2.1. *Research procedure*: [Explain the core aspect of your research design that stakeholders need to understand to agree to participate – *100 words.*]

    2.2. *Participants*: [Describe what kind of participants you are aiming to recruit and that you will seek their consent first – *50 words.*]

3. **Benefits to partner organizations**:

    3.1. *Reports*: [Explain all the reports and briefs they will receive and why they will be useful – *100 words.*]

    3.2. *Capability building*: [Describe any organizational process changes or upskilling of staff that will result from your program of research – *100 words.*]

4. **Funding model** (required commitment from participating organizations): [*150 words in total.*]

    4.1. *Cash contribution*: [If any is needed, explain how much money the organization would have to contribute, the instalments, and why the cash contribution is needed – make a business case for it.]

    4.2. *In-kind contribution*: [If any is needed, explain the type of non-cash material and staff support you expect to get from the organization in order to successfully complete the project and why this support is needed.]

    4.3. *Note*: [Explain whether and how the cash and in-kind contributions can be negotiated.]

    4.4. *University contribution*: [Explain what kind of contribution you and your university will be making to the project.]

5. **Contact**: [Provide title, full name, email address, and phone number of the main contact with authority to discuss the project – *10 words.*]

References

Adamovic, M., Sojo, V., Schachtman, R., & Vargas, A. (2022). Explaining the relationship between ethnicity and depressive symptoms: The roles of climate for inclusion, job self-efficacy, and job demands. *Asia Pacific Journal of Management, 40*, 903–928. https://doi.org/10.1007/s10490-022-09834-9

Aguinis, H., Ramani, R. S., & Villamor, I. (2019). The first 20 years of organizational research methods: Trajectory, impact, and predictions for the future. *Organizational Research Methods, 22*(2), 463–489. https://doi.org/10.1177/1094428118786564

Aguinis, H., & Vandenberg, R. J. (2014). An ounce of prevention is worth a pound of cure: Improving research quality before data collection. *Annual Review of Organizational*

Psychology and Organizational Behavior, *1*, 569–595. https://doi.org/10.1146/annurev-orgpsych-031413-091231

Antonakis, J., Banks, G. C., Bastardoz, N., Cole, M. S., Day, D. V., Eagly, A. H., et al. (2019). The Leadership Quarterly: State of the journal. *Leadership Quarterly*, *30*(1), 1–9. https://doi.org/10.1016/j.leaqua.2019.01.001

Aquino, K., & Lamertz, K. (2004). A relational model of workplace victimization: Social roles and patterns of victimization in dyadic relationships. *Journal of Applied Psychology*, *89*, 1023–1034. http://dx.doi.org/10.1037/0021-9010.89.6.1023.

Australian Bureau of Statistics. (2022). Business longitudinal analysis data environment (BLADE). www.abs.gov.au/about/data-services/data-integration/integrated-data/business-longitudinal-analysis-data-environment-blade (retrieved October 17, 2022).

Beal, D. J. (2015). ESM 2.0: State of the art and future potential of experience sampling methods in organizational research. *Annual Review of Organizational Psychology and Organizational Behavior*, *2*(1), 383–407. https://doi.org/10.1146/annurev-orgpsych-032414-111335

Becker, T. E. (2005). Potential problems in the statistical control of variables in organizational research: A qualitative analysis with recommendations. *Organizational Research Methods*, *8*(3), 274–289. https://doi.org/10.1177/1094428105278021

Beckman, N., Birney, D., Beckman, J., Wood, R., Sojo, V., & Bowman, D. (2020). Inter-individual differences in intra-individual variability in personality within and across contexts. *Journal of Research in Personality*, *85*, 1–22. https://doi.org/10.1016/j.jrp.2019.103909

Bellé, N. (2015). Performance-related pay and the crowding out of motivation in the public sector: A randomized field experiment. *Public Administration Review*, *75*(2), 230–241. https://doi.org/10.1111/puar.12313

Black, T. R. (2002). *Understanding Social Science Research*. SAGE Publications. https://dx.doi.org/10.4135/9780857020208.n3

Bono, J. E., & McNamara, G. (2011). Publishing in AMJ – Part 2: Research design. *Academy of Management Journal*, *54*(4), 657–660. https://doi.org/10.5465/amj.2011.64869103

Brewerton, P., & Millward, L. (2001). *Organizational Research Methods*. SAGE Publications. https://doi.org/10.4135/9781849209533

Calderwood, L., & Lessof, C. (2009). Enhancing longitudinal surveys by linking to administrative data. In R. M. Groves, G. Kalton, J. N. K. Rao, N. Schwarz, C. Skinner, & P. Lynn (eds.), *Methodology of Longitudinal Surveys* (pp. 55–72). https://doi.org/10.1002/9780470743874.ch4

Callegaro, M., Baker, R., Bethlehem, J., Göritz, A. S., Krosnick, J. A., and Lavrakas, P. J. (2014). Online panel research. In M. Callegaro, R. Baker, J. Bethlehem, A. S. Göritz, J. A. Krosnick, and P. J. Lavrakas (eds.), *Online Panel Research* (pp. 1–22). Wiley. https://doi.org/10.1002/9781118763520.ch1

Campbell, D. T., & Stanley, J. C. (1963). *Experimental and Quasi-Experimental Designs for Research*. Houghton Mifflin.

Caplow, T. (1964). *Principles of Organization*. Harcourt Brace & World.

Chandler, J., Mueller, P., & Paolacci, G. (2014). Nonnaïveté among Amazon Mechanical Turk workers: Consequences and solutions for behavioral researchers. *Behavior Research Methods*, *46*(1), 112–130. https://doi.org/10.3758/s13428-013-0365-7

Charlesworth, S., McDonald, P., & Cerise, S. (2011). Naming and claiming workplace sexual harassment in Australia. *Australian Journal of Social Issues*, *46*(2), 141–161. https://doi.org/10.1002/j.1839-4655.2011.tb00211.x

Clark, E., & McCann, T. V. (2005). Researching students: An ethical dilemma. *Nurse Researcher*, *12*(3), 42–51. https://doi.org/10.7748/nr2005.01.12.3.42.c5947

Cortina, L. M., Fitzgerald, L. F., & Drasgow, F. (2002). Contextualizing Latina experiences of sexual harassment: Preliminary tests of a structural model. *Basic and Applied Social Psychology*, *24*(4), 295–311. https://doi.org/10.1207/S15324834BASP2404_5

Cortina, J. M., & Landis, R. S. (2013). Introduction: Transforming our field by transforming its methods. In J. M. Cortina & R. S. Landis (eds.), *Modern Research Methods for the Study of Behavior in Organizations* (pp. 1–25). Routledge. https://doi.org/10.4324/9780203585146

Cunliffe, A. L. (2022). Must I grow a pair of balls to theorize about theory in organization and management studies? *Organization Theory*, *3*(3), 26317877221109277.

Eden, D. (2017). Field experiments in organizations. *Annual Review of Organizational Psychology and Organizational Behavior*, *4*(1), 91–122. https://doi.org/10.1146/annurev-orgpsych-041015-062400

Edwards, J. R. (2010). Reconsidering theoretical progress in organizational and management research. *Organizational Research Methods*, *13*(4), 615–619. https://doi.org/10.1177/1094428110380468

Eldridge, J. E. T., & Crombie, A. D. (2013). *A Sociology of Organisations*. Routledge.

Fisher, G. G., & Sandell, K. (2015). Sampling in industrial–organizational psychology research: Now what? *Industrial and Organizational Psychology*, *8*, 232–237. https://doi.org/10.1017/iop.2015.31

Garud, N., Pati, R., Sojo, V., Bell, S. J., Hudson, R., & Shaw, H. (2022). 3 ways hospitals can boost worker engagement. *Harvard Business Review*, February 16. https://hbr.org/2022/02/3-ways-hospitals-can-boost-worker-engagement.

Goodman, J. K., & Paolacci, G. (2017). Crowdsourcing consumer research. *Journal of Consumer Research*, *44*(1), 196–210. https://doi.org/10.1093/jcr/ucx047

Grosser, T. J., Lopez-Kidwell, V., & Labianca, G. (2010). A social network analysis of positive and negative gossip in organizational life. *Group & Organization Management*, *35*(2), 177–212. https://doi.org/10.1177/1059601109360391

Gulati, R., Lawrence, P. R., & Puranam, P. (2005). Adaptation in vertical relationships: Beyond incentive conflict. *Strategic Management Journal*, *26*(5), 415–440. https://doi.org/10.1002/smj.458

Harley, B. (2018). Sociology, the labour process and employment relations. In A. Wilkinson, T. Dundon, J. Donaghey, & A. Colvin (eds.), *The Routledge Companion to Employment Relations* (pp. 81–92). Routledge. https://doi.org/10.4324/9781315692968

Hauser, D. J., & Schwarz, N. (2016). Attentive Turkers: MTurk participants perform better on online attention checks than do subject pool participants. *Behavior Research Methods*, *48*(1), 400–407. https://doi.org/10.3758/s13428-015-0578-z

Heath, C., & Sitkin, S. (2001). Big-B versus Big-O: What is organizational about organizational behavior? *Journal of Organizational Behavior*, *22*, 43–58. https://doi.org/10.1002/job.77

Heath, C., & Staudenmayer, N. (2000). Coordination neglect: How lay theories of organizing complicate coordination in organizations. *Research in Organizational Behavior*, *22*, 153–191. https://doi.org/10.1016/S0191-3085(00)22005-4

Hedrick, T. E., Bickman, L., & Rog, D. J. (1993). *Applied Research Design*. SAGE Publications. https://dx.doi.org/10.4135/9781412983457

Holman, M. (2022). Citations as power. *#MHAWS: Mirya Holman's Aggressive Winning Scholars Newsletter.* https://miryaholman.substack.com/p/citations-as-power (retrieved April 28, 2022).

Hunter, S. B., Miles, J. N. V., Paddock, S. M., & D'Amico, E. J. (2013). Evaluating treatment efficacy. In P. M. Miller (ed.), *Interventions for Addiction: Comprehensive Addictive Behaviors and Disorders* (pp. 589–597). Academic Press. https://doi.org/10.1016/B978-0-12-398338-1.00061-0

Jeong, S.-H., Mooney, A., Zhang, Y., & Quigley, T. J. (2022). How do investors really react to the appointment of Black CEOs? *Strategic Management Journal, 44*(7), 1733–1752. https://doi.org/10.1002/smj.3454

Johns, G. (2018). Advances in the treatment of context in organizational research. *Annual Review of Organizational Psychology and Organizational Behavior, 5*(1), 21–46. https://doi.org/10.1146/annurev-orgpsych-032117-104406

Kerlinger, F. N., & Lee, H. B. (1999). *Foundations of Behavioral Research*. Harcourt College.

Kozlowski, S. W. J., & Ilgen, D. R. (2006). Enhancing the effectiveness of work groups and teams. *Psychological Science in the Public Interest, 7*(3), 77–124. https://doi.org/10.1111/j.1529-1006.2006.00030.x

Landers, R. N., & Behrend, T. S. (2015). An inconvenient truth: Arbitrary distinctions between organizational, Mechanical Turk, and other convenience samples. *Industrial and Organizational Psychology, 8*(2), 142–164. https://doi.org/10.1017/iop.2015.13

MacKenzie, S. B. (2003). The dangers of poor construct conceptualization. *Journal of the Academy of Marketing Science, 31*(3), 323–326. https://doi.org/10.1177/0092070303031003011

Maurer, C. C., & Qureshi, I. (2021). Not just good for her: A temporal analysis of the dynamic relationship between representation of women and collective employee turnover. *Organization Studies, 42*(1), 85–107. https://doi.org/10.1177/0170840619875480

McAdams, D. P., & Olson, B. D. (2010). Personality development: Continuity and change over the life course. *Annual Review of Psychology, 61*(1), 517–542. https://doi.org/10.1146/annurev.psych.093008.100507

Minbashian, A., Wood, R. E., & Beckmann, N. (2010). Task-contingent conscientiousness as a unit of personality at work. *Journal of Applied Psychology, 95*(5), 793–806. https://doi.org/10.1037/a0020016

Mitchell, T. R. (1985). An evaluation of the validity of correlational research conducted in organizations. *Academy of Management Review, 10*(2), 192–205. https://doi.org/10.5465/amr.1985.4277939

Mulfinger, N., Sander, A., Stuber, F., Brinster, R., Junne, F., Limprecht, R., et al. (2019). Cluster-randomised trial evaluating a complex intervention to improve mental health and well-being of employees working in hospital – a protocol for the SEEGEN trial. *BMC Public Health, 19*(1), 1694. https://doi.org/10.1186/s12889-019-7909-4

Osis, J., & Donins, U. (2017). Structure analysis and design. In Osis & Donins (eds.), *Topological UML Modeling* (pp. 205–224). Elsevier. https://doi.org/10.1016/B978-0-12-805476-5.00008-3

Overbeck, J. R., Neale, M. A., & Govan, C. L. (2010). I feel, therefore you act: Intrapersonal and interpersonal effects of emotion on negotiation as a function of social power. *Organizational Behavior and Human Decision Processes, 112*(2), 126–139. https://doi.org/10.1016/j.obhdp.2010.02.004

Park, M., Leahey, E., & Funk, R. J. (2023). Papers and patents are becoming less disruptive over time. *Nature, 613*(7942), 138–144. https://doi.org/10.1038/s41586-022-05543-x

Porter, C. O. L. H., Outlaw, R., Gale, J. P., & Cho, T. S. (2019). The use of online panel data in management research: A review and recommendations. *Journal of Management, 45*(1), 319–344. https://doi.org/10.1177/0149206318811569

Porter, M. E. (1991). Towards a dynamic theory of strategy. *Strategic Management Journal, 12*(S2), 95–117. https://doi.org/10.1002/smj.4250121008

Reed, M. (2006). Organizational theorizing: A historically contested terrain. In S. Clegg, H. Cynthia, T. Lawrence, & W. Nord (eds.), *The SAGE Handbook of Organization Studies* (pp. 19–54). SAGE Publications. https://doi.org/10.4135/9781848608030.n2

Roe, R. (2008). Time in applied psychology. *European Psychologist, 13*(1), 37–52. https://doi.org/10.1027/1016-9040.13.1.37

Schwab, D. P. (2004). *Research Methods for Organizational Studies*. Routledge.

Schwerdt, G., & Woessmann, L. (2020). Empirical methods in the economics of education. In S. Bradley & C. Green (eds.), *The Economics of Education*, 2nd ed. (pp. 3–20). Academic Press. https://doi.org/10.1016/B978-0-12-815391-8.00001-X

Smith, N., Sabat, I., Martinez, L., Weaver, K., & Xu, S. (2015). A convenient solution: Using MTurk to sample from hard-to-reach populations. *Industrial and Organizational Psychology, 8*(2), 220–228. https://doi.org/10.1017/iop.2015.29

Sojo, V., & Roberts, V. L. (2019). From apples and cases to barrels and orchards: Macro-level drivers of workplace abuse. *Academy of Management Proceedings, 2019*(1), 12323. https://doi.org/10.5465/AMBPP.2019.12323symposium

Sojo, V., Wood, R., & Genat, A. (2016). Harmful workplace experiences and women's occupational well-being: A meta-analysis. *Psychology of Women Quarterly, 40*(1), 10–40. https://doi.org/10.1177/0361684315599346

Spector, P. E. (2006). Method variance in organizational research: Truth or urban legend? *Organizational Research Methods, 9*(2), 221–232. https://doi.org/10.1177/1094428105284955

Spector, P. E., Zapf, D., Chen, P. Y., & Frese, M. (2000). Why negative affectivity should not be controlled in job stress research: Don't throw out the baby with the bath water. *Journal of Organizational Behavior, 21*(1), 79–95. https://doi.org/10.1002/(SICI)1099-1379(200002)21:1<79::aid-job964>3.0.CO;2-G

Stratemeyer, M., Sojo, V., Wheeler, M., Rozenblat, V., Lee, I., Peter, D., et al. (2018). *Recruit Smarter* [technical report]. Victorian Government (Australia). www.vic.gov.au/recruit-smarter

Trzebiatowski, T. M., Wanberg, C. R., & Dossinger, K. (2020). Unemployed needn't apply: Unemployment status, legislation, and interview requests. *Journal of Management, 46*(8), 1380–1407. https://doi.org/10.1177/0149206318823952

Van Quaquebeke, N., Salem, M., van Dijke, M., & Wenzel, R. (2022). Conducting organizational survey and experimental research online: From convenient to ambitious in study designs, recruiting, and data quality. *Organizational Psychology Review, 12*(3), 268–305. https://doi.org/10.1177/20413866221097571

Vantilborgh, T., Hofmans, J., & Judge, T. A. (2018). The time has come to study dynamics at work. *Journal of Organizational Behavior, 39*(9), 1045–1049. https://doi.org/10.1002/job.2327

Vetter, T. R., & Chou, R. (2014). Clinical trial design methodology for pain outcome studies. In H. T. Benzon, J. P. Rathmell, C. L. Wu, D. C. Turk, C. E. Argoff, & R. W. Hurley (eds.), *Practical Management of Pain* (pp. 1057–1065). Mosby. https://doi.org/10.1016/B978-0-323-08340-9.00080-3

Walter, S. L., Seibert, S. E., Goering, D., & O'Boyle, E. H. (2019). A tale of two sample sources: Do results from online panel data and conventional data converge? *Journal of Business and Psychology, 34*(4), 425–452. https://doi.org/10.1007/s10869-018-9552-y

Wang, M., Zhou, L., & Zhang, Z. (2016). Dynamic modeling. *Annual Review of Organizational Psychology and Organizational Behavior, 3*(1), 241–266. https://doi.org/10.1146/annurev-orgpsych-041015-062553

Wheeler, M., Wood, R., Sojo, V., & McGrath, M. (2016). *A Question of Ethics: Navigating Ethical Failure in the Banking and Financial Services Industry*. Chartered Accountants Australia and New Zealand and Centre for Ethical Leadership.

Wickert, C., Post, C., Doh, J. P., Prescott, J. E., & Prencipe, A. (2021). Management research that makes a difference: Broadening the meaning of impact. *Journal of Management Studies, 58*(2), 297–320. https://doi.org/10.1111/joms.12666

7 Integrating Culture in Research

Brien K. Ashdown and Angela T. Maitner

Abstract

All social and behavioral sciences research is conducted within a cultural context. This chapter highlights the role of culture in research, focusing on important ethical and methodological considerations. It is important to explicitly define culture when conducting culturally focused research and to include researchers with significant knowledge of a cultural context as partners in identifying ethical concerns, designing research studies, and contextualizing research findings. We identify a number of ethical concerns that are foundational to the design of cultural research and yet are rarely included in research training, such as recognizing power differences, developing awareness of local sensitivities and vulnerabilities, identifying appropriate review boards to evaluate and oversee culturally focused research, and considering elements of consent when working with diverse populations. We discuss the importance of operationalizing culture, translating words, methods, or constructs across cultures, specific considerations associated with identifying and recruiting participants, and collecting and analyzing data. Although explicitly identified as cross-cultural concerns, we argue that considering these issues is important for all researchers working in human sciences.

Keywords: Cross-Cultural Samples, Informed Consent, Cross-Cultural Ethics, Cultural Equivalence, Community-Based Research

Introduction

More than a hundred years ago, Wundt (1900) suggested that culture plays a significant role in human behavior and should be of interest to relevant scientists. However, Western, mainstream, hegemonic perspectives predominantly take a positivist approach to social and behavioral science, aiming to generate universal laws and generalizable research findings while using geographically and culturally limited samples (Gjorgjioska & Tomicic, 2019; Henrich et al., 2010). To adequately account for culture, researchers must *test* the generalizability versus the context-sensitive nature of findings and explicitly consider the way culture and mind dynamically influence one another (Adams et al., 2015; Shweder, 1990). Aligning with broader campaigns to calibrate effect sizes and identify moderators of "classic" research findings as well as to increase representation (Henrich et al., 2010; Ledgerwood et al., in press), culturally focused research is essential to creating a nuanced and inclusive understanding of *Homo sapiens* (Rad et al., 2018).

In 2008, Arnett estimated that only 5% of the world's population – sometimes referred to as the developed world but identified here as the Minority World because it constitutes a numerical minority of the world's population – was represented in psychological research published in American Psychological Association journals. This estimate had increased to 11% by 2020 (Thalmayer et al., 2021). Critiques related to the problems and consequences of underrepresentation have been published regarding evolutionary social sciences (Barrett, 2020), sex research (Klein et al., 2022), health and medical research (Gurven & Lieberman, 2020), anthropology (Clancy & Davis, 2019), religious studies (Newson et al., 2021), and behavioral science more generally (Henrich et al., 2010).

Although social and behavioral science is slowly including more research participants from the "Majority World" (sometimes referred to as the developing world; see Kağıtçıbaşı, 1996), researchers continue to overwhelmingly live and work in Minority World countries (Thalmayer et al., 2021). Being well-trained in Minority World research methods does not mean being well-trained in culturally focused research methods. Instead, many students are taught to apply hegemonic and positivist methods to samples from different cultures. Such training (or lack thereof) fails to prepare scientists to conduct ethical or meaningful culturally grounded scholarship.

To better test the extent to which social and behavioral sciences depict processes that are universal versus those that are context- or culture-sensitive, and to gain a better understanding of Majority World science, research must include more representative samples and more local and Indigenous researchers and methods (Henrich et al., 2010; Rad et al., 2018; Tiokhin et al., 2019). In addition, Minority World researchers must be better trained in culturally focused methods. Many techniques and considerations discussed in these volumes, including the basics of measurement reliability and validity, statistical power, and research ethics, are applicable to all social and behavioral research studies. However, there are some concerns that require special attention from researchers conducting culturally focused research. In this chapter, we discuss basic tenets that scholars conducting culturally focused research should consider and incorporate into their research.

In addition, we suggest that *all* human scientists should contextualize their research findings to prevent overgeneralizations from limited samples. Often, Majority World researchers are required to incorporate findings and conclusions from Minority World scholarship into their own work and to consider the role of context or culture in why they obtained the results they did, especially if they vary from those found in the Minority World. Yet Minority World researchers often do not incorporate work from the Majority World, nor are they likely to consider contextual or cultural features that influenced their results (Bou Zeineddine et al., 2021).

We consider this chapter a primer, focused on basic methodological considerations as well as ethical and technical aspects of working across cultures (Broesch et al., 2020; Fischer & Poortinga, 2018; Rad et al., 2018). Several advanced handbooks and textbooks more completely articulate these and other concerns (e.g., advanced statistical analyses for culturally focused research; establishing cultural equivalency). For more detailed and advanced information, we refer readers to those books and articles (e.g., Ember & Ember, 2009; Fischer & Poortinga, 2018; Matsumoto & van de Vijver, 2011).

Culture and How It Is Integrated into Social and Behavioral Research

Most definitions of culture include the caveat that it is difficult to define, a "fuzzy set" of values, beliefs, policies, behaviors, and worldviews that provide meaning to one's own behavior and an explanation for other people's behaviors (Spencer-Oatey, 2008, p. 3). Culture can include information that is socially learned or be used to identify groups of individuals sharing a system of meaning (Broesch et al., 2022). Hofstede (1994, p. 5) defined culture as "the collective programming of the mind which distinguishes the members of one group or category of people from another." Although culture can include tangible (e.g., food, dress, housing) and intangible (e.g., beliefs, values, worldviews) components, at its most basic level culture is something that is shared by a group of people that provides meaning and structure for shared ways of life. When researchers want to use culture as an explanatory construct, its intended meaning in that particular research context must be clarified and carefully operationalized (Fischer & Poortinga, 2018).

An analysis of empirical studies published in one of the leading culturally focused psychology journals, *Journal of Cross-Cultural Psychology*, suggests that compared to research in the twentieth century, more recently published culturally focused work (when evaluated in the early 2000s) was likely to be in the field of social psychology and to apply a hypothesis-testing approach (Brouwers et al., 2004). Although most articles predicting cross-cultural differences also found cross-cultural similarities, researchers tended to focus on differences. Fischer and Poortinga (2018) argue that this focus on difference distorts the cultural literature. Indeed, Berry has argued that culturally focused research should investigate whether existing theory applies in understudied cultural contexts (i.e., whether processes are universal or culturally dependent), as well as explore newly defined processes and phenomena in local cultural terms (Berry, 1999). These two suggestions have developed as parallel approaches to conducting culturally focused research.

The first focuses on comparing different cultural groups on dependent variables (DV) of interest and aims to draw conclusions about the impact of particular cultural values or attributes on the DV. Although the goal is often to explain why groups differ in cultural attributes, the quasi-experimental nature of these designs requires careful measurement of cultural constructs and meaningful control of extraneous variables (Fischer & Poortinga, 2018).

Methodically exploring how cultural values (as an independent variable; IV) impact DVs within a single group, reflects Berry's second suggestion for culturally focused social research. Similarly, multicultural approaches focus on an intersectional analysis of how cultural values (as IVs) impact people of different cultural or ethnic backgrounds (these can be considered moderating variables) within the same diverse multicultural society.

All of the above approaches can theoretically be conducted by any researcher, whether they are a member of the group being studied or not. Indigenous scholarship emerges when members of a particular cultural group develop a science of behavior from within that cultural group to explain the behavior of that group. The identity-conscious body of knowledge that results emerges from local understandings and realities that differ from those in other cultures and whose logic may appear foreign or elusive to outsiders. Finally, liberation approaches deepen the Indigenous focus, by recognizing that Western, hegemonic science is largely a science of (predominantly White) Western people, and thus aim to intellectually decolonize research in both focus and method (Adams et al., 2015).

Ethical Considerations

Because all social and behavioral research designs include ethical considerations, here we mention those unique to or particularly important for culturally based work. For example, who designs and conducts studies and who gives permission or has oversight of studies is an integral part of research design (Fischer & Poortinga, 2018). Researchers must take accountability for satisfactorily considering and resolving such issues regardless of the specific methodology they employ (Broesch et al., 2020; Davies, 2020; Neil & Saenz, 2020; Pratt et al., 2014; Presidential Commission for the Study of Bioethical Issues, 2011; Tusino & Furfaro, 2021).

Who Conducts Culturally Focused Research?

Any researcher can theoretically be involved in culturally focused work, and we ourselves, as Minority World raised and trained researchers, engage in this kind of work. We have encountered the challenges we outline below and have even run afoul or violated some of them in our own work. It is important to recognize, however, that Minority World researchers often work from a position of relative privilege (reflecting differences in resources, institutional support, etc.) and are trained in disciplines that have a colonial past whose legacy is often implicitly but intrinsically integrated into training and research processes (Broesch et al., 2020). The power and resources that such researchers may bring with them can represent opportunities and threats to many communities (Broesch et al., 2020). For example, based on some of our own experiences, some organizations in the Majority World are eager to work with Minority World scholars because of their resources and perceived expertise but are wary of research outcomes that might label the Majority World organizations and structures as insufficient or unacceptable from a Minority World perspective. Thus, to conduct cultural work ethically, any researcher working outside of their native culture needs to spend meaningful time and effort building relationships, infrastructure, and deep cultural and ethnographic knowledge before undertaking culturally focused work.

Context-Specific Samples

Ethnographic knowledge and cultural understanding can come from extensive background research or extended experiences with the culture of interest. However, projects are vitally enriched when a researcher works with local collaborators or communities; such projects are also more likely to include protection of the cultural capital of local communities (Ashdown et al., 2021). If a researcher is unwilling or unable to put in the time and effort to build their ethnographic knowledge and work with local research collaborators, they should avoid culturally focused scholarship.

Recruiting local collaborators simply to secure institutional support or collect data from local community members is insufficient and often represents an extractive practice (Broesch et al., 2020). Indeed, Minority World researchers sometimes treat Majority World samples or collaborators as little more than data points or research assistants (Bou Zeineddine et al., 2021), extracting information that is neither shared nor interpreted from a culturally sensitive or knowledgeable lens (Broesch et al., 2020; Foulks, 1989; Klausner & Foulks, 1979, 1980). In our own experience, we have received invitations to collect data associated with culturally sensitive or even illegal practices. At times when we have reported our concerns to project coordinators, they have listened and adjusted accordingly. Other times, they have replied that they simply want the data, even if these would reflect predictable self-report biases or put participants in vulnerable positions. For these reasons, when local collaborators are involved, it is critical to create an equitable team and have intentional conversations about the research process and everyone's role in it (Broesch et al., 2020). In this way, researchers decenter methodology from a single cultural perspective and consider not only how cultural variables could affect research methods and findings, but also whether the research process leads to different ethical costs across samples or members of the research team.

When collecting data from groups with which the researcher does not identify, it is critical to avoid tokenizing samples or treating outcomes or processes that are different from one's own as abnormal (Adams et al., 2015). It is important to denaturalize hegemonic perspectives and instead consider how cultural logics, systems, institutions, and other historical, political, or sociological forces might promote different outcomes across cultural contexts (Adams et al., 2015; Broesch et al., 2020).

With that in mind, it is important for *all* researchers, whether they are explicitly considering cultural variables or not, to clearly identify their samples (including, we argue, in the titles of resulting manuscripts), contextualize data, and consider potential limits to the generalizability of their findings as well as the role of historical or political forces in their results. Failure to do so reflects the privileged position of researchers in hegemonic contexts, and maintains systems of domination that effectively "other" the Majority World (Adams et al., 2015; Bou Zeineddine et al., 2021). For example, as in the case of the research invitations we referenced above, applying some Minority World concepts of gender identity and sexual orientation when designing culturally based work can increase political, financial, and social risk to participants and researchers from particular locales who may not be able to ask or answer such questions. This effectively erases the experiences and worldviews of these participants because their data is inaccurate or not collected.

Indeed, many research papers based on Minority World samples or written by scholars trained in the Minority World fail to adequately identify research samples (Cheon et al., 2020; Rad et al., 2018). This neglect can often lead to an overgeneralization of findings and a lack of awareness of cultural nuance and influence. However, whether explicitly considered or not, *all* data are collected within a cultural context. Identifying samples and considering how cultural or other contextual variables may underlie or affect processes of interest will go a long way in decentering the Minority World and contextualizing social and behavioral research. At the most basic level, researchers must avoid the implication, either by omission or the use of generic language, that their samples are generally reflective of humankind when their samples are culturally limited (Cheon et al., 2020; Ledgerwood et al., 2022).

Exploring Culturally Sensitive Topics

Developing ethnographic knowledge and building relationships is critical to recognizing sensitivities in research topics or methods. Sometimes, aspects of social and behavioral science can be limited or suppressed by legal codes, in which case asking about sensitive issues may put participants and researchers at risk. Other times, sensitivities reflect taboos or counter-normative practices, and asking about them may lead to significant self-report biases (van de Vijver & Tanzer, 2004). Such sensitivities and legal restrictions might be identified by institutional review boards (IRB) or other bodies overseeing research. However, these issues are better identified by collaborators with extensive knowledge of the cultural context to ensure measures are ethical and meaningful.

In some regions, institutions repress specific scientific inquiry because social and behavioral research is perceived as a threat to current power structures (Saab et al., 2020). Even reporting pre-existing, country- or culture-level data can put participants, collaborators, or institutions at risk; one of the authors had to ask to be removed from a large cross-cultural study when a country-level indicator, not included in any study descriptions or our IRB application, was later introduced. Culture- or country-level data (intentionally or unintentionally) often imply hierarchical rankings of groups. Failing to recognize the constructivist nature of the variable of interest – which was most likely identified and designed within a Western context – further naturalizes Minority World research at a cost to understanding and normalizing Majority World processes (Adams et al., 2015). However, even when a country- or culture-level variable is adequately contextualized, it may agitate sensitivities, increase risk, and damage research relationships or future opportunities. For this and other reasons, Broesch et al. (2020) recommend centering community desires in methodology, distribution of results, and data sharing. One approach to ensure the community and their culture, values, and needs are centered in the research is community-based participatory research (Wexler, 2011).

Community-Based Participatory Research

Community-based participatory research (CBPR) is often used in public health scholarship (e.g., Dulin et al., 2011; Rhodes et al., 2012; Tremblay et al., 2018) and involves all stakeholders in a research project or intervention (i.e., researchers, community leaders, community members) as equal partners in the scholarly work being conducted in a community. This approach challenges the hierarchy often inherent in many Western-based research procedures and ensures that decision-making and other aspects of the research process are equally influenced by all involved. Assuring equal participation of all stakeholders makes it less likely that errors of cultural misunderstanding, hegemony, or inappropriately positivist approaches result in incorrect or harmful interpretations or conclusions (Tremblay et al., 2018).

While there are various ways to approach CBPR, some aspects should be common to all cultural work. As is the case with all research, such issues include discussions about who deserves and will earn authorship on publications and presentations, who owns the data, who needs to approve how data is published or disseminated, who gives consent for research participation, and who should be involved in approving research methodology and data collection processes. These issues should be discussed and decided before seeking IRB and other approvals so as to be included in ethics reviews and to clearly delineate rights and responsibilities of the researchers, participants, and other involved community members.

While research ethics of a particular location or culture are often enforced by professional associations or institutions, those ethical guidelines or enforcing agencies do not always include or incorporate the ethical expectations of other locations (Broesch et al., 2022). It is vital to adhere to local expectations of ethical practices, whether they match with the expectations of the researcher's home institution or not. Engaging in CBPR and ensuring familiarity with local communities' expectations regarding research behavior will help researchers confirm that they are engaging in appropriate research practices.

A second issue that culturally focused researchers should consider before data collection begins is determining who "owns" the data after it has been collected. This issue was highlighted in the poorly navigated cross-cultural research known as the Barrow Alcohol Study (Klausner & Foulks, 1979, 1980). In this study, data about alcohol use and misuse among Alaska Native residents of a small, far north community was badly mismanaged, released to the media before community members had approved the conclusions, and resulted in a *New York Times* headline ("Alcohol Plagues Eskimos") that reified harmful stereotypes (Foulks, 1989). This all resulted in understandable mistrust by Alaska Native communities to further engage with non-Native researchers and a paucity of research and understanding of alcohol use among Native communities (Skewes & Lewis, 2016).

The Barrow Alcohol Study, which directly and indirectly led Native communities to establish more control over research conducted with their members, underscores the need for researchers to avoid misconstruing evidence. It also emphasizes the need to assure that the community members have a full voice in drawing conclusions from data based in the context of their own cultural worldviews. Researchers must recognize that a community's consent to participate is not blanket consent for their data to be published or disseminated without further review. Working with collaborators, community members, and leaders to establish who owns data and whose permission is required before data can be publicly discussed will help ensure that researchers avoid causing harm (Skewes & Lewis, 2016).

Who Evaluates and Gives Permission for Culturally Focused Research?

Who should evaluate and provide permission for culturally focused research depends on the research question being asked and the research design chosen to answer that question. Aspects of ethical review – such as institutional ethics review and informed consent – require unique consideration for each culturally focused research question and design.

Institutional Review

One question that researchers must answer is which institutional review board (IRB) or other ethical board has jurisdiction to review the ethical acceptability of protocols and procedures. Codes of ethics and institutional procedures vary across countries and expectations of one country may not be appropriate or sufficiently address issues that may be critical in another (Broesch et al., 2022). Failure to comply with the ethical guidelines and legal requirements of the country or location where one is conducting culturally focused work can lead to serious consequences for the researchers, their home institutions, and even journals that might publish their work.

Clark (2012) points out that IRBs in the US and ethics committees in much of Western Europe expect that all members of a research team be formally trained in research ethics in order to approve a project. However, such training is often complex, culturally specific, and only available in certain languages, raising questions about how appropriate it is to require members of a research team from outside Minority World nations to complete that training, especially when the data are not being collected in the Minority World countries that are requiring the training.

While US-based IRBs may require training deemed unnecessary in some contexts, they may simultaneously do an insufficient job protecting non-English-speaking and non-US-born participants (Perry, 2011; Schroeder et al., 2019). Because scholars should receive approval from their own institution's ethics committee for any work they plan to conduct, they may need to advocate for more flexible adoption of best practices to ensure that methods are culturally appropriate for all samples while still meeting expectations of ethical behavior that reflect the norms and values of their home ethics committee.

Formal and legal understandings of participants' rights in research is heavily based on notions of Western ethics (e.g., autonomy, justice, beneficence), such as the Belmont Report (National Commission for the Protection of Human Subjects of Biomedical and Behavioral Research, 1978), that might be constructed and understood differently across cultures and time periods (Friesen et al., 2017; White, 1999).

Thus, it is important that an ethics committee located in each country where data collection will occur evaluates the research protocol, as local bodies are best positioned to provide feedback, support, and approval for ethical research behavior (Klitzman, 2011, 2012; Klitzman et al., 2019). The appropriate committee will depend upon the location where data are being collected, and indeed some countries do not require IRB oversight for all research projects, whereas in other countries, all studies require government review (Rashwan & Jenkins, 2017). Discrepancies in ethical perspectives across cultures are likely unavoidable (Klitzman, 2011, 2012; Klitzman et al., 2019). Resolving such discrepancies in ways that ensure data are collected in valid, reliable, and ethical ways may require creativity, flexibility, and possibly different protocols and procedures across cultural contexts. One clear example of the flexibility required is reflected in informed consent.

Informed Consent

Many IRBs in Minority World countries require that formal (and often written) informed consent be secured from each participant individually before that participant is allowed to participate (Festinger et al., Volume 1 of this Handbook; Metro, 2014). Clearly, requiring written informed consent would not be appropriate for participants with low literacy (Clark, 2012; Leong & Lyons, 2010). Suggestions for handling such situations include collecting participants' thumbprints in place of signatures (Clark, 2012; Ssali et al., 2016). However, as Adams et al. (2007) point out, fingerprinting can carry connotations of coercion, state power, or corruption. Requiring identifiable consent in locations where signing papers has been associated with violence, loss of property, or coerced confessions may represent a similar form of epistemic violence (Broesch et al., 2020).

With that in mind, researchers need to consider whether active consent (i.e., participant actively agrees to participate) or passive consent (i.e., consent is assumed unless participant actively disagrees) is appropriate. While some previous work on consent has focused on whether the research topic should inform whether passive or active consent is required (Liu et al., 2017; Solberg & Eikemo, 2021; Spence et al., 2015), here we focus on determining who in a particular cultural group can provide consent for participation and whether that person or group should be expected to provide active or passive consent. In most Minority World countries, active consent is required from individual participants over a certain age, or from legal guardians. However, in various cultural groups, some people are not recognized as able to provide active consent because that consent can only be provided by group leaders, elders, or male family members regardless of the participant's age (Adams et al., 2007; Leong & Lyons, 2010). In such cases, researchers need to consider hosting community-level discussions before seeking individual consent (Broesch et al., 2020).

This can be a challenging concept for researchers to explain to IRBs in Minority World countries. In one of our own experiences, it proved challenging and time-intensive to convince a US-based IRB that active consent from school administrators, passive consent from parents, and verbal assent from student participants were appropriate and sufficient for collecting data from teenagers in a different country.

Balancing the expectations of Minority World IRBs with culturally specific understandings of consent takes time, effort, and flexibility, but forcing people from a culture with a different understanding of consent to follow Minority World-mandated protocols is itself unethical.

Instead, researchers and IRBs should focus on the primary goal of obtaining consent, ensuring that the participants (or those who consent on their behalf) fully understand what they are consenting to and allowing the specific type of consent to vary based on local practices. These latter points are critical as, regardless of the method used to collect informed consent, the failure of culturally focused researchers to adequately communicate with their samples too often undermines the participants' understanding and the researchers' ability to obtain fully informed consent (Clark, 2012; Ssali et al., 2016).

Methodological Considerations

Hruschka (2020) argues that "workflows we use to recruit participants, to give instructions, to present stimuli, and to observe and record behaviors are complex, culturally constructed social activities" (p. 458). Moreover, the culturally constructed nature of measurement tools and processes may render them invalid when administered outside of the context where they were originally developed (Broesch et al., 2020; Hruschka, 2020; Tucker 2017; van de Vijver & Tanzer, 2004). Thus, building relationships, infrastructure, and ethnographic knowledge are critical to conducting *successful* cultural research.

Researchers familiar with relevant cultural contexts can work collaboratively to select variables of interest and to design appropriate methods, considering infrastructure and cultural relevance (Fischer & Poortinga, 2018). Indeed, the Global Engagement Task Force from the Society for the Improvement of Psychological Science suggests that researchers "should focus first on understanding how scholars are already working and what their contexts and needs are rather than imposing a certain set of predetermined tools and practices on others" (Steltenpohl et al., 2021, p. 4).

When developing research studies, foreign researchers can take an etic (i.e., from outside) or emic (i.e., from inside) approach. Etic approaches are related to Berry's first goal (i.e., whether theories apply in understudied cultural contexts), and in practice often reflect Minority World researchers replicating already established effects or testing measurement equivalence in other contexts. Emic approaches reflect Berry's second goal for cultural research (i.e., exploring and discovering new processes and phenomena in local cultural terms). Culturally based research would ideally apply both approaches, aiming to create a more nuanced and comprehensive understanding of how culture affects humans (Berry, 1999).

Regardless of taking an emic or etic approach, we suggest five core issues that researchers should consider in any type of cultural work. First, researchers should be programmatic, transparent, and direct in how they operationalize or measure cultural attributes in their work (Broesch et al., 2022). Second, researchers should pay attention to translation issues, not just of language but also of constructs and meaning. Third, researchers must be aware of how and why they are recruiting specific participants (Broesch et al., 2020). Fourth, researchers must ensure that their methods are both culturally sensitive and empirically appropriate. Finally, researchers should employ data analysis strategies that answer the research question and lead to informed and culturally relevant conclusions.

Operationalizing or Measuring Culture

Defining culture is a complex task (Broesch et al., 2022; Hofstede, 1994; Spencer-Oatey, 2008). Importantly, how researchers conceptualize culture will influence how they operationalize culture. For example, culture can be measured at the individual level, the group level, or the national level (with nation often used as a proxy for culture; Akaliyski et al., 2021). Researchers might compare groups, identities, or nationalities as reflective of different cultural types, or they might measure endorsement of cultural values by people at the individual level. Whether a researcher defines culture as a constellation of individual-level beliefs or as group-level practices, the definition of culture and subsequent level of measurement used should be influenced by the research question and the methodology employed to answer that question (Broesch et al., 2022).

One common mistake is measuring cultural values at an individual level (i.e., comparing one person's level of a trait to another person's) but then drawing conclusions at a group level (i.e., assuming that results generalize to all people from collectivistic cultures; Hofstede, 2011). While not all researchers would agree about the seriousness of this mistake, the point Hofstede makes about the care required when measuring culture at one level of analysis (i.e., individuals) and making inferences or drawing conclusions at a different level of analysis (e.g., cultural or national groups) should be considered.

It is not always logical to assume that a variable (e.g., individualism) that was measured at one level (e.g., individuals) will behave similarly at a different level of measurement (e.g., national groups; Smith, 2002). For example, when subjective well-being is measured at a national level, national-level income is a strong predictor. However, when subjective well-being is examined *within* specific national groups, at an individual level, predictors vary between countries with different levels of per capita wealth (Diener & Diener, 1995; Oishi et al., 1999; Rosling et al., 2018). This suggests that, while income predicts group-level well-being, other constructs play important roles at the individual level, which vary by nation and culture. Broesch et al.'s (2022) suggestion bears repeating – the way that culture is defined and measured should be based on the research question under consideration. Research that aims to answer questions about group-level constructs should define and measure culture at the group level, and research that aims to answer questions about individual-level constructs should define and measure culture at the individual level.

A final point about measuring cultural variables is that national groups are not always meaningful substitutes for cultural groups. For decades, scholars have argued that culturally focused research too often conflates national residency or citizenship with cultural groups and values (Halttunen, 2017; Hollins, 1990). Recently, one of us published work that used pre-existing theoretical and empirical work arguing that the dominant cultural logic of multiple national contexts reflected dignity, face, or honor values to identify cultural groupings. This work aimed to investigate whether cultural context (rather than personal cultural values) affected emotions and behavior. However, our results, which showed some predicted cultural differences but also overarching similarities, may reflect the fact that individual participants may not always endorse or experience the dominant cultural logic of their national contexts (Maitner et al., 2022).

Too many researchers uncritically accept the assumption that national identity equals cultural identity, leading to incorrect and harmful misinterpretations of data and findings. This point is made compellingly clear by work in multicultural psychology showing people endorse different cultural values and beliefs within the same national context (Gaines et al., 1997; Vargas & Kemmelmeier, 2013). For example, Gaines et al. (1997) showed that Asian, Black, and Latinx Americans scored higher on measures of collectivistic value orientation than did European Americans. These findings also show that value orientations can be similar across cultural groups (i.e., Asian, Black, and Latinx Americans), underscoring the importance of utilizing appropriate cross-cultural approaches.

Translation

One of the central aspects of conducting high-quality culturally focused research is ensuring that measurement tools and other materials are understood equivalently across relevant cultural groups. Establishing the equivalence of constructs and measures used to collect data is vital for the validity and reliability of cross-cultural studies. Researchers conducting culturally focused work must establish that the constructs of interest show structural invariance, suggesting they are understood in an equivalent way across all participants and groups (Kankaraš & Moors, 2010).

The process of establishing measurement equivalence (i.e., any measurements used are measuring the construct of interest in equivalent ways across groups) is complicated and time-consuming. Statistically, equivalence can be established via different approaches (Cheung et al., 2011) and by utilizing various analyses (Putnick & Bornstein, 2016; Tay et al., 2011; Welzel & Inglehart, 2016). We encourage any researcher conducting cultural work to invest the time and energy to understand the importance and process of establishing construct and measurement equivalence by studying sources such as Davidov et al. (2014), Fischer and Fontaine (2011), Fischer and Poortinga (2018), Freitag and Bauer (2013), and Matsumoto and van de Vijver (2011). Culturally focused work conducted without established equivalence introduces bias that may undermine validity.

One aspect of construct and measurement equivalence that is often misunderstood focuses on the linguistic translation of measures. Some scholars (Cheung et al., 2011) argue that measures developed in the culture and language where they will be used are preferable to measures created in one culture and language being translated for use into another; however, it is common in cultural work to linguistically translate measures for use with different cultures. Often, the process of translation is inadequate and introduces bias and non-equivalence. One of the most common errors is to focus on linguistic translation with insufficient focus on cultural translation. As Abbasi et al. (2012) argue, good translation requires that translators not only translate surveys or other tools from one language to another, but are also aware of cultural values, group dynamics, regional dialects, and other variables that will influence the way items on a measure are interpreted by members of different cultural groups (Sun, 2011).

Back translation has long been considered the "gold standard" for translating measures and constructs from one language to another (Brislin, 1970; Brislin & Freimanis, 2001). There are various specific and unique ways to back-translate a measure. However, the basic process is that: (1) a measure is translated from its original language into the target language by one bilingual translator; (2) another bilingual translator translates the measure from the target language back into the original language; (3) differences in the two versions in the original language are identified as problematic; and (4) the survey in the target language is adjusted until the original survey and the survey back-translated into the original language match. Once the original and back-translated surveys match, the assumption is that the survey in the target language is equivalent to the original survey.

While back translation can help ensure linguistic equivalence, scholars now argue that it is not always the best or only way to ensure construct equivalence (Ozolins et al., 2020; Son, 2018). As an alternative, Douglas and Craig (2007) suggest iterative collaboration among translators. Other scholars make similar arguments, suggesting that there is not a single acceptable process for translating measures, and instead propose that the appropriate translation procedure depends on the research question and methodology (Cha et al., 2007) and should be understood as an inherently subjective process (Wong & Poon, 2010). Rather than demanding that one specific process be used for translation, researchers and editors should recognize that the goal of translation is to establish construct and measurement equivalence, and various translation processes can lead to this outcome (see Matsumoto & van de Vijver, 2011).

Recruiting Participants

If the goal of a research study is to investigate *replicability* or *generalizability* of a finding, researchers should recruit collaborators and samples from cultural contexts that vary maximally from their own. They should then update a previously investigated paradigm as appropriate for the new context to determine if the variables of interest function similarly in different cultural contexts (Tiokhin et al., 2019). However, if the goal is to investigate cultural *differences*, a researcher should aim to collect data from cultural contexts that vary primarily in the attribute hypothesized to underlie differences but that are otherwise as similar to each other as possible. In this way, differences on the variable of interest can be understood as effects of the identified cultural value(s) of interest. In either instance, researchers should have a clear theoretical justification for why they recruited their sample(s) of interest (Broesch et al., 2020).

As with research that is not (intentionally) culturally focused, sometimes the most appropriate sample will be a randomly selected representative sample of the population(s) of interest, and may involve sampling techniques like cluster sampling, stratified sampling, or systematic sampling. While recruiting representative samples across cultures can be particularly challenging, research questions that investigate relationships among variables or differences between groups with the goal of making universalist, etic claims should strive to recruit samples that are as representative as possible.

At other times, a "typical" sample might be more appropriate (Boehnke et al., 2011; see also Matsumoto & van de Vijver, 2011). In a typical sample, the distribution of variables of interest is typical of, or similar to, the distribution of those variables within the cultural group being studied. For example, a researcher interested in comparing predictors of self-esteem in two cultural groups may recruit samples that are "typical" of the distribution of self-esteem within each culture, ensuring that the samples reflect the variable of interest as it is distributed in each population. This is particularly important if the average levels of measured self-esteem are different in the populations. Creating typical samples requires non-random sampling procedures, such as purposive or quota sampling. However, by recruiting samples that reflect the typical distribution of self-esteem within each population, the researcher can focus on what predicts self-esteem as it is typically distributed within each population.

Researchers who do not conduct culturally focused research on a regular basis may choose to do so simply because they have gained access to a sample from outside their own cultural group and want to take advantage of that opportunity (such researchers are sometimes referred to as "safari researchers"; Ashdown et al., 2021). In such situations (which are not limited to culturally based work), access to a sample often guides the sampling technique and possibly the research question. This approach can easily lead to uninformed or even harmful conclusions, and reify culturally based stereotypes or misunderstandings. Instead, researchers should aim to recruit the type of sample best suited to answer their research question.

Interacting with Participants

As with determining the best way to measure culture, recruit and sample participants, and translate materials, the method of data collection in culturally focused work should primarily be based on the research question and constructs being investigated. However, it is important to note that researchers from different cultural contexts and participants from different cultural groups will have different training in, access to, and experience with data collection methods. For example, while in most Minority World countries people are trained how to respond to Likert-type rating surveys from a very early age, this is not the case globally. Using Likert-type surveys may undermine measurement validity in some parts of the world, particularly where cultural values might influence participants' patterns of responding and lead to issues such as acquiescence bias, dissent bias, or social desirability bias (Cheung & Rensvold, 2000; Ross & Mirowsky, 1984; Smith & Fischer, 2008; Tucker, 2017; van de Vijver & Tanzer, 2004).

Other issues that researchers should bear in mind include participants' comfort and experience with paper-and-pencil or computer-based forms. Filling out paperwork is not a universal experience, and in some places, there is a history of terror or corruption around the process of committing things to paper (see Adams et al., 2007; Broesch et al., 2020). Access to the internet or technology and literacy levels are also issues researchers must consider. Finally, researchers must also consider cultural response biases (e.g., acquiescence, dissent, extreme responding), such as participants' willingness to agree or disagree with another person (e.g., the researcher), even in survey-based research (Johnson et al., 2011; Morren et al., 2012; Smith et al., 2016).

The challenges of recruiting participants and translating measures usually receive more attention from culturally focused researchers than does the specific way data will be collected. This is often a result of researchers being culture-bound and culture-blind (Berry, 2013), assuming data collection methods common in their own cultural context are universal ways to collect data from any group around the world (see Tiokhin et al., 2019). Ideally, researchers should employ mixed methods, including methods indigenous to the relevant participating cultural groups, to establish convergent validity of research findings and support more nuanced and complete conclusions about the role of culture in social and behavioral sciences (Berry, 1999; Broesch et al., 2020; Fischer & Poortinga, 2018).

Data Analysis Strategies

While a detailed discussion of analysis issues related to culturally focused work is beyond the scope of this chapter, we urge researchers conducting cultural work to investigate the special considerations that culturally based data require for appropriate analysis, particularly when comparing cultural groups (Fischer & Poortinga, 2018). As discussed above, before comparing scores on measures across cultures, it is important to test their equivalence across groups. From that point, nearly all statistical analyses used to examine work that is not purposefully cultural in nature can be appropriately applied to cultural data (Matsumoto & van de Vijver, 2011). However, in order to ensure that conclusions are culturally sensitive and appropriate, statistics need to be interpreted with caution. For example, obtaining large effect sizes when comparing cultural groups on a DV of interest might suggest that the groups are different because of the culturally focused IV. Alternatively, it might mean the groups are different from each other for other, non-measured reasons which may or may not be cultural (Matsumoto et al., 2011). Similarly, some statistical analyses, such as multilevel modeling (Nezlek, 2011) and meta-analysis (Van Hemert, 2011), may need to be modified to include cultural variables beyond the constructs of interest when applied to cultural data.

Additional Issues to Consider

We think it is important to also mention issues related to international and cross-cultural collaborations that are not necessarily directly related to high-quality research designs but are related to ethical and professional behavior. As researchers who live and work outside the Minority World yet collaborate often with colleagues who live and work in the Minority World, we have experienced (and likely engaged in) collaborations that were managed in ways that impede high-quality research, and these issues deserve mention.

Discussions of authorship (e.g., what earns authorship, authorship order) should be discussed and determined before a project formally begins, with roles clearly defined. Clearly, authorship should reflect the amount of effort and contribution each person made toward the study and not be a matter of where members of the research team were trained, where they were born, or where they work. Relatedly, be aware of cultural differences among members of the research team regarding approaches to collaborative work, leadership, and hierarchy, as well as work obligations across contexts.

Finally, pay attention to the technical aspects of working across time zones, resources, and languages. Rotate virtual meeting times so that the same team member is not always meeting late at night or early in the morning; recognize that not all team members will have access to the same databases for literature searches; question why surveys are always translated from English to another language (rather than using surveys created in a language other than English and translated into English if necessary). Clear and open communication, self-reflection, and flexibility in international collaborative relationships will make them more successful and lead to higher-quality research projects.

Conclusion

Whether they recognize it or not, *all* researchers conduct research that is grounded in a particular cultural context, and researchers should be aware of the ethical and contextual assumptions that underlie their methodological choices and their interpretations of results. No matter where they work and live, researchers must take the time and effort to make those assumptions explicit – a burden that is already required of Majority World researchers (Bou Zeineddine et al., 2021; Cheon et al., 2020). Exploring and reflecting on those assumptions, as well as educating oneself about best practices in conducting culturally focused and international work – the practices discussed in this chapter as well as those found in the reference list below – will create more equitable, ethical, meaningful, nuanced, and context-specific social and behavioral science.

References

Abbasi, G., Zadeh, S. S., Janfaza, E., Assemi, A., & Dehghan, S. S. (2012). Language, translation, and culture. *International Conference on Language, Medias and Culture, 33*(2), 83–87.

Adams, G., Dobles, I., Gómez, L. H., Kurtiş, T., & Molina, L. E. (2015). Decolonizing psychological science: Introduction to the special thematic section. *Journal of Social and Political Psychology, 3*, 213–238. https://doi.org/10.5964/jspp.v3i1.564

Adams, V., Miller, S., Craig, S., Sonam, Nyima, Droyoung, et al. (2007). Informed consent in cross-cultural perspective: Clinical research in the Tibetan Autonomous Region, PRC. *Culture, Medicine and Psychiatry, 31*, 445–472. https://doi.org/10.1007/s11013-007-9070-2

Akaliyski, P., Welzel, C., Bond, M. H., & Minkov, M. (2021). On "nationology": The gravitational field of national culture. *Journal of Cross-Cultural Psychology, 52* (8–9), 1–23. http://doi.org/10.1177/00220221211044780

Arnett, J. J. (2008). The neglected 95%: Why American psychology needs to become less American. *American Psychologist, 63*(7), 602–614. https://psycnet.apa.org/doi/10.1037/0003-066X.63.7.602

Ashdown, B. K., Dixe, A., & Talmage, C. A. (2021). The potentially damaging effects of developmental aid and voluntourism on cultural capital and well-being. *International Journal of Community Well-Being, 4*(1), 113–131. https://doi.org/10.1007/s42413-020-00079-2

Barrett, H. C. (2020). Deciding what to observe: Thoughts for a post-WEIRD generation. *Evolution and Human Behavior, 41*(5), 445–453. https://doi.org/10.1016/j.evolhumbehav.2020.05.006

Berry, J. W. (1999). Emics and etics: A symbiotic conception. *Culture & Psychology, 5*(2), 165–171. https://doi.org/10.1177/1354067X9952004

(2013). Global psychology. *South African Journal of Psychology, 43*(4), 391–401. https://doi.org/10.1177%2F0081246313504517

Boehnke, K., Lietz, P., Schreier, M., & Wilhelm, A. (2011). Sampling: The selection of cases for culturally comparative psychological research. In Matsumoto & van de Vijver (pp. 101–129).

Bou Zeineddine, F., Saab, R., Lášticová, B., Kende, A., & Ayanian, A. H. (2021). "Some uninteresting data from a faraway country": Inequity and coloniality in international social psychological publication. *Journal of Social Issues, 78*(2), 320–345. https://doi.org/10.1111/josi.12481

Brislin, R. W. (1970). Back-translation for cross-cultural research. *Journal of Cross-Cultural Psychology, 1*(3), 185–216. https://doi.org/10.1177%2F135910457000100301

Brislin, R. W., & Freimanis, C. (2001). Back-translation: A tool for cross-cultural research. In C. Sin-Wai & D. E. Pollard (eds.), *An Encyclopedia of Translation* (pp. 22–40). Chinese University Press.

Broesch, T., Crittenden, A. N., Beheim, B. A., Blackwell, A. D., Bunce, J. A., Colleran, H., et al. (2020). Navigating cross-cultural research: Methodological and ethical considerations. *Proceedings of the Royal Society B: Biological Sciences, 287* (1935), 20201245. https://doi.org/10.1098/rspb.2020.1245

Broesch, T., Lew-Levy, S., Kärtner, J., Kanngiesser, P., & Kline, M. A. (2022). A roadmap to doing culturally grounded developmental science [Unpublished manuscript].

Brouwers, S. A., van Hemert, D. A., Breugelmans, S. M., & van de Vijver, F. J. R. (2004). A historical analysis of empirical studies published in the *Journal of Cross-Cultural Psychology* 1970–2004. *Journal of Cross-Cultural Psychology, 35*(3), 251–262. https://doi.org/10.1177%2F0022022104264121

Burton, M., & Kagan, C. (2005). Liberation social psychology: Learning from Latin America. *Journal of Community & Applied Social Psychology, 15*(1), 63–78. https://doi.org/10.1002/casp.786

Cha, E.-S., Kim, K. H., & Erlen, J. A. (2007). Translation of scales in cross-cultural research: Issues and techniques. *Journal of Advanced Nursing, 58*(4), 386–395. https://doi.org/10.1111/j.1365-2648.2007.04242.x

Cheon, B. K., Melani, I., & Hong, Y. (2020). How USA-centric is psychology? An archival study of implicit assumptions of generalizability of findings to human nature based on origins of study samples. *Social Psychological and Personality Science, 11*(7), 928–937. https://doi.org/10.1177/1948550620927269

Cheung, F. M., van de Vijver, F. J. R., & Leong, F. T. L. (2011). Toward a new approach to the study of personality in culture. *American Psychologist, 66*(7), 593–603. https://psycnet.apa.org/doi/10.1037/a0022389

Cheung, G. W., & Rensvold, R. B. (2000). Assessing extreme and acquiescence response sets in cross-cultural research using structural equations modeling. *Journal of Cross-Cultural Psychology, 31*(2), 187–212. https://doi.org/10.1177/0022022100031002003

Clancy, K. B. H., & Davis, J. L. (2019). Soylent is people, and WEIRD is white: Biological anthropology, whiteness, and the limits of WEIRD. *Annual Review of Anthropology, 48*, 169–186. https://doi.org/10.1146/annurev-anthro-102218-01133

Clark, M. J. (2012). Cross-cultural research, challenge and competence. *International Journal of Nursing Practice, 18*(s2), 28–37. https://doi.org/10.1111/j.1440-172X.2012.02026.x

Davidov, E., Meuleman, B., Cieciuch, J., Schmidt, P., & Billiet, J. (2014). Measurement equivalence in cross-national research. *Annual Review of Sociology, 40*, 55–75. https://doi.org/10.1146/annurev-soc-071913-043137

Davies, S. E. H. (2020). The introduction of research ethics review procedures at a university in South Africa. Review outcomes of a social science research ethics committee. *Research Ethics, 16*(1–2), 1–26. https://doi.org/10.1177/1747016119898408

Diener, E., & Diener, M. (1995). Cross-cultural correlates of life satisfaction and self-esteem. *Journal of Personality and Social Psychology, 68*, 653–663. https://doi.org/10.1037/0022-3514.68.4.653

Douglas, S. P., & Craig, C. S. (2007). Collaborative and iterative translation: An alternative approach to back translation. *Journal of International Marketing, 15*(1), 30–43. https://doi.org/10.1509%2Fjimk.15.1.030

Dulin, M. F., Tapp, H., Smith, H. A., Urquieta de Hernandez, B., & Furuseth, O. J. (2011). A community based participatory approach to improving health in a Hispanic population. *Implementation Science, 6*, Article 38. https://doi.org/10.1186/1748-5908-6-38

Ebert, T., Gebauer, J. E., Brenner, T., Bleidorn, W., Gosling, S. D., Potter, J., & Rentfrow, P. J. (2022). Are regional differences in psychological characteristics and their correlates robust? Applying spatial-analysis techniques to examine regional variation in personality. *Perspectives on Psychological Science, 17*(2), 407–441. https://doi.org/10.1177/1745691621998326

Ember, C. R., & Ember, M. (2009). *Cross-Cultural Research Methods*, 2nd ed. Altamira Press.

Fischer, R., & Fontaine, J. R. J. (2011). Methods for investigating structural equivalence. In Matsumoto & van de Vijver (pp. 179–215).

Fischer, R., & Poortinga, Y. H. (2018). Addressing methodological challenges in culture-comparative research. *Journal of Cross-Cultural Psychology, 49*(5), 691–712. https://doi.org/10.1177/0022022117738086

Fontaine, J. R. J., & Fischer, R. (2011). Data analytic approaches for investigating isomorphism between the individual-level and the cultural-level internal structure. In Matsumoto & van de Vijver (pp. 273–298).

Foulks, E. F. (1989). Misalliances in the Barrow Alcohol Study. *American Indian and Alaska Native Mental Health Research, 2*(3), 7–17.

Fraser, G. (2018). Evaluating inclusive gender identity measures for use in quantitative psychology research. *Psychology & Sexuality, 9*(4), 343–357. https://doi.org/10.1080/19419899.2018.1497693

Freitag, M., & Bauer, P. C. (2013). Testing for measurement equivalence in surveys: Dimensions of social trust across cultural contexts. *Public Opinion Quarterly, 77*(S1), 24–44. https://doi.org/10.1093/poq/nfs064

Friesen, P., Kearns, L., Redman, B., & Caplan, A. L. (2017). Rethinking the Belmont Report? *American Journal of Bioethics, 17*, 15–21. https://doi.org/10.1080/15265161.2017.1329482

Gaines, S. O., Jr., Marelich, W. D., Bledsoe, K. L., Steers, W. N., Henderson, M. C., Granrose, C. S., et al. (1997). Links between race/ethnicity and cultural values as mediated by racial/ethnic identity and moderated by gender. *Journal of Personality and Social Psychology, 72*(6), 1460–1476. https://doi.org/10.1037//0022-3514.72.6.1460

Gjorgjioska, M. A., & Tomicic, A. (2019) The crisis in social psychology under neoliberalism: Reflections from social representations theory. *Journal of Social Issues, 75*, 169–188. https://doi.org/10.5964/jspp.v1i1.97

Gurven, M. D., & Lieberman, D. E. (2020). WEIRD bodies: Mismatch, medicine and missing diversity. *Evolution and Human Behavior, 41*(5), 330–340. https://doi.org/10.1016/j.evolhumbehav.2020.04.001

Halttunen, L. (2017). Whose culture? Monolithic cultures and subcultures in early childhood settings. *Journal of Early Childhood Research, 15*(1), 73–82. https://doi.org/10.1177%2F1476718X15579742

Hambleton, R. K., & Zenisky, A. L. (2011). Translating and adapting tests for cross-cultural assessments. In Matsumoto & van de Vijver (pp. 46–70).

Henrich, J., Heine, S. J., & Norenzayan, A. (2010). The weirdest people in the world? *Behavioral and Brain Sciences, 33*(2–3), 61–83. https://doi.org/10.1017/S0140525X0999152X

Hofstede, G. (1994). *Cultures and Organizations: Software of the Mind*. HarperCollins.

(2011). Dimensionalizing cultures: The Hofstede Model in context. *Online Readings in Psychology and Culture, 2*(1). https://doi.org/10.9707/2307-0919.1014

Hollins, E. A. (1990). Debunking the myth of a monolithic White American culture; or, moving toward cultural inclusion. *American Behavioral Scientist, 34*(2), 201–209. https://doi.org/10.1177%2F0002764290034002008

Hruschka, D. J. (2020). "What we look with" is as important as "what we look at". *Evolution and Human Behavior, 41*(5), 458–459. https://doi.org/10.1016/j.evolhumbehav.2020.07.011

Hruschka, D. J., Munira, S., Jesmin, K., Hackman, J., & Tiokhin, L. (2018). Learning from failures of protocol in cross-cultural research. *Proceedings of the National Academy of Sciences, 115*(45), 11428–11434. https://doi.org/10.1073/pnas.1721166115

Johnson, T. P., Shavitt, S., & Holbrook, A. L. (2011). Survey response styles across cultures. In Matsumoto & van de Vijver (pp. 130–175).

Kağıtçıbaşı, Ç. (1996). *Family and Human Development across Cultures: A View from the Other Side*. Psychology Press.

Kankaraš, M., & Moors, G. (2010). Researching measurement equivalence in cross-cultural studies. *Psihologija, 43*(2), 121–136.

Klausner, S., & Foulks, E. (1979). *Alcohol and the Future of Ukpiagvik*. Center for Research on the Acts of Man.

(1980). *Social Change and the Alcohol Problem in the Alaskan North Slope*. Center for Research on the Acts of Man.

Klein, V., Savas, Ö., & Conley, T. D. (2022). How WEIRD and androcentric is sex research? Global inequities in study populations. *Journal of Sex Research, 59*(7), 810–817. https://doi.org/10.1080/00224499.2021.1918050

Klitzman, R. (2011). How local IRBs view central IRBs in the US. *BMC Medical Ethics*, 12, Article 13. https://doi.org/10.1186/1472-6939-12-13

(2012). US IRBs confronting research in the developing world. *Developing World Bioethics, 12*(2), 63–73. https://doi.org/10.1111/j.1471-8847.2012.00324.x

Klitzman, R., Pivovarova, E., Murray, A., Appelbaum, P. S., Stiles, D. F., & Lidz, C. W. (2019). Local knowledge and single IRBs for multisite studies: Challenges and solutions. *Ethics & Human Research, 41*(1), 22–31. https://doi.org/10.1002/eahr.500003

Ledgerwood, A., da Silva Frost, A., Kadirvel, S., Maitner, A. T., Wang, Y. A., & Maddox, K. B. (in press). Methods for advancing an open, replicable, and inclusive science of social cognition. Chapter to appear in K. Hugenberg, K. Johnson, & D. E. Carlston (eds.), *Oxford Handbook of Social Cognition*. Oxford University Press.

Ledgerwood, A., Hudson, S. T. J., Lewis, N. A., Maddox, K. B., Pickett, C. L., Remedios, J. D., et al. (2022). The pandemic as a portal: Reimagining psychological science as truly open and inclusive. *Perspectives on Psychological Science, 17*(4), 937–959. https://doi.org/10.1177/17456916211036654

Leong, F. T. L., & Lyons, B. (2010). Ethical challenges for cross-cultural research conducted by psychologists from the United States. *Ethics & Behavior, 20*(3–4), 250–264. https://doi.org/10.1080/10508421003798984

Liu, C., Cox, Jr., R. B., Washburn, I. J., Croff, J. M., & Crethar, H. C. (2017). The effects of requiring parental consent for research on adolescents' risk behaviors: A meta-analysis. *Journal of Adolescent Health, 61*(1), 45–52. https://doi.org/10.1016/j.jadohealth.2017.01.015

Maitner, A. T., DeCoster, J., Andersson, P. A., Eriksson, K., Sherbaji, S., Giner-Sorolla, R., et al. (2022). Perceptions of emotional functionality: Similarities and differences among dignity, face, and honor cultures. *Journal of Cross-Cultural Psychology, 53*(3–4), 263–288. https://doi.org/10.1177/00220221211065108

Matsumoto, D., Kim, J. J., Grissom, R. J., & Dinnel, D. L. (2011). Effect sizes in cross-cultural research. In Matsumoto & van de Vijver (pp. 244–272).

Matsumoto, D., & van de Vijver, F. J. R. (eds.). (2011). *Cross-Cultural Research Methods in Psychology*. Cambridge University Press.

Metro, R. (2014). From the form to the face to face: IRBs, ethnographic researchers, and human subjects translate consent. *Anthropology & Education Quarterly, 45*(2), 167–184. https://doi.org/10.1111/aeq.12057

Morren, M., Gelissen, J. P. T. M., & Vermunt, J. K. (2012). Response strategies and response styles in cross-cultural surveys. *Cross-Cultural Research*, *46*(3), 255–279. https://doi.org/10.1177%2F1069397112440939

National Commission for the Protection of Human Subjects of Biomedical and Behavioral Research. (1979). *The Belmont Report: Ethical Principles and Guidelines for the Protection of Human Subjects of Research*. www.hhs.gov/ohrp/regulations-and-policy/belmont-report

Neil, M., & Saenz, C. (2020). Advancing research ethics systems in Latin America and the Caribbean: A path for other LMICs? *The Lancet: Global Health*, *8*(1), E23–E24. https://doi.org/10.1016/S2214-109X(19)30441-3

Newson, M., Buhrmester, M., Xygalatas, D., & Whitehouse, H. (2021). Go WILD, not WEIRD. *Journal for the Cognitive Science of Religion*, *6*(1–2), 80–106. https://doi.org/10.1558/jcsr.38413

Nezlek, J. B. (2011). Multilevel modeling and cross-cultural research. In Matsumoto & van de Vijver (pp. 299–345).

Oishi, S., Diener, E. F., Lucas, R. E., & Suh, E. M. (1999). Cross-cultural variations in predictors of life satisfaction: Perspectives from needs and values. *Personality and Social Psychology Bulletin*, *25*, 980–990. https://doi.org/10.1177/01461672992511006

Ozolins, U., Hale, S., Cheng, X., Hyatt, A., & Schofield, P. (2020). Translation and back-translation methodology in health research – a critique. *Expert Review of Pharmacoeconomics & Outcomes Research*, *20*(1), 69–77. https://doi.org/10.1080/14737167.2020.1734453

Perry, K. H. (2011). Ethics, vulnerability, and speakers of other languages: How university IRBs (do not) speak to research involving refugee participants. *Qualitative Inquiry*, *17*(10), 899–912. https://doi.org/10.1177%2F1077800411425006

Pratt, B., Van, C., Cong, Y., Rashid, H., Kumar, N., Ahmad, A., et al. (2014). Perspectives from South and East Asia on clinical and research ethics: A literature review. *Journal of Empirical Research on Human Research Ethics*, *9*(2), 52–67. https://doi.org/10.1525/jer.2014.9.2.52

Presidential Commission for the Study of Bioethical Issues. (2011). *Research across Borders: Proceedings of the International Research Panel of the Presidential Commission for the Study of Bioethical Issues*.

Putnick, D. L., & Bornstein, M. H. (2016). Measurement invariance conventions and reporting: The state of the art and future directions for psychological research. *Developmental Review*, *41*, 71–90. https://doi.org/10.1016/j.dr.2016.06.004

Rad, M. S., Martingano, A. J., & Ginges, J. (2018). Toward a psychology of *Homo sapiens*: Making psychological science more representative of the human population. *Proceedings of the National Academy of Sciences*, *115*, 11401–11405. https://doi.org/10.1073/pnas.1721165115

Rashwan, B., & Jenkins, J. C. (2017). Fatalism and revolution: Expanding our understanding of fatalism during a unique political opening in Egypt. *Journal of North African Studies*, *22*(4), 645–664. https://doi.org/10.1080/13629387.2017.1316716

Rhodes, S. D., Daniel, J., & Alonzo, J. (2012). A systematic community-based participatory approach to refining an evidence-based community-level intervention: The HOLA intervention for Latino men who have sex with men. *Health Promotion Practice*, *14*(4), 604–616. https://doi.org/10.1177%2F1524839912462391

Rosling, H., Rosling, O., & Rönnlund, A. R. (2018). *Factfulness*. Flatiron Books.

Ross, C. E., & Mirowsky, J. (1984). Socially-desirable response and acquiescence in a cross-cultural survey of mental health. *Journal of Health and Social Behavior, 25*(2), 189–197. https://doi.org/10.2307/2136668

Saab, R., Ayanian, A., & Hawi, D. (2020). The status of Arabic social psychology: A review of 21st-century research articles. *Social Psychological and Personality Science, 11*, 917–927. https://doi.org/10.1177/1948550620925224

Schroeder, D., Chatfield, K., Singh, M., Chennells, R., & Herissone-Kelly, P. (2019). *Equitable Research Partnerships: A Global Code of Conduct to Counter Ethics Dumping*. Springer.

Shweder, R. A. (1990). Cultural psychology: What is it? In J. E. Stigler, R. A. Shweder, & G. Herdt (eds.), *Cultural psychology: Essays on Comparative Human Development* (pp. 1–43). Cambridge University Press.

Sireci, S. G. (2011). Evaluating test and survey items for bias across languages and cultures. In Matsumoto & van de Vijver (pp. 216–240).

Skewes, M. C., & Lewis, J. P. (2016). Sobriety and alcohol use among rural Alaska Native elders. *International Journal of Circumpolar Health, 75*(1), Article 30476. https://doi.org/10.3402/ijch.v75.30476

Smith, P. B. (2002). Levels of analysis in cross-cultural psychology. *Online Readings in Psychology and Culture, 2*(2). https://doi.org/10.9707/2307-0919.1018

Smith, P. B., & Fischer, R. (2008). Acquiescence, extreme response bias and culture: A multilevel analysis. In F. J. R. van de Vijver, D. A. Van Hemert, & Y. H. Poortinga (eds.), *Multilevel Analysis of Individuals and Cultures* (pp. 285–314). Lawrence Erlbaum Associates.

Smith, P. B., Vignoles, V. L., Becker, M., Owe, E., Easterbrook, M. J., Brown, R., et al. (2016). Individual and culture-level components of survey response styles: A multi-level analysis using cultural models of selfhood. *International Journal of Psychology, 51*(6), 453–463. https://doi.org/10.1002/ijop.12293

Solberg, B., & Eikemo, H. (2021, January 11). Passive consent for passive participation? *Tidsskr Nor Legeforen, 141*. https://doi.org/10.4045/tidsskr.20.0654

Son, J. (2018). Back translation as a documentation tool. *Translation & Interpreting, 10*(2), 89–100.

Spence, S., White, M., Adamson, A. J., & Matthews, J. N. S. (2015). Does the use of passive or active consent affect consent or completion rates, or dietary data quality? Repeat cross-sectional survey among school children aged 11–12 years. *BMJ Open, 5*(1), Article e006457. https://doi.org/10.1136/bmjopen-2014-006457

Spencer-Oatey, H. (2008). *Culturally speaking: Culture, Communication and Politeness Theory*. Continuum.

Ssali, A., Poland, F., & Seeley, J. (2016). Exploring informed consent in HIV clinical trials: A case study in Uganda. *Heliyon, 2*(11), Article e00196. https://doi.org/10.1016/j.heliyon.2016.e00196

Steltenpohl, C. N., Montilla Doble, L. J., Basnight-Brown, D. M., Dutra, N. B., Belaus, A., Kung, C.-C., et al. (2021). Society for the Improvement of Psychological Science Global Engagement Task Force Report. *Collabra: Psychology, 7*(1). https://doi.org/10.1525/collabra.22968

Sun, H. (2011). On cultural differences and translation methods. *Journal of Language Teaching and Research, 2*(1), 160–163. https://doi.org/10.4304/jltr.2.1.160-163

Tay, L., Newman, D. A., & Vermunt, J. K. (2011). Using mixed-method item response theory with covariates (MM-IRT-C) to ascertain observed and unobserved measurement equivalence. *Organizational Research Methods*, *14*(1), 147–176. https://doi.org/10.1177%2F1094428110366037

Thalmayer, A. G., Toscanelli, C., & Arnett, J. J. (2021). The neglected 95% revisited: Is American psychology becoming less American? *American Psychologist*, *76*(1), 116–129. https://psycnet.apa.org/doi/10.1037/amp0000622

Tiokhin, L., Hackman, J., Munira, S., Jesmin, K., & Hruschka, D. (2019). Generalizability is not optional: Insights from a cross-cultural study of social discounting. *Royal Society Open Science*, *6*(2), 181386. https://doi.org/10.1098/rsos.181386

Tremblay, M.-C., Martin, D. H., McComber, A. M., McGregor, A., & Macaulay, A. C. (2018). Understanding community-based participatory research through a social movement framework: A case study of the Kahnawake School Diabetes Prevention Project. *BMC Public Health*, *18*, 487. https://doi.org/10.1186/s12889-018-5412-y

Tucker, B. (2017). From risk and time preferences to cultural models of causality: On the challenges and possibilities of field experiments, with examples from rural southwestern Madagascar. *Nebraska Symposium on Motivation*, *64*, 61–114.

Tusino, S., & Furfaro, M. (2021). Rethinking the role of research ethics committees in the lift of Regulation (EU) No 536/2014 on clinical trials and the COVID-19 pandemic. *British Journal of Clinical Pharmacology*, *88*(1), 40–46. https://doi.org/10.1111/bcp.14871

van de Vijver, F. J. R., & Leung, K. (2011). Equivalence and bias: A review of concepts, models, and data analytic procedures. In Matsumoto & van de Vijver (pp. 17–45).

van de Vijver, F. J. R., & Tanzer, N. K. (2004). Bias and equivalence in cross-cultural assessment: An overview. *European Review of Applied Psychology / Revue Européenne de Psychologie Appliquée*, *54*(2), 119–135. https://doi.org/10.1016/j.erap.2003.12.004

Van Hemert, D. A. (2011). Cross-cultural meta-analysis. In Matsumoto & van de Vijver (pp. 348–378).

Vargas, J. H., & Kemmelmeier, M. (2013). Ethnicity and contemporary American culture: A meta-analytic investigation of horizontal–vertical individualism–collectivism. *Journal of Cross-Cultural Psychology*, *44*(2), 195–222. https://doi.org/10.1177/0022022112443733

Welzel, C., & Inglehart, R. F. (2016). Misconceptions of measurement equivalence: Time for a paradigm shift. *Comparative Political Studies*, *49*(8), 1068–1094. https://doi.org/10.1177%2F0010414016628275

Wexler, L. (2011). Intergenerational dialogue exchange and action: Introducing a community-based participatory approach to connect youths, adults, and elders in an Alaska Native community. *International Journal of Qualitative Methods*, *10*(3), 248–264. https://doi.org/10.1177%2F160940691101000305

White, M. T. (1999). Guidelines for IRB review of international collaborative medical research: A proposal. *Journal of Law, Medicine & Ethics*, *27*(1), 87–94. https://doi.org/10.1111/j.1748-720X.1999.tb01440.x

Wong, J. P-H., & Poon, M. K-L. (2010). Bringing translation out of the shadows: Translation as an issue of methodological significance in cross-cultural qualitative research. *Journal of Transcultural Nursing*, *21*(2), 151–158. https://doi.org/10.1177%2F1043659609357637

Wundt, W. (1900). *Elemente der Völkerpsychologie / Elements of Folk Psychology*, trans. E. L. Schaub. George Allen & Unwin.

8 Mixed Methods and Multimethod Research

Judith Schoonenboom

Abstract

This chapter explains how researchers can design studies that include multiple methods. It starts by defining multiple-methods research as bringing together multiple perspectives at the methodological and other levels to obtain a deeper and more inclusive understanding of a phenomenon (and, in the end, to make a better-informed decision) than would be possible using one method alone. Using four real-life examples, Part I of the chapter shows the four consecutive steps of multiple-methods design: including multiple perspectives, exploring them, integrating their conclusions, and using this integrated conclusion to make a decision in practice. Part II shows that multiple-methods research is emergent and discusses the most important of these emergent elements: emerging aspects, focusing, searching for explanations, emerging data, and emerging subgroups. Part III discusses concepts that are relevant to combining qualitative and quantitative data sets: meaningful connections, purposes of mixing, theoretical drive, timing, and fully integrated research designs. The chapter concludes with recommendations for research with multiple methods.

Keywords: Definition of Mixed Methods Research, Emergent Research Design, Methods of Social Research, Mixed Methods Research, Multimethod Research, Multiperspective Research, Multiple-Methods Research, Research Design

Introduction

Designing social and behavioral science research is not easy. Researchers must identify a research gap and use that gap to formulate a research question. To answer that research question, they must select appropriate methods of data collection and analysis. Sometimes, even this is not enough. To obtain a more comprehensive understanding, researchers must sometimes combine perspectives (e.g., the perspectives offered by different methods, such as questionnaires, interviews, and observations). This is because different methods can reveal different aspects of a phenomenon. For example, as we will see, observations can offer a perspective on people's behavior, whereas interviews can offer a perspective on their motives. The question arises of how such research with multiple methods can be designed so the perspectives they offer can be meaningfully combined. That is the question this chapter aims to answer.

Based on earlier definitions (Bazeley, 2018; Creswell & Plano Clark, 2018; Johnson et al., 2007; Maxwell & Mittapalli, 2010), I define multiple-methods research as follows:

> *Multiple-methods research brings together multiple perspectives at the methodological and other levels to obtain a deeper and more inclusive understanding of a phenomenon (and, in the end, to make a better-informed decision) than would be possible using one method alone.*

As this definition shows, including these various perspectives is not enough. Multiple perspectives must be brought together; they must be brought into dialogue (Greene, 2008). Such *integration* is what leads to a deeper and more inclusive understanding of a phenomenon, and it is considered the hallmark of mixed methods research (Fetters & Molina-Azorin, 2017). Finally, a deeper and more inclusive understanding can support better decision-making (Ivankova, 2015; Mertens, 2018; Schoonenboom, 2018, 2023). It is to be expected, for example, that an intervention in a school has a higher chance of success when it is based on the perspectives of multiple stakeholders, such as students, teachers, and school managers.

How we label a study with multiple methods depends on the methods involved. A distinction is made between *quantitative methods*, such as questionnaires, that use calculations based on standardized methods of data collection, and *qualitative methods*, such as interviews, that rely on the interpretation of non-standardized data. Research that combines quantitative and qualitative methods is called *mixed methods research* (Bryman, 2008; Creswell & Plano Clark, 2018; Johnson et al., 2007). In *multimethod* research, multiple qualitative methods or multiple quantitative methods are combined (Flick, 2018), but not both (Tashakkori et al., 2021; for other uses of the term *multimethod*, see Anguera et al., 2018). Mixed methods and multimethod research are both discussed in this chapter because they share many design issues. For convenience, I will often use *multiple-methods research* as a shorthand for mixed methods and multimethod research.

This chapter offers three perspectives on multiple-methods research that each answer different design questions and that complement each other. Part I explains the steps of multiple-methods research and how to design them. Part II explains common changes that researchers encounter during the multiple-methods research process and how to use them to adapt and optimize their study design. The central question of Part III is how researchers can combine quantitative and qualitative research components (based on, among others, Bazeley, 2018; Creamer, 2018; Creswell & Plano Clark, 2018; Schoonenboom & Johnson, 2017; Tashakkori et al., 2021).

Part I. The Four Steps of Multiple-Methods Research Design

Four Research Design Steps

Multiple-methods research design can be divided into four design steps. A first design step is to include multiple "lenses" at one or more levels, each having the capability of providing a different perspective on a phenomenon. Examples are multiple stakeholders, such as students, teachers, and parents; multiple organizational levels, such as schools, classes, and individuals; and multiple methods, such as interviews and observations. Each stakeholder group, organizational level, or method constitutes a distinct lens that can offer another perspective. At the methodological level, for instance, observations can reveal aspects of a phenomenon that interviews cannot because they provide a lens on behaviors, whereas interviews provide a lens on opinions and values.

A second design step is to explore the perspective that each lens can offer. Researchers explore a perspective when they ask questions such as: What can we learn from students about the phenomenon? What can we learn from teachers? What can we learn from observations of the phenomenon, and what can we learn from interviews? In empirical research, explorations are performed through data collection and analysis. They result in separate research findings and conclusions for each perspective.

In the third design step, called *integration*, researchers ask how the conclusions from each perspective hang together. Possible answers include that one conclusion explains the other, that the conclusions agree, or that the conclusions are contradictory, as in the example: "Although teachers preferred student-centered teaching in their interviews, the observations showed a tendency toward teacher-centered teaching behavior." By integrating conclusions from various perspectives, researchers reach a more inclusive understanding than they would based on one perspective (e.g., observations or interviews only).

As an optional fourth step, the obtained inclusive understanding can form the basis for a decision in practice. In intervention and action research, for instance, research is performed to change unwanted situations in practice. Such interventions are assumed to have a better chance of success when they are based on an understanding of the perspectives of various stakeholders.

These four steps of inclusion, exploration, integration, and decision-making are helpful for design because these research activities are performed sequentially. Disparate lenses must first be *included* before their distinct perspectives can be *explored*. After separate exploration has yielded a conclusion for each perspective, these conclusions can be *integrated*, and only after that can researchers use the resulting deeper understanding to *make a decision* in practice. I explain below how this can be accomplished.

Step 1. Including Multiple Lenses at Multiple Levels

As a first step, multiple-methods researchers decide on the lenses they will include in their study. In addition to multiple methods, they often include multiple lenses at other levels, such as multiple research questions, stakeholders, locations, or groups differently affected by the phenomenon. These diverse lenses are discussed and exemplified below.

> **Box 8.1 Including Multiple Research Questions in a Study on Sexual Health Education**
>
> Finlay et al. (2015) studied sexual health education among young people with intellectual disabilities. They made video recordings of sexual health education sessions to examine the interactions between educators and learners, and they interviewed educators to learn about their views on sexual health education.

Including Multiple Research Questions

The sexual health education example (Box 8.1) includes two related but distinct research questions: "How do educators and learners interact during sexual health education?" and "What are educators' views on sexual health education?" In each research question, a different lens is provided on sexual health education, one focusing on interactions in the classroom and the other on educators' views.

Including Multiple Methods

By definition, a mixed methods or multimethod study includes multiple methods. The sexual health education example (Box 8.1) includes video observations and interviews. Each method constitutes another lens. Observations can show how people interact, and interviews can investigate their views. In the sexual health education example, methods and research questions are connected. Each method is used to answer one research question: Video recordings are used to learn about the interactions between educators and learners, whereas interviews are used to learn about educators' views of sexual health education. Because observations and interviews are both qualitative methods, the sexual health education example is a multimethod study, not a mixed methods study.

The sexual health education example demonstrates that it usually makes sense to start designing by formulating the research aim and overall research questions and then selecting appropriate methods. Researchers investigate how, using which methods, they can answer their research questions rather than seek questions that allow them to use their methods.

Including Multiple Stakeholder Perspectives

The preschool example (Box 8.2) includes lenses of multiple stakeholder groups: children, parents, and practitioners. The perspectives of the adult stakeholders, parents, and practitioners were obtained only through interviews. In addition to interviews and observations, the researchers used participatory tools, such as photographs and tours, to obtain a comprehensive view of the children's perspectives. The preschool example demonstrates that researchers usually start designing by including stakeholder groups and then selecting appropriate methods.

> **Box 8.2 Including Multiple Perspectives during the Redevelopment of a Preschool Outdoor Environment**
>
> A study by Clark and Moss (2005) accompanied the redevelopment of the outdoor environment of a preschool in the United Kingdom. The study investigated the perspectives on the outdoor environment of several stakeholders: 28 three- to four-year-olds, 4 parents, 4 preschool practitioners, and 1 manager. To discover the children's views of and experiences with the outdoor environment, the researchers observed the children and interviewed them. The children were also actively involved by taking photographs and organizing tours for researchers. Practitioners and parents were interviewed regarding their perspectives on how the children used the outdoor space. The researchers summarized the results for the objects in the outdoor space, particularly the playhouse, the caterpillar, and the fence.

Including Multiple Locations

In the preschool example (Box 8.2), each playground object provides a distinct perspective on the outdoor environment. The caterpillar, playhouse, and fence each form one unique location for children to play, and it is expected that children use the playhouse differently from the caterpillar. I call this including "multiple locations" because these objects refer to *where* the children play. Multiple locations can also be, for instance, the sites in a multi-site intervention, such as the individual schools that form part of a multi-school intervention.

The preschool example demonstrates that including multiple locations is often not about what locations to add but about what locations to distinguish within an until-then-undifferentiated environment. Because the preschool example (Box 8.2) included the entire outdoor environment, it automatically included the caterpillar, the playhouse, and the fence. It was the researchers' decision to identify these objects as diverse locations, each providing a varying lens on the children's play.

Including Multiple Organizational Levels

In the preschool example (Box 8.2), children, parents, and practitioners represent individuals with a specific perspective on the children's play. On other occasions, different groups of individuals represent different structural levels. For example, children could represent the individual level, practitioners the class level, and managers the school level. Such organizational levels are often included in multiple-methods research as well as in monomethod research. They form the basis of the well-known monomethod of quantitative [monomethod of quantitative multilevel analysis] multilevel analysis.

Including Groups Experiencing the Phenomenon to Varying Degrees

The procrastination example (Box 8.3) includes three groups of students that display different levels of procrastination: low, average, and high. The aim of this interview study is to investigate students' experiences with procrastination. It is to be expected

> **Box 8.3 Including Groups of Students with Different Levels of Academic Procrastination**
>
> Visser et al. (2018) studied academic procrastination (postponing study tasks) among first-year students in an elementary teacher education program in the Netherlands. In the study, 186 of 215 first-year students completed the Academic Procrastination State Inventory that measured procrastination levels. Based on the results, 22 students were invited for an interview: eight students with low, eight with average, and eight with high procrastination levels.

that these experiences will vary widely among students. In order to include a variety of experiences and to investigate whether there are systematic differences between groups of students, the researchers based their selection and their grouping on a criterion most likely strongly related to how often and how students experience procrastination: their procrastination level as measured by a quantitative questionnaire.

To summarize Step 1, multiple-methods researchers often include disparate methodological lenses to accommodate multiple lenses at other levels, such as multiple research questions, stakeholder perspectives, or structural levels. These multiple lenses are often complemented by including or distinguishing multiple locations or groups of individuals who experience the phenomenon to different degrees.

Step 2. In-Depth Exploration

After including multiple lenses, researchers explore the perspectives of each lens in depth. They do so by collecting and analyzing data for each perspective, for each lens, separately. In-depth exploration is necessary to obtain a deep understanding of each perspective. Understanding each perspective, in turn, is an essential requirement for obtaining an overall deep and inclusive understanding.

Exploration in the preschool example (Box 8.4) illustrated that one of the objects, the playhouse, was experienced differently by each stakeholder group. The children mentioned details about their play, but the parents did not. Children and parents did not mention aggressive play, but practitioners did. Different perspectives were also offered by different methods. Observations, photographs, and tours provided a perspective on how and how often the playhouse was used. The interviews provided information on how the playhouse was valued by the children, parents, and practitioners. The interviews supplemented the observations because observations could not have demonstrated that parents and practitioners considered the playhouse important or that children and practitioners valued the noise level and aggressive play negatively.

The procrastination example explored the perspectives of students with different levels of procrastination. For each group of low, average, and high procrastinators separately, Box 8.5 discusses how they viewed diverse aspects of procrastination:

> **Box 8.4 Exploration in the Preschool Example**
>
> One of the objects in the outdoor environment was the playhouse, comprising a wooden shed with a door and two windows into which four or more children could squeeze. Observations showed that the playhouse was used most of the time; it appeared in many photographs of the children and was included in the tours that the children organized for the researchers. The children's interviews provided details on their play in the playhouse but also mentioned its noise level. Parents considered the playhouse important for their children. Practitioners emphasized the significance of the playhouse but thought it promoted aggressive play because it was too small.

> **Box 8.5 Exploration in the Procrastination Example**
>
> Students with low procrastination levels had a strong motivation to become teachers; they enjoyed both the theoretical and practical aspects of their studies. Students with average procrastination were similarly motivated to become teachers. They were less interested in pedagogical theory and suffered from task aversion while working on theory-related tasks. Nevertheless, they kept studying, even when they disliked a task. Students with high levels of procrastination lacked a strong motivation to become teachers. They struggled with both theory-related and practical tasks and stopped learning.

their procrastination behaviors, their motivations to become teachers, and the theoretical and practical aspects of their studies.

In summary, in multiple-methods research, the inclusion of various lenses in Step 1 is followed by an exploration in Step 2, in which the perspective of each separate lens is explored in depth. Collecting and analyzing data from distinct perspectives results in separate conclusions for each perspective.

Step 3. Bringing the Perspectives Together – Integration

Step 2, exploration, results in separate conclusions for each perspective. In Step 3, these conclusions are brought together. In mixed methods research, this process is called *integration*, and its result is called *meta-inference*, a conclusion that surpasses (*meta*) individual qualitative and quantitative perspectives (Schoonenboom, 2022). Integration is considered the hallmark of mixed methods research (Bazeley, 2018; Moseholm & Fetters, 2017; Teddlie & Tashakkori, 2009). Without integration, we would not have a mixed methods study but separate studies for each perspective (Bryman, 2007) that happen to share some research components.

Box 8.6 contains the following meta-inference: "(1) Evidence showed comprehension that resulted from challenge and correction was superficial (2) *because* (3) educators expected comprehension to develop slowly and wanted to give attention to all the pupils." Box 8.6 shows how conclusions 1 and 3, obtained by exploring respective observations and interviews, are integrated. *Integration* means that these

> **Box 8.6 Integration in the Sexual Health Education Example**
>
> The observations by Finlay et al. (2015) demonstrated that when educators discussed comprehension problems with learners, they seemed satisfied with the superficial answers that learners gave and did not attempt to develop a deeper understanding. *The interviews provided a rationale for the educators' behavior.* Educators expected learners to pick up superficial "bits." They expected a deeper understanding to develop slowly and non-linearly, and they did not want to spend too much time on one individual at the expense of other group members and activities.

> **Box 8.7 Integration in the Preschool Example**
>
> One of the objects studied by Clark and Moss (2005) was the playhouse. Clark (2005, p. 34) stated the following:
>
> > Observing the children revealed the house to be a key resource for them. The children confirmed this through their photographs, the tour and their interviews. Parents also mentioned the house as an important space in the preschool. However, the interviews with practitioners showed that the house was a source of tension. They felt it was too small. The review with children, practitioners, and Learning through Landscapes **recognised these opposing views**.

conclusions are connected by a word that describes their relationship. The connecting word (2), *because*, reveals that conclusion 3 provides an *explanation* for conclusion 1.

Explanation is only one of the various ways in which conclusions can be integrated. In the preschool example (Box 8.7), connecting the conclusions of separate explorations leads to *confirmation* and *contradiction*. Confirmation was established by comparing the conclusions from children's observations, photographs, tours, and interviews with children and parents. They all confirmed the conclusion that the house was an important resource for the children, indicated in Box 8.7 by the words *confirmed* and *also*. Box 8.7 revealed a contradiction between the perspectives of the children and parents, who considered the playhouse a key resource, and the perspectives of the practitioners, who considered the playhouse a source of tension because it was too small. This contradiction is indicated in Box 8.7 by the word *however*. This contradiction was identified in the preschool study, as the review "recognised these *opposing views*."

In summary, in multiple-methods research, Step 2, Exploration, is followed by Step 3, Integration, in which the separate conclusions from each perspective are connected. Possible relationships include, but are not limited to, explanation, confirmation, or contradiction. Notably, integration does not necessarily mean creating one coherent whole in which the two conclusions align. One possible outcome is contradiction (Uprichard & Dawney, 2019), as the preschool example has demonstrated.

Step 4. Making a Decision in Practice

Integrating conclusions results in an inclusive understanding that can be used to inform a fourth step: making decisions in practice. A practical decision can, but need not, be part of a multiple-methods study.

In the integration step of the preschool example (Box 8.7), the perspectives on the playhouse proved to be contradictory. These opposing views are brought together in a practical decision to create a new space for the children where they can build their own temporary structures (Box 8.8). This decision preserves the positively valued function of the playhouse as a shelter in which children like to "sit, talk, and cook." Simultaneously, the problems of the playhouse's small size are avoided because children can set up several playhouses simultaneously.

The preschool example demonstrates how this decision in practice would not have been possible without exploring various perspectives. That the playhouse was too small was not mentioned in the children's interviews (because they did not say that it was too small, only that there was too much noise) or from the parents' perspective (possibly because they did not watch the children using the playhouse often enough). However, it was mentioned by the practitioners who had to deal with the playhouse daily. Without the inclusion of the practitioners' perspectives, the decision probably would have been to keep the playhouse as is, as both children and parents mentioned it as an important object but failed to notice that it was too small.

In summary, the deep understanding achieved through integration in Step 3 can be used in Step 4 to make a decision in practice. Such a decision is assumed to be of higher quality because it is based on more perspectives compared to a decision based on only one perspective.

Box 8.8 Making a Decision in Practice in the Preschool Example

The review with the stakeholders led to discussions about the playhouse. On one hand, the playhouse was recognized as an important object. On the other hand, it was considered too small and overcrowded, it encouraged aggressive play, and needed constant supervision by the practitioners. Based on these discussions, a decision was made to create "a newly turfed outdoor space for the children to build temporary structures where they can 'sit, talk, and cook'."

(Clark, 2005, p. 42)

Part II. Emergent Design

Multiple-Methods Research Design Is Emergent

Part I leaves the impression that multiple-methods studies proceed in a specific order. First, all lenses are included; subsequently, their perspectives are explored. Next, the conclusions of these explorations are brought together, and finally, the resulting insights are used to make a decision in practice. Such a fixed order would be a great help in designing a multiple-methods study because researchers could develop a complete study at the beginning and perform the study by simply executing their design.

This impression is false. Multiple-methods research designs are not fixed but *emergent*. Although some parts of a multiple-methods study can and should be planned in advance, others cannot. These non-plannable parts will considerably alter the initial plan and the study. Below, I discuss a few important emergent design elements and depict how they relate to the four research steps of Part I. I define as *emergent* any research activity that (1) requires that some data have been collected and analyzed previously and (2) builds on these data and conclusions. In particular, I discuss the following emergent elements: emerging aspects, focusing, searching for explanations, emerging data, and emerging subgroups.

Emerging Aspects

Aspects of a phenomenon are emergent when their importance was not known at the beginning of the study but discovered after a first exploration of the data, and these aspects are subsequently used as separate lenses. Emerging aspects occurred in all three real-life examples discussed in Part I. At the beginning of the sexual health education study, Finlay et al. (2015) did not know what interactions would be important. A first exploration of the observations showed that comprehension issues were important, and a decision was made to focus further analysis on this issue. At the beginning of the preschool study, Clark and Moss (2005) did not know which objects were important for the children; a first exploration of the data revealed that these were the playhouse, the caterpillar, and the fence. Hence, a decision was made to focus on in-depth explorations of these objects. At the beginning of the procrastination study, Visser et al. (2018) did not know which of all the known factors of procrastination proved to be notable in the students' experiences. These proved to be the motivation to become a teacher, the appreciation of pedagogical theory, and the appreciation of teaching practice. These aspects were explored in all three procrastination groups, and the conclusions were later connected.

Emerging Foci

Identifying emerging aspects will sometimes demonstrate that resources will not be sufficient to explore the initial research question for all the identified aspects in

Box 8.9 Focusing in the Sexual Health Education Example

According to Finlay et al. (2015, p. 330), "The interview schedule and resulting thematic analysis were partly informed by our analysis of the video data. In particular, we identified interactional trouble as an important issue in the sessions, and as a result the topic of comprehension formed one of the foci of the interviews and resulting analysis."

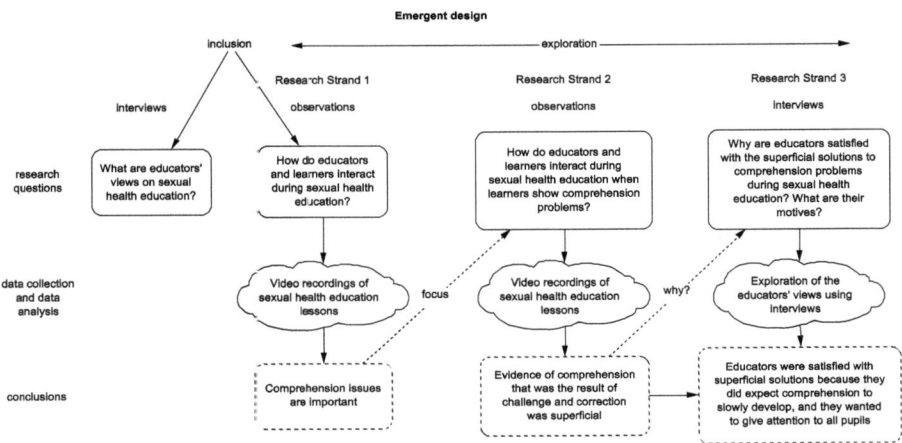

Figure 8.1 *Visualizing an emergent design: the sexual health education example.*

depth. That is why identifying emerging aspects can also lead to focusing when researchers decide to target studies on some aspects and not on others.

Box 8.9 illustrates how focusing on comprehension problems in the sexual health education example fulfills the two requirements of emerging elements. First, comprehension problems were not identified as a relevant category from the beginning, but they emerged as a critical issue during the initial explorations of the observations. Second, the importance of comprehension issues influenced other elements of the research process. Comprehension problems were selected as the focus of the remainder of the study. Therefore, they changed other elements of the design – in this case, the research question. Interview data *collection* centered on the research question, "How do educators and learners interact during sexual health education?" Nonetheless, the *analysis* used the data to answer the focused research question, "How do educators and learners interact during sexual health education when learners show comprehension problems?"

Figure 8.1 delineates how emerging elements affect which perspectives are explored and in what order. In Step 1, two research questions are included and, to answer them, two methods: interviews and observations. Next, Figure 8.1 shows how, in Step 2, three perspectives are *explored* separately. Each exploration constitutes one *research strand* – that is, one act of answering one research question by exploring a data set and drawing conclusions. For now, I focus on Research Strands 1 and 2. Although both involve observations, Research Strands 1 and 2 represent two perspectives that are explored separately. The reason is that their research questions are different: "How do educators and learners interact during sexual health education?" for Research Strand 1 and "How do educators and learners interact during sexual health education when learners show comprehension problems?" for Research Strand 2. Between Research Strand 1 and Research Strand 2, comprehension issues were identified as important, and the researchers decided to focus their research question on comprehension issues, indicated by an arrow between the conclusions of Research Strand 1 and the research question of Research Strand 2. In technical terms, the emerging element *focus* altered the research question used to explore the observations. Indeed, Research Strand 2 answers this focused research question, not the general research question of Research Strand 1: Evidence showed comprehension that was the result of challenge and correction was superficial.

Figure 8.1 represents a long tradition of visualizing mixed methods research designs. Ivankova et al. (2006) presented a visualization of a mixed methods research design as one vertical succession of research decisions and activities. Figure 8.1 builds on Teddlie and Tashakkori (2009), where research strands start in a different "column" and are connected by arrows. See, for a horizontal variant, Creswell and Plano Clark (2018) and, for other visualizations of mixed methods research designs, Bazeley (2018), Creamer (2018), Maxwell (2013), and Maxwell and Loomis (2003).

Searching for an Explanation

Figure 8.1 shows a second form of emergence in the sexual health education example. An arrow *why?* runs from the conclusions of Research Strand 2 to the research question of Research Strand 3, indicating that the researchers tried to find an explanation for their conclusions of their observations by analyzing the interviews. As already discussed under Integration (Box 8.6), the educators' satisfaction with superficial solutions (observations) can be explained by their view that they expected a deeper understanding to develop slowly and non-linearly and that they did not want to spend too much time on one individual at the expense of other group members and activities (interviews).

In multiple-methods research, searching for an explanation often emerges after unexpected results have been generated. In the sexual health education example, the superficiality of the answers in the observations was apparently judged to merit explanation. Overall, the sexual health education example is emergent because it contains two research decisions that could not be planned: the decision to focus on comprehension issues and the decision to search for an explanation for superficial solutions.

Finding an explanation plays an important role in much multiple-methods research. Sometimes, an explanation is sought for a striking phenomenon, as was the case in the sexual health education example. Often, an explanation is sought for

> **Box 8.10 Explaining Differences in the Procrastination Example**
>
> The results showed that students with low and intermediate levels of procrastination had a strong motivation to become a teacher, whereas students with high levels of procrastination lacked this motivation. Students with low procrastination levels enjoyed theory-related tasks, whereas students with average levels of procrastination suffered from task aversion for theory-related tasks, as did students with high levels of procrastination. Faced with theory-related tasks, their strong motivation to become teachers helped students with average levels of procrastination overcome their task aversion and continue studying. *Because* they lacked this motivation, students with high procrastination levels stopped learning.

> **Box 8.11 Emerging Data in the Preschool Example**
>
> In the preschool study, children were involved in data collection. According to Clark (2005, p. 31), "children use cameras to document 'what is important here'; they take the researcher on a tour and are in charge of how this is recorded and make maps using their photographs and drawings." One important object was the playhouse, as became visible in their photographs: "The house was in 12 of the 60 photographs taken by the children and chosen for inclusion in their books" (p. 41).

differences and contradictions between perspectives; this is a key reason for including these perspectives in the first place.

In the procrastination example, researchers had noticed during their explorations (Box 8.5) that the three groups with different procrastination levels diverged in their motivation to become a teacher, interest in didactic theory, interest in the practice of teaching, task aversion, and study behavior in the face of task aversion. In Box 8.10, these elements are brought together as the strong motivation to become a teacher is identified as a factor through which these differences in behavior can be explained: "Facing task aversion, students with a high procrastination level stopped learning *because* they lacked this strong motivation."

Emerging Data: Transforming Qualitative Data into Quantitative Data

Another emergent element is data resulting from the transformation of other data. In the preschool example (Box 8.11), the researchers transformed the qualitative photographs into quantitative data. Each photograph became one record with the variables "playhouse," "caterpillar," "fence," and so forth, that could be either absent or present. Such quantitative data are emergent because they are derived from qualitative data collected previously (i.e., the photographs). Called "quantitizing qualitative data" (Nzabonimpa, 2018; Sandelowski et al., 2009), this is a powerful method in mixed methods research. In the preschool example, the researchers determined the importance of each object by counting the number of times it was present in the photographs: The more often an object occurred, the higher its assumed importance for the children.

Emerging Subgroups: Simultaneously Creating and Exploring Perspectives

In the procrastination example, the three subgroups of low, average, and high procrastinators were determined before their perspectives were explored. In other studies, establishing groups and exploring them can go hand in hand, and it does so in, for instance, grounded theory and other qualitative research approaches (Morse et al., 2021).

Box 8.12 illustrates how subgroups can emerge through an analysis in which the quantitative and qualitative data of the same individuals are analyzed together. Based on the quantitative data, four groups emerged with different combinations of language test scores and GPAs: high/high, high/low, low/high, and low/low (where *high* means the highest score possible and *low* anything else). By exploring the qualitative data focusing on the low/high group, the researchers discovered that members of the low/high group recognized that they used strategies to compensate for their missing language knowledge, an awareness absent from the low/low group. Thus, by analyzing the quantitative and qualitative data simultaneously, Schoonenboom and Johnson discovered an emerging group: students who used strategies to compensate for their lack of language skills and, consequently, obtained the highest GPAs possible. (For a detailed description of this powerful technique, see Schoonenboom and Johnson, 2021.)

In summary, multiple-methods research is emergent. Elements such as emerging aspects, foci, data, subgroups, or searches for explanations arise during a study after initial explorations have yielded the first conclusions. Emerging elements alter the course of a study and lead to improvements; however, this also means that a study cannot be completely planned.

Box 8.12 Emerging Subgroups in a Study on the Relationship between Language Problems and Academic Achievement

Schoonenboom and Johnson (2021) used quantitative and qualitative data reported by Lee and Greene (2007), who studied international students at one university in the United States, to examine the relationships between language problems and academic achievement. From a quantitative viewpoint, these concepts were operationalized as a student's score on a language test at the beginning of their first semester and their grade point average (GPA) at the end of that semester. From a qualitative perspective, these relationships were examined in interviews with students. Schoonenboom and Johnson (2021) created a simple table containing one record for each student, along with their language test score, GPA, and a quote from their interview. They sorted and resorted their table to uncover patterns. One group of four students emerged. Despite their language problems, members of this group still obtained the highest GPAs. Further exploration of the quotes showed that three of the four students in this group referred to compensation strategies, while none of the students with language problems and less than the highest possible GPA did so. Correspondingly, Schoonenboom and Johnson (2021) were able to formulate a hypothesis for further research: Language problems affect international students' GPAs unless they deliberately use compensation strategies.

Part III. Combining Qualitative and Quantitative Data Research Components

Introduction

Part III completes this chapter on mixed methods and multimethod research. It considers mixed methods research from the question, "How can we combine qualitative and quantitative research components, especially qualitative and quantitative data?" The answers to this question make use of various concepts, including meaningful connections, purposes of mixing, theoretical drive, timing, and fully integrated research designs. This section introduces these concepts and connects them to the four steps of the mixed methods design process of Part I, the emerging element of Part II, and the four real-life examples discussed throughout.

Meaningful Connections

Commonly, mixed methods research is defined as (1) a combination of quantitative and qualitative data collection and data analysis that (2) are meaningfully connected or integrated (Bryman, 2006, 2008; Creswell & Plano Clark, 2018; Mertens et al., 2016). Such meaningful connections between different data sets are visible in all four real-life examples. In the procrastination example, quantitative data are used to draw a sample with three groups for the qualitative interviews. In the language problems example, quantitative and qualitative data are combined in a table and subsequently analyzed together. In the preschool example, different perspectives on the playhouse, involving both qualitative and quantitative data, were scrutinized for agreement and distinctions. The sexual health education example is an exception because it contains meaningful connections between two qualitative data sets: The views expressed in the interviews were used to explain the observed behavior in the observations. Therefore, it is not a mixed methods study but a multimethod study.

Purposes of Mixing

Including both qualitative and quantitative data starts with the question: "What is the purpose of combining qualitative and quantitative data sets in this study?" Such *purposes of mixing* have been classified in various ways (Bryman, 2006; Greene et al., 1989). According to Greene et al. (1989), mixing can serve five purposes. Four combine qualitative and quantitative data sets that are analyzed independently. *Triangulation* involves comparing conclusions from two or more sets of data to determine whether they are the same or different. Triangulation occurred in the preschool example, where the perspectives of parents, children, and practitioners on the playhouse were compared. The comparison revealed that children's and parents' perspectives agreed, as indicated by the words of confirmation, and the practitioners' perspectives disagreed, as indicated by the word *although*.

For the purpose of *expansion*, different methods are used to study different aspects of a phenomenon. This occured in the sexual health education example, where interviews were used to study the views of educators and observations to research their behavior. This example also includes the purpose of *complementarity*, in which the results from the interviews were used to enhance, elaborate, and clarify the results of the observations – in this case, by providing an explanation. The purpose of *initiation* is to seek new and fresh perspectives and contradictions. Initiation occurred in the language problems example, where existing data were analyzed by searching for groups with contrasting behaviors.

For the purpose of *development*, one data set is not analyzed but instead used to develop a component of a research strand that includes a data set of the other type. For instance, a development purpose underlies the transformation of qualitative data into quantitative data, because its aim is to create a data set, not to analyze data. A similar development purpose underlies the use of quantitative data to develop a sample for a qualitative study, as was done in the procrastination example. Again, the quantitative data were not analyzed but were used to create three groups with varying levels of procrastination. Using quantitative data for sampling is a powerful technique in mixed methods research (also called "connecting"; see Guetterman & Fetters, 2022). Had Visser et al. (2018) solely included a convenience sample of students with high procrastination levels (as previous qualitative studies had done), they could not have identified the essential distinctions that play a role in procrastinating.

Purposes of mixing are useful but come with a caveat. Although originally conceptualized as a way to classify mixed methods studies, Greene et al. (1989) already recognized that a mixed methods study can have several purposes for mixing. Schoonenboom et al. (2018) went further by stating that mixed methods studies usually include several purposes of mixing and that purposes of mixing should be used to describe what is happening *within* a study, not as a classification *of* a study. Thus, researchers should describe purposes of mixing within their study.

Timing

An often-used dimension to distinguish mixed methods designs is *timing*: the order of and dependence between qualitative and quantitative data collection and data analysis (Creswell & Plano Clark, 2018; Guest, 2013; Schoonenboom & Johnson, 2017; Teddlie & Tashakkori, 2009). Related to timing, the procrastination example is a *sequential* design because the quantitative questionnaire precedes the qualitative interviews, and the design of the qualitative interviews depends on the results from the questionnaire. The preschool example would be called *concurrent* because its various data were collected simultaneously and independently. Only at the end of the study were they brought together in a review (Box 8.8).

Describing mixed methods designs as concurrent or sequential can be useful for giving a first impression of a study. If we look more closely, however, we see that this dimension is too broad to capture a design as a whole. In the health education example, for instance, data collection is concurrent. The interview and observational data were collected at once and were independent. The data analysis, however, proceeded sequentially. The outcomes of the observations first provided a focus and later a research question for the data analysis of the interviews: What were the motives and reasons for educators' satisfaction with superficial solutions? (See Figure 8.1.)

As we have argued in Part II, a mixed methods research design is emergent. Emergence always means a change compared to the initial design and, thus, constitutes a sequential element. What to do next depends on the outcomes of what was analyzed first. Accordingly, purely concurrent designs do not exist because they assume that everything can be planned beforehand. Restricted to data collection, though, the distinction between concurrent and sequential can be very helpful because it relates to an important design decision: Do we want to collect our data concurrently, at the same time (as in sexual health education, the preschool, and the language problems example), or sequentially, one after the other (as in the procrastination example)? Such timing is an important consideration in any study in which more than one data set is collected.

Theoretical Drive

Mixed methods studies vary in the extent to which one of the components, qualitative or quantitative, is dominant, also called its "theoretical drive" (Morse & Niehaus, 2009). In a study with a quantitative theoretical drive, the quantitative component forms a complete study on its own, and the qualitative component plays a minor supplementary role. In a qualitative-dominant study, this situation is reversed. A qualitative theoretical drive can be found in the preschool and procrastination examples. In the preschool example, the quantitative component of counting the photographs formed a very small part of the entire study. In the procrastination example, a quantitative questionnaire was used to distinguish student groups in an otherwise qualitative study. Identifying a theoretical drive can be useful in deciding what to call and how to advertise a study. Visser et al. (2018), for instance, called their procrastination study a qualitative study, not a mixed methods study, because the role of the quantitative data was secondary.

Sometimes, however, it is not really possible to establish a theoretical drive. In the language problems example, both quantitative and qualitative data play a major role in analyzing the data. The quantitative data play a role in discovering different student groups; however, they can do so because of the resemblances and variations in the qualitative data – the student quotes. Such a study, in which neither the qualitative nor the quantitative component is dominant, is called an equal-status mixed methods study (Johnson et al., 2007).

Fully Integrated Mixed Methods Research Designs

As mentioned earlier, integration is considered the hallmark of mixed methods research. Without integration, we would not have a mixed methods study but separate studies for each perspective (Bryman, 2007) that happen to share some research components. Several authors have extended this idea by stating that the more integration or "mixing" a study contains, the better it is (Bazeley & Kemp, 2012; Creamer, 2018; Teddlie & Tashakkori, 2009). Researchers should strive for a "fully integrated" mixed methods design, in which mixing occurs in all stages of a study. This includes mixing methods, paradigms, methodologies, rationales, worldviews, research questions, units of analysis, sampling, instrument development, data collection, data analysis, conclusions (resulting in a meta-inference), etc. (Creamer, 2018; Fetters & Molina-Azorin, 2017; Yin, 2006).

Developing a fully integrated design can be worthwhile if one proceeds cautiously. I agree that it often makes sense to include multiple perspectives at various levels. However, I do not think that more mixing – that is, including more perspectives – is always better. For instance, the preschool example is not a better study than the procrastination study because the former includes disparate lenses at the level of stakeholder perspectives, research questions, methods, and locations, whereas the latter includes only lenses at the level of groups affected differently by the phenomenon. To understand the added value of including multiple perspectives, it is often helpful to compare them to including only one perspective. From that viewpoint, the procrastination study is "better" because it included the perspectives of students differently affected by procrastination, whereas former qualitative studies only included convenience samples of students who experienced procrastination.

Summary and Recommendations

This chapter has demonstrated how researchers can design mixed methods and multimethod research. Part I explained the four design steps of inclusion, exploration, integration, and making a decision in practice. Part II showed that multiple-methods research is emergent and discussed the most important emergent elements. Part III described the most important concepts for combining qualitative and quantitative data sets.

The conclusions of each part can be summarized in a list of recommendations provided in Box 8.13.

I started this chapter by remarking that designing a study with multiple perspectives is difficult. I do not think that this chapter has made this task easier, but I hope to have made designing multiple-methods studies more manageable. I hope that the

---

Box 8.13 Recommendations for Designing Mixed Methods and Multimethod Research

Decisions at the Beginning of a Study

Decisions about how and why to combine qualitative and quantitative data (Part III):

- Consider whether you want to collect data concurrently or sequentially.
- Consider your theoretical drive (if you have one).
- Consider several purposes of mixing that might be relevant to your study.

Box 8.13

Decisions related to the four steps of multiple-methods design (Part I):

- Decide at what level you wish to include different lenses.
  - Will you include varying research questions or stakeholder perspectives?
  - How does this affect the use of disparate methods?
  - Will you include distinct locations, levels, and groups differently affected by the phenomenon?

Decisions Relatively Early in a Study (Parts I and II)

- Explore each perspective separately.
- Use your first exploration and data to:
  - notice emerging aspects or emerging groups for separate exploration;
  - focus on one aspect or group if limited resources require this.

Decisions Relatively Late in a Study (Parts I and II)

- Bring the conclusions of your separate explorations together in a meta-inference.
  - Notice contrasting or contradictory findings that need further exploration and explanation.

Decision at the End of a Study (Part I)

- (If applicable) Use the resulting deeper understanding to make a decision in practice.

Decision at All Stages

- Visualize your design.

Box 8.13

To make these guidelines more concrete, we will now apply them to one of the real-life examples of this chapter, the preschool study.

Decisions at the Beginning of a Study

Decisions about how and why to combine qualitative and quantitative data (Part III):

- Consider whether you want to collect data concurrently or sequentially.

In the preschool study, various types of data are collected and analyzed over a longer period of time. The data sources are collected and analyzed simultaneously and independently from one another, making this a concurrent design.

- Consider your theoretical drive (if you have one).

The goal of this study is to understand how children use the playground objects and how this use is valued by various stakeholders. This understanding will be used in making a decision on how to further develop the outdoor environment. Thus, the emphasis is on understanding rather than generalization, making the theoretical drive qualitative.

Box 8.13

- Consider several purposes of mixing that might be relevant to your study.

The preschool study involves a triangulation purpose because it investigates the extent to which the perspectives of the various stakeholder groups on the playhouse are the same or different. It also involves an expansion purpose because different methods are used for answering different research questions: The use of the playground objects is investigated using observational methods, the value of the playground objects using interviews. In addition to searching for confirmation (triangulation), the study explores dissonance among stakeholder groups, and it therefore includes an initiation purpose.

Decisions Related to the Four Steps of Multiple-Methods Design (Part I)

- Decide at what level you wish to include different lenses.
  - Will you include varying research questions or stakeholder perspectives?

The preschool example includes the perspectives of children, practitioners, parents, and preschool management. It includes two related research questions: How do children use "important objects" in the outdoor environment? and How do stakeholders value how children use the important objects?

  - How does this affect the use of disparate methods?

Observational methods (researchers' observations, children's photographs, and tours) are used to investigate how children use important objects, whereas interviews are used to investigate how stakeholders valued their object use. These methods complement each other: observations are very useful to observe how the children use the playground objects, but tell us little about how they are valued, whereas interviews are very useful to find out how the playground objects are valued. Their role in finding out how children use the playground objects is limited.

The use of methods is also affected by the different stakeholder groups. Given children's limited and diverse abilities to express themselves in language, the interviews are adapted to the children's linguistic capabilities, and photographs are included as a method of data collection that enables children to express their vision on the playground objects.

  - Will you include distinct locations, levels, and groups differently affected by the phenomenon?

Yes, each playground object is considered on its own and analyzed separately.

Decisions Relatively Early in a Study (Parts I and II)

- Explore each perspective separately.

The photographs, tours, observations, and interviews are conducted separately and analyzed separately.

- Use your first exploration and data to:
  - Notice emerging aspects or emerging groups for separate exploration.

> **Box 8.13**
>
> *No emerging aspects or groups are identified.*
>
> - Focus on one aspect or group if limited resources require this.
>
> In the first rounds of data analysis, important objects are identified, and these form the focus of further investigation.
>
> **Decisions Relatively Late in a Study (Parts I and II)**
>
> - Bring the conclusions of your separate explorations together in a meta-inference.
>
> *The conclusions of exploring the photographs, the tour, the children's interviews, and the interviews with parents are compared, which results in the conclusion that they point in the same direction: the playhouse is an often used and positively valued playground object. Comparison with the practitioners' views leads to a more nuanced overall conclusion or meta-inference: in addition to being often used and a positively valued playground object, the playhouse is also a source of tension because it is too small.*
>
> - Notice contrasting or contradictory findings that need explanation.
>
> *The conclusions from interviewing the practitioners contradict those from observing and interviewing the children and parents. This is noticed, but in the end, no attempt is made to find an explanation. Instead, the contradiction forms the basis for a decision.*
>
> **Decision at the End of the Study (Part I)**
>
> - (If applicable) Use the resulting deeper understanding to make a decision in practice.
>
> *A decision is made to create a new space for the children where they can build their own temporary structures (Box 8.8). This decision preserves the positively valued function of the playhouse as a shelter in which children like to "sit, talk, and cook." Simultaneously, the problems of the playhouse's small size are avoided because children can set up several playhouses simultaneously.*

discussion of its four steps, emerging elements, the concepts for combining quantitative and qualitative data sets, and the resulting recommendations will support researchers in designing multiple-methods studies that obtain a deeper and more inclusive understanding than would be possible using one method alone.

References

Anguera, M. T., Blanco-Villaseñor, A., Losada, J. L., Sánchez-Algarra, P., & Onwuegbuzie, A. J. (2018). Revisiting the difference between mixed methods and multimethods: Is it all in the name? *Quality & Quantity, 52*(6), 2757–2770. https://doi.org/10.1007/s11135-018-0700-2

Bazeley, P. (2018). *Integrating Analyses in Mixed Methods Research*. SAGE Publications.

Bazeley, P., & Kemp, L. (2012). Mosaics, triangles, and DNA: Metaphors for integrated analysis in mixed methods research. *Journal of Mixed Methods Research*, *6*, 55–72. https://doi.org/10.1177/1558689811419514

Bryman, A. (2006). Integrating quantitative and qualitative research: How is it done? *Qualitative Research*, *6*(1), 97–113. https://doi.org/10.1177/1468794106058877

Bryman, A. (2007). Barriers to integrating quantitative and qualitative research. *Journal of Mixed Methods Research*, *1*(1), 8–22. https://doi.org/10.1177/2345678906290531

Bryman, A. (2008). Why do researchers integrate/combine/mesh/blend/mix/merge/fuse quantitative and qualitative research? In M. M. Bergman (ed.), *Advances in Mixed Methods Research* (pp. 87–100). SAGE Publications. https://doi.org/10.4135/9780857024329.d9

Clark, A. (2005). Ways of seeing: Using the Mosaic approach to listen to young children's perspectives. In A. Clark, A. T. Kjørholt, & P. Moss (eds.), *Beyond Listening: Children's Perspectives on Early Childhood Services* (pp. 29–49). Policy Press.

Clark, A., & Moss, P. (2005). *Spaces to Play: More Listening to Young Children Using the Mosaic Approach*. National Children's Bureau.

Creamer, E. G. (2018). *An Introduction to Fully Integrated Mixed Methods Research*. SAGE Publications.

Creswell, J. W., & Plano Clark, V. L. (2018). *Designing and Conducting Mixed Methods Research*, 3rd ed. SAGE Publications.

Fetters, M. D., & Molina-Azorin, J. F. (2017). The journal of mixed methods research starts a new decade: The mixed methods research integration trilogy and its dimensions. *Journal of Mixed Methods Research*, *11*(3), 291–307. https://doi.org/10.1177/1558689817714066

Finlay, W. M. L., Rohleder, P., Taylor, N., & Culfear, H. (2015). "Understanding" as a practical issue in sexual health education for people with intellectual disabilities: A study using two qualitative methods. *Health Psychology*, *34*(4), 328–338. https://doi.org/10.1037/hea0000128

Flick, U. (2018). *Doing Triangulation and Mixed Methods*. SAGE Publications.

Greene, J. C. (2008). Is mixed methods social inquiry a distinctive methodology? *Journal of Mixed Methods Research*, *2*(1), 7–22. https://doi.org/10.1177/1558689807309969

Greene, J. C., Caracelli, V. J., & Graham, W. F. (1989). Toward a conceptual framework for mixed-method evaluation designs. *Educational Evaluation and Policy Analysis*, *11*(3), 255–274. https://doi.org/10.2307/1163620

Guest, G. (2013). Describing mixed methods research: An alternative to typologies. *Journal of Mixed Methods Research*, *7*(2), 141–151. https://doi.org/10.1177/1558689812461179

Guetterman, T. C., & Fetters, M. D. (2022). Data visualization in the context of integrated analyses. In J. H. Hitchcock & A. J. Onwuegbuzie (eds.), *The Routledge Handbook for Advancing Integration in Mixed Methods Research* (pp. 301–323). Routledge. https://doi.org/10.4324/9780429432828-6

Ivankova, N. V. (2015). *Mixed Methods Applications in Action Research: From Methods to Community Action*. SAGE Publications.

Ivankova, N. V., Creswell, J. W., & Stick, S. L. (2006). Using mixed-methods sequential explanatory design: From theory to practice. *Field Methods*, *18*(1), 3–20. https://doi.org/10.1177/1525822x05282260

Johnson, R. B., Onwuegbuzie, A. J., & Turner, L. A. (2007). Toward a definition of mixed methods research. *Journal of Mixed Methods Research*, *1*(2), 112–133. https://doi.org/10.1177/1558689806298224

Lee, Y.-J., & Greene, J. (2007). The predictive validity of an ESL placement test: A mixed methods approach. *Journal of Mixed Methods Research*, *1*(4), 366–389. https://doi.org/10.1177/1558689807306148

Maxwell, J. A. (2013). *Qualitative Research Design: An Interactive Approach*, 3rd ed. SAGE Publications.

Maxwell, J. A., & Loomis, D. M. (2003). Mixed methods design: An alternative approach. In A. Tashakkori & C. Teddlie (eds.), *Handbook of Mixed Methods in Social & Behavioral Research* (pp. 241–271). SAGE Publications.

Maxwell, J. A., & Mittapalli, K. (2010). Realism as a stance for mixed methods research. In A. Tashakkori & C. Teddlie (eds.), *SAGE Handbook of Mixed Methods in Social & Behavioral Research*, 2nd ed. (pp. 145–167). SAGE Publications.

Mertens, D. M. (2018). *Mixed Methods Design in Evaluation*. SAGE Publications.

Mertens, D. M., Bazeley, P., Bowleg, L., Fielding, N., Maxwell, J., Molina-Azorin, J. F., & Niglas, K. (2016). *The Future of Mixed Methods: A Five Year Projection to 2020*. Mixed Methods International Research Association task force report. https://mmira.wildapricot.org/resources/Documents/MMIRA%20task%20force%20report%20Jan2016%20final.pdf

Morse, J. M., Bowers, B. J., Charmaz, K., Clarke, A. E., Corbin, J., & Porr, C. J. (eds.). (2021). *Developing Grounded Theory: The Second Generation Revisited*, 2nd ed. Routledge.

Morse, J. M., & Niehaus, L. (2009). *Mixed Method Design: Principles and Procedures*. Left Coast Press.

Moseholm, E., & Fetters, M. D. (2017). Conceptual models to guide integration during analysis in convergent mixed methods studies. *Methodological Innovations*, *10*(2), 1–11. https://doi.org/10.1177/2059799117703118

Nzabonimpa, J. P. (2018). Quantitizing and qualitizing (im-)possibilities in mixed methods research. *Methodological Innovations*, *11*(2), 1–16. https://doi.org/10.1177/2059799118789021

Sandelowski, M., Voils, C. I., & Knafl, G. (2009). On quantitizing. *Journal of Mixed Methods Research*, *3*(3), 208–222. https://doi.org/10.1177/1558689809334210

Schoonenboom, J. (2018). Mixed methods in early childhood education. In M. Fleer & B. van Oers (eds.), *International Handbook of Early Childhood Education* (pp. 269–293). Springer. https://doi.org/10.1007/978-94-024-0927-7_11

(2022). Developing the meta-inference in mixed methods research through successive integration of claims. In J. H. Hitchcock & A. J. Onwuegbuzie (eds.), *The Routledge Handbook for Advancing Integration in Mixed Methods Research* (pp. 55–70). Routledge. https://doi.org/10.4324/9780429432828-6

(2023). Ten mixed methods integration strategies for obtaining a detailed understanding. In R. Tierney, F. Rizvi, K. Ercikan, & G. Smith (eds.), *International Encyclopedia of Education*, 4th ed. Elsevier. https://doi.org/10.1016/B978-0-12-818630-5.11045-0

Schoonenboom, J., & Johnson, R. B. (2017). How to construct a mixed methods research design. *Kölner Zeitschrift für Soziologie und Sozialpsychologie*, *69*(2), 107–131. https://doi.org/10.1007/s11577-017-0454-1

(2021). The case comparison table: A joint display for constructing and sorting simple tables as mixed analysis. In A. J. Onwuegbuzie & R. B. Johnson (eds.), *The*

Routledge Reviewer's Guide to Mixed Methods Analysis (pp. 277–288). Routledge. https://doi.org/10.4324/9780203729434-24

Schoonenboom, J., Johnson, R. B., & Froehlich, D. E. (2018). Combining multiple purposes of mixing within a mixed methods research design. *International Journal of Multiple Research Approaches*, *10*(1), 271–282. https://doi.org/10.29034/ijmra.v10n1a17

Tashakkori, A. M., Johnson, R. B., & Teddlie, C. B. (2021). *Foundations of Mixed Methods Research: Integrating Quantitative and Qualitative Approaches in the Social and Behavioral Sciences*, 2nd rev. ed. SAGE Publications.

Teddlie, C. B., & Tashakkori, A. (2009). *Foundations of Mixed Methods Research: Integrating Quantitative and Qualitative Approaches in the Social and Behavioral Sciences*. SAGE Publications.

Uprichard, E., & Dawney, L. (2019). Data diffraction: Challenging data integration in mixed methods research. *Journal of Mixed Methods Research*, *13*(1), 19–32. https://doi.org/10.1177/1558689816674650

Visser, L., Korthagen, F. A., & Schoonenboom, J. (2018). Differences in learning characteristics between students with high, average, and low levels of academic procrastination: Students' views on factors influencing their learning. *Frontiers in Psychology*, *9*(808). https://doi.org/10.3389/fpsyg.2018.00808

Yin, R. K. (2006). Mixed methods research: Are the methods genuinely integrated or merely parallel? *Research in the Schools*, *13*(1), 41–47.

PART II

Important Methodological Considerations

9 Reliability

Tenko Raykov

Abstract

This chapter is concerned with reliability as a key indicator of measurement quality in behavioral and social science research. It commences with a discussion of the basics and a definition of the reliability coefficient. The following section deals with the meaning, interpretation, and utility of the reliability concept. Subsequently, the focus is on the evaluation of reliability as well as its discrepancy from the popular coefficient alpha that has been widely used for a number of decades as an index related to reliability. The large-sample behavior of the alpha and scale reliability estimates is then discussed, as is the relationship between the reliability coefficient and that of standardized reliability. The conclusion points out the limitations of the procedures for reliability evaluation discussed in the chapter.

Keywords: Classical Test Theory, Congeneric Test Model, Estimation, Population Discrepancy, Reliability, Unidimensionality

Introduction

Reliability is a key quality index of behavioral and social science measurement as well as of measurement in most empirical sciences. Informally speaking, reliability of a measuring instrument, such as a psychometric scale or a single item, has to do with the repeatability of the results obtainable with the instrument. I provide below a formal definition of this foundational concept for the chapter, but already at the outset I would like to mention that high reliability is in general a necessary condition for a high-quality measurement process.

Chapter 10 in this volume discusses validity, which is of utmost importance for measurement of human behavior, and one may well say also for any evaluation process in a science where measurement is of relevance. I address the relationship between reliability and validity later in this chapter. It is worth pointing out here though that while high reliability is not sufficient for high validity, the latter cannot be achieved without reliable measurement in the vast majority of settings of theoretical and empirical importance in the social and behavioral disciplines (e.g., Raykov & Marcoulides, 2011).

The plan of this chapter is as follows. I begin with a discussion of the basics and a definition of reliability. In the following section, I am concerned with the meaning, interpretation, and utility of the reliability concept. Subsequently, I focus on the evaluation of reliability as well as its discrepancy from the popular coefficient alpha that has been widely used for a number of decades in many disciplines. I then address the large-sample behavior of alpha and scale reliability estimators, as well as the relationship between the reliability coefficient and that of standardized reliability. In the conclusion, I deal with the limitations of the procedures for reliability evaluation covered in the chapter.

The Basics and Definition of Reliability

Reliability can be approached within a factor analysis (FA) framework or a classical test theory (CTT) framework. A coherent discussion of reliability benefits substantially from the use of CTT. CTT is more than a century old and its origins can be seen as closely linked to the far-reaching work by Charles Spearman around the turn of the twentieth century (Spearman, 1904). The fullest coverage of CTT is found in Zimmerman (1975; see also Lord & Novick, 1968).

I commence the process of defining reliability at the population level with the observation that most measurements in the social and behavioral sciences, before they have been conducted, can be considered random variables. Denote by X a measurement of interest that is defined as the observed result obtainable when measuring a given personal or related characteristic under consideration (or of a unit of analysis) in a study of a behavioral phenomenon. For example, when evaluating anxiety, X can be a patient's response to a given question in a well-established scale of anxiety, or alternatively the overall scale score.

Perhaps the first feature of X that can be noted is that in contemporary empirical research X is bounded from both below and above in any population Π of interest. For example, with discrete measurement, a five-response-options Likert item has lowest and highest numbered categories, once numerically coded; these categories are usually symbolized as 1 and 5, or alternatively 0 and 4, respectively. They represent, along with the integer numbers between them, the available corresponding answer categories such as "strongly disagree," "disagree," "neither agree nor disagree," "agree," and "strongly agree." As an alternative example of continuous measurement (or one that could be treated as such), reaction time to a cognitive stimulus can never be negative. In addition, for a population of concern, one could find a sufficiently large number that cannot be meaningfully exceeded by a member of that population. Similarly, a question in an anxiety scale, that is scored from 1 to 7, cannot have a score lower than 1 or larger than 7.

Further examples can be easily given from other experimental or observational settings that all share the same property. Specifically, the individual realization of the pertinent random variable X representing the recorded measurement – that is usually referred to as observed score – cannot be smaller than a lower bound (a number denoted L) or larger than an upper bound (denoted U). According to a well-known result in statistics (e.g., Arnold, 1990), the mean of a random variable like X that is bounded from below and above always exists (i.e., is a finite number). Denoting it by

T [i.e., $T = \mathcal{E}(X)$ where $\mathcal{E}(.)$ symbolizes this mean (expectation)], and referring to the latter as the true score associated with X, we observe that

$$X = \mathcal{E}(X) + (X - \mathcal{E}(X)) \tag{1}$$

always holds as a simple tautology relationship. In Equation (1), the difference $E = X - \mathcal{E}(X)$ has a mean of 0 and is referred to as error score associated with the observed score X and its true score T (e.g., Raykov & Marcoulides, 2011). That is, based on (1) and the preceding discussion, the relationship

$$X = T + E \tag{2}$$

is an identity that is always valid in contemporary social and behavioral research.

In this chapter, and in much of the measurement literature, Equation (2) is referred to as the CTT decomposition, or the CTT equation. I hasten to add that (2) is not a model in any strict sense (and certainly not the CTT model), despite references to it as such in some substantive and quantitative sources (e.g., Embretson & Reise, 2000). The reason is that Equation (2) does not represent an assumption or statement that can in principle be wrong. Rather, the decomposition (2) is always true and thus cannot be disconfirmed. Models for multiple random variables like X can be constructed, however, that can be referred to as CTT-based models. They are counterparts of useful factor analysis models for behavioral measurement and are discussed in detail elsewhere (e.g., Raykov, 2012).

The next readily made observation is that, in empirical research, it is rather unusual that a set of individual measurements carried out in a given population or sample, designated X_i, are all the same (where the subindex i denotes observation – i.e., unit of analysis: respondent, patient, client, student, or aggregates of such). Thus, practically always – unless with very low and unacceptable quality measurement – there are individual differences associated with the observations arising in behavioral measurement. A key numerical index capturing these differences is the well-known variance, denoted $Var(X)$ (for the variable X; e.g., Casella & Berger, 2002). I also note that, due to X being bounded from below and above, as mentioned earlier, the variance of X similarly exists and is a finite number (e.g., Arnold, 1990). As just discussed, this variance is typically also positive. For example, a scale of neuroticism is unlikely to yield the same scale score for all persons studied, and hence its sample (population) variance will exist and will typically be positive.

With the preceding developments in mind, on the assumption of $Var(X) > 0$ advanced for the rest of the chapter, the reliability coefficient associated with the measurement X in a population under consideration, Π, is defined as

$$r_X = Var(T)/Var(X), \tag{3}$$

where $Var(T)$ is the associated true score variance in Π (and "/" stands for division). I stress that the reliability coefficient (3) is well-defined. This is because the true variance $Var(T)$ exists as well (i.e., is a finite number), due to the mean of X being similarly bounded from below and above in Π (in fact, by the same aforementioned numbers L and U, respectively; cf. Arnold, 1990).

In the rest of this chapter, there is no need to assume that true individual differences always exist (i.e., that $Var(T) > 0$ is the case). In fact, if $Var(T) = 0$ holds, then the reliability coefficient ρ_X results as 0 from Equation (3) and is thus well-defined. In the remainder, we will not be interested in the less widely used notion of reliability index, defined as the positive square root of (3) (e.g., Raykov & Marcoulides, 2011). Therefore, I will frequently utilize the reference "reliability" for the reliability coefficient throughout the chapter.

Taking a look again at the definitional Equation (3), it is worth stressing its implication that reliability depends on both the behavioral measure X of interest and the population Π in which it is considered. For example, different items in a multi-component measuring instrument – such as a scale, test, inventory, composite, self-report, subscale, test-battery, testlet, subtest, questionnaire, survey or a part thereof – can and usually will have different reliability in any population of concern as well as across populations. Also, different measuring instruments can and usually will have distinct reliabilities in any population or in different populations under investigation. This feature of the reliability coefficient, depending on both measure and population rather than being determined by the given measure only, has been incorrectly implied in some literature to be a deficiency of the coefficient (cf. McDonald, 1999). However, it would not be logically possible to agree with such a view. The reason is that also, say, the mean, variance, or standard deviation do depend on the random variable (measure) *and* population under consideration. That is, this dependence on measure and population cannot be logically seen as a deficiency of the reliability concept, and in fact is to be expected from it.

In conclusion of this section, I wish to emphasize also that the reliability coefficient is defined for any measure with positive observed variance. That is, irrespective of whether the measure X is (i) a highly discrete item such as say a binary or binary scored item (question, problem, or task), or (ii) a polytomous ordinal item such as a Likert type question, or (iii) a continuous measure or scale/test component, its reliability coefficient does exist as long as its variance is positive.

The Meaning, Interpretation, and Utility of Reliability

The definition of reliability in Equation (3) implies that it is the proportion of true individual differences in observed differences. Hence, reliability is the degree to which the manifest measure X captures the extent to which there is variability in the underlying latent dimension of interest. Further, if considering the regression model $X = a + bT + u$, where u is the residual term and α and β its intercept and slope, it can be shown that the reliability coefficient is the R-square index if "predicting" X based on T (cf., e.g., Raykov & Marcoulides, 2011; Agresti & Finlay, 2008; see next). Conversely, based on the similarly contemplated model $T = g + dX + v$, with v being its residual term and γ and δ its intercept and slope, reliability is also the R-square index when "predicting" T based on X. None of these two conceptual regressions or "predictions" can be carried out in an empirical setting, since unlike the manifest score X its true score T is not observed. However, keeping these contemplated regressions in mind is useful in more than one way. Specifically, they help us observe that reliability is closely tied to a key index of model fit, such as the R-square, in the widely used regression analysis framework in the social and behavioral sciences.

An alternative expression of reliability also follows from Equation (3), when one realizes that, due to its above definition, the true score T is unrelated to the error score E (e.g., Zimmerman, 1975). As a consequence, that equation entails the following observed variance decomposition:

$$Var(X) = Var(T) + Var(E), \quad (4)$$

with $Var(E)$ standing for error variance. I explicitly state here this instructive variance decomposition, due to its relevance for much of the remainder of the chapter. Next, with Equation (4) in mind, from (3) one readily sees that

$$r_X = 1 - Var(E)/Var(X) \quad (5)$$

holds as well. The last expression (5) shows that once multiplied by 100, reliability is also the complement to 100 of the percentage of observed variance that remains unexplained by true individual differences.

Equation (5) further relates reliability to the widely utilized noise to signal ratio (NSR) in the technical, engineering, and physics disciplines. Indeed, if one considers the NSR as the ratio of error variance to observed variance, then (5) simply shows reliability as the complement to 1 of the NSR. In other words, reliability is a "reverse" function of the NSR and thus increases only when the NSR decreases, since their sum is 1, as stated by Equation (5). If alternatively interested in the true signal to noise ratio (TSNR), denoted τ and defined as the ratio of true variance to error variance, then on the assumption of positive error variance it follows directly from (5) that

$$\tau = Var(T)/Var(E) = r_X/(1 - r_X), \quad (6)$$

or conversely

$$r_X = \tau/(1 + \tau). \quad (7)$$

Equations (6) and (7) show that the reliability and TSNR coefficients are non-linearly related. Thereby, this non-linear relationship is represented by a monotonically increasing function (i.e., the true signal to noise ratio increases if and only if reliability does so, and vice versa).

Furthermore, from Equation (3) it can be shown that the reliability coefficient in fact equals the correlation of two parallel measures when their error scores are uncorrelated (see, e.g., Raykov, Marcoulides, & Patelis, 2015, for the importance of this uncorrelatedness assumption for "classical" psychometrics). Indeed, suppose

X and Y represent two parallel measures evaluating the same true score T with uncorrelated error scores E_X and E_Y that possess the same variance. Then, their parallelism entails that $T = X–E_X = Y–E_Y$ and $Corr(X, Y) = r_X$, where $Corr(.,.)$ denotes correlation (for details, see, e.g., Raykov & Marcoulides, 2011).

The importance of the last equation, $Corr(X, Y) = r_X$, lies in the fact that it provides a natural link between psychometrics and the experimental disciplines. The reason is that experimental replications may well be seen as the counterpart of parallel measures in the experimental and "hard" sciences, where these replications play a foundational role (e.g., Bevington & Robinson, 2003). Moreover, this same equation is the basis of the interpretation of reliability as degree of consistency or repeatability of the results obtained with a given measure (say X) when used more than once (yielding Y, say, when repeated). Therefore, the equation $Corr(X, Y) = r_X$ may be seen as providing also an important philosophy of science interpretation, and thus attests to the high relevance of the reliability notion.

The preceding developments relate reliability to concepts of key import in statistics and the technical, physical, and experimental disciplines as well as epistemology. In addition, the popular attenuation/disattenuation formula in traditional psychometrics and its applications also connects reliability to true correlations that are typically of actual interest in research (cf. Bartholomew, 1996). Indeed, if U and V, say, represent a pair of observed measures with respective reliabilities ρ_U and ρ_V (assumed positive), on the assumption of uncorrelated errors the correlation between their corresponding true scores, T_U and T_V, is

$$Corr(T_U, T_V) = Corr(U, V)/\sqrt{(r_U r_V)}, \qquad (8)$$

where $\sqrt{(.)}$ denotes positive square root (e.g., Raykov & Marcoulides, 2011). That is, the reliability coefficient further relates the observed correlation between behavioral measurements with their true relationship (more precisely, linear relationship index) that is usually of real concern to a behavioral scholar.

In summary, the reliability coefficient is a concept of special relevance in more than one way for both theoretical and empirical research, rather than an index of mainly historical import or merely facilitating evaluation of the standard error of measurement (cf. McDonald, 1999). In particular, with its above relations to key notions in the statistical, technical, physical, and experimental disciplines as well as traditional psychometrics and philosophy of science, reliability can be viewed as a concept of particular importance not only in the social and behavioral sciences but also well beyond them.

Evaluation of Reliability

The discussion so far in the chapter has evolved at the population level. In an empirical study, assuming the availability of a representative sample from a studied population, a naturally arising question is how to point and interval estimate the reliability (for that population) of a behavioral measure under consideration. In the extant literature, the issue of reliability estimation for a single measure (i.e., one not further divisible into constituent components) has been addressed in numerous treatments over the past several decades (e.g., Crocker & Algina, 1986). For instance, test-retest correlations, alternative form applications, combination of both approaches, split-half or analysis of variance related methods, can be used for point estimation of what may at times be better referred to as coefficients of stability. Under relatively strong assumptions, these coefficients can inform a researcher about the reliability of a measure in question, and I refer to various prior sources for detailed discussions of these procedures (e.g., McDonald, 1999).

At the same time, however, most of them in my view need not be considered satisfactory or acceptable, strictly speaking, from today's perspective in many empirical settings. For example, test-retest correlations in effect assume parallel repeated measures with uncorrelated errors that are generally very difficult to construct in practice (e.g., Raykov, Marcoulides, & Patelis, 2015, and references therein). This requirement remains valid for the alternative form applications and their combination with a test-retest approach. Split-half procedures typically produce multiple ambiguous if not conflicting estimates of reliability that depend on split, with no helpful criterion for selection among them. They are also associated with significant challenges when interested in interval estimation of reliability, as a researcher generally must also be. Last but not least, analysis of variance-based approaches typically presume lack of interaction between subjects and instrument components, which in the usual setting of measure application is not a testable assumption.

The rest of this chapter is therefore predicated on the key realization that most concepts of theoretical and empirical concern in the social and behavioral sciences cannot be fully represented by a single number (e.g., Rao, 1973). As a result, they cannot be meaningfully captured by a single measurement or observation. Rather, their substantive nature typically calls for simultaneous measurement of their multiple facets, aspects, sides, dimensions, manifestations, or directions of expression; these may but need not be fully representable themselves by single numbers or measurements (see also Raykov, 2023). For these and related reasons, multiple-component measuring instruments have been enjoying increasing popularity over the past several decades across many disciplines. In the latter, it is easily observed that experimental replication – seen as the "modus operandi" in the experimental or hard sciences – is not really meaningfully possible for a variety of important reasons. Instead, joint evaluation of (presumed) multiple indicators, proxies, or manifestations of the studied concepts, frequently represented by latent variables, is much if not most of the time recommendable in these "soft" sciences. These reflections on the complexity of social phenomena create a strong motivation for widespread use of multi-component measuring instruments in empirical research.

Given the above limitations of the procedures for single measure reliability estimation, as well as the need for multi-item psychometric scales, the rest of this chapter is concerned with reliability evaluation for such instruments. These activities are often referred to as "scale reliability evaluation" in the literature (e.g., Raykov, 2012). To this end, I introduce here a slight modification of the earlier notation, which is undertaken in order to emphasize the multiplicity of measures of relevance for a studied concept that are in fact dependent variables. Accordingly, the individual k components of a considered instrument are denoted in the sequel as $Y_1, Y_2, \ldots, Y_k (k > 1)$. Relatedly, their sum score, which is often of special interest in empirical research, is symbolized as

$$Y = Y_1 + Y_2 + \ldots + Y_k. \tag{9}$$

Extensions of the following discussion to weighted composites (weighted scale scores) can be obtained along the lines of that used for maximal reliability in Raykov (2012). They are beyond the confines of this chapter and will thus not be of interest below. Instead, the remainder will be concerned with the reliability of the sum score (9) that is very frequently utilized in present-day studies.

In the next several subsections, I discuss first a model-free means of scale reliability estimation. I then move on to model-based reliability evaluation. Subsequently, I elaborate on the necessity to avoid in general estimation of standardized reliability in empirical research. The reason is that standardized reliability has acquired, in my opinion, undue popularity in recent years but can be seriously misleading for social and behavioral scientists. Within each of the next three subsections, the discussion develops initially at the population level and then specializes to corresponding empirical estimation procedures.

The Longevity of Coefficient Alpha

Coefficient alpha (referred to as "alpha" below and denoted α; Cronbach, 1951) is one of the earliest indices of reliability of a multi-component measuring instrument. In fact, what may be seen as first references to alpha could be found nearly a century ago (Kelley, 1927). Since then, α has become one of the most popular measurement-related coefficients and continues to be often used across disciplines. In addition, α is one of the most frequently discussed indices in the psychometric and substantive literature, and thus it will receive due attention next.

The Population Definition of Alpha as a Model-Free and Assumption-Free Index of Reliability

To discuss coefficient alpha more specifically, one must commence with its population definition (e.g., Cronbach, 1951; see also (9)):

$$\alpha = \frac{k}{k-1}\left[1 - \sum_{i=1}^{k} Var(Y_i)/Var(Y)\right]. \tag{10}$$

From Equation (10), it is obvious that α is well-defined in any population as soon as there are individual differences on the sum score Y – that is, $Var(Y) > 0$ holds there – and no further assumptions of any kind are needed for the definition of α (realizing of course that $k > 1$ when a sum score is of relevance). Currently, this sum score positive variability is essentially always the case in empirical research, and thus alpha exists practically always (cf. Raykov & Marcoulides, 2019).

I stress that as immediately seen from (10), (i) there is no model assumed in the definition of alpha; (ii) no hypothesis, and certainly not that of unidimensionality, needs to be true (or retainable) for the considered instrument; and (iii) there are no distributional assumptions with respect to any variables appearing in alpha's definition or underlying the observed measures. In fact, the scale components can be dichotomous, polytomous (ordinal), or continuous, or a mixture of such. In all these cases, alpha is well-defined and meaningful as an index informing about scale reliability. More specifically, no assumption of normality for the observed components Y_1 through Y_k or for their true scores or error scores is needed for alpha's definition (see McNeish, 2018, for such incorrect assumptions). With this feature of being practically always well-defined and existing, α represents a widely applicable model-free and in effect assumption-free coefficient informing about a given scale's reliability (as long as the variance of the sum score Y is positive; this is essentially always the case in contemporary empirical studies).

How Close Is Alpha to Scale Reliability?

For more than a half century, a great deal of research has been conducted on the relationship of coefficient alpha and scale reliability at the population level. Based on it, what one can say is that this relationship is rather complicated. As a result, no single recommendation for using one instead of the other could be given that would be applicable to the large majority of social and behavioral research. In fact, numerous settings of theoretical and empirical relevance in these and cognate disciplines can be readily found where (a) alpha markedly underestimates reliability, or alternatively (b) alpha is practically identical or very close to reliability at the population level. This near identity can hold even with differing strength of relationship between the instrument components and an underlying common source of latent variability (see below). For these reasons, this subsection aims at shedding needed light on the complex relationship between the alpha and scale reliability coefficients.

As perhaps the first landmark paper on the topic, Novick and Lewis (1967) showed that, as long as the error scores of a considered instrument's components are uncorrelated, (i) alpha cannot exceed reliability and (ii) alpha equals reliability only when these components are tau-equivalent – that is, evaluate the same common true score with the same units of measurement (see also further below). It is likely this far-reaching result that has led to the reference to alpha as a "lower bound" of reliability. However, I emphasize that this property of α holds only if the errors of the individual components (i.e., of the Ys in the right-hand side of Equations (9) and (10)) are uncorrelated. Whenever these errors correlate though, it is also possible that population alpha becomes an upper rather than lower bound to reliability at large (or even equals the latter; see, e.g., Raykov, 2001a, and Equation (11) below).

The population relationship between alpha and reliability is possibly most frequently discussed in the context of the popular congeneric measure model (CMM; Jöreskog, 1971). This widely applicable model stipulates that the instrument components $Y_1, \ldots, Y_k$ are congeneric (i.e., share the same common true score that they evaluate with possibly different units of measurement and precision). Formally, the CMM is defined as follows:

$$\underline{Y} = \underline{a} + BT + \underline{E}, \tag{11}$$

where $\underline{Y}$ is the $k \times 1$ vector of observed measures, $\underline{a}$ that of intercepts, T the common true score (see next), $B = (b_1, b_2, \ldots, b_k)'$ is the $k \times 1$ matrix of their loadings on (or slopes/relationships to) that true score, and $\underline{E}$ is the $k \times 1$ vector of error scores of the scale components. (Transposition is denoted by priming and vector by underlining in this chapter.) In other words, the CMM assumes that the true scores of $Y_1, \ldots, Y_k$, designated correspondingly $T_1, \ldots, T_k$, are all perfectly linearly related to a common true score T (that can be taken to be, say, that of Y_1, i.e., T_1). That is, the CMM posits that $T_j = a_j + b_j T$ holds for the component true scores ($j = 1, \ldots, k$; evidently, $a_1 = 0$ and $b_1 = 1$ with the last mentioned choice of T).

The CMM is testable (with k > 3) and empirically indistinguishable from the widely used single-factor model in the single-occasion, single-population setting underlying this chapter. Either of these models represents practically equivalently the popular unidimensionality hypothesis for a multi-component measuring instrument (McDonald, 1999; see, e.g., Raykov & Marcoulides, 2016a, for settings with multiple assessment occasions). The reason is that the CMM and the single-factor model have then the same implications for the observed means, variances, covariances, and correlations, as well as third- and fourth-order moments. These are all moments (statistics) needed in the model estimation approaches currently available within the overarching structural equation modeling framework used to fit the CMM as well as factor analysis and related models.

A main implication of the key result by Novick and Lewis (1967) is that, with no error correlations, population alpha equals population scale reliability if

$$b_1 = b_2 = \ldots = b_k \tag{12}$$

holds in the CMM (11) for the components of a scale under consideration, such as an anxiety or neuroticism multi-item measuring instrument. That is, under the CMM with uncorrelated errors, $\alpha < \rho_Y$ is true in the population unless the equalities (12) are fulfilled for the b-loadings (factor loadings) in (11); in addition, their identity (12) on the assumption of this model being correct guarantees that alpha and reliability are identical there.

While Novick and Lewis (1967) discussed the qualitative population relationship between α and reliability, Raykov (1997) quantitatively evaluated the population discrepancy between these two coefficients (see Table 1 and pp. 342–344 there). Accordingly, when the components are unidimensional, with uncorrelated errors, and possess unequal but uniformly high loadings b_1 through b_k, coefficient alpha differs from scale reliability to a practically negligible extent. The last cited source implies that there are infinitely many cases with unequal loadings b_1 through b_k where coefficient alpha and scale reliability, while unequal in the population, are in effect identical there for most if not all practical purposes (see also Raykov, Anthony, and Menold, 2023).

The discussion in this subsection indicates that, in general, the population alpha to reliability discrepancy (PARD) can be (a) positive (Raykov, 2001a); or (b) zero (when the above Equation (12) holds; Novick and Lewis, 1967); or (c) negative (Raykov, 1997). Examples of theoretically and empirically relevant settings where alpha is substantially lower than reliability and the PARD markedly negative, are found in Raykov (1997, 2001b). In such settings, it could be potentially seriously misleading to use α as an index of reliability and especially as a guide to scale revision (e.g., utilizing the "Alpha if item deleted" statistic routinely provided by canned software). The reason is that if α is used as such an index, the deletion of the suggested component(s) by this removal statistic can in fact lead to notable losses in reliability and validity (criterion validity; e.g., Raykov, 2007, 2008). For this reason, use of the index "Alpha if item deleted," which is readily available in canned software like SPSS, SAS, or Stata, is generally discouraged.

Alternatively, as indicated above, sufficient (but not necessary) conditions for the PARD being negligible are given in Raykov (1997, Table 1, pp. 342–344). They can be described as the requirements of instrument unidimensionality, uncorrelated errors, and the b-loadings in Equation (11) being uniformly high while not identical (see also Raykov & Marcoulides, 2018 on necessary and sufficient conditions within a related measurement context). At the same time, it is possible that there are other settings, in fact infinitely many, where the b-loadings in (11) are markedly unequal yet the PARD is so small as to be ignorable for most practical purposes (e.g., Raykov et al., 2023). I reiterate that when Equation (12) holds in a CMM with uncorrelated errors, PARD = 0 (i.e., α equals scale reliability at large; Novick and Lewis, 1967).

In more general quantitative terms, the PARD is discussed in detail in Raykov (1997), Raykov and Marcoulides (2023), and Raykov et al. (2023). The first source obtains the PARD as a non-linear function of the CMM parameters (with uncorrelated errors). Raykov (2001a) extends that discussion to the case with correlated errors that has also attracted considerable interest from a number of researchers over the past half century or so (e.g., Maxwell, 1967; Zimmerman, 1972).

Summarizing the developments in this subsection, the population relationship of coefficient alpha and scale reliability is far more complicated than could be reflected in (a) overly simplistic attempts at general statements about it, and (b) certainly misleading general calls or implied such for abandoning the use of coefficient alpha (e.g., McNeish, 2018; cf. Sijtsma, 2009). The present subsection, along with other publications (e.g., Raykov, 1997; Raykov et al., 2023; Raykov & Marcoulides, 2019; Raykov, West, & Traynor, 2015), renders such general statements or calls as flawed.

The preceding discussion actually demonstrates that despite those general calls (McNeish, 2018; cf. Sijtsma, 2009), coefficient alpha continues to be needed after nearly a century of being available. This is because, as seen from the last and earlier cited sources, α can indeed be an informative and dependable index of reliability, as it will be in the settings outlined earlier (i.e., whenever Equation (12) holds or the aforementioned sufficient conditions do for the PARD to be practically negligible; Raykov, 1997; Raykov et al., 2023). Raykov and Marcoulides (2023) discuss procedures for testing these conditions.

Point and Interval Estimation of Coefficient Alpha and Its Discrepancy from Scale Reliability

This subsection has focused thus far on population relationships. For a given sample from a studied population, Raykov and Marcoulides (2015a) and Raykov, Anthony, and Menold (2023) provide a readily used point and interval estimation procedure for coefficient alpha, with relevant software code (in their Appendices). The procedure is model-free and practically assumption-free, and is applicable with dichotomous, polytomous (ordinal), or continuous components (items). That is, it is applicable regardless of the distribution of the individual instrument components (as long as the scale score Y has positive variance), and without assuming the validity of any model, in particular not assuming that of unidimensionality. That approach for evaluation of α is extended to the case of nationally representative (large-scale or complex design) studies in Raykov, West, and Traynor (2015). Raykov and Marcoulides (2023) have recently described a readily and widely applicable point and interval estimation procedure for the PARD (with unidimensionality and uncorrelated errors), along with software code accomplishing these aims (see also Appendix to this chapter).

I emphasize that the PARD is an important discrepancy measure that is helpful and useful to empirical scientists. This is because α is a model-free and effectively assumption-free index of reliability that can be used in a trustworthy way in the settings mentioned in this subsection where the PARD is negligible. In addition, alpha represents an informative lower bound of reliability in all other settings and empirical studies, where either the CMM (single-factor model) with uncorrelated errors or a multidimensional model with such errors is correct or plausible. Hence, coefficient alpha can be the reliability index of choice when a behavioral scholar is dealing with an empirical setting characterized by positive scale score variance, the testable assumption of uncorrelated component errors, and is not willing to make any other assumptions – in particular not such of a specific model (e.g., that of unidimensionality). In those cases, α can be utilized as a helpful lower bound of reliability and can also be useful with measuring instruments consisting of discrete items. When, in addition to uncorrelated errors, the above testable sufficient conditions are fulfilled (or plausible), coefficient alpha can be employed as a dependable reliability measure.

Point and Interval Estimation of the Scale Reliability Coefficient

As shown in Bollen (1980), for the CMM with uncorrelated errors, the reliability coefficient of the sum score Y in Equation (9) can be expressed as the following non-linear function of model parameters:

$$\rho_Y = \frac{(b_1 + \ldots + b_k)^2}{(b_1 + \ldots + b_k)^2 + \theta_1 + \ldots + \theta_k} \qquad (13)$$

where θ_1 through θ_k denote the error variances associated with its components Y_1 through Y_k, respectively. The validity of Equation (13) is readily seen by realizing that, under the CMM, the true score associated with the overall scale score Y is $a_1 + \ldots + a_k + (b_1 + \ldots + b_k)T$, while its error score is $E_1 + \ldots + E_k$ (see (11)). When employing well-known rules of covariance algebra then (e.g., Raykov & Marcoulides, 2006), and on the assumption of unit latent variance for model identification (i.e., $Var(T) = 1$), the true variance is directly found as the numerator of (13), while observed variance results as its denominator.

With multinormal data, the maximum likelihood (ML) model fitting and parameter estimation method is applicable and yields from (13) the ML scale reliability estimator as

$$\hat{\rho}_Y = \frac{(\hat{b}_1 + \ldots + \hat{b}_k)^2}{(\hat{b}_1 + \ldots + \hat{b}_k)^2 + \hat{\theta}_1 + \ldots + \hat{\theta}_k} \qquad (14)$$

where a caret denotes ML estimator of the respective parameter. The rationale behind the ML scale reliability estimator (14) lies in the invariance property of ML estimators (e.g., Casella & Berger, 2002). With correlated errors, reliability is similarly expressed as follows, since the observed variance needs to be extended then by twice the sum of the non-zero error covariances (assuming model identification; Bollen, 1980):

$$\rho_Y = \frac{(b_1 + \ldots + b_k)^2}{(b_1 + \ldots + b_k)^2 + \theta_1 + \ldots + \theta_k + 2\sum_{j<s} Cov(E_j, E_s)} \qquad (15)$$

Furthermore, since the right-hand sides of Equations (13) and (15) are continuously differentiable functions of the model parameters, the popular bootstrap methodology (e.g., Efron & Tibshirani, 1993) can be used to furnish a confidence interval for scale reliability (with or without correlated errors) at a pre-specified confidence level. The software code rendering these ML point and interval estimates can be found in Raykov and Marcoulides (2011; see also Raykov & Marcoulides, 2016a, for a more general setting, and below).

The discussion so far has assumed unidimensionality and normality, as well as lack of clustering effects and substantial unobserved heterogeneity. These assumptions can be relaxed, and scale reliability can be point and interval estimated along largely the same lines as above (see Raykov & Shrout, 2002; Raykov & Marcoulides, 2011). These relaxations, singly or in combination, are discussed in detail in Raykov and Marcoulides (2016a). Those authors also provide software code for accomplishing these aims in an empirical setting (see also Appendix to this chapter).

In particular, when normality is violated, robust ML could be used for estimation of scale reliability (and is also applicable with limited clustering effects), and as an alternative the popular delta-method could be utilized for its interval estimation (Raykov & Marcoulides, 2004). This approach can arguably be employed with scale components that are continuous but with (not excessively) skewed and/or kurtotic distributions, as well as in cases when they represent or contain discrete items with at least five to seven possible response options and not too asymmetric distributions (Rhemtulla et al., 2012). With binary scored items, the procedure in Raykov, Dimitrov, and Asparouhov (2010) can be utilized for reliability evaluation. With items that have up to possibly five response options, the method in Yang and Green (2009) can be considered for the same aims (see also Raykov & Marcoulides, 2011, for a potential alternative). With very large samples, likely in the thousands (e.g., Hu, Bentler, & Kano, 1992), the asymptotically distribution-free method (Bollen, 1989) can be used for scale reliability estimation regardless of the individual continuous component distribution. The software implementation of the procedure for point and interval estimation of scale reliability in a general setting, indicated in this paragraph, is provided in the Appendix to this chapter.

The scale reliability evaluation approaches discussed in this subsection rest on the assumption of a single-class population, as mentioned above. In such a population, there is no excessive heterogeneity as would be the case with substantial unobserved individual differences (e.g., Raykov, Marcoulides, & Chang, 2016). In recent decades, the realization has been becoming increasingly widespread that many populations of interest in the social and behavioral sciences are unlikely to represent single-class entities. Rather, they could instead be expected to consist of two or more underlying subpopulations (or latent classes) that are relatively homogeneous within but not between themselves.

This fact is due to the increasing unobserved heterogeneity in studied characteristics. That heterogeneity is posing a serious challenge to methodologists and substantive researchers involved in statistical modeling, including reliability and validity evaluation. Owing to the increasing relevance of this issue, recent discussions have attended to it by mostly raising the above concern and referring to procedures for handling it (e.g., Raykov, 2023). In particular, Raykov and Marcoulides (2015b) deal with reliability estimation in the pertinent mixture setting. Their approach represents an extension of the above estimation procedures to the case where a studied population consists of an unknown number of subpopulations or latent classes, where subpopulation membership is also unknown for the individual units of analysis. Whether one is indeed dealing, in a particular empirical study, with considerable population heterogeneity can be examined with the method in Raykov, Marcoulides, and Chang (2016).

To conclude this subsection, I would like to reiterate that the scale reliability coefficient depends both on the multi-item measuring instrument (set of components/items under consideration) as well as on the population in which it is used. In general, it would be very difficult to argue that a population of interest in contemporary social and behavioral research does not undergo development over time. In fact currently, most populations of concern in these disciplines are arguably experiencing notable change. As a consequence, many of their characteristics are changing within what may be seen as relatively limited time intervals. For this reason, it is recommendable that scale/test/measuring instrument manuals should not be consulted routinely with respect to reliability coefficient estimates when a scholar considers use of a scale that has been developed in prior research.

This recommendation is based on the realization that the likelihood is high that the estimate(s) reported in that documentation may be outdated due to such population dynamics and temporal development. Rather, what is recommendable is (i) collecting whenever possible own data at the relevant time point with a considered instrument for the population under investigation, and (ii) obtaining (e.g., as above) scale reliability point and interval estimates that are thus of importance at that time, instead of relying on possibly no longer applicable or relevant prior reliability estimates for that instrument and population (prior population studied).

This recommendation may become even more important when realizing that the latent structure of a given multi-component measuring instrument may also change with time (e.g., Raykov, 2023). If the latter is the case, that change would most likely render misleading earlier reliability estimates, some of which may have been based on the assumption of unidimensionality made at the time. In addition, a population that in prior years could have been reasonably seen essentially as a single-class entity may have increased its heterogeneity with time to such an extent that it would be more appropriate to treat it now as consisting of multiple latent classes (subpopulations). This fact would render inappropriate also the consideration of a single reliability coefficient or estimate for it. As a consequence, this observation calls for potential consideration of several reliabilities for a given scale and respective estimates of them for each of these subpopulations within the overall population under investigation (e.g., Raykov & Marcoulides, 2016b; Raykov, 2023; see also Raykov, Marcoulides, & Li, 2016, with respect to validity in mixtures, and Raykov, 2023). These estimates provide a fuller picture of how the used instrument is functioning in the population of initial interest and in particular reflect the complexity of behavioral and social science measurement in heterogeneous populations of increasing relevance for contemporary research.

Strong Convergence of the Coefficient Alpha and Scale Reliability Estimators with Increasing Sample Size

Social and behavioral scientists involved in scale construction and development are typically interested in working with parameter estimators that approach and converge on the population parameter value with the use of additional data from a studied population. In particular, when concerned with measuring instrument reliability estimation, they typically wish to use such estimators that with large enough samples in effect become identical to or practically indistinguishable from the true scale reliability coefficient in that population.

As can be shown using pertinent results from relevant large-sample statistical theory (e.g., DasGupta, 2008), the scale reliability estimator in Equation (13) is a consistent estimator of the population scale reliability coefficient (under the CMM with uncorrelated errors; see also Equation (14) and Raykov, 2012, for the correlated errors case when this consistency property also holds). That is, the probability of the reliability estimator being arbitrarily close to the true population value approaches 1 as sample size increases. However, this large-sample behavior does not guarantee that the resulting reliability estimates themselves approach, as a real number sequence, that population value when sample grows unboundedly (e.g., Apostol, 2006; Raykov et al., 2022).

As it turns out, the latter stronger and highly desirable convergence property holds with probability 1 for the coefficient alpha estimator (10) (under fairly weak regularity conditions such as variable independence and finite variance as well as fourth-order moments, which as indicated earlier is practically always the case in empirical research; e.g., DasGupta, 2008). In other words, as sample size increases, the resulting alpha estimates, for a given scale and studied population, practically always converge as a real number sequence on the population coefficient alpha. Hence, these estimates converge almost surely on the population scale reliability coefficient whenever the b-loading equalities (12) hold (e.g., Raykov, 2019a). Similarly, under some regularity conditions (that hold under normality of the scale components and in a considerably wider class of distributions for them), the above scale reliability coefficient estimates also demonstrate this strong convergence property. That is, with increasing sample size these reliability estimates converge with probability 1 on the population reliability coefficient (e.g., Raykov, 2019b). Therefore, empirical scholars can presume in their work (under those fairly mild conditions) that the alpha and the scale reliability estimates possess the highly desirable property of practically always converging on the population alpha and reliability coefficients, respectively, as sample size increases without limit.

How One Can Go Wrong with Standardized Scale Reliability

The preceding discussion in this chapter was concerned with the reliability of the sum score Y of the original measuring instrument components, $Y_1, \ldots, Y_k$. Thereby, at no point have we hinted at standardized scores (z-scores) or at any need, perceived or otherwise, to standardize these components prior to estimating scale reliability. Suppose one wished for some reason though to standardize them, leading to their standardized versions $^*Y_1, \ldots, ^*Y_k$, respectively. The reliability of their sum score, denoted $^*Y$, is frequently referred to as standardized scale reliability (cf. McDonald, 1999). Specifically, the standardized reliability coefficient results from the above reliability definition Equation (3) when applied to $^*Y = {^*Y_1} + \ldots + {^*Y_k}$. In the same way, one can obtain a standardized alpha coefficient that will be the alpha for the measures $^*Y_1$ through $^*Y_k$ (i.e., coefficient alpha associated with $^*Y$). We may note that obviously $^*Y_1$ through $^*Y_k$ are themselves observed variables with error scores that correlate if and only if those of the original components Y_1 through Y_k do.

Further, if the CMM holds for the original components, then it is also valid for the standardized components (which evidently possess the same common true score as that of the Ys since the latter components' true scores are linear functions of the original components' true scores). Therefore, based on the preceding developments in this section, one can say that as long as the error scores of the instrument components $Y_1, \ldots, Y_k$ do not correlate, standardized alpha will never exceed the standardized reliability coefficient in the population. In fact, standardized alpha will only equal the latter when the CMM holds for the standardized components with equal pertinent loadings (cf. Equation (11)).

Standardized model solutions and associated coefficients (e.g., within the widely used regression analysis framework) have been quite popular among applied researchers over the past several decades. A main reason has been the widespread realization that the units of measurement underlying the observed variables in these disciplines are oftentimes arbitrary, irrelevant, or very difficult to interpret. As a consequence, standardized solutions have been receiving considerable attention from scholars primarily due to the resulting comparability, free of original metrics, of the relationships between various variables of interest. However, there are a number of potentially serious statistical and related limitations of standardized solutions that should be kept in mind when considering their use (see, e.g., Judd, McClelland, & Ryan, 2017, for elaborated discussions). These limitations suffice to recommend against them in many empirical settings.

Perhaps as a result of what may be seen a strong "inertia" from the twentieth century, this interest in standardized solutions seems to have led to enhanced interest in standardized reliability that continues to be used in contemporary behavioral research. Unfortunately, recent publications contribute further to this generally misleading trend (as, e.g., in McNeish, 2018). More concretely, as elaborated in Raykov and Marcoulides (2021), there are serious pitfalls that typically await scientists engaging in the use of standardized reliability coefficients. This can be the case when estimating, reporting, or interpreting standardized reliability, and especially if basing on the latter (or on standardized alpha) one's decisions related to retaining or dropping components in tentative versions of multi-item measuring instruments under consideration (see below).

Specifically, as shown in Raykov and Marcoulides (2021), in the widely used unidimensionality setting (with uncorrelated errors), the population standardized reliability can be markedly higher, or alternatively substantially lower, than its unstandardized scale reliability counterpart ρ_Y (Equation (3)). This coefficient ρ_Y has been the only reliability coefficient used and referred to throughout this chapter (apart from this subsection). Yet, it is this unstandardized scale reliability coefficient that is typically of interest for evaluation in empirical research. This is because ensuing analyses typically use the initial instrument components and/or their sum score (unweighted or weighted; Raykov, 2023) or extend models of interest with latent variables and their original measurement indicators reflecting theoretical concepts of concern in pertinent research questions and modeling efforts.

Hence, if a scientist employs, estimates, reports, and/or interprets the standardized reliability coefficient in their work, they can in fact (i) end up promoting lower-quality scales possessing deficient actual reliability (and possibly validity) than that reflected in their spuriously high standardized coefficient. Alternatively, they may also (ii) miss a scale (version) having "satisfactory" reliability by being instead concerned only with its markedly lower standardized reliability coefficient, leading them to suboptimal scale revisions. Furthermore, based on the developments in the previous subsection dealing with the large-sample behavior of the scale reliability estimator, one can only logically state the following: advice to use standardized reliability or a discussion implying such a recommendation (e.g., McNeish, 2018) will then be wrong with probability 1 and hence could be correct merely with probability 0 (for details, see also Raykov & Marcoulides, 2019, 2021).

With the preceding in mind, this chapter recommends generally avoiding the estimation, use, reporting, or interpretation of standardized scale reliability estimates unless researchers have strong reasons for employing standardized scale components to begin with. These reasons need to be first convincingly argued for by the potential user of standardized reliability and would seem to be rarely of relevance in contemporary social and behavioral research.

Discussion and Conclusion

This chapter focuses on reliability as a major coefficient of quality of measurement in the social and behavioral sciences. As indicated in the introductory section, and discussed in more detail elsewhere (e.g., Raykov & Marcoulides, 2011), high reliability is a necessary although not sufficient condition for high validity. This is due to the fact that the reliability index is an upper bound of criterion validity (with uncorrelated errors of measure and criterion). For this reason, a main section of the chapter discussed readily and widely applicable procedures for point and interval estimation of reliability of multi-component measuring instruments that are highly popular in the behavioral and related disciplines (see also Appendix). Furthermore, I pointed out extensions of them to general structure scales, clustering effects, and population heterogeneity that are of growing relevance for current and likely future empirical studies.

In addition, an earlier section dealt with the population relationship between scale reliability and the popular coefficient alpha, indicating a multitude of settings where alpha is a trustworthy index of reliability due to being practically indistinguishable from the scale reliability coefficient. Similarly, I attended to the relationship between scale reliability and standardized reliability and generally recommended against use of the latter. Unfortunately, standardized reliability is an index that is still enjoying popularity among certain circles of behavioral researchers, mostly due to recent publications encouraging its use despite its serious disadvantages as a potentially misleading reliability coefficient in contemporary research.

The reliability estimation procedures indicated in this chapter have several limitations. As mentioned, they have been developed within the comprehensive latent variable modeling framework, and hence necessitate large samples of units of analysis (cf. Raykov, 2012, 2022). To date, there are no specific guidelines for determining needed sample size that would be generally applicable. This is mostly due to the fact that necessary sample size depends on multiple factors as well as their potential interactions. As possibly the only generally valid observation, sample size depends on overall fitted model complexity as well as latent structure of, and extent of measurement error in, the scale components. A related and somewhat underrated limitation is the possibility of capitalization on chance, particularly if the estimation procedures are used to inform tentative scale revisions that themselves are evaluated subsequently on the same data set. For this reason, it is highly recommendable to use large initial samples, split them into two (or more) random parts, and conduct exploratory and confirmatory (model testing) analyses on different subsamples (for details, see Raykov, 2012, 2023). Even then, much more trust can be placed in the "final results and findings" of the procedures in a given empirical study, after replication studies are conducted on independent samples from the same studied populations (see also Chapter 15, this volume, for a further exposition of the importance of replication).

I would like to conclude this chapter by emphasizing that the full benefit of the reliability procedures discussed in it can be materialized only when they are utilized in tandem with well-informed substantive considerations and expertise. This synergy may best occur within a creative process based on all accumulated knowledge and prior research in the pertinent substantive research domain.

Acknowledgments

I am indebted to G. A. Marcoulides, D. M. Dimitrov, D. J. Hand, P. M. Bentler, S. Penev, R. E. Millsap, and R. Steyer for valuable discussions on reliability estimation and related topics. I am also grateful to J. Edlund and A. Nichols for critical comments on an earlier version of the chapter, which have contributed substantially to its improvement.

Appendix

Point and Interval Estimation of Scale Reliability

Title:	USING MPLUS TO POINT AND INTERVAL ESTIMATE SCALE RELIABILITY (SEE EQUATION 14); CF. RAYKOV (2009); RAYKOV, ANTHONY, & MENOLD (2023); see also Note below).
DATA:	FILE = <name of raw data file>;
VARIABLE:	NAMES = Y1-Y5;
ANALYSIS:	ESTIMATOR = MLR;
MODEL:	F BY Y1*(B1) Y2-Y5 (B2-B5) ! THESE ARE THE b'S IN EQUATION (14); Y1-Y5 (T1-T5); ! THESE ARE THE *theta*'s IN EQUATION (14).
MODEL CONSTRAINT:	
	NEW(SC_REL); ! THIS IS THE SCALE RELIABILITY ! COEFFICIENT SC_REL = (B1+B2+B3+B4+B5)^2/ ((B1+B2+B3+B4+B5)^2+ T1+T2+T3+T4+T5);
OUTPUT:	CINTERVAL; ! PRODUCES A SYMMETRIC CONFIDENCE ! INTERVAL ! OF SCALE RELIABILITY.

Note: This source code (given here for the case of five components, as an example) with the highly popular latent variable modeling software Mplus can be used with continuous or approximately continuous components, or with discrete items possessing at least five response options and not excessively asymmetric distributions (see Rhemtulla et al., 2012; Raykov & Marcoulides, 2011). For source code using the estimation approach via the bootstrap methodology for interval estimation, see Raykov and Marcoulides (2015a).

References

Agresti, A., & Finlay, B. (2008). *Statistical Methods for the Social Sciences*. CRC Press.
Arnold, S. F. (1990). *Mathematical Statistics*. Prentice Hall.
Bartholomew, D. J. (1996). *The Statistical Approach to Social Measurement*. Academic Press.
Bevington, P. R., & Robinson, D. K. (2003). *Data Reduction and Error Analysis for the Physical Sciences*. McGraw-Hill.
Bollen, K. A. (1980). Issues in the comparative measurement of political democracy. *American Sociological Review, 45*, 370–390.
— (1989). *Structural Equations with Latent Variables*. Wiley.
Casella, G., & Berger, J. O. (2002). *Statistical Inference*. Wadsworth.
Crocker, L., & Algina, J. (1986). *Introduction to Classical and Modern Test Theory*. Harcourt College Publishers.
Cronbach, L. J. (1951). Coefficient alpha and the internal structure of tests. *Psychometrika, 16*, 297–334.
DasGupta, A. (2008). *Asymptotic Theory of Statistics and Probability*. Springer.
Efron, B., & Tibshiriani, R. J. (1993). *An Introduction to the Bootstrap*. Chapman Hall/CRC.
Embretson, S. E., & Reise, S. P. (2000). *Item Response Theory for Psychologists*. Lawrence Erlbaum Associates.
Hu, L.-T., Bentler, P. M., & Kano, Y. (1992). Can test statistics in covariance structure analysis be trusted? *Psychological Bulletin, 112*(2), 351–362.
Jöreskog, K. G. (1971). Statistical analysis of sets of congeneric tests. *Psychometrika, 36*, 109–133.
Judd, C. M., McClelland, G. H., & Ryan, C. S. (2017). *Data analysis: A Model Comparison Approach to Regression, ANOVA, and Beyond*, 3rd ed. Routledge.
Kelley, T. L. (1927). *Interpretation of Educational Measurement*. World Book Company.
Lord, F. M., & Novick, M. (1968). *Statistical Theories of Mental Test Scores*. Wesley.
Maxwell, A. E. (1967). The effect of correlated errors on estimates of reliability coefficients. *Education and Psychological Measurement, 28*, 803–811.
McDonald, R. P. (1999). *Test Theory: A Unified Treatment*. Lawrence Erlbaum Associates.
McNeish, D. (2018). Thanks coefficient alpha, we'll take it from here. *Psychological Methods, 23*, 412–433.
Novick, M. R., & Lewis, C. (1967). Coefficient alpha and the reliability of composite measurements. *Psychometrika, 32*, 1–13.
Rao, C. R. (1973). *Linear Statistical Inference and Its Applications*. Wiley.
Raykov, T. (1997). Scale reliability, Cronbach's coefficient alpha, and violations of essential tau-equivalence for fixed congeneric components. *Multivariate Behavioral Research, 32*, 329–354.
— (2001a). Bias of coefficient alpha for congeneric measures with correlated errors. *Applied Psychological Measurement, 25*, 69–76.
— (2001b). Estimation of congeneric scale reliability via covariance structure models with nonlinear constraints. *British Journal of Mathematical and Statistical Psychology, 54*, 315–323.
— (2007). Reliability if deleted, not "alpha if deleted": Evaluation of scale reliability following component deletion. *British Journal of Mathematical and Statistical Psychology, 60*, 201–216.

(2008). "Alpha if item deleted": A note on loss of criterion validity in scale development if maximising coefficient alpha. *British Journal of Mathematical and Statistical Psychology, 61*, 275–285.

(2009). Evaluation of scale reliability for unidimensional measures using latent variable modeling. *Measurement and Evaluation in Counseling and Development, 42*, 222–232.

(2012). Scale development using structural equation modeling. In R. Hoyle (ed.), *Handbook of Structural Equation Modeling* (pp. 472–492). Guilford Press.

(2019a). Strong consistency of reliability estimators for multiple-component measuring instruments. *Structural Equation Modeling, 26*, 750–756.

(2019b). Strong convergence of the coefficient alpha estimator for reliability of multiple-component measuring instruments. *Structural Equation Modeling, 26*, 430–436.

(2023). Psychometric scale evaluation using structural equation and latent variable modeling. In R. Hoyle (ed.), *Handbook of Structural Equation Modeling*, 2nd ed. Guilford Press.

Raykov, T., Anthony, J. C., & Menold, N. (2023). On the importance of coefficient alpha for measurement research: Loading equality is not necessary for alpha's utility as a scale reliability index. *Educational and Psychological Measurement, 83*(4), 766–781.

Raykov, T., Dimitrov, D. M., & Asparouhov, T. (2010). Evaluation of scale reliability with binary measures using latent variable modeling. *Structural Equation Modeling, 17*, 122–132.

Raykov, T., Doebler, P., & Marcoulides, G. A. (2022). Applications of Bayesian confirmatory factor analysis in behavioral measurement: Strong convergence of a Bayesian parameter estimator. *Measurement: Interdisciplinary Research and Perspectives, 20*(4), 215–227.

Raykov, T., & Marcoulides, G. A. (2004). Using the delta method for approximate interval estimation of parametric functions in covariance structure models. *Structural Equation Modeling, 11*, 659–675.

(2006). *A first Course in Structural Equation Modeling*. Lawrence Erlbaum Associates.

(2011). *Introduction to Psychometric Theory*. Routledge.

(2015a). A direct latent variable modeling-based procedure for evaluation of coefficient alpha. *Educational and Psychological Measurement, 75*, 146–156.

(2015b). Scale reliability evaluation in heterogeneous populations. *Educational and Psychological Measurement, 75*, 875–892.

(2016a). Scale reliability evaluation under multiple assumption violations. *Structural Equation Modeling, 23*, 302–313.

(2016b). On examining specificity in latent construct indicators. *Structural Equation Modeling, 23*, 845–855.

(2018). *A Course in Item Response Theory and Modeling with Stata*. Stata Press.

(2019). Thanks, coefficient alpha – we still need you! *Educational and Psychological Measurement, 79*, 200–210.

(2021). On the pitfalls of estimating and using standardized reliability coefficients. *Educational and Psychological Measurement*, 791–810.

(2023). Evaluating the discrepancy between scale reliability and Cronbach's coefficient alpha using latent variable modeling. *Measurement: Interdisciplinary Research and Perspectives, 21*(1), 29–37.

Raykov, T., Marcoulides, G. A., & Chang, C. (2016). Studying population heterogeneity in finite mixture settings using latent variable modeling. *Structural Equation Modeling, 23*, 726–730.

Raykov, T., Marcoulides, G. A., & Li, T. (2016). Measurement instrument validity evaluation in finite mixtures. *Educational and Psychological Measurement, 76*, 1026–1044.

Raykov, T., Marcoulides, G. A., & Patelis, T. (2015). The importance of the assumption of uncorrelated errors in psychometric theory. *Educational and Psychological Measurement, 75*, 634–647.

Raykov, T., & Shrout, P. E. (2002). Reliability of scales with general structure: Point and interval estimation using a structural equation modeling approach. *Structural Equation Modeling, 9*, 195–212.

Raykov, T., West, B. T., & Traynor, A. (2015). Evaluation of coefficient alpha for multiple component measuring instruments in complex sample designs. *Structural Equation Modeling, 22*, 429–438.

Rhemtulla, M., Brosseau-Liard, P. E., & Savalei, V. (2012). When can categorical variables be treated as continuous? A comparison of robust continuous and categorical SEM estimation methods under suboptimal conditions. *Psychological Methods, 17*, 354–373.

Sijtsma, K. (2009). On the use, the misuse, and the very limited usefulness of Cronbach's alpha. *Psychometrika, 74*, 107–120.

Spearman, C. (1904). "General intelligence," objectively determined and measured. *American Journal of Psychology, 15*, 201–292.

Yang, Y., & Green, S. B. (2009). Reliability of summed item scores using structural equation modeling: An alternative to coefficient alpha. *Psychometrika, 75*, 155–167.

Zimmerman, D. W. (1972). Test reliability and the Kuder-Richardson formulas: Derivation from probability theory. *Educational and Psychological Measurement, 32*, 939–954.

(1975). Probability spaces, Hilbert spaces, and the axioms of test theory. *Psychometrika, 40*, 395–412.

10 Measurement Validity in the Social and Behavioral Sciences: Some "Whys" and "Hows"

John J. Skowronski

Abstract

This chapter argues that research-focused social and behavioral scientists also need to be good research technicians. This statement reflects the belief that this technical skill is needed because an accurate understanding of the social and behavioral sciences depends crucially on the use of valid measures of variables that are of interest and importance. The chapter also argues that the establishment of measurement validity is not an easy task, requiring researchers to gather evidence for measurement validity diligently, persistently, and constantly. Described in the chapter are some ways in which such evidence can be obtained and some of the pitfalls that confront researchers when they evaluate their evidence.

Keywords: Measurement Validity, Properties of Valid Measurements, Sources of Measurement Invalidity, Measure Validation and Assessment of Measure Validity, Practices to Maximize Measurement Validity

This chapter addresses the topic of the *validity* of measures in the social and behavioral sciences. The use of valid measures is central to the science conducted in these areas. Most importantly, using valid measures in scientific research leads to the development of *trust in the results* derived from that research. The development of such trust allows the science conducted in the social and behavioral sciences to progress toward its goal of *systematically accumulating trustworthy knowledge* (for more detailed discussion of this assertion, see Vazire et al., 2022). Such trustworthy knowledge can *facilitate the generation of good scientific theories*. Moreover, trustworthy knowledge can also lead to the *development and implementation of effective interventions*.

In contrast, if invalid measures are employed in research, that research will not (a) yield trustworthy knowledge, (b) prompt the emergence of good scientific theories, or (c) lead to the development and implementation of effective interventions. Moreover, when a large corpus of findings comes from research using invalid measures, a lot of time and many resources may be required to debunk the flawed research results and poor theory generated from the flawed findings. Indeed, as will be illustrated later in this chapter, experience has shown that the debunking process is quite difficult, and pessimists might suggest that full and permanent debunking might not even be possible.

The implications of these points are clear and of the upmost importance: *both the capacity of science to produce trustworthy results and the capacity to act effectively on those results crucially depend on the use of valid methods in scientific research.* For these reasons, many scholars continue to ponder and study the elements of measurement validity (for examples, see Buntins et al., 2017; Camargo et al., 2018; Foster & Cone, 1995; Lissitz, 2009; Sackett et al., 2012).

The Perils of Method Invalidity: An Example

Sadly, history provides many examples of the perils of doing research using invalid methods. One such case involves the study of phrenology (see Combe, 1851; Hollander, 1902; for modern perspectives, see Eling & Finger, 2021). Studies in this area were based on the idea that the size of various bumps on the skull reflected something about mental attribute use (typically frequency of use and/or attribute potency). Early phrenology theorizing attributed differences in brain bump sizes to the actions of muscles, but later reasoning linked such differences to the magnitude of, or frequency of, neural activity across various parts of the brain.

Regardless of the exact theory that was proposed, the basic ideas in phrenology were (a) that more of a psychological trait led to more activity in a given part of the brain, and (b) these activity differences should be manifest in bump size differences on the exterior of the skull. Hence, according to phrenology, one could discern a person's characteristics and personality by working backward from the skull bumps. That is, if one wanted to know about the extent to which a person was combative, all one had to do was to measure the size of the skull bump in the "combativeness" skull location; if one wanted to know the extent to which a person was benevolent, all one had to do was to measure the size of the skull bump in the "benevolence" skull area. Researchers "knew" where these various areas were by consulting one or more of the various published "skull maps."

Within academia, phrenology's ideas became well known and were often described and explored. For example, publication outlets focusing on phrenology were *Phrenological Journal* (1823–1847) and *American Phrenological Journal and Life Illustrated* (1838–1911). However, phrenology's ideas also escaped from the halls of academe and were widely disseminated to the general public. For example, one major treatise highlighting phrenology, Combe's *The Constitution of Man*, sold more than 300,000 copies between 1828 and 1868 (for one of the various editions, see Combe, 1835). If the book received similar market penetration today (given world population estimates provided by the Worldometer website: www.worldometers.info/world-population/world-population-by-year), that would translate to roughly 2,100,000 contemporary copies.

The widespread dissemination of phrenology's ideas is also reflected in the extent to which the ideas appeared in products produced by popular culture. For example, consider the Sherlock Holmes fictional story *The Adventure of the Final Problem* (Conan Doyle, 1981). In that story, during a meeting, Professor Moriarty remarked about Holmes (p. 331), "You have less frontal development than I should have expected." This statement was likely included in the story to reflect that, not only was Moriarty a criminal mastermind, but that he was a very well-informed man whose knowledge base included the study of phrenology. Yet another illustration of phrenology's public popularity lies in a device named the psychograph that appeared at the 1934 Century of Progress Exposition in Chicago. This machine examined the skull and produced a phrenological reading that included a printout. This device was said (as reported in *Vintage Everyday*, 2017) to have netted its owners approximately $200,000 at the fair. That net total translates to $3,602,874.25 in today's money.

The public's apparent trust in results produced from the study of phrenology was misplaced: Many authors have reviewed the existing evidence showing that the methods used by phrenologists are now known via research to be invalid (e.g., Gardner, 1957; Greenblatt, 1995). The size of the bumps on a skull's exterior is not at all related to an individual's psychological characteristics (for a modern debunking, see Parker Jones et al., 2018).

There is irony in this debunking. It is entirely reasonable to argue that the dismissal of phrenology is actually a success story for scientific psychology. After all, scientists often claim that the application of scientific methods to an area allows ideas that do not work to be definitively discarded. This is exactly what has happened with phrenology. The ideas underlying phrenology are wrong, and the methods used to explore phrenology are now known to be bunk.

However, it clearly took a long while and a lot of effort for this scientific debunking to be definitive. Moreover, one can also argue that, despite the definitive scientific debunking of phrenology, the failure to assess critically the validity of phrenology's methods and ideas early in phrenology's life cycle has produced lasting damage. For example, phrenology gave rise to ideas in (a) craniometry that tried to link head shape to personality, intelligence, and character, and (b) physiognomy that tried to establish similar links for facial features. One especially unfortunate consequence of these efforts is that both areas of study were linked to the so-called "races," and were often used to justify the superiority of those whose cranial appearance led to them being classified as "Aryan" or "White." For example, head and face appearance cues, some of which were emphasized as differing across the so-called "races," were linked to the propensity to engage in criminal behavior (see Thompson, 2021).

Perhaps even more troubling is that, despite the scientific success of the debunking efforts (e.g., recent DNA studies – see Fuentes et al., 2019; Goodman et al., 2020 – showing that the notion of separate and definable "races" is genetically implausible), these phrenologically inspired ideas about the so-called "races" continue to persist in many quarters of modern cultures (see Ghandoosh, 2014). Indeed, despite the successful debunking efforts, versions of links between appearance-based cues, including cranial cues, and various individual differences (such as intelligence), continue to be promoted in modern treatises that purport to be "scientific" (e.g., Herrnstein & Murray, 1994).

It might be easy for modern social and behavioral scientists to discount methodologically invalid areas of research, such as phrenology, as relics of the ancient past. Unfortunately, stories that echo the history of phrenology have frequently emerged in the "modern" age. One example lies in the proposed individual difference known as GRIT (Duckworth et al., 2007). GRIT's proponents suggested that the GRIT individual difference characteristic reflected the combined action of the personality traits of perseverance and passion and was especially relevant to understanding outstanding performances. A second example lies in attempts to measure attitudes, such as racial prejudice, via the Implicit Association Test (IAT; e.g., Rudman et al., 1999). The test is attractive as a potential method of measuring attitudes because the purpose of the test is not immediately obvious (as it is in self-report). A third example lies in the study of microaggressions (Sue et al., 2007). Microaggressions are comments or actions that are thought to subtly and often unconsciously or unintentionally express a prejudiced attitude toward a member of a marginalized group (such as a racial minority). These subtle behaviors are obviously attractive to the study of interactions because they serve as explanations for why marginalized group members can often feel uncomfortable and underperform in settings in which they are clearly a marginalized group member.

These areas of study share several characteristics with the phrenology area. First, being provocative, the ideas in each area stimulated considerable research and became widespread in academe. Second, the ideas in each area rapidly escaped from the halls of academe and made their way into popular culture. Third, these first two effects occurred, despite the fact that the validity of the scientific procedures and measures used to explore these areas is still uncertain. This uncertainty has contributed to the fact that the study of the validity of the methods and measures used in these areas continues to be a hot topic of research for scientists (for GRIT, see Ponnock et al., 2020; Tynan, 2021; for the IAT, see Falk et al., 2015; Schimmack, 2021; for microaggression, see Lilienfeld, 2017; Thomas & Skowronski, 2020).

I hasten to add that, in my opinion, these three areas do not yet share phrenology's status as bunk. Ultimately, the ideas from each area may be shown to have at least some degree of utility. However, in my opinion, given the state of the ongoing research, it is still much too early to draw conclusions about the extent to which, or the circumstances under which, the methods used in these areas are valid. Consequently, I find it disconcerting that people in the real world might be making practical decisions (e.g., making choices about hiring and promotion based on scores from a GRIT test; designing intervention programs to minimize microaggressive behaviors) based on research results in which the validity of the methods used is still being hotly debated in the scientific literature.

Given the points that I have so far raised in this chapter, I hope that you now appreciate *why* I think that it is a good idea to place the establishment of methodological validity at the center of whatever research program a researcher chooses to pursue. Validating methods is a part of what makes research results obtained from such methods trustworthy, useful to good theory development, and practically usable. Failure to validate methods, or using methods of questionable validity, makes research results obtained using those methods untrustworthy, misleading for (or irrelevant to) good theory development, and practically useless (or even dangerous).

What Are the Desirable Properties Exhibited by Valid Measures?

Scientists make observations. Observing often involves formally measuring the attributes of various "things" (e.g., objects, properties, or constructs), whether the things be concrete (e.g., a light's luminosity) or abstract (e.g., the extent to which a person feels anxious). Scientists always want these measures to be *valid*: *the instrument must measure what it purports to measure and must do a good job of doing so*. If one is trying to measure how much voltage is running through a wire, then one's measuring tool ought to reflect actual electrical current. If one is trying to measure the extent to which a person is furious, then one's measuring tool ought to reflect a person's actual anger.

Measures judged high in validity exhibit at least three desirable properties. First, to be valid, results from a measure of an attribute of a "thing" should be as *accurate* as possible. The concept of accuracy assumes that the value obtained by the measure reproduces the "real" value of the target attribute being measured. For example, if it takes exactly 100 ms for a research participant to push a key in response to a probe, a measuring tool assessing response latency would be perfectly accurate if it provided a reading of exactly 100 ms.

Of course, measures are almost never perfectly accurate all the time. There will usually be some degree of inaccuracy in the extent to which the value output by a measure will reflect a target attribute's real value. However, it is highly desirable for these inaccuracies to be small. When measurement inaccuracies are, indeed, small, the measure is said to be high in *precision* – the second desirable property in measurement.

The third property that scientists desire in a measure is that the measure's inaccuracies should be unsystematic (or *unbiased*). That is, measurement inaccuracies ideally should be divided equally between overestimates of the target attribute's real value and underestimates of the target attribute's real value.

While it is easy to think about measures in a binary way (a measure is either valid or not), given these three properties, it is probably better to think about validity as a continuum. Some measures might exhibit high validity, some might exhibit moderate validity, and some might exhibit low validity.

One implication of this *continuum of validity* concept is that even flawed measures can sometimes be scientifically useful. For example, consider results obtained from a scale that always reports a weight measure that is 10 lbs. under the actual weight. The measures thus produced by the scale are only somewhat valid because they exhibit a degree of inaccuracy, are somewhat imprecise, and are biased. However, despite being only somewhat valid, the flawed weight measure can retain a measure of utility. That is, the results produced by such a scale may correctly report the ordinal relations among the measures (e.g., the weights of people weighed on the scale will be placed in the correct order). In addition, if a treatment is available that leads to weight reduction, even the flawed scale could be useful in documenting this change. Although the exact weights reported by the scale would be inaccurate, the post-treatment weights would reflect the fact that weight does go down in response to the treatment, perhaps (if a researcher is especially lucky) even correctly reflecting the pre-treatment vs. post-treatment change in weight.

However, despite their utility, it would be a mistake to get too comfortable with flawed measures. For example, the measures produced by the flawed scale might not be especially useful, and might even be misleading, to scientific research and theory that demands a high standard of validity. For example, imagine that a researcher wants to develop activity level guidelines that could help people control their weight. In one study, a researcher might conduct a study in which a person's body mass index (weight in kg / height in m^2) is predicted by the number of steps the person takes daily, averaged over a month, as recorded by a smartwatch. From such data, the researcher could calculate an estimate of the number of steps needed daily (on average) to keep a person's BMI in the normal range. This may lead to the development of theories about weight as it relates to energy expenditure. However, because of the flawed weight measurements produced by our flawed scale, this study would produce incorrect estimates of the needed step rates; this could lead to flawed ideas about the energy expended during activity. Moreover, not only can a flawed measure be scientifically misleading, it can also be troublesome, or even dangerous, in applied settings. For example, anesthesiologists often use weight as a guideline when deciding dosages. Underreported weights might prompt overdoses of anesthetic.

General Elements that Affect Measurement Validity

Social and behavioral science researchers often adopt (either implicitly or explicitly) an *effect indicator model* approach to measurement (see Borsboom et al., 2004). This model assumes that some attribute (e.g., height, weight, extremity, intensity) of a measurement target *causally affects* the results obtained from the use of a given measurement tool to measure the attribute. From the effect indicator model perspective, ideally a "real" 12 inch long board would cause a 12 inch reading to emerge from a device that measures length; ideally, a "real" 12 second duration in running a 100 yard dash would cause a 12 second reading to be output by a timing device.

In the routine measurements that people make in their day-to-day lives, people often simply assume that a strong version of this causal model holds true. In this strong version, the attribute is the dominant causal influence on the measurement. Usually, that is probably a safe assumption. For example, when measuring object lengths with rulers or tape measures, the many, many times these tools have successfully been used to measure object lengths in routine circumstances tends to preclude doubts that object lengths cause measurements that approximate the actual values of those lengths. However, in many measurement circumstances, the causal link between a property and a measurement, and thus the validity of the measure, is not as high as in these common instances. This is because of at least four factors that weaken the causal link between the attribute being measured and the readout produced by the measuring tool.

First, consider *elements that lie largely within the measuring tool* that might detract from its validity. For example, some tools might exhibit manufacturing flaws that cause its readings to be somewhat unreliable even when these tools are new. For example, diabetics often find that their testing paraphernalia produce glucose readings that are not exact relative to readings produced from laboratory testing (for insight, see Bode et al., 2021). Moreover, equipment that ages or that is abused might have originally produced valid readings, but those readings might become increasingly unreliable as the tool degrades with use. For example, a weight scale that employs springs in its mechanisms might develop inaccuracies as the properties of the springs change with use. These two examples illustrate cases in which the causal link between an attribute and a measurement produced by a tool is weakened by tool-related factors that causally affect the measurement tool and interfere with the validity of the causal link between the attribute of a "thing" and the measurement produced by the tool.

A second source of measurement tool invalidity can be introduced by the *measurement tool users*. Maximizing validity in measurement requires that users have high ability to use measurement tools. Thus, even when a measurement tool that has high potential validity is put to use, measurement invalidity might be introduced via user errors. One example of user error comes from user carelessness (e.g., when a user does not take enough time to procure a correct measurement). A second example of user error lies in lack of user ability. For example, a visually impaired user may not be able to discriminate among closely spaced length markings on a tape measure. A third example of user error is a user's lack of knowledge about proper measurement tool use. An example of this kind of error is a user who has not received adequate training on how to use a coding system for recording observations.

A third source of measurement invalidity can be introduced by *the conditions in which a measurement is made*. One way in which this kind of invalidity emerges is when *conditions add variability* to measurements. For example, imagine that a wooden ship has sprung a leak in a storm and that a shipwright needs to cut a precisely measured patch to repair the leak. However, cutting a good patch might be hard because the ship is being buffeted about by the storm – there might be a lot of variability in the shipwright's measures, despite concerted efforts to produce valid measures. Conditions can also introduce measurement invalidity when those conditions *produce interference* with a measurement tool. Consider a psychophysics experiment in which an observer is trying to detect the presentation of a low-luminosity light source. That observer (the measurement tool) might be a highly valid low-luminosity light detector in a pitch-black room, but might not be a valid detector of that same light source in a bright room since the ambient light in a bright room interferes with the observer's ability to detect the light source.

A fourth source of measurement invalidity lies in the *characteristics and properties of the target of measurement*. For example, heat might cause an object to expand, causing a measure of that object's size or volume to vary with temperature. Indeed, target properties may often change when the targets being measured are human participants. For example, assume that a researcher wants to use a tool that measures the extent to which an individual might be prejudiced against Klingons (an alien in the *Star Trek* television shows and movies). That tool asks the respondents to self-report responses to items (e.g., "I hate Klingons") presented on a questionnaire. It is reasonable to assume that prejudice against Klingons might causally contribute to participant responses. However, it is also reasonable to assume that other factors may also contribute to an individual's responses. Examples of these include an individual's desire (a) to please the experimenter, (b) to "screw up" the experiment (e.g., via random responding), (c) to not appear prejudiced to themselves or to other people, (d) to appear dangerous to themselves or others by excessively denigrating Klingons, or (e) to conform to their society's prevailing opinion about Klingons. These alternatives might each be prompted by various elements of the measurement context (e.g., imagine that a Klingon is proctoring the test). The extent to which the Klingon prejudice measurement tool is subject to such alternative causal influences limits the validity of the measurement tool (see Vazire et al., 2022).

Properties of Measures to Consider When Assessing Measure Validity

Researchers in the social and behavioral sciences might be able to better anticipate threats to the validity of measures by attending to some of the properties of those measures. For example, some things that psychologists try to measure are quite *concrete*. Examples are:

- the length of a line produced by a research participant in response to a request to draw a 100 cm line;
- the amount of cortisol in a research participant's saliva;
- the time it takes for a research participant to pedal a bicycle from point A to point B;
- the minimum number of lumens output by a light source needed for a research participant to detect the light.

However, at times the attribute being measured might only be a concept or an idea (the psychometrics literature refers to these as *hypothetical constructs*). Examples of these are:

- the extent to which an individual is narcissistic;
- the extent to which an individual feels stress;
- the extent to which an individual is at risk of engaging in physical abuse of a child;
- the stability of an individual's self-concept.

Measurement tools also vary in terms of the *directness of the relation* between the measurement tool and the attribute being measured. In some cases, the relation seems quite direct. In these *direct measures*, use of the measurement tool requires only that the tool be properly "read" to provide an accurate measure of the attribute. Examples of these are:

- using a ruler to measure the length of a line drawn by a research participant;
- using a chemical assay to determine the amount of cortisol in saliva;

- using a stopwatch to measure the time it takes to cover 20 miles on a bicycle;
- using a light meter to determine the intensity of a light.

However, some measurement tools provide *indirect assessments* of an attribute. In such circumstances, researchers measure one attribute, then use that measurement *to make an inference* about a second attribute (the attribute of interest). This description is probably a bit obtuse, so let me clarify it with an illustrative example.

Consider the use of carbon-14 (or radiocarbon) dating to determine the age of bones unearthed in an archaeological dig. In carbon-14 dating, the property of the target that is *actually* measured is the amount of carbon-14 in the bone. However, this is not the attribute of interest in this measurement. This carbon-14 measurement is used to *make an inference* about a second bone property – the bone's age (for recent updates about carbon dating, see Jones, 2020). The inference relies on the chain of reasoning that follows in the next few sentences. While alive, animals absorb carbon, including a variant known as radioactive carbon-14. When the animal dies, they stop absorbing carbon. The radioactive carbon accumulated while the animal is alive decays at a rate that is relatively stable across time. Thus, given some assumptions about the rate of carbon-14 uptake while an animal was alive, measuring the amount of carbon-14 remaining in a found bone (must be less than 50,000 years old) can provide an estimate as to how long the animal has been dead. This "how long dead" estimate yields an estimate of the age of the bone. Thus, in carbon 14 dating, bone age (the construct of interest) *is not directly measured.* Instead, bone age *is inferred* from the influence that the age construct is thought to have on a second construct (the amount of carbon 14 in a bone – what is actually measured) that is thought to be related to age.

Social scientists often measure one attribute and use those measurements to make an inference about a second attribute. Examples include:

- measuring cortisol in saliva because researchers think that cortisol is an indicator of stress;
- examining the time it takes respondents to make a decision (response latency) about whether a black man holding a cell phone is perceived to be a threat to the respondent because researchers believe that response latencies in this scenario reflect respondent stereotypes or prejudices that influence processing ease;
- after respondents read a passage, measuring the number of word recognition errors a respondent makes on a later word recognition task because researchers believe that such errors reflect the extent to which people spontaneously thought of the words (that were not actually presented) when the respondents engaged in the initial reading task.

Despite the method differences reflected in these latter three examples, they are united by the fact that in all of these cases the measurement obtained is not the main interest. Instead, the measurement is thought to be an indicator of an attribute in which the researcher is interested. Cortisol levels in saliva are thought to fluctuate in response to psychological stress. Response latency is thought to fluctuate in response to the ease with which a stimulus can be understood. Erroneously recognizing words that did not actually appear in a text passage may reflect spontaneous activation and use of those words while reading the passage. In each of these three cases, then, each measure (cortisol, response latency, false recognition rate) is thought to reflect, or index, the action of an underlying psychological factor (stress, processing ease, construct activation level).

Having described these various properties, let me now turn to the reasons that explain why I suggest that researchers consider properties such as the concreteness/abstractness of a measure and the direct/indirect properties of a measure in their research programs. This suggestion follows from my belief that considering these properties will have an impact on an investigator's research program as that program pursues evidence for the validity of the measures used in the program. Here's the reasoning.

First, I believe that method validation ought to be an ongoing activity that is central to any research program. Second, I conjecture that this process of measure validation will **tend to be easier** for measures that assess concrete (vs. ideational or conceptual) attributes, and for measures that directly (vs. indirectly) assess attributes. These beliefs are grounded in the additional belief that the "mushiness" of hypothetical constructs (vs. concrete constructs) and the extra inferential step needed for the validation of indirect (vs. direct) construct measures *both tend to increase the risk of measure invalidity.*

In my view, these points suggest that a researcher will need to do extra work to validate measures of hypothetical constructs and measures that are indirect. The reasoning underlying this belief of heightened validation need for indirect (vs. direct) measures is straightforward. Simply stated, *there is more that can go wrong for indirect measures than can go wrong for direct measures.*

In direct measures, the primary source of error lies in the measurement process itself. For example, (a) machine error may cause response latency to be mismeasured, or (b) coder error may produce an erroneous count of negative reactions emitted during an interaction.

Such errors can also plague indirect measures. For example, in assessing how rapidly people can respond to incongruity in a stimulus, the latency measure itself can be erroneous (e.g., due to machine error). However, with such measures, *even more can go wrong*. For example, the extent to which the latency measure reflects the difficulty of stimulus processing caused by incongruity might be clouded by the fact that latency may also reflect other, non-incongruity factors. One such factor is that latencies might lengthen as respondents ponder how their responses make them look to themselves or others (e.g., because of a high need to appear socially desirable). Alternatively, latencies might decrease for respondents who become bored as they proceed through a lengthy procedure and quit meaningfully processing the stimuli presented to them. Thus, while response latencies might sometimes, and for some people, primarily reflect difficulty in processing an incongruity-containing stimulus, response latencies can also reflect self-presentation concerns, boredom, and a host of other constructs.

To be clear, constructs such as processing difficulty, self-presentation concerns, and boredom can also affect direct measures. However, for direct measures, these kinds of constructs can affect validity of measurement only via their impact on measurement accuracy, precision, and/or bias. In other words, these constructs can introduce measurement invalidity *via their influence on the process of measurement.* These constructs can degrade the validity of indirect measures in a similar fashion. However, these kinds of constructs can introduce invalidity for an indirect measure via a second route – *affecting what the measurement "means."* That is, the inference of an attribute from the measurement (e.g., processing difficulty caused by incongruity) provides an opportunity to introduce invalidity that goes beyond simple inaccuracy in the response latency measures. Instead, to the extent that response latencies are affected by social desirability concerns, those latencies are rendered less valid as a measure of processing incongruity. Thus, in these kinds of cases, *indirect measures might exhibit some degree of invalidity even though the measured attribute may have been measured perfectly (e.g., with perfect accuracy, with perfect precision, and without bias).*

The implication, then, is clear. With indirect measures, not only does a researcher need to document that the process of measurement produces a reasonably accurate measurement, but the researcher also needs to document that the implications for the measure (latency) for a second construct (processing difficulty caused by incongruency in a stimulus) are also valid. The next section describes just some of the methods that can be used to obtain such documentation.

Measurement Validity in the Research Program: Some Positive Practices

The points made in this chapter so far suggest that measurement validity ought to occupy a central role in a research program. What follows is a list of ideas and suggestions about how this centrality can be reflected in a research program.

Choose measurement tools known to be valid and/or that exhibit especially high validity. Researchers often have options about the manner in which an attribute of interest can be measured. For example, imagine that participants respond to a question by making a tick mark on a continuous line. How far this tick mark is from the starting point of the line can be measured with various devices. These include a ruler, a tape measure, a rolling wheel, or a laser measuring device. Which one should be used?

Obviously, measure choice will be affected by practical constraints imposed by budgets, elements of method (responses made via computer vs. made on paper), the characteristics of the respondents, the characteristics of the research team members, and the circumstances in which the research is conducted. However, the position advocated here is that because higher-validity measures tend to produce more useful results than lower-validity measures, an investigator should choose the highest-validity measure possible within their constraints.

A priori determination of measure validity can be obtained from various sources. For example, imagine that a researcher wants to assess the state depression of respondents via administration of a self-report depression measure. A search of the literature will reveal that many such measures exist (see American Psychological Association, 2019) and that extensive efforts have been made to validate many of them. Thus, in many circumstances, a researcher could reasonably choose as a starting point for their research a pre-validated measure that is a good fit to their practical constraints.

Develop and validate your own measurement tool. However, it is sometimes the case that a search of the literature does not yield a measure that a researcher thinks is satisfactory. In such cases, a researcher might choose to develop their own measure. In the case of such a desire, it is desirable to obtain a corpus of evidence documenting the validity of a measure before it is used in a research program. There are many examples of how this can be done. For example, Joel Milner, a researcher at Northern Illinois University, wanted to use a self-report questionnaire measure to assess a parent's risk of physically abusing their child. Not finding one that he thought was satisfactory, he went about developing his own measure. Descriptions of the extensive efforts to develop and validate the measure, and results from those efforts, appear in a number of publications (e.g., Milner, 1994, 2022a, 2022b; Milner & Crouch, 2012, 2017).

One point to be derived from Milner's story (and similar stories from other measures) is that that initial measure development and validation is typically not an easy task. Nonetheless, it is a crucial task. As noted earlier in this chapter's discussion of phrenology, considerable damage can be done when research uses invalid methods. Thus, before using a measure in a wide-ranging research program, it is essential to establish that a measurement method validly assesses a given attribute.

Pursuing and Assessing Measurement Validity

To this point, the present chapter has not addressed some of the nuts-and-bolts of pursuing measurement validity: documenting an existing measure's validity, documenting the validity of a new measure, or documenting the validity of an existing measure that is being used in a new context. The points raised in the present section will provide an overview that should help to remedy this omission. One important aspect of validity focuses on doing one's best to make sure to minimize error that might be introduced by the process of measurement. Useful techniques to minimize such error follow.

Calibration. *Frequently calibrate measurement tools* to confirm their accuracy, precision, and lack of bias. For example, to confirm a weight scale's accuracy, precision, and lack of bias, a researcher might conduct a method experiment in which they place a series of weights, one at a time, on the scale and measure the extent to which the scale's reading matches each known weight value. Data from such studies may show that instruments may need to be recalibrated or replaced. Moreover, because instrument accuracy, precision, and bias can change in response to factors such as instrument age, usage frequency, or fluctuating environmental conditions (such as changes in room temperature), it is desirable to conduct such calibration studies as often as is practicable.

Training. *Extensively train measurement tool users* so that they use the tools correctly and so that between-user differences are minimized. For example, in studies that obtain physiological measurements from research participants, research assistants may need to be trained extensively so that they always apply the equipment sensors in exactly the same manner to exactly the same locations. A second example illustrating the need for extensive training comes from studies in which research assistants view videos and record behaviors based on what they see. It is advisable to train the research assistants extensively prior to the start of the research so that (a) they code the behaviors in the prescribed manner and (b) between-coder differences in coding are minimized. It is also advisable to do periodic checks on the coding results provided by a given coder to ensure that the coder's performance has not drifted away from previous good performance.

Do your best to keep control over variables that might contaminate the measurement procedure. As has been noted earlier in this chapter, the accuracy and/or precision of results from a measurement procedure can sometimes be affected by seemingly minor alterations in equipment, technique, or environment. These include things like the characteristics of computers used to present stimuli, the gels used to attach electrodes, or the appearance of research assistants who administer psychological tests. Thus, to the extent possible, it is best to try to keep measurement circumstances as stable as possible across the various data collection sessions. If changes are made (e.g., equipment, supplies, or personnel), it is good practice, before proceeding with new research, to re-evaluate the performance of the measure in these new circumstances to ensure comparability with results previously obtained.

Take multiple measurements. It is often the case that the performance of a measure can be maximized by the collection of multiple measures. This can be accomplished in several ways. For example, when a property of something of interest is relatively stable across time, one might be able to use the same measurement tool repeatedly to assess the property (e.g., carpenters often say that you should measure twice before you cut). In addition, one can choose to perform repeated measurements using different measurement tools. For example, to determine the line length, indicated by a tick mark drawn through a line on a continuous response scale, reflecting the amount of anger a person is feeling, a researcher might repeatedly measure the placement of the tick mark relative to the starting anchor point using different rulers. This procedure (a method pursuing *convergent validity*) would help to minimize measurement bias that might be associated with any given ruler (due to either ruler bias or user bias).

One can also minimize user-based threats to accuracy by using multiple measurers. For example, in "olden days," to measure sprint speed, many observers with their own stopwatch separately recorded the time it took a runner to sprint 100 yards. They then used some mathematical method (e.g., median, mean, mean after discarding high and low times) to combine their observations. Statistical theory suggests that combining such observations can (though not always) produce more accurate data than a randomly selected single observation.

In addition, to maximize the accuracy, precision, and unbiasedness of measurement, researchers also need to use procedures that work to ensure that the meaning of measures, especially indirect measures, is as clear as possible. When pursuing evidence of the meaning of indirect measures, one can sometimes gather validity evidence from other researchers, or one can gather one's own validity evidence. Regardless of whether a researcher relies on validity evidence collected by others, or the researcher gathers their own validity data, a researcher's basic approach to this measure validation task is not hard to understand. I find that a useful way to approach the issue is to ask the question "Does this measure behave in the way that one would expect if the measure was actually assessing (some property)?" If research data leads one to answer "yes" to this question, then the measure has at least some validity (for a more elaborate discussion, see Foster & Cone, 1995).

One source of this kind of validation data is predictive/correlational. There are two components to this type of data. One component of correlational validation-supportive data would show *that a measure correlates with or predicts the things it "should"* – that the measure has *criterion validity*. The psychometrics literature suggests that one can discriminate among many different, somewhat specific, "flavors" of criterion validity. For example, the term *predictive validity* refers to a measure's capacity to predict something it should theoretically be able to predict. The term *concurrent validity* refers to a measure's capacity to assess correctly an attribute that is known to differ between groups. The term *convergent validity* refers to a measure's capacity to converge with data from other measures that supposedly measure the same thing as the target measure.

Here are examples of these kinds of criterion validity. For example, imagine that a researcher is trying to measure a respondent's prejudice toward Klingons via a self-report measure. Validity evidence for the measure would come from studies showing: (a) the measure predicts how often the respondent has discriminated against Klingons in the past, present, or future (an example of *predictive validity*); (b) strong correlations with other measures of anti-Klingon prejudice obtained from the respondent in the past, present, or future (an example of convergent validity); or (c) the ability to, with a reasonable degree of accuracy, discriminate between those who are known to be prejudiced against Klingons and those who are known to not be prejudiced against Klingons (an example of *concurrent validity*).

The other important element of correlational data indicative of validity shows that the measure is *not* correlated with the things it should not be correlated with it if were measuring a given construct. This is called *discriminant validity.* For example, one might be concerned that the self-report measure aimed at measuring prejudice against Klingons might not simply reflect prejudice against Klingons, but it might instead reflect the extent to which a respondent is prejudiced against any ethnic group other than the respondent's own. Such an explanation would be countered by data showing that a result from the self-report measure indicating high prejudice against Klingons is *not* associated with high levels of prejudice toward members of other groups (e.g., alternative *Star Trek* groups such as Aenars, Bajorans, Deltans, Ferengi). A similar approach can be used to show that people's responses to the Klingons prejudice measure do not largely reflect their attempts to provide socially desirable responses. This possibility can be discounted by showing low correlations between the anti-Klingon prejudice measures and other measures that assess an individual's tendency to behave in socially desirable ways. The bottom line is that validation of what a measure means sometimes comes from data showing that the measure indeed *does not predict what it shouldn't*.

There is also a non-correlational source of validity evidence for a measure – a measure's *elasticity* in response to manipulation. This term means that a measure should change appropriately in response to an experimental manipulation. For example, one would become more confident that a measure reflects prejudice against Klingons if scores on the measure decrease after exposure to a manipulation thought to reduce anti-Klingon prejudice (e.g., being helped by a Klingon in an emergency situation or being part of a successful working group that contained a diligent and effective Klingon).

One might wonder which of these kinds of validity evidence is "best." In my view, the answer is "all." That is, in my view, the best case for validity comes from successful validation studies that tap into *as many of these different forms of validation* using *as many different methods* as possible. This is the essence of the classic Campbell and Fiske (1959) multitrait/multimethod approach to validity.

Measure Validation Is Harder than It Looks

The argument that I offered in the prior paragraphs implies that measure validation will not be easy. Even when results are consistent across studies, many studies will be needed to be confident in a measure's validity. This suggests that, even under the best of circumstances, validating a measure will be a long and labor-intensive process. However, researchers do not always operate in the best of circumstances. Inevitably, sometimes, perfect cross-study convergence does not occur. A measure that looks to be valid in one set of studies might not look to be as valid when assessed in different studies.

Sometimes, this inconsistent validity evidence is caused by the different criterion measures used across studies. For example, in the attitude measurement literature, a given attitude (i.e., the focal measure) tends to be more valid as a predictor of other attitudes than of attitude-related behaviors (for context, see Ajzen, 2005). Explanations for this difference across studies often center on the different characteristics of the different criterion variables used in the different studies (i.e., the attitudes being predicted vs. the behaviors being predicted). In other words, some researchers in this area believe that this discrepancy across studies is not caused by differences in the quality of the focal attitude measure across studies, but by differences in the criterion measures used across studies.

To generalize this conclusion, sometimes a measured variable might be equally valid as a measure of a "thing" (e.g., object, property, or construct) across studies, but may vary in its predictive power across studies *because of qualities of the other variables being assessed in those studies and the properties of the measures used to assess those variables* Indeed, such inconsistency across studies may characterize even a perfectly measured "thing." These kinds of inconsistency effects can be a difficult problem for measure validation. However, even here, one expects that with a sufficient amount of research, one should eventually be able to show that this kind of cross-study inconsistency is not caused by the measure that one is attempting to validate, but instead by the properties of the variables (or measures of those variables) that one is employing for the purposes of validation.

However, it will sometimes be the case that the validity of a measure "truly" varies across studies. To this end, I remind readers that, earlier in this chapter, I argued that discrepant results across validation studies may sometimes be caused by differences in the *research contexts* that are present in those studies. Change the context in which a measure is used, and the validity of the measure may change from the validity exhibited by the measure when used in its original circumstances.

Context Effects Revisited

I believe that many researchers may not appreciate the relatively high likelihood with which these context effects may occur. I hope to change this perception by noting just some of the mechanisms by which context can alter a measure's validity. As in the shipwright example used earlier in this chapter, one mechanism works via alterations in the physical ability of a researcher to make measurements across contexts. For example, researchers who use some physiological measures will make their measurements in special shielded rooms that minimize electromagnetic signals that originate from outside the room. Doing so minimizes variability in the data provided by the devices that are trying to capture the electromagnetic "signals" of interest. Hence, readings from a physiological measure that might exhibit high validity when taken in a shielded room may not exhibit similarly high validity when taken in an unshielded room.

This is not the only relatively obvious reason that measure validity might fluctuate across circumstances. Another example comes from research showing that people might sometimes act differently depending on whether they know they are being observed or are especially concerned about being observed (e.g., Costa-Gomes et al., 2019). For example, imagine a study in which a parent's behaviors toward their child are recorded and coded by observers so that an inference can be made about the parent's risk of being a child abuser. A parent's behaviors may provide a reasonably valid measure of child abuse risk when parental behavior is recorded secretly. However, it is easy to imagine that a parent who is actually at high risk of child abuse might try to hide this fact by being on their "best behavior" when they know that they are being evaluated for child abuse risk. Thus, the validity of the observational measure of child abuse risk might decrease substantially when the parent knows that their behavior is being evaluated.

Another example of the effects of measurement circumstances on measure validity involves the extent to which a context causes an individual to focus on the task at hand and/or take that task seriously. For example, imagine that during the development and validation of a self-report scale, the scale was administered in clinical or laboratory settings and yielded relatively high validity in such settings. It is not hard to imagine that such high validity levels might not be achieved when the self-reports are collected and respondents are in their home. One can imagine that, in such circumstances, respondents might not be fully attentive to the self-report measure; their responses may be influenced by many factors (e.g., interruptions and distractions from people and devices or haste prompted by a lack of supervision and a desire to complete the self-report measure as quickly as possible). These influences can all weaken the validity of the inference from the measured participant responses to the hypothetical attribute that the self-report intended to measure.

However, the effect of contexts on measurement validity may not always be so obvious.

One real example of a subtle context effect comes from the experience of a graduate student who was trying to measure non-verbal mimicry – the tendency of one partner in a dyadic interaction to match the non-verbal movements of the second partner in the interaction (see Chartrand & Lakin, 2013). Many researchers had independently replicated the phenomenon, but for a time, the graduate student could not do so. Diligent sleuthing by the graduate student discerned that the reason lay in a small detail of procedure. In the procedure, the two interaction partners had to look at photos in a folder and then discuss them; this is where the mimicry was supposed to happen. The graduate student's original procedure left the folder open. His sleuthing revealed that, in the procedures that found evidence of mimicry, the folder was closed. To his chagrin, the graduate student realized that, when the folder was open, the partners looked at the photos and not at each other, suggesting that gazing at the partner was necessary for mimicry. Accordingly, when the graduate student changed the procedure so the folder was closed, the non-verbal mimicry phenomenon emerged. The important lesson here is that even small, seemingly insignificant context changes may substantially alter the validity of a measure.

Another illustration of how such small context changes might matter greatly to measure validity comes from research examining standardized testing situations (e.g., ACT or SAT testing). In such circumstances, it is believed that performance on the test reveals something about the knowledge possessed by, and/or mental capabilities of, the test-taker. However, the results of testing might not be equally valid across testing circumstances.

The phenomenon of stereotype threat (e.g., Inzlicht et al., 2006) illustrates this effect. The stereotype threat phenomenon shows that the performance of some people on standardized tests might sometimes be suppressed. This suppression may occur when (a) the test-taker belongs to a group that is associated with a stereotype containing beliefs about poor performance in the domain assessed by the test, and (b) the conditions of testing make the stereotype salient to the test-taker.

To illustrate this phenomenon, imagine that Klingons are a minority group associated with the stereotype of mental incompetence. When before the test a Klingon test-taker is exposed to a pre-standardized test task that might activate the Klingon/mental incompetence stereotype (e.g., by being asked to check "Klingon" in a pretest demographic survey), the Klingon's performance on the test may be suppressed. Hence, as with the non-verbal mimicry example described earlier in this chapter, our

Klingon test-taker's test results may differ based on seemingly trivial changes in measurement circumstances. More importantly, these differences suggest that the test is *not an equally valid assessment* of knowledge and mental capabilities across those circumstances.

One other subtle contextual variable that requires researcher awareness reflects systematic differences in the characteristics of people across research samples. I suggest that it is dangerous to assume that a measure that exhibited high validity when used with one set of individuals will exhibit similarly high validity when used with a different set of individuals. In making this point, I am obviously considering different respondent populations to constitute different measurement contexts.

It should be intuitively reasonable that the validity of a measure may vary across systematic differences in the characteristics of the individuals being measured. These systematic differences may sometimes reflect demographics. For example, a self-report measure exhibiting high validity when used on individuals from Western countries may not exhibit the same validity when used with individuals from Eastern countries. These differences can also occur at the level of individual personalities. That is, a self-report measure exhibiting high validity when used with highly conscientious respondents may not exhibit similarly high variability when the respondents are low in conscientiousness. Finally, these differences can also reflect experiences or expertise. A measure that exhibits high validity when used with chess novices may not exhibit equal validity when used with chess masters.

The implication of this discussion of these contextual variables for measure validation is extremely important, especially because contexts in research programs are *always* changing. Even when a researcher attempts, to the best of their ability, to replicate exactly a previously used measurement procedure, the new study reflects at least one contextual change: there is a passage time between the initial study and the replication. Thus, because the contexts in which measurements occur are *always* changing, researchers *always* need to consider the possibility that the validity of a measure might change across these contexts.

I suggest that researchers ought to keep this possible context-validity relation in mind when evaluating the extent to which a corpus of research provides inconsistent support for the validity of a measure. I also suggest that researchers ought to expect that at least some of this inconsistency can be explained by alterations of contexts across studies, and that a systematic analysis of the contexts might be useful as a guide to the generation of new measure validation research.

Coda

I would guess that most research-focused social and behavioral scientists entered their field because they were interested in elements of their field's foci. For example, when trying to understand human thought and behavior, sociologists may emphasize the study of cultures, geographers may emphasize the study of locations, and psychologists may emphasize the study of the mind. However, despite this diversity, the scientific endeavors of these different scholars are united by the fact that regardless of their foci, research-focused social and behavioral scientists need to be good research technicians: they have to do a good job in measuring variables that are central to their foci.

Why this emphasis on measurement? In this chapter, I have made the case that the reason for this emphasis on good measurement practice is that an accurate understanding of the social and behavioral sciences *depends crucially* on the use of valid measures of variables that are of interest and importance. In this chapter, I also aimed to argue effectively that the establishment of measurement validity is not an easy task, as a measure's validity can sometimes be a slippery beast. Thus, in my view, establishing measure validity should *always* be a central goal in a research program. In pursuit of this goal, researchers need to gather evidence for measure validity diligently, persistently, and constantly. Finally, I also hope that this chapter helps readers to think about when to, and how to, use the variety of available techniques that contribute to documentation of the validity of a measure.

Acknowledgments

Thanks to David Valentiner, Alecia Santuzzi, Randy McCarthy, and Joel Milner for the kind assistance that they provided during the writing of this chapter.

References

Ajzen, I. (2005). The influence of attitudes on behavior. In D. Albarracín, B. T. Johnson, & M. P. Zanna (eds.), *The Handbook of Attitudes* (pp. 173–221). Lawrence Erlbaum Associates.

American Psychological Association (2019, August). *Depression Assessment Instruments*. www.apa.org/depression-guideline/assessment

Bode, B., King, A., Russell-Jones, D., & Billings, L. K. (2021). Leveraging advances in diabetes technologies in primary care: A narrative review. *Annals of Medicine*, 53(1), 805–816. https://doi.org/10.1080/07853890.2021.1931427

Borsboom, D., Mellenbergh, G. J., & Van Heerden, J. (2004). The concept of validity. *Psychological Review*, 111(4), 1061–1071. https://doi.org/10.1037/0033-295X.111.4.1061

Buntins, M., Buntins, K., & Eggert, F. (2017). Clarifying the concept of validity: From measurement to everyday language. *Theory & Psychology*, 27(5), 703–710. https://doi.org/10.1177/0959354317702256

Camargo, S. L., Herrera, A. N., & Traynor, A. (2018). Looking for a consensus in the discussion about the concept of validity: A Delphi study. *Methodology: European Journal of Research Methods for the Behavioral and Social Sciences*, 14(4), 146–155. https://doi.org/10.1027/1614-2241/a000157

Campbell, D. T., & Fiske, D. W. (1959). Convergent and discriminant validation by the Multitrait-Multimethod Matrix. *Psychological Bulletin*, 56(2), 81–105. http://dx.doi.org/10.1037/h0046016

Chartrand, T. L., & Lakin, J. L. (2013). The antecedents and consequences of human behavioral mimicry. *Annual Review of Psychology, 64*, 285–308. https://doi.org/10.1037/h0046016

Combe, G. (1835). *The Constitution of Man, Considered in Relation to External Objects*. John Anderson Jr.

——— (1851). *A System of Phrenology*. Benjamin B. Mussey.

Conan Doyle, A. (1981). The *Original Illustrated* Sherlock Holmes. Castle Books.

Costa-Gomes, M.A., Ju, Y., & Li, J. (2019). Role reversal consistency: An experimental study of the golden rule. *Economic Inquiry, 57*(1), 685–704. https://doi.org/10.1111/ecin.12708

Duckworth, A. L., Peterson, C., Matthews, M. D., & Kelly, D. R. (2007). Grit: Perseverance and passion for long-term goals. *Journal of Personality and Social Psychology, 92* (6), 1087–1101. https://doi.org/10.1037/0022-3514.92.6.1087

Eling, P., & Finger, S. (eds.) (2021). *Gall, Spurzheim, and the Phrenological Movement: Insights and Perspectives*. Routledge.

Falk C. F., Heine S. J., Takemura K., Zhang C. X., & Hsu, C.-W. (2015). Are implicit self-esteem measures valid for assessing individual and cultural differences? *Journal of Personality, 83*, 56–68. https://doi.org/10.1111/jopy.12082

Foster, S. L., & Cone, J. D. (1995). Validity issues in clinical assessment. *Psychological Assessment, 7*(3), 248–260. https://doi.org/10.1037/1040-3590.7.3.248

Fuentes, A., Ackermann, R. R., Athreya, S., Bolnik, D., Lasisi, T., Lee, S., et al. (2019). AAPA statement on race and racism. *American Journal of Physical Anthropology, 169* (3), 400–402. https://doi.org/10.1002/ajpa.23882

Gardner, M. (1957). From bumps to handwriting. In Gardner, *Fads and Fallacies in the Name of Science*. Dover.

Ghandnoosh, N. (2014, September 3). Race and punishment: Racial perceptions of crime and support for punitive policies. *The Sentencing Project*. www.sentencingproject.org/publications/race-and-punishment-racial-perceptions-of-crime-and-support-for-punitive-policies

Goodman, A. H., Moses, Y. T., & Jones, J. L. (2020). *Race: Are We So Different?* 2nd ed. John Wiley & Sons / American Anthropological Association.

Greenblatt, S. H. (1995). Phrenology in the science and culture of the 19th century. *Neurosurgery, 37*(4), 790–805. https://doi.org/10.1227/00006123-199510000-00025

Herrnstein, R. J., & Murray, C. (1994). *The Bell Curve: Intelligence and class Structure in American Life*. Free Press.

Hollander, B. (1902). *Scientific Phrenology: Being a Practical Mental Science and Guide to Human Character*. Grant Richards.

Inzlicht, M., McKay, L., & Aronson, J. (2006). Stigma as ego depletion: How being the target of prejudice affects self-control. *Psychological Science, 17*(3), 262–269. https://doi.org/10.1111/j.1467-9280.2006.01695.x

Jones, N. (2020). Carbon dating, the archaeological workhorse, is getting a major reboot. *Nature News*, May 19. https://doi.org/10.1038/d41586-020-01499-y

Lilienfeld, S. O. (2017). Microaggressions: Strong claims, inadequate evidence. *Perspectives on Psychological Science, 12*(1), 138–169. https://doi.org/10.1177/1745691616659391

Lissitz, Robert W. (ed.). (2009). *The Concept of Validity: Revisions, New Directions, and Applications*. IAP Information Age.

Milner, J. S. (1994). Assessing physical child abuse risk: The Child Abuse Potential Inventory. *Clinical Psychology Review, 14*(6), 547–583. https://doi.org/10.1016/0272-7358(94)90017-5

(2022a). *The Child Abuse Potential Inventory: Manual.* Psytec.

(2022b). *An Interpretive Manual for the Child Abuse Potential Inventory*, rev. ed. Psytec.

Milner, J. S., & Crouch, J. L. (2012). Psychometric characteristics of translated versions of the Child Abuse Potential Inventory. *Psychology of Violence, 2*(3), 239–259. https://doi.org/10.1037/a0026957

(2017). Child physical abuse risk assessment: Parent and family evaluations. In J. C. Campbell & J. T. Messing (eds.), *Assessing Dangerousness: Domestic Violence Offenders and Child Abusers*, 3rd ed. (pp. 55–88). Springer.

Parker Jones, O., Alfaro-Almagro, F., & Jbabdi, S. (2018). An empirical, 21st century evaluation of phrenology. *Cortex, 106*, 28–35. https://doi.org/10.1016/j.cortex.2018.04.011

Ponnock, A., Muenks, K., Morell, M., Seung Yang, J., Gladstone, J. R., & Wigfield, A. (2020). Grit and conscientiousness: Another jangle fallacy. *Journal of Research in Personality, 89*, 1–5. https://doi.org/10.1016/j.jrp.2020.104021

Rudman, L. A., Greenwald, A. G., Mellott, D. S., & Schwartz, J. L. K. (1999). Measuring the automatic components of prejudice: Flexibility and generality of the Implicit Association Test. *Social Cognition, 17*(4), 437–465. https://doi.org/10.1521/soco.1999.17.4.437

Sackett, P. R, Putka, D. J, & McCloy, R. A. (2012). The concept of validity and the process of validation. In N. Schmitt (ed.), *The Oxford Handbook of Personnel Assessment and Selection* (pp. 91–118). Oxford University Press.

Schimmack, U. (2021). The Implicit Association Test: A method in search of a construct. *Perspectives on Psychological Science, 16*(2), 396–414. https://doi.org/10.1177/1745691619863798

Sue, D. W., Capodilupo, C. M., Torino, G. C., Bucceri, J. M., Holder, A. M. B., Nadal, K. L., & Esquilin, M. (2007). Racial microaggressions in everyday life: Implications for clinical practice. *American Psychologist, 62*(4), 271–286. https://doi.org/10.1037/0003-066X.62.4.271

Thomas, C., & Skowronski, J. J. (2020). The study of microaggressive behavior: Reflections on the construct, construct-relevant research, and possible future research. In J. T. Nadler & E. C. Voyles (eds.), *Stereotypes: The Incidence and Impacts of Bias* (pp. 45–69). Praeger.

Thompson, C. E. (2021). *An Organ of Murder: Crime, Violence, and Phrenology in Nineteenth-Century America*. Rutgers University Press.

Tynan, M. C. (2021). Deconstructing Grit's validity: The case for revising Grit measures and theory. In L. E. van Zyl, C. Olckers, & E. van der Vaart (eds.), *Multidisciplinary perspectives on Grit: Contemporary Theories, Assessments, Applications and Critiques* (pp. 137–155). Springer.

Vazire, S., Schiavone, S. R., & Bottesini, J. G. (2022). Credibility beyond replicability: Improving the four validities in psychological science. *Current Directions in Psychological Science, 31*(2), 162–168. https://doi.org/10.1177/09637214211067779

Vintage News Daily. (2017, September 20). Bad invention: Psychograph, a phrenology machine to measure the shape of your head from the early 20th century. https://vintagenewsdaily.com/bad-invention-psychograph-a-phrenology-machine-to-measure-the-shape-of-your-head-from-the-early-20th-century

11 Statistical Power: How Not to Miss What's Right in Front of You

Erin M. Buchanan

Abstract

In this chapter, we discuss the definitions of power and how to interpret power in Null Hypothesis Significance Testing. Next, the main determinants of power are outlined, including the sample size, effect size (and variability), α, and the type of statistical test. Each influence on power is demonstrated with example studies on statistics education and data literacy. Different types of power analyses, planning for sample sizes and sensitivity, are illustrated using power tables, popular programs, simulation, and accuracy in parameter estimation. Last, the limitations of power – especially what it does not tell you and what you should not do – are outlined to warn you about the potential misuses of power analyses. Suggestions on appropriate power planning are provided at the end of the chapter.

Keywords: Power, Effect Size, Sample Size, Software, Programming

Statistical power is one of the most difficult aspects of designing and implementing a research project, as it is often confusing and overly technical to many scientists. One reason for this confusion is the number of facets that serve a role in understanding or calculating power, which all need to be considered simultaneously for the best outcomes in a research project. First, let's cover the definition of power and related statistical concepts, so you can understand how to use power analyses to plan your research studies. Three example studies related to statistics education and literacy will help solidify how to apply the concepts of power and calculate power analyses for future studies.

What Is Power?

When using Null Hypothesis Significance Testing (NHST), statistical power represents the ability to discover an effect *if* it truly exists. NHST, in the modern era, is a combination of the works from Neyman-Pearson and Fisher used to test opposing hypotheses (Dienes, 2008). The null (or nil) hypothesis is generally the default consideration that no effect/relationship exists. The alternative (or research) hypothesis suggests that something did happen in the study. For example, in one study (outlined below), we might propose:

H_0 Null Hypothesis: The classes taught with *R* and *JASP* do not have different final exam scores.

H_A Research Hypothesis: The classes taught with *R* and *JASP* have different final exam scores.

In this setup, the hypothesis does not predict a specific direction (i.e., *R* students performed better than *JASP* students), but rather simply predicts that some difference between their final exams may be found. We could use an independent *t*-test as our statistical test to determine whether we find any differences between classroom final exam means. Statistical tests can be imagined as a ratio of our model hypothesis to the amount of error in the study. For example, we want to detect whether there's a larger difference in the final exams between classes (model hypothesis) than we might expect considering individual students are all different (error). Power is the ability to find a high enough ratio to detect the difference.

Within the NHST framework, the researcher must decide to either "reject" the null hypothesis as very unlikely given a large enough ratio of model to error or "fail to reject" the null hypothesis when the ratio of model to error is small or equal. In Figure 11.1, we show our decision on the left-hand side, and on the top, the real world, if one could know the real outcome, is displayed. If we failed to reject the null hypothesis, we would make the correct decision if there was no real difference in final exams. However, if we fail to reject the null hypothesis (do not detect those differences), and there truly are differences in *R* and *JASP* classrooms, we have "missed" detecting the effect (i.e., β or a Type II error; top right corner). On the other side, if we reject the null hypothesis, and say there are differences in final exam scores, we could make a Type I error (represented by α) if there was no actual difference in reality. Last, power reflects the probability that we would reject the null hypothesis when we should, as there is a difference to be found between final exam scores.

Let's provide an analogy to help solidify this type of thinking. Imagine you are a detective who is trying to solve a crime. Your statistical test is the amount of evidence that you can collect that points to who committed the crime (model) compared to the evidence that does not clearly support that they did the crime, or

		Real World	
		H_0 True No Effect	H_A True An Effect
Our Decision	H_0 Fail to Reject No Effect Detected	Correct Decision	β Type II
	H_0 Rejected Effect Detected	α Type I	Power

Figure 11.1 *Decision errors, power, and correct rejections for null hypothesis testing.*

the evidence is wrong (error). A Type I error would occur if person A was found guilty of the crime, as it appeared there was enough evidence, but in reality, person A did not commit the crime. A Type II error would occur if person A committed the crime, but you could never find enough evidence to convict them. Last, power would be the ability of the detective to find the evidence to convict the right person for the crime. Another famous example is of pregnancy tests: a Type I error would occur if a someone who is not pregnant was told they were pregnant at the doctor's office, while a Type II error would occur if the pregnancy test was negative and did not detect an actual pregnancy.

Our ability to know the "real" answer is generally limited, especially in scientific studies. Therefore, α, β, and power are generally represented as theoretical concepts used to control and plan research studies. Each of these values is expressed as a probability. Researchers will generally set the probability of α to $\leq .05$ to avoid a Type I error, as it is perceived as more problematic than a Type II error and is a strong research norm. Several fields, such as medicine and physics, require lower α values for their studies, usually α to $\leq .001$. β is commonly set to $\leq .20$ – a 20% probability of missing a true effect. Power is the direct opposite of β, and therefore, by choosing .20, power becomes .80 – an 80% likelihood of detecting an effect that exists (i.e., power $= 1 - \beta$). Note that the probabilities listed here are common practice in current research but are not necessarily "correct," and each should be carefully considered and justified within the context of any research study (Lakens et al., 2018). Within the current credibility revolution – the drive for improved quality in scientific studies (Vazire, 2018) – power plays an important role, and many have suggested setting this value to a higher standard (i.e., power > 90%) to improve the evidence provided within an individual study.

The rest of this chapter focuses on power analyses as defined for NHST frameworks. Other statistical frameworks, such as Bayesian analysis, still require power analyses (Dienes, 2023; McElreath, 2020). However, they may not use traditional or popular programs that others use for power purposes that we will outline below. Readers interested in learning more about Bayesian analyses can check out Dienes (2023).

Study Examples

To help illustrate these issues, we will consider three different research studies focusing on statistics education that highlight the nuance required for statistical power analysis.

In our first research project, shown in Figure 11.2, a statistics teacher is interested to know whether students differ in their final exams scores based on the software used within an introduction to statistics course. Several professors have implemented the software *R* – a programming-based computer language that was designed to calculate statistics (R Core Team, 2022). Learning a programming language is often daunting to students, and the statistics teacher also recruits several instructors who use *JASP* (Jeffreys's Amazing Statistics Program) – a point-and-click statistics

Figure 11.2 *Study 1 illustrates two separate statistics classrooms each learning a different software to determine the influence of computer programs on final grades.*

Figure 11.3 *Study 2 illustrates a survey design where students' data literacy is assessed to understand its relationship with future employment in data analytics.*

program designed to calculate statistics using R with no programming knowledge (JASP Team, 2022). Both programs are desirable to students, as they are both free, unlike their rivals.

Our second study, in Figure 11.3, illustrates a survey in which students' data literacy and digital competence are measured at the end of their college career in a university exit exam (Gümüş & Kukul, 2023). Digital competence refers to the ability of individuals to process, understand, and apply information found in digital sources (e.g., social media, news outlets, research; Pangrazio et al., 2020). Not only are these skills necessary for day-to-day activities (i.e., interpreting the weather report), they are increasingly necessary for employment. Trends in job descriptions and hiring advertisements indicate that employers are increasingly interested in data analytics and digital competence (US Bureau of Labor Statistics, n.d.; Matli & Ngoepe, 2020). Data analytics can be leveraged across the workforce, from research careers in analyzing study data, to improving student learning in education, to business practices to optimize performance, increase profits, and improve customer relations. Software toolkits, such as R and *JASP*, are featured in data analytics as well as the ability to comprehend, process, and apply statistical skills. In this study, the correlation is examined between students' data literacy scores and self-reported income in their first job after graduation.

Figure 11.4 *A depiction of Study 3 that examines the implementation of gamification in a statistics classroom to improve data literacy.*

Finally, our last study, shown in Figure 11.4, extends into a newer methodology: ecological momentary assessment (EMA; Shiffman et al., 2008). In EMA studies, participants are asked to fill out smaller surveys or questionnaires over a period of time (e.g., once a day for two weeks, once a week for a semester). This type of design has surged in popularity, as survey platforms and special smartphone apps have made it easier for both the researcher and participant to complete the study (Porras-Segovia et al., 2020). As noted, data literacy is increasingly imperative for future employment, yet many students have anxiety when taking a statistics course (Aerts et al., 2021; Ralston, 2020). In this study, statistics courses were "gamified" by adding challenges and leader boards to the course to mimic game play found in many popular phone and video games (Legaki et al., 2020). Students were encouraged to maximize their points and compete in teams to improve on the leader board, and these game modules served as practice to improve data literacy skills and improve student performance on exams (Seaborn & Fels, 2015). Students were assessed on data literacy throughout the semester using the EMA design, and these scores were predicted by the game module points in the course.

In this chapter, we will use these three studies as examples to outline the definitions and influences on power. In the next section, we will explore what factors can influence power. These influences will be applied when demonstrating how to calculate power and how the same design can lead to different answers when exploring power. Last, we will warn you about what a power analysis *does not* tell you, as a cautionary tale to understand the limitations of power.

Determinants of Power

In this section, we will review the factors that influence power, including sample size, the effect size, α, and the type of statistical test. For each, you will see an example of the factor's effect on overall power. Remember, while we discuss these individually, they tend to interact within a study – as each factor changes, the power will change accordingly. That said, researchers tend to fix most of these values and focus on one influencing factor at a time, when conducting a power analysis, to decrease complexity of calculation.

Sample Size

Sample size is often considered the main determinant of power in a study, especially because sample size is the main factor that a researcher has control over when planning and executing a study. As such, it is typical to see a published or pre-registered "power analysis" focus on determining sample size necessary for their study.

So why does sample size have such a large influence on power? Remember that statistical tests are generally calculated by using a formula of model variability to the amount of error variability. Error variability is generally some form of standard error and is calculated by $\frac{SD}{\sqrt{(N)}}$ or a similar form depending on test. This formula represents the standard deviation – the amount of variation around the mean – divided by the square root of the sample size (N). With this formula, as N increases, the overall standard error decreases. When you divide your model variability by a smaller error variability (standard error), the ratio of model to error increases, and the ability to find a significant effect also increases. In fact, this influence is so well known, it is a common statistical joke to note that with large enough sample sizes "everything is significant." As we will note in our limitations section, large power and significant results are not necessarily practically important results.

Large sample sizes have additional bonuses beyond increasing power. First, we have increased our precision in measurement (see the Newer Methods: AIPE section below) for our study and hopefully sampled a larger diversity of participants. Larger samples mean that individual data points have less influence on statistical parameters, such as the mean and standard deviation. Last, the "big-team" science movement has made collecting large sample sizes easier on individual researchers. In these studies, multiple research labs, often across the globe, join to collect data (Coles et al., 2022; Cuccolo et al., 2021; Koch & Jones, 2016) to improve power, generalizability, and scientific knowledge.

In our second study, we will examine the correlation between data literacy and first job income. If we set all the other variables that affect power, how does the sample size increase our ability to detect a correlation? As you can see in Figure 11.5, larger sample sizes increase power in a curvilinear fashion (often called a power curve!) that eventually approaches nearly 100% power.

Effect Size

Effect size is our second factor that influences power. Effect size is a standardized measurement of the magnitude of the results in our study – that is, how "big" the results were in the study (Lakens, 2013). Some common effect sizes include d (the standardized mean difference between groups or measurements), r (the correlation between two measurements), and η^2 (the proportion of overlap between the independent variable(s) and the dependent variable). Effect sizes can aid researchers in comparing between studies with different variables, interpreting the size or impact of their study variables, and planning future studies.

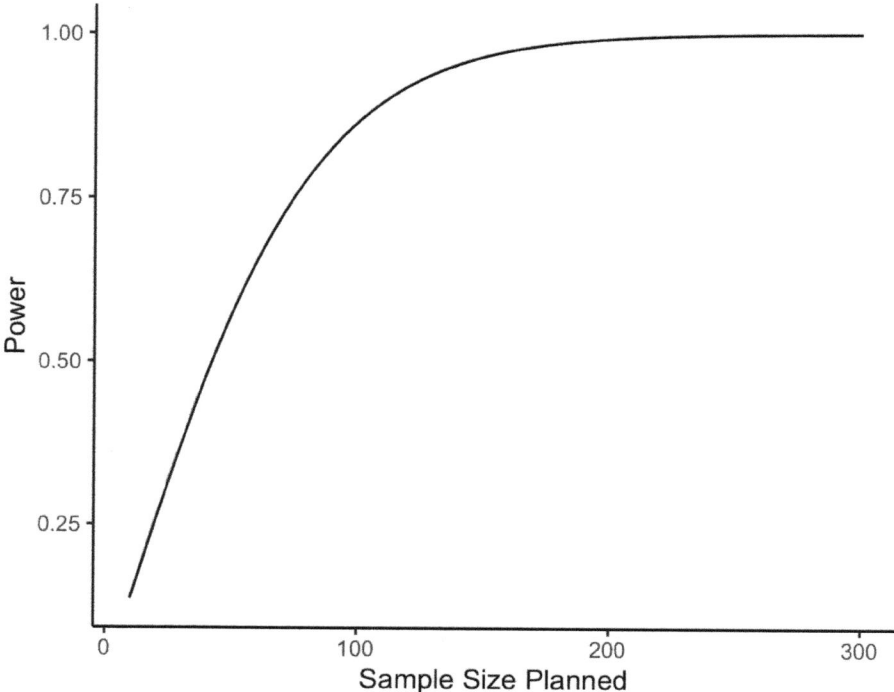

Figure 11.5 *The relationship between planned sample size and power in the correlation study measuring data literacy skills and future income. This curve represents the power and sample size for a correlation of* r = *.30 using* α *of .05.*

Effect sizes are generally impacted by two components: (1) the size of the model variability, and (2) the size of the error variability. As noted earlier, these two pieces are the formula for most statistical tests and part of our explanation for why sample size is a large factor in power analyses. The difference between the statistical test formula and effect size formula is the sample size: if the statistical test is approximated by $\frac{Model}{SE}$ then the effect size would be $\frac{Model}{SD}$, as effect sizes are designed to represent the magnitude of the model without the influence of sample size (i.e., *SE* is calculated by dividing *SD* by the square root of *N*). Note that this explanation gives you the basic idea of the concept for effect sizes, as the real formulas for effect size are influenced by the number of variables and type of research design.

Power will increase with larger effect sizes, as it's always easier to find effects that are larger. As the size of the model variability increases, we see increases in power; correspondingly, as the model error decreases, we also see increases in power (because it's in the denominator of the formula). If we add a few different effect sizes to our data literacy study (rather than just *r* = .30), we can see the impact of effect size and sample size simultaneously (Figure 11.6). As the different correlations increase in size (the lines on the figure), the power increases at each sample size. We can see how they interact, as

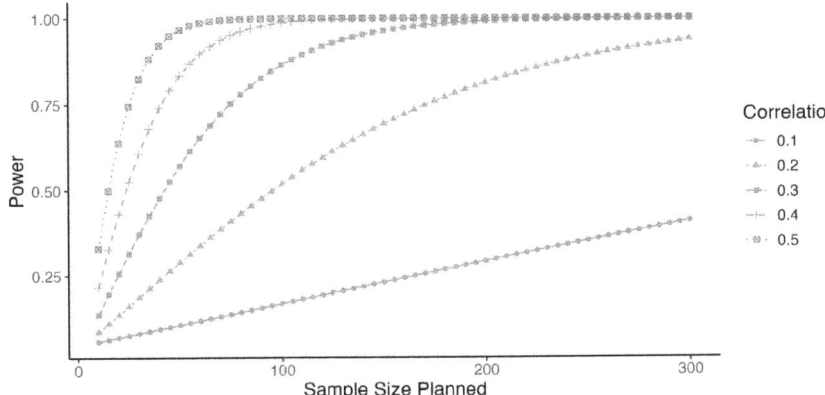

Figure 11.6 *The relationship between sample size planned, power, and effect size (the lines) for our correlation study measuring data literacy and income using α = .05.*

larger effect sizes show a sharper increase in power as sample size increases because the lines reach nearly 100% power faster (e.g., they are steeper).

Sample Size and Effect Size Together

We noted in the previous section that many power analyses are used for study planning to determine the sample size necessary for the study to achieve a certain level of power. Alternatively, if our sample size is limited due to money, time, or a small study population, we can use a sensitivity analysis to determine the smallest detectable effect given all other considerations (Vevea & Woods, 2005). These analyses have become more popular to illuminate whether the study has or had adequate power to detect a certain effect, especially if the study did not find the effect size researchers planned. For example, if the study was planned with a medium effect but found a small one, did they have enough power to detect the small or medium effect? These sensitivity analyses may be especially important when considering publication bias – the issue that studies are significantly more likely to be published if they contain significant effects (Franco et al., 2014). If we use previously published results to help estimate our effect size for a newly planned study's power analysis, it is likely that we will use a number nearly twice the real effect size (Open Science Collaboration, 2015) because the studies that did not show larger effects did not get published. Both sensitivity analyses and smallest detectable effects will be demonstrated below in the power analysis section.

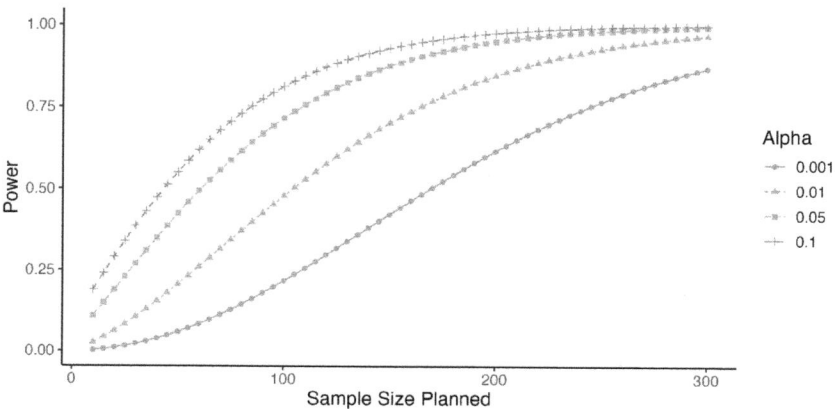

Figure 11.7 *The relationship between sample size planned, power, and the α criterion for our data literacy correlation study where* r ~ .25.

Alpha

As described earlier, α is the Type I error rate (i.e., the probability of incorrectly rejecting the null hypothesis when the null is true). The most common α value found in social and behavioral science literature is $\alpha \leq .05$, although there is no particular reason why it should be set to .05. Some scientists recently suggested this value should be lowered to control for the number of studies that were published with false positives (Benjamin et al., 2018), while others suggested that the rule was not the problem – the mindless use of the rule was the issue (Lakens et al., 2018). Of note, physics and the medical field often use lower criteria of .01 or .001 (Meehl, 1967), so alternative alpha levels are not unheard of. Each individual researcher should examine what they would consider as their threshold before the research is conducted based on their desire to balance Type I to Type II errors (Miller & Ulrich, 2019).

As α increases (e.g., as it approaches one), power also increases. Using our sample size example from above, we can plot the power for several α values in comparison with power (Figure 11.7). The interpretation here is that if you give yourself a 10% chance of falsely rejecting the null ($\alpha = .10$), you will increase power versus only giving yourself a .1% chance of falsely rejecting the null ($\alpha = .001$). It is usually not recommended to simply increase α to increase power, especially as the scientific community worries that too many false positives already exist.

Test Type

The last main influence on power is the type of research design and statistical test. Although many statistics books pretend that a specific research design is always analyzed with a corresponding specific statistical test, reality is much more complicated. A research study called the "Many Analysts" paper gave multiple teams of researchers the same data and hypothesis and asked each to analyze the data. The study investigators then compiled the number of ways the data was analyzed, and the effect size found in each team analysis. These teams came up with over twenty ways to analyze the data with a wide range of final effect sizes reported (Silberzahn et al., 2018). Therefore, we see that different types of statistical tests can be performed on the same data. The main idea is that some statistical tests are more sensitive, meaning they are likely to give you more power to detect effects that exist in comparison to other statistical tests.

The influence of research design is a bit easier to conceptualize: repeated measures designs have more power than between-subjects designs. Please note that these often have multiple names – repeated measures can be called dependent or within-subject designs; between-subjects can be called independent designs. Our third study is a repeated measures design because each person is measured on their data literacy multiple times within the same study; the first study is a between-subjects design as each person is only measured in one classroom for their final exams. Repeated designs have more power for similar reasons as larger sample size and effect size have more power – the amount of error variability is *generally* smaller in repeated designs. When people are measured multiple times, we have to mathematically control for their non-independence (e.g., that each response is dependent on a previous response) and controlling for their individual variability tends to reduce the error variability in the model to error ratio.

To help you understand why this happens, imagine you know that some students are great students, and some students are average students. You can control for their individual differences and just look at the change in their scores across time. If you did not know why some students scored higher than others because you only measured them once, all those differences are considered error in your study. The

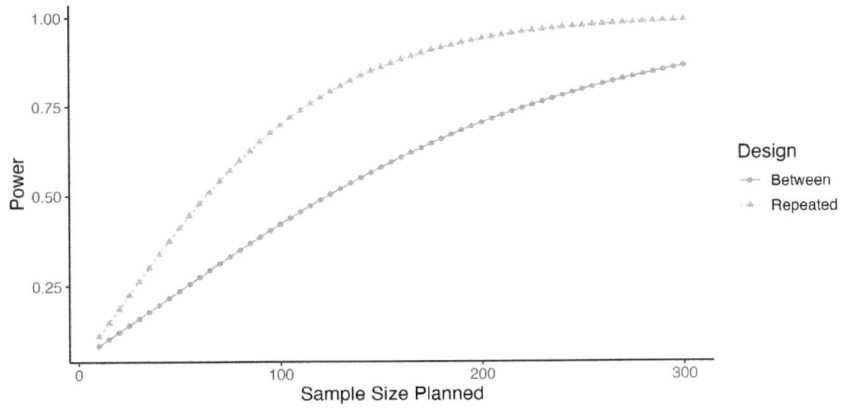

Figure 11.8 *The relationship between sample size planned, power, and the type of research design if we could measure our study on statistics classrooms in both a between and repeated measures design.*

first study is a between-subjects design – you compare two different sets of individuals in two separate classrooms. However, you could convert this design to repeated measures by comparing exam scores from two different semesters for the same people (i.e., they learn R in one semester and *JASP* in another semester). As shown in the figure below, the repeated measures design would achieve much higher power for nearly all sample sizes.

Power Analyses

Using Tables

In the days before we all carried tiny computers in our pockets, calculating power or estimating the ideal sample size usually involved a table or chart printed in a large textbook (Cohen, 2013) or rules of thumb such as $N > 30$ for groups and $N > 100$ for correlations. These tables usually included sample size estimates for a range of power and effect size estimates. For example, in Table 11.1, if you wanted to estimate the number of participants necessary for 80% power with an effect size of $d = 0.50$, you would find the necessary row and column to determine you need $n = 64$ participants. These tables were printed for different levels of α and types of tests but were very tedious to search through for a specific combination of requirements.

Using Programs (Sample Size)

Increases in computing power have improved our ability to estimate and determine information about the power in our studies. Computer programs can use exact formulas to calculate values for sample size, effect size, or precise power values given input by the researcher. The most popular point-and-click program is G*Power (Erdfelder et al.,

Table 11.1 *A traditional power table outlining effect size, power, and planned sample size for independent* t-*tests*

Power	Effect size (d)										
	0.1	0.2	0.3	0.4	0.5	0.6	0.7	0.8	1	1.2	1.4
0.25	332	84	38	22	14	10	8	6	5	4	3
0.50	769	193	86	49	32	22	17	13	9	7	5
0.60	981	246	110	62	40	28	21	16	11	8	6
0.67	1,144	287	128	73	47	33	24	19	12	9	7
0.70	1,235	310	138	78	50	35	26	20	13	10	7
0.75	1,389	348	155	88	57	40	29	23	15	11	8
0.80	1,571	393	175	99	64	45	33	26	17	12	9
0.85	1,797	450	201	113	73	51	38	29	19	14	10
0.90	2,102	526	234	132	85	59	44	34	22	16	12
0.95	2,600	651	290	163	105	73	54	42	37	19	14
0.99	3,675	920	409	231	148	103	76	58	38	27	20

Table 11.2 *Where to find common statistical tests in G*Power menus*

Common test name	Test family	Statistical test
Correlation	Exact	Correlation: Bivariate normal model
Single sample t-test	t tests	Means: Difference from constant (one sample case)
Independent t-test	t tests	Means: Difference between two independent means (two groups)
Dependent t-test	t tests	Means: Difference between two dependent means (matched pairs)
Between-subjects ANOVA (one variable)	F tests	ANOVA: Fixed effect, omnibus, one-way
Between-subjects ANOVA (multiple variables)	F tests	ANOVA: Fixed effects, special, main effects, and interactions
Repeated measures ANOVA (multiple variables)	F tests	ANOVA: Repeated measures, within factors
Mixed ANOVA (main effect)	F tests	ANOVA: Repeated measures, between factors
Mixed ANOVA (interaction)	F tests	ANOVA: Repeated measures, within-between interaction
Multiple regression (overall model)	F tests	Linear multiple regression: Fixed model, R2 deviation from zero
Multiple regression (individual predictor)	F tests	Linear multiple regression: Fixed model, R2 increase

1996; Faul et al., 2007), which is both simple and free. Users like G*Power because it contains most common statistical tests and has a user-friendly interface for entering the necessary information to calculate a specific value. A table of G*Power inputs for common statistical tests taught in statistics is provided in Table 11.2. Web-based tools such as https://powerandsamplesize.com and https://designingexperiments.com harness the power of computational languages (e.g., *R*) to create online applications for power estimation with simple text entries (Anderson et al., 2017).

To demonstrate how these tools work, let's calculate the power for our statistics classroom example. If we set our α to .05, power to .80, and our expected effect size to $d = 0.30$ – our best guess for the predicted effect size based on previous research – how many students would we need to recruit for the study? This study design is between-subjects, as each classroom consists of different individuals, and we have two groups. Therefore, we would select an independent *t*-test for our analysis, using a two-tailed test, as we did not make a prediction whether the *R* or *JASP* class would do better. As shown in the output in Figure 11.9, we would need to enroll at least 352 students across the two groups in our study! The allocation ratio section is useful if you know one group will be larger than another – you can account for it here, otherwise leave as one. For example, if you know that the classes recruited for the *JASP* students will be larger than the *R* classes, you would take the ratio of general enrollment sizes (i.e., 40/25 = 1.6) and use that number in that box. One suggestion would be to estimate various possible effect sizes, power, and test type combinations to get a full picture of what may happen in your study.

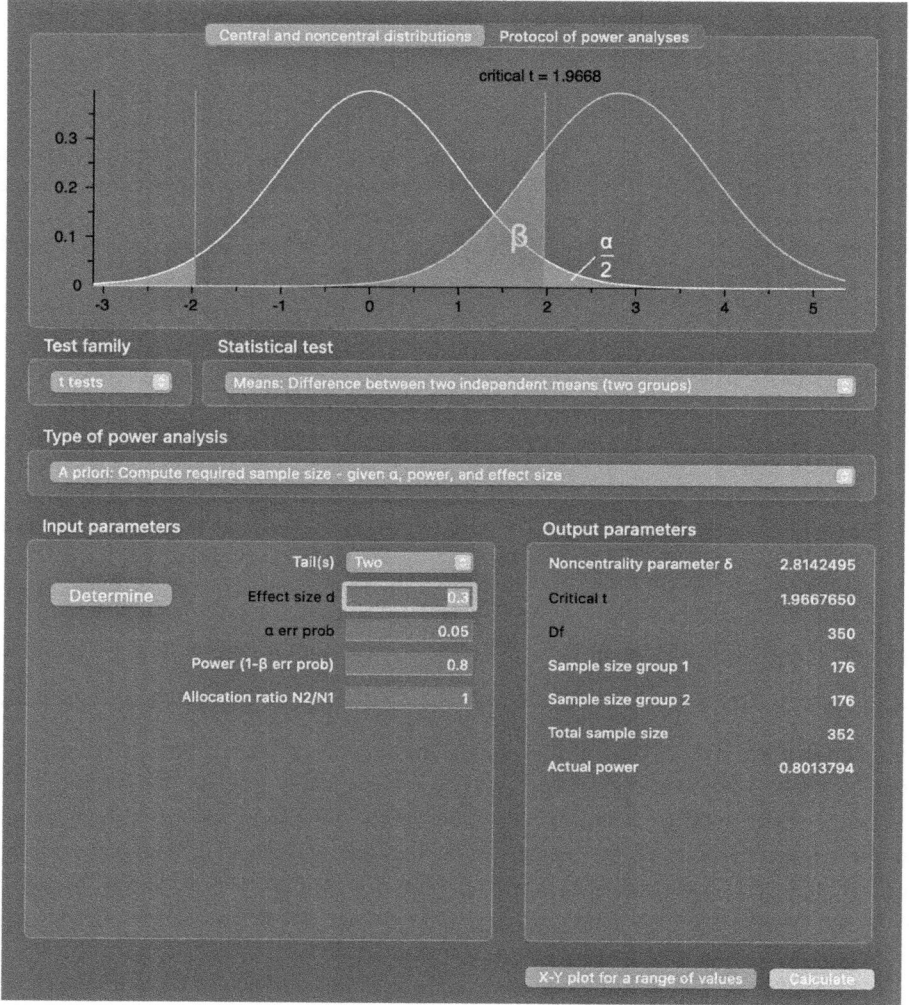

Figure 11.9 *A screen capture of G*Power for estimating the required sample size for the first study on statistics classrooms. The bottom left panel would be filled in with the effect size, α, power, and allocation ratio. The bottom right section indicates the number of participants required in each group and overall for these settings.*

Using Programs (Sensitivity)

What if we do not have the capability of recruiting that many students? The beauty of these programs is that we can switch from estimating the required sample size to determining the *potential* power or sensitivity of our study, given any research ability constraints. If you only have six classes with thirty students

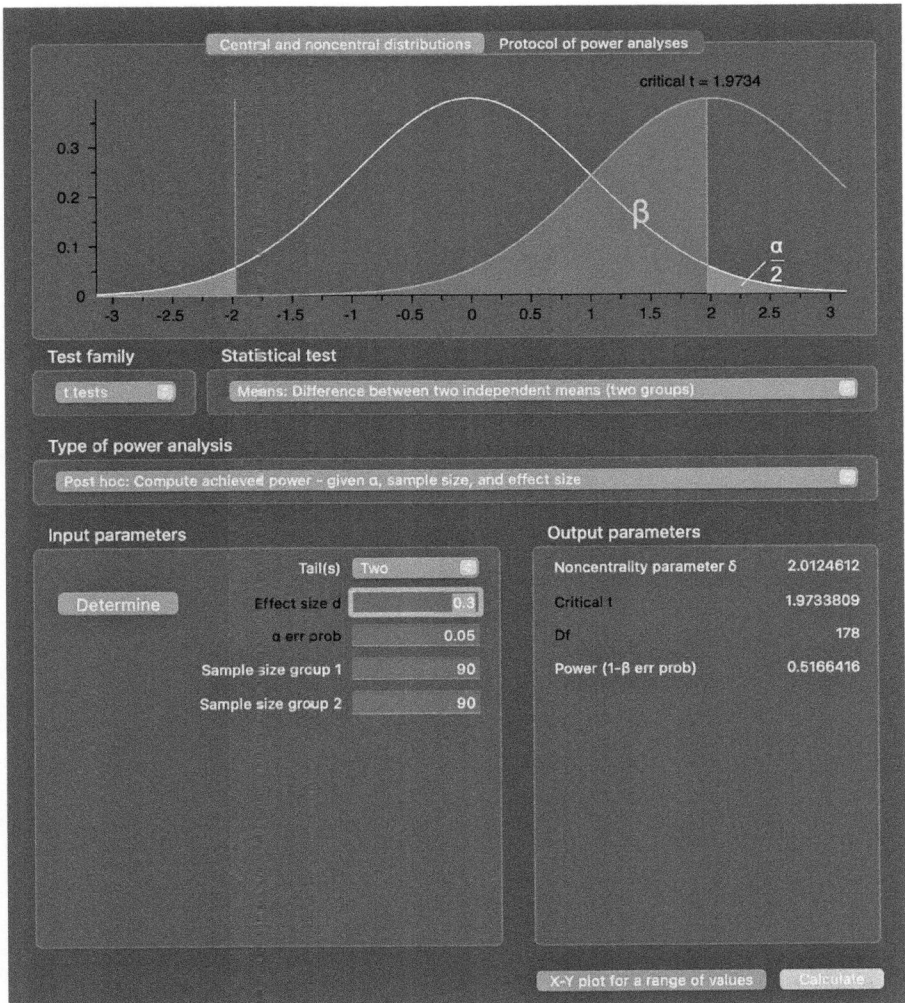

Figure 11.10 *An estimation of prospective power (i.e., calculated before the study is conducted) for our first study on statistics classrooms using the same criterion as the previous power estimation but a specific sample size we know we can collect in the left-hand panel. The output is the likely power that can be detected with this sample size and effect size.*

in class (i.e., 180 students total) per year for your experiment, what would your power be for the study with α set to .05 and an effect size set to $d = 0.30$? As shown in Figure 11.10, we would expect power to be approximately 52% – not very encouraging.

Instead, we may decide to calculate a sensitivity analysis that would indicate what effect size you could reasonably expect to detect with α set to .05 and power set to .80. When we recalculate, we find that the study would be able to

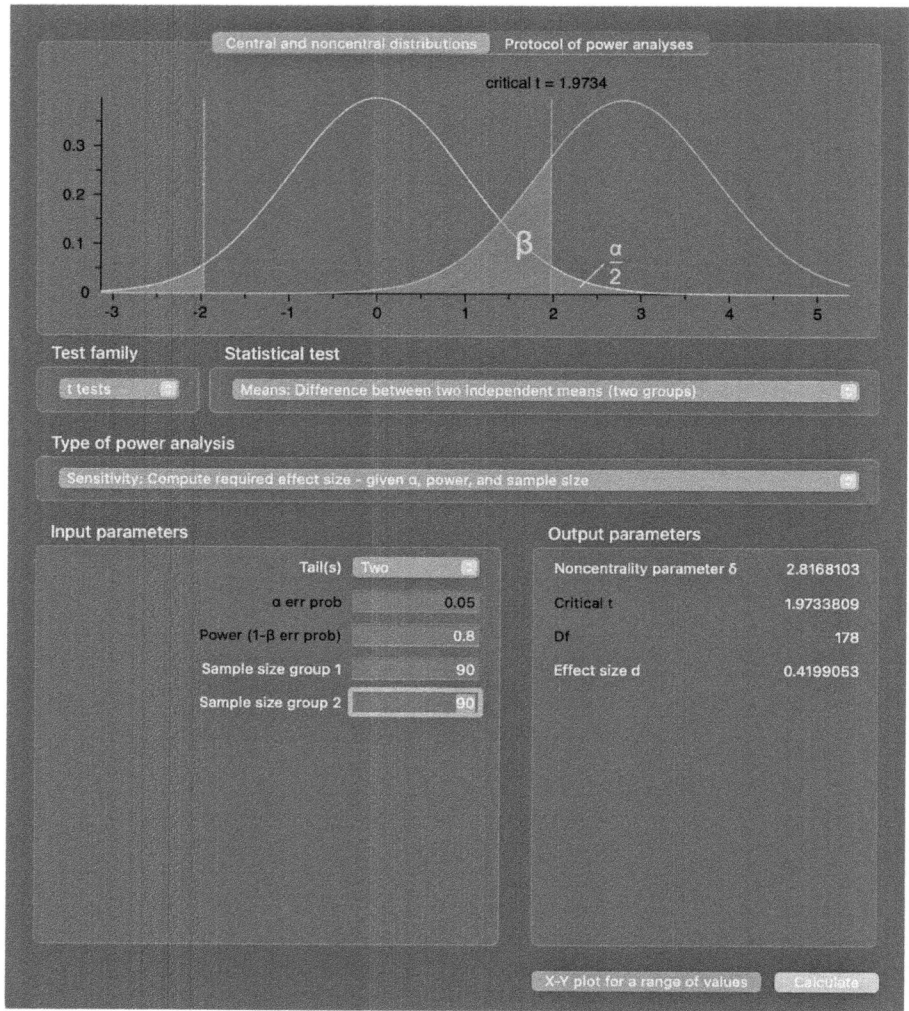

Figure 11.11 *An estimation of sensitivity for our first study on statistics classrooms using the same criterion as the previous power estimation but a specific sample size we know we can collect in the left-hand panel. The output is the effect size that can be detected with that sample size and power values entered.*

detect an effect size of $d = 0.42$; this result is not extremely different from our estimated effect size (Figure 11.11). Given that we sample exactly 90 students in each group, the final study will not have the power to detect smaller effects.

Our second study is also relatively straightforward to calculate in G*Power using a correlation between data literacy and first job income of $r = .30$ – often considered a medium effect size in social and behavioral sciences (Gignac & Szodorai, 2016). With this effect size and the same α and power we've used

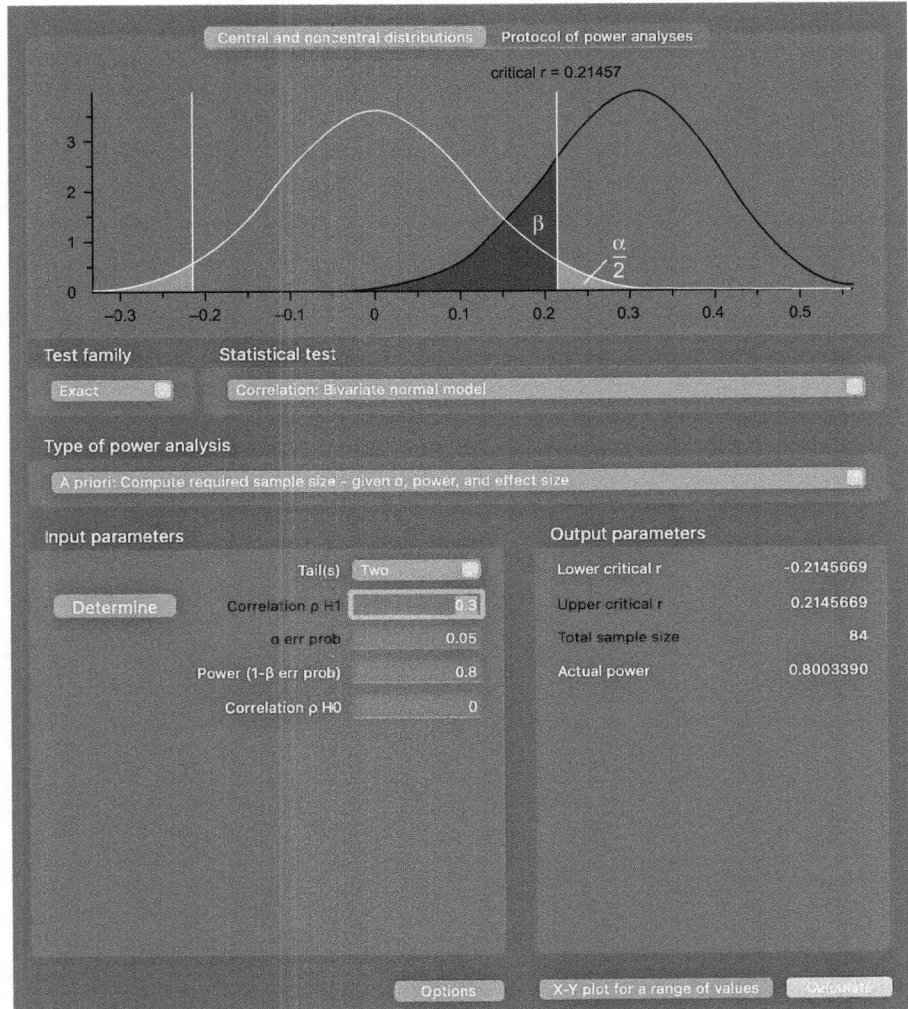

Figure 11.12 *Sample size estimation for Study 2 examining the correlation between data literacy and income. In the bottom left panel, you would enter the correlation, α, power, and the population correlation as comparison. The total sample size and power would appear in the bottom right-hand panel.*

previously, we would need $n = 84$ participants to detect the effect shown in Figure 11.12. If we wanted to correlate other skills found on the graduation exit exam with first job income, we should determine the expected lowest effect size that may occur to ensure enough power to detect all the possible correlations individually.

Using *R*: Packages and Simulations

Finally, we turn to our last study that examines student data literacy and the scores on the game modules presented in class. These students were measured once a week for the entire semester – 14 assessments excluding exam weeks. The study design is repeated measures, as we are measuring the same participants multiple times throughout the semester. As noted earlier, repeated measures designs usually have more power than the counterpart between-subjects designs, which makes them desirable to many researchers. However, the caveat to research designs with multiple measurement times is that the statistical analyses can potentially increase in complexity along with the data collection. For example, no simple point-and-click program can adequately capture the intricacy of an ecological momentary assessment design; this complexity then leads to the necessity of statistical programming skills for both power planning and analysis of the data.

Before we estimate our sample size for the third study, let's examine one of the most popular power planning packages available in *R* – *pwr* (Champely et al., 2017). The basic installation of *R* (called base *R*) comes with several functions and options for computing statistics and creating diagrams. The open source community of programmers and researchers provide add-ons to base *R* (called packages) that allow you to customize your analyses. Nearly 20,000 *R* packages are available for download from the official *R* collection, and even more are accessible through GitHub – a collaborative code-hosting platform. Using *pwr*, we can perform the same analyses as we did in G*Power and reach the same conclusions about the sample size given the effect size, power, and α shown in Figures 11.13 and 11.14.

```
library(pwr)
pwr.t.test(
  n = NULL, # estimate N
  d = 0.3, # effect size
  sig.level = .05, # alpha
  power = .80, # power level
  type = "two.sample", # independent t is two.sample
  alternative = "two.sided" # two tailed test
)

##
##     Two-sample t test power calculation
##
##              n = 175.3847
##              d = 0.3
##      sig.level = 0.05
##          power = 0.8
##    alternative = two.sided
##
## NOTE: n is number in *each* group
```

Figure 11.13 *The code used from the* pwr *library in R to estimate the sample size for the classroom comparison study. Next to each code section, the purpose of the section is noted. The output notes that estimation is for each group separately, and therefore, we would have to multiply by the number of groups to get our final sample size.*

```
pwr.r.test(
  n = NULL, # estimate N
  r = 0.3, # effect size
  sig.level = .05, # alpha
  power = .80, # power level
  alternative = "two.sided" # two tailed test
)

##
##     approximate correlation power calculation (arctangh
       transformation)
##
##              n = 84.07364
##              r = 0.3
##      sig.level = 0.05
##          power = 0.8
##    alternative = two.sided
```

Figure 11.14 *The code used from the* pwr *library to estimate the sample size needed for the correlation study on data literacy and job income.*

Once our design becomes too complex for G*Power, it often becomes too complex for most available programs, website applications, and *pwr*. In this scenario, researchers can simulate the study using other available packages in *R*. Simulation effectively involves *making up* plausible data that match your study, estimating power at various sample and/or effect sizes, and then repeating this task multiple times to determine the average power at each combination of variables. The end result is sometimes a table much like the one we started this section with – the number of participants proposed, and the power found for each sample size. Thankfully, there are multiple packages that can be used to create fake data (e.g., *faux*, DeBruine, 2021; and *simstudy*, Goldfeld and Wujciak-Jens 2020; see Figure 11.15).

Our study on gamification in the classroom not only includes multiple assessments measuring participants across the semester but also includes multiple variables using multiple game module scores to predict data literacy. As shown in Table 11.3, we could simulate the power of having multiple game modules predicting data literacy at a medium effect size for sample sizes of 30 to 100 participants. We also simulated the number of weeks we might need to measure participants to achieve a certain level of power (7, 10, and 14 weeks). As noted in our type-of-test section, repeated measures designs often show more power than between-subjects designs, and each subsequent measurement may also increase power. For each sample size, the results indicate that we increase our power by increasing the number of days we measure each participant. We can use a simulation test similar to this one to manipulate multiple factors that influence our study (sample size, measurement days) at once and compare what might be the best scenario for our project. Participants may drop out of the study if it becomes too long

```
set.seed(5839052)
library(faux)
library(nlme)
# define parameters
subj_n = 10  # number of subjects
item_n = 7   # number of days, change from 7, 10, 14
b0 = 0       # intercept
b1 = 2       # fixed score for coefficients
u0s_sd = .5  # random intercept SD for subjects
u0i_sd = .5  # random intercept SD for days
u1i_sd = .5  # random b1 slope SD for days
r01i = 0     # correlation between random effects 0 and 1 for days
sigma_sd = 2 # error SD

sample_sizes <- c(30, 40, 50, 60, 70, 80, 90, 100)
p_values <- data.frame(sample_sizes = 1:(length(sample_sizes)*100),
                       p = 1:(length(sample_sizes)*100))

row <- 1
for (i in sample_sizes) {

  for (r in 1:100) {

  # set up data structure
  DF <- add_random(subj = i, item = item_n) %>%
    # add both variables
    add_within("subj", measure = c("game_1", "game_2")) %>%
    # add random effects
    add_ranef("subj", u0s = u0s_sd) %>%
    add_ranef("item", u0i = u0i_sd, u1i = u1i_sd, .cors = r01i) %>%
    add_ranef(sigma = sigma_sd) %>%
    # calculate DV
    mutate(dv = b0 + u0s + u0i + (b1 + u1i) + sigma) %>%
    pivot_wider(id_cols = c("subj", "item"),
                names_from = "measure",
                values_from = "dv") %>%
    mutate(positive = scale(positive))

  # save study results
  save <- summary(lme(negative ~ positive,
      data = DF,
      random = list(~1|subj)))
  p_values[row,] <- c(i, save$tTable[2, 5])

  row <- row + 1

  }

}
# calculate power
day_data <- p_values %>%
  group_by(sample_sizes) %>%
  summarize(Power = sum(p <= .05)/100)

# export data to save
export(day_data, "seven_days.csv", row.names = F)
```

Figure 11.15 *The code for simulating the data and estimating power for our repeated measures study on data literacy and gamification.*

Table 11.3 *Simulation estimation of power for several potential sample sizes and number of measurement days for the gamification of data literacy study*

Sample size	7 days	10 days	14 days
30	0.55	0.59	0.72
40	0.52	0.65	0.79
50	0.68	0.78	0.89
60	0.61	0.87	0.92
70	0.75	0.88	0.96
80	0.69	0.88	0.94
90	0.86	0.92	1.00
100	0.83	0.97	0.97

without incentive, so we could compromise to collect $n = 60$ participants over ten days to achieve at least 80% power. Table 11.3 shows the estimated power and this value appears to represent the best compromise of number of days and participants needed.

With this example, hopefully you can see how complex power can be to estimate. The goal is often to pinpoint an appropriate sample size for a research study, or the sensitivity of the study given a fixed sample size. The desire would be to have one set estimate when planning the study, but as one considers all the potential influences on power, the number of "right" answers for power estimation can increase substantially. Estimations are often our best guess by fixing a known set of variables (α, effect size, study type, etc.) that may not represent the true values found in the population of study. Estimating across multiple best guesses can provide you with a range of potential outcomes to consider.

Newer Methods: AIPE

In light of these considerations, a newer method of power and sample size planning involves accuracy in parameter estimation (AIPE; Maxwell et al., 2008; Kelley, 2007; Kelley et al., 2018). Power, traditionally defined, focuses on finding a significant effect – that is a p-value less than your set cut-off criterion (i.e., α). Not all studies involve a specific hypothesis test to use in the power analysis; often, studies include multiple hypothesis tests, complicated statistics that may not fit into point-and-click programs, or simply no hypothesis test at all (e.g., a collection for a database of values that other researchers will use for their study planning or exploratory analyses; Buchanan et al., 2019). Instead, using AIPE, researchers can estimate sample size or sensitivity of their planned design to create an "accurately measured" parameter of interest. Parameters are simply something you want to measure (e.g., means, effect size, or regression slopes).

But what does "accurately measured" actually mean? First, a researcher would specify the parameter they want to measure and estimate from their study. Next, they would decide what a "sufficiently narrow" window of measurement around that parameter would be by using confidence intervals. Confidence intervals are a range of values around a parameter that represent an estimate of the true population parameter; they help us understand the uncertainty in our measurement. For example, the mean in our Study 1 *R* class could be 82 points, while the mean for the *JASP* class is 78 points. It would appear that the *R* class did better! However, when we add a confidence interval around the mean for each class, we can see that each has a good bit of variability, and they likely are not that different – *R*: 95% CI [75, 89] and *JASP*: 95% CI [68, 88]. In fact, these two confidence intervals show that the scores in the classrooms are very similar because they overlap each other. The percentage (95%) presented with the confidence interval represents the percent of time that one might expect the true population mean to be between the lower and upper numbers.

Therefore, the researcher would define the amount of variability (i.e., the width of the confidence interval around their parameter they are willing to accept) as "sufficiently narrow". Conveniently, the *MBESS* package in *R* can make these calculations straightforward for researchers (Kelley, 2022) with the caveat that it can be tricky to know exactly what width to use for confidence intervals, as this procedure is fairly new to most researchers. This area can be paired with determining the smallest effect size of interest (i.e., the smallest effect size a researcher would determine as practically important or useful for their study; Anvari & Lakens, 2021; Riesthuis et al., 2022). Previously, we used an effect size of $d = 0.30$ for our study examining the differences in statistics classrooms. We may decide that the smallest effect of interest is $d = 0.10$ – a small change in grades when using one statistical program over another. If the study shows anything smaller than that effect size, we would suggest the difference between classrooms was not useful enough to make instructors switch to a new instruction method. Using *MBESS*, we would find that the suggested sample size is over 700 participants (Figure 11.16)!

We can similarly use this procedure to estimate how many participants would be necessary for our second study on data literacy and job income. We previously used $r = .30$ and could similarly suggest that we would not be interested if the correlation was below $r = .10$. This sample size is also very large in comparison to our previous power estimations – over 2,800 participants (see Figure 11.17).

```
library(MBESS)
ss.aipe.smd(delta = 0.30, # the effect size
            conf.level = 0.95, # confidence interval
            width = 0.20) # our suggested width

## [1] 777
```

Figure 11.16 *AIPE estimation code and sample size output from* MBESS *used to estimate the number of participants needed to find a* d *value between 0.10 and 0.50 (0.30 ± 0.20 width).*

```
ss.aipe.R2(Population.R2 = 0.30^2, # our correlation squared
           conf.level = 0.95, # confidence interval
           width = 0.20^2, # the width squared
           p = 1) # one predictor X to Y
## [1] "The approximate sample size is given below; you should
consider using the additional"
## [1] "argument 'verify.ss=TRUE' to ensure the exact sample
size value is obtained."

## $Required.Sample.Size
## [1] 2863
```

Figure 11.17 *AIPE estimation code and sample size output for the correlation study. In this example, we use R^2 – the estimated correlation r squared —, and we similarly square the width of the confidence interval we are looking for.*

```
pwr.t.test(
   n = NULL, # estimate N
   d = 0.3, # effect size
   sig.level = .05, # alpha
   power = .95, # power level
   type = "two.sample", # independent t,
   alternative = "two.sided" # two tailed test
)

##      Two-sample t test power calculation
## 
##               n = 289.7353
##               d = 0.3
##       sig.level = 0.05
##           power = 0.95
##     alternative = two.sided
##
## NOTE: n is number in *each* group
```

Figure 11.18 *The code for 95% power using the* pwr *package in R for our statistics classroom example. In comparison to our previous 80% power, we find that we need more people; this matches the AIPE estimations.*

One thing to remember is that we used a power level of 80% in the previous estimations, yet the AIPE procedure generally uses a confidence interval of 95%. If we recalculate the power at 95% for our first study, we find a much larger number of 580 participants total (290 for each group) in Figure 11.18 (as compared to 777 from *MBESS* in Figure 11.16 and 350 total from *pwr* at 80% power in Figure 11.13). However, the sample size estimate for our correlation study is much smaller in sample size estimate for 95% power at 138 participants in Figure 11.19 (compared to *MBESS* estimation of 2863 in Figure 11.17 and 84 from *pwr* at 80% power in Figure 11.14). These two estimation methods

```
pwr.r.test(
  n = NULL, # estimate N
  r = 0.3, # effect size
  sig.level = .05, # alpha
  power = .95, # power level
  alternative = "two.sided" # two tailed test
)
##
##       approximate correlation power calculation (arctangh
          transformation)
##
##                  n = 137.7587
##                  r = 0.3
##          sig.level = 0.05
##              power = 0.95
##        alternative = two.sided
```

Figure 11.19 *The code for 95% power for the data literacy and job income correlation example. The AIPE estimations are still much larger than the estimations using normal power approximations.*

are not meant to give the same answer, as they have different goals to achieve (i.e., a specific *p*-value versus a specific confidence interval). One caution with using accuracy in parameter estimation, though, is that while AIPE is advertised as a way to estimate sample size regardless of hypothesis test, confidence intervals still use the framework of null hypothesis significance testing. Therefore, a 95% confidence interval for a correlation *r* of [.10, .50] would also usually be "significant" using *p*-value criterion and $\alpha \leq .05$ because the confidence interval does not include zero (i.e., the estimation of the true population *r* does not include zero because the entire confidence interval is greater than zero).

Limitations

What Power Does Not Say

Let's go back to the definition of power. It is the likelihood of detecting a significant effect, given the effect size, α, sample size, and so on, *if that effect exists* (e.g., if the null hypothesis is actually false). When using NHST, we usually want the null hypothesis to be false (i.e., supporting our research hypothesis). Power does not tell you whether the null hypothesis is in reality false – just the likelihood of rejecting the null if it is. We often do not know if the null is truly false (and therefore, we should move on from our study idea); this ambiguity can create a scenario where you might think the effect exists, but maybe you did not have enough power to detect it (and continue to look for something that does not exist). This scenario happens to researchers quite a bit – samples cost time, money, and effort to collect. You cannot always get as many data points as you would like, and even if you do, the other factors estimated within a power analysis may be the wrong guess.

If you overestimate your effect size, you likely will not have enough power to find the smaller effect size that truly exists in the population. Additionally, it is important to remember publication bias – the published background research likely overestimates the true effect size as only the "significant" findings will be published (Franco et al., 2014). Therefore, the values you might find in published research are likely only the best case scenario. Last, effect sizes *also* have variance, just like any other statistical parameter (e.g., the mean has a standard deviation). Therefore, when a researcher runs a study, even if they estimated the right effect size for their power analysis, they could find something higher or lower depending on their particular sample (Pek et al., in press). Thus, even with our best intentions, power analyses do not guarantee that we will detect a true effect, and estimates that we used in the power analysis often differ from the final study values.

Post Hoc Power

As you might have noticed, this chapter has mainly focused on calculating the necessary sample size to plan a study or the sensitivity of a study with a specific sample size. In practice, we could calculate the amount of power found in a study after it is complete (i.e., *post hoc* power or retrospective power; Dziak et al., 2020). Reviewers of research papers may request this information to know whether the study was "powered appropriately" for a non-significant result. However, once the data is collected, we know whether we have found a significant effect or not, and any post hoc power analysis will reflect the same answer as the p-value from the study (i.e., if the result is non-significant, the power analysis will say there was not enough power).

For example, let's examine our study focusing on job income and data literacy using a correlation of $r = .30$. If we only had twenty participants, we might find that post hoc power was .26. If we collected 100 participants, then power jumps to .86. This analysis seems like it says something useful right? However, *post hoc* power is only a representation of the p-value found in the study, which here, was influenced by the change in sample size. Therefore, all we have learned is something we knew from earlier in this chapter: sample size has a large influence on power. Figure 11.20 shows this relationship for our $r = .30$. As sample size increases, power increases, and p-values decrease. Therefore, if you had 300 participants, the post hoc power would be high and the p-value would be low, which does not tell you much about the actual ability to detect your effect in a new study. Instead, one should provide a sensitivity analysis or simply the effect size found in the study with the 95% confidence

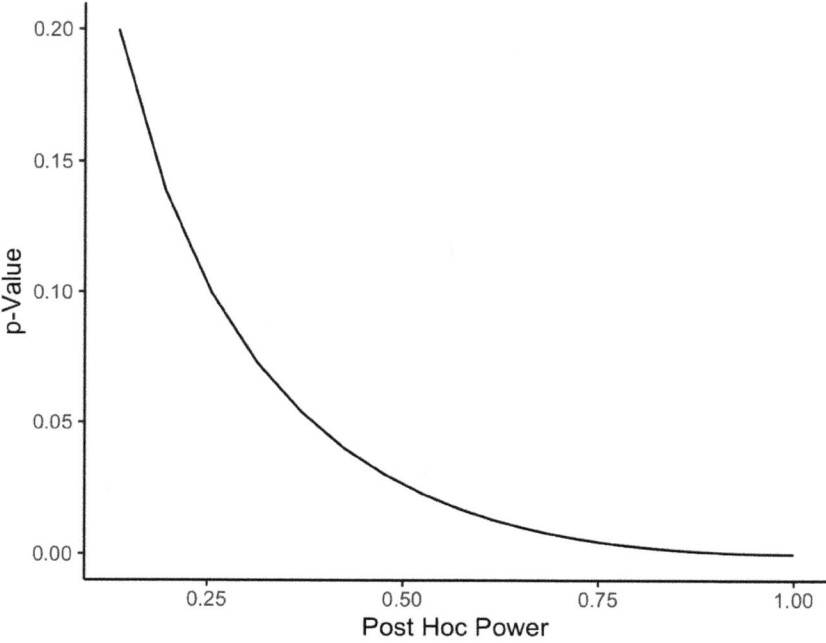

Figure 11.20 *The relationship between post hoc power and p-values for* r = .30. *As shown, the power increases exponentially with decreasing p-values.*

interval to understand the potential range of the effect found with the study parameters (Heckman et al., 2022).

Suggestions

Given all that you've learned in this chapter, what guidelines should you use when performing power analyses?

- Use previous literature in your study area to estimate possible effect sizes; however, keep in mind that not all studies are published, and the potential effect size may be only half the size of what is published (Open Science Collaboration, 2015). Use the smallest effect size you find to help overestimate sample size for adequate power.
- Select and justify the choices of α, β, and power when planning your research study.
- If possible, calculate necessary sample size from several sources (calculators, programs, simulation, AIPE) and with several parameters (different effect sizes, study manipulations) to explore the potential power outcomes for your study.
- Try to achieve the largest sample size suggested by different power analyses, as sample size is one of the largest influences on power.

- Consider multiple types of research designs and statistical analyses for their impact on the power of the study.
- When sample size is predetermined by resources, calculate the sensitivity of your study to detect various effect sizes.

Acknowledgments

Special thanks to Twitter and Joe Simons for suggesting great titles for this chapter.

References

Aerts, M., Molenberghs, G., & Thas, O. (2021). Graduate education in statistics and data science: The why, when, where, who, and what. *Annual Review of Statistics and Its Application*, *8*(1), 25–39. https://doi.org/10.1146/annurev-statistics-040620-032820

Anderson, S. F., Kelley, K., & Maxwell, S. E. (2017). Sample-size planning for more accurate statistical power: A method adjusting sample effect sizes for publication bias and uncertainty. *Psychological Science*, *28*(11), 1547–1562. https://doi.org/10.1177/0956797617723724

Anvari, F., & Lakens, D. (2021). Using anchor-based methods to determine the smallest effect size of interest. *Journal of Experimental Social Psychology*, *96*, 104159. https://doi.org/10.1016/j.jesp.2021.104159

Benjamin, D. J., Berger, J. O., Johannesson, M., Nosek, B. A., Wagenmakers, E.-J., Berk, R., et al. (2018). Redefine statistical significance. *Nature Human Behaviour*, *2*(1), 6–10. https://doi.org/10.1038/s41562-017-0189-z

Buchanan, E. M., Valentine, K. D., & Maxwell, N. P. (2019). LAB: Linguistic annotated bibliography a searchable portal for normed database information. *Behavior Research Methods*, *51*(4), 1878–1888. https://doi.org/10.3758/s13428-018-1130-8

Champely, S., Ekstrom, C., Dalgaard, P., Gill, J., Weibelzahl, S., Anandkumar, A., et al. (2017). *Pwr: Basic functions for power analysis* [software]. https://cran.r-project.org/web/packages/pwr

Cohen, J. (2013). *Statistical Power Analysis for the Behavioral Sciences*. Routledge. https://doi.org/10.4324/9780203771587

Coles, N. A., Hamlin, J. K., Sullivan, L. L., Parker, T. H., & Altschul, D. (2022). Build up big-team science. *Nature*, *601*(7894), 505–507. https://doi.org/10.1038/d41586-022-00150-2

Cuccolo, K., Irgens, M. S., Zlokovich, M. S., Grahe, J., & Edlund, J. E. (2021). What crowdsourcing can offer to cross-cultural psychological science. *Cross-Cultural Research*, *55*(1), 3–28. https://doi.org/10.1177/1069397120950628

DeBruine, L. (2021). Faux: Simulation for Factorial Designs [software]. Zenodo. https://doi.org/10.5281/ZENODO.2669586

Dienes, Z. (2008). *Understanding Psychology as a Science*. Palgrave Macmillan.

(2023). Testing theories with Bayes factors. In A. L. Nichols & J. E. Edlund (eds.), *Cambridge Handbook of Research Methods and Statistics for the Social and Behavioral Sciences* (vol. 1, pp. 494–512). Cambridge University Press.

Dziak, J. J., Dierker, L. C., & Abar, B. (2020). The interpretation of statistical power after the data have been gathered. *Current Psychology, 39*(3), 870–877. https://doi.org/10.1007/s12144-018-0018-1

Erdfelder, E., Faul, F., & Buchner, A. (1996). GPOWER: A general power analysis program. *Behavior Research Methods, Instruments, & Computers, 28*(1), 1–11. https://doi.org/10.3758/BF03203630

Faul, F., Erdfelder, E., Lang, A.-G., & Buchner, A. (2007). G*Power 3: A flexible statistical power analysis program for the social, behavioral, and biomedical sciences. *Behavior Research Methods, 39*(2), 175–191. https://doi.org/10.3758/BF03193146

Franco, A., Malhotra, N., & Simonovits, G. (2014). Publication bias in the social sciences: Unlocking the file drawer. *Science, 345*(6203), 1502–1505. https://doi.org/10.1126/science.1255484

Gignac, G. E., & Szodorai, E. T. (2016). Effect size guidelines for individual differences researchers. *Personality and Individual Differences, 102*, 74–78. https://doi.org/10.1016/j.paid.2016.06.069

Goldfeld, K., & Wujciak-Jens, J. (2020). *Simstudy*: Illuminating research methods through data generation. *Journal of Open Source Software, 5*(54), 2763. https://doi.org/10.21105/joss.02763

Gümüş, M. M., & Kukul, V. (2023). Developing a digital competence scale for teachers: Validity and reliability study. *Education and Information Technologies, 28*(3), 2747–2765. https://doi.org/10.1007/s10639-022-11213-2

Heckman, M. G., Davis, J. M., & Crowson, C. S. (2022). Post hoc power calculations: An inappropriate method for interpreting the findings of a research study. *Journal of Rheumatology, 49*(8), 867–870. https://doi.org/10.3899/jrheum.211115

JASP Team. (2022). *JASP* (version 0.16.3)[software]. https://jasp-stats.org

Kelley, K. (2007). Sample size planning for the coefficient of variation from the accuracy in parameter estimation approach. *Behavior Research Methods, 39*(4), 755–766. https://doi.org/10.3758/BF03192966

(2022). *MBESS: The MBESS r package* [software]. https://CRAN.R-project.org/package=MBESS

Kelley, K., Darku, F. B., & Chattopadhyay, B. (2018). Accuracy in parameter estimation for a general class of effect sizes: A sequential approach. *Psychological Methods, 23*(2), 226–243. https://doi.org/10.1037/met0000127

Koch, C., & Jones, A. (2016). Big science, team science, and open science for neuroscience. *Neuron, 92*(3), 612–616. https://doi.org/10.1016/j.neuron.2016.10.019

Lakens, D. (2013). Calculating and reporting effect sizes to facilitate cumulative science: A practical primer for t-tests and ANOVAs. *Frontiers in Psychology, 4*. https://doi.org/10.3389/fpsyg.2013.00863

Lakens, D., Adolfi, F. G., Albers, C. J., Anvari, F., Apps, M. A. J., Argamon, S. E., et al. (2018). Justify your alpha. *Nature Human Behaviour, 2*(3), 168–171. https://doi.org/10.1038/s41562-018-0311-x

Legaki, N.-Z., Xi, N., Hamari, J., Karpouzis, K., & Assimakopoulos, V. (2020). The effect of challenge-based gamification on learning: An experiment in the context of statistics education. *International Journal of Human-Computer Studies, 144*, 102496. https://doi.org/10.1016/j.ijhcs.2020.102496

Matli, W., & Ngoepe, M. (2020). Capitalizing on digital literacy skills for capacity development of people who are not in education, employment or training in South Africa. *African Journal of Science, Technology, Innovation and Development, 12*(2), 129–139. https://doi.org/10.1080/20421338.2019.1624008

Maxwell, S. E., Kelley, K., & Rausch, J. R. (2008). Sample size planning for statistical power and accuracy in parameter estimation. *Annual Review of Psychology, 59,* 537–563. https://doi.org/10.1146/annurev.psych.59.103006.093735

McElreath, R. (2020). *Statistical Rethinking: A Bayesian Course with Examples in R and STAN,* 2nd ed. Routledge.

Meehl, P. E. (1967). Theory-testing in psychology and physics: A methodological paradox. *Philosophy of Science, 34*(2), 103–115. https://doi.org/10.1086/288135

Miller, J., & Ulrich, R. (2019). The quest for an optimal alpha. *PLOS ONE, 14*(1), e0208631. https://doi.org/10.1371/journal.pone.0208631

Open Science Collaboration. (2015). Estimating the reproducibility of psychological science. *Science, 349*(6251), aac4716. https://doi.org/10.1126/science.aac4716

Pangrazio, L., Godhe, A.-L., & Ledesma, A. G. L. (2020). What is digital literacy? A comparative review of publications across three language contexts. *E-Learning and Digital Media, 17*(6), 442–459. https://doi.org/10.1177/2042753020946291

Pek, J., Pitt, M. A., & Wegener, D. T. (in press). Uncertainty limits the use of power analysis. *Journal of Experimental Psychology: General.*

Porras-Segovia, A., Molina-Madueño, R. M., Berrouiguet, S., López-Castroman, J., Barrigón, M. L., Pérez-Rodríguez, M. S., et al. (2020). Smartphone-based ecological momentary assessment (EMA) in psychiatric patients and student controls: A real-world feasibility study. *Journal of Affective Disorders, 274,* 733–741. https://doi.org/10.1016/j.jad.2020.05.067

R Core Team. (2022). *R: A Language and Environment for Statistical Computing.* R Foundation for Statistical Computing. www.gbif.org/tool/81287/r-a-language-and-environment-for-statistical-computing

Ralston, K. (2020). "Sociologists shouldn't have to study statistics": Epistemology and anxiety of statistics in sociology students. *Sociological Research Online, 25*(2), 219–235. https://doi.org/10.1177/1360780419888927

Riesthuis, P., Mangiulli, I., Broers, N., & Otgaar, H. (2022). Expert opinions on the smallest effect size of interest in false memory research. *Applied Cognitive Psychology, 36*(1), 203–215. https://doi.org/10.1002/acp.3911

Seaborn, K., & Fels, D. I. (2015). Gamification in theory and action: A survey. *International Journal of Human-Computer Studies, 74,* 14–31. https://doi.org/10.1016/j.ijhcs.2014.09.006

Shiffman, S., Stone, A. A., & Hufford, M. R. (2008). Ecological momentary assessment. *Annual Review of Clinical Psychology, 4*(1), 1–32. https://doi.org/10.1146/annurev.clinpsy.3.022806.091415

Silberzahn, R., Uhlmann, E. L., Martin, D. P., Anselmi, P., Aust, F., Awtrey, E., et al. (2018). Many analysts, one data set: Making transparent how variations in analytic choices affect results. *Advances in Methods and Practices in Psychological Science, 1*(3), 337356.

US Bureau of Labor Statistics. (n.d.). *Occupational Outlook Handbook.* www.bls.gov/ooh/math/data-scientists.htm

Vazire, S. (2018). Implications of the credibility revolution for productivity, creativity, and progress. *Perspectives on Psychological Science, 13*(4), 411–417. https://doi.org/10.1177/1745691617751884

Vevea, J. L., & Woods, C. M. (2005). Publication bias in research synthesis: Sensitivity analysis using a priori weight functions. *Psychological Methods, 10*, 428–443. https://doi.org/10.1037/1082-989X.10.4.428

12 Interdisciplinary and Integrative Research

Rick Szostak

Abstract

This chapter describes a common set of challenges faced in interdisciplinary research and strategies for addressing each of these challenges. These strategies are shown to be quite distinct from the disciplinary methods addressed in other chapters in this Handbook. Importantly, strategies are outlined for several distinct steps in the interdisciplinary research process. A set of challenges associated with team research is also identified, and a set of strategies for addressing these is presented. Having described how interdisciplinary research is performed, we are then able to clarify our definition of interdisciplinarity. The chapter closes with discussions of the relationship between interdisciplinarity and creativity, appropriate standards for evaluating interdisciplinary research, important concerns regarding the impact of interdisciplinary research on career progress, and the value of employing integrative strategies within disciplines. In all, the chapter urges a symbiotic relationship between specialized and interdisciplinary research.

Keywords: Interdisciplinarity, Integration, Mixed Methods, Team Research, Creativity, Complexity

Introduction

Although there are an increasing number of interdisciplinary PhD programs (especially in North America; Holley and Szostak, 2022), much interdisciplinary research is still performed by scholars trained within disciplines. Whereas disciplinary scholars are usually given detailed training on how to employ methods common in their discipline, interdisciplinary scholars often lack any formal instruction on how to do interdisciplinary research. However, just as specialized scholars benefit from a detailed understanding of the methods employed in their disciplines, interdisciplinary scholars can benefit from familiarity with strategies that have proven useful in interdisciplinary research. Without this training, they may not even appreciate that there are important differences between specialized and interdisciplinary research.

It should be stressed that interdisciplinary research is both important and risky. Major scientific advances often come from integrating insights from different disciplines. The publications of interdisciplinary research teams get more citations than publications of individual scholars and are far more likely to get thousands of citations (Okamura, 2019). At the same time, interdisciplinary research, and especially interdisciplinary team research, often fails to produce any valuable results. These failures can often be traced to one or more of the common challenges to be discussed below (Fam and O'Rourke 2021). It seems likely that researchers could have avoided failure if aware of strategies that have proven successful in the past.

How can we best summarize these strategies? The next section describes an iterative 10-step interdisciplinary research process and strategies for performing each step. The subsequent section looks at challenges and strategies associated with team research. Although individuals can perform interdisciplinary research, it is often pursued by interdisciplinary teams. Having identified a wide range of both challenges and strategies, I then make a handful of key observations about interdisciplinary strategies in general. The succeeding section addresses further aspects of interdisciplinary research such as creativity, complexity, and implications for career progress. I close with some brief concluding remarks.

It is far easier to define the essence of interdisciplinarity below, *after* addressing in detail how interdisciplinary analysis is best pursued. Yet a provisional definition can be provided here: interdisciplinary research integrates insights generated by specialized research.

The Interdisciplinary Research Process

Repko and Szostak (2020) outline a 10-step process for performing interdisciplinary research. This process is grounded in decades of research by scholars of interdisciplinarity as well as research in cognate fields such as common ground theory and complexity science. It is an iterative process, such that researchers are expected to revisit earlier steps in the process as they perform later steps. Importantly, interdisciplinary researchers have identified strategies that work well for performing each step. Some of these strategies may seem obvious. Yet as was noted above, interdisciplinary research projects often fail because researchers were unaware of successful strategies. The value of these various strategies can only be appreciated in their employment, just as the intricacies of any disciplinary method can only be both mastered and valued when applied. It is critical, when teaching this material to students, that they apply it in their own research.

The Question

The first steps involve choosing a good research question and justifying its interdisciplinary nature. I would again stress the iterative nature of the research process here, for researchers will often revisit their guiding question as they proceed. It is nevertheless quite useful to follow some simple guidelines at the outset. Clarity is one important guideline; even more so than in specialized research, the interdisciplinary scholar needs to ask a question that they and others – from multiple disciplines – can readily comprehend. The interdisciplinary researcher should generally eschew disciplinary jargon when stating their question or carefully define this if jargon proves unavoidable. Unbiasedness is another guideline – it is all too easy for a scholar to state a question in a way that privileges the understandings of one discipline over others. For decades, economists interpreted the question "What are the causes of economic growth?" narrowly such that they only sought answers in a handful of economic variables such as levels of investment. Only slowly did they come to appreciate that they needed to engage with institutions (and how these are created politically), cultural values, and geography, among other things.

Many scholars never seriously engage with the question of why their project is interdisciplinary. Are they dissatisfied with disciplinary treatments of the subject, and if so why? Alternatively, are they asking a question that no discipline addresses, and if so why? Are they examining causal connections among phenomena studied by different disciplines? Are they drawing on methods or theories employed in different disciplines or perhaps applying the theories or methods of one discipline to the phenomena studied in another discipline? With a bit of reflection, researchers may realize that there are multiple reasons why their project requires an interdisciplinary approach, and each needs to be consciously addressed in the research plan.

A simple exercise of drawing a flow chart of one's research question can be immensely valuable (here and in later steps). What phenomena (i.e., things that we collectively study) are important in your research question, and what sort of causal influences do you seek to investigate among these? Researchers will often have to limit their investigations to a subset of the phenomena that matter, but it is nevertheless useful to sketch a diagram that includes all potentially relevant phenomena. The researcher can then reflect on which phenomena and relationships are studied by which disciplines and what theories and methods are commonly applied to each (and which relationships are ignored). The researcher can then readily identify what is novel about their research plan and how they can build upon but transcend existing disciplinary insights. For an interdisciplinary research team, such a diagram can be a useful team exercise that helps identify the tasks that each team member can perform, how team members will interact in understanding particular relationships, and perhaps whether the team needs to add certain members to address certain relationships.

Evaluating Disciplinary Insights

The next steps involve identifying and evaluating the insights generated by disciplines. Interdisciplinary literature surveys are challenging precisely because our libraries are organized around disciplines rather than the things we study (see Szostak et al., 2016, for suggestions on how we could better organize our libraries). Researchers need to be prepared to use different search terms in different disciplines. Talking to researchers in other disciplines is also invaluable. Universities sometimes seek to introduce colleagues from different disciplines in the hopes of fostering interdisciplinary collaboration; such introductions are more likely to be fruitful if researchers discuss the sorts of questions they are interested in and methods they apply.

The interdisciplinary researcher can engage in a form of evaluation that complements that which occurs within disciplines. Disciplinary editors and referees will evaluate works to ensure that disciplinary theories and methods are properly employed, yet they rarely, if ever, will ask if alternative theories or methods might shed a quite different light on the subject. They will almost never ask whether assumptions common to the discipline are driving the results. In addition, they will rarely ask why the paper reaches conclusions different from those reached in other disciplines. The interdisciplinary researcher, by asking such questions, can identify paths for novel research that can usefully inform disciplinary conversations. We will discuss below the challenges and opportunities for communicating back to disciplines.

Specialized researchers, having spent years of their lives mastering one discipline, sometimes wonder at the very possibility of interdisciplinary research. How can any researcher master multiple disciplines well enough to do rigorous research? One answer is to assemble an interdisciplinary research team (see below), yet even there the team members must learn about each others' disciplines so they can work together. Moreover, individuals perform much valuable interdisciplinary research. The simple fact is that one does not have to have a practitioner level of expertise to draw upon the insights of a discipline. One should, though, understand the overall perspective of each discipline that one draws upon.

Each discipline has a set of phenomena they study and a set of preferred theories and methods for doing so. These evolve over time as disciplines take on new questions and shed old. At any point in time, though, there is coherence – disciplines choose theories and methods that are particularly good at investigating "their" phenomena. Disciplines will also have a (largely subconscious, perhaps) set of epistemological attitudes that cohere well with their theories and methods – disciplines that pursue quantitative methods tend to believe that precise and objective understandings are possible while more qualitative disciplines tend to doubt that precision and objectivity are possible. An interdisciplinary researcher who understands a discipline's perspective will be well prepared to ask to what extent a particular disciplinary research result reflects that perspective.

I noted above that there are both advantages and costs associated with disciplinary preferences. I can note here that results can be biased by the fact that disciplines choose methods that work well with their theories. For decades, my home discipline of economics was dominated by rational choice theory that argues humans make their economic decisions rationally. One little-appreciated advantage of such a theory is that scholars do not then have to worry too much about how humans actually make decisions – if we know their options and their goals, we can assume that they will choose the option that best achieves their goals. Economists could further assume that most agents want to maximize income or minimize costs of production. As a result, economists then exclusively employed mathematical models and statistical analysis, and these produced good enough approximations of reality that rational choice theory was unquestioned. Slowly, though, experiments and occasional surveys suggested that humans did not always behave rationally. There is now an important field of "behavioral economics" that explores how non-rational decision-making influences economic outcomes. There is a lesson in this story for all interdisciplinary researchers – we may get very interesting results when we apply different methods than those commonly employed in a discipline. Likewise, we should be wary of taking disciplinary theory for granted.

Interdisciplinary researchers can usefully evaluate disciplinary insights if they have a good idea of the discipline's overall perspective and the strengths and weaknesses of its favored theories and methods. A handbook such as this can be very useful in the latter respect. It shows that the social scientist has access to several well-developed methods (and a larger set of more precise techniques within these methods). Some methods provide detailed insight into how a few agents behave while others provide some idea of how large numbers of agents behave. Some methods have lots of inductive potential while others are almost entirely deductive in nature. Some methods can follow agents through time or space while others can only study them in a particular time and place. Some methods are conducive to broad generalizations while others are better at describing the uniqueness of particular situations (see Szostak 2004 for comparisons of 12 key methods according to these and other distinctions). The interdisciplinary researcher can reflect on which methods are best suited to particular research questions. They will generally find that multiple methods have something useful to contribute (see below).

In addition to evaluating individual disciplinary research insights in terms of the discipline's perspective, the interdisciplinary researcher should read widely enough in the discipline's literature to understand any key debates regarding the phenomena and relationships of interest to the researcher. We want to avoid a superficial kind of research in which the interdisciplinary scholar "cherry-picks" research results that they find congenial. Sound interdisciplinary research should be grounded in a careful evaluation of disciplinary debates. The interdisciplinary researcher should justify which elements of disciplinary insights s/he finds valuable.

Disciplines, especially in the human sciences, often reach different conclusions. Though the gap is narrowing, sociologists are still far more likely than economists to emphasize non-rational forms of decision-making. Similarly, political scientists, on average, like government interventions in markets more than economists. Comparing the insights of different scholars is an important evaluative tool. It guides the interdisciplinary researcher to identify the sources of disagreement. Are they using different methods? Different theories? Are they studying different sets of phenomena? Are they making different assumptions – whether the explicit assumptions made in particular papers or the implicit assumptions taken for granted in a discipline?

A good starting assumption for interdisciplinary research is that every discipline drawn upon will have something useful to contribute to an understanding of the research question but that no disciplinary insight is likely to be perfect. By engaging in interdisciplinary forms of evaluation, we hope to identify the best parts of disciplinary insights. Only then should we try to integrate these insights into a more comprehensive understanding.

Integration

The process of evaluating disciplinary insights sets the stage for integration. While integration is an inherently creative act (see below), there are a handful of clear strategies that can be employed to integrate insights from different disciplines (or indeed from different authors within disciplines). The first involves clarification of terminology. Each discipline has its own jargon, and the inevitable result is that the same word may carry quite different meanings in different disciplines. Economists attach a very narrow definition to the word "investment" – only expenditures on buildings or machines or other items that increase our ability to produce goods and services in future. Some business professors would prefer a definition close to common parlance wherein any transaction with a goal of making money in the future counts as investment. The two can disagree violently over a statement like "investment encourages economic growth" simply because they are defining "investment" differently. The interdisciplinary researcher is guided to interpret the research findings that they draw upon in terms of a shared vocabulary. This strategy, I might note, is particularly important for interdisciplinary research teams. These are often observed to stumble due to miscommunication (O'Rourke et al., 2014). One useful substrategy here is for team members to try to repeat, in their own words, what others have said.

Each discipline inevitably emphasizes the phenomena that they study. A sociologist looking at youth crime will worry about peer pressure, a psychologist will wonder about personality traits, and an economist will consider the costs and benefits of criminal activity. The interdisciplinary researcher in such cases may be able to combine these insights (after carefully evaluating them). One strategy here is to identify the broadest theory employed at present and ask if the phenomena and causal arguments addressed in other disciplines can be added to that theory. This strategy of "theory extension" works best when the phenomena studied in different disciplines exert independent influences on the phenomenon of interest (e.g., youth crime in the example above).

It will often be the case, though, that the phenomena studied in different disciplines exert important influences on each other. In the example above, one might easily imagine that peer pressure will result in different outcomes based on personality traits. The sort of flow chart diagram that was urged above when designing our research question (see Figure 12.1 for an example) can be useful again here. On this diagram, a researcher can plot all of the phenomena identified across disciplines as being important to their research question. The researcher can then hypothesize and investigate how these phenomena influence each other. We may at times be able to mathematically model this set of interactions, but it is still useful to start with a visual diagram. It will often be the case that disciplinary researchers will have paid little, if any, attention to the links between the phenomena studied in different disciplines.

The three strategies addressed so far deal with situations in which disagreements between disciplines are more apparent than real. In the first case, apparent differences flow from terminological confusion. Our second and third strategies deal with situations in which different disciplines merely emphasize different phenomena.

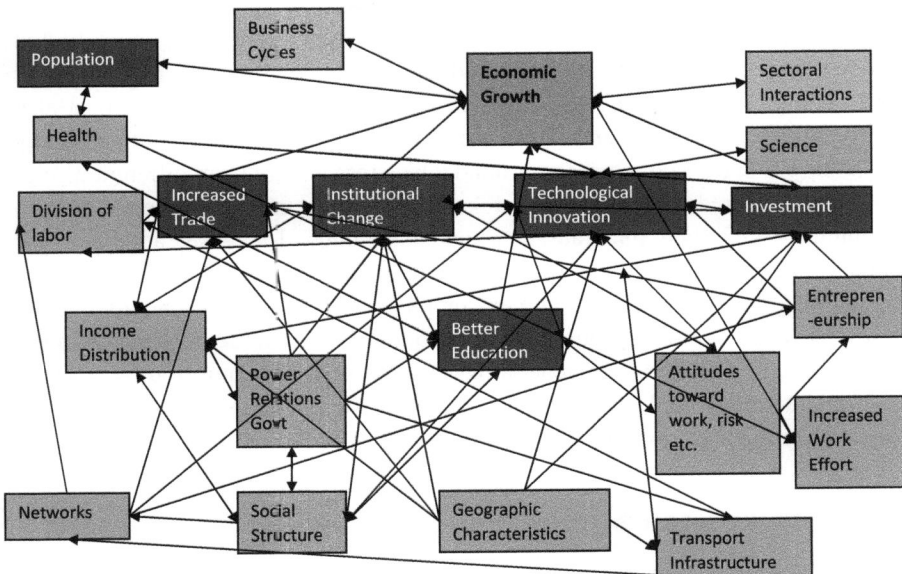

Figure 12.1 *Influences on economic growth. Reproduced from Repko, Szostak, and Buchberger (2020).*

What, though, can be done when disciplines talk about the same causal relationship and disagree about the effect of one phenomenon upon another? The broad answer involves interrogating the assumptions that each brings to bear on any research question.

An economist asked about the effect of an increase in the legal penalty for a particular crime might employ rational choice theory and conclude that an increase in the cost of crime will lead to a decrease in crime. A sociologist who assumes that criminals are driven by impulse or peer pressure, rather than rational calculation, may conclude the exact opposite. The interdisciplinary researcher need not choose between these opposing conclusions. They can instead speculate (and perhaps investigate) that potential criminals are neither perfectly rational nor completely non-rational, and thus the likely impact falls somewhere between the conclusions reached by the two scholars. That is, the interdisciplinary researcher can recognize a continuum between the assumptions of the two authors (in this example a continuum of degrees of rationality) and draw on each analysis to the appropriate degree. It will often be the case, as in this example, that one can imagine different agents operating at different places along the continuum.

I would stress again that integration is a creative act. It may be that none of these strategies will work in a particular piece of research, though each of them has proven useful in many previous research inquiries (see Repko, Newell, and Szostak, 2012). It is usually not immediately obvious how each strategy might be applied to a particular research question.

We noted above that interdisciplinary analysis draws upon "common ground theory." The idea here is that individuals from different backgrounds need to first identify some "common ground" of shared understanding, after which they will be able to communicate about related issues. Interdisciplinary integration must also identify some common ground (Bromme, 2000). A shared understanding of key terminology is one sort of common ground. Once researchers from different disciplines have a shared understanding of key terms, they are much better able to communicate and then integrate their understandings. Likewise, a theory that embraces phenomena studied in different disciplines can serve as common ground. A visual diagram of how the phenomena emphasized by different scholars interact can also serve as common ground. As noted above, it can guide researchers to see how they might collaborate in generating a shared understanding of a large set of causal interactions. Finally, a continuum between competing assumptions can also provide a common ground that allows researchers to transcend a false dichotomy.

Mixed Methods Research

Some interdisciplinary research may go no further than integrating the insights of previous disciplinary research. This, on its own, can be incredibly valuable in generating a more comprehensive, more nuanced understanding of the issue at hand. In performing this kind of research, the interdisciplinary researcher need not have a practitioner-level understanding of the theories or methods employed in the research that they draw upon. They need to understand the core assumptions of the theories they draw upon and the strengths and weaknesses of the methods employed in investigating those theories. Their expertise and contribution lie in employing interdisciplinary strategies for evaluation and integration.

Often, though, interdisciplinary researchers will take a further step. They will employ disciplinary methods to further investigate the hypotheses developed in previous steps. This will usually involve the application of multiple methods. Since Chapter 8 in this volume of the Handbook addresses the use of multiple methods in research, I can be brief here (see also Hesse-Bulber & Johnson, 2015). I can stress that a core assumption at the heart of interdisciplinary research is the idea that no method is perfect. It follows that we can be most confident in any hypothesis if evidence from different methods supports it. Some types of mixed methods research build directly on this insight – different methods are applied to the same precise research question, and the results are compared. If the results differ, the researcher draws upon their understanding of the different methods to "triangulate" (a word borrowed from surveyors) toward the most likely result. Economists have effectively been triangulating between the results of statistical analysis and experiments in revising their attitudes toward rational choice theory (see above).

Other types of mixed methods research apply different methods sequentially, as when the results of a survey are used to guide follow-up interviews. Here again, we appreciate that different methods have different strengths and drive results that we can have greater confidence in than if we had merely employed one method. The interviews flesh out survey results while survey results place the interviews in context. A third type of mixed methods research applies different methods to different causal relationships within the broader research question (an approach that is best pursued after the sort of mapping exercise outlined above). Here, we need to reflect carefully on why we rely on particular methods for particular tasks.

We noted above that disciplines choose methods that are readily applied to their theories. Interdisciplinary researchers are encouraged to query disciplinary preferences and wonder what insights alternative methods might provide. They should be alert to the likelihood that different methods will reach different conclusions. I noted in the preceding section that authors and disciplines may disagree about a particular causal relationship because they make different theoretical assumptions. We can appreciate here that authors and disciplines may also disagree because they employ different methods. A research design that combines methods employed in different disciplines may shed light on the source of disagreements between those disciplines. Furthermore, a research design that employs methods not common to either discipline may shed a quite novel light on the problem at hand.

Reflecting and Testing

One important purpose of interdisciplinary research is to counteract the biases inherent in disciplinary specialization. In doing so, interdisciplinary researchers must police their own biases. Especially for those who were trained in a discipline, they must be careful that they do not favor the theories, methods, or phenomena of one discipline over another. They should strive, indeed, to find some good in the theories they are skeptical of and to critique the theories they find attractive. Moreover, they should make sure that an interdisciplinary approach is truly justified and that no single discipline can adequately address the question at hand. That is, they should not assume, without reflection, that a particular research inquiry requires an interdisciplinary approach.

If interdisciplinary research is called for, they should then ask themselves why they chose – or did not choose – particular strategies for interdisciplinary research. Did they choose the best strategies? On what basis did they choose strategies? Have they given adequate attention to each step in the interdisciplinary research process? In particular, did they achieve and display an adequate understanding of each discipline's insights into their research question? Finally, like any good researcher, they should reflect on the limitations of their study and suggest avenues for further research.

All researchers should reflect on the nature of their research and the biases that they may have (Lumsden, 2019). Yet this reflective task is particularly important for interdisciplinary researchers precisely because they need to be aware of the biases that can afflict both disciplinary and interdisciplinary research. One key question is to what extent researchers should report on their reflective processes. There is a tendency across the academy for us to write up the results of our research as if we had proceeded flawlessly from research question to supportive argument and evidence and onward to a conclusion. We leave out all of the juicy details of how we flailed around coming up with a question, revised it multiple times as we could not find the evidence or results that we hoped for, and adjusted our research plan as we ran into dead ends. Our finished research leaves few clues of the messy process behind the scenes.

There is an obvious advantage to this subterfuge – our published works can provide clear exposition of hypotheses, arguments, evidence, and conclusion. However, the subterfuge makes it harder to evaluate the work. Unless we know how the author went about all of these tasks, how can we know that the author used the best methods and strategies, applied these appropriately (e.g., did not arbitrarily exclude certain data points or studies), surveyed the literature appropriately, evaluated the work of others in an unbiased manner, and thus reached reasonable conclusions? I am wary of cluttering our research reports with a lot of reflection as this practice risks making the author loom larger than the research subjects do. Yet there is perhaps a place for a reflective appendix much like the data appendices that commonly accompany quantitative analyses.

The complexity of most interdisciplinary research makes it hard to test any guiding hypothesis with one empirical test. The common use of multiple methods reinforces this challenge, yet we can evaluate the evidence generated by any method or interdisciplinary strategy for any component of our research question. We will generally have to employ judgment in ascertaining whether we have compelling evidence regarding any hypotheses regarding the entire set of interactions we have studied. We need to ask in what ways our interdisciplinary analysis generates understandings that differ from disciplinary analyses and what kinds of evidence we can provide in support of these different conclusions.

Communicating

Interdisciplinary researchers will often wish to reach multiple audiences. They will likely have something to say to each discipline that they have drawn upon in their research. In addition, they may have audiences among policy-makers or the wider public in mind. They may try to reach multiple audiences simultaneously by publishing in the growing number of interdisciplinary journals or by writing a book. Alternatively, they may target different audiences with different publications. It is entirely legitimate, and one of the potential rewards of interdisciplinary research, to publish different versions of the results of your research in multiple venues, indicating how they inform different disciplinary conversations. I confess to having done so multiple times in my career. Whatever the precise communication plan, interdisciplinary researchers need to recognize that each audience requires a different strategy.

Novice researchers especially, whether disciplinary or interdisciplinary, often mistakenly assume that their brilliant research will sell itself. The researcher found it interesting, and so surely others will too. Yet scholarship is a conversation, and academics are busy, so we can only interest others in our amazing research by convincing them that it informs conversations in which they are involved. That is, we must tell them how our research answers questions that they care about, suggests further research that might interest them, and intersects with their own research interests. Above, I urged interdisciplinary researchers to be aware of debates in each discipline they draw upon regarding their research question. I now urge researchers to explicitly explain how their research informs disciplinary debates or conversations when reporting their results back to disciplines. Since each discipline has its own unique conversations, interdisciplinary researchers must reflect on how they might add to conversations in each discipline they have drawn upon.

I noted above that each discipline has a way of looking at the world. We should not underestimate the challenge of communicating to a discipline the value of alternative theories or methods or of studying relationships to phenomena studied in other disciplines. Nevertheless, the task is not impossible. Economists were once quite hostile to the idea of experiments or surveys, but now the fact that these methods question the dominance of rational choice theory is widely appreciated in the discipline.

Interdisciplinary researchers can potentially provide policy advice that is less biased and more comprehensive, simply by integrating across the insights of others. Policy-makers too need to be convinced of the value of research before they will bother consulting it. Here too, it is necessary to understand the particular challenges that they are facing and thus the questions that they themselves are asking. The best way to do this is to interact regularly with policy-makers and even involve them in the research from the beginning. If they have had a role in shaping research questions and research strategies, they will see the value in the research results (see British Academy, 2021).

I would argue that the purpose of communication is persuasion: we want others to see the value and importance of our research. We should then appreciate that persuasion is itself a creative act. We can be justifiably proud of all of the hard work that we have devoted to our research, yet it may well be that an evocative anecdote or clever metaphor will do more to persuade others than all of the argument and evidence that we have so painstakingly compiled. At the very least, the anecdote or metaphor may encourage others to take a closer look at our arguments and evidence. All researchers need to appreciate the importance of persuasion, but it is particularly important that interdisciplinary researchers do so. Disciplinary researchers may subconsciously absorb the persuasive strategies common in their discipline, but the interdisciplinary researcher needs consciously to persuade multiple audiences. Moreover, in communicating to disciplines about insights from theories, or methods, or the study of phenomena engaged in other disciplines, the persuasive burden is much higher than for a disciplinary scholar engaging familiar theories, methods, and phenomena.

Team Research

Interdisciplinary team research faces two great intellectual challenges. The first is terminological confusion. The second is differences in overall disciplinary perspective. There are strategies for addressing both.

I outlined one strategy for addressing terminology above. We need to ensure that team members share a similar understanding of key terms used by the research team.

One way of doing so is for team members to define the term in their own words. The team may find it useful to define terms quite differently to how any of their disciplines do to facilitate conversation (see Galison, 1997, for an interesting comparison between the "pidgin" languages developed by some research teams and the pidgin languages that develop when people from different linguistic backgrounds interact).

A second strategy involves a recognition that the greatest ambiguity is attached to complex terms. If a research team employs the term "globalization," it may be that the economist on the team thinks of globalization in terms of trade and investment flows, the political scientist thinks of international organizations, and the sociologist thinks of the cultural impacts of foreign movies. While the team may struggle to achieve a common understanding of "globalization," it can readily achieve shared understandings of "trade" and "foreign movies."

Every interdisciplinary research team needs to confront the simple fact that each discipline has an overall perspective that includes favored theories, methods, phenomena, and epistemological attitudes. Unless differences in perspective are brought into the open, some team members will fail to appreciate the suggestions made by others. The Toolbox Project, funded by the National Science Foundation in the United States, has held workshops with dozens of interdisciplinary research teams. These were given questionnaires with epistemological and methodological questions such as "Does research always involve testing hypotheses?" The diverse answers given by team members were then discussed. When the questionnaire was administered a second time, there was greater consensus, and team members often indicated that they better understood other team members (O'Rourke et al. 2014). In the absence of conversations, such as those guided by the Toolbox project, concerns about subjectivity may seem bizarre to those from disciplines that only rarely worry about this, and insistence on hypothesis testing may offend those from disciplines in which thick description is advocated. Team members are more likely to respect and build upon the ideas put forth by others if they know where they are coming from.

We can segue here from a discussion of intellectual challenges to a set of more practical challenges to team research. One common mistake that is made in assembling research teams is to focus entirely on gathering people with the necessary expertise. The team must cohere, and thus it is just as important to gather people with desirable personalities. Most obviously, we need team members who are open-minded enough to appreciate both the value that other disciplines bring and the limitations of their own discipline. We need team members who are confident enough to ask questions when they do not understand what other team members are saying but not so arrogant as to dominate every discussion. We also need team members who are responsible, for the team needs to trust that others will perform their tasks in a timely manner. In addition, we need team members who are respectful of others, who do not believe that their discipline is inherently superior, and with the curiosity and the intellectual courage to stray far from familiar theories and methods and phenomena. We could also benefit from team members who are willing to engage in constructive conversations rather than try to win debates and who will try to see things from the perspective of other team members rather than dismiss what they have to say. Since interdisciplinary team research is challenging and takes time, we ultimately need team members who will persevere against early challenges.

We need team meetings that get things done, or team members will lose confidence that the team will ever accomplish anything. However, the very purpose of a research team is to generate novelty through interaction. The team must thus find time in its meetings for brainstorming. Team members should feel comfortable throwing out "crazy" ideas, yet an entire meeting devoted to such ideas may cause some team members to reassess their commitment to the team. The team needs to develop a clear idea of its research direction at the start (with subtasks identified and assigned and a timeline suggested) but needs also to be able to alter that direction in response to both early research results and the brainstorming efforts of team members. Many teams fail to strike a productive balance between moving things forward and innovating. Social events, I might note, can be important both for cementing personal connections among team members and for providing a venue for the pursuit of brainstorming.

Importantly, we may want diversity of many types – not just disciplinary but cultural, gender, racial, and personality diversity. Diversity may increase our communication challenges and make it harder to achieve group cohesion, yet diversity of any sort increases the likelihood of novelty – that one team member will bring an insight that others have never considered. Note that the group can only achieve novelty from diversity if it is successful in forging common ground and achieving integration.

There is a host of even more practical questions. How is any budget allocated? Whose names go on which publications and in which order? Different disciplines have different practices here: economists usually list authors in alphabetical order while anthropologists generally list in order of contribution. If there are students, who supervises them? Again, supervisory practices differ across disciplines, especially between lab-based disciplines and those that perform research in the field. How will decisions be made within the team? It is generally best to answer these questions early. Otherwise, teams may be riven with conflict later on (Hall et al., 2019).

Challenges and Strategies Revisited

Interdisciplinary researchers face a set of common challenges such as deciding which theories, methods, or disciplines to engage or determining how to integrate insights generated by different theories or methods (in addition to a set of challenges specific to particular research questions). Not surprisingly, interdisciplinary researchers have identified a set of useful strategies for addressing such challenges. Scholars unfamiliar with these strategies may waste valuable time "reinventing the wheel" by developing such strategies on their own. Worse yet, they may fail to do so, and their research may fail as a result. Yet the very diversity of interdisciplinary research – which addresses topics linking every discipline in the academy – often blinds researchers to the simple fact that they can learn much from the decades of interdisciplinary research that has gone before (Repko and Szostak, 2020).

I should stress here a distinction between strategies and methods. Most of the chapters in this Handbook will discuss methods employed within various disciplines. Interdisciplinary researchers will draw upon or employ these methods also. Interdisciplinary researchers need to be as careful in employing disciplinary methods as disciplinary scholars are. However, interdisciplinary research involves many tasks that are not guided by disciplinary methods. It is in the performance of these important tasks that interdisciplinary research strategies are key.

There are, I should note, some interdisciplinary scholars who worry about efforts to identify interdisciplinary research strategies. Many scholars became interdisciplinary because they felt constrained by their home disciplines. They worry about efforts to limit the freedom inherent in interdisciplinary research. There are a few critical points to make here. Foremost, it cannot be stressed too much that interdisciplinarity cannot provide an excuse to perform shoddy research. As noted just above, interdisciplinary researchers must be as careful in their use of disciplinary methods as disciplinary researchers are. Likewise, if certain strategies have been found useful in interdisciplinary research in the past, then interdisciplinary researchers are well advised to use them also. From time to time, they may identify novel strategies (or more likely adjustments to existing strategies). These will need to be justified, just as disciplinary scholars need to justify any deviations from the methods common in their disciplines (Szostak, 2012). The principle of interdisciplinary freedom is invaluable but need not and should not guide us away from performing rigorous research.

What sort of freedom does interdisciplinarity then need to embrace? Interdisciplinary scholars should be free to draw upon any disciplinary theory or method that they find relevant to their research question. Importantly, the strategies that were outlined in this chapter (and the wider literature) in no way limit the disciplinary theories or methods that an interdisciplinary scholar may choose to draw upon. Disciplines at any point in time tend to have strong preferences for particular theories and methods. Scholars often become interdisciplinary precisely because they are attracted to alternative theories or methods. We can embrace this sort of "freedom" wholeheartedly as long as these theories and methods are applied judiciously.

We should appreciate that disciplinary preferences serve an important purpose. A scholar employing the theories and methods favored by their discipline need not explain the basics of these theories or methods to others in their discipline. They can focus on any minor changes they may propose to theory or method and on the precise application or test that they are proposing. Disciplinary conversations can be very productive precisely because there is a common basis from which to proceed. However, this common basis necessarily comes with a cost – disciplinary scholars will tend to ignore alternative theories or methods or interactions between the phenomena they study and those studied in other disciplines.

Interdisciplinary research naturally reflects both the strengths and weaknesses of disciplinary research. Interdisciplinary researchers build on the insights generated by disciplinary research, yet interdisciplinary research then performs tasks that disciplinary research cannot. It evaluates disciplinary research in a manner that is complementary to disciplinary evaluation. It may also apply a theory and/or method common in one discipline to the subject matter of another. More commonly, it may investigate the relationship between phenomena studied in two or more disciplines. Note that there is a symbiotic relationship here – interdisciplinary research draws upon the specialized research performed within disciplines but places this in a larger context and points out to specialized researchers what they might learn from drawing upon alternative theories or methods or studying the relationships with phenomena studied in other disciplines.

We can also note here a very practical advantage of appreciating the nature of interdisciplinary research and of strategies for performing this. Granting agencies often seek to encourage interdisciplinarity and ask researchers to explain the interdisciplinary nature of their research project. Yet both researchers and adjudication committees often have a very limited understanding of the characteristics of a good interdisciplinary research project. Both researchers and granting agencies can benefit from a more nuanced understanding of what interdisciplinary research necessarily involves and how it can best be pursued (see McLeish and Strang 2016).

The Nature of Interdisciplinary Research

Defining Interdisciplinarity

I postponed the task of defining interdisciplinarity at the start of this chapter. We are much better placed to do so now after having discussed how interdisciplinarity is best pursued. It is a general – though not unanimous – view in the literature that the distinguishing feature of interdisciplinarity is integration of insights from relevant disciplines. If we merely juxtapose insights from different disciplines, without combining these, then we are pursuing *multidisciplinarity*. This can also be valuable but does not usually generate a more comprehensive understanding of any issue.

Philosophers have long warned us that our abilities at definition are limited and that words can only be understood in context. Our understanding of "interdisciplinarity" is thus enhanced by our discussion above. Interdisciplinary research will sometimes involve applying the theories or methods of one discipline to the subject matter of another but most often involves studying interactions among phenomena studied in multiple disciplines. It also generally involves the evaluation and integration of theories employed in different disciplines and the use of methods favored in multiple disciplines. Team research, at least, involves a further kind of integration as researchers transcend barriers of perspective and terminology to work as a coherent team.

We should also mention the word "transdisciplinarity." This word has had many meanings over the years and often signaled an effort to transcend disciplines in pursuit of a unified theory of everything. Its most common meaning today involves the pursuit of a form of interdisciplinarity that involves stakeholders from beyond the academy. A transdisciplinary environmental research project might involve local farmers and policy-makers, for example. There is a vast literature on how to perform transdisciplinary research. The best starting point is the website of the Swiss-based td-net (https://transdisciplinarity.ch/en; see also Bergmann et al., 2012; Hirsh Hadorn et al., 2008). The key challenge is to manage the inherent conflict between the interest of academics in publications and the interest of stakeholders in practical policy proposals. The key lesson is that external stakeholders need to be involved at all stages of the research planning process.

Interdisciplinarity and Creativity

We have noted above that interdisciplinary research is inherently creative. It is worth exploring the links between interdisciplinarity and creativity in more depth. Creativity (in art or science) is generally understood as having two components: the creation of something novel and that novelty being judged to have merit by at least some observers. Interdisciplinary integration will generate an understanding that is novel and that could not have been achieved by any one discipline. It thus fits the definition of creativity as long as some community of scholars values this more comprehensive understanding.

The literature on creativity describes a process very similar to the interdisciplinary research process that was outlined above. The creative person must first recognize a question, problem, or challenge. Then, they reflect consciously on this and gather relevant information. Only then are they capable of an act of inspiration in which an idea from their subconscious thought processes becomes conscious. Note here that experts on creativity disdain the common misperception that inspirations just happen but appreciate instead that considerable preparation is necessary before inspiration is possible. They also appreciate that our inspirations are usually imperfect and need to be consciously evaluated and revised. The various strategies outlined above pave the way for acts of inspiration and allow these to be further revised.

The literature on creativity appreciates that the degree of novelty achieved depends critically on the range of information gathered beforehand. New ideas combine existing ideas in novel ways. If we have explored what distant disciplines (e.g., psychology and art history) have to say about our research question, then we create a potential for great novelty. We also run the risk of total failure. There is a trade-off then – looking far and wide for inputs into the creative process has both a huge potential upside and a downside. Yet the interdisciplinary researcher can hope that, by combining insights that have never previously been integrated, they should have a reasonable likelihood of achieving a valuable novelty.

Creativity is commonly attributed to creative "geniuses," yet all humans have creative abilities. Importantly, we can be trained to be more creative (see Sternberg, 2006). As we have just seen, searching for diverse insights into any research question itself paves the way for creativity. Another interdisciplinary strategy – perspective-taking – also encourages creativity. If we can try to see an issue from multiple perspectives, whether those of multiple stakeholders or multiple members of a research team, we increase the chances of creative insight. Buzan (2010) has argued that the sort of visual diagramming that I have recommended multiple times above can stimulate creativity, perhaps because our subconscious thought processes operate visually. Buzan urges us to put all relevant ideas on a diagram, consciously draw connections that we can readily appreciate, and then give our subconscious thought processes time to identify connections that had not previously occurred to us.

It is easier to identify strategies for the conscious gathering of information and revision of inspirations than for facilitating the act of inspiration itself (Buzan, 2010 can be seen as one exception to this rule). Yet it seems clear that acts of inspiration occur generally when the mind is at rest – when the creative person is taking a bath or walking in the park. Creativity, then, requires some degree of balance. The creative person must actively collect information but must also take the occasional break in which it is easier for their subconscious thought processes to both operate and manage to render ideas conscious. Some creative people find certain kinds of music or aromas or other stimuli useful, but there seems to be (at least at our present state of understanding) no set of stimuli that works for everyone. As with any skill, creativity benefits from practice. If we can set our students tasks that demand a little bit of creativity, they can both gain confidence in their creative ability while learning how best to encourage their own individual creative processes (see Ulibarri et al., 2019).

Writers on creativity emphasize the need to persuade others of the value of one's creative insight. The history of both art and science is littered with people who had great ideas but were unable to convince others of their value. Those who achieve acclaim for their creativity are not necessarily those with the best ideas but those who are the most persuasive. I noted above that interdisciplinary researchers face particular communicative challenges. I recognized that anecdotes and metaphors may advance a case as much or more than careful argument and evidence. We can appreciate here that acts of persuasion are themselves creative acts. The interdisciplinary researcher is advised to devote time and energy – but also periods of inaction in which ideas may bubble up from subconscious thought processes – to the question of how to persuade others of the value of their insights (see Szostak 2017a).

Interdisciplinarity and Complexity

Newell (2001) argued that interdisciplinarity was required to deal with complexity. Most scholars of interdisciplinarity might be unwilling to argue, as he did, that interdisciplinarity was only necessary in complex situations. It is nevertheless true that interdisciplinary research often addresses interactions among large numbers of phenomena. One definition of complexity would refer to sets of phenomena that interact in an unpredictable manner. Such sets of interactions (sometimes deserving to be called systems) can be challenging to study. It may at times be possible to mathematically model all of the (most important) interactions. Often, though, different methods are called for in understanding different causal linkages. Interdisciplinary scholars should, like specialized researchers, aim for coherence in their analysis but should be prepared to generate answers that involve multiple theoretical understandings of different relationships.

There may at times be negative feedback loops that lend stability to some set of interactions. Often, though, the dynamics of the set of interactions is unstable. One important cause of instability is that any set of phenomena will also interact with other phenomena not included in a particular research study. Szostak (2017b) noted that most social science disciplines study systems that exhibit a fair bit of stability: economic stability, political stability, social stability, personality stability. However, all of these systems can be shocked from outside. For example, a war can disrupt each of these types of stability. As social and behavioral scientists, we need to understand both the forces guiding stability and instability. Indeed, we might argue that it is even more important to understand instability, for it is in periods of instability that we are most in need of enlightened policy advice. Yet disciplines, due to the natural tendency to emphasize interactions among the set of phenomena studied in that discipline, are likely to stress the forces of stability. Interdisciplinary researchers, in looking at interactions among phenomena studied in different disciplines, are likely to inform our understanding of instability. We may not always need to understand how epidemics can disrupt economic (and other kinds of) stability, but it is occasionally extremely valuable to have that sort of understanding.

Evaluating Interdisciplinary Research

Though there are a growing number of interdisciplinary journals, interdisciplinary researchers may still want to publish in disciplinary journals to communicate their findings to that disciplinary audience. Referees and editors with a strong preference for one theory or method may harshly judge interdisciplinary research that integrates different theories and methods. Interdisciplinary research will simply not look like the specialized research that referees and editors are accustomed to dealing with, since disciplines have not only favored theories and methods but also preferences regarding how papers are structured, references are cited, and so on.

Journals that wish to encourage interdisciplinary research need to consciously encourage openness to alternative theories, methods, and phenomena (and styles of argument) in their refereeing process. They should also appreciate the value of employing interdisciplinary research strategies correctly. Note that our discussion of the interdisciplinary research process above itself suggests a series of evaluative questions: Is the question clear and unbiased? Does the author display adequate understanding of all disciplines, theories, and methods? Are appropriate evaluative and integrative strategies employed? Is it clear which phenomena and relationships are addressed? Is a valuable integration achieved? Did the author reflect on possible biases? And is the research connected to important disciplinary conversations? Editors and referees should appreciate the symbiosis between specialized and interdisciplinary research and thus ask whether a particular piece of interdisciplinary analysis generates a useful novelty and suggests new lines of research for specialized researchers to undertake (Laursen, Motzer, and Anderson, 2022, survey the literature on interdisciplinary evaluation).

It is important to stress that we can and should evaluate interdisciplinary research as rigorously as we evaluate specialized research, yet the precise standards employed will necessarily differ. Interdisciplinary researchers should be free to draw upon the full range of disciplinary theories and methods but should be expected to apply these – and interdisciplinary research strategies – rigorously and appropriately. If we are not aware of the correct standards, then we will reject solid work while publishing superficial analyses. The latter sort of error will encourage those who worry about the quality of interdisciplinary research.

Career Progress

One unsurprising characteristic of interdisciplinary research is that scholars often publish outside of their home discipline, whether in the journals of other disciplines or in the increasing number of interdisciplinary journals. It should be equally unsurprising, then, that those interdisciplinary researchers can suffer in career progress decisions if evaluated according to disciplinary preferences for publications in certain journals. Universities that wish to encourage interdisciplinary research should thus ensure that this research is appropriately rewarded (see Lyall et al. 2011 and Lyall 2019 for advice).

Another relevant characteristic of interdisciplinary research is that it takes time. First, the individual needs to gain some level of adequacy in more than one discipline. In addition, interdisciplinary research teams necessarily spend some time at the outset getting acquainted and plotting research strategies. This time investment at the start can be richly rewarded by impressive outcomes later. Especially for junior scholars, though, this time commitment may be unfeasible due to the need to accumulate a certain number of publications before a decision such as tenure or contract renewal can be made.

Integration within Disciplines

Though we have defined interdisciplinary research as involving theories, methods, or phenomena from multiple disciplines, it is important to recognize that many of the strategies reviewed above can also be employed within disciplines. There are, after all, disagreements within disciplines that can potentially be transcended through integrative research strategies. Moreover, there are fields within disciplines that focus on different subsets of the phenomena studied in a discipline, and these can likewise be usefully linked by integrative research.

There is a further important advantage of integration within disciplines. Specialized scholarship tends to be very forgetful. Scholars routinely survey only a small number of other works at the start of any paper. It is quite easy, then, for discoveries to be forgotten as research agendas move off on a slightly different tangent. The occasional survey article in a field is not enough to keep researchers aware of all relevant research in the field. Inevitably, then, researchers often reinvent the wheel, making discoveries that are not in fact novel. A greater body of integrative research would limit such wasteful behavior. It would likely also serve to identify promising lines of future research. Moreover, it can alleviate a common problem in the social sciences – replication (see Chapter 13 in this volume). There are very few efforts to replicate research results, and thus we are forced to rely on whether multiple research projects in the same area provide some sort of broad support for particular hypotheses.

Integrative research within disciplines might also serve as a bridge between specialized research and interdisciplinary research. Integrative research within a discipline can aid interdisciplinary researchers in grasping key debates within the discipline. It could also advertise, to specialized researchers, the potential value of alternative theories or methods, or links to phenomena studied by other disciplines (Szostak 2022).

Concluding Remarks

Interdisciplinary researchers can benefit immeasurably from familiarity with strategies for addressing a set of common challenges in interdisciplinary and team research. Many research projects fail due to lacking awareness of such strategies. Others waste valuable time developing such strategies. However, successful researchers can be very creative, producing research results that are widely cited and that influence academic conversations in multiple disciplines.

There is much confusion in today's academy around the nature of interdisciplinarity and how this is best pursued. From time to time, this leads to misplaced critiques, such as confusing interdisciplinarity with anti-disciplinarity (Jacobs, 2013) or doubting that interdisciplinary scholars appreciate the power differentials among disciplines (Frickel et al., 2016). A wider appreciation of the symbiotic relationship between disciplines and interdisciplinarity would be invaluable. A greater appreciation of the nature of interdisciplinary research – and especially the career progress challenges – would also allow universities to better support it. Finally, a more detailed understanding of the strategies conducive to quality interdisciplinary research would both allow granting agencies to better target their funding and referees and editors to better judge research quality.

References

Bergmann, M., Jahn, T., Knobloch, T., Krohn, W., Pohl, C., & Schramm, E. (2012). *Methods for Transdisciplinary Research: A Primer for Practice*. Campus.
British Academy. (2021). *Knowledge Exchange in the SHAPE Disciplines*. www.thebritishacademy.ac.uk/publications/knowledge-exchange-in-the-shape-disciplines
Bromme, R. (2000). Beyond one's own perspective: The psychology of cognitive interdisciplinarity. In P. Weingart and N. Stehr (eds.), *Practicing Interdisciplinarity* (pp. 115–133). University of Toronto Press.
Buzan, T. (2010). *The Mindmap Book*. BBC Books.

Fam, D., & O'Rourke, M. (eds.). (2021). *Interdisciplinary and Transdisciplinary Failures: Lessons Learned from Cautionary Tales*. Routledge.

Frickel, S., et al. (eds.). (2016). *Investigating Interdisciplinary Collaboration: Theory and Practice across Disciplines*. Rutgers University Press.

Galison, P. (1997). *Image and Logic: A Material Culture of Microphysics*. University of Chicago Press

Hall, K. L., Vogel, A. L., & Croyle, R. T. (eds.). (2019). *Strategies for Team Science Success: Handbook of Evidence-Based Principles for Cross-Disciplinary Science and Practical Lessons Learned from Health Researchers*. Springer.

Hesse-Bulber, S., & Johnson, R. B. (eds.). (2015). *Oxford Handbook of Multimethod and Mixed Methods Research Inquiry*. Oxford University Press.

Hirsch Hadorn, G., Hoffmann-Riem, H., Biber-Klemm, S., Grossenbacher-Mansuy, W., Joye, D., Pohl, C., et al. (eds.). (2008). *Handbook of Transdisciplinary Research*. Springer.

Holley, K., & Szostak, R. (2022). Interdisciplinary education and research in North America. In J. T. Klein and B. V. Baptista (eds.), *Interdisciplinarity and Transdisciplinarity: Institutionalizing Collaboration across Cultures and Communities*. Routledge.

Jacobs, Jerry A. (2013). *In Defense of Disciplines: Interdisciplinarity and Specialization in the Research University*. University of Chicago Press.

Laursen, B. K., Motzer, N., & Anderson, K. J. (2022). Pathway profiles: Learning from five main approaches to assessing interdisciplinarity. *Research Evaluation*, *32*(2), 213–227. https://doi.org/10.1093/reseval/rvac036

Lumsden, K. (2019). Introduction: The reflexive turn and the social sciences. In K. Lumsden, J. Bradford, & J. Goode (eds.), *Reflexivity: Theory, Method, and Practice* (pp. 1–36). Routledge.

Lyall, C. (2019). *Being an Interdisciplinary Academic: How Institutions Shape Careers*. Palgrave Macmillan.

Lyall, C., Bruce, A., Tait, J., & Meagher, L. (2011). *Interdisciplinary Research Journeys*. Bloomsbury Academic.

McLeish, T., and Strang, V. (2016). Evaluating interdisciplinary research: The elephant in the peer-reviewers' room. *Palgrave Communications*, *2*, 16055.

Newell, W. H. (2001). A theory of interdisciplinary studies. *Issues in Integrative Studies*, *19*, 1–25.

Okamura, K. (2019). Interdisciplinarity revisited: Evidence for research impact and dynamism. *Palgrave Communications*, *5*, 141.

O'Rourke, M., Crowley, S., Eigenbrode, S. D., & Wulfhorst, J. D. (eds.). (2014). *Enhancing Communication and Collaboration in Interdisciplinary Research*. SAGE Publications.

Repko, A. F., Newell, W. H., & Szostak, R. (eds.). (2012). *Case Studies in Interdisciplinary Research*. SAGE Publications.

Repko, A., & Szostak, R. (2020). *Interdisciplinary Research: Process and Theory*, 4th ed. SAGE Publications.

Repko, A., Szostak, R., & Buchberger, R. (2020). *Introduction to Interdisciplinary Studies*. SAGE Publications.

Sternberg, R. J. (2006). The nature of creativity. *Creativity Research Journal*, *18*(1), 87–98.

Szostak, R. (2004). *Classifying Science: Phenomena, Data, Theory, Method, Practice*. Springer.

(2012). The interdisciplinary research process. In A. F. Repko, W. H. Newell, & R. Szostak (eds.), *Case Studies in Interdisciplinary Research* (pp. 3–19). SAGE Publications.

(2017a). Interdisciplinary research as a creative design process. In F. Darbellay, Z. Moody, & T. Lubart (eds.), *Creative Design Thinking from an Interdisciplinary Perspective* (pp. 17–33). Springer.

(2017b). Stability, instability, and interdisciplinarity. *Issues in Interdisciplinary Studies, 35*, 65–87.

(2022). *Integrating the Human Sciences: Enhancing Cohesion and Progress across the Social Sciences and Humanities*. Routledge.

Szostak, R, Gnoli, C., & López-Huertas, M. (2016). *Interdisciplinary Knowledge Organization*. Springer.

Ulibarri, N., Cravens, A. E., Nabergoj, A. S., Kernbach, S., & Royalty, A. (2019). *Creativity in Research: Cultivate Clarity, Be Innovative, and Make Progress in your Research Journey*. Cambridge University Press.

13 The Importance of Replication

Jon E. Grahe and Kelly M. Cuccolo

Abstract

This chapter offers a broad review of why replication is important to science by considering all aspects of the construct from definition to publication. The chapter introduces critical considerations about how to discuss replication given the complexity of its meaning as well as the challenges in conducting and interpreting it. Additionally, the chapter describes why replications are critical for any single construct as well as their contribution to generalizability across scientific disciplines. By conducting high-quality replications before and after effects are published, researchers can remain confident in their contributions to science.

Keywords: Replication, Reproducibility, Methodology, Definitions, Examples, Characteristics

A Difficult Term to Define

This chapter presents a justification for why replication is important to science as well as suggestions for how to properly engage in the process of replication. As such, a good starting point is to define the construct of replication. The most basic conception of a replication is that it is a repetitive reproduction of something. In science, this basic conception of a replication is that it reflects a study that is repeating another study. The problem is that the term has many different uses and could be used as a subject, verb, adverb, or object within a sentence. Consider the following:

A group of replicators replicated a study with questionable replicability and yielded a successful replication of the original effect.

The preceding sentence might read absurdly, but it helps to demonstrate that understanding the construct requires understanding its meaning within a sentence. Here, replicators are people engaging in the process of replication, at least in this study. As they engage in the action of replicating a study, the term becomes a verb. In this sentence, the original effect is qualified by using the term as an adverb. The outcome of the process is a study that is described as a replication. Thus, replication is a process that envelops people, actions, and objects, so speakers should be careful to be clear about what it means.

Further complicating the matter, not all replications are the same. Later in the chapter, the explicit differences between exact, direct, close, and conceptual types of replications will be discussed. In short, they differ based on the degree to which the replication matches the original study. Furthermore, the replication might not be focused on the entire study or the entire process. If the original study examined multiple hypotheses, a replication might only focus on one effect. Alternatively, a replication might re-examine only the data collected in the original study. In this case, the replication is a new process but does not represent new data. And so, replications as verbs and objects must be clearly identified when they are being discussed.

The final area where replications can cause confusion is how they are interpreted. Specifically, what does it mean to say that a replication has been successful? It could mean that the findings reproduced the original effect. By defining success like this, a failed replication could represent a study that finds null or contradictory results to the original. However, it could also represent a successful process of reproducing the original study. Here, success reflects finding the original materials and procedure, executing them with enough participants, and applying correct analysis protocols to the resulting data. Failure would not reflect the size or direction of the effect but rather the interruption of the completion of some step in the research process. When considering the evaluation of multiple replication studies, we may consider success as alignment between effect sizes across sites; however, this may not capture the core of what we are looking for – evidence supporting or refuting an effect (Nosek & Errington, 2020)

The other area where interpretation of replications can be confusing is determining whether a finding has been replicated according to the statistical analyses performed (Hedges & Schauer, 2019; Lakens, 2013). The question that emerges is whether an original effect that is statistically significant is the same or different from a replication effect that is interpreted as being non-significant (Anderson & Maxwell, 2016; Anderson, 2020). In some cases, the difference might be so large that conclusions are obvious, but consider an example expressed in p-values from a Null Hypothesis Significance Test (NHST) approach. What if the original effect reported $p = .04$ and the replication effect reported $p = .06$? From an NHST approach, the original effect is statistically significant, but the replication effect is not. From an effect size perspective, if the original effect reported $r = .19$ and the replication effect reported $r = .21$, it might be concluded that they are equivocal and that the replication supports the conclusion from the original study.

This example demonstrates two points. First, the analysis approach, NHST, Bayesian, or effect size estimation, could impact the decisions about success. Secondly, it is a reminder that all effect estimates are only that, estimates. There is no absolute truth in science, only successive iterations of the truth. This applies to physics (e.g., the continued search for the meaning of gravity) and medicine (e.g., the changing understanding of healthy behavior and treatment) as much as it does to social and behavioral sciences (Rohlfing & Zuber, 2021). The original effect has no more truth than the replication, although one might be a better estimate depending on the process involved in collecting and analyzing the data. As such, it is almost impossible to determine the success or failure of a single effect size, whether it is the original or replication (Cumming, 2013; Hedges, 2019).

A Basic Step in Science

Replication is a basic tenet of the scientific method. Replication allows researchers to systematically evaluate specific claims and is essential for the falsification of hypotheses – a central tenet of science (Popper, 1963; Zwaan et al., 2018). Through replication, we can engage in falsification because replications offer the possibility of finding alternative results, providing a systematic way to "rule out" other explanations. Replications also increase confidence about the original findings' validity. If different researchers identify the same finding at different times using different samples, the replications suggest that the original finding was not a random event. It is important to consider the probabilistic nature of research. For example, researchers typically aim to control for false positives (Type I error), but through replications, false positives become increasingly less likely (Forstmeier et al. 2017; Schmidt, 2009).

Replication helps distinguish science from pseudoscience as it allows for falsifiability, promotes self-correction (e.g., flushing out Type I errors), allows for connectivity (i.e., allows researchers to build on existing constructs), and clarifies the conditions under which the effect may be found (see Edlund et al., 2022). All in all, replications bolster the credibility of research findings, spark conversations that advance science, and are important for public perceptions of science (Edlund et al., 2022; Hendriks et al., 2020; Wingen et al., 2020).

A Dangerous Task in Science

Exact Is Not Possible

Focusing on replications as a primary research area has challenges. While replication in science is both fundamental and critical to the progression toward better knowledge, it is not always valued as a career activity. The *Replication Crisis* that sparked the Open Science Revolution 2.0 in psychology (Spellman, 2012) is often attributed to publication bias and loose publishing standards (Pashler & Wagenmakers, 2012). These causes were intertwined with a publish-or-perish environment in academia that valued high profile, novel, catchy findings, further discouraging replication science (Bakker et al., 2012; Nosek et al., 2012). This reduction in conducting (or publishing) replications of published effects partly influenced the low reproducibility of major effects (Begley & Ellis, 2012; Smith, 2018). The phrase "Replication is a dangerous task in science" is intended to highlight these challenges.

If a researcher does engage in replications, the first challenge in social and behavioral sciences (compared to physical sciences) is that the conditions of the study will never be identical. Different types of replications reflect this reality. Before characterizing the types, consider the task of replication. Imagine that researchers wish to determine whether Manipulation X causally impacts

Measured Variable Y using a randomized-control, two-group design. A convenience sample from a local population experiences one of two levels of the manipulation (X1 or X2) and their responses are recorded on the Measured Variable (Y). Furthermore, imagine the two levels of X are a Smile or Frown from a confederate, and the measured variable is whether the participant smiles, frowns, or has a neutral response. This imagined example was an actual replication used as a teaching tool (Grahe et al., 2000) though it had a slightly more complex experimental design. The experiment seems simple enough, but an exact replication of the original experiment is impossible. Before proceeding to the next paragraph, consider variable or experimental parameters that can never be exactly replicated (e.g., confederates' smiles, environmental conditions, and locations of the trials).

Readers likely recognize the challenge of reproducing a smile in exactly the same way between individuals, even within the same person. Grahe et al. (2000) used the same operational definitions as the original experiment (Hinsz & Tomhave, 1991) that instructed confederates how to move their mouths, faces, and foreheads to elicit specific expressions. The finding that approximately 50% return a smile with a smile and 25% return a frown with a frown was robust across the samples, making it a good teaching exercise. This research on non-verbal displays during passing encounters (Patterson, 2008; Patterson & Tubbs, 2005) could also be studied from many social science lenses such as anthropology and sociology as they are influenced by cultural factors. Even with practice, different confederates are not able to depict identical smiles or frowns. In the same vein, the measured variable (the degree to which the person smiles or frowns back) can be operationally defined, but two people might not see the same intended facial expressions.

Consider the environmental conditions present in this interpersonal exchange of facial expressions (e.g., location, weather, time of day, surroundings). Moreover, the populations would be different. This includes both cultural factors or settings such as urbanization density and the time of data collection. Even if conducted within the same time frame (e.g., just a few years apart), the locations in which they take place often vary, and thus the replications are inherently different (Grahe et al., 2000). Although there are ways to make some variables more exact, such as using computerized displays and standardizing behavioral measures, the settings and people involved will differ.

Even researchers replicating their own work are not identical to their prior selves. As mentioned above, stimuli, environment, and locations are never identical between the original and the replications. Many other aspects of an experiment can never be identical to the original. Time and experience change us in subtle ways – from our appearance to our construals of the world. For instance, the COVID-19 pandemic significantly changed the way people think about and approach healthcare, public spaces, education, and tourism (Honey-Rosés et al., 2021; Kelly & Cuccolo, 2022; Rahman et al., 2021; Vindrola-Padros et al., 2020). Though slight and subtle, these changes all result in the fact that exact replications are impossible in behavioral and social sciences.

Close as We Can Get

Sometimes, the term "direct replication" is used synonymously with "close replication," and sometimes with "exact replication," so it is better to stick with using "close." Close replications reflect the reality of this perpetual ambiguity. Close replications try to match the original study wherever possible. They use the same materials as in the original study, including the recruitment and application protocols. For example, Kraus and Tan (2015) reported that Americans overestimate class mobility, especially when comparing themselves to similar others and if they perceive themselves to be of high social class. Given the important implications of these results, Kraus (2015) conducted a "pre-registered exact replication of Study 3" using "a roughly identical online sample of workers from Amazon's Mechanical Turk" and "identical methods as the original study." Although researchers recruited participants in the same way as the original study, it is important to note that the sample was new and that the researchers themselves were not the same as when the original work was published.

As a further example, consider replication in the context of making an artistic copy of an image. A perfect copy is never possible because the moment is unique, even if one should use a camera. Cameras would take better pictures than a human drawing or painting, but none offers an exact copy. If cameras represent the attempt to copy the image using close replication procedures, other media tools would reflect the attempt to copy the image using conceptual replication procedures. Even an expert artist's work with pencil, marker, or paint will look qualitatively different from the original image (see Figure 13.1; color versions can be found in Grahe & Cuccolo, 2023). Imagine the quality of a replication as the degree to which the reproduction matches the original.

Conceptual Replications Introduce Confounds

Conceptual replications are qualitatively different from the original. Whereas close replications use identical materials to the original, conceptual replications study the generalizability of the original effect, often with new materials. Using the example from above, Grahe et al. (2000) represent a close replication of Hinsz and Tomhave (1991) because they employed identical operational definitions and measurement protocols to the original. However, instructors can invite students to complete conceptual replications for classes where they manipulate different types of smiles (e.g., happy versus nervous) and different types of frowns (e.g., angry versus sad).

Conceptual replications received some blame for the replication crisis (Wiggins & Christopherson, 2019) because researchers often interpreted them in the same manner as close replications. Close replications are critical for identifying systematic and unsystematic error and drawing conclusions about the reproducibility of the original effect (Simons, 2014) by recreating critical aspects of the study in question (e.g., procedure, measures). Because of the wider scope that conceptual replications can take on, their estimates of

Figure 13.1 *Replications of "Willow Sitting in Front of Piano." The photo metaphorically represents a close replication, while the painting and drawing offer metaphorical examples of conceptual replications. Readers should consider the challenge of replicating the event of "Testing an Original Effect" and consider the details that are needed to establish a close rather than conceptual replication.*

reproducibility are confounded with other factors. Researchers can never be sure if the outcome matches the original result because the result could be a function of the different manipulations and has no bearing on the original estimate. In fact, Nosek and Errington (2020) argue that conceptual replications should not be considered replications at all because their failure to demonstrate an effect would not offer negative evidence regarding the original effect. At best, the conceptual replication can suggest a boundary condition where the original effect does or does not generalize to the new situation.

To help distinguish between replication types, Brandt et al. (2014) provide a "replication recipe" for researchers to help communicate about their work. Before data collection, they recommend researchers answer 27 questions about the following categories: nature of the effect, designing the replication study, documenting differences from the original, and analysis and replication evaluation. The goal is to help researchers understand the differences from the original so that boundary conditions can be further tested in the future.

Hard to Repeat

Another challenge with replication is that even the perfect replication of an effect might not have the same outcome. To understand this, replication outcomes measured as effect sizes must be considered as data points estimating population parameters and understood through the Central Limit Theorem. The Central Limit Theorem states that, for samples of adequate size ($N > 30$), sample means should be normally distributed around the population mean even if the original scale was not normally distributed (Islam, 2018; Zhang et al., 2022). When considering effect sizes in this context, estimates could occur anywhere along the X axis of the sampling distribution around the population mean. Because the normal distribution is so well understood, we can further estimate how much variability there will be in effect size estimates from future replications.

Certain characteristics of the normal distribution inform why replication outcomes can radically differ even when the effect is real and correctly measured. First, each observation is independent. Second, all outcomes exist somewhere along the normal distribution. For instance, the 68, 95, 99.7 percent rule reflects the percentage of scores between plus and minus 1, 2, and 3 standard deviations about the mean. Third, the normal distribution is asymptotic – the ends never touch the axis. Thus, while only 0.3% of estimates lie beyond +/- 3 standard deviations of the mean, it is always possible to find a randomly determined effect estimate that is so far removed from the true score that it looks like it comes from a different population of estimates.

Together, these characteristics mean that correct estimates could occur anywhere in the distribution, and suggest radically different and seemingly contrary outcomes. Further, larger samples with more reliable measures should yield distributions with more data points that are more closely packed in the center of the distribution, also called a leptokurtic distribution. In contrast, small samples will yield distributions that are flatter and more spread out, reflecting a platykurtic distribution. Because of random variability of these statistics, all effect sizes approximate rather than truly define the parameter. In conclusion, all estimates include some amount of error and some chance of being very wrong.

Understanding replication outcomes as randomized effect sizes that are subject to statistical principles helps to characterize that a series of unbiased estimates should be normally distributed around the true effect, not the original effect. There are two critical points here. First, the original effect should not be considered primary, or more true, than replications as they are all equally likely to include error and bias. Second, effects should be interpreted through the aggregation of all effects rather than by considering whether subsequent effects supported or rejected the original effect. This process of aggregation is called meta-analysis (see Volume 1, Chapter 27). It is important to note that meta-analytic findings and interpretations are more successful when the replications are very close to each other and the original.

Limited Influence

The process of science includes sharing findings for the iterative benefit of science. However, once an effect gets published, it begins to be treated as truth. Published research provides the content that comprises textbooks and instructional materials. When a replication is considered beside the original effect, they should be considered equal with each estimate offering the same level of evidence. However, in practice, for an established effect to be reconsidered, the replication effects are expected to be much more powerful. For example, the original study that demonstrated an effect related to the facial feedback hypothesis had a total of 152 participants in five studies (Zajonc et al., 1989). However, it took multiple highly powered replications failing to demonstrate the same effect (Wagenmakers et al., 2016) to introduce doubt regarding the presence of this effect.

The preceding paragraph notes the limits to the persuasive influence of published replications. Historically, it was even harder to get a replication published, particularly for findings that were non-significant. This problem was so pervasive that Rosenthal (1979) termed this the File Drawer Problem and suggested that meta-analyses should be attenuated with the expectation of a certain portion of unpublished studies with null or contrary effects. Journal editors are driven to publish 'good' research papers that will increase readership and citations. As such, there is a bias for novel findings that are particularly interesting or counterintuitive (Easley et al., 2013; Ferguson & Heene, 2012; Neuliep, 1990).

Replications, particularly close replication studies, are not novel; nor are they likely to increase readership or get cited often. These increased challenges to publication and limited post-publication influence decreased the likelihood that researchers would engage in them – particularly researchers focused on getting good jobs or receiving tenure and promotion. The devaluing of replication might start with doctoral training where students are focused on their supervisors' research. Additionally, they might pursue "novel" results that offer a better chance at publication. Applying for external funding (e.g., grants) for one's work may also discourage replication if such funding applications put emphasis on the researchers' novel findings and line of research (Giner-Sorolla, 2012).

A Fascinating Stage of Science

Present Crisis

Currently, many are grappling with the state of science, discussing the overall "health" and functionality of the systems. While more recent papers argue that science is doing well (e.g., Edlund et al., 2022), others were less optimistic about the enterprise not so long ago (Lehrer, 2011). Ioannidis (2005) raised many concerns about rates of replicability in various sectors of science. Across disciplines, even when using methodology that is consistent with that of the original studies, rates of successful replication are low (Dafoe, 2014; Ioannidis et al., 2018; Prinz et al., 2011,

Open Science Collaboration, 2015; Świątkowski & Dompnier, 2017). Scientists are not ignorant about this issue either, with 52% of those surveyed agreeing there is a significant crisis (32% a slight crisis) of replicability (Baker, 2016). The failure of previous work to replicate raises questions about the original study. Such issues include the integrity of the research process, the possible unreported boundary conditions in the original study, and whether the published decision represented a false positive rather than true effect.

Ioannidis (2005) emphasizes that significant findings should be interpreted cautiously in light of factors that make significance difficult to achieve (e.g., small sample and effect sizes). Measurement error and researcher degrees of freedom in the original work may obscure or misrepresent statistical significance and effect sizes, affecting decisions about what to replicate and how (Loken & Gelman, 2017). Publication bias (i.e., the phenomenon where significant findings, e.g., $p < .05$, are more likely to be published than null findings, e.g., $p > .05$) may compound the impact of false positives on research endeavors. The over-representation of significant findings in empirical journals may mislead researchers' future work as the population's estimates of the accumulated effect are inaccurate (Giner-Sorolla, 2012).

Another possible reason a study may not replicate is due to the (intentional or unintentional) use of questionable research practices (QRPs) surrounding researcher degrees of freedom (John et al., 2012; Wicherts et al., 2016). Researcher degrees of freedom represent choices that researchers can make across the research process. Wicherts et al. (2016) document 32 different decisions across the entire research and reporting process. Researcher degrees of freedom are not inherently egregious, but the lack of transparency about their occurrence can alter the course of a research project and associated outcomes. These become QRPs when researchers intentionally or unintentionally obscure their decisions.

Simmons et al. (2011) demonstrated common QRPs that include the following: failing to report all of a study's outcome measures, deciding to collect more data after looking to see whether the results were significant, and hypothesizing after results are known ("HARKing"). HARKing (Kerr, 1998) represents a particularly dangerous practice because it dismantles the scientific criterion of falsification (Popper, 1963). QRPs are additionally related to increased risks for false positives (John et al., 2012; Schooler, 2011; Simmons et al., 2011). One step beyond QRPs, fraud can also contribute to the inability to replicate an effect (see Świątkowski & Dompnier, 2017; Crocker & Cooper, 2011).

To address questions about failed replications, there is a need for a larger number of replications across populations and locations. However, attempting replications is not a seamless process. In an ideal world, a methods section includes all the information needed to conduct a replication. Alternatively, researchers should be able to contact the authors to easily obtain necessary instructions, materials, data, or other information important to the experiment. Historically, however, this was often not the case (Savage & Vickers, 2009). In this regard, open science facilitates replication. Open science is an approach to the scientific process with the goal of making the whole research cycle open/transparent (Hesse, 2018; Kidwell et al.,

2016). For example, open science initiatives aim to remove barriers that inhibit access to necessary "ingredients" for conducting a replication. Researchers can store materials in open science repositories (such as the Open Science Framework, Dataverse, or Figshare) and make them available for use by others.

Offers New Opportunities

There are many intended solutions to the replication crisis engendered by the larger open science movement. Though most are beyond the scope of this chapter, the Berkeley Initiative for Transparency in the Social Sciences (BITSS, 2019) offers a Resource Library to address each stage of the research process. These projects often also follow open science protocols such as data, materials, design, and analysis transparency. These projects are also relatively new as research tools, with the first emerging at the beginning of the new millennium (see the School Spirit Study Group et al., 2004). These different projects offer distinct solutions due to design choices or research foci.

The Reproducibility Project: Psychology (RP:P; Open Science Collaboration, 2015) represents an important pilot test of the field by demonstrating the capacity to engage hundreds of psychology researchers to focus on a single project. They replicated 100 studies that were published in three top journals during a predetermined time period. Though the RP:P researchers compiled their own replications, the Many Labs projects represent a distinct model in that leaders of studies organized the procedures and materials centrally and addressed specific meta-science questions. For example, Many Labs 1 (Klein et al., 2014) measured 15 effects selected by organizer interest. Many Labs 2 (Klein et al., 2018) measured 32 effects testing cultural boundary effects. Many Labs 3 (Ebersole et al., 2016) measured 10 effects across the academic term to test timing boundary conditions. Many Labs 4 (Klein et al., 2022) and Many Labs 5 (Ebersole et al., 2020) measured possible researcher expertise effects on replications.

The Psychological Science Accelerator (PSA; Moshontz et al., 2018) represents the most recent, and arguably the most sophisticated of these crowd projects. This model offers replications to examine novel questions in addition to existing published effects. The decentralized leadership model also offers a sustainable organization that can adapt and produce for many years. While the PSA is the top-line project for established researchers, the Collaborative Replications and Education Project (CREP; Wagge et al., 2019) is built explicitly to help train undergraduates. Additionally, the Network for International Collaborative Exchange (NICE; Cuccolo et al., 2021) is a Psi Chi Project that is scaffolded to support undergraduate researchers while focusing on international cross-cultural research. These various projects offer many new opportunities to engage in large-scale, high-impact projects for researchers at all expertise levels.

These projects offer benefits to the research community that participates in them. For instance, though the projects are often focused on a primary research question, the sheer size of the project, and the complexity of the designs, often offer potential secondary research questions that offer further publication experiences.

Additionally, the large collection of researchers includes a collection of diverse skills that allows contributors to make limited and specialized contributions rather than try to manage all stages of the process on their own. As such, these projects allow researchers to make large impacts from limited contributions.

Offers New Connections

Crowdsourcing may bear some resemblance to other scientific efforts that focus on the recruitment of a "team" (e.g., citizen science; Eitzel et al., 2017). Crowdsourced projects can have a variety of goals such as engaging in replication or facilitating cross-cultural research (Cuccolo et al., 2021; Klein et al., 2018). To achieve the goals of the project, different iterations/flavors of crowdsourcing may be used. With a crowd of researchers, the combination yields varying skills, abilities, backgrounds, and/or interests. Together, the researchers' diverse backgrounds allow for the crowd's goal to be achieved. When the crowds are the participants, projects typically focus on automating some aspect of the participant recruitment process and increasing the diversity or size of one's sample.

Crowdsourcing projects vary in the frequency and intensity of communication, as well as the timeline for the project itself. For example, while each iteration of NICE Crowd runs for approximately one academic year, Psychological Science Accelerator (PSA) projects can span multiple years; both require frequent communication. Communication is necessary on a variety of levels. The project organizers must transparently convey the goals, hypotheses, methods, and analytic plan. In the interest of transparency, this is often done through pre-registration. To facilitate quality data collection, all contributors must have a clear understanding of, and access to, study materials, measures, and protocols. This is often achieved through standardized operating procedures shared via open science repositories (e.g., Open Science Framework). To leverage the diverse expertise and experiences of collaborators, it is imperative that organizers make space for collaborators to be involved in all stages of the project, voice concerns, and share feedback. Finally, once a projects' findings are formally written up, results should be shared in a timely and accessible manner. This may be done through posting the manuscript in a repository without a paywall, for example. Data may also be made publicly available to facilitate transparency, and additional empirical research (Kass-Hout et al., 2016; Napoli & Karaganis, 2010; Wallach et al., 2018).

Through project-related discourse, researchers may also make new connections across locations and disciplines (subfields). Indeed, the PSA has members from 73 countries and 6 continents (see https://psysciacc.org). Moreover, contributors tend to be involved in more than one project, facilitating the expansion of one's professional network. Having such a network offers individuals connections to those with expertise and interests different from one's own. Such connections benefit science as they increase rigor and decrease the likelihood of the research being influenced by individual bias or error (Moshontz et al., 2018). Furthermore, these connections are perceived favorably by those who participate in crowdsourcing initiatives.

A survey sent out to researchers participating in the first iteration of NICE Crowd identified networking as a benefit of participation (Cuccolo et al., 2021).

Crowdsourcing also offers both formal and informal professional development opportunities as collaborators are often communicating with professionals outside of their institutions, working with persons who have varying expertise and interests, gaining skills and knowledge related to the scientific method, and contributing to project presentations and publications. In addition to formal professional development benefits such as authorship, NICE Crowd collaborators reported informal professional development benefits, including networking and mentorship opportunities (Cuccolo et al., 2021).

A Critical Step to Advance Science

Expanding Sampled Populations

Henrich et al. (2010) asserted that the vast majority of research samples historically came from Westernized, educated, industrialized, rich, and democratic (i.e., WEIRD) populations. However, this only represents less than half of the world population. Replication projects can help by focusing on populations that were not previously included. Any published work that includes only one population is inherently biased. When papers include internal replications from the same institution, it is possible that any effects are limited and cannot generalize beyond that single population. Direct replications test the generalizability of effects on new sample populations. Further, crowd projects test the generalizability of effects across many populations at one time. Collectively, these types of projects could offer important tests of the generalizability of psychology to non-WEIRD populations.

Establishing Better Methods

The focus on replication in the past decade has led to advances in the methods of replication work. In one way, the argument about the presence of effects and the evidence offered to support or reject the hypothesis refined our understanding of how closely a replication needs to match the original test. The development of the replication recipe (Brandt et al., 2014) and various registration templates represented drives to increase the precision of documenting research protocols to increase the effectiveness of direct replications. Further, the debate highlighted the issue that conceptual replications provide no falsifiability of the original effect (Nosek & Errington, 2020). While clarifying the expectations for single-sample replications, the field also developed new methodologies around large-scale research projects. The methodologies around these projects improved from the decentralized RP:P to the highly refined and evolving PSA. All these developments reflect how science is adapting through critical evaluation of replication.

Estimating Parameters

Science estimates approximations of true findings through a series of iterative estimations. No single estimate represents a population parameter, yet it is possible to have better or worse estimates. The quality of an estimate is a function of validity (see Chapter 10, this volume), reliability (see Chapter 9, this volume), and generalizability. They each impact the degree to which an estimate approaches or misrepresents a parameter. Each of these is under the control of the researcher. Further, generalizability emerges from applying valid and reliable methods across multiple samples. While this is more difficult to attain by a single researcher, each replication offers another estimate to help clarify the estimation of a true effect.

A Thing to Do Correctly

Selection

Not all research is worth conducting, and engaging in pointless research is ethically questionable since it is not valuing the participants' time. The criteria for deciding whether a study needs to be replicated or not are not firm, but guidelines suggest an original effect should be important and require additional study, among other conditions (Field et al., 2019; Hardwicke et al., 2018). Because of some concern that replication scientists target effects aggressively and inappropriately (Bohannon, 2014), researchers should take care to make their selection process known.

An individual researcher will offer such a justification as part of the introduction of a manuscript. However, crowd projects make selection based on criteria. For instance, the RP:P selected three premier journals (*Journal of Personality and Social Psychology*, *Journal of Experimental Psychology*, *Psychological Science*) and a certain time period (January to June, 2010) and tried to replicate each study published in that time. In a different approach, the Many Labs projects selected effects to address methodological questions. For instance, Many Labs 2 specifically sought effects that would be responsive to cultural differences (Klein et al., 2018), Many Labs 3 sought effects that would be responsive to time-of-semester effects (Ebersole et al., 2016), and Many Labs 4 used a single effect that contained manipulations that could be modified by replication scientists (Klein et al., 2022). All these projects represented many studies being replicated simultaneously.

Sometimes, a research question is so compelling that a crowd of researchers focuses on a single effect. These are called registered replication reports; RRRs modify the peer-review process to encourage high-quality replication studies. Researchers will first submit a detailed methodological and analysis plan for review to journal editors, and in some cases, authors from the original study. Researchers receive feedback and, upon completion of any necessary edits, the protocol gets publicly posted so that others may also engage in efforts to replicate. After data collection and analysis are completed, the manuscript is published – regardless of the outcome – as long as the studies demonstrate compliance with pre-registered protocols (Simons et al., 2014). Crowd projects that use replication for the study of novel effects, such as the PSA and the NICE, both detail the process for submitting proposals for the crowd to consider.

Planning and Preparation

Once a question is identified, project planning follows. It might help to make a spreadsheet and estimate the completion of each step; see Table 13.1 for an imaginary example checklist. This imaginary project started late in the spring academic term and progressed through the following year for a submission for publication the year after. This imaginary project should not be extrapolated to address local questions such as research question (developmental or groups research takes longer) or time to complete ethics review, data collection, or writing times. Notably, some of these tasks can occur simultaneously. For instance, the introduction and methods can both be written (and might be easiest to write) simultaneously with the ethical approval (e.g., IRB) process. At this point, the researcher knows exactly how the study will be conducted. The results could also be drafted in a results-blind approach since the researcher should already be clear on how the data will be cleaned, coded, and tested.

Executing the Process

In a replication, the first step is to fully understand the original effect. This might require reading one or more papers multiple times and thinking through the theory deeply. In addition to understanding the original effect, the researcher should collect the materials and procedures that repeat the original study as closely as possible. If the original publication did not include materials, a polite email to the authors might be useful. If the paper and the author do not yield materials as needed, the researcher

Table 13.1 *Possible planning and tracking project completion*

	Start date	Reviewed	Completed
Ethics proposal/approval	Sept. 30, 23	Oct. 15, 23	Nov. 15, 23
Population identified	Aug. 5, 23	Aug. 10, 23	Aug. 29, 23
Recruitment planned	Aug. 5, 23	Aug. 10, 23	Aug. 29, 23
Materials finalized	Apr. 30, 23	May. 15, 23	June 15, 23
Procedure	Apr. 30, 23	May. 15, 23	June 15, 23
Pre-registration	Sept. 30, 23	Oct. 22, 23	Nov. 18, 23
Data collection	Nov. 21, 23	n/a	Mar. 28, 24
Data cleaning and analysis	Apr. 4, 24	Apr. 11, 24	Apr. 18, 24
Writing introduction	Sept. 30, 23	Oct. 23, 23	Nov. 18, 23
Writing methods	Sept. 30, 23	Oct. 23, 23	Nov. 18, 23
Writing results	Sept. 30, 23	Apr. 11, 24	May 15, 24
Writing discussion	Sept. 30, 23	May 15, 24	May 22, 24
Submission	June 3, 24	??	??

may struggle to conduct a close replication because slight changes in materials or procedures would create a conceptual replication that only provides support, not negation, of the original effect. Finally, transparent science expects researchers to pre-register the hypotheses, methods, and analyses. There are different options to choose from depending on the intended publication outlet, but they all are consistent in documenting the study methods before data collection begins. Researchers can further document their process by making a video of the experimental procedure. In this way, replications can more closely match the situational conditions by seeing the room itself.

As with the materials and procedure, ideally the same data-cleaning steps and analyses as the original will be followed. However, this is not always possible. For instance, if the first study was comparing two groups using a t-test, a replication with many samples might need to examine the size of the effect statistics to match the study conditions. In any case, the test should be as close as possible to the original. When conducting the analyses, the researcher will conduct an analysis of the existing data and compare the outcomes to the original. As mentioned above, when there are multiple estimates, each estimate can be treated as a data point, and the outcomes can be compared to each other to determine whether they have similar conclusions.

When drawing conclusions, the researcher should generalize the replication effect to the sample population. If there are contrary outcomes, it might be that the populations differed from each other, or it is possible that one of the decisions was an error (Type I or II). However, contrary evidence is not evidence of fraud. Randomness and human error are both more likely explanations for outcome variability. Remember, that science only presents iterations of the truth – it does not reveal truth.

A Repeatable Consideration

The three Scientific Utopia papers, written in response to the growing discourse surrounding inaccessible scientific communication standards, describe an idealized vision of the scientific enterprise. They imagine a future science that is fully transparent and reproducible. Their collective suggestions are too broad for this chapter, but each paper makes recommendations about replication. Scientific Utopia I suggested better mechanisms to communicate about science, including the removal of barriers such as those that inhibit publication of replications (Nosek & Bar-Anan, 2012). Scientific Utopia II suggested changes to the process of science and the associated rewards, including recognizing the value of replications in tenure and promotion and suggesting the value of crowdsourcing projects (Nosek et al., 2012). Scientific Utopia III focused on the contribution of crowdsourcing projects that focus on replication work whether they are replicating novel or previously published effects (Uhlmann et al., 2019). Collectively these papers reimagine the future of science, and replication is a critical part of that future.

Although replication research may never be as glamorous as transformative novel research, meta-science is critical to the advancement of our science. The lack of publishing opportunities persists despite the increased call for replications. However, the landscape has been changing. The advent of open access journals offers broader publication opportunities for any study; this may be particularly appealing to researchers conducting previously hard-to-publish replication studies. Additionally, crowd projects such as the RP:P and Many Labs projects yielded extremely high citation counts. This suggests an increased valuing of seeing such work published, at least in the case of high-quality, large-scale work.

Another attempt at valuing replications is the Transparency and Openness Promotion Guidelines (Nosek et al., 2015) that represent eight areas that could be more transparent in scientific publishing: citation standards, data, analytic methods, research materials, design and analysis, study pre-registration, analysis plan pre-registration, and replication. The TOP guidelines recommend that journals review the degree to which their explicit instructions and implicit expectations recognize, encourage, or require transparency in these areas. By recognizing, or even requiring replication in publication, journals then improve the replication rate. One journal, the *Psi Chi Journal*, created a "Replication" open science badge to offer in addition to the data, materials, and pre-registration badges used by many other journals (Rouse, 2017).

Whether it be through heightened focus from journals and editors or the success of large-scale crowd projects, replication science is emerging as a new subfield of research. This research must focus on two areas of replication. On the small scale, researchers need clear guidelines about what conditions of an experiment need to be more closely monitored for variance from the original. Brandt et al. (2014) offer a replication recipe, but the work needs to identify whether some differences are more problematic than others rather than just which characteristics to monitor.

Beyond how to conduct a good replication, researchers also need clear guidance about how to interpret and report on the outcomes. Anderson and Maxwell (2016) suggest that there are six replication goals that require different statistical evidence to interpret. For instance, Goal 1 is to determine whether the effect exists – this would require NHST testing. Goal 4 is to evaluate the cumulative effect – meta-analyses are more appropriate here. Goals 5 (testing whether the replication is inconsistent with original) and 6 (testing whether the replication is consistent with the original) require confidence intervals examining either the differences or equivalence. Additionally, researchers can struggle with proper application of statistics to replications that include multiple samples and other complexities that can be assisted by reviewing (Cumming, 2013; Lakens 2013; Lakens, Scheel, & Isager, 2018). Studying the different motivations for conducting replications, as well as the effectiveness of different analysis techniques, collectively offers a better understanding of the evidentiary value of the work.

A Redux

Ideally, readers now understand replication to be a complex term that requires clear operational definitions. There are many choices and approaches to replication science, such as close versus conceptual or analytic decisions. Though we might not be sure of how all the differences in replications impact results, the more divergence between the original and the replication, the less evidentiary value of the replication. As such, researchers should remain educated about choices and approaches. Luckily, there are organizations that collect resources on this topic, such as the Center for Open Science, the Berkeley Institute for Transparency in Social Sciences, and the Society for the Improvement of Psychological Sciences.

Additionally, it is valuable to remember that replications are estimates of the true effect with the same possible power as the original. Often an original effect has the momentum of being established, suggesting it was a truer estimate. However, a replication that uses the same materials and quality of research protocol but has more participants is actually a more convincing estimate than the original. However, public perception in sciences can sometimes diverge from this fact. If an effect is interesting and/or important, there should be many tests of the effect – not just one, or two. In this way, replications are the basic unit in the iterative process of science.

References

Anderson, S. F. (2020). Misinterpreting p: The discrepancy between p values and the probability the null hypothesis is true, the influence of multiple testing, and implications for the replication crisis. *Psychological Methods*, *25*(5), 596–609. https://doi.org/10.1037/met0000248

Anderson, S. F., & Maxwell, S. E. (2016). There's more than one way to conduct a replication study: Beyond statistical significance. *Psychological Methods*, *21*(1), 1–12. https://doi.org/10.1037/met0000051

Baker, M. (2016). 1,500 scientists lift the lid on reproducibility. *Nature News*, *533*(7604), 452–454. https://philpapers.org/rec/BAKSL-2

Bakker, M., Van Dijk, A., & Wicherts, J. M. (2012). The rules of the game called psychological science. *Perspectives on Psychological Science*, *7*(6), 543–554. https://doi.org/10.1177/1745691612459060

Begley, C. G., & Ellis, L. M. (2012). Raise standards for preclinical cancer research. *Nature*, *483*(7391), 531–533. https://doi.org/10.1038/483531a

BITSS (Berkeley Initiative for Transparency in the Social Sciences). (2019, October 12). *Resource Library*. www.bitss.org/resource-library (retrieved December 16, 2022).

Bohannon, J. (2014). Psychology. Replication effort provokes praise – and "bullying" charges. *Science*, *344*(6186), 788–789.

Brandt, M. J., IJzerman, H., Dijksterhuis, A., Farach, F. J., Geller, J., Giner-Sorolla, R., et al. (2014). The replication recipe: What makes for a convincing replication? *Journal of Experimental Social Psychology*, *50*, 217–224. https://doi.org/10.1016/j.jesp.2013.10.005

Crocker, J., & Cooper, M. L. (2011). Addressing scientific fraud. *Science*, *334*(6060), 1182. https://doi.org/10.1126/science.1216775

Cuccolo, K., Irgens, M. S., Zlokovich, M. S., Grahe, J., & Edlund, J. E. (2021). What crowdsourcing can offer to cross-cultural psychological science. *Cross-Cultural Research*, *55*(1), 3–28. https://doi.org/10.1177/1069397120950628

Cumming, G. (2013). *Understanding the New Statistics: Effect Sizes, Confidence Intervals, and Meta-Analysis*. Routledge.

Dafoe, A. (2014). Science deserves better: The imperative to share complete replication files. *PS: Political Science & Politics*, *47*(1), 60–66. https://doi.org/10.1017/S104909651300173X

Easley, R. W., Madden, C. S., & Gray, V. (2013). A tale of two cultures: Revisiting journal editors' views of replication research. *Journal of Business Research*, *66*(9), 1457–1459. https://doi.org/10.1016/j.jbusres.2012.05.013

Ebersole, C. R., Atherton, O. E., Belanger, A. L., Skulborstad, H. M., Allen, J. M., Banks, J. B., & Nosek, B. A. (2016). Many Labs 3: Evaluating participant pool quality across the academic semester via replication. *Journal of Experimental Social Psychology*, *67*, 68–82. https://doi.org/10.1016/j.jesp.2015.10.012

Ebersole, C. R., Mathur, M. B., Baranski, E., Bart-Plange, D. J., Buttrick, N. R., Chartier, C. R., et al. (2020). Many Labs 5: Testing pre-data-collection peer review as an intervention to increase replicability. *Advances in Methods and Practices in Psychological Science*, *3*(3), 309–331.

Edlund, J. E., Cuccolo, K., Irgens, M. S., Wagge, J. R., & Zlokovich, M. S. (2022). Science through replication studies. *Perspectives on Psychological Science*, *17*(1), 216–225. https://doi.org/10.1177/1745691620984385

Eitzel, M. V., Cappadonna, J. L., Santos-Lang, C., Duerr, R. E., Virapongse, A., West, S. E., et al. (2017). Citizen science terminology matters: Exploring key terms. *Citizen Science: Theory and Practice*, *2*(1), 2. http://doi.org/10.5334/cstp.96

Ferguson, C. J., & Heene, M. (2012). A vast graveyard of undead theories: Publication bias and psychological science's aversion to the null. *Perspectives on Psychological Science*, *7*(6), 555–561. https://doi.org/10.1177/1745691612459059

Field, S. M., Hoekstra, R., Bringmann, L., & van Ravenzwaaij, D. (2019). When and why to replicate: As easy as 1, 2, 3? *Collabra: Psychology*, *5*(1), 46. https://doi.org/10.1525/collabra.218

Forstmeier, W., Wagenmakers, E.-J., & Parker, T. H. (2017). Detecting and avoiding likely false-positive findings – a practical guide. *Biological Reviews*, *92*(4), 1941–1968. https://doi.org/10.1111/brv.12315

Gernsbacher, M. A. (2018). Writing empirical articles: Transparency, reproducibility, clarity, and memorability. *Advances in Methods and Practices in Psychological Science*, *1*(3), 403–414. https://doi.org/10.1177/2515245918754485

Giner-Sorolla, R. (2012). Science or art? How aesthetic standards grease the way through the publication bottleneck but undermine science. *Perspectives on Psychological Science*, *7*(6), 562–571. https://doi.org/10.1177/1745691612457576

Grahe, J. E., & Cuccolo, K. (2023, May 19). Replications of Willow in color. https://osf.io/deu8y

Grahe, J. E., Williams, K. D., & Hinsz, V. B. (2000). Teaching experimental methods while bringing smiles to your students' faces. *Teaching of Psychology*, *27*(2), 108–111. https://doi.org/10.1207/S15328023TOP2702_06

Hardwicke, T. E., Tessler, M. H., Peloquin, B. N., & Frank, M. C. (2018). A Bayesian decision-making framework for replication. *Behavioral and Brain Sciences*, *41*, e132.

Hedges, L. V. (2019). The statistics of replication. *Methodology: European Journal of Research Methods for the Behavioral and Social Sciences*, *15*(S1), 3–14. https://doi.org/10.1027/1614-2241/a000173

Hedges, L. V., & Schauer, J. M. (2019). Statistical analyses for studying replication: Meta-analytic perspectives. *Psychological Methods*, *24*(5), 557–570. https://doi.org/10.1037/met0000189

Hendriks, F., Kienhues, D., & Bromme, R. (2020). Replication crisis = trust crisis? The effect of successful vs failed replications on laypeople's trust in researchers and research. *Public Understanding of Science*, *29*(3), 270–288. https://doi.org/10.1177/0963662520902383

Henrich, J., Heine, S. J., & Norenzayan, A. (2010). Most people are not WEIRD. *Nature*, *466*(7302), 29. https://doi.org/10.1038/466029a

Hesse, B. W. (2018). Can psychology walk the walk of open science? *American Psychologist*, *73*(2), 126. https://doi.org/10.1037/amp0000197

Hinsz, V. B., & Tomhave, J. A. (1991). Smile and (half) the world smiles with you, frown and you frown alone. *Personality and Social Psychology Bulletin*, *17*(5), 586–592. https://doi.org/10.1177/0146167291175014

Honey-Rosés, J., Anguelovski, I., Chireh, V. K., Daher, C., Konijnendijk van den Bosch, C., Litt, J. S., et al. (2021). The impact of COVID-19 on public space: An early review of the emerging questions – design, perceptions and inequities. *Cities & Health*, *5*(S1), S263–S279. https://doi.org/10.1080/23748834.2020.1780074

Ioannidis, J. P. (2005). Why most published research findings are false. *PLOS Medicine*, *2*(8), e124. https://doi.org/10.1371/journal.pmed.0020124

Ioannidis, J. P. A., Kim, B. Y. S., & Trounson, A. (2018). How to design preclinical studies in nanomedicine and cell therapy to maximize the prospects of clinical translation. *Nature Biomedical Engineering*, *2*, 797–809. https://doi.org/10.1038/s41551-018-0314-y

Islam, M. R. (2018). Sample size and its role in Central Limit Theorem (CLT). *International Journal of Physics and Mathematics*, *1*(1), 37–47. https://doi.org/10.31295/ijpm.v1n1.42

John, L. K., Loewenstein, G., & Prelec, D. (2012). Measuring the prevalence of questionable research practices with incentives for truth telling. *Psychological Science*, *23*(5), 524–532. https://doi.org/10.1177/0956797611430953

Kass-Hout, T. A., Xu, Z., Mohebbi, M., Nelsen, H., Baker, A., Levine, J., et al. (2016). OpenFDA: An innovative platform providing access to a wealth of FDA's publicly available data. *Journal of the American Medical Informatics Association*, *23*(3), 596–600. https://doi.org/10.1093/jamia/ocv153

Kelly, A. E., & Cuccolo, K. (2022). Supporting college students during times of transition: Pedagogical recommendations based on pandemic learning data. *College Teaching*, *72*(1), 15–27. https://doi.org/10.1080/87567555.2022.2071825

Kerr, N. L. (1998). HARKing: Hypothesizing after the results are known. *Personality and Social Psychology Review*, *2*(3), 196–217. https://doi.org/10.1207/s15327957pspr0203_4

Kidwell, M. C., Lazarević, L. B., Baranski, E., Hardwicke, T. E., Piechowski, S., Falkenberg, L. S., et al. (2016). Badges to acknowledge open practices: A simple, low-cost, effective method for increasing transparency. *PLOS Biology*, *14*(5), e1002456. https://doi.org/10.1371/journal.pbio.1002456

Klein, R. A., Cook, C. L., Ebersole, C. R., Vitiello, C., Nosek, B. A., Hilgard, J., et al. (2022). Many Labs 4: Failure to replicate mortality salience effect with and without original author involvement. *Collabra: Psychology*, *8*(1), 35271. https://doi.org/10.1525/collabra.35271

Klein, R. A., Ratliff, K. A., Vianello, M., Adams Jr, R.B., Bahník, Š., Bernstein, M. J., et al. (2014). Investigating variation in replicability: A "many labs" replication project. *Social Psychology, 45*(3), 142–152. https://doi.org/10.1027/1864-9335/a000178

Klein, R. A., Vianello, M., Hasselman, F., Adams, B. G., Adams Jr, R. B., Alper, S., et al. (2018). Many Labs 2: Investigating variation in replicability across samples and settings. *Advances in Methods and Practices in Psychological Science, 1*(4), 443–490. https://doi.org/10.1177/2515245918810225

Kraus, M. W. (2013). Look everyone: A social priming finding with direct replications! *Psych Your Mind* [blog], November 6. https://psych-your-mind.blogspot.com/2013/11/look-everyone-social-priming-finding.html

(2015). Americans still overestimate social class mobility: A pre-registered self-replication. *Frontiers in Psychology, 6*, 1709. https://doi.org/10.3389/fpsyg.2015.01709

Kraus, M. W., & Tan, J. J. (2015). Americans overestimate social class mobility. *Journal of Experimental Social Psychology, 58*, 101–111. https://doi.org/10.1016/j.jesp.2015.01.005

Lakens, D. (2013). Calculating and reporting effect sizes to facilitate cumulative science: A practical primer for t-tests and ANOVAs. *Frontiers in Psychology, 4*, 863. https://doi.org/10.3389/fpsyg.2013.00863

Lakens, D., Scheel, A. M., & Isager, P. M. (2018). Equivalence testing for psychological research: A tutorial. *Advances in Methods and Practices in Psychological Science, 1*(2), 259–269. https://doi.org/10.1177/2515245918770963

Lehrer, J. (2011). Trials and errors: Why science is failing us. *Wired*, December 16. www.wired.com/2011/12/ff-causation

Loken, E., & Gelman, A. (2017). Measurement error and the replication crisis. *Science, 355*(6325), 584–585. www.science.org/doi/full/10.1126/science.aal3618

Moshontz, H., Campbell, L., Ebersole, C. R., IJzerman, H., Urry, H. L., Forscher, P. S., et al. (2018). The Psychological Science Accelerator: Advancing psychology through a distributed collaborative network. *Advances in Methods and Practices in Psychological Science, 1*(4), 501–515. https://doi.org/10.1177/2515245918797607

Napoli, P. M., & Karaganis, J. (2010). On making public policy with publicly available data: The case of US communications policymaking. *Government Information Quarterly, 27*(4), 384–391. https://doi.org/10.1016/j.giq.2010.06.005

Neuliep, J. W. (1990). Editorial bias against replication research. *Journal of Social Behavior and Personality, 5*(4), 85–90.

Nosek, B. A., Alter, G., Banks, G. C., Borsboom, D., Bowman, S. D., Breckler, S. J., et al. (2015). Scientific standards: Promoting an open research culture. *Science, 348*(6242), 1422–1425. https://doi.org/10.1126/science.aab2374

Nosek, B. A., & Bar-Anan, Y. (2012). Scientific Utopia: I. Opening scientific communication. *Psychological Inquiry, 23*(3), 217–243. https://doi.org/10.1080/1047840X.2012.692215

Nosek, B. A., & Errington, T. M. (2020). What is replication? *PLOS Biology, 18*(3), e3000691. https://doi.org/10.1371/journal.pbio.3000691

Nosek, B. A., Spies, J. R., & Motyl, M. (2012). Scientific Utopia: II. Restructuring incentives and practices to promote truth over publishability. *Perspectives on Psychological Science, 7*(6), 615–631.

Open Science Collaboration. (2015). Psychology. Estimating the reproducibility of psychological science. *Science, 349*(6251), aac4716.

Pashler, H., & Wagenmakers, E.-J. (2012). Editors' introduction to the special section on replicability in psychological science: A crisis of confidence? *Perspectives on Psychological Science*, *7*(6), 528–530. https://doi.org/10.1177/1745691612465253

Patterson, M. L. (2008). Back to social behavior: Mining the mundane. *Basic and Applied Social Psychology*, *30*(2), 93–101. https://doi.org/10.1080/01973530802208816

Patterson, M. L., & Tubbs, M. E. (2005). Through a glass darkly: Effects of smiling and visibility on recognition and avoidance in passing encounters. *Western Journal of Communication*, *69*(3), 219–231. https://doi.org/10.1080/10570310500202389

Popper, K. R. (1963). Science as falsification. *Conjectures and Refutations*, 1, 33–39.

Prinz, F., Schlange, T., & Asadullah, K. (2011). Believe it or not: How much can we rely on published data on potential drug targets? *Nature Reviews Drug Discovery*, *10* (712). https://doi.org/10.1038/nrd3439-c1

Rahman, M. K., Gazi, M. A. I., Bhuiyan, M. A., & Rahaman, M. A. (2021). Effect of Covid-19 pandemic on tourist travel risk and management perceptions. *PLOS ONE*, *16*(9), e0256486. https://doi.org/10.1371/journal.pone.0256486

Rohlfing, I., & Zuber, C. I. (2021). Check your truth conditions! Clarifying the relationship between theories of causation and social science methods for causal inference. *Sociological Methods & Research*, *50*(4), 1623–1659. https://doi.org/10.1177/0049124119826156

Rosenthal, R. (1979). The File Drawer Problem and tolerance for null results. *Psychological Bulletin*, *86*(3), 638–641. https://doi.org/10.1037/0033-2909.86.3.638

Rouse, S. V. (2017). The red badge of research (and the yellow, blue, and green badges, too). *Psi Chi Journal of Psychological Research*, *22*(1), 2–9.

Savage, C. J., & Vickers, A. J. (2009). Empirical study of data sharing by authors publishing in *PLOS* journals. *PLOS ONE*, *4*(9), e7078. https://doi.org/10.1371/journal.pone.0007078

Schmidt, S. (2009). Shall we really do it again? The powerful concept of replication is neglected in the social sciences. *Review of General Psychology*, *13*(2), 90–100. https://doi.org/10.1037/a0015108

Schooler, J. (2011). Unpublished results hide the decline effect. *Nature*, *470*(7335), 437–438. https://doi.org/10.1038/470437a

School Spirit Study Group, Sandra, A. H., Rowatt, T., Brooks, L., Magid, V., Stage, R., et al. (2004). Measuring school spirit: A national teaching exercise: The School Spirit Study Group. *Teaching of Psychology*, *31*(1), 18–21. https://doi.org/10.1207/s15328023top3101_5

Simmons, J. P., Nelson, L. D., & Simonsohn, U. (2011). False-positive psychology: Undisclosed flexibility in data collection and analysis allows presenting anything as significant. *Psychological Science*, *22*(11), 1359–1366. https://doi.org/10.1177/0956797611417632

Simons, D. J. (2014). The value of direct replication. *Perspectives on Psychological Science*, *9*(1), 76–80. https://doi.org/10.1177/1745691613514755

Simons, D. J., Holcombe, A. O., & Spellman, B. A. (2014). An introduction to registered replication reports at *Perspectives on Psychological Science*. *Perspectives on Psychological Science*, *9*(5), 552–555. https://doi.org/10.1177/1745691614543974

Smith, R. J. (2018). The continuing misuse of null hypothesis significance testing in biological anthropology. *American Journal of Physical Anthropology*, *166*(1), 236–245. https://doi.org/10.1002/ajpa.23399

Spellman, B. A. (2012). Introduction to the special section on research practices. *Perspectives on Psychological Science*, *7*(6), 655–656. https://doi.org/10.1177/1745691612465075

Świątkowski, W., & Dompnier, B. (2017). Replicability crisis in social psychology: Looking at the past to find new pathways for the future. *International Review of Social Psychology*, *30*(1), 111–124. https://doi.org/10.5334/irsp.66

Uhlmann, E. L., Ebersole, C. R., Chartier, C. R., Errington, T. M., Kidwell, M. C., Lai, C. K., et al. (2019). Scientific Utopia: III. Crowdsourcing science. *Perspectives on Psychological Science*, *14*(5), 711–733. https://doi.org/10.1177/1745691619850561

Vindrola-Padros, C., Andrews, L., Dowrick, A., Djellouli, N., Fillmore, H., Gonzalez, E. B., et al. (2020). Perceptions and experiences of healthcare workers during the COVID-19 pandemic in the UK. *BMJ Open*, *10*(11), e040503. http://dx.doi.org/10.1136/bmjopen-2020-040503

Wagenmakers, E.-J., Beek, T., Dijkhoff, L., Gronau, Q. F., Acosta, A., Adams Jr, R. B., et al. (2016). Registered replication report: Strack, Martin, & Stepper (1988). *Perspectives on Psychological Science*, *11*(6), 917–928. https://doi.org/10.1177/1745691616674458

Wagge, J. R., Brandt, M. J., Lazarevic, L. B., Legate, N., Christopherson, C., Wiggins, B., & Grahe, J. E. (2019). Publishing research with undergraduate students via replication work: The collaborative replications and education project. *Frontiers in Psychology*, *10*, 247. https://doi.org/10.3389/fpsyg.2019.00247

Wallach, J. D., Boyack, K. W., & Ioannidis, J. P. (2018). Reproducible research practices, transparency, and open access data in the biomedical literature, 2015–2017. *PLOS Biology*, *16*(11), e2006930. https://doi.org/10.1371/journal.pbio.2006930

Wicherts, J. M., Veldkamp, C. L., Augusteijn, H. E., Bakker, M., Van Aert, R., & Van Assen, M. A. (2016). Degrees of freedom in planning, running, analyzing, and reporting psychological studies: A checklist to avoid p-hacking. *Frontiers in psychology*, *7*. https://doi.org/10.3389/fpsyg.2016.01832

Wiggins, B. J., & Christopherson, C. D. (2019). The replication crisis in psychology: An overview for theoretical and philosophical psychology. *Journal of Theoretical and Philosophical Psychology*, *39*(4), 202–217. https://doi.org/10.1037/teo0000137

Wingen, T., Berkessel, J. B., & Englich, B. (2020). No replication, no trust? How low replicability influences trust in psychology. *Social Psychological and Personality Science*, *11*(4), 454–463. https://doi.org/10.1177/1948550619877412

Zajonc, R. B., Murphy, S. T., & Inglehart, M. (1989). Feeling and facial efference: Implications of the vascular theory of emotion. *Psychological Review*, *96*(3), 395–416. https://doi.org/10.1037/0033-295X.96.3.395

Zhang, X., Astivia, O. L. O., Kroc, E., & Zumbo, B. D. (2022). How to think clearly about the Central Limit Theorem. *Psychological Methods*, *28*(6), 1427–1445. https://doi.org/10.1037/met0000448

Zwaan, R. A., Etz, A., Lucas, R. E., & Donnellan, M. B. (2018). Making replication mainstream. *Behavioral and Brain Sciences*, *41*, 3120. https://doi.org/10.1017/S0140525X17001972

14 The Inner Workings of Registered Reports

Zoltan Dienes

Abstract

Registered Reports provide one way to address shortcomings in the current way we manage research – from the design of studies to their publication. The format requires pre-specifying (1) why a design may crucially test a theory, (2) what auxiliary assumptions are required for the experiment to be such a test, (3) what outcome-neutral tests are required to test those assumptions, (4) what specific crucial tests will be used to test the theory (of the many tests that could be used), and (5) why those tests could provide evidence for no effect of interest given the proposed numbers of trials and participants. Reviewers and authors are then constructively involved in optimizing the study before it is performed. The agreement between reviewers and authors, as adjudicated by the editors, defines, in advance, the proposed method and analytic protocol, virtually guaranteeing acceptance of the paper, no matter what position, if any, the results support. In this chapter, I go through what problems the format solves and why it must be approached in a way that is little understood by people coming to it for the first time. Common pitfalls are also discussed. In all, the paper provides a roadmap for how readers, authors, and editors can approach Registered Reports.

Keywords: Registered Reports, Open Science, Pre-Registration, Analytic Flexibility, Bias Control

Science involves discovering objective relations between theories, predictions, and evidence (Popper, 1972). However, we are humans, and in assessing the relations between theory and evidence, we are subject to biases (Chavalarias & Ioannidis, 2010; Kerr, 1998; Ritchie, 2020). Thus, it behoves us to assess these relations under conditions that minimize bias. A way of addressing bias is to make judgments that are subject to critical public scrutiny and to make judgments without knowing whether those judgments would lead to the results that would support a theory or not (Wagenmakers et al., 2012). One way to accomplish this is by performing a Registered Report (Chambers, 2013, 2019), in which the motivation, method, and analytic protocol are settled by critical discussion before the data are collected.

Registered Reports as a concept were first used in parapsychology in the 1970s and then clinical trials in the 2000s (Chambers & Tzavella, 2020). However, in none of these cases were papers accepted before results were in; at least in the latter case, adherence to the principles has not been rigorous (Goldacre et al., 2018). The first attempt to enforce their rigorous use was in the explicitly labeled article type Registered Reports in *Cortex* and the independently conceived Registered Replication Reports of *Perspectives on Psychological Science* (Simons et al., 2014). As of 2022, over 300 journals use the Registered Reports format as either a regular article type or a format for special issues (Center for Open Science, 2023). Registered Reports can now be submitted for any scientific discipline.

Initially, in the Registered Report process, a submitted manuscript, providing introduction, method, and planned analysis sections, is, after editorial triage, sent to review. Reviewers and authors then work together to revise the theory, derivation of predictions, method, and analytical protocol to optimize all aspects of the study as best they can. Once the editor judges that revisions have produced a workable study, a Stage 1 In Principle Acceptance (IPA) is granted. The authors then run the study. The data are next analyzed according to the agreed protocol; in addition, the authors can introduce new analyses in a different subsection of the results section. The paper is finally accepted at Stage 2 if the authors followed the procedure they said they would, reported the analyses they said they would, planned quality control checks are passed, and the discussion is appropriate. In this chapter, the way a Registered Report overcomes various biases is discussed to motivate how a Registered Report should be approached. Common mistakes in writing a Registered Report are addressed and guidance is provided for authors, reviewers, and editors.

Although the chapter discusses the Registered Report, a weaker but still valuable process is pre-registration. Pre-registration is not an article type; it is something any author can do for any paper. In pre-registration, the author writes up a plan in as much detail as is seen fit and it is posted in a public repository such as OSF. Then, the study is conducted and submitted through the normal process to a journal. Reviewers may disagree with the planned analysis, but at least they know what was planned and what was not, and that can inform judgment.

The pre-registration misses out on many of the benefits of a Registered Report, which we now discuss, while gaining, for better or worse, in flexibility (the pre-registration is completely under the authors' control). For example, when mere pre-registration is used rather than a Registered Report, the extent to which authors write clear pre-registrations and then follow what they prescribed is not enforced (Ikeda et al., 2019). In a Registered Report, the pre-registration is not simply up to the author but is a collaborative product of the authors, reviewers, and editor. This changes the review process from being a battle over the merits of what has already been done to a constructive consideration of what is best to do. Furthermore, unlike with a simple pre-registration, in a Registered Report the pre-registered analyses will be the ones used for drawing conclusions because the reviewers have already agreed to them.

In this chapter, I first present a view of the workings of science as seen at the scale of a single study or a small sequence of studies. The possible fault lines are discussed and why the Registered Report helps address the problems is indicated. Then, I go through each aspect of this account to indicate how a Registered Report can be approached. The chapter aims to provide a framework for understanding the nature of Registered Reports; for simple practical guidance, see *PCI RR* (2023).

A View of Science

Seen at a certain scale, science consists of testing a substantial theory, by deriving predictions of phenomena and using well-tested and otherwise simple assumptions; data then provide evidence for or against the phenomena (Figure 14.1). A substantial theory is a claim that could be found wrong by the study and from which various predictions may follow (Popper, 1959). The theory functions as an explanation of those predictions. For example, the claim that "extrinsic motivation impairs intrinsic motivation because of a shift in attributions about the causes of behavior" is a substantial theory (Deci & Ryan, 2000). Various interesting phenomena can be derived from it as predictions. For example, "rewarding children for eating their greens by giving them dessert reduces the desirability of the greens" (cf. Newman & Taylor, 1992) is a phenomenon predicted by the theory.

In Figure 14.1, A represents an ideal view of science as objective relations between theory, predictions, and data. From a substantial theory, predictions of phenomena can be derived, using auxiliary assumptions. Data provide evidence for or against the predictions and, therefore, count for or against the theory. As shown in Figure 14.1B, seeing data first may tempt one to corrupt the perceived relation between theory and predictions. The predictions stated may no longer be those that follow from the theory with simple and safe assumptions. Figure 14.1C demonstrates how seeing data first may tempt one to give up on using theory because one can guarantee finding some phenomenon or other if one pokes around long

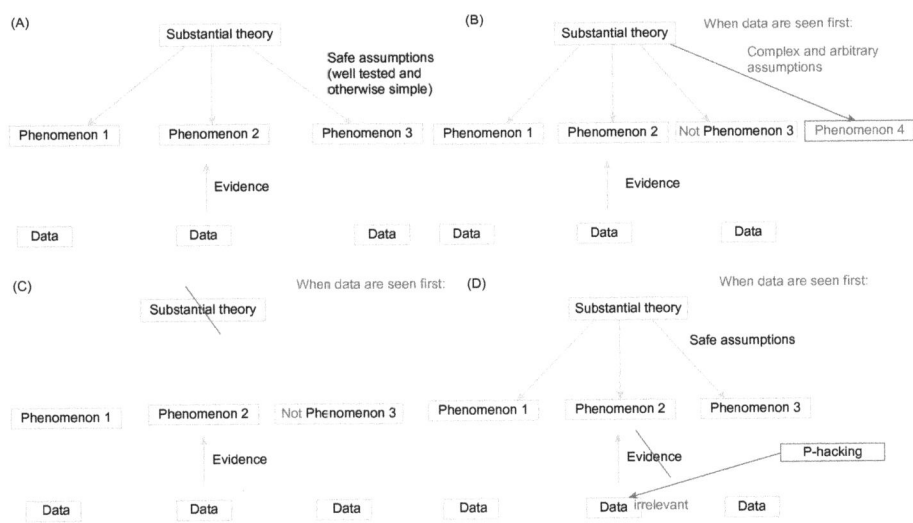

Figure 14.1 *Biases that may arise from seeing data first.*

enough. Finally, Figure 14.1D illustrates how seeing data first may tempt one to corrupt the perceived relation of data to predictions by hacking. Data may seem to support predictions when, in fact, the data provide no evidence for them.

A phenomenon is an empirical generalization (Haig, 2014); Popper (1959) calls it a low-level hypothesis claiming what the results are. "Extroverts drink more coffee than introverts in the morning" is a phenomenon. A substantial theory of extroversion may predict it. The theory will do so on the basis of assumptions. For example, if the theory of extroversion refers to arousal, an assumption is that caffeine is relevant to the sort of arousal postulated by the theory. In fact, the study can only test the prediction by making assumptions (e.g., by making the assumption that the extroversion questionnaire measured extroversion; Flake et al., 2022). Ideally, such assumptions have been well tested or are simple.

Consider Figure 14.2. If the assumptions can be taken as safe (e.g., caffeine does increase the right type of arousal; the questionnaire can be taken to measure extroversion), then if the evidence counts against the phenomenon (i.e., it turns out that extroverts do not drink more coffee than introverts in the morning), the substantial theory also takes a hit (i.e., the evidence counts against the theory that extroverts have low levels of cortical arousal). Conversely, if the evidence supports the phenomenon, the substantial theory is corroborated. These relations are objective in that scientists can be wrong about their nature; that is, we need to *find out* what predictions follow from a theory in a simple way with well tested assumptions and *find out* what the data say about the predictions (Popper, 1972).

A theory that cortical arousal is lower in extroverts than introverts could be tested by making prediction of a phenomenon – extroverts drink more coffee than introverts. This prediction follows only by making assumptions (e.g., that coffee increases the sort of arousal postulated by the theory). If data count against the

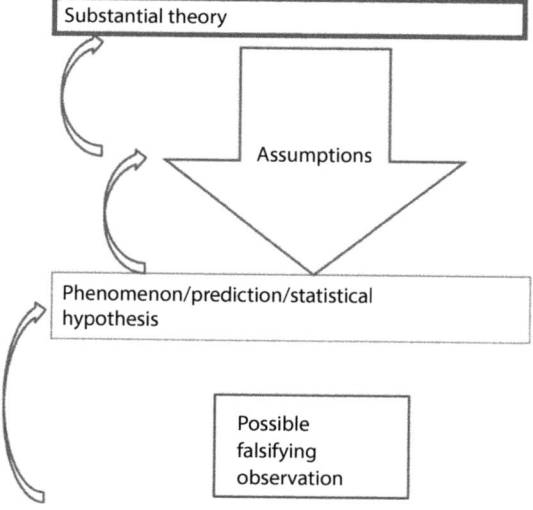

Figure 14.2 *How evidence counts against a theory.*

prediction (e.g., maybe it is found that introverts drink more coffee than extroverts), the counter evidence only transmits back to the theory, as evidence against the theory, if the assumptions are safe. Instead of taking the evidence to count against the theory, one might argue that coffee does not raise that sort of arousal or extroversion was not measured properly. In this way, the theory can be protected. However, if the assumptions are safe, the evidence against the prediction counts against the theory itself.

If we can be wrong about the actual theoretical and evidential relationships, these relations should be assessed under conditions where bias in their assessment is minimized. When the relations are assessed in the light of the data, several biases are possible. First, when data are seen first before deriving predictions from a theory, complex assumptions may be introduced to make the theory fit the phenomena (Figure 14.1B); the data are then no longer evidential regarding the theory. Gelman and Loken (2014) present examples in which papers have "predicted" complex effects (that were statistically significant), but the stated theory, in fact, makes simpler predictions (that were not statistically significant); for example, a main effect is just as well predicted by the theory as an interaction, but the non-significant main effect is not reported. Kerr (1998) also describes several variants of this practice.

Second, one may give up on postulating any substantial theory and simply declare whatever phenomenon is found as a discovery (Figure 14.1C; Kerr, 1998). In the absence of theory, the temptation is to want to find phenomena of low prior plausibility (i.e., surprising or "sexy" findings, Fiedler, 2017) for which a conventionally low evidential threshold may be inappropriate (Benjamin et al., 2017). Further, without coherent explanatory research programs, such research can veer away from science to mere phenomena-chasing (Klein, 2014). A common comment in the question time of talks, or in discussing someone's research over coffee, is to say: "I wonder what would happen if you manipulated this variable?" And the question is left there as if that were the end in itself. Some pursuit of phenomena themselves is a crucial part of science (e.g., Haig, 2014; for an ingenious systematic way of exploring phenomena, see Baribault et al., 2018). However, pursuing phenomena should not replace theory testing, as it is only in the context of a theoretical research program that science develops (Alger, 2019; Deutsch, 2011; Guest & Martin, 2021; Lakatos, 1970).

Finally, when data are seen before planning analyses, p-hacking (or B-hacking for Bayes factors) may make support for the predictions sufficiently probable regardless of the data; the data, as analyzed, are no longer evidential regarding phenomena (Figure 14.1D; Chuard et al., 2019; Dienes, 2023; Mayo, 2018; Simmons et al., 2011).

A single paper need not cover all these aspects of science. A paper is valuable if it helps in any aspect of developing a substantial theory, e.g., in exploring data (McIntosh, 2017; Yanai & Lercher, 2020), in determining what assumptions are safe in making predictions (establishing phenomena), or in showing how predictions may be severely tested (developing methodology). Registered Reports are an article type that can be used when all these aspects happen to come together. Specifically, in a standard Registered Report, a paper is accepted before data are collected based on

(1) a substantial theory being tested; (2) assumptions connecting theory to predictions being safe; and (3) analytic flexibility being tied down while ensuring sensitive results. In this way, the Registered Report seeks to reduce biases that potentially corrupt the scientific process. In the following section, I discuss these three desired features.

A Substantial Theory

A substantial theory functions as an explanation of the phenomena it predicts. It is also a claim that could be shown wrong by the results of the study. Exactly what is needed here varies by journal. *Peer Community In Registered Reports* (*PCI RR*, 2023) and *Royal Society Open Science* (2020) indicate only that submissions will be evaluated with respect to "the scientific validity of the research question(s)." *Nature Human Behaviour* (2020), on the other hand, states as the criterion "the importance of the research question(s) and relevance for a broad, multidisciplinary audience." Although these criteria do not mention a substantial theory as such, in my experience, as both editor and reviewer of Registered Reports, the lack of a clear substantial theory has been grounds for revision at Stage 1; so, if you do not present a substantial theory initially, you may be asked to do so.

In principle, a Registered Report may be used to test the existence of a phenomenon or to estimate its size. The minimal theory in this case may be that the phenomenon exists. However, if the phenomenon is interesting because it bears on theory, at some point a substantial theory will need to be postulated to explain the phenomenon. If one is postulated at Stage 1, the formulation of the theory and its relation to predicted phenomena may benefit from critical discussion before the results are known. In this situation, an appropriate strategy is to conjecture the most general bold claim that could still be tested and shown wrong by the specific study. For an example of a Registered Report whose sole aim was to estimate a practically important quantity in an unbiased way (related to the accuracy of measuring the presence of SARS-CoV-2 because of mutations in the virus potentially causing a mismatch to what the PCR test can detect), see Khan and Cheung (2020). In this case, a substantial theory was not explicitly stated, though there was relevant theory at play in setting up the parameter to be estimated, and there was a key theory at stake – that the size of the parameter estimated rendered the measurement relevant to its practical function.

Safe Assumptions Connecting Theory to Predictions: Outcome-Neutral Tests

All tests of theories involve assumptions – claims that must be true for the test to be a test of the substantial theory (Popper, 1963). For example, one must assume that the independent variable manipulates/measures what it is claimed to, and the dependent variable measures what it is claimed to. The truth of these assumptions is independent of the truth of the substantial theory. Thus, tests of these assumptions are called outcome-neutral tests. An example of an outcome-neutral test is a positive control, such as a manipulation check; for example, a check that a manipulation of mood changes mood ratings.

More generally, a positive control is a control that the manipulation should affect if the procedure works as it should. An example of a positive control would be showing one's manipulation affects something it is known to affect; in testing the claim that mental pain can be reduced in the same way as physical pain, a positive control would be showing that a painkiller is given at a dose that reduces physical pain to a sufficient extent to prove the protocol is being employed correctly. An example of a positive control that is not a manipulation check is showing that one's measuring instrument detects a relevant difference where one is known to exist; for example, showing that an indirect measure of pain is sensitive to a relevant noxious stimulus. Outcome-neutral tests include checks of implementation fidelity or intervention fidelity (Carroll et al., 2007). For example, for the delivery of a therapy: Were there intervention manuals and were therapists shown to know their contents?

According to the *PCI RR* (2023) guide to Registered Reports, one should consider whether there are "sufficient outcome-neutral conditions (e.g., absence of floor or ceiling effects, positive controls, other quality checks) for ensuring that the obtained results are able to test the stated hypotheses or answer the stated research question(s)." A Registered Report likely includes outcome-neutral tests. For example, if a mood manipulation is involved, test that the mood was changed appropriately, independent of the substantial theory tested. Imagine that a substantial theory predicts that a negative mood speeds up learning of a certain sort. A researcher might say "I don't need a separate manipulation check; I know the mood changed if the learning was sped up. That is the only reason the learning could change." There is a way to save the theory if the prediction fails. If learning does not speed up, instead of the substantial theory being disconfirmed, the researcher can say "the prediction failed because mood did not change." The researcher is then free to try again with a new mood manipulation and then again, until learning changes; they maintain confidence in the substantial theory, despite successive predictive failures. By using appropriate outcome-neutral tests, this scenario is avoided.

In addition to assuming the independent variable manipulated/measured what it claims to, the dependent variable is also assumed to measure what it claims to, and this may need to be established (Flake & Fried, 2020). Outcome-neutral tests can also be used to rule out the problem of post hoc disregarding of data from particular experimenters because their failure to get the effect shows they are unskilled (e.g., Baumeister, 2016); if the outcome-neutral tests are passed, the data from that experimenter should be included. If predictions are not confirmed, key assumptions should be safe, so that the substantial theory takes the blame.

In a Registered Report, some outcome-neutral tests are specified as ones that must be passed for them to test the substantial theory (e.g., mood was changed). These can be distinguished from checks that are useful but not essential (e.g., did participants take equal time to read the positive and negative mood-inducing statements?). To deal with this, if the time difference is within stated bounds, time might be added as a covariate. An advantage of Registered Reports is that reviewers and the editor can help identify and shape the outcome-neutral tests that genuinely test key assumptions.

Outcome-neutral tests may be useful even for studies not testing a substantial theory per se, e.g., estimating an important parameter. There will still be auxiliary assumptions for the estimation to be useful, and these assumptions should be carefully considered to determine whether any need to be tested by outcome-neutral tests for the estimation to be regarded as relevant. For example, if estimating the degree of racism, or anything socially sensitive, a researcher could check for indications of honesty in a pilot by comparing the standard test to one in which the person is sometimes instructed to roll a die and report the opposite response for binary answers; this procedure means the participant is aware that the researcher does not know whether that participant's answer is true.

If your study design does not contain one or more outcome-neutral tests, consider what tests might be needed. Include checks of study or data quality broadly construed, such as absence of floor or ceiling effects. Explicitly list the outcome-neutral tests that are crucial (i.e., that must be passed for the results to count for or against the theory) and those that are just desirable (e.g., might just change the key analyses). Some quality control checks may simply be a basis for excluding participants (e.g., checks on whether the participant was concentrating). According to many journal guidelines, guaranteed publication at Stage 2 may depend on the crucial outcome-neutral tests being passed. However, I am unaware of any Stage 2 submissions that were not published for this reason; even a failed outcome-neutral test can be useful in showing a standard procedure does not perform as it should.

Analytic Flexibility Being Tied Down while Ensuring Sensitive Results

There is always a range of equally legitimate analyses to address a research question (Carp, 2012; Simonsohn et al., 2019; Steegen et al., 2016). Steegen et al. call this space of analyses the multiverse. There are always various ways of coding the variables, excluding outliers, dealing with assumptions, including covariates, modeling structure, and so on. The factorial combination of all these different possible analytic methods is the multiverse (i.e., the complete set of possible analyses given the stated different possible variants of each stage of analysis). The multiverse will typically allow a range of conclusions. For example, in Figure 14.3A, Bayes factors are used that allow the potential conclusions of good enough evidence for H0, good enough evidence for H1, and no evidence to speak of. If the data speak

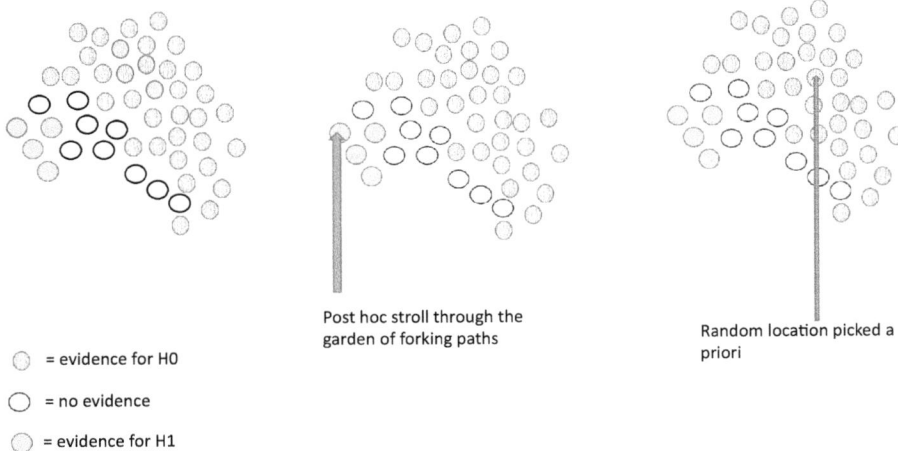

○ = evidence for H0

○ = no evidence

○ = evidence for H1

Figure 14.3 *Picking a point in the multiverse.*

relatively clearly to a question, one conclusion may predominate; in Figure 14.3A, it is that there is evidence for H0.

However, if researchers have the data in front of them while making analytic decisions, they can take a stroll through the garden of forking paths (i.e., make coding and analysis choices in the light of data; Gelman & Loken, 2014) and justify each analytic choice post hoc given the way it pushes toward a desired result. There is always a compelling reason for any choice – it is tougher one way / tougher another way / more conservative / more inclusive / more widely used / more recently used, and so on. Thus, a researcher, while thinking they are making decisions for scientific reasons, may be fooling themselves; they may be making decisions because these support the conclusion they personally want. As illustrated in Figure 14.3B, they may end up in a small region of the multiverse that gives an uncharacteristic conclusion (see Steegen et al., 2016, for a real example).

In Figure 14.3A, there is a multiverse of different possible analyses. A majority of analyses favor H0. For example, the test could be whether learning differs between positive and negative mood. Learning could be measured in different ways, outliers could be excluded in different ways, and different variations on robust analyses could be tried. In each combination of these possibilities, a Bayes factor is calculated that may favor H1, H0, or neither. In fact, in this example, most Bayes factors favor H0. Figure 14.3B illustrates that, if one took a stroll through the garden of forking paths (i.e. checking which way to go in the light of how much a theory is supported), one may end up with an outcome that few analyses show. Finally, Figure 14.3C illustrates that choosing the location of the multiverse in advance probably yields the most common conclusion – objective evidential relation between data and hypotheses are probably respected.

One solution is to conduct a multiverse analysis – that is, perform all analyses implied by any combination of coding and analytic choices that have been identified. This can be a good solution, but it is not generally practical. In general, one cannot, for every test, conduct potentially thousands of analyses and then examine how to interpret them. Further, there is not one objective list of possible analyses for any given effect of interest; there is a multiverse of these multiverses. Instead, there is a shortcut (Dienes, 2016, p. 86). If, in advance, one point in a multiverse was randomly picked, the result probably yields the most common outcome and probably reflects the objective evidential relation of the data to the prediction. This can be achieved by specifying the analytic protocol in advance of the data while making sure there is no analytic flexibility left.

Removing all analytic flexibility takes more specification of the analytic protocol than researchers have typically been used to. When specifying your analyses, ask yourself if you left any wriggle room to bias the results in light of the data. If so, you need to make sure where you end up in the multiverse is independent of where your prejudices would want you to be. Analytic decisions can still be conditional on properties of the data (Devezer et al., 2021) but in pre-specified ways so that they are not conditional on the outcome. Consider how all variables will be coded, how assumptions will be checked, what you will do about assumption violation, on what precise grounds individuals or trials will be removed, and how structure will be modeled. It is often useful to run a small pilot. The pilot need not be the full design of the study, but making sure you understand the sort of data you are dealing with in advance of specifying full analyses can be very helpful.

One might decide that not all analytic decisions can be decided in advance due to the complexity of the data. A useful tool in this case may be blind analyses (e.g., Dutilh et al., 2017; MacCoun & Perlmutter, 2015). The analyst is presented with several data sets. One data set is real; the others have had one or more key variables shuffled or otherwise transformed. The analyst does not know which set is the real set. The analyst can then analyze all data sets until they are satisfied that the same analysis is appropriate for all data sets and that the analysis deals with assumptions and unexpected features adequately. If the blinding has been successful, the analyst makes decisions without knowing how those decisions produce different conclusions. *PCI RR* and various journals allow blinding procedures as part of the analytical protocol for a Registered Report. How blinding is to be done, and when it will be broken, needs to be clearly specified.

Obtaining sensitive results

The extent to which the analysis allows conclusions contrary to predictions should be determined. For example, if the theory predicts a difference, to what extent does the analysis allow the conclusion that there is no effect? This is crucial to determine for the study to count against the theory. Three (non-exhaustive) ways of answering this question are by use of power, inference by intervals (including equivalence testing), and Bayes factors (see Dienes, 2021a, for all three). Each method is considered next.

Power

Part of tying down flexibility is specifying a stopping rule for frequentist statistics – that is, stating the precise conditions under which one will stop collecting data. The simplest method is to calculate the number of participants to achieve a relevant power. According to *PCI RR* (2023), "Studies involving Neyman-Pearson inference should include a priori statistical power analysis, with estimated effect sizes justified with reference to the existing literature or theory. Since publication bias overinflates published estimates of effect size, power analysis should be based on the lowest available or meaningful estimate of the effect size." Note that specific power and significance requirements will vary by journal.

In testing a theory, the effect size used for calculating power should be the one that defines the minimal plausible effect of interest for that theory or practical context. To control the long-run probability of missing an effect of interest (i.e., a Type II error), power must be calculated for the smallest effect one does not want to miss out on detecting Otherwise, a non-significant result does not in itself count against a theory predicting an effect. Dienes (2021a) presents heuristics for determining a theoretically relevant minimally interesting effect size. One heuristic is calibration. Calibration is the process of converting from one scale, about which it is hard to judge what is of interest, to another scale for which we can judge. For example, a dependent variable for measuring distress in an animal may be how distracted it is (e.g., the proportion of time it wanders close to stimuli it would typically avoid; Braithwaite, 2010).

What proportion of time is of minimal interest? This can't be answered in the abstract nor with standardized effect sizes. Instead, the question is, how much distress do we care about? That question may have a reasonable answer. For example, given a scale of painful stimuli including "non-painful squeeze," "slight pinch," "slight bruising of skin," "broken skin," the level of distress caused by a "slight bruising of skin" may be relevant for welfare considerations. From a plot of proportion of time distracted against the scale of painful stimuli, the proportion corresponding to "slight pinch" can be determined; then, any proportion of time up to and including this can be treated as theoretically irrelevant, so we are happy to miss out on detecting such differences. Note that this process involves finding out answers to real questions, and data may have to be collected. Notice also that, if calibration were not used, and the minimal interesting effect was a standardized effect size plucked from the air (e.g., Cohen's $d = 0.5$), there is no meaningful scientific reason why this should be relevant. See Dienes (2021b) for other examples and heuristics.

Inference by Intervals

Another method for allowing the conclusion that there is no relevant effect is to define a null interval – the interval of effects less than a minimally interesting one, m. If a confidence or credibility interval lies within the interval [-m, +m], there is support for the null interval hypothesis (Greenwald, 1975; in the frequentist case, this is known as equivalence testing, Westlake, 1972). The same principles for finding minimally interesting effect sizes apply for this method as for power (see Dienes 2021a, 2021b for further examples in a Bayesian context). Having determined the relevant null interval, in planning the study size, use simulations to determine how severely H1 is tested. That is, one needs to find out that if H1 were false, how likely would the evidence indicate H1 were false (Popper, 1963)? To do this, find the number of participants needed to achieve an X% chance (e.g., 90%) of the 95% CI being within the null interval if the null interval hypothesis were true. This process ensures one can in practice test the substantial theory severely. A stopping rule can be running until the 95% CI (or 90% CI, etc.) is either completely inside or completely outside the null interval (cf. Dienes, 2016, and Kruschke, 2018, for discussion). For advice on writing up inference by intervals, see Dienes (2021b).

Bayes Factors

It may be easier not to determine a minimally interesting effect size; instead, a roughly expected effect size, or range of effect sizes, may be best. The minimally interesting effect size is typically the most arbitrary aspect of the range of effect sizes predicted by a theory and can often be approximated as 0. The roughly expected effect size, or its plausible range, is what is required for a Bayes factor. A Bayes factor compares the ability of a model of H1 to predict data compared to a model of H0 (Jeffreys, 1939; Wagenmakers et al., 2017). The Bayes factor is then the evidence for that model of H1 relative to H0 provided by the data.

For the Bayes factor to be relevant to testing a theory, the model of H1 must be an adequate model of the predictions of that theory (Dienes, 2023). That is, the effect size used to scale the predictions of the model of H1 must be the effect size predicted by the theory. Dienes (2019, 2021a, 2021b) provides heuristics for determining what rough effect size a theory predicts. This may involve collecting some pilot data – not necessarily for the full design. For example, if the aim of the study is to determine whether a manipulation removes or impairs an effect of caffeine, the pilot could estimate the caffeine effect (call that c); the manipulation can then be predicted to produce an effect no bigger than this (i.e., an effect plausibly in the range [0, c]). When using Bayes factors, report how one modeled H1 (see Dienes, 2021b, for advice on this and also on writing up Bayes factors). H0 is typically modeled as a point (or spike of probability) at zero slope (or zero difference between means, etc.). However, H0 could be something else, so the model of H0 (cf. Palfi & Dienes, 2019a) should be explicitly stated too (see also Dienes, 2023).

In planning the study, estimate roughly how many participants may be needed to achieve the desired cut-off (see Schönbrodt et al., 2017, and Schönbrodt & Wagenmakers, 2018, for using simulations to estimate the required sample size). Make sure the simulations use the same model of H1 as you will use. A very quick way of calculating an approximate likely number of participants, which involves no simulation, is provided by Palfi and Dienes (2019b, version 3, Table 1). According to PCI RR (2023), "If the stopping rule is dependent on the Bayes factor, authors should indicate a maximum feasible sample size after which sampling will stop, regardless of the Bayes factor. In this case, reviewers should judge whether the maximum possible sample size is sufficiently large that an inconclusive Bayes factor at that sample size would nevertheless provide an important message for the field."

Whichever method one uses, obtaining support for no effect is always relative to the size of effect that is relevant to detect, and that is a matter of scientific context. For example, in the case of minimally interesting effect sizes, the minimal acceptable level of distress may vary according to context (farming versus toxicology). In the case of Bayes factors, if the theory claims that happiness will reduce learning, and a control condition performs 10% above chance on the learning task, the difference between the happy and control condition can be modeled as a uniform [0, 10%]; that is, the difference between the two cannot be more than 10%. On the other hand, if the control performed at 5%, the difference between happy and control conditions can be modeled as a uniform distribution [0, 5%]. The different contexts make different predictions, and that changes how easy it is to obtain evidence for no effect. There is no such thing as evidence for no effect in the absence of theory and scientific context, so make sure minimally interesting effects (for power or inference by intervals) or expected effect sizes (for Bayes factors) are justified for reasons relevant to the theory being tested. Only by using theoretically relevant effects can the theory be severely tested (Dienes, 2023).

Lining Up Predictions and Tests

Consider a planned study measuring Stroop interference (a reaction time difference) at four points in time (four blocks of trials, within-participants) and testing two groups – anxious versus non-anxious. The stated prediction is "Interference will decrease over blocks more slowly for anxious than non-anxious participants." The authors will analyze the data with a 2 (group: anxious vs. non-anxious) × 4 (time: block1 vs. block2 vs. block3 vs. block4) analysis of variance (ANOVA). The number of participants is determined by a power analysis: "The power to detect Stroop interference being above zero is 0.90 with N = 30 for α = .02." However, N = 30 has been chosen by a power analysis on a different test (testing the mere existence of interference) from the test of their prediction (differential change in interference over time), so the Registered Report is sent back at triage. It comes back with a new calculation: "The power for the two-way interaction group × time (df = 3) is 0.90 with N = 150 for α = .02." Now, the sample size has been determined by reference to the group × time interaction, and the prediction is indeed about how the change over time is different for the different groups. The paper is still sent back at triage for revising this precise point. Why?

The prediction is about something decreasing – that is, it is about one thing moving as a whole. It is a one degree of freedom prediction. The suggested test has three degrees of freedom; that is, it is a test of a complex pattern in which three independent things can move in three different directions at once. Therefore, the test is not precisely a test of the prediction. The prediction refers to the extent to which interference decreases over blocks. This can be measured by a linear contrast. Let B1 be the interference in block1, B2 the interference in block2, and so on. Then let $L = (-3/4) \times B1 + (-1/4) \times B2 + (1/4) \times B3 + (3/4) \times B4$ $L = (-3/4) \times B1 + (-1/4) \times B2 + (1/4) \times B3 + (3/4) \times B4$. This measures the linear change in interference over blocks. Note that the positive coefficients sum to 1 and the negative ones to -1; the expected size of L in raw units is just a bit smaller than the expected difference between the two extreme conditions. Thus, the heuristics discussed in Dienes (2019, 2021a, 2021b) for the difference between conditions may be useful for such contrasts. One useful rule of thumb is that, when calculating a contrast, make positive coefficients sum to 1, negative to -1; then, it may be easy to think about expected effect sizes for the contrast in raw units.

We can now phrase the test of prediction: $L_{anxious} - L_{non\text{-}anxious} > 0$, where $L_{non\text{-}anxious}$ is the linear contrast L for the non-anxious group, and $L_{anxious}$ is L for the anxious group. This test is just a t-test, and power should be determined for this test. Consider what test precisely tests your prediction. In general, if your prediction says something will be greater or lesser than something else, it is one degree of freedom, and so the test should be likewise. This is partly a matter of tying down analytic flexibility – if you allow a multi-degree of freedom test to be the test of a one degree of freedom prediction, you are allowing a range of outcomes to support your theory. Consider also that you will have more power for the same number of participants for a one degree of freedom test than a multi-degree of freedom test. Further, any multi-degree of freedom result will need to be unpacked into single degree of freedom effects. Therefore, you must consider what the theory really predicts, and in particular, whether the prediction is one degree of freedom.

You should also line up all your predictions, both for outcome-neutral tests and for testing the substantial theory. For each prediction, determine a precise test that tests exactly that prediction. For each of those tests, you need to show you have sufficient sensitivity (i.e., a sufficient sample size for adequate power or probability of achieving conclusions with inference by intervals or by Bayes factors). According to *PCI RR* (2023) guidelines, "For full Stage 1 manuscripts ... describing quantitative research that involves the testing of hypotheses, inclusion of a study design template is a mandatory requirement; for all other quantitative and qualitative research modes it is strongly encouraged but not required."

Each hypothesis is represented by one row in the Design Template table with the following columns:

- **Question**: Articulate each research question being addressed in one sentence.
- **Hypothesis**: Where applicable, a prediction arising from the research question should be stated in terms of specific variables rather than concepts. Where the testability of one or more hypotheses depends on the verification of auxiliary assumptions (e.g., positive controls, tests of intervention fidelity, manipulation checks, or any other quality checks), any tests of such assumptions should be listed as hypotheses. Stage 1 proposals that do not seek to test hypotheses can ignore or delete this column.
- **Sampling plan**: For proposals using inferential statistics, the details of the statistical sampling plan for the specific hypothesis should go here (e.g., power analysis, Bayes Factor Design Analysis, ROPE). For proposals that do not use inferential statistics, include a description and justification of the sample size.
- **Analysis plan**: For hypothesis-driven studies, the specific test(s) that will confirm or disconfirm the hypothesis. For non-hypothesis-driven studies, the test(s) that will answer the research question.
- **Rationale for deciding the sensitivity of the test for confirming or disconfirming the hypothesis**: For hypothesis-driven studies that employ inferential statistics, an explanation of how the authors determined a relevant effect size for statistical power analysis, equivalence testing, Bayes factors, or other approach.
- **Interpretation given different outcomes**: A prospective interpretation of different potential outcomes, making clear which outcomes would confirm or disconfirm the hypothesis.
- **Theory that could be shown wrong by the outcomes**: Where the proposal is testing a theory, make clear what theory could be shown to be wrong, incomplete, or otherwise inadequate by the outcomes of the research.

(PCI RR 2023)

Design template

Theory	Prediction	Specific test	Sampling Plan	Interpretation of different outcomes
The manipulation is effective in changing mood	Sad group will rate their mood more negative than the happy group on the PANAS	One tailed Robust Bayesian t-test; H0 U[0, 1 Likert units] H1 a half-normal (mean = 1, SD = 1 Likert units)	Run until B > 6 or < 1/6 or until N = 50	If B < 1/6 the theory will be rejected; the manipulation is not good enough; if B > 6 the manipulation check is passed
The more negative the mood the greater the focus on detail				

Pros and Cons of RRs

Registered Reports have been useful in providing apparently unbiased evidence for whether well-known phenomena predicted by a theory exist. The worry arises that, with too much analytic flexibility and selective publishing, whole literatures might arise around non-existent effects, or overestimated ones; meta-analyses of those literatures will be distorted and thus not answer the question of what effect there is (e.g., Friese & Frankenbach, 2020). For example, in the first Registered Replication Report, Alogna et al. (2014) investigated the "verbal overshadowing effect." Originally, Schooler and Engstler-Schooler (1990) found that verbally summarizing a just-witnessed event harms later visual identification – a finding that triggered a small literature. In two studies, involving 31 and 22 labs respectively, with a minimum of 50 and 30 participants per lab, respectively, Alogna et al. found evidence for the effect, with a precise estimate of its size.

Similarly, a special issue of *Comprehensive Results in Social Psychology* investigated various claimed effects of power posing (Cesario et al., 2017). Carney et al. (2010) suggested that holding an expansive versus contractive posture for two minutes would change one's psychological and hormonal states toward those that co-occur with having a position of power. The theory triggered many subsequent studies; an analysis of the pattern of p-values (p-curve analysis) suggested to Simmons and Simonsohn (2015) that selective reporting of studies of an actually non-existent phenomenon might be at work. This is, of course, a problem that Registered Reports can address. Seven registered reports were submitted to the special issue addressing different aspects of the theory. No study found evidence for any of the hormonal and behavioral predictions of the theory. In a meta-analysis of all seven studies, Gronau et al. (2017) concluded there was evidence for people subjectively feeling (or rating themselves as feeling) more powerful after expansive rather than contractive poses. In conclusion, the Registered Reports helped indicate the effect was considerably more limited than originally claimed, but that a core phenomenon remained.

One argument for Registered Reports is that it reduces the bias that can arise in every stage of the process of testing a theory when decisions about setting up the test can be made in the light of the data obtained from the test. It is an empirical matter whether bias is actually reduced by Registered Reports as they are in practice implemented. There is no guarantee that these biases do often arise just because data are seen first and no guarantee that Registered Reports will reduce bias (Devezer et al., 2021). So far, the evidence supports the claim that Registered Reports reduce biases that arise in conventional publishing. In a pre-registered study, Scheel et al. (2020) found that published Registered Reports obtained results supporting predictions 44% of the time, whereas that rate was 96% in the corresponding standard literature. Similarly, Allen and Mehler (2019) estimated that only 39.5% of predictions in Registered Reports were supported, compared to 80–95% in the standard literature.

Further, there is higher reproducibility of the main results from the original data than for regular articles (Obels et al., 2020). Methodological rigor and quality of Registered Reports rated higher than non-Registered Reports papers by judges given sections to read, blind to the status of the article (Soderberg et al., 2021). There is not a single answer to the question of how much Registered Reports reduce bias; the answer depends on context and on how Registered Reports are actually performed. How much the different biases postulated in this paper are each addressed is unknown. The meta-scientific exploration of Registered Reports should be ongoing, but we already have evidence that the pursuit of Registered Reports is worthwhile.

Peer Community In Registered Reports (*PCI RR*, https://rr.peercommunityin.org) has introduced some publishing innovations to deal with limitations of previous Registered Reports. One difficulty people have faced is the long lead-in from submitting the Stage 1 to being able to start collecting data, as there will be some back and forth between reviewers and the author before the Stage 1 receives In Principle Acceptance. *PCI RR* has a "scheduled review," in which in the first instance the authors submit a "snapshot" or one-page summary of the proposed research, and they promise to deliver a Stage 1 manuscript a fixed period of time later (e.g., in six weeks). The editor (or "recommender" as they are called in *PCI RR*) then recruits reviewers who guarantee a review within a few days of the fixed date of Stage 1 submission. This dramatically cuts down the initial review period to only a few days.

PCI RR also has programmatic reports, where a single Stage 1 can set out several studies, each of which can be submitted as a separate Stage 2 paper, thereby also reducing the total time involved in getting out the final Stage 2 papers. *PCI RR* allows for the fact that some of the benefits of Registered Reports can be achieved for existing data sets. One just needs to make explicit the degree of bias control achieved and note whether it is less depending on the situation. For example, the existing data may have been inaccessible by the authors; in contrast, the authors could, in principle, have accessed the data but claim they have not (thus a lower degree of bias control needs to be noted). *PCI RR* explicitly marks six different levels of bias control.

One argument against Registered Reports might be that the timing of a prediction relative to data is metaphysically irrelevant. Imagine there are 10 different possible differences that could be obtained. Ten people pick one difference as the key one they predict, based only on a gut reaction they have. Andy predicts difference 1, Bonnie predicts difference 2, . . . Jenny predicts difference 10. Data are collected and there is evidence for difference 2; there is evidence against all other differences. What are we to make of this? First, from the point of view of advancing science, it is irrelevant that Bonnie predicted difference 2. That is, predicting in advance is not in itself important.

Now, change the scenario so that 10 different theories potentially explaining a phenomenon, not necessarily mutually exclusive, each predict one of the differences. It is very relevant that theory 2 predicts difference 2. We have learned a lot; theory 2 is supported and the rest of the theories disconfirmed. What is important for science is the objective relation between theory, predictions, and data. The timing of the different components is not metaphysically important. However, notice that the (effectively time-independent) objective relations between theory, predictions, and data were the view of science on which this paper based its arguments for Registered Reports. In sum, we as humans must judge the relations between the components, and that may be one reason why using data to support a theory that came later has a bad name – introducing data first motivates biased judgments. Thus, the argument from bias motivates the use of Registered Reports, regardless of any metaphysical status accorded timing.

Conclusion

In preparing a Registered Report, ask yourself these questions: (1) What is the most general theory that could be disconfirmed? (2) What is the prediction – is it one degree of freedom? (3) How does the prediction follow from theory? (4) Do these assumptions need to be tested? (5) Is there sensitivity to establish everything that needs to be established? Then, choose a statistical test for each prediction and each assumption. Make sure you have resources to obtain an adequate sample size for each prediction and each assumption. A study design template lining up each prediction and assumption with an appropriate test is likely to be useful.

When one considers the components that go into testing a theory, tries to make each component as rigorous as possible to reform the scientific mess we are in, and puts the pieces together, the result is a tighter integration than some of us may have been used to, where, for example, theory penetrates even the statistical tests conducted. Go through this process perhaps even only once, and you might find you do not look upon science quite the same again.

Acknowledgments

Thanks to Chris Chambers, Rob McIntosh, John Edlund, and Austin Lee Nichols for many helpful suggestions.

References

Alger, B. E. (2019). *Defense of the Scientific Hypothesis: From Reproducibility Crisis to Big Data*. Oxford University Press.

Allen, C., & Mehler, D. M. A. (2019). Open science challenges, benefits and tips in early career and beyond. *PLOS Biology, 17*(5), e3000246.

Alogna, V. K., Attaya, M. K., Aucoin, P., Bahnik, S., Birch, S., Birt, A. R., et al. (2014). Registered replication report: Schooler & Engstler-Schooler (1990). *Perspectives on Psychological Science, 9*, 556–578.

Baribault, B., Donkin, C., Little, D. R., Trueblood, J., Oravecz, Z., van Ravenzwaaij, D., et al. (2018). Metastudies for robust tests of theory. *Proceedings of the National Academy of Sciences, 115*, 2607–2612.

Baumeister, R. F. (2016). Charting the future of social psychology on stormy seas: Winners, losers, and recommendations. *Journal of Experimental Social Psychology, 66*, 153–158

Benjamin, D. J., Berger, J. O., Johannesson, M., Nosek, B. A., Wagenmakers, R. B., Bollen, K. A., et al. (2017). Redefine statistical signfiicance. *Nature Human Behaviour, 2*, 6–10. https://doi.org/10.1038/s41562-017-0189-z

Braithwaite, V. (2010). *Do Fish Feel Pain?* Oxford University Press.

Carney, D. R., Cuddy, A. J. C., & Yap, A. J. (2010). Power posing: Brief nonverbal displays affect neuroendocrine levels and risk tolerance. *Psychological Science, 21*, 1363–1368.

—— (2015). Review and summary of research on the embodied effects of expansive (vs. contractive) nonverbal displays. *Psychological Science, 26*, 657–663.

Carp, J. (2012). On the plurality of (methodological) worlds: Estimating the analytic flexibility of fMRI experiments. *Frontiers in Neuroscience, 6*. http://doi.org/10.3389/fnins.2012.00149

Carroll, C., Patterson, M., Wood, S. Booth, A., Rick, J., & Balain, S. (2007). A conceptual framework for implementation fidelity. *Implementation Science, 2*, 40. https://doi.org/10.1186/1748-5908-2-40

Center for Open Science. (2023). Registered Reports: Peer review before results are known to align scientific values and practices [webpage]. www.cos.io/initiatives/registered-reports (viewed March 16, 2023.

Cesario, J., Jonas, K. J., & Carney, D. R. (2017). CRSP special issue on power poses: What was the point and what did we learn? *Comprehensive Results in Social Psychology, 2*(1), 1–5. https://doi.org/10.1080/23743603.2017.1309876

Chambers, C. D. (2013). Registered reports: A new publishing initiative at Cortex. *Cortex, 49*, 609–610.

—— (2019). What's next for registered reports? *Nature, 573*(7773), 187–189.

Chambers, C. D., & Tzavella, L. (2020).The past, present and future of Registered Reports. *MetaArXiv Preprints.* https://doi.org/10.31222/osf.io/43298

Chavalarias, D., & Ioannidis, J. P. A. (2010). Science mapping analysis characterizes 235 biases in biomedical research. *Journal of Clinical Epidemiology, 63*, 1205–1215.

Chuard, P. J. C, Vrtílek, M., Head, M. L., & Jennions, M. D. (2019). Evidence that non-significant results are sometimes preferred: Reverse P-hacking or selective reporting? *PLOS Biology, 17*(1): e3000127. https://doi.org/10.1371/journal.pbio.3000127

Deci, E. L., & Ryan, R. M. (2000). The "what" and "why" of goal pursuits: Human needs and the self-determination of behavior. *Psychological Inquiry, 11*, 227–268.

Deutsch, D. (2011). *The Beginning of Infinity: Explanations that Transform the World.* Penguin.

Devezer, B., Navarro, D. J., Vandekerckhove, J., & Buzbas, E. O. (2021). The case for formal methodology in scientific reform. *Royal Society Open Science, 8*, 200805. https://doi.org/10.1098/rsos.200805

Dienes, Z. (2016). How Bayes factors change scientific practice. *Journal of Mathematical Psychology, 72*, 78–89.

—— (2019). How do I know what my theory predicts? *Advances in Methods and Practices in Psychological Science, 2*, 364–377. https://doi.org/10.1177/2515245919876960

—— (2021a). Obtaining evidence for no effect. *Collabra: Psychology, 7*(1), 28202. https://doi.org/10.1525/collabra.28202

(2021b). How to use and report Bayesian hypothesis tests. *Psychology of Consciousness: Theory, Research, and Practice*, *8*, 9–26.

(2023). Testing theories with Bayes factors. In A. L. Nichols & J. E. Edlund (eds.), *Cambridge Handbook of Research Methods and Statistics for the Social and Behavioral Sciences* (vol. 1, pp. 494–512). Cambridge University Press.

Dienes, Z., Palfi, B., & Lush, P. (2022). Controlling phenomenology by being unaware of intentions. In J. Weisberg (ed.), *Qualitative Consciousness: Themes from the Philosophy of David Rosenthal* (pp. 229–242). Cambridge University Press.

Dutilh, G., Vandekerckhove, J., Ly, A., Matzke, D., Pedroni, A., Frey, R., et al. (2017). A test of the diffusion model explanation for the worst performance rule using preregistration and blinding. *Attention, Perception, & Psychophysics*, *79*, 713–725. https://doi.org/10.3758/s13414-017-1304-y

Fiedler, K. (2017). What constitutes strong psychological science? The (neglected) role of diagnosticity and a priori theorizing. *Perspectives on Psychological Science*, *12*, 46–61.

Flake, J. K., Davidson, I. J., Wong, O., & Pek, J. (2022). Construct validity and the validity of replication studies: A systematic review. *American Psychologist*, *77*(4), 576–588.

Flake, J. K., & Fried, E. I. (2019). Measurement schmeasurement: Questionable measurement practices and how to avoid them. *Advances in Methods and Practices in Psychological Science*, *3*(4), 456–465. https://doi.org/10.1177/2515245920952393

Francis, G. (2012). Too good to be true: Publication bias in two prominent studies from experimental psychology. *Psychonomic Bulletin & Review*, *19*, 151–156.

Friese, M., & Frankenbach, J. (2020). p-Hacking and publication bias interact to distort meta-analytic effect size estimates. *Psychological Methods*, *25*(4), 456–471.

Gelman, A., & Loken, E. (2014). The statistical crisis in science: Data-dependent analysis – a "garden of forking paths" – explains why many statistically significant comparisons don't hold up. *American Scientist*, *102*(6), 460. https://doi.org/10.1511/2014.111.460

Goldacre, B, DeVito, N. J., Heneghan, C., Irving, F., Bacon, S., Fleminger, J., & Curtis, H. (2018). Compliance with requirement to report results on the EU Clinical Trials Register: Cohort study and web resource. *BMJ*, *362*, k3218.

Greenwald, A. G. (1975). Consequences of prejudice against the null hypothesis. *Psychological Bulletin*, *82*(1), 1–20. https://doi.org/10.1037/h0076157

Gronau, Q. F., van Erp, S., Heck, D. A., Cesario, J., Jonas, K. J., & Wagenmakers, E.-J. (2017). Bayesian model-averaged meta-analysis of the power pose effect with informed and default priors: The case of felt power. *Comprehensive Results in Social Psychology*, *2*, 123–138.

Guest, O., & Martin, A. E. (2021). How computational modeling can force theory building in psychological science. *Perspectives on Psychological Science*, *16*(4), 789–802. https://doi.org/10.1177/1745691620970585

Haig, B. D. (2014). *Investigating the Psychological World: Scientific Method in the Behavioural Sciences*. MIT Press.

Ikeda, A., Xu, H., Fuji, N., Zhu, S., & Yamada, Y. (2019). Questionable research practices following pre-registration. *Japanese Psychological Review*, *62*(3), 281–295.

Jeffreys, H. (1939). *The Theory of Probability*. Oxford University Press.

Kerr, N. L. (1998). HARKing: Hypothesizing after the results are known. *Personality & Social Psychology Review*, *2*, 196–217.

Khan, K. A., & Cheung, P. (2020). Presence of mismatches between diagnostic PCR assays and coronavirus SARS-CoV-2 genome. *Royal Society Open Science, 7*, 200636. http://doi.org/10.1098/rsos.200636

Klein, S. B. (2014). What can recent replication failures tell us about the theoretical commitments of psychology?*Theory & Psychology, 24*(3), 326–338. https://doi.org/10.1177/0959354314529616

Kruschke, J. K. (2018). Rejecting or accepting parameter values in Bayesian estimation. *Advances in Methods and Practices in Psychological Science, 1*, 270–280.

Lakatos, I. (1970). Falsification and the methodology of scientific research programmes. In I. Lakatos & A. Musgrave (eds.), *Criticism and the Growth of Knowledge* (pp. 91–196). Cambridge University Press.

MacCoun, R., & Perlmutter, S. (2015). Hide results to seek the truth. *Nature, 526*, 187–189.

Mayo, D. G. (2018). *Statistical Inference as Severe Testing: How to Get Beyond the Statistics Wars*. Cambridge University press.

McIntosh, R. D. (2017). Exploratory reports: A new article type for Cortex. *Cortex, 96*, A1–A4.

Nature Human Behaviour. (2020). *Registered Reports* [webpage]. www.nature.com/nathumbehav/submission-guidelines/registeredreports (retrieved April 20, 2020).

Newman, J., & Taylor, A. (1992). Effect of a means-end contingency on young children's food preferences. *Journal of Experimental Child Psychology, 64*, 200–216.

Obels, P., Lakens, D., Coles, N. A., Gottfried, J., & Green, S. A. (2020). Analysis of open data and computational reproducibility in Registered Reports in psychology. *Advances in Methods and Practices in Psychological Science, 3*(2), 229–237. https://doi.org/10.1177/2515245920918872

Palfi, B., & Dienes, Z. (2019a). When and how to calculate the Bayes factor with an interval null hypothesis. *PsyArXiv Preprints*. https://doi.org/10.31234/osf.io/9chmw

(2019b). The role of Bayes factors in testing interactions. *PsyArXiv Preprints*. https://doi.org/10.31234/osf.io/qjrg4

(2020). Why Bayesian "evidence for H1" in one condition and "evidence for H0" in another does not mean Bayesian evidence for a difference between conditions. *Advances in Methods and Practices in Psychological Science, 3*, 300–308.

PCI RR (Peer Community In Registered Reports). (2023). *Guide for Authors* [webpage]. https://rr.peercommunityin.org/help/guide_for_authors

Popper, K. R. (1959). *The Logic of Scientific Discovery*. Hutchinson.

(1963). *Conjectures and Refutations: The Growth of Scientific Knowledge*. Routledge & Kegan Paul.

(1972). *Objective Knowledge: An Evolutionary Approach*. Oxford University Press.

Ritchie, S. (2020). *Science Fictions: How Fraud, Bias, Negligence, and Hype Undermine the Search for Truth*. Metropolitan Books.

Royal Society Open Science. (2020). *Registered Reports* [webpage]. https://royalsocietypublishing.org/rsos/registered-reports (retrieved April 20, 2020).

Scheel, A. M., Schijen, M., & Lakens, D. (2020). An excess of positive results: Comparing the standard psychology literature with Registered Reports. *Advances in Methods and Practices in Psychological Science, 4*(2). https://doi.org/10.1177/25152459211007467

Schönbrodt, F. D., & Wagenmakers, E.-J. (2018). Bayes factor design analysis: Planning for compelling evidence. *Psychonomic Bulletin & Review, 25*, 128–142.

Schönbrodt, F. D., Wagenmakers, E.-J., Zehetleitner, M., & Perugini, M. (2017). Sequential hypothesis testing with Bayes factors: Efficiently testing mean differences. *Psychological Methods, 22,* 322–339.

Schooler, J. W., & Engstler-Schooler, T. Y. (1990). Verbal overshadowing of visual memories: Some things are better left unsaid. *Cognitive Psychology, 22,* 36–71.

Simmons, J., Nelson, L., & Simonsohn, U. (2011). False-positive psychology: Undisclosed flexibility in data collection and analysis allow presenting anything as significant. *Psychological Science, 22,* 1359–1366.

Simmons, J., & Simonsohn, U. (2015, May). Power posing: Reassessing the evidence behind the most popular TED talk. *Data Colada,* May 8. http://datacolada.org/2015/05/08/37-power-posing-reassessing-the-evidence-behind-the-most-popular-ted-talk

Simons, D. J., Holcombe, A. O., & Spellman, B. A. (2014). An introduction to Registered Replication Reports at *Perspectives on Psychological Science. Perspectives on Psychological Science, 9,* 552–555.

Simonsohn, U., Simmons, J. P., & Nelson, L. D. (2019). Specification curve: Descriptive and inferential statistics on all reasonable specifications. *SSRN.* http://doi.org/10.2139/ssrn.2694998

Soderberg, C. K., Errington, T. M., Schiavone, S. R., Bottesini, J., Thorn, F. S., Vazire, S., et al. (2021). Initial evidence of research quality of registered reports compared with the standard publishing model. *Nature Human Behaviour, 5*(8), 990–997.

Steegen, S., Tuerlinckx, F., Gelman, A., & Vanpaemel, W. (2016). Increasing transparency through a multiverse analysis. *Perspectives on Psychological Science, 11,* 702–712.

Wagenmakers, E.-J., Verhagen, A. J., Ly, A., Matzke, D., Steingroever, H., Rouder, J. N., & Morey, R. D. (2017). The need for Bayesian hypothesis testing in psychological science. In S. Lilienfeld & I. Waldman (eds.), *Psychological Science under Scrutiny: Recent Challenges and Proposed Solutions* (pp. 123–138). John Wiley and Sons.

Wagenmakers, E.-J., Wetzels, R., Borsboom, D., van der Maas, H. L. J., & Kievit, R. A. (2012). An agenda for purely confirmatory research. *Perspectives on Psychological Science, 7,* 627–633.

Westlake, W. J. (1972). Use of confidence intervals in analysis of comparative bioavailability trials. *Journal of Pharmaceutical Sciences, 61,* 1340–1341. https://doi.org/10.1002/jps.2600610845

Yanai, I., & Lercher, M. (2020). A hypothesis is a liability. *Genome Biology, 21,* 231. https://doi.org/10.1186/s13059-020-02133-w

PART III

Self-Report Measures

15 Self-Report Measures

Ting Yan

Abstract
Self-report measures are questions that are answered by respondents about themselves. They are essential to researchers and policy-makers; they provide a direct window for researchers and policy-makers to learn what people know, what they do, and how they think about an issue, a person, or an event. This chapter begins with an overview of how people go about answering survey questions. To answer a survey question, respondents must first understand what the question asks. Next, they retrieve relevant information required by the question and integrate it into an estimate or a judgment. Then, they map the estimate or the judgment to one of the response options provided to them. At each stage of this survey response process, respondents could run into problems that would negatively impact the accuracy and completeness of their answers. Lastly, the chapter discusses how the context in which a survey item is asked and the mode of data collection affect self-report measures. The chapter concludes with recommendations on how to improve the quality of self-report measures.

Keywords: Survey Response Process, Context Effects, Interviewer Effects, Comprehension, Retrieval, Judgment, Mapping, Data Quality

Self-report measures are questions that are answered by respondents about themselves. Social and behavioral science often relies on self-report measures obtained directly from people to learn what people know, what they do, and how they think about an issue, an event, or a person. For example, the American National Election Studies (ANES) samples US citizens aged 18 or older living in the 50 states or Washington, DC, and recruits them to participate in two surveys: a pre-election survey before the election day and a post-election survey after the election day (American National Election Studies, 2021). Respondents provide answers to survey questions about a wide variety of topics covering attitudes, behaviors, and experiences, such as health insurance, voting experiences, attitudes toward public health officials and organizations, perception of foreign countries, social media use. The answers provided by these respondents are self-report measures.

Some self-report measures are considered objective as, in theory, they can be verified by external records (Tourangeau et al., 2000). Age and number of doctor visits in the past 12 months are examples of objective self-report measures. In theory, self-reports of age can be verified by respondents' birth certificates or their driver's licenses. The number of doctor visits in the past 12 months is verifiable if medical records are available. Of course, the actual verification process can be challenging and even infeasible. External records are not always available or accessible. In addition, the linkage to external records may not always be accurate, and records themselves are not always error-free.

By contrast, subjective self-report measures are not verifiable. Examples include people's opinions, attitudes, perceptions, and evaluations. Although administrative data might provide information on what people know and what they do, no data can confirm peoples' attitudes, opinions, judgments, and perceptions. As a result, no external records exist that can be used to verify a respondent's self-report of his or her attitude about, for example, the US President.

Furthermore, some self-report measures are sensitive in nature because they touch on private topics, have disclosure risks, or are prone to social desirability bias (Tourangeau & Yan, 2007; Yan, 2021). Examples of sensitive measures include number of sexual partners, use of illicit drugs, abortions and miscarriages, sexual orientation, voter registration and voter turnout, and so on. Sensitive self-report measures are especially prone to measurement error, as described in the later sections.

Regardless, for researchers and policy-makers to rely on self-report measures, these measures have to pass the ultimate test of validity and reliability (see Chapters 9 and 10 in this volume for a detailed exposition on these topics). In other words, researchers and policy-makers count on respondents' ability to know their behaviors and attitudes and to report on them accurately and reliably. However, survey literature suggests that self-report measures are sensitive to minor variations in question wording, question format, question order, position and shading of response options, and even images shown next to survey questions in a web survey, leading to false or inconsistent reports of attitudes and behaviors (e.g., Tourangeau et al., 2000; Schwarz, 2019). To understand sources of measurement error in self-report measures, this chapter begins with an overview of a well-known theoretical framework of survey response process that describes the steps taken by respondents to generate their answers to a survey question and to produce self-report measures (Tourangeau, 1984; Tourangeau et al., 2000). The subsequent sections describe what could go wrong at each step of the survey response process and the implications for the quality of self-report measures, as well as the impact of context and mode of data collection on self-report measures. The chapter concludes with recommendations on how to improve the quality of self-report measures and the use of alternative data sources to supplement self-report measures.

Overview of Survey Response Process

According to the most influential conceptual framework of survey response process (Tourangeau, 1984; Tourangeau et al., 2000), respondents undergo four stages of cognitive processing when answering a survey question. The *first stage* is comprehension. Respondents must understand the meaning of the survey question, its instructions, and its response options, as intended by the question writer, to provide a meaningful answer. They also must understand the intent of the survey question (i.e., what the question writer wants to know).

After respondents determine what a survey question is asking (e.g., "How much did your household spend on household furniture in the past three months?"), they experience the *second stage* of cognitive processing – retrieval of relevant information from memory. To provide an accurate response, the respondent must search for relevant information about purchases of household furniture in their long-term memory, and move the retrieved information from their long-term memory to their short-term memory.

Sometimes respondents are able to retrieve a previously formed attitude or an estimate and report it directly as their answer. But other times, respondents need to integrate relevant information retrieved to form an attitude or an estimate using a judgment or estimation strategy – the *third stage* of cognitive processing.

The *fourth stage* is to map the resultant judgment or estimate to one of the response options provided to respondents. Measurement error occurs if the response option selected by the respondent does not reflect his or her judgment or estimate (Groves et al., 2009; Tourangeau et al., 2000). For instance, a woman respondent reported "No" to a survey question asking whether she has had an abortion, despite having had one in her lifetime (Yan & Tourangeau, 2022).

Ideally, respondents follow the four stages sequentially and conscientiously to produce reliable and accurate answers. However, in reality, the four stages could overlap in time. For instance, people often start the retrieval stage before they are finished reading the survey question and are finished with the comprehension step. As a result, information is integrated into a judgment even as more information is being retrieved. Furthermore, people sometimes backtrack from a later step to an earlier one. For instance, as respondents are retrieving information, they may go back to the comprehension stage to adjust their understanding of the survey question. Sometimes people take cognitive shortcuts by skipping one or more steps or by carrying out a superficial job at a certain step. Survey methodologists label this behavior as "survey satisficing" (Krosnick, 1991, 1999). Satisficing leads to answers that are less well thought-out and have a poorer quality. Examples of satisficing include providing "Don't know" answers (instead of going through the four stages conscientiously to come up with an answer), straightlining (selecting the same response option to a batch of survey items without differentiation based on the question content), agreeing with a statement regardless of the content (also referred to as "acquiescence bias"), selecting the extreme scale point, and selecting the middle response option (Krosnick, 1991, 1999; Chapter 17 in this volume).

Comprehension

Comprehension of a survey question occurs at three levels: syntactical, semantic, and pragmatic (Tourangeau, et al., 2000; Tourangeau & Bradburn, 2010). The syntactical process involves grammatical analysis of the question to identify its presupposition (What assumption does the question presuppose?) and focus (What information is requested of respondents?). Survey questions with a complex syntactical structure are difficult for respondents to process and to answer. Studies using eye-tracking and response times show that longer questions, questions with multiple clauses, and negatively phrased questions are more burdensome and take a longer time for respondents to understand and to answer (Kamoen et al., 2017; Lenzner et al., 2011; Yan & Tourangeau, 2008).

Semantic comprehension of a survey question involves understanding the meaning of each word in the question. What is crucial to the accuracy of self-report measures is that respondents understand the meaning of the words in the question as intended by the question writer. There are several hurdles to semantic comprehension. First, some words have multiple meanings. For instance, the word "table" can refer to a coffee table, an Excel table, or tabling a discussion. Second, even words commonly used are subject to different understandings. When question concepts (e.g., expenses on household furniture) match people's life circumstances (e.g., an end table was bought), comprehension tends to be straightforward and accurate. However, when the matching between question concepts (e.g., expenses on household furniture) and people's life (e.g., a floor lamp was purchased) becomes complicated, comprehension is at a stake, leading to low accuracy of self-reported measures (Schober & Conrad, 1997; Schober et al., 2004). As an example, Suessbrick et al. (2000) asked respondents about their understanding of one question used in the Current Population Survey – "Have you smoked at least 100 cigarettes in your entire life?" Approximately half of their respondents (54%) understood the word "smoking" as including any puffs whether inhaled or not – the meaning intended by the question writer. However, the other half (46%) thought that smoking in this question was asking about only puffs that one inhaled and provided an answer based on that misunderstanding. Consequently, self-report of cigarette smoking is underreported for these respondents.

Respondents also need to understand the intent of survey questions; this involves the determination of the pragmatic meaning of the questions. To infer the pragmatic meaning, respondents resort to conversational principles that they engage in everyday conversations, treating a survey as a conversational situation (Conrad et al., 2014; Tourangeau et al., 2000). They draw on contextual cues to make inferences about the intent behind survey questions and generate answers based on inferred intentions, producing context effects. Context effects are discussed in detail in a later section.

Retrieval

Retrieval involves searching for relevant information in long-term memory and moving the retrieved information from long-term memory to short-term memory to report the response on the survey. Two major sources of error at this stage of retrieval are forgetting and misdating. People are more likely to forget events or experiences that occurred a long time ago (Jobe et al., 1993). Mundane and frequent events are harder to recall than distinctive and salient events. For instance, people are more likely to remember details about the purchase of a home than the details of a trip to a grocery store. Forgetting is a major cause of respondents underreporting information and a leading cause of the resultant self-reported measures underestimating the phenomenon being studied (e.g., Neter & Waksberg, 1964). In addition, people often misremember dates, which can lead to telescoping. Telescoping refers to respondents reporting an event or experience that occurred outside the reference period, yielding an overestimation of the event or experience (Neter & Waksberg, 1964).

Furthermore, people do not necessarily encode everything that has happened in their life. Some information may never be stored in long-term memory. One study suggested that parents did not commit to their memories the immunizations their children received, and thus, were unable to accurately report them (Lee et al., 1999). Another encoding problem affecting retrieval is that information being sought after could be encoded into a different category and/or with a different label than what it is used in survey questions. For example, respondents may remember walking their dog every day, but they may not encode that piece of information as an instance of physical exercise. As a result, they would not necessarily recall that piece of information when answering a question regarding exercise.

Judgment and Estimation

Sometimes respondents directly use the retrieved information as their answer. This happens when respondents have an existing attitude or perception or encode a running tally of events. For instance, people typically retrieve their answer directly from their memory when asked how many children they have or how they feel about broccoli. However, in the absence of an existing attitude or an estimate, respondents will have to form a judgment or derive an estimate in the moment by applying one of the following three estimation strategies to integrate information retrieved: bottom-up, top-down, or impression-based (Tourangeau, 2018; Tourangeau & Bradburn, 2010; Tourangeau et al., 2000). The particular type of integration strategy used by respondents affects the quality of self-report measures.

With the bottom-up strategy, respondents use specific information retrieved to add up to an estimate or to derive a judgment. To answer a survey question on the number of dental visits in the last 12 months, for instance, respondents add up specific episodes of dental visits retrieved (e.g., "I had dental cleaning in February and two cavities filled in August") to yield an estimate ("2"). Similarly, when using the bottom-up strategy to generate answers to attitudinal questions, respondents combine specific beliefs or feelings retrieved about a candidate, for example, to derive an overall judgment about the Republican candidate (see Tourangeau, 2021, for a discussion of the belief-sampling model of forming an attitude on the fly).

By contrast, with the top-down strategy, respondents project general information retrieved (e.g., a rate or a general value) to the specific situation requested by the survey question. For instance, when answering the same question on the number of dental visits in the last 12 months, respondents apply a retrieved rate (e.g., "twice a year") to the last 12 months to derive an answer ("2"), regardless of what actually happened during that period of time. In the same way, respondents use a general value retrieved (e.g., "I don't like Republicans") to derive their answer to the question about how they feel about that Republican candidate. The choice of the bottom-up or top-down strategy, especially when answering questions about behavioral frequency, depends on the nature of the behavior, such as salience or importance of the behavior, frequency of the behavior, and regularity of the behavior (Brown, 2002; Sudman et al., 1996).

The last strategy respondents often use is an impression-based method – often used when the respondent is only able to retrieve an impression or stereotype about the survey measure. For instance, respondents apply an impression ("I never have dental problems") to yield an answer of zero to the question about dental visits in the last 12 months and a stereotype ("all politicians are corrupt") to derive a negative rating to the question asking about their attitudes toward a Republican candidate.

Survey literature shows that the quality of self-reported behavioral frequency measures is the best when respondents can directly retrieve their answer from long-term memory and the worst when respondents adopt the impression-based strategy. The bottom-up strategy tends to underestimate self-reported behavioral frequency measures because retrieval of specific episodes is likely be incomplete (Burton & Blair, 1991). The top-down strategy is more likely to overestimate the self-reported behavior due to exceptions to the rate and rate misestimation (Burton & Blair, 1991). To improve self-reports of behavioral frequency, respondents are encouraged to take their time and to resort to records if possible (Bradburn et al., 2004). In addition, survey questions starting with "how many times" encourage the use of the bottom-up strategy, unlike questions starting with "how often," which are more likely to elicit the use of the top-down strategy (Blair & Burton, 1987).

Mapping

The fourth stage is to report the judgment or estimate derived at the end of the judgment stage in a specific format. Survey questions generally require people to self-report their answers in one of three manners. Respondents may be asked to provide a verbatim answer to an open-ended question. For example, a common open-ended question asks respondents what they think is the most important issue facing this country, and respondents usually are free to report or to enter anything they like. There may be no restriction or requirement on the format or length of their answers. Another question format asks respondents to provide a numeric response to an open-ended question (e.g., the number of adults aged 18 or older living in their household). For this type of question, there may be an anticipated range of acceptable responses, and if the response provided is outside of that range, the survey may prompt the respondent to revisit their answer.

Lastly, respondents may be presented with a list of response options and respondents must map their resultant judgment or estimate to one of the response options provided to them. An exact match is desired to ensure validity and reliability of self-report measures, but mapping is not always an easy or straightforward process. Kamoen et al. (2011), for instance, showed that mapping a judgment to response options to negatively worded survey questions was more difficult than mapping to positively worded ones. Similarly, Chessa and Holleman (2007) analyzed response times data and found that respondents took longer to map their opinion to the "yes" option to survey questions asking if a certain issue should be forbidden than to the "no" option, leading to the well-documented "forbid/allow asymmetry."

There are several measurement issues with the mapping stage. One issue is when respondents deliberately do *not* choose the response option that best matches their answer. This happens with two types of survey items. The first type has to do with sensitive questions. Some questions (e.g., about sex partners and income) are sensitive because they are considered private and out of bounds of daily conversation (Tourangeau & Yan, 2007; Yan, 2021). These questions risk offending all respondents regardless of their answers. Questions on identifying information such as social security number and citizenship are sensitive because of the threats or risks of disclosing the information to the survey organization or a third party involved (Tourangeau & Yan, 2007; Yan, 2021). Lastly, some questions are sensitive because of social desirability concerns (Tourangeau & Yan, 2007; Yan, 2021). For these questions, there are societal norms that prescribe some attitudes and behaviors as socially desirable and others as socially undesirable. Respondents tend to answer these questions in a socially desirable manner.

As a result, self-report measures are subject to social desirability bias in the form of overreporting socially desirable behaviors and attitudes (e.g., voter turnout) and underreporting socially undesirable behaviors and attitudes (e.g., binge drinking). For instance, good citizens are expected to vote but not to binge drink. Consequently, self-report measure of voter turnout overestimates actual voter turnout whereas self-report measure of binge drinking underestimates actual binge drinking. The "Mode Effects" section below discusses how the mode of data collection affects respondents' answers to sensitive questions.

Second, sometimes surveys use filter questions to determine whether follow-up questions are applicable to respondents. Respondents may deliberately choose a response option to these filter questions that disqualifies themselves or their household from being eligible for the survey or to avoid additional follow-up questions, regardless of whether that selected response option reflects their true opinion or situation. This is also called motivated misreporting. Research suggests that a grouped question format (i.e., asking all filter questions together first and then asking follow-up questions) reduces motivated misreporting more than an interleafed format (asking the first filter question, followed by follow-up questions, and then the second filter question, followed by follow-up questions) (e.g., Eckman et al., 2014; Daikeler et al., 2022).

Another potential issue with the mapping stage is when the order in which response options are presented to respondents affects their selection of a particular option, producing response order effects. Sometimes, response options presented toward the beginning of the list are more likely to be selected, resulting in primacy effects. In other situations, response options toward the end of the list are more likely to be selected, yielding recency effects. Whether a primacy effect or a recency effect is expected depends on the nature of the response option list (i.e., whether or not there is an inherent order in the response lists) and the mode of data collection. A later section of the chapter further reviews differential response order effects observed for a list of unordered options by mode of data collection and scale direction effects when the response options are ordered.

A third potential issue with the mapping stage is if respondents report or select their answer in certain ways, regardless of question content and the judgment or estimate generated at the end of the judgment stage. This is called response style and contributes to systematic error in self-report measures (Van Vaerenbergh & Thomas, 2013). Well-known examples of response styles include acquiescence response style (ARS), extreme response style (ERS), and mid-point response style (MRS). ARS refers to the tendency of respondents to select agree options. As the name implies, ERS refers to the tendency to select the end points of a response scale. MRS is the tendency to select the mid-point of the scale.

These three types of response styles are sometimes considered to be the result of survey satisficing – selecting the first response that applies rather than taking the time to consider all of the options (Krosnick, 1991, 1999). However, satisficing alone cannot explain the role that culture plays in response styles (Van Vaerenbergh & Thomas, 2013). ARS is consistently documented to be higher among respondents from collectivist societies than from individualist cultures (e.g., Johnson et al., 2005; Kemmelmeier, 2016). Literature on cultural variability in ERS is less consistent, but ERS is also higher among Hispanics and African Americans than among White Americans (e.g., Johnson et al., 2010) and higher among Western respondents than Asians (e.g., Johnson et al., 2010). MRS is believed to reflect the process of response moderation (He & van de Vijver, 2015) and is also preferred by respondents from a collectivist culture (Chen et al., 1995).

Context Effects

Many studies have shown that responses to self-report measures can be highly sensitive to context. Sometimes even normatively unimportant and irrelevant features of the questionnaire can affect the resultant self-report measures, thus producing context effects (see Schwarz, Knäuper, Hippler, Noelle-Neumann, & Clark, 1991, for a review). For instance, contextual information demonstrated to have affected responses to self-report measures include the sponsor and title of the survey (Galesic & Tourangeau, 2007), the letterhead on which the questions are presented (Norenzayan & Schwarz, 1999, the content of prior questions (Schwarz, Strack, & Mai, 1991; Tourangeau & Rasinski, 1988), formal features of the questions, including the range of response options (Schwarz et al., 1985; Schwarz et al., 1988), numbers attached to scale points (Schwarz, 1991; Yan, 2006), the color and shade of response options on a screen (Tourangeau et al., 2007), and the use of images to illustrate survey concepts (Couper et al., 2007), to name just a few.

Context effects were once regarded as noises, contributing to unreliability of self-report measures, but they are now considered to reflect respondents' active use of conversational principles and Gricean maxims in the question-answering process (Schwarz, 2019). Respondents do not treat each question as a separate event. Instead, they treat their interaction with the whole questionnaire as an extended conversation and apply Grice's maxims as they do in daily conversation. According to Grice, speakers in a conversation should only say things that are relevant to the topic of the conversation (Maxim of Relation). They should not say what they believe to be false or say that for which they don't have adequate evidence (Maxim of Quality). Their contributions to the conversation should be informative, but not redundant (Maxim of Quantity). Lastly, they should be clear in what they say and should avoid being vague, ambiguous, or lengthy (Maxim of Manner).

Respondents expect that question writers are cooperative speakers following these maxims. As a result, respondents believe that all contextual cues are relevant (the Maxim of Relation). This includes that all information involved in their reaction with the questionnaire is meaningful (Maxim of Quality), informative (Maxim of Quantity), and clear (Maxim of Manner). Respondents infer the intent of survey questions using these maxims. Even when a question appears to be redundant or nonsensical, respondents will go beyond the semantic meaning of the question to look for what is implied by the question. Two classic context effects – question order effects and use of frequency scales – are elaborated next.

Question Order Effects

As the name implies, question order effects refer to the impact of earlier survey items on answers to subsequent items. Unless they are told otherwise, respondents perceive questions as relevant to each other and, in particular, relevant to the goal of completing the questionnaire. Consequently, they use earlier questions to ground their understanding of the intent of subsequent questions and provide answers to subsequent questions accordingly. According to Tourangeau and Rasinski (1988), prior items affect all four stages of survey response processing. The prior items can provide a framework for interpreting subsequent questions (especially when later questions are vague, ambiguous, or seemingly redundant), prime information for more accessible retrieval, suggest a norm or standard of comparison to be used as the basis for forming a judgment, and create pressures for respondents to be consistent in their answers.

Strack et al. (1991) conducted an experiment to demonstrate how respondents used a prior question to disambiguate the meaning of the subsequent question (also see Tourangeau & Rasinski, 1988). They asked German college students about their attitude toward a fictitious "educational contribution" law. The experiment varied the content of the question prior to this target question. The target question was preceded by either a question about the average tuition students pay in the United States or a question about the stipend Swedish students receive from their government as financial support for others. Strack et al. (1991) showed that students made sense of the fictitious law ("educational contribution") based on the prior question. Those receiving the US tuition question inferred that the law was about students paying money whereas those who got the Swedish financial support question took the law to be about students receiving money. Not surprisingly, their attitude toward the law was in line with the inferred meaning of the law – more positive attitudes were expressed when the law was perceived to have to do with receiving money than with paying money. This finding supports the recommendation of grouping related questions together in a questionnaire (Krosnick & Presser, 2010).

Researchers have also found that the correlation of self-reported measures of a specific domain (e.g., marriage satisfaction) and a general domain (e.g., life satisfaction) varies depending on the order of the two questions. The correlation of answers to the specific and general questions are higher when the specific question is asked before the general question than when the general question precedes the specific question (Strack et al., 1988; Schwarz, Strack, & Mai, 1991; Tourangeau et al., 1991; also see Mason et al., 1994). This is because answering the specific question on marriage satisfaction has made information about marriage highly accessible in working memory. Since marriage is an important part of life, the highly accessible information about marriage is also used to form a judgment about life satisfaction, yielding a high correlation between the two self-report measures. This is also called part–whole question order effect.

However, when the specific and general questions are introduced by a joint lead-in ("We now have two questions about your life. The first pertains to your marital satisfaction and the second to your general life satisfaction"), asking the specific question before the general question reduces the correlation of the two self-report measures compared to when no joint lead-in is used. The joint lead-in evokes the Gricean Maxim of Quantity that enjoins people to not provide redundant information. As a result, respondents exclude information about marriage when answering the general question about life satisfaction. Essentially, respondents infer the general question on life satisfaction to mean satisfaction with "other aspects of life aside from marriage." Furthermore, when multiple specific questions (e.g., satisfaction with leisure time, satisfaction with work, and satisfaction with marriage) are asked before the general life satisfaction question, the general question is inferred to mean "taking-all-aspects-together" (Schwarz, Strack, & Mai, 1991). Based on these findings, it is recommended to ask the general question first when both general and specific questions are asked about a topic (Bradburn et al., 2004; Tourangeau et al., 2000).

Use of Frequency Scales

Similar to how prior items affect respondents' question-answering process for later items, response options presented for a survey item can also impact respondents' interpretation of the intent of the survey item, the use of an estimation strategy to derive an answer, mapping the resultant estimate to a response option, and the formulation of comparative judgments. Respondents assume that the question writer knows the topic very well and has chosen the response options with care. The range and formal features of response options are meaningful and relevant to the task of question-answer process, legitimizing respondents' use of them when answering the survey item. This section discusses how respondents take advantage of frequency scales in their interpretation of the question, their reports of the behavior frequency, and related judgments.

Schwarz et al. (1988) asked respondents how often they typically came across situations in which they felt "really annoyed." Some respondents received a frequency scale ranging from "less than once a year" to "more than once every three months" (the low-frequency scale condition) whereas others saw a high-frequency scale ranging from "less than twice a week" to "several times a day." Schwarz et al. (1988) found support for respondents' use of the range of the frequency scale to interpret what the question writer must have meant by "feeling annoyed." Those presented with the low-frequency scale inferred that the question writer asked about major annoyances (because major annoyances occur less frequently) whereas those shown the high-frequency scale thought of minor irritations that happen more often. This interpretation led respondents to retrieve different episodes of annoyance; those in the low-frequency scale reported instances of more severe annoyance than those in the high-frequency scale.

The impact of the range of frequency scales extends beyond question interpretation. Respondents also use the range as a frame of reference in estimating their own or other people's behavioral frequencies. Respondents assume that the middle range of the frequency scale reflects "typical" or "average" behavior frequencies whereas the extremes of the scale reflect the extremes of the distribution. They then use this information to estimate how much they engage in a behavior as compared to the "average" frequency. For example, people may not encode the exact number of hours spent watching TV. They tend to encode impressions such as I watch a bit more TV than average or I watch as much TV as everyone else. They then use the frequency scale provided to them to help figure out the number of hours they spend watching TV.

Schwarz et al. (1985) asked respondents how much TV they watched along either a low-frequency or a high-frequency scale. The low-frequency scale goes from "up to ½ hour" to "more than 2 ½ hours." The middle two options are "1 to 1 ½ hours" and "1 ½ to 2 hours." By contrast, the high-frequency scale ranges from "up to 2 ½ hours" to "more than 4 ½ hours" with the two middle options being "3 to 3 ½ hours" and "3 ½ hours to 4 hours." Not surprisingly, the low-frequency scale resulted in lower estimates of TV watching than the high-frequency scale. Similarly, Tourangeau and Smith (1996) showed that respondents reported having more sexual partners when presented with a high-frequency scale than with a low-frequency scale.

The frequency range of the response alternatives has also been found to affect subsequent comparative judgments. When selecting a point along the frequency scale, respondents essentially have placed themselves in the distribution of the behavior of interest. For instance, respondents who watched TV for 2.5 hours are on the high end of the low-frequency scale, implying that they have watched a lot more TV than average people. However, they would be at the low end of the high-frequency scale, watching much less TV than average people. This relative location on the scale is subsequently used to form comparative judgments. Respondents in the low-frequency scale reported that TV played a more important role in their leisure time and that they were less satisfied with the variety of things they did in their leisure time than those provided with a high-frequency scale (Schwarz et al., 1985).

Not surprisingly, the impact of frequency ranges is more pronounced for mundane behaviors of high frequency that are less well represented in memory and for respondents who are cognitively limited or have a poor memory (Schwarz, 1999, 2019; Conrad et al., 2014; Knäuper et al., 2016).

Mode Effects

The mode of data collection is one of the most important design decisions of a survey as it has important implications for questionnaire design, development of survey protocols (e.g., how to contact sampled persons), quality of resultant survey estimates, and the cost and timeline of data collection. Researchers and practitioners have a wide variety of modes that they can select from. Common modes of data collection include mail surveys, web surveys, computer-assisted telephone interviewing (CATI), computer-assisted personal interviewing (CAPI), and audio computer-assisted self-interviewing (ACASI).

Survey literature compares and contrasts modes of data collection along a few dimensions such as degree of interviewer involvement, degree of interaction with respondents, degree of privacy, channels of communication, and use of technology (Groves et al., 2009). They all have implications for the quality of data obtained. For instance, when questionnaires are computerized (as in CATI, CAPI, ACASI, and web), skip logics can be programmed to reduce both omission errors (errors of not answering questions that should be answered) and commission errors (errors of answering questions that are not applicable to respondents).

Answers to computerized modes of data collection can be checked in real time for inconsistency and out-of-range values, producing data of higher quality than those obtained from mail surveys. Furthermore, researchers have better control over the measurement process for modes with higher interaction with respondents such as CATI and CAPI. For mail and web modes, sometimes it is not even clear who answers the survey. The other three (channels of communication, degree of interviewer involvement, and degree of privacy) are particularly relevant to the collection of self-report measures and will be discussed below.

Response Order Effects

Modes of data collection differ in channels of communication – in particular, how survey questions are delivered to respondents and how answers are communicated to researchers. Interviewer-administered modes of data collection (CATI and CAPI) are mostly aural – questions are read to respondents and respondents answer orally. For web surveys, questions are presented visually on a computer or mobile device, and respondents enter their answers through a keyboard or a keypad. For mail surveys, questions are presented visually on paper, and respondents write their answers on paper. For ACASI surveys, questions are displayed on a screen and are read aloud to respondents through recordings. Respondents enter answers through a keyboard.

Survey research has documented a key mode difference due to channels of communications between visual and auditory modes. When respondents are visually presented a list of unordered response options on paper, a showcard, or a computer screen, responses at the beginning of the list are more likely to be selected, leading to a primacy effect. However, when respondents are read the same list through an interviewer-administered mode, options toward the end of the list are more likely to be endorsed, resulting in a recency effect (Krosnick & Alwin, 1987; Krosnick & Presser, 2010).

Several mechanisms have been proposed to explain response order effects, including plausibility of response option and perceptual contrast effects (see Schwarz & Hippler, 1991; Schwarz et al., 1992). A popular explanation discussed in the survey literature is satisficing (Krosnick, 1991, 1999; Krosnick & Presser, 2010). Based on the satisficing notion, satisficers do not carefully evaluate each of the options before selecting the one that is the most appropriate. Instead, they simply choose the first one that appears to be satisfactory enough. Consequently, response order effects are also considered to be a manifestation of "weak satisficing" (Krosnick, 1991, 1999; Krosnick & Presser, 2010).

The satisficing account may explain primacy effects. When respondents are presented a list of unordered options on a paper questionnaire, computer screen, or show-card, they tend to process the list sequentially from top to bottom and left to right. Satisficers simply terminate their evaluation altogether once they come upon an alternative that seems to be a reasonable answer. As a result, options presented earlier (toward the top of a vertical list or on the left side of a horizontal scale) tend to be selected more often in self-administered modes (Krosnick & Alwin, 1987; Holbrook et al., 2007). Eye-tracking research provided direct support for the presence of primacy effects in answers obtained from a self-administered mode (Galesic et al., 2008; Galesic & Yan, 2011). However, the satisficing account alone is not sufficient to predict recency effects. Working memory is believed to play a role as well. When respondents are read a list of unordered response options, options that are read last are more likely to be retained in working memory when interviewers are done reading. As a result, they are more likely to be processed and, thus, selected.

Response order effects are shown to affect even dichotomous response options (Holbrook et al., 2007), but research has shown that they are more pronounced with longer response option lists and people with limited working memory such as older respondents (Knäuper et al., 2016). Response order effects are also observed for response scales comprised of a list of ordered options (e.g., an agreement scale running from strongly agree to strongly disagree), leading to scale direction effects. However, scale direction effects mostly take the form of primacy effects. That is, scale points closer to the start of a scale are more likely to be selected, regardless of the mode of data collection.

Scale effects are observed for both self-administered modes (Keusch & Yan, 2018, 2019) and interviewer-administered modes (Yan & Keusch, 2015). Although scale direction effects are stronger for longer scales and complex questions (Yan et al., 2018), satisficing does not fully explain the phenomenon. As a matter of fact, Keusch and Yan (2018) found that scale direction effects are observed across the board. For example, Yan and Keusch (2015) found support for the "anchoring-and-adjustment" heuristic as the underlying mechanism.

Interviewer Effects

A major difference between interviewer-administered modes of data collection and self-administered modes of data collection is the role of interviewers. Interviewers generally read questions to respondents and record answers provided by respondents. However, they are also treated by cooperative respondents as another part of the conversation, no matter how unusual a survey is (Schaeffer, 1991; Conrad et al., 2014). Respondents are often able to make accurate judgments about the interviewer's sex, age, racial background, and attractiveness even from the interviewer's voice alone (Bradburn, 2016). It is not surprising that characteristics of interviewers are found to affect both respondents' decision to participate in a survey and how they answer survey questions. For instance, interviewer sex is found to affect self-report measures of gender-related attitudes (e.g., Liu & Stainback, 2013; also see West & Blom, 2017, for a review). In a similar way, interviewer race has an impact on self-report measures of race-related attitudes (e.g., Davis et al., 2010; Schaeffer, 1980; West & Blom, 2017; see also Chapter 26 in this volume).

Interviewers affect obtained self-report measures by introducing another variance component to the variance of self-report measures (West & Blom, 2017). This is because interviewers tend to obtain similar self-report measures from the people they've interviewed, yielding correlated self-report measures by interviewers. This can result in reduced precision of self-report measures. Attitudinal, sensitive, ambiguous, complex, and open-ended questions are more prone to variable interviewer effects (West & Blom, 2017). Since interviewers are not present for self-administered modes such as mail surveys and web surveys, self-report measures from these surveys are not subject to interviewer bias and variance.

Sensitive Questions

Another important mode difference between interviewer-administered modes of data collection and self-administration lies in answers to sensitive questions (Tourangeau & Yan, 2007; Yan, 2021; Yan & Cantor, 2019). Some consider misreporting to sensitive questions the result of respondent satisficing (e.g., Holtgraves, 2004). That is, respondents skip the retrieval and judgment stages completely and give an answer that seems socially desirable without bothering to consult their actual behavior or attitudes (e.g., Johnson et al., 2010). However, Tourangeau and Yan (2007) argue that misreporting to sensitive questions is a motivated process in which respondents edit their answer prior to reporting it. The purpose of this deliberate editing process is to avoid embarrassing themselves in the presence of an interviewer or to avoid repercussions from third parties.

The editing account is supported by literature demonstrating that social desirability bias is reduced in self-administered modes of data collection (Tourangeau & Yan, 2007; Yan, 2021; Yan & Cantor, 2019). Yan and colleagues (Yan et al., 2012; Yan &

Tourangeau, 2022), for instance, examined women's self-report of abortion and miscarriage using data from the National Survey of Family Growth (NSFG). Both abortion and miscarriage are sensitive topics for women. The NSFG asks about abortion and miscarriage twice, once by an interviewer (in the CAPI part of the questionnaire) and the other in the ACASI part of the questionnaire when the interviewer is still in the same room but not actively involved in the question-answering process. Yan and colleagues found that self-reported abortion and miscarriage are consistently lower in the CAPI mode than in the ACASI mode. Furthermore, self-report measures of abortion and miscarriage using CAPI have a higher false negative rate than with ACASI. These findings provide one more piece of evidence demonstrating the difference between interviewer-administered modes and self-administered modes in answers to sensitive questions.

Improving Self-Report Measures

Researchers must have a clear conceptualization of what a self-report measure is supposed to measure (Yan, 2017). A common mistake made by researchers is not asking the right questions. For instance, the concept of unemployment involves both not having a job and wanting one. A survey question that only asks respondents whether or not they currently have a job does not fully capture the meaning of "unemployment." For example, retirees do not work, but they are not unemployed since they are not actively looking for work. As a result, using that question alone cannot produce an accurate measure of unemployment. The path from a concept to survey questions is not always straightforward (Hox, 1997; Schwarz, 1997). Concepts are abstract and multidimensional in nature, but survey questions need to be specific and concrete enough for people to answer. Having a list of clearly defined concepts will prevent researchers from producing survey questions measuring either the wrong concept or a part of the concept.

Once concepts are clarified and clearly defined, researchers can write questions that follow well-established principles for survey questions. Several textbooks and articles on questionnaire design are available that base guidelines and best practices on methodological research (e.g., Bradburn et al., 2004; Fowler, 1995; Krosnick & Presser, 2010; Schaeffer & Presser, 2003; Tourangeau et al., 2000; also see Chapter 16 on questionnaire design). In addition to general guidelines, survey literature also provides evidence-based recommendations on specific methods and approaches one can employ to improve self-report measures.

Studies have demonstrated that answer accuracy for ambiguous and complicated concepts was dramatically improved when definitions were provided to respondents (Schober & Conrad, 1997; Conrad & Schober, 2000; Ehlen et al., 2007). Methods to improve recall include using bounded interviews in panel surveys (Neter & Waksberg, 1964), providing a landmark event (either public or private events that respondents can recall well) marking the beginning of a reference period (Loftus & Marburger, 1983), providing richer recall cues (Tourangeau, 2018), and adopting an event history calendar approach (Belli et al., 2001). To improve answers to sensitive questions, research can employ various techniques such as using a self-administered mode (Tourangeau & Yan, 2007), bogus pipeline technique (Tourangeau et al.,1997), honesty pledge (e.g., McDonald et al., 2017), and use of forgiving introduction and wording (e.g., Holtgraves et al., 1997; Peter & Valkenburg, 2011; see Tourangeau & Yan, 2007; Yan & Cantor, 2019; Yan, 2021, for additional techniques and methods). Furthermore, shorter questions and questions with fewer response options are consistently shown to produce more reliable answers than longer questions (Alwin, 2007; Saris & Gallhofer, 2007a, 2007b; Tourangeau, Yan, & Sun, 2020) and those with more response options (Alwin et al., 2018; Revilla et al., 2014; Tourangeau, Yan, & Sun, 2020).

Aside from writing good questions in the first place, it is critical to evaluate and test survey questions to further minimize measurement error. A wide variety of question evaluation methods are available; they differ in when they can be used for question evaluation, the focus of question evaluation, whether or not data collection is needed, and budget and timeline (Tourangeau, Maitland, Steiger, & Yan, 2020). Some methods, such as focus groups, are extremely useful for the conceptualization phase and for understanding what general people think about the topic of interest as well as the terms and phrases people use when thinking about the topic. Methods such as expert review and cognitive interviews tend to be used before the survey questionnaire is fielded. Both are advantageous in identifying problems general people may have with answering particular questions. Methods including behavior coding and examination of response time data should also be conducted as the survey is carried out. Advanced statistical modeling methods are usually conducted after data collection is over to investigate the quality of self-report measures, including reliability and validity.

Even though different evaluation methods do not necessarily converge on the identification of specific issues a survey question may have (Maitland & Presser, 2016, 2018; Yan et al., 2012; Tourangeau et al., 2021), research consistently shows that using multiple methods is better than using one single method, and any method of question evaluation is better than no evaluation (Yan et al., 2012; Maitland & Presser, 2016, 2018). Tourangeau Maitland, Steiger, and Yan (2020) suggested a framework for making decisions on which question evaluation method(s) to select.

Lastly, researchers should select survey design features that are shown to improve self-report measures when making survey design decisions such as mode of data collection. As mentioned earlier, self-administrated modes of data collection should be selected when the survey asks sensitive questions (Yan, 2021; Yan & Cantor, 2019). However, an interviewer-administered mode of data collection is preferred when a survey asks complicated questions that involve complex mapping (Conrad & Schober, 2000). Recall aids (e.g., a calendar) can be used when the survey involves recall of past behaviors and events. Diaries are used for respondents to self-report consumer expenditures (US Bureau of Labor Statistics, n.d.), food acquisition and purchase (2019), and travel behaviors (Simas et al., 2019).

Furthermore, studies can collect additional and/or alternative data to supplement and improve self-report measures. For instance, purchase receipts can be collected to supplement respondents' self-reports of purchases and expenditures, as in the First

National Household Food Acquisition and Purchase Survey (US Department of Agriculture, n.d.).

GPS location data passively collected by a smartphone can be used to improve respondents' self-report of traveling behavior (McCool et al., 2021). Sensor data passively collected through wearables or smartphones can be used to derive measures of physical activity and sedentary behavior (Huber & Ghosh, 2021; Maher et al., 2018).

Researchers are encouraged to evaluate the appropriateness of using self-reports to obtain measures of interest before writing survey questions and to utilize best practices and principles of questionnaire design and evaluation to improve self-report measures collected through survey questions.

References

Alwin, D. F. (2007). *Margins of Error: A Study of Reliability in Survey Measurement*. John Wiley.

Alwin, D. F., Baumgartner, E. M., & Beattie, B. A. (2018). Number of response categories and reliability in attitude measurement. *Journal of Survey Statistics and Methodology, 6*, 212–239.

American National Election Studies. (2021). ANES 2020 time series study full release [data set and documentation]. July 19, 2021 version. www.electionstudies.org

Belli, R. F., Shay, W. L., & Stafford, F. P. (2001). Event history calendars and question list surveys: A direct comparison of interviewing methods. *Public Opinion Quarterly, 65*, 45–74.

Blair, E., & Burton, S. (1987). Cognitive processes used by survey respondents to answer behavioral frequency questions. *Journal of Consumer Research, 14*, 280–288.

Bradburn, N. (2016). Surveys as social interactions. *Journal of Survey Statistics and Methodology, 4*, 94–109.

Bradburn, N., Sudman, S., & Wansink, B. (2004). *Asking questions: The Definitive Guide to Questionnaire Design*. Wiley & Sons.

Brown, N. R. (2002). Encoding, representing, and estimating event frequencies: Multiple strategy perspective. In P. Sedlmeier & T. Betsch (eds.), *Frequency Processing and Cognition* (pp. 37–54). Oxford University Press.

Burton, S., & Blair, E. (1991). Task conditions, response formulation processes, and response accuracy for behavioral frequency questions in surveys. *Public Opinion Quarterly, 55*, 50–79.

Carp, F. (1974). Position effects on interview response. *Journal of Gerontology, 29*, 581–587.

Chen, C., Lee, S. Y., & Stevenson, H. W. (1995). Response style and cross-cultural comparisons of rating scales among East Asian and North American students. *Psychological Science, 6*, 170–175.

Chessa, A. G., & Holleman, B. C. (2007). Answering attitudinal questions: Modelling the response process underlying contrastive questions. *Applied Cognitive Psychology, 21*(2), 203–225.

Conrad, F. G., & Schober, M. F. (2000). Clarifying question meaning in a household telephone survey. *Public Opinion Quarterly, 64*, 1–28.

Conrad, F. G., Schober, M. F., & Schwarz, N. (2014). Pragmatic processes in survey interviewing. In T. M. Holtgraves (ed.), *The Oxford Handbook of Language and Social Psychology* (pp. 420–437). Oxford University Press. https://doi.org/10.1093/oxfordhb/9780199838639.013.005

Couper, M. P., Conrad, F. G., & Tourangeau, R. (2007). Visual context effects in Web surveys. *Public Opinion Quarterly, 71*(4), 623–634. https://doi.org/10.1093/poq/nfm044

Daikeler, J., Bach, R. L., Silber, H., & Eckman, S. (2022). Motivated misreporting in smartphone surveys. *Social Science Computer Review, 40*(1), 95–107. https://doi.org/10.1177/0894439319900936

Davis, R. E., Couper, M. P., Janz, N. K., Caldwell, C. H., & Resnicow, K. (2010). Interviewer effects in public health surveys. *Health Education Research, 25*, 14–26.

Eckman, S., Kreuter, F., Kirchner, A., Jäckle, A., Tourangeau, R., & Presser, S. (2014). Assessing the mechanisms of misreporting to filter questions in surveys. *Public Opinion Quarterly, 78*(3), 721–733. https://doi.org/10.1093/poq/nfu030

Ehlen, P., Schober, M. F., & Conrad, F. G. (2007). Modeling speech disfluency to predict conceptual misalignment in speech survey interfaces. *Discourse Processes, 44*(3), 245–265.

Fowler Jr, F. J. (1995). *Improving Survey Questions: Design and Evaluation.* SAGE Publications.

Galesic, M., & Tourangeau, R. (2007). What is sexual harassment? It depends on who asks! Framing effects on survey responses. *Applied Cognitive Psychology, 21*(2), 189–202.

Galesic, M., Tourangeau, R., Couper, M. P., & Conrad, F. G. (2008). Eye-tracking data: New insights on response order effects and other cognitive shortcuts in survey responding. *Public Opinion Quarterly, 72*(5), 892–913.

Galesic, M., & Yan, T. (2011). Use of eye tracking for studying survey response processes. In M. Das, P. Ester, & L. Kaczmirek (eds.), *Social and Behavioral Research and the Internet: Advances in Applied Methods and Research Strategies* (pp. 349–370). Routledge.

Grice, H. P. (1975). Logic and conversation. In P. Cole and J. Morgan (eds.), *Syntax and Semantics: Speech Acts* (vol. 3, pp. 41–58). Seminar Press.

Groves. R. M., Fowler Jr., F. J., Couper, M. P., Lepkowski, J. M., Singer, E. & Tourangeau, R. (2009). *Survey Methodology.* Wiley.

He, J., & van de Vijver, F. J. R. (2015). Effects of a general response style on cross-cultural comparisons: Evidence from the Teaching and Learning International Survey. *Public Opinion Quarterly, 79*, 267–290.

Holbrook, A. L., Krosnick, J. A., Moore, D., & Tourangeau, R. (2007). Response order effects in dichotomous categorical questions presented orally: The impact of question and respondent attributes. *Public Opinion Quarterly, 71*(3), 325–348.

Holtgraves, T. (2004). Social desirability and self-reports: Testing models of socially desirable responding. *Personality and Social Psychology Bulletin, 30*, 161–172.

Holtgraves, T., Eck, J., & Lasky, B. (1997). Face management, question wording, and social desirability. *Journal of Applied Social Psychology, 27*, 1650–1671.

Hox, J. (1997). From theoretical concepts to survey questions. In L. Lyberg et al. (eds.). *Survey Measurement and Process Quality* (pp. 47–69). Wiley.

Huber, R., & Ghosh, A. (2021). Large cognitive fluctuations surrounding sleep in daily living. *iScience, 3*(19), 102159.

Jobe, J. B., Tourangeau, R., & Smith, A. F. (1993). Contributions of survey research to the understanding of memory. *Applied Cognitive Psychology, 7*, 567–584.

Johnson, T., Kulesa, P., Cho, Y. I., & Shavitt, S. (2005). The relation between culture and response styles: Evidence from 19 countries. *Journal of Cross-Cultural Psychology, 36*, 264–277.

Johnson, T., Shavitt, S., & Holbrook, A. (2010). Survey response styles across cultures. In D. Matsumoto & F. Van de Vijver (eds.), *Cross-Cultural Research Methods in Psychology* (pp. 130–176). Cambridge University Press.

Kamoen, N., Holleman, B., Mak, P., Sanders, T., & Van Den Bergh, H. (2011). Agree or disagree? Cognitive processes in answering contrastive survey questions. *Discourse Processes, 48*, 355–385.

(2017). Why are negative questions difficult to answer? On the processing of linguistic contrasts in surveys. *Public Opinion Quarterly, 81*, 613–635.

Kemmelmeier, M. (2016). Cultural differences in survey responding: Issues and insights in the study of response biases. *International Journal of Psychology, 51*, 439–444.

Keusch, F., & Yan, T. (2018). Is satisficing responsible for response order effects in rating scale questions? *Survey Research Methods, 12*(3), 259–270.

(2019). Impact of response scale features on survey responses to factual/behavioral questions. In P. J. Lavrakas et al. (eds.), *Experimental Methods in Survey Research: Techniques that Combine Random Sampling with Random Assignment* (pp. 131–150). Wiley & Sons.

Knäuper, B., Carrière, K., Chamandy, M., Xu, Z., Schwarz, N., & Rosen, N. O. (2016). How aging affects self-reports. *European Journal of Ageing, 13*(2), 185–193.

Krosnick, J. A. (1991). Response strategies for coping with the cognitive demands of attitude measures in surveys. *Applied Cognitive Psychology, 5*, 213–236.

(1999). Survey research. *Annual Review of Psychology, 50*, 537–567.

Krosnick, J. A., & Alwin, D. F. (1987). An evaluation of a cognitive theory of response-order effects in survey measurement. *Public Opinion Quarterly, 51*, 201–219.

Krosnick, J. A., & Presser, S. (2010). Questionnaire design. In J. D. Wright & P. V. Marsden (eds.), *Handbook of Survey Research*, 2nd ed. (pp. 263–313). Elsevier.

Lee, L., Brittingham, A., Tourangeau, R., Willis, G., Ching, P., Jobe, J., & Black, S. (1999). Are reporting errors due to encoding limitations or retrieval failure? Surveys of child vaccination as a case study. *Applied Cognitive Psychology, 13*(1), 43–63.

Lenzner, T., Kaczmirek, L., & Galesic, M. (2011). Seeing through the eyes of the respondent: An eye-tracking study on survey question comprehension. *International Journal of Public Opinion Research, 23*, 361–373.

Liu, M., & Stainback, K. (2013). Interviewer gender effects on survey responses to marriage related questions. *Public Opinion Quarterly, 77*(2), 606–618.

Loftus, E. F., & Marburger, W. (1983). Since the eruption of Mt. St. Helens, has anyone beaten you up? Improving the accuracy of retrospective reports with landmark events. *Memory & Cognition, 11*, 114–120.

Maher, J. P., Rebar, A. L., & Dunton, G. F. (2018). Ecological momentary assessment is a feasible and valid methodological tool to measure older adults' physical activity and sedentary behavior. *Frontiers in Psychology, 9*, 1485.

Maitland, A., & Presser, S. (2016). How accurately do different evaluation methods predict the reliability of survey questions? *Journal of Survey Statistics and Methodology, 4*, 362–381.

(2018). How do question evaluation methods compare in predicting problems observed in typical survey conditions? *Journal of Survey Statistics and Methodology*, 6, 465–490.

Mason, R., Carlson, J. E., & Tourangeau, R. (1994). Contrast effects and subtraction in part–whole questions. *Public Opinion Quarterly*, 58, 569–578.

McCool, D., Schouten, J. D., & Lugtig, P. (2021). An app-assisted travel survey in official statistics: Possibilities and challenges. *Journal of Official Statistics*, 37, 149–170.

McDonald, J. A., Scott, Z. A., and Hanmer, M. J. (2017). Using self-prophecy to combat vote overreporting on public opinion surveys. *Electoral Studies*, 50, 137–141.

Mingay, D., & Greenwell, M. (1989). Memory bias and response-order effects. *Journal of Official Statistics*, 5(3), 253–263.

Neter, J., & Waksberg, J. (1964). A study of response errors in expenditure data from household interviews. *Journal of the American Statistical Association*, 59, 18–55.

Norenzayan, A., & Schwarz, N. (1999). Telling what they want to know: Participants tailor causal attributions to researchers' interests. *European Journal of Social Psychology*, 29, 1011–1020.

Peter, J., & Valkenburg, P. M. (2011). The influence of sexually explicit internet material on sexual risk behavior: A comparison of adolescents and adults. *Journal of Health Communication*, 16(7), 750–765.

Peytchev, A., Conrad, F., Couper, M., & Tourangeau, R. (2010). Increasing respondents' use of definitions in web surveys. *Journal of Official Statistics*, 26, 633–650.

Revilla, M., Saris, W. E., & Krosnick, J. A. (2014). Choosing the number of categories in agree/disagree scales. *Sociological Methods & Research*, 43, 73–97.

Saris, W. E., & Gallhofer, I. (2007a). *Design, Evaluation, and Analysis of Questionnaires for Survey Research*. John Wiley.

(2007b). Estimation of the effects of measurement characteristics on the quality of survey questions. *Survey Research Methods*, 1, 29–43.

Schaeffer, N. C. (1980). Evaluating race-of-interviewer effects in a National Survey. *Sociological Methods and Research*, 8, 400–419.

(1991). Conversation with a purpose or conversation? Interaction in the standardized interview. In P. P. Biemer, R. M. Groves, L. E. Lyberg, N. A. Mathiowetz, & S. Sudman (eds.). *Measurement Errors in Surveys* (pp. 367–391). Wiley & Sons.

Schaeffer, N.C., & Presser, S. (2003). The science of asking questions. *Annual Review of Sociology*, 29, 65–88.

Schober, M. F., & Conrad, F. G. (1997). Does conversational interviewing reduce survey measurement error? *Public Opinion Quarterly*, 61, 576–602.

Schober, M. F., Conrad, F. G., & Fricker, S. S. (2004). Misunderstanding standardized language in research interviews. *Applied Cognitive Psychology*, 18, 169–188.

Schwarz, N. (1997). Questionnaire design: The rocky road from concepts to answers. In L. Lyberg et al. (eds.), *Survey Measurement and Process Quality* (pp. 29–45). Wiley.

(1999). Self-reports: How the questions shape the answers. *American Psychologist*, 54, 93–105.

(2019). Surveys, experiments, and the psychology of self-report. In F. R. Kardes, P. M. Herr, & N. Schwarz (eds.), *Handbook of Research Methods in Consumer Psychology* (pp. 17–40). Routledge. https://doi.org/10.4324/9781351137713-2

Schwarz, N., & Hippler, H. J. (1991). Response alternatives: The impact of their choice and presentation order. In P. Biemer, R. M. Groves, L. E. Lyberg, N. A. Mathiowetz, & S. Sudman (eds.), *Measurement Error in Surveys* (pp. 41–56). Wiley.

Schwarz, N., Hippler, H. J., Deutsch, B., & Strack, F. (1985). Response categories: Effects on behavioral reports and comparative judgments. *Public Opinion Quarterly, 49*, 388–395.

Schwarz, N., Hippler, H. J., & Noelle-Neumann, E. (1992). A cognitive model of response-order effects in survey measurement. In N. Schwarz & S. Sudman (eds.), *Context Effects in Social and Psychological Research*, 187–201. Springer.

Schwarz, N., Knäuper, B., Hippler, H. J., Noelle-Neumann, E., & Clark, F. (1991). Rating scales: Numeric values may change the meaning of scale labels. *Public Opinion Quarterly, 55*, 570–582.

Schwarz, N., Strack, F., & Mai, H. P. (1991). Assimilation and contrast effects in part–whole question sequences: A conversational logic analysis. *Public Opinion Quarterly, 55*, 3–23.

Schwarz, N., Strack, F., Müller, G., & Chassein, B. (1988). The range of response alternatives may determine the meaning of the question: Further evidence on informative functions of response alternatives. *Social Cognition, 6*, 107–117.

Simas, M., Cates, A., & Fucci, A. (2019). Who uses these apps? Paper presented at the Biannual Conference of European Survey Research Association.

Strack, F., Martin, L. L., & Schwarz, N. (1988). Priming and communication: Social determinants of information use in judgments of life satisfaction. *European Journal of Social Psychology, 18*(5), 429–442. https://doi.org/10.1002/ejsp.2420180505

Strack, F., Schwarz, N., & Wänke, M. (1991). Semantic and pragmatic aspects of context effects in social and psychological research. *Social Cognition, 9*, 111–125.

Sudman, S., Bradburn, N. M., & Schwarz, N. (1996). *Thinking about Answers: The Application of Cognitive Processes to Survey Methodology*. Jossey-Bass.

Suessbrick, A. L., Schober, M. F., & Conrad, F. G. (2000). Different respondents interpret ordinary questions quite differently. In *2000 Proceedings of the Section on Survey Research Methods: Papers Presented at the Annual Meeting of the American Statistical Association* (pp. 907–912). American Statistical Association.

Tourangeau, R. (1984). Cognitive science and survey methods. In T. Jabine, M. L. Straf, J. M. Tanur, and R. Tourangeau (eds.), *Cognitive Aspects of Survey Design: Building a Bridge between Disciplines* (pp. 73–100). National Academy Press.

(2000). Remembering what happened: Memory errors and survey reports. In A. A. Stone, J. S. Turkkan, C. A. Bachrach, J. B. Jobe, H. S. Kurtzman, & V. S. Cain (eds.), *The Science of Self-Report: Implications for Research and Practice* (pp. 29–47). Lawrence Erlbaum Associates.

(2018). The survey response process from a cognitive viewpoint. *Quality Assurance in Education, 26*, 169–181.

(2021). Survey reliability: Models, methods, and findings. *Journal of Survey Statistics and Methodology, 9*, 961–991.

Tourangeau R., & Bradburn, N. (2010). The psychology of survey response. In J. D. Wright & P. V. Marsden (eds.), *Handbook of Survey Research*, 2nd ed. (pp. 315–346). Elsevier.

Tourangeau, R., Couper, M. P., & Conrad, F. (2007). Color, labels, and interpretive heuristics for response scales. *Public Opinion Quarterly, 71*(1), 91–112. https://doi.org/10.1093/poq/nfl046

Tourangeau, R., Maitland, A., Steiger, D., & Yan, T. (2020). A framework for making decisions about question evaluation methods. In P. Beatty et al. (eds.). *Advances in Questionnaire Design, Development, Evaluation and Testing* (pp. 47–73). Wiley.

Tourangeau, R., & Rasinski, K. (1988). Cognitive processes underlying context effects in attitude measurement. *Psychological Bulletin, 103*, 299–314.

Tourangeau, R., Rasinski, K. A., & Bradburn, N. (1991). Measuring happiness in surveys: A test of the subtraction hypothesis. *Public Opinion Quarterly, 55*, 255–266.

Tourangeau, R., Rips, L. J., & Rasinski, K. (2000). *The Psychology of Survey Response*. Cambridge University Press.

Tourangeau, R., & Smith, T. W. (1996). Asking sensitive questions: The impact of data collection mode, question format, and question context. *Public Opinion Quarterly, 60*, 275–304.

Tourangeau, R., Smith, T. W., & Rasinski, K. (1997). Motivation to report sensitive behaviors on surveys: Evidence from a bogus pipeline experiment. *Journal of Applied Social Psychology, 27*, 209–222.

Tourangeau, R., Sun, H., & Yan, T. (2021). Comparing methods for assessing reliability. *Journal of Survey Statistics and Methodology, 9*, 651–673.

Tourangeau, R., & Yan, T. (2007). Sensitive questions in surveys. *Psychological Bulletin, 133*, 859–883.

Tourangeau, R., Yan, T., & Sun, H. (2020). Who can you count on? Understanding the determinants of reliability. *Journal of Survey Statistics and Methodology, 8*, 903–931.

Van Vaerenbergh, Y., & Thomas, T. (2013). Response styles in survey research: A literature review of antecedents, consequences and remedies. *International Journal of Public Opinion Research, 25*(3), 195–217.

US Bureau of Labor Statistics. (n.d.). *Consumer Expenditure Surveys* [webpage]. www.bls.gov/cex

US Department of Agriculture. (n.d.). *FoodAPS National Household Food Acquisition and Purchase Survey* [webpage]. www.ers.usda.gov/data-products/foodaps-national-household-food-acquisition-and-purchase-survey

West, B. T., & Blom, A. G. (2017). Explaining interviewer effects: A research synthesis. *Journal of Survey Statistics and Methodology, 5*, 175–211.

Yan, T. (2006). How successful I am depends on what number I get: The effects of numerical scale labels and the need for cognition on survey responses. In *2006 Proceedings of the Section on Survey Research Methods: Papers Presented at the Annual Meeting of the American Statistical Association* (pp. 4262–4269). American Statistical Association.

(2017). Survey questionnaire design. In N. Balakrishnan et al. (eds.), *Wiley StatsRef: Statistics Reference Online*. John Wiley & Sons. https://doi.org/10.1002/9781118445112.stat06642.pub2

(2021). Consequences of asking sensitive questions. *Annual Review of Statistics and Its Application, 8*, 109–127.

Yan, T., & Cantor, D. (2019). Asking survey questions about criminal justice involvement. *Public Health Reports, 134*, 46s–56s.

Yan, T., & Keusch, F. (2015). The effects of the direction of rating scales on survey responses in a telephone survey. *Public Opinion Quarterly, 79*, 145–165.

Yan, T., Keusch, F., & He, L. (2018). The impact of question and scale characteristics on scale direction effects. *Survey Practice, 11*(2). https://doi.org/10.29115/SP-2018-0008

Yan, T., Kreuter, F., & Tourangeau, R. (2012). Latent class analysis of response inconsistencies across modes of data collection. *Social Science Research, 41*, 1017–1027.

Yan, T., Machado, J., Simas, M., Heller, A., & Denbaly, M. (2019). The feasibility of using smartphones to record food purchase and acquisition. Paper presented at the Annual Conference of the American Association of Public Opinion Research.

Yan, T., & Tourangeau, R. (2008). Fast times and easy questions: The effects of age, experience, and question complexity on web survey response times. *Applied Cognitive Psychology*, *22*, 51–68. https://doi.org/10.1002/acp.1331

(2022). Detecting underreporters of abortions and miscarriages in the National Study of Family Growth, 2011–2015. *PLOS ONE*, *17*(8), e0271288. https://doi.org/10.1371/journal.pone.0271288.

16 Question and Questionnaire Design

Sierra Davis Thomander and Jon A. Krosnick

Abstract

The process of questionnaire design has been done intuitively by investigators for decades despite a large literature being available to guide the process to yield maximally reliable and valid measurement tools. This chapter offers two conceptual frameworks involving (1) the cognitive processes involved in answering questions optimally, and (2) conversational conventions that govern everyday communication. We use these frameworks to explain a range of empirical evidence documenting the impact of question manipulations on responses. Topics covered include open vs. closed questions, rating vs. ranking, rating scale length and scale point labels, acquiescence response bias, multiple select questions, response order effects, treatment of non-substantive response options, social desirability response bias, question wording and order, questionnaire length, and considerations for internet surveys. In all, we provide a set of best practices that should be useful to all researchers.

Keywords: Questionnaires, Questions, Survey Methods, Measurement

Questionnaires have been used by social and behavioral scientists for at least a century to gather information. Questionnaire design has been done in remarkably varied ways. And numerous studies have shown that small changes in question wording, formatting, and order can substantially change findings; so design choices are consequential. Just as telescopes reveal details about the universe, questionnaires reveal details about people's thinking and action. Yet questionnaires cannot do this clearly if the "lens" of the question is dirty. Just as astronomers clean lenses after investing in an expensive telescope, so too should social scientists ensure that their questionnaires provide precise measurements. This chapter provides empirically based guidelines on how to do so.

For many decades, research methods textbooks have offered guidelines, yet these guidelines were largely based on intuition without empirical validation. For example, researchers have been advised to use simple, familiar words/phrases while avoiding technical terms, jargon, and slang (e.g., Poffenberger, 1932; Oppenheim, 1992). Other recommendations have been to use simple syntax with proper grammar (e.g., Saris & Gallhofer, 2014), avoid words with ambiguous meanings (e.g., Tourangeau et al., 2000), make response options exhaustive and mutually exclusive (Salant & Dillman, 1994), avoid leading or loaded questions that push respondents toward an answer (e.g., Oppenheim, 1992), avoid single and double negations (e.g., Edwards, 1957), make early questions easy and pleasant to answer so as to build rapport with respondents (e.g., Brace, 2018, pp. 45–48), group questions on the same topic together (e.g., Dillman, 2000), ask general questions before specific questions on the same topic (e.g., Mathers et al., 2007), ask sensitive questions at the end of a questionnaire (e.g., Tourangeau et al., 2000), and include filter questions to avoid asking inapplicable questions (e.g., de Vaus, 2016, p. 208).

This sort of advice leaves unaddressed many decisions that questionnaire designers must make. In this chapter, we outline what 100 years of research have shown about best practices in questionnaire design to maximize reliability and validity. We begin by offering two theoretical perspectives that constitute a useful foundation for understanding a range of empirical evidence and, on that basis, offer guidelines for optimal design decisions.

Cognitive Processes

Decades ago, psychologists proposed accounts of the cognitive processes underlying optimal question answering (e.g., Cannell et al., 1981; Tourangeau & Rasinski 1988). When answering questions, respondents are thought to execute four steps. First, they must identify the intent of a question. Second, they must search their memories for all relevant information. Third, they must integrate whatever information comes to mind into a single judgment in a balanced way. Finally, respondents must translate that judgment into a response.

Because each step requires cognitive effort, respondents must be sufficiently motivated to expend that effort. The more motivated respondents are, the more likely they are to execute the four steps comprehensively and in an unbiased manner. When a respondent performs the necessary cognitive tasks ideally, the respondent is *optimizing*. Unfortunately, not all respondents do this. Some people may agree to complete a questionnaire due to a relatively automatic compliance process (e.g., Cialdini, 1993), financial inducement, or external requirement. Thus, they may merely agree to provide answers yet lack intrinsic motivation to make those answers high-quality. Other respondents may satisfy whatever desires motivated them to participate after answering earlier questions yet later grow fatigued, uninterested, or distracted.

To avoid expending the effort needed for optimal answering, respondents may take subtle shortcuts. They may execute all four steps, but less diligently than when optimizing – a process called *weak satisficing* (Krosnick, 1991). Alternatively, respondents may take dramatic shortcuts, skipping the retrieval and judgment steps altogether (e.g., reading questions superficially and selecting seemingly reasonable answers). Rather than basing answer choices on relevant internal psychological cues, respondents may look to question wording for a cue – pointing to a response that is easily selected (and easily defended, if necessary). Absent such a cue, respondents may arbitrarily select an answer. We call this behavior *strong satisficing* (Krosnick,

1991). Optimizing and strong satisficing are the two ends of a continuum indicating how thoroughly respondents perform the four response steps.

Three major factors determine a person's likelihood to satisfice when answering a question: task difficulty, respondent ability, and respondent motivation (Krosnick, 1991). Task difficulty is a function of question-specific attributes (e.g., the difficulty of question interpretation or retrieval of requested information) and attributes of questionnaire administration (e.g., interviewer pace). Ability derives from the extent to which respondents can adeptly perform complex mental operations, are practiced at thinking about the particular question topic, and are equipped with preformulated judgments on the relevant issue. Motivation is influenced by (1) the personality attribute called need for cognition (Cacioppo et al., 1996), (2) accountability, a state created by informing respondents that they will be asked to justify answers, (3) the degree to which the topic of a question is personally important, (4) the respondent's beliefs about whether the survey will have useful consequences, (5) respondent fatigue (e.g., Bowling et al., 2021), and (6) aspects of questionnaire administration process that encourage optimizing (e.g., interviewer behavior).

This understanding of optimizing and satisficing provides a basis for evaluating questionnaire design choices. Generally, efforts to minimize task difficulty and maximize respondent motivation are likely to pay off by minimizing satisficing and maximizing the accuracy of self-reports. The theory of satisficing provides a useful framework for understanding why some design decisions can improve answer quality, as we shall see.

Conversational Norms and Conventions

Conversational norms and conventions provide another useful framework that informs best practices, because the process of answering a questionnaire is functionally equivalent to participating in a conversation between two people: the researcher and the respondent. In general, people follow certain conversational patterns to effectively communicate: conversational norms (rules speakers follow and assume listeners follow that communicate additional information) and conversational conventions (arbitrary customs speakers follow that communicate no additional information). Deviating from these conversational patterns can lead to confusion, distraction, and misunderstanding. Despite this, a remarkable number of questionnaires do indeed deviate – putting measurements at risk (e.g., Dumitrescu & Martinsson, 2016).

Open versus Closed Questions

Whether to make questions open-ended (permitting respondents to answer in their own words) or closed-ended (requiring respondents to select an answer from a given choice set) is a crucial decision. Researchers commonly opt for closed questions because of time and money savings, easier analysis, respondent preferences, and less bias from interviewer probing and coding. However, open questions have been shown to yield superior measurements of some constructs. First, open questions better measure quantities (e.g., "How many times last year did you visit the zoo?") because respondents must first answer numerically in their own mind in order to then select from offered answer choices (e.g., fewer than 2 times, 3–5 times). Furthermore, offering a set of ranges can nudge respondents toward the middle range due to conversational conventions; respondents assume that the middle range is the most common or optimal answer (Schwarz et al., 1985). Thus, open questions are preferable to closed items for measuring quantities.

Open questions are also optimal for measuring categorical or nominal judgments (e.g., "What is the most important problem facing the country today?") if a researcher does not know the universe of possible answers respondents might offer. It might seem appealing to offer a set of answer choices and then offer an "other" option. However, this approach is generally ineffective; respondents tend to restrict their answers to the explicitly offered substantive choices due to conversational conventions (Lindzey & Guest, 1951; Schuman & Scott, 1987). The advantage of open questions is especially likely in interviewer-administered surveys that avoid the burden of respondents having to type lengthy open-ended answers (e.g., Mavletova, 2013).

Furthermore, answering a closed question of this type again requires the respondent to answer the open version of the question first in his or her own mind, so simply reporting that initial open-ended answer is simpler for respondents. Researchers should measure categorical variables with closed categorical questions only if the answer choice set is comprehensive. This will usually require large-scale pretesting with an open version of the question and a representative sample of the population of interest.

Some researchers might be tempted to include examples in open-ended questions to clarify the acceptable answer type (e.g., "What is your ancestry or ethnic origin? For example: German, Polish, Brazilian, etc."). Examples may clarify intended scope or specificity (e.g., food categories, types of wine) or remind respondents of easily forgotten yet applicable answers (e.g., calories consumed in beverages rather than just food; Tourangeau et al., 2014, 2017). However, the conversational conventions perspective cautions against offering examples because they are likely to bias respondent attention on the provided examples.

In addition to measuring opinions, questionnaires sometimes administer quiz questions in order to assess levels of respondent knowledge. Mondak (2001) found that open questions measuring political knowledge were more valid when respondents were encouraged to answer even in the face of uncertainty (see also Sturgis et al., 2008; Tourangeau et al., 2016). Therefore, open questions are preferable for measuring knowledge.

Ratings vs. Rankings

Researchers are often interested in the way respondents rank competing objects, such as candidates running for President or brands of toothpaste. Questionnaires may ask respondents directly to implement a ranking task to tap this ordering directly, but such ranking is often time-intensive and cognitively challenging for respondents. Therefore, some researchers ask not for complete rankings of all objects and instead ask respondents to identify the one, two, or three products, for example, that he or she is most likely to purchase. Even so, the practical challenges of ranking tempt some researchers to ask respondents instead to rate each of the competing options (e.g., in terms of likelihood of voting for the person or likelihood of purchasing the product), allowing derivation of rankings. However, empirical evidence shows that rankings yield higher data quality than do ratings in contexts where life forces choices, such as when parents must decide what values to emphasize during child-rearing or when voters must vote for only one candidate (Alwin & Krosnick, 1985; Krosnick & Alwin, 1988; Miethe, 1985; Wright et al., 2012). Rankings outperform ratings partly because satisficing causes some respondents to answer a battery of ratings by selecting the same point over and over, thus failing to differentiate the objects from one another.

In contexts where life does not force choices (e.g., a person can like chicken and beef equally), rating the individual objects is preferred. However, there are at least two inherent dangers to watch out for. First, different respondents interpret the meanings of rating scale points differently, so two people who actually view an object identically might nonetheless give different ratings to that object. In addition, non-differentiation due to satisficing masks differences between objects in the mind of the respondent. Therefore, steps should be taken to minimize the difficulty of the questions and to maximize motivation to optimize – to minimize non-differentiation when batteries of rating questions are asked.

Researchers have sometimes administered both rating and ranking tasks to force differentiation and measure absolute evaluations of objects. For example, the *least-most* method offered respondents a list of objects and asked them to pick the two objects with the most and least of some attribute, followed by rating the entire set of objects (see, e.g., Smyth et al., 2018). When implementing the *rank-then-rate* method, respondents first rank items, then rate each item as usual. Both methods provide more differentiation and less "end-piling" toward one end of the scale than simple rating procedures (McCarty and Shrum, 1997, 2000).

The rise of internet survey data collection facilitates the use of ranking tasks because dynamic visual displays can overcome challenges posed by paper questionnaires or oral administration. Specifically, when a long list of objects is to be considered and ranked, hearing and holding the list in working memory can be challenging; visual display obviates the need for that. Furthermore, software can make an item disappear from a screen after a respondent ranks it, making the remaining list of items to be ranked shorter and shorter. This is preferable to a static list presented on a paper questionnaire.

Number of Points on Rating Scales and Labels for Those Points

Rating scales may range from just two points (e.g., "Do you like or dislike pizza?") to more than one hundred points (e.g., the American National Election Study's

101-point feeling thermometers). And labels for points on rating scales can be numbers, words, graphics, or some combination (e.g., labeling endpoints verbally and labeling all points with numbers or with emojis). In this section, we review relevant literature.

Theory

Rating scales should be designed so that respondents can interpret scale point meanings with ease and clarity and interpret the meaning of each scale point identically. As much as possible, labels should validly differentiate respondents from one another. Finally, a rating scale should include points that correspond to all relevant points on the underlying construct's continuum (e.g., Beckstead, 2014).

Number of Scale Points

A literature exists helping to guide the choice of scale point length. Increasing the number of scale points from two to three to four etc. improves reliability, but gains slow down and eventually stop as scales get longer and longer (e.g., Givon & Shapira, 1984; Lissitz & Green, 1975). Likewise, validity improves with increasing scale length (e.g., Matell & Jacoby, 1971; Schuman & Presser, 1981, pp. 175–176), though gains level off with increasing scale length (Green & Rao, 1970; Lehmann & Hulbert, 1972; Lissitz & Green, 1975; Martin, 1973). Taken together, the body of available evidence suggests using five points for unipolar scales (where the conceptual zero point, meaning none of the construct, is at one end, such as "not at all certain") and seven points for bipolar scales (where the zero point is in the middle, in scales ranging from "like a great deal" to "dislike a great deal," where "neither like nor dislike," the zero point, is in the middle).

Middle Alternatives

Middle alternatives can take a few forms, including a "neither" option or a "status quo" endorsement (e.g., government spending on the military should stay the same rather than being increased or decreased). Importantly, offering midpoints does not encourage satisficing (e.g., Krosnick et al., 1997; Truebner, 2021). Some respondents truly belong at the midpoint, and forcing those people to take a side leads them to just select a point near the implied scale midpoint (Schuman & Presser, 1981; Krosnick, 2002) and yields random measurement error (O'Muircheartaigh et al., 2000). Omitting the middle alternative does not improve data quality for unipolar scales and compromises data quality for bipolar questions (Wang & Krosnick, 2020). This evidence reinforces support for five-point unipolar and seven-point bipolar scales.

Sliders

An alternative approach used by some researchers is what are sometimes called "slider scales" or "visual analog scales" that use graphic displays on computer screens to offer an infinite number of scale points. Sliders may feel novel and high-tech (Chyung et al., 2018), but ratings are biased toward the initial pointer position offered to respondents and by labels and decorations (Matejka et al., 2016). Sliders also have higher break-off rates and longer response times (Funke et al., 2011; Liu & Conrad, 2019), so sliders are best avoided.

Verbal Labels

The accumulated evidence suggests that rating scales are best designed with verbal labels on all points and numbers on none. In addition, some studies demonstrated higher reliability when all points are labeled with words than when only the end points are labeled (e.g., Krosnick & Berent, 1993; Peters & McCormick, 1966). More verbal labels also yield greater validity (e.g., Krosnick & Berent, 1993; Peters & McCormick, 1966; Wedell et al., 1990). Respondents also prefer fully verbally labeled scale points (e.g., Dickinson & Zellinger, 1980). Finally, verbal labels also perform best across survey modes.

Scales with more verbal labels also take less time to complete and administer than entirely numerically labeled scales (e.g., Menold, 2020). For example, removing verbal labels in favor of numeric labels in web surveys (to save screen space) increases time spent and causes respondents to cluster at the verbally labeled scale endpoints (Gummer & Kunz, 2021). Furthermore, combining numeric and verbal labeling often causes more harm than good when the meanings of the words and numbers contradict one another due to conversational conventions (e.g., Schwarz et al., 1991; Schwarz & Hippler, 1991). In sum, the most valid and reliable rating scales have verbal labels on all scale points, avoid overly specific or lengthy verbal labels, and have no numbers (Saris & Gallhofer, 2014).

Selecting Verbal Labels

Ideally, verbal labels are equally spaced and provide clear meaning to respondents. Past research has asked people to translate verbal phrases into numbers, revealing the meanings ascribed to those phrases. Based on the results of those studies, for unipolar scales, the modifiers "extremely, very, moderately, slightly, not at all," and "a great deal, a lot, a moderate amount, a little, none at all" work well. For bipolar scales, the modifiers "extremely, moderately, slightly" can be used (e.g., extremely good, moderately good, slightly good, neither good nor bad, slightly bad, moderately bad, extremely bad). Another workable scale is "like a great deal, like a moderate amount, like a little, neither like nor dislike, dislike a little, etc." If one wishes to ascertain judgments of quality using five points, "excellent, good, fair, poor, very poor" are about equally spaced (see Krosnick & Fabrigar, forthcoming).

Ratings on dimensions with no natural metric (e.g., importance, friendliness, liking) must be measured with rating scales. However, dimensions with natural metrics (e.g., frequency, amount, size) should not be measured using rating scales composed of "vague quantifiers" (e.g., "moderately often," "quite heavy") and should instead be measured with open-ended questions tapping the natural metric (e.g., 5 days a week, 18 pounds). People's interpretations of the meanings of vague quantifiers vary across people and contexts (Budescu & Wallsten, 1985; Lichtenstein & Newman, 1967; Theil, 2002) and communicate biasing expectations, both for respondents and researchers.

One unresolved issue is whether to measure perceived probabilities with numbers (e.g., a 70% chance) or verbal labels (e.g., "very likely"). Regardless, if one does elicit probability judgments on a scale from 0% to 100%, it is important to recognize that some respondents select 50 to convey "don't know" rather than a 50% probability. Therefore, people who select 50 should be asked whether they said that because they truly meant 50% or because they meant they don't know the probability (Wallsten et al., 1993).

Branching

Questions with bipolar rating scales benefit from branching (i.e., the conversion of one question into two), because they improve reliability and validity and take less time to answer (Krosnick and Berent, 1993). Branching questions begin with a question asking on which side of neutral an attitude falls (e.g., positive or negative, increase or decrease), and then another question ascertains extremity (e.g., extremely, moderately, or slightly, or a great deal, a moderate amount, or a little). Thus, rather than offering seven response options all at once to a respondent and asking him or her to choose one of them, respondents are asked two questions that sequentially place respondents into one of seven ordinal categories.

Acquiescence Response Bias

We turn next to three common sets of answer choices for survey questions: agree-disagree, true-false, and yes/no questions. The first two of these question types involve making a statement to the respondent and asking for a reaction to that statement (e.g., "Soccer is the best sport"). Yes-no questions also focus on one point of view, such as "Do you favor increasing taxes on soda?" Such questions are fatally flawed by acquiescence response bias – the tendency to endorse assertions regardless of content. More people agree with an assertion than disagree with the opposite assertion, despite the questions appearing to be mirror images of one another. That is, more respondents will *agree* with the statement "I *like* pineapple" than will *disagree* with the statement "I *dislike* pineapple" (e.g., Javeline, 1999; Schuman & Presser, 1981).

This seems to occur as the result of satisficing (see Krosnick, 1991), conversational norms (Grice, 1975), social conditioning to avoid confrontation (Leech, 1983), a desire to defer to higher-status individuals (Lenski & Leggett, 1960), or a general personality disposition of agreeableness (e.g., Billiet & Davidov, 2008). Acquiescence and other problems undermine the performance of these three question formats (see Krosnick & Fabrigar, 1999 for review; Saris et al., 2010), so researchers should instead use balanced construct-specific response options that mention the construct being measured explicitly, as in: "Have you ever purchased a car, or have you never done that?" (e.g., Shaeffer et al., 2005).

Multiple Select Questions

When requesting similar evaluations of a series of items (e.g., which magazines a respondent read), researchers can use what is called a multiple select question format (e.g., "Which of the following magazines have you read? Check all that apply") or may instead ask a series of separate balanced, forced-choice questions (e.g., "Did you read magazine X, or did you not do that? Did you read magazine Y, or did you not do that?"). Reliability is higher when using balanced forced-choice questions (Dolnicar et al., 2012), and this format encourages deeper processing (Smyth et al., 2008), so it is preferable.

Response Order Effects

The order in which response options are presented to respondents can also affect people's answers. Some studies have documented primacy effects (i.e., earlier presented response options are selected more often), and others documented recency effects (i.e., the last or later presented response options are selected more often); some documented no order effects. Satisficing theory explains this body of evidence well (e.g., Krosnick, 1999). Weak satisficers select the first reasonable response option offered by categorical questions that they consider, yielding primacy effects with visual presentation (e.g., Becker, 1954; Bishop et al., 1988; Krosnick & Alwin, 1987; Schwarz et al., 1992; Smyth et al., 2019) and recency effects under oral presentation (e.g., Berg & Rapaport, 1954; Bishop et al., 1988; Krosnick, 1992; McClendon, 1986; Schuman & Presser, 1981; Schwarz et al., 1992). However, when using rating scales, weak satisficers manifest primacy effects regardless of presentation mode (e.g., Carp, 1974; Chan, 1991; Kalton et al., 1978; Mingay & Greenwell, 1989; Quinn & Belson, 1969).

Randomization across respondents of the order of response options can be done with categorical questions. As with rating scales, each respondent may be randomly assigned to receive either one order or the reverse. However, randomizing and rotating create systematic measurement error, so multivariate analyses should model and control for this error. However, researchers should not vary order across respondents if doing so will violate conversational norms (Holbrook et al., 2000) or if predicting a non-survey behavior wherein options are presented in a particular order (e.g., voting on ballots that list candidate names in alphabetical order).

Non-Substantive Response Options (NSROs)

How should people answer a question when they lack any relevant knowledge required to do so? Ideally, these people will indicate as much, but they may instead wish to appear informed, opting to answer substantively to convey a desired image of themselves (Converse, 1964). To discourage this behavior, researchers have often offered NSROs (non-substantive response options), such as "don't know" (e.g., Converse & Presser, 1986). Explicitly offering NSROs gives respondents permission to say they lack relevant knowledge or opinion. However, a large body of evidence indicates that NSRO selection typically results not from a genuine lack of opinions but more often from satisficing as well as question ambiguity, ambivalence, intimidation, and self-image protection (see Krosnick, 2002; also Fonda, 1951; Johanson et al., 1993; Rosenberg et al., 1955).

Pressing respondents to report their opinions can reveal valuable information, yet NSROs discourage just that. Best practice is to avoid NSROs and instead ask follow-up questions about the strength of attitudes and opinions (e.g., Krosnick, 2002; Krosnick et al. 2002; Visser et al., 2000). Instead of offering NSROs, opinion questions should be followed by questions measuring the strength of those opinions (see Krosnick et al., 1993 and Wegener et al., 1995 for further discussion).

Social Desirability

In the course of daily life, people take steps to create images of themselves in the eyes of others and in their own minds (Goffman, 1959; Schlenker & Weingold, 1989). Because a favorable image can increase social rewards and reduce social punishments, people are generally motivated in these ways (see Paulhus, 1984, 1986). Many social and behavioral science studies have reported evidence that researchers claimed documented social desirability response bias in self-reports, such as in reports of voter turnout (e.g., Belli et al., 1999) or racial attitudes (e.g., Finkel et al., 1991). However, a careful look at these studies reveals that they often did not provide definitive evidence of intentional misreporting by respondents. For example, what seems to be voter misreporting is attributable to higher rates of non-response in surveys among non-voters than among voters (for a review, see Berent et al., 2016). Furthermore, evidence that more convincingly documents intentional misreporting often documents very little bias.

Nonetheless, a variety of techniques have been explored to minimize social desirability response bias. For example, administering questionnaires anonymously can increase reporting of socially undesirable characteristics (Paulhus, 1984; Gordon, 1987) but also causes less respondent effort in reporting and less accuracy of reports (Lelkes et al., 2012). The *randomized response technique* (Warner, 1965) asks a respondent to answer one of two questions (determined by a secret coin flip done by the respondent) and derives the distribution of respondent attributes on a socially sensitive topic mathematically from the responses obtained. However, this method has been shown not to work well either (Holbrook & Krosnick, 2010). The Implicit Association Test and the Affect Misattribution Procedure are popular alternatives, but questions have been raised about these procedures as well (Clayton et al., 2021; Ditonto et al., 2013).

A more effective technique is the *item count technique* (e.g., Blair & Imai, 2012; Tourangeau and Yan, 2007). Respondents read or hear a list of items and are asked to say how many of those items have a particular characteristic. For example, some respondents (chosen randomly) can be asked how many (not which) of the following make them angry: waiting in long lines at stores, hearing politicians give speeches they disagree with, and seeing people allowing their dogs to run freely in areas that require leashes at all times. Other respondents are also asked how many items make them angry, but the list of items has an addition, such as "affirmative action to increase college admissions of African Americans." By comparing the average number given by respondents who read or hear the short list and the long list, it is possible to compute the proportion of respondents who are angered by affirmative action, even though no respondents ever explicitly reported disapproving of that policy.

Another approach is to explicitly legitimize socially undesirable responses by telling respondents that socially undesirable responses are acceptable (e.g., "In talking to people about elections, we often find that a lot of people were not able to vote because they weren't registered, were sick, or just didn't have time"). This sort of wording increases reports of presumably undesirable behaviors but has not been shown to increase validity of reports (Holbrook and Krosnick 2010). Another approach is to ask multiple questions allowing respondents to report socially desirable attributes before being asked to report an undesirable attribute (e.g., Belli et al., 1999), but no evidence yet shows this technique to eliminate social desirability response bias either.

Question Wording

Once all of the above-discussed decisions have been made about item structure, researchers must then choose specific words to express the ideas of interest in questions. In general, the existing literature suggests choosing words that have unambiguous meanings (rather than two or more different definitions), that are familiar to people, and that have fewer letters and syllables. Furthermore, sentences in questions should have the fewest words necessary to convey the intended idea clearly and uniformly to respondents. Likewise, questions should include as few sentences as are needed to convey ideas as intended. This means that shorter questions are not necessarily superior to longer ones – the optimal length is the shortest length needed to convey ideas effectively (see Lenzner, 2012). Gauging effectiveness of communication with questions can be usefully done by cognitive pretesting (e.g., Willis, 2005).

Question Order

A number of past studies have demonstrated that asking one question can change answers to later questions. Fortunately, though, Smith's (1988) large-scale analysis of many experiments showed that "overall the number of [question order] effects ... are minuscule; 11–12 probable order effects out of over 500 variables."

Likewise, a similar analysis by Schuman and Presser (1981) with 113 experiments found 8 statistically significant question order effects. Therefore, the threat of question order effects appears to be quite minimal.

Consistent with satisficing theory, respondent fatigue grows as more and more questions have been answered; so the risk of satisficing increases accordingly (see, e.g., Backor et al., 2007). Therefore, researchers are incentivized to ask as few questions as are needed. Researchers sometimes believe it is necessary to measure a single construct with a long battery of questions, such as Rosenberg's (1965) 10-item self-esteem battery. Fortunately, a growing literature is showing that single-item measurement can work quite well (e.g., see Brailovskaia & Margraf, 2020; Riordan et al., 2018; Robins et al., 2001).

Conclusion

This chapter provides guidance for optimal questionnaire design. We have offered evidence-based recommendations ranging from optimal design of rating scale points to managing response choice order effects. The two guiding conceptual frameworks, the theory of satisficing and norms of conversation, not only help explain and justify the advice provided here but also constitute useful tools for guiding other design decisions. By creating conditions that minimize satisficing (i.e., increasing motivation and minimizing task difficulty), reliability and validity may be improved. In addition, by respecting conversational norms and conventions, questionnaire designers can avoid confusing, distracting, and misleading respondents. More generally, by following best practices, researchers can maximize the return on their investment in collecting and analyzing data with questionnaires.

References

Alwin, D. F., & Krosnick, J. A. (1985). The measurement of values in surveys: A comparison of ratings and rankings. *Public Opinion Quarterly, 49*, 535–552.

Backor, K., Golde, S., & Nie, N. (2007). Estimating survey fatigue in time use study. Paper presented at the 2007 International Association for Time Use Research Conference, Washington, DC.

Becker, S. L. (1954). Why an order effect. *Public Opinion Quarterly, 18*, 271–278.

Beckstead, J. W. (2014). On measurements and their quality: Verbal anchors and the number of response options in rating scales. *International Journal of Nursing Studies, 51*, 807–814.

Belli, R. F., Traugott, M. W., Young, M., & McGonagle, K. A. (1999). Reducing vote overreporting in surveys: Social desirability, memory failure, and source monitoring. *Public Opinion Quarterly, 63*, 90–108.

Berent, M. K., Krosnick, J. A., & Lupia, A. (2016). Measuring voter registration and turnout in surveys. *Public Opinion Quarterly, 80*, 597–621.

Berg, I. A., & Rapaport, G. M. (1954). Response bias in an unstructured questionnaire. *Journal of Psychology, 38*, 475–481.

Billiet, J. B., & Davidov, E. (2008). Testing the stability of an acquiescence style factor behind two interrelated substantive variables in a panel design. *Sociological Methods & Research*, *36*, 542–562.

Bishop, G. F., Hippler, H. J., Schwarz, N., & Strack, F. (1988). A comparison of response effects in self-administered and telephone surveys. In R. M. Groves, P. P. Biemer, L. E. Lyberg, J. T. Massey, W. L. Nicholls II, & J. Waksberg (eds.), *Telephone Survey Methodology* (pp. 321–340). Wiley.

Blair, G., & Imai, K. (2012). Statistical analysis of list experiments. *Political Analysis*, *20*, 47–77.

Bowling, N. A., Gibson, A. M., Houpt, J. W., & Brower, C. K. (2021). Will the questions ever end? Person-level increases in careless responding during questionnaire completion. *Organizational Research Methods*, *24*, 718–738.

Brace, I. (2018). *Questionnaire Design: How* to Plan, Structure, and Write Survey Material for Effective Market Research, 4th ed. Kogan Page.

Brailovskaia, J., & Margraf, J. (2020). How to measure self-esteem with one item? Validation of the German Single-Item Self-Esteem Scale (G-SISE). *Current Psychology*, *39*, 2192–2202.

Budescu, D. V., & Wallsten, T. S. (1985). Consistency in interpretation of probabilistic phrases. *Organizational Behavior and Human Decision Processes*, *36*, 391–405.

Cacioppo, J. T., Petty, R. E., Feinstein, J. A., & Jarvis, W. B. G. (1996). Dispositional differences in cognitive motivation: The life and times of individuals varying in need for cognition. *Psychological Bulletin*, *119*, 197–253.

Cannell, C. F., Miller, P.V., & Oksenberg, L. (1981). Research on interviewing techniques. *Sociological Methodology*, *11*, 389–437.

Carp, F. M. (1974). Position effects in single trial free recall. *Journal of Gerontology*, *29*, 581–587.

Chan, J. C. (1991). Response-order effects in Likert-type scales. *Educational and Psychological Measurement*, *51*, 531–540.

Chyung, S. Y., Swanson, I., Roberts, K., & Hankinson, A. (2018). Evidence-based survey design: The use of continuous rating scales in surveys. *Performance Improvement*, *57*, 38–48.

Cialdini, R. B. (1993). *Influence: Science and Practice*, 3rd ed. HarperCollins.

Clayton, K., Horrillo, J., and Sniderman, P. (2021). The BIAT and the AMP As measures of racial prejudice in political science: A methodological assessment. *SSRN*. https://doi.org/10.2139/ssrn.3744338.

Converse, J. M., & Presser, S. (1986). *Survey Questions: Handcrafting the Standardized Questionnaire*. SAGE Publications.

Converse, P. E. (1964). The nature of belief systems in mass publics. In D. E. Apter (ed.), *Ideology and Discontent* (pp. 206–261). Free Press.

de Vaus, D. (2016). Survey research. In T. Greenfield & S. Greener (eds.), *Research Methods for Postgraduates*, 3rd ed. (pp. 202–213). Wiley & Sons.

Dickinson, T. L., & Zellinger, P. M. (1980). A comparison of the behaviorally anchored rating mixed standard scale formats. *Journal of Applied Psychology*, *65*, 147–154.

Dillman, D. A. (2000). *Mail and Internet Surveys: The Tailored Design Method*, 2nd ed. Wiley.

Ditonto, T. M., Lau, R. R., & Sears, D. O. (2013). AMPing racial attitudes: Comparing the power of explicit and implicit racism measures in 2008. *Political Psychology*, *34*(4), 487–510.

Dolnicar, S., Rossiter, J. R., & Grün, B. (2012). "Pick any" measures contaminate brand image studies. *International Journal of Market Research, 54*, 821–834.

Dumitrescu, D., & Martinsson, J. (2016). Surveys as a social experience: The lingering effects of survey design choices on respondents' survey experience and subsequent optimizing behavior. *International Journal of Public Opinion Research, 28*, 534–561.

Edwards, A. L. (1957). *Techniques of Attitude Scale Construction*. Appleton-Century-Crofts.

Finkel, S. E., Guterbock, T. M., & Borg, M. J. (1991). Race-of-interviewer effects in a pre-election poll: Virginia 1989. *Public Opinion Quarterly, 55*, 313–330.

Fonda, C. P. (1951). The nature and meaning of the Rorschach white space response. *Journal of Abnormal Social Psychology, 46*, 367–377.

Funke, F., Reips, U., & Thomas, R. K. (2011). Sliders for the smart: Type of rating scale on the Web interacts with educational level. *Social Science Computer Review, 29*, 221–231.

Givon, M. M., & Shapira, Z. (1984). Response to rating scales: A theoretical model and its application to the number of categories problem. *Journal of Marketing Research, 21*, 410–419.

Goffman, E. (1959). *The Presentation of Self in Everyday Life*. Doubleday/Anchor.

Gordon, R. A. (1987). Social desirability bias: A demonstration and technique for its reduction. *Teaching of Psychology, 14*, 40–42.

Green, P. E., & Rao, V. R. (1970). Rating scales and information recovery: How many scales and response categories to use? *Journal of Marketing, 34*, 33–39.

Grice, P. (1975). Logic and Conversation. In P. Cole & J. Morgan (eds.), *Syntax and Semantics*, vol. 3: *Speech Acts* (pp. 41–58). Academic Press.

Gummer, T., & Kunz, T. (2021). Using only numeric labels instead of verbal labels: Stripping rating scales to their bare minimum in Web surveys. *Social Science Computer Review, 39*, 1003–1029.

Holbrook, A. L., & Krosnick, J.A. (2010). Measuring voter turnout by using the randomized response technique: Evidence calling into question the method's validity. *Public Opinion Quarterly, 74*, 328–343.

Holbrook, A. L., Krosnick, J. A., Carson, R. T., & Mitchell, R. C. (2000). Violating conversational conventions disrupts cognitive processing of attitude questions. *Journal of Experimental Social Psychology, 36*, 465–494.

Javeline, D. (1999). Response effects in polite cultures: A test of acquiescence in Kazakhstan. *Public Opinion Quarterly, 63*, 1–28.

Johanson, G. A., Gips, C. J., & Rich, C. E. (1993). If you can't say something nice: A variation on the social desirability response set. *Evaluation Review, 17*, 116–122.

Kalton, G., Collins, M., & Brook, L. (1978). Experiments in wording opinion questions. *Applied Statistics, 27*, 149–161.

Krosnick, J. A. (1991). Response strategies for coping with the cognitive demands of attitude measures in surveys. *Applied Cognitive Psychology, 5*, 213–236.

(1992). The impact of cognitive sophistication and attitude importance on response order effects and question order effects. In N. Schwarz & S. Sudman (eds.), *Order Effects in Social and Psychological Research* (pp. 203–218). Springer.

(1999). Survey research. *Annual Review of Psychology, 50*, 537–567.

(2002). The causes of no-opinion responses to attitude measures in surveys: They are rarely what they appear to be. In R. M. Groves, D. A. Dillman, J. N. Eltinge, & R. J. A. Little (eds.), *Survey Nonresponse* (pp. 88–100). Wiley-Interscience.

Krosnick, J. A., & Alwin, D. F. (1987). An evaluation of a cognitive theory of response-order effects in survey measurement. *Public Opinion Quarterly, 51*, 201–219.

(1988). A test of the form-resistant correlation hypothesis: Ratings, rankings, and the measurement of values. *Public Opinion Quarterly, 52*, 526–538.

Krosnick, J. A., & Berent, M. K. (1993). Comparisons of party identification and policy preferences: The impact of survey question format. *American Journal of Political Science, 37*, 941–964.

Krosnick, J. A., Boninger, D. S., Chuang, Y. C., Berent, M. K., & Carnot, C. G. (1993). Attitude strength: One construct or many related constructs? *Journal of Personality and Social Psychology, 65*, 1132–1151.

Krosnick, J. A., & Fabrigar, L. R. (1999). *Designing Good Questionnaires: Insights from Psychology*. Oxford University Press.

(forthcoming). *The Handbook of Questionnaire Design*. Oxford University Press.

Krosnick, J. A., Holbrook, A. L., Berent, M. K., Carson, R. T., Hanemann, W. M., Kopp, R. J., et al. (2002). The impact of "no opinion" response options on data quality: Nonattitude reduction or invitation to satisfice? *Public Opinion Quarterly, 66*, 371–403.

Krosnick, J. A., Narayan, S. S., & Smith, W. R. (1997). Satisficing in surveys: Initial evidence. In M. T. Braverman & J. K. Slater (eds.), *Advances in Survey Research* (pp. 29–44). Jossey-Bass.

Leech, G. N. (1983). *Principles of Pragmatics*. Longman.

Lehmann, D. R., & Hulbert, J. (1972). Are three-point scales always good enough? *Journal of Marketing Research, 9*, 444–446.

Lelkes, Y., Krosnick, J. A., Marx, D. M., Judd, C. M., & Park, B. (2012). Complete anonymity compromises the accuracy of self-reports. *Journal of Experimental Social Psychology, 48*, 1291–1299.

Lenski, G. E., & Leggett, J. C. (1960). Caste, class, and deference in the research interview. *American Journal of Sociology, 65*, 463–467.

Lenzner, T. (2012). Effects of survey question comprehensibility on response quality. *Field Methods, 24*, 409–428.

Lichtenstein, S., & Newman, J. R. (1967). Empirical scaling of common verbal phrases associated with numerical probabilities. *Bulletin of the Psychonomic Society, 9*, 563–564.

Lindzey, G. G., & Guest, L. (1951). To repeat – check lists can be dangerous. *Public Opinion Quarterly, 15*, 355–358.

Lissitz, R. W., & Green, S. B. (1975). Effect of the number of scale points on reliability: A Monte Carlo approach. *Journal of Applied Psychology, 60*, 10–13.

Liu, M., & Conrad, F. G. (2019). Where should i start? On default values for slider questions in Web surveys. *Social Science Computer Review, 37*, 248–269.

Martin, W. S. (1973). The effects of scaling on the correlation coefficient: A test of validity. *Journal of Marketing Research, 10*, 316–318.

Matejka, J., Glueck, M., Grossman, T., & Fitzmaurice, G. (2016). The effect of visual appearance on the performance of continuous sliders and visual analogue scales. In *Proceedings of the 2016 CHI Conference on Human Factors in Computing Systems (CHI '16)* (pp. 5421–5432). ACM.

Matell, M. S., & Jacoby, J. (1971). Is there an optimal number of alternatives for Likert scale items? Study I: Reliability and validity. *Educational and Psychological Measurement, 31*, 657–674.

Mathers, N., Fox, N., & Hunn, A. (2007). *Surveys and Questionnaires*. Trent RDSU.

Mavletova, A. (2013). Data quality in PC and mobile Web surveys. *Social Science Computer Review, 31*, 725–743.

McCarty, J. A., & Shrum, L. J. (1997). Measuring the importance of positive constructs: A test of alternative rating procedures. *Marketing Letters, 8*, 239–250.

— (2000). The measurement of personal values in survey research: A test of alternative rating procedures. *Public Opinion Quarterly, 64*, 271–298.

McClendon, M. J. (1986). Response-order effects for dichotomous questions. *Social Science Quarterly, 67*, 205–211.

Menold, N. (2020). Rating-scale labeling in online surveys: An experimental comparison of verbal and numeric rating scales with respect to measurement quality and respondents' cognitive processes. *Sociological Methods & Research, 49*, 79–107.

Miethe, T. D. (1985). Validity and reliability of value measurements. *Journal of Psychology, 119*, 441–453.

Mingay, D. J., & Greenwell, M. T. (1989). Memory bias and response-order effects. *Journal of Official Statistics, 5*, 253–263.

Mondak, J. J. (2001). Developing valid knowledge scales. *American Journal of Political Science, 45*, 224–238.

O'Muircheartaigh, C., Krosnick, J. A., & Helic, A. (2000). Middle alternatives, acquiescence, and the quality of questionnaire data. Working Papers 0103, Harris School of Public Policy Studies, University of Chicago.

Oppenheim, A. N. (1992). *Questionnaire Design, Interviewing, and Attitude Measurement*. Pinter.

Paulhus, D. L. (1984). Two-component models of socially desirable responding. *Journal of Personality and Social Psychology, 46*, 598–609.

— (1986). Self-deception and impression management in test responses. In A. Angleitner & J. Wiggins (eds.), *Personality Assessment via Questionnaires: Current Issues in Theory and Measurement* (pp. 143–165). Springer.

Peters, D. L., & McCormick, E. J. (1966). Comparative reliability of numerically anchored versus job-task anchored rating scales. *Journal of Applied Psychology, 50*(1), 92–96.

Poffenberger, A. T. (1932). *Psychology in Advertising*. McGraw-Hill.

Quinn, S. B., & Belson, W. A. (1969). *The Effects of Reversing the Order of Presentation of Verbal Rating Scales in Survey Interviews*. Survey Research Center.

Riordan, B. C., Cody, L., Flett, J. A. M., Conner, T. S., Hunter, J., & Scarf, D. (2018). The development of a single item FoMO (fear of missing out) scale. *Current Psychology, 39*, 1215–1220.

Robins, R. W., Hendin, H. M., & Trzesniewski, K. H. (2001). Measuring global self-esteem: Construct validation of a single-item measure and the Rosenberg Self-Esteem Scale. *Personality and Social Psychology Bulletin, 27*, 151–161.

Rosenberg, M. (1965). *Society and the Adolescent Self-Image*. Princeton University Press.

Rosenberg, N., Izard, C. E., & Hollander, E. P. (1955). Middle category response: Reliability and relationship to personality and intelligence variables. *Educational and Psychological Measurement, 15*, 281–290.

Salant, P., & Dillman, D. A. (1994). *How to Conduct Your Own Survey*. John Wiley.

Saris, W. E., & Gallhofer, I. N. (2014). *Design, Evaluation, and Analysis of Questionnaires for Survey Research*. John Wiley & Sons.

Saris, W. E., Revilla, M., Schaeffer, E., & Krosnick, J. A. (2010). Comparing questions with agree/disagree response options to questions with item-specific response options. *Survey Research Methods, 4*, 61–79.

Shaeffer E. M., Krosnick J. A., Langer G. E., & Merkle, D. M. (2005). Comparing the quality of data obtained by minimally balanced and fully balanced attitude questions. *Public Opinion Quarterly, 69*, 417–428.

Schlenker, B. R., & Weingold, M. F. (1989). Goals and the self-identification process: Constructing desired identities. In L. A. Pervin (ed.), *Goal Concepts in Personality and Social Psychology* (pp. 243–290). Lawrence Erlbaum Associates.

Schuman, H., & Presser, S. (1981). *Questions and Answers in Attitude Surveys: Experiments on Question Form, Wording and Context.* Academic Press.

Schuman, H., & Scott, J. (1987). Problems in the use of survey questions to measure public opinion. *Science, 236*, 957–959.

Schwarz, N., & Hippler, H. J. (1991). Response alternatives: The impact of their choice and presentation order. In P. P Biemer, R. M. Groves, L. E. Lyberg, N. A. Mathiowetz, & S. Sudman (eds.), *Measurement Errors in Surveys* (pp. 41–56). Wiley & Sons.

Schwarz, N., Hippler, H. J., Deutsch, B., & Strack, F. (1985). Response scales: Effects of category range on reported behavior and subsequent judgments. *Public Opinion Quarterly, 49*, 388–395.

Schwarz, N., Hippler, H. J., & Noelle-Neumann, E. (1992). A cognitive model of response-order effects in survey measurement. In N. Schwarz & S. Sudman (eds.), *Context Effects in Social and Psychological Research* (pp. 187–201). Springer.

Schwarz, N., Knäuper, B., Hippler, H. J., Noelle-Neumann, E., & Clark, L. (1991). Rating scales: Numeric values may change the meaning of scale labels. *Public Opinion Quarterly, 55*, 570–582.

Smith, T. W. (1988). Context effects in the general social survey. In P. P. Biemer, R. M. Groves, L. E. Lyberg, N. A. Mathiowetz, & S. Sudman (eds.), *Measurement Errors in Surveys* (pp. 57–72). Wiley & Sons.

Smyth, J. D., Christian, L. M., & Dillman, D. A. (2008). Does "yes or no" on the telephone mean the same as "check-all-that-apply" on the Web? *Public Opinion Quarterly, 72*, 103–113.

Smyth, J. D., Israel, G. D., Newberry, M. G., & Hull, R. G. (2019). Effects of stem and response order on response patterns in satisfaction ratings. *Field Methods, 31*, 260–276.

Smyth, J. D., Olson, K., & Burke, A. (2018). Comparing survey ranking question formats in mail surveys. *International Journal of Market Research, 60*, 502–516.

Sturgis, P., Allum, N., & Smith, P. (2008). An experiment on the measurement of political knowledge in surveys. *Public Opinion Quarterly, 72*, 90–102.

Theil, M. (2002). The role of translations of verbal into numerical probability expressions in risk management: A meta-analysis. *Journal of Risk Research, 5*, 177–186.

Tourangeau, R., Conrad, F. G., Couper, M. P., & Ye, C. (2014). The effects of providing examples in survey questions. *Public Opinion Quarterly, 78*, 100–125.

Tourangeau, R., Maitland, A., & Yan, H. Y. (2016). Assessing the scientific knowledge of the general public: The effects of question format and encouraging or discouraging don't know responses. *Public Opinion Quarterly, 80*, 741–760.

Tourangeau, R., & Rasinski, K. A. (1988). Cognitive processes underlying context effects in attitude measurement. *Psychological Bulletin, 3*, 299–314.

Tourangeau, R., Rips, L. J., & Rasinski, K. (2000). *The Psychology of Survey Response.* Cambridge University Press.

Tourangeau, R., Sun, H., Conrad, F. G., & Couper, M. P. (2017). Examples in open-ended survey questions. *International Journal of Public Opinion Research, 29*, 690–702.

Tourangeau, R., & Yan, T. (2007). Sensitive questions in surveys. *Psychological Bulletin, 133*, 859–883.

Truebner, M. (2021). The dynamics of "neither agree nor disagree" answers in attitudinal questions. *Journal of Survey Statistics and Methodology, 9*, 51–72.

Visser, P. S., Krosnick, J A., Marquette, J. F., & Curtin, M. F. (2000). Improving election forecasting: Allocation of undecided respondents, identification of likely voters, and response order effects. In P. L. Lavrakas & M. Traugott (eds.), *Election Polls, the News Media, and Democracy* (pp. 224–260). Chatham House.

Wallsten, T. S., Budescu, D. V., & Zwick, R. (1993). Comparing the calibration and coherence of numerical and verbal probability judgments. *Management Science, 39*, 176–190.

Wang, R., & Krosnick, J. A. (2020). Middle alternatives and measurement validity: A recommendation for survey researchers. *International Journal of Social Research Methodology, 23*, 169–184.

Warner, S. L. (1965). Randomized response: A survey technique for eliminating evasive answer bias. *Journal of the American Statistical Association, 60*, 63–69.

Wedell, D. H., Parducci, A., & Lane, M. (1990). Reducing the dependence of clinical judgment on the immediate context: Effects of number of categories and type of anchors. *Journal of Personality and Social Psychology, 58*, 319–329.

Wegener, D. T., Downing, J., Krosnick, J. A., & Petty, R. E. (1995). Measures and manipulations of strength-related properties of attitudes: Current practice and future directions. In R. E. Petty & J. A. Krosnick (eds.), *Attitude Strength: Antecedents and Consequences* (pp. 455–487). Lawrence Erlbaum Associates.

Willis, G. B. (2005). *Cognitive Interviewing: A Tool for Improving Questionnaire Design*. SAGE Publications.

Wright, M., Citrin, J., & Wand, J. (2012). Alternative measures of American national identity: Implications for the civic-ethnic distinction. *Political Psychology, 33*, 469–482.

PART IV

Behavioral Measures

17 Reaction Time Measures
Jeremy D. Heider

Abstract

The term *reaction time* (RT) describes the interval between the initial appearance of a stimulus and an organism's response to that stimulus. Because RT data are notorious for substantial individual differences and positive skew, the overarching goal of this chapter is to equip researchers with sufficient knowledge to design RT studies that enhance experimental control, thereby reducing unwanted error variability. To accomplish this goal, the chapter discusses five major themes: (1) an overview of the evolution of RT research; (2) a discussion of the state of RT knowledge today, with a focus on moderating variables that researchers could control; (3) a review of some of the most common RT measures employed by contemporary social and behavioral scientists; (4) a description of specific technological tools that can be used to administer those measures; and (5) a discussion of basic considerations for statistical analysis of RT data.

Keywords: Reaction Time, Recognition Reaction Time, Choice Reaction Time, Evaluative Priming, Implicit Association Test

I think it necessary to mention that my assistant, Mr. David Kinnebrook, who observed the transits of the stars and planets very well ... began, from the beginning of August last, to set them down half a second of time later than he should do, according to my observations; and in January ... he increased his error to eight-tenths of a second.

(Maskelyne, as quoted in Howse, 1989, p. 169)

It only took eight-tenths of a second to set in motion a series of events that would eventually lead to the widespread use of *reaction time* measures among social and behavioral scientists. What is reaction time? How is it measured and analyzed, and why should such measures be included in the social and behavioral scientist's toolbox? To address these key questions, this chapter will unfold in five major sections: (1) an overview of how reaction time research has evolved; (2) a description of the state of reaction time knowledge today; (3) a review of several common reaction time measures employed in the contemporary social and behavioral sciences; (4) a description of specific technologies that can be used to administer those measures; and (5) a discussion of basic considerations when statistically analyzing reaction time data.

A Brief History of (Reaction) Time

The term *reaction time* (RT) describes the interval between the initial appearance of a stimulus and an organism's response to that stimulus (Luce, 1986). Though they share certain basic characteristics, RTs are distinct from *reflexes* – involuntary reactions that protect organisms from harm. RT measures have a long history in the social and behavioral sciences, but their prominence began in astronomy and physiology (Schultz & Schultz, 2016). Decades before Austrian physiologist Sigmund Exner (1873) coined the term *Reaktionszeit* (reaction time), the aforementioned Kinnebrook made a series of "errors" that cost him his job and also inspired the study of RT as we know it (Schultz & Schultz, 2016).

The "Incompetent" Astronomer's Assistant

Kinnebrook was the assistant to Nevil Maskelyne, Royal Astronomer of England. When studying stellar transit, Kinnebrook's observations became consistently slower than Maskelyne's, and the assistant was fired (Boring, 1950). Approximately 20 years later, German astronomer Friedrich Bessel determined such "errors" were merely normal variation among human observers. He developed the *personal equation* to adjust for systematic differences between observers (Boring, 1950). For example, if Kinnebrook's observations were consistently 0.8 seconds slower than Maskelyne's, their figures could be equated by subtracting 0.8 seconds from each Kinnebrook observation (Hergenhahn, 2013). The personal equation was important for two reasons: (1) it showed subjective psychological phenomena could be quantified, nullifying the philosophical argument that mental processes could not be studied experimentally; and (2) it provided evidence from a "real" (i.e., respected as objective) science that subjective perception is critical to understand, meaning the role of the human observer must be appreciated in all sciences (Schultz & Schultz, 2016).

The Role of Ninetenth-Century Physiologists

Around the time astronomers discovered RT, physiologists were studying the rate of nerve conduction. Johannes Müller believed nervous transmission was virtually instantaneous – perhaps as fast as the speed of light – and thus impossible to measure (Müller, 1833–1840). However, Müller's pupil, Hermann von Helmholtz, disagreed. Helmholtz used his newly invented *myograph* to determine that the rate of human nerve conduction was approximately 50–100 meters per second (slower than sound, let alone light; Boring, 1950). Unfortunately, substantial variability in conduction rates, both between and within persons, led Helmholtz to abandon the study of RT. Nonetheless, his work was refined by other physiologists, including Franciscus Donders, who first studied *simple reaction time*, gauging the basic lag between stimulus and response. Later, he conducted investigations of *recognition reaction time* – presenting numerous stimuli to participants at once but with instructions to only respond to one of them – and *choice reaction time*, presenting several stimuli but with instructions to respond to each one differently. He established that simple RTs are the shortest, followed by recognition and choice RTs, respectively (Hergenhahn, 2013).

Wundt Incorporates RT into Social and Behavioral Science

Germany's Wilhelm Wundt, often considered the founding father of psychology, was himself a trained physiologist. Thus, being influenced by Müller, Helmholtz, and Donders, it is no surprise that Wundt incorporated RT into his experiments (Hergenhahn, 2013). Wundt detailed seven types of reactions ranging from fastest (*reflexes*) to slowest (*judgment reactions*). By subtracting one type from another, he could establish the time it took a person to engage in various cognitive processes (Boring, 1950). Wundt coined the term *mental chronometry* to designate such studies as an entire subdiscipline of psychology. Of course, much like Helmholtz before him, Wundt encountered considerable variability in RTs across participants, time, sensory modality, stimulus intensity, and other variables; he eventually stopped studying RT altogether. Still, by this point it was clear that RT was fully infused into the new psychology and was there to stay (Hergenhahn, 2013).

What We Know about the Study of Reaction Time Today

Why is the study of reaction time important to social and behavioral scientists? From an information-processing perspective, RT studies allow us to examine the human cognitive system during optimal performance. Other cognitive processes, such as memory, are often only understood when they fail (e.g., Atkinson & Shiffrin, 1968). Also, as Wundt first demonstrated, RT studies are valuable in determining the relative length of various cognitive processes and the manner in which they are temporally organized (i.e., whether they occur serially or in parallel).

Of course, there are also many real-world implications of RT, many of which have potentially serious consequences. RT impacts a driver's ability to appropriately recognize stimuli on the road, the speed with which a law enforcement officer determines the level of threat posed by a suspect, and the particular associations that activate when a teacher encounters a student of another race. Each of these processes could, in turn, have behavioral implications. For example, the driver might turn the steering wheel to avoid an obstruction, the officer might draw their firearm to deter the suspect from further threatening behaviors, or the teacher might try to suppress negative stereotypes associated with the student's race. Conversely, each person's cognitive system might fail to initiate such behaviors.

Contemporary studies of RT can be classified in much the same way Donders classified them in the nineteenth century: simple reaction time, recognition reaction time, and choice reaction time (Luce, 1986). Simple RT measures involve a single stimulus and a single response. For example, if a participant pressed the spacebar on a keyboard as quickly as possible each time a red "X" appeared on the computer screen – and the red "X" was the only type of stimulus presented – they would be completing a simple RT task.

Recognition RT measures incorporate some stimuli that require a response and other stimuli that require non-response. An example of this type of measure is the Go/No-go Association Task (GNAT; Nosek & Banaji, 2001), in which participants respond with a key press (the "go" response) to stimuli representing a category (e.g., science) or an attribute (e.g., positivity) but do *not* press a key (the "no-go" response) for any stimuli not associated with the category or attribute. Finally, choice RT measures present participants with multiple potential active responses. An example is the Implicit Association Test (IAT; Greenwald et al., 1998), in which participants categorize stimuli by pressing one key in response to stimuli from social and/or evaluative categories on the left side of a screen and a different key in response to stimuli from categories on the right side of the screen.

As was the case in Donders's laboratory, RT studies continue to show RTs vary reliably according to the nature of the task, such that simple RTs < recognition RTs < choice RTs. There is some debate about whether these differences are purely the result of differential cognitive processing time (Miller & Low, 2001) or whether other potential mechanisms such as motor reactions are involved (Danek & Mordkoff, 2011), but the general pattern is robust. There are also well-established differences in RT across sensory modalities, such that auditory RTs (i.e., reactions to sounds) are faster than touch RTs (i.e., reactions to tactile sensations), which are faster than visual RTs (i.e., reactions to stimuli that are seen). Importantly, these differences across the three senses emerge regardless of whether one employs simple, recognition, or choice tasks (Sanders, 1998). Taste and smell RTs (i.e., reactions to gustatory or olfactory stimuli) are rarely studied, as they involve inherently less precision in both stimulus onset and detection (see Kling & Riggs, 1971; Robinson, 1934). However, for examples of such studies, see Delwiche et al. (1999) and Overbosch et al. (1989).

Of course, many other variables besides task type moderate the length of RTs. The primary goal of presenting this information is to equip researchers with sufficient knowledge to design RT studies that enhance experimental control, thereby reducing unwanted error variability. RT data are notorious for revealing substantial individual differences and exhibiting considerable positive skew (Whelan, 2008). Awareness of variables that moderate RT should allow researchers to minimize the impact of such factors by incorporating them into their experimental designs.

Intensity and Complexity of Stimuli

Aside from task type and sensory modality, perhaps the best understood moderators of reaction time are *stimulus intensity* and *stimulus complexity*. Numerous lines of evidence converge on two complementary conclusions: (1) increased stimulus intensity decreases RTs and (2) increased stimulus complexity increases RTs (Luce, 1986; Pins & Bonnet, 1996; Stafford et al., 2011). In other words, people respond more quickly to intense stimuli (e.g., a bright light rather than a dim one) and more slowly to more complex stimuli (e.g., five words on a screen rather than a single word). However, the intensity–RT relationship is curvilinear, such that the tendency for intensity to decrease RT levels off after the stimulus reaches a sufficient degree of intensity.

The complexity–RT relationship, on the other hand, seems to vary according to the type of task. In recognition RT tasks, the complexity–RT relationship is often linear (e.g., Sternberg, 1969). Conversely, it is often curvilinear in choice RT tasks. Specifically, RTs tend to increase along with the number of stimuli up to a point, after which the amount of increase in RT with each additional stimulus gets smaller and smaller (e.g., Hick, 1952). The important lesson here is that researchers need to control for intensity and complexity either by holding such variables constant or by carefully manipulating them.

Physiological Arousal

Physiological arousal has also received considerable attention in the RT literature, with many findings paralleling the *Yerkes-Dodson Law* (Yerkes & Dodson, 1908) regarding the relationship between arousal and performance. According to this law, the arousal–performance relationship follows an inverted-U pattern, whereby performance is best at moderate levels of arousal and worst at very low or very high levels of arousal. With occasional exceptions in which some participants exhibit a pattern opposite to the traditional inverted-U (e.g., VaezMousavi et al., 2009) or no relationship between arousal and performance (e.g., Damanpak et al., 2014), the vast majority of RT studies show participants respond with optimum speed, to a wide range of stimuli, when arousal is moderate (e.g., Arent & Landers, 2003; see Levitt & Gutin, 1971, for a demonstration of optimal heart rate for RT tasks). For this purpose, note that *greater* performance equates to *lower* RT, such that examination of the raw RTs themselves yields a standard-U pattern rather than the inverted-U.

Durlach et al. (2002) found moderately increased arousal via doses of caffeine decreased RTs and increased attentional focus. In the opposite direction, it is well known that sleep deprivation and fatigue worsen RT on both simple and choice RT tasks (Jaśkowski & Włodarczyk, 1997; Pavelka et al., 2020). Because of these patterns, we recommend creating conditions of moderate arousal to optimize participant performance. In other words, unless one is purposely studying varying levels of arousal, it is important to avoid conditions in which arousal might be too low (e.g., due to sleep deprivation or other forms of fatigue) or too high (e.g., a highly stressful situation).

Focus of Attention

Numerous studies have documented substantially faster visual reaction times to stimuli presented foveally (i.e., focused centrally on the retina) compared to those presented parafoveally (i.e., in one's peripheral vision; Babkoff et al., 1985). This effect can be attenuated through practice, whereby practice with parafoveal stimuli decreases the foveal–parafoveal RT difference (Ando et al., 2002, 2004). In addition, Johns et al. (2009) presented evidence that visual RTs increase significantly –

sometimes by as much as two-tenths of a second – when blinks and/or saccadic eye movements occur either immediately before or immediately after the presentation of a stimulus. Yet other studies clearly show that distractor stimuli increase response latency (e.g., Elliott et al., 2014).

For these reasons, studies of visual RT (and other forms of RT, for that matter) typically utilize a "warning" system to orient the participant's attention prior to stimulus presentation. A common feature of such systems is the use of a visual fixation point. Participants are instructed to look directly at that point, as it is the exact location where the target stimulus will appear. Although nothing is guaranteed with this approach, it does increase the likelihood that participants will orient their attention at the right place and time compared to approaches that do not use such a warning system (see Chapter 18 of this volume for a detailed discussion of eyetracking in the social and behavioral sciences).

The Influence of Practice

As noted previously, Ando et al. (2002, 2004) found practice with foveal and parafoveal stimuli improved reaction time. Ando et al. (2004) further documented that the practice gains were still present after a three-week interval. However, these studies hardly represent the only evidence of practice effects (see Dutilh et al., 2009, and Evans et al., 2018, for models of the processes underlying practice effects). Dutilh et al. (2009) used a lexical decision task (i.e., distinguishing words from nonwords) to study practice effects, but others have used experience with a specific activity as a proxy for practice and found similar patterns of results. For example, Fontani et al. (2006) found more experienced practitioners of karate were faster on a simple RT task than those with less experience. However, this pattern did not replicate among volleyball players. Less experienced volleyball players actually had faster RTs; it is important to note that they also committed more errors – lending support to the notion that practice is a crucial component of overall performance.

Practice effects are most noticeable when the RT task is complex and the practice is extended over a period of days or weeks, but such effects can also be accomplished with brief "warmup" periods within a single session. Such "warmups" are common to the specific RT measures we will review later in this chapter. For example, the IAT (Greenwald et al., 1998), which typically takes participants only 10–15 minutes to complete, incorporates blocks of both practice trials and critical trials. The practice blocks are intended to orient the participant to the nature of the categorization task, thus reducing error variability during the critical blocks. Thus, for most applications of RT tasks, we highly recommend using practice blocks prior to administering critical blocks. Nonetheless, there is also a downside to practice effects. For example, if a participant becomes "too good" at a particular RT task, it may cease to be a valid indicator of how members of the population at large process information (e.g., by creating ceiling/floor effects). The key is to provide enough opportunities for practice to reduce spurious error variability while maintaining appropriate individual differences among participants.

Age of the Participant

Large volumes of research show a curvilinear relationship between reaction time and age that resembles the U-shaped relationship discussed earlier with respect to arousal. RTs are slowest at very young (i.e., infancy, toddlerhood) and very old (i.e., elderly) ages, with speed for most individuals peaking in their 20s and 30s and declining most dramatically after age 70 (Welford, 1981). These differences across age groups are more pronounced with complex RT tasks than simple RT tasks (Der & Deary, 2006). Another key difference is that RTs become more variable among older individuals in addition to the increase in mean RTs (Dykiert et al., 2012; Medic-Pericevic et al., 2020), and this effect is only exacerbated by neurodegenerative conditions such as Alzheimer's disease (Gorus et al., 2008). For this reason, so-called *intra-individual variability in reaction time* (RT IIV) has been suggested as a potential measure of central nervous system integrity (Dykiert et al., 2012). At a minimum, researchers must be aware of the greater RTs (e.g., means) and RT variability (e.g., standard deviations) that come with studying older populations. A significant challenge for RT researchers is to develop techniques – both methodological and statistical – that distinguish whether changes in RT as a person ages are a function of ordinary aging or more serious clinical conditions.

Before we move on to our discussion of widely used RT measures in the social and behavioral sciences, we should reiterate that the treatment of potential moderators in this section was not meant to be exhaustive. Thus, we encourage readers to examine other possible moderators, such as sex (e.g., RTs are slightly slower and more variable among female participants; Der & Deary, 2006), learning disorders (e.g., RTs are slower among dyslexic children; Vakil et al., 2015), brain injury (e.g., RTs are delayed among concussed athletes; Lavoie et al., 2004), personality traits (e.g., neuroticism positively correlates with RT variability; Robinson & Tamir, 2005), and hemispheric specialization (e.g., minor differences appear if visual stimuli are only processed in the left or right visual field; Hernandez et al., 1992). Again, the primary goal of familiarizing oneself with such patterns is to aid in designing RT studies that reduce unwanted noise.

Reaction Time Measures Commonly Used by Social and Behavioral Scientists

The ubiquity of reaction time measures in social and behavioral science research makes it difficult to describe all possible measures. In fact, many modern software applications (including those described in the next section of this chapter) make it possible to record RTs for literally every response a participant provides during a computer-based procedure. One possibility, then, is to simply use RT as a dependent variable to gauge cognitive processing time for any kind of response. As noted above, the practical applications of such information are numerous (e.g., speed of response when law enforcement officers encounter suspects). However, many specific RT tasks have gained immense popularity among social and behavioral scientists in their examinations of cognitive processing. In this section, we examine five such tasks: the Stroop test, the Eriksen flanker task, evaluative priming, the Implicit Association Test, and the Go/No-go Association Task. Although alternative methods of administration are possible, we will focus on computer-based administration as it is the most frequent manner by which all five tasks are executed.

The Stroop Test

The *Stroop Color and Word Test* (SCWT), more commonly known as the *Stroop test* (Stroop, 1935), is a choice reaction time task that examines participants' ability to process two separate stimulus features simultaneously – typically the semantic meaning of a color word (e.g., "blue") and the color in which the word is presented (this may or may not match the semantic meaning). Unlike many other choice RT tasks, the speed of participants' cognitive responding is typically not measured on a per-stimulus basis. Rather, the total amount of time participants take to process an entire set of stimuli is the focus because participants typically state their responses verbally rather than responding with a mechanical key press. Such verbal responses are inherently more difficult to measure with millisecond-level precision.

Despite many variations, Stroop's (1935) original test involves the participant processing three stimulus sets as quickly as possible: (1) color words presented in black lettering; (2) basic shapes (e.g., squares) presented in different colors; and (3) color words presented in lettering of an incongruent color (e.g., the word "blue" presented in red lettering; see Figure 17.1). The first two sets are considered congruent – there is no interference between stimulus features. However, the third stimulus set requires participants to inhibit a relatively automatic process (reading the word) to engage a more effortful process (naming the color of the lettering; see MacLeod & Dunbar, 1988). Stroop (1935) found only a 5.6% increase in processing time of the third stimulus set, compared to the first set, when participants read the

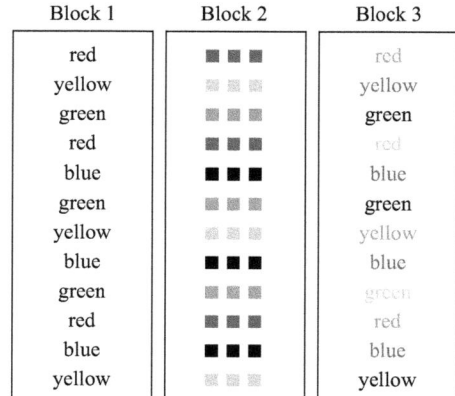

Figure 17.1 *Sample stimuli for the Stroop Color and Word Test (SCWT). www.sciencedirect.com/topics/neuroscience/stroop-effect. From Baghdadi, Towhidkhah, and Rajabi (2021). Reprinted with permission of publisher.*

color words themselves, but a 74.3% increase when participants had to name the color of the lettering – having to inhibit the automatic process in favor of the effortful one. This increase in processing time has been termed the *Stroop effect*.

An interesting application of the Stroop test, typically known as the *emotional Stroop test*, involves naming the colors of words that are emotionally negative or neutral. Gotlib and McCann (1984) found that clinically depressed participants reacted more slowly when naming colors of the negative emotional words. Thus, although the Stroop test was originally designed to assess cognitive processing, it can be used to gauge emotional processing as well. More recently, Satorres et al. (2020) found that patients with degenerative neurocognitive disorders (described as probable Alzheimer's disease diagnoses) performed poorly compared to controls on the emotional Stroop test. These and other similar findings (e.g., Volkan & Hadjimarkou's 2019 study of post-traumatic stress) suggest the emotional Stroop also holds promise for studying clinical populations beyond depression and possibly even use as a diagnostic tool in the future.

The Eriksen Flanker Task

The *Eriksen flanker task,* alternatively called the *Eriksen task* or *flanker task*, is a choice RT task that examines the effects of peripheral "flanker" stimuli that surround target stimuli (Eriksen & Eriksen, 1974). Much like the Stroop test, the flanker task involves interference between competing cognitive processes. However, two key differences are that the flanker task records RTs on a per-stimulus basis and it avoids the potentially confounding influence of other variables (e.g., verbal ability).

In a typical procedure, participants are presented with a group of stimuli and instructed to press either a left key or right key depending on the nature of the central (target) stimulus. For example, if "H" is the target stimulus in the center of the stimulus group, the participant is to press the left key. If any other letter appears centrally, the participant presses the right key. In either case, the central stimulus will be "flanked" by irrelevant stimulus letters. All else being equal, the task is easier in terms of both RT and accuracy when flanker stimuli are consistent with the target (e.g., "HHHHH") than when they are inconsistent (e.g., "SSHSS"). The difference in average per-trial RT between consistent and inconsistent trials is known as the *Eriksen effect* or *flanker effect*.

A large number of variations of the flanker task have been implemented in the literature; in most variations, the target and flanker stimuli are of the same type, such as letters. However, other types of stimuli, such as shapes or symbols, have also been used (e.g., Peschke et al., 2013; see Figure 17.2 for examples of differing types of target and flanker stimuli). Some researchers have also found the same basic flanker effect when placing flankers in varying patterns around the target stimulus (e.g., Eriksen & St. James, 1986).

Importantly, the flanker task has a number of potential applications. Similar to the aforementioned research using the emotional Stroop test (e.g., Satorres et al., 2020), the flanker task has also been used as an indicator of the integrity of cognitive functioning in populations with neurodegenerative conditions. Wylie et al. (2009)

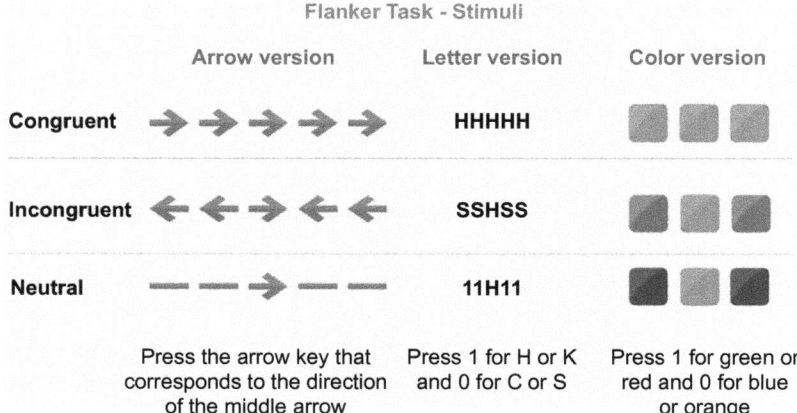

Figure 17.2 *Sample stimuli for the Eriksen flanker task. Image retrieved from www.testable.org/experiment-guides/executive-function/flanker-task. This webpage also includes a programming template for running the flanker task. Flanker Task Overview © 2022 by Testable Research Inc. is licensed under CC BY 4.0.*

gave patients with Parkinson's disease (PD) flanker task instructions that emphasized either speed or accuracy. Compared to control participants who had no neurodegenerative diagnoses, PD patients showed greater interference effects on the flanker task when the instructions emphasized speed. Analysis of the distribution pattern of RTs suggested PD patients had a harder time suppressing incorrect responses under these conditions (see Rodriguez-Raecke et al., 2022, for evidence of appropriate medications mitigating differential flanker effects in PD patients).

Evaluative Priming

The remaining measures in this section have primarily been used by social and behavioral scientists to study implicit attitudes (i.e., relatively non-conscious evaluations) of various social groups in domains such as race/ethnicity, gender, sexual orientation, and religion, though they do have various other applications (e.g., the measurement of implicit self-esteem; see Greenwald & Farnham, 2000). The first of these techniques is primarily known as *evaluative priming* (Fazio et al., 1986), though Fazio et al. (1995) provided the alternative moniker "bona fide pipeline" as a play on words relating to the classic *bogus pipeline* designed to reveal hidden attitudes (Jones & Sigall, 1971). Evaluative priming is a choice RT task in which participants make a series of decisions regarding the evaluative connotation of words (i.e., whether each word is positive/good or negative/bad in meaning). On each trial, the target word is preceded by a prime. Depending on the researcher's goals, the primes can be presented either supraliminally (i.e., above the threshold of conscious perception – approximately 50 milliseconds for most people, Fazio et al., 1995); or subliminally (i.e., below the threshold of conscious perception, Dovidio et al., 1997; Dovidio et al., 2002).

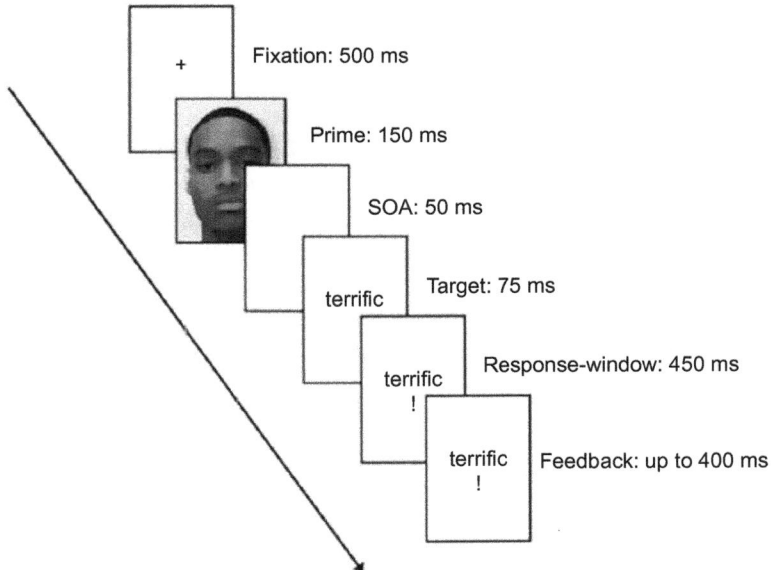

Figure 17.3 *Sample procedure for the race-based evaluative priming task. SOA = stimulus onset asynchrony. From Van Bavel and Cunningham (2010). Reprinted with permission of publisher.*

Perhaps the most common application of evaluative priming has been in the assessment of implicit racial attitudes. In this context, the primes are typically facial photographs of African American and Caucasian targets (any other social groups can easily be substituted; see Figure 17.3 for an example schematic of a race-based evaluative priming procedure). Among samples that consist of entirely or at least primarily Caucasian participants, responses to negative adjectives are often facilitated (as in faster RTs) following an African American prime relative to a Caucasian prime (and, to some extent, responses to positive adjectives are inhibited following an African American prime). These differential RTs have, in turn, been related to discriminatory behavior in interracial interactions (e.g., Fazio et al., 1995).

Evaluative priming tasks (EPTs) have been used to measure other constructs as well, such as implicit self-esteem. For example, Zayas et al. (2022) used the standard evaluative priming procedure of Fazio et al. (1986) to demonstrate that priming the self-concept simultaneously activates both positive and negative implicit self-evaluations. To adapt the evaluative priming task to the measurement of self-esteem, Zayas et al. (2022) simply used the participant's own name or strings of letters (e.g., "AAA") as primes in place of the African American and Caucasian targets used for the racial attitudes version of the EPT. The target words remained a standard set of positive- and negative-meaning terms such as *honor*, *diamond*, and *freedom* (positive) and *evil*, *disaster*, and *rotten* (negative).

The Implicit Association Test

In terms of sheer frequency of use, the undisputed king of modern-day reaction time measures is the *Implicit Association Test,* or IAT. As a testament to its widespread use, the original article reporting the development of the IAT (Greenwald et al., 1998) has been cited several thousand times, making it the most-cited paper in the history of the *Journal of Personality and Social Psychology.* The IAT is a choice RT task that, much like evaluative priming, has mostly been used to assess implicit attitudes (and implicit racial attitudes in particular). However, unlike evaluative priming, the IAT is a relative task that gauges differences in average RT between "compatible" trials (those involving judgments that are attitude-consistent for most respondents) and "incompatible" trials (those involving judgments that are attitude-inconsistent for most).

The basic reasoning is that participants should be able to provide the same response to two concepts that are similar in evaluative connotation more easily than providing the same response to two concepts with contrasting evaluative connotations. In the context of race, an implicit preference for Caucasians over African Americans is indicated when the participant exhibits faster average RTs when responding with one key to Caucasian stimuli (typically facial photographs) and positive words while responding with another key to African American stimuli and negative words. Conversely, an implicit preference for African Americans over Caucasians is indicated by faster average RTs when the participant uses one key in response to African American names and positive words and a different key in response to Caucasian names and negative words (see Figure 17.4 for a visual example of the IAT procedure).

Much like evaluative priming, the IAT also has numerous applications outside the realm of racial attitudes, including the measurement of implicit self-esteem. Typically, the IAT procedure is modified by alternately pairing the categories *me* and *not-me* with the positive and negative words (Greenwald & Farnham, 2000). The *me* and *not-me* categories are populated by asking participants for self-descriptive terms such as their first name, last name, hometown, birth month, and others. The

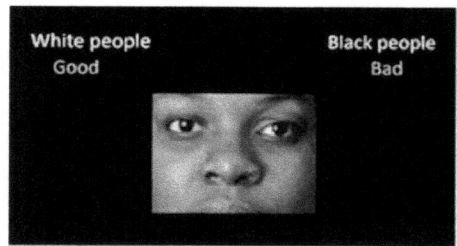 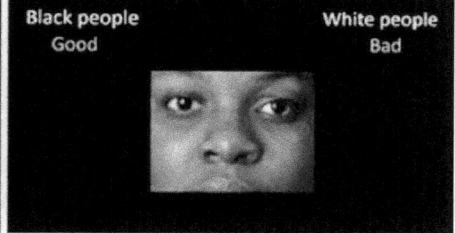

(a) White-Good/Black-Bad condition.   (b) Black-Good/White-Bad condition.

Figure 17.4 *Visual example of the race-based Implicit Association Test. https://courses2.cit.cornell.edu/sociallaw/student_projects/Definingbias.html Both "compatible" (a) and "incompatible" (b) trials are depicted. From Epifania et al. (2023). This article is licensed under CC BY 4.0.*

self-descriptive terms constitute the *me* category, and a parallel set of similar yet non-self-descriptive stimuli is developed for the *not-me* category (e.g., first names, last names, and hometowns. other than the participant's). This approach has the advantage of using idiographic stimuli that are customized at the level of the individual participant.

One recent application involved comparing self-esteem IAT performance among dysphoric and control participants (Lou et al., 2021). Although IAT scores did not significantly differ between the two groups, participants with dysphoria showed greater brain reactivity – as indicated by increased late positive component (LPC) amplitude – during *me-negative* blocks compared to *me-positive* blocks, suggesting more efficient categorization of self-negativity compared to the control group. Lou et al. suggested that, despite the apparent lack of difference in the overall IAT effect, the LPC data could have indicated lower implicit self-esteem within the participants with dysphoria. In other applications, the IAT has been shown to relate to a wide range of important behavioral outcomes, many of which have potential practical significance. For example, Senholzi et al. (2015) found IAT scores were positively related to amygdala activation (indicative of a fear reaction) in response to images of armed African Americans.

Importantly, the enormous popularity of the IAT should not be taken to mean it is universally accepted as a measure of implicit attitudes. As is often the case when something becomes so widespread, criticisms of the IAT abound. One of the simpler criticisms is that differences in RTs between the compatible and incompatible portions of the test are relative, not absolute (Brendl et al., 2001). For example, a result suggesting an implicit preference for African Americans could mean one of three things: (1) the participant has a positive implicit attitude toward African Americans and a negative implicit attitude toward Caucasians; (2) the participant has a positive implicit attitude toward both groups but the positive attitude toward African Americans is more pronounced; or (3) the participant has a negative implicit attitude toward both groups but the negative attitude toward African Americans is less pronounced. Whatever the case, the only meaningful conclusion one can draw is that the participant has an evaluative preference for one group over the other. Other criticisms of the IAT are more extensive, such as questioning whether the associations it measures are actually rooted within the person taking the test (Olson & Fazio, 2004).

The Go/No-go Association Task

Largely due to the aforementioned relative nature of the IAT, Nosek and Banaji (2001) developed the Go/No-go Association Task (GNAT) – a similar computer-based task that assesses implicit attitudes without requiring a contrast category. The GNAT measures the positivity or negativity of the participant's implicit evaluation of any one social group, independent of his or her implicit evaluation of any other group. As its name implies, the GNAT is a recognition RT task in which participants actively respond to some stimuli (the "go" response) but do *not* respond to other stimuli (the "no-go" response). In a standard GNAT procedure measuring implicit attitudes, participants are presented with stimuli from both the social category (e.g., African American) and positive or negative words. In some trial blocks, participants press the designated "go" key if the stimulus belongs to the social or positive word category; no response is given if any other stimulus appears. In other trial blocks, participants respond "go" to stimuli from the social and negative word categories but do not respond to any other stimuli. The GNAT can also be adapted to measure other constructs (e.g., implicit self-esteem) using an approach similar to that described above for the IAT (i.e., using *me* and *not-me* in place of social categories; see Valiente et al., 2011, for a clinical application of the implicit self-esteem GNAT).

Besides a contrast category being unnecessary in the GNAT, its scoring also distinguishes it from the IAT. First, though the GNAT involves recording per-trial RTs, and such RTs can certainly be used (see Nosek & Banaji, 2001), its primary scoring method is grounded in signal detection theory (SDT; Green & Swets, 1966). To the extent that the social category and attribute dimension (positive or negative) are more strongly associated, sensitivity (i.e., discriminating signal from noise, indicated by d' [d-prime]) should increase. Therefore, differences in sensitivity between the two critical trial types indicate the nature of the participant's implicit evaluation of the social category (Nosek & Banaji, 2001). In our example, greater sensitivity when African American and positive stimuli are paired together suggests a positive implicit attitude toward African Americans; greater sensitivity when African American and negative stimuli are paired suggests a negative implicit attitude toward African Americans.

Software for Reaction Time Research

Reaction time tasks require equipment capable of presenting stimuli and recording responses with millisecond-level precision. In most social and behavioral research, this equipment takes the form of computer hardware and software. Because hardware is often specific to certain tasks involving RT and software is continuously advancing, this chapter focuses on software for the presentation and recording of RTs commonly available for use on most personal computers.

The rapid development of RT software is a double-edged sword. Advances in the capabilities of such software provide researchers with a myriad of options for design and implementation. This amount of choice also highlights the importance of making informed decisions about which software is most appropriate for one's research. Thankfully, discussion of RT software can focus on important commonalities among the available options. Most well-known and widely used examples of software can be used on most personal computers and with the various RT tasks described earlier in this chapter.

Software programs used in RT research are often commercially available products since companies, as compared to individuals, are likely to have the time and resources to focus on timely development, distribution, and maintenance of such software. The software developers give explicit consideration to the critical issues of the reliability and validity of RT presentation and response. Although a variety of

Table 17.1 *Comparison of product features across DirectRT, E-Prime, and SuperLab*

Product feature	DirectRT	E-Prime	SuperLab
Publisher	Empirisoft (empirisoft.com)	Psychology Software Tools (pstnet.com)	Cedrus (cedrus.com)
Operating system	Windows	Windows	Windows, MacOS
Programming style	Excel/spreadsheet	Drag-and-drop or syntax	Point-and-click interface
Input hardware	Standard (e.g., keyboard, mouse) or specialized (e.g., button box)	Standard (e.g., keyboard, mouse) or specialized (e.g., button box)	Standard (e.g., keyboard, mouse) or specialized (e.g., button box)
Output type	.txt or import to Excel/SPSS	.txt converted to .edat or .edat2 in E-DataAid	.txt or import to Excel/SPSS
Compatibility with mobile devices	None	Tablets, touchscreens	None
Compatibility with other software	MediaLab and/or PowerPoint integration	None	None
Pre-programmed sample tasks	Yes (40+)	Yes (80+)	Yes (25)
Sound/graphic stimulus presentation	Yes	Yes	Yes
Record button release times (in addition to button presses)	Yes	Yes	No

Note: Paid licenses are required for all three programs. Licenses can be purchased on a per-device basis or as site licenses at the laboratory, departmental, and institutional levels. See each publisher's website for pricing details.

such software exists, it is most illustrative to focus on specific examples that have been extensively used in published research and professional presentations: DirectRT, E-Prime, and SuperLab (see Table 17.1 for a direct comparison of product features). Of note, these do not require specialized knowledge of programming languages and offer user-friendly interfaces.

DirectRT

DirectRT (Empirisoft Corporation, 2020a) is software that runs on devices using Windows operating systems to allow researchers to quickly and easily create tasks that require precision timing. The primary strength of DirectRT involves cognitive/perception "blocks of trials" (e.g., priming/lexical decision style) tasks that require measures of stimulus presentation and response times reliable and accurate to the millisecond. DirectRT allows users to create, copy, paste, and modify single or multiple trials in research designs, similar to working in a spreadsheet. DirectRT uses DirectX to present sound, video, images, and text with exacting precision.

Using either standard hardware (e.g., a USB keyboard, serial mouse, joystick, or sound card microphone) or specialized millisecond-accurate keyboards and button boxes from the Empirisoft Corporation, DirectRT obtains accurate, millisecond-level responses from participants. DirectRT also can be used in conjunction with other software (e.g., MediaLab; Empirisoft Corporation, 2020b) to add its RT-related capabilities to larger research designs. Output files are saved in a .txt format that is compatible with most spreadsheet and data analysis software; data files can also be manipulated and merged using the Data Restructuring utility of DirectRT.

E-Prime

E-Prime (Psychology Software Tools, 2016) uses a collection of applications on devices using Windows operating systems to create and present RT tasks. Researchers can create different tasks involving reaction time using a graphical drop-and-drag interface. Specifically, E-Prime uses "objects" to control different functions (e.g., presentation of stimuli, the creation of blocks of trials, presentation of feedback, and the order of presentation of these events). E-Prime collects input using both standard (i.e., keyboard and mouse) and specialized (i.e., button boxes) peripheral devices. Among its extensive documentation, E-Prime provides users with detailed information about the testing procedure to ensure the reliability and validity of its RT-based functions (see https://support.pstnet.com/hc/en-us/categories/204686967-E-Prime). Similar to DirectRT, E-Prime provides users with tools for debugging problems that might arise while testing program files. Output files are similarly saved in a .txt format; data files can also be viewed and cleaned in the E-DataAid application of E-Prime. In addition, a distinguishing feature of E-Prime relative to other software is the ability to use the program with tablets and touchscreens.

SuperLab

SuperLab (Cedrus Corporation, 2022) runs on devices using Windows or Macintosh operating systems. It uses a point-and-click interface that allows researchers to control the presentation of stimuli such as images, sound, and video files. Software users can create a variety of tasks in blocks of trials that feature millisecond-level presentation of stimuli and recording of response input. SuperLab collects input using both standard (i.e., keyboard and mouse) and specialized (i.e., button boxes) peripheral devices. Timing of stimulus presentation is coordinated with the refresh rate of the device display; timing of inputs is recorded to the nearest millisecond from various user-defined events (e.g., trial onset or stimulus presentation). Output files are saved in a .txt format; data files can also be viewed and cleaned in the Data Viewer function of SuperLab.

Online and Open Source Tools

Another feature common to these three examples of software is that their use is primarily confined to the machine on which the software is installed. Understandably, adding anything between the actual hardware of the computer and the software used to run RT tasks introduces possible variability in the execution of said tasks. Despite this valid concern, some software companies have taken up this challenge and successfully developed software to conduct RT research online. Though some concerns may arise due to variations in participants' internet connection speeds, many researchers have found considerable success with this approach (e.g., Nosek et al., 2007). Projects such as Project Implicit (https://implicit.harvard.edu/implicit) allow for online versions of specific tasks involving reaction time (e.g., the IAT).

Inquisit (Millisecond Software, 2022) is software with a version that can run locally on devices using a Window or Macintosh operating system with many of the same functions for RT research as described in our previous examples. However, Inquisit also has a version for use on the internet for research tasks involving RT. A primary difference is that creation of these tasks in Inquisit involves a user-friendly scripting language resembling HTML (www.millisecond.com/products/features). Although the programming and creation of tasks in Inquisit may be more involved, the ability to run the tasks online is an attractive feature.

Use of the internet to implement RT tasks has also contributed to the creation and proliferation of open source software available to researchers. Open source software is attractive to researchers for its great potential to include numerous capabilities and features, often at little to no monetary cost to the researcher. Importantly, the open source software has evidence of reliable and accurate timing functions (de Leeuw & Motz, 2016). However, these open source programs are likely to use more complex programming languages to create reaction time tasks and may be troublesome for researchers without proficiency in computer programming. Open source software is also heavily dependent on development teams and users to continually support the software; the software is only as good as the effort its users put into its maintenance and maturation. This recent addition to the toolboxes of RT researchers and its potential contributions bear watching.

Statistical Analysis of Reaction Time Data

Although it is beyond our scope to discuss all the possible nuances of analyzing reaction time data, we do want to provide a basic overview of analytical approaches to give the reader a sense of some of the challenges that RT data pose. Thankfully, other authors have written extensive treatments of this subject (e.g., Whelan, 2008). We encourage the reader to examine such sources when dealing with one's own RT data sets (including making informed decisions during the study design process).

Of note, many researchers use analysis of variance (ANOVA) to compare mean RTs across different conditions (Van Zandt, 2002). Although this approach can occasionally be statistically sound, usually it is not (Whelan, 2008). Factors such as fatigue and inattention (even sporadic inattention) typically yield RT data with a high degree of positive skew, making the statistician's job a bit trickier. In this section, we will compare two general approaches to analyzing RT data: one that utilizes standard measures of central tendency and another that examines the full scope of RTs across the entire distribution (see Whelan, 2008 for discussion of a third approach that involves aggregation of RT data).

Measures of Central Tendency

As noted above, tests of mean differences (e.g., ANOVA) are frequently employed with RT data. However, it is also well known that such tests are underpowered when examining non-normal distributions such as those yielded by most RT measures (Wilcox, 1998). Ratcliff (1993) examined various strategies to increase statistical power; these strategies can be loosely categorized into three areas: trimming outliers, data transformations, and using alternate parameters. Trimming outliers involves setting cutoff points for extremely fast (e.g., below 100 ms) and/or slow RTs (e.g., greater than a predetermined number of standard deviations above the mean). Although this technique is intuitive and does often increase power, it should not be used in isolation because it can also *decrease* power in some circumstances (e.g., when experimental manipulations differentially affect only the slow or fast RTs across conditions; Ratcliff, 1993).

As such, using data transformations to normalize distribution shapes (e.g., inverse transformations, log transformations) alongside trimming outliers has become common practice. Transformations typically lessen the impact of slow outliers and thus improve statistical power (Osborne, 2002). Lastly, many researchers use parameters other than the mean and standard deviation to reflect central tendency and variability, respectively. For example, the median and interquartile range are less influenced by outliers, although the median can be a biased estimator when conditions are based on different numbers of trials (Whelan, 2008).

Full RT Distributions

One clear limitation of the central tendency approach is that two or more distributions can have the same mean RT but differ dramatically in overall shape (e.g., differing patterns of slow vs. fast responses). As a result, contemporary RT researchers are increasingly turning to analyses that incorporate the full distribution of responses. Although this approach usually requires a large number of observations, both per participant and per condition, it can reveal overall patterns of responses that a single metric, such as the mean, cannot (Whelan, 2008).

For example, Hervey et al. (2006) compared RT performance between children diagnosed with attention-deficit hyperactivity disorder (ADHD) and a control group. The standard metrics suggested the children with ADHD were both slower and more variable (i.e., a larger mean and standard deviation). However, an examination of the full distribution found the children with ADHD actually had slightly *faster* mean RTs in the relatively normal portion of the distribution but also had more RTs in the tail (i.e., the skewed portion containing the slowest RTs). Based on these findings, Hervey et al. suggested children with ADHD were not necessarily slower than the control group. It seems they were simply more prone to lapses in attention on certain trials.

Conclusion

In many ways, the history of reaction time research is the history of social and behavioral science. Both borrowed and refined the study of physical sensations from traditional "hard sciences" for the study of human behavior. Both occupy a centrally situated role in contemporary empirical research on human behavior that is unlikely to go away any time soon. Both underwent a paradigm shift with the invention and proliferation of computer technology. Of course, RT research faces challenges in further defining its role. For example, advances in technology (e.g., smartwatches and fitness trackers) that change the placement of displays from the traditional location of eye level affect RTs (Harrison et al., 2009). Researchers using such devices will need to take explicit care to compare and validate new technology with the existing body of RT research.

Future RT research should also consider the relationship between implicit and explicit thoughts and/or behaviors. The large body of empirical research on implicit and explicit thoughts and behaviors clearly demonstrates its variations for a number of topics of study such as attitudes (Nosek, 2007), emotion regulation (Gyurak et al., 2011), and self-esteem (Krizan & Suls, 2008). It also demonstrates the centrality of RT in such research using the internet instead of more traditional methods (Nosek et al., 2002). Researchers studying RT should be aware of possible moderators and mediators – including the RT measure itself – of the phenomena under investigation.

Acknowledgments

The author would like to thank Jason Reed for his invaluable contributions to an earlier version of this chapter, particularly with respect to software. Gratitude is also in order for the editors of this volume, John Edlund and Austin Nichols, for their tireless (and often thankless) efforts to make this book a reality.

References

Ando, S., Kida, N., & Oda, S. (2002). Practice effects on reaction time for peripheral and central visual fields. *Perceptual and Motor Skills*, *95*(3), 747–752. http://dx.doi.org/10.2466/pms.2002.95.3.747

(2004). Retention of practice effects on simple reaction time for peripheral and central visual fields. *Perceptual and Motor Skills*, *98*(3), 897–900. http://dx.doi.org/10.2466/PMS.98.3.897-900

Arent, S. M., & Landers, D. M. (2003). Arousal, anxiety, and performance: A reexamination of the inverted-U hypothesis. *Research Quarterly for Exercise and Sport*, *74*(4), 436–444. http://dx.doi.org/10.1080/02701367.2003.10609113

Atkinson, R. C., & Shiffrin, R. M. (1968). Human memory: A proposed system and its control processes. In K. W. Spence & J. T. Spence, *The Psychology of Learning and Motivation* (vol. 2, pp. 89–195). Academic Press.

Babkoff, H., Genser, S., & Hegge, F. W. (1985). Lexical decision, parafoveal eccentricity and visual hemifield. *Cortex*, *21*(4), 581–593. http://dx.doi.org/10.1016/S0010-9452(58)80006-4

Baghdadi, G., Towhidkhah, F., & Rajabi, M. (2021). *Neurocognitive Mechanisms of Attention*. Elsevier.

Boring, E. G. (1950). *A History of Experimental Psychology*, 2nd ed. Appleton-Century-Crofts.

Brendl, C. M., Markman, A. B., & Messner, C. (2001). How do indirect measures of evaluation work? Evaluating the inference of prejudice in the Implicit Association Test. *Journal of Personality and Social Psychology*, *81*(5), 760–773. http://dx.doi.org/10.1037//0022-3514.81.5.760

Cedrus Corporation. (2022). Download SuperLab [webpage]. https://cedrus.com/superlab/download.htm

Damanpak, S., Mokhtari, P., & Mousavi, S. M. V. (2014). Relationship between arousal and choice reaction time. *Biosciences Biotechnology Research Asia*, *11*(2), 803–806. http://dx.doi.org/10.13005/bbra/1341

Danek, R. H., & Mordkoff, J. T. (2011). Unequal motor durations under simple-, Go/No-go, and choice-RT tasks: Extension of Miller and Low (2001). *Journal of Experimental Psychology: Human Perception and Performance*, *37*(4), 1323–1329. https://doi.org/10.1037/a0023092

de Leeuw, J. R., & Motz, B. A. (2016). Psychophysics in a Web browser? Comparing response times collected with JavaScript and Psychophysics Toolbox in a visual search task. *Behavior Research Methods*, *48*(1), 1–12. http://dx.doi.org/10.3758/s13428-015-0567-2

Delwiche, J. F., Halpern, B. P., & Desimone, J. A. (1999). Anion size of sodium salts and simple taste reaction times. *Physiology & Behavior*, *66*(1), 27–32. https://doi.org/10.1016/S0031-9384(98)00273-X

Der, G., & Deary, I. J. (2006). Age and sex differences in reaction time in adulthood: Results from the United Kingdom Health and Lifestyle Survey. *Psychology and Aging*, *21*(1), 62–73. http://dx.doi.org/10.1037/0882-7974.21.1.62

Dovidio, J. F., Kawakami, K., & Gaertner, S. L. (2002). Implicit and explicit prejudice and interracial interaction. *Journal of Personality and Social Psychology*, *82*(1), 62–68. http://dx.doi.org/10.1037/0022-3514.82.1.62

Dovidio, J. F., Kawakami, K., Johnson, C., Johnson, B., & Howard, A. (1997). On the nature of prejudice: Automatic and controlled processes. *Journal of Experimental Social Psychology*, *33*(5), 510–540. http://dx.doi.org/10.1006/jesp.1997.1331

Durlach, P. J., Edmunds, R., Howard, L., & Tipper, S. P. (2002). A rapid effect of caffeinated beverages on two choice reaction time tasks. *Nutritional Neuroscience* *5*(6), 433–442. https://doi.org/10.1080/1028415021000039211

Dutilh, G., Vandekerckhove, J., Tuerlinckx, F., & Wagenmakers, E.-J. (2009). A diffusion model decomposition of the practice effect. *Psychonomic Bulletin and Review*, *16*(6), 1026–1036. http://dx.doi.org/10.3758/16.6.1026

Dykiert, D., Der, G., Starr, J. M., & Deary, I. J. (2012). Age differences in intra-individual variability in simple and choice reaction time: Systematic review and meta-analysis. *PLOS ONE*, *7*(10). https://doi.org/10.1371/journal.pone.0045759

Elliott, E. M., Morey, C. C., Morey, R. D., Eaves, S. D., Shelton, J. T., & Lutfi-Proctor, D. A. (2014). The role of modality: Auditory and visual distractors in Stroop interference. *Journal of Cognitive Psychology*, *26*(1), 15–26. http://dx.doi.org/10.1080/20445911.2013 859133

Empirisoft Corporation. (2020a). *v2020 Downloads* [DirectRT 2020.1.111]. www.empirisoft.com/download.aspx

Empirisoft Corporation. (2020b). *v2020 Downloads* [MediaLab 2020.1.111]. www.empirisoft.com/download.aspx

Epifania, O. M., Robusto, E., & Anselmi, P. (2023). Is the performance at the Implicit Association Test sensitive to feedback presentation? A Rasch-based analysis. *Psychological Research*, *87*, 737–750. https://doi.org/10.1007/s00426-022-01703-w

Eriksen, B. A., & Eriksen, C. W. (1974). Effects of noise letters upon the identification of a target letter in a nonsearch task. *Perception and Psychophysics*, *16*(1), 143–149. http://dx.doi.org/10.3758/BF03203267

Eriksen, C. W., & St. James, J. D. (1986). Visual attention within and around the field of focal attention: A zoom lens model. *Perception and Psychophysics*, *40*(4), 225–240. http://dx.doi.org/10.3758/BF03211502

Evans, N. J., Brown, S. D., Mewhort, D. J. K., & Heathcote, A. (2018). Refining the law of practice. *Psychological Review*, *125*(4), 592–605. https://doi.org/10.1037/rev0000105

Exner, S. (1873). Experimentelle Untersuchung der einfachsten psychischen Processe: Erste Abhandlung. *Archiv für die Gesammte Physiologie des Menschen und der Thiere*, *7*, 601–660. https://doi.org/10.1007/BF01613351

Fazio, R. H., Jackson, J. R., Dunton, B. C., & Williams, C. J. (1995). Variability in automatic activation as an unobtrusive measure of racial attitudes: A bona fide pipeline? *Journal of Personality and Social Psychology*, *69*(6), 1013–1027. http://dx.doi.org/10.1037/0022-3514.69.6.1013

Fazio, R. H., Sanbonmatsu, D. M., Powell, M. C., & Kardes, F. R. (1986). On the automatic activation of attitudes. *Journal of Personality and Social Psychology*, *50*(2), 229–238. http://dx.doi.org/10.1037/0022-3514.50.2.229

Fontani, G., Lodi, L., Felici, A., Migliorini, S., & Corradeschi, F. (2006). Attention in athletes of high and low experience engaged in different open skill sports. *Perceptual and Motor Skills*, *102*(3), 791–805. http://dx.doi.org/10.2466/PMS.102.3.791-805

Gorus, E., De Raedt, R., Lambert, M., Lemper, J.-C., & Mets, T. (2008). Reaction times and performance variability in normal aging, mild cognitive impairment, and Alzheimer's disease. *Journal of Geriatric Psychiatry and Neurology*, *21*(3), 204–218.

Gotlib, I. H., & McCann, C. D. (1984). Construct accessibility and depression: An examination of cognitive and affective factors. *Journal of Personality and Social Psychology*, *47*(2), 427–439. http://dx.doi.org/10.1037/0022-3514.47.2.427

Green, D. M., & Swets, J. A. (1966). *Signal Detection Theory and Psychophysics*. John Wiley.

Greenwald, A. G., & Farnham, S. D. (2000). Using the Implicit Association Test to measure self-esteem and self-concept. *Journal of Personality and Social Psychology, 79*(6), 1022–1038. http://dx.doi.org/10.1037/0022-3514.79.6.1022

Greenwald, A. G., McGhee, D. E., & Schwartz, J. L. K. (1998). Measuring individual differences in implicit cognition: The Implicit Association Test. *Journal of Personality and Social Psychology, 74*(6), 1464–1480. http://dx.doi.org/10.1037/0022-3514.74.6.1464

Gyurak, A., Gross, J. J., & Etkin, A. (2011). Explicit and implicit emotion regulation: A dual-process framework. *Cognition and Emotion, 25*(3), 400–412. http://dx.doi.org/10.1080/02699931.2010.544160

Harrison, C., Lim, B. Y., Shick, A., & Hudson, S. E. (2009, April). Where to locate wearable displays? Reaction time performance of visual alerts from tip to toe. In *Chi '09: Proceedings of the SIGCHI Conference on Human Factors in Computing Systems* (pp. 941–944). ACM. https://doi.org/10.1145/1518701.1518845

Henrich, J., Heine, S. J., & Norenzayan, A. (2010). The weirdest people in the world? *Behavioral and Brain Sciences, 33*(2–3), 61–83. https://doi.org/10.1017/S0140525X0999152X

Hergenhahn, B. R. (2013). *An Introduction to the History of Psychology*, 7th ed. Wadsworth.

Hernandez, S., Nieto, A., & Barroso, J. (1992). Hemispheric specialization for word classes with visual presentations and lexical decision task. *Brain and Cognition, 20*(2), 399–408. http://dx.doi.org/10.1016/0278-2626(92)90029-L

Hervey, A. S., Epstein, J. N., Curry, J. F., Tonev, S., Arnold, L. E., Conners, C. K., et al. (2006). Reaction time distribution analysis of neuropsychological performance in an ADHD sample. *Child Neuropsychology, 12*(2), 125–140. https://doi.org/10.1080/09297040500499081

Hick, W. E. (1952). On the rate of gain of information. *Quarterly Journal of Experimental Psychology, 4*, 11–26. http://dx.doi.org/10.1080/17470215208416600

Howse, D. (1989). *Nevil Maskelyne: The Seaman's Astronomer*. Cambridge University Press.

Jaśkowski, P., & Włodarczyk, D. (1997). Effect of sleep deficit, knowledge of results, and stimulus quality on reaction time and response force. *Perceptual and Motor Skills, 84*(2), 563–572. http://dx.doi.org/10.2466/pms.1997.84.2.563

Johns, M., Crowley, K., Chapman, R., Tucker, A., & Hocking, C. (2009). The effect of blinks and saccadic eye movements on visual reaction times. *Attention, Perception, and Psychophysics, 71*(4), 783–788. http://dx.doi.org/10.3758/APP.71.4.783

Jones, E. E., & Sigall, H. (1971). The bogus pipeline: A new paradigm for measuring affect and attitude. *Psychological Bulletin, 76*(5), 349–364. https://doi.org/10.1037/h0031617

Kling, J. W., & Riggs, L. A. (1971). *Woodworth & Schlosberg's experimental psychology*, 3rd ed. Holt, Rinehart, & Winston.

Krizan, Z., & Suls, J. (2008). Are implicit and explicit measures of self-esteem related? A meta-analysis for the Name-Letter test. *Personality and Individual Differences, 44*(2), 521–531. http://dx.doi.org/10.1016/j.paid.2007.09.017

Lavoie, M. E., Dupuis, F., Johnston, K. M., Leclerc, S., & Lassonde, M. (2004). Visual P300 effects beyond symptoms in concussed college athletes. *Journal of Clinical and Experimental Neuropsychology, 26*(1), 55–73. http://dx.doi.org/10.1076/jcen.26.1.55.23936

Levitt, S., & Gutin, B. (1971). Multiple choice reaction time and movement time during physical exertion. *Research Quarterly of the American Association for Health,*

Physical Education, and Recreation, 42(4), 405–410. https://doi.org/10.1080/10671188.1971.10615088

Luce, R. D. (1986). *Response Times: Their Role in Inferring Elementary Mental Organization*. Oxford University Press.

MacLeod, C. M., & Dunbar, K. (1988). Training and Stroop-like interference: Evidence for a continuum of automaticity. *Journal of Experimental Psychology: Learning, Memory, and Cognition, 14*(1), 126–135. http://dx.doi.org/10.1037/0278-7393.14.1.126

Medic-Pericevic, S., Mikov, I., Glavaski-Kraljevic, M., Spanovic, M., Bozic, A., Vasovic, V., & Mikov, M. (2020). The effects of aging and driving experience on reaction times of professional drivers. *Work: Journal of Prevention, Assessment & Rehabilitation, 66*(2), 405–419. https://doi.org/10.3233/WOR-203181

Miller, J. O., & Low, K. (2001). Motor processes in simple, Go/No-go, and choice reaction time tasks: A psychophysiological analysis. *Journal of Experimental Psychology: Human Perception and Performance, 27*(2), 266–289. http://dx.doi.org/10.1037/0096-1523.27.2.266

Millisecond Software. (2022). Download Inquisit Lab [Inquisit Lab 6.6.1]. www.millisecond.com/download

Müller, J. (1833–1840). *Handbuch der Physiologie des Menschen für Vorlesungen*. J. Hölscher.

Nosek, B. A. (2007). Implicit–explicit relations. *Current Directions in Psychological Science, 16*(2), 65–69. http://dx.doi.org/10.1111/j.1467-8721.2007.00477.x

Nosek, B. A., & Banaji, M. R. (2001). The Go/No-go Association Task. *Social Cognition, 19*(6), 625–666. http://dx.doi.org/10.1521/soco.19.6.625.20886

Nosek, B. A., Banaji, M. R., & Greenwald, A. G. (2002). Harvesting implicit group attitudes and beliefs from a demonstration web site. *Group Dynamics: Theory, Research, and Practice, 6*(1), 101–115. http://dx.doi.org/10.1037/1089-2699.6.1.101

Nosek, B. A., Smyth, F. L., Hansen, J. J., Devos, T., Lindner, N. M., Ranganath, K. A., et al. (2007). Pervasiveness and correlates of implicit attitudes and stereotypes. *European Review of Social Psychology, 18*, 36–88. http://dx.doi.org/10.1080/10463280701489053

Olson, M. A., & Fazio, R. H. (2004). Reducing the influence of extrapersonal associations on the Implicit Association Test: Personalizing the IAT. *Journal of Personality and Social Psychology, 86*(5), 653–667. http://dx.doi.org/10.1037/0022-3514.86.5.653

Osborne, J. W. (2002). Notes on the use of data transformations. *Practical Assessment, Research, and Evaluation, 8*(6). https://doi.org/10.7275/4vng-5608

Overbosch, P., de Wijk, R., de Jonge, T. J., & Köster, E. P. (1989). Temporal integration and reaction times in human smell. *Physiology & Behavior, 45*(3), 615–626. https://doi.org/10.1016/0031-9384(89)90082-6

Pavelka, R., Třebický, V., Fialova, J. T., Zdobinsky, A., Coufalova, K., Havlicek, J., & Tufano, J. J. (2020). Acute fatigue affects reaction times and reaction consistency in mixed martial arts fighters. *PLOS ONE, 15*(1), e0227675. https://doi.org/10.1371/journal.pone.0227675

Peschke, C., Hilgetag, C. C., & Olk, B. (2013). Influence of stimulus type on effects of flanker, flanker position, and trial sequence in a saccadic eye movement task. *Quarterly Journal of Experimental Psychology, 66*(11), 2253–2267. https://doi.org/10.1080/17470218.2013.777464

Pins, D., & Bonnet, C. (1996). On the relation between stimulus intensity and processing time: Piéron's law and choice reaction time. *Perception & Psychophysics*, *58*(3), 390–400. https://doi.org/10.3758/BF03206815

Psychology Software Tools. (2016). Psychology Software Tools homepage [E-Prime 3.0]. www.pstnet.com

Ratcliff, R. (1993). Methods for dealing with reaction time outliers. *Psychological Bulletin*, *114*(3), 510–532. https://doi.org/10.1037/0033-2909.114.3.510

Robinson, E. S. (1934). Work of the integrated organism. In C. Murchison (ed.), *A Handbook of General Experimental Psychology* (pp. 571–650). Clark University Press.

Robinson, M. D., & Tamir, M. (2005). Neuroticism as mental noise: A relation between neuroticism and reaction time standard deviations. *Journal of Personality and Social Psychology*, *89*(1), 107–114. http://dx.doi.org/10.1037/0022-3514.89.1.107

Rodriguez-Raecke, R., Schrader, C., Tacik, P., Dressler, D., Lanfermann, H., & Wittfoth, M. (2022). Conflict adaptation and related neuronal processing in Parkinson's disease. *Brain Imaging and Behavior*, *16*, 455–463.

Sanders, A. F. (1998). *Elements of Human Performance: Reaction Processes and Attention in Human Skill*. Lawrence Erlbaum Associates.

Satorres, E., Oliva, I., Escudero, J., & Meléndez, J. C. (2020). Conflict monitoring on an emotional Stroop task: Comparison of healthy older adults and patients with major neurocognitive disorders due to probable AD. *Journal of Clinical and Experimental Neuropsychology*, *42*(5), 485–494. https://doi.org/10.1080/13803395.2020.1761946

Schultz, D. P., & Schultz, S. E. (2016). *A History of Modern Psychology*, 11th ed. Cengage Learning.

Senholzi, K. B., Depue, B. E., Correll, J., Banich, M. T., & Ito, T. A. (2015). Brain activation underlying threat detection to targets of different races. *Social Neuroscience*, *10*(6), 651–662. http://dx.doi.org/10.1080/17470919.2015.1091380

Stafford, T., Ingram, L., & Gurney, K. N. (2011). Piéron's law holds during Stroop conflict: Insights into the architecture of decision making. *Cognitive Science*, *35*(8), 1553–1566. https://doi.org/10.1111/j.1551-6709.2011.01195.x

Sternberg, S. (1969). Memory-scanning: Mental processes revealed by reaction-time experiments. *American Scientist*, *57*(4), 421–457.

Stroop, J. R. (1935). Studies of interference in serial verbal reactions. *Journal of Experimental Psychology*, *18*(6), 643–662. http://dx.doi.org/10.1037/h0054651

Testable. (2021, September 14). *Flanker Task*. www.testable.org/experiment-guides/execu tive-function/flanker-task

VaezMousavi, S. M., Barry, R. J., & Clarke, A. R. (2009). Individual differences in task-related activation and performance. *Physiology and Behavior*, *98*(3), 326–330. http://dx.doi.org/10.1016/j.physbeh.2009.06.007

Vakil, E., Lowe, M., & Goldfus, C. (2015). Performance of children with developmental dyslexia on two skill learning tasks – Serial Reaction Time and Tower of Hanoi Puzzle: A test of the specific procedural learning difficulties theory. *Journal of Learning Disabilities*, *48*(5), 471–481. http://dx.doi.org/10.1177/0022219413508981

Valiente, C., Cantero, D., Vázquez, C., Sanchez, Á., Provencio, M., & Espinosa, R. (2011). Implicit and explicit self-esteem discrepancies in paranoia and depression. *Journal of Abnormal Psychology*, *120*(3), 691–699. https://doi.org/10.1037/a0022856

Van Bavel, J. J., & Cunningham, W. A. (2010). A social neuroscience approach to self and social categorisation: A new look at an old issue. *European Review of Social Psychology*, *21*(1), 237–284. https://doi.org/10.1080/10463283.2010.543314

Van Zandt, T. (2002). Analysis of response time distributions. In H. Pashler & J. Wixted (eds.), *Stevens' Handbook of Experimental Psychology: Methodology in Experimental Psychology*, 3rd ed. (vol. 4, pp. 461–516). John Wiley & Sons.

Volkan, E., & Hadjimarkou, M. M. (2019). Undivided trauma in a divided Cyprus: Modified emotional Stroop study. *Psychological Trauma: Theory, Research, Practice, and Policy, 14*(6), 989–997. https://doi.org./10.1037/tra0000527

Welford, A. T. (1981). Signal, noise, performance, and age. *Human Factors, 23*(1), 97–109.

Whelan, R. (2008). Effective analysis of reaction time data. *Psychological Record, 58*(3), 475–482.

Wilcox, R. R. (1998). How many discoveries have been lost by ignoring modern statistical methods? *American Psychologist, 53*(3), 300–314. https://doi.org./10.1037/0003-066X.53.3.300

Wylie, S. A., van den Wildenberg, W. P. M., Ridderinkhof, K. R., Bashore, T. R., Powell, V. D., Manning, C. A., & Wooten, G. F. (2009). The effect of speed-accuracy strategy on response interference control in Parkinson's disease. *Neuropsychologia, 47*(8–9), 1844–1853. https://doi.org/10.1016/j.neuropsychologia.2009.02.025

Yerkes, R. M., & Dodson, J. D. (1908). The relation of strength of stimulus to rapidity of habit formation. *Journal of Comparative Neurology and Psychology, 18*, 459–482. http://dx.doi.org/10.1002/cne.920180503

Zayas, V., Wang, A. M., & McCalla, J. D. (2022). Me as good and me as bad: Priming the self triggers positive and negative implicit evaluations. *Journal of Personality and Social Psychology, 122*(1), 106–134. http://dx.doi.org/2048/10.1037/pspp0000332

18 Eyetracking Research

Anjali K. Jogeshwar and Jeff B. Pelz

Abstract

This chapter describes the use of eyetracking as an advanced research tool in the social and behavioral sciences. It covers the correlation of eye movements to behavior, the basic anatomy of the eye and its movements, and different kinds of eyetrackers that can be used to capture a range of behaviors. It also explains how one should select an eyetracker, and how to obtain good-quality data. Data quality always affects the final result, and this chapter explains how the accuracy and precision of gaze data affect behavioral analysis along with giving examples about the real-life application of eyetracking in social and behavioral research. The potential of eyetracking as a technology is vast, providing a window to the visual perception which is likely to make eyetracking a very important tool in the years to come.

Keywords: Eyetracking, Eye Movements, Data Analysis, Data Visualization, Real-World Applications, Behavior Analysis

Erasmus Darwin dedicated his book, *Zoonomia; or, The Laws of Organic Life* (Darwin, 1794) to "all those who study the Operations of the Mind as a Science." Darwin was fascinated by the movements of the eyes and devoted a section of his book to "The Motions of the Retina Demonstrated by Experiments." His descriptions of eye movements were of course not the first; Darwin referenced work done by William Porterfield, a physician in Edinburgh, who published an "Essay Concerning the Motions of Our Eyes." In that essay, Porterfield described the dramatic anisotropy across the visual field, "yet no thing is distinctly and clearly seen but what the Eye is directed to" (Porterfield, 1735, p. 185). He described the need to make eye movements to inspect objects in detail: "Hence it is that to view any Object, and thence to receive the strongest and most lively Impressions it is always necessary we turn our Eyes directly towards it, that its Picture may fall precisely upon this most delicate and sensible Part of the Organ, which is naturally in the Axis of the Eye" (Porterfield, 1735, p. 184). He also pointed out the fact that people are typically not aware of the lack of detailed vision away from central vision, nor of the eye movements they make to compensate for that loss, describing that lack of awareness as a "vulgar error": "in viewing any large Body, we are ready to imagine that we see at the same Time all its Parts equally distinct and clear: But this is a vulgar Error, and we are led into it from the quick and almost continual Motion of the Eye, whereby it is successively directed towards all the Parts of the Object in an Instant of Time" (Porterfield, 1735, p. 186).

The "vulgar error" that Porterfield described, the commonly held belief (or "illusion") that our visual system supports continuous high acuity across the visual field, is what makes eyetracking such a powerful tool. This process that seems to support perception across the field in parallel is in fact a rapid serial process; humans make over 100,000 rapid eye movements per day to successively bring objects to the high-acuity central region of the retina. The ability to track an observer's direction-of-gaze position offers the researcher a unique window into behavior, attention, and performance. Because the acuity of the human visual system varies so dramatically across the visual field, with high acuity only available in the fovea (a small region in the center of the retina with the highest density of cones), humans have evolved a rich suite of oculomotor behaviors to move the eyes and reorient the fovea to regions requiring high acuity, and to stabilize the retinal image on the fovea during those tasks. Perhaps more important for eyetracking research, humans also tend to move their eyes to foveate regions of interest, even when high acuity is not required for a given task. As a result, tracking the eyes offers a method of tracking visual attention because while visual attention and gaze can be disassociated, they rarely are (Spering & Carrasco, 2015). As a result, eyetracking provides a powerful tool for monitoring performance, exploring task strategies, and understanding human behavior. Its use in the social sciences continues to grow, with applications from neuroscience to human factors (Mele & Federici, 2012).

Most people are completely unaware of the hundreds of rapid eye movements they make each minute to bring objects of interest to the high-acuity fovea (which covers less than 1/100th of 1% of the visual field) (Foulsham & Kingstone, 2013; Clarke et al., 2017). Orienting the eyes toward objects and regions allows people to examine them in detail. Even though it is impossible not to pay attention to the target of an eye movement (Shepherd et al., 1986), observers perform poorly when asked to report on their own eye movements. Marti et al. (2015) found that in addition to being unaware of many of their fixations, observers also reported many fixations in locations that were not fixated.

The value of eyetracking is therefore evident; a record of observers' gaze patterns provides a record of objects and regions attended even more accurate than known to the observers. Monitoring these eye movements provides an external marker of visual attention more accurate than alternate methods such as verbal report and posttests intended to infer attention, which are often unreliable and can change the behavior one is trying to understand. Eyetrackers have been used across the social and behavioral sciences, with applications across the fields of anthropology, criminal justice, economics, human factors, linguistics, neuro-marketing, and sociology. They can be used to determine what objects are attended to, how long objects, regions, or people are looked at, and alternately what regions are *not* attended to. Some examples of those applications are described in the Real-World Applications section below.

Understanding Eye Movements

Even without an eyetracker, looking carefully at someone performing a task reveals that the eyes typically alternate between periods of relative stability (*fixations*) and movements of the eyes from one direction to another (*eye movements*). The underlying mechanical and neural systems that control these events are complex. The oculomotor system of humans (and non-human primates) consists of neural control architecture and six extraocular muscles attached to each eye. The muscles are arranged in three agonist-antagonist pairs, as seen in Figure 18.1. The first pair, attached on the left and right of each eye, are the lateral rectus (on the temporal, or outer side of the eye) and the medial rectus (on the nasal, or inner side of the eye). Together, the lateral and medial recti rotate the eyes outward and inward. The second pair of muscles, attached on the top and bottom of each eye, are the superior rectus (on the top of the eye) and the inferior rectus (on the bottom). Together, the superior and inferior recti rotate the eyes up and down. The final pair, also attached on the top and bottom of each eye, are the superior oblique (on the top) and the inferior oblique (on the bottom). The oblique muscles are so named because they are attached in such a manner that they rotate the eye primarily about the optical axis rather than redirect that axis. Together, the superior and inferior obliques rotate the eyes (Leigh & Zee, 2015, pp. 27–31) about an axis approximate to the optical axis ("torsional" eye movements), as illustrated in Figure 18.2.

The extra-ocular muscles can be seen as serving two primary purposes: (1) stabilizing the image on the retina to optimize the information available to the visual system (especially in central vision), and (2) moving the retina to a new location to gather different information.

It is useful to parse oculomotor events into categories based on motion of the observer and of the target being viewed. In the simplest case both observer and target are stationary. When the eyes are stable in the head, the static target (or scene) is stable on the retina, and the eyes are said to be in *fixation*. When an observer shifts the orientation of the eyes to bring a new location to the retina to gather different information, optimal performance requires that the shift take place as quickly as possible to minimize the time during which the retinal image is unstable. The rapid

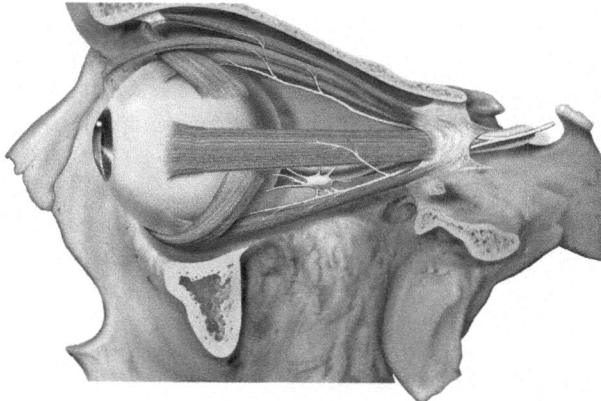

Figure 18.1 *Extraocular muscles. Adapted from Patrick Lynch, Yale University CC 2.5 2006*

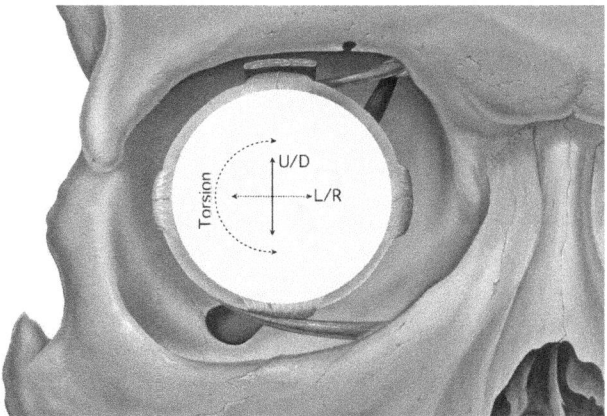

Figure 18.2 *Directions of eye movements. Adapted from Patrick Lynch, Yale University*

movement of the eyes from one place to another is known as a *saccade*, a French term introduced by Javal in 1878 to describe the intermittent "jerks" or "twitches" he observed in movements of the eyes (Tatler & Wade, 2003). The term was adopted widely in the literature decades later after Raymond Dodge reintroduced the term in a review of international literature and suggested that it was preferable to the then-current term 'Type I' eye movement, and that "it seems worth adopting" (Dodge, 1916, pp. 422–423).

The orientation of the eyes can be shown on a plot where the x-axis represents time (typically in milliseconds; thousandths of a second) and the y-axis represents the orientation of the eye in the horizontal (left-right) and vertical (up-down) direction. Figure 18.3 shows a record of the horizontal (thin line) and vertical (thick line) orientation of gaze measured in degrees. Looking straight ahead is 0 degrees. The data in Figure 18.3 is from an eyetracker that sampled the eye's orientation over a one-second interval. Fixations are evident as periods where the orientation is constant (e.g., from 0 to 60 milliseconds); saccades as periods where the orientation changes at a high rate (e.g., between 80 and 130 milliseconds). Saccadic eye movements are distinguished from other movements by their velocity, reaching rotational velocities of over 500°/sec. (Becker, 1989). The relationship between saccadic amplitude and peak velocity has been characterized over a wide range, from a small fraction of a degree to over 45 degrees. Bahill et al. (1981) showed that there is a quasi-linear relationship between amplitude and peak velocity and termed the relationship the *main sequence*. Over a relatively large range of saccadic amplitudes (e.g., 5–45°) one can estimate the duration of a saccade with the simple linear relationship $D = D_0 + d*A$, where D is the duration of the saccade, D_0 is the minimum duration for small saccades, d is the increase in duration per degree of saccadic amplitude, and A is saccadic amplitude (Becker, 1989). Values for D_0 vary from 20–30 milliseconds, and d varies from 1.5 to 3.0 milliseconds/degree, but a simple approximation can be obtained as $D = 20 + 2A$.

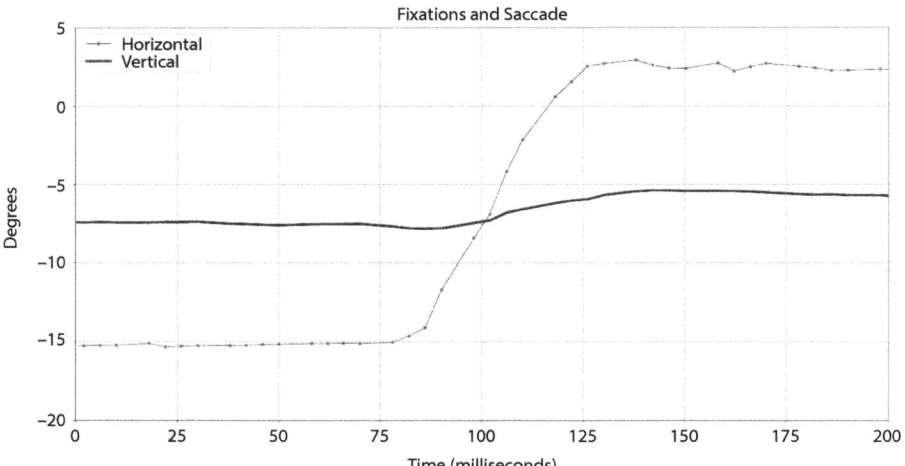

Figure 18.3 *Horizontal and vertical eye position as a function of time. Fixations and saccades are evident.*

The first saccade in Figure 18.3 is approximately 17° in amplitude, so its estimated duration would be 20 + 2(17) = 54 msec. Inspection of the plot verifies the estimate.

In the simplest case when both observer and target are stationary, the two oculomotor events are fixations and saccades. The next case considered is when the observer is stationary, but the target is moving within the observer's field of view. If gaze did not follow the target, vision would suffer both because the target of interest would drift away from the high-acuity fovea, and because the relative motion of the image on the retinal surface would result in blur.

Both potential faults are compensated by matching the eyes' rotation to the angular position of the target in the visual field with *smooth pursuit* eye movements. The result is a stable (or nearly stable) image projected on the retina. Unlike the fixations described above, where both eye and object are stationary, the image is stabilized by the lack of "relative" motion between the image and the retina. Note that smooth pursuit movements are rarely perfectly matched to object motion, resulting in some *retinal slip* (Grossberg et al., 2012). Figure 18.4 shows a record of the horizontal (thin line with dots) and vertical (thick line) orientation of gaze over a one-second interval. The vertical axis is scaled in degrees of visual angle. Smooth pursuit is evident throughout the one-second period with angular velocity ranging over ~30–35°/sec. Because smooth pursuit eye movements are often unable to exactly compensate for target motion, retinal errors can accumulate, moving the target away from the center of the retina. Small catch-up saccades are frequently executed to recenter the target, as evident between 300 and 700 milliseconds in Figure 18.4.

While smooth pursuit eye movements compensate for target motion with a stationary observer, relative motion between the image and the retina can also result from observer motion, even with a stationary target. If the target is static, but

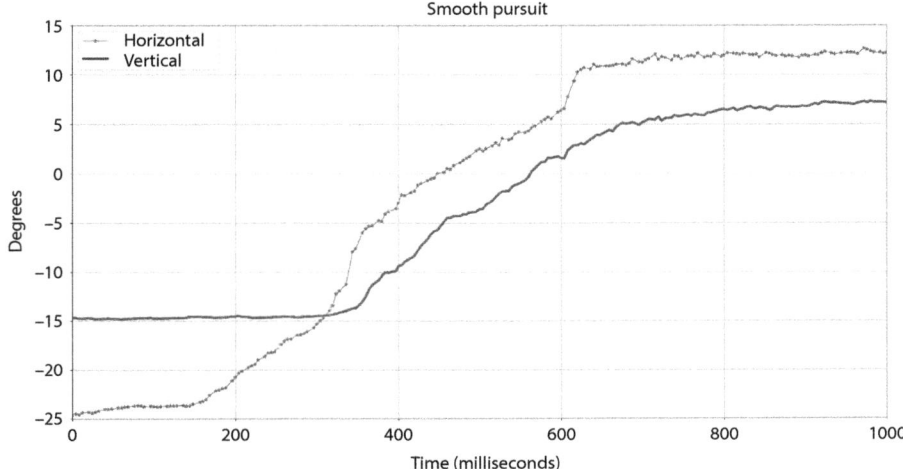

Figure 18.4 *Smooth pursuit eye movement with "catch-up" saccades.*

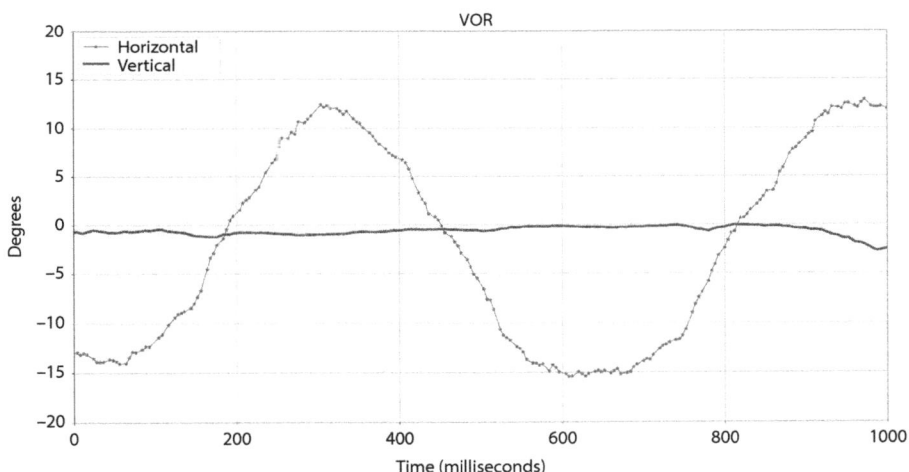

Figure 18.5 *Vestibular-ocular response (VOR) eye movements.*

the head rotates, vision would again suffer because the retinal image would be blurred, and it would drift away from the center of the retina.

The *vestibular-ocular response* (VOR) compensates for head rotations by counter-rotating the eyes to stabilize the retinal image (Lisberger, 2010). Figure 18.5 shows VOR movements resulting from an observer shaking their head "no." While gaze was fixed on a target location, the eyes counter-rotated to the head, i.e., if the head went from right to left, the horizontal component of gaze (thin line with dots) went right (toward more positive values). Saccades, smooth pursuit, and VOR are the

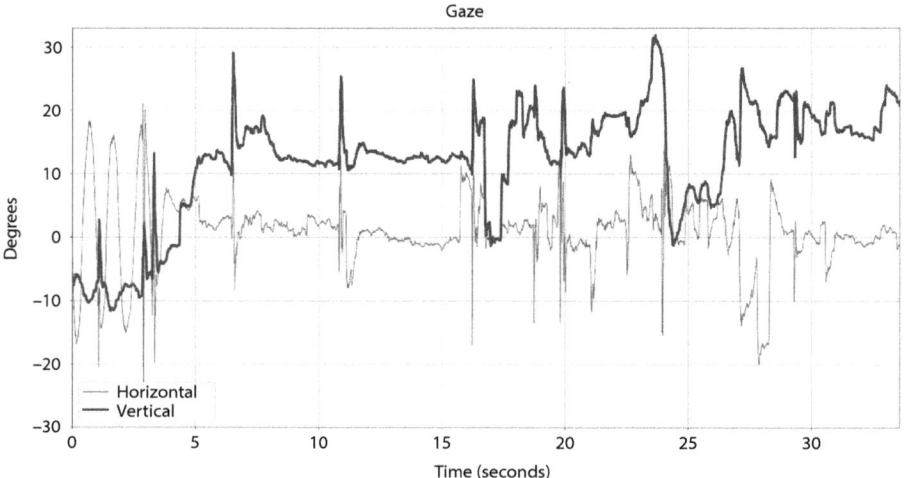

Figure 18.6 *Gaze orientation record for over one minute.*

most important classifications of conjugate eye movements – movements that drive both eyes in the same direction.

Other classifications include *vergence eye movements* (Kowler, 1995), where the angle between the two eyes varies based on the distance of the fixation point from the observer; *miniature eye movements* (or movements of fixation), made up of tremor, drift, and microsaccades (Rucci & Victor, 2015); and the *optokinetic reflex* (OKR), which is related to smooth pursuit, but driven by large-field motion instead of a small target (Leigh & Zee, 2015). It is important to note that while all of these classifications are convenient and valuable for discussion, during a real task they are often seen together in complex combination, as seen in Figure 18.6, which shows a 35-second segment from a task in which an observer was inspecting a pen.

All of the oculomotor events discussed so far – fixations, saccades, smooth pursuit, and VOR eye movements – are evident, and they are not easily separated because the classifications that are convenient in controlled experiments are typically indistinct in natural tasks.

Types of Eyetrackers

Many methods have been used to monitor eye movements over the years, from relatively crude mechanical linkages – such as the "mirror, attached to the cocainized cornea by an aluminum capsule" described earlier by Dodge (1911, p. 383) – to modern high-speed video devices that use computer-vision algorithms to track features of the eye or machine learning to infer gaze direction directly from images. The goal has always been the same: to obtain high-quality, low-noise measures of eye position (or velocity) over time without unduly affecting the underlying behavior.

Modern video-based eyetrackers can be classified into five broad categories: (1) *remote eyetrackers* that can monitor an observer's gaze position from a distance without requiring any contact with the observer, (2) *tower eyetrackers* – a subclass of remote eyetrackers that place the camera(s) near the observer and limit head movements, (3) *head-mounted eyetrackers* in which cameras are worn by the observer and are tethered to a laboratory computer, (4) *wearable eyetrackers* that are unconstrained and can be used outside of the laboratory, and (5) *head-mounted display* (HMD) eyetrackers that are integrated into VR/AR displays. The category boundaries can be blurred, but the categories are useful to introduce the hardware and systems in common use today. All of these systems rely on one or more video cameras to capture images of the observer's eye(s), and some method of representing the scene that the observer is viewing.

Remote Eyetrackers

This class of eyetracker is typically built into (or mounted below) computer displays (Figure 18.7), though they can be used without displays to monitor the gaze position of observers viewing other scenes. The primary advantages of remote eyetrackers are that nothing needs to be attached to the observer, and gaze position can be output directly in the fixed reference frame of display coordinates. The disadvantage is that the observer must typically stay relatively still (within a few inches in any direction) throughout the data collection if the camera(s) capturing the observer's eye(s) are static. Some systems address this issue by using dynamic eye cameras that follow the observer's movements, extending the effective headbox (Figure 18.8). In addition to uses in research, common uses for remote eyetrackers are market research and as assistive technologies for individuals with mobility or communication challenges.

Figure 18.7 *Tobii Pro Spectrum – Remote eyetracker mounted below computer monitor. Image ©, reprinted with permission from Tobii.*

Figure 18.8 *EyeGaze Edge – Remote eyetracker mounted below computer display. Image ©, reprinted with permissions from EyeGaze Inc.*

Tower Eyetrackers

Tower eyetrackers are designed to optimize performance at the expense of observer movement and flexibility. Figure 18.9 shows an EyeLink 1000 tower eyetracker. The illuminator and eye camera are mounted on the "tower" above the observer, and a "hot mirror" is placed between the observer and the stimulus monitor. The hot mirror serves as a beam splitter, allowing most of the visible light from the computer monitor to pass to the observer, while reflecting most of the near-infrared (NIR) power to illuminate and image the observer's eye. Because the participant's position is more strictly limited than with remote eyetrackers, the system design allows careful illumination and image capture of the observer's eye at high magnification and good focus. As a result, tower eyetrackers can provide among the highest-quality gaze data of all video-based eyetrackers. The trade-off, of course, is that tasks are limited to those that can be performed under these restricted conditions, and motion of the observer can limit data quality. Like remote eyetrackers, the tower eyetracker has the advantage that gaze position output is directly in the fixed reference frame of computer display coordinates because the tower eyetracker, display, and observer are stationary in that space.

Headband-Mounted Eyetrackers

Headband-mounted eyetrackers build the illumination and eye-capture hardware into a device that is worn by the observer and tethered to a laboratory computer. They offer high speed like the tower eyetracker, without placing severe limitations on head movements (and useful field-of-view). The Eyelink II offers gaze sampling at 500 Hz using only the pupil image, and at 250 Hz when also using corneal reflection tracking to compensate for small head movements. Because the illuminators and eye cameras are attached to the headband, they move with the participant's

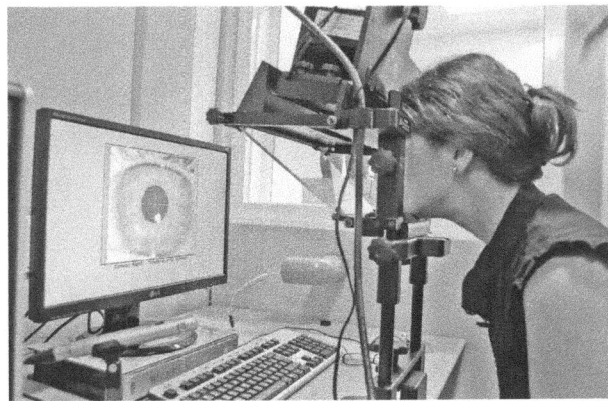

Figure 18.9 *Tower eyetracker (EyeLink 1000 Tower).*

head, extending the useful field-of-view to 360°. Unlike remote and tower eye-trackers, however, there is no fixed reference frame for the gaze output, so native gaze output from headband-mounted eyetrackers is limited to relative angle with respect to the headband (and observer's head, assuming no slippage). Headband-mounted eyetrackers typically include a "scene" (or "world") camera mounted to the headband that captures a video of the scene from the observer's (dynamic) viewpoint. Because the scene camera moves with the observer (and eye camera(s)), gaze can be output in the reference frame of the scene camera. Note that motion of the scene camera represents head (and full-body) motion of the observer, so mapping from scene-camera coordinates to world coordinates is a non-trivial problem.

While scene and eye cameras are mounted to the headband, processing and/or recording of the video streams is typically done on a tethered laboratory computer, limiting the range of motion, mobility, and tasks that can be performed with headband-mounted eyetrackers.

Wearable Eyetrackers

Wearable eyetrackers are designed to allow the entire system required for recording eye and scene videos, and optionally real-time processing, to be worn by the participant. The systems are lighter and less obtrusive than typical headband-mounted eyetrackers and are typically built into eyeglass-style frames, making it possible to take tasks outside of the laboratory. Figures 18.10–12 show wearable systems from Positive Science, Tobii, and Pupil Labs. Like headband-mounted eyetrackers, eye- and scene-cameras move with the participant's head, so all eye-movement records are with respect to the then current head position: in an "eye-in-head" reference frame, not in a world reference frame. The systems typically output a video record captured from the scene camera with a cursor (such as a circle or a cross) overlaid that indicates the observer's point of gaze on each frame, as shown in Figure 18.13 for a system from Positive Science.

Figure 18.10 *Positive Science – wearable eyetracker. Image ©, reprinted with permission from Positive Science.*

Figure 18.11 *Tobii Pro Glasses 3 – wearable eyetracker. Image ©, reprinted with permission from Tobii.*

Gaze data from wearable (and headband-mounted) eyetrackers can be analyzed by examining the output video stream (Vansteenkiste et al., 2015), mapping the eye-in-head gaze to gaze-in-world coordinates by incorporating head position measurements (Evans et al., 2012), or by incorporating markers in the environment to automatically map the scene by calculating the transformation necessary to map gaze position in the scene camera reference frame to the reference frame defined by the markers (Pfeiffer & Renner, 2014).

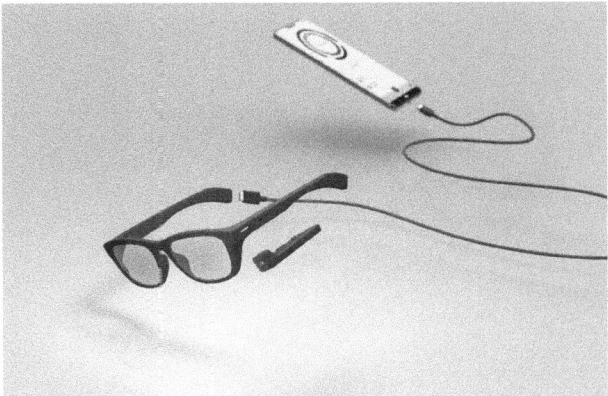

Figure 18.12 *Pupil Labs Invisible – wearable eyetracker. Image ©, reprinted with permission from Pupil Labs.*

Figure 18.13 *Frame of output video from wearable eyetracker (Positive Science). Image ©, reprinted with permission from Positive Science.*

Head-Mounted Display (HMD) Eyetrackers

HMDs displaying virtual-reality (VR) and augmented-reality (AR) content are becoming more widespread. While eyetracking in HMDs has been done since the 1990s (Geisler & Perry, 1998; Pelz et al., 1999; Duchowski et al., 2000), the cost of HMDs has plummeted in the last five years with the advent of commodity HMDs such as the Vive Pro Eye (Ha et al., 2022) and the Oculus Rift. Figure 18.14 shows a VR-integratable eye-tracker from Pupil Labs. The arrival of such eyetrackers brought the cost of high-quality, binocular HMDs down by an order of magnitude, and dramatically broadened the field of eyetracking in VR/AR. In its simplest form,

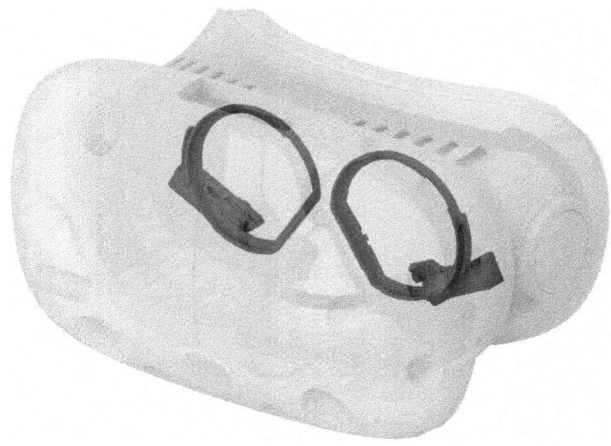

Figure 18.14 *HTC Vive with integrated eyetracker (Pupil Labs).*

Figure 18.15 *Virtual environment (Binaee and Diaz, 2019).*

gaze "inside" a virtual environment can be tracked in eye-in-head coordinates and analyzed manually by viewing the video record showing gaze position overlaid on the virtual scene. But VR systems require head tracking to update the display based on observer movements, so it is possible to map the eye-in-head signal onto the virtual environment, yielding a "gaze-in-(virtual)-world" signal (Diaz et al., 2013).

Figure 18.15 shows the left and right gaze vectors in the virtual environment, along with the virtual ball. The participant is seen striking a virtual ball in the left panel, and their view is shown in the right panel with left and right eye vectors.

Selecting an Eyetracker

Selecting an eyetracker category is typically based on the required accuracy, precision, and temporal sampling rate, the type of task and stimulus to be presented to the observer, the degree to which the experimenter is willing to limit the movements of the observer, and the display (or environment) to be used. Accuracy and precision are described in detail in the next section. In general, the more restrictions that are placed on the observer (and task), the greater is the likelihood of capturing accurate, precise, and repeatable results. For example, tower eyetrackers are capable of providing very high-quality data at sampling rates exceeding 1,000 samples per second (1 kHz), with the trade-off that observers typically use a chinrest that limits movement, and the field-of-view is limited by the apparatus. At the other extreme, wearable eyetrackers can be worn by observers as they perform natural tasks outside of the laboratory with an unlimited field of view. However, data rates are limited to ~250 Hz, data quality does not match that of a tower tracker, and the field-of-view over which data can be collected reliably is smaller than the total field-of-view. In some cases, the task requirements require the flexibility of a wearable eyetracker, and the experimental paradigm must be adapted to the available data quality. In other cases, the required accuracy and precision may dictate a simpler task (and more restrictive environment for the observers).

Data Quality

Whether data is collected in a laboratory, "in the wild," or in a virtual environment, it is critical to understand the effects of eyetracking data quality. The primary metrics of data quality are *accuracy* and *precision*. A useful definition of accuracy in the context of eyetracking data quality is the agreement between an averaged gaze position and the actual gaze position during that period. If an observer is asked to fixate a known target for half a second to validate a calibration, and the average of the reported gaze position differs from the known target position by 1° of visual angle, the system can be said to have an accuracy (or more formally an inaccuracy) of 1°. Precision can be defined as the dispersion of reported gaze position over time when gaze is not changing.

Figure 18.16 shows a calibration board. The left image shows a view from the scene camera with the calibration on a monitor screen, and on the right, we see

(a) View from scene camera   (b) Calibration board

Figure 18.16 *Gaze on calibration board.*

a high-resolution image of the same calibration board with gaze in the same position as in the real world. In this case, the calibration routine involves looking at all the crosses in a sequential pattern. Once the calibration routine is complete, the gaze-mapping is applied to data collection, which enables the researchers to view the observers' gaze at all times.

Accuracy

In the top panel, Figure 18.17 illustrates the raw gaze positions while the observer was reading text; the record is said to have "high accuracy" (or low inaccuracy) – less than 0.25° of visual angle in this illustration. The bottom panel of Figure 18.17 illustrates a case where the reported raw gaze positions consistently deviate from the actual target position by approximately 1° of visual angle. Accuracy is typically reported in degrees of visual angle and is usually specified as a single value. Unless specified, it is unclear whether the reported accuracy is the average, median, or maximum deviation from the targets. Both these images show variance in accuracy while being highly precise, i.e., the reported values over a location are very close to each other.

There is not wide agreement in the field about how to define, measure, or report accuracy in eyetracking research, and it is not unusual for publications to appear that simply report the manufacturers' claims of accuracy, which are often best-case values measured under ideal conditions (Reingold, 2014). Ideally, researchers should report accuracy ranges based on position in the visual field and over trial duration. Measures of accuracy made during an experiment end up measuring the accuracy of the entire system, including the eyetracker and the observer's ability to fixate a calibration point. To measure the eyetracker without including the influence of an observer's ability to hold fixation during calibration and validation, an artificial eye may be used. Wang et al. (2017) evaluated several eyetrackers using several artificial eyes provided by eyetracker manufacturers and adapted a commercially available model-eye designed for ophthalmic image training.

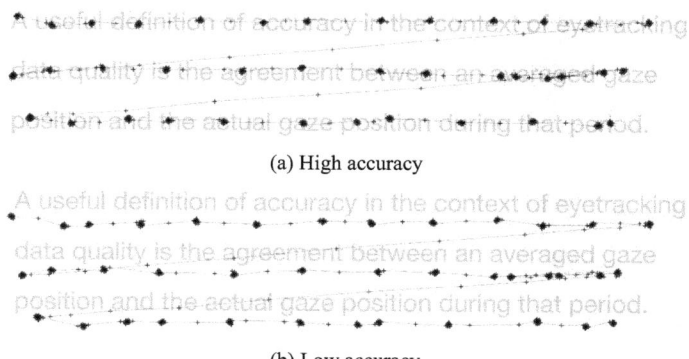

Figure 18.17 *Average gaze location with 0.05° average precision and 0° (top) and 1° (bottom) inaccuracy.*

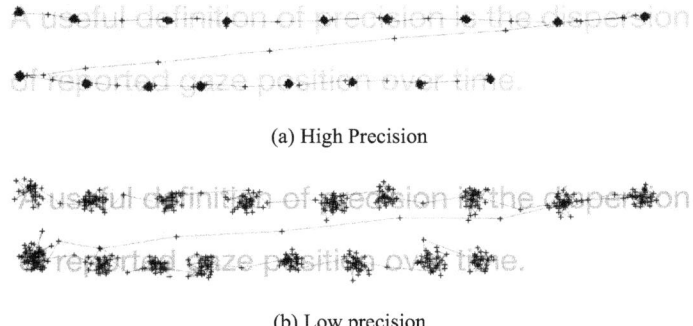

(a) High Precision

(b) Low precision

Figure 18.18 *Gaze locations with 0° average inaccuracy and high (top) and low (bottom) precision.*

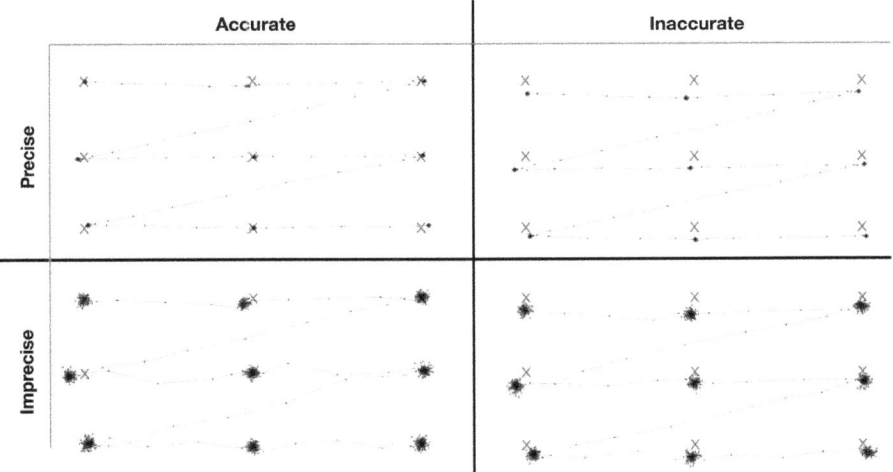

Figure 18.19 *Accuracy and precision in eyetracker data.*

Individual gaze records of a system with "high accuracy" (or low inaccuracy) may still vary widely on a short timescale; accuracy only refers to the time-averaged position, not the instantaneous position or the dispersion of reported values. Figure 18.18 shows two cases that both have high accuracy. The top panel has average inaccuracy less than $\sim 0.25°$ and low dispersion of $0.05°$, while the bottom panel has the same average inaccuracy but a much larger dispersion. Accuracy and precision are independent; it is possible for an eyetracker to be accurate and imprecise, inaccurate and precise, etc., as illustrated in Figure 18.19.

Precision

Reports of precision in eyetracking research are complicated by the fact that there are several different definitions of precision in use in the community. Blignaut and

Beelders (2012) reviewed many of the precision measures in use and proposed a new measure. Two commonly reported measures of precision are the standard deviation of position over time (σ), and the sample-to-sample root-mean-square distance (RMS-S2S). The two measures share a computational form (both are root-mean-square measures) but measure different characteristics of an eyetracker signal. Most important, σ ignores the temporal sequence (and data rate) of the gaze data with the resultant value being a function only of the spatial layout of the samples, while RMS-S2S is very sensitive to temporal sequences and data rate. In other words, σ measures the dispersion of data from the centroid of the distribution while RMS-S2S measures the dispersion of data from its preceding data point.

The two panels in Figure 18.20 show a sequence of 37 gaze positions with the same horizontal and vertical range, reported over a period of 300 msec. The left panel shows the reported gaze "drifting" from upper left to lower right; the right panel shows a more random pattern between the same points. The precision of the two cases is similar when reported in terms of standard deviation (0.4°), but the RMS-S2S is dramatically different: 0.1° for the "drifting" in the left of Figure 18.20 and 0.7° for the more random pattern in the right. The figure also shows why the RMS S2S measure is sensitive to data rate: more frequent samples would reduce the sample-to-sample difference but would not affect the range.

Spatial accuracy and precision are the most commonly reported measures of eyetracker data quality, but other measures are important. Nyström et al. (2013) reviewed other measures, including temporal precision (the eyetracking system's ability to accurately report the timing and duration of events), data loss (number of observers excluded and the fraction of data loss in included participants), and robustness to a number of factors that can affect data quality.

Nyström et al. (2013) list factors that influence data quality, including the physical characteristics of the participants (e.g., spectacle correction, complexion, makeup),

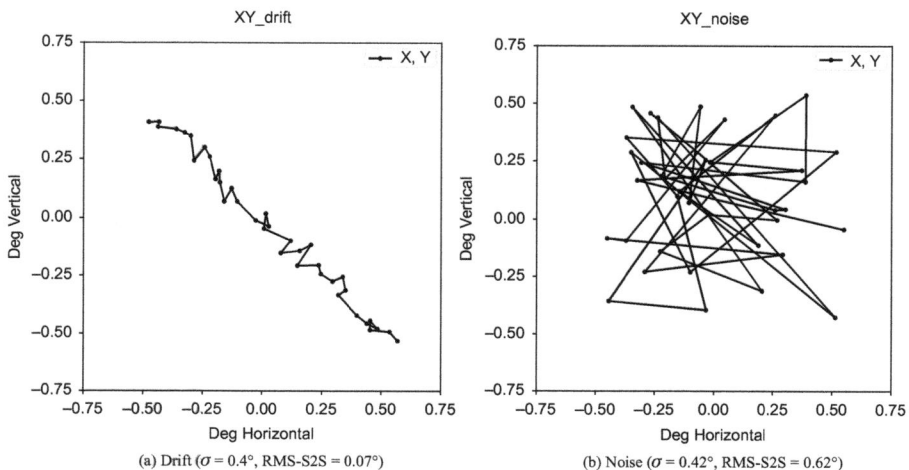

Figure 18.20 *Raw plots for drift and noise in gaze.*

operator (e.g., experience), task (e.g., difficulty, stimulus), environment (e.g., lighting, vibration), and eyetracker design (e.g., camera temporal and spatial resolution, algorithm design). Researchers should also consider the influence of gaze position within the visual field. Feit et al. (2017) reported the effect of position on accuracy and precision in user–interface design, but the results are at least as important to researchers.

Data-Quality-Based Analysis

Eyetracking data is widely used and some crucial developments are in gaze-estimation algorithms and gaze-analysis tools. These advances apply to all types of eyetrackers and are greatly impacted by the quality of data acquired.

Gaze-estimation algorithms, gaze analysis tools, and gaze visualization pipelines are three main components of eyetracking development. The gaze-estimation algorithms aid in obtaining reliable gaze measurements, while the analytical tools aid in understanding the features of gaze in detail, and visualization pipelines aid in seeing data in new ways. Data visualization requires analysis but not vice versa.

To utilize gaze data for analysis, gaze events (especially fixations and saccades) must be identified in the raw gaze data. Salvucci and Goldberg (2000) described a range of event-detection algorithms and introduced a taxonomy to describe them. Researchers and practitioners have since proposed a number of *event detectors* to parse raw gaze data, as reviewed by Startsev and Zemblys (2022), and current approaches have started incorporating machine learning models, e.g., Kothari et al. (2020).

Algorithms used to classify oculomotor events (fixations, saccades, smooth pursuit, VOR) are often very sensitive to noise (i.e., low-precision data). There are many filtering methods that can be used to reduce the apparent noise in gaze data. The simplest is a moving average that smooths the data in a sliding, fixed-width window. While effective in reducing noise, smoothing over multiple samples reduces the temporal detail, lowering the effective sample rate and potentially masking small, rapid movements like small saccades. A moving median filter takes the median within the sliding window, replacing the value in the center of the window with the median, removing point outliers from noise. The Savitzky/Golay filter (Savitzky & Golay, 1964) is a filter that is used to reduce noise without some of the negative effects of other moving-window filters. It uses a simplified least-squares approach to construct a trend line for the signal within the window to reduce noise. Filtering tools are available for Python (scipy.signal.savgol_filter), C++(e.g., arntanguy/sgsmooth), and Matlab (sgolayfilt).

Figure 18.21 illustrates the parsing of raw gaze data from a reading task into *fixation* and *saccade* events. Each row in the figure shows the resulting fixation plot on the left, with the horizontal ("rows") and vertical ("cols") fixation positions plotted as a function of time as the observer reads three lines of text. The raw plot on the right illustrates the raw gaze data from the brief temporal window highlighted on the fixation plot with a rectangular box. The fixations shown here are identified

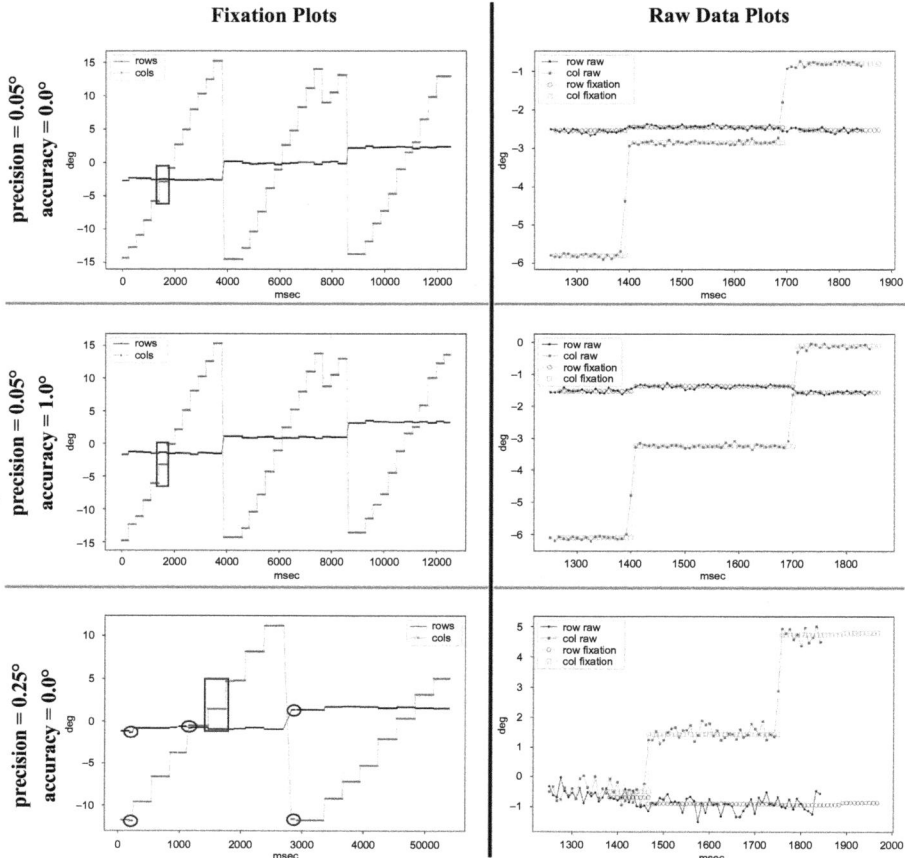

Figure 18.21 *Plots showing fixations throughout a reading task.*

with an algorithm that locates a series of raw gaze points whose values vary by less than a defined dispersion (< $dispersion_{max}$) over a period that lasts longer than a defined time (> $time_{min}$). In this case, $dispersion_{max} = 0.1°$ and $time_{min} = 100 msec$.

Shifted data is observed in the plots when the accuracy error is 1° as compared to no error (i.e., 0°). A jitter is also seen in the data when precision error is 0.25° as compared to 0.05° error. If the dispersion (from the eyetracker or the gaze-estimation algorithm) is too high, close proximity points can result in pseudo-fixations also known as phantom fixations. This is observed in the last row of Figure 18.21 and is marked in ellipses. There exists some noise in the hardware and software of the entire eyetracking pipeline, resulting in some uncertainty with gaze estimation, which can be tackled with a cone model (Jogeshwar et al., 2020).

Gaze-estimation algorithms have become increasingly accurate and precise over time. To estimate gaze, one must understand all of the factors that go into answering the question *Where is the observer looking?* Creating eye models or tracking different components of the eye are two popular methods for estimating gaze. Recording higher-quality video data, tracking numerous imaged features of the eye (Merchant, 1967), creating accurate mathematical eye models (Kassner et al., 2014), and better segmenting and tracking the components of the eye (Chaudhary & Pelz, 2020a) are all methods for improving the overall gaze-estimation algorithm performance. One of the recent approaches to boost performance has been to include machine learning or neural networks in these improvement strategies. Tonsen et al. (2020) explored a gaze-estimation model based on neural networks that drives calibration-free eyetracking. This, however, presents privacy issues about neural networks learning to identify and recognize people based on their eye features or eye dynamics (Kröger et al., 2019). A new stream of vision research is coming up to address these privacy concerns by understanding how to strengthen gaze-estimation without mistakenly disclosing a person's identity (Chaudhary & Pelz, 2020b). As much as the gaze obtained is precise, the errors from gaze-estimation algorithms directly affect gaze analysis and visualization.

Data Visualization

Tools and pipelines have been developed over the years to analyze and view events in gaze data in order to better understand human behavior. These tools heavily depend on the kind/format of data provided by the eyetracker. Two questions are frequently answered while analyzing data under the gaze: *Where is the person looking?* and *What is the person looking at?* A commonly used strategy for addressing these questions is to overlay the gaze (as a circle or crosshair) on the scene and observe it hover over various objects/environmental components over time. This type of visualization assists in comprehending all of the objects/areas with which the observer interacts; however, it is restricted to information in the scene. For example, if the environment is a monitor, then the entire interaction is bound to two dimensions. If we observe the interaction from a video-based wearable eyetracker, then the environment is in two dimensions.

It would be useful for researchers to be able to visualize an extended duration of interaction in a single, static image. A recent approach by Koch et al. (2022) stitches the 2D scene-snippets into spirals that help visualize all the Regions of Interest (ROIs). Simulating the environment in 3D and projecting gaze on an environmental model, as seen in Munn and Pelz (2009); Maurus et al. (2014); Jensen et al. (2017); Li et al. (2020); Jogeshwar (2020); Jogeshwar and Pelz (2021), Jogeshwar, A. (2023) allows a researcher to see all the gaze interactions in the entire environment at once, opening a portal to visualize enhanced data such as highlighted ROIs, gaze patterns, body pose, and current activity.

Real-World Applications

A few sample applications from the social and behavioral sciences are highlighted in this section. Eyetracking has been applied to multiple sectors such as marketing, healthcare, design, education, consulting, psychology, and more. Eyetracking applications have increased dramatically across many disciplines due to the advancements made in technology, making hardware and software tools more accessible (in terms of cost, ease of use, and data quality) than ever.

In work by Mühlenbeck et al. (2017), a remote eyetracker was used to explore the origins of manmade markings on Paleolithic-era artifacts. The researchers recorded the eye movement patterns of human observers as they viewed images of archeological artifacts (hand axes and sticks) with and without markings and incisions. The human observers were from two groups: adolescent "city dwellers" (from Hamburg and Berlin), and an age-matched group from a tribe of hunter-gatherers in Namibia. The groups differed in their cultural backgrounds and in the visual surroundings in which they spend most of their time, as the Indigenous hunter-gatherers lived on the southern African savannah and the German adolescents in industrialized cities. The results of the eyetracking study showed that the marked objects were fixated longer by both groups, though neither group judged the marked objects as more attractive than the unmarked objects.

In addition to the human subjects, the researchers also measured the eye movements of a group of orangutans who were trained to perform a similar task while their eye movements were tracked. Unlike the two human groups, the orangutans showed no increased fixation on the marked objects, leading the researchers to conclude that the function of early markings was to direct attention rather than to increase the appeal of the objects.

While Mühlenbeck et al. (2017) used eyetracking to study the intersection of anthropology, archeology, psychology, and art, others have applied the tools of eyetracking to the study of business practices and economic theory. Criminal justice and crime scene analysis are other areas where eyetracking has offered insights into long-standing questions. Lasky et al. (2017) recruited two "active shoplifters" and used a wearable eyetracker to monitor their eye movements while they simulated shoplifting in retail stores. The results provide a unique opportunity to examine the efficacy of security measures. Watalingam et al. (2017) explored criminal behavior from the perspective of the crime scene analyst. They used a wearable eyetracker to monitor the eye movement patterns of 32 crime scene analysts (categorized as "experts" or "trained novices") as they examined a mock crime scene. The experts were more efficient and effective (achieving higher scores in the same time). The authors also noted differences in the eye movement patterns between the two groups: comparisons of total contiguous fixation time in a region ("dwell time") and time in areas of interest (AOIs) revealed significant differences based on expertise. Notably, experts had more variation in dwell time on critical evidence (e.g., blood spatter and cartridge case) but had less variation in their search patterns.

Linguistics and language acquisition are two other application areas where eyetracking has proved to be a valuable tool. Eberhard et al. (1995) started a rich line of research in this area with their paper titled "Eye movements as a window into real-time spoken language comprehension in natural contexts" where they eyetracked observers performing real-time instructed natural tasks to study rapid mental processes that enable people to comprehend spoken language. In the "Visual World

Paradigm" (Salverda and Tanenhaus, 2017), observers listen to (or produce) spoken language while their gaze is tracked as they view objects related to the audio stream. The fixations revealed a detailed record of the temporal process of spoken language comprehension (or production). This record can be at the level of a phrase ("the brown dog brush") or a single word ("carpet"). In the first case, if a scene contains a brown box, a brown dog, and a brown dog brush, it is instructive to watch the pattern of eye movements of an observer viewing the scene as the phrase is spoken. Theories about when the meaning of the phrase can be understood can be tested by examining when gaze moves reliably to the brush. In the second case, if a scene contains a camera, a car, a card, and a carpet, the time-course of word disambiguation can be understood by monitoring gaze over the short time-period of a single word's utterance. In addition to the established literature in linguistics, researchers in language acquisition and second-language research are also making use of eye-tracking (Conklin & Pellicer-Sánchez, 2016).

Eyetracking has also been applied to the study of survey methodology in sociological research. Surveys continue to play an important role in such research, despite our awareness that survey results can be affected by subjects' concern over how their answers will appear to others – the "social desirability bias" (Belli et al., 2001). Kaminska and Foulsham (2016) used a wearable eyetracker to monitor the gaze of observers as they filled out surveys in one of three modes: Web, self-administered questionnaire (SAQ), and face-to-face. By measuring the relative time observers spent looking at the questions, the response options, and the interviewer (in the face-to-face mode), the researchers were able to examine the influence of mode, response option position, and question time.

A commercial application of eyetracking in the field of social science is in user experience design where researchers explore how humans behave with certain products to design/develop them better. One other way of viewing the problem is by understanding the cognitive load required to interact with a product. Cognitive load can be inferred from changes in eye movement patterns. Joseph et al. (2021) recorded the eye movement parameters while their participants performed complex tasks on a mobile phone. They observed that participants over the age of 50 showed higher cognitive load while using mobile phones, irrespective of the complexity of the task, as their fixation durations were longer.

Summary

Eyetracking is a powerful tool that provides quantitative measures of behavior, performance, stress, and attention that are otherwise difficult to obtain (Kovesdi et al., 2018; Macatee et al., 2017). Gaze offers an external marker of attention, and by guiding gaze it may be possible to guide behavior (Grant & Spivey, 2003). Recent advances have led to miniature, robust systems that can be used in real and virtual environments, extending the reach of eyetracking into new domains. The price of entry into eyetracking has fallen significantly in the last decade. While it used to cost tens of thousands of US dollars for an entry-level system, it is now possible to equip a laboratory with a basic system for less than 5,000 US dollars. The use of eyetracking across a broad range of application areas demonstrates the value of the methodology. Predicting future research directions is always dangerous, but it is evident that a few areas are ripe for methodological development that will allow new insights in the social sciences. The creation of sophisticated data analysis tools to support the resultant complicated data is an ongoing research subject with plenty of space for innovation, particularly with multidimensional data (Jogeshwar & Pelz, 2021; Jogeshwar, A., 2023). The AR/VR sector is already on the increase, with eyetrackers incorporated to research human behavior in tightly controlled circumstances that researchers would otherwise be unable to examine – for example, simulating a stressful driving environment to learn how humans manage high cognitive load while doing a hard activity. However, the present AR/VR field's scope includes coping with nausea difficulties caused by high-resolution displays. When the observer looks at objects in the virtual world at varying distances, they are all effectively at the same depth, i.e., the headset display, and therefore all appear in sharp focus instead of some of the objects being out of focus (which is the natural way of seeing the environment). This causes a vergence-accommodation conflict in which the eyes produce vergence-movement to look at distant objects while simultaneously not accommodating the lens since the objects are already in focus. While vergence and accommodation coexist in the actual world, conflict in the virtual world frequently causes discomfort and nausea (Ukai & Howarth, 2008). Further miniaturization of the instrumentation to capture high spatial and temporal resolution gaze data will allow more natural behaviors to be studied. Wireless and/or high-density portable storage will support long-term monitoring, allowing "experiments" extending for hours or days instead of minutes and seconds. Lastly, data privacy concerns will be prioritized and addressed by developing sophisticated human recognition concealment tools.

References

Bahill, A., Brockenbrough, A., & Troost, B. (1981). Variability and development of a normative data base for saccadic eye movements. *Investigative Ophthalmology & Visual Science, 21*(1), 116–125.

Becker, W. (1989). The neurobiology of saccadic eye movements: Metrics. *Reviews of Oculomotor Research, 3*, 13–67.

Belli, R. F., Traugott, M. W., & Beckmann, M. N. (2001). What leads to voting overreports? Contrasts of overreporters to validated voters and admitted nonvoters in the American National Election Studies. *Journal of Official Statistics, 17*(4), 479–498.

Binaee, K., & Diaz, G. (2019). Movements of the eyes and hands are coordinated by a common predictive strategy. *Journal of Vision, 19*(12).

Blignaut, P., & Beelders, T. (2012). The precision of eye-trackers: A case for a new measure. In *Proceedings of the 2006 Symposium on Eye Tracking Research and Applications* (pp. 289–292). ACM.

Chaudhary, A. K., & Pelz, J. B. (2020a). pi t –enhancing the precision of eye tracking using iris feature motion vectors [preprint]. *ArXiv.* https://doi.org/10.48550/arXiv.2009.09348

(2020b). Privacy-preserving eye videos using rubber sheet model. In *ETRA '20 Short Papers: ACM Symposium on Eye Tracking Research and Applications* (pp. 1–5). ACM.

Clarke, A. D., Mahon, A., Irvine, A., & Hunt, A. R. (2017). People are unable to recognize or report on their own eye movements. *Quarterly Journal of Experimental Psychology, 70*(11), 2251–2270.

Conklin, K., & Pellicer-Sanchez, A. (2016). Using eye-tracking in applied linguistics and second language research. *Second Language Research, 32*(3), 453–467.

Darwin, E. (1794). *Zoonomia or the Laws of Organic Life* (vol. 1). Printed for J. johnson.

Diaz, G., Cooper, J., Kit, D., & Hayhoe, M. (2013). Real-time recording and classification of eye movements in an immersive virtual environment. *Journal of Vision, 13*(12).

Dodge, R. (1911). Visual motor functions. *Psychological Bulletin, 8*(11), 382–385.

(1916). Visual motor functions. *Psychological Bulletin, 13*(11), 421–427.

Duchowski, A. T., Shivashankaraiah, V., Rawls, T., Gramopadhye, A. K., Melloy, B. J., & Kanki, B. (2000). Binocular eye tracking in virtual reality for inspection training. In *Proceedings of the 2000 Symposium on Eye Tracking Research and Applications* (pp. 89–96). ACM.

Eberhard, K. M., Spivey-Knowlton, M. J., Sedivy, J. C., & Tanenhaus, M. K. (1995). Eye movements as a window into real-time spoken language comprehension in natural contexts. *Journal of Psycholinguistic Research, 24*(6), 409–436.

Evans, K. M., Jacobs, R. A., Tarduno, J. A., & Pelz, J. B. (2012). Collecting and analyzing eye tracking data in outdoor environments. *Journal of Eye Movement Research, 5*(2).

Feit, A. M., Williams, S., Toledo, A., Paradiso, A., Kulkarni, H., Kane, S., & Morris, M. R. (2017). Toward everyday gaze input: Accuracy and precision of eye tracking and implications for design. In *Proceedings of the 2017 CHI Conference on Human Factors in Computing Systems* (pp. 1118–1130). ACM.

Foulsham, T., & Kingstone, A. (2013). Fixation-dependent memory for natural scenes: An experimental test of scanpath theory. *Journal of Experimental Psychology: General, 142*(1):41–56.

Geisler, W. S., & Perry, J. S. (1998). Real-time foveated multiresolution system for low-bandwidth video communication. In *Human Vision and Electronic Imaging III* (pp. 294–305). SPIE.

Grant, E. R., & Spivey, M. J. (2003). Eye movements and problem solving: Guiding attention guides thought. *Psychological Science, 14*(5), 462–466.

Grossberg, S., Srihasam, K., & Bullock, D. (2012). Neural dynamics of saccadic and smooth pursuit eye movement coordination during visual tracking of unpredictably moving targets. *Neural Networks, 27*, 1–20.

Ha, J., Park, S., & Im, C.-H. (2022). Novel hybrid brain-computer interface for virtual reality applications using steady-state visual-evoked potential-based brain–computer interface and electrooculogram-based eye tracking for increased information transfer rate. *Frontiers in Neuroinformatics, 16*.

Harris, D. J., Wilson, M. R., Holmes, T., de Burgh, T., & Vine, S. J. (2022). Eye movements in sports research and practice: Immersive technologies as optimal environments for the study of gaze behavior. In S. Stuart (ed.), *Eye Tracking: Background, Methods, and Applications* (pp. 207–221). Springer.

Jensen, R. R., Stets, J. D., Suurmets, S., Clement, J., & Aanæs, H. (2017). Wearable gaze trackers: Mapping visual attention in 3d. In *Scandinavian Conference on Image Analysis* (pp. 66–76). Springer.

Jogeshwar, A. K. (2020). Analysis and visualization tool for motion and gaze. In *ETRA '20 Short Papers: ACM Symposium on Eye Tracking Research and Applications* (pp. 1–3). ACM.

Jogeshwar, A. K., Diaz, G. J., Farnand, S. P., & Pelz, J. B. (2020). The cone model: Recognizing gaze uncertainty in virtual environments. *Electronic Imaging, 32*, 1–8.

Jogeshwar, A. K., & Pelz, J. B. (2021). GazeEnViz4D: 4-d gaze-in-environment visualization pipeline. *Procedia Computer Science, 192*, 2952–2961.

Jogeshwar, A. (2023). *Look at the Bigger Picture: Analyzing Eye Tracking Data With Multi-Dimensional Visualization*. Rochester Institute of Technology.

Joseph, A. W., Jeevitha Shree, D., Saluja, K. P. S., Mukhopadhyay, A., Murugesh, R., & Biswas, P. (2021). Eye tracking to understand impact of aging on mobile phone applications. In *Design for Tomorrow* (vol. 1, pp. 315–326). Springer.

Kaminska, O., & Foulsham, T. (2016). Eye-tracking social desirability bias. *Bulletin of Sociological Methodology / Bulletin de Methodologie Sociologique, 130*(1), 73–89.

Kassner, M., Patera, W., & Bulling, A. (2014). Pupil: An open source platform for pervasive eye tracking and mobile gaze-based interaction. In *Proceedings of the 2014 ACM International Joint Conference on Pervasive and Ubiquitous Computing: Adjunct Publication* (pp. 1151–1160). ACM.

Koch, M., Weiskopf, D., & Kurzhals, K. (2022). A spiral into the mind: Gaze spiral visualization for mobile eye tracking. *Proceedings of the ACM on Computer Graphics and Interactive Techniques, 5*(2), 1–16.

Kothari, R., Yang, Z., Kanan, C., Bailey, R., Pelz, J. B., & Diaz, G. J. (2020). Gaze-in-wild: A dataset for studying eye and head coordination in everyday activities. *Scientific Reports, 10*(1), 1–18.

Kovesdi, C., Spielman, Z., LeBlanc, K., & Rice, B. (2018). Application of eye tracking for measurement and evaluation in human factors studies in control room modernization. *Nuclear Technology, 202*(2–3), 220–229.

Kowler, E. (1995). Cogito ergo moveo: Cognitive control of eye movement. In *Exploratory Vision: The Active Eye*, pages 51–77. Springer.

Kröger, J. L., Lutz, O. H.-M., & Müller, F. (2019). What does your gaze reveal about you? On the privacy implications of eye tracking. In *Privacy and Identity Management: Data for Better Living* (pp. 226–241). Springer.

Lasky, N. V., Fisher, B. S., & Jacques, S. (2017). "Thinking thief" in the crime prevention arms race: Lessons learned from shoplifters. *Security Journal, 30*(3), 772–792.

Leigh, R., & Zee, D. (2015). *The Neurology of Eye Movements*, 5th ed. Oxford University Press.

Li, T.-H., Suzuki, H., & Ohtake, Y. (2020). Visualization of user's attention on objects in 3D environment using only eye tracking glasses. *Journal of Computational Design and Engineering, 7*(2), 228–237.

Lisberger, S. G. (2010). Visual guidance of smooth-pursuit eye movements: Sensation, action, and what happens in between. *Neuron, 66*(4), 477–491.

Macatee, R. J., Albanese, B. J., Schmidt, N. B., & Cougle, J. R. (2017). Attention bias towards negative emotional information and its relationship with daily worry in the context of acute stress: An eye-tracking study. *Behaviour Research and Therapy, 90*, 96–110.

Marti, S., Bayet, L., & Dehaene, S. (2015). Subjective report of eye fixations during serial search. *Consciousness and Cognition, 33*, 1–15.

Maurus, M., Hammer, J. H., & Beyerer, J. (2014). Realistic heatmap visualization for interactive analysis of 3D gaze data. In *ETRA '14: Proceedings of the Symposium on Eye Tracking Research and Applications* (pp. 295–298). ACM.

Mele, M. L., & Federici, S. (2012). Gaze and eye-tracking solutions for psychological research. *Cognitive Processing, 13*(1), 261–265.

Merchant, J. (1967). *The Oculometer* [technical report]. NASA.

Mühlenbeck, C., Jacobsen, T., Pritsch, C., & Liebal, K. (2017). Cultural and species differences in gazing patterns for marked and decorated objects: A comparative eye-tracking study. *Frontiers in psychology, 8*.

Munn, S. M., & Pelz, J. B. (2009). Fixtag: An algorithm for identifying and tagging fixations to simplify the analysis of data collected by portable eye trackers. *ACM Transactions on Applied Perception (TAP), 6*(3), 1–25.

Nyström, M., Andersson, R., Holmqvist, K., & Van De Weijer, J. (2013). The influence of calibration method and eye physiology on eyetracking data quality. *Behavior Research Methods, 45*(1), 272–288.

Pelz, J. B., Hayhoe, M. M., Ballard, D. H., Shrivastava, A., Bayliss, J. D., & von der Heyde, M. (1999). Development of a virtual laboratory for the study of complex human behavior. In *Stereoscopic Displays and Virtual Reality Systems VI* (pp. 416–426). SPIE.

Pfeiffer, T., & Renner, P. (2014). Eyesee3D: A low-cost approach for analyzing mobile 3D eye tracking data using computer vision and augmented reality technology. In *ETRA '14: Proceedings of the Symposium on Eye Tracking Research and Applications* (pp. 369–376). ACM.

Porterfield, W. (1735). An essay concerning the motions of our eyes. Part I. Of their external motions. *Edinburgh Medical Essays and Observations, 3*, 160–260.

Reingold, E. M. (2014). Eye tracking research and technology: Towards objective measurement of data quality. *Visual Cognition, 22*(3–4), 635–652.

Rucci, M., & Victor, J. D. (2015). The unsteady eye: An information-processing stage, not a bug. *Trends in Neurosciences, 38*(4), 195–206.

Salverda, A. P., & Tanenhaus, M. K. (2017). The visual world paradigm. In A. de Groot & P. Hagoort (eds.), *Research Methods in Psycholinguistics and the Neurobiology of Language: A Practical Guide* (pp. 89–110). Wiley-Blackwell.

Salvucci, D. D., & Goldberg, J. H. (2000). Identifying fixations and saccades in eye-tracking protocols. In *Proceedings of the 2000 symposium on Eye Tracking Research and applications* (pp. 71–78). ACM.

Savitzky, A., & Golay, M. J. (1964). Smoothing and differentiation of data by simplified least squares procedures. *Analytical Chemistry, 36*(8), 1627–1639.

Shepherd, M., Findlay, J. M., & Hockey, R. J. (1986). The relationship between eye movements and spatial attention. *Quarterly Journal of Experimental Psychology, 38*(3), 475–491.

Spering, M., & Carrasco, M. (2015). Acting without seeing: Eye movements reveal visual processing without awareness. *Trends in Neurosciences, 38*(4), 247–258.

Startsev, M., & Zemblys, R. (2022). Evaluating eye movement event detection: A review of the state of the art. *Behavior Research Methods, 55*(4), 1653–1714.

Tatler, B. W., & Wade, N. J. (2003). On nystagmus, saccades, and fixations. *Perception, 32*(2), 167–184.

Tinker, M. A., & Paterson, D. G. (1939). Influence of type form on eye movements. *Journal of Experimental Psychology*, *25*(5), 528–531.

Tonsen, M., Baumann, C. K., & Dierkes, K. (2020). A high-level description and performance evaluation of pupil invisible [preprint]. *ArXiv.* https://doi.org/10.48550/arXiv.2009.00508

Ukai, K., & Howarth, P. A. (2008). Visual fatigue caused by viewing stereoscopic motion images: Background, theories, and observations. *Displays*, *29*(2), 106–116.

Vansteenkiste, P., Cardon, G., Philippaerts, R., & Lenoir, M. (2015). Measuring dwell time percentage from head-mounted eye-tracking data–comparison of a frame-by-frame and a fixation-by-fixation analysis. *Ergonomics*, *58*(5), 712–721.

Wang, D., Mulvey, F. B., Pelz, J. B., & Holmqvist, K. (2017). A study of artificial eyes for the measurement of precision in eye-trackers. *Behavior Research Methods*, *49*(3), 947–959.

Watalingam, R. D., Richetelli, N., Pelz, J. B., & Speir, J. A. (2017). Eye tracking to evaluate evidence recognition in crime scene investigations. *Forensic Science International*, *280*, 64–80.

PART V

Physiological Measures

19 Measuring Hormones: Considerations for Biospecimen Collection, Assay, and Analysis

Shannin N. Moody, Amali I. Stephens, Jenny Mai Phan, Olga Miocevic, Amita Kapoor, Wen Wang, Allissa L. Van Steenis, Scott Le, Lotte van Dammen, and Elizabeth A. Shirtcliff

Abstract

This chapter presents a broad overview of the measurement of hormones, spanning from their collection in different biospecimens and the assay of hormones across laboratory strategies to a brief overview of statistical treatment and analysis that extracts the hormone of interest. We organize each section into a description of measurement tools followed by an agnostic analysis of the tools for their strengths, weaknesses, prospects, and pitfalls. We do not view any single approach as "best" or "optimal." This view is commensurate with the production and cellular conversion of hormones – adaptive physiological processes that are not "best" or "optimal" but rather constantly changing biobehavioral markers that shift according to the demands of the environment. Measuring the hormone is just the beginning of exploring the multifaceted ways that hormones can inform health, development, morbidity, and mortality.

Keywords: Hormone Biomarkers, Hormone Statistics, Hormone Collection Methods, Hormone Assays, Hormone Analysis

Introduction: Overview of Prospects and Pitfalls of Measuring Hormones in Social and Behavioral Sciences

One of the biggest challenges of measuring hormones in research is that hormones are molecules, not constructs. Yet, most social and behavioral scientists are trained to approach hormones as social and behavioral constructs. Hormones provide the substantive realism of biological measurement that is capable of *informing* us about actions, habits, emotions, and characteristics deeply rooted in social and behavioral sciences. Hormones promise insights into stress and health, love and hate, masculinity and femininity. However, these concepts may and often do shift to retrofit evolving definitions as fields advance while hormonal biomarkers remain defined by their molecular structure and are agnostic about changing scientific concepts. This often leaves a state of science in which measuring hormones feels like grappling with a misbehaving unruly teenager, failing to conform to the psychological constructs that we have imbued them with.

Hormonal biomarkers may fail to conform because they are often conceptualized as valenced entities. Cortisol is bad because it is linked with stress. Oxytocin is good because it is linked with a concept of love and "cuddles." These valenced mnemonics are shortcuts to make sense of the direction of regression weights, but it is nonsensical for the body to generate a strictly "good" or "bad" biological measure. Regulation implies balance and there will always be trade-offs to maintaining balance. Hormones are good *and* bad and everything in between. Just as oxytocin has become synonymous with "love" (Magon & Kalra, 2011) it may also be a biological catalyst for ethnocentrism and racism (De Dreu et al., 2011; Yong, 2012).

Hormonal biomarkers also may seem to misbehave because hormonal regulation is adaptive, but adaptive and desirable are not the same thing. The search for a "biomarker" is a quest to discover something "bad" (Ou et al., 2021). Public health needs and funding priorities dictate that problems are meant to be solved, risks identified, and damage mitigated (Institute of Medicine et al., 2012). When molecules change to meet the demands of their environment, they do so without valence, directional awareness, or public health priority. Biomarkers adapt to their environment, and regulation occurs with both costs and benefits. Public health priorities may do better to vilify high-cost adaptation to a disadvantaged environment than to further invest effort into identification of good and bad biomarkers.

It is with the overarching philosophy that biomarkers are first and foremost molecules which may *inform* social and behavioral constructs, that we approach the measurement of hormones. From what, how, and when hormones are collected can impact how we develop its construct. There is no gold standard for processes and collection, but there are plenty of wrong answers that will not pass the gauntlet of peer review. First, we present practical foundational information about hormonal measurement that stems from thoughtful collection, biomarker selection, and measurement. Second, we consider techniques for measuring hormones. These sections are grounded in the practical knowledge of molecules and their measurement. Assuming that the measurement of the molecule has gone well, the next section provides a brief overview of statistics that converts molecular findings into interpretable values. Our goal is to give an overview of how hormones are collected and processed to avoid "misbehavior" at a methodological and statistical level, well before becoming an unruly construct.

Biospecimen Collection

Hormones are molecules that are released into the bloodstream to impact an organ – often at a distance from the organ that released the hormone. The purpose of a hormone is often to trigger the release, or manufacture of, another hormone. The action of hormones likely occurs within cells, especially cell nuclei, where they function to change gene expression across a wide variety of timescales. The same molecule could operate as a neurotransmitter if the conduit weren't blood, or as a pheromone if the target organs belonged to someone else. Hormones are indiscriminate chemical messengers, but their message is only received within organs that have receptors to receive those messages. In addition, they go everywhere and do a lot, though rarely anything specific. This section is organized according to the feasibility and practicality of biospecimens collection and ranges in levels of invasiveness.

Invasive Sampling

Blood

Blood, as well as serum or plasma derived from blood samples, is well-established as a biospecimen for assessment of human hormones in research and medical settings (Awad et al., 2006; Eskander et al., 2012; Hurtado de Catalfo et al., 2007). Hormones are transported in blood or plasma (Belfiore & LeRoith, 2018). Depending on hormone molecular structure (e.g., derived from tyrosine, peptide hormone), blood may be the only option for reliable quantification. Blood sampling allows researchers and medical professionals to capture an extensive set of hormones such as oxytocin, vasopressin, insulin, estrogens, androgens, corticosteroids, progesterone, adrenalin, pituitary hormones, and many others (Gray et al., 1961). Thus, blood has a long history as a reliable biospecimen for assessment of a wide range of hormones (Hofman, 2001). Researchers interested in acute, short-term changes in hormone levels often favor blood as a biospecimen because it allows for the ability to capture hormone concentrations in single time-points and, if necessary, the rhythmic qualities of hormones through continuous or frequent sample collection (Veldhuis et al., 1987).

Minimally Invasive Sampling

Dried Blood Spots

Dried blood spots (DBS) have been used for over a century, originating as a method of absorbing blood onto paper to measure glucose levels (Hannon & Therrell, 2014). DBS is cost-effective by eliminating phlebotomy personnel and equipment costs. DBS can be completed in a wide variety of settings, including remote contexts in which freezing or storing samples on ice is impractical. Simplicity of room temperature storage and shipping has made DBS the "go-to" biospecimen for biological anthropology fieldwork. Although with fewer validated biomarkers than blood, DBS holds a wide set of potential biomarkers as concentrations are somewhat comparable to blood sampling. Given that hormones are defined according to blood transport, DBS has intuitive logical appeal (Lim, 2018). Potential drawbacks are that the lancet prick can be painful and merely the anticipation of pain can exaggerate perceptions of invasiveness (Dubey et al., 2019). This may be especially true for finger pricks or where multiple biomarkers are of interest and larger lancets or multiple pricks are needed. Another drawback is that some biomarkers are degraded by the filter paper, and extracting blood from the filter paper can be time-consuming in the lab. Insufficient saturation is an unfortunate source of error variability (Crimmins et al., 2020).

Tasso

To address concerns about filter paper degradation and to further minimize pain, Tasso is an emergent technology for minimally invasive blood collection. Tasso collection involves a small prick or needle stroke within an enclosed device (Roadcap et al., 2020; TASSO-SST, n.d.). Tasso is a proprietary method attached to the upper arm (Figure 19.1) or hip which have fewer sensitive nerve endings than fingers. As such, it is typically reported as less painful and stressful. Tasso collects capillary blood over a small span of time that allows smaller punctures for equivalent volumes (compared to DBS). Strengths of Tasso include convenient collection, storage, and shipping of capillary blood samples. Participants can easily collect capillary blood samples following the instructions without risk of bloodborne pathogen exposure (Hendelman et al., 2021). Like DBS, Tasso can be considered minimally invasive because it provides virtually painless collection experience; an additional benefit of Tasso is that lancets are not visible so they may be preferred for people with needle phobia, pediatrics, or vulnerable populations (Menestrina Dewes et al., 2022).

There are also challenges with Tasso. As Tasso is a relatively novel and emerging collection method, there are a limited number of validated hormones. Capillary blood samples take minutes (not seconds) to collect, so there is inherently a longer time-window of hormonal metrics. The volume of blood collected is necessarily small, so large panels of hormonal biomarkers may be impractical. Short samples may be especially prevalent in pediatric populations or other populations with low

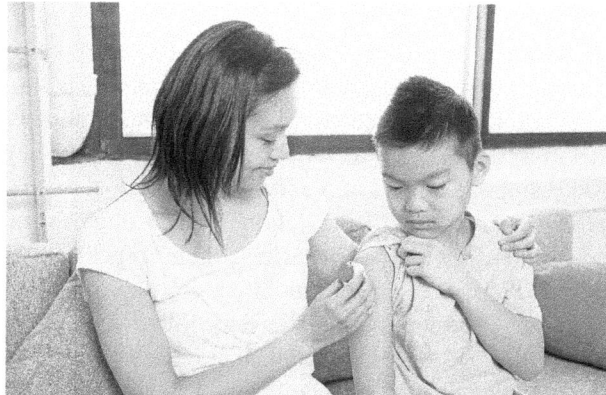

Figure 19.1 *Tasso device on upper arm.*

Figure 19.2 *Tasso collection and processing kit.*

blood flow (Gustafsson et al., 2021). When multiple samples are needed within one experimental setting, multiple Tasso kits (Figure 19.2) and punctures are necessary. This may have negative effects on research consent rate and increase the financial burden of research projects.

Non-invasive Sampling

Saliva

Through multiple collections taken at specific time points, saliva captures biologically active "free" steroidal hormones released in response to specific contexts (e.g., stress tests, exercise). Collecting multiple saliva biospecimens over days can also capture diurnal or trait-level hormones (Gildner, 2021). Saliva is non-invasive and allows for repeated samples that can take place in a variety of settings. Ease of collection means that most participants are able to collect samples themselves in point-of-care settings, including the home (Miočević et al., 2017).

Saliva is often collected through passive drool that involves directly expectorating in a vial or tube. Alternatively, saliva can be collected with the aid of a device such as a straw, larger collection funnel (Padilla et al., 2020), or absorbent cotton/polyester (Fernandes et al., 2013), and other types of filters (Neu et al., 2007). These collection devices have enhanced ease of collection in populations who cannot readily spit into small vials. Emerging collection devices, such as "wearable" pacifiers for infants, are being pilot tested and validated prior to widespread use (García-Carmona et al., 2019). Decisions about collection strategies should be considered if the device itself introduces error to salivary biomarkers (Harmon et al., 2007; Shirtcliff et al., 2001). Furthermore, the location of saliva collection in the oral cavity, as proximity to and stimulation of salivary glands, can contribute to the composition of the final collection. Often, the preference is for whole saliva that is pooled at/near the lips from the entire oral cavity.

While saliva as a biospecimen solves many of the limitations of invasive venipuncture, over time and with repeated narrowly timed sampling, saliva collection may seem inconvenient. Participants must actively be involved with saliva collection to varying degrees and collection takes time; although on average it may only be a minute or two, some individuals with dry mouth may take a long time to provide a sufficient sample. As saliva can be viscous, odorous, or discolored, there is the potential for embarrassment. Researchers may inadvertently introduce stress if attending too closely to participants; this can add to concerns with dry mouth (a common symptom of sympathetic nervous system stress activation). The need for daily multiple sampling contributes to missing data and systematic error due to collection protocol non-adherence (Fernandes et al., 2013).

Sample contamination can also be a concern, specifically with oral leakage of blood (Kivlighan et al., 2004) as well as other contaminants, such as food and drink (Navazesh, 1993; Padilla et al., 2020). Studies have been mixed on the utility of oral stimulants to encourage salivation (e.g., sweet tarts, flavored drinks) with some concluding that stimulants do not introduce major error (Talge et al., 2005). Statistical models can correct somewhat for contamination (Behr et al., 2017). The decision to include salivary stimulants should be contemplated when considering populations (e.g., medical conditions that may cause dry mouth, children, infants). If collection is taking place in a healthy adult group, minimum interference is best (e.g., passive drool). Regardless of final decisions, minimizing contamination is important to consider during study design and, to the extent possible, best practices in collection methods should be preferred, such as waiting an allotted time period after brushing and collecting samples before eating. Best practices can also be creative! For instance, while medication event monitoring system (MEMS) caps can capture times of sample tubes being opened (Fernandes et al., 2013), "selfies" can be fun for participants and also gather precise times of data collection (Stalder et al., 2022). Saliva rates can even be enhanced by introducing the smell of bacon (Peres et al., 2015).

Hair

Hair has grown into an established biospecimen that can be collected non-invasively to measure cumulative hormone concentrations at an approximate rate of one month's worth of circulation per centimeter (Meyer & Novak, 2012). This minimizes costs for obtaining a large number of repeated samples statistically converted to basal concentrations (Russell et al., 2012). Hair can be measured for a variety of steroids, such as cortisol (Russell et al., 2012) and sex hormone measurement (Marceau et al., 2021; Peng et al., 2022; Wang et al., 2019). Collection of hair samples is relatively simple and can be obtained in many settings (e.g., home, field, laboratory). Hair samples (Figure 19.3) are usually collected from the posterior vertex of the head, close to the scalp, but without leaving visible spots.

Figure 19.3 *Hair sample processing.*

Hair remains stable over long periods of time at room temperature (Russell et al., 2012), and hormones have remained detectable over millennia (Webb et al., 2015); therefore, it is convenient to transport and store hair samples. Hair allows researchers to eliminate financial fees and hazard costs from shipping with dry ice. In-home collection is feasible because it is easy to obtain hair collection tools (e.g., scissors, rubber bands). Hair as a biospecimen may be robust against attrition as ample information is gained with a single collection.

Biospecimens that call for repeated precisely timed samples show systematic non-compliance (Hall et al., 2011). For example, lower socio-economic status populations show reduced compliance due to the inconvenience and challenges of logging and obtaining samples (Hill Golden et al., 2014). Individuals with schedules that are less flexible (e.g., multiple jobs, student workers, busy caregivers) may be more willing to provide a single hair sample over several daily salivary samples. In addition, hair cannot capture short-term psychological stressors or physiological responses (e.g., exercise or pain), nor does hair measure circadian rhythmicity or momentary daily hormonal changes (Engert et al., 2018). However, this can be advantageous when controlling for variations in hormone release, such as menstrual cyclicity (Wang et al., 2019), and when capturing chronic exposures to stressors without requiring multiple collections.

Hair collection methodologies also present some challenges. Insufficient sample weights can indicate poor sample quality and result in systematic error, as distal segments do not correlate as strongly with proximal scalp-region segments (Wang et al., 2020). This error can be minimized with clear instructions and training for participants or researchers to collect "tiny snips" of hair taken from various parts of the scalp. Multiple tiny sample points may alleviate discomfort from the perception of hair loss or "noticeable divots." Bias can be introduced from external variables, including exposure to heat, chemical treatment (e.g., dye, perms, relaxers), exposure to natural sunlight and UV (Sauvé et al., 2007; Wester et al., 2016). Despite this, external hair exposures are not yet routinely reported as control measures, leaving ambiguity about the interpretation of hormone concentrations.

Given that hair varies in absorption of lipids (Martí et al., 2016), and that steroidal hormones are lipid-soluble (Kudielka et al., 2012), it is also unclear whether hormone absorption differs by hair type (Figure 19.4; Moody et al., 2022). Hair

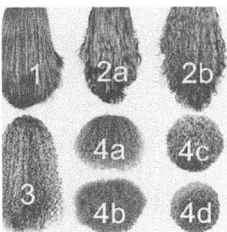

Figure 19.4 *Hair types.*

absorption studies are largely limited to forensic research in illicit drug use (Boumba et al., 2006) and show greater lipid absorption with "African" hair (Coderch et al., 2019). However, it is unclear whether this is due to hair thickness and or shape – both of which influence lipid absorption. Studies that have reported differences in hormone absorption, such that higher concentrations of cortisol were found in curlier hair types, found this only within Black and multiracial participants; White and Latine/x individuals showed a decrease in cortisol with curlier hair types (Moody et al., 2022). Finally, further research that considers whether hair on various parts of the body is well correlated may reduce attrition due to worry in hair loss when hair can be collected from less noticeable areas (e.g., back of the neck, leg hair, arm hair).

Urine

Urine is minimally invasive (Mericq & Cutler, 1998) and captures hormones over a cumulative period – typically lasting over a 24-hour period or for a set number of days. Urine has a benefit of capturing larger molecules, such as peptides (MacLean et al., 2019) (e.g., vasopressin and oxytocin). This makes urine ideal for research seeking to examine larger molecules as well as steroid hormones. Urine is a relatively copious biospecimen that makes assessments of wide panels of hormones feasible.

After collection, urine should be stored at cold temperatures (-20 to -80 degrees) to avoid sample degradation due to microbial growth (Tsivou et al., 2009). Because urine is processed through the kidneys, it can also be susceptible to error due to blood contamination, as well as fluctuation of steroidal hormones, when large amounts of water are consumed (Mericq & Cutler, 1998). While sample collection is fairly straightforward for adults and also a common procedure conducted during regular physical examinations, urine sample collection involving infants or children can be more challenging (Ammenti et al., 2020). This is largely because urine is most stable when collected from mid-sample stream (Zhu et al., 2021). The collection instructions can also be difficult to communicate to vulnerable populations. Urine sampling may also still be considered mildly uncomfortable for participants as well as researchers, and the measured hormones are often less reliable than other biospecimens (Schiffer et al., 2019) because molecules are metabolized prior to urination (Eriksson & Gustafsson, 1972).

Emerging Biospecimens: Nails and Feces

Nails

Following similar rationale as hair, nails are a minimally invasive way to capture hormone levels over long periods of time. Nails have successfully been extracted for testosterone, cortisol, and dehydroepiandrosterone (Voegel et al., 2018) and are used with a variety of assays – most commonly mass spectrometry (Phillips et al., 2021). It is not yet clear whether nails can measure the broad spectrum of hormones that hair can, as protocols are not yet established for nails. When hair collection makes participants unable (e.g., newborn infants or participants with short hair) or unwilling (e.g., longitudinal collection, thinning hair, cultural importance of hair) to provide hair samples, nails present a reasonable alternative.

Nails are susceptible to differences in growth rates depending on the digit or hand (Binz et al., 2018) and age (Shi et al., 2018). An added source of measurement error for nails is that clippings are from distal growth, where many hormones may become less reliable and where impact of individual differences in growth rates may be magnified. In humans, it is impossible to "nail down" when the nail clippings deposit the hormones without removing the nail from its bed. Nails may be more suitable during certain periods across the lifespan. For instance, while a pregnant woman experiences changes in hair growth and morphology derived in part from hormones, nails do not appear to reflect such changes (Altan Ferhatoğlu et al., 2018).

Furthermore, populations may be unable to provide nail samples, such as individuals who bite/cut nails short or have acrylic/manicured nails. While there is emerging literature that explores the impact of external exposures on steroidal sample degradation in hair, there are very few studies that look at the impact of hand creams, nail polish, and nail polish remover on hormones in nails (Phillips et al., 2021). Like other biospecimens, nails have both advantages and disadvantages when used to gauge hormones in humans.

Feces

Fecal samples can be useful for assessing hormones in a complementary biospecimen that is proximal to the microbiome. Like serum, the total fraction of hormones is represented in fecal samples and may also include byproducts of microbial communities (Sheriff et al., 2010). Although the range of hormones extends beyond cortisol, one of the primary advantages of fecal cortisol is to shed light on the stress endocrinology of the microbiome (Figure 19.5). Fecal biospecimens lend an important connection to biological stress as well as the systemic, transcriptomic, and metabolomic changes occurring in conjunction with one's own biological stress (Bailey et al., 2011). Experimental designs can connect glucocorticoids and other significant hormones to microbial analysis and can elucidate the internal microbial environment – the

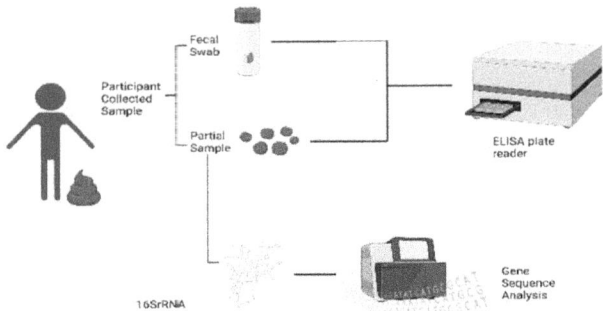

Figure 19.5 *Feces collection and processing.*

microbiome – and incidences of stress-related diseases. Another strength is that fecal samples are non-invasive and potentially passive collection that minimizes participant burden (Partrick, 2018). Samples as small as 1 g (a teaspoon amount of feces) can be used to assess biologically relevant hormones (Smith & Gaya, 2012).

Fecal biospecimens also have weaknesses – the most obvious being the overall "ick" factor. While some populations benefit from passive collection of fecal sampling in humans (e.g., infant diapers) and several animal models (e.g., mouse, hamster, non-human primate, whale), for many human populations, collecting fecal samples may require participant involvement where individuals have to collect their own sample. Participants and researchers must also navigate the safe and effective storage of fecal samples for processing. These efforts, though requiring more time, have been done effectively in large-scale, cross-site collection in young adults (Tavalire et al., 2021). Some biological realities can also influence whether fecal biospecimens can be collected. Food insecurity (Nguyen et al., 2021), stress (van Thiel et al., 2020), access to clean water (Spiller & Garsed, 2009), and overall diet (Rej et al., 2019) may impact fecal sampling due to diarrhea, bowel irregularity, or irritation.

In sum, there are an increasingly large number of biospecimens available to address questions about how hormones work. There is no single right answer for which biospecimen is best in every scenario. Each biospecimen has its own unique strengths and weaknesses, and the selection of biospecimens depends on the hormone of interest as well as feasibility for the population and research question. Weighing the strengths and weaknesses (see Tables 19.1 and 19.2) should take into account whether participants will ultimately be able and willing to comply with sampling protocols.

Table 19.1 *Sample specimen pros and cons*

Sample type	Pros	Cons
Blood	Well-established; rich source of many biomarkers (e.g., cholesterol, inflammation markers)	Temperature control for long-term storage; costly; specialized collection training; highly invasive
DBS	Well-established; cost-effective; simplicity	Painful; difficulty in abstraction; degradation of hormone; limited volume for assays
Tasso	Minimally invasive; convenient storage and shipping; low risk of pathogen exposure; no visible lancet	Limited validated hormones; longer time window for collection; small sample; proprietary
Saliva	Acute, basal, and diurnal; can capture other markers (e.g., inflammation biomarkers)	Lower concentration of biomarkers; messy; dry mouth; collection difficulties (e.g., babies)
Hair	Stable over long periods and at room temperature; easy transport; simple collection	Only captures long-term hormone release; limited validated hormones; external variable influence (e.g., sunlight and hair type)
Urine	Abundant sample supply; easy collection	Dilution from metabolization may require concentration techniques; hydration inference

Table 19.1 (cont.)

Sample type	Pros	Cons
Nails	Stable over long periods and at room temperature; easy transport; simple collection	Limited availability and expertise for analysis
Feces	Reflects gut microbiome and metabolites	Unpleasant collection, storage, and assay process; susceptible to diet interference

Table 19.2 *Cost and ease of collection, transport, and storage*

Sample type	Collection cost	Storage cost	Easy collection	Easy transport
Blood	Moderate to high	Moderate to high	No	No
DBS	Low	None	Yes	Yes
Tasso	Varies	Varies	Yes	Varies
Saliva	Low to moderate	Moderate to high	Varies	No
Hair	Low	Low	Yes	Yes
Urine	Low	Moderate to high	Yes	No
Nails	Low	Low	Yes	Yes
Feces	Moderate to high	Moderate to high	No	No

Hormone Assays

The next section describes common techniques for the measurement of hormones. Assays are tools that allow for the quantitative or qualitative measurement or concentration of a target entity or analyte – in our case, hormonal concentration. The principle of many assays is the same. It is impossible to measure a hormone directly; instead, you must place a precisely known amount of something that is tagged or labeled in some way. Decisions such as extraction, elution, and dilution are designed to enhance the signal-to-noise ratio of the molecule of interest compared to everything else in the biospecimen. Validation steps to demonstrate rigor and reproducibility are also empirical tests of the reliability of signal-to-noise. It is beyond our scope to fully address validation steps and performance characteristics, but specific assay selection should consider assay performance characteristics in addition to methodology.

Radioimmunoassay (RIA)

Radioimmunoassays (RIA)s have a long history of use, and at their inception won their inventor Rosalyn Yalow a Nobel prize for physiology (Thompson, 2012, p. 146). RIAs determine the concentration of an antigen (i.e., hormone) in a sample. This process involves antibodies and radiolabeled isotopes. Antibodies coat the wells on a multi-well plate or in a series of vials or tubes. Radiolabeled isotopes (commonly I-125 and I-131, Sadeghalvad & Rezaei, 2022) are added to bind to the antibodies. Unbound isotopes are removed from the well by washing or aspiration. A known volume of the sample added allows the unknown amount of antigens to bind to the antibodies, removing the radiolabeled isotopes competitively. As the number of bound antigens increases, the radioactivity in the well decreases. Radioactivity in the well can be compared to a standard graph to determine the concentration (Yalow & Berson, 1960). Succinctly, immunoassays expose the amount of a molecule by sticking to its counterpart. What doesn't stick is washed away and what's left over is then compared to a known value.

RIA's biggest advantage is that it is a widely applicable technique to measure the concentrations of peptides and non-peptide hormones, drugs, enzymes, viruses, bacterial antigens, tumor antigens, and other organic substances of biological interest (Yalow, 1982). RIAs are highly sensitive and specific, so they are able to detect very low sample concentrations when using antibodies of high affinity (Forghani et al., 1976). A primary disadvantage is that it requires a gamma counter and exposure (minimal) to radioactive isotopes. Laboratory safety protocols must also regularly minimize and record radioactive exposure for all users. Furthermore, many RIAs require aspiration as a step in which unbound liquid is removed manually in a way that may introduce error if the bound quantity is also aspirated. Lastly, radioactivity degrades over time, so RIA shelf-life is influenced by half-life.

Enzyme Immunoassay (EIA) or Enzyme Linked Immunosorbent Assays (ELISA)

Enzyme immunoassay (EIA) is a method first described in 1971 to measure steroid hormones (Engvall & Perlmann, 1972). It is based on the same principles as RIA, but instead of labeling with a radioactive isotope, EIAs use color-changing substances as labels. Broadly, the antigen and antibodies are incubated – forming antigen-antibody complexes. The complexes are separated from the free antigen and antibody, and the activity in the fraction(s) is measured (Figure 19.6) (Engvall & Perlmann, 1972). There are two major types of EIA that are currently used today: non-competitive and competitive.

Non-competitive. For this technique, a labeled antibody is used that is directed toward the analyte (antigen) of interest. The most popular type of EIA is the sandwich assay. Two antibodies are used that bind to different sites on the antigen. The captured antibody, which is highly specific for the antigen, is attached to a solid surface; the detection antibody binds the antigen at a different epitope than the capture antibody. As a result, the antigen is "sandwiched" between two antibodies (Cox et al., 2019). Many peptide hormone assays are of the sandwich type, but due to the small size of steroid hormones, they are not always good candidates for sandwich assays.

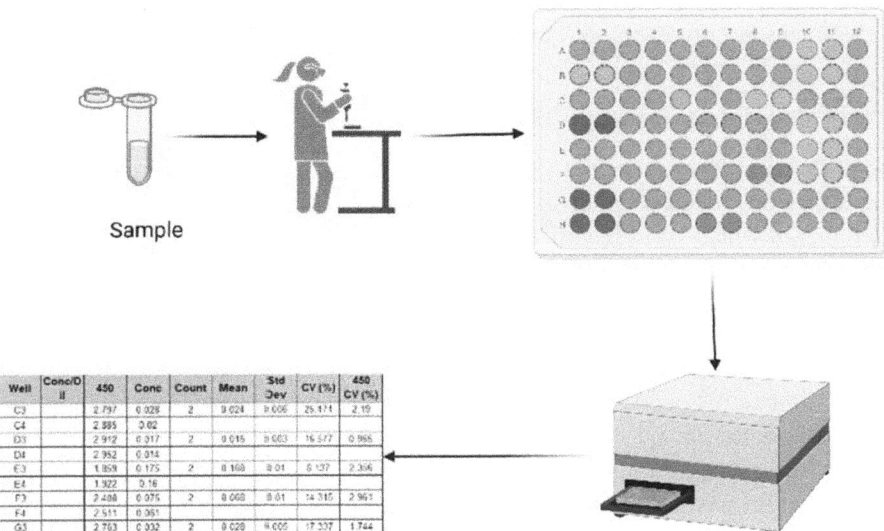

Figure 19.6 *ELISA assay process.*

Competitive. This assay type is based on the competition of labeled and unlabeled versions of the analyte of interest for a limited number of antibody binding sites. This assay type is often for small molecules, such as steroid hormones, and when a matched pair of antibodies to the analyte does not exist. A fixed amount of labeled molecule or hormone and a variable amount of unlabeled molecule of interest are incubated with the antibody. According to the law of mass action, the amount of bound labeled molecule is a function of the total concentration of labeled and unlabeled molecules (Hulme & Trevethick, 2010). Alternatively, an antigen can be coated on the plate with the antibody and the sample in solution. Fewer antibodies will be available to bind the coated antigen as the amount of antigen in the sample increases (Cox et al., 2019; Gan & Patel, 2013).

Strengths of EIAs are that they are a simple technique to learn and can easily be incorporated into laboratories. They generally do not require sample preparation as the biological specimens are added directly to the plates. Specifically for sandwich assays, they are also highly specific, as two antibodies are used to detect the antigen, and are known for their sensitivity and robustness.

There are also weaknesses of EIAs. It can be difficult and expensive to develop new methods since antibodies must be tested and validated in specimens and human testing. When antibodies come from commercial assays, rather than in-house sources, the antibody can be depleted and replaced; this requires extensive revalidation. Another weakness is that there is no way to know whether the assay will be successful prior to running it and troubleshooting can only occur after output of the data at the end of the assay. It is only after the run, and a potential failure, that many problems can be diagnosed, such as poor standard curve or poor correspondence between expected and measured control concentrations. This can be a serious issue if biospecimens are irreplaceable.

Lateral Flow Immunoassays (LFIA)

Lateral flow immunoassay (LFIA) is a popular method for detection and measurement of a variety of target molecules (Mirica et al., 2022). LFIAs are designed for use in settings in which rapid measurement of hormones and other molecules may be necessary (e.g., point-of-care) and have become more accessible over the last few decades (Miočević et al., 2017). Medical and research fields have seen a rise in LFIA applications in research, screening, monitoring, and diagnosis of various diseases, as well as potential for easy and affordable testing at home (Mirica et al., 2022).

LFIAs utilize polymeric strips suitable for a variety of biospecimens with prior applications with saliva, urine, whole blood, and sweat (Koczula & Gallotta, 2016). The fluid sample is dropped onto the strip through which it then migrates via capillary action across a number of sections – one of which contains antibodies for the biomarker in question (Koczula & Gallotta, 2016). Measurement is on the basis of a color change or instrument-detected change that indicates the presence or absence of molecules (Dalirirad & Steckl, 2019; Miočević et al., 2017). The detected change can be quantified to reflect hormone concentrations in the sample (Khelifa et al., 2022) or, in the case of the commonly used over-the-counter pregnancy tests that measure presence of human chorionic gonadotropin, used as a one-stop detection of the analyte (Koczula & Gallotta, 2016; Posthuma-Trumpie et al., 2009).

The simplicity of this method, from the user's perspective (e.g., patient at home, in POC contexts (Miočević et al., 2017)), is its most notable advantage. Over-the-counter tests (e.g., pregnancy, fertility, HIV) are great examples of the simplicity and user-friendliness of this method. In addition to being easy to use by the "untrained" layperson or professional, results are available within 5 to 30 minutes, and the cost of obtaining and processing samples is reduced compared to traditional assays (Khelifa et al., 2022). LFIAs have also been used for measurement of hormones for diagnostic purposes (Khelifa et al., 2022) and technology has shown great promise in supplementing invasive methods for measurement of hormones. LFIAs can be especially useful for measurement of hormones in a variety of contexts and biofluids, including saliva (Miočević et al., 2017), especially when ease of use and rapid results are essential.

One major drawback is that this technology is still emerging even though hCG is well established; further hormones remain in need of additional testing, validation, and commercialization (Khelifa et al., 2022; Miočević et al., 2017). For LFIAs to become a well-established method, it is necessary to evaluate them on several important parameters, including sensitivity and detection ranges across the variety of devices and analyte of interest. Depending on the hormone that is measured and its respective mechanism, LFIA may not provide the necessary sensitivity for detection compared to more established methods (Khelifa et al., 2022). Additional confirmatory testing may be desirable, in which case the affordability of LFIAs is reduced as it only serves as initial test prior to further assessment or diagnosis or confirmatory quantification. The most notable drawback of LFIAs is the underlying complexity of the technology as evidenced by the need for specialized laboratory and manufacturing equipment for development of the strips and quality control testing (Miočević et al., 2017).

Liquid-Chromatography Tandem Mass Spectrometry (LC-MS/MS)

Liquid-chromatography triple quadrupole mass spectrometry (LC-MS/MS) is highly specific for measurement of hormones due to the direct measurement of the mass to charge (m/z) ratio of the analyte. The main principle of triple quadrupole MS is that the sample flows through the mobile phase to the ionization source where gas ions are formed. These ions, known as the precursors, then travel to the first mass analyzer where they are separated in electric fields according to their m/z ratio (Figure 19.7). The relative abundance of precursors to production ions is quantified (Field, 2013).

The MS/MS principle is uniform across hormone types (e.g., peptide or steroid), but there are differences at the LC and sample preparation steps. These differences all relate to enhancing selectivity in complex samples for the analytes of interest. One of the difficulties of LC-MS/MS is low sensitivity if there are compounds present that will ionize and mask the signal. This is often observed as high background signal and matrix effects and becomes a serious issue when the analyte is in low concentration.

Some strengths of LC-MS/MS are the specificity and sensitivity of measurement. Since the detection is based on the molecular weight of the analyte of interest, panels can be created that can measure multiple hormones in one sample. This is especially beneficial in situations where sample volumes are limited, such as in young children or for some biospecimens (e.g., hair and nails). Development of new methods can be relatively simple and can be completed quickly. In contrast to immunoassays, system suitability tests can be run prior to running valuable samples, so the risk of assay failure is lower. Depending on the concentration of the analyte, sample preparation can be as simple as "dilute and shoot" or protein precipitation.

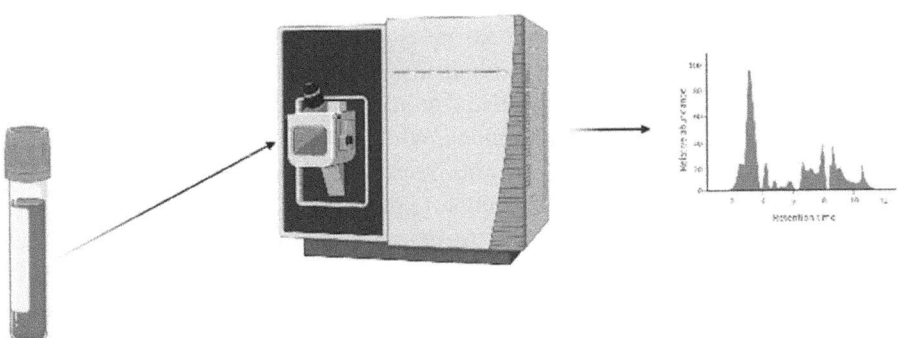

Figure 19.7 *Liquid-chromatography mass spectrometry.*

Table 19.3 *General pros and cons to each approach*

Method	Pros	Cons
RIA	High sensitivity and specificity	Requires the use of radioisotopes; radiation exposure
EIA and ELISA	Wide range of applications; well-established and widely used	Limited dynamic range and sensitivity; longer assay time compared to LFIA
LFIA	Rapid results with minimal equipment; portable and easy to use	Lower sensitivity and specificity compared to ELISA; expensive to develop and manufacture
LC-MS/MS	Highly sensitivity and specificity; wide dynamic range; acute quantification	Expensive instruments require technical expertise; specialized training and data analysis; complex sample preparation; high maintenance

The main weakness of LC-MS/MS is the complexity of the instrument. Specialized training to learn how to operate and maintain the instrument is required and has a steep learning curve. In addition, the expense of the instrument itself and the laboratory setup required can make incorporation of LC-MS/MS cost-prohibitive. Another weakness includes the amount of maintenance that is required to keep the instrument producing high-quality data. In sum, there are a variety of measurement tools that can convert a hormone from an unknown quantity in a biospecimen into a measurable concentration.

It is important to remember that the methods above do not provide direct measurements of the molecules but instead use assay principles to infer or interpolate hormone concentrations in a specific biological sample. These methods have both advantages and disadvantages which vary depending on the type of biological sample utilized. Table 19.3 broadly summarizes general pros and cons to each.

Statistical and Collection Method Considerations

Lastly, we consider three of the most common statistical constructs that are probed from measured hormones. Often these constructs relate to an interplay between time and timing of a hormonal measurement and its derivatives. These constructs can present differently depending on *how* and *when* a hormone is collected as well as *what* statistical method is utilized to interpret results, which will influence the final number used to quantify a hormone. While waking levels of a hormone may indicate a different construct than how a hormone reacts to a stressful situation, each method will also differ in cost of execution (e.g., using two samples over one day versus four samples across four days to derive a diurnal slope) and statistical complexity (e.g., area under the curve versus hierarchical linear modeling). Finally, because of metabolic rates and differences in the way hormones are deposited, not all specimens are suitable for or capable of addressing all research questions.

Diurnal Slopes, Waking, and Awakening Response

Many hormones show a circadian rhythm that, when limited to waking hours, is termed the diurnal (daytime) rhythm or slope. Diurnal hormones require a minimum of two samples (although the best practice minimum is four samples for quadratic findings) within a day to track individual differences in hormonal changes between waking and bedtime. Many hormones are highest in the morning, then decline across the day.

Steep patterns in diurnal rhythms are thought to reflect adequate regulation, as the normative rise and fall of hormones indicates a flexible system. Conversely, flattened patterns may indicate dysregulation when hormones do not show a steep rise or remain elevated throughout the day (Edwards et al., 2001). For cortisol, as an example, daily physiological activities (Aakvaag & Opstad, 2019), sex (Juster et al., 2016), race (Cohen et al., 2006), socio-economic status, psychosocial encounters (Telford et al., 2012), and age all impact diurnal patterns. While cortisol's diurnal rhythm is best known, other hormones also show rhythms. For instance, testosterone diurnal patterns may be impacted by varying psychosocial changes, such as competition (Carré & Archer, 2018), menstruation (Gildner, 2021), loss (Stanton et al., 2009), relationship status (Brarett et al., 2015), and parenthood (Meijer et al., 2019).

There are many analytical methods that can be chosen to calculate diurnal measures, including mean calculation, change scores, and area under the curve (AUC) (Pruessner et al., 2003). Diurnal rhythms are subject to day-to-day variations that make it valuable to collect samples across multiple and, if possible, consecutive days. When such repeated hormone measures are available across multiple days, growth curve models allow for extraction of the stability/change in hormones from one time point to the next as well as within-person variability in hormones beyond the diurnal rhythm (Dmitrieva et al., 2013). It is beneficial to model the diurnal slope with a strong consideration for the metric of time that best matches rhythmicity for that population and research question. Often, we favor time-since-waking over "clock time" (i.e., time of day) as the predicted level for a hormone that is meaningful (waking levels) and centered on that person's own rhythm. However, clock time also impacts hormones – samples collected later in the day are often lower, even when an equivalent number of waking hours into a person's day (Shirtcliff et al., 2012). Furthermore, diurnal patterns can vary significantly between weekdays and weekends (Söderström et al., 2006).

Diurnal slopes as well as other measures of daily hormone response, including waking (first measure of the day) and awakening response (peak level of daily hormone), depend heavily on accurate reported data on timing of sample as well as reported timing of awakening. Inaccurate reporting of time and delayed sample collection times influence the valuation of the area under the curve used to measure diurnal hormones. As little as an eight-minute delay of saliva collection after waking can lead to changes in the AUC of the entire diurnal slope (Stalder et al., 2022). Best practices for measuring awakening response have been established and heavily cited (Stalder et al., 2016), yet there has been little improvement in adherence to these best practice guidelines (Stalder et al., 2022). Technological advances allow for more accurate reporting or verification of awakening time and sampling time and collection (e.g., smart watches, MEMS caps, cryovial selfies), but implementing these verification steps still remains a challenge; what to do with "somewhat compliant sampling" also remains an important question. We generally favor approaches that model within-individual variability in time and timing so these samples can be salvaged. In some cases, it may be better to utilize less time-sensitive biospecimens, such as hair.

Reactivity and Recovery

Studies vary in selection of biospecimen and assay, but much of the science of measuring hormones has to do with decisions about when (and where) samples are collected. Laboratory tasks have been designed to elicit stress responses across different stages of development to produce a reactive measurement of steroidal hormones. In infants, the Strange Situation Task separates children from their caregiver while placing them in a novel situation and is frequently used to cause an HPA axis activation in young children (Gunnar et al., 1989).

In older youth and adults, the Trier Social Stress Task utilizes a combination of social evaluative threat and a mathematical challenge to elicit a stress or challenge response for hormones such as cortisol, testosterone, and DHEA responses (Kirschbaum et al., 1993) as well as salivary oxytocin (Bernhard et al., 2018). Although tasks that induce social threat seem to produce the most consistent reactivity (Labuschagne et al., 2019), exercise (Casto & Edwards, 2016) and pain (Mechlin et al., 2007) can also elicit a reactive hormonal response. For example, more recent studies have shown that jumping from a plane during skydiving successfully elicited a range of salivary hormone reactions, regardless of previous experience with parachuting (White et al., 2019). Novel task development continues across interdisciplinary landscapes, such as through use of virtual reality (van Dammen et al., 2022).

Hormone reactivity and recovery can be statistically analyzed with such analyses as time trends, change scores, and area under the curve (Dai et al., 2007). These methods can vary in results even when used within the same study, and there has been a call for open methodological practices in statistical analysis of hormones to increase reproducibility in hormonal research (Meier et al., 2022; see also Chapter 15, this volume). We often favor multilevel/growth-curve models that allow variation in sampling time and timing, that isolate or center the peak hormones, and that can be dynamically expanded across multiple hormones (Marceau et al., 2014). Methods that measure the rise and fall of hormones as a reaction to a task can be measured by calculating the time before and after hormones peak; this accounts for individual differences in the rise and fall of hormones. Assuming peak values occur at a set number of minutes, reactivity can also be calculated as the rise in hormones leading up to a particular sample and subsequent fall. These methods can also be used to model coupling patterns between two hormones (see below).

Ratios and Coupling

Many hormones work in conjunction with other hormones. Such co-release or co-activation has traditionally been measured via ratios that, unfortunately, often have extreme distributional shifts that invalidate their measure, or where one hormone excessively drives ratios. It is also difficult to understand "when" a ratio occurs, as hormones are released at different timescales.

Conceptualized coupling is another way of dynamically reflecting multiple hormones working together. For example, the HPG and HPA axes were historically thought to inhibit one another during challenging or stressful situations (termed "inverse coupling"). Inverse coupling can be statistically conceptualized as a significant negative correlation between an HPA-associated hormone (typically cortisol) and an HPG-associated hormone (e.g., testosterone) (Zakreski et al., 2018). Hormones also show positive coupling (or positive correlation) such that there is co-activation or parallel increases. Alternatively, hormones may exhibit no significant correlation (or less correlation; e.g., "decoupled") (Phan et al., 2021).

Positive coupling of the HPG- and HPA-derived hormone levels during stressful or challenging contexts is a more common occurrence than previously thought (Zakreski et al., 2018). Coupling can shed light on how the HPA axis calibrates with the HPG axis and may broaden understanding of which hormones get "under the skin" to influence behavior and development (Zakreski et al., 2018) as well as mental (Marceau et al., 2015) and physical health (Son et al., 2022). Given the increasing evidence that hormone coupling is a unique construct, continued probes for advancing our understanding of coupling will elucidate novel biological mechanisms underlying stress exposures, the physiologic stress responses, and broad developmental impacts on stress.

Table 19.4 *Comparisons of pros and cons*

Sample type	Acute reactivity	Diurnal and/or basal	Statistical analysis
Blood	Yes	Yes (costly)	Complex
DBS	No	Yes	Simple
Tasso	Yes	Yes (costly)	Simple
Saliva	Yes	Yes (costly)	Complex
Hair	No	Yes	Simple
Urine	Yes	Yes	Complex
Nails	No	Yes	Simple
Feces	Yes	No	Simple

Recommendations and Conclusion

Careful attention to what hormones do and do not offer can allow insight into psychological constructs and ideas to self-correct. For example, the concept of stress has been refined from a nebulous unseen impregnable force to have key elements of action. Through the measure of cortisol, we have learned that stress is not good or bad and is not easily identified or reported; stress, and the hormones that reflect it, can get under the skin to influence health whether we know it or want it to. These challenging molecules, like unruly teenagers, are exceptional reflections – whether we like it or not – of precisely the environment they come from.

Measuring hormones also presents unique challenges and opportunities compared to other data sources (Table 19.4). Hormones are, fundamentally, molecules that are measured through assays and often misbehave when we, as scientists, expect these molecules to behave like psychological constructs and ideas. Molecules are agnostic about cutting-edge theories and generally will, instead, change or adapt to allow the organism to best fit in its environment. In addition, the measure of hormones does not include measurement of the molecule itself but is rather the interpolated byproduct of an assay and statistical analysis derived from collection of a biospecimen. When seeking to incorporate hormones into research, "best practices" will shift based on budget, study design, specimen storage capability, time constraints, and feasibility of sample collection. Most importantly, when incorporating hormones into study designs, we recommend to always utilize collaborations with experts in the field of hormonal molecules and their many constructs.

Acknowledgments

Figures 19.5–19.7 created with BioRender.com

References

Aakvaag, A., & Opstad, P. K. (2019). Hormonal response to prolonged physical strain, effect of calorific deficiency and sleep deprivation. In K. Fotherby & S. B. Pal (eds.), *Exercise Endocrinology* (pp. 25–46). De Gruyter.

Altan Ferhatoğlu, Z., Göktay, F., Yaşar, Ş., & Aytekin, S. (2018). Morphology, growth rate, and thickness of the nail plate during the pregnancy. *International Journal of Dermatology, 57*(10), 1253–1258.

Ammenti, A., Alberici, I., Brugnara, M., Chimenz, R., Guarino, S., La Manna, A., et al. (2020). Updated Italian recommendations for the diagnosis, treatment and follow-up of the first febrile urinary tract infection in young children. *Acta Paediatrica, 109*(2), 236–247. https://doi.org/10.1111/apa.14988

Awad, H., Halawa, F., Mostafa, T., & Atta, H. (2006). Melatonin hormone profile in infertile males. *International Journal of Andrology, 29*(3), 409–413.

Bailey, M. T., Dowd, S. E., Galley, J. D., Hufnagle, A. R., Allen, R. G., & Lyte, M. (2011). Exposure to a social stressor alters the structure of the intestinal microbiota: Implications for stressor-induced immunomodulation. *Brain, Behavior, and Immunity, 25*(3), 397–407.

Barrett, E. S., Tran, V., Thurston, S. W., Frydenberg, H., Lipson, S. F., Thune, I., & Ellison, P. T. (2015). Women who are married or living as married have higher salivary estradiol and progesterone than unmarried women. *American Journal of Human Biology, 27*(4), 501–507.

Behr, G. A., Patel, J. P., Coote, M., Moreira, J. C. F., Gelain, D. P., Steiner, M., & Frey, B. N. (2017). A statistical method to calculate blood contamination in the measurement of salivary hormones in healthy women. *Clinical Biochemistry, 50*(7–8), 436–439.

Belfiore, A., & LeRoith, D. (2018). *Principles of Endocrinology and Hormone Action*. Springer.

Bernhard, A., van der Merwe, C., Ackermann, K., Martinelli, A., Neumann, I. D., & Freitag, C. M. (2018). Adolescent oxytocin response to stress and its behavioral and endocrine correlates. *Hormones and Behavior, 105*, 157–165.

Binz, T. M., Gaehler, F., Voegel, C. D., Hofmann, M., Baumgartner, M. R., & Kraemer, T. (2018). Systematic investigations of endogenous cortisol and cortisone in nails by LC-MS/MS and correlation to hair. *Analytical and Bioanalytical Chemistry, 410*(20), 4895–4903.

Boumba, V. A., Ziavrou, K. S., & Vougiouklakis, T. (2006). Hair as a biological indicator of drug use, drug abuse or chronic exposure to environmental toxicants. *International Journal of Toxicology, 25*(3), 143–163.

Carré, J. M., & Archer, J. (2018). Testosterone and human behavior: The role of individual and contextual variables. *Current Opinion in Psychology, 19*, 149–153.

Casto, K. V., & Edwards, D. A. (2016). Before, during, and after: How phases of competition differentially affect testosterone, cortisol, and estradiol levels in women athletes. *Adaptive Human Behavior and Physiology, 2*(1), 11–25.

Coderch, L., Oliver, M. A., Carrer, V., Manich, A. M., & Martí, M. (2019). External lipid function in ethnic hairs. *Journal of Cosmetic Dermatology, 18*(6), 1912–1920.

Cohen, S., Schwartz, J. E., Epel, E., Kirschbaum, C., Sidney, S., & Seeman, T. (2006). Socioeconomic status, race, and diurnal cortisol decline in the Coronary Artery Risk Development in Young Adults (CARDIA) Study. *Psychosomatic Medicine, 68*(1), 41–50.

Cox, K. L., Devanarayan, V., Kriauciunas, A., Manetta, J., Montrose, C., & Sittampalam, S. (2019). Immunoassay methods. In S. Markossion, A. Grossman, K. Brimacombe et al. (eds.), *Assay Guidance Manual* [e-book]. Eli Lily. www.ncbi.nlm.nih.gov/books/NBK92434

Crimmins, E. M., Zhang, Y. S., Kim, J. K., Frochen, S., Kang, H., Shim, H., et al. (2020). Dried blood spots: Effects of less than optimal collection, shipping time, heat, and humidity. *American Journal of Human Biology, 32*(5), e23390.

Dai, X., Thavundayil, J., Santella, S., & Gianoulakis, C. (2007). Response of the HPA-axis to alcohol and stress as a function of alcohol dependence and family history of alcoholism. *Psychoneuroendocrinology, 32*(3), 293–305.

Dalirirad, S., & Steckl, A. J (2019). Aptamer-based lateral flow assay for point of care cortisol detection in sweat. *Sensors and Actuators B: Chemical, 283*, 79–86.

De Dreu, C. K. W., Greer, L. L., Van Kleef, G. A., Shalvi, S., & Handgraaf, M. J. J. (2011). Oxytocin promotes human ethnocentrism. *Proceedings of the National Academy of Sciences, 108*(4), 1262–1266.

Dmitrieva, N. O., Almeida, D. M., Dmitrieva, J., Loken, E., & Pieper, C. F. (2013). A day-centered approach to modeling cortisol: Diurnal cortisol profiles and their associations among U.S. adults. *Psychoneuroendocrinology, 38*(10), 2354–2365.

Dubey, A., Sonker, A., & Agarwal, P. (2019). A comparison of lancets and evaluation of various manoeuvres in reducing finger prick pain during pre-donation haemoglobin estimation. *Transfusion Medicine, 29*(4), 279–283.

Edwards, S., Evans, P., Hucklebridge, F., & Clow, A. (2001). Association between time of awakening and diurnal cortisol secretory activity. *Psychoneuroendocrinology, 26*(6), 613–622.

Engert, V., Ragsdale, A. M., & Singer, T. (2018). Cortisol stress resonance in the laboratory is associated with inter-couple diurnal cortisol covariation in daily life. *Hormones and Behavior, 98*, 183–190.

Engvall, E., & Perlmann, P. (1972). Enzyme-linked immunosorbent assay, Elisa. 3. Quantitation of specific antibodies by enzyme-labeled anti-immunoglobulin in antigen-coated tubes. *Journal of Immunology, 109*(1), 129–135.

Eriksson, H., & Gustafsson, J.-Å. (1972). Excretion of steroid hormones in adults steroids in urine from adults. *Clinica Chimica Acta, 41*, 79–90. https://doi.org/10.1016/0009-8981(72)90498-6

Eskander, E. F., Estefan, S. F., & Abd-Rabou, A. A. (2012). How does long term exposure to base stations and mobile phones affect human hormone profiles? *Clinical Biochemistry, 45*(1–2), 157–161.

Fernandes, A., Skinner, M. L., Woelfel, T., Carpenter, T., & Haggerty, K. P. (2013). Implementing self-collection of biological specimens with a diverse sample. *Field Methods, 25*(1). https://doi.org/10.1177/1525822X12453526

Field, H. P. (2013). Tandem mass spectrometry in hormone measurement. *Methods in Molecular Biology, 1065*, 45–74.

Forghani, B., Schmidt, N. J., & Lennette, E. H. (1976). Sensitivity of a radioimmunoassay method for detection of certain viral antibodies in sera and cerebrospinal fluids. *Journal of Clinical Microbiology, 4*(6), 470–478.

Gan, S. D., & Patel, K. R. (2013). Enzyme immunoassay and enzyme-linked immunosorbent assay. *Journal of Investigative Dermatology, 133*(9), e12.

García-Carmona, L., Martín, A., Sempionatto, J. R., Moreto, J. R., González, M. C., Wang, J., & Escarpa, A. (2019). Pacifier biosensor: Toward noninvasive saliva biomarker monitoring. *Analytical Chemistry, 91*(21), 13883–13891.

Gildner, T. E. (2021). Reproductive hormone measurement from minimally invasive sample types: Methodological considerations and anthropological importance. *American Journal of Human Biology, 33*(1), e23535.

Gray, C. H., & Bacharach, A. L. (1961). *Hormones in Blood*. Academic Press.

Gunnar, M. R., Mangelsdorf, S., Larson, M., & Hertsgaard, L. (1989). Attachment, temperament, and adrenocortical activity in infancy: A study of psychoendocrine regulation. *Developmental Psychology, 25*(3), 355.

Gustafsson, H. C., Young, A. S., Stamos, G., Wilken, S., Brito, N. H., Thomason, M. E., et al. (2021). Innovative methods for remote assessment of neurobehavioral development. *Developmental Cognitive Neuroscience, 52*, 101015.

Hall, D. L., Blyler, D., Allen, D., Mishel, M. H., Crandell, J., Germino, B. B., & Porter, L. S. (2011). Predictors and patterns of participant adherence to a cortisol collection protocol. *Psychoneuroendocrinology, 36*(4), 540–546.

Hannon, W. H., & Therrell Jr., B. L. (2014). Overview of the history and applications of dried blood samples. In W. Li & M. S. Lee (eds.), *Dried Blood Spots: Applications and Techniques* (pp. 1–15). John Wiley & Sons.

Harmon, A. G., Hibel, L. C., Rumyantseva, O., & Granger, D. A. (2007). Measuring salivary cortisol in studies of child development: Watch out – what goes in may not come out of saliva collection devices. *Developmental Psychobiology, 49*(5), 495–500.

Hendelman, T., Chaudhary, A., LeClair, A. C., van Leuven, K., Chee, J., Fink, S. L., et al. (2021). Self-collection of capillary blood using Tasso-SST devices for Anti-SARS-CoV-2 IgG antibody testing. *PLOS ONE, 16*(9), e0255841.

Hill Golden, S., Sánchez, B. N., Desantis, A. S., Wu, M., Castro, C., Seeman, T. E., et al. (2014). Salivary cortisol protocol adherence and reliability by socio-demographic features: The Multi-Ethnic Study of Atherosclerosis. *Psychoneuroendocrinology, 43*, 30–40.

Hofman, L. F. (2001). Human saliva as a diagnostic specimen. *Journal of Nutrition, 131*(5), 1621S–1625S.

Hulme, E. C., & Trevethick, M. A. (2010). Ligand binding assays at equilibrium: Validation and interpretation. *British Journal of Pharmacology, 161*(6), 1219–1237.

Hurtado de Catalfo, G. E., Ranieri-Casilla, A., Marra, F. A., de Alaniz, M. J. T., & Marra, C. A. (2007). Oxidative stress biomarkers and hormonal profile in human patients undergoing varicocelectomy. *International Journal of Andrology, 30*(6), 519–530.

Institute of Medicine, Board on Population Health and Public Health Practice, & Committee on Public Health Strategies to Improve Health. (2012). *For the Public's Health: Investing in a Healthier Future*. National Academies Press.

Juster, R.-P., Raymond, C., Desrochers, A. B., Bourdon, O., Durand, N., Wan, N., et al. (2016). Sex hormones adjust "sex-specific" reactive and diurnal cortisol profiles. *Psychoneuroendocrinology, 63*, 282–290.

Khelifa, L., Hu, Y., Jiang, N., & Yetisen, A. K. (2022). Lateral flow assays for hormone detection. *Lab on a Chip, 22*(13), 2451–2475.

Kirschbaum, C., Pirke, K.-M., & Hellhammer, D. H. (1993). The "Trier Social Stress Test" – a tool for investigating psychobiological stress responses in a laboratory setting. *Neuropsychobiology, 28*(1–2), 76–81.

Kivlighan, K. T., Granger, D. A., Schwartz, E. B., Nelson, V., Curran, M., & Shirtcliff, E. A. (2004). Quantifying blood leakage into the oral mucosa and its effects on the measurement of cortisol, dehydroepiandrosterone, and testosterone in saliva. *Hormones and Behavior, 46*(1), 39–46.

Koczula, K. M., & Gallotta, A. (2016). Lateral flow assays. *Essays in Biochemistry, 60*(1), 111–120.

Kudielka, B. M., Gierens, A., Hellhammer, D. H., Wüst, S., & Schlotz, W. (2012). Salivary cortisol in ambulatory assessment – some dos, some don'ts, and some open questions. *Psychosomatic Medicine, 74*(4), 418–431.

Labuschagne, I., Grace, C., Rendell, P., Terrett, G., & Heinrichs, M. (2019). An introductory guide to conducting the Trier Social Stress Test. *Neuroscience and Biobehavioral Reviews, 107*, 686–695.

Lim, M. D. (2018). Dried blood spots for global health diagnostics and surveillance: Opportunities and challenges. *American Journal of Tropical Medicine and Hygiene, 99*(2), 256–265.

MacLean, E. L., Wilson, S. R., Martin, W. L., Davis, J. M., Nazarloo, H. P., & Carter, C. S. (2019). Challenges for measuring oxytocin: The blind men and the elephant? *Psychoneuroendocrinology, 107*, 225–231.

Magon, N., & Kalra, S. (2011). The orgasmic history of oxytocin: Love, lust, and labor. *Indian Journal of Endocrinology and Metabolism, 15* (Suppl. 3), S156–S161.

Marceau, K., Rolan, E., Robertson, O. C., Wang, W., & Shirtcliff, E. A. (2021). Within-person changes of cortisol, dehydroepiandrosterone, testosterone, estradiol, and progesterone in hair across pregnancy, with comparison to a non-pregnant reference group. *Comprehensive Psychoneuroendocrinology, 5*, 100024.

Marceau, K., Ruttle, P. L., Shirtcliff, E. A., Essex, M. J., & Susman, E. J. (2015). Developmental and contextual considerations for adrenal and gonadal hormone functioning during adolescence: Implications for adolescent mental health. *Developmental Psychobiology, 57*(6), 742–768.

Marceau, K., Shirtcliff, E. A., Hastings, P. D., Klimes-Dougan, B., Zahn-Waxler, C., Dorn, L. D., & Susman, E. J. (2014). Within-adolescent coupled changes in cortisol with DHEA and testosterone in response to three stressors during adolescence. *Psychoneuroendocrinology, 41*, 33–45.

Martí, M., Barba, C., Manich, A. M., Rubio, L., Alonso, C., & Coderch, L. (2016). The influence of hair lipids in ethnic hair properties. *International Journal of Cosmetic Science, 38*(1), 77–84.

Mechlin, B., Morrow, A. L., Maixner, W., & Girdler, S. S. (2007). The relationship of allopregnanolone immunoreactivity and HPA-axis measures to experimental pain sensitivity: Evidence for ethnic differences. *Pain, 131*(1–2), 142–152.

Meier, M., Lonsdorf, T. B., Lupien, S. J., Stalder, T., Laufer, S., Sicorello, M., et al. (2022). Open and reproducible science practices in psychoneuroendocrinology: Opportunities to foster scientific progress. *Comprehensive Psychoneuroendocrinology, 11*, 100144.

Meijer, W. M., van IJzendoorn, M. H., & Bakermans-Kranenburg, M. J. (2019). Challenging the challenge hypothesis on testosterone in fathers: Limited meta-analytic support. *Psychoneuroendocrinology, 110*, 104435.

Menestrina Dewes, M., Cé da Silva, L., Fazenda Meireles, Y., Viana de Freitas, M., Frank Bastiani, M., Feltraco Lizot, L., et al. (2022). Evaluation of the Tasso-SST® capillary blood microsampling device for the measurement of endogenous uracil levels. *Clinical Biochemistry, 107*, 1–6.

Mericq, M. V., & Cutler Jr., G. B. (1998). High fluid intake increases urine free cortisol excretion in normal subjects. *Journal of Clinical Endocrinology and Metabolism, 83*(2), 682–684.

Meyer, J. S., & Novak, M. A. (2012). Minireview: Hair cortisol: A novel biomarker of hypothalamic-pituitary-adrenocortical activity. *Endocrinology, 153*(9), 4120–4127.

Miočević, O., Cole, C. R., Laughlin, M. J., Buck, R. L., Slowey, P. D., & Shirtcliff, E. A. (2017). Quantitative lateral flow assays for salivary biomarker assessment: A review. *Frontiers in Public Health, 5*, 133.

Mirica, A.-C., Stan, D., Chelcea, I.-C., Mihailescu, C. M., Ofiteru, A., & Bocancia-Mateescu, L.-A. (2022). Latest trends in lateral flow immunoassay (LFIA) detection labels and conjugation process. *Frontiers in Bioengineering and Biotechnology, 10*, 922772.

Moody, S. N., van Dammen, L., Wang, W., Greder, K. A., Neiderhiser, J. M., Afulani, P. A., et al. (2022). Impact of hair type, hair sample weight, external hair exposures, and race on cumulative hair cortisol. *Psychoneuroendocrinology, 142*, 105805.

Navazesh, M. (1993). Methods for collecting saliva. *Annals of the New York Academy of Sciences, 694*, 72–77.

Neu, M., Goldstein, M., Gao, D., & Laudenslager, M. L. (2007). Salivary cortisol in preterm infants: Validation of a simple method for collecting saliva for cortisol determination. *Early Human Development, 83*(1), 47–54.

Nguyen, N. H., Khera, R., Ohno-Machado, L., Sandborn, W. J., & Singh, S. (2021). Prevalence and effects of food insecurity and social support on financial toxicity in and healthcare use by patients with inflammatory bowel diseases. *Clinical Gastroenterology and Hepatology, 19*(7), 1377–1386.

Ou, F.-S., Michiels, S., Shyr, Y., Adjei, A. A., & Oberg, A. L. (2021). Biomarker discovery and validation: Statistical considerations. *Journal of Thoracic Oncology, 16*(4), 537–545.

Padilla, G. A., Calvi, J. L, Taylor, M. K., & Granger, D. A. (2020). Saliva collection, handling, transport, and storage: Special considerations and best practices for interdisciplinary salivary bioscience research. In D. A. Granger & M. K. Taylor (eds.), *Salivary Bioscience: Foundations of Interdisciplinary Saliva Research and Applications* (pp. 21–47). Springer.

Partrick, K. (2018). Acute and repeated exposure to social stress reduces gut microbiota diversity in Syrian hamsters. *Physiology & Behavior, 176*(1), 100–106.

Peng, F.-J., Palazzi, P., Mezzache, S., Bourokba, N., Soeur, J., & Appenzeller, B. M. R. (2022). Profiling steroid and thyroid hormones with hair analysis in a cohort of women aged 25 to 45 years old. *European Journal of Endocrinology, 186*(5), K9–K15.

Peres, J. C., Rouquette, J. L., Miočević, O., Warner, M. C., Slowey, P. D., & Shirtcliff, E. A. (2015). New techniques for augmenting saliva collection: Bacon rules and lozenge drools. *Clinical Therapeutics, 37*(3), 515–522.

Phan, J. M., Van Hulle, C. A., Shirtcliff, E. A., Schmidt, N. L., & Goldsmith, H. H. (2021). Longitudinal effects of family psychopathology and stress on pubertal maturation and hormone coupling in adolescent twins. *Developmental Psychobiology, 63*(3), 512–528.

Phillips, R., Kraeuter, A.-K., McDermott, B., Lupien, S., & Sarnyai, Z. (2021). Human nail cortisol as a retrospective biomarker of chronic stress: A systematic review. *Psychoneuroendocrinology, 123*, 104903.

Posthuma-Trumpie, G. A., Korf, J., & van Amerongen, A. (2009). Lateral flow (immuno) assay: Its strengths, weaknesses, opportunities and threats. A literature survey. *Analytical and Bioanalytical Chemistry, 393*(2), 569–582.

Pruessner, J. C., Kirschbaum, C., Meinlschmid, G., & Hellhammer, D. H. (2003). Two formulas for computation of the area under the curve represent measures of total hormone concentration versus time-dependent change. *Psychoneuroendocrinology, 28*(7), 916–931.

Rej, A., Aziz, I., Tornblom, H., Sanders, D. S., & Simrén, M. (2019). The role of diet in irritable bowel syndrome: Implications for dietary advice. *Journal of Internal Medicine, 286*(5), 490–502.

Roadcap, B., Hussain, A., Dreyer, D., Carter, K., Dube, N., Xu, Y., et al. (2020). Clinical application of volumetric absorptive microsampling to the gefapixant development program. *Bioanalysis, 12*(13), 893–904.

Russell, E., Koren, G., Rieder, M., & Van Uum, S. (2012). Hair cortisol as a biological marker of chronic stress: Current status, future directions and unanswered questions. *Psychoneuroendocrinology, 37*(5), 589–601.

Sadeghalvad, M., & Rezaei, N. (2022). Introduction on laboratory tests for diagnosis of infectious diseases and immunological disorders. In N. Rezaei (ed.), *Encyclopedia of Infection and Immunity*. Elsevier.

Sauvé, B., Koren, G., Walsh, G., Tokmakejian, S., & Van Uum, S. H. M. (2007). Measurement of cortisol in human hair as a biomarker of systemic exposure. *Clinical and Investigative Medicine, 30*(5), E183–E191.

Schiffer, L., Barnard, L., Baranowski, E. S., Gilligan, L. C., Taylor, A. E., Arlt, W., et al. (2019). Human steroid biosynthesis, metabolism and excretion are differentially reflected by serum and urine steroid metabolomes: A comprehensive review. *Journal of Steroid Biochemistry and Molecular Biology, 194*, 105439.

Sheriff, M. J., Krebs, C. J., & Boonstra, R. (2010). Assessing stress in animal populations: Do fecal and plasma glucocorticoids tell the same story? *General and Comparative Endocrinology, 166*(3), 614–619.

Shi, J., Lv, Z., Nie, M., Lu, W., Liu, C., Tian, Y., et al. (2018). Human nail stem cells are retained but hypofunctional during aging. *Journal of Molecular Histology, 49*(3), 303–316.

Shirtcliff, E. A., Allison, A. L., Armstrong, J. M., Slattery, M. J., Kalin, N. H., & Essex, M. J. (2012). Longitudinal stability and developmental properties of salivary cortisol levels and circadian rhythms from childhood to adolescence. *Developmental Psychobiology, 54*(5), 493–502.

Shirtcliff, E. A., Granger, D. A., Schwartz, E., & Curran, M. J. (2001). Use of salivary biomarkers in biobehavioral research: Cotton-based sample collection methods can interfere with salivary immunoassay results. *Psychoneuroendocrinology, 26*(2), 165–173.

Smith, L. A., & Gaya, D. R. (2012). Utility of faecal calprotectin analysis in adult inflammatory bowel disease. *World Journal of Gastroenterology, 18*(46), 6782–6789.

Söderström, M., Ekstedt, M., & Akerstedt, T. (2006). Weekday and weekend patterns of diurnal cortisol, activation and fatigue among people scoring high for burnout. *Scandinavian Journal of Work, Environment & Health, 32*(2), 35–40.

Son, Y. L., Ubuka, T., & Tsutsui, K. (2022). Regulation of stress response on the hypothalamic-pituitary-gonadal axis via gonadotropin-inhibitory hormone. *Frontiers in Neuroendocrinology, 64*, 100953.

Spiller, R., & Garsed, K. (2009). Infection, inflammation, and the irritable bowel syndrome. *Digestive and Liver Disease, 41*(12), 844–849.

Stalder, T., Kirschbaum, C., Kudielka, B. M., Adam, E. K., Pruessner, J. C., Wüst, S., et al. (2016). Assessment of the cortisol awakening response: Expert consensus guidelines. *Psychoneuroendocrinology, 63*, 414–432.

Stalder, T., Lupien, S. J., Kudielka, B. M., Adam, E. K., Pruessner, J. C., Wüst, S., et al. (2022). Evaluation and update of the expert consensus guidelines for the assessment of the cortisol awakening response (CAR). *Psychoneuroendocrinology, 146*, 105946.

Stanton, S. J., Beehner, J. C., Saini, E. K., Kuhn, C. M., & Labar, K. S. (2009). Dominance, politics, and physiology: Voters' testosterone changes on the night of the 2008 United States presidential election. *PLOS ONE, 4*(10), e7543.

Talge, N. M., Donzella, B., Kryzer, E. M., Gierens, A., & Gunnar, M. R. (2005). It's not that bad: Error introduced by oral stimulants in salivary cortisol research. *Developmental Psychobiology, 47*(4), 369–376.

Tasso, Inc. (n.d.). *Tasso-SST* [webpage]. www.tassoinc.com/tasso-sst (retrieved October 31, 2022).

Tavalire, H. F., Christie, D. M., Leve, L. D., Ting, N., Cresko, W. A., & Bohannan, B. J. M. (2021). Shared environment and genetics shape the gut microbiome after infant adoption. *mBio, 12*(2). https://doi.org/10.1128/mBio.00548-21

Telford, C., McCarthy-Jones, S., Corcoran, R., & Rowse, G. (2012). Experience sampling methodology studies of depression: The state of the art. *Psychological Medicine, 42*(6), 1119–1129.

Thompson, G. (2012). *Nobel Prizes that Changed Medicine*. World Scientific.

Tsivou, M., Livadara, D., Georgakopoulos, D. G., Koupparis, M. A., Atta-Politou, J., & Georgakopoulos, C. G. (2009). Stabilization of human urine doping control samples: II. Microbial degradation of steroids. *Analytical Biochemistry, 388*(1), 146–154.

van Dammen, L., Finseth, T. T., McCurdy, B. H., Barnett, N. P., Conrady, R. A., Leach, A. G., et al. (2022). Evoking stress reactivity in virtual reality: A systematic review and meta-analysis. *Neuroscience and Biobehavioral Reviews, 138*, 104709.

van Thiel, I. A. M., de Jonge, W. J., Chiu, I. M., & van den Wijngaard, R. M. (2020). Microbiota-neuroimmune cross talk in stress-induced visceral hypersensitivity of the bowel. *American Journal of Physiology: Gastrointestinal and Liver Physiology, 318*(6), G1034–G1041.

Veldhuis, J. D., Carlson, M. L., & Johnson, M. L. (1987). The pituitary gland secretes in bursts: Appraising the nature of glandular secretory impulses by simultaneous multiple-parameter deconvolution of plasma hormone concentrations. *Proceedings of the National Academy of Sciences, 84*(21), 7686–7690.

Voegel, C. D., La Marca-Ghaemmaghami, P., Ehlert, U., Baumgartner, M. R., Kraemer, T., & Binz, T. M. (2018). Steroid profiling in nails using liquid chromatography–tandem mass spectrometry. *Steroids, 140*, 144–150.

Wang, W., Moody, S. N., Kiesner, J., Tonon Appiani, A., Robertson, O. C., & Shirtcliff, E. A. (2019). Assay validation of hair androgens across the menstrual cycle. *Psychoneuroendocrinology, 101*, 175–181.

Wang, W., van Dammen, L., Moody, S. N., Kiesner, J., Neiderhiser, J. M., Dismukes, A., et al. (2020). The validation of estradiol extraction and analysis from hair [preprint]. *PsyArXiv.* https://doi.org/10.31234/osf.io/knuxs

Webb, E. C., White, C. D., Van Uum, S., & Longstaffe, F. J. (2015). Integrating cortisol and isotopic analyses of archeological hair: Reconstructing individual experiences of health and stress. *American Journal of Physical Anthropology, 156*(4), 577–594.

Wester, V. L., van der Wulp, N. R. P., Koper, J. W., de Rijke, Y. B., & van Rossum, E. F. C. (2016). Hair cortisol and cortisone are decreased by natural sunlight. *Psychoneuroendocrinology, 72*, 94–96.

White, S. F., Lee, Y., Phan, J. M., Moody, S. N., & Shirtcliff, E. A. (2019). Putting the flight in "fight-or-flight": Testosterone reactivity to skydiving is modulated by autonomic activation. *Biological Psychology, 143*, 93–102.

Yalow, R. S. (1982). The limitations of radioimmunoassay (RIA). *Trends in Analytical Chemistry, 1*(6), 128–131.

Yalow, R. S., & Berson, S. A. (1960). Plasma insulin concentrations in nondiabetic and early diabetic subjects: Determinations by a new sensitive immuno-assay technic. *Diabetes, 9*, 254–260.

Yong, E. (2012). Dark side of the love hormone. *New Scientist, 213*(2851), 39–41.

Zakreski, E., Dismukes, A. R., Tountas, A., Phan, J. M., Moody, S. N., & Shirtcliff, E. A. (2018). Developmental trajectories of HPA-HPG dual axes coupling: Implications for social neuroendocrinology. In O. Schultheiss & P. Mehta (eds.), *Routledge International Handbook of Social Neuroendocrinology* (pp. 608–632). Routledge.

Zhu, C., Yuan, C., Ren, Q., Wei, F., Yu, S., Sun, X., & Zheng, S. (2021). Comparative analysis of the effects of collection methods on salivary steroids. *BMC Oral Health*, *21*(1).

20 Cardiovascular Measures for Social and Behavioral Research

Mary G. Carey

Abstract

Cardiovascular measures for social and behavioral research have been historically popular because they are often non-invasive, inexpensive, and capture the dynamic nature of cardiac physiology. Among adults, many measures are static, like height – they do not change over time – but importantly, cardiovascular measures change moment-to-moment. For example, measuring the heart rate is easy and valuable for documenting different health conditions and can be predictive of overall longevity and disease. Electronic medical records provide access to retrospective high-quality cardiac measures; plus, now that consumer wearable devices are ubiquitous, it is even easier to prospectively collect cardiovascular measures that are continuous and automatically obtained. Thus, cardiovascular measures are important metrics of overall health, and their dynamic nature is important to capture with both established and novel scientific instruments. This chapter will focus on physiological measures that validate psychometric data, describe types of cardiovascular measures of health, and present future directions of cardiovascular measures in research.

Keywords: Research, Social Science, Behavioral Science, Cardiac Disease, Cardiovascular Measures

Introduction of Cardiovascular Measures of Health in Social and Biobehavioral Research

Historically, cardiovascular measures for social and behavioral research have been quite common because they cause little subject burden due to their nature of being non-invasive, are inexpensive, and are able to capture the dynamic nature of cardiac physiology. Literally, everybody has a heart. In other words, not everyone will experience Alzheimer's disease or cancer but everyone has a heart and heart disease is part of normal aging; so, contributions to the existing evidence by social and behavioral scientists are important. In fact, because of the planet's aging population, it is important to improve our understanding of the effect of aging on the heart, so understanding how to include cardiovascular measures for research is important. For example, aging is the largest significant effect on the heart and arterial system because of the buildup of fatty deposits in the walls of arteries over many years that can result in increased atherosclerosis, hypertension, myocardial infarction, and stroke (North & Sinclair, 2012); in fact, the most important determinant of cardiovascular health is a person's age (Lakatta & Levy, 2003). Thus, including cardiovascular measures in research protocols provides important metrics of overall health, and their dynamic nature is important to capture with both established and novel scientific methods.

Types of Cardiovascular Measures of Health

For research purposes, there are numerous modalities currently available to collect cardiac measures, both for clinical use as well as for research purposes. This section provides the most common methodologies used for cardiac measures.

Non-invasive Measures

Blood Pressure

The blood pressure includes two numbers: systolic blood pressure (SBP) – a measure of pressure while the heart is contracting – and diastolic blood pressure (DPB) – a measure of pressure while the heart rests between heartbeats. It is most commonly measured with a sphygmomanometer and reported in millimeters of mercury (mmHg) where 1mmHG is equivalent to a pressure of about 133 pascal or 0.00133 bar; newer electronic devices actually do not contain mercury. In general, the interpretation of blood pressure values is:

(1) Normal: <120/80 mmHg
(2) Elevated: SBP 120–129 and diastolic <80 mmHg
(3) High, Hypertension Stage 1: SBP 130–139 or diastolic 80-89 mmHg
(4) High, Hypertension State 2: SBP >140 or diastolic >90 mmHg

Higher blood pressure levels increase risks for health problems, including heart disease, heart attack, and cerebral stroke. Importantly, blood pressure is different for every individual, and the measure can fluctuate up and down rapidly.

Measurement considerations include resting time before the measures, posture of the subject, placement of the BP cuff over clothing or on bare skin, and whether the subject is talking – these all affect the accuracy of the measures. Thus, blood pressure should be measured in a resting state, ideally with the arm positioned roughly at the same level as the heart. If possible, the skin should be bare and not include heavy apparel, e.g., sweatshirt. While the patient is not talking, two measures should be taken over a five-minute period to ensure reliability or reproducibility of the values, and then the two readings should be averaged. Because blood pressure has a circadian pattern, that is, it changes over the day (often being lowest first thing in the morning), the measure should be obtained at the same time of day (e.g., morning, afternoon, evening).

Special Considerations. Currently, in both clinical practice and with field research, manual measurements are considered equivalent to automatic measures. However, in some cases, because of age, gender, and arm circumference, the accuracy of the measures may vary. Importantly, clinical experience is positively correlated to more accurate measures of blood pressure. In other words, the measure may be operator-dependent. Thus, many research investigators use research nurses because they have the clinical expertise to accurately obtain cardiovascular measures (e.g., blood pressure; Carey et al., 2011); however, if the data collectors are not skilled clinicians, then blood pressure should be obtained using an automated blood pressure cuff. Regardless, accuracy of BP measurements is important in research. Blood pressure is a dynamic measure, changing all the time, and is influenced by the environment, behavior of the individual, measurement approach, device, and operator. For research purposes, where investigators have more control, special consideration should be taken in regard to accurately measuring blood pressure. For example, environmental factors, including the temperature of the room, can interfere with accurate measures, for instance if the participant is shivering or if their cell phone is ringing. Also, investigators should control for behaviors influencing blood pressure measures such as physical exercise, drinking coffee, falling asleep, or having an uncomfortable full bladder.

A recent meta-analysis compared automated blood pressure measurements obtained with the patient resting alone in a quiet place versus a routine office BP measure with a clinician, based on more than 30 articles (Roerecke et al., 2019). It recommended that automated blood pressure measurements obtained with the patient resting alone avoided the "white coat effect" (an artificially elevated BP because of the emotional stress of seeing a clinician) and were more accurate. For epidemiological research among patients with hypertension, it is not recommended to use automated BP cuffs (Lim et al., 2014) because measures contributing to prevalence data require the best accuracy possible. Thus, as a cardiovascular measure for research purposes, blood pressure is very valuable for describing a sample's characteristic overall health status and provides predictive information for overall survival and potential for cardiac events.

Electrocardiography

Variables. Electrocardiography (ECG) yields numerous measures that can be very valuable to a variety of research questions. Table 20.1 provides 15 examples of ECG parameters with their corresponding measure and operational definition. Depending on the cardiovascular measure of interest, the variable can be calculated manually or automatically through computerization. Strategically, it is common for social and behavioral scientists to include some form of ECG monitoring in prospective studies to complement their non-physiological psychometric measures, e.g., self-report data. For example, Li et al. (2021) demonstrated the feasibility of measuring workplace stress among nurses using heart rate variability (HRV) analysis via a wireless ECG heart rate monitor and correlated the measure with the Nursing Stress Response scale. If more advanced ECG measures are obtained for research purposes (e.g., 12-lead

Table 20.1 *12-lead ECG measures for research: both resting and 24-hour Holter*

	ECG parameter	Measure	Definition
1	QRS duration	Conduction defect	Duration from QRS onset to QRS offset averaged among all leads over 10 s
2	Heart-rate corrected QT interval	Sympathetic tone	Duration from QRS onset to T offset averaged among all leads over 10 s then corrected for heart rate using Bazzett's formula (QT/RR)
3	Fragmented QRS	Conduction defect	(1) RSR morphology ≥ 2 R or (2) notching in the nadir off S wave with a narrow QRS (<120 ms) or (3) ≥ 2 R or ≥ 2 notches in the nadir of S wave with a widened QRS
4	Q waves	Prior infarction	The presence of pathologic Q waves (>40 ms) in at least two leads corresponding to the same coronary territory
5	Left bundle branch block	Conduction defect	The presence of this pattern as per American Heart Association
6	Left ventricular hypertrophy	Myocardial strain	The presence of this pattern as per Cornell voltage criteria
7	Spatial QRS-T angle	Electrical depolarization and repolarization	The three-dimensional spatial angle between the mean R and T vectors estimated directly from the 12-lead ECG
8	Minimum heart rate	Sympathetic tone	The minimum 5 min averaged heart rate during the 24 h Holter monitoring period
9	Heart rate variability	Sympathetic tone	The standard deviation of normal-to-normal R-R intervals of all R-R intervals averaged over 24 h
10	Atrial fibrillation	Cardiac rhythm	A heart rhythm with irregular RR interval with absent P wave at any time during the 24 h Holter recording
11	Non-sustained ventricular tachycardia	Cardiac rhythm	A least one episode of ≥ 3 consecutive ventricular beats at a rate of ≥ 120 beats/minute
12	Ventricular ectopic activity	Cardiac ectopy	The presence of frequent premature ventricular contractions at rate of ≥ 10/hour for the duration of the Holter recording
13	ST depression	Myocardial ischemia	The presence of at least one episode of ST depression of ≥ 0.5 mm in leads V2-V3 or ≥ 1 mm in all other leads in ≥ 2 contiguous leads for at least 5 min at any time during the Holter reading
14	QT/RR slope	Sympathetic tone	The linear regression slope between all beat-to-beat QT and R-R intervals over a 24 h period
15	Persistent pacing	Cardiac rhythm	100% of the total monitoring period with prolonged QRS complexes due to single chamber right ventricular (RV) pacemaker spikes. Bi-ventricular packing, although it limits the interpretation of other ECG parameters, was not considered a high-risk parameter.

Source: Al-Zaiti et al. (2014)

ECG), the investigators should consider budgeting the expense of a national ECG Core Lab to provide the professional analysis of the ECG data for consistent and valid results (Kleiman et al., 2016).

Below are the two most common cardiac measures extracted from the ECG.

Heart rate (HR) is measured as the number of times your heart beats in a minute. Although it is a basic vital sign, it is very influential because it is central to cardiac output – the amount of blood pumped with every heart beat – and predicts longevity. The relationship between heart rate and longevity is inverse – that is, the higher the heart rate, the lower the survival (Böhm et al., 2015). Heart rate also predicts cardiovascular diseases, including heart failure. Different measures of continuous heart rate monitoring include resting heart rate, average heart rate of the monitoring period (e.g., 24 hours), and maximum and minimum heart rate over the monitoring period. Individuals with average heart rates that exceed 75 beats over 24 hours are at risk for future cardiac events (Böhm et al., 2015). Of all the measures, heart rate is among the easiest to obtain for both the researcher and participant; thus, it should be seriously considered.

Heart rate variability (HRV) is among the most popular cardiovascular measures in social and behavioral science because it is a non-invasive approach to measuring autonomic nervous system activity by power spectral analysis of the heart rate time series. Researchers use HRV when studying conditions related to cardiovascular health or mental health issues like depression and anxiety. HRV provides an indirect assessment of the autonomic nervous system balance, such that lower high-frequency domain (HF) indicates decreased parasympathetic modulation of the heart (Al-Zaiti et al., 2019; Thayer et al., 2010). Parasympathetic nervous system activation will conversely act on the SA and AV nodes to decrease the heart rate and will decrease cardiac output.

Theoretically, the natural pacemaker of the heart, the sinus node, paces the heart very regularly, but there are very small differences, measured in fractions of seconds between heart beats (Figure 20.1). These fluctuations are undetectable by human eyes, but computers easily detect differences and provide a quantified value. HRV may also be referred to as: "R–R variability" and "cycle length variability." Among young healthy adults, the normal HRV is between 55 and 105 milliseconds; with age

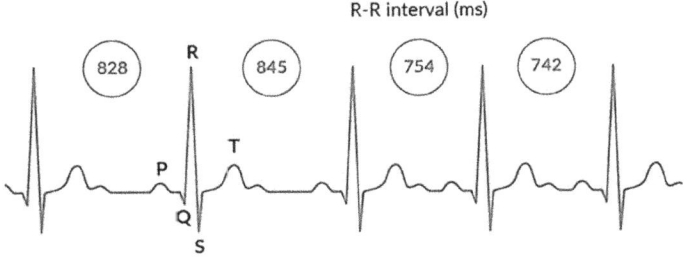

Figure 20.1 *Heart rate variability. Very small variation between each heart beat is measured in milliseconds by the computer and is a measure of sympathetic tone.*

the HRV naturally decreases, and among older adults (>60 years) the HRV ranges between 25 and 45 milliseconds. Thus, a low HRV indicates the sympathetic or fight-or-flight response is dominating; a high HRV indicates the parasympathetic or relaxation response is dominating.

High-performance athletes tend to have high HRVs (Bellenger et al., 2016) because their physical behaviors increase HRV: they exercise regularly, eat high-quality diets, adequately hydrate, avoid alcohol, sleep well, are regularly exposed to natural light, practice cold thermogenesis (which stimulates the vagus nerve and simulates the parasympathetic branch of the autonomic nervous system which controls HRV), practice intentional breathing and mindfulness meditation, and often keep a gratitude journal. Overall, HRV is an indirect measure of the autonomic nervous system and HRV parameters are shown to be related to cardiovascular risk, including sudden cardiac death (Cygankiewicz & Zareba, 2013). Steps to apply HRV to research methods may seem complex to users without adequate background knowledge. Thus, Pham et al. (2021) provides a tutorial for the application of HRV in psychology.

Methods. The electrocardiogram (ECG) records the electrical activity of the heart. The ECG recording is one of the most commonly performed diagnostic tests to examine the condition of the heart for both health and disease states, including cardiac arrhythmias and myocardial ischemia. Newer artificial intelligence approaches using computers aim at improving prediction models (e.g., predicting an individual's risk of acquiring a new arrhythmia; Khurshid et al., 2022).

The 12-lead ECG is the "gold standard" for electrocardiography. The skin electrodes are placed on the chest and limbs to capture the electrical signal of the heart that is then transformed into 12 ECG waveforms and printed on graph paper to allow for rapid and standard measurements of the electrical conduction (Figure 20.2). Each heart beat generates a QRS complex, and measures between heart beats are called

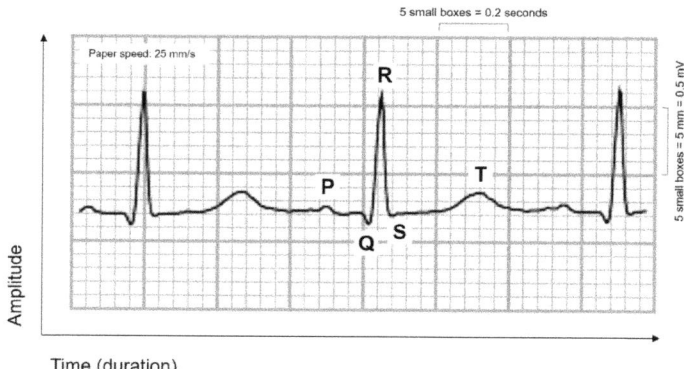

Figure 20.2 *An electrocardiogram. An example of an electrocardiogram (ECG) on the standard ECG graph paper calibrated at 25 mm/second paper speed with a 10 mm/millivolt (mV) amplitude. The y-axis measures the amplitude of the signal; the x-axis measures the speed of the ECG signal.*

"R-waves" (i.e., QRS complexes). The exact locations of the electrodes are: one electrode on each forearm or wrist (right arm, RA; left arm, LA); one on each leg above the ankles (left leg, LL; right leg, RL); and six electrodes placed across the precordium, or the chest – known as precordial leads (V_1–V_6). The ECG waveforms have several different labels, representing the sequence of the electrical conduction system of the heart; they include leads I, II, III, aVR, aVL, aVF, V1, V2, V3, V4, V5, and V6. Ideally, the standard, resting 12-lead ECG is recorded with the research subject or patient in a resting state (for at least five minutes before initiating the recording) and in the supine position.

A Holter monitor is a continuous ECG recording device that allows the collection of ECG waveforms for a specific period of time – commonly 24 or 48 hours – and is often used in the ambulatory setting. Holters can be single or multiple leads, although the 12-lead Holter is commonly used for research purposes. The placement of the limb leads for a 12-lead Holter is a modified version of that for the standard 12-lead ECG, where the limb leads are placed on the torso instead of distal extremities to minimize artifact due to movement. The ECG lead configuration is called the Mason-Likert (Figure 20.3). Although one can have a printout or digital record of the standard 12-lead ECG available immediately for manual review or analysis, Holter recordings may require the data to be downloaded from the Holter device into a computer for a retrospective annotation using a specific software or analytic tool. Therefore, the ECG interpretation will not become available immediately. In contrast, continuous ECG can also be monitored and stored in real time using physiologic monitors or telemetry devices in hospital settings. Currently, various multiple-lead options are available for clinicians and researchers depending on the vendors.

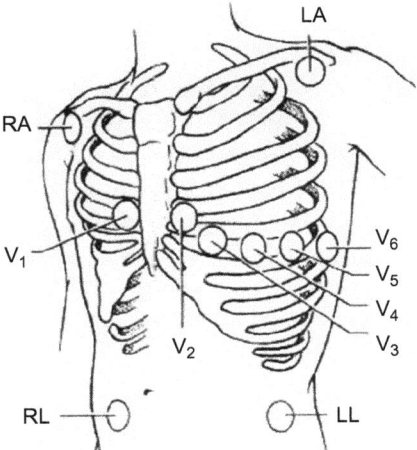

Figure 20.3 *ECG lead Mason-Likert configuration. A configuration used for continuous ECG monitoring where the ECG leads of the limbs are shifted from the limbs to the torso to reduce motion artifact.*

Echocardiography

Echocardiography is another commonly used non-invasive imaging modality, involving ultrasound primarily to quantify the structure and function of the heart (Galderisi et al., 2017); in other words, it is an assessment of "pump function." The echocardiogram shows how much blood pumps out of a filled heart chamber with each heartbeat – called ejection fraction (EF). It also shows how much blood the heart pumps in a minute – called cardiac output. Among elite athletes, many researchers are interested in the effects of exercise on the function of the heart. For example, among a sample of Chinese soccer players, Chen (2020) reported that the heart structure changed, including thickening of the heart wall, interventricular septum, and left ventricular wall– all seen on echocardiography. He concluded that Chinese soccer players have a higher function of heart pumping blood because performing high-level sports can change the shape and function of the heart, enhance the heart's reserve ability, and help the body to produce beneficial fitness adaptive changes. With the rapid advancement and affordability of cardiac imaging technology, echocardiography is widely used in the ambulatory clinic, the emergency room, and the intensive care unit. Plus, the advancement of artificial intelligence helps minimize observer variation in the interpretation and provides numerous high-quality, reproducible measures for advances in research (Kusunose, 2021).

Invasive Measures

Historically, social and behavioral scientists did not include invasive cardiovascular physiological measures because these were beyond the scope of their discipline. However, as scientific teams have become more interdisciplinary (Carey & Brunner, 2023), and there is increased availability of hospital medical records for retrospective data, there is a growing ability to include more sophisticated measures in social and behavioral research. To improve the scientific quality of results, some "gold standard" measures can be included. A gold standard test is the diagnostic test or benchmark that is the best available under reasonable conditions (Rutjes et al., 2007). For example, instead of depending on self-report, if a researcher wanted to know whether a subject has coronary artery disease, the gold standard test would be angiography; if the subject had an angiography, then the results would be available in the electronic medical records. Two of the invasive studies summarized in this chapter are coronary angiography and electrophysiology study. One strategy to remember the difference is that angiography assesses the "plumbing" of the heart while electrophysiology assesses the "electrical system" of the heart. They are very specialized disciplines, and clinicians study many years to gain expertise in these important, life-saving areas of cardiology.

Coronary Angiography

Coronary angiography is the gold standard imaging modality for a comprehensive assessment and measurement of the coronary arteries and, importantly, the coronary perfusion or blood flow (Fihn et al., 2012). Primarily, the goals of coronary angiography are to examine the presence and extension of coronary artery occlusion. To help standardize operational definitions of cardiovascular disease for both clinical and research purposes, a coronary occlusion greater than 70% of the lumen is considered to be coronary disease. Because atherosclerosis is a normal aging process, coronary occlusions are expected, so the interventionalist is looking for a "culprit" occlusion, or something that is causing the patient's symptoms (Reisman et al., 1997).

The three cardiovascular measures of interest include the location of the occlusions among the three major coronary arteries (left anterior ascending, left circumflex artery, and right coronary artery). The second measure is the extent of the occlusion based on the number of occluded vessels (e.g., single vessel disease, double vessel disease, triple vessel disease). Finally, the severity of the occlusion is quantified by the percentage reduction of the coronary occlusion. For researchers who are studying older subjects who may have cardiovascular disease, it is important to understand that stress commonly induces angina, or chest pain, but in a stable state angina typically resolves if the stress is reduced.

Electrophysiology

An electrophysiology (EP) study is an invasive procedure primarily aimed to evaluate cardiac electrical disorders (i.e., arrhythmias), allowing a comprehensive evaluation of the origin and underlying mechanisms of cardiac arrhythmias and informing decisions on the best treatment approach. Oftentimes, when feasible and necessary, catheter ablation is performed during the EP study to treat the arrhythmias. EP studies are also used to risk stratify certain often complex cardiac conditions, such as ventricular electrical storm (i.e., incessant ventricular tachycardia) or structural heart disease in a presence of lethal arrhythmias (Buxton et al., 2006; Muresan et al., 2019). During EP studies, surface ECGs and intracardiac electrograms are recorded, and diagnostic evaluations focus on the overall functions of the conduction system (the sinus node, atrium, atrioventricular (AV) node, His-Purkinje system, accessory pathway, and ventricles).

Important research measures from these recordings may include sinoatrial (SA) conduction and sinus recovery time, intra-atrial conduction, atrio-His (AH) interval (time interval from activation of right atrium to the His bundle), His bundle duration, His-ventricular (HV) interval (measured between His bundle and the earliest ventricular activation), and intraventricular conduction time. In addition to ablation, other procedures may be performed during EP studies, such as pacemaker or implantable cardioverter-defibrillator (ICD) implantation, intracardiac lead extraction, and cardioversion (Buxton et al., 2006). Of note, these invasive studies are not conducted for research purposes, but have been conducted for clinical reasons and are available to investigators retrospectively, with institutional review board approval, through electronic medical records. All of these measures provide high-quality assessment of the electrical conduction system and can be obtained for research purposes such as predictive strategies (e.g., early identification for risk of atrial fibrillation).

Summary of the Types of Cardiovascular Measures of Health

Of all available methodologies to measure cardiac health, perhaps the ECG, both resting and continuous Holter, is the most frequently used method in social and behavioral studies because it is non-invasive, inexpensive, and easy to perform in almost all settings. For example, my previous work even included demonstrating the feasibility of obtaining high-quality 12-lead ECGs for on-duty professional firefighters (Carey & Thevenin, 2009). The initial proof-of-concept work led to numerous studies applying ECG to the high-risk cardiovascular population because firefighters have twice the rate of sudden cardiac death compared to other first responders (Kales et al., 2007). Based on this work, two important cardiovascular markers emerged among firefighters: (1) elevated average heart rates and (2) poor heart rate recovery after exertion; both contribute to their inflated cardiovascular mortality (including sudden cardiac death; Carey et al., 2010).

In addition, ECG provides extensive data for researchers to establish a diagnosis or to risk stratify, serves as a proxy for certain human behaviors, and helps researchers understand the human response to environment. For example, Tell et al. (2021) investigated the association between altered autonomic nervous system and proinflammatory response to acute stress, where the altered autonomic nervous system was measured by heart rate variability calculated from 5-lead Holter ECG recordings. They concluded that exposure to stress altered the autonomic nervous system reactivity and resulted in a blunted HRV among a sample of young African American men – young men lost their cardio-protective heart rate variability because of exposure to stress (i.e., they are at higher risk for cardiovascular events, including chest pain.

In a different study, researchers also investigated the complex stress systems in response to social-evaluative threat, in which cardiovascular measures obtained from ECG were collected to evaluate the sympathetic index as part of the complex response system (Poppelaars et al., 2019). Cardiac measures from echocardiography that are commonly used in social and behavioral studies include left ventricular ejection fraction, stroke volume, or cardiac index. Yamazaki et al. (2021) recently investigated CV measures, such as stroke volume, cardiac index, LV ejection time, and other measures obtained from echocardiography, as novel candidate biomarkers in differentiating neurobehavioral resilience and vulnerability to sleep deprivation and psychological stress.

Oftentimes, cardiac functions are not measured as the primary outcome of interest but instead to study the association of cardiac conditions under certain social and behavioral conditions. For example, there are studies that investigated function and quality of life in patients after transcatheter aortic valve replacement procedure, in which left ventricular systolic function was an important factor measured from echocardiography (Kim et al., 2014). They reported the high-risk cardiac procedure improved cardiac and physical function but found modest benefits in psychological and general health measures. In a different study of patients with coronary artery disease, Denollet et al. (2010) investigated the risk for future cardiac events among patients with a Type D personality – a personality with a tendency to experience distress or inhibit self-expressions. They concluded that, among the sample of Type D personality patients, participants had a fourfold rate of suppressed anger, and they were at an increased risk of cardiac events. In their analysis, they included the following cardiovascular measures: left ventricular ejection fraction, severity of coronary artery disease, and invasive treatment with coronary artery bypass surgery or percutaneous coronary intervention (e.g., coronary stent).

Physiological Measures to Validate Psychometrics Data

Psychometrics, also known as psychological measurement, is the process of assigning values to represent specified behaviors or attributes (Rust & Golombok, 2009). Psychometrics is the cornerstone of empirical research and practice. For data to be useful, measurement validity is essential (see Chapter 10, this volume). The higher the measurement validity, the better the data and the stronger the conclusions of the research (Boateng et al., 2018). Psychometric data is typically collected using three major methods: behavioral observation data, self-report data, and trace data. Among the three strategies, behavioral observation is the most reliable and valid because the investigator observes and documents the data. Self-report is less valid and reliable because of all the reasons someone may misreport (see Chapter 16, this volume), while trace data is less susceptible to participatory dishonesty. Studying behaviors that leave only "trace data," rather than directly observable evidence, requires more elaborate data collection methods and coding techniques but is considered to be more valid than self-report. The most important quality of trace data is that it is unobtrusive and non-reactive: the data are not directly collected so there is no observer present to affect the participant's behavior. In addition to digital vendors and governments, academic scientists are quickly becoming interested in how these data can be used to better understand contemporary social behaviors.

Traditionally, constructs are not physical measurements such as time, length, height, and weight (see Chapters 9 and 10 in this volume). An example of a cardiovascular measure used for social and behavioral research is cardiovascular reactivity because it is a measure of physiological response to psychological stress. An exaggerated physiological response to psychological stress is associated with long-term negative cardiovascular health consequences (Chida & Steptoe, 2010). For example, in our research with professional firefighters, we applied continuous 12-lead ECG Holter monitoring, and importantly, sometimes the highest heart rates were recorded when the firefighters were driving to the emergency (Carey et al., 2010). In other words, this was not when their physiological demands were highest (i.e., when they were actually extinguishing fires) but rather while listening to radio calls about the fire because of the mental stress of anticipating fighting the fire and the expectation to protect and rescue life. Thus, cardiovascular measures contribute to our understanding of cardiovascular health and disease but also social and behavioral responses.

Electronic Medical Records for Obtaining Cardiovascular Measures

Electronic medical records (EMR) are electronic records of health-related information about an individual that are created, gathered, managed, and accessed by the individual and authorized clinicians and researchers. It covers a wide range of data, including demographics, medical history, vital signs, medication and allergies, immunization status, and laboratory tests and images (e.g., radiology including X-rays). Despite its challenges, studies have demonstrated that the EMR can improve quality of care. For example, in one study in 2011 regarding diabetes care, published in the *New England Journal of Medicine*, patients with Type 2 diabetes reduced their sugar levels because the EMR helped them manage their diabetes by involving them actively in its management (Cebul et al., 2011). For social and behavioral scientists, the EMR provides access to high-quality, large samples of physiological data. Typically, the access to EMR data is first managed through an institutional review board (IRB) for the protection of human subjects of research (see Volume 1, Chapter 2). Once IRB approval for a research protocol has been granted, the researchers submit a request to a "data guardian" who professionally searches for the variables of interest and returns a file with de-identified data (Kubiak, 2014). In this way, researchers can creatively include numerous CV measures that are ubiquitous throughout the medical records.

Current & Future Directions of CV Measures of Health in Social and Behavioral Research

Point-of-Care Tests in Social and Behavioral Research

Point-of-care tests (POCT) are rapid diagnostics that are performed in person with the individual rather than in a traditional laboratory. For example, at the onset of the COVID-19 pandemic, individuals would have to present to a medical clinic to be tested and wait for the results. However, within 18 months of the start of the pandemic, the US Food and Drug Administration authorized SARS-CoV-2 rapid at-home self-tests for individuals with and without symptoms (Woloshin et al., 2022). This rapid advancement in POCT was due to marketplace technology, consumer demands, and relaxed federal regulation because of the seriousness of the pandemic. In regard to POCT cardiovascular measures, some include blood glucose and cholesterol levels, and there is ongoing work developing troponin assays for early identification of myocardial damage or heart attacks (El-Osta et al., 2017). While there are some concerns regarding the cost of a POCT system, there is evidence showing cost savings and economic improvements to clinical workflow and health resource utilization (El-Osta et al., 2017).

There is evidence that POCT is a subject satisfier (Al Hayek et al., 2021); thus, it is fair to assume that same satisfaction with POCT would also translate to research subjects in regard to recruitment and retention during clinical studies. For example, in the author's research experience among professional firefighters, she used POCT to test fasting blood sugar, triglycerides, and high-density lipoproteins (Carey et al., 2011) in the actual fire house. The research was a prospective low-glycemic nutritional fitness program to revise metabolic syndrome (i.e., serum testing). As stakeholders, the firefighters were consulted regarding the design of the study, and they were not enthusiastic about a venous puncture with a needle and a blood sample being sent to the laboratory for results at a later time. However, when presented with POCT testing of the blood serum, only using a needle prick for a drop of blood with immediate results, they were supportive of that approach. The serological cardiovascular measures correlated with the physiological cardiovascular measures, including waist circumference and blood pressure. This approach was important because the study was longitudinal and design was dependent on the firefighters participating continuously throughout the 12 weeks.

Mobile Technologies in Social and Behavioral Research

Historically, the field of cardiology has used wearable medical devices to capture transient cardiac events. For example, Apple Watch (Series 4) recently launched a novel feature that enables consumers to record a rhythm strip and assist in the self-diagnosis of atrial fibrillation (Isakadze & Martin, 2020). As a result, if a subject experiences symptoms (e.g., dizziness) during a medical exam, but the symptom is not reproducible, the cardiologist would send the patient home with an ECG recorder in the hope of catching the transient event (e.g., paroxysmal atrial fibrillation). Since 2000, commercially available consumer wearables have saturated the popular market and have become of particular interest to researchers, with a rapid increase in publications citing the methodological approach of using "wearables" (Nelson et al., 2020). The consumption was accelerated with the COVID-19 pandemic, which resulted in remote, decentralized, and personalized self-care.

Many commercial wearables are now able to capture certain biological measurements. Watch products, such as Apple Watch 3 and Fitbit Charge 2, are now capable of measuring heart rate (Nelson & Allen, 2019). In addition, patches, such as Zio^{XT} Patch (iRhythm, USA), have also been used in clinical studies for continuous ECG monitoring in patients with undiagnosed atrial fibrillation (Steinhubl et al., 2018). Historically, the standard 12-lead ECG is obtained in a healthcare setting, with the patient lying down and a technician applying 10 adhesive electrodes to the chest and limbs. Then, while the individual is resting quietly, a 10-second ECG tracing is obtained and the electrodes are removed. In 2020, after the onset of the COVID-19 pandemic, an ECG monitoring company, QT Medical, Inc., provided home ECG testing kits for cardiac patients who needed routine annual ECGs for their cardiologist. The ECG kit was mailed to their homes and included instructions, an ECG patch (small, medium, large, or extra-large), ECG recorder, and a return envelope (Figure 20.4). ECG data was transmitted from the mobile application to the ECGcloud, where it was stored, accessed, and downloaded by the cardiologist. The mobile application was secured by requiring

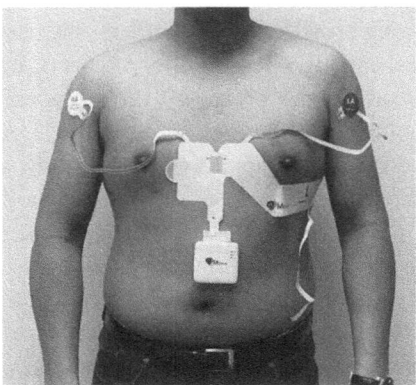

Figure 20.4 *A novel 12-lead ECG patch with recorder, "QT ECG." (QT Medical, Diamond Bar, California, USA)*

login credentials specific to the user. The computer app can only transmit the ECG data to the cloud and did not store any data. Of the 1,000 patients who participated, 93% successfully recorded and uploaded a clinical-quality ECG, and failure to complete the ECG recording due to technical issues was only 1.4% (Chang, 2022). Thus, at-home testing for the 12-lead ECG, the gold standard for electrocardiography, is feasible, reliable, and affordable.

Another new technology that may become available for researchers, albeit not in the form of a wearable device, is the use of toilet-seat-based cardiovascular monitoring targeted to monitor heart failure patients at home (Conn et al., 2019). With clinical studies still underway, such technology has great potential to improve the monitoring of heart failure patients without significant changes to their daily routine; therefore, it is likely to be easily adapted by patients at home. The advancement of sensor technologies and software algorithms has allowed the application of wearable devices both to make complex biological measurements and to assist in patients' risk assessment, cardiac diagnosis and management, and cardiac rehabilitation in an outpatient setting (Bayoumy et al., 2021).

Challenges with Wearables

As with any advancement, there are challenges to wearables. In general, there is some measurement error – up to 10%, compared to hospital-grade equipment used to measure during ideal conditions (Wang et al., 2017). The measurements may also be compromised with individuals with tattoos, darker skin tones, higher body mass indices, and during exertion (Pevnick et al., 2018). Plus, most of the literature focuses on younger healthier research subjects versus those with disease conditions and elders. A recent survey of nearly 1,500 older adults examined the use of wearable devices and their willingness to share their health data with providers. They reported that men were less likely to use wearables; however, those who shared their health information and searched for online health information were more likely to use wearables. Overall, more than 80% were willing to share their health information with their providers (Chandrasekaran et al., 2021).

Although smart wearables generate metadata, they are not interfaced with clinical practice because of concerns regarding accuracy, patient privacy, cost, and health equity (Bayoumy et al., 2021). In regard to accuracy, even with hospital-grade equipment, there is always a balance between actionable data versus noise or artifact. For example, with cardiac monitoring, if asystole, or flat-lining occurs, the patient's pulse is double-checked and, if absent, CPR is initiated. If the ECG data came from a wearable, the responsible clinician would have to locate and assess the patient, yet it is likely that the wearable's battery just failed. Overall, the pace of marketplace technology is much faster than the validation of the tools in clinical settings, so some caution is recommended.

Improving Health Equity

Nearly 40 years ago, the Department of Health and Human Services published the Heckler Report on Black and Minority Health, exposing for one of the first times that race and ethnicity may be an independent contributor to health outcomes (US Department of Health and Human Services, 1985). In regard to cardiovascular healthcare, Black Americans had fewer appointments, interventions, and diagnoses compared to White Americans. Health disparity is a heath difference that adversely affects disadvantaged groups, based on at least one health outcome including higher incidence, earlier onset of disease, higher prevalence of risk factors, higher rates of symptoms, premature or excessive mortality, and greater global burden of disease (Borrell & Vaughan, 2019).

While equity involves delivering resources and opportunities to these groups to achieve equal health outcomes, compared to the general population Black people suffer higher rates of uncontrolled cardiovascular risk factors and higher rates of cardiovascular-related death (Carnethon et al., 2017). Participating in digital health, researchers can reduce and prevent cardiovascular disease by obtaining continuous, longitudinal, high-quality patient data to increase access to care by decreasing healthcare delivery barriers and cost. To prevent increasing the health equity divide, extraordinary efforts are needed to include underrepresented groups in all stages of the development of these devices, including research and development, clinical research, and digital health distribution. For example, researchers from other disciplines, outside of healthcare, can easily add non-invasive, inexpensive cardiovascular measures to their research protocols.

Literature has highlighted the importance of the social determinants of health – economic stability, access to food, education, neighborhood and physical environment, healthcare system, etc. – in the development of cardiovascular disease. In recent years, the effort to modify some clinical risk stratification methods to include measures of social determinants of health has gained momentum. Moreover, with a widely used electronic health record system, many healthcare systems see major opportunities to incorporate social determinants of health measures as part of standard assessments. These will further facilitate personalized care plans during and after hospitalization (Jilani et al., 2021; Powell-Wiley et al., 2022). Research addressing indirect risk factors, such as environmental exposures and health behaviors, may also shed light on effective interventions that could inhibit the progression of cardiovascular diseases (Jilani et al., 2021). Research incorporating these determinants of health can help shape policy, practice, and care delivery, and ultimately reduce cardiovascular risk and improve outcomes.

Conclusions

Cardiovascular measures in the social and behavioral sciences are well established and are quickly expanding to include inexpensive wearables providing continuous physiological measures. When researchers improve the rigor of their research by the addition of obtaining cardiovascular measures, they contribute to the growing body of evidence regarding the importance of understanding the cardiovascular system – specifically, how the cardiovascular system is connected to other important physiological and psychological systems of the human body and their experience.

References

Al Hayek, A. A., Al-Saeed, A. H., Alzahrani, W. M., & Al Dawish, M. A. (2021). Assessment of patient satisfaction with on-site point-of-care hemoglobin A1c testing: An observational study. *Diabetes Therapy, 12*(9), 2531–2544. https://doi.org/10.1007/s13300-021-01126-7

Al-Zaiti, S. S., Fallavollita, J. A., Canty Jr., J. M., & Carey, M. G. (2014). Electrocardiographic predictors of sudden and non-sudden cardiac death in patients with ischemic cardiomyopathy. *Heart and Lung, 43*(6), 527–533. https://doi.org/10.1016/j.hrtlng.2014.05.008

Al-Zaiti, S. S., Pietrasik, G., Carey, M. G., Alhamaydeh, M., Canty, J. M., & Fallavollita, J. A. (2019). The role of heart rate variability, heart rate turbulence, and deceleration capacity in predicting cause-specific mortality in chronic heart failure. *Journal of Electrocardiology, 52*, 70–74. https://doi.org/10.1016/j.jelectrocard.2018.11.006

Bayoumy, K., Gaber, M., Elshafeey, A., Mhaimeed, O., Dineen, E. H., Marvel, F. A., et al. (2021). Smart wearable devices in cardiovascular care: Where we are and how to move forward. *Nature Reviews Cardiology, 18*(8), 581–599. https://doi.org/10.1038/s41569-021-00522-7

Bellenger, C. R., Fuller, J. T., Thomson, R. L., Davison, K., Robertson, E. Y., & Buckley, J. D. (2016). Monitoring athletic training status through autonomic heart rate regulation: A systematic review and meta-analysis. *Sports Medicine, 46*(10), 1461–1486. https://doi.org/10.1007/s40279-016-0484-2

Boateng, G. O., Neilands, T. B., Frongillo, E. A., Melgar-Quiñonez, H. R., & Young, S. L. (2018). Best practices for developing and validating scales for health, social, and behavioral research: A primer. *Frontiers in Public Health, 6*, 149. https://doi.org/10.3389/fpubh.2018.00149

Böhm, M., Reil, J. C., Deedwania, P., Kim, J. B., & Borer, J. S. (2015). Resting heart rate: Risk indicator and emerging risk factor in cardiovascular disease. *American Journal of Medicine, 128*(3), 219–228. https://doi.org/10.1016/j.amjmed.2014.09.016

Borrell, L. N., & Vaughan, R. (2019). An AJPH supplement toward a unified research approach for minority health and health disparities. *American Journal of Public Health, 109*(S1), S6–S7. https://doi.org/10.2105/ajph.2019.304963

Buxton, A. E., Calkins, H., Callans, D. J., DiMarco, J. P., Fisher, J. D., Greene, H L., et al. (2006). ACC/AHA/HRS 2006 key data elements and definitions for electrophysiological studies and procedures: A report of the American College of Cardiology / American Heart Association Task Force on Clinical Data Standards (ACC/AHA/HRS Writing Committee to Develop Data Standards on Electrophysiology). *Journal of the American College of Cardiology, 48*(11), 2360–2396. https://doi.org/10.1016/j.jacc.2006.09.020

Carey, M., Al-Zaiti, S., Liao, L., Butler, R., & Martin, H. (2010). Characteristics of the standard 12-lead Holter ECG in professional firefighters. *Computing in Cardiology, 3*, 122–138.

Carey, M. G., Al-Zaiti, S. S., Liao, L. M., Martin, H. N., & Butler, R. A. (2011). A low-glycemic nutritional fitness program to reverse metabolic syndrome in professional firefighters: Results of a pilot study. *Journal of Cardiovascular Nursing, 26*(4), 298–304. https://doi.org/10.1097/JCN.0b013e31820344d7

Carey, M., & Brunner, W (2023). Building fruitful collaborations. In A. L. Nichols & J. E. Edlund (eds.), *Cambridge Handbook of Research Methods and Statistics for the Social and Behavioral Sciences* (vol. 1, pp. 695–713). In Cambridge University Press.

Carey, M. G., & Thevenin, B. J. (2009). High-resolution 12-lead electrocardiograms of on-duty professional firefighters: A pilot feasibility study. *Journal of Cardiovascular Nursing, 24*(4), 261–267. https://doi.org/10.1097/JCN.0b013e3181a4b250

Carnethon, M. R., Pu, J., Howard, G., Albert, M. A., Anderson, C. A. M., Bertoni, A. G., et al. (2017). Cardiovascular health in African Americans: A scientific statement from the American Heart Association. *Circulation, 136*(21), e393–e423. https://doi.org/doi:10.1161/CIR.0000000000000534

Cebul, R. D., Love, T. E., Jain, A. K., & Hebert, C. J. (2011). Electronic health records and quality of diabetes care. *New England Journal of Medicine, 365*(9), 825–833. https://doi.org/10.1056/NEJMsa1102519

Chandrasekaran, R., Katthula, V., & Moustakas, E. (2021). Too old for technology? Use of wearable healthcare devices by older adults and their willingness to share health data with providers. *Health Informatics Journal, 27*(4), 14604582211058073. https://doi.org/10.1177/14604582211058073

Chang, R. K. (2022). Resting 12-lead ECG tests performed by patients at home amid the COVID-19 pandemic – results from the first 1000 patients. *Journal of Electrocardiology, 73*, 108–112. https://doi.org/10.1016/j.jelectrocard.2022.06.006

Chen, X. (2020). Analysis of athlete's heart pumping function and echocardiography. *Investigacion Clinica, 61*(1).

Chida, Y., & Steptoe, A. (2010). Greater cardiovascular responses to laboratory mental stress are associated with poor subsequent cardiovascular risk status. *Hypertension, 55*(4), 1026–1032. https://doi.org/doi:10.1161/HYPERTENSIONAHA.109.146621

Conn, N. J., Schwarz, K. Q., & Borkholder, D. A. (2019). In-home cardiovascular monitoring system for heart failure: Comparative study. *JMIR Mhealth and Uhealth, 7*(1), e12419. https://doi.org/10.2196/12419

Cygankiewicz, I., & Zareba, W. (2013). Heart rate variability. *Handbook of Clinical Neurology, 117*, 379–393. https://doi.org/10.1016/b978-0-444-53491-0.00031-6

Denollet, J., Gidron, Y., Vrints, C. J., & Conraads, V. M. (2010). Anger, suppressed anger, and risk of adverse events in patients with coronary artery disease. *American Journal of Cardiology, 105*(11), 1555–1560. https://doi.org/10.1016/j.amjcard.2010.01.015

El-Osta, A., Woringer, M., Pizzo, E., Verhoef, T., Dickie, C., Ni, M. Z., et al. (2017). Does use of point-of-care testing improve cost-effectiveness of the NHS Health Check programme in the primary care setting? A cost-minimisation analysis. *BMJ Open, 7*(8), e015494. https://doi.org/10.1136/bmjopen-2016-015494

Fihn, S. D., Gardin, J. M., Abrams, J., Berra, K., Blankenship, J. C., Dallas, A. P., et al. (2012). ACCF/AHA/ACP/AATS/PCNA/SCAI/STS guideline for the diagnosis and management of patients with stable ischemic heart disease. *Circulation, 126*(25), e354–471. https://doi.org/10.1161/CIR.0b013e318277d6a0

Galderisi, M., Cosyns, B., Edvardsen, T., Cardim, N., Delgado, V., Di Salvo, G., et al. (2017). Standardization of adult transthoracic echocardiography reporting in agreement with recent chamber quantification, diastolic function, and heart valve disease recommendations: An expert consensus document of the European Association of Cardiovascular Imaging. *European Heart Journal – Cardiovascular Imaging, 18*(12), 1301–1310. https://doi.org/10.1093/ehjci/jex244

Isakadze, N., & Martin, S. S. (2020). How useful is the smartwatch ECG? *Trends in Cardiovascular Medicine, 30*(7), 442–448. https://doi.org/10.1016/j.tcm.2019.10.010

Jilani, M. H., Javed, Z., Yahya, T., Valero-Elizondo, J., Khan, S. U., Kash, B., et al. (2021). Social determinants of health and cardiovascular disease: Current state and future directions towards healthcare equity. *Current Atherosclerosis Reports, 23*(9). https://doi.org/10.1007/s11883-021-00949-w

Kales, S. N., Soteriades, E. S., Christophi, C. A., & Christiani, D. C. (2007). Emergency duties and deaths from heart disease among firefighters in the United States. *New England Journal of Medicine, 356*(12), 1207–1215.

Khurshid, S., Friedman, S., Reeder, C., Di Achille, P., Diamant, N., Singh, P., et al. (2022). ECG-based deep learning and clinical risk factors to predict atrial fibrillation. *Circulation, 145*(2), 122–133. https://doi.org/10.1161/circulationaha.121.057480

Kim, C. A., Rasania, S. P., Afilalo, J., Popma, J. J., Lipsitz, L. A., & Kim, D. H. (2014). Functional status and quality of life after transcatheter aortic valve replacement: A systematic review. *Annals of Intern Medicine, 160*(4), 243–254. https://doi.org/10.7326/M13-1316

Kleiman, R., Litwin, J., & Morganroth, J. (2016). Benefits of centralized ECG reading in clinical oncology studies. *Therapeutic Innovation and Regulatory Science, 50*(1), 123–129. https://doi.org/10.1177/2168479015597729

Kubiak, R. (2014). The right to information. *Anaesthesiology Intensive Therapy, 46*(3), 180–194. https://doi.org/10.5603/ait.2014.0033

Kusunose, K. (2021). Steps to use artificial intelligence in echocardiography. *Journal of Echocardiography, 19*(1), 21–27. https://doi.org/10.1007/s12574-020-00496-4

Lakatta, E. G., & Levy, D. (2003). Arterial and cardiac aging: Major shareholders in cardiovascular disease enterprises: Part I: Aging arteries: A "set up" for vascular disease. *Circulation, 107*(1), 139–146. https://doi.org/10.1161/01.cir.0000048892.83521.58

Li, X., Zhu, W., Sui, X., Zhang, A., Chi, L., & Lv, L. (2021). Assessing workplace stress among nurses using heart rate variability analysis with wearable ECG device – a pilot study. *Frontiers in Public Health, 9*, 810577. https://doi.org/10.3389/fpubh.2021.810577

Lim, Y. H., Choi, S. Y., Oh, K. W., Kim, Y., Cho, E. S., Choi, B. Y., et al. (2014). Comparison between an automated device and a manual mercury sphygmomanometer in an epidemiological survey of hypertension prevalence. *American Journal of Hypertension, 27*(4), 537–545. https://doi.org/10.1093/ajh/hpt100

Muresan, L., Cismaru, G., Martins, R. P., Bataglia, A., Rosu, R., Puiu, M., et al. (2019). Recommendations for the use of electrophysiological study: Update 2018. *Hellenic Journal of Cardiology, 60*(2), 82–100. https://doi.org/10.1016/j.hjc.2018.09.002

Nelson, B. W., & Allen, N. B. (2019). Accuracy of consumer wearable heart rate measurement during an ecologically valid 24-hour period: Intraindividual validation study. *JMIR Mhealth and Uhealth, 7*(3), e10828. https://doi.org/10.2196/10828

Nelson, B. W., Low, C. A., Jacobson, N., Areán, P., Torous, J., & Allen, N. B. (2020). Guidelines for wrist-worn consumer wearable assessment of heart rate in biobehavioral research. *npj Digital Medicine, 3*(1), 90. https://doi.org/10.1038/s41746-020-0297-4

North, B. J., & Sinclair, D. A. (2012). The intersection between aging and cardiovascular disease. *Circulation Research, 110*(8), 1097–1108. https://doi.org/10.1161/circresaha.111.246876

Pevnick, J. M., Birkeland, K., Zimmer, R., Elad, Y., & Kedan, I. (2018). Wearable technology for cardiology: An update and framework for the future. *Trends in Cardiovascular Medicine, 28*(2), 144–150. https://doi.org/10.1016/j.tcm.2017.08.003

Pham, T., Lau, Z. J., Chen, S. H. A., & Makowski, D. (2021). Heart rate variability in psychology: A review of HRV indices and an analysis tutorial. *Sensors, 21*(12). https://doi.org/10.3390/s21123998

Poppelaars, E. S., Klackl, J., Pletzer, B., Wilhelm, F. H., & Jonas, E. (2019). Social-evaluative threat: Stress response stages and influences of biological sex and neuroticism. *Psychoneuroendocrinology, 109*, 104378. https://doi.org/10.1016/j.psyneuen.2019.104378

Powell-Wiley, T. M., Baumer, Y., Baah, F. O., Baez, A. S., Farmer, N., Mahlobo, C. T., et al. (2022). Social determinants of cardiovascular disease. *Circulation Research, 130*(5), 782–799. https://doi.org/10.1161/CIRCRESAHA.121.319811

Reisman, M., Buchbinder, M., Warth, D., Sundling, N., Harms, V., & Whitlow, P. L. (1997). Comparison of patients with either < 70% diameter narrowing or > or = 70% narrowing of the right coronary artery when performing rotational atherectomy on > or = 1 narrowing in the left coronary arteries. *American Journal of Cardiology, 79*(3), 305–308. https://doi.org/10.1016/s0002-9149(96)00752-7

Roerecke, M., Kaczorowski, J., & Myers, M. G. (2019). Comparing automated office blood pressure readings with other methods of blood pressure measurement for identifying patients with possible hypertension: A systematic review and meta-analysis. *JAMA Internal Medicine, 179*(3), 351–362. https://doi.org/10.1001/jamainternmed.2018.6551

Rust, J., & Golombok, S. (2009). *Modern Psychometrics: The Science of Psychological Assessment*, 3rd ed. Routledge.

Rutjes, A. W., Reitsma, J. B., Coomarasamy, A., Khan, K. S., & Bossuyt, P. M. (2007). Evaluation of diagnostic tests when there is no gold standard: A review of methods. *Health Technology Assessment, 11*(50). https://doi.org/10.3310/hta11500

Steinhubl, S. R., Waalen, J., Edwards, A. M., Ariniello, L. M., Mehta, R. R., Ebner, G. S., et al. (2018). Effect of a home-based wearable continuous ECG monitoring patch on detection of undiagnosed atrial fibrillation: The mSToPS randomized clinical trial. *JAMA, 320*(2), 146–155. https://doi.org/10.1001/jama.2018.8102

Tell, D., Burr, R. L., Mathews, H. L., & Janusek, L. W. (2021). Heart rate variability and inflammatory stress response in young African American Men: Implications for cardiovascular risk. *Frontiers in Cardiovascular Medicine, 8,* 745864. https://doi.org/10.3389/fcvm.2021.745864

Thayer, J. F., Hansen, A. L., & Johnsen, B. H. (2010). The non-invasive assessment of autonomic influences on the heart using impedance cardiography and heart rate variability. In A. Steptoe (ed.), *Handbook of Behavioral Medicine: Methods and Applications* (pp. 723–740). Springer. https://doi.org/10.1007/978-0-387-09488-5_47

US Department of Health and Human Services. (1985). *Report of the Secretary's Task Force on Black and Minority Health.* US Department of Health and Human Services.

Wang, R., Blackburn, G., Desai, M., Phelan, D., Gillinov, L., Houghtaling, P., & Gillinov, M. (2017). Accuracy of wrist-worn heart rate monitors. *JAMA Cardiology, 2*(1), 104–106. https://doi.org/10.1001/jamacardio.2016.3340

Woloshin, S., Dewitt, B., Krishnamurti, T., & Fischhoff, B. (2022). Assessing how consumers interpret and act on results from at-home COVID-19 self-test kits: A randomized clinical trial. *JAMA Internal Medicine, 182*(3), 332–341. https://doi.org/10.1001/jamainternmed.2021.8075

Yamazaki, E. M., Rosendahl-Garcia, K. M., Casale, C. E., MacMullen, L. E., Ecker, A. J., Kirkpatrick, J. N., & Goel, N. (2021). Left ventricular ejection time measured by echocardiography differentiates neurobehavioral resilience and vulnerability to sleep loss and stress. *Frontiers in Physiology, 12,* 795321. https://doi.org/10.3389/fphys.2021.795321

21 Electrodermal Activity: Applications and Challenges

Md-Billal Hossain, Youngsun Kong,
Hugo F. Posada-Quintero, and Ki H. Chon

Abstract
Electrodermal activity (EDA) is a conductance measure that can be used to assess the sympathetic nervous system arousal and for the diagnosis of stress, pain, sleepiness, seizure prediction, neuropathies, depression, and other states. EDA has potential for ambulatory research applications, as it can be collected using wearable devices, but motion artifacts are an issue. While EDA was discovered in 1879 by Vigouroux, the signal was traditionally observed in most of the studies as the mean value of the signal in response to a given stimulus, which provides static information but does not account for time-varying dynamics of the signal. The new technologies for EDA collection and the development of novel and robust signal processing algorithms have increased the interest in EDA for many new and emerging fields, including affective computing, seizure prediction, and pain monitoring. We aim to summarize the characteristics of EDA, describe current and future applications, and outline challenges when using EDA.

Keywords: Electrodermal Activity, Physiomarkers, Motion Artifact Detection, Pain Detection, Stress and Emotion Detection, Wearable Devices and Ambulatory Monitoring, Seizure Detection and Prediction

Introduction

Electrodermal activity (EDA) refers to changes in the capacity of the skin to conduct electrical current resulting from the amount of sweat produced by the sweat glands. Originally discovered by Vigouroux in 1879, scientists have called it different names through history, such as galvanic skin response, skin conductance, and skin resistance. Given the relatively recent interest in EDA for biological applications, attempts to standardize the terminology and the techniques for collecting and processing the signals have been made, and EDA is currently more widely accepted (Boucsein et al., 2012).

Since its discovery, EDA has been primarily used in psychophysiological research, and most researchers have used EDA to measure the body's autonomic response to emotional and cognitive stimuli. However, given that sweat glands are controlled directly and uniquely by the sympathetic nervous system, EDA can be used as an indication of both psychological responses and general sympathetic arousal. Furthermore, in a similar fashion to photoplethysmography, accelerometry, and skin temperature, EDA is feasible for deployment in wearable sensors. Its direct link to sympathetic arousal and its ease of collection make EDA a feasible sensor for a wide range conditions, including stress, pain, sleepiness, exercise recovery, epilepsy, neuropathies, and depression. It can also be deployed in currently hot fields like affective computing, marketing, human–computer interaction, and social-media analysis.

Advances in smart wearable devices, novel signal processing of EDA data, and the recent popularity of machine learning have been the main drivers of new insights and some impressive diagnostic capabilities in the above-mentioned applications. Hence, in this chapter we will discuss the morphology of EDA signals, popular EDA indices used as physio-markers, challenges in EDA signal processing (e.g., motion artifact detection), various applications of EDA signals in real life and clinical settings, wearable implementations, and smartphone applications for data collection and analysis. Some limitations and challenges of EDA interpretations will also be discussed.

Technically speaking, EDA refers to the variation in the electrical properties of the skin. Sweat gland activities are modulated by sympathetic stimuli (i.e., stress, pain, and emotional behavior), and the changes are captured in the EDA signal (Sato et al., 1989). As sodium and chloride (major components in sweat) are the most abundant electrolytes, they are responsible for increased conductance of the skin by creating low-resistance parallel paths along the skin surface (Poh, Loddenkemper, Swenson, et al., 2010; Sato et al., 1989). There have been multiple theories about how the sweat glands are innervated. Although it was initially thought that both the sympathetic and parasympathetic nervous systems contribute to innervating sweat glands (Boucsein, 2012), subsequent research confirmed that only the sympathetic nervous system innervates the sweat glands. Thus, sympathetic arousal due to emotion, cognition, and attention can be measured by variations in the EDA signal; they reflect the modulation of the sympathetic nervous system.

Due to their indication of the modulation of sympathetic activities, EDA measurements have been applied extensively in psychological applications such as stress detection (Gjoreski et al., 2016; Healey et al., 2010; Hernandez et al., 2011; Momin et al., 2020; Setz et al., 2010), autism examination (Prince et al., 2017; Schupak et al., 2016), panic disorder studies (Wendt et al., 2008), detection of depression (A. Y. Kim et al., 2018), and recognition of emotional states (Jang et al., 2015; Jaques et al., 2015). Diverse medical studies using EDA have included sleep monitoring (H. Kim et al., 2021; Romine et al., 2019; Sano et al., 2014), objective measurement of pain (Kong et al., 2020, 2021b, 2021a; Posada-Quintero et al., 2020; Posada-Quintero, Kong, & Chon, 2021; Sugimine et al., 2020; Susam et al., 2018), and hypoglycemia detection in diabetes (Elvebakk et al., 2018), as well as neurological applications such as seizure detection (Poh et al., 2012; Poh, Loddenkemper, & Swenson, 2010; Posada-Quintero et al., 2022), attention-deficit hyperactivity disorder (ADHD) studies (Beauchaine et al., 2015; Dupuy et al., 2014; von Polier et al., 2014), and dementia monitoring (Melander et al., 2018; Perugia et al., 2017).

EDA Data Collection

Typically, the EDA signal is recorded using two main approaches: (1) the exosomatic method, in which a constant current or voltage is applied between two electrodes and the corresponding variation in electrical conductance is measured over time; and (2) the endosomatic approach, in which an AC voltage or current source replaces the DC voltage/current source. However, because of the simplicity of their circuit implementation, DC-source devices are generally the most popular for EDA data collection. In addition, EDA data can be collected using both wired and wireless wearable sensors, as shown in Figure 21.1. In both cases, a pair of electrodes is placed on the middle and index fingers, typically, or on the wrist. Some studies reported a low correlation of wrist EDA with finger EDA; the latter is regarded as the gold standard since there are more sweat glands on the fingers.

Two types of electrodes are widely used for EDA data collection: dry stainless steel electrodes and wet (gel) Ag/AgCl electrodes. While gel electrodes offer better sensitivity and good signal quality, they are also not feasible for long-term monitoring since the gel may degrade, get detached, or cause skin irritation. Dry electrodes, on the other hand, depend on sufficient sweat and may require a longer time to capture the signal (hydration time), especially in cold and dry conditions. The easiest

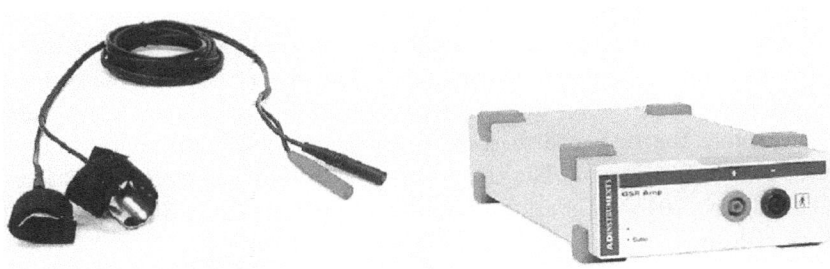

Figure 21.1a *EDA data collection setup for laboratory environment. (Images obtained from ADInstruments.)*

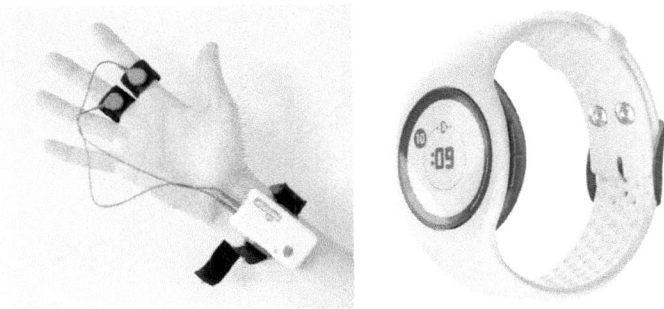

Figure 21.1b *Examples of wearable EDA devices. (Images obtained from Shimmer and embracePLUS.)*

way to check the quality of the EDA signal is by providing a momentary stimulus such as a deep breath and observing the corresponding change in EDA. In an ideal scenario, there should be a rise in the EDA signal corresponding to the initiation of the stimulus. In most EDA studies, baseline data is recorded for a few minutes in the beginning. During the baseline, the subjects are instructed to rest without talking. Since caffeine or any other stimulant may affect the sympathetic activities, it is often recommended that the subjects do not consume any caffeine at least 24 hours before the experiment.

Another crucial factor for EDA data collection is the electrode placement site (Hossain, Kong, et al., 2022). Because of high sweat gland density, palms and fingers are usually the primary site for EDA data collection (Frewin & Downey, 1976; Harker, 2013; Saga, 2002). However, as some applications may rule out using palmer sites or fingers, alternative sites such as the foot, forehead, wrists, and lower calves are proposed in many research papers (Hossain, Kong, et al., 2022; Kasos et al., 2018, 2020; van Dooren et al., 2012). However, when considering alternative sites for EDA data collection, hydration time (i.e., conduction time) should be considered, as some of the sites have fewer sweat pores (Hossain, Kong, et al., 2022; Kasos et al., 2020).

Basic EDA Morphology

A raw EDA signal, plotted as amplitude versus time, is often characterized by oscillatory transient events, also known as skin conductance responses (SCRs). These SCRs are of two types: (1) event-related SCRs that are used to capture the response to some given external stimuli, and (2) non-specific SCRs that are due to changes in the phasic signal not related to any stimuli (Theodoros, 2014). Figure 21.2 shows a typical SCR with time-based quantitative measures.

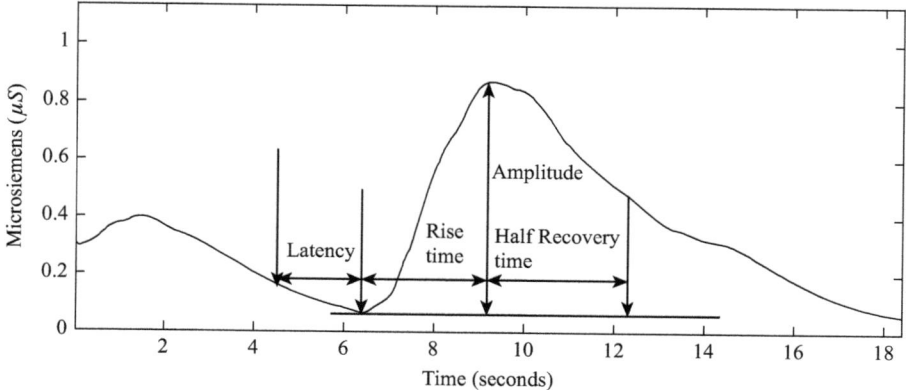

Figure 21.2 *Morphology of typical skin conductance response (SCR).*

An ideal event-related SCR starts with a given stimulus that initiates the response in the EDA signal. The time interval between the stimulus being applied and the beginning of the SCR peak is regarded as the latency and ranges between 1 and 3 seconds (Boucsein, 2012). The amplitude of SCRs can reach several μS, and a minimum threshold of 0.05 or 0.04 is set to identify event-related or significant SCRs (Boucsein, 2012; Posada-Quintero & Chon, 2020). The time between the onset of an SCR and the peak is termed the rise time and typically ranges between 0.5 and 5 s (Theodoros, 2014). The amplitude and the rise time may vary depending on the type of stimulus being provided (Posada-Quintero & Chon, 2020). Soon after the peak, there is a slow and exponential decay in the amplitude until the phasic signal value reaches the baseline. The time interval needed for 50% decay of the peak amplitude is regarded as the half recovery time (as shown in Figure 21.2.). Typically, the half recovery period may vary between 2 and 10 s depending on the experimental conditions, such as electrode placement and the environmental temperature (Boucsein, 2012; Posada-Quintero & Chon, 2020), since EDA response can vary slightly depending on the surrounding temperature and sweat gland density of the recording site.

EDA Signal Processing

Typically, EDA signals are decomposed into two major components. In addition to the skin conductance responses just discussed, consisting of rapid and transient events in the EDA signal that represent the dynamics of the sympathetic stimuli, there is also the skin conductance level (SCL) – the slow and smooth overall trend in the EDA signal that represents the response to tonic stimuli. The baseline value of the SCL varies within and between different individuals (Braithwaite et al., n.d.); this is why SCL is not typically used for analysis (Boucsein, 2012; Topoglu et al., 2020). However, changes in normalized skin conductance level (nSCL) can be an important indicator of the intensity of sympathetic stimuli (Munsters et al., 2012).

There are several different approaches for decomposing EDA into phasic and tonic components (see Figure 21.3). The most popular approaches include continuous and discrete decomposition analysis (Boucsein, 2012), dynamic causal modeling (Bach et al., 2011), convex optimization (CvxEDA; Greco et al., 2016), and sparse deconvolution (sparsEDA; Hernando-Gallego et al., 2018). CvxEDA models the EDA signal as the sum of three components – phasic, tonic, and additive noise. CvxEDA then uses Bayesian statistics and the convex optimization technique to obtain the phasic and the tonic components from the noisy observation data by minimizing the error. SparsEDA models the phasic component (the skin conductance response: SCR) as a standard linear convolution between a sudomotor sympathetic nervous system innervation and the response triggered by that driver. SparsEDA is known to be a computationally fast and easily interpreted method. Both cvxEDA and SparsEDA decomposition methods are open source and available online (cvxEDA, SparsEDA).

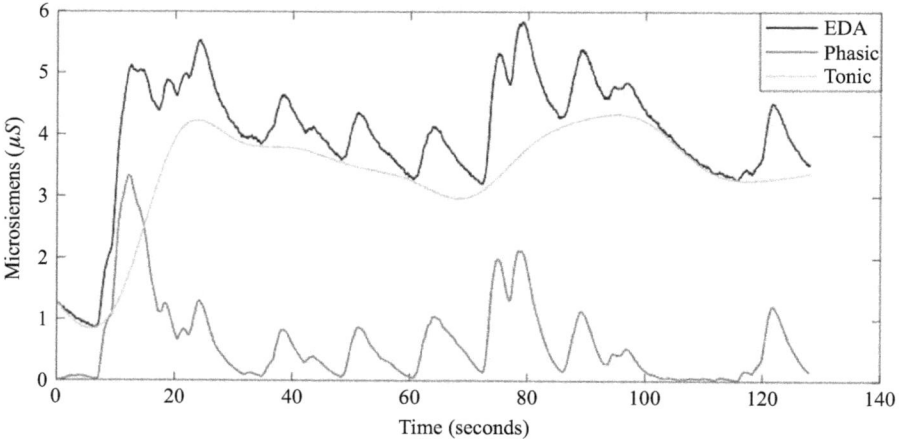

Figure 21.3 *Decomposition of EDA into tonic and phasic components.*

EDA Physiomarkers

There have been several EDA indices developed by researchers for different applications. These EDA indices can be broadly classified into time domain and frequency domain measures. Most EDA indices are based on the phasic and tonic decomposition of EDA in the time domain, as mentioned earlier. The time domain EDA indices include amplitudes, number of SCRs, rise time, and falling time. Moreover, a number of statistical features such as mean and median values of EDA, approximate entropy, and sample entropy are calculated from either the raw EDA signal or the phasic component calculated from the EDA signal. In addition, a number of automated sympathetic arousal tracking methods, such as the sparse decomposition approach with physiological priors (Amin & Faghih, 2021; Amin & Faghih, 2022) and marked process filtering (Wickramasuriya & Faghih, 2020), have been developed by researchers.

There have been several research projects on frequency domain and time-frequency domain EDA indices. Most of the spectral analyses of EDA have been developed recently and were motivated by spectral analyses of the heart rate variability (HRV). The high frequency content of HRV – the parasympathetic activity – typically resides in the frequency band 0.15 to 0.4 Hz. The low frequency content – in the frequency band 0.04 to 0.15 Hz – represents both sympathetic and parasympathetic activities. In the presence of different stressors, the spectral power of EDA lies in a similar frequency band as the low frequency components in HRV (Posada-Quintero et al., 2016). Based on this observation, a sensitive index, named EDASymp, was proposed by Posada-Quintero et al. (2016).

Detection and Correction of Motion Artifacts

Despite its popularity, EDA is often affected by severe noise and motion artifacts (MA), especially when data collection involves wearable devices or is in a non-controlled setting (Boucsein, 2012). The sources of noise and motion artifacts include unstable electrode contact (Boucsein, 2012; Healey et al., 2010), environmental temperature and humidity (Boucsein, 2012; Shaffer et al., 2016), and the subject's activities (Boucsein, 2012; Kleckner et al., 2018; Zhang et al., 2017). All these factors corrupt EDA signals, thereby leading to unusable data. Typically, motion artifacts are detected using accelerometers or simple algorithms, and those corrupted portions of data segments are discarded (Posada-Quintero & Chon, 2020). There have been significant efforts toward automatic detection of motion artifacts in EDA signals. They can be broadly classified as simple rules-based (Kleckner et al., 2018) and machine-learning-based methods (Hossain, Posada-Quintero, Kong, McNaboe, & Chon, 2022; Subramanian et al., 2021; Taylor et al., 2015; Xia et al., 2015; Zhang et al., 2017). While detecting and discarding MA-corrupted data is one option, it is not always the best solution, especially when most of the data are needed. In this case, recovering a clean EDA signal from the MA-corrupted segments would be more beneficial. Unfortunately, there is little research on this topic.

Since manual handling of motion artifacts is time-consuming and inefficient, several automatic motion artifact algorithms have been developed. An automated quality assessment for EDA signals was proposed by Kleckner et al. (2018) in which the authors identified noisy EDA data based on some simple rules such as EDA out of range, EDA values changing too quickly, or thermocouples indicating that an EDA electrode was not making good contact. This method works well when there are large amplitude spikes or obvious discernible motion artifacts. Several machine-learning-based algorithms were proposed for automatic MA detection in EDA in recent years (Subramanian et al., 2021; Taylor et al., 2015; Zhang et al., 2017). Machine learning methods use different statistical features such as the mean, median, and standard deviation derivatives, maxima and minima of EDA, and spectral features calculated using wavelet transforms to assess the data quality.

The performance of machine learning methods is largely dependent on accurate labeling of EDA (e.g., clean or corrupted); this can be complicated given the aperiodic nature of EDA signals. To overcome this limitation, a reference EDA signal was suggested for accurate modeling of the EDA signal (Hossain et al., 2021; Hossain, Posada-Quintero, Kong, McNaboe, & Chon, 2022). In our recent studies, we collected reference EDA signals and used them as a supporting tool when labeling the EDA signal (Hossain et al., 2021; Hossain, Kong, Posada-Quintero, & Chon, 2022; Hossain, Posada-Quintero, Kong, McNaboe, & Chon, 2022). Independent validation on an unseen data set was performed to test the generalizability of the method. Figure 21.4 shows one example of MA detection in an EDA signal using the machine learning method (Hossain, Posada-Quintero, Kong, McNaboe, & Chon, 2022). However, this approach requires an additional EDA sensor on a different and more stable body location that is not optimal for practical implementation.

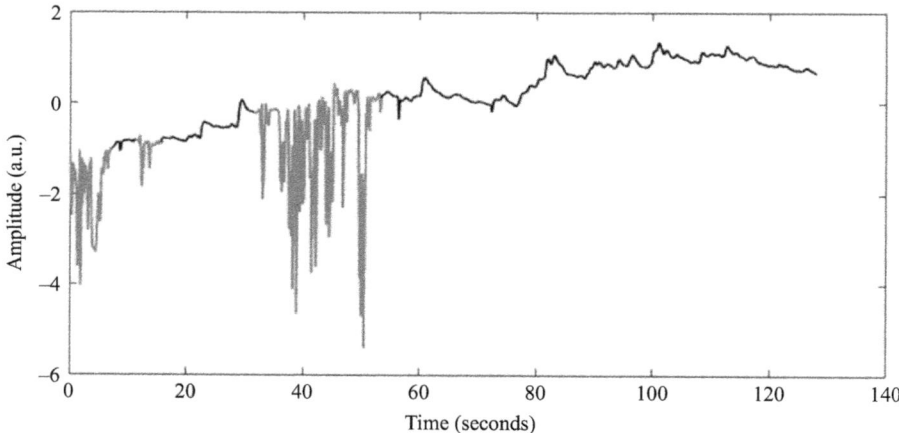

Figure 21.4 *Motion artifact detection in EDA using machine learning method. (The B&W marked portion represents motion artifact.)*

MA detection algorithms can be of great value, especially when handling long-term EDA recordings. However, in the case of short-duration collection or limited data, it is often desirable to recover moderately MA-affected EDA data. Fortunately, automated algorithms for EDA reconstruction can recover a considerable amount of data. There are several notable automated motion artifact correction algorithms developed in recent years. Chen et al. (2015) proposed an automatic motion artifact removal technique based on the wavelet transform, in which the authors decomposed the EDA segments using the stationary wavelet transform (SWT). This approach involved modeling each wavelet coefficient using the Gaussian mixture model (GMM), computing an automated threshold using the cumulative distribution of GMM to mask the MA components in each wavelet coefficient, and finally using the inverse SWT to reconstruct a clean EDA. This method works well when the MA-corrupted data segments are relatively small and MA-corrupted values have significantly higher amplitudes than the clean signal.

The other approaches (Llanes-Jurado et al., 2021; Subramanian et al., 2021, 2022) use motion artifact detection first, remove the motion artifacts, and use linear/non-linear interpolation to replace the corrupted data portions. The main disadvantage of these methods is that they only work well when MA-corrupted segments are only a small portion of the signal. Moreover, the interpolation procedure used for replacing the MA-corrupted segments is not advisable for relatively longer artifact segments, as the linearity assumption becomes invalid.

Given the availability of large data sets and the ever-growing efficiency of computational processing, it is timely to apply advanced deep learning methods for automatic reconstruction of EDA segments corrupted with MA. In our most recent work (Hossain, Posada-Quintero, & Chon, 2022a; Hossain, Posada-Quintero, & Chon, 2022b), a deep convolutional denoising autoencoder (DCAE) has been used to automatically remove motion artifacts from EDA signals. The application of this

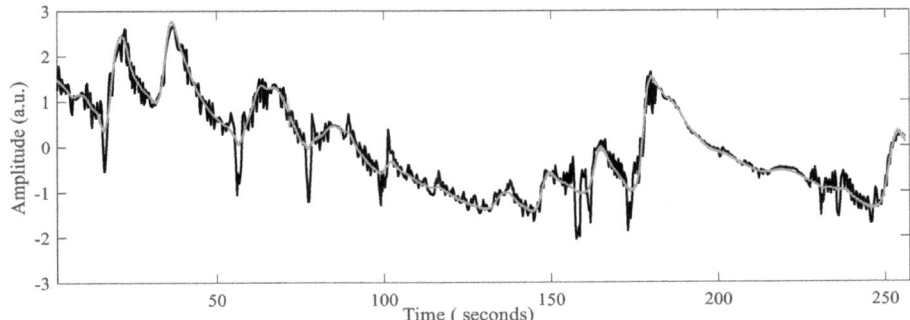

Figure 21.5 *DCAE reconstruction of EDA signal B&W from MA-corrupted data (black).*

denoising autoencoder has led to impressive reconstruction performance on EDA signals. A denoising autoencoder is one of the state-of-the-art MA removal techniques widely used in different applications such as signal reconstruction (Vincent et al., 2010), dimensionality reduction (Wang et al., 2016), and biomedical signal denoising and classification (Chiang et al., 2019; Feng et al., 2014; Lee et al., 2019; Li et al., 2015; Reljin et al., 2020).

A representative plot of DCAE reconstruction is shown in Figure 21.5. The black line represents MA-corrupted EDA data, and the red line shows the reconstructed EDA using the DCAE network. As shown, DCAE is able to effectively remove most of the high-frequency MA dynamics.

Applications of EDA

As previously noted, EDA has been widely used in different psychological, physiological, and neurological applications. We describe a few EDA applications in this section.

Pain Detection

It is well established that dynamics of the sympathetic nervous system (SNS) are elevated in proportion to pain intensity (Nahman-Averbuch & Coghill, 2017; Nickel et al., 2017). Thus, EDA can be used as a pain detector since EDA is a physiomarker of SNS dynamics. Dubé et al. (2009) showed the brain activities associated with elevated EDA dynamics during acute heat pain; the authors identified brain stimulation related to the resultant EDA dynamics by modeling the predicted blood oxygen level dependent (BOLD) signal. Munsters et al. (2012) observed that changes in skin conductance can be used to detect and differentiate pain and discomfort in newborn infants. Sugimine et al. (2020) measured the number of fluctuations (NFSC) in EDA and normalized skin conductance level (nSCL) during different pain stimuli such as heat, mechanical, and cold stimulation, and other sympathetic stimuli consisting of abrupt sound and painful images and found that both NFSC and nSCL increased during these stimulations. The authors concluded that nSCL could better differentiate than NFSC between physical pain stimuli and other sympathetic-induced responses. Similarly, Susam et al. (2018) used timescale decomposition to extract salient features from EDA signals and applied machine learning to distinguish between pain and no pain. As a result of their approach, the authors achieved a moderate level of accuracy in detecting pain, indicating the feasibility of developing medical applications in objective pain assessment, currently reliant on self-report or observation, which can be affected by personal bias.

Time-varying spectral features have been used extensively in pain detection studies and are reported to have higher sensitivity compared to time-domain indices (Kong et al., 2021a). Posada-Quintero, Kong, et al. (2020) used the time-varying spectral index (TVsymp) of EDA to quantify a multilevel pain stimulation evoked by thermal grill. This work showed that TVsymp was significantly affected by thermal grill pain-inducing stimulations. Kong et al. (2021a) collected EDA signals during different levels of electrical stimulation. This work computed several sensitive EDA indices using a derivative of the phasic EDA signal and time-varying spectral analysis. The authors also proposed modification of a previously developed time-varying spectral index (MTVsymp) that enabled more accurate detection and quantification of pain. The method showed a robust 87% balanced accuracy in classifying high versus no pain stimulations. These examples demonstrate the merits of using time-varying spectral indices for detecting and quantifying pain induced by different stimuli. Their high level of accuracy indicates that utilizing the differential characteristics of EDA enhances the detection of fast and sharp responses, such as pain. By leveraging these distinct features of EDA signals, their approach proves to be particularly effective in capturing rapid physiological changes associated with pain, potentially leading to more efficient and precise pain assessment techniques.

Stress Detection

Stress is sensed in the amygdala of the brain, activating the sympathetic nervous system (Scharmüller et al., 2015; Yang et al., 2007). Since EDA can be used as a noninvasive surrogate marker of SNS activity, a corresponding change is expected in the EDA signal during stress. This is the motivation to use EDA for stress detection. Liu et al. (2015) found that participants showed increased SCL following stress. They also observed that sleep-deprived people had higher SCL responses to stress than did well-rested subjects. Ruiz-Robledillo and Moya-Albiol (2015) performed an interesting study comparing parents of children with autism spectrum disorder (ASD) to parents of children without ASD. The authors observed that the parents of the ASD patients showed lower EDA response to acute stress compared to the parents of the children without ASD; this could reflect an adaptive habituation of parents of the ASD patients to stress.

Setz et al. (2010) did an interesting study in which they induced mild cognitive load and two stress factors (cognitive and psychological) on the participants; cognitive stress was induced by solving arithmetic problems under time pressure and psychological stress was induced by a social-evaluative threat. Mild cognitive stress was also induced by solving arithmetic problems without a time limit. The authors obtained a classification accuracy of 82.8% between cognitive load and stress using EDA features such as peak height and instantaneous peak rate. Posada-Quintero et al. (2018) collected EDA on subjects while they were fully immersed in water and performing the Stroop test (a moderate cognitive-stress-inducing experiment; Scarpina & Tagini, 2017). This study did not observe any significant changes in time domain indices such as SCL and non-specific SCRs during cognitive stress. However, the frequency domain indices, such as EDAsymp and TVsymp, showed significant differences between baseline and cognitive stress.

Most of the stress-related experiments were performed in a controlled laboratory environment. However, there have been some studies that were performed in real-life settings. Liu and Du (2018) used electrodermal activity features with a simple linear discriminant analysis classifier to classify the stress levels on drivers. They used the MIT Media Lab driver stress database that contains EDA data from 24 drivers while they were driving in different stressful scenarios such as on highways and in a city and also during resting moments. Their machine learning method obtained a classification accuracy of 81.8%. Hernandez et al. (2011) also used EDA signals with a support vector machine (SVM) to classify stressful versus non-stressful calls in a call center and obtained a good accuracy of around 75%. Choi et al. (2012) used the heart rate variability (HRV) with EDA features in association with logistic regression to discriminate between mental stress and relaxation in an ambulatory setting.

EDA in Sleep Applications

Since different stages of sleep and wakefulness produce different levels of SNS activation (Murali et al., 2003; Silvani & Dampney, 2013; Somers et al., 1993), EDA can be a potential tool for analyzing sleep stages. In addition, EDA can be easily collected while sleeping using wearable devices to capture information pertaining to sleep stages and sleep quality. Moreover, SNS activity reduces by more than half from wakefulness through light to deep sleep stages (Murali et al., 2003; Somers et al., 1993). These observations have motivated several sleep research studies using EDA. Most of the sleep research studies were performed in the laboratory while some were performed in natural settings such as at home. Early studies using EDA-based sleep analysis reported more frequent "storm" patterns, and elevated EDA responses, during slow wave sleep (SWS) (Koumans et al., 1968). One of the studies reported lower EDA peak frequencies during the first cycle of the night (Freixa i Baqué, 1983). Koumans et al. (1968) studied skin potential and skin resistance level and observed that those levels could differentiate between being awake and asleep.

Recently there have been several works on sleep applications using EDA. Sano et al. (2014) collected EDA data from both wrist and palmer surfaces with concurrent polysomnography (PSG) during nighttime. The authors compared the EDA obtained from the wrist and the palm and observed higher and more frequent EDA peaks from the wrist compared to the palm. This study also compared EDA peaks across different sleep stages – N1, N2, SWS, REM – and found that 80% of the EDA peaks occurred in non-REM sleep. Herlan et al. (2019) performed a study on 48 patients with sleep disorders and 43 healthy subjects, collecting EDA signals during nighttime. The authors computed EDA-smoothed features called EDASEF, and the number of EDA peaks (EDAcounts), and compared them across wakefulness and different stages of sleep. The authors found significant differences between wakefulness and sleep stages, such as awake versus non-REM stage 1 (N1), awake versus N2, awake versus SWS, and awake versus REM. Moreover, the authors reported a significant difference in EDA counts between normal healthy subjects and patients with sleep disorder in the stage N1. Also, higher variances in EDAcounts and EDASEF were observed in the sleep-disordered group.

Emotion Recognition

Since EDA is considered a non-invasive surrogate measure of SNS activity, it can be applied to recognize emotional arousal that is controlled by the autonomic nervous system (Dutta et al., 2022; Shu et al., 2018). Wu et al. (2010) used EDA, blood oxygen saturation, and heart rate as inputs to a random forests machine learning method to recognize five different emotions. The authors computed several statistical features such as the mean and standard deviation of EDA, number of SCRs, and the average amplitude and duration of SCRs. The machine learning method yielded an overall accuracy of 74%. Das et al. (2016) combined EDA and electrocardiogram (ECG) features to classify sad, happy, and neutral emotions. The authors concluded that features calculated using power spectral density (PSD) from both ECG and EDA were effective in classifying the happy, sad, and neutral emotions. The authors obtained maximum classification accuracy of 93.32% when differentiating opposite emotions such as sad and happy. The accuracies for sad vs. neutral and happy vs. neutral emotions were 91.42% and 90.12%, respectively. These show promise of EDA in human–brain computer interaction.

Several researchers used a publicly available data set (A Dataset for Emotion Analysis using Physiological Signals – DEAP; Koelstra et al., 2012) for emotion recognition. This multimodal data set consists of several physiological signals, including electroencephalogram (EEG), EDA, electromyogram (EMG), and ECG. The measurements were obtained while playing varied emotional content on videos to induce different emotions in the participants. For example, Ganapathy et al. (2021) used the DEAP data set and applied a multiscale deep convolutional neural network on EDA signals to differentiate various emotional states. This approach achieved an accuracy of 69.33% in classifying valence and 71.43% for classifying arousal.

Veeranki et al. (2021) used EDA signals and explored different time-frequency decomposition methods such as the short-time Fourier transform, Choi Williams distribution, and smoothed pseudo-Wigner-Ville distribution in association with various machine learning algorithms to classify and annotate happy and sad events obtained from different publicly available data sets. The authors reported that smoothed pseudo-Wigner-Ville distribution with a random forests classifier yielded the highest F measure of 8.74%. Likewise, Shukla et al. (2019) used EDA signals from a publicly available emotion data set named AMIGOS (Miranda-Correa et al., 2021), and extracted 40 different features from the time-frequency domain of EDA. They used different feature selection techniques and machine learning to classify emotional valence and arousal. The authors reported that the Mel-Frequency Cepstral Coefficients (MFCC) outperformed other features. In summary, time-frequency features of EDA in association with machine learning can be a potentially powerful tool for automatic emotion recognition.

Seizure Detection

Epileptic seizures cause significant changes in ANS function and often cause symptoms such as flushing, sweating, and piloerection (Loddenkemper et al., 2004; Wannamaker, 1985). Poh, Loddenkemper, et al. (2010) collected EDA data in patients and observed that epileptic seizures induced a surge in EDA amplitudes. This study also found that a generalized tonic-clonic seizure induced a massive sympathetic discharge. Their work was the first to illustrate the use of EDA for seizure detection. Meisel et al. (2020) collected multimodal data such as EDA, body temperature, and blood volume pulse from epilepsy patients' wristbands and used machine learning techniques, including 1D-convolutional neural network and long short-term memory (LSTM), to predict epileptic seizure. There have been a few other studies (Nasseri et al., 2021; van Andel et al., 2017; Vandecasteele et al., 2017) that used ambulatory EDA alone or with other modalities such as ECG and PPG for seizure prediction.

Recently our group published interesting results on prediction of seizures in rats caused by exposure to hyperbaric oxygen (Posada-Quintero et al., 2022). This study collected EDA data on rats while they were breathing 100% oxygen at hyperbaric pressure which caused central nervous system oxygen toxicity leading to generalized seizures. This study captured the EDA dynamics over time using TVsymp and observed a significant increase in its amplitude approximately two minutes before the seizure occurred, as noted by the experts. This result motivated us to explore similar predictive capability using EDA on humans. Our group performed hyperbaric oxygen experiments on human subjects until either a maximum time of 120 minutes or when the subject started showing symptoms associated with oxygen toxicity (Posada-Quintero, Derrick, et al., 2021). This study reported similar sudden and large increase in EDA amplitudes as observed in rats, about one minute prior to expert adjudication noting the symptoms associated with oxygen toxicity. These findings are exciting, as the EDA device can potentially be used for prediction of seizures related to oxygen toxicity while scuba diving after prebreathing oxygen to prevent decompression sickness.

Challenges and Limitations of Using EDA

The main challenges and limitations of technologies based on EDA can be summarized by two factors: reduced specificity due to motion artifacts and other confounding sympathetic-induced reactions seen in EDA, and lack of validation involving large populations. First, the sensitivity of EDA to sympathetic arousal is at the same time linked to its main limitation. When a pain assessment based on EDA is examined, for example, in many instances the observed reaction in the EDA signal is also a byproduct of expectations and stress as well as pain itself. The challenge in this case is developing features based on signal processing tools that are more specifically linked to the phenomena being assessed (e.g., SCRs with abnormal amplitude, slope, spectral content) and using multimodal approaches (e.g., incorporating heart rate) to rule out other sources of sympathetic reaction using the patterns of reaction produced in different signals.

Secondly, none of the tools for pain, seizures, stress, emotions, etc., have been validated in large populations. Different scenarios can create data corruption and MA that need to be identified and corrected before the technologies can be used with confidence. Furthermore, studies involving large populations will allow better generalizability of the chosen machine/deep learning models. Finally, although there is some preliminary evidence of the production of SCRs from the innervation of sympathetic nerves, a more in-depth understanding of the functioning of the physiology behind the tonic and phasic changes of EDA is necessary to foster better acceptability and generalization of the technique.

Conclusions

EDA has become increasingly popular over the last few decades and has found its way into many exciting applications. However, as previously discussed in this chapter, motion and noise artifacts are a big challenge in EDA analysis. With the advancement of deep learning techniques, such as the convolutional autoencoder, a significant amount of corrupted data can be recovered. Innovations should be made in terms of data collection as well. For example, finding the best recording sites and incorporating accelerometers that could be used for identifying and removing MA continue to be active research areas. Regarding EDA analysis, time-varying spectral features have been particularly useful, as the dynamics of the signal are transient and related to the duration of the stimuli. Application of machine learning has enabled more accurate classification of different psychophysiological events. With ambulatory monitoring being so popular nowadays, and allowing collection of even greater amounts of data, it is timely to explore more advanced deep learning techniques in EDA research. Moreover, given the success of EDA research over the last few years, it is also timely to develop the next generation of wearables. There have been a number of exciting developments in EDA applications involving wearables and smartphones recently, but the number of research works is still limited. We envision that wearable and smartphone applications for EDA will be an exciting and growing research area in the coming years.

References

Amin, Md. R., & Faghih, R. T. (2021). Identification of sympathetic nervous system activation from skin conductance: A sparse decomposition approach with physiological priors. *IEEE Transactions on Biomedical Engineering, 68*(5), 1726–1736. https://doi.org/10.1109/TBME.2020.3034632

(2022). Physiological characterization of electrodermal activity enables scalable near real-time autonomic nervous system activation inference. *PLOS Computational Biology, 18*(7), e1010275. https://doi.org/10.1371/journal.pcbi.1010275

Bach, D. R., Daunizeau, J., Kuelzow, N., Friston, K. J., & Dolan, R. J. (2011). Dynamic causal modeling of spontaneous fluctuations in skin conductance. *Psychophysiology, 48*(2), 252–257. https://doi.org/10.1111/j.1469-8986.2010.01052.x

Beauchaine, T. P., Neuhaus, E., Gatzke-Kopp, L. M., Reid, M. J., Chipman, J., Brekke, A., et al. (2015). Electrodermal responding predicts responses to, and may be altered by, preschool intervention for ADHD. *Journal of Consulting and Clinical Psychology, 83*, 293–303. https://doi.org/10.1037/a0038405

Boucsein, W. (2012). *Electrodermal Activity*, 2nd ed. Springer. https://doi.org/10.1007/978-1-4614-1126-0

Boucsein, W., Fowles, D. C., Grimnes, S., Ben-Shakhar, G., Roth, W. T., Dawson, M. E., et al. (2012). Publication recommendations for electrodermal measurements. *Psychophysiology, 49*(8), 1017–1034. https://doi.org/10.1111/j.1469-8986.2012.01384.x

Braithwaite, J., Watson, D., Robert, J., & Mickey, R. (2015). *A Guide for Analysing Electrodermal Activity (EDA) & Skin Conductance Responses (SCRs) for Psychological Experiments*, rev. ed. Technical Report, Selective Attention & Awareness Laboratory, Behavioural Brain Sciences Centre, University of Birmingham. www.birmingham.ac.uk/documents/college-les/psych/saal/guide-electrodermal-activity.pdf

Chen, W., Jaques, N., Taylor, S., Sano, A., Fedor, S., & Picard, R. W. (2015). Wavelet-based motion artifact removal for electrodermal activity. In *37th Annual International Conference of the IEEE Engineering in Medicine and Biology Society* (pp. 6223–6226). IEEE. https://doi.org/10.1109/EMBC.2015.7319814

Chiang, H.-T., Hsieh, Y.-Y., Fu, S.-W., Hung, K.-H., Tsao, Y., & Chien, S.-Y. (2019). Noise reduction in ECG signals using fully convolutional denoising autoencoders. *IEEE Access, 7*, 60806–60813. https://doi.org/10.1109/ACCESS.2019.2912036

Choi, J., Ahmed, B., & Gutierrez-Osuna, R. (2012). Development and evaluation of an ambulatory stress monitor based on wearable sensors. *IEEE Transactions on Information Technology in Biomedicine, 16*(2), 279–286. https://doi.org/10.1109/TITB.2011.2169804

Das, P., Khasnobish, A., & Tibarewala, D. N. (2016). Emotion recognition employing ECG and GSR signals as markers of ANS. In *2016 Conference on Advances in Signal Processing (CASP)* (pp. 37–42). IEEE. https://doi.org/10.1109/CASP.2016.7746134

Dubé, A.-A., Duquette, M., Roy, M., Lepore, F., Duncan, G., & Rainville, P. (2009). Brain activity associated with the electrodermal reactivity to acute heat pain. *NeuroImage*, *45*(1), 169–180. https://doi.org/10.1016/j.neuroimage.2008.10.024

Dupuy, F. E., Clarke, A. R., Barry, R. J., Selikowitz, M., & McCarthy, R. (2014). EEG and electrodermal activity in girls with Attention-Deficit/Hyperactivity Disorder. *Clinical Neurophysiology*, *125*(3), 491–499. https://doi.org/10.1016/j.clinph.2013.09.007

Dutta, S., Mishra, B. K., Mitra, A., & Chakraborty, A. (2022). An analysis of emotion recognition based on GSR signal. *ECS Transactions*, *107*(1), 12535. https://doi.org/10.1149/10701.12535ecst

Elvebakk, O., Tronstad, C., Birkeland, K. I., Jenssen, T. G., Bjørgaas, M. R., Frøslie, K. F., et al. (2018). Evaluation of hypoglycaemia with non-invasive sensors in people with Type 1 diabetes and impaired awareness of hypoglycaemia. *Scientific Reports*, *8*(1). https://doi.org/10.1038/s41598-018-33189-1

Feng, X., Zhang, Y., & Glass, J. (2014). Speech feature denoising and dereverberation via deep autoencoders for noisy reverberant speech recognition. In *2014 IEEE International Conference on Acoustics, Speech and Signal Processing (ICASSP)* (pp. 1759–1763). IEEE. https://doi.org/10.1109/ICASSP.2014.6853900

Freixa i Baqué, E. (1983). Reliability of spontaneous electrodermal activity in humans as a function of sleep stages. *Biological Psychology*, *17*(2), 137–143. https://doi.org/10.1016/0301-0511(83)90014-5

Frewin, D. B., & Downey, J. A. (1976). Sweating – physiology and pathophysiology. *Australasian Journal of Dermatology*, *17*(3), 82–86. https://doi.org/10.1111/j.1440-0960.1976.tb00794.x

Ganapathy, N., Veeranki, Y. R., Kumar, H., & Swaminathan, R. (2021). Emotion recognition using electrodermal activity signals and multiscale deep convolutional neural network. *Journal of Medical Systems*, *45*(4), 49. https://doi.org/10.1007/s10916-020-01676-6

Gjoreski, M., Gjoreski, H., Luštrek, M., & Gams, M. (2016). Continuous stress detection using a wrist device: In laboratory and real life. In *Proceedings of the 2016 ACM International Joint Conference on Pervasive and Ubiquitous Computing: Adjunct* (pp. 1185–1193). ACM. https://doi.org/10.1145/2968219.2968306

Greco, A., Valenza, G., Lanata, A., Scilingo, E. P., & Citi, L. (2016). cvxEDA: A convex optimization approach to electrodermal activity processing. *IEEE Transactions on Biomedical Engineering*, *63*(4), 797–804. https://doi.org/10.1109/TBME.2015.2474131

Harker, M. (2013). Psychological sweating: A systematic review focused on aetiology and cutaneous response. *Skin Pharmacology and Physiology*, *26*(2), 92–100. https://doi.org/10.1159/000346930

Healey, J., Nachman, L., Subramanian, S., Shahabdeen, J., & Morris, M. (2010). Out of the lab and into the fray: Towards modeling emotion in everyday life. In P. Floréen, A. Krüger, & M. Spasojevic (eds.), *Pervasive Computing* (pp. 156–173). Springer. https://doi.org/10.1007/978-3-642-12654-3_10

Herlan, A., Ottenbacher, J., Schneider, J., Riemann, D., & Feige, B. (2019). Electrodermal activity patterns in sleep stages and their utility for sleep versus wake classification. *Journal of Sleep Research*, *28*(2), e12694. https://doi.org/10.1111/jsr.12694

Hernandez, J., Morris, R. R., & Picard, R. W. (2011). Call center stress recognition with person-specific models. In S. D'Mello, A. Graesser, B. Schuller, & J.-C. Martin (eds.), *Affective Computing and Intelligent Interaction* (pp. 125–134). Springer. https://doi.org/10.1007/978-3-642-24600-5_16

Hernando-Gallego, F., Luengo, D., & Artés-Rodríguez, A. (2018). Feature extraction of galvanic skin responses by nonnegative sparse deconvolution. *IEEE Journal of Biomedical and Health Informatics, 22*(5), 1385–1394. https://doi.org/10.1109/JBHI.2017.2780252

Hossain, M.-B., Kong, Y., Posada-Quintero, H. F., & Chon, K. H. (2022). Comparison of electrodermal activity from multiple body locations based on standard EDA indices' quality and robustness against motion artifact. *Sensors, 22*(9). https://doi.org/10.3390/s22093177

Hossain, M. B., Posada-Quintero, H., & Chon, K. (2022a). A deep convolutional autoencoder for automatic motion artifact removal in electrodermal activity. *IEEE Transactions on Biomedical Engineering, 69*(12), 3601–3611. https://doi.org/10.1109/TBME.2022.3174509

(2022b). A deep convolutional autoencoder for motion artifact removal in electrodermal activity signals: A preliminary study. *IEEE Transactions on Biomedical Engineering, 69*(12), 3601–3611.

Hossain, M. B., Posada-Quintero, H. F., Kong, Y., McNaboe, R., & Chon, K. (2021). A preliminary study on automatic motion artifacts detection in electrodermal activity data using machine learning. In *43rd Annual International Conference of the IEEE Engineering in Medicine and Biology Society* (pp. 6920–6923). IEEE. https://doi.org/10.1109/EMBC46164.2021.9629513

(2022). Automatic motion artifact detection in electrodermal activity data using machine learning. *Biomedical Signal Processing and Control, 74*, 103483. https://doi.org/10.1016/j.bspc.2022.103483

Jang, E.-H., Park, B.-J., Park, M.-S., Kim, S.-H., & Sohn, J.-H. (2015). Analysis of physiological signals for recognition of boredom, pain, and surprise emotions. *Journal of Physiological Anthropology, 34*(1). https://doi.org/10.1186/s40101-015-0063-5

Jaques, N., Taylor, S., Azaria, A., Ghandeharioun, A., Sano, A., & Picard, R. (2015). Predicting students' happiness from physiology, phone, mobility, and behavioral data. In *2015 International Conference on Affective Computing and Intelligent Interaction (ACII)* (pp. 222–228). IEEE. https://doi.org/10.1109/ACII.2015.7344575

Kasos, K., Kekecs, Z., Csirmaz, L., Zimonyi, S., Vikor, F., Kasos, E., et al. (2020). Bilateral comparison of traditional and alternate electrodermal measurement sites. *Psychophysiology, 57*(11), e13645. https://doi.org/10.1111/psyp.13645

Kasos, K., Kekecs, Z., Kasos, E., Szekely, A., & Varga, K. (2018). Bilateral electrodermal activity in the active-alert hypnotic induction. *International Journal of Clinical and Experimental Hypnosis, 66*(3), 282–297. https://doi.org/10.1080/00207144.2018.1460551

Kim, A. Y., Jang, E. H., Kim, S., Choi, K. W., Jeon, H. J., Yu, H. Y., & Byun, S. (2018). Automatic detection of major depressive disorder using electrodermal activity. *Scientific Reports, 8*(1). https://doi.org/10.1038/s41598-018-35147-3

Kim, H., Kwon, S., Kwon, Y.-T., & Yeo, W.-H. (2021). Soft wireless bioelectronics and differential electrodermal activity for home sleep monitoring. *Sensors, 21*(2). https://doi.org/10.3390/s21020354

Kleckner, I. R., Jones, R. M., Wilder-Smith, O., Wormwood, J. B., Akcakaya, M., Quigley, K. S., et al. (2018). Simple, transparent, and flexible automated quality assessment procedures for ambulatory electrodermal activity data. *IEEE Transactions on Biomedical Engineering*, *65*(7), 1460–1467. https://doi.org/10.1109/TBME.2017.2758643

Koelstra, S., Muhl, C., Soleymani, M., Lee, J.-S., Yazdani, A., Ebrahimi, T., et al. (2012). DEAP: A database for emotion analysis; using physiological signals. *IEEE Transactions on Affective Computing*, *3*(1), 18–31. https://doi.org/10.1109/T-AFFC.2011.15

Kong, Y., Posada-Quintero, H. F., & Chon, K. H. (2020). Pain Detection using a Smartphone in Real Time*. *2020 42nd Annual International Conference of the IEEE Engineering in Medicine Biology Society (EMBC)*, 4526–4529. https://doi.org/10.1109/EMBC44109.2020.9176077

(2021a). Sensitive physiological indices of pain based on differential characteristics of electrodermal activity. *IEEE Transactions on Biomedical Engineering*, 3122–3130. https://doi.org/10.1109/TBME.2021.3065218

(2021b). Real-time high-level acute pain detection using a smartphone and a wrist-worn electrodermal activity sensor. *Sensors*, *21*(12). https://doi.org/10.3390/s21123956

Koumans, A. J. R., Tursky, B., & Solomon, P. (1968). Electrodermal levels and fluctuations during normal sleep. *Psychophysiology*, *5*(3), 300–306. https://doi.org/10.1111/j.1469-8986.1968.tb02826.x

Lee, J., Sun, S., Yang, S. M., Sohn, J. J., Park, J., Lee, S., & Kim, H. C. (2019). Bidirectional recurrent auto-encoder for photoplethysmogram denoising. *IEEE Journal of Biomedical and Health Informatics*, *23*(6), 2375–2385. https://doi.org/10.1109/JBHI.2018.2885139

Li, J., Struzik, Z., Zhang, L., & Cichocki, A. (2015). Feature learning from incomplete EEG with denoising autoencoder. *Neurocomputing*, *165*, 23–31. https://doi.org/10.1016/j.neucom.2014.08.092

Liu, J. C. J., Verhulst, S., Massar, S. A. A., & Chee, M. W. L. (2015). Sleep deprived and sweating it out: The effects of total sleep deprivation on skin conductance reactivity to psychosocial stress. *Sleep*, *38*(1), 155–159. https://doi.org/10.5665/sleep.4346

Liu, Y., & Du, S. (2018). Psychological stress level detection based on electrodermal activity. *Behavioural Brain Research*, *341*, 50–53. https://doi.org/10.1016/j.bbr.2017.12.021

Llanes-Jurado, J., Carrasco-Ribelles, L. A., Alcañiz, M., & Marín-Morales, J. (2021). Automatic artifact recognition and correction for electrodermal activity in uncontrolled environments [preprint].

Loddenkemper, T., Kellinghaus, C., Gandjour, J., Nair, D. R., Najm, I. M., Bingaman, W., & Lüders, H. O. (2004). Localising and lateralising value of ictal piloerection. *Journal of Neurology, Neurosurgery & Psychiatry*, *75*(6), 879–883. https://doi.org/10.1136/jnnp.2003.023333

Meisel, C., El Atrache, R., Jackson, M., Schubach, S., Ufongene, C., & Loddenkemper, T. (2020). Machine learning from wristband sensor data for wearable, noninvasive seizure forecasting. *Epilepsia*, *61*(12), 2653–2666. https://doi.org/10.1111/epi.16719

Melander, C. A., Kikhia, B., Olsson, M., Wälivaara, B.-M., & Sävenstedt, S. (2018). The impact of using measurements of electrodermal activity in the assessment of problematic behaviour in dementia. *Dementia and Geriatric Cognitive Disorders Extra*, *8*(3), 333–347. https://doi.org/10.1159/000493339

Miranda-Correa, J. A., Abadi, M. K., Sebe, N., & Patras, I. (2021). AMIGOS: A dataset for affect, personality and mood research on individuals and groups. *IEEE Transactions* on *Affective Computing, 12*(2), 479–493. https://doi.org/10.1109/TAFFC.2018.2884461

Momin, A., Bhattacharya, S., Sanyal, S., & Chakraborty, P. (2020). Visual attention, mental stress and gender: A study using physiological signals. *IEEE Access, 8*, 165973–165988. https://doi.org/10.1109/ACCESS.2020.3022727

Munsters, J., Wallström, L., Ågren, J., Norsted, T., & Sindelar, R. (2012). Skin conductance measurements as pain assessment in newborn infants born at 22–27weeks gestational age at different postnatal age. *Early Human Development, 88*(1), 21–26. https://doi.org/10.1016/j.earlhumdev.2011.06.010

Murali, N. S., Svatikova, A., & Somers, V. K. (2003). Cardiovascular physiology and sleep. *Frontiers in Bioscience-Landmark, 8*(6). https://doi.org/10.2741/1105

Nahman-Averbuch, H., & Coghill, R. C. (2017). Pain-autonomic relationships: Implications for experimental design and the search for an "objective marker" for pain. *PAIN, 158*(11), 2064–2065. https://doi.org/10.1097/j.pain.0000000000001035

Nasseri, M., Pal Attia, T., Joseph, B., Gregg, N. M., Nurse, E. S., Viana, P. F., et al. (2021). Ambulatory seizure forecasting with a wrist-worn device using long-short term memory deep learning. *Scientific Reports, 11*(1), 1–9.

Nickel, M. M., May, E. S., Tiemann, L., Postorino, M., Ta Dinh, S., & Ploner, M. (2017). Autonomic responses to tonic pain are more closely related to stimulus intensity than to pain intensity. *PAIN, 158*(11), 2129–2136. https://doi.org/10.1097/j.pain.0000000000001010

Perugia, G., Rodríguez-Martín, D., Díaz Boladeras, M., Mallofré, A. C., Barakova, E., & Rauterberg, M. (2017). Electrodermal activity: Explorations in the psychophysiology of engagement with social robots in dementia. In *26th IEEE International Symposium on Robot and Human Interactive Communication (RO-MAN)* (pp. 1248–1254). IEEE. https://doi.org/10.1109/ROMAN.2017.8172464

Poh, M.-Z., Loddenkemper, T., Reinsberger, C., Swenson, N. C., Goyal, S., Sabtala, M. C., et al. (2012). Convulsive seizure detection using a wrist-worn electrodermal activity and accelerometry biosensor. *Epilepsia, 53*(5), e93–e97. https://doi.org/10.1111/j.1528-1167.2012.03444.x

Poh, M.-Z., Loddenkemper, T., Swenson, N. C., Goyal, S., Madsen, J. R., & Picard, R. W. (2010). Continuous monitoring of electrodermal activity during epileptic seizures using a wearable sensor. In *2010 Annual International Conference of the IEEE Engineering in Medicine and Biology Society* (pp. 4415–4418). IEEE. https://doi.org/10.1109/IEMBS.2010.5625988

Poh, M.-Z., Swenson, N. C., & Picard, R. W. (2010). A wearable sensor for unobtrusive, long-term assessment of electrodermal activity. *IEEE Transactions on Biomedical Engineering, 57*(5), 1243–1252. https://doi.org/10.1109/TBME.2009.2038487

Posada-Quintero, H. F., & Chon, K. H. (2020). Innovations in electrodermal activity data collection and signal processing: A systematic review. *Sensors, 20*(2). https://doi.org/10.3390/s20020479

Posada-Quintero, H. F., Derrick, B. J., Winstead-Derlega, C., Gonzalez, S. I., Claire Ellis, M., Freiberger, J. J, & Chon, K. H. (2021). Time-varying spectral index of electrodermal activity to predict central nervous system oxygen toxicity symptoms in divers: Preliminary results. In *43rd Annual International Conference of the IEEE Engineering in Medicine Biology Society* (pp. 1242–1245). IEEE. https://doi.org/10.1109/EMBC46164.2021.9629924

Posada-Quintero, H. F., Florian, J. P., Orjuela-Cañón, A. D., Aljama-Corrales, T., Charleston-Villalobos, S., & Chon, K. H. (2016). Power spectral density analysis of electrodermal activity for sympathetic function assessment. *Annals of Biomedical Engineering, 44*(10), 3124–3135. https://doi.org/10.1007/s10439-016-1606-6

Posada-Quintero, H. F., Florian, J. P., Orjuela-Cañón, A. D., & Chon, K. H. (2018). Electrodermal activity is sensitive to cognitive stress under water. *Frontiers in Physiology, 8*. https://doi.org/10.3389/fphys.2017.01128

Posada-Quintero, H. F., Kong, Y., & Chon, K. H. (2021). Objective pain stimulation intensity and pain sensation assessment using machine learning classification and regression based on electrodermal activity. *American Journal of Physiology – Regulatory, Integrative and Comparative Physiology, 321*(2), R186–R196. https://doi.org/10.1152/ajpregu.00094.2021

Posada-Quintero, H. F., Kong, Y., Nguyen, K., Tran, C., Beardslee, L., Chen, L., et al. (2020). Using electrodermal activity to validate multilevel pain stimulation in healthy volunteers evoked by thermal grills. *American Journal of Physiology – Regulatory, Integrative and Comparative Physiology, 319*(3), R366–R375. https://doi.org/10.1152/ajpregu.00102.2020

Posada-Quintero, H. F., Landon, C. S., Stavitzski, N. M., Dean, J. B., & Chon, K. H. (2022). Seizures caused by exposure to hyperbaric oxygen in rats can be predicted by early changes in electrodermal activity. *Frontiers in Physiology, 12*. https://doi.org/10.3389/fphys.2021.767386

Prince, E. B., Kim, E. S., Wall, C. A., Gisin, E., Goodwin, M. S., Simmons, E. S., et al. (2017). The relationship between autism symptoms and arousal level in toddlers with autism spectrum disorder, as measured by electrodermal activity. *Autism, 21*(4), 504–508. https://doi.org/10.1177/1362361316648816

Reljin, N., Lazaro, J., Hossain, M. D., Noh, Y. S., Cho, C. H., & Chon, K. H. (2020). Using the redundant convolutional encoder–decoder to denoise QRS complexes in ECG signals recorded with an armband wearable device. *Sensors, 20*(16). https://doi.org/10.3390/s20164611

Romine, W., Banerjee, T., & Goodman, G. (2019). Toward sensor-based sleep monitoring with electrodermal activity measures. *Sensors, 19*(6). https://doi.org/10.3390/s19061417

Ruiz-Robledillo, N., & Moya-Albiol, L. (2015). Lower electrodermal activity to acute stress in caregivers of people with autism spectrum disorder: An adaptive habituation to stress. *Journal of Autism and Developmental Disorders, 45*(2), 576–588. https://doi.org/10.1007/s10803-013-1996-3

Saga, K. (2002). Structure and function of human sweat glands studied with histochemistry and cytochemistry. *Progress in Histochemistry and Cytochemistry, 37*(4), 323–386. https://doi.org/10.1016/s0079-6336(02)80005-5

Sano, A., Picard, R. W., & Stickgold, R. (2014). Quantitative analysis of wrist electrodermal activity during sleep. *International Journal of Psychophysiology, 94*(3), 382–389. https://doi.org/10.1016/j.ijpsycho.2014.09.011

Sato, K., Kang, W. H., Saga, K., & Sato, K. T. (1989). Biology of sweat glands and their disorders. I. Normal sweat gland function. *Journal of the American Academy of Dermatology, 20*(4), 537–563. https://doi.org/10.1016/S0190-9622(89)70063-3

Scarpina, F., & Tagini, S. (2017). The Stroop color and word test. *Frontiers in Psychology, 8*, 557. https://doi.org/10.3389/fpsyg.2017.00557

Scharmüller, W., Wabnegger, A., & Schienle, A. (2015). Functional brain connectivity during fear of pain: A comparison between dental phobics and controls. *Brain Connectivity*, *5*(3), 187–191. https://doi.org/10.1089/brain.2014.0297

Schupak, B. M., Parasher, R. K., & Zipp, G. P. (2016). Reliability of electrodermal activity: Quantifying sensory processing in children with autism. *American Journal of Occupational Therapy*, *70*(6), 1–6. https://doi.org/10.5014/ajot.2016.018291

Setz, C., Arnrich, B., Schumm, J., Marca, R. L., Tröster, G., & Ehlert, U. (2010). Discriminating stress from cognitive load using a wearable EDA device. *IEEE Transactions on Information Technology in Biomedicine*, *14*(2), 410–417. https://doi.org/10.1109/TITB.2009.2036164

Shaffer, F., Combatalade, D., Peper, E., & Meehan, Z. M. (2016). A guide to cleaner electrodermal activity measurements. *Biofeedback*, *44*(2), 90–100. https://doi.org/10.5298/1081-5937-44.2.01

Shu, L., Xie, J., Yang, M., Li, Z., Li, Z., Liao, D., et al. (2018). A review of emotion recognition using physiological signals. *Sensors*, *18*(7). https://doi.org/10.3390/s18072074

Shukla, J., Barreda-Angeles, M., Oliver, J., Nandi, G. C., & Puig, D. (2019). Feature extraction and selection for emotion recognition from electrodermal activity. *IEEE Transactions on Affective Computing*, 857–869. https://doi.org/10.1109/TAFFC.2019.2901673

Silvani, A., & Dampney, R. A. L. (2013). Central control of cardiovascular function during sleep. *American Journal of Physiology– Heart and Circulatory Physiology*, *305*(12), H1683–H1692. https://doi.org/10.1152/ajpheart.00554.2013

Somers, V. K., Dyken, M. E., Mark, A. L., & Abboud, F. M. (1993). Sympathetic-nerve activity during sleep in normal subjects. *New England Journal of Medicine*, *328*(5), 303–307. https://doi.org/10.1056/NEJM199302043280502

Subramanian, S., Tseng, B., Barbieri, R., & Brown, E. N. (2021). Unsupervised machine learning methods for artifact removal in electrodermal activity. In *43rd Annual International Conference of the IEEE Engineering in Medicine Biology Society* (pp. 399–402). IEEE. https://doi.org/10.1109/EMBC46164.2021.9630535

(2022). An unsupervised automated paradigm for artifact removal from electrodermal activity in an uncontrolled clinical setting. *Physiological Measurement*, *43*(11) https://doi.org/10.1088/1361-6579/ac92bd

Sugimine, S., Saito, S., & Takazawa, T. (2020). Normalized skin conductance level could differentiate physical pain stimuli from other sympathetic stimuli. *Scientific Reports*, *10*(1). https://doi.org/10.1038/s41598-020-67936-0

Susam, B. T., Akcakaya, M., Nezamfar, H., Diaz, D., Xu, X., de Sa, V. R., et al. (2018). Automated pain assessment using electrodermal activity data and machine learning. In *40th Annual International Conference of the IEEE Engineering in Medicine and Biology Society* (pp. 372–375). IEEE. https://doi.org/10.1109/EMBC.2018.8512389

Taylor, S., Jaques, N., Chen, W., Fedor, S., Sano, A., & Picard, R. (2015). Automatic identification of artifacts in electrodermal activity data. In *37th Annual International Conference of the IEEE Engineering in Medicine and Biology Society* (pp. 1934–1937). IEEE. https://doi.org/10.1109/EMBC.2015.7318762

Theodoros, A. (2014). Electrodermal activity: Applications in perioperative care. *International Journal of Medical Research & Health Sciences*, *3*(3).

Topoglu, Y., Watson, J., Suri, R., & Ayaz, H. (2020). Electrodermal activity in ambulatory settings: A narrative review of literature. In H. Ayaz (ed.), *Advances in*

Neuroergonomics and Cognitive Engineering (pp. 91–102). Springer. https://doi.org/10.1007/978-3-030-20473-0_10

van Andel, J., Ungureanu, C., Arends, J., Tan, F., Van Dijk, J., Petkov, G., et al. (2017). Multimodal, automated detection of nocturnal motor seizures at home: Is a reliable seizure detector feasible? *Epilepsia Open, 2*(4), 424–431.

van Dooren, M., de Vries, J. J. G., & Janssen, J. H. (2012). Emotional sweating across the body: Comparing 16 different skin conductance measurement locations. *Physiology & Behavior, 106*(2), 298–304. https://doi.org/10.1016/j.physbeh.2012.01.020

Vandecasteele, K., De Cooman, T., Gu, Y., Cleeren, E., Claes, K., Van Paesschen, et al. (2017). Automated epileptic seizure detection based on wearable ECG and PPG in a hospital environment. *Sensors, 17*(10).

Veeranki, Y. R., Ganapathy, N., & Swaminathan, R. (2021). Electrodermal activity based emotion recognition using time-frequency methods and machine learning algorithms. *Current Directions in Biomedical Engineering, 7*(2), 863–866. https://doi.org/10.1515/cdbme-2021-2220

Vincent, P., Larochelle, H., Lajoie, I., Bengio, Y., & Manzagol, P.-A. (2010). Stacked denoising autoencoders: Learning useful representations in a deep network with a local denoising criterion. *Journal of Machine Learning Research, 11*, 3371–3408.

von Polier, G. G., Biskup, C. S., Kötting, W. F., Bubenzer, S., Helmbold, K., Eisert, A., et al. (2014). Change in electrodermal activity after acute tryptophan depletion associated with aggression in young people with attention deficit hyperactivity disorder (ADHD). *Journal of Neural Transmission, 121*(4), 451–455. https://doi.org/10.1007/s00702-013-1119-5

Wang, Y., Yao, H., & Zhao, S. (2016). Auto-encoder based dimensionality reduction. *Neurocomputing, 184*, 232–242. https://doi.org/10.1016/j.neucom.2015.08.104

Wannamaker, B. B. (1985). Autonomic nervous system and epilepsy. *Epilepsia, 26*(s1), S31–S39. https://doi.org/10.1111/j.1528-1157.1985.tb05722.x

Wendt, J., Lotze, M., Weike, A. I., Hosten, N., & Hamm, A. O. (2008). Brain activation and defensive response mobilization during sustained exposure to phobia-related and other affective pictures in spider phobia. *Psychophysiology, 45*(2), 205–215. https://doi.org/10.1111/j.1469-8986.2007.00620.x

Wickramasuriya, D. S., & Faghih, R. T. (2020). A marked point process filtering approach for tracking sympathetic arousal from skin conductance. *IEEE Access, 8*, 68499–68513. https://doi.org/10.1109/ACCESS.2020.2984508

Wu, G., Liu, G., & Hao, M. (2010). The analysis of emotion recognition from GSR based on PSO. In *2010 International Symposium on Intelligence Information Processing and Trusted Computing* (pp. 360–363). IEEE. https://doi.org/10.1109/IPTC.2010.60

Xia, V., Jaques, N., Taylor, S., Fedor, S., & Picard, R. (2015). Active learning for electrodermal activity classification. In *2015 IEEE Signal Processing in Medicine and Biology Symposium* (pp. 1–6). https://doi.org/10.1109/SPMB.2015.7405467

Yang, T. T., Simmons, A. N., Matthews, S. C., Tapert, S. F., Bischoff-Grethe, A., Frank, G. K. W., et al. (2007). Increased amygdala activation is related to heart rate during emotion processing in adolescent subjects. *Neuroscience Letters, 428*(2), 109–114. https://doi.org/10.1016/j.neulet.2007.09.039

Zhang, Y., Haghdan, M., & Xu, K. S. (2017). Unsupervised motion artifact detection in wrist-measured electrodermal activity data. In *Proceedings of the 2017 ACM International Symposium on Wearable Computers* (pp. 54–57). ACM. https://doi.org/10.1145/3123021.3123054

22 Surface Electromyography

Joseph S. Baschnagel, Moet Aita, and Michael McTighe

Abstract

Surface electromyography (EMG) measurements provide a non-invasive way to measure physical behavior in a way that is more sensitive and less prone to bias compared to observational methods. This chapter covers the use of EMG in social and behavioral research. First, the biological underpinnings of muscle activity are briefly reviewed to give the reader a basic understanding of the signal being measured. Next, the steps for obtaining the EMG signal are covered, including equipment and signal processing. Finally, some common use cases of EMG measures in social and behavioral research are reviewed. With modern-day equipment, EMG measures can be collected both in the traditional laboratory setting and, when signal noise concerns are acknowledged, in the "real world."

Keywords: Electromyography, EMG, Psychophysiology, Muscle, Movement

In the social and behavioral sciences, there are three primary areas of assessment that can be used to study human behavior and experience – self-report measures, behavioral measures, and psychophysiological measures. Self-report measures, such as interviews and surveys, enable us to sample cognitive processes and individual experiences that we cannot directly observe (see Chapters 15 and 16 in this volume). Behavioral measures, such as reaction time or approach/avoidance behaviors, allow us to quantify observable phenomena performed by the individuals under study. Both of these approaches provide valuable information to those aiming to understand human experience, but both also share limitations. The primary limitation is the degree to which self-report and behavior can be voluntarily modified based on external influences, such as social desirability (Paulhus, 1984). When asking a person fearful of spiders how afraid they are of a spider presented to them, depending on the situation, they may be motivated to report very little fear to maintain an image of being a strong person and adjust their behavior accordingly. However, if we were to measure their physiology, we might see a high level of arousal present. While one might change their behavior in a specific context to act in a more socially acceptable manner, it is much harder to control one's automatic physiological responses. One of the strengths of measuring physiological responses is that they are much more difficult to voluntarily influence.

There are many peripheral psychophysiological measures one can use in studying behavior. One commonly used measure is electromyography (EMG). EMG is a measure of the electrical potential generated when muscles contract. This measure can be used to assess reflexes, voluntary movements, muscle tonus and tension, and fatigue in skeletal muscles. The use of EMG can be a useful addition to observational methods, as EMG can be measured continuously without participant effort, potentially be more reliable than observer coding, allow for time course analyses, and potentially indicate responses that would be imperceptible to visual observation (Tassinary et al., 2007). The EMG measure can be used to study various constructs and behaviors, such as emotional states, facial expressions, attention, reaction time, and human–machine interactions. The following chapter reviews the neurobiological bases of skeletal muscle activity, discusses the basics of surface EMG signal measurement, and highlights a few applications of EMG measurement in behavioral research.

Neurobiological Bases of Skeletal Muscle Activity

Neuro-control of the skeletal muscular system is complex, and a full review is beyond the scope of this chapter. However, we give a brief overview of the neurobiological bases of muscle activity here. Muscle activity can be either under voluntary control or elicited as part of a reflex. At the central nervous system level, muscle control is overseen by two main tracts: the pyramidal tract and the extrapyramidal tract. The pyramidal tract is important for initiation of movements and control of fine motor movements. This tract originates in the primary motor cortex – a cortical area that maps out the body and where most complex motor movements are initiated (AbuHasan & Munakomi, 2022). The primary motor cortex codes for behavioral intent, and neuronal activity can be seen in this region in patients who are paralyzed when they are thinking of specific motor movements (Sabbah et al., 2002).

Many movements that are automatic, such as the constant changes in muscle tension needed to balance while walking, are controlled through reflexes and central pattern generators; these are mostly mediated through relatively simple neuronal circuits in the spinal cord. These actions are triggered by either external stimuli or sensory receptors that monitor the relative tension and stretch of our muscles. The reflexes can often be moderated by central nervous system input. Later in this chapter, we will discuss the startle reflex which is commonly used in psychophysiological research on attention and emotion.

Motor neurons that project from the spinal cord synapse at neuromuscular junctions of muscle fibers (i.e., muscle cells) where they release acetylcholine as the neurotransmitter. The ratio of motor neurons synapsing on muscle fibers impacts the precision of movement possible, with lower ratios (e.g., 1 motor neuron to 3 muscle fibers) resulting in more precise movements, such as that seen in eye movements, and higher ratios (e.g., 1 motor neuron to 1,000 muscle fibers) resulting in lower precision, as seen in larger muscles, such as a bicep. The combination of the motor neuron and all of the muscle fibers it enervates is referred to as a motor unit.

Muscles are made up of multiple fasciculi – groups of muscle fibers bundled together. Each muscle fiber is made up of a large number of myofibrils – groups of protein molecules called myosin filaments and actin filaments (see Figure 22.1).

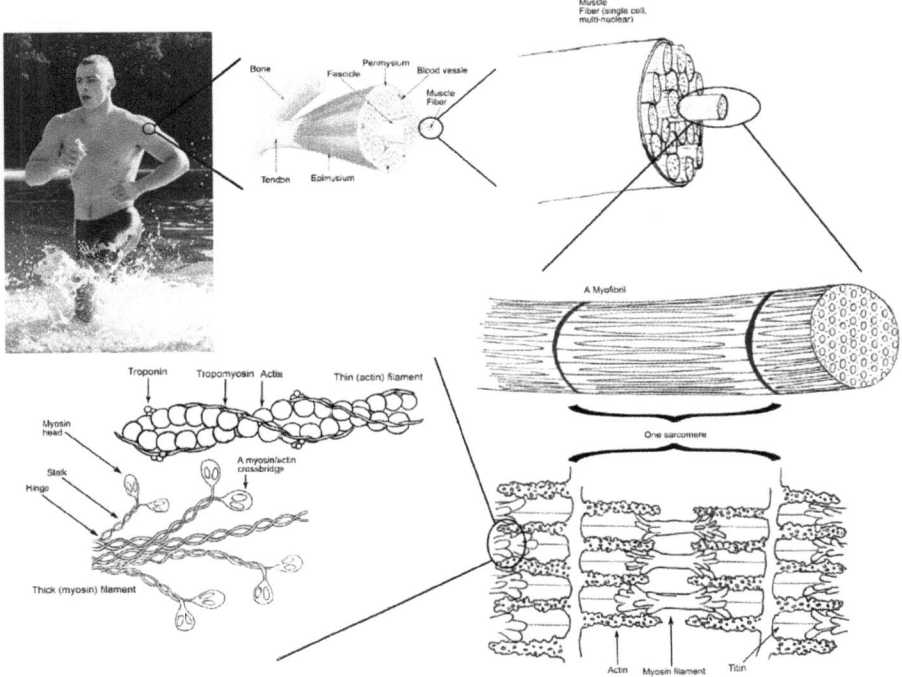

Figure 22.1 *Skeletal muscle anatomy.*

When a motor unit is activated, acetylcholine released by the motor neuron makes the muscle fiber membrane (i.e., sarcoplasm) more permeable to sodium. This leads to a depolarization of the muscle cell, allowing calcium ions into the sarcoplasm; that in turn causes the actin filaments to slide into spaces next to the myosin fibrils. This results in a muscle contraction (Jacob and Francone, 1970). The enzyme acetylcholinesterase breaks down acetylcholine at the neuromuscular junction, allowing the process to start over again. The electrical potentials that are generated by this muscle contraction are what is measured in electromyography.

Electromyography

There are multiple ways to measure EMG signals. The activity of single motor units can be measured invasively with needle electrodes inserted into the muscle. This form of measurement is typically used in clinical medicine and/or physiology research but not often used when studying behavioral and psychological processes due to its invasive nature. Most behavioral scientists will use a more minimally invasive and safer alternative method of measurement that uses surface electrodes; we will focus on that here. Note that this section provides the procedures one would use to apply EMG measurement and is the basis of all applications of

Table 22.1 *A summary of steps for implementing EMG measurement*

Step 1: Determine the purpose of the study and the muscles to be measured.
Step 2: Prepare the participant by cleaning the skin at the site where electrodes will be placed.
    a. Lightly abrade skin with exfoliating gel.
    b. Rub a thin layer of electrode gel into the skin where each electrode will be placed. Wipe off any excess so the electrode tabs will stick to the skin and make sure the gel does not bridge the two electrodes.
Step 3: Apply surface EMG electrodes to the skin overlying the muscles of interest.
    a. Place electrode tabs to electrodes.
    b. Fill electrodes with electrode gel.
    c. Place electrodes. Be sure electrodes run along the length of the muscle fibers, not across muscle fibers.
Step 4: Connect the electrodes to an EMG amplifier and ensure that the signal is being recorded properly.
    a. Set amplifier gain. Higher gain for smaller muscles, lower gain for larger muscles.
    b. Set filter settings on hardware or software.
    a. Low-pass filter – 500 Hz (though may depend on your specific needs).
    b. High-pass filter – 28 Hz
    c. Set sampling rate – at least 2× the highest frequency in your signal. Typically 1,000 Hz when using a low-pass filter of 500 Hz.
Step 5: Instruct the participant to perform specific movements or tasks to elicit muscle activity.
    a. Minimize extraneous body movements.
Step 6: Record the EMG data during the task or movement.
Step 7: Filter and process the EMG signal to remove noise and extract relevant features.
    a. Use a 50 or 60 Hz digital notch filter to reduce electromagnetic noise
    b. Follow your software's guidelines for rectifying and integrating your signal.
Step 8: Analyze the EMG data to quantify muscle activity, such as amplitude and timing characteristics.
    a. For amplitude, subtract the baseline measure (i.e., average EMG a few seconds before response onset) from the response peak.
    b. For timing, measure delay from stimulus onset to response onset, or stimulus onset to response peak.
    c. Compare EMG responses across your experimental conditions.
Step 9: Interpret the results and draw conclusions based on the research question or hypothesis.

EMG covered in the application section that follows. Table 22.1 provides an outline of the procedure.

Surface electrodes are attached to the skin with adhesive electrode gel or double-sided adhesive tabs that stick the electrode to the skin over the muscle of interest. Modern electrodes are typically made from silver-silver chloride (Ag-AgCl) material encased in a small plastic cup that is attached to a wire lead. These electrodes come in reusable forms or as one-use disposable options. They are designed to minimize electric potentials that are generated at the surface of the skin by the electrodes themselves. These come in variable-sized diameters that can range from 2 millimeters up to a centimeter, with smaller sizes used to measure smaller muscles or smaller numbers of motor units and larger sizes for larger muscles or for measuring a larger group of motor units.

Electrode Placement

The EMG signal is a measurement of the electrical potential difference between a pair of electrodes. These electrodes can be placed in either a monopolar or a bipolar arrangement. In a monopolar arrangement, one electrode is placed over the active measurement site, and the other is placed on a relatively non-active site, such as over a bone. In the more commonly used bipolar placement, the focus of this chapter, both electrodes are placed over the active muscle. Because these electrodes are placed on the surface of the skin, they pick up the sum of electrical potentials from a number of motor units, and potentially other biological potentials, located below and between the two electrodes. Thus, placement of the electrodes is important, as the position of the electrodes and the distance between them will determine which muscles will contribute to the measurement as well as the magnitude of the signal that is collected.

Choice of electrode size and distance of electrode placement will be dictated by the size of the muscle of interest and the purpose of measurement. Closer placement allows for more precise measurement of fewer motor units or smaller-sized muscles (e.g., eye muscle when measuring startle eye-blink responses); farther placement allows for better measurement of full muscle tension (e.g., shoulder muscles when studying muscle tension in biofeedback applications). The direction of the muscle fibers runs from the one muscle insertion point to the other, and an electrode pair should be placed over the same muscle, parallel to the muscle fibers. When using EMG as part of a study collecting data across participants, placement should be standardized using anatomical landmarks. For example, if measuring the bicep muscle, electrodes should be placed in the same ratio distance from the elbow and the shoulder in each participant. There have been efforts to standardize EMG electrode placement, and examples can be seen in Tassinary et al. (2007) and the SENIAM project (www.seniam.org; Hermens et al. 2000). See Figure 22.2 for suggested placement of facial EMG electrodes.

Given that surface electrodes are measuring electrical potentials from any muscles below and between them, attributing the EMG signal to any specific muscle group can be difficult. This is particularly true in areas where many muscle groups overlap, such as the back. For this reason, accurate and reliable electrode placement becomes important, and when describing EMG signals it is best to label the measured activity as originating from a region of measurement (e.g., over the corrugator muscle region) versus a specific muscle (Stern et al., 2001).

Surface Preparation

Once the electrode placement site is decided upon, the area of the skin needs to be prepared. Rubbing alcohol or a specifically made abrading gel (e.g., NuPrep, by Weaver and Co.), contained on a manufactured pad or applied to a facial tissue, is used to rub the area of skin of the electrode placement site. This is done to exfoliate

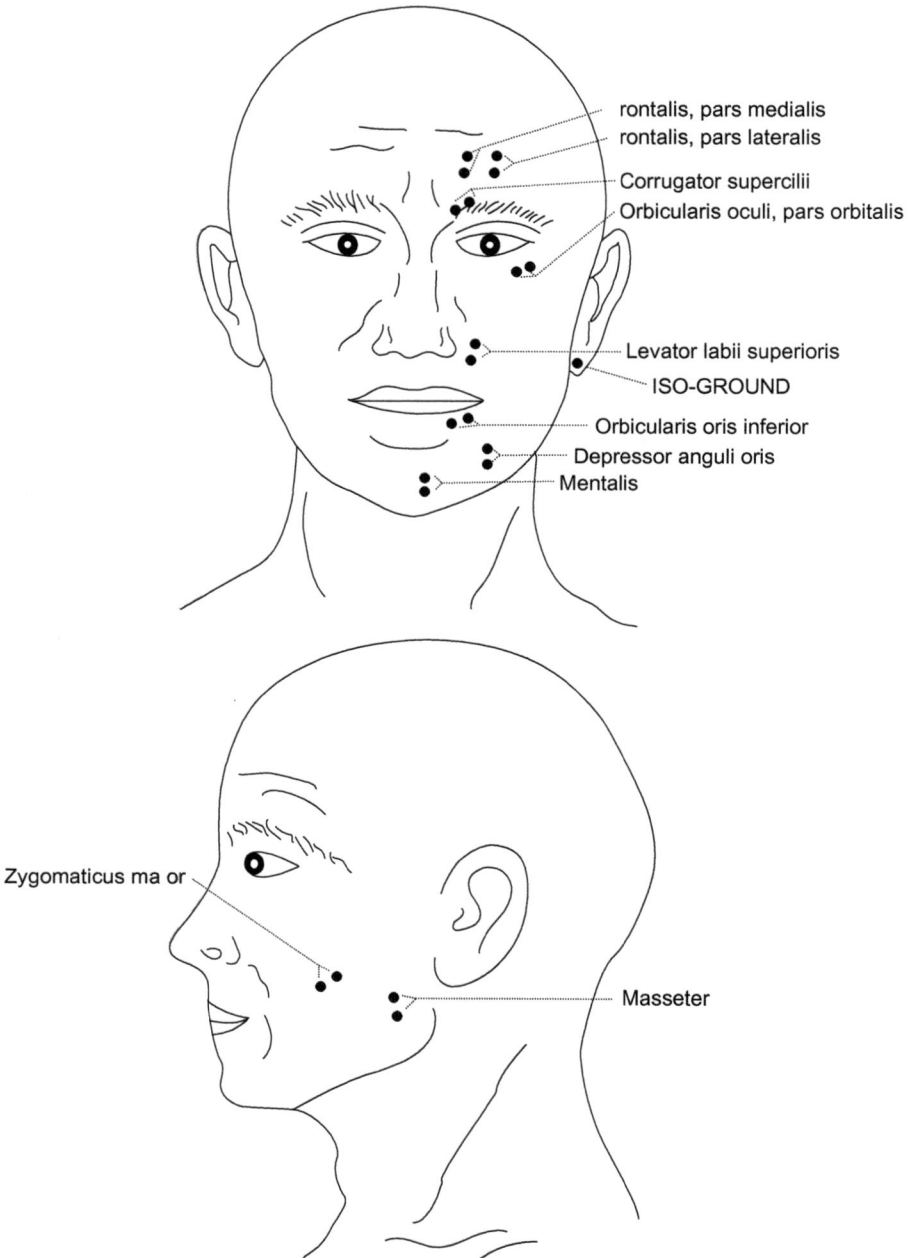

Figure 22.2 *Facial EMG electrode placement. (From Tassinary et al., 2007.)*

and remove dirt and excess oil from the skin. Excess hair may also need to be removed. A thin layer of saline electrode gel or paste is then rubbed into the skin. It is important not to apply too much gel, as this can impact the ability of the electrode tabs to stick to the skin. It is recommended to avoid bridging this layer of gel between the two electrodes as this will reduce the magnitude of the measured signal.

Proper surface preparation helps to reduce surface impedance and reduces signal noise – allowing for a cleaner EMG signal. Once the measurement site is prepped, the electrodes can be placed. It is good practice to check the impedance between electrodes with an impedance meter. A value less than 5,000 Ohms is recommended, with lower values generally better, to maximize signal fidelity. However, impedance values below 1,000 Ohms should be checked for gel bridging between the electrodes or electrodes that are placed too close together (Andreassi, 2013; Fridlund & Cacioppo, 1986).

Equipment and Signal Processing

The typical EMG signal can range from less than 1 μV to 50 μVs but can range higher at times depending on the muscle size and amplification settings. Given the generally small magnitude of EMG signals, they need to be amplified with a bioamplifier to a level that can be adequately converted to a digital signal by an analog to digital converter (i.e., A-D converter). A list of major bioamplifier manufacturers is presented in Table 22.2. Gain settings can typically range between 500 to 5,000×, with smaller signals, such as from smaller facial muscles, requiring greater gain settings than larger signal sources, such as from a bicep. The frequency bandwidth of EMG signals ranges between 15 and 1,000 Hz, with most of the signal power falling between 10 and 200 Hz (Fridlund & Cacioppo, 1986).

Most amplifiers designed for EMG signal amplification will have hardware filters allowing the user to filter the data signal. Low-pass filters are designed to let signal data below a set frequency pass to the A-D converter; high-pass filters allow signal data above a set frequency to pass. Both filters allow for reduction of signal noise generated from other sources, such as other bio-signals (e.g., low-frequency heart rate signals) or from noise generated by the amplifier circuit. Filter settings will vary depending on the application, but generally HP filters of 1,000 Hz, 500 Hz, or 250 Hz and LP filters 10 to 100 Hz can be used. For most recordings, allowing a passband between 10 and 500 Hz is recommended.

After amplification, the EMG signal is then fed to an A-D converter that digitizes the signal for storage and manipulation on a computer. When digitizing an analog

Table 22.2 *Manufacturers of commonly used bioamplifers used in research settings*

ADInstruments, www.adinstruments.com
Biopac, www.biopac.com
Great Lakes NeuroTechnologies, www.glneurotech.com
Medical Expo, www.medicalexpo.com
MindWare Technologies, www.mindwaretech.com

signal, signal resolution (i.e., bit-depth and sampling rate) are important considerations. Luckily for the modern researcher, bit-depth is determined by the equipment manufacturer and is more than sufficient for EMG work. In most equipment, however, the end-user typically still has the option to set the sampling rate of the data acquisition. Sampling rate refers to the number of samples an A-D converter will take over a given period of time, in Hz (i.e., samples per second).

The choice of sampling rate will mainly be determined by the Nyquist frequency – the highest frequency in the signal to be recorded. The minimum sampling rate needs to be two times the maximum frequency in a signal, so if an EMG signal is low-pass filtered by the bioamplifier at 500 Hz, then the minimum sampling rate can be no lower than 1,000 Hz to avoid aliasing artifacts in the signal. In the past, and to a lesser extent currently, the other main determinant of sampling rate choice is digital storage space and processing power. Higher sampling rates result in larger data files that require more storage space and more processing power to analyze. Even with today's powerful computers, unless there is a specific need for high-resolution signals, recording at 2× the Nyquist signal is typically sufficient. Sampling rates are typically set within the data acquisition software.

In addition to setting low- and high-pass filters on the hardware, software researchers often will have the option to apply additional digital filters to the signal. It is important to note that hardware filters are destructive to the signal – that is, once you filter the signal, data is lost. Digital signals can be non-destructive as you can apply them to a copy of the saved raw signal. Oftentimes, notch filters – filters that drastically reduce the signal at a specific frequency – will be applied digitally, as digital filters can be more precise than hardware filters for this purpose. Notch filters are often used to reduce signal noise as mentioned below.

The raw EMG signal will have both negative and positive components to it (see Figure 22.3a). A raw EMG signal can be analyzed by counting individual motor unit spikes in the signal, but this becomes untenable when the motor unit spikes occur frequently close in time and begin to merge together. In most social and behavioral research applications, the raw signal will be full-wave rectified and then smoothed or integrated (see Figure 22.3b). Full-wave signal rectification is the process of taking the absolute value of the waveform values, so all negative components of the signal become positive.

The signal is then typically smoothed with low-pass filters or integrated, where the area under the curve of the rectified signal is calculated by taking the mathematical integration of set fixed timed slices of the rectified signal. From here, amplitude and time-based parameter extraction can occur. It is also possible to do frequency power analysis on the raw EMG signal with a power spectral density function. This frequency analysis might be used for studying the time course of EMG activity changes, particularly when studying muscle fatigue over time. For most psychological-based phenomena being studied with EMG, the output of more complicated frequency-based analyses is similar to simpler amplitude and time-based measures. Therefore, most research will use the later approaches, described below.

For the average social or behavioral scientist, this signal processing is often done through dedicated software created by the hardware manufacturer (e.g., Biopac's

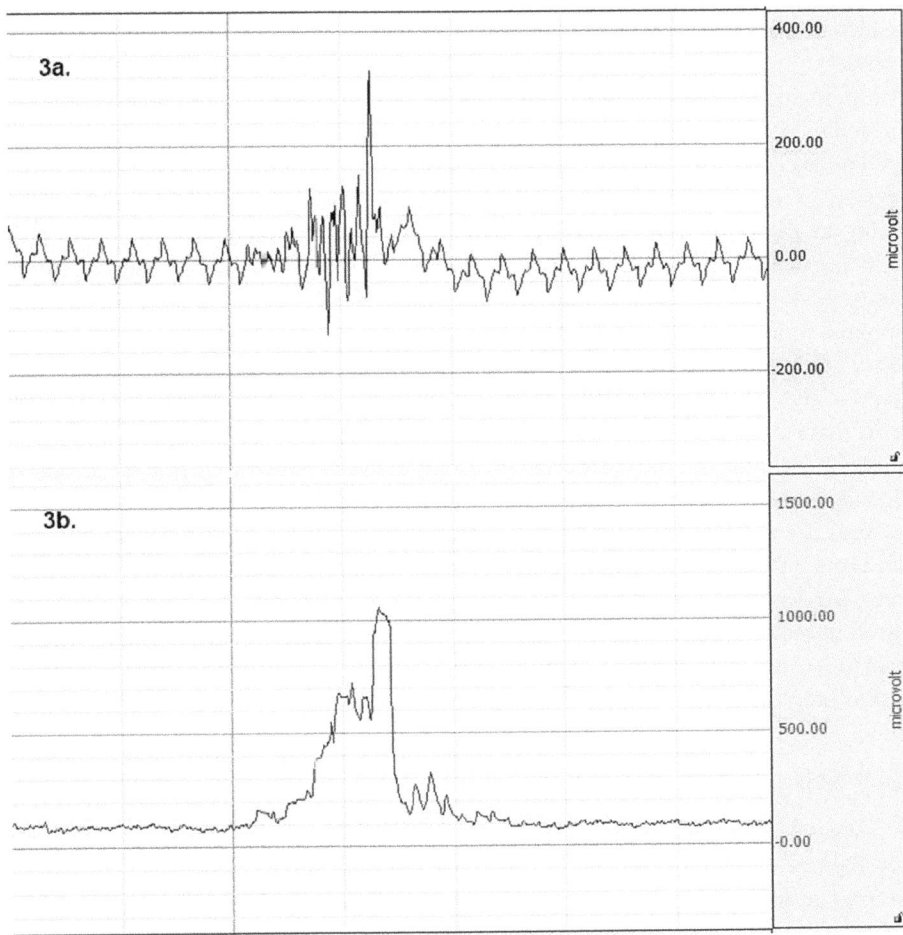

Figure 22.3 *EMG signal measured from the orbicularis oculi muscle: (a) Raw EMG signal and (b) EMG signal after band pass filtering (28–500 Hz), rectification, and RMS integration.*

Acqknowledge or Mindware's EMG Analysis Application), though there are options available for signal processing in programs such as Matlab. Many of these programs will also have options for data scoring, with some processes that can be automated. It is advised to reference the supporting documentation for any software that you use to be sure you understand what the software is doing to the signal. In addition, it is suggested to avoid proprietary software where validation documentation is not open to review by the end user.

Once the EMG signal has been transformed, the next step is to mark or remove observations that are artifacts. Artifacts include parts of the signal that are not part of the natural response, such as electrical noise generated by extraneous movement. Next, quantification of responses or parameter extraction is conducted. There are various parameters that can be extracted from the EMG response, and which parameters one extracts will depend on the experimental design and hypotheses to be tested.

Response onset latency is the time from the onset of a trial or stimulus to the point at which the EMG signal starts to exceed a preset value. Another latency measure is peak latency – the time from either the response onset or stimulus onset to the peak response in the waveform. Latency measures are particularly useful in studies looking at response reaction times, such as assessing whether a threat stimulus results in faster responding than non-threat stimuli. Another parameter is maximum peak to peak EMG amplitude during a specified epoch. This measurement can be compared to another epoch from different experimental conditions or to a baseline control condition. The average amplitude signal during an epoch can also be derived either through an averaged rectified value or a root mean square amplitude (Garcia & Vieira, 2011).

Amplitude values from smoothed signals are reported in microvolts, while amplitude values from integrated signals are expressed in microvolt seconds. Amplitude measures are used in the majority of social and behavioral research applications, such as quantifying eye-blink reflex responses in an attentional gating experiment. In some cases, the integrated EMG signal can be directly linked to a stimulus presentation, as in biofeedback where a stimulus parameter changes based on the change in signal over time, or used by a computer as control input in human–computer interface applications.

Signal Noise Reduction

One aspect of psychophysiology measures that needs attention is the potential for electrical noise in the signal. Noise can come from different sources. AC electrical systems can introduce 50 or 60 Hz noise into the signal. The specific frequency is determined by the electrical system of the particular locale one is in (e.g., 60 Hz in North America or 50 Hz in Europe). This noise can be introduced through the electromagnetic fields generated by main electrical wiring in the walls or fluorescent lights. To reduce electromagnetic noise, an electrically shielded participant chamber and non-fluorescent lighting can be used for data collection. Additionally, a third electrode, referred to as a ground electrode, is often placed over an inactive site and helps reduce electrical signal noise that may enter the system. A 50 or 60 Hz notch filter can be used to reduce some of this noise from the signal. However, because this frequency falls within the band in which much of the power of the EMG signal resides, one needs to be careful to not remove too much of the signal. This is typically done by using a narrow digital notch filter to minimize reduction of the surrounding frequencies.

Another source of noise is movement artifact. This is electrical noise that is generated in the electrode wires when there is excessive movement of the wires or of the electrodes on the surface of the skin. To reduce this noise, one can design experimental tasks that reduce unnecessary movements. One can also reduce excessive movement of the wires by taping the wires down to the participant's torso or shoulders depending on the EMG signal being recorded. Low-frequency movement-related noise can be reduced with a 20 Hz high-pass filter. Reducing skin–electrode impedance through proper skin preparation, as mentioned above, also greatly reduces noise. Signal noise can also originate from other physiological sources, such as the electrical activity generated by heart contractions, or from other muscles near the site of the target muscle. These sources of noise can be reduced with high-pass filters and proper electrode placement. When collecting EMG data with a mobile system outside of a controlled laboratory setting, increased noise will be a trade-off for increased mobility. In general, noise becomes more likely for smaller amplitude signals from smaller muscles compared to larger amplitude signals likely to be generated by large muscles.

EMG Applications

We now review some specific applications of the EMG measure. This includes the use of EMG to measure the startle eye-blink reflex to study affective and attentional processes, using EMG to study emotion through the measure of facial expressions, the use of EMG in clinical biofeedback techniques, and EMG in human–machine interfaces.

Startle Eye-Blink Reflex

One of the most popular uses of surface EMG, in the field of psychology, is the measurement of the startle eye-blink reflex. In general, the startle reflex is a whole-body protective response to a sudden, intense stimulus and includes the drawing in of the limbs to the torso, hunching over, tucking the chin to the chest, and blinking of the eyes. Of the different behavioral manifestations of the startle reflex, the eye-blink component is the slowest to habituate, has the fastest onset, and is the most reliable (Landis & Hunt, 1939). Early work studying the startle eye-blink measured the response with high-speed photography, but today most researchers utilize EMG to measure the magnitude of contraction of the orbicularis oculi muscle – the primary muscle involved in blinking. Reflexive responses can be modified by psychophysiological processes (Bowditch & Warren, 1890; Yerkes, 1905), and the startle eye-blink is no different. Researchers have used the startle eye-blink response to study both attentional and emotional processes, as highlighted below.

In the laboratory, the startle eye-blink response can be elicited by an intense flash of light, a sudden tactile stimulus (e.g., a puff of air to the temple), or a short loud burst of noise. Today, acoustic stimuli are the most widely used startle stimuli (i.e., startle probe) – typically in the form of a 50 ms burst of white noise, with instantaneous rise and fall times, presented at 85–105 dB over a pair of headphones (Blumenthal et al., 2005). This stimulus is created using sound editing software (e.g., Audacity, www.audacityteam.org). Use the editing options in the software to save a 50 ms portion of the noise. Rise time means that the stimulus goes from no sound to full intensity immediately. Taking a random slice of the white noise will achieve this. The auditory stimulus can then be presented over headphones via a headphone amplifier. To set the final volume of the startle probe, take a longer section of the white noise file and play it through the headphones. Measure the sound level with a sound meter placed over one of the headphone speakers, and adjust the headphone amplifier gain until the sound gets to your target dB setting. Now, when you play the 50 ms stimulus over the headphones, it will be at the correct setting.

To measure the EMG response, two small 4 mm electrodes are taped under the eye over the orbicularis oculi muscle (see Figure 22.2) – one in line with the pupil and the other in line with the outer canthus (i.e., corner of the eye). The electrode tabs used to adhere the electrodes typically need to be trimmed to fit the electrodes close to the eyelid. Because the orbicularis oculi muscle is relatively small, careful skin preparation is important to obtain the best signal to noise ratio. After the raw EMG signal is recorded, amplitude and latency data are extracted from an epoch of the integrated or smoothed waveform between 21 and 120 ms post startle probe onset. The amplitude data can be averaged across trials as a mean amplitude or mean magnitude measure. Mean amplitude only includes trials with a blink response; mean magnitude includes trials with a non-blink response (Blumenthal et al., 2005). Because startle blink magnitudes can vary greatly across participants, the data is often standardized within subjects using z or T scores or using a relative metric based on changes from control trials for blink modulation measures (e.g., percent change scores, see example below).

Startle and Attention

The startle eye-blink reflex can be modulated by attentional processes, and the prepulse inhibition (PPI) of the startle reflex has been used extensively to study attention for many years. Prepulse inhibition of the startle reflex is a phenomenon where a non-startling pre-stimulus (i.e., 20 ms 64 dB white noise with 5 ms rise/fall times), presented 30–500 ms prior to the onset of the startle probe, causes the startle magnitude to be reduced compared to startles elicited by the startle probe alone.

This is theorized to reflect an automatic sensory gating effect (i.e., the ability to filter out distracting stimuli) whereby the brain protects the ongoing processing of the prepulse stimulus to ascertain its relevance. This, in turn, reduces cognitive resources available to process the startle probe. The reduction of attentional resources to the startle probe results in the inhibition of the elicited reflexive response (Braff & Geyer, 1990). Note, to make the prepulse stimulus, follow the same procedure for making the startle probe stimulus. The main difference is that you should not change the headphone amp gain setting to set the stimulus intensity; instead, the stimulus intensity will need to be set by reducing the wave file gain in the sound editing software (e.g., using a software's amplify options).

The PPI effect is fairly robust and has been used to study attentional gating in both humans and animals; albeit the effect is typically not studied with EMG in animals. Prepulse inhibition is best quantified as a proportion of the difference from control (Blumenthal et al., 2004), where the average startle response in control (i.e., probe alone) trials is subtracted from the average of prepulse trials and then divided by the average of the control responses. This is often converted to a percent change score by multiplying by 100, with negative percentages indicating inhibition. For example, if the average startle response during probe alone control trials for a participant was 30 mV, and the average startle response during prepulse trials was 15 mV, that participant demonstrated a 50% inhibition of the startle reflex due to the prepulse (e.g., (15-30/30) × 100% = -50%).

Startle and Emotion

In addition to using the startle eye-blink reflex to study attention, it can also be used to study emotion. Startle responses are potentiated during negative mood states and attenuated during positive mood states (Vrana et al., 1988; Bradley et al., 1990). This is thought to be due to what is termed mismatch negativity; when matched between the averseness of the startle probe with a negative emotion state, it exacerbates the effect of the startle probe, while a mismatch with a positive emotion state reduces the startling effect of the probe (Lang et al., 1990).

This affective modification of startle effect is most often studied in a paradigm that presents pictures from the International Affective Picture System (IAPS; Lang et al., 2008) – a standardized set of pictures rated on valence, arousal, and dominance. Pictures are chosen based on valence and arousal settings to be included in positive and negative emotion conditions and are typically shown for 6 seconds with startle probes occurring between 3 and 5 seconds from picture onset. Startles are presented on a majority of picture trials but not all, as well as occasionally during the inter-trial interval to reduce the predictability of the probe. Mean startle responses are then compared across emotion condition. This affective modification effect can also be studied using other emotion induction paradigms, including emotional words (Herbert & Kissler, 2010) and imagery (Miller et al., 2002).

The affective modification of startle has been used to study basic aspects of emotional processing such as the influence of valence, arousal, and attention (Bradley et al., 2001). It has also been used to study emotional processing in specific contexts such as in clinical disorders, including borderline personality disorder (Baschnagel et al., 2013) and autism spectrum disorder (Dichter et al., 2010). Other examples include studying sex differences in emotional reactions to jealousy (Baschnagel & Edlund, 2016), differentiating fear and disgust reactions (Yartz & Hawk, 2002), studying trait behavioral inhibition and approach (Hawk & Kowmas, 2003), and studying the reactions to ingroup and outgroup facial expressions (Paulus et al., 2019).

Some affective modification of startle paradigms specifically focus on reactions to threat stimuli, where the effect is often referred to as fear-potentiated startle. This fear-potentiated startle effect has been used to study fear responses in animals and humans in paradigms often developed to understand anxiety disorders. A common paradigm for fear-potentiated startle involves either the application or the threat of application of an aversive stimulus, such as a shock or strong air puff to the throat. Typically, these paradigms will include conditioning the threat to a neutral stimulus, allowing for the study of conditioned fear responses.

One example using the threat-of-shock paradigm to study post-traumatic stress disorder demonstrated how combat veterans with PTSD showed exaggerated startles to an explicit threat cue, similar to the control group. However, this exaggerated startle generalized to the testing environment even when the shock electrodes were not attached to the participants (Grillon et al., 1998). The exaggerated startle in the PTSD group was not evident in a prior testing session where there was no threat of shock, suggesting that one of the diagnostic criteria for PTSD is context-specific. The contextual variation in the fear-potentiated startle effect has even been shown to be a prospective marker of PTSD development after exposure to a traumatic event (Pole et al., 2009).

Facial EMG and Emotion

Another use of EMG measurement is in the study of emotion as conveyed through facial expressions. Assessing facial expressions is a generally accepted objective measure of underlying emotional state (Keltner & Ekman, 2000). Emotion recognition can be as simple as recognizing a person's happiness when they smile or identifying their sadness when they frown. Facial EMG provides an objective measure of affect beyond self-report and subjective observation by measuring the electrical activity in the muscles associated with specific emotions.

The most common area of investigation of this type is in the dimensional domain of positive and negative affect (Dimberg, 1988). When a person frowns during the experience of a negative emotion, there is sizable activity in the corrugator supercilii – the muscles located around the eyebrow (Larsen et al., 2003). Similarly, during the experience of a happy emotion or a smile, there is a proportional increase in the activity of the zygomaticus major – a muscle that extends from the corner of the mouth to the upper arch of the cheekbone (Larsen et al., 2003). Facial electromyography can be used to observe positive and negative affect during the presentation of a specific stimulus or during the course of a behavioral experiment.

Foundational work by Dimberg (1990) demonstrated the methodological utility of facial electromyography as an unbiased and expeditious observation of underlying emotion. To measure facial EMG, the basic procedures outlined above apply. Typically, 4 mm electrodes will be used and placed over the muscles of interest (see Figure 22.2). The electrode tabs can be trimmed to allow for close placement of the electrodes over the muscles. Then, one measures the EMG activity during emotion induction trials and compares it to measurements during control trials.

Over the past two decades, facial EMG has been used to investigate individual differences in various psychopathologies, prejudices, and biases of the social and racial variety, cognitive and perceptual experiences, and other psychological constructs that can be operationally defined via muscular activity of the face. A common area of clinical study involves the investigation of facial reactivity and expressivity in populations dealing with mental and emotional disorders. Facial EMG measures have been used to study emotional expressions following the presentation of affective stimuli in populations with autism spectrum disorders (Rozga et al., 2013), borderline personality disorder (Matzke et al., 2014), and schizophrenia (Varcin et al., 2019). This method has also been used to observe differences in affective reactions in substance users who are presented with substance-related cues (Lang & Yegiyan, 2014).

Some social psychologists have measured the activity of the cheek and the eyebrow as a proxy variable for implicit racial bias (Vanman et al., 2004) while others have stated that it is an efficacious method of observing anti-gay bias (Morrison et al., 2019). Moreover, researchers interested in perception have attempted to use EMG as a measurable experience of pain (Reicherts et al., 2013), all while market research has validated this technique as useful in distinguishing emotional responses to vacation destination advertising (Li et al., 2018).

Biofeedback

Biofeedback is an example of an applied use of surface EMG. This application is typically used as part of clinical treatments and in clinical research. Biofeedback describes an information feedback system where individuals receive extrinsic information about their physiological functions in real time, such as their heart rate, skin temperature, or muscle activity, in the form of visual and/or auditory signals (Wolf, 1978). Through biofeedback training, individuals can increase their awareness of their internal physiological processes, develop control over these processes, and learn to regulate their physiological functions without relying on external information (Bowles et al., 1979).

Research on the implementation of biofeedback training emerged in the 1960s to provide a complementary treatment for rehabilitation programs related to neuromuscular and psychiatric disorders (Monteiro et al., 2022). One of the most widely researched and implemented biofeedback modalities is through EMG activity (Giggins et al., 2013). EMG biofeedback training is meant to enhance musculoskeletal and neurological rehabilitation, with its efficacy explored for symptoms and conditions ranging from headaches, psychiatric disorders, attention-deficit disorders, and pain. EMG biofeedback training can help individuals learn how to relax overactive muscles or activate flaccid or weak muscles. The most common muscles targeted through EMG biofeedback training are the frontalis (forehead) and trapezius muscles (Bowles et al., 1979).

EMG biofeedback training is conducted by measuring skeletal muscle activity using surface electrodes placed on the region of the target muscle. The electrical signals are converted into visual or auditory signals, proportional to the degree of muscular activity, and fed back to the individual (Giggins et al., 2013). Visual feedback is often depicted as transformed EMG signal amplitudes or using light; auditory feedback is typically depicted through changing tones or sound volume (Rokicki et al., 2003). Further, by manipulating the gain settings, the biofeedback training can induce either muscle relaxation or activation. A high-gain setting will be highly sensitive to muscle activity, lending itself to relaxation exercises, while a low-gain setting is less sensitive and therefore useful in training muscle recruitment (Watson, n.d.). Beyond the basic procedure for measuring EMG described above, researchers need to have a data collection software that allows the incoming signal data to be displayed in some form, either through the same software or by outputting the EMG data stream to another software. Researchers with programming skills can create biofeedback stimuli in programs such as Matlab. Those without programming skills should consider ready-made software options that work with their bioamplifiers or buy dedicated biofeedback devices.

EMG Biofeedback for Tension-Type Headaches

Tension-type headaches (TTH) are recurrent episodes of headache, characterized by dull, pressure-like pain that is usually bilateral in location (Chowdhury, 2012). Since TTH is accompanied by muscle contractions in the face, scalp, and neck (Tunis & Wolff, 1954), Budzynski et al. (1973) first explored the benefits of EMG biofeedback training for patients suffering from TTH. Since the 1980s, the efficacy of EMG biofeedback as a non-pharmacological therapy for TTH is well supported. During the training, patients are taught to consciously reduce muscle tension and autonomic arousal that typically accompany their headaches. Over the course of the training sessions, patients learn to control and relax their pericranial muscles (Chowdhury, 2012).

EMG Biofeedback for Anxiety Disorders

Anxiety disorders are often accompanied by physiological arousal that can present itself through elevated heart rate, increased electrodermal activity, and somatic symptoms like restlessness and muscle tension (Agnihotri et al., 2008). Given the close association between anxiety disorders and physiological arousal, researchers have examined how biofeedback training might target such autonomic nervous system responses (Bazanova et al., 2018). One of the ways researchers apply EMG biofeedback for anxiety disorders is by training patients to relax the frontalis muscle (Schoenberg & David, 2014). The frontalis muscle is considered one of the more difficult muscles to voluntarily relax, therefore the training is expected to improve overall relaxation skills for the whole body (Agnihotri et al., 2008). Researchers should keep in mind that, although biofeedback training can result in an overall reduction in stress levels, if muscle activity is not responsible for the specific anxiety symptom, it may not lead to improved symptomology (Schoenberg & David, 2014). Therefore, it is suggested that EMG biofeedback training use should be in alignment with the individual patient's specific psychophysiological symptoms (Agnihotri et al., 2008).

EMG Biofeedback for Attention Disorders

Research on the applications of EMG biofeedback training for attention-deficit hyperactivity disorder (ADHD) emerged due to a strong demand for non-pharmacological, behavioral treatments (Maurizio et al., 2014). As ADHD is characterized by hyperactivity and impulsivity symptoms, along with comorbid motor coordination problems, EMG biofeedback presents an opportunity to improve fine motor skills and motor regulation by training the control of EMG activity of the forearms (Maurizio et al., 2014). Research also shows that since children with ADHD exhibit difficulties controlling muscle tension-relaxation, training to reduce forehead muscle tension can effectively target hyperactivity (Barth et al., 2017).

Broadly speaking, evidence supports the use of EMG biofeedback to improve muscle relaxation and reduce hyperactivity in children with ADHD (Cobb & Evans, 1981; Lee, 1991). Moreover, EMG biofeedback training provides a well-matched active control condition to electroencephalogram (EEG) neurofeedback research. EEG neurofeedback is aimed at reducing excess theta activity and increasing beta activity at fronto-central locations based on early research that suggests elevated theta/beta ratios can provide a prognostic measure of ADHD (Arns et al., 2013). Alternatively, EMG biofeedback targets forehead muscle relaxation and motor regulation (Bakhshayesh et al., 2011). In studies comparing EEG neurofeedback and EMG biofeedback, both groups demonstrated significant improvements in ADHD symptoms (Bakhshayesh et al., 2011; Bazanova et al., 2018). In particular, EMG biofeedback was associated with a reduction in hyperactivity and impulsivity symptoms based on parent ratings while neurofeedback training was associated with overall improvements in hyperkinetic symptoms (Bakhshayesh et al., 2011).

EMG-based Human-Machine Interfaces

The versatility in the application of EMG signals is evident in the emerging field of EMG-based human–machine interfaces (HMI) designed to control ground and aerial vehicles (McCoggle et al., 2022). Researchers have tested EMG-based systems to control electric wheelchairs, drones, tractors, and cars using hand gestures (Vigliotta et al., 2021; Kundu et al., 2018; Gomez-Gil et al., 2011; McCoggle et al., 2022). Although EMG-based control systems are primarily developed to allow people with disabilities, or motor or sensory limitations, to control vehicles with minimal muscle motion, other applications include advancing assistive technology such as steering assistance interfaces (Choromański et al., 2021; Nacpil et al., 2019).

EMG-based HMIs allow for the communication between EMG signals and various interfaces through (1) signal acquisition; (2) signal filtering and amplification; and (3) classification (Vigliotta et al., 2021). EMG signals are measured, filtered to reduce signal-to-noise ratio, and amplified (McCoggle et al., 2022). Then, detection algorithms are implemented to classify and identify the specific muscle activity performed (McCoggle et al., 2022). The classifier can map, identify, and estimate different patterns from EMG signal features to then act on the device (Shair et al., 2022). A commonly used classifier is the artificial neural network (ANN), which uses adaptive learning to detect patterns and trends from vague or complex EMG signals and classifies them into a variety of muscle groups (Karlik, 2014). Another neural network is the self-organizing map (SOM), which uses an unsupervised learning technique that takes unlabeled data sets and organizes them into a two-dimensional map (Yousefi & Hamilton-Wright, 2014). SOMs are useful for their comparison ability (e.g., discriminating EMG signals by human body percentile categories) since arm circumferences influence the amplitudes of EMG signals (Jali et al., 2014). More transparent classifiers (e.g., the decision tree and fuzzy classifiers) are advantageous because they provide explanations for the input/output data behavior and increase model comprehension (Yousefi & Hamilton-Wright, 2014).

Other assistive technologies include steering assistance interfaces that use surface EMG signals from bicep brachii muscles intended to execute hands-free steering rotation at a faster speed than able-bodied drivers (Nacpil et al., 2019). With even more minimal muscle movements, applications of EMG signals from 14 finger movements are studied to command in-car electronic equipment to minimize biomechanical driver distraction that results from releasing the hand(s) from the steering wheel to physically attend to something else (Shair et al., 2022). While a large majority of research and proposed EMG-based control systems intend to serve the medical field, the field continues to expand, with interest in its applications seen in industrial, civilian, and commercial markets.

Conclusion

This chapter has reviewed the biological underpinnings of muscle activity, equipment, and signal processing involved in electromyography, and provided some common use cases of EMG measures in social and behavioral research. Surface EMG measurements provide a non-invasive way to measure somatic behavior in a way that is more sensitive and less prone to bias compared to observational methods. With modern-day equipment, EMG measures can be collected both in the traditional laboratory setting and, when signal noise concerns are acknowledged, in the "real world." Many specific EMG measures have been developed to study attention and emotion, and EMG measures are increasingly being utilized in applied settings. As a result, electromyography continues to be a useful tool for social and behavioral scientists.

References

AbuHasan, Q., & Munakomi, S. (2022). *Neuroanatomy, Pyramidal Tract*. StatPearls Publishing. Available from www.ncbi.nlm.nih.gov/books/NBK545314

Agnihotri, H., Paul, M., & Sandhu, J. S. (2008). The comparative efficacy of two biofeedback techniques in the treatment of generalized anxiety disorder. *Pakistan Journal of Social and Clinical Psychology, 6*(1), 35–46.

Andreassi, J. L. (2013). *Psychophysiology: Human behavior & physiological response*, 4th ed. Psychology Press.

Arns, M., Conners, C. K., & Kraemer, H. C. (2013). A decade of EEG theta/beta ratio research in ADHD: A meta-analysis. *Journal of Attention Disorders, 17*(5), 374-383.

Bakhshayesh, A. R., Hänsch, S., Wyschkon, A., Rezai, M. J., & Esser, G. (2011). Neurofeedback in ADHD: A single-blind randomized controlled trial. *European Child & Adolescent Psychiatry, 20*, 481–491.

Barth, B., Mayer, K., Strehl, U., Fallgatter, A. J., & Ehlis, A. C. (2017). EMG biofeedback training in adult attention-deficit/hyperactivity disorder: An active (control) training? *Behavioural Brain Research, 329*, 58-66.

Baschnagel, J. S., Coffey, S. F., Hawk Jr., L. W., Schumacher, J. A., & Holloman, G. (2013). Psychophysiological assessment of emotional processing in patients with borderline personality disorder with and without comorbid substance use. *Personality Disorders: Theory, Research, and Treatment, 4*(3), 203–213.

Baschnagel, J. S., & Edlund, J. E. (2016). Affective modification of the startle eyeblink response during sexual and emotional infidelity scripts. *Evolutionary Psychological Science, 2*, 114–122.

Bazanova, O. M., Auer, T., & Sapina, E. A. (2018). On the efficiency of individualized theta/beta ratio neurofeedback combined with forehead EMG training in ADHD children. *Frontiers in Human Neuroscience, 12*, 3. https://doi.org/10.3389/fnhum.2018.00003

Blumenthal, T. D., Cuthbert, B. N., Filion, D. L., Hackley, S., Lipp, O. V., & van Boxtel A. (2005). Committee report: Guidelines for human startle eyeblink electromyographic studies. *Psychophysiology, 42*(1), 1-15. https://doi.org/10.1111/j.1469-8986.2005.00271.x

Blumenthal, T. D., Elden, A., & Flaten, M. A. (2004). A comparison of several methods used to quantify prepulse inhibition of eyeblink responding. *Psychophysiology, 41*(2), 326–332.

Bowditch, H. P., & Warren, J. W. (1890). The knee-jerk and its physiological modifications. *Journal of Physiology, 11*(1–2), 25–64. https://doi.org/10.1113/jphysiol.1890.sp000318

Bowles, C., Smith, J., & Parker, K. (1979). EMG biofeedback and progressive relaxation training: A comparative study of two groups of normal subjects. *Western Journal of Nursing Research, 1*(3), 179–189. https://doi.org/10.1177/019394597900100304

Bradley, M. M., Codispoti, M., Cuthbert, B. N., & Lang, P. J. (2001). Emotion and motivation I: Defensive and appetitive reactions in picture processing. *Emotion, 1*(3), 276–298.

Bradley, M. M., Cuthbert, B. N., & Lang, P. J. (1990). Startle reflex modification: Emotion or attention? *Psychophysiology, 27*(5), 513–522.

Braff, D. L., & Geyer, M. A. (1990). Sensorimotor gating and schizophrenia: Human and animal model studies. *Archives of General Psychiatry, 47*, 181–188.

Budzynski, T. H., Stoyva, J. M., Adler, C. S., & Mullaney, D. J. (1973). EMG biofeedback and tension headache: A controlled outcome study. *Psychosomatic Medicine, 35*(6), 484-496. https://doi.org/10.1097/00006842-197311000-00004

Choromański, W., Grabarek, I., & Kozłowski, M. (2021). Integrated design of a custom steering system in cars and verification of its correct functioning. *Energies, 14*(20), 1–9.

Chowdhury, D. (2012). Tension type headache. *Annals of Indian Academy of Neurology, 15* (Suppl. 1), S83–S88. https://doi.org/10.4103/0972-2327.100023

Cobb, D. E., & Evans, J. R. (1981). The use of biofeedback techniques with school-aged children exhibiting behavioral and/or learning problems. *Journal of Abnormal Child Psychology, 9*, 251–281.

Dichter, G. S., Benning, S. D., Holtzclaw, T. N., & Bodfish, J. W. (2010). Affective modulation of the startle eyeblink and postauricular reflexes in autism spectrum disorder. *Journal of Autism and Developmental Disorders, 40*, 858–869.

Dimberg, U. (1988). Facial electromyography and the experience of emotion. *Journal of Psychophysiology, 2*(4), 277–282.

(1990). Facial electromyography and emotional reactions. *Psychophysiology*, *27*(5), 481–494. https://doi.org/10.1111/j.1469-8986.1990.tb01962.x

Fridlund, A. J., & Cacioppo, J. T. (1986). Guidelines for human electromyographic research. *Psychophysiology*, *23*(5), 567–589.

Garcia, M. C., & Vieira, T. M. M. (2011). Surface electromyography: Why, when and how to use it. *Revista andaluza de medicina del deporte*, *4*(1), 17–28.

Giggins, O. M., Persson, U. M., & Caulfield, B. (2013). Biofeedback in rehabilitation. *Journal of Neuroengineering and Rehabilitation*, *10*, 60. https://doi.org/10.1186/1743-0003-10-60

Gomez-Gil, J., San-Jose-Gonzalez, I., Nicolas-Alonso, L. F., & Alonso-Garcia, S. (2011). Steering a tractor by means of an EMG-based human–machine interface. *Sensors*, *11*(7), 7110–7126.

Grillon, C., Morgan III, C. A., Davis, M., & Southwick, S. M. (1998). Effects of experimental context and explicit threat cues on acoustic startle in Vietnam veterans with post-traumatic stress disorder. *Biological Psychiatry*, *44*(10), 1027–1036.

Hawk, L. W., & Kowmas, A. D. (2003). Affective modulation and prepulse inhibition of startle among undergraduates high and low in behavioral inhibition and approach. *Psychophysiology*, *40*(1), 131–138.

Herbert, C., & Kissler, J. (2010). Motivational priming and processing interrupt: Startle reflex modulation during shallow and deep processing of emotional words. *International Journal of Psychophysiology*, *76*(2), 64–71.

Hermens, H. J., Freriks, B., Disselhorst-Klug, C., & Rau, G. (2000). Development of recommendations for SEMG sensors and sensor placement procedures. *Journal of Electromyography and Kinesiology*, *10*(5), 361–374.

Jacob, S. W., & Francone, C.A. (1970). *Structure and Function in Man*. Saunders.

Jali, M. H., Bohari, Z. H., Sulaima, M. F., Nasir, M. N. M., & Jaafar, H. I. (2014). Classification of EMG signal based on human percentile using SOM. *Research Journal of Applied Sciences, Engineering and Technology*, *8*(2), 235–242.

Karlik, B. (2014). Machine learning algorithms for characterization of EMG signals. *International Journal of Information and Electronics Engineering*, *4*(3), 189–194.

Keltner, D., & Ekman, P. (2000). Facial expression of emotion. In M. Lewis, & J. Haviland-Jones (eds.), *Handbook of Emotions*, 2nd ed. (pp. 236–249). Guilford Press.

Kundu, A. S., Mazumder, O., Lenka, P. K., & Bhaumik, S. (2018). Hand gesture recognition based omnidirectional wheelchair control using IMU and EMG sensors. *Journal of Intelligent & Robotic Systems*, *91*, 529–541.

Landis, C., & Hunt, W. (1939). *The Startle Pattern*. Farrar & Rinehart.

Lang, A., & Yegiyan, N.S. (2014). Mediated substance cues: Motivational reactivity and use influence responses to pictures of alcohol. *Journal of Health Communication*, *19*, 1216–1231.

Lang, P. J., Bradley, M. M., & Cuthbert, B. N. (1990). Emotion, attention, and the startle reflex. *Psychological Review*, *97*(3), 377–395.

(2008). *International Affective Picture System (IAPS): Instruction Manual and Affective Ratings*. Technical Report A-8. Center for Research in Psychophysiology, University of Florida.

Larsen, J. T., Norris, C. J., & Cacioppo, J. T. (2003). Effects of positive and negative affect on electromyographic activity over zygomaticus major and corrugator supercilii. *Psychophysiology*, *40*(5), 776–785. https://doi.org/10.1111/1469-8986.00078

Lee, S. W. (1991). Biofeedback as a treatment for childhood hyperactivity: A critical review of the literature. *Psychological Reports*, *68*(1), 163–192.

Li, S., Walters, G., Packer, J., & Scott, N. (2018). Using skin conductance and facial electromyography to measure emotional responses to tourism advertising. *Current Issues in Tourism*, *21*, 61–1783. https://doi.org/10.1080/13683500.2016.1223023

Matzke, B., Herpertz, S. C., Berger, C., Fleischer, M., & Domes, G. (2014). Facial reactions during emotion recognition in borderline personality disorder: A facial electromyography study. *Psychopathology*, *47*(2), 101–110. https://doi.org/10.1159/000351122.

Maurizio, S., Liechti, M. D., Heinrich, H., Jäncke, L., Steinhausen, H.-C., Walitza, S., et al. (2014). Comparing tomographic EEG neurofeedback and EMG biofeedback in children with attention-deficit/hyperactivity disorder. *Biological Psychology*, *95*, 31–44. https://doi.org/10.1016/j.biopsycho.2013.10.008

McCoggle, M., Wilson, S., Rivera, A., Alba-Flores, R., & Soloiu, V. (2022). Biosensors based controller for small unmanned aerial vehicle navigation. In *SoutheastCon 2022*. IEEE. https://doi.org/10.1109/southeastcon48659.2022.9764015

Miller, M. W., Patrick, C. J., & Levenston, G. K. (2002). Affective imagery and the startle response: Probing mechanisms of modulation during pleasant scenes, personal experiences, and discrete negative emotions. *Psychophysiology*, *39*(4), 519–529. https://doi.org/10.1017/S0048577202394095

Monteiro, P., Tavares, D. L., Mourão, L., Nouws, H. P., & Maia, G. (2022). Biosensors, biofeedback, and neurofeedback. In A. Marques & R. Queirós (eds.), *Digital Therapies in Psychosocial Rehabilitation and Mental Health* (pp. 303–320). IGI Global. https://doi.org/10.4018/978-1-7998-8634-1.ch015

Morrison, M. A., Trinder, K. M., & Morrison, T. G. (2019). Affective responses to gay men using facial electromyography: Is there a psychophysiological "look" of anti-gay bias. *Journal of Homosexuality*, *66*(9), 1238–1261. https://doi.org/10.1080/00918369.2018.1500779

Nacpil, E. J. C., Zheng, R., Kaizuka, T., & Nakano, K. (2019). A surface electromyography controlled steering assistance interface. *Journal of Intelligent and Connected Vehicles*, *2*(1), 1–13.

Paulhus, D. L. (1984). Two-component models of socially desirable responding. *Journal of Personality and Social Psychology*, *46*(3), 598–609.

Paulus, A., Renn, K., & Wentura, D. (2019). One plus one is more than two: The interactive influence of group membership and emotional facial expressions on the modulation of the affective startle reflex. *Biological Psychology*, *142*, 140–146.

Pole, N., Neylan, T. C., Otte, C., Henn-Hasse, C., Metzler, T. J., & Marmar, C. R. (2009). Prospective prediction of posttraumatic stress disorder symptoms using fear potentiated auditory startle responses. *Biological psychiatry*, *65*(3), 235–240.

Reicherts, P., Gerdes, A. B., Pauli, P., & Wieser, M. J. (2013). On the mutual effects of pain and emotion: Facial pain expressions enhance pain perception and vice versa are perceived as more arousing when feeling pain. *Pain*, *154*(6), 793–800. https://doi.org/10.1016/j.pain.2013.02.012

Rokicki, L. A., Houle, T. T., Dhingra, L. K., Weinland, S. R., Urban, A. M., & Bhalla, R. K. (2003). A preliminary analysis of EMG variance as an index of change in EMG biofeedback treatment of tension-type headache. *Applied Psychophysiology and Biofeedback*, *28*(3), 205–215. https://doi.org/10.1023/a:1024633230584

Rozga, A., King, T. Z., Vuduc, R. W., & Robins, D. L. (2013). Undifferentiated facial electromyography responses to dynamic, audio-visual emotion displays in individuals with autism spectrum disorders. *Developmental Science*, *16*(4), 499–514. https://doi.org/10.1111/desc.12062

Sabbah, P., De Schonen, S., Leveque, C., Gay, S., Pfefer, F., Nioche, C., et al. (2002). Sensorimotor cortical activity in patients with complete spinal cord injury: A functional magnetic resonance imaging study. *Journal of Neurotrauma*, *19*(1), 53–60.

Schoenberg, P. L., & David, A. S. (2014). Biofeedback for psychiatric disorders: A systematic review. *Applied Psychophysiology and Biofeedback*, *39*(2), 109–135. https://doi.org/10.1007/s10484-014-9246-9

Shair, E. F., Razali, R. H., Abdullah, A. R., & Jamaluddin, N. F. (2022). EMG pattern recognition using TFD for future control of in-car electronic equipment. *International Journal of Fuzzy Logic and Intelligent Systems*, *22*(1), 11–22.

Stern, R. M., Ray, W. J., & Quigley, K. S. (2001). *Psychophysiological Recording*. Oxford University Press.

Tassinary, L. G., Cacioppo, J. T., & Vanman, E. J. (2007). The skeletomotor system: Surface electromyography. In J. T. Cacioppo, L. G. Tassinary, & G. G. Berntson (eds.), *Handbook of Psychophysiology* (pp. 267–299). Cambridge University Press.

Tunis, M. M., & Wolff, H. G. (1954). Studies on headache: Cranial artery vasoconstriction and muscle contraction headache. *AMA Archives of Neurology & Psychiatry*, *71*(4), 425–434.

Vanman, E. J., Saltz, J. L., Nathan, L. R., & Warren, J. A. (2004). Racial discrimination by low-prejudiced whites: Facial movements as implicit measures of attitudes related to behavior. *Psychological Science*, *15*(11), 711–714.

Varcin, K. J., Nangle, M. R., Henry, J. D., Bailey, P. E., & Richmond, J. L. (2019). Intact spontaneous emotional expressivity to non-facial but not facial stimuli in schizophrenia: An electromyographic study. *Schizophrenia Research*, *206*, 37–42. https://doi.org/10.1016/j.schres.2018.12.019

Vigliotta, J., Cipleu, J., Mikell, A., & Alba-Flores, R. (2021). EMG controlled electric wheelchair. *Lecture Notes in Networks and Systems*, *296*, 439–449. https://doi.org/10.1007/978-3-030-82199-9_29

Vrana, S. R., Spence, E. L., & Lang, P. J. (1988). The startle probe response: A new measure of emotion? *Journal of Abnormal Psychology*, *97*(4), 487–491. https://doi.org/10.1037/0021-843X.97.4.487

Watson, T. (n.d.). *EMG Biofeedback – The Principles*. Herman & Wallace Pelvic Rehabilitation Institute. https://hermanwallace.com/images/Tim_Watson_Biofeedback_Intro.pdf (retrieved February 20, 2023).

Wolf, S. L. (1978). Essential considerations in the use of EMG biofeedback. *Physical Therapy*, *58*(1), 25–31. https://doi.org/10.1093/ptj/58.1.25

Yartz, A. R., & Hawk Jr., L. W. (2002). Addressing the specificity of affective startle modulation: Fear versus disgust. *Biological Psychology*, *59*(1), 55–68.

Yerkes, R. M. (1905). The sense of hearing in frogs. *Journal of Comparative Neurology and Psychology*, *15*, 279–304. https://doi.org/10.1002/cne.920150402

Yousefi, J., & Hamilton-Wright, A. (2014). Characterizing EMG data using machine-learning tools. *Computers in Biology and Medicine*, *51*, 1–13.

23 EEG and ERP

Christian Panitz, Richard T. Ward, Jourdan Pouliot, and Andreas Keil

Abstract

Electroencephalography (EEG) and its measures, such as event-related brain potentials (ERPs) and time-frequency analysis (TFA), are powerful tools for investigating cognitive and behavioral processes in humans and therefore are increasingly attracting attention in the social and behavioral sciences. This chapter has been written for readers who are interested in getting involved in EEG research or who may already have some experience and wish to expand their toolbox of EEG methods. It aims to address both needs by providing a brief overview of human electrophysiology, with new users in mind, followed by a discussion of common challenges and typical applications. We conclude by describing current trends and potential for future developments.

Keywords: Electroencephalography, Event-Related Potentials, Neural Time Series, Neurophysiology, Large-Scale Brain Dynamics, Mind–Body–Brain Interactions Psychophysiology

I. Brain Electrophysiology as a Research Tool

Since their discovery in the late 1920s (Berger, 1929), human brain wave recordings have attracted the interest of a variety of scientific disciplines. This interest is rooted in the notion that brain states can be inferred by brain wave recordings, and that these brain states are systematically linked with human behavior and experience (e.g., Ray & Cole, 1985). Brain activity as captured by electroencephalography (EEG) is crucial for the full range of human experience and behavior, including constructs such as cognition, memory, perception, emotion, proprioception, and movement (e.g., Buzsáki & Draguhn, 2004). Measures of brain activity are also widely used in assessing potential disorders related to these constructs, in disciplines such as neurology or psychiatry. Therefore, EEG measures, such as event-related brain potentials (Section V) and time-frequency analysis (Section VI), are powerful tools for investigating neurocognitive and behavioral processes in humans.

II. What Does the EEG Signal Represent?

For scientists using brain wave recordings, it is helpful to understand the neurophysiological and biophysical processes that produce the scalp-recorded EEG signal. Seminal works by Nunez and Srinivasan (2006), Freeman (1975), and Kappenman and Luck (2012) provide introductory overviews and in-depth discussions of these processes. In brief, the EEG signal reflects the synchronized activity of large populations of so-called pyramidal neuronal cells in the cortex (Biasiucci et al., 2019). Pyramidal neurons have an elongated shape, and occur as large populations (i.e., tens of thousands to millions of neurons) often aligned in a neatly parallel fashion as shown in Figure 23.1B (Biasiucci et al., 2019). They make up the majority (i.e., 80–90%) of neurons in the cerebral cortex, the outer layer of the brain that is crucial for many aspects of human behavior and experience. Their interactions with one another involve a number of electrical processes, the most widely known being the action potential.

The action potential is the electrical signal propagating down a neuron's axon when it "fires" in a binary, all-or-nothing fashion. However, action potentials are not reflected in scalp-recorded EEG because they do not generate electrical fields that can be measured away from the immediate environment of the axon. The EEG is

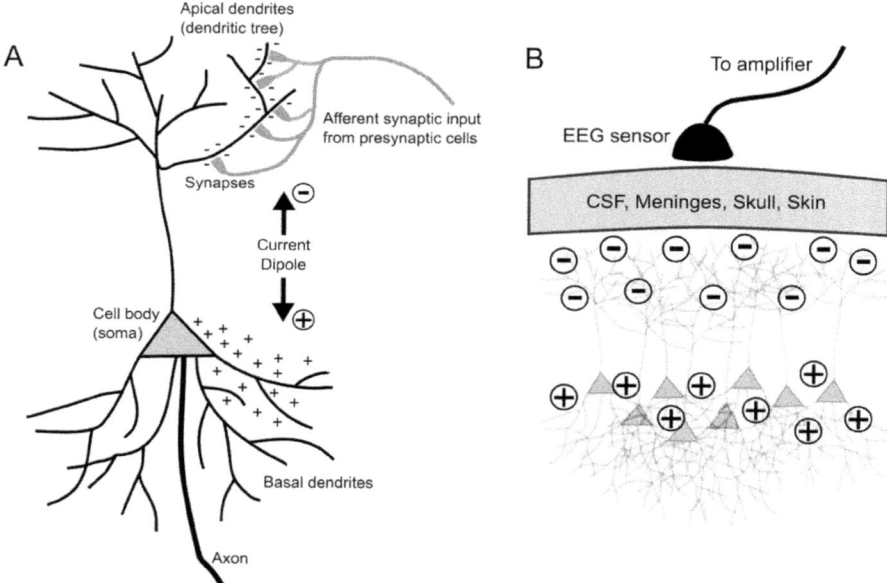

Figure 23.1 *Generation of the EEG signal. (A) Influx of neurotransmitters at the dendritic tree creates post-synaptic currents in apical dendrites (top left). In the case of excitatory input, positive current will flow inside the dendrites, leaving a negative charge in the extracellular environment of the dendrites. The extracellular environment at the base of the neuron will become positively charged. This creates a current dipole between the top of the neuron and its base. (B) Many pyramidal neurons undergo this change simultaneously, creating a larger dipolar field that may be strong enough to be detected by EEG electrodes outside of the brain after this signal has passed through cerebrospinal fluid, meninges, the skull, and skin. CSF = cerebrospinal fluid.*

instead composed of extracellular currents that arise from so-called post-synaptic potentials – in which neurons send graded information to other neurons by releasing neurotransmitters from a sending (i.e., pre-synaptic) neuron to a target (i.e., post-synaptic) neuron (e.g., Olejniczak, 2006).

One may think of these post-synaptic potentials as the signature of neural communication – post-synaptic signals are exchanged between neurons when prompted by an action potential in a pre-synaptic neuron, but they may also result in action potentials in the post-synaptic neuron. Most cortical pyramidal neurons receive modulatory signals through tree-like structures (i.e., dendrites), a portion of the neuron that points to the outer edge of the cortex, near the skull. Influx of neurotransmitters at this apical portion causes a voltage gradient between this outer portion and the deeper portion of the neuron, turning the neuron into a miniature battery for a short moment in time (Figure 23.1A). It is possible to measure the electrical activity that is generated jointly by several thousands of pyramidal neurons if their synaptic modulation occurs simultaneously and if the neurons are oriented in the same direction. This is why many researchers refer to the EEG signal as a neural population signal or neural mass activity (Nunez et al., 1997). However, a major constraint of EEG is that the electrical currents inside the brain must travel through neuronal tissue layers of the cortex, cerebrospinal fluid, the meninges, bone, and the scalp before reaching the EEG electrodes. As the electrical current passes through these tissues, volume conduction effects lead to blurring and distortion of the original electrical field changes generated by pyramidal neurons. As a consequence, the EEG signal cannot be used to unambiguously infer the nature of the underlying microscopic processes, such as excitatory versus inhibitory potentials, number of neurons involved, or the cortical region and cortical layer in which the processes occur. However, new methodological developments aim to overcome these challenges, and are briefly discussed later in this chapter.

III. Strengths and Weaknesses of EEG in Comparison with Other Neuroimaging Methods

EEG is arguably the oldest tool for studying brain activity in humans. It thus may be helpful to demarcate its properties in comparison to other, more recently developed brain imaging techniques (see Table 23.1). For example, positron emission tomography (PET) measures metabolic activity within the brain by radioactively tagging a molecule of interest, such as glucose, or neurotransmitters (Hooker & Carson, 2019). PET renders spatially highly resolved maps that indicate the distribution of the target molecule, averaged across several minutes. This allows researchers to evaluate differences between long-lasting behavioral states (e.g., rest versus doing a task) or between groups (e.g., people with schizophrenia versus control participants). However, PET involves the injection of a radioactively labeled substance, making it challenging in terms of logistics and research ethics (see Volume 1, Chapter 2). Functional magnetic resonance imaging (fMRI), a more widely used neuroimaging modality, also allows for the visualization of metabolic

Table 23.1 *Properties of different brain imaging methods relative to EEG*

	EEG	MEG	fMRI	PET
What is measured?	Changes in voltage due to post-synaptic potentials	Magnetic fields produced by post-synaptic potentials	Differences in proportion of oxygenated blood	Distribution of radioactive tracers indicating blood flow, glucose metabolism, or other processes
Temporal Resolution	+	+	–	–
	(sub) milliseconds	(sub) milliseconds	seconds	seconds
Mobility	+	–	–	–
	Can be used stationary or mobile	Stationary	Stationary	Stationary
Safety & tolerability	+	+	–	–
	Safe and tolerable for participants	Safe and tolerable	Safe if safety protocols are adhered to. Loud environment and participants cannot move.	Similar to fMRI, with the additional risks from radioactive tracers
Costs	$	$$	$$$$	$$$$
Spatial resolution & range	–	–	+	+
	Lower spatial resolution, mostly restricted to cortical sources	In some cases better resolution than EEG but also mostly restricted to cortical sources	Good spatial precision for the entire brain	Good spatial precision for the entire brain

Note: + and – signs indicate relative strengths and weaknesses of each method. Greater cost is indicated by a greater number of $ signs.

activity with high spatial accuracy (Logothetis, 2008). Specifically, fMRI measures blood-oxygen-level-dependent (BOLD) signals in the brain. These arise from hemodynamics, the flow of oxygenated blood into active brain regions, a process that changes at a timescale of several seconds. Thus, the physiological processes indexed by PET and fMRI are relatively slow and are only indirectly related to the primary activity of brain cells.

EEG's biggest advantage is its high temporal resolution. EEG allows researchers to track neural activity in real time and on a submillisecond scale (Freeman, 1975). It shares this advantage with magnetoencephalography (MEG) that measures magnetic fields that are created by the previously described post-synaptic potentials. Both methods are ideal for testing hypotheses regarding the time courses of a wide range of psychological processes and their underlying brain processes. However, only EEG also has high mobility compared to other measures of brain activity imaging. Although strong movement produces unwanted artifacts in the EEG (see Section IV), recent technical advancements have increased the ambulatory usage of EEG (Jacobsen et al., 2020), as well as usage in more ecologically valid situations, including sleep studies. These properties allow for investigating populations that are usually not compliant with requirements of fMRI (e.g., infants and small children) or cannot tolerate movement restrictions (e.g., individuals with claustrophobia in the MRI scanner). EEG assessment is non-invasive, unlike intracranial recordings or PET scanning that uses radioactive tracers. Compared to the MRI environment, EEG recordings do not involve loud noises and do not include safety risks associated with strong magnetic fields. See Table 23.1 for strengths and weaknesses of different methods.

Researchers interested in EEG research face comparably low monetary costs, both for the initial purchase and for maintenance. High-quality stationary EEG systems cost between 10,000 and 200,000 USD depending on the manufacturer and other specifications (see Ledwidge et al., 2018 for advice on setting up a basic EEG laboratory). Although it is easy to spend over 100,000 USD on a new EEG lab, fMRI and magnetoencephalography (MEG, see below) are much more expensive. This not only makes EEG attractive for smaller budgets, but it makes collection of larger samples more feasible.

One significant limitation of EEG is its spatial resolution. The EEG signal is a mix of many underlying neural sources, and thus it is often difficult to associate scalp-recorded EEG signals with a specific brain area. As described in Section II, EEG reflects mostly signals from cortical but not subcortical structures, further restricting its spatial scope. If hypotheses are about where in the cortex certain responses occur, source estimation methods can be used (i.e., algorithms to estimate the origin of scalp voltages; Asadzadeh et al., 2020). Although they typically do not achieve the same spatial precision and range as fMRI or PET, it is possible to combine EEG with simultaneous fMRI/PET measures to exploit each method's strengths (Ullsperger & Debener, 2010).

To summarize, a key strength of EEG is its very fine temporal resolution. Furthermore, EEG recordings are much more affordable than other neuroimaging techniques and are non-invasive. However, the spatial resolution of EEG signals is limited in most cases, compared to fMRI and PET. In the remainder of this chapter, we will highlight the utility of using EEG for conducting social and behavioral science research. Below, we describe some of the biophysical properties of EEG recordings, discuss recording setups and analytical techniques, and consider how EEG may be related to psychological phenomena.

IV. EEG Research: From Recording to Publication

EEG recordings are usually performed in an experimental chamber or room that is shielded from external electrical fields. During the recording procedure, participants are often encouraged to avoid eye and body movements, as these lead to artifacts, confounding signals in voltages (Berg & Scherg, 1994; Junghöfer et al., 2000). These instructions alone may impact behavior and cognition, and there is a vigorous debate as to how this issue should be resolved (Keil et al., 2014). Typical EEG recording and data pre-processing involves the following steps: (1) EEG electrodes are placed on the scalp, and impedances (i.e., electrical resistance between the electrode and scalp) are measured; (2) filtering, digitization, and recording of the data occurs; (3) artifacts are removed offline (i.e., after the recording) from the data; (4) meaningful time segments are chosen from the data and further analyzed. In the following, we discuss some of these steps.

The Electrode Array

Over the past decades, the application of EEG electrodes on the scalp has become more convenient and comfortable for participants due to technical innovations, such as all-in-one electrode caps that can hold hundreds of electrodes and are placed on the head using a cap or net structure. Other examples include active electrode systems with built-in preamplifiers that significantly reduce preparation time and improve the signal-to-noise ratio of recorded data. For instance, Figure 23.2A illustrates a dense sensor-array net, in which the electrodes have a sponge and can conduct electrical current if dipped in a saline solution prior to recording.

The 10-20 international system is widely used to denote electrode locations (Figure 23.2B). This system labels electrodes that are placed over the frontal pole (Fp), frontal (F), central I, temporal (T), parietal (P), and occipital (O) cortex; even numbers label electrodes over the right hemisphere, odd numbers label electrodes over the left hemisphere, and "z" (i.e., "zero") labels midline locations (e.g., Fz is frontal midline). The numbers attached to electrodes provide information regarding their distance from the midline – larger numbers indicate greater distances.

Because voltage is a relative measure, or a difference in electrical potential that exists between two sites, amplitude at any specific electrode is always measured with respect to pre-specified reference electrodes. One reference montage often used in EEG research is that each of the recording electrodes measures the voltage gradient against a common reference electrode. The location of the common reference electrode is critical to the interpretation of the resulting scalp distribution of the

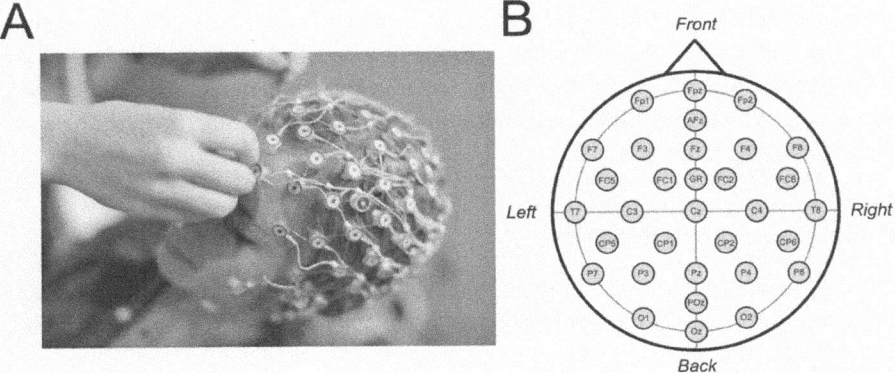

Figure 23.2 *EEG electrodes. (A) Dense sensor-array nets allow for hundreds of electrodes to be placed on the head. (B) The 10-20 international system electrode array arrangement for a 32-sensor montage. GR = ground electrode.*

measured voltage, with traditional recommendations to place the reference at a site that is presumed to be electrically "silent" (e.g., the nose or earlobes). During offline data processing, an average reference can be computed as the mean differences across all electrodes. Use of this average reference avoids biases due to the reference electrode location if the montage provides extensive coverage over the entire head (Junghöfer et al., 1999). The choice of reference can greatly affect the timing and shape of the final EEG waveform and topography across the scalp.

Amplifiers, Filters, and Sampling Rate

In addition to the selection of a reference site, other variables affect the quality and appearance of EEG signals during and after recording. The measured voltage at each electrode is typically amplified by appropriate hardware and can increase the amplitude of the EEG signal by factors of several thousands, making it highly sensitive to both scalp noise and high impedances. Traditional recordings of EEG have attempted to keep scalp electrode impedance below 5 Kilo Ohms (kΩ); this can be measured after the electrodes are applied to the head. Recent developments in EEG technology include the creation of very high-input-impedance amplifiers that allow clean recordings even with scalp impedances much higher than 5 kΩ (Jackson & Bolger, 2014).

Filters are also used during and after EEG recording to further suppress unwanted electrical noise that can interfere with data processing and distort observed voltage changes. Filtering is particularly effective if the desired, or the unwanted, electrical signals are characterized by a certain frequency (e.g., AC line noise at 60 Hz). The selection of filters for reducing noise in specific frequency bands will greatly affect the resulting EEG waveforms (Cook III & Miller, 1992; Widmann et al., 2015).

The sampling rate at which the EEG is digitized into a numeric representation using an analog-to-digital converter will also influence the extent to which slow or fast-going signals are accurately represented in the recordings. For many applications, sample rates of 500 Hertz (Hz) and above will allow veridical reconstruction of an analog EEG signal. For some applications that occur at rapid timescales, much higher sample rates are necessary. Many introductory texts explain the underlying principles guiding these decisions regarding signal processing and digitization (Cacioppo et al., 2007; Luck, 2014).

Artifact Control and Rejection

EEG data contain neurogenic signals and several types of artifacts, i.e., voltage deflections that reflect processes other than brain activity. As discussed later in this chapter, there are different ways of mitigating the effects of artifacts on EEG data. However, from a data quality perspective, "There is no substitute for good data" (Joe Hansen's axiom; Luck, 2014). Thus, we will review the most common types of artifacts in EEG data together with strategies to avoid them (Table 23.2). Although avoiding artifacts is always better than dealing with them after recording, in practice, there will always be some amount of artifacts; we therefore will review approaches to dealing with contaminated data.

Physiological EEG artifacts stem from sources including eyes (e.g., blinks and eye movements; Lins et al., 1993), the heart (e.g., cardiac field and pulse artifacts; Dirlich et al., 1997), muscles (e.g., myogenic artifacts; Goncharova et al., 2003) and sweat glands (e.g., cephalic skin potentials; Corby et al., 1974; Picton & Hillyard, 1972). Non-physiological artifacts are caused by participants' movement, external sources of electromagnetic noise, suboptimal sensor attachment, or hardware malfunction. Table 23.2 gives an overview of the most common artifacts in EEG data and how to avoid them. Figure 23.3 shows examples of how some common artifacts present in EEG data.

Researchers may use different strategies to deal with data containing artifacts. They may try to correct the data by (i) estimating artifacts and mathematically removing them from the data while retaining the cleaned data (i.e., artifact correction, data cleaning); (ii) estimating the signal from surrounding channels, replacing electrodes with artifacts (i.e., topographical interpolation); or (iii) excluding data (i.e., time segments or electrodes) with artifacts from analyses (artifact rejection), or a combination of these methods.

Artifact Correction

One approach to reducing the impact of artifacts is by correcting the data, with the aim of obtaining a cleaned-up signal, or a representation of EEG data as if there had not been an artifact present. Widely used methods include regression, template subtraction, and Independent Component Analysis (ICA). Regression- and template-based artifact subtraction techniques require researchers to identify and estimate the artifacts that are to be removed, often using non-EEG information. For example, electrodes near the eyes may be used to measure eye artifacts such as blinks and eye

Table 23.2 *List of common EEG artifacts and strategies to avoid them*

Artifact	Description	How to Avoid
Physiological		
Eye blinks	Eye blinks produce large, positive-going deflections with steep slopes at frontal electrodes (Figure 23.3).	Participants are often instructed to blink as little as possible.
Eye movements	Vertical eye movements produce similar artifacts to blinks. Lateral eye movements are most dominant at sensors around the temples with more positive voltage to the side of the gaze (Figure 23.3).	Participants can be instructed to look at a fixation point at the beginning of or during each trial. Visual stimuli should not be larger than necessary to reduce scanning eye movements.
Muscle activity	Potentials from muscles have a broad frequency spectrum. The strongest artifacts are typically found on electrodes near temples, jaw, and neck (Figure 23.3).	Participants should be reminded to sit in a relaxed position. Paradigms should include sufficient breaks to move and stretch. Participants may not chew gum during the experiment.
Cardiovascular	Cardiac field artifacts reflect the electrocardiogram. Slower pulse wave artifacts result from the blood rhythmically expanding blood vessels beneath the electrodes.	There are no effective measures for avoiding this artifact. For certain applications (EEG-fMRI, heartbeat-evoked potentials), specific correction methods have been developed.
Skin potentials	Phasic activation of sweat glands leads to slow drift artifacts (≤ 4 Hz). Their shape may resemble skin conductance responses as recorded on palms.	The air in the test room should be kept dry and the temperature should be controlled (ca. 70°F / 21°C). Low electrode impedances help to reduce the impact of skin potentials.
Non-physiological		
Participant movement	Movement of the head or face or due to respiration causes movement of electrodes or cables. Artifacts have different shapes including slow, large drifts across multiple channels.	Participants are often instructed to sit as still and relaxed as possible. Test sessions should not be too long and have sufficient breaks.
Electromagnetic noise	The most commonly observed electromagnetic artifact is AC line noise. EEG sensors can pick up a regular sine wave signal of 50 or 60 Hz, depending on the country's standards. Similarly, monitors can produce noise at the frequency of their refresh rate.	Avoid proximity to main power lines. The test room may be built within a Faraday cage that shields the space from electromagnetic waves. Researchers should then not bring sources of electromagnetic noise into the Faraday cage. Active electrodes, shielded electrode cables, and amplifiers with high input impedance help to reduce electromagnetic noise.

Table 23.2 (cont.)

Artifact	Description	How to Avoid
Unstable or changing impedances	Unstable contact between scalp and sensors may lead to so-called electrode pops – sudden, steep voltage changes at single electrodes. In addition, chemical or physical changes at the sensor sites (e.g., sweating) may affect impedances.	Researchers may use caps or nets that sit tight on the head. They should prepare the sensor sites carefully and keep impedances low. Amplifiers should have high voltage resolution to prevent signal saturation due to slow voltage drifts. It is also recommended to let electrode gel "settle" for a couple of minutes before recording.
Bridging	Electrical bridging occurs when there is a low-impedance connection between electrodes. This can be caused by short-circuits in the hardware or, most commonly, when electrode gel connects different contacts on the head. Two connected channels show a nearly identical signal (flatline if the reference sensor is involved).	Researchers should not use excessive amounts of electrode gel or saline, especially when using high-density sensor arrays.
Damaged wires or electrodes	Broken wires can cause strong, unsystematic voltage changes in the area of millivolts (loose contacts) or flat lines (no contact at all). Some EEG systems will not work at all with broken circuits.	Equipment should be handled with care and faulty hardware repaired as soon as possible.

Note: Brief overview of common EEG artifacts. EEG is more susceptible to artifacts than many other physiological measures, and a significant portion of replication issues with EEG data stems from noisy data or lack of signal.

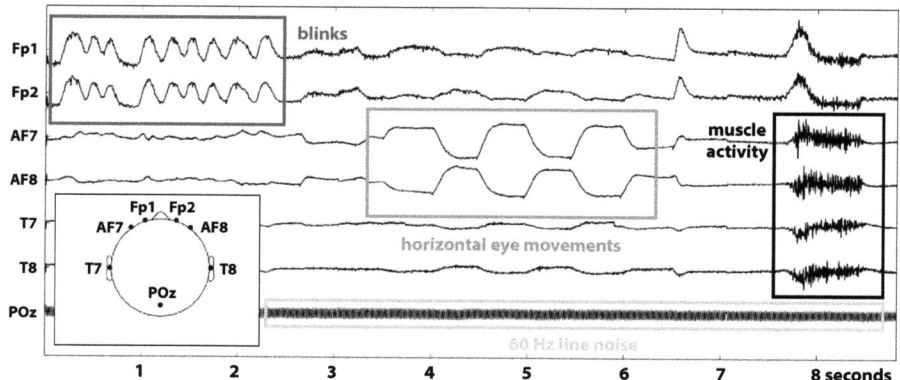

Figure 23.3 *Examples of common artifacts in EEG data. Artifacts commonly display greater magnitude compared to the ongoing EEG signal, illustrated by the impact of blinks (top left), horizontal eye movements (middle), muscle artifact (right), and line noise (bottom) on the EEG recording.*

movements. The recorded artifact data then is subtracted from the EEG channels (Gratton et al., 1983; Schlögl et al., 2007).

ICA is a family of blind signal separation algorithms that has been used for a variety of signal processing purposes (Hyvärinen & Oja, 2000; Tharwat, 2018). Unlike the previously described correction procedures, ICA tries to estimate different independent contributions to the EEG signal using the EEG data itself. Similar to the more widely known principal component analysis, ICA decomposes an observed signal into a set of latent components by finding spatial patterns of activity that are statistically independent from each other over time. Components that reflect artifact contributions can be identified based on their shape over time and the distribution of their weights across channels (Chaumon et al., 2015). For example, blink artifacts are most prominent at medial frontopolar sites. ICA can be used to correct for both physiological artifacts (e.g., ocular, cardiovascular, and to some degree muscle), and non-physiological artifacts, such as line noise (McMenamin et al., 2010). Researchers who want to use ICA for their data processing should make sure that the data contain sufficient electrodes (ideally 64 or more; Klug & Gramann, 2020). ICA requires more processing power than many other artifact control methods and should be run on computers with sufficient computing resources.

Interpolation

EEG signals can also be topographically interpolated. That is, the signal from a given electrode is estimated using data from surrounding electrodes (Perrin et al., 1989; Soong et al., 1993). Given the current-conducting properties of the head, neighboring electrodes have correlated signals and overlap in the neural generators they are sensitive to. Interpolation is recommended primarily when artifacts cannot be handled via other methods or if no actual signal was recorded in the first place (e.g., broken or detached electrodes; estimating the signal at the ground electrode position). Often, topographical interpolation is done for the entire time series of select channels, although it can also be done on a trial-by-trial basis with different channels in each trial (Peyk et al., 2011).

Artifact Rejection

After, or instead of, using correction and interpolation methods, data segments or individual channels may be excluded from further analyses. An excluded segment of channel will contain a mixture of desirable signal and undesirable noise. Researchers aim to find a good balance between excluding noise and retaining signal. Rejection of artifacts can be implemented manually or by suitable algorithms. Manual artifact detection gives full control to the researcher and assists in learning about the data in great detail. However, this approach is labor-intensive, requires thorough training of artifact scorers, and puts limits to reproducibility of analyses.

On the other hand, there are many algorithms to automatically detect and flag suspicious data. Advantages of automated procedures include their reproducibility and convenience; disadvantages include the black box characteristics of many algorithms. Manual artifact screening should be conducted blind to experimental conditions or groups whenever possible. Similarly, parameters of automated procedures should be either consistent or, if different thresholds are used for different participants, be applied blind to experimental groups. Readers can find a detailed overview of artifact detection and correction methods, along with recommendations, in Islam and colleagues' comprehensive review (2016).

V. Doing Research with EEG, Part 1: Using the Event-Related Potential (ERP) Technique

The event-related potential (ERP) technique is the most widely used EEG-based technique (Luck & Kappenman, 2011). ERPs are derived from ongoing EEG activity and measure specific neural activity following or preceding an anchoring event that is under the control of the experimenter; it is typically repeated many times during a recording session. Common anchoring events include the onset of a word, picture, sound, or other visual, auditory, olfactory, or somatosensory stimulus. Other anchoring events can include the execution of specific motor behaviors, a stimulus that cues preparation of motor behaviors, or even a cue to perform covert mental operations (e.g., mental imagery, retrieval, anticipation). ERPs reflect the prototypical brain electric changes in response to these anchoring events. They are readily interpretable as elicited by the anchoring event of interest and are highly compatible with experimental tasks with repeated trials. As a consequence, ERPs have been used to index a broad spectrum of social phenomena, including perception, attention, emotion, action, response preparation, motor planning, and memory. For example, researchers may wish to study how pictures of faces are processed in the visual part of the brain in the back of the head, depending on an observer's familiarity with the face, or depending on the observer's level of social anxiety.

By averaging EEG activity over many trials (Figure 23.4A), a representative temporal waveform of brain voltage changes can be obtained (Figure 23.4B) that characterizes the neuronal population response to the event of interest. Trial averaging is essential for ERPs because continuously recorded EEG is noisy. Its magnitude tends to be on the scale of hundreds of microvolts (μV), whereas the ERP is characterized by voltage fluctuations in the range of a few microvolts, often well below 10 μV. Random activity not related to the anchoring event of interest will cancel out as the number of trials used to average increases, leading to greater suppression of non-stimulus-related EEG signal. Subtraction of a pre-stimulus baseline is typically used to center the signal at zero μV and measure voltage deflections relative to the voltage level prior to stimulus onset (see Figure 23.4B).

As an example, education researchers may be interested in assessing the noticeability of an unexpected numerical symbol in a stream of digits. They record continuous EEG while students view several hundreds of expected and unexpected digits. They then segment the EEG into periods that are time-locked to the onset of the expected and unexpected digit and average the segments separately for unexpected and expected events. This enables them to compare the amplitude of the

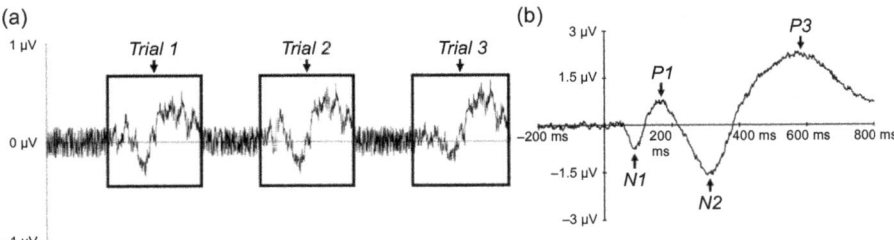

Figure 23.4 *Event-related potential (ERP). (A) Event-related EEG responses from single trials used to compute ERPs are often obscured by larger ongoing EEG signals that are not related to the event of interest. By averaging trials together, random voltage deflections in EEG signals are reduced, with the final waveforms reflecting ERPs tied to specific target events of interest. (B) The resulting output is a temporal series of negative and positive voltage deflections time and time-locked to the event of interest.*

symbol-evoked ERP for expected versus unexpected digits. They may now test hypotheses such as notions regarding the timing of neural processes (at what time ERP differences between expected and unexpected digits become apparent) or regarding inter-individual differences (e.g., they may hypothesize that students whose ERP does not differ between expected and unexpected did not understand the task as well as students with pronounced differences).

Depending on the nature and size of the ERP of interest, recommendations for the number of trials necessary for extracting meaningful ERPs range between 15 and 20 trials (e.g., for extracting large responses to salient visual target stimuli) to thousands of trials (e.g., for extracting the brainstem's response to specific sounds). A sizable and growing literature has discussed the number of trials needed to achieve robust ERP signals that are sufficiently distinct from noise. Researchers are encouraged to consider this literature, as it is crucial for the design of reproducible studies (Boudewyn et al., 2018; Gibney et al., 2020; Thigpen et al., 2017).

The pronounced positive and negative voltage deflections in an ERP that are reliably present within a specific experimental context are often called *components* and are typically labeled by letter–number pairs indicating their polarity and temporal position in the sequence of event-related components (Figure 23.4B). For example, N1 or N100, refers to the first negative deflection, whereas P2 or P200, is the second positive deflection. Historically, the numerical index reflected the temporal latency of a component in ms rather than its temporal position. However, in recent years, labeling an ERP component by its temporal position of voltage deflections (e.g., 1, 2, 3) is preferred, as the specific timing of a component can vary broadly depending upon the experimental context. Hence, a classical ERP component originally labeled as "P"00" (i.e., a positive deflection around 300 ms after a stimulus onset) is often also referred to as a "P3" component. Whereas the P3 typically tends to be the third positive peak in studies of visual attention and perception, its temporal maximum is not always at 300 ms.

Slower ERP components include longer-lasting deflections that often lack a clear peak; they are typically labeled, depending upon their polarity, as positive or negative slow waves or potentials (e.g., the Late Positive Potential or the Contingent Negative Variation). Occasionally, ERP components that occur very reliably in specific paradigms are named based on their topographical computation (e.g., the Lateralized Readiness Potential). This is an ERP that is maximal over contralateral electrodes (i.e., electrodes on the opposite hemisphere in which an action, motor or visual, is made) when preparing to make a motor movement on one side of the body. Difference waveforms between two experimental conditions can highlight neural differences between events that are ideally identical, except for a variable of interest that was manipulated in the experiment.

In addition to amplitude and latency values of different ERP components, ERP studies also reveal topographical information that specifies the electrode locations at which selected positive and negative voltage deflections are maximal. Because EEG records activity arising from large cell assemblies, whose original locus is spatially smeared by conductance properties of the scalp and other brain matter, the topographical information associated with a measured ERP component does not specify the original source of this neural activity. Moreover, any specific scalp topography could theoretically be generated by many different configurations of potential sources of neural activity, meaning the topography of any voltage distribution measured at the scalp does not uniquely identify the underlying sources (the so-called inverse problem). Thus, topographical information in an ERP study primarily allows more precise labeling of an ERP component that is useful for comparison across paradigms and as a means of differentiation from other components that may occur in the same time interval, but measured at other sites. To conclude this section, Table 23.2 gives an overview of some of the most widely used ERP components and how they are used in empirical research.

Table 23.3 *Common ERP components*

ERP component	Peak latency (ms)	Neurophysiological generators	Basic interpretation
Auditory			
Auditory Nerve and Brainstem Potentials I, II, III, IV, & V	~1–10 ms	Cochlea (I), auditory nerve and brainstem (II), brainstem (III), and upper pons (IV & V)	Lowest stimulus detection threshold and temporal properties of a stimulus
Middle-Latency Potentials N0, P0, Na, Pa, & Nb	~10–40 ms	Brainstem (N0), postauricular muscles (P0), Midbrain, thalamus, or thalamocortical radiations (Na), and primary auditory cortices (Pa, Nb)	High-intensity auditory stimulation, temporal properties of a stimulus, first major response of the auditory cortex

Table 23.3 (cont.)

ERP component	Peak latency (ms)	Neurophysiological generators	Basic interpretation
P50	~50 ms	Primary auditory cortex	Sensory activation and gating
N1	~100 ms	Auditory cortex and auditory association cortices	Acoustic changes in the environment, or deviation from previous auditory input
P2	~150–250 ms	Auditory cortex and auditory association cortices	Stimulus classification and attentional allocation
Mismatch Negativity (MMN)/N2	~100–200 ms	Bilateral supratemporal cortices and right frontal regions	Stimulus discrimination/ mismatches and perception
P3	~250–500 ms	Frontal (P3a) and parietal (P3b) regions, and some evidence for medial temporal lobe (P3b)	Higher-order cognitive processes (e.g., context updating, attentional resource allocation, probability and stimulus categorization)
N400	~100–500 ms	Potentially left inferior frontal cortex	Violation of semantic context
Visual			
C1	~50–70 ms	Striate cortex, specifically the calcarine fissure	Luminance, contrast, and spatial frequency of visual stimulus
P1	~60–130 ms	Extrastriate cortex and lateral extrastriate cortex	Spatial attention, simple feature-based attention
N1/N170	~100–200 ms	Extrastriate cortex and lateral extrastriate cortex (N1), and the lateral occipital cortex and fusiform gyrus (N170)	Spatial and feature-based attention (N1), and facial perception (N170)
P2	~100–175 ms	Re-entrant V1 activity, intraparietal sulcus, and V6	Processing of target features in stimuli
N2	~200–400 ms	Anterior cingulate cortex	Conflict monitoring and stimulus incongruency detection

Table 23.3 (cont.)

ERP component	Peak latency (ms)	Neurophysiological generators	Basic interpretation
N2 posterior contralateral (N2pc)	~200–300 ms	V4 and lateral occipital complex	Covert attentional selection
P3	~300–800 ms	Frontal (P3a) and parietal (P3b) regions, and some evidence for medial temporal lobe (P3b)	Higher-order cognitive processes (e.g., context updating, attentional resource allocation, probability and stimulus categorization)
N400	~300–600 ms	Potentially left inferior frontal cortex	Violation of semantic context
Contralateral Delay Activity (CDA)	~400–900 ms	Intraparietal sulcus	Items maintained in working memory
Late Positive Potential (LPP)	~300–1,500 ms	Occipitotemporal, parietal, and inferior temporal cortices	Sustained attention to affective stimuli or affective processes
Motor/Response-Based			
Contingent Negative Variation (CNV)	Within several seconds between the onset of an initial warning stimulus (S1) and subsequent target stimulus (S2)	No consensus, likely various regions involving attention and motor preparation	Processing a warning stimulus for motor preparation to a subsequent target stimulus
Stimulus Preceding Negativity (SPN)	Preceding an upcoming target stimulus that was previously cued by a warning stimulus	Right hemispheric prefrontal cortex, insula, and parietal cortex	Increasing anticipation for the occurrence of an informative/ subsequent stimulus
Lateralized Readiness Potential (LRP)	Preceding movement onset	Primary motor cortex	Motor preparations
Error-Related Negativity (ERN)	~0–150 ms post-response	Anterior cingulate cortex and supplementary motor area	Recognition of incorrect responses and potential conflict monitoring

Note: The visual N1 and N170 components are considered to be the same component by some. The auditory MMN and N2 are also considered synonymous.

VI. Doing Research with EEG, Part 2: Spectral and Time-Frequency Analysis

Brain oscillations – rhythmic aspects of the EEG measured by the number of cycles per second (i.e., Hz) – provide another useful means to analyze EEG signals, complementing ERP studies. Traditionally, brain oscillations have been categorized as spontaneous, evoked, emitted, or induced (Galambos, 1992). Spontaneous oscillations occur during waking or sleeping at any point in time, and many are used in neurological assessment as well as in sleep staging (Babiloni et al., 2020). Evoked oscillations are elicited by a time-locked event and can be analyzed similar to ERPs. In contrast, emitted oscillations may occur when a time-locked event is expected but does not occur.

Induced oscillations are elicited by a specific event but are neither time- nor phase-locked to its onset. Thus, they require specific analytical methods, other than time-domain averaging as used for ERP analysis. Oscillations are typically quantified through frequency domain analyses that decompose the EEG signal's variability over time into a frequency spectrum to produce power and phase information regarding each frequency – the repetition rate of an oscillation. In these analyses, power refers to the overall strength or magnitude of a given frequency, while phase reflects an observed frequency's relative position in time compared to a given reference point for when that oscillation is believed to occur. As such, oscillations vary in frequency, power, and phase.

The most basic form of frequency-domain decomposition is the Fourier transformation that uses sine and cosine basis functions to quantify oscillatory activity. Typically, spectra contain frequencies represented on an x-axis and power or phase displayed on a y-axis (Figure 23.5A). Traditionally, the EEG power spectrum is divided into canonical frequency bands, referred to as delta (< 3 Hz), theta (4–7 Hz), alpha (8–12 Hz), beta (13–30 Hz), and gamma (> 30 Hz) oscillations. In the past, canonical bands were related to specific cognitive or behavioral processes, but this practice is increasingly rare because (i) the demarcation of the frequency bands varies greatly between participants and between experimental contexts, and (ii) changes in power or phase in each of the canonical bands are likewise highly sensitive to small differences in setting and task demands. Thus, it is not possible

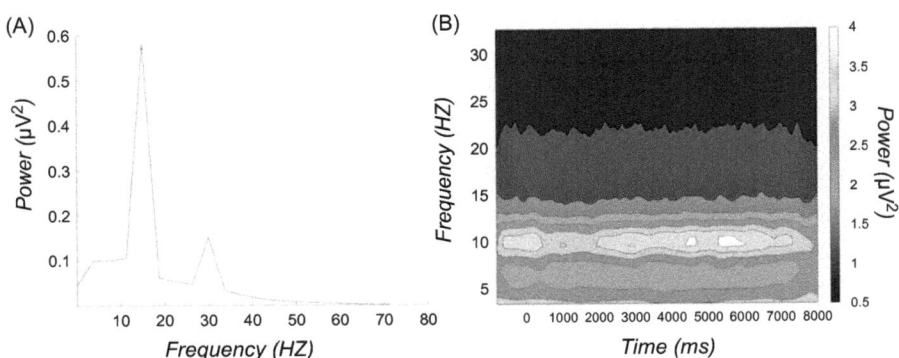

Figure 23.5 *Spectrum and spectrogram. (A) Spectral analyses often include an illustration of power over a range of frequencies or spectrum. (B) Time-frequency analyses are instead represented by a spectrogram. This allows for the visualization of changes in power over time for each analyzed frequency.*

to unambiguously link the presence of power in a given frequency band to a specific cognitive or behavioral state (Keil et al., 2022). It is also important to note that spectral power and phase measurements reflect both oscillatory and non-oscillatory activity (e.g., broadband noise, such as "white" and "pink" noise; see Keil et al., 2022 for further details). This is because the Fourier spectrum, and comparable methods, are sensitive to all changes in amplitude in the original EEG signal, rhythmic and non-rhythmic (Donoghue et al., 2020).

Many excellent introductory texts are available for those interested in applying spectral analysis. Cohen's book on neural time series analysis (2014) is a widely used volume that also covers more advanced techniques, such as time-frequency analysis (TFA), discussed next. An edited volume on EEG frequency analysis (Gable et al., 2022) represents a collection of foundational topics and advanced applications. Finally, readers interested in publication guidelines and best practices are referred to a recent paper by Keil and colleagues (2022).

More advanced spectral analytical strategies also allow for the assessment of temporal information relative to an event of interest – often represented through spectrograms with an x-axis displaying time, a y-axis showing frequency, and a third dimensional color map reflecting power for each frequency at a given time point (Figure 23.5B). TFA are similar to ERPs in that they provide information regarding changes in EEG signal that unfold in time, with respect to an event of interest. However, unlike ERPs, TFA can provide information regarding other properties of the oscillations of interest, such as phase consistency of oscillations across trials and phase synchrony across electrode sites. Thus, spectra and TFA provide a unique lens for examining information in the EEG that may not be captured through ERP analyses.

VI. EEG Signals and Social Processes

ERPs and frequency domain analyses are powerful tools for identifying underlying processes associated with information processing and behavior in human participants. They also are useful for understanding individual differences due to psychopathology, brain insult or injury, aging, and other clinically relevant phenomena. EEG/ERP measures are used to make inferences about the presence or absence of neural processes within a specific experimental context, and to draw conclusions regarding the timing and ordering of these processes.

For example, researchers interested in error processing may separately average EEG segments recorded during trials with correct versus incorrect responses and compare the waveforms. Researchers interested in social cognition may record EEG as participants perform evaluative judgments of text vignettes and measure the frequency content of the EEG signal, comparing trials with positive as opposed to neutral or negative evaluations. It is important to note that the interpretation of the resulting EEG/ERP measures depends on the predictions and manipulations of the experimental design used in the study under consideration. By contrast, linking EEG phenomena unconditionally to a cognitive construct regardless of what was being manipulated may result in the fallacy of reverse inference (Poldrack, 2011). This inference takes the general form: previous studies have shown that X cognitive process causes B brain response, and the present study found B brain response, therefore X cognitive process was present. As noted by Sinnott-Armstrong and Simmons (2021), reverse inference is deductively invalid because it commits the fallacy of affirming the consequent; the truth of the premises does not necessarily obtain the truth of the conclusion.

VII. Emerging Trends in EEG Research

The field of EEG research is subject to rapid advancements, both methodological and conceptual. In this section we briefly summarize emerging trends in the field.

Multimodal Imaging and Advanced Signal Processing

Given its robust signal, unobtrusive nature, and low cost, EEG is highly suitable to combine with other imaging modalities. This trend is facilitated by dramatic progress in advanced signal processing methods, including algorithms for estimating the sources underlying the scalp EEG. Although expensive, and somewhat cumbersome, concurrent recordings of EEG and fMRI are now increasingly feasible and yield reliable data (Huster et al., 2012). Ongoing efforts are focusing on improving algorithms for EEG-fMRI fusion as well as combining the use of EEG with other modalities with the goal of maximizing the added value of concurrent recordings, increasing interpretability and neurophysiological validity.

Mobile EEG

As stated in Section I, miniaturization of amplifiers, along with shrinking microcircuits for sampling and processing and improved electrode technology, has enabled development of increasingly mobile EEG systems. These systems may take different forms and now include around-ear arrays (Debener et al., 2015), barely visible to bystanders, or dry electrode arrays, worn like a cap or light bicycle helmet. Although caution is warranted, these developments have opened avenues for using EEG in environments not previously accessible, such as clinics, sports arenas, or classrooms (Lau-Zhu et al., 2019). Future work may use these ecologically valid recordings to test novel hypotheses regarding brain electric changes in social, environmental, competitive, or educational contexts.

Machine Learning and Artificial Intelligence

Computational tools have dramatically evolved over the past decade, including network architectures that have superior pattern recognition capabilities, such as artificial neural networks (e.g., deep and recurrent architectures). Emerging applications of these tools include improved artifact detection and elimination and modeling of EEG signals. These models include generative models that may mimic some of the main properties of EEG and may be used as a testbed for methodological, clinical, or experimental work (Neymotin et al., 2011). Methods such as support vector machines are also increasingly used to quantify the amount of information in EEG signals that is diagnostic for classifying experimental conditions or groups of participants, a process known as decoding (Bae & Luck, 2018). These analyses are also relevant in basic and clinical science, in the context of so-called brain–computer interfaces, where EEG signals are used to control devices (Abiri et al., 2019), and in the context of neurofeedback training, where participants learn to modulate aspects of their own brain electric activity (Sitaram et al., 2017).

Computer Modeling

The fine temporal resolution of EEG/ERP signals adds to computer models of neurocognitive processes. Such models involve the mathematical/statistical description of cognitive functions, often linking environmental variables to predicted behavioral performance data. Example approaches include the Rescorla-Wagner model of associative learning (Riels et al., 2022) and drift-diffusion models of choice behavior (Nunez et al., 2017).

Reproducibility, Pre-registration, and Pipeline Sharing

Paralleling developments in other areas of science, a growing number of EEG researchers have begun to implement changes in scientific practice that aim to heighten reproducibility (for an extended discussion of this, see Chapter 13, this volume), as well as provide greater access to the research materials and products (Garrett-Ruffin et al., 2021). In addition to widely adopted practices, such as pre-registration, archive publishing, and data sharing (Kappenman et al., 2021), EEG research has also begun to systematically widen accessibility to data analysis scripts. Sharing these so-called pipelines is expected to heighten the reproducibility of increasingly complex data analysis schemes, relying on sophisticated computational tools. Efforts also include making data formats more compatible so that different groups of researchers may access shared data; this assists in meta-analyses and also allows gathering of large samples across different laboratories.

VIII. Closing Remarks

EEG recordings are among the most versatile brain imaging techniques available to social and behavioral scientists. Widely available, relatively inexpensive, and increasingly compatible with a wide range of study environments and paradigms, EEG can be used to test many different hypotheses about brain function. This includes hypotheses regarding the extent to which a social or behavioral manipulation affects neurocognitive processes, and the time course of neurocognitive processes. Efforts for data sharing, multi-site collaboration, and pipeline integration (Pavlov et al., 2021) benefit from EEG's clear data structure, long research tradition, and established quality indices. It is likely that calls for more replication, improved science practices, and transparent data analysis – now prevalent across all sciences – will further benefit EEG research (Clayson et al., 2022). In summary, EEG will remain an essential tool in the social and behavioral sciences for decades to come.

References

Abiri, R., Borhani, S., Sellers, E. W., Jiang, Y., & Zhao, X. (2019). A comprehensive review of EEG-based brain–computer interface paradigms. *Journal of Neural Engineering*, *16*(1), 011001. https://doi.org/10.1088/1741-2552/aaf12e

Asadzadeh, S., Yousefi Rezaii, T., Beheshti, S., Delpak, A., & Meshgini, S. (2020). A systematic review of EEG source localization techniques and their applications on diagnosis of brain abnormalities. *Journal of Neuroscience Methods*, *339*, 108740. https://doi.org/10.1016/j.jneumeth.2020.108740

Babiloni, C., Barry, R. J., Başar, E., Blinowska, K. J., Cichocki, A., Drinkenburg, W. H. I. M., et al. (2020). International Federation of Clinical Neurophysiology (IFCN) – EEG research workgroup: Recommendations on frequency and topographic analysis of resting state EEG rhythms. Part 1: Applications in clinical research studies. *Clinical Neurophysiology*, *131*(1), 285–307. https://doi.org/10.1016/j.clinph.2019.06.234

Bae, G.-Y., & Luck, S. J. (2018). Dissociable decoding of spatial attention and working memory from EEG oscillations and sustained potentials. *Journal of Neuroscience*, *38*(2), 409–422. https://doi.org/10.1523/JNEUROSCI.2860-17.2017

Berg, P., & Scherg, M. (1994). A multiple source approach to the correction of eye artifacts. *Electroencephalography and Clinical Neurophysiology*, *90*(3), 229–241.

Berger, H. (1929). Über das Elektrenkephalogramm des Menschen. *Archiv für Psychiatrie und Nervenkrankheiten*, *87*, 527–570.

Biasiucci, A., Franceschiello, B., & Murray, M. M. (2019). Electroencephalography. *Current Biology*, *29*(3), R80–R85.

Boudewyn, M. A., Luck, S. J., Farrens, J. L., & Kappenman, E. S. (2018). How many trials does it take to get a significant ERP effect? It depends. *Psychophysiology*, *55*(6), e13049. https://doi.org/10.1111/psyp.13049

Bressler, S. L., & Menon, V. (2010). Large-scale brain networks in cognition: Emerging methods and principles. *Trends in Cognitive Sciences*, *14*(6), 277–290. https://doi.org/10.1016/j.tics.2010.04.004

Bridwell, D. A., Cavanagh, J. F., Collins, A. G. E., Nunez, M. D., Srinivasan, R., Stober, S., & Calhoun, V. D. (2018). Moving beyond ERP components: A selective review of approaches to integrate EEG and behavior. *Frontiers in Human Neuroscience*, *12*. https://doi.org/10.3389/fnhum.2018.00106

Buzsáki, G., & Draguhn, A. (2004). Neuronal oscillations in cortical networks. *Science*, *304* (5679), 1926–1929. https://doi.org/10.1126/science.1099745

Cacioppo, J. T., Tassinary, L. G., & Berntson, G. (2007). *Handbook of Psychophysiology*. Cambridge University Press.

Chaumon, M., Bishop, D. V. M., & Busch, N. A. (2015). A practical guide to the selection of independent components of the electroencephalogram for artifact correction. *Journal of Neuroscience Methods*, *250*, 47–63. https://doi.org/10.1016/j.jneumeth.2015.02.025

Clayson, P. E., Keil, A., & Larson, M. J. (2022). Open science in human electrophysiology. *International Journal of Psychophysiology*, *174*, 43–46. https://doi.org/10.1016/j.ijpsycho.2022.02.002

Cohen, M. X. (2014). *Analyzing Neural Time Series Data: Theory and Practice*. MIT Press.

Cook III, E. W., & Miller, G. A. (1992). Digital filtering: Background and tutorial for psychophysiologists. *Psychophysiology*, *29*(3), 350–367. https://doi.org/10.1111/j.1469-8986.1992.tb01709.x

Corby, J. C., Roth, W. T., & Kopell, B. S. (1974). Prevalence and methods of control of the cephalic skin potential EEG artifact. *Psychophysiology*, *11*(3), 350–360. https://doi.org/10.1111/j.1469-8986.1974.tb00554.x

Debener, S., Emkes, R., De Vos, M., & Bleichner, M. (2015). Unobtrusive ambulatory EEG using a smartphone and flexible printed electrodes around the ear. *Scientific Reports*, *5*(1), 16743. https://doi.org/10.1038/srep16743

Dirlich, G., Vogl, L., Plaschke, M., & Strian, F. (1997). Cardiac field effects on the EEG. *Electroencephalography and Clinical Neurophysiology*, *102*(4), 307–315. https://doi.org/10.1016/S0013-4694(96)96506-2

Donoghue, T., Haller, M., Peterson, E. J., Varma, P., Sebastian, P., Gao, R., et al. (2020). Parameterizing neural power spectra into periodic and aperiodic components. *Nature Neuroscience*, *23*(12), 1655–1665. https://doi.org/10.1038/s41593-020-00744-x

Freeman, W. J. (1975). *Mass Action in the Nervous System: Examination of the Neurophysiological Basis of Adaptive Behavior through the EEG*. Academic Press.

Gable, P., Miller, M., & Bernat, E. (2022). *The Oxford Handbook of EEG Frequency*. Oxford University Press.

Galambos, R. (1992). A comparison of certain gamma-band (40 Hz) brain rhythms in cat and man. In E. Basar & T. Bullock (eds.), *Induced Rhythms in the Brain* (pp. 103–122). Springer.

Garrett-Ruffin, S., Hindash, A. C., Kaczkurkin, A. N., Mears, R. P., Morales, S., Paul, K., et al. (2021). Open science in psychophysiology: An overview of challenges and emerging solutions. *International Journal of Psychophysiology*, *162*, 69–78. https://doi.org/10.1016/j.ijpsycho.2021.02.005

Gibney, K. D., Kypriotakis, G., Cinciripini, P. M., Robinson, J. D., Minnix, J. A., & Versace, F. (2020). Estimating statistical power for event-related potential studies using the late positive potential. *Psychophysiology*, *57*(2), e13482. https://doi.org/10.1111/psyp.13482

Goncharova, I. I., McFarland, D. J., Vaughan, T. M., & Wolpaw, J. R. (2003). EMG contamination of EEG: Spectral and topographical characteristics. *Clinical Neurophysiology*, *114*(9), 1580–1593. https://doi.org/10.1016/S1388-2457(03)00093-2

Gratton, G., Coles, M. G. H., & Donchin, E. (1983). A new method for off-line removal of ocular artifact. *Electroencephalography and Clinical Neurophysiology*, *55*(4), 468–484. https://doi.org/10.1016/0013-4694(83)90135-9

Hooker, J. M., & Carson, R. E. (2019). Human positron emission tomography neuroimaging. *Annual Review of Biomedical Engineering*, *21*(1), 551–581. https://doi.org/10.1146/annurev-bioeng-062117-121056

Huster, R. J., Debener, S., Eichele, T., & Herrmann, C. S. (2012). Methods for simultaneous EEG-fMRI: An introductory review. *Journal of Neuroscience*, *32*(18), 6053–6060. https://doi.org/10.1523/JNEUROSCI.0447-12.2012

Hyvärinen, A., & Oja, E. (2000). Independent component analysis: Algorithms and applications. *Neural Networks*, *13*, 411–430. https://doi.org/10.1016/S0893-6080(00)00026-5

Islam, M. K., Rastegarnia, A., & Yang, Z. (2016). Methods for artifact detection and removal from scalp EEG: A review. *Neurophysiologie Clinique / Clinical Neurophysiology*, *46*(4–5), 287–305. https://doi.org/10.1016/j.neucli.2016.07.002

Jackson, A. F., & Bolger, D. J. (2014). The neurophysiological bases of EEG and EEG measurement: A review for the rest of us. *Psychophysiology*, *51*(11), 1061–1071. https://doi.org/10.1111/psyp.12283

Jacobsen, N. S. J., Blum, S., Witt, K., & Debener, S. (2020). A walk in the park? Characterizing gait-related artifacts in mobile EEG recordings. *European Journal of Neuroscience*, 54(12), 8421–8440. https://doi.org/10.1111/ejn.14965

Junghöfer, M., Elbert, T., Tucker, D. M., & Braun, C. (1999). The polar average reference effect: A bias in estimating the head surface integral in EEG recording. *Clinical Neurophysiology*, *110*(6), 1149–1155. https://doi.org/10.1016/S1388-2457(99)00044-9

Junghöfer, M., Elbert, T., Tucker, D. M., & Rockstroh, B. (2000). Statistical control of artifacts in dense array EEG/MEG studies. *Psychophysiology*, *37*(4), 523–532. https://doi.org/10.1111/1469-8986.3740523

Kappenman, E., Farrens, J., Zhang, W., Stewart, A. X., & Luck, S. J. (2021). ERP CORE: An open resource for human event-related potential research. *NeuroImage*, *225*, 117465. https://doi.org/10.31234/osf.io/4azqm

Kappenman, E. S., & Luck, S. J. (2012). ERP components: The ups and downs of brainwave recordings. In S. J. Luck & E. S. Kappenman (eds.), *The Oxford Handbook of ERP Components*. Oxford University Press.

Keil, A., Bernat, E. M., Cohen, M. X., Ding, M., Fabiani, M., Gratton, G., et al. (2022). Recommendations and publication guidelines for studies using frequency-domain and time-frequency-domain analyses of neural time series. *Psychophysiology*, *59*(5), e14052. https://doi.org/10.1111/psyp.14052

Keil, A., Debener, S., Gratton, G., Junghöfer, M., Kappenman, E. S., Luck, S. J., et al. (2014). Committee report: Publication guidelines and recommendations for studies using electroencephalography and magnetoencephalography. *Psychophysiology*, *51*(1), 1–21. https://doi.org/10.1111/psyp.12147

Klug, M., and Gramann, K. (2020). Identifying key factors for improving ICA-based decomposition of EEG data in mobile and stationary experiments. *European Journal of Neuroscience*, *54*(12), 8406–8420. https://doi.org/10.1111/ejn.14992

Lau-Zhu, A., Lau, M. P. H., & McLoughlin, G. (2019). Mobile EEG in research on neurodevelopmental disorders: Opportunities and challenges. *Developmental Cognitive Neuroscience*, *36*, 100635. https://doi.org/10.1016/j.dcn.2019.100635

Ledwidge, P., Foust, J., & Ramsey, A. (2018). Recommendations for developing an EEG laboratory at a primarily undergraduate institution. *Journal of Undergraduate Neuroscience Education*, *17*(1), A10–A19.

Linden, D. E. (2005). The p300: Where in the brain is it produced and what does it tell us? *Neuroscientist*, *11*(6), 563–576.

Lins, O. G., Picton, T. W., Berg, P., & Scherg, M. (1993). Ocular artifacts in EEG and event-related potentials I: Scalp topography. *Brain Topography*, *6*(1), 51–63. https://doi.org/10.1007/BF01234127

Logothetis, N. K. (2008). What we can do and what we cannot do with fMRI. *Nature*, *453* (7197), 869–878. https://doi.org/10.1038/nature06976

Luck, S. J. (2014). *An Introduction to the Event-Related Potential Technique*, 2nd ed. MIT Press.

Luck, S. J., & Kappenman, E. S. (2011). *The Oxford Handbook of Event-Related Potential Components*. Oxford University Press.

McMenamin, B. W., Shackman, A. J., Maxwell, J. S., Bachhuber, D. R. W., Koppenhaver, A. M., Greischar, L. L., & Davidson, R. J. (2010). Validation of ICA-based myogenic artifact correction for scalp and source-localized EEG. *NeuroImage*, *49*(3), 2416–2432. https://doi.org/10.1016/j.neuroimage.2009.10.010

Neymotin, S. A., Jacobs, K. M., Fenton, A. A., & Lytton, W. W. (2011). Synaptic information transfer in computer models of neocortical columns. *Journal of Computational Neuroscience*, *30*(1), 69–84. https://doi.org/10.1007/s10827-010-0253-4

Nunez, M. D., Vandekerckhove, J., & Srinivasan, R. (2017). How attention influences perceptual decision making: Single-trial EEG correlates of drift-diffusion model parameters. *Journal of Mathematical Psychology*, *76*, 117–130. https://doi.org/10.1016/j.jmp.2016.03.003

Nunez, P. L., & Srinivasan, R. (2006). *Electric Fields of the Brain*, 2nd ed. Oxford University Press.

Nunez, P. L., Srinivasan, R., Westdorp, A. F., Wijesinghe, R. S., Tucker, D. M., Silberstein, R. B., & Cadusch, P. J. (1997). EEG coherency. I: Statistics, reference electrode, volume conduction, Laplacians, cortical imaging, and interpretation at multiple scales. *Electroencephalography and Clinical Neurophysiology*, *103*(5), 499–515.

Olejniczak, P. (2006). Neurophysiologic basis of EEG. *Journal of Clinical Neurophysiology*, *23*(3), 186–189. https://doi.org/10.1097/01.wnp.0000220079.61973.6c

Pavlov, Y. G., Adamian, N., Appelhoff, S., Arvaneh, M., Benwell, C. S. Y., Beste, C., et al. (2021). #EEGManyLabs: Investigating the replicability of influential EEG experiments. *Cortex*, *144*, 213–229. https://doi.org/10.1016/j.cortex.2021.03.013

Perrin, F., Pernier, J., Bertrand, O., & Echallier, J. F. (1989). Spherical splines for scalp potential and current density mapping. *Electroencephalography and Clinical Neurophysiology*, *72*(2), 184–187. https://doi.org/10.1016/0013-4694(89)90180-6

Peyk, P., De Cesarei, A., & Junghöfer, M. (2011). Electromagnetic encephalography software: Overview and integration with other EEG/MEG toolboxes. *Computational Intelligence and Neuroscience*, *2011*, 861705. https://doi.org/10.1155/2011/861705

Picton, T. W., & Hillyard, S. A. (1972). Cephalic skin potentials in electroencephalography. *Electroencephalography and Clinical Neurophysiology*, *33*, 419–424.

Poldrack, R. A. (2011). Inferring mental states from neuroimaging data: From reverse inference to large-scale decoding. *Neuron*, *72*(5), 692–697. https://doi.org/10.1016/j.neuron.2011.11.001

Ray, W. J., & Cole, H. W. (1985). EEG alpha activity reflects attentional demands, and beta activity reflects emotional and cognitive processes. *Science*, *228*(4700), 750–752.

Riels, K., Ramos Campagnoli, R., Thigpen, N., & Keil, A. (2022). Oscillatory brain activity links experience to expectancy during associative learning. *Psychophysiology*, *59* (5), e13946. https://doi.org/10.1111/psyp.13946

Schlögl, A., Keinrath, C., Zimmermann, D., Scherer, R., Leeb, R., & Pfurtscheller, G. (2007). A fully automated correction method of EOG artifacts in EEG recordings. *Clinical Neurophysiology*, *118*(1), 98–104. https://doi.org/10.1016/j.clinph.2006.09.003

Sinnott-Armstrong, W., & Simmons, C. (2021). Some common fallacies in arguments from M/EEG data. *NeuroImage*, *245*, 118725. https://doi.org/10.1016/j.neuroimage.2021.118725

Sitaram, R., Ros, T., Stoeckel, L., Haller, S., Scharnowski, F., Lewis-Peacock, J., et al. (2017). Closed-loop brain training: The science of neurofeedback. *Nature Reviews Neuroscience*, *18*(2), 86–100. https://doi.org/10.1038/nrn.2016.164

Soong, A. C. K., Lind, J. C., Shaw, G. R., & Koles, Z. J. (1993). Systematic comparisons of interpolation techniques in topographic brain mapping. *Electroencephalography and Clinical Neurophysiology*, *87*(4), 185–195. https://doi.org/10.1016/0013-4694(93)90018-Q

Tharwat, A. (2018). Independent component analysis: An introduction. *Applied Computing and Informatics*, *17*(2), 222–249. https://doi.org/10.1016/j.aci.2018.08.006

Thigpen, N. N., Kappenman, E. S., & Keil, A. (2017). Assessing the internal consistency of the event-related potential: An example analysis. *Psychophysiology*, *54*(1), 123–138. https://doi.org/10.1111/psyp.12629

Ullsperger, M., & Debener, S. (2010). *Simultaneous EEG and fMRI: Recording, Analysis, and Application*. Oxford University Press.

Widmann, A., Schröger, E., & Maess, B. (2015). Digital filter design for electrophysiological data – a practical approach. *Journal of Neuroscience Methods*, *250*, 34–46. https://doi.org/10.1016/j.neumeth.2014.08.002

PART VI

Qualitative Data Collection Sources

24 Open-Ended Survey Questions
Gloria Fraser

Abstract
Open-ended survey questions (OESQs) are a flexible and efficient method of collecting qualitative data but have received little attention in qualitative methods research and teaching. Here, I discuss OESQs as a stand-alone data collection method, a demographic data collection method, and an adjunct to researcher-derived survey responses. I explore the advantages and disadvantages of OESQs, review previous research using them, and provide practical guidance for survey design, data collection, and data analysis. When used thoughtfully, OESQs have potential to collect rich data from large samples and allow for exciting new directions in qualitative and survey research.

Keywords: Qualitative Survey, Open-Ended Survey Questions, Qualitative Research, Survey Design, Qualitative Methodology

Introduction

In every new research methods class, I ask students which data collection methods come to mind when they think about qualitative research – "interviews" and "focus groups" come up first without fail. Other qualitative data collection methods – including open-ended survey questions (OESQs) – have received comparatively little attention in research and teaching despite all they can offer qualitative researchers across research paradigms and career stages (note, for example, the absence of guidance on OESQs in several leading qualitative methods handbooks: Denzin & Lincoln, 2017; Hennink et al., 2020; Leavy, 2014).

OESQs provide research participants with an open space to craft a response in their own words, rather than selecting from a researcher-derived list of responses. Here, I discuss the advantages and disadvantages of OESQs, review research on demographic and survey design factors influencing non-response rates, and provide guidance on conducting qualitative research using OESQs. Throughout the chapter, I use my research on *Rainbow Mental Health Support Experiences in Aotearoa New Zealand* to provide worked examples and to reflect on learnings about collecting data with this very exciting (and arguably underutilized) method (see Fraser, 2020; Fraser et al., 2021, 2022).

Defining OESQs

OESQs serve three main purposes: (1) they can stand alone to collect data relating to a research question or feedback on the study as a whole (e.g., Bogetz et al.,

2020; Gauld & Horsburgh, 2014; Toerien & Wilkinson, 2004); (2) they can stand alone to collect demographic information (Fraser, 2018; Fraser et al., 2020); or (3) they can be paired with a researcher-derived list of responses for use in cases where a participant's response is not listed, or to clarify or expand upon their response (e.g., Harrison et al., 2012; see Figure 24.1 for examples of each question type). OESQs are most commonly used in pen and paper, online, and email surveys. Some researchers use instant messaging sites, such as Facebook Messenger, to collect data; however, this might be best considered under the broader umbrella of

Standalone demographic question

What is your sexual orientation?

Standalone open-ended question

We know that research often focusses on the negative experiences of sex, sexuality, and gender diverse people. What is **amazing** about being queer, trans, and/or intersex?

Additional response to list of researcher-derived questions

Do any of these also describe you? We acknowledge the above questions might only pick up on **some** of the things that make you who you are, or are important to know about you. Is there anything else you'd like us to know about you?
Tick all that apply

☐ Non-monogamous and/or polyamorous
☐ Physically disabled or impaired
☐ Neurodiverse
☐ Refugee migrant
☐ Migrant
☐ Sex worker
☐ Faith and/or religion (specify if you wish)
☐ Low socioeconomic status
☐ Homeless, or in unstable housing
☐ Not listed here, but I'd like you to know that...

Figure 24.1 *Examples of the three most common types of OESQs. From Fraser (2020).*

interviewing (given the opportunities available for follow-up questions by the researcher and dialogue between researcher and participant), so is not discussed in the current chapter.

For the purposes of this chapter, I distinguish between *small q* and *Big Q* qualitative research, introduced by Kidder and Fine (1987) and further explored by Braun and Clarke (2013, 2021a). *Small q* research refers to the collection and analysis of qualitative data within a *dominant* or *quantitative* paradigm. *Small q* research typically uses a hypothetico-deductive approach, adopts a realist ontological position, and attempts to control for potential sources of bias (this could, for example, include recruiting researchers of the same age and gender in face-to-face studies, to account for their potential impact on research findings). The quality of *small q* research is often assessed by its ability to produce replicable and generalizable findings (Braun & Clarke, 2021a). Such research might code qualitative data for use in quantitative research, measure interrater reliability between multiple coders, or conduct a qualitative analysis with a view to presenting a representative account of participants' talk.

In contrast, *Big Q* research refers to the collection and analysis of qualitative data within a *qualitative* paradigm. Such research is more likely to adopt a relativist ontological position and views knowledge as partial and shaped by the context in which it is produced (Braun & Clarke, 2013). Researchers' identities and positions inform the collection and interpretation of data but are understood as a source of richness and depth, rather than bias. *Big Q* research aims to gain in-depth understanding of a topic and often explores how we construct our social realities through language (Willig, 2021). It does not aim for representativeness or generalizability.

The *small q/Big Q* distinction is, in some ways, an oversimplified dichotomy; in reality, researchers routinely conduct *Big Q* research from a realist ontological position (e.g., qualitative studies informed by critical realism), and *small q* researchers can (and do) acknowledge how their identities and subject positions influence their knowledge production. It is important to note that no research paradigm is better or worse than any other; rather, selection of research paradigm is based on researchers' beliefs and assumptions about reality (ontology) and knowledge (epistemology), on their values (axiology), and on the type of questions they are interested in addressing. For further discussion of research paradigms, refer to Al-Ababneh (2020).

Strengths of Using OESQs

Perhaps the greatest strength of open-ended questions is their flexibility. Open-ended survey data can be collected using a range of methods (e.g., pen and paper, online, and email) as part of predominantly quantitative studies, combined with quantitative measures in mixed-methods studies, or as a stand-alone method (although purely qualitative surveys remain relatively rare; Terry & Braun, 2017).

Researchers can invite responses of various lengths, and the data can be analyzed using a range of qualitative analysis methods or form the basis of quantitative analyses. Terry and Braun's (2013) study of gender and body hair removal practices in Aotearoa New Zealand exemplifies the flexibility and myriad uses of OESQs. Their survey was developed within a qualitative research paradigm – the majority of the 92 questions were open-ended explorations of participants' views on hair and hair removal, and quantitative measures were included to identify participants' practices of hair removal. Terry and Braun's (2013) research challenges the typical mixed methods approach to surveying, where OESQs can seem an afterthought in a survey dominated by quantitative measures. I discuss this further in the "Survey Type" section of this chapter.

Data collection with open-ended questions is typically less time- and resource-intensive for researchers than methods such as interviews and focus groups, because researchers can collect data from multiple participants simultaneously, participants often complete surveys in their own time, and data typically does not require transcription (pen and paper being the exception). The time- and resource-efficiency of surveys means that researchers using open-ended questions can often collect data from larger samples, presenting an opportunity to gain a broad understanding (or what some researchers have called a "wide-angle" picture) of a phenomenon of interest (Toerien & Wilkinson, 2004, p. 70). Because responses are not limited to a Likert scale or researcher-derived list of responses, OESQs have the potential to collect surprising, imaginative, and unusual responses (Albudaiwi, 2018). Research participants often respond in a location and time of their choosing that, together with the anonymity of survey research, makes OESQs suitable for collecting data about sensitive topics (Braun et al., 2021). Similar to other forms of qualitative data collection, OESQs are well suited for exploratory studies aimed toward meaning-making and increased understanding (Terry & Braun, 2017).

Historically, demographic information has predominantly been collected using closed-ended questions (either with or without an additional open-ended response embedded); however, researchers are increasingly using stand-alone open-ended questions for demographic questions that require a very long list of potential responses or where there is reason to believe they could not feasibly list all possible responses (e.g., gender, sexual orientation, ethnicity; see Fraser, 2018 for discussion). Our previous work on collecting gender and sexual orientation data using stand-alone OESQs highlights the feasibility of coding such data in large samples (Fraser et al., 2020; Greaves et al., 2017). Of note, researchers can develop their own coding schemes for coding demographic data or can refer to existing coding schemes and guiding documents for gender (Fraser et al., 2020), sexual orientation (Greaves et al., 2017), and ethnicity (Yao et al., 2021). For example, Beaudry and colleagues (2022) have developed "gendercoder," a freely available R package for coding open-ended gender data. Gendercoder is intended to support inclusive collection of gender data and to reduce the time required to manually code gender in large data sets.

Challenges of Using OESQs

Although many researchers view OESQs as a "qualitative data dream" (Miller & Lambert, 2014, p. 1) and "short but often sweet" (Terry & Braun, 2017, p. 15), OESQs come with several potential pitfalls. They are famous for their high non-response rates, and previous literature is dominated by discussion of the "non-response nightmare" (Miller & Lambert, 2014, p. 1) – OESQs yield non-response rates as high as 75% (see, for example, Zhou et al., 2017; a review of factors influencing non-response rates is outlined below). The content and order of OESQs are predetermined, and there are rarely opportunities for follow-up or probing questions about participants' responses (these are considered key advantages of interviews and focus groups; Edley & Litosseliti, 2018). Another prominent concern about open-ended survey data, particularly in studies with large sample sizes, is the laborious and time-consuming nature of data coding. Analyses with hundreds (if not thousands) of data points can become unwieldy and challenging to write into a coherent narrative. However, challenging does not mean impossible, and the field of "computer-supported qualitative research" explores how software (e.g., Leximancer and NVivo) can support researchers to organize and structure large volumes of qualitative data (see, for example, Cogin & Ng, 2016).

A final criticism of note is that OESQs cannot produce data of adequate depth to generate rigorous qualitative insights. LaDonna and colleagues (2018), for example, argue that "free-text responses to survey or assessment items rarely produce data rich enough either to achieve sincerity, credibility, and resonance or to make a substantial contribution" (p. 347). The authors go on to note that data consisting of a few sentences "usually cannot get at the 'how?' and 'why?' questions that are the core business of qualitative research" (p. 348). Proponents of open-ended questions challenge this assumption, noting that data collected using OESQs can be rich and in-depth when viewed as a whole, even if individual responses are brief (Braun et al., 2021; Terry & Braun, 2017). For a summary of the advantages and disadvantages of using OESQs, see Table 23.1.

Table 24.1 *Advantages and disadvantages of using OESQs*

Advantages	Disadvantages
Flexibility in data collection method, length, method of analysis, type of survey	Higher non-response rates than closed-ended survey questions
Typically, less time- and resource-intensive than other qualitative data collection methods	Typically, no opportunities for probing or clarifying responses
Larger sample sizes can gain a broad understanding of a topic of interest	Analysis can be laborious and time-consuming
Responses can be surprising, imaginative, or unusual	Can be difficult to summarize disparate responses into a coherent narrative
Suitable for sensitive topics	Have been criticized for lack of depth needed to generate rigorous qualitative insights

Previous Research Using OESQs

Research with Large Samples

Gauld and Horsburgh (2014) analyzed 3,205 open-ended survey responses as part of a wider study on New Zealand healthcare professionals' perceptions of local implementation of a national clinical governance policy. They explored key barriers in clinical governance implementation, including interpersonal tension between managers and healthcare professionals and lack of time for clinicians to involve themselves in leadership and clinical governance. As well as providing valuable insights from practicing healthcare professionals, this study demonstrates the feasibility of open-ended survey research in large samples.

Research on Sensitive Topics

Bogetz and colleagues (2020) surveyed bereaved parents of children who received palliative care services at a Boston hospital, to understand their perspectives on preparedness at end of life, for children with complex chronic conditions. Their analysis of 110 parents' responses to 21 OESQs produced nuanced and complex perspectives, with parents discussing the "pretense of preparedness" (Bogetz et al., 2020, p. 1157) and the circumstances and emotional experiences surrounding their child's death. Bogetz and colleagues' (2020) research highlights the potential for OESQs to provide space to reflect on sensitive and distressing experiences and challenges claims that OESQs are unlikely to generate conceptually rich data when included in a larger, predominantly quantitative project (LaDonna et al., 2018).

Research Exploring Social Norms

Data analysis with open-ended survey data is not only suited to summarizing descriptions of participants' perspectives and experiences – it can be used in critical work to explore the constructions of social norms. Opperman and colleagues (2014) conducted a fully qualitative survey with 119 British young adults about their experiences of orgasm and sexual pleasure, including questions about the meaning of orgasm, orgasm frequency and timing, self versus partner orgasm, faking orgasm, and descriptions and evaluations of typical or last orgasm experiences. They argued that participants' experiences, interpretations, and meanings around orgasm and sexual pleasure "are already strongly socially patterned and are underpinned by dominant systems of meaning related to sex, heterosex, and orgasm ... sexual norms can create anxieties about abnormality, distress, and indeed enactments to achieve the perceived normality" (p. 511).

Factors Influencing Response Rates

OESQs typically yield higher non-response rates than closed-ended survey questions (including multi-item lists, ordinal and nominal scales, and yes/no questions; Andrews, 2005; Darby, 2007; Millar & Dillman, 2012; Reja et al., 2003; Zhou et al., 2017). Disparities in non-response rates are generally attributed to the additional time taken to respond to open-ended questions as well as higher cognitive demands on participants (Israel, 2010). Predictors of response rates include demographic factors, survey completion mode, the size of OESQ answers boxes, question order, and the presence of motivational statements.

Demographic Factors

Miller and Lambert (2014) highlight several demographic predictors of open-ended question non-response, with lower response rates among men, single people, as well as those aged under 50, with dependent children, in employment, and with higher incomes. Andrews (2005) found a different pattern of results on a large-scale government employee survey; participants more likely not to respond included those with less formal education, aged under 60, and of non-white ethnicity. The most common explanations for group differences in non-response are (1) time burdens fall more heavily on some groups than others (e.g., participants with dependent children; Miller & Lambert, 2014) and (2) dissatisfied participants are more likely to respond to open-ended questions (Poncheri et al., 2008) which might explain higher response rates among marginalized groups and those with lower incomes.

Completion Mode

Lambert and Miller's (2015) study of completion device and survey responses found that participants using desktop or laptop computers were more likely to respond to OESQs than participants using a smartphone or tablet and provided longer responses. This presumably speaks to the effort required to type out responses on a touch screen (particularly a small touch screen) versus typing out responses on a keyboard. Comparisons of open-ended responses across pen and paper versus online are mixed. Millar and Dillman (2012) report higher non-response rates for open-ended questions in online surveys, but Denscombe (2009) reports higher non-response rates among paper questionnaires.

Size of Answer Box

In Zuell and colleagues' (2015) study, large answer boxes for open-ended questions show higher non-response rates than small answer boxes, whereas other studies (Emde & Fuchs, 2012; Israel, 2010; Smyth et al., 2009) report no reduction in response rate with larger boxes. It is interesting to note that large answer boxes seem to produce longer and more complex responses (Christian & Dillman, 2004).

Consistent with this, a study of responses to open-ended questions with answer boxes of seven different heights showed answer length increased linearly with box size (Israel, 2010).

Question Order

There is evidence to suggest that non-response rates on OESQs are higher when questions are placed near the end of the survey compared to questions placed near the beginning or in the middle of the survey (Darby, 2007; Miller & Lambert, 2014; Schmidt et al., 2020). Darby (2007) explored participants' reasons for not completing the OESQs in a mixed methods survey: the most common was participants feeling they had expressed all they needed to in the forced-choice questions, followed by participants reporting they "could not be bothered to complete it" (p. 407). OESQs placed earlier in the survey are likely less vulnerable to survey fatigue.

Motivational Statements

Motivational statements that emphasize the importance of an open-ended question increase the frequency of responses to OESQs (Chaudhary & Israel, 2016; Zuell et al., 2015) as well as response length (Smyth et al., 2009). For example, Zuell and colleagues (2015) found an increase in the response rate for a question prefaced with the statement "The following question is very important for my work and helps you to express your opinion and wishes. Please take your time to answer the question" (p. 118). The mechanism for the success of motivational statements remains unclear; however, I suspect that they humanize the researcher and appeal to participants' desire to be helpful.

Doing Research with OESQs: Survey Design

Researchers have numerous decisions to make during the survey design process. These decisions are influenced by their research paradigm, resulting research questions, and practical constraints such as the time and resources available for data collection and analysis. Table 24.2 provides an overview of key survey design decisions when using open-ended questions.

Data Collection Method

As noted above, OESQs can be included in pen and paper, online, and email surveys. These methods can also be combined; for example, survey participants have the option of printing a survey and completing it by hand then scanning and returning it by email. Pen and paper surveys are increasingly less common, as they come with printing and often postal fees and require transcription of open-ended responses. They do, however, present an opportunity to recruit participants less likely to take part in online and email surveys (e.g., older participants and people without regular

Table 24.2 *Survey design decisions when using open-ended questions*

Survey design decision	Options
Method of data collection	Pen and paper Online Email
Type of survey	Purely qualitative Qualitative-dominated Fully mixed Quantitative-dominated
Ordering of questions	Front-load with open-ended questions Back-load with open-ended questions Place mid-way or scatter throughout
Space provided to respond	Set predetermined space on hard copy or online survey Set character limit on online survey Suggest word count for email survey Use adaptive questionnaire design to create custom-size box
Purpose of question	Stand-alone open-ended question Stand-alone demographic question Provide additional response to list of researcher-derived responses
Method of analysis	Big Q qualitative analysis small q qualitative analysis Code for use as quantitative data

access to a computer, tablet, or phone). The New Zealand Attitudes and Values Study (NZAVS) is one of New Zealand's few remaining large-scale national studies collecting data using both online and pen and paper postal questionnaires, and these multiple data collection methods increase sample representativeness across regions and demographic groups (see Sibley, 2022).

Pen and paper surveys are also useful when researchers have a captive audience who might not have devices available to complete an online survey (e.g., classes of school students). Online surveys have the benefit of automatically storing participants' responses as they progress through the survey, so if a survey is left unfinished, researchers have access to partial data. In contrast, researchers cannot access a partially completed email or pen and paper survey if the participant does not submit it.

Survey Type

Surveys containing open-ended questions exist on a spectrum, ranging from purely qualitative surveys to surveys in which open-ended questions make up a small portion of the overall study. Terry and Braun (2017) provide a useful typology of more- to less-qualitative surveys; surveys fall into four categories: (1) the *'fully' qualitative* survey that only includes qualitative questions (e.g., McEvoy et al., 2021;

Opperman et al., 2014), (2) the *qualitative-dominated* survey, where collection and analysis of qualitative data is the primary focus (e.g., Davey et al., 2019), (3) the *fully mixed* survey, where both qualitative and quantitative data collection is required to address the research questions, and qualitative and quantitative questions are somewhat balanced in number (e.g., Terry & Braun, 2013) and (4) the *quantitative-dominated* survey, where collection and analysis of quantitative data is the primary focus (e.g., Broodryk & Robinson, 2022).

Researchers interested in explanation, prediction, and relationships between variables will likely steer clear of the fully qualitative or qualitative-dominated survey, and researchers interested in building an understanding of phenomena of interest might lean more heavily on these types of surveys. The fully mixed survey can be useful for mixed methods researchers interested in both qualitative and quantitative approaches. Including *at least* one open-ended survey question in every survey ensures participants have an opportunity to give feedback on the survey, clarify their responses, and elaborate on their experiences.

Question Order

Because question order influences non-response rates for OESQs, researchers must consider whether they will front-load their survey with open-ended questions, include them at the end of the survey, or scatter open-ended questions throughout. Non-response rates for open-ended questions are highest for those placed at the end of surveys, so open-ended questions that are central to addressing your research questions are best placed in the first half of the survey. Miller and Lambert (2014) warn against starting surveys with open-ended questions because they may deter participants from continuing; instead, researchers might consider "warming up" participants with easily answered quantitative measures, or a demographic information section.

Within a positivist or quantitative paradigm, placing demographic questions first in a survey can be discouraged due to priming effects (see, for example, Klar et al., 2020). Researchers within a qualitative paradigm, however, are interested in locating participants within their context, and typically have no problem with participants holding their identities and subject positions in mind as they respond. Researchers must be aware that regardless of where demographic questions are placed, they will impact participants' responses, so should be positioned thoughtfully.

Surveys are typically structured in sections or blocks, either by topics of interest or by scales. For example, our research began with a section of demographic questions, followed by sections about experiences of accessing mental health support, experiences of accessing gender-affirming healthcare, and general questions about rainbow strengths and survey feedback (Fraser, 2020). We included some stand-alone open-ended questions throughout the survey but placed most of them at the end, as they were not of central importance to addressing our research questions.

Terry and Braun (2017) emphasize the importance of a survey's flow; there must be a clear and logical progression through the different sections of a survey. One option for including OESQs, which I recommend, is placing relevant open-ended questions at the end of a section or block, so participants are not faced with a raft of open-ended questions at the end of the survey. Open-ended questions inviting participants to provide feedback on the survey or providing a space to elaborate on their experiences are best placed at the end of the survey.

Space Provided to Respond

Previous research exploring the effect of answer size on open-ended survey response rates is mixed; some studies find no relationship (Emde & Fuchs, 2012; Smyth et al., 2009) while others report higher non-response rates with larger answer boxes (Zuell et al., 2015). In some cases, larger response size predicts longer and more complex responses (Christian & Dillman, 2004; Israel, 2010). It might be that participants assume the size of the box indicates the expected length of their response; participants who do not wish to spend the time and effort opt out of responding, while participants eager to provide detailed responses take the opportunity. As such, researchers might create boxes that reflect the length of the response they desire – a single line for a demographic question and space for a paragraph in response to questions designed to elicit an in-depth response. If the box provided is too small, this can create frustration for participants when they attempt to scroll backwards to review their answer. This is particularly difficult on smartphones when the response box is only big enough for a single line of text. Researchers should also be aware of character limits on some survey platforms. Qualtrics and Survey Monkey, for example, have a 20,000-character limit within a single text entry field (350–400 words). In our survey, this meant some participants' responses were inadvertently cut off.

Emde and Fuchs (2012) highlight an exciting new development in web surveys – adaptive questionnaire design. They conducted an experiment in which the response length of an initial open-ended question was used to create a custom-size answer box to a later open-ended question (where initial responses led to a larger answer box later in the survey). They found this decreased non-response rates among participants who did not answer the first question while "prolific writers" (p. 1) had space to provide more detailed answers. Although adaptive questionnaire design is not yet offered by major survey platforms (e.g., Qualtrics and Survey Monkey), it provides a promising future direction for increasing response rates on OESQs.

Question Design

Perhaps the most important aspect of designing open-ended questions is *clearly communicating* what information you wish to gather from participants. OESQs will inevitably be interpreted in different ways by different people, but ambiguity can be reduced by adhering to the following guidelines.

- Avoid jargon or wordy questions and provide definitions for key survey terms. Terms with definitions can be boldened or underlined in online surveys, prompting participants to hover their mouse or click to see the definition (see Figure 24.2). Researchers need not define all terms but might provide definitions for terms not in common use or that have multiple or conflicting definitions. Sometimes, leaving terms undefined is useful for exploring participants' understanding of particular terms, and some researchers warn against providing definitions too frequently, as they might narrow the range of participants' responses (Terry & Braun, 2017).
- Only ask one question at a time. Providing one space to respond to multiple questions can result in participants attending to some questions but not others.
- Provide motivational statements that encourage participants to respond. Motivational statements can be used to emphasize that OESQs are an important part of the research, that OESQs provide an opportunity for research participants to freely share their opinions and wishes, and that participants are encouraged to take their time to respond. Although there is a dearth of research exploring the use of multiple motivational statements throughout a survey, I recommend that motivational statements be used sparingly – if every open-ended question is prefaced with a motivational statement, they might lose their impact!
- Think about the overall survey length. Longer surveys typically yield higher non-completion rates (Sinkowitz-Cochran, 2013). Researchers can gather estimates of their survey length by piloting their survey before publishing it and removing questions if it is too long. It is also important to provide participants with an indication of how long the survey will take; an estimate can be included in the survey information sheet.

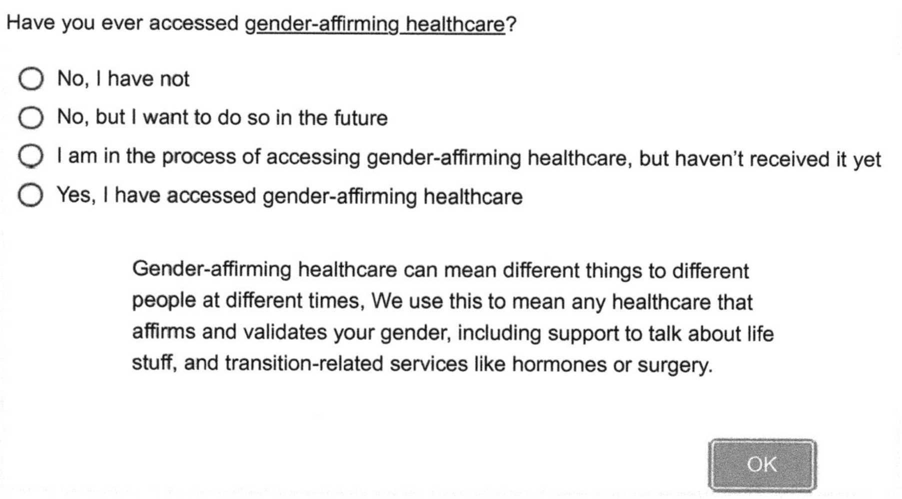

Have you ever accessed gender-affirming healthcare?

- ○ No, I have not
- ○ No, but I want to do so in the future
- ○ I am in the process of accessing gender-affirming healthcare, but haven't received it yet
- ○ Yes, I have accessed gender-affirming healthcare

> Gender-affirming healthcare can mean different things to different people at different times, We use this to mean any healthcare that affirms and validates your gender, including support to talk about life stuff, and transition-related services like hormones or surgery.
>
> [OK]

Figure 24.2 *Defining key survey terms.*

Ethical Considerations

Volume 1, Part I of this Handbook devotes a chapter to research ethics, so I make only a few brief notes about ethical considerations when collecting and analyzing open-ended survey data. Regarding confidentiality and anonymity, researchers must de-identify their data before allowing other researchers access to protect their participants' identities. This is particularly important when working in small and interconnected communities or when researchers have formed relationships with research community members. De-identifying data is the manual process of researchers closely reading the data and redacting any information that could individually identify participants, including their names or others' names, contact details, and place names. Related to this, researchers using open-ended questions must carefully consider publishing qualitative data on open access data repositories due to the potential for participants to be identified based on contextual information (for discussion see Chauvette et al., 2019).

When collecting sensitive information or conducting research that has potential to cause participants distress, researchers should include a debriefing section that directs participants to sources of support (see Figure 24.3 for an example debriefing

---

Ngā mihi nui ki a koe! Thank you so much for helping us out with this survey. You're all done, and your responses have been submitted.

Click here if you want to do any of the following:
- enter the prize draw for a $50 voucher
- receive a copy of the findings and updates about the project
- help us develop the resource for mental health professionals using results from this survey
- receive invitations to participate in more research
- share the survey with others

This is in a separate window to make sure your contact details are not linked in any way to your survey responses.

If you have any questions, please feel free to contact Gloria at ▇▇▇▇▇▇▇▇▇ Alternatively, you can contact her supervisors: ▇▇▇▇▇▇▇▇▇▇▇▇▇▇▇▇▇▇▇▇▇▇▇▇▇▇▇▇▇▇▇▇▇ To get in touch with our community partners, ▇▇▇▇▇▇▇▇▇▇▇▇▇

We know that talking about mental health support or past negative experiences can be tough, or can bring up some stuff for lots of people. If you wish to talk further about the topics and issues raised in this survey, you can contact OUTLine, a confidential support service staffed by LGBTIQ+ identifying volunteers, by calling 0800 688 5463 or emailing info@outline.org.nz. You can also free call or text the National Telehealth Service on 1737 any time, 24 hours a day, to talk to a trained counsellor.

If you want to talk to someone face to face, a visit to your family doctor or general practitioner (GP) is often the first step in getting help - they may be able to refer you to mental health services. If you are at school or in tertiary study, contact your school nurse, school counsellor, or your education institution's student support services. If you are in crisis, contact your local crisis assessment team - click here for the contact details of your local service.

If you have any concerns about the ethical conduct of the research you may contact the Victoria University HEC Convener: ▇▇▇▇▇▇▇▇▇▇▇▇▇▇▇▇▇▇▇▇▇▇▇▇▇▇▇▇

Figure 24.3 *Example debriefing sheet. From Fraser (2020).*

section). We also strongly recommend that participants are offered an opportunity to receive a report on the research findings and something to acknowledge the time they spent participating in the research. This might be a voucher or entry into a prize draw. Readers might note that the debriefing sheet in Figure 24.3 directs participants to a separate survey to collect contact information for the purpose of a prize draw, to take part in future research, or to receive a report of study results. For example, we included this as an additional step to protect participants' identities; by collecting survey data and participants' contact details, we as researchers could not match up survey responses to participants' names and contact information.

Research ethics require that we minimize harm to research participants as well as to ourselves and our research colleagues. Reading and analyzing open-ended data can take an emotional toll on researchers (e.g., in our survey, many participants described distressing experiences of discrimination, serious mental health problems, and difficulties accessing mental health support). Researchers should read and analyze data with plenty of time scheduled for breaks and have a place they can discuss survey content that is impacting them. Research supervisors should discuss with their students the potential for open-ended survey data to bring up difficult emotions and normalize this experience.

Survey Recruitment

Effective survey recruitment strategies capture the attention of potential participants and pique their interest in the project. This is critical for researchers using OESQs, which are known to be more demanding on research participants than closed-ended questions (Israel, 2010). Moreover, marginalized groups are often recruited for qualitative studies and can experience "research fatigue" that comes with being over-researched (Ashley, 2021).

Figure 24.4 shows two examples of eye-catching and culturally informed research recruitment on Instagram; they were used to recruit Māori (Indigenous New Zealanders), for a study on young adults' experiences of well-being (Rukuwai, 2022, left of figure), and migrant youth, for a study on migrant youth well-being (Aryan, 2022, right of figure). These posts highlight the importance of using prospective participants' own imagery and language to draw their attention and interest. Rukuwai (2022) uses (and credits) the work of Indigenous artist @maori_mermaid, and Aryan (2022) greets participants in 23 languages from around the world.

Unexpected (and delightful) recruitment methods have the potential to increase recruitment rates in survey research (see, for example, Figure 24.5, where we tweeted photos of our research team's pets to reach participants). Our survey was part of a wider community-based research project, meaning we consulted and collaborated with rainbow organizations at each stage of the research process. Our relationships with community organizations also supported our survey recruitment, as our research partners posted our flyer on their social media pages and in their physical spaces. As well as helping to increase sample size and connect with hard-to-reach populations, collaborating with community members ensures that research is

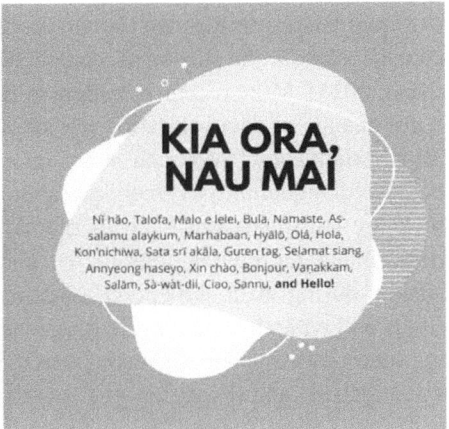

Figure 24.4 *Example research recruitment posts.*

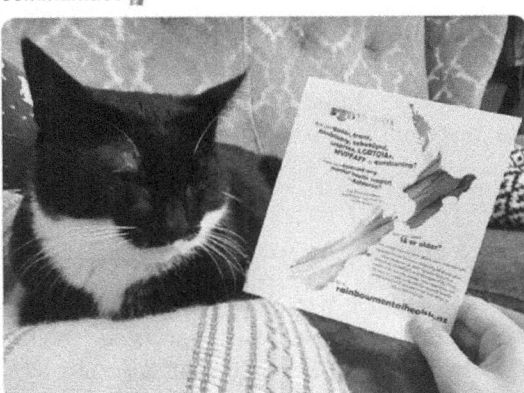

Figure 24.5 *Recruitment materials for the Rainbow Mental Health Support Experiences study.*

relevant to communities that researchers wish to engage with and that it has *real-world utility* (for more information, see Strand et al., 2003).

Finally, sample size is worth discussing. The ideal sample size of a qualitative study depends on a number of factors. Unlike quantitative studies, which generally take a "more is more" approach to data (as bigger samples increase statistical power), qualitative research attempts to reach a "sweet spot" of sample size – having enough data for rich analysis but not so much that it becomes unwieldy. Previously, the concept of data saturation was considered the "gold standard" for guiding decisions about qualitative sample size (Braun & Clarke, 2021b). Data saturation states that data collection should stop when no new information is yielded from the data (Fusch & Ness, 2015). More recently, leaders in *Big Q* qualitative research have questioned the dominance of data saturation (Braun & Clarke, 2021b), arguing that an "information redundancy" approach is not consistent with the *Big Q* paradigm. Instead, they posit that qualitative researchers should come up with a provisional sample size guided by considerations such as practical constraints, the focus of the research question, and the conventions of the discipline. Then, they should make a final decision during data collection (Braun & Clarke, 2021b). Researchers using OESQs will typically end up with bigger sample sizes than other qualitative methods (e.g., interviews and focus groups), as OESQs are less time- and resource-intensive for researchers, and responses tend to be brief.

Data Analysis

Researchers using OESQs draw on a wide range of data analytic strategies. Readers can refer to Volume 3 of this Handbook for in-depth exploration of a range of advanced qualitative approaches. In this section, I provide examples of potential data analytic approaches using my research on *Rainbow Mental Health Support Experiences in Aotearoa New Zealand*. I first provide an overview of a *small q* approach; this was used to code open-ended demographic data for numerical analysis and to summarize responses to "not listed" questions. I then provide a very brief overview of a *Big Q* approach. Here, I direct readers to the previously reviewed OESQ research in this chapter that tends to draw on *Big Q* approaches (e.g., reflexive thematic analysis).

Analyzing Demographic Data Using a *small q* Approach

Small q approaches collect qualitative data and apply qualitative techniques using a (post)positivist or quantitative paradigm, rather than a qualitative paradigm (for discussion, see Braun & Clarke, 2013). One example of *small q* qualitative research is converting qualitative data to numerical representation, and this is common when analyzing open-ended demographic data. Demographic data is typically coded into numerical data for the purposes of presenting descriptive statistics or for use in statistical analysis. Coding participants' gender and sexual orientation was particularly important for our survey, given our focus on *rainbow* peoples' mental health support experiences. We collected this data using two stand-alone open-ended questions.

Gender and sexual orientation data are routinely collected using closed-ended questions. This approach has been criticized because researchers cannot capture the diversity of possible responses with an itemized list (Fraser, 2018). Stand-alone open-ended items have been recognized as one of several inclusive measures to collect demographic information about gender (Fraser, 2018), and coding schemes for gender and sexual orientation data are available (Fraser et al., 2020; Greaves et al., 2017). The *Rainbow Mental Health Support Experiences* study was my first experience coding gender and sexual orientation in an exclusively rainbow sample, rather than a population, random, or adolescent community sample, and it was a much more complex task than anticipated. This was partially due to the sheer number of identity labels; there were 323 unique responses to the item assessing sexual orientation and 285 unique responses to the item assessing gender. On top of this, many participants used multiple terms to describe their gender and/or sexual orientation (e.g., "nonbinary/genderfluid"), and it was unclear which terms should be prioritized in coding. I was aware of the need to code participants' data, both to examine the experiences of groups within the rainbow community and to compare between groups. At the same time, I was concerned about the potentially unethical practice of asking about identity using open boxes only to impose my own understanding of participants' identities by labeling them with potentially irrelevant or incorrect terms.

In an attempt to strike a balance – to code participants in a way that was useful for analysis while respecting the terms they had chosen – I formed a team of three researchers to code gender and sexual orientation data to ensure all decisions around coding were informed by a range of perspectives. We first used dummy coding, meaning that multiple identity terms could be coded. For example, a participant who described their gender as "non binary trans masc/male" would be coded as 1 in the categories 'nonbinary,' 'trans,' 'male,' and 'masculine,' and would be coded as 0 in all other gender categories. We created 28 gender dummy codes including terms for codes such as "cis" and "trans." We then created 30 sexual orientation dummy codes. After completing dummy coding, we coded the gender and sexual orientation data into nominal variables – each participant was placed into a single category. Table 24.3 lists the dummy codes for gender and sexual orientation as well as the nominal variables participants' responses were then coded into. Many responses are in te reo Māori (the Indigenous language of New Zealand). We tend to use the nominal variable codes for ease of analysis but note the limited utility of our "something else" variable given the diversity of self-labels not captured in our other nominal gender and sexual orientation variables.

Our research had a particular interest in gender and sexual orientation, so most surveys will generate far fewer unique responses to open-ended demographic questions than ours produced. Researchers also have the option of taking a "not listed here" approach to collecting demographic data (e.g., closed-ended responses of trans woman, cis woman, trans man, cis man, and nonbinary could be provided along with an open-ended "not listed here" option). Hopefully, our example of coding demographic data demonstrates the diversity and nuance in responses that can be lost with closed-ended items. Although more time-intensive to code for researchers, open-ended demographic items invite participants to describe themselves in their own words rather than placing themselves in a box that might not reflect their identity or experience.

Table 24.3 *Dummy and nominal codes for gender and sexual orientation*

	Gender	Sexual orientation
Dummy codes	Woman/female/wahine/F	Bisexual
	Nonbinary/NB	Pansexual
	Cis/cisgender/cisgendered	Gay
	Masculine/masc/mostly male	Lesbian
	Feminine/femme/female-ish	Queer
	Queer	Asexual
	Gender nonconforming	Questioning
	Trans/FTM/AFAB/transsexual	Demisexual
	Genderfluid/fluid	Homosexual
	Agender/don't have one/none	Specifies who they are attracted to
	Questioning/female maybe/unsure	Takatāpui
	Genderqueer	Straight
	Demigirl/demiwoman	Biromantic
	Demiboy/demiboi	Homoflexible
	Neutrois/neutral/null	Aromantic
	Takatāpui	Grey
	Bigender	Heterosexual
	Genderflux	Panromantic
	Androgyne	Heteroflexible
	Gender indifferent	Homoromantic
	Intersex	Curious
	Ira tangata kōwhiri kore	Demiromantic
	Tāhine	Heteromantic
	Ze/it	Polysexual
	Third gender	Omnisexual
	Blended	Rainbow
	Zigzag	Polyamorous
		Demipolysexual
		Androsexual
		Gynesexual
Nominal variable codes	Cis woman	Gay/lesbian
	Trans woman	Multiple gender attracted
	Cis man	Asexual
	Trans man	Queer
	Nonbinary	Something else
	Something else	

Analyzing "Not Listed Here" Responses Using a *small q* Approach

We analyzed "not listed here" responses throughout our survey using summative content analysis (see Hsieh & Shannon, 2005). Summative content analysis identifies and quantifies content in text to understand its *contextual* use; that is, it goes beyond counting instances of words or phrases by interpreting and coding for meaning. One example of a "not listed here" response is seen in Figure 24.6. We

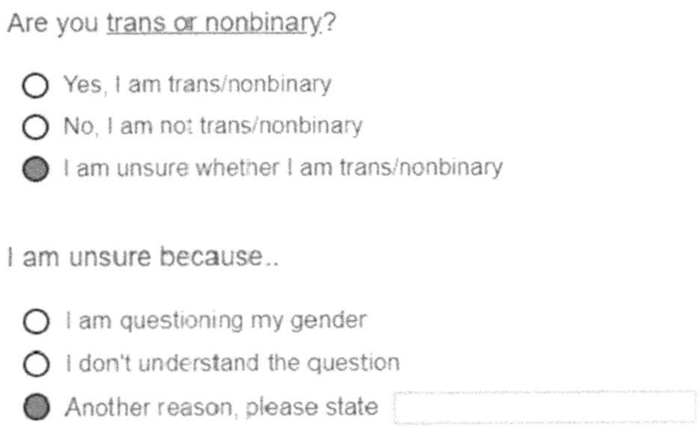

Are you trans or nonbinary?

○ Yes, I am trans/nonbinary
○ No, I am not trans/nonbinary
● I am unsure whether I am trans/nonbinary

I am unsure because...

○ I am questioning my gender
○ I don't understand the question
● Another reason, please state [   ]

Figure 24.6 *Addition of an open-ended response to list of researcher-derived responses.*

asked participants whether they are trans or nonbinary; if they reported they were unsure, they were asked a follow-up question exploring the reason for this (e.g., "I am 100% female, but not conforming to gender stereotypes," "I prefer to not use labels," and "Sometimes I'm nonbinary, sometimes not"). We read and reread the list of open-ended responses, created codes to summarize patterns of meaning, and coded each response using this list.

We identified six categories of response (e.g., a mismatch between participants' experience of their gender and the labels they use to describe it, comments on the confusing and constructed nature of gender, and uncertainty about "counting" as trans or nonbinary). We reported the number of participants in each category, and our emphasis on the frequency of participants' responses makes this a *small q*, rather than a *Big Q* approach. These responses highlight the limitations of asking about a complex phenomenon such as gender using quantitative measures and small open boxes; when understandings of terms like "transgender" and "nonbinary" differ between people, or shift depending on context, it is impossible for many people to simply place themselves in one box or another.

Data Analysis Using a *Big Q* Approach

Big Q analytic approaches are *inductive* and oriented to exploring *meaning* in qualitative data rather than quantifying participants' responses or fitting the data to predetermined themes or codebooks (Braun & Clarke, 2013). Reflexive thematic analysis (TA) is one of the most popular and widely used *Big Q* approaches for analyzing open-ended survey data (see, for example, Grogan & Mechan, 2017; North et al., 2021; Taylor et al., 2021). Outlined by Braun and Clarke (2013, 2021a), reflexive TA belongs to a broader family of pattern-based analytic approaches for qualitative data. The *reflexive* part of reflexive TA refers to the fact that "themes cannot exist separately from the researcher – they are generated by the researcher through data engagement mediated by all that they bring to this process (e.g., their research values, skills, experience and training)" (Braun & Clarke, 2021a, p. 39). For in-depth and practical guidance for doing reflexive TA, see Braun and Clarke (2021c). For further examples of *Big Q* analyses using OESQs, refer to the work previously cited in this chapter (Bogetz et al., 2020; Davey et al., 2019; Gauld & Horsburgh, 2014; McEvoy et al., 2021; Opperman et al., 2014; Terry & Braun, 2013; Toerien & Wilkinson, 2004).

Data Analysis of "Any Other Comments" Questions

Before we conclude, a final note about some of the most widely used OESQs: "any other comments" questions (see Figure 24.7). Such "leftover" or "any other comments" questions are commonly included in survey research, but analyses of this data are rarely published (O'Cathain & Thomas, 2004; for exceptions, see Chambers & Chiang, 2012; Ellonen et al., 2018). O'Cathain and Thomas (2004) highlight a lack of clarity about how to analyze and report data from "any other comments" questions but argue they can be useful if researchers have a clear understanding of the purpose of collecting it (e.g., to conduct in-depth analysis, produce quantifiable data, or scan for key concerns; Singer & Couper, 2017). They note that ignoring open-ended data due to the resource-intensive nature of coding can present an ethical dilemma, and they suggest that researchers should not collect open-ended data unless they are prepared to analyze it.

I end with this example, as it speaks to my broader argument about using OESQs – their strengths make OESQs an incredibly promising tool in qualitative research, particularly for researchers eager to gain a wide-angle lens on a phenomenon of interest. However, researchers must be *thoughtful* about (1) their rationale for including OESQs, (2) survey design, and (3) data analytic strategy to avoid high non-response rates and the too-often-seen outcome of collecting open-ended data that remains unused. We can only speculate about the goldmine of data generated from OESQs that researchers lack the time, resources, or inclination to analyze and publish!

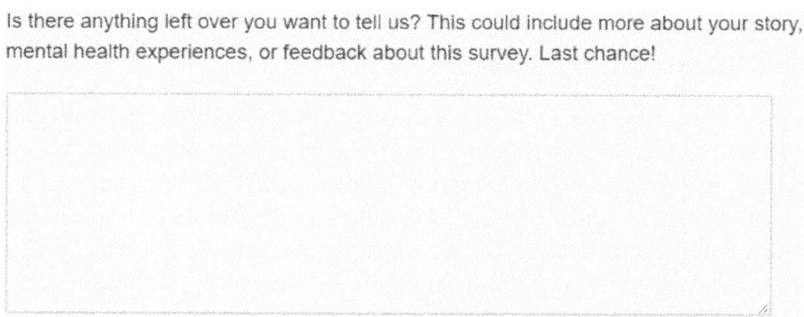

Figure 24.7 *Example of an "any others comments" question.*

Conclusion

In the field of qualitative research, OESQs have lived in the shadow of interviews and focus groups despite their exciting potential to gain an in-depth understanding of a wide range of topics, collect inclusive demographic data using participants' own words, and save researchers valuable time and resources during data collection. OESQs can be used across research paradigms and offer researchers considerable flexibility in survey design and data analysis. Research using OESQs does not come with hard and fast rules; rather, researchers must ensure their decisions regarding data collection and analysis flow logically from their chosen research paradigm and have a clear rationale. My hope is that this chapter has inspired you to consider OESQs for your next qualitative study.

References

Al-Ababneh, M. (2020). Linking ontology, epistemology and research methodology. *Science & Philosophy*, 8(1), 75–91.

Albudaiwi, D. (2018). Surveys, advantages, and disadvantages. In M. Allen (ed.), *The SAGE Encyclopedia of Communication Research Methods* (pp. 1735–1736). SAGE Publications.

Andrews, M. (2005). Who is being heard? Response bias in open-ended responses in a large government employee survey. In *60th Annual Conference of the American Association for Public Opinion Research* (pp. 3760–3766). AAPOR. www.asasrms.org/Proceedings/y2005/files/JSM2005-000924.pdf

Aryan, N. (2022). An immigrant paradox or a mental health crisis: Understanding the psychological wellbeing of migrant youth in Aotearoa. Manuscript in preparation.

Ashley, F. (2021). Accounting for research fatigue in research ethics. *Bioethics*, 35(3), 270–276.

Beaudry, J., Kothe, E., Singleton Thorn, F., McGuire, R., Tierney, N., & Ling, M. (2022). *gendercoder: Recodes Sex/Gender Descriptions into a Standard Set*. [R package version 0.0.0.9000]. Retrieved from https://github.com/ropensci/gendercoder

Bogetz, J. F., Revette, A., Rosenberg, A. R., & DeCourcey, D. (2020). "I could never prepare for something like the death of my own child": Parental perspectives on preparedness at end of life for children with complex chronic conditions. *Journal of Pain and Symptom Management*, 60(6), 1154–1162.

Braun, V., & Clarke, V. (2013). *Successful Qualitative Research: A Practical Guide for Beginners*. SAGE Publications.

(2021a). Can I use TA? Should I use TA? Should I not use TA? Comparing reflexive thematic analysis and other pattern-based qualitative analytic approaches. *Counselling and Psychotherapy Research*, 21(1), 37–47.

(2021b). To saturate or not to saturate? Questioning data saturation as a useful concept for thematic analysis and sample-size rationales. *Qualitative Research in Sport, Exercise and Health*, 13(2), 201–216.

(2021c). *Thematic Analysis: A Practical Guide*. SAGE Publications.

Braun, V., Clarke, V., Boulton, E., Davey, L., & McEvoy, C. (2021). The online survey as a qualitative research tool. *International Journal of Social Research Methodology, 24*(6), 641–654.

Broodryk, T., & Robinson, K. (2022). Dataset describing Aotearoa New Zealand young adults' psychological well-being and behaviour during nationwide lockdown. *Data in Brief, 40*, 107808.

Chambers, T., & Chiang, C. H. (2012). Understanding undergraduate students' experience: A content analysis using NSSE open-ended comments as an example. *Quality & Quantity, 46*(4), 1113–1123.

Chaudhary, A. K., & Israel, G. D. (2016). Influence of importance statements and box size on response rate and response quality of open-ended questions in web/mail mixed-mode surveys. *Journal of Rural Social Sciences, 31*(3), 140–159.

Chauvette, A., Schick-Makaroff, K., & Molzahn, A. E. (2019). Open data in qualitative research. *International Journal of Qualitative Methods, 18*.

Christian, L. M., & Dillman, D. A. (2004). The influence of graphical and symbolic language manipulations on responses to self-administered questions. *Public Opinion Quarterly, 68*(1), 57–80.

Cogin, J., & Ng, J. L. (2016). Computer-supported qualitative research. In *Handbook of Qualitative Research Methods on Human Resource Management*. Edward Elgar.

Darby, J. A. (2007). Open-ended course evaluations: A response rate problem? *Journal of European Industrial Training, 31*(5), 402–412.

Davey, L., Clarke, V., & Jenkinson, E. (2019). Living with alopecia areata: An online qualitative survey study. *British Journal of Dermatology, 180*(6), 1377–1389.

Denscombe, M. (2009). Item non-response rates: A comparison of online and paper questionnaires. *International Journal of Social Research Methodology, 12*(4), 281–291.

Denzin, N. K., & Lincoln, Y. S. (eds.). (2017). *The SAGE Handbook of Qualitative Research*. SAGE Publications.

Edley, N., & Litosseliti, E. (2018). Critical perspectives on using interviews and focus groups. In L. Litosseliti (ed.), *Research Methods in Linguistics*. (pp. 195–227). Bloomsbury.

Ellonen, N., Fagerlund, M., & Pösö, T. (2018). Free-text comments as a tool for developing the self-report method: Parents' responses to a survey on violence against children. *Australian & New Zealand Journal of Criminology, 51*(1), 58–75.

Emde, M., & Fuchs, M. (2012). Using adaptive questionnaire design in open-ended questions: A field experiment. Paper presented at the American Association for Public Opinion Research (AAPOR) 67th Annual Conference. https://memde.de/Emde_Fuchs_using_adaptive_questionnaire_design_AAPOR_paper_2012.pdf

Fraser, G. (2018). Evaluating inclusive gender identity measures for use in quantitative psychological research. *Psychology & Sexuality, 9*(4), 343–357.

(2020). *Rainbow Experiences of Accessing Mental Health Support in Aotearoa New Zealand: A Community-Based Mixed Methods Study* [unpublished PhD thesis]. Victoria University of Wellington.

Fraser, G., Brady, A., & Wilson, M. S. (2021). "What if I'm not trans enough? What if I'm not man enough?": Transgender young adults' experiences of gender-affirming healthcare readiness assessments in Aotearoa New Zealand. *International Journal of Transgender Health, 22*(4), 454–467.

(2022). Mental health support experiences of rainbow rangatahi youth in Aotearoa New Zealand: Results from a co-designed online survey. *Journal of the Royal Society of New Zealand, 52*(4), 1–18.

Fraser, G., Bulbulia, J., Greaves, L. M., Wilson, M. S., & Sibley, C. G. (2020). Coding responses to an open-ended gender measure in a New Zealand national sample. *Journal of Sex Research, 57*(8), 979–986.

Fusch, P. I., & Ness, L. R (2015). Are we there yet? Data saturation in qualitative research. *Qualitative Report, 20*(9), 1408–1416.

Gauld, R., & Horsburgh, S. (2014). Measuring progress with clinical governance development in New Zealand: Perceptions of senior doctors in 2010 and 2012. *BMC Health Services Research, 14*(1), 1–7.

Greaves, L. M., Barlow, F. K., Lee, C. H., Matika, C. M., Wang, W., Lindsay, C. J., et al. (2017). The diversity and prevalence of sexual orientation self-labels in a New Zealand national sample. *Archives of Sexual Behavior, 46*(5), 1325–1336.

Grogan, S., & Mechan, J. (2017). Body image after mastectomy: A thematic analysis of younger women's written accounts. *Journal of Health Psychology, 22*(11), 1480–1490.

Harrison, J., Grant, J., & Herman, J. L. (2012). A gender not listed here: Genderqueers, gender rebels, and otherwise in the National Transgender Discrimination Survey. *LGBTQ Public Policy Journal at the Harvard Kennedy School, 2*(1), 13–24.

Hennink, M., Hutter, I., & Bailey, A. (2020). *Qualitative Research Methods*. SAGE Publications.

Hsieh, H. F., & Shannon, S. E. (2005). Three approaches to qualitative content analysis. *Qualitative Health Research, 15*(9), 1277–1288.

Israel, G. D. (2010). Effects of answer space size on responses to open-ended questions in mail surveys. *Journal of Official Statistics, 26*(2), 271–285.

Kidder, L. H., & Fine, M. (1987). Qualitative and quantitative methods: When stories converge. *New Directions for Program Evaluation, 1987*(35), 57–75.

Klar, S., Leeper, T., & Robison, J. (2020). Studying identities with experiments: Weighing the risk of posttreatment bias against priming effects. *Journal of Experimental Political Science, 7*(1), 56–60.

LaDonna, K. A., Taylor, T., & Lingard, L. (2018). Why open-ended survey questions are unlikely to support rigorous qualitative insights. *Academic Medicine, 93*(3), 347–349.

Lambert, A. D., & Miller, A. L. (2015). Living with smartphones: Does completion device affect survey responses? *Research in Higher Education, 56*(2), 166–177.

Leavy, P. (ed.). (2014). *The Oxford Handbook of Qualitative Research*. Oxford University Press.

McEvoy, C., Clarke, V., & Thomas, Z. (2021). 'Rarely discussed but always present': Exploring therapists' accounts of the relationship between social class, mental health and therapy. *Counselling and Psychotherapy Research, 21*(2), 324–334.

Millar, M., & Dillman, D. (2012). Do mail and internet surveys produce different item nonresponse rates? An experiment using random mode assignment. *Survey Practice, 5*(2), 1–6.

Miller, A. L., & Lambert, A. D. (2014). Open-ended survey questions: Item nonresponse nightmare or qualitative data dream? *Survey Practice, 7*(5), 1–11.

North, M., Kothe, E., Klas, A., & Ling, M. (2021). How to define "Vegan": An exploratory study of definition preferences among omnivores, vegetarians, and vegans. *Food Quality and Preference, 93*, 104246.

O'Cathain, A., & Thomas, K. J. (2004). "Any other comments?" Open questions on questionnaires – a bane or a bonus to research? *BMC Medical Research Methodology, 4*(1), 1–7.

Opperman, E., Braun, V., Clarke, V., & Rogers, C. (2014). "It feels so good it almost hurts": Young adults' experiences of orgasm and sexual pleasure. *Journal of Sex Research*, *51*(5), 503–515.

Poncheri, R. M., Lindberg, J. T., Thompson, L. F., & Surface, E. A. (2008). A comment on employee surveys: Negativity bias in open-ended responses. *Organizational Research Methods*, *11*(3), 614–630.

Reja, U., Manfreda, K. L., Hlebec, V., & Vehovar, V. (2003). Open-ended vs. close-ended questions in web questionnaires. *Developments in Applied Statistics*, *19*(1), 159–177.

Rukuwai, E. (2022). The role of identity and culture in perfectionism and non-suicidal self-injury within rangatahi Māori. Manuscript in preparation.

Schmidt, K., Gummer, T., & Roßmann, J. (2020). Effects of respondent and survey characteristics on the response quality of an open-ended attitude question in Web surveys. *Methods, Data, Analyses*, *14*(1), 3–34.

Sibley, C. G. (2022). Sampling procedure and sample details for the New Zealand Attitudes and Values Study. *PsyArXiv Preprints*. https://doi.org/10.31234/osf.io/wgqvy

Singer, E., & Couper, M. P. (2017). Some methodological uses of responses to open questions and other verbatim comments in quantitative surveys. *Methods, Data, Analyses*, *11*(2), 115–134.

Sinkowitz-Cochran, R. L. (2013). Survey design: To ask or not to ask? That is the question.... *Clinical Infectious Diseases*, *56*(8), 1159–1164.

Smyth, J. D., Dillman, D. A., Christian, L. M., & McBride, M. (2009). Open-ended questions in web surveys: Can increasing the size of answer boxes and providing extra verbal instructions improve response quality? *Public Opinion Quarterly*, *73*(2), 325–337.

Strand, K., Marullo, S., Cutforth, N., Stoecker, R., & Donohue, P. (2003). Principles of best practice for community-based research. *Michigan Journal of Community Service Learning*, *9*(3), 5–15.

Taylor, A., Caffery, L. J., Gesesew, H. A., King, A., Bassal, A. R., Ford, K., et al. (2021). How Australian health care services adapted to telehealth during the COVID-19 pandemic: A survey of telehealth professionals. *Frontiers in Public Health*, *9*, 648009.

Terry, G., & Braun, V. (2013). To let hair be, or to not let hair be? Gender and body hair removal practices in Aotearoa/New Zealand. *Body Image*, *10*(4), 599–606.

(2017). Short but often sweet: The surprising potential of qualitative survey methods. In V. Braun, V. Clarke, & D. Gray (eds.), *Collecting Qualitative Data: A Practical Guide to Textual, Media and Virtual Techniques* (pp. 15–44). Cambridge University Press.

Toerien, M., & Wilkinson, S. (2004). Exploring the depilation norm: A qualitative questionnaire study of women's body hair removal. *Qualitative Research in Psychology*, *1*(1), 69–92.

Willig, C. (2021). *Introducing Qualitative Research in Psychology*. Open University Press.

Yao, E. S., Meissel, K., Bullen, P., Carr, P. A., Clark, T. C., & Morton, S. M. (2021). Classifying multiple ethnic identifications. *Demographic Research*, *44*, 481–512.

Zhou, R., Wang, X., Zhang, L., & Guo, H. (2017). Who tends to answer open-ended questions in an e-service survey? The contribution of closed-ended answers. *Behaviour & Information Technology*, *36*(12), 1274–1284.

Zuell, C., Menold, N., & Körber, S. (2015). The influence of the answer box size on item nonresponse to open-ended questions in a web survey. *Social Science Computer Review*, *33*(1), 115–122.

25 Qualitative Archival Data: A Call to Creativity

Constance Jones and Andrea Wiemann

Abstract

Not all empirical investigations require fresh data collection. Abundant sources of data, amenable for systematic evaluation, already exist in the form of archival data. Meaning may be extracted from a variety of data sources surrounding us (primary archival data – e.g., obituaries, blogs, yearbooks) or from data previously collected by other researchers (secondary archival data – e.g., computerized archives). Examples of both primary and secondary archival data are provided, with an emphasis on qualitative sources. Common techniques for analyzing qualitative data are then described, and a suggested set of steps for proceeding with a study employing archival data is detailed. The chapter ends with a list of important qualitative secondary archival data sets.

Keywords: Archival Data, Data Reuse, Qualitative Data, Example Qualitative Secondary Archival Data Sets

> *Return again, return again*
> *return to the land of your soul*
> *Return to who you are*
> *return to what you are*
> *return to where you are*
> *born and reborn again*
>
> ***Return Again* © Rabbi Shlomo Carlebach, BMI**
> *Used with permission*

Archival data may be broadly defined as any sort of information, previously created or collected by others, that is amenable to systematic study (Jones, 2010). Social and behavioral scientists – including psychologists, sociologists, demographers, political scientists, anthropologists, and economists – are all in the business of describing, explaining, and predicting human behavior and are fortunate to be surrounded by huge arrays of data that can generate and/or confirm insights. The range of data sources, types, and characteristics available, along with the myriad of techniques to analyze those data, is extraordinary, with something to capture almost any researcher's imagination. The use of archival data forces a thoughtful recentering both upon the individuals who originally provided the data and also often upon the original researchers and the socio-historical context in which the two came together. This return to data – with new truths "born" and "reborn again" – can produce genuinely creative, exciting, and nuanced scientific work.

Given the broad definition of archival data, we will first provide definitions and examples of different sources of data (primary versus secondary) by characteristics of data (qualitative versus quantitative). Once the range of data options is illustrated, we move to a discussion of the range of techniques currently available to analyze those data. We conclude with a brief outline of how one might initiate a study using archival data, and provide a list of important qualitative secondary archival data sets.

Primary Archival Data

Primary archival data are data sources that have been created for non-research purposes but may be harvested and converted to answer specific empirical research questions. The sources of such data are incredibly far-ranging, as will be illustrated below.

Qualitative Data

Qualitative data are defined as "non-numerical" data, such as text and images. Sources of primary qualitative data, ready to give fresh insights into human behavior, are abundant. Humans leave traces of their behavior and attitudes in astounding manners, particularly in the exponentially increasing virtual world.

As a first example, consider published obituaries. Obituaries provide a rich but succinct detailing of an individual's life, highlighting the values of the individual person and the eras in which that individual lived. Hume (2003) performed an analysis of the *New York Times* "Portraits of Grief," commemorating those who perished in the September 11, 2001 terrorist attacks to capture the American zeitgeist of that terrible time. She studied 427 portraits published nearly immediately following the attacks until the end of December 2001. She discovered several important themes in the obituaries, including devotion to family, outside-work passions, strong work ethic, generosity, good health, and cultural values. Because all individuals died at essentially the same moment, of essentially the same cause, certain issues normally highlighted in obituaries were not detailed. Sadly, there is now a parallel set of obituaries in the *New York Times* for those who have succumbed to COVID-19.

As another example of the use of text to capture a country's zeitgeist, consider published books and magazines. Dale and colleagues (2016) analyzed 58 children's princess books, written in English, published between 1978 and 2010, and analyzed content being delivered to primarily young girls. They found princesses were often coded as being in distress and naïve, with these female-stereotyped qualities remaining high even in more recently published books. They note books marketed to children contain sparse child-appropriate content (e.g., joy) and excessive adult-appropriate content (e.g., finding a husband).

Online diaries, known as blogs, were explored to understand nurses' experiences working on the frontline of the COVID-19 pandemic in Wuhan, China (Chen et al., 2022). Rather than travel to Wuhan, or burden already overworked nurses with questionnaires or interviews, blogs of 12 nurses with a relatively wide readership, who were writing between January 2020 and April 2020, were examined. Entries with similar length were extracted, producing a total of 205 diary entries. Inductive content analysis uncovered two primary themes – constructing a better self and constructing a strong support network. Both themes illustrate the resilience of nurses working in crisis conditions.

Significantly more private than blogs, Joiner et al. (2002) coded a sample of 80 suicide notes. They used an evolutionary-psychological perspective to explore reasons why individuals would desire an end to their own life path. Of several other potential variables (hopelessness, emotional pain), they found that those who wrote notes rated higher in burdensomeness were less likely to survive their suicide attempt and were more likely to employ risky lethal methods in their attempts (e.g., gunshot versus cutting). The perception of burdensomeness as a driver of suicide has both theoretical evolutionary and practical clinical implications.

Text need not be extensive or intensely personal to yield valuable information. The 140-character-long "post" (still commonly called a "tweet") provides fascinating insight into publicly shared opinions and attitudes. Kamiński and colleagues (2021) analyzed 17,331 tweets related to COVID-19 posted by health agencies, government authorities, universities, scientific journals, medical associations, and celebrities. The authors tracked number of likes and number of retweeted messages, along with message content, classified as positive or negative. An example positive tweet relating to COVID comes from Paris Hilton: "So proud that the @HiltonFoundation just donated $10Million in additional funding toward relief efforts & support for communities most impacted by #COVID19 here in #LosAngeles & abroad. It is our collective responsibility in philanthropy to work together during this time! ♡🙏"

An example negative tweet relating to COVID comes from Oprah Winfrey: "As #COVID19 continues to shake up the world, it has had a more deadly impact on the African American community here in the US. So I've gathered leaders, journalists like @VanJones68, and families who are facing this crisis head on to discuss this. #OprahTalks." Analyses of COVID-related tweets indicate that celebrities and politicians posted more positive messages than the scientifically informed organizations, and that more positive messages received more likes than negative messages.

As a final example of publicly available text ripe for analysis, consider bathroom graffiti. Fisher and Radtke (2014) explored 20 clubs and bars in Toronto and took photographs of all graffiti in women's and men's bathrooms. They gathered a total of 371 graffiti items from the women's bathrooms and 479 from the men's bathrooms. Using a thematic analysis approach, the top women's themes were love, competition, heterosexual sexual behavior, alliances, and same-sex sexual behavior. The top men's themes were tagging (leaving stylized initials), philosophy/politics, and heterosexual sexual behavior. Taking an evolutionary perspective, the authors note that men's typical graffiti – tagging – can be seen as a sign of territoriality; women's typical graffiti involve messages of relationships.

Graffiti can include both text and imagery. Quickly drawn doodles, produced with very little text, can also be analyzed for thematic content. For example, 195 nursing students studying at a comprehensive university in the Philippines were asked to draw rough doodles of an effective clinical nursing instructor (e.g., picture of an angel) and an ineffective clinical nursing instructor (e.g., picture of an angry face), along with a brief written description. Themes of an enlightening, engaging, and embracing effective instructor and a detrimental, dangling, and disturbing ineffective instructor emerged from these sources of information (de Guzman et al., 2008).

Moving to pure images, "selfies" (pictures of oneself) posted on social media can be systematically and scientifically studied (rather than silently judged). Babič and colleagues (2018), using samples from Bangkok, Berlin, London, Moscow, New York, and Sao Paolo, analyzed 2,754 selfies posted to Instagram to explore gender differences in facial prominence. Those portrayed with greater facial prominence – defined as the proportion of head seen in the photograph to the whole – are judged to be more dominant, assertive, and ambitious than those who are portrayed displaying more of the rest of their body. Generally, men are found to be portrayed with greater facial prominence than women, but the authors found this only for selfies posted from a subset of cities: Berlin, London, and Sao Paolo. Connections between country-level indicators of values (e.g., gender equality, efficacy of government) and extent of difference between genders were explored, but no significant results were obtained.

Consider also the amount of information that may be gleaned from family photo albums. Rather than asking individuals how they hold their babies, or providing a baby and asking individuals to pose with them, Manning (1991) examined gender differences in "left-side infant holding" by obtaining a sample of 1,696 family photographs of individuals holding a baby. Results indicate women prefer left-holding over men, all without intruding upon a large sample of men or women or hapless babies. They hypothesized that holding the infant on the left side of the body gives greater information to the right hemisphere of the brain – associated with emotional processing.

Another treasure trove of images are yearbooks. Rather than ask managing partners of America's top 100 law firms to reflect upon their appearances and personality in college, Rule and Ambady (2011) retrieved and analyzed the partners' college yearbook photographs. They found that college-aged appearances of power (dominance and facial maturity) positively predicted the partners' firm's profit margin, profitability, and profits per equity partner decades later.

Quantitative Data

Quantitative data are "numerical" data. Because this chapter focuses on qualitative data, a single brief example of primary archival quantitative data will be provided here, to clarify the advantages and disadvantages of qualitative data. Global stock indices are a rich publicly available set of primary data of great interest to economists and others monitoring the financial reactivity/health of countries. Ngwakwe (2020) explored the impact of the COVID-19 pandemic on four such indices: SSE Composite Index (China), Euronext 100 (European Union), the Dow Jones Industrial Average, and the Standard and Poor's 500 (United States of America). They examined data for 50 days before the pandemic and 50 days during the COVID-19 pandemic. The effect of the pandemic was quite varied across and within countries, with the Euronext 100 and the S&P 500 holding steady, SSE Composite Index increasing, and the Dow Jones Industrial Average decreasing. Stock index numbers are more easily computerized and may be more swiftly analyzed, but possess less richness than the qualitative data examples described above.

Secondary Archival Data

The second source of archival data involves reanalysis of data collected by previous researchers. Reuse/reanalysis of data collected by other researchers has been termed secondary analysis (Bernard et al., 2016). In the past, secondary analysis of quantitative data has been more common than secondary analysis of qualitative data (e.g., Heaton, 2008; Ruggiano & Perry, 2019; Sharp & Munly, 2022), but the increasing emphasis on open science and data sharing, along with advances in computer programs to analyze qualitative data, are changing this imbalance.

Qualitative Data

Given the boggling abundance of data available, it is reasonable for a researcher to become quickly overwhelmed with the choices. For example, the Henry A. Murray Archive, at Harvard University, is an important source of qualitative secondary data. Studies available for reanalysis include work on children of gay fathers, bulimia in college students, faith development and moral development in old age, immigration, family life, and achievement motivation in Latino adolescents, and the Intergenerational Studies (more details below). The time required to search for, and completely understand, the correct set of data, to answer one's research question, eliminates all notions that analysis of archival data, of any type, is easier or faster than collecting fresh data of one's own. A list of important sites holding primarily qualitative secondary archival data sets is given near the end of this chapter.

A first example of using, and then interestingly expanding upon, qualitative secondary archival data comes from Lyon and Crow (2020). Pahl, a sociologist, collected, analyzed, then contributed to the UK Data Archive a set of children's essays written in 1978. All children were living on the Isle of Sheppey in Kent, England and were asked to write an essay describing what their lives were like, imagining themselves near the end of their lives. The economic future at the time appeared bleak, with limited opportunities for the 16-year-olds about to depart school.

Pahl (1978) analyzed these essays then archived them. Lyon and Crow (2020), who discovered the essays nearly 30 years later, thought to replicate the research design and collect similar-themed essays from similar-aged children in the same location (unfortunately once again facing a bleak economy) in 2010. The similarities in data collection and location, separated by time, provides a rich opportunity for comparative analysis. An example finding was the convergence between boys and girls in aspirations for education and employment, with greater similarities in ambitions in 2010 versus 1987. In part in reaction to the difficulties of coaxing essays from the more modern cohort, even more innovative methods to gather data along the same theme were generated by Lyon and Crow, including holding focus groups, with discussion prompted by evocative images.

A second example illustrates the power of re-examining secondary archival data with a fresh eye and tying old data to new data about the same individual. Terman (1968) began a study of intellectually gifted schoolchildren in California in 1921, collecting voluminous qualitative and quantitative data from boys and girls in an attempt to predict their life choices and outcomes in adulthood. Friedman and Martin revisited those data decades later, crafted new measures of personality from the old data, then linked childhood personality to death records to uncover powerful predictors of longevity from childhood. For example, it becomes clear, working with data describing individuals from childhood all the way through to their death, that greater conscientiousness in childhood powerfully predicts a longer life (Friedman & Martin, 2012; Martin et al., 2007).

As a final example, consider the Intergenerational Studies (IGS), a set of three originally separate longitudinal studies of childhood and adolescent development – the Berkeley Growth Study, the Berkeley Guidance Study, and the Oakland Growth Study. The IGS illustrate multiple themes of secondary qualitative archival data, including forced creativity in working with previously collected data, and the value of expanding and linking data to the same individuals across time and to different individuals at the same time. The three original studies began at the Institute of Human Development (then termed the Institute of Child Welfare) in the late 1920s and early 1930s. Addressing the fact that very little empirical information about infant and child development – physical, cognitive, or social – existed at the time, researchers systematically collected data from infants and children living in the west coast of the United States, in Berkeley, CA, and in Oakland, CA. Taking a simultaneously atheoretical and multidisciplinary approach to data collection, a huge mass of both quantitative (height and weight) and qualitative (transcriptions of interviews with the children's parents) data were laid down, with new information collected every six months or every year in the early years of the studies.

The three studies were merged together in the 1960s due to a new researcher's desire to work with a larger, more powerful sample size. Because data collection procedures were not identical across the three studies, Block (1971) returned to the qualitative transcripts of interviews, in conjunction with other materials, and crafted a new measure of personality termed the California Q-sort. Trained clinicians read and pondered the collection of information available for a certain person at a certain age (e.g., age 14) then converted the qualitative data to a quantitative measure, ranging from 1–9, on a set of 100 descriptive terms (e.g., *calm; values independence; uncomfortable with uncertainty; overcontrolled; warm*). This conversion of roughly parallel qualitative data to exactly parallel quantitative data, particularly because the process was repeated for multiple ages, greatly expanded the power and replicability of the now larger combined data set.

In part due to the extremely rich data collected from the participant children and their families, the original principal investigators developed both a personal and scientific curiosity about the children they came to know so well. Many of the

Table 25.1 *Major texts demonstrating secondary data analysis of Intergenerational Studies data*

Citation	Discipline of researcher	Participants	Studies used	Summary
Block, 1971	Psychologist	OP	BGu, OG	Types of personality development
Elder, Jr., 1974	Sociologist	OP	OG	Impact of the Great Depression on development
Clausen, 1993	Sociologist	OP, SP	BGr, BGu, OG	American lives in historical context
Weiss, 2000	Historian	OP, SP	BGu, OG	American marriages in historical context
Setttersten, Jr. et al., 2021	Sociologists	PP	BGu	American lives in historical context

OP = original participant; SP = spouse of original participant; PP = parent of original participant.
BGr = Berkeley Growth Study; BGu = Berkeley Guidance Study; OG = Oakland Growth Study.

children, as adolescents, became similarly attached to the principal investigators. With fresh funding, additional waves of data were collected from the original participants as they grew into adulthood, middle age, and old age. And importantly, by deciding to include spouses and then children of the original participants in data collection, historical changes in spousal and parental relationships became ripe for exploration.

Over the years, a huge number of publications have been generated using the expansive Intergenerational Studies data set. Many more will follow, given the data are now formally archived at the Henry Murray Center. Examples of the power of secondary analysis of qualitative data, working across multiple studies, are given in Table 25.1. Note the range of publication dates, the range of disciplines of primary researchers, and the different choices of participants. Each of these texts can be used as a powerful example of the power of secondary analysis of qualitative data.

Quantitative Data

A single brief example of secondary quantitative data is provided, to highlight differences from qualitative data. California Q-sort data (described above) from the Intergenerational Studies, available for early and late adolescence, and early, middle, and late adulthood, were first analyzed by Haan and colleagues (1986). Using repeated-measures ANOVA, they created nomothetic patterns of lifetime change – purportedly true for all individuals in the sample – for six principal components extracted from California Q-sort data. With the advent of new statistical procedures that allow investigation of inter-individual differences in intra-individual change – idiothetic patterns of lifetime change – Jones and Meredith (1996) reanalyzed essentially the same data with latent curve analysis (Meredith & Tisak, 1990) and discovered a single pattern of change or stability for five of six components; this also included important individual differences in the amount and even direction of change. No systematic pattern of change could be found for the remaining component. New analyses of the same data produced a more nuanced and accurate view of change in personality across the lifespan.

Analyses and Interpretation of Archival Data

It is important to differentiate between archival data and analyses of those archival data; both of these can be either qualitative or quantitative in nature (Bernard et al., 2016). For social and behavioral scientists, data approximate the human experience collected in numbers, words, stories, and a variety of other measurements. For example, an economist may focus on the financial health and well-being of a county using macroeconomic data, housing market trends, and the like, collected by government agencies. Those data contain pieces of the people and culture that they came from, but like a box of proverbial chocolates, you don't know what you have until you take the time and often enormous effort to analyze it.

"Telling the story" of the data has become such a common method for describing data analysis that there are references to it in textbooks across fields, memes, X, and Reddit threads, and many introductory methods courses. This idea of the data as the content and the analysis as the story is simplistic but helps in understanding the broad variety of methodologies and the influence of an analyst's field, training, experiences, and biases. Just as data may be qualitative or quantitative, the analysis of data may also be qualitative or quantitative; because each type has strengths and weaknesses, it is also becoming increasingly popular to combine the two. For simplicity, qualitative analysis refers to the process of identifying meaning and patterns from data and is considered a more subjective approach that excludes the use of numbers. Quantitative analysis uses mathematical equations and probabilities to learn about the various responses or observations and their relevance to the real world (Goodwin & O'Connor, 2020). The decisions regarding methodology depend on type of data and research question, among other considerations. The sections below focus on the differentiation between qualitative analysis of qualitative data and quantitative analysis of qualitative data, with a brief contrast to quantitative and qualitative analysis of quantitative data.

Qualitative Analysis of Qualitative Archival Data

Before deciding how to analyze qualitative archival data, an important step is to identify how those data were collected and understand the goals of the individuals involved. This is expanded upon in the recommendations at the of the chapter. Original researcher motivation and study design can influence qualitative data (and quantitative data) in unexpected ways when not properly accounted for. This information is often referred to as metadata and refers to how the data was collected, where, by whom, and for what purpose (e.g., Irwin, 2020). For example, if researchers conduct interviews about experiences with racism, the interpretation changes considering when they were conducted, whether the interviewers were racially concordant with the interviewees, etc. Once the process of understanding where the data comes from and how is complete, the actual analysis process should be chosen based on the goals and limitations of the planned study.

Bernard et al. (2016), in a helpful introductory text, list 11 different ways to analyze qualitative data; Saldaña (2013) classifies 24 separate methods to perform initial coding. Methods for qualitative analysis of qualitative archival data range from the very low tech (involving index cards or different colored highlighter pens) to the moderately technical (using word processor systems or spreadsheets) to high-tech qualitative data analysis software (QDAS), such as NVivo, Dedoose, or MAXQDA. Johns Hopkins Sheridan Libraries (2023) suggests decision-making factors such as how well the program supports the planned methodology, visualization and analysis capabilities, and cost. Ultimately, researchers should identify what they need to accomplish and find a program or method that fits the data collection method and the analysis method while staying within their allotted time and budget for the analysis.

As discussed earlier, qualitative archival data come in formats ranging from interview transcripts to blogs to graffiti. For example, an introductory course on qualitative methods in sociology may focus on a set of ethnographic field notes about everyday interactions, one-on-one interviews regarding discrimination from different time periods, or a number of other methods. It is important to note that grounded theory, developed by Glaser and Strauss (1967), though one of the most generally used techniques for qualitative analysis, is not typically used for the analysis of archival data. This is because new interviews (or other data collection methods) are meant to build on the ideas of the previous interviews until something called saturation is reached. This is the point at which no additional information is gleaned from interviews and at which interviewing or data collection stops. As such, no examples of grounded theory analyses are included below.

Instead, we focus on narrative analysis. Narrative analysis is commonly used to identify patterns in how people or entities construct stories from their experiences, including written historical narratives, oral narratives of personal experience (Riessman, 2005), and even Instagram stories. Bernard et al. (2016) identifies three narrative traditions in the social sciences: sociolinguistic methods focus on the structure of the narrative itself; hermeneutic methods focus on the content and bigger picture of the narrative; and phenomenological methods focus on the experience of the narrator. By exploring individuals' "stories of their lives" in a systematic manner, rich patterns of similarities and differences emerge.

In one example of a narrative analysis, Purcell et al. (2020) explored transcripts of one-on-one interviews with a total of 138 women who had undergone an abortion, pulling data across five separate data sets. Using a narrative inquiry methodology, transcripts were carefully examined and discussed by multiple lead authors. Identified themes included non-negative framings of the experience (e.g., "the whole experience was actually OK, I wasn't like traumatized by it," p. 1354), positive framings (e.g., "I was so happy, you know, so happy," p. 1355), and negation statements (e.g., "I didn't feel like, y'know, ashamed of what I was doing," p. 1357).

In general, personal statements about lived experience contradicted the stigmatizing messages of abortion found in some religious or political commentaries.

As another example, Boudens (2005) collected narratives from Terkel's (1972) *Working* and Bowe et al.'s (2000) *Gig*. The narratives were simplified into "core stories," sorted into groups sharing a common theme by a first rater, then assigned to an independent coder to verify reliability of the sorting process. Example themes include "inequitable situations," "discrimination," and "cross-level conflict." Within themes, emotional content was identified. Emotion themes for "inequitable situations," for example, included "resigned acceptance of the way things are" and "feeling unappreciated." Stepping back and examining the many work themes and emotions expressed, the author identified three overarching themes: balance (i.e., in relationships and with their work), silence (i.e., the unspoken experiences that occur within organizations and subtly shape them), and boundaries (i.e., the challenges experienced when maintaining boundaries).

Moving into the world of video games, Kohlburn et al. (2022) studied perceptions of LGBTQ+ inclusive video games by performing a content analysis of publicly available reviews on Steam – a web store for online games and digital applications. Using inductive and deductive coding of the reviews, the authors identified common themes, including both positive discussion of LGBTQ+ representation (e.g., "As an LGBTQ player, it's good that we have games with Gay characters like this . . . I hope we have more LGBTQ games for more representation," p. 12) and negative discussion of the same (e.g., "Awful. SJW garbage made by worthless hipster trash. Suckered into buying this," p. 12). The authors used this and other themes and co-occurrence of themes to support the importance of representation in gaming. They found the most frequently identified theme in reviews is the storyline/narrative of the game and the ethics of the games' creation.

Social media platforms provide a plethora of opportunities for qualitative exploration. Sowles et al. (2018) conducted content analysis in a pro-eating-disorder community, groups that promote eating disorders and share their experiences and recommendations. Before or instead of seeking treatment, some individuals enjoy the refuge of connection with others suffering from eating disorders. By evaluating discussion threads on Reddit, an anonymous social networking platform, the authors coded discussion posts and identified common themes. The most common expressions consistent with eating disorder psychopathology were eating concerns (e.g., "I'm so anxious about having to eat two meals today. I have a work lunch meeting and a family dinner. If I can't come up with something, I'll be purging this evening," p. 140) and shape concerns (e.g., "I seriously can't wait for more bones! I really like how my muscles are starting to show, but bones would be nice. Still very insecure about my arms," p. 141). They also found that the majority of responses to posts provided emotional support to the commenter.

The examples presented above illustrate researchers working with one set of texts and converting them to a second set of texts. Consider the innovation of Sharp, a family scholar, and Durham-DeCesaro, a choreographer, who undertook a genuinely transdisciplinary project. Sharp provided two sets of her qualitative data – one involving women describing their wedding and another involving single women – to DeCesaro, who read the transcripts then extracted key phrases that struck her as having "kinesthetic possibilities" or that produced in her "kinesthetic reactions." She then wrote dance pieces to highlight themes she uncovered, not via text, but via movement (Sharp & Durham-DeCesaro, 2015). This methodology demonstrates the various ways that qualitative data can be interpreted and shared.

Quantitative Analysis of Qualitative Archival Data

Quantitative analysis of qualitative data refers to assigning numerical values to represent text or other non-quantitative original data. As one example, Danner et al. (2001) used content analysis to identify words with positive and negative connotations in essays. American Catholic nuns who were taking their final vows in 1930 were asked to write a short autobiography. Discovered years later, these essays were analyzed for number of positive (e.g., gratitude), negative (e.g., shame), and neutral (e.g., surprise) emotion content words. Tied to death certificates six decades later, a clear positive relationship was found between the number of positive words used in their autobiographies and longevity.

In another recent study, researchers explored the use of social media, specifically Instagram stories and Instagram feeds, by elite female athletes. The top 37 women soccer athletes were selected from across the world, and their Instagram posts were harvested. After an extensive coding process and evaluation of inter-rater agreement between researchers, Li and colleagues (2021) counted the number of posts falling into certain categories, such as "information sharing," "opinion expression," and "behind the scenes stories." They then used traditional inferential statistics, such as t-tests and chi-squared tests, to find differences between the type of post on their Instagram stories compared to the Instagram feeds of the general population. Analyses revealed that the elite female athletes used Instagram messages more often for the expression of their opinions; Instagram stories were more often used for promotion and sharing behind-the-scenes content.

Quantitative Analysis of Quantitative Archival Data

To compare with our discussion of the qualitative and quantitative analysis of qualitative data, we present a brief description of quantitative analysis of quantitative data. For example, archival data analysis might involve calculating the mean and standard deviation of a sample of community-dwelling adults' Beck Depression Inventory scores. Other examples include conducting analyses with data from the Office of Statewide Health Planning and Development (OSHPD) to investigate preventable hospitalizations across California, or exploring poverty rates by county.

This process of quantitatively analyzing quantitative archival data involves importing a data set, often in Excel or CSV format for archival data, and using a software package to correctly extract summary statistics and perform inferential tests using one's preferred approach. There are a wide variety of methods for quantitative analysis that depend on the measurement and distribution of the variables of interest, and these methods can be applied to archival data. For all users and levels, mastering a statistical program, whichever it may be, is just the beginning of the analysis and interpretation process. While most students can duly report statistics, such as mean and standard deviation for a set of archival Beck Depression Inventory scores, truly understanding the meaning of those numbers and writing about them intelligibly is a whole other matter. For example, are those in the sample, in general, quite depressed or relatively cheerful? Are they quite similar to one another with respect to score or quite disparate? Are there people in the sample who need immediate mental health care? What does it all really mean?

As a final example, Lee and colleagues (2021) conducted a retrospective study of 43,519 elderly diabetes mellitus patients, using archival data from the 2012 Maryland (United States) Clinical Public Use Data. The researchers compared four types of insurance with three outcomes (length of hospital stay, whether or not they were readmitted within 30 days, and whether or not the patient was hospitalized as having end-stage renal disease). A series of t-tests and regressions identified significant differences in health outcomes by insurance type; those with Medicare Fee-For-Service had significantly longer length of stay, higher likelihood of being readmitted, and a higher likelihood of being hospitalized with end-stage renal disease than those with Medicare Managed Care, Private Fee-For-Service, and Private Medicare Plans. It is notable that the researchers chose Maryland specifically, as healthcare subscribers can choose between fee-for-service and managed care plans for both government and private insurance. In the land of no universal healthcare, that is an uncommon option. The context of applicable healthcare policies combined with a strong conceptual understanding of the meaning of the data was necessary for the researchers to successfully complete the project.

Qualitative Analysis of Quantitative Archival Data

Qualitative analysis of quantitative data might sound contradictory, but in some cases, it refers to exploring and interpreting the underlying meanings, patterns, and insights from numerical data. It involves going beyond the raw numbers and statistical analysis to better understand the data's implications and context. This type of analysis helps to answer "why" and "how" questions that cannot be adequately addressed solely through quantitative methods. This process includes exploring data through various techniques and looking for patterns and relationships, evaluating context, and interpreting and sharing the information in a way that fits the intended audience.

As noted above, Lee and colleagues (2021) used quantitative methods to analyze quantitative archival data to investigate the relationship between health insurance and health outcomes. After presenting their analysis, the researchers provided additional context by sharing what other researchers found in past related studies and discussed the limitations of a cross-sectional study. Rather than use the results (incorrectly) to shout from the rooftops that Medicare Fee-For-Service causes poor health outcomes, the researchers used the analysis to suggest future research in targeted areas to better understand this relationship and ultimately help understand the benefits and challenges of different health insurance options.

Qualitative analysis of quantitative data can be instrumental in social sciences, market research, and business analytics, where understanding the underlying factors, motivations, and context can significantly enhance the understanding and applicability of the numerical results. It is not about converting quantitative data into qualitative data but rather augmenting quantitative findings with qualitative insights to provide a more holistic understanding of the studied phenomenon.

Analysis of archival data, whether qualitative or quantitative, requires a multifaceted approach, encompassing qualitative and quantitative perspectives. Qualitative analysis of qualitative data delves into the nuanced meanings and contextual richness embedded in the records, providing a deeper understanding of the events and experiences captured. On the other hand, quantitative analysis of qualitative data transforms textual information into measurable variables, enabling systematic exploration and statistical inference. When examining numerical records, quantitative analysis of quantitative data employs statistical methods to identify patterns, trends, and correlations within the data. Lastly, qualitative analysis of quantitative data delves beyond the numbers, unraveling the underlying insights and implications that extend beyond the raw data points. Integrating these four analyses enables a better understanding of archival data, unlocking valuable historical, social, and cultural insights that contribute to a richer appreciation of the past and its significance for the present and future.

Issues to Address When Beginning an Investigation Using Qualitative Archival Data: A Rough Guideline

- Read the existing scientific literature deeply and widely to identify a broad research question. That is, do not work backwards, exploring qualitative primary data or secondary data sets and generating potential research questions. New researchers, in anxious haste to publish and not perish, may be tempted to commit too quickly to data. Let gaps in the scientific literature guide decisions rather than expediency of data access.
- Once settled upon a preliminary research question, confirm that the "answer" to the research question is not fairly well settled already. For example, consider the question: Are women more prone to depression than men? This generic question has already been extensively studied. However, if there is a new measure of depression, a new sample of females (very young children / very old women / animal models), or a new era (analysis of novels written in the 1800s), a new study may reasonably be undertaken.
- With greater commitment to a research question and a hunch that data may already be available to answer that question, a political pitstop is now in order. University faculty are, of course, free to study research topics of their own choosing, using whatever scientific methods are deemed acceptable, but a general read of relevant personnel promotion committees might be prudent. Similarly, students should check with their mentor/committee members to gauge their level of support for the use of archival data.

- Other researchers unfamiliar with the use of archival data may initially think investigators are "cheating" by not collecting their own fresh data. The traditional deductive "cycle of science," for example, implies researchers should select an appropriate theory, create a research question and research hypothesis, then collect fresh data and analyze those data to confirm or deny their hypothesis, subsequently tying results back to their selected theory. However, if one expands the definition of data to include pre-existing data – either amassed coincidentally by others or for others' research purposes – scientific innovation, flexibility, and creativity come to the forefront.
- In the face of resistance from research colleagues/mentors in positions of power, the following arguments for the use of archival data may be presented:
  - Using archival data is not quicker or easier than collecting fresh data. It instead involves redistributing efforts from data collection to data discovery, data exploration, and data reconfiguration/reuse (e.g., Jones, 2010; Neale, 2020).
  - Secondary qualitative data analytic work is in fact becoming more common (Bishop & Kuula-Luumi, 2017). In addition, reuse of any kind of data fits with the move toward open science (Allen & Mehler, 2019), in part in reaction to the "failure to replicate crisis" (Open Science Collaboration, 2015). Scientists and the public alike benefit from the transparent sharing of data, lifting back the veil, making the scientific process less mysterious and more accessible.
  - Data collection can be extraordinarily time-consuming and expensive. Consider the cost, for example, of identifying participants, contacting participants, scheduling participants to arrive at a location to be interviewed, hiring interviewers, recording the interviews, transcribing the interviews, and storing the interview transcripts to be ready for analysis. It is terribly wasteful to presume that the initial principal investigators are the only individuals who should be allowed to use the data, and that they can only use the data once. Fresh researchers, with fresh academic disciplines and research tools, can pull new information from data created by others with very little additional cost (e.g., DuBois et al., 2018; Hughes & Tarrant, 2020).
  - Some forms of data collection can be truly grueling for participants. For example, rather than asking rape survivors to give the details of the crime perpetrated upon them, repeatedly for each researcher interested in their story, surely data can be collected once and protected for others to learn from (e.g., Sharp & Munly, 2022). Consider other potentially fragile populations: Holocaust survivors, parents of children murdered in mass school shootings, early widowers, the grisly list goes on. Skillfully interviewing such individuals *once*, and asking some fairly free-form questions then transcribing answers would create data useful to many in the future.
  - Open Science, involving the sharing of data with fellow researchers, on the one hand, can be thought of as something deeply invasive. The idea of rivals "checking" work, to make sure results are "correct," prompts natural fears of humiliating "gotcha" scenarios. And while Open Science can reduce fraudulent research claims, the primary purpose is to infuse fresh insight into data. No single mind, no matter how brilliant, is capable of considering all the angles of

data, all the contexts, all the possibilities. Particularly given a rich set of qualitative data, secondary analysis can highlight the genuine strengths of a "thick" study of human behavior. Fresh insights can be drawn from the same set of data for literally decades, with the advent of new methodologies, theories, disciplines, knowledge, and scientific and historical understanding. There is awesome power in "multilogicality" – the inclusion of more than one thoughtful, interpretive lens for data analysis (e.g., Sharp & Munly, 2022).

- Once it becomes clear that relevant colleagues see the value of archival data, a return to the literature is an efficient next step. Did any previous studies addressing the selected research question employ archival data? If so, which types of data or which data sets? Create an account of sample size, data harvested, analytical methods employed, and strengths and weaknesses of each previous study.
- Once each potential data set meets initial acceptability, take a deep dive. It is difficult to remember details regarding a data set created for one's own research purposes. Minor procedural issues (e.g., what type of participants were excluded and why? Which items were omitted from a standardized questionnaire and why? Did data collection begin in August or September?) call for detailed documentation that often seems unnecessary at the beginning of a project. However, one step removed, and a secondary data analyst is completely dependent upon the "metadata" produced by the original principal investigator to understand the larger context of the study (e.g., Hughes & Tarrant, 2020). Where were the data collected? When? How? Why? What were the surrounding socio-historical contexts for these data? By definition, secondary analysis of data involves engaging with data collected in the past (e.g., Duncan, 2012). Whether it be the far past (e.g., 65,000-year-old cave paintings) or the near past (e.g., the last election cycle), consideration of old data forces a contemplation of the person originally providing the data, the researchers collecting the data, and their socio-historical context at the time of data collection. It becomes shockingly easy to imagine that data freshly collected for one's own research purposes are "generic" or "time-free," with results "permanently true." Secondary data analysis forces researchers to consider data in the context of time and to acknowledge the fallacy of "permanent truth," particularly with respect to most topics of focus for psychologists.
- Inexperienced researchers may not know to worry about or ask about important details and may feel the desire to rush to the data before fully pondering context. This is a grievous error. Good secondary analysts spend their time getting to know their data, including metadata, replacing the time they might have spent collecting the data in the first place. After learning as much as possible about the data set(s), a very cautious initial use of a subset of data is in order. This is not to "peek" and explore whether the research question will be supported. This is, instead, to confirm the data can be coded and analyzed as intended. For example, imagine re-exploring 52-year-old women's answers to the following four questions: (1) What were your goals for yourself in your twenties and thirties? (2) What are your goals for yourself now? (3) What do you feel were the values you lived by in your

twenties and thirties? (4) What values do you think you will live by from here on? If your values have changed, why? (Harker & Solomon, 1996; Helson & Mitchell, 2020). Perhaps the plan was to count the number of positive (e.g., proud) and number of negative (e.g., embarrassed) emotion content words in the responses to each of the four questions and tie those numbers to marital and child status. Are the responses handwritten or converted to text? If handwritten, are the majority legible? How difficult will it be to convert data to be ready for analysis? If raters are to be employed, train the raters and have them rate a set of essays. Check that reliability and validity are sufficient. Deeply ponder whether results are properly capturing the essence of the data.

- After committing to a data set, further considerations can involve the possibility of tying data sets together. Several approaches are possible:

  - One possibility is to tie old data to new data. Collecting fresh data from participants (e.g., reinterviewing them) or fresh data about participants (e.g., collecting their date of death from Ancestory.com) and tying those data to previously provided data can be enormously powerful. Such longitudinal data allow a lifespan perspective, drawing out the arc of understanding and prediction of human behavior. By continuing to follow participants from childhood and adolescence until their adulthood, for example, researchers from the Zurich Longitudinal Studies can search back for pre-adult predictors of adult health and aging (e.g., Wehrle et al., 2021). Archival longitudinal data sets, in particular, allow new researchers access to information they could never personally collect in their professional lifetime.
  - Alternatively, while working with a single foreign data set is difficult, to combine multiple data sets and work to understand similarities and opportunities for connection is even more difficult, but can pay off in a broadened perspective and larger sample size. Davidson and colleagues (e.g., Davidson et al., 2019; Edwards et al., 2020) describe a "breadth and depth" method of working across multiple similar qualitative data sets. Their four steps involve surveying the available data, recursively identifying themes, performing preliminary analyses, then expanding with in-depth analyses. Their tips are useful for those ready to move across multiple archival qualitative data sets.

- Be careful. For those data involving participants' disclosure of very personal information (e.g., transcripts of life review interviews), concerns involving anonymity are valid and important to consider. Certainly, full names can be redacted, but if other identifying information remains, anonymity can be lost. For example, a nameless person or person with a pseudonym who describes how she invented a novel cloning technique, committed a heinous crime, or became the first CEO of a Fortune 500 company may be fairly easily identified (e.g., Ruggiano & Perry, 2019). For example, early investigators with the Intergenerational Studies blundered horribly by allowing publication of nude photographs of teenage participants, with faces blacked out, including one of a girl wearing a bracelet that she always wore, thereby identifying her to her classmates also involved in the studies.

- Finally, submit your final research plan to the relevant Institutional Review Board (IRB). When data are collected by the original principal investigators, it is assumed their proposal will be reviewed and approved by the relevant IRB before data collection begins. For maximum security, proposals to use archival data should also undergo IRB review. Although anonymized quantitative data sets (e.g., SAT scores for all students taking the examination across the state of Maryland) will generally be classified as "no risk," the same may not be true for qualitative data. Ideally, participants initially providing both quantitative and qualitative data could be asked for permission to release their data to other researchers in the future (e.g., Ruggiano & Perry, 2019).

All scientific investigations require thoughtful precision, creativity, and a solid disposition. Our contention is that the use of archival data requires those qualities and more – involving a recentering both upon the individuals who originally provided or created the data, the original researchers if secondary data are involved, and the socio-historical context in which all came together. But truths "born" and "reborn again" from archival data can push science forward in truly exciting ways. Below we offer a list of example qualitative secondary archival data sets, for those who are intrigued

Example Qualitative Secondary Archival Data Sets

The Australian Data Archive
Consortium of European Social Science Data Archives
Family Rhythms Project
Finnish Social Science Data Archive
Growing up in Ireland
Henry A. Murray Research Archive
Inter-University Consortium of Political and Social Research
Irish Qualitative Data Archive
Life Histories and Social Change
Northern Ireland Qualitative Archives
Qualidata Archive
The Schlesinger Library
Swiss Data and Research Information Services
Swiss Foundation for Research in Social Sciences
The Timescapes Archive
The UK Data Archive

References

Allen, C., & Mehler, D. M. A. (2019). Open science challenges, benefits and tips in early career and beyond. *PLOS Biology, 17*(5).

Babič, N. Č., Ropert, T., & Musil, B. (2018). Revealing faces: Gender and cultural differences in facial prominence of selfies. *PLOS ONE*, *13*(10), 1–12.

Bernard, H. R., Witich, A., & Ryan, G. W. (2016). *Analyzing Qualitative Data: Systematic Approaches*. SAGE Publications.

Bishop, L., & Kuula-Luumi, A. (2017). Revisiting qualitative data reuse: A decade on. *SAGE Open*, *7*(1). https://doi.org/10.1177/2158244016685136

Block, J. (1971). *Lives through Time*. Bancroft Books.

Boudens, C. J. (2005). The story of work: A narrative analysis of workplace emotion. *Organization Studies*, *26*(9), 1285–1306.

Bowe, J., Bowe, M., & Streeter, S. (2000). *Gig*. Crown.

Chatfield, S. L. (2020). Recommendations for secondary analysis of qualitative data. *Qualitative Report*, *25*(3), 833–842. https://doi.org/10.46743/2160-3715/2020.4092

Chen, H., Wang, Y., & Liu, Z. (2022). The experiences of frontline nurses in Wuhan: A qualitative analysis of nurse online diaries during the COVID-19 pandemic. *Journal of Clinical Nursing*, *31*, 2465–2475.

Clausen, J. A. (1993). *American Lives: Looking Back at the Children of the Great Depression*. University of California Press.

Dale, L. P., Higgins, B. E., Pinkerton, N., & Couto, M. (2016). Princess picture books: Content and messages. *Journal of Research in Childhood Education*, *30*, 185–199.

Danner, D. D., Snowdon, D. A., & Friesen, W. V. (2001). Positive emotions in early life and longevity: Findings from the Nun Study. *Journal of Personality and Social Psychology*, *80*, 804–813.

Davidson, E., Edwards, R., Jamieson, L., & Weller, S. (2019). Big data, qualitative style: A breadth-and-depth method for working with large amounts of secondary qualitative data. *Quality and Quantity*, *53*, 363–376.

de Guzman, A., Pablo, L. A., Prieto, R. J., Purificacion, V. N., Que, J. J., & Quia, P. (2008). Understanding the persona of clinical instructors: The use of students' doodles in nursing research. *Nurse Education Today*, *28*, 48–54.

DuBois, J. M., Strait, M., & Walsh, H. (2018). Is it time to share qualitative research data? *Qualitative Psychology*, *5*, 380–393.

Duncan, S. (2012). Using elderly data theoretically: Personal life in 1949/1950 and individualization theory. *International Journal of Social Research Methodology*, *15*, 311–319.

Edwards, R., Weller, S., Jamieson, L., & Davidson, E. (2020). Search strategies: Analytic searching across multiple datasets within combined sources. In K. Hughes and A. Tarrant (eds.), *Qualitative Secondary Analysis*. SAGE Publications.

Elder, Jr., G. H. (1974). *Children of the Great Depression: Social Change in Life Experience*. University of Chicago Press.

Fisher, M. L., & Radtke, S. (2014). Sex differences in the topics of bathroom graffiti. *Human Ethology Bulletin*, *29*(2), 68–81.

Friedman, H. S., & Martin, L. R. (2012). *The Longevity Project: Surprising Discoveries for Health and Long Life from the Landmark Eight-Decade Study*. Plume.

Glaser, B. G., & Strauss, A. L. (1967). *The Discovery of Grounded Theory: Strategies for Qualitative Research*. Aldine.

Goodwin, J., & O'Connor, H. (2020). Imagination and the analytical potential of working with non-interview or unusual data. In K. Hughes and A. Tarrant (eds.), *Qualitative Secondary Analysis*. SAGE Publications.

Haan, N., Millsap, R., & Hartka, E. (1986). As time goes by: Change and stability in personality over fifty years. *Psychology and Aging, 1*, 220–232.

Harker, L., & Solomon, M. (1996). Change in goals and values of men and women from early to mature adulthood. *Journal of Adult Development, 3*, 133–143.

Heaton, J. (2008). Secondary analysis of qualitative data: An overview. *Historical Social Research, 33*, 33–45.

Helson, R., & Mitchell, V. (2020). *Women on the River of Life*. University of California Press.

Hughes, K., & Tarrant, A. (2020). An introduction to qualitative secondary analysis. In K. Hughes and A. Tarrant (eds.), *Qualitative Secondary Analysis*. SAGE Publications.

Hume, J. (2003). "Portraits of Grief," reflectors of values: The *New York Times* remembers victims of September 11. *Journalism & Mass Communication Quarterly, 80*(1), 166–182.

Irwin, S. (2020). Qualitative secondary analysis: Working across datasets. In K. Hughes and A. Tarrant (eds.), *Qualitative Secondary Analysis*. SAGE Publications.

Johns Hopkins Sheridan Libraries. (2023, June 20). *Qualitative data analysis software*. https://guides.library.jhu.edu/QDAS

Joiner, Jr., T. E., Pettit, T. E., Walker, J. W., Voelz, R. L., Cruz, Z. R., Rudd, J., & Lester, D. (2002). Perceived burdensomeness and suicidality: Two studies on the suicide notes of those attempting and those completing suicide. *Journal of Social and Clinical Psychology, 21*, 531–545.

Jones, C. (2010). Archival data: Advantages and disadvantages for research in psychology. *Social and Personality Psychology Compass, 4*, 1008–1017.

Jones, C. J., & Meredith, W. (1996). Patterns of personality change across the life span. *Psychology and Aging, 11*, 57–65.

Kamiński, M., Szymańska, C., & Nowak, J. K. (2021). Whose tweets on COVID-19 gain the most attention: Celebrities, political, or scientific authorities? *Cyberpsychology, Behavior, and Social Networking, 24*, 123–128.

Kohlburn, J., Cho, H., & Moore, H. (2022). Players' perceptions of sexuality and gender inclusive video games: A pragmatic content analysis of Steam reviews. *Convergence, 29*(2), 379–399.

Lee, S. H., Brown, S. L., & Bennett, A. A. (2021). The relationship between insurance and health outcomes of diabetes mellitus patients in Maryland: A retrospective archival record study. *BMC Health Services Research, 21*(1), 1–10.

Li, B., Scott, O. K., Naraine, M. L., & Ruihley, B. J. (2021). Tell me a story: Exploring elite female athletes' self-presentation via an analysis of Instagram Stories. *Journal of Interactive Advertising, 21*(2), 108–120.

Lyon, D., & Crow, G. (2020). Doing qualitative secondary analysis: Revising young people's imagined futures in Ray Pahl's Sheppey studies. In K. Hughes and A. Tarrant (eds.), *Qualitative Secondary Analysis*. SAGE Publications.

Manning, J. T. (1991). Sex differences in left-side infant holding: Results from "family album" photographs. *Ethology and Sociobiology, 12*, 337–343.

Martin, L. R., Friedman, H. W., & Swartz, J. E. (2007). Personality and mortality risk across the life span: The importance of conscientiousness as a biopsychosocial attribute. *Health Psychology, 26*, 428–436.

Meredith, W., & Tisak, J. (1990). Latent curve analysis. *Psychometrika, 55*, 107–122.

Neale, B. (2020). Documents of lives and times: Revising qualitative data through time. In K. Hughes and A. Tarrant (eds.), *Qualitative Secondary Analysis*. SAGE Publications.

Ngwakwe, C. C. (2020). Effect of COVID-19 pandemic on global stock market values: A differential analysis. *Acta Universitatis Danubius. Œconomica, 16*(2), 255–269.

Open Science Collaboration. (2015). Psychology: Estimating the reproducibility of psychological science. *Science, 349*(6251), 943–944. https://doi.org/10.1126/science.aac4716

Pahl, R. E. (1978). Living without a job: How school leavers see the future. *New Society, 2*, 259–262.

Purcell, C., Maxwell, K., Bloomer, F., Rowlands, S., & Hoggart, L. (2020). Toward normalizing abortion: Findings from a qualitative secondary analysis study. *Culture, Health, & Sexuality, 22*, 1329–1364.

Riessman, C. K. (2005). Narrative analysis. In *Narrative, Memory & Everyday Life* (pp. 1–7). University of Huddersfield.

Ruggiano, N., & Perry, T. E. (2019). Conducting secondary analysis of qualitative data: Should we, can we, and how? *Qualitative Social Work, 18*, 81–97.

Rule, N. O., & Ambady, N. (2011). Judgments of power from college yearbook photos and later career success. *Social Psychological and Personality Science, 2*, 154–158.

Saldaña, J. (2013). *The Coding Manual for Qualitative Researchers*, 2nd ed. SAGE Publications.

Settersten, Jr., R. A. Elder, Jr., G. H., & Pearce, L. D. (2021). *Living on the Edge: An American Generation's Journey through the Twentieth Century*. University of Chicago Press.

Sharp, E. A., & Durham-DeCesaro, G. (2015). Modeling innovative methodological practices in a dance/family studies transdisciplinary project. *Journal of Family Theory and Review, 7*, 367–380.

Sharp, E. A., & Munly, K. (2022). Reopening a can of *words*: Qualitative secondary data analysis. *Journal of Family Theory and Review, 14*, 44–58.

Snowdon, D. A., Kemper, S. J., Mortimer, J. A., Greiner, L. H., Wekstein, D. R., & Markesbery, W. R. (1996). Linguistic ability in early life and cognitive function and Alzheimer's disease in late life: Findings from the Nun Study. *Journal of the American Medical Association, 275*, 528–532.

Sowles, S. J., McLeary, M., Optican, A., Cahn, E., Krauss, M. J., Fitzsimmons-Craft, E. E., et al. (2018). A content analysis of an online pro-eating disorder community on Reddit. *Body image, 24*, 137–144.

Terkel, S. (1972). *Working*. New Press.

Terman, L. M. (1968). *Genetic Studies of Genius*, vol. III: *The Promise of Youth: Follow-up Studies of a Thousand Gifted Children*. Stanford University Press.

Wehrle, F. M., Caflisch, J., Eichelberger, D. A., Haller, G., Latal, B., Largo, R. H, et al. (2021). The importance of childhood for adult health and development – Study protocol of the Zurich Longitudinal Studies. *Frontiers in Human Neuroscience, 14*, 1–23.

Weiss, J. (2000). *To Have and to Hold: Marriage, the Baby Boom, and Social Change*. University of Chicago Press.

26 Interviews: Processes, Strategies, and Reflections

Zoë B. Corwin and Jordan Harper

Abstract

Interviews can shed light on how people make sense of their daily lives and their experiences with phenomena through the intentional exchange of questions and responses and thematic explorations. The process of preparing for, conducting, and wrapping up an interview requires a delicate dance in which both the researcher and the interview participant engage. Furthermore, decisions made during each phase of the interview process have significant implications for the trustworthiness of findings and the relationships between researchers and interview participants. In this chapter, we highlight key steps in the interview process that facilitate producing a high-quality interview, transcript, and related analyses and deliverables. We also consider new and emerging reflections that emphasize innovation, reciprocity, care, and critical knowledge.

Keywords: Interviews, Data Collection, Qualitative Methods, Sample, Trustworthiness

Introduction to Interviews

Interviews have the potential to unlock participants' unique interior and exterior experiences and, as a result, help researchers understand, unearth, clarify, and see the world differently (Josselson, 2013; Kvale & Brinkmann, 2009; Mishler, 1986; Seidman, 2006; Weis, 1994). Interviews entail an intentional exchange of questions and responses, often involving thematic explorations. The process and product are riddled with beautiful complexity, depth, and nuance that require careful attention and direction. As such, interviewing is a *craft* where researchers must pay "close attention to its technical execution" (Holstein & Gubrium, 2003, p. 2) to engage in a shared meaning-making experience that serves a larger purpose, such as understanding phenomena or shedding light on social problems.

Historically, interviews were used to learn about those with high social standing (Benney & Hughes, 1956; Madge, 1965). These elite members of society were seen as some of the most competent storytellers and knowledge bearers – they spoke the language of the elite and had presumed elite knowledge; this is precisely what others in society wanted to acquire and know more about (Alasuutari, 1998; Platt, 2012). Henry Mayhew (1851) challenged the "elites-only" traditional approach to interviewing and underlying assumptions by interviewing the London poor. The London poor spoke about their experiences with poverty using "unvarnished language" (p. iii). Learning from the quotidian and mundane unearthed the extraordinary – a perspective that had yet to be properly communicated to the masses. Mayhew was able to amplify the experiences that resonated with the majority of society and lay the groundwork for materially improving their lives and circumstances. Mayhew's resistance to the status quo forged a new path for social science research and solidified interviews as a viable method to learn about life and people's experiences, garnering rich insights accordingly. His work helped situate the everyday citizen as a knowledge bearer and storyteller. In recent decades, critical race and feminist methodologists have continued exploring ordinary perspectives through traditional and innovative techniques to excavate historically silenced and shunned perspectives (please see Esposito & Evans-Winters, 2021; Evans-Winters, 2019; Gubrium & Holstein, 2002; McGarth et al., 2013; Tachine & Nicolazzo, 2022 for compelling examples). We consider some of those perspectives throughout the chapter.

The interview process positions the researcher as a key instrument in the research process. In 1996, Steinar Kvale likened the interviewer to two contrasting metaphors – the interviewer as the miner and an interviewer as a traveler. As a miner, the interviewer attempts to unearth knowledge that is seen as valuable material. In this pursuit, the interviewer is responsible for tapping into the un/subconscious to get at the true essence of one's experience. As a traveler, the interviewer packs their bags with all the necessary tools and resources to embark on a journey to tell a rich and compelling story that drives deeper understanding of phenomena and the human experience. The interviewer talks to people along the way and shares with others what they heard and found. Since then, interviewers have been referred to as salsa dancers (Luker, 2008) and participants as vessels of answers (Gubrium & Holstein, 2002). Building on the salsa dancing metaphor, we contend that interviewers and participants must move in a choreographed, delicate, and careful way that is mutually beneficial and respectful – advancing new understandings about social life and experiences through careful and considerate interviews.

This chapter takes on a knowingly ambitious project – to unpack the craft of interviews and interview research in a concise space. Conducting high-quality interviews takes considerable preparation, reflection, and time. Although the structure and flow of interviews can vary extensively, most interviews follow a fairly standardized process.

We have organized the chapter around key steps in preparing for, conducting, and wrapping up interviews. In doing so, we pay close attention to the tools, strategies, and skills for effectively navigating each phase. We conclude the chapter with important considerations for interviews and interview research, emphasizing that transparency and specificity around decisions made during each phase of the interview are critical when asserting the trustworthiness of a study. We carry with us throughout the chapter the idea that interviewing is a craft. If the craft is strongly cultivated, and researchers enter interviews with proper training and intense readiness, participants, guided by the careful attention of the interviewer, will be more likely to open "the sluice gates of dammed hurts and dreams" (Terkel, 1972, p. xxv) that have the possibility to unlock portals to social change.

Preparing for the Interview

While an interview might have a finite time frame (e.g., you request 60 minutes to meet with a participant), preparing for that interview entails a series of important activities, including determining the interview type, obtaining institutional review board (IRB) approval (see Volume 1, Chapter 2 of this Handbook for a detailed exposition of these issues), conducting a thorough review of the literature and/or other background information to inform the interview, composing an interview guide, thoughtfully selecting who you will interview, recruiting participants (including interfacing with gatekeepers), scheduling a time to meet with the participant(s), and traveling to a location or setting up the technology for a virtual interview. Below, we expand on these key steps (see Figure 26.1) that interviewers take before entering the field.

Align Interview Type with Research Methodology and Study Goals

Researchers will first need to decide what type of interview they will conduct. Interview type is in large part determined by a researcher's epistemological stance and methodological choices. Interview type manifests in the level of structure of the interview (i.e., structured, semi-structured, open-ended), which is connected to the degree to which participants are empowered to steer the trajectory of the interview (Holstein & Gubrium, 2003). Survey interviews, for example, involve highly structured questions and are designed to obtain responses that are tightly aligned with the questions posed. In contrast, life history interviews have an open-ended, in-depth structure where a researcher's line of inquiry is responsive to stories that participants share.

Below, we outline a few types of interviews to provide a sense of how researchers might engage with participants. The interview types vary considerably with regard to the structuredness of interview questions and the depth of respondents' reflections. In our experience, we have sometimes had to experiment with different types of interviews and different levels of structuredness before landing on a primary type of interview method to employ in a given study. We have also utilized multiple interview types and varying levels of structured questions embedded within one particular study. These design decisions often evolve in response to reactions in the field and lessons learned during iterative data analysis.

Highly Structured Interviews

Highly structured interviews have a strict set of questions that should be designed to address the overall research questions/hypotheses. Survey interviews are perhaps the most structured of all interview types. They aim to minimize bias in the interview and "control the interview encounter so that nothing other than the questions serves as the

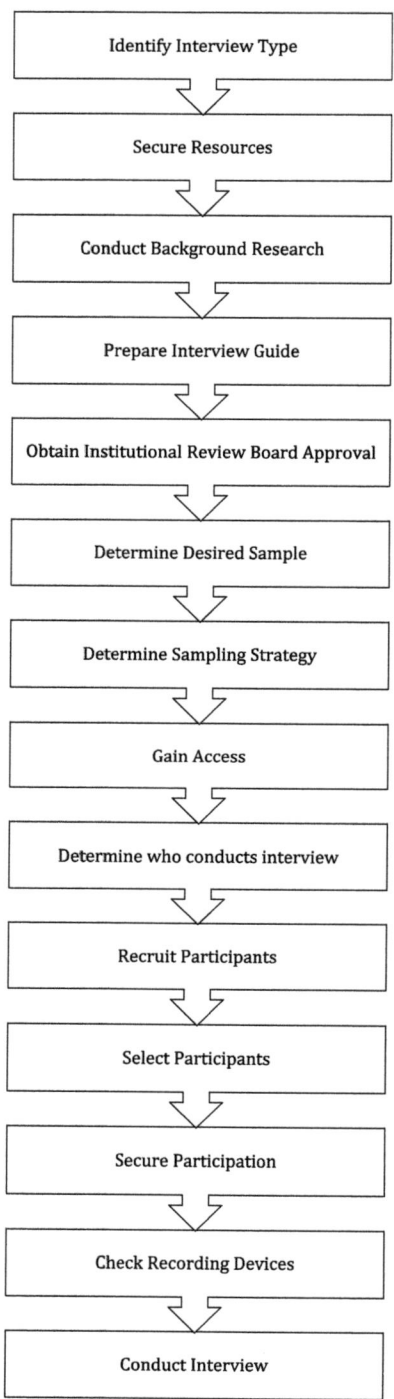

Figure 26.1 *Key steps in preparing for the interview.*

trigger or stimulus for producing the answers" (Marvasti & Tanner, 2020, p. 332). Structured interviews tend not to involve significant follow-up, and the interview is driven primarily by the interviewer.

In one study, for example, Corwin worked with a team of researchers to learn more about how students from low-income backgrounds, who were enrolled in a pre-college high school program, made sense of the financial aid process during their final year in high school. Researchers interviewed over 300 students at three times during the year. Questions were designed to get a sense of (a) students' knowledge about financial aid options, (b) how they planned to afford college, and (c) how their actual plans developed based on financial aid secured. The goal was to collect highly structured information across a large sample to identify trends and to inform future, more nuanced qualitative data collection. Due to the scope and goals of the project, responses were collected on a standardized interview spreadsheet. Later, the research team conducted in-depth interviews with a much smaller group of students. This two-pronged approach informed a decade of subsequent work on college access.

Semi-Structured Interviews

More flexible than structured interviews, semi-structured interviews tend to involve open-ended questions, a cycle of question and response between interviewer and participant, and reliance on an interview protocol with pre-established wording and flow of questions (Rubin & Rubin, 2012). A useful technique related to semi-structured interviews is "exploring" (also commonly referred to as "probing") – the interviewer follows up on a pre-planned question in direct response to what a participant shares (Seidman, 2006). Explorations require the researcher to be nimble and highly attentive to a participant's responses, while also continuing to guide the exchange.

One example of a semi-structured interview is the phenomenological interview. Phenomenological interviews seek to capture an individual's lived experience with a phenomenon (Moustakas, 1994; Vagle, 2018). Commonly, scholars who use the phenomenological approach to interviewing attempt to unearth often taken-for-granted aspects of participants' respective worlds. Phenomenological interviews respect and embrace stories, with the researcher playing a supportive role in helping participants articulate the meanings attached to their experiences (Van Manen, 2014). As such, the researcher and the participant must share the responsibility to lead and steer the conversation, making a semi-structured approach ideal given the fluid and reciprocal nature of the exchange as well as the researcher's need to keep the interview focused on the phenomena under exploration.

Focus group interviews tend to take a semi-structured approach but can also take a structured shape (Chapter 28, this volume). When conducting focus group interviews, researchers must contend with a range of discursive practices and the surprising yet interesting discussion threads that will undoubtedly emerge (Kamberelis & Dimitriadis, 2013). For example, imagine a researcher conducts a focus group about job stress with a group of medical residents. At one point, a participant mentions a transformational experience she had with a mentor who assuaged her work-related stress at a critical moment. The resident's reflection has a snowball effect, and the other focus group participants start talking about positive experiences with mentors. The researcher quickly recognizes the value in veering off the interview guide because the topic is aligned closely enough with the study's overarching research question and the focus group participants are engaged in responding. As a result, the researcher encourages all participants to share examples about mentors and requests they highlight experiences with mentors who have expertise in the medical field so that programs can learn from their perspectives. The responses to the unanticipated discussion point provide the researcher with valuable insights into the role mentors can play in supporting medical residents in navigating stress.

Open-Ended Interviews

Open-ended interviews have little to no structure. Interviews that often rely on participants' narrative understanding are loosely designed because "narrative understanding is emergent" (Josselson, 2007, p. 557). For this reason, narrative interviews and life history interviews are likely to take an open-ended approach because the researcher knows little to nothing about the participant and their individualized experience before interview data collection commences. Participants' stories will largely shape the interview, and the interviewer's role is to facilitate rather than direct the conversation. In narrative and life history interviews, for example, participants live and retell key, and even quotidian, aspects of their lives with the researcher (Connelly & Clandinin, 1990). Life history interviews, in particular, consider how events, behaviors, memories, relationships, aspirations, and regrets have shaped and continue to shape the participant and the subjective account of their life (Bertaux, 1981; Cole & Knowles, 2001; Olive, 2014).

To capture narratives in their richness and complexity, researchers often plan for multiple interviews with participants and engage in careful rapport-building. In 2018, Corwin – a middle-aged, middle-income, white, non-skateboarding woman – embarked on a study to learn about how skateboarders from racially minoritized and/or low-income backgrounds navigated community, education, career, and their well-being. The rapport-building process was critical in her ability to secure interview participants and engage in meaningful data collection. Building rapport entailed maintaining a visible presence in skate sites prior to interview recruitment, introductions to skaters through community partners, and multiple conversations with the skaters. After building rapport and recruiting participants, Corwin chose to employ an open-ended interview approach to let the skateboarders guide the direction of what she would learn through the interviews. Open-ended prompts inspired by Spradley's (1979) grand-tour approach invited skaters to reflect on the community they had formed through skateboarding. Responses varied substantially and ultimately illustrated key differences by region, race, and gender; they also revealed core similarities around the stigmatization of skaters, the prevalence of positive cross-cultural and intergenerational communication in skate parks, and the role skateboarding plays in strengthening mental health.

Longitudinal Interviews

Structured, semi-structured, and open-ended interviews can either consist of one instance or multiple interviews over time. Longitudinal interviews are a series of interviews that are multilayered and explore narratives, phenomena, and experiences over time (Thomson & Holland, 2003). They can take varied approaches and structures. For example, they can be part phenomenological and part ethnographic; they can also be semi-structured or completely unstructured. Ethnographic studies often utilize longitudinal interviews with various actors over an Extended period (e.g., Punch, 2012).

Longitudinal interviews move beyond capturing snapshots of time and allow the researcher to document multiple critical moments that impact participants' lives, thus offering the potential to develop a more nuanced understanding of a phenomenon, space, or person. Yücel et al. (2022) used longitudinal interviews to examine community college students' support networks before and after transferring into four-year institutions. They stated that the benefit to a longitudinal approach was their ability to capture how, why, and to what extent students grew their networks over time to attain their educational goals; this would not have been possible to explain if it had not been for the longitudinal approach.

Hybrid and Innovative Interview Types

In recent decades, methodologists have experimented with innovative approaches to interviews, many of which combine different elements of structure and type. Episodic narrative interviews, for example, involve narrative research inquiry where participants tell stories yet are focused on particular phenomena and a specific event or series of events (Mueller, 2019). Walking interviews are also a particularly innovative approach that has gained traction in recent years. They operate from a semi-structured perspective and prioritize gaining a deep understanding of context and self in context; participants and researchers navigate particular spaces to highlight power dynamics and spatial practices (Harris, 2016).

Furthermore, critical scholars have begun developing and taking up decolonial narrative interview methods (e.g., testimonios and pláticas/queer pláticas) as a way to challenge white supremacy and (re)humanize historically disenfranchised individuals. Testimonios are an extension of narrative interviews but invite the participant to reflect on a particular phenomenon critically and encourage participants to share stories of oppression (Delgado Bernal et al., 2017; Flores Carmona, 2014). Queer/pláticas take up a similar project but carry a more conversational and relational process and approach to interviewing by recovering and remembering experiences and relationships toward liberation (Fierros and Delgado Bernal, 2016; Gonzalez et al., 2023).

In conclusion, there are numerous interview types and interview structures. Choices regarding interview types and structures will depend on the study's methodological underpinnings and the goals the research sets out to reach. Table 26.1 offers examples of questions with differing degrees of structure (i.e., closed and

Table 26.1 *Examples of interview questions highlighting varying structures and types*

Type of interview	Level of structure	Example question/prompt	How and why this interview type and structure is effective
Survey	Highly structured	• Do you have a faculty mentor? • How frequently do you meet with your mentor? • What topics do you discuss during your meetings?	• Allows for a clear answer (i.e., Y/N, 5–10 times per semester) • Allows space for open-ended responses that do not necessarily require an immediate follow-up by the researcher or participant
Narrative	Open-ended	• Tell me a story about when a faculty mentor provided critical support to you.	• Opening with a broad, open-ended question gives the participant the ability to shape the conversation in ways relevant to their experiences; the researcher then follows suit and asks follow-ups to communicate the participant's narrative effectively.
Decolonial narrative	Semi-structured	• When you think of racialized campus spaces, where comes to mind? • Let's discuss how a mentor helped you to navigate a racialized space on campus.	• There's a specific undertone in the questions that give space for the participant to communicate their feelings regarding oppression or empowerment. • The questions loosely guide the participants in their response (i.e., aligned with a particular topic) but also allow the researcher to deviate from the script according to how the participant responds.

open-ended) for different types of interviews. The context of these example questions/prompts is from studies on student success and mentorship. For more examples, we encourage readers to peruse appendices in publicly available doctoral dissertations, as students often publish their interview protocols alongside their approaches and structures.

Take Stock of and Secure Resources

Once the interview type has been identified, it is important to ensure that the interviewer has the resources to conduct an interview study successfully. If working with a research team, one must first determine who will conduct the interview and whether tailored training is necessary. Training could entail familiarizing interviewers with new recording equipment, sharing different methodological approaches, or reviewing how to reflect on the research process.

Interview research is time-consuming; researchers need to determine how much time it will take to prepare for, conduct, transcribe, and analyze each interview. Potential costs include using a professional transcription service – costs that can be mitigated by using free online tools (e.g., Otter.ai, Zoom transcriptions) – and/or paying for online qualitative data analysis software (e.g., Dedoose, ATLAS.ti). If researchers plan to record interviews, they will need to ensure that a device's microphone will be reliable in their interview setting (i.e., will the recording pick up too much background noise?), verify that they have sufficient battery power for the length of the interview, and confirm they have a strong Wi-Fi connection if conducting a video interview.

On the latter point, we recommend having a backup way to connect in case Wi-Fi connection fails, such as a phone number to complete the interview. Interviewers might consider operating a backup recording device (such as a voice memo on a cell phone) to account for any recording errors or battery failure. If the interviewer does not plan on recording the interview but rather taking notes, they will also need to prepare appropriate materials to record the dialogue (i.e., notebook and writing instrument). We discuss other essential tools later in the chapter.

Conduct Background Research

To conduct an effective interview, interviewers should familiarize themselves with information about the person (or people) they will speak with and/or the social setting where they will conduct the interview. In addition to conducting a literature review of foundational and current peer-reviewed scholarly material about the topic, another helpful strategy is to familiarize yourself with current news, social media, and popular cultural materials related to your participants or topic. Having a solid, relevant understanding of issues and research on the topic is critical. For novice researchers, it can be helpful to listen closely to how journalists and podcast hosts incorporate background information into their interviews to facilitate robust conversations and exchange of ideas.

Determine Who to Interview and Why

The caliber of interview data relies heavily on who is interviewed. The majority of qualitative interviews involve a relatively small sample of participants, making reaching data saturation challenging (Saunders et al., 2018). Identifying the size and composition of a sample is strongly connected to the overall research design and resources available (Hesse-Biber & Leavy, 2011).

The majority of qualitative interviews involve purposive sampling, where researchers exercise intentionality in whom they recruit to participate in interviews. Stratified purposive sampling adds another element of intentionality to sampling procedures to ensure that participants have specific characteristics that would be helpful to understanding and answering research questions.

When selecting participants for a study on postsecondary transfer students, for instance, a researcher might utilize stratified purposive sampling to ensure there is a subgroup of commuter students in the sample, thus ensuring a diversity of perspectives in the data that includes a key, often overlooked group of students. Other common sampling procedures (Creswell & Creswell, 2018; Glaser & Strauss, 1967; Hesse-Biber & Leavy, 2011) include:

- *convenience sampling* – the sample is determined by who is willing, able, and qualified to participate in an interview
- *snowball sampling* – participants suggest new people for the interviewer to connect with given how they understand the goals of the research project; this is a particularly useful strategy for hard-to-reach groups
- *random sampling* – participants are randomly selected with equal probability from a participant pool
- *theoretical sampling* – recruitment and selection evolve during the research process in response to prior data collected (i.e., recruiting more individuals from the same group or beginning to talk to different groups of individuals that differ from those originally interviewed)

Regardless of which sample or sampling strategy is chosen, documenting decisions around both is critical when writing up research methods to help the reader interpret your findings.

Prepare an Interview Guide

Interview guides are important tools that should be thought through before the interview begins. Broad & Joos (2004) posit that interview guides are meant to be "conversational agendas" rather than a "procedural directive" (p. 933). In fact, Patton (2014) warns against having a laundry list of questions, as doing so results in the researcher "miss[ing] the dynamics of the unfolding relationship that is at the heart of interactive interviewing" (p. 676). Depending on the type of interview and methodology, interview guides may be altered and modified *during interviews* according to participants' responses and sharpened throughout data collection. Administering a high-quality interview to obtain thick and rich descriptions and responses may sometimes call for the disruption of routinized interviews (Honan, 2014). However, researchers must be forewarned that this view is not universal.

One particularly helpful way to shape and create an interview guide is to bucket interview questions into themes relevant to the established research question(s). In a study on how established committees worked to design and implement cultural changes for non-tenure-track faculty, Culver et al. (2022) created and used a themed interview guide that framed their focus group interviews. The three themes were (1) design (e.g., how did the group that developed the changes come into being?), (2) implementation (e.g., tell us about challenges you faced with regard to implementing the change), and (3) connections between design, implementation, and design thinking framework (e.g., which parts of the process that you just described align with the design thinking model?). During the interviews, they were able to signal to focus group participants when the direction of the interview was shifting toward and away from these distinct themes. Participants were also able to cater their responses to the themes presented, even if they did not have specific answers to stated questions.

Protect Participants

Obtaining appropriate consent to participate in research is essential before starting the interview. Researchers whose studies are required to undergo review by their institutional review board (IRB) must contend with how they will protect their participants and obtain the necessary permissions to collect data (Creswell & Creswell, 2018). In most cases, obtaining consent involves reviewing IRB forms that describe the study and cover the risks and benefits of involvement (Volume 1, Chapter 2 of this Handbook). It must also ensure that participants understand they can withdraw from the interview at any time and that their identity will remain confidential unless otherwise stated. Participants should review and consent to the research before the interview begins. Importantly, researchers must not coerce participants into signing these forms. In addition, if the researcher decides to use an audio or video recording device, it is important to ask participants' permission before the researcher begins recording. Although interviews conducted for classroom assignments often do not require IRB approval, student-researchers should still maintain strict ethics in protecting their participants.

The enactment of IRB safeguards serves to (1) protect the well-being of the participant, and (2) create an interview environment where the participant feels comfortable sharing insights openly (see Moses, 2021, for a compelling case for institutional naming in research studies). Imagine, for example, a researcher is studying a sensitive topic – such as navigating LGTBQ+ identity in a conservative locale – and is conducting interviews virtually. Beyond obtaining consent to begin the interview, the researcher should ensure the appropriateness of the interview location. For instance, is the interview situated in a private location, without the threat of intrusion, to protect their identity? Private locations can also help build rapport and facilitate the open sharing of insights. The IRB process helps researchers think through how to keep participants safe and how to communicate procedures to participants. Ultimately, these procedures enhance the likelihood of collecting high-quality data and improve the trustworthiness of the study.

Recruit Participants

Thoughtful plans around sample and sampling strategy are rendered moot if a researcher is unable to recruit interview participants successfully. Effective recruitment entails figuring out the best way to connect with your target audience.

Recruiting college students, for example, might best be facilitated by social media posts, but connecting with elderly residents in a retirement community might be best facilitated through physical postcards; human trafficking survivors, on the other hand, might be best recruited through word-of-mouth invitations from trusted individuals. Other approaches include using infographics, YouTube videos, and leveraging listservs to connect with potential participants. Recruitment can sometimes necessitate multiple rounds of outreach and creative troubleshooting.

Select Participants

Ultimately, the power of interview data derives from who participates in the interviews. When selecting participants, researchers might decide to include participants who represent mainstream points of view in a given social situation – or perhaps select people with marginalized or fringe experiences. Take, for instance, a study designed to improve how a school district food pantry might most effectively deliver food to local families. Interview participants randomly selected from a pool of students facing food insecurity would offer a wide range of perspectives to inform the service provision. However, imagine that the random sampling strategy failed to identify students with experiences in foster care who might have different needs, daily rhythms, and transportation constraints to the mainstream school population. What researchers might learn about basic needs provision would be limited by a sample that focused on general, rather than particular, points of view.

Secure Participation

After participants have been selected for the study, a critical step is to translate recruitment and selection efforts into actual participation. Effective outreach in this regard includes clearly communicating about the study and parameters of participation (points likely already described in the study's IRB application and often conveyed through a study information sheet). This high-stakes phase of the interview process is seldom discussed and can lead to grave challenges in moving forward if not implemented well. Direct, culturally appropriate language in all outreach materials and respectful follow-through are key. For example, if English is not the preferred language in the community where you are conducting interviews, translate materials into the primary language, and be clear about the availability of translators. If no translation is available, then clearly state that. In some situations, brief face-to-face conversations (in person or virtual) enhance the likelihood of a participant committing to the interview. Negotiating a mutually agreeable time and location can also entail significant flexibility on the researcher's part and can be quite time-intensive.

Determine Who Will Conduct the Interview

It is worth mentioning that, in some situations, an interview might be much more effective if conducted by someone who shares similar identities to the person being interviewed. For example, if the goal of an interview is to learn more about racialized campus climate, a researcher who shares a similar identity to the participant may be best suited to conduct the interview. To accomplish this, a pre-interview demographic survey or a preliminary conversation with the participant prior to the official interview may help.

Regardless, intense reflexivity about positionality and potential biases is essential. We have both conducted interviews with participants who hold different identities and experiences to our own. In some cases, due to the focus of the interview, we have chosen not to name our differing positionalities (e.g., when Harper was interviewing senior university administrators about their leadership styles). In other cases, it made sense to name the differences to build rapport, signal awareness of potential perceived power dynamics and possible blindspots (e.g., when Corwin interviewed students with experiences in foster care). In their book chapter, *Race, Subjectivity and the Interview Process*, Dunbar, Jr. et al. (2001) offer a particularly interesting discussion about the role of social and historical factors in how interviews are conducted and analyzed and the complexities inherent in interviewing across racial or cultural differences. They write that ignoring this element of procedural consciousness "cheats the experiences of those whose lives are not lived in accord with, or may even be lived against, the standard" (p. 295).

Check Recording Devices

Whether interviews take place in person or remotely, it is advantageous for researchers to record their interviews – via audio, video, note-taking, or a combination (Creswell & Creswell, 2018; Kvale, 2012). Using recording devices during interviews makes it easier to analyze data and share participant quotes when the time comes. Additionally, recording devices – especially audio and video – allow the researcher to stay in the moment and listen attentively without feeling the need to jot down what the participant shares.

When deciding what type of recording devices to use, it is important that researchers consider the study's needs and the participant's comfort. This means thinking through how the presence of a camera may sway participants' responses (e.g., would an interview participant in a study about abortion care conducted in a conservative setting feel comfortable sharing opinions transparently if being recorded) or how only choosing to take notes during an interview may make the data analysis process more tedious and difficult. If the researcher decides to take notes, it is important to consider *how* they take notes. That is, what note-taking tools are they using (e.g., computer, smartphone, pen and paper) and how often are they taking notes. It is important to note that the presence of technology (e.g., laptop, tablet) to support note-taking can be a barrier to connecting with participants; it can possibly create a disingenuous environment prone to distractions. Above all else, however, participants should be comfortable with the recording devices the researcher decides to use, and they should always have a choice regarding whether or not to record.

Conducting the Interview

The context of an interview can be unpredictable as can the interviewer's and interviewee's reaction to the interview process. Thus, we offer a few strategies that we believe help to cultivate a strong, nimble interviewer. Some of these strategies can be developed through roleplay scenarios with AI technology, or practicing in a safe-to-fail environment such as the classroom or by interviewing trusted friends and family. Listening to journalists conduct extended interviews, as are prevalent in podcast settings, can also be instructive.

Build and Sustain Rapport

James Spradley (1979) describes rapport as "a harmonious relationship" where "a basic sense of trust has developed that allows for the free flow of information" (78). Building rapport is a critical first step in the interview because the more comfortable a participant feels, the more likely they are to share information and insights, thus leading to high-quality data. A key strategy for building rapport involves clearly communicating the study's purpose and how the interview will contribute to the larger research project. Transparency in explaining the rationale for the interview can help participants feel comfortable with the researcher and is integral in obtaining high-quality data. Other strategies include explaining why the research topic is important to the researcher, emphasizing that there are no correct responses to questions, and acknowledging that their stories matter. If a participant understands why their perspectives are valuable to the study, they will likely speak openly and not just share the information *they think the interviewer wants to hear*. In general, building and sustaining rapport also requires great intentionality on the researcher's part to identify and deconstruct power dynamics (Harper, 2015; Hoffman, 2007)

Spradley (1979) suggests four phases of rapport-building that can apply to various forms of interviews: (1) *apprehension* – when both the participant *and* interviewer work through initial nerves and uncertainty related to the interview process; (2) *exploration* – generally evident after initial questions have put both people at ease when a sense of calm permeates the interview (often demonstrated by laughter or comfort with pauses); (3) *cooperation* – when the participant and the interviewer know what to expect of each other and play a more active role in steering the interview; and (4) *participation* – when participants bring information to the interview and co-construct the interview with the interviewer.

Pose Questions with Intentionality

Equipped with a solid interview guide or protocol, a mechanism for recording responses, and a genuine interest in learning from the interview participant, researchers can now begin the most important part of the interview – posing questions and listening actively to responses. The *duration and flow* of the interview are informed by the study's methodology and will often be determined by the flexibility afforded by the type of interview and the time allotted to the interview.

In interviews that are minimally structured (i.e., open-ended, semi-structured), interviewers are well-served by the following techniques outlined by Seidman (2006):

- Listen more, talk less (actively listen to content, stay aware of when a participant might be guarded, pay attention to process).
- Follow up on what the participant says, don't interrupt (request details when clarification is needed).
- Ask questions when you do not understand (circle back to unclear concepts using the participant's language).
- Ask to hear more about a subject (when appropriate, veer away from protocol to learn more from a participant's story).
- Explore, don't probe (strike a balance between pursuing clarification and inviting the participant to expand on ideas).
- Avoid leading questions.
- Ask open-ended questions.
- Introduce creative approaches such as asking participants to talk to you as if you were someone else or asking participants to tell a story.
- Do not take the ebbs and flows of interviewing too personally.
- Follow your hunches.
- Share experiences on occasion.
- Ask participants to reconstruct, not to remember.
- Avoid reinforcing participants' responses.
- Explore laughter.
- Tolerate silence.

Listen Actively

Being a good listener is one of the most important skills interviewers must possess. Through active listening, the researcher approximates what Holstein and Gubrium (2003) refer to as "a discourse of empowerment" (p. 19), where the interviewer and interviewee collaborate on meaning-making during the interview. Given this importance, Seidman (2006) posits that qualitative researchers must do three types of listening: (1) listening to what the participant is saying, (2) listening for the inner voice, and (3) listening to make sense of progress. Lareau (2021) offers a fourth, listening to yourself.

Listening to What the Participant Says

This type of listening requires a reorientation away from the way we normally converse. At some level, humans love to talk, listen, and talk back (Soss, 2015). As such, we may often find ourselves trying to impose our viewpoints on others or steer the conversation in ways that support our assumptions and subsequent knowledge. In contrast, Seidman (2006) claims that researchers "must concentrate on the substance [of the interview] to make sure that they understand it and to assess whether what they are hearing is as detailed and complete as they would like it to be" (p. 78). This approach constitutes listening to understand as opposed to listening to respond. By attending to a participant's insights and the content of what is shared, the researcher is more easily able to connect the dots between what the participant says and what theory, literature, and phenomena imply.

Listening for a Participant's Inner Voice

What participants say may be quite different from what they truly feel. For example, feminist scholars (e.g., DeVault, 1990) have argued that language expressed in interview settings, especially when it is known that elements of the interview (i.e., quotes) will be made "public" (i.e., published in academic journals, used in publIora), is sometimes incongruent with how one actually feels. As such, paying close attention to a participant's outer voice can facilitate a researcher's ability to unearth the inner, unuttered subtext of an experience. It requires paying close attention to how their bodies react or moods shift as you introduce new questions and topics to the interview.

Seidman offers some ways to uncover the inner voice. For example, researchers can explore using very particular words and phrases such as "What you said about X was really *fascinating*. I'd love to hear more about that." This further exploration enables the participant to grapple with what they just said and tussle with the complexity out loud, out in the open, and with the researcher. The researcher then makes them feel comfortable to openly express their inner voice and even helps them begin to grapple with the discomfort that may arise between the inner voice and the outer, more public voice. While this type of listening is useful for all types of interviews, it is particularly useful when interviewing elites who have strong ties to powerful institutions and organizations (for more on interviewing elites, see Kezar, 2003; Rice, 2010).

Listening to Make Sense of Progress

An additional offering from Seidman (2006) is for researchers to listen for progress – being aware of what has already been shared, keeping track of time during interviews, and examining what other questions to ask given what has already been shared and how much time is left. The key here is respecting the participants' contributions and their time and being aware of the flow of the interview. Seidman (2006) notes that listening for progress "requires that, for a good part of the time, we [researchers] quash our normal instinct to talk. At the same time, interviewers must be ready to say something when a navigational nudge is needed" (p. 79). Sometimes it is best to give the participant some agency while listening for progress. This could involve allowing them the time and opportunity to conclude the interview of their own accord. For example, Shamus Khan suggests a final question – "In this interview, I was interested in [name research question here]. Is there anything you didn't tell me that you wish you did? Is there anything I should have asked that I didn't?" (Khan, n.d., as cited in Lareau, 2021, p. 98).

Listening to Yourself

Lareau (2021) adds another key listening element that we believe is worth adding to Seidman's contributions – listening to yourself. Listening to yourself means knowing when to pivot, having a plan for self-care while navigating the interview process, and trusting your instincts. Lareau notes that interviewing is an emergent process – you often think and act as you go and even act like you know what you're doing. Interviewing is not a rigid process – it requires flexibility. As such, researchers must listen to themselves to do what is best for the study, the issue and phenomena being studied, and themselves. As such, Lareau argues that researchers must think broadly about the role the study plays in their life.

Be Ready to Improvise

Researchers should use interviews to garner rich, deep, and even surprising data (Timmermans & Tavory, 2022). To do so, researchers are well served by improvising. Each participant is going to behave and respond uniquely. The researcher's job, then, is to improvise accordingly to create a safe and comfortable environment for both parties. Improvisation and being a good and careful listener are inextricably linked. To be a good improviser, researchers have to be good and careful listeners. It can become easy to simply rely on the pre-written questions and move through the interview with less of a flow and more of a prescriptive manner. However, this can result in unhelpful responses that may lack depth and abundance, as well as feel uncomfortable for the interviewee.

Engage in Critical Reflection

When conducting interviews with members of historically disenfranchised communities or related to sensitive topics (e.g., racism, incarceration, abortion), it is important that researchers approach the interview with a sense of critical consciousness and reflection. A term popularized by Paulo Freire (1973) – critical consciousness – refers to awareness of and action against oppressive systems toward the advancement of social justice. In the context of critical consciousness, awareness is the pre-work while action emerges from conducting the interview, subsequent data analysis, and how the researcher shares findings (and to what tune they offer recommendations).

As such, researchers must be deeply informed about the issues they are conducting interviews about and understand that, with critical consciousness, there is an expectation that the researcher will also know how to navigate emotion and move throughout the interview with empathetic regard. It is also expected that researchers think through the possible ways that their interviews can cause harm to participants and their communities. The action component of critical consciousness involves the researcher deciding how to use interview data in ways that inform new social change efforts as well as contribute to already existing efforts (Canella et al., 2016; Denzin, 2017).

Analytic Memos

Analytic memos are a particularly useful tool for practicing critical reflection (Saldaña, 2020; Saldaña & Omasta, 2016). Often loosely structured, memos help the researcher keep assumptions at a minimum, draw connections to larger theory/concepts that guide the study, and even "record and develop their ideas at each stage of the research project" (Bryant & Charmaz, 2007, p. 375). Researchers can be creative when writing their analytic memos (e.g., writing the memos as letters to yourself or the community, drawing concept maps). Memos can and should be reworked as the interview process evolves. Some questions that may guide the analytic memo process include:

- How did I feel while conducting the interview? What emotions emerged?
- What words or phrases came up during the interview that stuck with me or stood out to me?
- What surprised me? What remained consistent with the conceptual/theoretical framework and the literature? What differed?
- How did this particular interview help me think about the study's research questions?

Pay Attention to Context

Understanding an interview's context is connected to understanding how interview participants make sense of their everyday experiences. When sharing physical proximity, an interviewer can take notes on surroundings, including the sounds, scents, and other environmental details, and ask a participant to elaborate on contextual details. When conducting remote interviews, either online or via telephone, the researcher is challenged to capture contextual details and must rely on the interviewee to describe the context.

It is also imperative to understand the cultural context in which the researcher is interviewing. Traditional interview approaches, even those we mention throughout this chapter, may not work when engaging people from all cultures. The researcher should be educated on the cultural apparatus in which participants exist, navigate, and negotiate. Part of understanding the participants' culture can be learned and understood in the rapport-building phase of the interview. The researcher should keep culture in mind when engaging in the actual interview and the data analysis process.

Practice Reciprocity

As with any research activity, the interviewer runs the risk of exploiting an interview participant. To avoid reinforcing unequal power dynamics, researchers might consider the reciprocity of the interview exchange (Corbin & Morse, 2003). Indigenous research methods and decolonizing approaches offer thoughtful mechanisms to ensure that participants and communities benefit from research and to hold Euro-Western researchers accountable for perpetuating extractive approaches to data collection (Chilsia, 2012; Kara, 2015; Wilson et al., 2018).

Exercise Care when Exiting the Field

Exercising care should be implemented throughout the interview process, but especially while exiting the field. Some activities that allow the researcher to exercise care when exiting the field include:

- factoring in adequate time to leave the interview setting and doing so in a way that honors the participant's time and willingness to participate in the interview
- composing correspondence to express gratitude for the time spent participating in the interview
- if applicable, paying participants for their participation in a timely manner
- following up on action items identified during the interview (e.g., sharing of information or resources)
- writing up field notes that capture context and describe participants
- composing analytic memos

Preparing for Analysis and Dissemination

In this section, we review a few strategies that result in strong data analysis and thoughtful dissemination.

Develop high-quality transcripts

The quality of an interview transcript has implications for a study's analytic rigor and, consequently, the study's trustworthiness (Kvale, 2012; Poland, 1995). Transcripts allow the researcher to revisit the previously recorded exchange with extended time for reflection (Dortins, 2002). If a researcher transcribes an interview on their own, they are likely to become immersed in the data during the transcription process. When interviews are sent to a professional transcription service or transcribed using digital technologies, the researcher inevitably loses an opportunity to engage deeply with the actual recording and must exercise intentionality when reviewing the transcript. Developing high-quality transcripts includes making key decisions about how language will be transcribed (i.e., verbatim oral vs. written style), ensuring the reliability of transcripts (e.g., by having two researchers transcribe the same interview to assess quality control), and determining how to capture language so that it responds to research purposes (Kvale, 2012).

Write up Findings with Attention Paid to Research Goals and Participant Perspectives

Through the interview process, researchers and participants co-construct knowledge (Gubrium & Holstein, 2002). After interview data are collected and analyzed, the researcher engages in a series of decisions about how to write up and disseminate findings. Decisions are tightly connected to the research methodology and goals of the project and must be vehemently guided by ethics (e.g., maintain participants' confidentiality). Survey interview findings, for example, might be presented using tables and involve numerical displays that convey the frequency of responses. On the other hand, narrative or life history interviews might include robust segments of a participant's quotes. Regardless of decisions made around conveying findings, it is incumbent on the researcher to ensure that data are written up, shared, and disseminated in ways that resonate with the insights conveyed by participants.

Documenting the Process

Throughout the interview process – from preparation to analysis – it is important for researchers to document decisions around each step in the process. That is, for example, why they chose to use interviews as a primary or tertiary method, how they selected their sample, or the rationale behind their coding strategy. This helps to contribute to the trustworthiness of the findings and keeps the researcher accountable. In many ways, documenting the process also helps the researcher capture their own "interior monologue" (Richardson, 1997) that can sometimes be forgotten in the chaos of attempting to plan and implement interviews.

Disseminating Findings in Interesting and Non-Traditional Ways

As noted earlier, researchers should be continuously and critically thinking about how and where they disseminate the findings that emerge from interviews. Beyond the traditional outlets that the academy supports and rewards (e.g., journal articles, research books, lectures), we also encourage researchers to consider interesting and non-traditional ways to disseminate their findings. As Smith (2021) mentions, there is not a singular "right" way to share findings. Instead, the question of how and where a researcher disseminates interview findings "are simply part of a larger set of judgments" (p. 10). Said differently, how and where a researcher disseminates interview findings are dependent on what and who they deem important, valuable, and worth engaging with.

Does every study need to be shared with the academy by way of academic journals and lectures? Does each study have to contribute to the researcher's career promotion in some way? Disseminating research in ways that extend far beyond what the academy values can be transformational. Researchers can hold town halls and community conversations and write opinion editorials (op-eds) for various public and accessible outlets. Corwin and team, for example, found accessible ways to share findings from their skateboarding studies through video compilations, zines (succinct graphic-laden magazines), research briefs, and community gatherings. These accessible formats positioned the research in front of non-academic audiences who then used the research to advocate for skate parks in municipal and state legislative environments and to inform practice in non-profit settings.

Concluding Thoughts

The craft of interviewing is a creative and complex endeavor. We believe that the interview process is enhanced when a researcher approaches the interview with curiosity, strategic background knowledge, a strong capacity to listen actively, and a deep respect for the people who have agreed to participate. As we have outlined above, conducting effective interviews requires ample time, serious intentionality in preparing for and navigating the conversation, a variety of resources, and the ability to reflect on the research experience. The structure, type of interview, and questions posed will depend on what the researcher is attempting to learn and how they intend to use the interview data. If done right, the interviewer and the interviewee have the potential to produce new insights that influence the way we understand social life and impact social change.

References

Alasuutari, P. (1998). *An Invitation to Social Research*. SAGE Publications.
Atkinson, P., & Silverman, D. (1997). Kundera's Immortality: The Interview Society and the Invention of the Self. *Qualitative Inquiry*, 3(3), 304–325.
Benney, M., & Hughes, E. C. (1956). Of sociology and the interview: Editorial preface. *American Journal of Sociology*, 62(2), 137–142.
Bertaux, D. (1981). *Biography and Society: The Life History Approach in the Social Sciences*. SAGE Publications.
Broad, K. L., & Joos, K. E. (2004). Online inquiry of public selves: Methodological considerations. *Qualitative Inquiry*, 10(6), 923–946.
Bryant, A., & Charmaz, K. (eds.). (2007). *The SAGE Handbook of Grounded Theory*. SAGE Publication.
Burawoy, M. (1998). The extended case method. *Sociological Theory*, 16(1), 4–33.
Cannella, G. S., Pérez, M. S., & Pasque, P. A. (2016). The 'new materialisms': A thorn in the flesh of critical qualitative inquiry? In G. S. Cannella, M. S. Pérez, & P. A. Pasque

(eds.), *Critical Qualitative Inquiry: Foundations and Futures* (pp. 93–112). Routledge.

Chilsia, B. (2012). *Indigenous Research Methodologies*. SAGE Publications.

Clemens, R. F., & Tierney, W. G. (2020). The uses and usefulness of life history. In M. R. M. Ward & S. Delamont (eds.), *Handbook of Qualitative Research in Education* (pp. 270–284). Edward Elgar.

Cole, A. L., & Knowles, J. G. (2001). *Lives in Context: The Art of Life History Research*. Rowman Altamira.

Connelly, F. M., & Clandinin, D. J. (1990). Stories of experience and narrative inquiry. *Educational Researcher*, *19*(5), 2–14.

Corbin, J., & Morse, J. M. (2003). The unstructured interactive interview: Issues of reciprocity and risks when dealing with sensitive topics. *Qualitative Inquiry*, *9*(3), 335–354.

Creswell, J. W., & Creswell, J. D. (2018). *Research Design: Qualitative, Quantitative, and Mixed Methods Approaches*. SAGE Publications.

Culver, K. C., Harper, J., & Kezar, A. (2022). Engaging design thinking in professional bureaucracies: Improving equity for non-tenure track faculty in higher education. *Journal of Higher Education Policy and Leadership Studies*, *3*(1), 68–89.

Delgado Bernal, D. D., Burciaga, R., & Carmona, J. F. (eds.). (2017). *Chicana/Latina Testimonios as Pedagogical, Methodological, and Activist Approaches to Social Justice*. Routledge.

Denzin, N. K. (2017). Critical qualitative inquiry. *Qualitative Inquiry*, *23*(1), 8–16.

DeVault, M. L. (1990). Talking and listening from women's standpoint: Feminist strategies for interviewing and analysis. *Social Problems*, *37*(1), 96–116.

Dortins, E. (2002). Reflections on phenomenographic process: Interview, transcription and analysis. *Quality Conversations: Research and Development in Higher Education*, *25*, 207–213.

Dunbar, Jr., C., Rodriguez, D., & Parker, L. (2001). Race, subjectivity, and the interview process. In J. Gubrium & J. Holstein (eds.), *The Handbook of Interviewing* (pp. 279–298). SAGE Publications.

Eder, D., & Fingerson, L. (2003). Interviewing children and adolescents. In J. A. Holstein & J. F. Gubrium (eds.), *Inside interviewing: New Lenses, New Concerns* (pp. 33–54) SAGE Publications.

Esposito, J., & Evans-Winters, V. (2021). *Introduction to Intersectional Qualitative Research*. SAGE Publications.

Evans-Winters, V. E. (2019). *Black Feminism in Qualitative Inquiry: A Mosaic for Writing Our Daughter's Body*. Routledge.

Fierros, C. O., & Delgado Bernal, D. (2016). Vamos a platicar: The contours of pláticas as Chicana/Latina feminist methodology. *Chicana/Latina Studies*, *15*(2), 98–121.

Flores Carmona, J. (2014). Cutting out their tongues: Mujeres' testimonios and the Malintzin researcher. *Journal of Latino/Latin American Studies*, *6*(2), 113–124.

Freire, P. (1973). *Education for Critical Consciousness*. Continuum.

Glaser, B. G., & Strauss, A. L. (1967). *The Discovery of Grounded Theory: Strategies for Qualitative Research*. Routledge.

Gonzalez, Á. D. J., Orozco, R. C., & Gonzalez, S. A. (2023). Joteando y mariconadas: Theorizing queer pláticas for queer and/or trans Latinx/a/o research. *International Journal of Qualitative Studies in Education*, *36*(4), 1–16.

Gubrium, J. F., & Holstein, J. A. (eds.) (2002). *Handbook of Interview Research: Context and Method*. SAGE Publications.

Harper, S. R. (2015). Success in these schools? Visual counternarratives of young men of color and urban high schools they attend. *Urban Education*, *50*(2), 139–169.

Harris, J. (2016). Utilizing the walking interview to explore campus climate for students of color. *Journal of Student Affairs Research and Practice*, *53*(4), 365–377.

Hesse-Biber, S. N., & Leavy, P. (2011). *The Practice of Qualitative Research*. SAGE Publications.

Hoffmann, E. A. (2007). Open-ended interviews, power, and emotional labor. *Journal of Contemporary Ethnography*, *36*(3), 318–346.

Holstein, J., & Gubrium, J. F. (2003). *Inside Interviewing: New Lenses, New Concerns*. SAGE Publications.

Honan, E. (2014). Disrupting the habit of interviewing. *Reconceptualizing Educational Research Methodology*, *5*(1), 1–17.

Josselson, R. (2007). The ethical attitude in narrative research: Principles and practicalities. In D. J. Clandinin (ed.), *Handbook of Narrative Inquiry: Mapping a Methodology* (pp. 537-566). SAGE Publications.

(2013). *Interviewing for Qualitative Inquiry: A Relational Approach*. Guilford Press.

Kamberelis, G., & Dimitriadis, G. (2013). *Focus Groups: From Structured Interviews to Collective Conversations*. Routledge.

Kara, H. (2015). *Creative Research Methods in the Social Sciences: A Practical Guide*. Policy Press.

Kezar, A. (2003). Transformational elite interviews: Principles and problems. *Qualitative Inquiry*, *9*(3), 395–415.

Kvale, S. (1996). *InterViews: An Introduction to Qualitative Research Interviewing*. SAGE Publications

(2012). *Doing Interviews*. SAGE Publications.

Kvale, S., & Brinkmann, S. (2009). *InterViews: Learning the Craft of Qualitative Research Interviewing*. SAGE Publications.

Lareau, A. (2021). *Listening to People: A Practical Guide to Interviewing, Participant Observation, Data Analysis, and Writing It All Up*. University of Chicago Press.

Lawrence-Lightfoot, S., & Davis, J. H. (1997). *The Art and Science of Portraiture*. Jossey-Bass.

Luker, K. (2008). *Salsa Dancing into the Social Sciences*. Harvard University Press.

Madge, J. (1965). *The Tools of Social Science*. Longmans, Green.

Marshall, C., & Rossman, G. B. (2014). *Designing Qualitative Research*. SAGE Publications.

Marvasti, A., & Tanner, S. (2020). Interviews with individuals. In M. R. M. Ward & S. Delamont (eds.). *Handbook of Qualitative Research in Education* (pp. 329–337). Edward Elgar.

Maxwell, J. A. (2013). *Qualitative Research Design: An Interactive Approach*. SAGE Publications.

Mayhew, H. (1851). *London Labour and the London Poor*. Penguin.

McGrath, P., Rawson, N., & Adidi, L. (2013). Challenges associated with qualitative interviewing for Indigenous research: Insights from experience. *International Journal of Multiple Research Approaches*, *7*(2), 260–270.

Mertens, D. M. (2008). *Transformative Research and Evaluation*. Guilford Press.

Mishler, E. G. (1986). The analysis of interview-narratives. In T. R. Sarbin (ed.), *Narrative Psychology: The Storied Nature of Human Conduct* (pp. 233–255). Praeger.

Moses, M. W. (2021). Methodological interest convergence: Research site anonymity's maintenance of structural racism. *International Journal of Qualitative Studies in Education, 34*(9), 886–900.

Moustakas, C. (1994). *Phenomenological Research Methods*. SAGE Publications.

Mueller, R. A. (2019). Episodic narrative interview: Capturing stories of experience with a methods fusion. *International Journal of Qualitative Methods, 18*, 1–11.

Olive, J. L. (2014). Reflecting on the tension between emic and etic perspectives in life history research: Lessons learned. *Forum: Qualitative Social Research, 15*(2).

Patton, M. Q. (2014). *Qualitative Research & Evaluation Method: Integrating Theory and Practice*. SAGE Publications.

Platt, J. (2012). The history of the interview. In J. F. Gubrium, J. A. Holstein, A. B. Marvasti, & K. D. McKinney (eds.), *The SAGE Handbook of Interview Research: The Complexity of the Craft*, 2nd ed. (pp. 9–27). SAGE Publications.

Poland, B. D. (1995). Transcription quality as an aspect of rigor in qualitative research. *Qualitative inquiry, 1*(3), 290–310.

Punch, S. (2012). Studying transnational children: A multi-sited, longitudinal, ethnographic approach. *Journal of Ethnic and Migration Studies, 38*(6), 1007–1023.

Rice, G. (2010). Reflections on interviewing elites. *Area, 42*(1), 70–75.

Richardson, L. (1997). *Fields of Play: Constructing an Academic Life*. Rutgers University Press.

Rodriguez, D., & Parker, L. (2002). Race, subjectivity, and the interview process. In J. F. Gubrium & J. A. Holstein (eds.), *Handbook of Interview Research: Context and Method*, 279–298. SAGE Publications.

Rubin, H. J., & Rubin, I. S. (2012). *Qualitative Interviewing: The Art of Hearing Data*, 3rd ed. SAGE Publications.

Saldaña, J. (2020). Qualitative data analysis strategies. In P. Leavy (ed.), *The Oxford Handbook of Qualitative Research* (pp. 876–911). Oxford University Press.

Saldaña, J., & Omasta, M. (2016). *Qualitative Research: Analyzing Life*. SAGE Publications.

Saunders, B., Sim, J., Kingstone, T., Baker, S., Waterfield, J., Bartlam, B., et al. (2018). Saturation in qualitative research: Exploring Its Conceptualization and Operationalization. *Quality & Quantity, 52*(4), 1893–1907.

Seidman, I. (2006). *Interviewing as Qualitative Research: A Guide for Researchers in Education and the Social Sciences*. Teachers College Press.

Smith, L. T. (2021). *Decolonizing Methodologies: Research and Indigenous Peoples*. Bloomsbury.

Soss, J. (2015). Talking our way to meaningful explanations: A practice-centered view of interviewing for interpretive research. In D. Yanow & P. Schwartz-Shea (eds.), *Interpretation and Method* (pp. 161–182). Routledge.

Spradley, J. P. (1979). *The Ethnographic Interview*. Waveland Press.

Squire, D. D., & Nicolazzo, Z. (2019). Love my naps, but stay woke: The case against self-care. *About Campus, 24*(2), 4–11.

Tachine, A. R., & Nicolazzo, Z. (eds.). (2022). *Weaving an Otherwise: In-Relations Methodological Practice*. Stylus.

Terkel, S. (1972). *Working: People Talk about What They Do All Day and How They Feel about What They Do*. New Press.

Thomson, R., & Holland, J. (2003). Hindsight, foresight and insight: The challenges of longitudinal qualitative research. *International Journal of Social Research Methodology, 6*(3), 233–244.

Thorne, B. (2001). Learning from kids. In R. M. Emerson (ed.) *Contemporary Field Research: Perspectives and Formulations*, 2nd ed. (pp. 224–238). Waveland Press.

Timmermans, S., & Tavory, I. (2022). *Data Analysis in Qualitative Research: Theorizing with Abductive Analysis*. University of Chicago Press.

Vagle, M. D. (2018). *Crafting Phenomenological Research*. Routledge.

Van Manen, M. (2014). *Phenomenology of Practice: Meaning-Giving Methods in Phenomenological Research and Writing*, 1st ed. Routledge.

Weiss, R. S. (1994). *Learning from Strangers: The Art and Method of Qualitative Interview Studies*. Simon & Schuster.

Wengraf, T. (2001). *Qualitative Research Interviewing: Biographic Narrative and Semi-Structured Methods*. SAGE Publications.

Wilson, E., Kenny, A., & Dickson-Swift, V. (2018). Ethical challenges of community based participatory research: Exploring Researchers' Experience. *International Journal of Social Research Methodology, 21*(1), 7–24.

Yücel, E., Jabbar, H., & Schudde, L. (2022). Navigating transfer through networks: How community college students seek support from social ties throughout the transfer process. *Review of Higher Education, 45*(4), 487–513.

27 Case Studies: A Personal Account of Choices and Dilemmas

Christine Meyer

Abstract

This chapter is a personal account of choices and dilemmas I have faced when conducting case studies. From the very start of my career as a researcher, I have been attracted to getting my hands dirty and conducting case studies in the field. Case studies are not a straightforward research strategy, however. There are multiple choices and dilemmas on the way and there is no "right way" of doing them. Nevertheless, my long career as a case researcher has given me the courage to compile some reflections and recommendations. Throughout the chapter, I draw on some of the most prominent case researchers in the field and present their various approaches to conducting case studies. To give life to the text, I have included examples and illustrations from my own work, being as honest and open as I can about my choices and the difficulties and ethical dilemmas I met on my way.

Keywords: Case Studies, Personal Experiences, Epistemological Approaches, Design Choices, Role of Researchers

Back in the 1990s, I was a young PhD student who was fascinated by the prospect of doing case studies to explore real mergers and acquisitions (M&As). There was only one catch – no one at my business school had used case study methodology for their PhDs, as all research and teaching there were based on quantitative methodology. Fortunately, my supervisor was amenable to an alternative approach, but to succeed in my research, he advised me to spend time abroad with a co-supervisor who was an expert in qualitative case studies.

Since my PhD, I have immersed myself in qualitative research and explored numerous ways of conducting a case study. Case studies have not been that easy to publish, and it has often remained a real challenge to write up and make sense of the vast amounts of data. However, I have learned so much from my work on the numerous studies and treasure the opportunity to understand what really goes on beneath the surface in organizations. In the following paragraphs, I will lay out different approaches to conducting case studies, explore design choices, envisage roles for researchers, and look at how to collect and analyze data.

What Is a Case Study?

In the sixth edition of Yin's book on case studies (Yin, 2018), a book I would highly recommend to all students and scholars planning to conduct a case study, Yin distinguishes between the popular case study and the research case study. What we are grappling with in this chapter is a research case study, and this requires methodic inquiry and transparency about the procedures involved and theorizing. Case study research is all about understanding – in a way that provides a comprehensive impression of what is going on. We are not interested in the mere micro elements but in understanding the big picture.

Yin (2018) defines a case study as an empirical method that "investigates a contemporary phenomenon (the 'case') in depth and within its real-world context." The case study approach is suitable for exploring new processes and behaviors that are little understood (Hartley, 1994) and is particularly useful for responding to "how" and "why" questions (Leonard-Barton, 1990). The aim of most case studies is to build rather than test theory (Eisenhardt, 1989).

Case studies are often categorized as qualitative research but are importantly different from other qualitative methods (see also Volume 1 Chapter 20 of this Handbook). Creswell and Poth (2018) compare four other qualitative approaches to case studies: narrative research, phenomenology, grounded theory, and ethnography. The most defining character that distinguishes case studies from other approaches is their research focus – to develop an in-depth description and analysis of one or more cases. This is in contrast to the other approaches where the focus is on the exploration of the life of an individual (narrative research), understanding the essence of the experience (phenomenology), developing a theory grounded in field data (grounded theory), or describing and interpreting a culture-sharing group (ethnography). The cases in question can be events, programs, activities, or organizations where it is possible to set some boundaries around the object of study and distinguish between what is on the inside and outside.

The distinction between the different qualitative approaches is useful in fleshing out the distinct features of case studies. However, when conducting case study research, the differences between the methodologies may not be so clear cut. Some case studies apply grounded theory, and many more apply the coding procedures from this methodological approach. Moreover, case studies may use narratives as a way of presenting the findings and can also incorporate more ethnographic features; we will come back to this in the discussion of the different roles researchers can play.

The Different Epistemological Approaches

In a symposium at the Academy of Management Conference in 2017, professors Ann Langley, Steven Corley, and Kathleen Eisenhardt presented their approaches to qualitative research. In the debate that followed, the difference between epistemological approaches clearly surfaced. Eisenhardt expressed a realist or positivist orientation – searching for the objective truth and comparing and contrasting multiple case studies. Many have been inspired by Eisenhardt's work, and her approach to conducting case study research has also been referred to as the Eisenhardt template (Langley & Abdallah, 2011).

Langley on her part, known for process studies and attention to richness and detail, challenged this position and argued that there is an alternative to the positivistic approach – a relativist or interpretivist orientation. The realist perspective assumes the existence of a single reality that is independent of any observer (Yin, 2018). This approach attempts to capture the different perspectives of the participants while acknowledging that different researchers may observe different realities. Prominent researchers advocating this approach are Gioia and colleagues (Gioia, 2004; Gioia & Chittipeddi, 1991; Corley & Gioia, 2004; Gioia et al., 2010) and, as with Eisenhardt, there is also a template for the Gioia method (Langley & Abdallah, 2011). Rather than looking for variations across many cases and observations, this interpretivist approach focuses more on how people construct and understand their experience set in the context of situational phenomena (Gioia et al., 2012).

What is important is that the researchers conducting the case study research are self-aware and conscious of where they stand. The approach they choose or adhere to will have implications for how the study is designed and how the data are collected and analyzed. If you belong to the positivist tradition, you will normally choose multiple cases and compare the cases to find patterns that can explain different outcomes. If you instead identify yourself more with the interpretivist approach, you will probably choose one or a few cases, to be more attentive to the richness of the data, and try to put yourself in the informants' shoes. The interpretivist approach allows you to pay much more attention to the complexities and subtleties in the specific contexts and to understand how context is interwoven in the case (Pettigrew, 1990).

To guide case study researchers in their choices, Langley and Abdallah (2011) have compared the two templates stemming from Eisenhardt's and Gioia's research. The epistemological foundation is one of the important features that guides the choice of approach. The templates contrast single and multiple case studies. However, case study researchers may find themselves somewhere in the middle – selecting a few case studies or not fully adhering to one template or the other. Nevertheless, it is useful to highlight the distinct features of the different approaches.

Blindfolded or Theoretical Glasses?

An important aspect of case studies is the clarity of the research problem and theoretical perspectives before entering the field. Independent of the purpose of a case study, it is recommendable to have an initial definition of the research question (Gioia et al., 2012). The research question frames the case study and sets out a purpose for the data collection. However, the precision of the research question and choice of concepts and theory are likely to vary depending on the purpose.

Table 27.1 *Two templates for qualitative case studies*

	The "Eisenhardt method"	The "Gioia method"
Epistemological foundations	*Post-positivistic assumptions* *Purpose:* To develop theory in the form of testable propositions; to search for facts *Product:* Nomothetic theory	*Interpretive assumptions* *Purpose:* To capture and model the informants' meanings; to search for informants' understanding of organizational events *Product:* Process model/novel concept
Logic of method	*Design to maximize credible novelty* Multiple cases (4–10) chosen to be sharply distinct on one dimension while similar on others Interview data with diverse informants Identify elements that distinguish high- and low-performing cases building on cross-case comparison Validity and reliability from multiple researchers, triangulation of data	*Design for revelation, richness, and trustworthiness* Single case chosen for its revelatory potential and richness of data Real-time interviews and observation Build "data structure" by progressive abstraction starting with informants' first-order codes and building to second-order themes and aggregate dimensions Trustworthiness from insider–outsider roles, member checks, triangulation
Rhetoric of writing	*Establishing novelty:* Contrasting findings with previous research *Providing evidence:* Data presentation in two steps: (a) data tables, (b) narrative examples of high and low cases	*Establishing the gap:* Show how this study fills a major gap *Distilling the essence:* Present the data structure emphasizing second-order themes and overarching dimensions

Extracted from Table 27.1 in Langley and Abdallah (2011), pp. 205–206.

Often, the initial formulation of the research question is quite broad and vague. This allows the researcher to be open to emergent findings and make sense of the data during data collection. This is often regarded as one of the major strengths of case study research. However, vague formulation of the research question can also mean that the researcher needs to spend more time in the field, possibly pursuing several dead ends and collecting large amounts of data. At the opposite end of the scale, we find case studies with questions of a narrow scope within the context of existing theory. Here, the justification is that qualitative data can offer insights into complex social processes that quantitative data is unable to capture (Eisenhardt, 1989).

The problem can also be turned upside down during the study. We rarely get to know about these turnarounds, but in an interesting paper in *Academy of Management Discoveries* (Barley, 2015), the author gives a rare account of how the research question changed two years into the study. Barley and his team conducted participant observation in two car dealerships in Northern California over an 18-month period, expecting to find interesting differences between the two dealerships selling Toyota and Chevrolet vehicles, respectively. After spending months reading, coding and analyzing the field notes, Barley and the team concluded that there were no important differences between the two dealerships in terms of how the cars were sold. However, during their data collection, they discovered that there were significant differences in the channels through which the cars were sold (i.e., internet sales or floor sales). This discovery led to the team shifting its attention and going back to the field to collect more systematic data.

A key question in case study research is whether the researchers should engage with literature before entering the field. Early advocates for the grounded theory approach (Glaser & Strauss, 1967) argued that it was important to let the data speak for themselves and to rid yourself of theoretical preconceptions that might influence your fieldwork. Since grounded theory was first introduced, the strict order of data first, then theory, has been somewhat relaxed, with greater acceptance of the fact that researchers often have theoretical preconceptions when entering the field (Gioia et al., 2012). This approach has been adopted by many case study researchers when coding their data.

Eisenhardt (Eisenhardt, 1989; Eisenhardt & Graebner, 2007) is an advocate for engaging with theory before entering into the field. She argues that a priori specification of constructs can be valuable in helping the researcher to find a firmer empirical grounding. Bougeois and Eisenhardt (1988), for example, explicitly measure the constructs identified in the literature in their interview protocols and questionnaires. Even if there is a lack of theory, the researcher should justify their research by clearly and explicitly identifying the gap in the existing literature.

Regardless of the approach and theoretical predisposition, it is important to be open to serendipitous findings and new insights when entering the field. New insights will often spur the search for new theoretical perspectives, and these are often presented in articles stemming from case study research. Further, do not be fooled by the way in which the studies are written up. The theoretical perspectives often communicated toward the beginning of the paper may have come about late in the process and might even have been suggested by the reviewers.

All the Design Choices

I was quite surprised when I learned how many design choices there are in case studies. In contrast to surveys and grounded theory, however, there is very little guidance on how to conduct them. However, since I wrote my doctoral thesis in the 1990s, case studies have become more prevalent in the top journals, and there are clearer guidelines to be found on how to code and analyze the data (see Table 27.1). Design choices, however, are still very much up to the individual researchers. The lack of requirements guiding case study research represents both a strength and a weakness. On the one hand, it allows the researcher to tailor the design to the specific research question, while on the other, it may result in poor case studies and difficulty publishing your research.

Choosing Cases

One of the most important design choices is the selection of cases. The logic in case studies is theoretical rather than statistical sampling. The aim is normally to develop theory, not test it, although on rare occasions, case studies are conducted to test theory. The selection of case(s) is also guided by the aim to replicate or extend emergent theories, create theoretical insights, or explore an unusual phenomenon (Eisenhardt, 1989; Eisenhardt & Graebner, 2007). The process of selecting cases does not take place in a vacuum, however. There is often a long negotiation process for access, and the access you do obtain may be somewhat limited or not ideal timewise.

In my doctoral research, I wanted to study the implementation of mergers and acquisitions. The ideal form of access would have been to obtain access to track the process in real time from the offset to learn how the past, present, and future were interlinked (Pettigrew, 1997). However, this was unrealistic due to secrecy and sensitivity at this stage, as very few people know about these processes before the M&A is announced. This led me to search for cases where the decision to merge or acquire had recently been made.

The choice of cases may also be more opportunistic (Pettigrew, 1990) and can be based on preferential access. The researcher may have a long-standing relationship with the organization (e.g., as an employee or a consultant). Many of the case studies I have conducted have been opportunistic. In one merger case, I was involved as a consultant to the major incumbent telecom company in Norway that was planning to merge with its Swedish counterpart (Meyer & Altenborg, 2008). In this case, I gained access to the merger negotiations and planned to use this information to inform my study of the post-merger integration process. I have also been an insider in top positions in the Norwegian public sector, both as a junior minister and as a general director, and chose to write up my experiences after I left the organization in both these cases (Meyer & Stensaker, 2009, Meyer, 2013, Meyer & Stensaker, 2020). I will elaborate more on the different roles and ethical considerations involved in these cases below.

How Many Cases

A key question is how many cases the researcher should select. Eisenhardt typically selects multiple case studies and bases her selection on a replication logic (Eisenhardt, 1989; Eisenhardt & Graebner, 2007). Each case stands as an independent analytical unit, and the multiple cases serve as a series of related experiments. By adding new cases, it is possible to replicate, contrast, and build on emerging theory. In line with a realist or positivist orientation, Eisenhardt argues that multi-case studies provide a stronger foundation for theory building, as the "theory is better grounded, more accurate, and more generalizable ... and adding three cases to a single case study is modest in terms of numbers, but offers four times the analytical power" (Eisenhardt & Graebner, 2007, p. 27). Eisenhardt's studies are often based on variation in the outcome variables, and in her sampling of cases, she is clear on what other features she wants to keep as constant as possible and where to seek variation.

From a realist perspective, it is more common to choose one or a few cases that are chosen because they are unusually revelatory, extreme exemplars, or opportunities for unusual research access (Pettigrew, 1990; Eisenhardt & Graebner, 2007). One or a few cases give the opportunity for rich and contextual data (Siggelkow, 2007), and adding more cases may harm the ability to explore the depth and understand the context, process, and complexities of the case. One prominent example of how the richness of a case study can be portrayed is Alison's (1971) classic study of the decisions made in the Cuban Missile Crisis. Alison applied alternative explanatory templates to look at the case from three different angles, including the rational actor model, the political model, and the organizational process model.

Holistic or Embedded

The structure within each case is equally important. Some researchers apply a holistic design – focusing on the global nature of the phenomenon; others choose an embedded design where more attention is given to the subunits and how the different levels of an organization are interrelated (Yin, 2018). This latter approach makes it possible to compare and contrast units and time periods within the case. Again, the choices are dependent on your research approach, but there is also reason for some caution when choosing the embedded research approach.

The embedded approach is often favored by qualitative researchers who seek multiple comparisons and contrasts and assign numbers to the different observations. However, if the researcher goes too far in that direction, there is a danger of losing the richness and contextuality. I chose an embedded design for my PhD, but this did not mean that I was only concerned with the subunits. My focus was both on the variations between subunits and different time periods and on the case as a whole. For example, I quickly realized that one of the most intense rivalries was between former head office locations, and this tension was at times more prevalent than the tension between the merging parties.

Sampling Time

Time often plays an important role in case studies, especially if you choose to conduct a process study (Pettigrew, 1997; Langley et al., 2013). Time sets a reference for what changes can be seen and how these changes can be explained (Pettigrew, 1990). When conducting case studies, there are several important decisions the researcher must make. The first concerns whether time should be captured in real time, retrospectively, or both. Both approaches have their strengths and weaknesses. Often, the only option is to collect data retrospectively because you are not granted real-time access. Moreover, collecting retrospective data can also be important to set the study in time and map the recent history.

Collecting data retrospectively allows the interviewees to reflect on their experiences and sort out their emotions. However, retrospective recollections are also prone to forgetfulness, faulty recollections, and rationalization of what happened. However, real-time data may be difficult to access and can also be quite messy. Having the chance to go back to the field and ask the respondents to reflect on past experiences can therefore provide some interesting insights. In the M&As I studied for my PhD, I collected data both in real time and retrospectively. I first entered the field shortly after the post-merger integration had started, then re-entered the field two years later. I vividly remember the anger and negative emotions of one of the interviewees I talked to when expressing that they had been taken over by the other party. Two years down the road, however, I interviewed the same person, and this time, their emotions had cooled down and the interviewee had a very different recollection of the same time period. Having both real-time and retrospective data opened a more complete picture of the merger integration and also allowed me to understand how people both forget and try to rectify impressions of events in hindsight.

For this reason, the researcher needs to think about whether data should be collected at different points of time. When mapping processes over time, it is a strength to do more than one round of data collection, and there are quite a few strong exemplars that illustrate how this can be done. Vuori and Huy (2020) studied the regulation of top managers' emotions during strategy-making sessions in Nokia. They collected data during two periods, and many of the interviewees were interviewed more than once, making up a total of 121 in-depth interviews. Interviewing respondents repeatedly gives the opportunity to build trust and have a more open and trustworthy conversation. Moreover, real-time and retrospective data can be collected simultaneously.

One of the most difficult decisions, however, is when to *exit* the field, particularly when conducting process studies. Processes seldom have abrupt or finite ends and will continue after the researcher has left the field. For example, if a researcher is focused on marital relationships or alliances between business partners, they are likely to exit this context while the relationship is still ongoing. Moreover, the phenomenon you observe is set in the time you choose, and this phenomenon may look fundamentally different in a different period. Trajectories of processes are probabilistic and uncertain in their nature due to changing contexts and human actions (Pettigrew, 1990). The recommendation for the case researcher is to be explicit and transparent about their process choices.

The Different Roles Researchers Can Play

With the explicit danger of entering into other qualitative research approaches (Creswell & Poth, 2018), it is important to understand the different roles researchers can play in the field when conducting case studies. In particular,

I will explore the roles of being a pure researcher, a consultant, a complete participant, and a combination of participant and researcher. I should add that the different roles are also addressed elsewhere in this volume (see Chapters 25, 26, 27, 28), but I wanted to share some of my unique experiences from being in these different roles and the ethical precautions I took (for further discussion of ethical considerations, see Volume 1, Chapter 2 of this Handbook).

Pure Researcher

The first approach to field research is to be an outsider as a pure researcher. The vast majority of case studies fall under this category. The strength of this approach is that the researchers are able to keep their distance, without adopting the informant's view, and are able to theorize from the data (Gioia et al., 2012). However, there is a danger of "going native," particularly if you spend a lot of time in the field interviewing and observing. Even if you do not go native, you might still feel loyal to the informants, making it more challenging for you personally to expose the negative aspects of the stories or characters.

I have grappled with these challenges many times and have also received feedback from people I interviewed who felt negatively exposed, even though the citations were anonymous. To avoid the pitfall of getting too close and loyal to the participants, Gioia et al. (2012) recommend always having a member of the team who adopts the outsider perspective and acts as a devil's advocate – questioning the assumptions and interpretations of the other team members. In one study, I had a more senior professor sit in on a few interviews. One of the interviews with a CEO was not going very well; I was asking critical questions and the CEO was brushing me off time after time. I felt very uncomfortable throughout the interview and expressed this to the senior professor afterwards. His response was that my probing questions had revealed interesting aspects of the CEO's personality and his views of the organization as a well-functioning machine – a helpful and insightful observation I had not captured, having been caught up in the tense atmosphere.

Consultant

Another role is to enter the field as a consultant. This is a role many of my academic colleagues combine with their roles as researchers, but most often, the roles are kept separate. Compared to being a pure researcher, the access to and openness of information is distinctly different (Gummesson, 1988). In one of my field studies, mentioned above (Meyer & Altenborg, 2008), I entered as purely a consultant, and the opportunity to publish from my consultancy work was a welcome surprise after the fact. The backdrop was a planned merger between the largest Norwegian telecom company and its Swedish counterpart. I was hired as a consultant on the pre-merger process – working closely with one of the insiders to the process – but I also had an aim to negotiate access to study the post-merger process – an aim I was open about.

I vividly remember that I had just spent some time in Sweden negotiating access and establishing trust with the Swedish organization when I learned that the merger had fallen through. My first thought was that all this work to gain access and learn about the merger was a waste of time. However, what I learned about pre-merger processes from my role as consultant was unique, and this knowledge was not wasted (although admittedly it could not be published). To my surprise, when I met the CEO of the company some months later, he asked me what I intended to do with what I had learned. I replied that my role in the process made it unethical to publish the study. He was quite an unusual CEO, and very favorable to research, so he relieved me of my duty of confidentiality and said he would welcome publication of the failed merger (Meyer & Altenborg, 2008).

Nevertheless, we needed to take some ethical measures in relation to the informants in the study. Firstly, when acting as a consultant, I did not record the interviews, and felt it would be wrong to cite from these interviews since the intention to publish was not communicated to the informants. We, therefore, used this material to inform our fieldwork and went back to the field to conduct 12 new interviews. In addition, we included a lot of documentation from the merger and from the media where the scandal of the demerger had received a lot of attention. We also sent an early draft of the paper to the head of staff and included his insights and comments in the paper.

Complete Participant

On two occasions, I have been a complete participant and have written up my experiences from the field – first as a junior minister in the Norwegian government and then as general director for Statistics Norway. In the first study, I wrote about the political decision-making involved in getting a controversial reform through the Cabinet and Parliament (Meyer, 2013; Meyer & Stensaker, 2009). In the second study, I wrote about two change processes I initiated as general director – one successful and one that led to my resignation (Meyer & Stensaker, 2020). On both occasions, I returned to academia after holding these positions and used the opportunity serendipitously to reflect on and put my experiences into writing.

Reflecting on one's own experiences as a complete participant can be characterized as auto-ethnography (Ellis, 1991, 1993; Ellis & Bochner, 2000) and is based on personal experience (Denzin, 1989) and auto-observation (Adler & Adler, 1994). This use of the self as a research tool for understanding is deeply rooted in the early origins of sociology. In this form of auto-observation, the researcher becomes both the subject and the object of the study. There are two approaches to auto-ethnography: planned and opportunistic (Adler & Adler, 1994). I applied the latter, where the researcher opportunistically turns settings in which they are members, or experiences they are having, into topics of auto-observation. At the time I participated in the field, I was not a researcher but a complete participant (Adler & Adler, 1987) with the single purpose of being a complete participant.

The single-purpose role as a complete participant has some important advantages over the other roles of observation. In my case, I had no explicit goal to observe, and the question of whether observation happens overtly or covertly (Adler & Adler, 1994) became irrelevant. Since I had no research purpose, I did not influence the field as the research instrument. However, as I was part of the process, I could not set myself outside the field setting. Both as a junior minister and as a general director, I had substantial influence over decisions and processes.

The downside of not being able to combine the roles of researcher and complete participant was that a lot of observational information was lost and the observations, to a large extent, were unfocused (Silverman, 2000). Moreover, the research question emerged after I had left the field, and there was no opportunity to probe into emerging findings (Denzin & Lincoln, 1994, 2000). In other instances, the lack of detailed and written recollections of observational data could be compensated for by going back to the field to collect new data by interviewing key participants, observing, and collecting documentary material. Indeed, this was what I had done when I was a consultant in the merger study described above. Because of my roles, however, I felt that it was unethical to go back into the field to conduct interviews with the employees who had been under my supervision. Nevertheless, I had obtained and used a lot of documents as well as extensive newspaper clippings relating to both studies.

Since I was so immersed in my own data, I also took measures to distance myself from the field. In two of the three papers I wrote, I invited an academic colleague to take part in writing up the research. She was very important in making sense of the data and bringing the analysis to a higher theorical level. She also questioned a number of my interpretations, feeling that they were too skewed toward defending my own position. Moreover, she encouraged me to bring in more documentation to corroborate my story.

Participant and Researcher

Though still rare to spot in top journals, there is a rising trend of people combining the roles of complete participant and researcher. In the Nordic countries, for example, we are encouraging experienced employees to take industrial or public sector PhDs, where the company or public sector body and the university collaborate on a doctoral project. The PhD student has a dual role as an employee in the private or public sector organization and a student under the supervision of the university. I have supervised a couple of these PhD students and have experienced both the advantages of being employed by the organization and some dilemmas around having these combined roles.

When you are an employee of an organization with some tenure, you have a head start and do not have to spend a lot of time familiarizing yourself with the context and the organization. In addition, you already know a lot of people, and this gives you unique access to the organization. Further, because they know that you are knowledgeable about the inner workings, it is not as easy for them to get away with superfluous explanations or rosy pictures. You also have a unique opportunity to collect rich data through your unique access to the organization.

However, there are also some challenges. Firstly, learning to theorize and distancing yourself from the field might prove to be quite a challenge. It is also likely that you have some preconceptions you need to reflect carefully on when entering the field. Based on my observations, there is an even more challenging side of the industrial PhDs – to manage the expectations of your employer. Because you have all the insights into the organization, there is a greater danger of them being exposed when the research is published, and this may restrain the access and make it more difficult to publish. One way of making this work is to take the step into action research, where the researcher has a much more active and consultative role during the data collection (for an example of action research, see Lüscher & Lewis, 2008). Another step is to try to keep a distance but still accept that you need to give something back during the field studies to keep your employer happy. The pressure on giving back is not, incidentally, unique to this role but something many qualitative researchers feel when spending a long time in the field. Balancing these different considerations is difficult, but it is important to be transparent about how it is done.

Collecting Data

What is typical for case studies is that they involve a mix of different types of data: interviews, observations, documentation, archival records, physical artifacts and other visuals (Yin, 2018). Increasingly, it is also becoming more common to include quantitative data by applying mixed method data collection. A study by Rouzies and Colman (2012) is one prominent example, where the authors combine three repeated surveys with 147 interviews and secondary data studying post-merger integration. Depending on the template and the role of the researcher in the field, the balance between the different data sources is likely to be distinct. In single case studies, observation is more common than in multiple case studies, and an obvious reason for this is that observation is very time-consuming. As mentioned above, access to the cases may also limit the extent of observation, even though that may be the preferred method of data collection.

The role of the different data collection methods is also likely to serve a different purpose when you pursue multiple case studies rather than single case studies. If you are on a truth-finding mission, the purpose of multiple data sources is often to triangulate the data. This allows you, for example, to check whether information provided from an interview is consistent with information in documents. Often, the interviewees give quite rough time estimates, and by checking the documents, you can find the exact times. If you, on the other hand, are interested in different perceptions, your expectation is to find differences and explore the reasons why. In our studies on employees' reactions to change, for example, we found key differences between the inexperienced and the experienced employees (Stensaker & Meyer, 2012). When the employees were inexperienced, their reactions were much more emotional, but they also displayed a wider variety of reactions – ranging from paralysis to actively supporting the change. More experienced employees were more similar in their reactions – supporting the change but differing as to whether this represented a coping strategy to survive or a genuine willingness to change.

Observations

As discussed above, there are multiple ways to conduct observations in the field. These observations can be overt or covert, although covert observations are unusual and raise major ethical concerns. One example of a covert study is journalist James Bloodworth's six-month undercover study of jobs in low-wage Britain (Bloodworth, 2018). Bloodworth spent six months working for several employers, including Amazon and Uber. His story of how Amazon workers urinated in coke bottles because they were afraid to take toilet breaks received substantial attention and negatively affected Amazon's reputation. An example of a semi-covert study is Pratt's (2000) study of Amway, a network marketing company. Pratt's objective was to study the practices and processes involved in managing the members' organizational identification. He found two types of practices for managing identification, sensebreaking and sensegiving. Pratt was open to his co-workers about his dual role as an employee and a researcher but not to his customers. This semi-overt observation allowed him the opportunity to ask questions that might otherwise seem unusual coming from a co-worker.

The observer can also be an overt complete participant, as I was in my roles as junior minister and general director. However, I did not have a dual role as a participant and a researcher, since the intention to do research came after I left the field. The dual role is more common in collaborative action research where the insider is also part of the research (Shani & Coghlan, 2014). A less active role is to be a participant observer; this is the role I took on when I worked as a consultant in the failed telecom merger. The most passive role is the role of pure observer. However, as discussed above, spending a long time in the field might create some pressure to participate (or at least to give some feedback to the informants). As Pettigrew so aptly puts it, "Social scientists have no given right to expect other people's organizations to be their laboratories" (Pettigrew, 1997).

Interviews

Interviews play a major role in most case studies. Although selecting interviewees in advance might seem preferable, it is very useful to allow for snowballing when the problem is broadly defined, as the interviewees refer you to people you should talk to. How to conduct the interviews depends on the approach and purpose of each interview. Langley and Meziani (2020) have identified five different approaches to conducting interviews.

Although the investigative approach is associated with the quest to find the truth, it might also supplement other approaches (e.g., to map the chronology in a process study or identify key events). The apprentice approach is often useful as part of the studies to build an understanding of the context or phenomenon. In one recent study of the innovative journey of a major Norwegian bank, I sought to understand how the bank's old IT systems made innovation more cumbersome and difficult. These systems were constructed in the 1980s and 1990s when storage and processing capacity were limited. Since then, layer after layer had been added, making the

Table 27.2 Five interview genres: purposes and practices

INTERVIEW GENRE	INVESTIGATIVE	APPRENTICE	INTERPRETIVE	DISCURSIVE	INTERVENTIONIST
PRIMARY PURPOSE	Tracing events	Articulating tacit knowledge	Constructing meaning	Revealing communicative practices	Stimulating reflexivity
ONTOLOGICAL ASSUMPTIONS	Neo positivist	Practice perspective	Phenomenological	Discursive/ Constructionist	Clinical
VOCABULARY	Events Facts	Practice Doing Tasks Routines	Subjective experience Meaning Representation	Story Identity work Language Co-construction	Action Transformation Reflexivity
SPECIFIC TECHNIQUES AND PRACTICES	Event tracking Courtroom questioning Indirect questioning	Think aloud interviews Critical incident technique Interview to the double	Introspection Clean language interview Topic label avoidance	Narrative methods Constructionist analysis	Dialogical inquiry Appreciative interviews

Source: extract from Langley and Meziani (2020).

systems extremely complex and intricate. When interviewing people who were knowledgeable about these legacy systems, I took the role as a novice and asked them to explain how the systems hindered innovation and what could be done about it. It was often very helpful that they used analogies to explain the problem to me:

We have so much spaghetti ... It's like a heart transplant ...

If you have a ramshackle house and you invest in fiber (to communicate to the outside world), then things do not fundamentally change. The API (application programming interface) may be fantastic, but if no one wants to come and visit or live in your house, it doesn't amount to much.

An important assumption in the interpretivist approach is that people are perceived as knowledgeable agents. They know what they are trying to do and are capable of explaining their thoughts, intentions, and actions (Gioia et al., 2012). This has important implications for how we collect our data. We do not want to impose our concepts or understandings on the informants; this may sound easy but is in fact very hard to do throughout long and intense interviews. However, by adopting this approach, it is easier to represent the voice of the informants in the research and to discover new concepts (rather than just confirm what we already know).

As one example, in our research on change in two large organizations (Stensaker et al., 2002), the new concept of excessive change arose from the interviews with employees. They shared their experiences and reflections on the continuous and never-ending changes taking place in their respective organizations:

There are too many changes. There's instability everywhere and we didn't have to start everything at the same time. Nobody has control over it.

When something new was introduced, it had a starting point, but the different pieces were never in place, they are supposed to fall into place as we go along. But before they do, there is something new again. There is never anything that gets implemented. You get started and then you're cut off ...

The interviewees did not specifically use the expression "excessive change" in the interviews; instead, this was a concept that was grounded in the data. In the interpretive approach, it is the combination of knowledgeable agents and researchers that makes it possible to discover new and interesting concepts (Gioia et al., 2012). The reader can also consult Chapter 26 in this volume for a detailed exposition on interviews.

Documents

Documents are most often collected for other purposes, and this is important to consider when applying them in data collection. There are a great variety of documents, and in the last decades, social media and other internet sources have become increasingly important. The role of documents can also differ quite substantially depending on the purpose of the research. In my research, documents have always been important, either to familiarize myself with the context, map the

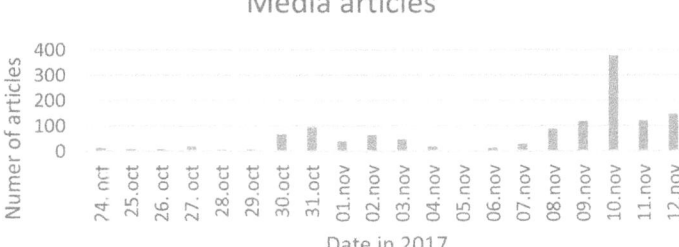

Figure 27.1 *Media articles covering the change processes in Statistics Norway in 2017.*

chronology and identify key events, or to corroborate the findings when other sources were inadequate. In the two studies previously mentioned, I was a complete participant with a single purpose, and I felt it was unethical to return to the field and conduct interviews because of my former role. Moreover, the observations I had made were not noted. I, therefore, needed to back up my observations with documents and archival records. In both cases, the documentation was substantial.

As another example, in the study of two change processes in Statistics Norway (Meyer & Stensaker, 2020), I made use of newspaper articles to present the employees' and unions' sides of the story, citing the different articles in the paper. This extensive media coverage proved valuable when I was building the case at a later point of time. Figure 27.1 shows the extensive media coverage, where the spike on 10 November was the day before I resigned from my position as general director as a result of a conflict with the Minister of Finance.

Analyzing the Data

In most case studies, it is important to start analyzing the data when in the field, and the simultaneous process of collecting and analyzing data is a key feature in qualitative case studies. As a result, the interview guides and the focus of observation often change throughout the course of the data collection as new features surface, are pursued, and new informants are added. Moreover, coming up with novel theory and concepts often takes time, and writing up emerging concepts and theories when collecting data in the field gives more time to reflect and probe and follow leads.

Case studies and qualitative research have often been criticized for lack of rigor, or as Michael Pratt (2009) says, qualitative research lacks a boilerplate. To assist qualitative researchers in their analysis of data, different templates for conducting case studies have emerged. Templates guide the researchers in their analysis of often messy and vast amounts of data and helps to build qualitative rigor into the process. Although the different templates are very useful to obtain more rigorous case analyses, there is also a need to be cautious and not lose the benefits of qualitative research – to tailor the research to the research question and be flexible.

The Eisenhardt Template

Eisenhardt has a very clear template for analyzing case studies (see Table 27.1; Eisenhardt, 1989; Eisenhardt & Graebner, 2007). Eisenhardt starts by analyzing each case to become familiar with the data and consider how the data could generate new theory. She then searches for patterns across the cases, looking beyond the initial impressions and seeing the evidence through multiple lenses. Her next step is to shape hypotheses. She builds constructs and searches for evidence of the "why" behind the relationships, contrasting and comparing the data and looking for evidence that confirms, extends, and sharpens theory. The third step is to engage with existing theory by comparing the emerging new theories with theories that are both conflicting and similar. For researchers planning to conduct case studies in the Eisenhardt tradition, it is also useful to read Eisenhardt and colleagues' many empirical papers to study how she analyses the data, builds up a story, and constructs new theory, concepts, and propositions (see, for example, Hannah & Eisenhardt, 2019; McDonald & Eisenhardt, 2020).

When building up the analysis for my PhD study of mergers, I was very much in the Eisenhardt tradition and also very much influenced by Andrew Pettigrew and his approach to comparative, longitudinal case studies. I started by making myself familiar with the extensive field of M&A and, in particular, what was written on post-merger integration. I then went through several stages of reducing and analyzing the data; this included establishing the chronology, coding, writing up the data according to phases and themes, introducing organizational integration into the analysis, comparing the cases, and applying the theory (see Table 27.3).

Table 27.3 *Steps of an analysis*

STEP	ACTIVITY
Establish chronology	Track events in internal and external documents
	Included in the appendices
Code data	Color-code the interviews and documents based on themes and phases of post-merger integration
Write up each case	Scan information on each theme and phase, build up the facts, and fill in with perceptions and reactions in a show-and-tell logic
Make cases more analytical	Introduce three dimensions of organizational integration: integration of tasks, unification of power, and cultural integration, and organize the themes into these categories
Compare cases	Compare and contrast the findings from each case
Analytical generalization	Compare the emergent findings on themes, concepts, and relationships with literature on M&A and other relevant fields. Ask what is similar, what contradicts, and why

Source: Meyer (2001)

The Gioia Template

One of the main differences between the Eisenhardt and Gioia templates for analysis is the use of theory. Eisenhardt is much more driven by theoretical perspectives throughout the analysis, whereas the Gioia method has clear recommendations regarding when to introduce theory and distinguishes between first- and second-order coding. In first-order coding, the analysis focuses on using informant-centric codes. Here, is it important to stay close to the informants' terms, and this implies that the number of categories tends to explode, making it very easy to lose track and get completely lost. In second-order coding, the researchers make sense of the first-order codes by searching for themes, dimensions, and new concepts (Gioia et al., 2012). As a result, we as researchers interpret what is going on and try to make sense of the first-order codes.

Gioia et al. (2012) emphasize making a conscious choice not to engage too much with the literature during data collection and the initial analysis. Instead, they suggest to put blinders on until the first steps of coding have been completed. Note that this does not imply that the result of the analysis is not theoretical – the engagement with theory happens at a later stage. Moreover, not engaging with theory at an early stage does not mean that the researchers are uninformed; they try to take deliberate actions to not be clouded by their theoretical preconceptions and let the data guide which theoretical perspectives they choose.

The data structure for the Gioia template can be illustrated by Corley and Gioia, 2004 (see Figure 27.2).

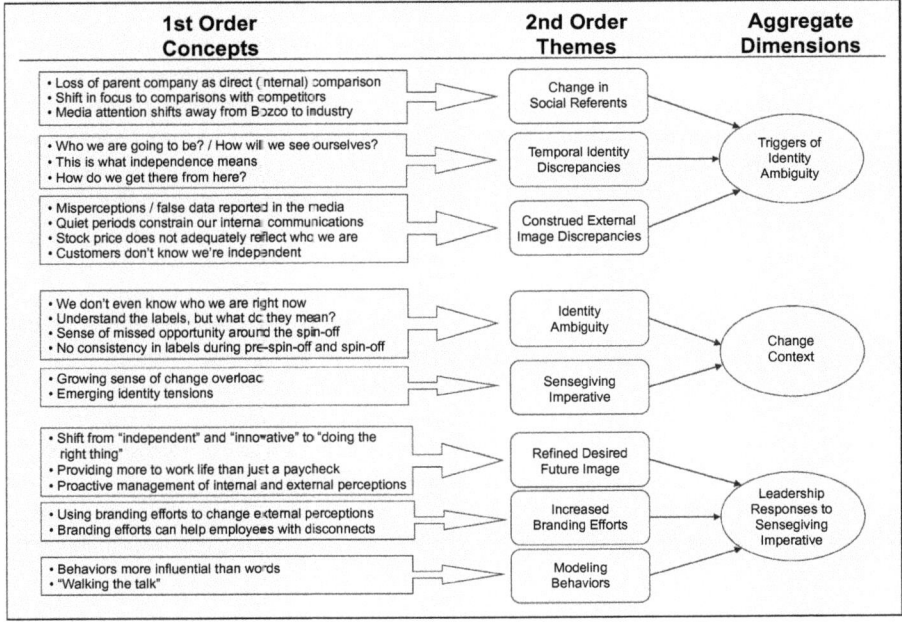

Figure 27.2 *Illustration of the Gioia data structure template.*

In our paper from the early 2000s investigating excessive change (Stensaker et al., 2002), different researchers discovered the same phenomenon in two companies. This discovery convinced us that the issue was worth investigating further. As a result, the two cases were supplemented with a third case from one of the organizations. We used an inductive approach, exploring how individuals perceived and dealt with excessive change. To aid us with the coding, we used a software program, and all four researchers were involved in the process. In Table 27.4 we have illustrated the first- and second-order concepts (what we would have labelled these categories today) and citations illustrating and backing these concepts.

Table 27.4 *Analyzing data for excessive change*

Second-order concepts	First-order concepts	Interview data
MUSICAL CHAIRS	Rotation of managers	*We call it musical chairs. We change places and some have to leave.* *In the past six months we have had six managers, one manager twice.*
	Voluntary and involuntary turnover	*It's easy to play hide and seek ... They (poor managers) can surf on the waves. Nobody has time to follow them up.* *There is little continuity at the level that is supposed to implement the strategy.* *When you delegate responsibility to the level with least continuity, well, then no one remembers the strategy.*
ORCHESTRATING WITHOUT A CONDUCTOR	Employees lack direction due to non-functional and inconsistent middle management	*I must admit this has been a hard time. The manager hasn't had the time to take care of his own group of employees.* *The managers hardly know what we are doing.* *The CEO said one thing and his subordinate another. They were inconsistent, and we began to wonder what was going on ...* *I could just as well have used a secretary (instead of a manager). If I need help, I make a phone call or ask a colleague*
SHAKY FOUNDATIONS	Lack of routines and unclear responsibilities	*The name of the game is the more change the better. Everything gets very turbulent.*

Table 27.4 (cont.)

Second-order concepts	First-order concepts	Interview data
		Everything has happened all at once. We have had no time to sit down and draw the map. We have had to go out and draw the map. We have had to go out and draw the terrain without any guidelines. I feel we have had an inhuman task to cope with.
		Lists have been lost and not even been handed to the pay office. There is such a lack of routines and when this starts to show up on people's pay checks, they really get upset.

Source: Extracted from Stensaker et al. (2002)

Analyzing Processes in Case Study Research

Process research addresses questions about how and why things emerge, develop, grow, or terminate over time (Langley et al., 2013). Pettigrew (1997, p. 338) defines a process as "A sequence of individual and collective events, actions, and activities unfolding over time in context." However, this is only the first step of defining what a process is. In all process studies, time and history are of the essence, and the role of the researcher is to catch the reality in flight. The aim of processual research, however, is not to produce a case history but a case story. Pettigrew outlines three steps of processual research with two cases (p. 339):

(1) Search for patterns in the process and compare and contrast the shape, character, and incidence of this pattern in case A with case B.
(2) Find the underlying mechanisms which shape the patterns.
(3) Compare and contrast the inductive pattern recognition with theory deduction.

As for interpretive single case studies (e.g., Gioia's studies), the role of context is crucial in the analysis. "If the process is our stream of analysis, the terrain around the stream which shapes the flow of events and is in turn shaped by them is a necessary part of the process of investigation" (Pettigrew, 1997, p. 340). A key feature of process studies is the opportunity for longitudinal replication (Langley et al., 2013). As such, the sample size for the process study is not the number of cases or units within the case – it is the number of temporal observations. This can be in the form of events or temporal bracketing where comparative units of analysis are identified within the stream of data. In my study of the public reform (Meyer, 2013), I divided the process into three distinctive periods (see Figure 27.3). In phase 1, the purpose

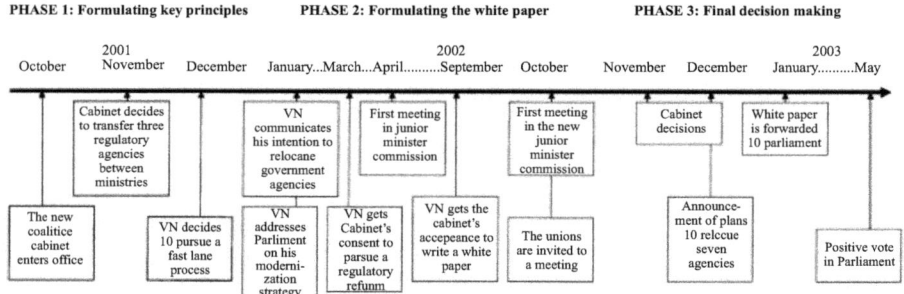

Figure 27.3 *Temporal bracketing in reform case.*

was to formulate the principles for the white paper. In the second and most demanding phase for the survival of the reform, the aim was to get a white paper approved by the Cabinet. The next step was the parliamentary process, but here there was a lower risk due to the expected majority in parliament supporting the reform.

In the study of two change processes in Statistics Norway, the events were the driving focus behind the process. In this paper, it made less sense to divide the processes into brackets, but there were key events that raised either the change or stasis momentum in the two processes. Hence, we plotted the events along two timelines and showed how they differed between the two changes – one that succeeded while the other failed.

Although the above steps in the various templates may look neat, they are the result of a lot of back-and-forth between the emergent data, concepts, themes, and relevant literature. This also reflects the fact that there is no clear boundary between data collection in the field and analysis of the data; one of the strengths of this type of research is indeed the ability to move back and forth between these processes. Our study of excessive change illustrates this point. We discovered the phenomenon during two separate studies of strategy implementation before going back to the field with a more focused research question to build up a stronger analysis.

Wrapping Up

My academic career has been marked by many different ways of conducting case studies, and there has never been a single dull moment. Case studies have opened up opportunities to study organizations and businesses in their natural habitat and learn from their practices. As a case study researcher one gets to meet many interesting and knowledgeable people, who let you into their thinking and doing, deepen your understanding of the phenomena, and give you true eureka and thrilling moments. Through case study design, there is an opportunity to take different roles in the field, and also to reflect on one's own experiences. Though dual roles can pose some challenges in the field and in writing up your work, they also open up closer connections between academia and practice and bring new knowledge to the table.

Hopefully, sharing these insights from my journey will also help to pass on what I have learned along the way and some of my enthusiasm for studying cases to the readers of this chapter.

References

Adler, P. A., & Adler, P. (1987). *Membership Roles in Field Research*. SAGE Publications.
— (1994). Observational techniques. In N. K. Denzin & Y. S. Lincoln (eds.), *Handbook of Qualitative Research* (pp. 377–392). SAGE Publications.
Alison, G. T. (1971). *Essence of Decision*. Boston: Little, Brown.
Barley, S. R. (2015). Why the internet makes buying a car less loathsome: How technologies change role relations. *Academy of Management Discoveries*, *1*(1), 5–35.
Bloodworth, J. (2018). *Hired: Six Months Undercover in Low-Wage Britain*. Atlantic Books.
Bourgeois III, L. J., & Eisenhardt, K. M. (1988). Strategic decision processes in high velocity environments: Four cases in the microcomputer industry. *Management Science*, *34*(7), 816–835.
Colman, H. L., & Rouzies, A. (2019). Postacquisition boundary spanning: A relational perspective on integration. *Journal of Management*, *45*(5), 2225–2253.
Corley, K. G., & Gioia, D. A. (2004). Identity ambiguity and change in the wake of a corporate spin-off. *Administrative Science Quarterly*, *49*(2), 173–208.
Creswell, J. W., & Poth, C. N. (2018). *Qualitative Inquiry and Research Design: Choosing among Five Approaches*, 4th ed. SAGE Publications.
Denzin, N. K. (1989). *Interpretive Biography*. SAGE Publications.
Denzin, N. K., & Lincoln, Y. S. (eds.). (1994). *Handbook of Qualitative Research*. SAGE Publications.
— (eds.). (2000). *Handbook of Qualitative Research*, 2nd ed. SAGE Publications.
Eisenhardt, K. M. (1989). Building theories from case study research. *Academy of Management Review*, *14*(4), 532–550.
Eisenhardt, K. M., & Graebner, M. E. (2007). Theory building from cases: Opportunities and challenges. *Academy of Management Journal*, *50*(1), 25–32.
Ellis, C. (1991). Emotional sociology. In N. K. Denzin (ed.), *Studies in Symbolic Interaction: A Research Annual*, vol. 12 (pp. 123–145). JAI.
— (1993). "There are survivors": Telling a story of sudden death. *Sociological Quarterly*, *34*, 711–730.
Ellis, C., & Bochner, A. (2000). Autoethnography, personal narrative, reflexivity: Researcher as subject. In N. K. Denzin & Y. S. Lincoln (eds.), *Handbook of Qualitative Research*, 2nd ed. (733–768). SAGE Publications.
Gioia, D. A. (2004). A renaissance self: Prompting personal and professional revitalization. In R. E. Stablein & P. J. Frost (eds.), *Renewing Research Practice: Scholars' Journeys* (pp. 97–114). Stanford University Press.
Gioia, D. A., & Chittipeddi, K. (1991). Sensemaking and sensegiving in strategic change initiation. *Strategic Management Journal*, *12*(6), 433–448.
Gioia, D. A., Corley, K. G., & Hamilton, A. L. (2012). Organizational research. *Organizational Research Methods*, *16*(1), 15–31.
Gioia, D. A., Price, K. N., Hamilton, A. L., & Thomas, J. B. (2010). Forging an identity: An insider-outsider study of processes involved in the formation of organizational identity. *Administrative Science Quarterly*, *55*(1), 1–46.

Glaser, B. G., & Strauss, A. L. (1967). *The Discovery of Grounded Theory: Strategies for Qualitative Research*. Aldine.

Gummesson, E. (1988). *Qualitative Methods in Management Research*. Studentlitteratur.

Hannah, D. P., & Eisenhardt, K. M. (2019). Bottlenecks, cooperation, and competition in nascent ecosystems. *Strategic Management Journal*, 40(9), 1333–1335.

Hartley, J. (1994). Case studies in organisational research. In C. Casell and G. Symon (eds.), *Qualitative Methods in Organisational Research: A Practical Guide* (pp. 208–229). SAGE Publications.

Langley, A., & Abdallah, C. (2011). Templates and turns in qualitative studies of strategy and management. In D. D. Bergh & D. J. Ketchen, Jr. (eds.), *Building Methodological Bridges* (pp. 201–235). Emerald.

Langley, A. N. N, & Meziani, N. (2020). Making interviews meaningful. *Journal of Applied Behavioral Science*, 56(3), 370–391.

Langley, A. N. N., Smallman, C., Tsoukas, H., & Van de Ven, A. H. (2013). Process studies of change in organization and management: Unveiling temporality, activity, and flow. *Academy of Management Journal*, 56(1), 1–13.

Leonard-Barton, D. (1990). A dual methodology for case studies: Synergistic use of a longitudinal single site with replicated multiple sites. *Organization Science*, 1(3), 248–266.

Lüscher, L. S., & Lewis, M. W. (2008). Organizational change and managerial sensemaking: Working through paradox. *Academy of Management Journal*, 51(2), 221–240.

McDonald, R. M., & Eisenhardt, K. M. (2020). Parallel play: Startups, nascent markets, and effective business-model design. *Administrative Science Quarterly*, 65(2), 483–523.

Meyer, C. B. (2001). A case in case study methodology. *Field Methods*, 13(4), 329–352.

(2013). When radical reforms are on the agenda: Managing politics in government. *Journal of Applied Behavioral Science*, 48(2), 194–224.

Meyer, C. B., & Altenborg, E. (2008). Incompatible strategies in international mergers: The failed merger between Telia and Telenor. *Journal of International Business Studies*, 39(3), 508–525.

Meyer, C. B., & Stensaker, I. G. (2009). Making radical change happen through selective inclusion and exclusion of stakeholders. *British Journal of Management*, 20(2), 219–237.

(2020). Momentum for change and stakeholder dynamics in the public sector. *Academy of Management Proceedings*, 2020(1), 16982.

Pettigrew, A. M. (1990). Longitudinal field research on change: Theory and practice. *Organization Science*, 1(3), 267–292.

(1997). What is a processual analysis? *Scandinavian Journal of Management*, 13(4), 337–348.

Pratt, M. G. (2000). The good, the bad, and the ambivalent: Managing identification among Amway distributors. *Administrative Science Quarterly*, 45(3), 456–493.

(2009). From the Editors: For the lack of a boilerplate: Tips on writing up (and reviewing) qualitative research. *Academy of Management Journal*, 52(5), 856–862.

Rouzies, A., & Colman, H. L. (2012). Identification processes in post-acquisition integration: The role of social interactions. *Corporate Reputation Review*, 15(3), 143–157.

Shani, A. B., & Coghlan, D. (2014). Collaborate with practitioners: An alternative perspective. A rejoinder to Kieser and Leiner (2012). *Journal of Management Inquiry*, 23(4), 433–437.

Siggelkow, N. (2007). Persuasion with case studies. *Academy of Management Journal, 50*(1), 20–24.

Silverman, D. (2000). *Doing Qualitative Research: A Practical Handbook.* London: SAGE Publications.

Stensaker, I. G., Falkenberg, J., Meyer, C. B., & Haueng, A. C. (2002). Excessive change: Coping mechanisms and consequences. *Organizational Dynamics, 31*(3), 296–312.

Stensaker, I. G., & Meyer, C. B. (2012). Change experience and employee reactions: Developing capabilities for change. *Personnel Review, 41*(1), 106–124.

Vuori, T. O., & Huy, Q. N. (2020). Regulating top managers' emotions during strategy making: Nokia's socially distributed approach enabling radical change from mobile phones to networks in 2007–2013. *Academy of Management Journal, 65*(1).

Yin, R. K. (2018). *Case Study Research and Applications: Design and Methods*: SAGE Publications.

28 Focus Groups

Noa Amir, Chandana Guha, Simon Carter, and Allison Jauré

Abstract

Focus groups are a qualitative research method that involves a facilitated group discussion to elicit the perspectives of participants. They use group dynamics and encourage communication among research participants. Thus, focus groups are particularly useful for brainstorming ideas and to understand the reasons for differing opinions. They also have broad applicability in social and behavioral science, and the resulting findings can be used to inform practice and policy. This chapter provides an overview of focus group methods, including design, participant selection, conduct, and analysis. It also provides a guide to ensure rigor in conducting and reporting focus group studies. Considerations in conducting focus groups in specific populations, including children and culturally and linguistically diverse populations, will also be discussed along with considerations for using online platforms to conduct such studies.

Keywords: Focus Groups, Group Methods, Qualitative Research, Nominal Group Technique, Group Dynamics

Introduction to Focus Groups

Definition and Key Features

Focus groups are facilitated small group discussions that generate information regarding participants' beliefs, ideas, and opinions about a given topic. The groups are "focused" on a set of questions on a specific topic. The aim of focus groups is to generate a range of perspectives and they may be used to understand the reasons for differences or similarities of opinion among the group. They are conducted to facilitate interaction among participants, whereby respondents react to and build on the previous responses of group members. The participants work alongside the researcher to challenge or defend statements, clarify views, and generate other questions to provide further insights on the topic. Focus groups harness participant interaction to stimulate thought and prompt participants to generate ideas, ask questions, exchange experiences and opinions, and comment on those of others. The insights drawn from verbal and non-verbal interpersonal communication generate rich and nuanced understandings of group norms and values (Du Bois, 1983; Pope & Mays, 2019).

History of Focus Groups

Focus group methods originated in the field of sociology in the 1920s (Bogardus, 1926; Basch, 1987). Their early use was within media and communication studies to describe audience perspectives on film and television programs. The work of Merton and Kendal (1946), focused on eliciting participant reactions to wartime propaganda, led to broader recognition for this method as a tool for market research, gauging political opinions, and informing policy formulation. Focus groups are now commonly used as a qualitative research tool for data collection across many fields, including the social sciences, health, education, and political science. For example, focus groups received significant media coverage in the 2008 US presidential elections as a way to inform preferences of undecided voters, identify desirable attributes, and convey these to the public (Kenski et al., 2010).

Use of Focus Groups and Their Application in Social and Behavioral Science

Focus groups can be used as a stand-alone study to generate data where there is little prior knowledge about the phenomenon of interest. Such exploratory focus groups adopt an inductive approach used to generate new hypotheses, research questions, and understandings of the social and behavioral processes driving reasoning and debate. For example, to generate hypotheses about the key drivers of addiction behaviors, focus groups were used for an exploratory study to elicit adolescent and young adult perspectives on gambling (Calado et al., 2014).

Often, focus groups are used as part of a mixed methods design to identify topics or research questions that require further investigation through surveys or interviews. They can also be used to ensure that the language and content of surveys is comprehensible, relevant, and culturally sensitive to the target study population (Pope & Mays, 2019). For example, Detmar et al. (2006) sought to understand children's perspectives on the main constituents of health-related quality of life through focus groups. Social functioning was identified as a key determinant, exceeding both physical and cognitive functioning. This study ultimately informed the design, language, and content of a health-related quality-of-life survey for children.

Focus groups are used widely in health sciences to inform the design, implementation, and evaluation of interventions and programs. In the design of a group-based weight-management intervention, Engström et al. (2016) sought to understand the key motivators for lifestyle change among obese adolescents. Through the use of focus groups, this study informed strategies to overcome the key psychological challenges, including the development of autonomous motivations, a sense of belonging, and empowerment through achievement.

In general, focus groups are flexible and allow for embedding activities, such as prioritization exercises, eliciting reactions to a collective activity, and hypothetical scenarios. In this setting, focus groups can help to elicit the diverse reasons that underpin participant reactions or choices. For example, in a nominal group study to identify and prioritize factors that shape community members' attitudes toward organ donation,

Irving et al. (2012) reported altruistic motives (e.g., "saving lives" and "giving is good") as most influential in decision-making. This subsequently shaped communication campaigns raising awareness of deceased organ donation.

Advantages of Focus Group Methods

Focus group methods are particularly valuable for collectively brainstorming ideas that may not otherwise emerge in individual interviews. Various forms of interpersonal communication examined through focus groups can generate understandings of group norms, cultural values, and the language and concepts used to structure participant experiences, thoughts, and opinions. This method is particularly powerful in understanding diverse perspectives across culturally and linguistically diverse populations. For example, focus group methods were used to examine cultural variations in young people's ways of thinking and planning for their future (Brannen & Nilsen, 2002). Focus groups are also increasingly used to highlight issues for disadvantaged or minority groups. Gould et al. (2013) conducted focus groups to elicit perspectives among Australian Aboriginal women on smoking in pregnancy and understand barriers to smoking cessation. Through this approach, Aboriginal women were empowered to share their narrative and develop recommendations for culturally appropriate interventions.

Limitations of Focus Group Methods

Understanding the limitations of focus groups is important so that these can be addressed in the design, conduct, analysis, interpretation, and reporting of studies. First, the social context of the focus group may impact the opinions expressed. For example, dominant and opinionated participants may silence others, particularly those who may not share the same views. Social desirability bias may lead to undesirable characteristics and behaviors being underreported. However, a skilled moderator can encourage participation of all group members to generate debate and express the underlying reasons for their diverse opinions. Participants may also be reluctant to disclose perspectives of a personal or sensitive nature due to stigma and shame (Mack, 2005). Another challenge is safeguarding participant anonymity and confidentiality, as information is shared among the group. This risk can be mitigated by asking participants to use first names only or an alias. Researchers can also brief participants about the ethical implications of breaching confidentiality, and privacy of group members, and the content discussed (Pope & Mays, 2019).

Designing Focus Groups

Research Question

The research question should be well framed, with a clear focus and scope, as this will inform the question guide, participation selection, group composition, analysis, and interpretation (see Breakwell et al., 2021 for a detailed exposition on this issue). Figure 28.1 describes the various research questions addressed using focus group methods, including practical examples.

Methodological Framework

A range of qualitative methodological frameworks exist that inform the choice of methods (e.g., interview or focus group). In this section, we will provide a brief definition of the three more commonly used methodologies in which focus groups

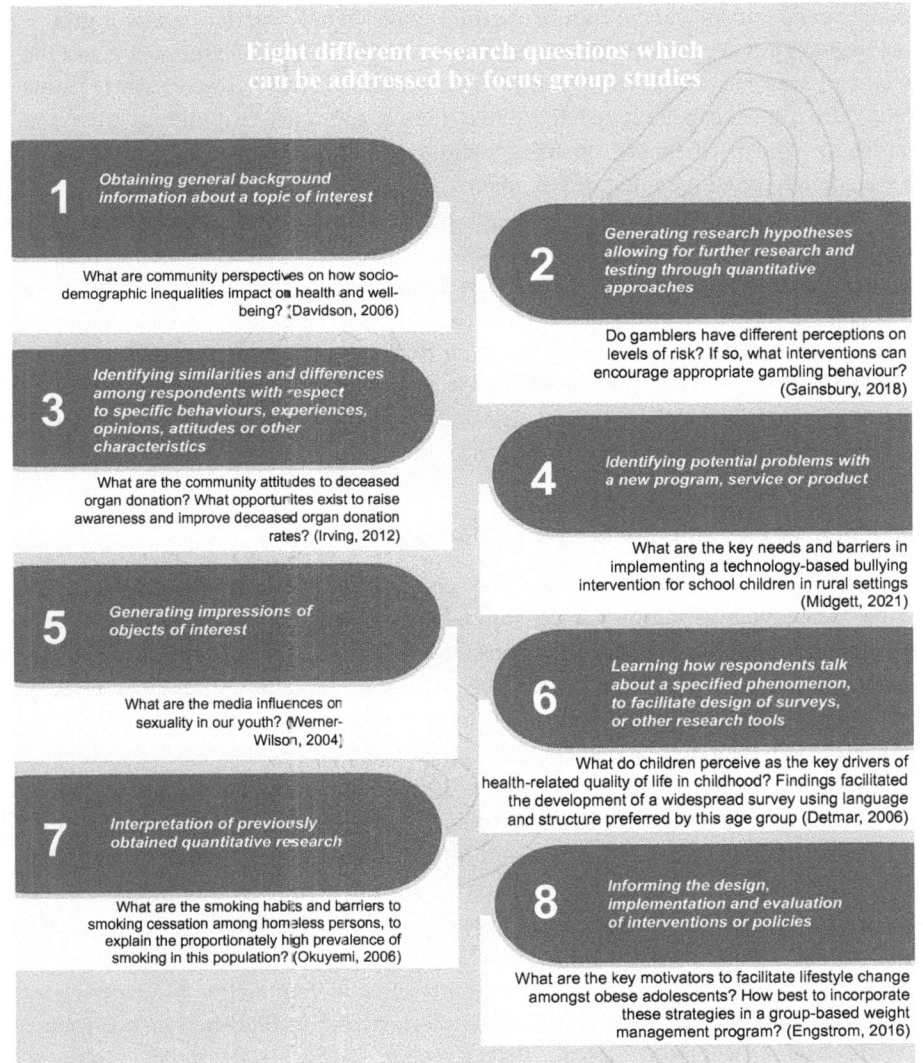

Figure 28.1 *Eight different research questions which can be addressed by focus group studies. Adapted from Bickman and Rog (2009).*

may be used. *Grounded theory* uses systematic and iterative approaches to data collection and analysis to build theory derived directly from the data. Grounded theory is well suited to focus groups, building theory about a phenomenon where there is little prior knowledge. For example, Parker et al. (2012) discuss the benefits of focus group interaction in a grounded theory study to elicit parental perspectives on emotions in the family context.

In contrast, *phenomenology* seeks to understand how individuals make sense of the world, providing insights into the "lived experiences" of participants. Palmer and colleagues (2010) describe the utility of focus group dynamics in eliciting experiential reflection in a phenomenological study describing the lived experiences of caregivers of people with mental illness. Finally, *ethnography* seeks to interpret behaviors and understand the culture of groups with shared experience. Focus groups used in ethnography studies emphasize the collective nature of experience and the social context of accounts (Smithson, 2008). As one example, Jowett and O'Toole (2006) describe the benefits of the ethnographic approach in building trust and familiarity with participants, enabling natural and spontaneous group discussion on the socially sensitive topic of feminism.

Although focus group studies may not adhere to a specific methodology, they largely involve an inductive approach, allowing theories or concepts to emerge from the data to generate hypotheses. This differs from the deductive methods, used more often in quantitative research, that center around testing a predetermined hypothesis. Focus group researchers generally adopt an iterative approach, in which the data collected may be used to inform study design, such as revising the research question, guiding participant selection, or making adjustments to the question guide to clarify meaning and formulate concepts as new insights emerge.

Participant Selection and Group Composition

It is recommended that each focus group be comprised of 6–8 participants. This size is sufficient to generate group discussion while ensuring group manageability and providing opportunities for all participants to voice their opinions (Amir et al., 2021). For the purposes of participant selection, purposive sampling strategy is usually recommended and involves selection of "information rich" participants who have a range of demographic, characteristics, experiences, and backgrounds relevant to the research question (Krueger & Casey, 2015). The intention of this sampling method is to gain diversity of perspectives and more comprehensive understandings of the phenomenon of interest (Schwandt & Core, 2007). For example, one focus group study seeking to understand parental beliefs about the role of emotions in the family unit purposively sampled participants across diverse cultures and socio-economic backgrounds (Parker et al., 2012).

It is recommended that participants share some commonality of experience, locality, or community so rapport may be more readily established to encourage open discussion (Ritchie & Lewis, 2003; Kreuger, 2015). For example, single-sex groups may be appropriate for addressing gender-specific topics, including sexuality, body image, and infertility. Groups of similar age are recommended in focus groups with children and adolescents. In particular, caution should be applied in heterogeneous, cross-cultural focus groups, whereby more dominant cultures risk silencing others – particularly in topics such as sexual habits and gender identity that may be perceived as more sensitive or private by certain cultural groups. Furthermore, hierarchy within a group is also an important consideration, since the perception of superiority of other group members may be intimidating and inhibit participation or induce others to engage in a way that seeks their approval.

On the other hand, there are certain advantages to diversity in group composition. Focus groups composed of participants of varying age, occupation, or life stage can generate a diverse range of perspectives (Smithson, 2008). Familiarity among group members may also inhibit discussion of sensitive topics, or expression of disagreement, through self-censorship and striving to achieve group consensus (Morgan & Scannell, 1998). For example, Smithson (2000) discusses how composition of mixed-sex groups was able to challenge typical male and female discourses in eliciting perspectives on parental roles in the provision of childcare. Roller and Lavrakas (2015) similarly considered heterogeneity in group composition as a catalyst for creating certain group tension, and heightened group dynamics, that can provoke conversations on sensitive topics such as racism and social injustice.

Although there is no "best mix" of focus group participants, group composition requires comprehensive and detailed planning to best nurture group dynamics. For example, to understand the cultural influences of breastfeeding, a relatively homogeneous group with shared culture and experiences will foster group dynamics to generate data directly addressing the research question. On the other hand, understanding community perspectives on the impact of health education on breastfeeding practices would benefit from a heterogeneous group composition. The heightened level of diversity in the data generated from heterogeneous groups can serve to uncover deeper insights into the varying influences within different population groups.

Conducting Focus Groups

Preparation and Setup

It is important to select a location, date, and time that are convenient for participants. Consider the time of day that will work best for the group (e.g., mornings for children and seniors, lunchtime and evenings for corporate workers). Reminders should be sent to participants, providing details about the session, location, and topic of discussion. Focus groups should be held in a relaxed setting, and participants should be comfortable, ideally seated, and undistracted from the task (e.g., phones should be on quiet mode). A quiet room with minimal background noise will ensure clarity of discussion and ease of transcription. Accessibility for participants with mobility issues (e.g., wheelchair access) should also be considered. Furthermore, participants should be seated where they may see each other (e.g., in a circle) to help establish rapport. Participants and the facilitators should have name tags, so that they can be correctly identified by the group. They should be offered refreshments, and reimbursements may be offered to cover travel expenses.

The Role of the Facilitator

The facilitator (or moderator) has a central role in the focus group discussion. Ideally, the facilitator should have experience in conducting focus groups and be skilled in group dynamics, able to manage dominant or silent participants and minimize separate concurrent discussions. The facilitator should also be perceptive to the feelings of group members, able to detect when participants are uncomfortable with any aspect of discussion, and manage this appropriately. S/he needs to employ a sensitive approach, using language that is clear, comprehensible, and culturally appropriate. The facilitator's position should be neutral (not agreeing or endorsing anyone's opinions or experiences), to minimize the researcher's influence on participant responses. In encouraging debate and discussion, the facilitator should probe the inconsistencies within the group, and within participants' own thinking, to understand the underlying reasons for these discrepancies (Kitzinger, 1995).

The facilitator is expected to encourage discussion and interaction among group members by clarifying and redirecting rather than having all responses directed to the facilitator (Sim, 1998). The role and subjectivity of the facilitator are central to the research context and impact the group dynamics and shape the data generated. Therefore, reflexivity is essential to acknowledge and examine the facilitator's own background, agenda, values, and assumptions that may influence the group and the research process (Wilkinson & Kitzinger 1996).

In general, the approach the facilitator employs will largely depend on the research question. An open and less directive approach, allowing the discourse to take direction from the group, may be appropriate when exploring a phenomenon that is new. Conversely, if the research question has a more focused objective, the facilitator should employ more specific and directive questions about the area of interest.

A co-facilitator should work alongside the facilitator and be responsible for note-taking. The notes record the key issues emerging in the group discussions and serve as a record of participant non-verbal interactions, group dynamics, participants' emotional disposition, facial expressions, body language, and contextual detail. The co-facilitator is also responsible for recording the focus group layout (e.g., where participants were seated in the room), managing latecomers, and providing support and reassurance to participants expressing some discomfort or anxiety relating to the discussion.

Structure

The structure of focus groups is largely determined by the research question but should allow for some flexibility to enable related topics to emerge. The duration of focus groups is typically one to two hours. Focus groups usually start with a welcome and introduction to the group, followed by introductory questions that transition to key questions, and end with a summary and final comments. It is important to allow sufficient time for the introductions as a means of establishing rapport, as well as the summary and closing comments, to ensure that all perspectives have been captured. A halfway break with refreshments should be planned, particularly for emotionally charged discussions and for those with difficulty sitting and focusing on discussion for the entire duration (e.g., children and those suffering from disabilities).

Welcome, Introduction, and Ice-Breaker

The facilitator commences the focus group discussion by presenting the main topic for discussion, introducing a set of ground rules, and presenting some important ethical issues. One common ground rule is that only one participant speaks at a time so that all views can be heard and captured in the transcription. The facilitator should convey that there are no right or wrong answers and ask participants to listen respectfully as different views are expressed. The key ethical issues, as detailed on the participant consent form, should be reiterated, reinforcing that participation is voluntary and that withdrawal from the study is possible at any stage. Permission is sought for audio or videorecording, describing how this data will be stored and used to ensure confidentiality. It is also important to emphasize the importance of confidentiality being respected by all participants in the group.

After the "round table" introductions, an ice-breaker can provide an effective strategy to engage participants and promote group interaction. A light-hearted question is recommended, requiring little deliberation (e.g., favorite food, color, or sporting activity), that does not highlight any power or status differences. This sets the scene and gives participants a sense of who they are interacting with while discussing a non-contentious issue (Pope & Mays, 2019).

Question Guide

The focus group question guide is used by the facilitator to ensure all relevant topics are addressed. The question guide introduces the broad areas for discussion and forms a reminder of all the topics that require probing. This guide should serve as a flexible tool and can be modified in response to the discussion and interaction among participants in the group. This allows freedom and variability in focus group discussions, allowing participants to speak on their own terms, and pursue their own priorities (McCracken, 1988).

In the typical focus group, there should be several key questions and prompts. The initial questions are more general, providing more background contextual perspectives. These are followed by more specific questions that focus on the research question. Prompts should be included to encourage participants to speak among each other, such as "Would anyone else like to add anything?" The five different question categories that can be used to design the focus group question guide are summarized in Table 28.1. Here, we provide practical examples for each question category adapted from a focus group study eliciting the beliefs and attitudes to organ donation within ethnic minorities (Ralph et al., 2016).

Table 28.1 *The five different questions that guide focus group discussion*

Introductory questions – open discussion on the main research area
These questions introduce the topic and encourage participants to start thinking about their connection with the topic. Introductory questions might ask participants to describe their experiences of a certain event or how they use a product or service. These questions provide the first clues about participant views.

"What sorts of things have you heard about transplantation?"
"What is the first thing that comes to your mind when I say 'organ donation'?"

Transition questions – moving between key topics
These questions direct the conversation into key areas that directly address the research question. Transition questions ask participants to go into more depth than the introductory questions – moving toward the key questions. These questions could ask participants to provide more detail of a certain aspect of their experience or the benefits and burdens of a particular decision.

"How might your understanding of organ allocation influence your views about organ donation?"

Key questions – central to the research topic
Typically, there are four to six key questions. The responses to these questions often require the greatest attention in the analysis. The facilitator should reserve sufficient time to allow for full discussion of these key questions; they may require 10–20 minutes each. It is in these questions that the facilitator will seek to further probe and clarify points.

"What role do you think family members have in decisions about organ donation?"
"What would influence your decision for or against organ donation and why?"

Ending questions – closure to the discussion
These questions allow an opportunity for participant reflection on prior comments or questions. This three-pronged approach to ending questions is as follows:

- Firstly, it is important to determine participants' final position on critical areas of concern. Participants can be asked to reflect on the discussion and then identify which aspects they deem most important or requiring action.

  "Reflecting on our discussion, what do you think are the key drivers or barriers to registering for deceased organ donation?"

- The facilitator should thereafter provide a short summary of the discussion and allow participants to comment about the adequacy of the summary.

  "From this summary, which aspects do you think are most important?"

- Finally, after providing an overview of the study, highlighting the key purpose of the work, the facilitator asks participants if there is anything missing or overlooked.

  "Is there anything else you think is important to add or that was missing from the summary?"

Source: adapted from Krueger and Casey (2015).

Recording and Transcription

Focus group discussions are typically captured using audio or video recordings. It is important to test recording equipment beforehand and have more than one device recording the group discussion. Video recordings should capture all participants in the group with sufficient clarity to observe non-verbal behaviors. Further, the recordings should link participant voices with their names to facilitate transcription and assist in analysis.

Transcription of the audio recordings facilitates further analysis and establishes a permanent record of the group discussion that can be shared with other interested parties (Stewart et al., 2007). Transcriptions are not always complete; there may be unexpected interruptions of speech, half-finished thoughts, odd phrases, gaps, and grammatical errors. Caution should be applied in editing the transcript, since the facilitator's memory may err, or be shaped by the content of the discourse later in the interview. Further, it is important that the transcript reflects the true flow of conversation and the character of the respondents' comments. Observational data through note-taking and/or video recording supplements the transcript and captures the non-verbal behavior of participants.

Embedding Activities

Activities, such as listing, ranking, or eliciting reactions to hypothetical scenarios or data, can be embedded into focus group design as a different approach to elicit opinions and encourage discussion. Embedded activities can be particularly beneficial for reflective participants who are less comfortable with immediate verbal responses (Cowan & Oliver, 2013). These approaches are inclusive and empowering for all participants and help avoid the discussion being dominated by outspoken participants (Carter et al., 2022). Activities can be used at various stages of the focus group (e.g., a warmup activity, transitioning to another area of interest, or to summarize the group discussion) and can generate ideas relating to the topic in question, promoting sharing, discussion, and prioritization. In the following, we provide an overview of the nominal group technique – a consensus research method that can be embedded into focus group design and is used widely for priority-setting in healthcare research.

Nominal Group Technique

The nominal group technique involves a structured group discussion used to achieve consensus among participants. The process involves four phases. First is the silent generation of ideas, whereby the facilitator presents the question to the group and asks participants to write down their responses or ideas individually and silently. This is followed by a round-robin recording of ideas that involves participants contributing at least one idea to the group. This phase proceeds until all participants have stated their ideas and no new ideas are generated. The subsequent group discussion on each of the ideas encourages participants to clarify their understanding and opinions of the ideas listed. Finally, in the voting phase, participants individually prioritize the list of ideas based on what they deem most important. Participants may be asked to select between five and ten important ideas and rank them in order of their importance.

Within social and behavioral science research, applications of the nominal group technique include guideline development, research priority-setting, establishing core outcomes, and identifying healthcare service and education needs (Carter et al., 2022). As an example of identifying health service and education needs, Irving et al. (2012) conducted 13 nominal groups to identify and prioritize factors that influence community attitudes toward organ donors. The first stage involved focus group discussion about participants' thoughts and attitudes toward organ donation. Thereafter, participants were asked to identify factors that would influence their decision to register as an organ donor and nominate their top five factors. After generating a comprehensive list of all the factors discussed by the group, the list was supplemented with factors identified from the literature. Participants then individually ranked all the factors in order of their importance. On completion of individual scoring, participants discussed their priorities with the group to better understand the reasons behind these choices. Altruism was the greatest motivator for organ donation. To increase community registration for organ donation, participants recommended positive media messages and recipient stories describing the benefits of organ donation, which could be targeted to specific age, religious, and cultural groups.

Focus Groups in Specific Populations

Focus Groups with Children

Focus groups with children and adolescents can offer a rich, interactive, and developmentally appropriate approach to collect data. For example, they have been used to understand adolescent experiences of alcohol use (Demant & Jarvinen, 2006), examine their transition to adulthood (Brannen & Nilsen, 2002), explore embarrassment as one of the often ignored emotions of young people (vanTeijlingen et al., 2007), and to help design health programs and instruments to assess quality of care (Kennedy et al., 2001).

Focus group studies with children require certain methodological considerations. Group composition should be homogeneous respective to age-group. It is generally accepted that focus groups are unsuitable for children under six years, due to limited social and language skills. The group size should be limited to four to six participants when working with younger children (six to ten years), while groups of eight are possible with older children (Gibson, 2007). The question guide should include short, concrete, specific questions in developmentally appropriate language.

An introductory activity, such as making and wearing participants' own name tags or drawing pictures, can serve as an ice-breaker to help children feel comfortable within the group (Adler et al., 2019). Each participant, including the facilitator, should have an opportunity to share some information about themselves with the group (e.g., age and primary interests). Activities (e.g., drawing, role-playing, puzzles, or short video clips) can also be embedded throughout the discussion to promote continued interest and engagement. Focus groups should be shorter in duration with young children to ensure the group remains attentive and focused on the study agenda. The facilitator should also have appropriate training and techniques to engage young participants, foster a safe peer environment, facilitate balanced discussions, and interact with the children on an equal footing.

Tatangelo and Ricciardelli (2017) sought to understand children's perceptions of peer and media influences on body image. This focus group study convened relatively homogeneous groups of same-gendered participants aged eight to ten years. Focus groups comprised of four participants and were 45 minutes in duration. The facilitator was selected for her prior experience working with children of this age group. The question guide referenced popular celebrities or sporting figures. This approach encouraged ongoing engagement and group dynamics, providing rich understandings of the operation of social comparisons and their influence on body image in children.

Culturally and Linguistically Diverse Groups

The involvement of culturally and linguistically diverse populations through focus groups is a powerful approach to understand diverse perspectives and develop culturally appropriate interventions (Kitzinger, 1995). Unique considerations are required in the design and conduct of focus groups in these populations. Firstly, it is important to translate all participant-related material (e.g., recruitment, consent, and question guide) and consult cultural representatives in the development of participant information, consent forms, and question guides to ensure the content is comprehensible, relevant, and culturally sensitive.

Focus groups should be composed of participants with shared cultural backgrounds, allowing the similarities to promote rapport among the group. Ideally, the facilitator should be fluent in the native language and familiar with cultural meanings and specific nuances (e.g., emotional tone, feelings, and reflexivity). In some cultures, for example, expression of dissent or overt criticism of authority is not deemed acceptable in public. Therefore, tailoring the approach (e.g., an embedded activity using a hypothetical scenario that challenges the perceived dominant viewpoint) is required to encourage culturally acceptable questioning and challenging to generate the desired data (Smithson, 2008). Transcription of the audio recordings should be performed in the native language and thereafter professionally translated to facilitate analysis.

As an example, Balasuriya and colleagues (2021) sought to identify barriers and motivators to COVID-19 vaccine acceptance among Black and Latinx communities in the United States. There were eight culturally homogeneous focus groups in total.

Representatives from these communities were involved in the adaptation of the question guide and participant recruitment materials. The four groups conducted in Spanish, with a native-speaker facilitator, were transcribed and then professionally translated into English. Emerging from this study was the concept of mistrust driven by the beliefs of ongoing pervasive mistreatment of these communities within healthcare. Priorities for COVID-19 vaccination acceptance and equitable vaccination uptake included provision of health information through trusted messengers within communities, open choice of vaccination, social support, and addressing structural barriers.

Online Focus Groups

Particularly since the COVID-19 pandemic, there has been widespread uptake of videoconferencing and a notable increase in conducting focus groups using online platforms. Online focus groups have some advantages, including the ability to access hard-to-reach populations (e.g., geographically remote) or those with severe disabilities (e.g., physical disability or hearing impairment) and require fewer resources (e.g., no venue or travel costs). For example, Holton et al. (2019) discuss the advantages of the online platform for focus group discussion in women with cystic fibrosis. In addition to including a geographically diverse group of women, the online mode eliminated the risk of cross-infection for at-risk group members and overcame a barrier to participation.

The heightened sense of anonymity in online focus groups creates a safe environment to discuss sensitive topics and express disagreement more freely (Nguyen & Alexander, 1996; Stewart & Williams, 2005). Woodyatt et al. (2016) provides an example of the benefit of anonymity offered by the online environment in a study comparing the quality and depth of data generated between online and in-person focus groups. The study recruited gay and bisexual men and compared the data from online and in-person group discussions on the topic of intimate partner violence. The anonymity of online groups was thought to facilitate in-depth discussion on firsthand experiences of intimate partner violence either as a victim or as a perpetrator. This theme did not emerge during in-person focus group analysis.

The web-based nature of this research allows for easier online recruitment, such as advertising through social media, websites, and emails. Moore et al. (2015) discuss the utility of promoting online focus groups on social networking sites, websites, or forums relevant to the target sampling population. However, this approach has the potential to exclude populations of socio-economic disadvantage, advancing age, and geographic remoteness through lack of either internet, technology, or digital literacy (Townsend et al., 2013). Multiple recruitment strategies, using online and offline approaches and enabling participation via phone, ensures that digitally excluded people have the opportunity to participate.

The heightened risk of non-attendance and technical difficulties with online groups can be minimized by contacting participants on several occasions prior to the group discussion. Participants should receive step-by-step instructions on accessing the videoconferencing platform. It is also preferable that participants test the platform prior to the group discussion. In addition, smaller groups are generally recommended (e.g., four to six participants per group) to establish rapport, facilitate discussion, and enable manageability of the group (Silverman & Patterson, 2021).

To address the issue of confidentiality with online focus groups, the videoconferencing platform should be hosted by a secure provider. The meeting room should be password protected, and participants should be identified by either their first name only or an alias. The consent form and dialogue during the introduction to the focus group should detail how the recording and the data generated will be stored and used securely to ensure confidentiality.

Given that some non-verbal cues (e.g., eye contact, turning toward or pointing to a participant) are not readily available to the facilitator in the online environment, participants may be called on for responses more often than in face-to-face settings. The facilitator must be more proactive and employ prompts to encourage engagement and probing questions for clarification. Group exercises are often utilized to encourage group interaction and discussion. For example, Moore et al. (2015) asked participants to share their motivations for taking part in the study. Through shared interest in the study topic, participants were encouraged to converse with each other directly. Other exercises include using photos, short film-clips, the chat box, or whiteboard to stimulate engagement and discussion. The content of the chat box or whiteboard can also be saved and incorporated alongside the audio recording into the data analysis (Silverman & Patterson, 2021).

Analyzing and Interpreting Data

As with other forms of qualitative data, analysis of focus groups should capture the breadth and depth of the data. Analysis should generate comprehensive, trustworthy, compelling, and original insights that align with the topic and scope of the research question. This is performed concurrently with data collection, adopting an inductive approach that allows the theories or concepts emerging from the data to generate hypotheses. Data analysis is a systematic, interpretive, and iterative process that involves reading the data, coding, and comparing codes throughout the data set. On completion of initial coding, the investigators group concepts into themes and identify patterns and relationships among themes. This iterative process aims to capture all concepts related to the phenomenon being investigated. The transition from descriptive to analytical processes ultimately aims to provide explanations for the patterns identified in the data.

Approaches to Analysis

There are different approaches to the analysis and interpretation of focus group data, and this may depend on the methodology (e.g., grounded theory, phenomenology, ethnography) and the research question. Three distinctive perspectives are relevant to qualitative analysis of focus group data. Social constructivism theorists argue that much of reality, and the meaning and categories that frame everyday life, is a social creation. Analysis that reflects this theory tends to view the group as a unit of analysis and emphasizes the collective and collaborative approach to construct shared meaning and opinions about the research question. For example, Yelden et al. (2017) used focus groups to understand perspectives of decision-makers in healthcare on withdrawal of care for minimally conscious patients. Since these real-life decisions tend to involve a collaborative approach of a multidisciplinary team, the analysis emphasized group interactions and influences shaping the opinions of the group.

The phenomenological approach, in contrast, recognizes the distinctions of individual opinion and seeks to understand differences of opinion by thoroughly exploring individual thoughts and feelings. For example, Palmer and colleagues (2010) utilized the social interaction and dynamics of focus groups to understand the lived experiences of caregivers of people with mental illness. The analytical approach involved acknowledging the wider socio-cultural factors of the group setting while eliciting individual experiential reflection.

Finally, interpretivism accepts perspectives of social constructivism and phenomenological analysts but focuses on human experiences and social contexts, such as individual actions, body language, and facial expressions; this approach is skeptical about taking focus group respondents' words at face value (Krueger & Casey, 2015; Stewart et al., 2007). Dodson and Schmalzbauer (2005) utilized an interpretive analytical approach to unearth withheld information in social research into the lives of marginalized low-income people. Focus groups with community members were held to co-analyze existing focus group data and took the following line of enquiry: "Are we hearing what is really going on in these people's lives? What else do you think is going on, that is not represented here?" This analytical approach enabled the construction of meaning behind silence and omissions, developing a compelling narrative of low-income America.

Regardless of the analytical orientation of the researchers, the approach to analysis must be shaped by the research question and purpose. There are, however, unique considerations and challenges to the analysis of focus group data. Analysis should recognize the three layers of data generated by focus groups: the individual, the group, and the group interaction. Differentiating individual participants' opinions and collective views of the group poses a great challenge. Analysis requires attention to the group dynamics, the type and range of speech, and the group influences on the content of discussion. Further, descriptions of the contextual nature and non-verbal behaviors (e.g., dominant personalities, humor, sarcastic tone, and gestures) of the focus group can have a role in analysis and interpretation of focus group data. For example, in a focus group study of public opinion on paying living kidney donors in Australia, Tong et al. (2015) illustrate the use of humor to highlight the perils of paying donors. Kitzinger and Farquhar (1999) similarly discuss the analytical potential of "sensitive moments" such as participants revealing experiences that are not freely disclosed in the public setting and may be indicated by hesitation, awkwardness, reactions of surprise, or defensiveness.

Analyzing Group Interaction

In the context of focus group analysis, internal inconsistency refers to changes in individual opinions that have been influenced by acquired understandings from group discussion and knowledge of group dynamics. This poses a certain quandary during the analysis, as the same individual has expressed contradictory opinions. Sim (1998) also warns that focus groups have the potential to overemphasize consensus. It is argued that consensus is shaped by group interaction rather than a reflection of participant opinions. As a result, analysis should focus on the content and process of such discussions instead of relying on the summary of the outcome reached.

Table 28.2 includes several analytical questions, guiding the analysis and interpretation of group interactions, helping to uncover meaning at a group level.

Coding

Codes are tags or labels used to assign units of meaning to the descriptive or inferential information compiled during a study. Codes are usually attached to segments of text of varying size and can include words, phrases, sentences, or whole paragraphs as well as non-verbal communication or parts of other media such as video/pictures (Miles & Huberman, 1994). This process is used in focus groups and more broadly in qualitative studies that use other methods of data collection. It is recommended that two or more analysts who have read and are familiar with the transcripts be involved in the coding. This approach, referred to as

Table 28.2 *Analyzing group interaction*

Group component	Aspect of interaction for analysis
What?	What topics/opinions produced consensus?
	What statements seemed to evoke conflict?
	What were the contradictions in the discussion?
	What common experiences were expressed?
	Did the collective interaction generate new insights or precipitate an exchange of information among participants?
Who?	Whose interests were being represented in the group?
	Were alliances formed among group members?
	Was a particular member or viewpoint silenced?
How?	How closely did the group adhere to the issues presented for discussion?
	How did group members respond to the ideas of others?
	How did the group resolve disagreements?
	How were emotions handled?
	How were non-verbal signs and behaviors used to contribute to the discussion?

Source: adapted from Stevens et al. (1996).

investigator triangulation, aims to enhance the authenticity of the findings through ensuring the coding and analytical framework capture all primary data.

The first step involves reading the transcript to identify concepts, themes, and ideas that are relevant to the research question. Coding is an iterative process that starts by highlighting relevant segments of words and classifying relevant words (e.g., setting and context, perspectives, meaning, relationship, and social structure). Codes are grouped into initial clusters of similar ideas or themes that are checked against the transcript to ensure they explain and capture participant perspectives. Preliminary codes and themes are successively refined by raising questions, seeking explanations, and recognizing relationships.

This process may warrant transcripts to be read multiple times as categories of topics evolve and as the analyst gains greater insight into the content of the group discussion. The impact of group dynamics can be recognized during the coding process by providing unique coding for certain types of narratives, such as jokes, anecdotes, and different types of interaction to indicate "questions," "challenges," "deferring to the opinion of others," "censorship," and "changes of mind" (Kitzinger, 1995).

Summary of Different Analytical Approaches to Focus Group Data

There are several analytical approaches to focus group data, the selection of which should be shaped by the research question and methodology. Below, we discuss four analytical techniques used in focus group data analysis: thematic analysis, grounded theory analysis, content analysis, and conversation analysis.

(a) *Thematic analysis* is a commonly used flexible form of qualitative analysis and involves the development of themes and subthemes from the data. A theme is a major thread, idea, or pattern that recurs throughout the data. Thematic analysis is typically inductive, rather than deductive, whereby the themes are generated from the data. This iterative process involves generating meaning for themes, identifying relationship between themes, and providing examples in the data (Thomas & Harden, 2008).

Smit et al. (2015) used thematic analysis to understand the emotional and behavioral impact of personalized genetic risk information on members of the public. This study built on existing theory, that suggests highly personalized genetic risk information may be a more powerful motivator of behavioral change than standard preventative approaches (McBride et al., 2010). Four focus groups were convened and presented with a hypothetical scenario implying an individual's genetic risk of melanoma. A coding framework was developed initially, and an iterative process was employed to identify additional themes and subthemes. These themes were analyzed to identify variations and patterns, providing links from the data. This study describes the perceived benefits of knowledge and of understanding genetic risk. However, the opportunity for preventative behaviors is offset by anxiety and concerns for occupational and insurance discrimination.

(b) *Grounded theory* analysis is an inductive process that generates innovative and substantive theoretical frameworks that emerge from the data (Glaser & Strauss, 1967). Distinct from thematic analysis, grounded theory involves a cyclical and iterative process of analysis that informs subsequent sampling, further data collection, and testing of emerging theories. Thus, theoretical sampling is an important component of grounded theory – allowing the researcher to deliberately select participants to test emerging analytical theories. Grounded theory analysis is characterized by three stages. First, open coding generates preliminary concepts from the data. Next, axial coding involves reviewing, developing, linking, and grouping concepts. Finally, selective coding involves organizing and formalizing relationships to construct conceptual links and a theoretical framework (Strauss & Corbin, 1998). Constant comparison analysis is used to identify similarities and differences within the data and across sources.

In a study addressing early breastfeeding cessation, Hunt and Thomson (2017) sought to elicit reasons underpinning underutilized support services for breastfeeding women. Grounded theory methodology guided the analytical approach to build theory on which there was little prior knowledge. Data analysis was concurrent with data collection, adopting an inductive approach. Barriers to accessing these services centered around women's perceptions of pressure and judgement relating to their feeding decisions. This was associated with women's perceptions of a dichotomous landscape to infant feeding as "one way or no way" and "success or failure."

© *Content analysis* involves three distinct approaches that are all used to interpret the content of qualitative data (Morgan, 1997). First, conventional analysis is an inductive approach describing the phenomenon through coding and identification of categories within the data. Directed content analysis employs a deductive approach to identify existing theories and extends or validates them within the data using predetermined coding strategies. Finally, summative content analysis involves a more quantitative approach – counting and comparing words and content before engaging in more interpretive analysis (Hsieh & Shannon, 2005).

Persson and colleagues (2021) used content analysis to describe experiences of pain among school-aged children. Content analysis was selected to describe similarities and differences in a textual format. Statements corresponding to the research question were extracted and then condensed while retaining their core meaning. These codes were further categorized by comparing the data and identifying conceptual similarities. As a result, pain was perceived as a unique experience for each child, requiring a personalized approach to distinguish between physical and emotional pain.

(d) *Conversation analysis* examines features of language to understand its role in constructing the social world (Kuper et al., 2008). Applied to focus groups, conversation analysis examines the conversational sequences, organization of turn-taking, and choice of words, as well as identifying asymmetry in social interaction between all group members. This allows for analysis of an array of interactions and emotions (e.g., joking, frowning, sarcasm, agreeing, and criticizing) and a focus on the participants' understanding of this social interaction (Onwuegbuzie et al., 2009).

Grønkjær et al. (2011) used conversation analysis to describe the cultural and contextual influences of alcohol use among a Danish sample. Five focus groups were convened, composed of adults within certain age groups. Conversation analysis was used to analyze a series of interactional events that took place during focus group data collection. This approach was chosen to understand how normality relating to alcohol consumption is constructed and negotiated through conversation, shared anecdotes, and emotions. This indicated a mutual understanding of the perceived legitimacy and social acceptance of alcohol-related behavior in various contexts.

Ensuring the Trustworthiness of Focus Group Studies

Focus group research should generate comprehensive and trustworthy insights. The following constructs proposed by Lincoln and Guba (1985) can guide the appraisal of qualitative research: *credibility* (can the findings be trusted?), *dependability* (is the process logical and auditable?), *transferability* (are the findings relevant to other contexts and settings?), and *confirmability* (are the findings and interpretations linked to the data?). Figure 28.2 provides a guide for assessing qualitative research according to these four constructs.

Reporting of Focus Group Studies

Several guidelines are available for reporting and appraising qualitative research. The Consolidated Criteria for Reporting Qualitative Research (COREQ; Tong et al., 2007) is one popular reporting guideline for focus groups studies. The COREQ checklist was developed to promote complete and transparent reporting on aspects of interview and focus group studies. This framework allows readers to better understand the design, conduct, analysis, and findings of published qualitative studies, through inclusion of key details such as the research team involved in each stage of the study, the study context, methods, findings, data analysis, and interpretations.

Conclusion

Focus group studies, conducted rigorously and systematically, can generate meaningful insights exploring opinions and how they are shaped by interpersonal interaction. This method of data collection is unique in that understandings from social interaction among participants, both verbal and non-verbal, form the cornerstone of analysis and interpretation. Focus groups should be conceptualized and designed to nurture group dynamics and optimize social interaction. This requires a carefully designed research question, strategies toward participant selection and group composition, and a skilled facilitator. There are various benefits to social

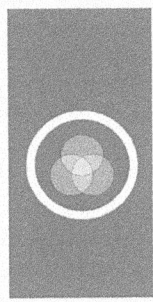

Figure 28.2 *The four constructs: strategies to ensure trustworthiness in focus group research.*

interaction and group dynamics that encourage and empower participants to generate and explore their own questions and develop their own agendas, and that inspire participant communication in various forms. Focus groups generate rich understandings of group norms, cultural values, and the operation of social processes in articulation of knowledge, thoughts, and opinions. Thus, focus groups are increasingly utilized in social and behavioral science with a valued role in informing practice and policy.

References

Adler, K., Salantera, S., & Zumstein-Shaha, M. (2019). Focus group interviews in child, youth, and parent research: An integrative literature review. *International Journal of Qualitative Methods*, *18*, 1–15. https://doi.org/10.1177/1609406919887274

Amir, N., McCarthy, H. J., & Tong, A. (2021). Qualitative research in nephrology: An introduction to methods and critical appraisal. *Kidney360*, *2*(4), 737–741. https://doi.org/10.34067/KID.0006302020

Balasuriya, L., Santilli, A., Morone, J., Ainooson, J., Roy, B., Njoku, A., et al. (2021). COVID-19 vaccine acceptance and access among Black and Latinx communities. *JAMA Network Open*, *4*(10), e2128575. https://doi.org/10.1001/jamanetworkopen.2021.28575

Basch, C. E. (1987). Focus group interview: An underutilized research technique for improving theory and practice in health education. *Health Education & Behavior*, *14*(4), 411–448. https://doi.org/10.1177/109019818701400404

Bickman, L., & Rog, D. J. (2009). *The SAGE Handbook of Applied Social Research Methods*, 2nd ed. SAGE Publications.

Bogardus, E. (1926). The group interview. *Journal of Applied Sociology*, *10*(4), 372–382.

Brannen, J., & Nilsen, A. (2002). Young people's time perspectives: From youth to adulthood. *Sociology*, *36*, 513–537. https://doi.org/doi:10.1177/0038038502036003002

Breakwell, G. M., Wright, D. B., & Barnett, J. (2020). Research questions, design, strategy and choice of methods. In Breakwell, Wright, & Barnett (eds.), *Research Methods in Psychology* (pp. 1-30). SAGE Publications.

Calado, F., Alexandre, J., & Griffiths, M. D. (2014). Mom, Dad it's only a Game! Perceived gambling and gaming behaviors among adolescents and young adults: An exploratory study. *International Journal of Mental Health and Addiction*, *12*(6), 772–794. https://doi.org/10.1007/s11469-014-9509-y

Carter, S. A., Tong, A., Craig, J., Teixeira-Pinto, A., & Manera, K. (2022). Consensus methods for health research in a global setting. In P. Liamputtong (ed.), *Handbook of Social Sciences and Global Public Health* (pp. 1–26). Springer.

Cowan, K., & Oliver, S. (2013). *James Lind Alliance Guidebook*, 5th ed. James Lind Alliance.

Davidson, R., Kitzinger, J., & Hunt, K. (2006). The wealthy get healthy, the poor get poorly? Lay perceptions of health inequalities. *Social Science & Medicine*, *62*(9), 2171–2182. https://doi.org/10.1016/j.socscimed.2005.10.010

Demant, J., & Jarvinen, M. (2006). Constructing maturity through alcohol experience – focus group interviews with teenagers. *Addiction Research & Theory*, *14*, 589–602. https://doi.org/10.1080/16066350600691683

Detmar, S. B., Bruil, J., Ravens-Sieberer, U., Gosch, A., Bisegger, C., & European KIDSCREEN Group. (2006). The use of focus groups in the development of the

KIDSCREEN ERQL questionnaire. *Quality of Life Research, 15*(8), 1345–1353. https://doi.org/10.1007/s11136-006-0022-z

Dodson, L., & Schmalzbauer, L. (2005). Poor mothers and habits of hiding: Participatory methods in poverty research. *Journal of Marriage and Family, 67*(4), 949–959. https://doi.org/10.1111/j.1741-3737.2005.00186.x

Du Bois, B. (1983). Passionate scholarship: Notes on values, knowing and method in feminist social science. In G. Bowles & R. D. Klein (eds.), *Theories of Women's Studies* (pp. 105–116). Routledge & Kegan Paul.

Engström, A., Abildsnes, E., & Mildestvedt, T. (2016). "It's not like a fat camp" – a focus group study of adolescents' experiences on group-based obesity treatment. *International Journal of Qualitative Studies on Health and Well-Being, 11*. https://doi.org/10.3402/qhw.v11.32744

Gainsbury, S. M., Abarbanel, B. L. L., Philander, K. S., & Butler, J. V. (2018). Strategies to customize responsible gambling messages: A review and focus group study. *BMC Public Health, 18*(1). https://doi.org/10.1186/s12889-018-6281-0

Gibson, F. (2007). Conducting focus groups with children and young people: Strategies for success. *Journal of Research in Nursing, 12*(5), 473–483. https://doi.org/10.1177/17449871079791

Glaser, B., & Strauss, A. (1967). *The Discovery of Grounded Theory: Strategies for Qualitative Research*. Aldine.

Gould, G. S., Munn, J., Avuri, S., Hoff, S., Cadet-James, Y., McEwen, A., & Clough, A. R. (2013). "Nobody smokes in the house if there's a new baby in it": Aboriginal perspectives on tobacco smoking in pregnancy and in the household in regional NSW Australia. *Women and Birth : Journal of the Australian College of Midwives, 26*(4), 246–253. https://doi.org/10.1016/j.wombi.2013.08.006

Grønkjær, M., Curtis, T., de Crespigny, C., & Delmar, C. (2011). Analysing group interaction in focus group research: Impact on content and the role of the moderator. *Qualitative Studies, 2*(1), 16–30.

Holton, S., Fisher, J., Button, B., Williams, E., & Wilson, J. (2019). Childbearing concerns, information needs and preferences of women with cystic fibrosis: An online discussion group. *Sexual & Reproductive Healthcare, 19*, 31–35. https://doi.org/10.1016/j.srhc.2018.11.004

Hsieh, H. F., & Shannon, S. E. (2005). Three approaches to qualitative content analysis. *Qualitative Health Research, 15*(9), 1277–1288. https://doi.org/10.1177/1049732305276687

Hunt, L., & Thomson, G. (2017). Pressure and judgement within a dichotomous landscape of infant feeding: A grounded theory study to explore why breastfeeding women do not access peer support provision. *Maternal and Child Nutrition, 13*(2).

Irving, M. J., Tong, A., Jan, S., Cass, A., Chadban, S., Allen, R. D., et al. (2012). Community attitudes to deceased organ donation: A focus group study. *Transplantation, 93*(10), 1064–1069. https://doi.org/10.1097/TP.0b013e31824db997

Jowett, M., & O'Toole, G. (2006). Focusing researchers' minds: Contrasting experiences of using focus groups in feminist qualitative research. *Qualitative Research, 6*(4), 453–472.

Kennedy, C., Kools, S., & Krueger, R. (2001). Methodological considerations in children's focus groups. *Nursing Research, 50*(3), 184–187. https://doi.org/10.1097/00006199-200105000-00010

Kenski, K., Hardy, B. W., & Jamieson, K. H. (2010). *The Obama Victory: How Media, Money, and Message Shaped the 2008 Election*. Oxford University Press.

Kitzinger, J. (1995). Qualitative research: Introducing focus groups. *BMJ, 311*(7000), 299–302. https://doi.org/10.1136/bmj.311.7000.299

Kitzinger, J., & Farquhar, C. (1999). The analytical potential of 'sensitive moments' in focus group discussions. In R. S. Barbour & J. Kitzinger (eds.), *Developing Focus Group Research: Politics, Theory and Practice*, 156–172. SAGE Publications.

Krueger, R. A., & Casey, M. A. (2015). *Focus Groups: A Practical Guide for Applied Research*, 5th ed. SAGE Publications.

Kuper, A., Lingard, L., & Levinson, W. (2008). Critically appraising qualitative research. *BMJ, 337*(7671). https://doi.org/10.1136/bmj.a1035

Lincoln, Y. S., & Guba, E. G. (1985). *Naturalistic Inquiry*, 6th ed. SAGE Publications.

Mack, N. (2005). *Qualitative Research Methods: A Data Collector's Field Guide*. Family Health International.

McBride, C. M., Koehly, L. M., Sanderson, S. C., & Kaphingst, K. A. (2010). The behavioral response to personalized genetic information: Will genetic risk profiles motivate individuals and families to choose more healthful behaviors? *Annual Review of Public Health, 31*, 89–103.

McCracken, G. D. (1988). *The Long Interview*. SAGE Publications.

Merton, R. K., & Kendall, P. L. (1946). The focused interview. *American Journal of Sociology, 51*, 541–557.

Midgett, A., Doumas, D. M., Myers, V. H., Moody, S., & Doud, A. (2021). Technology-based bullying intervention for rural schools: Perspectives on needs, challenges, and design. *Rural Mental Health, 45*(1), 14–30. https://doi.org/10.1037/rmh0000151

Miles, M. B., & Huberman, A. M. (1994). *Qualitative Data Analysis: An Expanded Sourcebook*, 2nd ed. SAGE Publications.

Morgan, D. L. (1997). *Focus Groups as Qualitative Research*, 2nd ed. SAGE Publications.

Morgan, D. L., & Scannell, A. U. (1998). *Planning Focus Groups*, 1st ed. SAGE Publications.

Moore, T., McKee, K., & McLoughlin, P. (2015). Online focus groups and qualitative research in the social sciences: Their merits and limitations in a study of housing and youth. *People, Place and Policy, 9*(1), 17–28. https://doi.org/10.3351/ppp.0009.0001.0002

Nguyen, D. T., & Alexander, J. (1996). The coming of cyberspace time and the end of the polity. In R. Shields (ed.), *Cultures of Internet: Virtual Spaces, Real Histories, Living Bodies* (pp. 99–124). SAGE Publications.

Okuyemi, K. S., Caldwell, A. R., Thomas, J. L., Born, W., Richter, K. P., Nollen, N., et al. (2006). Homelessness and smoking cessation: Insights from focus groups. *Nicotine & Tobacco Research, 8*(2), 287–296. https://doi.org/10.1080/14622200500494971

Onwuegbuzie, A. J., Dickinson, W. B., Leech, N. L., & Zoran, A. G. (2009). A qualitative framework for collecting and analyzing data in focus group research. *International Journal of Qualitative Methods, 8*(3), 1–21.

Palmer, M., Larkin, M., de Visser, R., & Fadden, G. (2010). Developing an interpretative phenomenological approach to focus group data. *Qualitative Research in Psychology. 7*, 99–121. https://doi.org/10.1080/14780880802513194

Parker, A. E., Halberstadt, A. G., Dunsmore, J. C., Townley, G., Bryant, A., Thompson, J. A., & Beale, K. S. (2012). "Emotions are a window into one's heart": A qualitative analysis of parental beliefs about children's emotions across three ethnic groups. *Monographs of the Society for Research in Child Development, 77*(3), 1–144.

Persson, S., Warghoff, A., Einberg, E.-L., & Garmy, P. (2021). Schoolchildren's experience of pain – a focus group interview study. *Acta Paediatrica*, *110*(3), 909–913.

Pope, C., & Mays, N. (2019). *Qualitative Research in Health Care*, 4th ed. Wiley-Blackwell.

Ralph, A. F., Alyami, A., Allen, R. D., Howard, K., Craig, J. C., Chadban, S. J., et al. (2016). Attitudes and beliefs about deceased organ donation in the Arabic-speaking community in Australia: A focus group study. *BMJ Open*, *6*(1), e010138. https://doi.org/10.1136/bmjopen-2015-010138

Ritchie, J., & Lewis, J. (2003). *Qualitative Research Practice: A Guide for Social Science Students and Researchers*. SAGE Publications.

Roller, M. R., & Lavrakas, P. J. (2015). *Applied Qualitative Research Design: A Total Quality Framework Approach*. Guilford Press.

Strauss, A., & Corbin, J. (1998). *Basics of Qualitative Research*. SAGE Publications.

Schwandt, T. A., & Core, S. R. M. (2007). *The SAGE Dictionary of Qualitative Inquiry*, 3rd ed. SAGE Publications.

Silverman, R. M., & Patterson, K. L. (2021). Online qualitative interviewing and focus groups. In R. M. Silverman & K. L. Patterson (eds.), *Qualitative Research Methods for Community Development*, 2nd ed. (pp. 103–111). Routledge. https://doi.org/10.4324/9781003172925

Sim, J. (1998). Collecting and analysing qualitative data: Issues raised by the focus group. *Journal of Advanced Nursing*, *28*(2), 345–352. https://doi.org/10.1046/j.1365-2648.1998.00692.x

Smit, A. K., Keogh, L. A., Newson, A. J., Hersch, J., Butow, P., & Cust, A. E. (2015). Exploring the potential emotional and behavioural impact of providing personalised genomic risk information to the public: A focus group study. *Public Health Genomics*, *18*(5), 309–317. https://doi.org/10.1159/000439246

Smithson, J. (2000). Using and analysing focus groups: Limitations and possibilities. *International Journal of Methodology: Theory and Practice*, *3*(2), 103–119.

(2008). Focus groups. In P. Alasuutari, L. Bickman, & J. Brannen (eds.), *The SAGE Handbook of Social Research Methods* (pp. 357–370). SAGE Publications. https://doi.org/10.4135/9781446212165

Stevens, P. E. (1996). Focus groups: Collecting aggregate-level data to understand community health phenomena *Public Health Nursing*, *13*(3), 170–176. https://doi.org/10.1111/j.1525-1446.1996.tb00237.x

Stewart, D. W., Shamdasani, P. N., & Rook, D. W. (2007). *Focus Groups: Theory and Practice*, 2nd ed. SAGE Publications.

Stewart, K., & Williams, M. (2005). Researching online populations: The use of online focus groups for social research. *Qualitative Research*, *5*, 395–416.

Tatangelo, G. L., & Ricciardelli, L. A. (2017). Children's body image and social comparisons with peers and the media. *Journal of Health Psychology*, *22*(6), 776–787. https://doi.org/10.1177/1359105315615409

Thomas, J., & Harden, A. (2008). Methods for the thematic synthesis of qualitative research in systematic reviews. *BMC Medical Research Methodology*, *8*(1). https://doi.org/10.1186/1471-2288-8-45

Tong, A., Sainsbury, P., & Craig, J. (2007). Consolidated criteria for reporting qualitative research (COREQ): A 32-item checklist for interviews and focus groups. *International Journal for Quality in Health Care*, *19*(6), 349–357. https://doi.org/10.1093/intqhc/mzm042

Tong, A., Ralph, A. F., Chapman, J. R., Wong, G., Gill, J. S., Josephson, M. A., & Craig, J. C. (2015). Focus group study of public opinion about paying living kidney donors in Australia. *Clinical Journal of the American Society of Nephrology*, *10*(7), 1217–1226. https://doi.org/10.2215/CJN.10821014

Townsend, A., Adam, P., Li, L. C., McDonald, M., & Backman, C. L. (2013). Exploring eHealth ethics and multi-morbidity: Protocol for an interview and focus group study of patient and health care provider views and experiences of using digital media for health purposes. *JMIR Research Protocols*, *2*(2). https://doi.org/10.2196/resprot.2732

vanTeijlingen, E., Reid, J., Shucksmith, J., Harris, F., Philip, K., Imamura, M., & Penney, G. (2007). Embarrassment as a key emotion in young people talking about sexual health. *Sociological Research Online*, *12*, 1–16.

Werner-Wilson, R. J., Fitzharris, J. L., & Morrissey, K. M. (2004). Adolescent and parent perceptions of media influence on adolescent sexuality. *Adolescence*, *39*(154), 303–313.

Wilkinson, S., & Kitzinger, C. (1996). *Representing the Other*. SAGE Publications.

Woodyatt, C. R., Finneran, C. A., & Stephenson, R. (2016). In-person versus online focus group discussions: A comparative analysis of data quality. *Qualitative Health Research*, *26*(6), 741–749. https://doi.org/10.1177/1049732316631510

Yelden, K., Sargent, S., & Samanta, J. (2018). Understanding the decision-making environment for people in minimally conscious state. *Neuropsychological Rehabilitation*, *28*(8), 1415–1426. https://doi.org/10.1080/09602011.2017.1310657

29 Observational Data

Lesley Baillie and Shanlee Higgins

Abstract

Observational data are valuable for many research studies across different fields and can be appropriate for various studies, including qualitative, quantitative, and mixed methods research. Observations can be structured, semi-structured, or unstructured and are often combined with other methods such as interviews and documentary analysis. In this chapter, we focus on the practical aspects of observational data, including identifying appropriate settings and gaining access, determining the role of the observer and the level of participation during observation, and planning how the data will be collected, recorded, and analyzed. We also emphasize the role of reflexivity – an important tool for the observer to ensure they are aware of how they are influencing the data observed. Although there are many benefits to observation as a data collection method, there are also challenges, limitations, and ethical issues to address; all these areas will be considered in this chapter.

Keywords: Observation, Field Notes, Data Collection, Ethics, Reflexivity

Introduction

Observation is frequently used for collecting data across a wide range of fields, including health and social care, psychology, anthropology, business, and education. Although observational data are collected within various research paradigms and methodologies, our focus in this chapter is mainly on observation as a qualitative data collection method. We consider practical aspects of collecting observational data, ethical concerns, limitations and challenges, and the role of reflexivity. Throughout the chapter, we provide illustrative examples from a range of research studies.

Observation as a Data Collection Method

Observation is a flexible method of collecting data; it can be structured, semi-structured, or unstructured, depending on the underlying paradigm, research questions, and methodology. Positivistic research generally uses structured observation, using predetermined observation schedules, developed from existing theory, to record quantitative data (Mulhall, 2003). This type of observation is frequently used in the social sciences and may be conducted in the natural environment, a laboratory, or another artificial setting. For example, Loop et al. (2017) observed child behavior during parent–child interactions using a structured observation tool to collect quantitative data. They observed artificial activities, mostly in an unnatural environment (university laboratory) rather than in naturally occurring environments. In contrast, within the constructivist or interpretivist paradigms, researchers usually use unstructured or semi-structured observation within natural settings (Mulhall, 2003) and gather these data through their senses (Bloomer et al., 2012). For example, Ferguson (2016) collected unstructured observational data where social workers carry out their child protection work, observing the social workers, their managers, and families in their natural settings, which included observing in the social work office, on the car journeys to the homes of the families, and within different areas of the home (kitchen, living room, bedrooms).

Of note, both structured and unstructured observation can be conducted in the same study. A researcher could use a structured observation tool to collect specific observational data while simultaneously conducting unstructured observation and writing field notes about contextual factors. As an example, Baillie and Thomas (2017) used a structured tool, the Quality of Interaction Schedule ("QUIS"; Dean et al., 1993), in an adapted version from Health Improvement Scotland that was used for measuring person-centered care for older people in acute hospitals. They also recorded open field notes to contextualize the interactions they were scoring and recorded data about the number of staff, the shift pattern they were working, and the skill mix. When reporting their results, Baillie and Thomas (2017) noted that, while the statistical analysis of the observational data gathered through the QUIS tool did not indicate significant differences in the quality of interactions between staff and patients in the two wards observed, the staffing details and field notes highlighted possible influencing factors. For example, on a shift where there were lower QUIS scores on one ward, staffing data recorded few permanent staff on duty, the field notes indicated the ward was particularly busy with many acutely ill patients, and staff were "struggling to meet patients' needs" (p. 160). This example illustrates how structured and unstructured observation can be combined and lead to new insights.

Advantages of Using Observation

There are many reasons why you might consider collecting observational data. Structured observation can be used to measure observed changes in behavior between two or more groups using validated tools or with the same group before and after an intervention is tested during a trial. Observation is also well suited for studying complex societies or situations, such as cultural practices (De Walt & De Walt, 2011). Through observation, you can capture the whole social setting in which people function, including influences of the physical environment and the context for behaviors and processes (Mulhall, 2003). Additionally, as observation is ongoing and dynamic, this method can provide evidence for continually evolving processes, including interactions (Mulhall, 2003). For example, Ferguson (2016) observed how social workers interacted with children at home through touch and play. He also observed how social workers gained access to talk to the children alone and put them at ease. Similarly, Seim (2021) spent one year riding along in ambulances, observing the interactions with patients and how ambulance crews worked with other frontline staff.

Participant observation also allows the researcher to experience the social activities between people in the specific setting where they occur (Berthelsen et al. 2017). For example, rather than relying on secondhand accounts from practitioners, Beaton et al. (2018) used participant observation to study the application of oral health interventions for people experiencing homelessness. Similarly, Saarnio et al. (2019) observed in nursing homes, observing how nursing assistants enabled the residents to feel at home. Residents and staff then completed short interviews after being observed, to clarify and explore the observations, the residents' experiences, and what the nursing staff's purpose and intention were during care of the residents. In this way, observation can be used to triangulate with interview data – to explore how what people are observed to do in practice relates to what they say they do during interview (van de Gaar et al., 2016). Mulhall (2003) argued that what people perceive they do and what they actually do are both valid accounts but represent different perspectives.

Furthermore, observation can help researchers to understand the worldview of people who may not be able to participate in other forms of data collection, such as people who do not use words to communicate (McCormack, 2017). Issues that are difficult for people to articulate can be revealed through their observed actions, thus allowing for the "unspoken to be recognized" (Gunson et al., 2016). As an example, Higgins (2021) found that observation enabled insights into hydration care for older people with dementia in hospital, without placing unnecessary burden on them or relying solely on their verbal communication, as that may be challenging for anyone who is unwell in the hospital. Higgins (2021) also found observation was a way of collecting data about how staff delivered care without being too demanding on their time, as some staff were too busy to take part in interviews.

Research Methodologies that Use Observation

Although a range of methodologies use observation, the type of observation varies across these methods. In experimental research, observation is usually structured using validated measurement tools. In contrast, ethnography is more likely to use unstructured observation. In participatory research, observation is also mainly unstructured but could include structured observation too. Finally, in grounded theory, observation is mainly unstructured but could become more structured during theory development. Thus, the way observational data are collected must be congruent with the epistemological and methodological approach. For example, within grounded theory, Berthelsen et al. (2017) suggested that participant observation will be conducted differently depending on whether a classic or constructivist grounded theory approach is adopted.

Observation is a flexible method of data collection and can also be combined with other data collection methods. For example, ethnography has traditionally used participant observation and interviews and accordingly, Ferguson (2016) used participant observation and interviews in an ethnographic study of encounters between social workers and families. In a participatory action research study focusing on local language as a medium of instruction, Akello and Timmerman (2018) included interviews, focus group discussions, reviews of exercise books, and lesson observations. In a contrasting design, Burke et al. (2017) conducted a mixed method evaluation using a pre-post experiment design to evaluate a "FRIENDS for Life" program among children presenting with autism spectrum disorder. They conducted narrative observation of FRIENDS sessions but also included pre- and post-quantitative anxiety scales, parental interviews, and a post-intervention children's evaluation questionnaire. In another mixed method study, which focused on palliative care communication, Gramling et al. (2015) used observation and audio-recorded palliative care consultations, patient/proxy/clinician self-report questionnaires both before and the day after consultation, post-consultation in-depth interviews, and analysis of medical/administrative records.

Higgins (2021) adopted Yin's (2018) case study approach for her study of person-centered hydration care for people with dementia in acute hospital wards. This methodology sets out that one can use multiple data collection methods; she collected data through observation, interviews, and documents. She found that observational data could support, expand, or contrast with other data collected. During interviews, nursing staff explained how the "hosts" – non-healthcare staff who delivered hot drinks – used minimal interactions with patients; her observations of the hosts in practice supported the interview data. Observations enabled Higgins to expand her understanding of hydration care as she observed how combining verbal and non-verbal communication with practical support to drink was a successful strategy for hydration; patients refused drinks from staff who did not use this combined approach. An example of observations contrasting with interviews was related to staff hydration roles. Higgins (2021) found that staff often expressed at interview that hydration care was "everyone's role" but the observations evidenced that different staff groups had separate and distinctive hydration roles, leading to compartmentalization.

Access to the Setting for Observation and Recruiting Participants

An important part of planning your study is identifying the setting, or settings, where you will collect observational data. You then need to negotiate access and plan how you will recruit participants to observe, to achieve your research goals. The procedures for gaining access to the setting and participants vary according to the specific circumstances. Sometimes, access is needed at several levels. For example, when conducting observation during an ethnographic study in UK Jobcentre Plus (welfare) offices, Grant (2017) described gaining organizational access at a national level (macro), access to individual offices (meso) and, at micro level, access to advisors. She discussed the many challenges involved in gaining and maintaining access and identified potential solutions, summarized in a useful table. While Grant's (2017) study settings were driven by the aim of observing a specific public service, in other studies, researchers purposefully select varied settings to ensure they are observing the phenomenon in different environments. For example, Hill et al. (2018), who were studying the characteristics of sites where alcohol is consumed in the UK, selected seven contrasting settings so they could compare their observational data: a country pub, a town pub, a sports bar, two nightclubs, and a resort holding an adults only weekend. Where possible, it is beneficial to spend time in the research setting, before starting to collect data, to become familiar with the environment and start getting to know the people present, who will become more relaxed in your presence, thus increasing the likelihood of behavior observed being natural. Hammersley and Atkinson (2019) suggested that "the value of pure sociability should not be underestimated as a means of building trust" (p. 70). Strategies for observing non-intrusively and note-taking can also be identified during this preparation.

As well as identifying the setting for observation, you will need to identify who your participants are and the sample size. In experimental studies using structured observation, samples are usually selected randomly from a population. In most other studies using observation, participants are selected purposefully and will be the people who meet certain inclusion criteria that you identify. There may be more than one participant group, and you need to be clear about who you are observing. For example, if observing in a classroom, is your focus on the teachers or the pupils or both? In Ferguson's (2016) study, he was observing the social workers, their managers, and the families they visited. Ferguson (2016) explained that managers agreed he could recruit social workers from their teams to his study of social work encounters with families. The recruitment of families was through the social workers. In some instances, parents declined involvement, and there were some parents whom social workers did not feel it was appropriate to ask. During your fieldwork, you may become increasingly purposeful about your sample. For example, you might aim to observe a range of grades of staff in a workplace, carrying out different activities at different times.

Role of the Observer in the Setting

You will need to plan the role you will undertake while you are observing in the selected setting and to what extent, if any, you will interact and participate with the people present. Hammersley and Atkinson (2019) argued that "all social research is a form of participant observation because we cannot study the social world without being part of it" (p. 24). As such, the term "participant observation," often associated with ethnography, is used for observing in the natural setting, while participating in some way. In 1958, Gold identified a typology of participant observer roles that included the complete participant, the participant as observer, the observer as participant, and the complete observer. The "complete participant" takes an entirely insider role and is fully part of the setting, for example, by being an employee in an organization; they often observe covertly, but this has ethical implications, as discussed later. The "participant as observer" gains access to a setting through having a natural and non-research reason for being part of the setting and is part of the group being studied. The "observer as participant" has only minimal involvement in the setting being studied and is not normally part of the social setting. The "complete observer" does not take part in the social setting at all. Takyi (2015) argued that the complete observer role results in limited access to data, but some researchers do adopt this type of role. During observation of mental health professionals' team meetings, Strand et al. (2015) reported being complete observers as they only observed and took notes. Finally, a researcher can adopt more than one role during observational data collection. For example, Higashida (2016) described his role during observation of social work as being "'the participant as observer,' albeit partly 'the complete participant'" (p. 3), as he took different roles according to the situation.

While Gold's (1958) typology is still widely used by researchers today, Takyi (2015) critiqued Gold's typology and argued that neither the complete observer or the complete participant roles are applicable to today's research environments due to both practical problems and violation of the ethical requirement for informed consent (See Volume 1, Chapter 2 of this Handbook). Regarding the observer-as-participant role, Takyi suggested that the limited involvement in the lives of the people under study prevents a full understanding of the context and can lead to suspicion and concealed or distorted data. He therefore argued for the participant-as-observer role, as the greater involvement of the researcher enables a deeper, more accurate understanding of the context.

In a recent critique of Gold's typology, Seim (2021) argued that participant observation should be reframed as "observant participation" – a deeper level of participation. For example, Seim described how his ethnographic study started with a year of being a participant observer in ambulances. He then became an emergency medical technician and continued his research as an observant participant for a further nine months, aiming to both extend and challenge his observations as a participant observer. He reflected that being an observant participant enabled him to access situations he could not otherwise have accessed, and the stronger relationships developed led to more open conversations. However, through being a participant observer, he could add breadth to his observations, for example, by observing supervisors, rather than being in a fixed position as an employee and observant participant. A further difference experienced was analytic gaze. Being a participant observer first led to an outward-looking gaze, as Seim was focused on other people as a mainly passive observer, only focusing on himself (inward gaze) as a secondary consideration. As an observant participant, Seim focused on his own experience of the field first (inward gaze), including his physical and emotional responses and interactions, followed by observing others (outward gaze). Seim referred to his use of both participant observation and observant participation as a hybrid approach; he considered this beneficial but acknowledged that it would not be feasible for every study.

There are some unique practical issues regarding covert participant observation (e.g., developing a cover story and collecting data surreptitiously). In addition, to conduct observation covertly, you would certainly have to make a strong case to a research ethics committee, on the grounds that the benefits to others from the research outweigh the participants' rights to informed consent. However, from a social science perspective, Roulet et al. (2017) argued that covert participant observation has led to important theoretical insights and is the only way that some topics, such as deviant behaviors and secretive organizations, can be studied. For example, in their study of a street gang, Przemieniecki et al. (2020) considered that it was essential for researchers to be able to observe covertly in order to access the "deviant world" of street gangs (p. 983). Furthermore, Roulet et al. (2017) argued that covert observation enables the researcher to be a "pure" insider who experiences the phenomenon as the participants do, while preventing participants from modifying their behavior. Roulet et al. provided useful practical information on covert observation issues.

Presentation of the Observer and Their Activities during Observation

Once you have established your role and extent of participation during observation, you then need to decide on how you will present yourself within the setting, and what activities, if any, you will undertake while observing. Hammersley and Atkinson (2019) highlighted the importance of researchers adopting appropriate manner of dress during observation. Considerations include what you will wear so you are unobtrusive yet that will not lead to others having expectations of you that you cannot fulfill in the researcher role. If you are observing in a school classroom, for example, you would probably wear similar clothes to other staff in that environment. In healthcare settings, where most staff wear uniforms, researchers have described wearing similar uniforms to the staff they were observing (van Meurs et al., 2018; Saarnio et al. 2019). For example, while conducting observation in older people's hospital wards, Baillie and Thomas (2017) wore clinical uniforms, kept to the clinical staff dress code in relation to jewelry and footwear, and wore hospital badges that identified them as researchers. In contrast, Przemieniecki et al. (2020) carried out participant observation in a street gang at a US rally. The observers deliberately ensured that they did not resemble members of the media, so they did not carry a camera or video/audio recorder. It is also important to make people aware that you are in a research role when introducing yourself. Furthermore, to increase awareness of their role, some researchers display a poster in the setting with their photo and a brief explanation of who they are.

It is important to consider what activities you will get involved in, if any, and the impact of that involvement on the setting and participants. Takyi (2015) highlighted that the balance between detachment and involvement in the role of an observer has been a challenge to qualitative researchers for many years. For example, Franco and Yang (2021) described undertaking participant observation in a retirement village when conducting research into older consumers' technology consumption experiences. The researcher took on the role of a volunteer technology helper with the "unintended consequence" of participants becoming dependent on the technological assistance. The impact of the researcher's withdrawal then took some careful planning to minimize potential distress. As another challenge, researchers who are professionals observing in their own professional practice settings can face difficulties with participants understanding their research role. For example, Faisal (2021), a pharmacist observing older patients' medication management practices, found participants often expected her to provide advice about their medication and deal with medication-related problems. Faisal described the discomfort she felt as she was observing as a researcher not a pharmacist, was not the participants' pharmacist, and did not have enough information about their individual health conditions and medication to be able to safely give advice. She developed ways of dealing with these situations in a safe and professional manner.

In some anthropological studies, participant observation is prolonged, and researchers are warned to guard against losing the observer role entirely and "going native" (Gold, 1958). For example, McCormack (2017) conducted participatory research with three adults with profound and multiple disabilities. The other participants were family members, friends, and support workers. Over an extensive period of fieldwork, she found the support workers started treating her as "one of the team" (p. 87), using her as a sounding board and including her in social arrangements. As a result, it became increasingly difficult to complete the fieldwork. Her reflexivity about the situation enabled her to maintain her researcher role and set out expectations and thus complete the fieldwork. We explore reflexivity later in this chapter. The observer in a healthcare setting also runs the risk of "going native" if, for example, due to staff shortages, they take on the full role of a staff member instead of being an observer. This risk is important to consider if you are conducting research in your own setting and you will need to carefully explain your role as a researcher conducting observation to people who know you in your usual role as a practitioner. Nevertheless, you could, at times, still feel under pressure ethically to participate in the work.

If your role as observer includes participation, it is important to consider carefully what activities you will and will not do and be able to justify this stance to yourself and others, from professional, ethical, and research integrity perspectives. Gramling et al. (2015) described the role of observer in palliative care consultations as "not to be a participant, nor is it to be completely inanimate" and described how observers had weeks of training in how to "navigate the nuance of being present but not disruptive" (p. 6). Decisions about actions were based on safety and risk. For example, if an infusion pump alarm was beeping during the conversation, the observer would not mute the sound, but if the patient asked the observer to pass them a cup of water or to help them find their nurse call button, then the observer would do so if no clinical team member was available at the time.

Similarly, Bloomer et al. (2012) suggested that, in a healthcare setting, observers need to be sensitive to the changing environment and plan in advance how they will behave if an emergency occurs. They identified the importance of observers determining their research limits at the outset and recommended involving service users in making these plans. As Bloomer et al. were observing end-of-life care, they needed, for example, to plan whether observation should be ceased at the moment of death, when the patient is receiving hygiene care, or when death is imminent. They emphasized the importance of clarifying the researcher's roles and responsibilities with the participants and of setting out a clear process of action and reporting, prior to commencing observation. Even with planning, you need to be aware that the reality of observing in practice may lead you to revise your plans, as situations can arise that you had not expected. It is important to document and justify your actions in your research diary.

It is also important to report your role in subsequent presentations and/or publications. When you read research articles where observation has been used, the role of the researcher and extent of participation should be clear. For example, Nisbet et al. (2015) stated that the researcher took the role of observer as participant in their study of interprofessional learning. The researcher observed healthcare professionals' team meetings in a hospital setting. Their observer role was known to the participants, but the researcher was not a member of the team observed nor were they participating in the team meetings. The researcher noted points during observation for follow-up in subsequent interviews, for example, opportunities for teaching and learning that participants could have taken up during meetings.

Observation Focus and Recording Data

The focus of your observations and how you record your observational data depend on your research question, whether you are conducting structured or more unstructured observation, and your observer role. For example, Loop et al. (2017) used video to record their data about child behavior during parent–child interactions, while Ferguson (2016) recorded data about social work practice through field notes and he audio-recorded the social worker's interviews with the families that he observed. In structured observation, a validated tool, that has been shown to measure what it intends, will be used for data collection. If you are planning to use such a tool, you need to check any permissions required and keep evidence of these. You should critically review tools for what populations they were validated with and whether it would be valid to use the tool with your intended population. In some circumstances, you might identify necessary adaptations to the tool, and you will need permissions for these. You must explain what adaptations you made and why, and you will need to pilot the adapted tool. You should also plan how you will use the tool, be clear about the version of the tool and rationale, and consider whether you will write any open field notes too. If there is more than one observer using a structured tool, the researchers need to practice and compare understanding of the tool and scoring. Baillie and Thomas (2017) explained how they piloted the Quality of Interactions

Scale (QUIS) tool together, by independently observing interactions between older people and staff in the same hospital ward bay and comparing their ratings. They discussed any variations and differences in interpretation of the interactions observed, and then repeated this process until ratings were consistent. McHugh (2012) argued that, if raters are experienced and little guessing is likely, researchers may safely rely on percent agreement to determine interrater reliability.

If you are conducting semi-structured or unstructured observations, you need to decide what you will observe and how to record your field notes. The research questions, methodology, and setting will all influence the approach taken. For example, in the field of end-of-life care, Bloomer et al. (2012) recommended the identification of a clearly defined observation field and consideration of how the setting works, the usual routines and practices, any political issues, the culture, and both internal and external influences that might impact upon the observation field. From an ethnographic perspective, Spradley (1980) proposed that participant observation begins with wide-focused descriptive observations that continue, but the emphasis moves to focused observations and then to selective observations. He also suggested a detailed framework that can ensure a systematic and comprehensive approach, including the space (e.g., layout, outside or inside), people involved, their activities, objects present (e.g., furniture), individual actions, particular events (e.g., meetings), sequence of events, goals (what people are aiming to achieve), and emotions in different contexts.

As a contrasting approach, in Strand et al.'s (2015) study, entailing observation of health team meetings in a psychiatric unit, observers aimed to record as literally as possible all discussions about patients' parents (the study topic), including the context and the professional role of the person talking. Their notes included nonverbal behaviors too. In other studies, researchers have used some pre-planned categories with scope for additional relevant content. For example, in the field of oral health practice, Beaton et al. (2018) recorded date, time, and location, other relevant contextual information, and wrote detailed field notes in a narrative style. Although there were some pre-identified items that they expected to observe, there was space for other unexpected but relevant items too. Similarly, in a cancer center, where researchers investigated shared decision-making in patient–physician consultations, observational data were recorded on a form with sections to record the name of the observer, time and place of the observation, a short description of the situational context and participating individuals, and then a section for the observation memo that was unstructured (Hahlweg et al., 2017).

When writing field notes during observation, you need to consider where you will write them, as well as what you will write. Mulhall (2003) considered that every observer has their own preferred strategies; although some researchers will write up their field notes in full at the end of each day, others attempt to record events in detail as they occur or by withdrawing to a private area to write up observations immediately afterwards. Others delay writing up comprehensive field notes until they have left the study site completely. Nåden (2010) proposed writing up observations and conversations immediately and finalizing the field notes on the same day, so research material was gathered as near as possible in memory to the actual events.

Similarly, Hill et al. (2018) described writing up notes made during observation immediately afterwards into a detailed report.

Writing field notes at the time of observation needs practical consideration about how to do this as well as ensuring the security of the data captured. One approach is to jot down key words that will trigger more detailed recollections when writing up fuller notes as soon as possible afterwards. In a grounded theory study of software development, Sedano et al. (2017) described using post-it notes or jotting notes in a notebook, as they considered this was more culturally appropriate than typing on a laptop. They gave an explanation to the participants about the notetaking that, "What you said was really insightful," so participants felt valued. They also found making verbal notes during breaks between observations to be a good strategy.

There is a balance to be achieved between observing and recording the observations. Hagan (2021) reflected on her concern about missing other things due to focusing on key points to write up soon after the event in her car. As a further influencing factor, the observer's role and the setting affect how and where field notes are recorded. For example, Seim (2021) explained how, as a participant observer in ambulances, he could jot down extensive notes at the time that he then wrote up on his computer afterwards. However, when he became an employee and an observant participant, he could rarely write notes at all; any notes he managed were mainly written on his phone, as he legitimately checked messages and emails. He then relied on memories combined with these brief phone notes to write up his field notes on his computer after his shift. It is important to note that field notes have been criticized as being only comprehensible to their author (Mulhall, 2003), but writing up the notes digitally soon afterwards leads to them being more accessible.

During observations in homecare settings, Hellesø et al. (2015) described some flexibility; the observers mainly wrote initial notes during the visit, or in the car between visits, but sometimes had to add information later as there was often insufficient time for writing full notes. They found that some patients wanted to talk to the researchers, and they felt it unethical to write notes during the visit. They also took photographs and collected documents in some instances; clearly this would need ethical approval. Also, in home settings, Lo et al. (2022) recorded stroke participants' activities chronologically in a self-developed checklist, including how the activities were performed, duration, difficulties encountered, assistance required, physical environment, persons contacted, participants' facial expressions, and key conversations. The observer also recorded field notes, photos, and the observer's impressions.

These different examples illustrate the multiple approaches that observers have used to record their observations, depending on their study focus, the setting, and their observation role. As Ferguson (2016) described, drawing diagrams of the environment and items and positioning of people and other objects present can be useful. As an example, in an ethnographic study using observation in people's homes, Baillie and Lankshear (2014) included a picture showing a patient's creativity in managing their peritoneal dialysis (a home treatment for kidney failure) in the home environment. In their study of places where alcohol is consumed, Hill et al. (2018) similarly report making sketches of each environment during observation.

Immediately afterwards, they used the sketches to produce a more detailed map of the establishment and they provide examples in their article.

Planning is key to effective field notes. Prior to commencing observation in hospital wards, Higgins (2021) developed an observational data extraction document that had sections to capture relevant structured and unstructured data during each observation period. The structured observation details included the time an interaction started, the length of time of the interaction, and the role of the staff member the interaction was with (e.g., a staff nurse), with a space alongside the structured data for unstructured field notes. Higgins carried out pilot observations from which she realized a much larger space was necessary for capturing the unstructured field notes, so she expanded this area in the data extraction document.

Analysis of Observational Data

Mulhall (2003) asserted that there are varied views regarding at what point analysis of unstructured observational data starts; some researchers argue that the very process of note-writing starts analysis. Observation can generate large amounts of data, so it is important to factor adequate time to analyze these data when designing the study. There are many approaches to analyzing observational data, and the analysis approach must align with the study's methodology. As observation is often used with other data collection methods, plans for data analysis and reporting should include a robust approach to analyzing and reporting on the whole data set, integrating data from different sources to promote triangulation.

Higgins (2021) used a combination of inductive and deductive codes to analyze multiple sources of data, using a framework analysis approach (Ritchie & Spencer, 1994). As a further example, Saarnio et al. (2019) also used multiple data collection methods but took an inductive approach, using Thorne's (2016) constant comparative analysis. You will need to justify the analysis approach used, in the context of your methodology. If conducting structured observation, you will record quantitative data and analyze these data statistically, using an appropriate statistical package to calculate descriptive statistics of frequencies and percentages and to conduct statistical tests appropriate to the research question(s)/hypotheses.

Ethical Issues

As with any data collection method, you should consider your participants and the setting and then identify the specific issues and how to address these to protect your participants and yourself. The research ethics committee will require details about this planning before giving approval to proceed (see Volume 1, Chapter 2 in this Handbook]. In this section, we focus on some ethical issues of particular relevance to observation. The individual characteristics of your participants and setting may trigger specific ethical issues too.

Researcher Safety and Well-Being during Observation

Researcher safety and well-being may be of particular concern during observation in some settings (e.g., private homes or prisons). Therefore, you need to conduct a risk assessment of the settings where observation will take place and plan strategies to ensure personal safety. The strategies could include how to support your mental well-being, if you are observing distressing events. You will also need to identify a confidential, supportive space to deal with your emotions and the personal impact. One of the ethical issues particularly pertinent to observation is that you could observe issues that give you concern (e.g., poor professional practice, possible harm, or illegal activity). Generally, the best approach is to include, in the participant information sheet, that, if you observe any incidents of concern, you will speak to the participant to discuss action. Any safeguarding concerns would also need to be reported, in accordance with local policy.

Privacy and Confidentiality during Observation

Although privacy and confidentiality are relevant to most research methods, there are particular issues to be aware of when planning and conducting observation. To assure confidentiality, you should anonymize all identifying details of the setting and people observed in your field notes, assigning participants anonymous identifiers (number or pseudonym) from the start, but ensuring identifiers are not associated with any documents that include personal details (e.g., consent forms). Furthermore, the nature of the setting has connotations for privacy. Zahle (2017) makes the distinction between situational privacy and informational privacy. Situational privacy is about the space where the observer is present – a public space or a private space. As an example of observing in a public place, Hill et al. (2018) observed in seven public licensed premises. Ferguson's (2016) study of social work practice, however, took place in private spaces as he was observing social workers in their offices, where they interacted with managers and colleagues, in the social worker's car journey to family homes, and in family homes, where the social workers worked with families.

Informational privacy relates to the type of information gathered about a participant; it may be public or non-public knowledge (Zahle, 2017). Observers who gather non-public information about their participants risk intruding on their privacy, particularly if they have not gained informed consent. Zahle (2017) gives the example of telling participants in a reading group that the researcher is observing how much and when they read, while actually observing how the participants express their political outlooks. Regardless of the type of observation undertaken, and whether you are observing in public or private spaces, you need to decide what observations are necessary to meet the study's aims without unnecessary intrusion. In addition, you must use your own judgment about when to withdraw from situations to provide privacy.

Informed Consent for Observation

For informed consent, a participant must be competent, informed about the research, and able to decide whether to take part (Zahle, 2017). However, it can be difficult to predict the individuals who will be present during observation and to gain consent from everyone in advance; this is particularly likely in public settings. For individuals who have not consented in advance, but appear unexpectedly during an observation period, you could refrain from observing them or you could provide the information needed and gain informed consent at that point. Higgins (2021), during observation of older people with dementia on hospital wards, always gained consent from patients she was going to observe in advance, but she could not predict in advance all the staff who might be present. Therefore, she gained consent to observe on the ward from the ward sister and asked for information sheets to be sent out to all staff by electronic mail (with the option to opt out). Additionally, she kept a folder stocked with participant information sheets and consent forms at hand to use with staff who were present with the consented patient during the observation period. Conversely, in van Meurs et al.'s (2018) study of how nurses explore spirituality with cancer patients, researchers gained consent in advance from purposively selected nurses, and then, on the day of observation, they approached the patients present, explained the study, and gained verbal consent; they did this while assuring them of the right to refuse to be observed with the nurse. This approach did not give the patients long to take in the information and make a decision about being observed but was a pragmatic approach, given that it could be problematic to predict which patients the nurse would care for on a shift.

If you are going to observe children, or participants with impaired mental capacity, you will need to plan your approach to informed consent with great care. Haines (2017) provided details about how he managed informed consent for people with profound intellectual disabilities who did not have capacity to give informed consent (see Volume 1, Chapter 10 of this Handbook for a detailed exposition on consent). In another population, Higgins (2021) explained how she gained consent to observe people with dementia who might have impaired mental capacity, as excluding people with dementia who do not have capacity to consent could be ethically unjust and may limit research findings. Recruiting participants for research who may lack capacity must comply with relevant legislation that involves adherence to Section 32 of the Mental Capacity Act (2005) in the United Kingdom. Higgins first asked nursing staff if they were caring for any patient with dementia who fit the inclusion criteria. If the patient was felt to have capacity to consent, the nursing staff approached the individual first; if they agreed, Higgins provided participant information and assessed the person's capacity independently, prior to them signing a consent form for observation, if they had capacity. If the person lacked capacity to consent, Higgins then approached their next-of-kin about acting as a consultee; a consultee does not consent on behalf of a person who lacks capacity but advises what the person's opinion may have been about taking part in research. In Higgins's study, if the next-of-kin was willing to be a consultee, and believed their relative would not have objected to being observed, they signed the consultee declaration form. During the observation, Higgins remained mindful that, if any participant with dementia expressed any form of dissent, particularly if it seemed her presence was causing distress, she would then consider that the person was withdrawing consent and stop the observation.

Exceptionally, observation may be carried out without informed consent, if agreed by a research ethics committee. Roulet et al. (2017) provided a detailed analysis of the ethical issues around covert participant observation and further argued that all observational studies lie on a continuum of consent, as few research projects are either fully overt or fully covert due to practical constraints and the ambiguous nature of consent. They contend that depth of consent ranges from full disclosure of the research purpose, process, risks, and benefits, to giving false information on all elements including risks and benefits; in between, there may be omission or misrepresentation of some elements. The breadth of consent ranges from all participants to no one at all; in-between, there may be consent from some participant groups only. In Hill et al.'s (2018) report of their non-participant observation in public licensed premises, there is no mention of consent at all, with the authors only referring to having gained ethical approval for the study.

Exiting Fieldwork Ethically

If you conduct lengthy periods of fieldwork, your withdrawal from the field needs a sensitive approach; otherwise, participants might experience distress. Franco and Yang (2021) suggested a negative impact of withdrawal is a particular risk where there are frequent interactions between the researcher and the participants over the fieldwork period, with close relationships developing, and especially where the participants are vulnerable. They recommended that researchers should aim to "exit with grace" in a way that considers the interests of themselves and the participants. They highlighted that exit planning should be part of the research protocol, considered before starting fieldwork, and at every stage afterwards – not just toward the end. Haines (2017) described how he ensured that participants understood the relationship would be time-limited and planned to withdraw in a "gradual, planned and respectful way, seeking in particular not to end contact suddenly or unexpectedly" (p. 228).

Limitations and Challenges of Observation

At the beginning of this chapter, we considered reasons why researchers select observation and the advantages. There are also limitations and challenges to be aware of when using observation, but most can be addressed in some way. As with ethical issues, what is important is to be aware of them and plan your strategies to address the issues. One of the most discussed limitations is probably the Hawthorn effect – the tendency for people to behave differently when they know they are being studied (Chiesa & Hobbs, 2008). This consideration is often how researchers justify covert observation. However, this issue may be overemphasized, as it is hard for people to maintain changed behavior over long periods and this is particularly so in busy work environments (Mulhall, 2003). Higgins's (2021) experience concurs, as she found that, shortly into each observation period in acute hospital wards, staff were too busy to pay much attention to her. Additionally, she found that staff did not associate her with a presence that required alteration of their behavior. For example, she observed some staff engaging in substandard behavior, such as their eyes closed or scrolling through their mobile phone for extended periods, while being assigned as a one-to-one staff member, caring for a person with dementia. She felt they knew this was not expected, as she witnessed them modifying their behavior quickly when doctors or senior nursing staff were present. However, the staff then returned to the substandard behavior after senior staff left, although Higgins, as the researcher, remained present and observing. Another concern is that being observed might elicit anxiety, but during observation on busy older people's hospital wards, Baillie and Thomas (2019) found that no staff declined to be observed; however, not all wished to be interviewed. It seemed that staff saw observation as not affecting their work; in contrast, interviews were perceived to take up additional time.

As another limitation, observations carried out might not be representative of the group as a whole or be typical behaviors. Glabinski (2016), reflecting on the conduct of participant observation to study the tourism activities of senior Polish tourists, identified that it was a serious challenge to identify whether the behaviors observed were typical of other older tourists. Maputle (2018) observed women in labor but only during day shifts; she acknowledged that behaviors of midwives on nightshifts may be different, limiting the transferability of results. To address concerns about representativeness of observations, you should try to cover a range of situations, people, and timings so that you gain a comprehensive overview of what is going on. Baillie and Thomas (2019) explained how they observed activities on older people's hospital wards during different days of the week, as ward activities can differ, particularly with fewer staff on duty at weekends. As a further example, Beaton et al. (2018) observed oral health practices in a range of settings – a service user's flat, a canteen, a mobile dental unit, and meeting rooms.

In unstructured observation, the researcher's own interpretive lens affects what they observe and record (Mulhall, 2003), so reflexivity is essential (see below). Furthermore, unstructured participant observation is unpredictable, unfolding through the research process, and it can be difficult to set out exact plans for research ethics applications (Gunson et al., 2016). Although being an insider researcher carries advantages, there are also challenges during observation. For example, it may be difficult to become aware of things that you normally take for granted (Mulhall, 2003). For some researchers, their dual identity in the setting can lead to tensions, and this could impact their study (Bloomer et al., 2012) as they try to maintain both roles. A key strategy for managing issues around impact of self on observational data is reflexivity; we explore this next.

Reflexivity

Takyi (2015) emphasized the importance of participant observers accounting for their own biases and possible effects on their observations and data gathered.

Reflexivity is a tool for achieving this and is defined as "the process of reflecting critically on the self as a researcher" (Lincoln et al., 2011). The aim of reflexivity is to manage the potential for you to influence how your data are collected and analyzed – consciously and/or unconsciously. Researchers who are reflexive will be open about their strengths and shortcomings, examine their effect on the research setting, and note others' reactions to them (Tracy, 2010). Finlay (1998) proposed four aspects to reflexivity: your assumptions, expectations, behavior or emotional reactions, and unconscious responses. Therefore, when planning observation, first reflect on your assumptions and expectations about what you will observe, so you are more consciously aware of these.

For example, Hellesø et al. (2015) reported that a nurse researcher carrying out observation during homecare visits was aware of her previous experience as a nurse in home settings. She was concerned that, with this nursing lens, she would jump to conclusions too quickly and miss important information. She, therefore, prepared herself to be mindful of these preconceptions, carefully considering situations that she might take for granted during the observations and that could, therefore, prevent her from obtaining an in-depth understanding of the phenomenon. Berger (2015) highlighted that the researcher's personal familiarity with the participants' experience impacts on all phases of the research – data collection, analysis, interpreting, and drawing conclusions. Berger explained that, while greater familiarity with the participants' experiences could enhance depth of understanding, the researcher must be constantly alert to how their own experiences could project onto and affect the lens through which they view the data. A research diary or journal is a key strategy for reflexivity. Hagan (2021) provided examples of how she used a research diary to help her recognize her judgments about the motivations and attitudes she observed during observation of volunteers. Similarly, Faisal (2021), as a pharmacist conducting observation of patients' medication management practices in their own homes, described use of a research journal to support reflexivity. After each observation episode, she recorded her thoughts, feelings, and frustrations in her research journal, and these prompted her to reflect critically on her emotions. She recognized her positionality as a researcher bringing four main positions: a pharmacist, a woman, an immigrant, and a person of color. She provided detailed accounts of how each of these positions affected her research role.

As a further example, Higgins (2021) explained how she used a reflective diary to document her assumptions, preconceptions, and developing thoughts and feelings throughout her observation of people with dementia on hospital wards. One aspect that became clear through this reflexivity was the emotional labor involved in observing care where people were left with unmet physical or psychological needs. She became aware of how the minutiae of absent interactions or insufficient care, which alone were not immediately harmful but accumulated over time, amounted to witnessing care that was uncomfortable to see. Higgins found that these emotions often resurfaced during analysis of the observational data, particularly as analyzing multiple observations at one time provided new insight into the accumulation of unmet needs and often led to a strong emotional response or feelings of discomfort and powerlessness.

Higgins's research diary became a strategy to manage and cope with these emotions, as well as to document them, in addition to supervision and allowing herself enough time to analyze the findings, taking breaks when needed. Higgins found it was important to regularly revisit her research objectives and questions to report the data that answered these and not only report the data that illustrated her emotional response. This was achieved through reflexivity and a systematic, rigorous analysis process.

Conclusion

This chapter on observational data has highlighted that there are a number of advantages as well as limitations to consider and challenges to be overcome. Observation is often used with other data collection methods and can be appropriately used in various different methodologies. The type of observation used should align with the methodology and underlying epistemology and, as such, observation may be conducted using validated, structured tools, or may be semi-structured or unstructured, though sometimes these types are combined. The role of the observer during data collection needs careful planning and ethical issues must be addressed with care. Reflexivity is also an important strategy that will promote the trustworthiness of your observational data.

References

Akello, L. D., & Timmerman, M. C. G. (2018). Local language a medium of instruction: Challenges and way forward. *Educational Action Research*, 26(2), 314–332.

Baillie, J., & Lankshear, A. (2014). Patient and family perspectives on peritoneal dialysis at home: Findings from an ethnographic study. *Journal of Clinical Nursing*, 24, 222–234.

Baillie, L., & Thomas, N. (2017). How does the length of day shift affect patient care on older people's wards? A mixed method study. *International Journal of Nursing Studies*, 75, 154–162.

Baillie, L., & Thomas, N. (2019). Changing from 12-hr to 8-hr day shifts: A qualitative exploration of effects on organising nursing care and staffing. *Journal of Clinical Nursing*, 28(1–2), 148–158.

Beaton, L., Anderson, I., Humphris, G., Rodriguez, A., & Freeman, R. (2018). Implementing an oral health intervention for people experiencing homelessness in Scotland: A participant observation study. *Dentistry Journal*, 6(4).

Berger, R. (2015). Now I see it, now I don't: Researcher's position and reflexivity in qualitative research. *Qualitative Research*, 15(2), 219–234.

Berthelsen, C. B., Lindhardt, T., & Frederiksen, K. (2017). A discussion of differences in preparation, performance and postreflections in participant observations within two grounded theory approaches. *Scandinavian Journal of Caring Sciences*, 31, 413–420.

Bloomer, M .J., Cross, W., Endacott, R., O'Connor, M., & Moss, C. (2012). Qualitative observation in a clinical setting: Challenges at end of life. *Nursing and Health Sciences*, 14, 25–31.

Burke, M.-K., Prendeville, P., and Veal, A. (2017). An evaluation of the "FRIENDS for Life" programme among children presenting with autism spectrum disorder. *Educational Psychology in Practice, 33*(4), 435–449.

Chiesa, M., & Hobbs, S. (2008). Making sense of social research: How useful is the Hawthorne effect? *European Journal of Social Psychology, 38*(1), 67–74.

Dean, R, Proudfoot, R, & Lindesay, J. (1993). The Quality of Interactions Schedule (QUIS): Development, reliability and use in the evaluation of two Domus units. *International Journal of Geriatric Psychiatry, 1003*(10), 819–826.

De Walt, K. M., & De Walt, B. R. (2011). *Participant Observation: A Guide for Fieldworkers*, 2nd ed. AltaMira Press.

Faisal, S. (2021). Lessons in reflexivity of a pharmacist conducting ethnographic research. *Research in Social and Administrative Pharmacy, 17*, 1849–1855.

Ferguson, H. (2016). Researching social work practice close up: Using ethnographic and mobile methods to understand encounters between social workers, children and families. *British Journal of Social Work, 46*, 153–168.

Finlay, L. (1998). Reflexivity: An essential component for all research? *British Journal of Occupational Therapy, 61*(10), 453–456.

Franco, P., and Yang, N. Y. (2021). Exiting fieldwork 'with Grace': Reflections on the unintended consequences of participant observation and researcher-participant relationships. *Qualitative Market Research: An international journal 24*(3), 358–374.

Glabinski, Z. (2016). Analysing the tourism activity of seniors by applying the method of participant observation. *Bulletin of Geography. Socio–economic Series, 33*, 55–70.

Gold, R. (1958). Roles in sociological field observation. *Social Forces, 36*, 217–223.

Gramling, R., Gajary-Coots, E., Stanek, S., Dougoud, N., Pyke, H., Thomas, M., et al. (2015). Design of, and enrolment in, the palliative care communication research initiative: A direct-observation cohort study. *BMC Palliative Care, 14*.

Grant, A. (2017). "I don't want you sitting next to me": The macro, meso, and micro of gaining and maintaining access to government organizations during ethnographic fieldwork. *International Journal of Qualitative Methods, 16*, 1–11.

Gunson, J. S., Warin, M., & Zivkovic, T., & Moore, V. (2016). Participant observation in obesity research with children: Striated and smooth spaces. *Children's Geographies, 14*(1), 20–34.

Hagan, J. (2021). The pitfalls and potential of participant-observation: Ethnographic enquiry in volunteering. *VOLUNTAS: International Journal of Voluntary and Nonprofit Organizations, 33*(2), 1179–1186.

Hahlweg, P, Härter, M, Nestoriuc, Y., & Scholl, I. (2017). How are decisions made in cancer care? A qualitative study using participant observation of current practice. *BMJ Open, 7*, e016360.

Haines, D. (2017). Ethical considerations in qualitative case study research recruiting participants with profound intellectual disabilities. *Research Ethics, 13*(3–4), 219–232.

Hammersley, M., & Atkinson, P. (2019). *Ethnography: Principles in Practice*, 4th ed. Routledge.

Hellesø, R., Melby, L., & Hauge, S. (2015). Implications of observing and writing field notes through different lenses. *Journal of Multidisciplinary Healthcare, 8*, 189–197.

Higashida, M. (2016). Integration of religion and spirituality with social work practice in disability issues: Participant observation in a rural area of Sri Lanka. *SAGE Open, 6*(1), 1–8.

Higgins, S. (2021). *Person-Centred Hydration Care for Older People Living with Dementia in Acute Hospital Wards: A Case Study* [unpublished PhD thesis]. London South Bank University. Available from https://openresearch.lsbu.ac.uk/item/8zvq4

Hill, K. M., Pilling, M., & Foxcroft, D. R. (2018). Affordances for drinking alcohol: A non-participant observation study in licensed premises. *European Journal of Social Psychology*, *48*, 747–755.

Lincoln, Y. S., Lynham, S. A., & Guba, E. G. (2011). Paradigmatic controversies, contradictions, and emerging confluences, revisited. In N. K. Denzin, & Y. S. Lincoln (eds.), *The Sage Handbook of Qualitative Research*, 4th ed. (pp. 97–128). SAGE Publications.

Lo, S. H. S., Chau, J. P. C., Lam, S. K. Y., & Saran, R. (2022). Understanding the priorities in life beyond the first year after stroke: Qualitative findings and non-participant observations of stroke survivors and service providers. *Neuropsychological Rehabilitation*, *33*(5), 794–820.

Loop, L., Mouton, B., Brassart, E., & Roskam, I. (2017). The observation of child behavior during parent-child interaction: The psychometric properties of the Crowell procedure. *Journal of Child and Family Studies*, *26*, 1040–1050.

Maputle, M. S. (2018). Support provided by midwives to women during labour in a public hospital, Limpopo Province, South Africa: A participant observation study. *BMC Pregnancy and Childbirth*, *18*.

McCormack, N. (2017). *Making Memory Sites: Extending Opportunities for People with Profound and Multiple Learning Disabilities to Participate in Life Story Work* [unpublished PhD thesis]. University of East London. Available from https://repository.uel.ac.uk/item/84wy3

McHugh, M. L. (2012). Interrater reliability: The kappa statistic. *Biochemistry Medicine*, *22*(3), 276–282.

Mulhall, A. (2003). In the field: Notes on observation in qualitative research. *Journal of Advanced Nursing*, *41*(3), 306–313.

Nåden, D. (2010). Hermeneutics and observation – a discussion. *Nursing Inquiry*, *17*, 74–80.

Nisbet, G., Dunn, S., & Lincoln, M. (2015). Interprofessional team meetings: Opportunities for informal interprofessional learning. *Journal of Interprofessional Care*, *29*(5), 426–432.

Przemieniecki, C. J., Compitello, S., & Lindquist, J. D. (2020). Juggalos – Whoop! Whoop! A family or a gang? A participant-observation study on an FBI defined 'hybrid' gang. *Deviant Behavior*, *41*(8), 977–990.

Ritchie, J., & Spencer, L. (1994). Qualitative data analysis for applied policy research. In J. Ritchie, L. Spencer, A. Bryman, & R. G. Burgess (eds.), *Analysing Qualitative Data* (pp. 305–329). Routledge.

Roulet, T. J., Gill, M. J., Stenger, S., & Gill, D. J. (2017). Reconsidering the value of covert research: The role of ambiguous consent in participant observation. *Organisational Research Methods*, *20*(3), 487–517.

Saarnio, L., Boström, A-M, Hedman, R., Gustavsson, P., & Öhlén, J. (2019). Enabling at-homeness for older people with life-limiting conditions: A participant observation study from nursing homes. *Global Qualitative Nursing Research*, *6*, 1–12

Sedano, T., Ralph, P., & Péraire, C. (2017). Lessons learned from an extended participant observation grounded theory study. In *CESI 17: Proceedings of the 5th International Workshop on Conducting Empirical Studies in Industry* (pp. 9–15). IEEE.

Seim, J. (2021). Participant observation, observant participation, and hybrid ethnography. *Sociological Methods & Research, 53*(4), 1–32.

Spradley, J. P. (1980). *Participant Observation*. Holt, Rinehart & Winston.

Strand, J., Olin, E., & Tidefors, I. (2015). Mental health professionals' views of the parents of patients with psychotic disorders: A participant observation study. *Health and Social Care in the Community, 23*(2), 141–149.

Takyi, E. (2015). The challenge of involvement and detachment in participant observation. *Qualitative Report, 20*(6), 864–872.

Thorne, S. (2016). *Interpretive Description*. Left Coast Press.

Tracy, S. J. (2010). Qualitative quality: Eight 'big-tent' criteria for excellent qualitative research. *Qualitative Inquiry, 16*(10), 837–851.

van de Gaar, V. W., Jansen, W., van der Kleij, M. J. J., & Raat, H. (2016). Do children report differently from their parents and from observed data? Cross-sectional data on fruit, water, sugar-sweetened beverages and break-time foods. *BMC Public Health, 16*.

van Meurs, J., Smeets, W., Vissers, K. C. P., Groot, M., & Engels, Y. (2018). Nurses exploring the spirituality of their patients with cancer: Participant observation on a medical oncology ward. *Cancer Nursing, 41*(4), E39–E45.

Yin, R. K. (2018). *Case Study Research: Design and Methods*, 6th ed. SAGE Publications.

Zahle, J. (2017). Privacy, informed consent and participant observation. *Perspectives on Science, 25*(4), 465–487.

Index

Please note: page numbers in *italic type* indicate figures or tables

23andme.com, 64

accuracy in parameter estimation (AIPE), 251–254
algorithms
  definition, 49
  Prolific's use of, 77
Amazon's Mechanical Turk, 129, *see* Mechanical Turk (mTurk)
animal testing, sampling and, 5
archival data
  analyses and interpretation of, 578–583
  definition, 571
  primary, 572
  secondary, 575
  qualitative data
    definition, 572
    primary, 572–574
    secondary, 575, *577*
      example sets, 587
    qualitative analysis, 578–581
    quantitative analysis, 581
    considerations when beginning an investigation using, 583–587
  quantitative data
    primary, 574–575
    secondary, 577
    qualitative analysis, 582–583
    quantitative analysis, 581–582
Atkinson, P., 669, 671
attention-check questions (ACQs), 29, 38, 52, 82–83, 84, 85–86, 88
Australian Bureau of Statistics, 130

Baillie, L., 666, 671, 673, 675, 680
Basil, M. D., 12
Beaton, L., 667, 674, 680
behavioral measures, limitations, 497
behavioral science research, designing, 163
Bello, D., 11, 12
Bernard, H. R., 579
Berry, J. W., 142, 149
Bessel, Friedrich, 374

Big Q approach
  comparison with small q research, 549
  data saturation and, 562
  open-ended survey questions, 565
Black Lives Matter movement, 58
Bloomer, M. J., 673, 674
Bollen, K. A., 200
Brandt, M. J., 288, 298
Braun, V., 549, 550, 555, 556, 566
Brexit, political micro-targeting and, 62
Broesch, T., 145, 150
Business Longitudinal Analysis Data Environment (BLADE), 130
Buzan, T., 277

California Consumer Privacy Act (CCPA), 65
Cambridge Analytica, 61–62
Canada, Personal Information Protection and Electronic Documents Act (PIPEDA), 65
cardiovascular measures of health, 455–456, 464
  overview, 455–456
  electronic medical records (EMR) and, 466
  improving health equity, 469–470
  invasive
    overview, 462
    angiography vs. electrophysiology, 462
    coronary angiography, 462–463
    electrophysiology (EP), 463
  mobile technologies and, 467–469
    challenges with wearables, 468–469
  non-invasive
    blood pressure, 456–457
      special considerations, 457
    echocardiography, 462
      research examples, 464
    electrocardiography (ECG)
      12-lead ECG measures for research, 458
      example electrocardiogram, 460
      heart rate variability (HRV), 459–460
      home testing kits, 467
      Mason-Likert lead configuration, 461
      methods, 460–461

research examples, 464
  variables, 457–460
  home ECG testing kits, 468
  toilet-seat-based monitoring, 468
point-of-care tests (POCT), 466–467
validation of psychometrics data, 465
case studies
  choices and dilemmas, 616
  case selection, 621
  comparison of quantitative approaches, 617
  data analysis, 631
    Eisenhardt template, 619, 632
    for excessive change, 634, 635
    Gioia template, 619, 633–634
  data collection, 627
    documents, 630
    interviews, 628–630
    observations, 628
  design choices, 620
  epistemological approaches, 617–618
  formulation of the research question, 618–620
  grounded theory approach, 620
  holistic or embedded design, 622
  number of cases, 621–622
  process analysis, 635–636
  researchers' roles, 623
    combines participant/researcher, 626–627
    complete participant, 625–626
    consultant, 624–625
    pure researcher, 624
  templates, 619
  the concept, 617
  time of sampling, 622–623
ChatGPT, 60
China, banning of Western social media
    applications, 49
Clark, A., 147, 167, 170, 172, 175
Clarke, V., 549, 566
CloudResearch
  approval ratings, 85
  comparison with other platforms, 80, 86–90
  data quality, 87–88
  mTurk and, 28, 30, 36
  participant vetting system, 28, 37, 87
cognitive interviewing, 107
convenience samples
  cost efficiency, 8
  exploratory purposes, 11
  history, 10
  testing relationships using, 12
Corwin, Z. B., 595, 596, 603, 611
COVID-19 pandemic
  point-of-care-tests (POCT), 466
  remote, personalized self-care, 467
  SARS-CoV-2 rapid at-home self-tests, 466
  tracking the psychological effects, 60
Creswell, J. W., 617
Crow, G., 575–576

CrowdFlower (Figure Eight), 86
crowdsourcing
  as solution to the replication crisis, 293–294
  coining of the term, 51
  for data collection
    drawbacks, 52
    participant recruitment, 51–52
    quality control, 52–53,
  See also individual platforms
cultural integration
  Barrow Alcohol Study, 146–147
  Belmont Report, 147
  emergence of Indigenous scholarship, 143
  ethical considerations, 143–149
    community-based participatory research
        (CBPR), 146–147
    conducting culturally focused research,
        143–147
    context-specific sampling, 144–145
    evaluating and giving permission for
        culturally focused research, 147–149
    exploring culturally sensitive topics, 145
    informed consent, 148–149
    institutional review, 147, 148
  in social and behavioral research, 142–143
  meaning of culture, 142–143
  methodological considerations, 149–155
    cultural translation, 151–152
    data analysis strategies, 154
    ethical and professional issues, 155
    interacting with participants, 153–154
    operationalization/measurement of culture,
        150–151
    recruitment of participants, 152–153
  multicultural approaches, 142
  overview, 140–142, 155
  percentage of the world's population
      represented in APA journals, 141
Cunliffe, A. L., 132

Dedoose, 579, 599
descriptive research, value of in medicine, 10
Diana, Princess of Wales, comparison in reactions
    to the death of across different samples,
    12
Dienes, Z., 234, 315, 317
Donders, Franciscus, 374, 375–376

Eisenhardt, K. M., 617, 620, 621, 622, 632
electrodermal activity (EDA)
  overview, 475–476
  applications
    emotion recognition, 486–487
    pain detection, 483–484
    psychological applications, 476
    seizure detection, 487
    sleep research, 485–486
    stress detection, 484–485

electrodermal activity (EDA) (cont.)
  basic morphology, 478–479
  challenges and limitations, 488
  data collection, 477–478
  detection and correction of motion artifacts, 481–483
  physiomarkers, 480
  signal processing, 479
  wearable devices, 477
electroencephalography (EEG)
  brain electrophysiology as research tool, 519
  comparison with other neuroimaging methods, 521–524
  EEG signals and social processes, 536–537
  generation of the signal, 520
  monetary costs, 523
  neurophysiological and biophysical processes represented by, 519–521
  recording procedure
    amplifiers, 525
    artifact control strategies, 526
    artifact correction, 526–529
    artifact rejection, 529–530
    electrode array, 524–525
    filters, 525
    interpolation, 529
    sampling rate, 525
  research techniques
    event-related potential (ERP) technique, 530, 534
      common components, 532–534
    spectral and time-frequency analysis, 534–536
  research trends, 537, 538
  spatial resolution, 523
  versatility, 538
electromyography (EMG)
  applications for EMG measurement
    biofeedback training, 511–512
      for anxiety disorders, 512
      for attention disorders, 512–513
      for tension-type headaches, 512
    facial EMG and emotion, 510–511
    human–machine interfaces (HMI), 513–514
    startle and attention, 508–509
    startle and emotion, 509–510
    startle eyeblink reflex, 507–508
  neurobiological bases of muscle activity, 498–499
  overview, 497–498
  procedures, 499–507
    electrode placement, 501
    equipment and signal processing, 503–506
    signal noise reduction, 506–507
    surface preparation, 501–503
  steps for implementing EMG measurement, 500
Ellison, Nicole, 49
European Union

digital rights legislation, 55
  General Data Protection Regulation (GDPR), 65
Evidence in Governance & Politics (EGAP), 109
Exner, Sigmund, 374
experimental research
  benefits of homogeneity, 13
  potential effects of sample manipulation and, 4
  use of in organizational research, 124–126
  use of observation, 667
  use of student samples in, 11, 12–14
eyetracking research
  accuracy, 412–413
  data analysis, 415
  data quality, 411–412
  gaze visualization, 417
  head-mounted eyetrackers, 406–407
  head-mounted eyetrackers, VR/AR, 409–410
  precision, 413–415
  real-world applications, 417–419
  remote eyetrackers, 405
  selecting an eyetracker, 410–411
  summary, 419–420
  tower eyetrackers, 406
  types of eyetrackers, 404
  understanding eye movements, 399–404
    fixations, 400
    saccadic, 401–402
    smooth pursuit, 402–403
    vestibular-ocular response (VOR), 403
  wearable eyetrackers, 407–408

Facebook, 53, 65
  and consent for use of data, 61–63
  manipulation of users' feeds, 62–63
  primary function, 49
  scraping and, 55, 98
Fair Crowd Work, 36
Fazio, R. H., 382, 383
Ferguson, H., 666, 668, 669, 673, 675, 677
field research
  advantages, 95
    breadth of research topics, 96
    causal testing, 96
    ecological validity, 95–96
    intervention program evaluation, 96–97
    social impact, 97
  assessing the naturalism of a study, 94–95
  challenges, 97–98
  definition of "field", 93
  descriptive surveys, 98
  design and implementation concerns
    attrition, 104–105
    noncompliance, 105–106
    spillover, 103–104
  example research designs, 94
  expansion of the field, 107–108
  experimental methods, 99–103

block randomization, 101–102
cluster randomization, 100–101
simple randomization, 99–100
waitlist design, 102–103
generalizability, 109
interest in social media, 110
Metaketa Initiative, 109
naturalistic observation, 98
non-experimental methods, 98, 99
overview, 93–95, 111
pilot testing, 106–107
qualitative interviews, 98
replicability, 109
role of construal, 106, 107
technological advancement and, 109–111
FindingFive, 28
Finlay, L., 681
Finlay, W. M. L., 166, 170, 172–173
Fischer, R., 142, 151
focus groups
　advantages of the method, 642
　application in social and behavioral science, 641–642
　conducting
　　example questions, 648
　　facilitator's role, 646
　　preparation and setup, 645
　　recording and transcription, 649
　　structure, 646–647
　data analysis and interpretation, 653
　　approaches to, 653–654, 656–658
　　　content analysis, 657
　　　conversation analysis, 657–658
　　　grounded theory analysis, 657
　　　thematic analysis, 656
　　coding, 655–656
　　of group interaction, 655
　definition and key features, 640
　design
　　methodological framework, 643–644
　　participant selection and group composition, 644–645
　　research questions, 642
　diversity in composition, 645
　embedded activities, 649
　　nominal group technique, 649–650
　ensuring trustworthiness of studies, 658
　grounded theory and, 644
　guidelines, 658
　history, 641
　in ethnography studies, 644
　limitations of the method, 642
　semi-structured approach, 595–596
　specific populations
　　children, 650–651
　　culturally and linguistically diverse groups, 651–652
　　online focus groups, 652–653

Franco, P., 672, 679
Freire, Paulo, 607
functional magnetic resonance imaging (fMRI)
　comparison with EEG, 521, 523
　properties relative to EEG, 522

gendercoder, 550
General Data Protection Regulation (GDPR), 65
Gephi software, 58
Gioia, D. A., 618, 619, 624, 633–634
Glaser, B. G., 579
Gold, R., 669–670
Google, 65
Google Forms, 53
Gorilla, 72, 79–81
Gosling, S. D., 64, 65
Grahe, J., 280, 286, 287
Gramling, R., 668, 672
Grant, A., 668–669
Greene, J. C., 176, 177–178

Hagan, J., 681
Haines, D., 678, 679
Hammersley, M., 669, 671
health, cardiovascular measures of, 455, see cardiovascular measures of health
Heckler Report on Black and Minority Health, 469
Heggestad, E. D., 12
Hellesø, R., 675, 681
Helmholtz, Hermann von, 374
Higgins, S., 667, 668, 676, 678–680, 681
Hill, K. M., 669, 675, 677, 679
Hilton, Paris, 573
Holleman, B. C., 332, 334
human behavior and experience, primary areas of assessment, 497
human behavior research, student samples in, 5

inferential statistics, 4, 13
interdisciplinary research
　career progress and, 279
　challenges and strategies, 273–275
　choice of research question, 262, 263
　communication to multiple audiences, 270–271
　complexity and, 277–278
　creativity and, 276–277
　defining interdisciplinarity, 275–276
　disciplinary insights, 263–265
　evaluating interdisciplinary research, 278–279
　integration, 266–268
　　within disciplines, 279–280
　mixed methods research, 268–269
　overview, 261–262, 280
　process, 262
　reflection and testing, 269–270
　team research, 271–273
interviews
　background research, 599

interviews (cont.)
  choice of interviewer, 603
  conducting the interview
    context, paying attention to, 608
    critical reflection, 607–608
    exiting the field, exercising care, 609
    improvisation, value of, 607
    listening actively
      for progress, 606
      for the participant's inner voice, 606
      to what the participant says, 606
      to yourself, 607
    posing questions with intentionality, 605
    rapport, building and sustaining, 604
    reciprocity of the interview exchange, 609
  data analysis and dissemination
    dissemination process, 610–611
    documenting the interview process, 610
    transcription process, 609
    writing up findings, 610
  overview, 591–592
  preparation for, 593
    choice of appropriate interview type, 593–598
    consent process, 601
    interview guide, 600–601
    key steps, 594
    location of interview, 601
    protection of participants, 601
    recording devices, 603–604
    recruitment of participants, 601
    sampling, 599–600
    securing participation, 602
    securing resources, 598–599
    selection of participants, 602
  question examples, 598
  role in case studies, 628–630
  types of interview
    focus group interviews, 595–596
    highly structured interviews, 593
    hybrid and innovative approaches, 597–598
    longitudinal interviews, 597
    open-ended interviews, 596
      see also open-ended survey questions (OESQs)
    phenomenological interviews, 595
    purposes and practices, 629
    semi-structured interviews, 595–596
Ioannidis, J. P., 290, 291

James, William, 95
Javal, Émile, 401
Johns Hopkins Sheridan Libraries, 579
Johnson, R. B., 176

Kiaer, Nicolai, 3
Kinnebrook, David, 374

Lambert, A. D., 553, 556
Langdon-Roosevelt poll, sampling bias, 8–9, 10, 14
Langley, A., 617–618
Language Inquiry Word Count (LIWC), 59–60, 63
Lee, S. H., 582
Lewin, Kurt, 17
Lewis, C., 197, 198
Leximancer, 551
LinkedIn, 49, 65
liquid-chromatography triple quadrupole mass spectrometry (LC-MS/MS), 441–442
Literary Digest presidential election poll (1936), 8–9, 10, 14
Loop, L., 666, 673
Lynch, J. G., 13, 14
Lyon, D., 575–576

Majority World, meaning of, 141
Marcoulides, G. A., 198, 199–200, 201, 202, 205
Maskelyne, Nevil, 374
MAXQDA, 579
Maxwell, J. A., 298
McCormack, N., 672
measuring hormones
  biospecimen collection, 428
    blood, 429
      dried blood spots (DBS), 429–430
      Tasso collection, 430–431
    feces, 435–436
    hair, 432–434
    nails, 434–435
    saliva, 431–432
    urine, 434
  pros and cons, 436
    cost and ease of collection, transport and storage, 437
  overview, 427–428
  purpose and action of hormones, 428
  statistical constructs, 442
    comparisons of pros and cons, 445
    diurnal hormones, 443–444
    ratios and coupling, 445
    reactivity and recovery, 444–445
  techniques
    assays, 437
    enzyme immunoassay (EIA), 438–440
    lateral flow immunoassays (LFIA), 440–441
    liquid-chromatography triple quadrupole mass spectrometry (LC-MS/MS), 441–442
    radioimmunoassay (RIA), 437–438
    pros and cons to each approach, 442
  recommendations and conclusions, 446
Mechanical Turk (mTurk), 129
  background, 24–25
  comparison with other platforms, 80, 86–90
  concept and function, 25–26

cost-effectiveness, 52
data quality, 88
    best practices, 37–38
    challenges, 29–30
disciplines benefiting from use of, 52
ethics
    best practices, 39
    challenges
        exploitation, 35–36
        requesters' treatment of participants, 36–37
        wages, 36
example code, 27
graphical user interface, 27
interacting with for research, 26–29
"micro-tasks", 89
number of participants advertised by Amazon, 30
participant activity as a share of worker experience, 34
participants per month, 40
recruitment, 51
replication study, 287
research potential, 39–40
sampling
    best practices, 38–39
    challenges
        demographic representation, 31–34
        experience and non-naiveté, 34–35
        population size, 30
    strengths, 39
third-party services, 28
worker dashboard, 26
Merunka, D., 11, 12
#MeToo movement, 60
Midjourney, 61
Miller, A. L., 553, 556
Milner, J., 211, 222
Minority World, meaning of, 141
mixed methods research
    definition, 164, 177
    design recommendations, 180–183
    focus groups, 641
    inclusion of multiple methods, 166
    integration, 179–180
    interdisciplinary research, 268–269
    meaningful connections, 177
    purposes of mixing, 177–178
    theoretical drive, 179
    timing, 178–179
    triangulation, 177
Mondak, J. J., 355
Moore, T., 652, 653
Moss, P., 167, 170, 172
Mühlenbeck, C., 418
Mulhall, A., 674, 676
Müller, Johannes, 374
multiple-methods research

definition, 164
design recommendations, 180–183
design steps, 164–165
emergent design, 172
    emerging aspects, 172
    emerging data, 175
    emerging foci, 172–174
    emerging subgroups, 176
    searching for an explanation, 174–175
examples
    academic procrastination study, 168, 169, 175
    emergent design, 173
    emerging data, 175
    explaining differences, 175
    exploration, 169
    focusing, 173
    including groups with varying experience, 168
    integration, 170
    making decisions in practice, 171
    multiple perspectives, 167
    preschool outdoor environment redevelopment study, 167, 169, 170–171, 175
    sexual health education study, 166, 170, 173
in-depth exploration, 168–169
integration, 169–171
lenses, 165–168
    including groups with varying experience, 167–168
    including multiple locations, 167
    including multiple methods, 166
    including multiple organizational levels, 167
    including multiple research questions, 166
    including multiple stakeholder perspectives, 166–167
making decisions in practice, 171
overview, 163–164
multiple methods, 163
MySpace, 49, 53

Neyman, Jerzy, 3
non-human animals, research on, 5
non-naïve participants, potential impact on research, 83
Nosek, B. A., 288, 385
Novick, M. R., 197, 198
null hypothesis significance testing (NHST), 232–233, 234, 254, 298
NVivo, 551, 579
Nyström, M., 414

observational data
    advantages, 666–667
    analysis of, 676
    ethical issues
        exiting the field, 679

observational data (cont.)
  informed consent, 678, 679
  privacy and confidentiality, 677
  researcher safety and well-being, 677
 focus and recording of observations, 673–676
 Hawthorn effect, 679
 identifying settings for observation and participant recruitment, 668–669
 limitations and challenges of observation, 679–680
 observation as data collection method, 665–666
 overview, 665
 presentation and activities of the observer, 671–673
 reflexivity and, 680–682
 research methodologies that use observation, 667–668
 role of the observer, 669–671
OkCupid, 55
online data collection, 25, 129–130
 sampling, 8, 25,
 See also crowdsourcing and individual platforms
online samples, 8
open-ended survey questions (OESQs)
 advantages and disadvantages, 551
 challenges, 551
 data analysis, 562
  "any other comments" questions, 566
  Big Q approach, 565
  small q approach
   demographic data, 562–563
   "not listed here" responses, 564
 definition and purposes, 547–549
 demographic questions, 550
 ethical considerations, 559–560
 examples, 548
 factors influencing response rates, *551*
  completion mode, 553
  demographic factors, 553
  motivational statements, 554
  order of questions, 554
  size of answer box, 553–554
 overview, 547
 previous research
  exploring social norms, 552
  large samples, 552
  sensitive topics, 552
 question design, 557–558
 status in the field of qualitative research, 567
 strengths, 549–550
 survey design
  data collection method, 554
  order of questions, 556–557
  space provided to respond, 557
   adaptive questionnaire design, 557
  type of survey, 555
 survey recruitment, 560–562

organizational research
 cluster randomized controlled trials (CRCT), 125
 correlational studies, 122–124
 cross-sectional studies, 120, 122
 data collection
  conceptual and contextual considerations, 126–127
  online panels, 129–130,
  See also crowdsourcing and individual platforms
  primary sources, 128–129
  sampling strategies, 127–128
  secondary data, 130
  sources of data, 128–130
 defining organizations, 116–117
 DEI perspective, 132–133
 design considerations, 118–120
 dynamism of processes, 120
 ethical considerations
  coercion risks, 131–132
  privacy risks, 131
  reputational risks, 131
 experimental studies, 124–126
 exploratory/descriptive studies, 121
 levels of analysis, 119
 overview, 116, 117, 133
 research design, 120–126
 structures and hierarchies, 119
 theory-driven, 117–118
 units of analysis, 119

Palmer, M., 644, 654
Paluck, E. L., 100, 103
Pelz, J. B., 378, 417
Pettigrew, A. M., 628, 632, 635
phrenology, study of as example of method invalidity, 212, 214
physiological measures
 strengths, 497,
 See also cardiovascular measures of health; electrodermal activity (EDA); electroencephalography (EEG); electromyography (EMG); measuring hormones
Poortinga, Y. H., 142, 151
Posada-Quintero, H., 484, 485
Positly, 28
positron emission tomography (PET)
 comparison with EEG, 521, 523
 properties relative to EEG, 522
Pratt, M. G., 628, 631
probability sampling, 13
Prolific
 advantages, 89
 comparison with other platforms, 80, 86–87, 89–90
 connectivity to research software, 79–82
 data quality

aspects of, 82–84
comparison with other platforms, 86–89
ex-ante steps, 84–85
ex-post steps, 85–86
high, 82–86
disadvantages, 90
number of participants and researchers, 73
overview, 72–76, 90–91
recruitment, 51
sampling on, 77–79
prescreened sampling, 77–79
representative sampling, 77
viral TikTok video, 77
Przemieniecki, C. J., 671
psiTurk, 28
psychological research, percentage of the world's population represented in APA journals, 141

quality control in data collection, attention checks, 52
Qualtrics, 129
character limit, 557
cost of a high-quality participant, 88
mTurk and, 26
Prolific and, 73, 79–82, 90
social media research and, 53, 54
questionnaire design
acquiescence response bias, 359
adaptive, 557
cognitive processes underlying optimal question answering, 353–354
conversational norms and conventions, 354
frequency scales, 338–340
implications of data collection mode, 340
internet survey data collection and, 356
multiple select questions, 360
non-substantive response options (NSROs), 360–361
open vs. closed questions, 354–355
order of questions, 362
overview, 352–353
question order effects, 337–338
rating scales
branching, 359
middle alternatives, 357
number of scale points, 357
points and labels, 356
slider scales, 357
theory, 357
verbal labels, 358
selecting, 358–359
ratings vs. rankings, 355–356
recommendations for improvement, 343–345
response order effects, 335–336, 360
satisficing behavior and, 353–354
social desirability response bias, 335, 361–362
wording of questions, 362

Raykov, T., 127, 196, 199, 201–202, 205
reaction time (RT)
brief history, 374–375
commonly used measures, 379–386
Eriksen flanker task, 381–382
sample stimuli, 382
evaluative priming tasks (EPTs), 382–383
sample procedure, 383
Go/No-go Association Task (GNAT), 385–386
Implicit Association Test (IAT), *384*, 384–385
visual example, 384
Stroop Color and Word Test (SCWT), 380–381
sample stimuli, 380
moderating factors
age, 379
arousal–performance relationship, 377
focus of attention, 377
influence of practice, 378
intensity and complexity of stimuli, 376–377
other possible moderators, 379
physiological arousal, 377
sleep deprivation, 377
neurodegenerative conditions and, 379
real-world implications, 375
research software, 386–389
comparison of product features, 387
DirectRT, 387–388
E-Prime, 388
Inquisit, 389
online and open source tools, 389
SuperLab, 388
statistical analysis of data, 389–391
study of, current knowledge, 375–379
Reddit, *56*, 60, 580
registered reports
analytic flexibility, 312–317
Bayes factors, 316–317
inference by intervals, 316
obtaining sensitive results, 314
power, 315
assumptions and outcome neutral tests, 310–312
guidance, 319
overview, 305, 307
planning a study, 317–318
planning considerations, 322
pre-registration, 306
pros and cons, 320–322
scientific background, 307–310
substantial theory, function of, 310
reliability of measures
basics and definition, 190–192
classical test theory framework, 190
coefficient alpha
closeness to scale reliability, 197–199

reliability of measures (cont.)
    discrepancy from scale reliability, 200
    longevity, 196
    population definition, 196–197
    evaluation of, 194–196
    interpretation and utility, 192–194
    overview, 189–190, 206–207
    relationship with validity, 189
    scale reliability coefficient
        convergence of coefficient alpha and, 203–204
        point and interval estimation, 200–203, 210
    standardized solutions, limitations, 204–205
replication, 283
    as basic tenet of the scientific method, 285
    as "dangerous task" in science, 285–290
    Central Limit Theorem and, 289
    close replications, 287
    conceptual replications, 287–288
    defining, 283–284
    difficulty of repeating outcomes, 289
    exact replication, impossibility of, 285–286
    execution of the process, 296–297
    expansion of sampled populations and, 294
    File Drawer Problem, 290
    interpretation challenges, 284
    limited influence, 290
    methodological improvement, 294
    overview and resources, 298–299
    parameter estimation approaches, 295
    project planning, 296
    questionable research practices (QRPs) and, 291
    recommendations, 297–298
replication crisis
    causes, 290–292
    solutions, 292–293
        Berkeley Initiative for Transparency in the Social Sciences (BITSS), 292
        Collaborative Replications and Education Project, 292
        crowdsourcing, 293–294
        Network for International Collaborative Exchange, 292
        Psychological Science Accelerator, 292–293
        Reproducibility Project, 292
    researcher choices and, 291
    role in falsifiability, 285
    selection criteria, 295–296
research design
    correlational studies examining relationships, 11–12
    descriptive studies, 8–10
    experimental research, 12–14
    exploratory research, 10–11
RiddleMeThis, 54
Roulet, T. J., 671, 679

Rouzies, A., 627
RTurk, 28
Russia, Internet Research Agency (IRA), 58

Saarnio, L., 667, 676
sampling
    bias, classic example of, 8–9, 10, 14
    concept of, 3
    context-specific sampling, 144–145
    convenience samples, 8
    different forms of, 5–6
    history of, 3–4
    in animal testing, 5
    on Prolific, 77–79
        prescreened sampling, 77–79
        representative sampling, 77
    online samples, 8
    organizational research, 127–128
    probability sampling, 13
    snowball sampling, 51
    sociological sampling, 6,
    See also student samples
SARS-CoV-2 rapid at-home self-tests, 466
satisficing
    acquiescence response bias and, 359
    examples of, 331
    influencing factors, 354
    meaning of, 331
    NSROs and, 361
    primacy effects and, 341
    respondent fatigue and, 363
    response order effects and, 341, 360
    response style and, 336
    strong, 353
    weak, 353
Schachter, Stanley, 24
Schoonenboom, J., 176, 178
Schwarz, N., 339
scientific method, replication as basic tenet, 285, see also replication
Sears, D. O., 6, 7, 16, 18
Seidman, I., 605, 606–607
Seim, J., 667, 670, 675
self-report measures
    American National Election Studies example, 329
    context effects, 336–340
        frequency scales, use of, 338–340
        question order effects, 337–338
    limitations, 497
    mode effects, 340–343
        interviewer effects, 342
        response order effects, 340–342
        sensitive questions, 342–343
    objective measures, 329
    overview, 329–330
    recommendations for improvement, 343–345
    sensitive measures, 330

subjective measures, 330
survey response process
  comprehension, 331–332
  cultural considerations, 336
  judgment and estimation, 333–334
  mapping, 334–336
  overview, 330, 331
  response order effects, 335–336
  retrieval, 332–333
  satisficing behavior, 331, 336, 341
  social desirability bias, 335
  validity testing, 224–225, 227, 228
  verifiability, 329–330
self-selection bias, avoiding, 13
Sim, J., 655
Simmons, J. P., 291, 320
Skowronski, John, 127
small q approach
  comparison with Big Q research, 549
  demographic data, 562–563
  "not listed here" responses, 564
snowball sampling, 51
social media research
  concept of social media, 49–50
  confidentiality and consent, 64
  data analysis
    Language Inquiry Word Count (LIWC), 59–60
    sentiment analysis, 59–60
    tracking the psychological effects of COVID-19 pandemic, 60
    viral spread of content, 57–59
  data collection
    anonymising of data, 64
    consent issues, 55, 64
    digital footprints, 54–57
    Google Trends, 56
    methods and tools, 53–57
    overview, 50
    pre-existing social media data sets, 57
    quality control, 52–53
    scraping, 55
    simulations, 54
    social media companies offering academic APIs, *56*
    surveys, 53–54
  ethical concerns
    manipulation of users' Facebook feeds, 62–63
    outdated guidelines and, 65
    political microtargeting, 61–62
    primary pitfalls, 63–64
  insights into human behavior, 48
  machine learning techniques, 60–61
  overview, 48–49
  participant recruitment, 50–53
    crowdsourced data collection, 51–52, *See also* crowdsourcing *and individual platforms*
    snowball sampling, 51
  privacy concerns, 64–66
  shared features of social media, 49
Society for the Improvement of Psychological Science, 149
sociological sampling, 6
Spradley, J. P., 596, 604, 674
Starbird, Kate, 57
statistical power
  definition and related concepts, 232–234
  examples, 234–236
  influencing factors
    alpha levels, 240
    effect size, 237–239
    research design and test type, 240
    sample size, 237
    sensitivity analyses, 239
  limitations, 254
  null hypothesis significance testing (NHST), 232–233, 234, 254, 298
  post hoc power, 255–256
  power analyses
    using AIPE, 251–254
    using programs (sample size), 242–243
    using programs (sensitivity), 244–247
    using R, 248–251
    using tables, 242
  pregnancy tests example, 234
  recommendations, 256–257
Stephan, F. F., 3, 10
Stephens-Davidowitz, Seth, 56
Strand, J., 670, 674
Stroop test, 380–381, 485
student samples
  characteristics which raise concerns, 6–7
  comparisons with other sample types, 11
  correlational studies examining relationships, 11–12
  descriptive studies, 8–10
  different forms of sampling, 5–6
  dimensions where students can vary from the public, 9
  evaluating use of, 4–5
  experimental research, 12–14
  exploratory research, 10–11
  external validity of experiments and, 13
  generalizability debate, 6–8, 11, 16, 17
  in human behavior research, 5
  overview, 3–5, 17–18
  percentage of marketing studies using, 11
  percentage of US social psychology studies using, 11
  potential effects on research findings, 7
  recommendations for interpretation, 16–17
  representativeness, 9–10
  role of theory, 15–16
  statistical analysis, 14
  validity and generalizability concerns, 6

StudyResponse, 129
surface electromyography, viii, *see* electromyography (EMG)
Survey Monkey, 51–52, 53, 557

Takyi, E., 670, 671, 680
Terry, G., 550, 555, 556
Thomas, N., 666, 671, 673, 680
TikTok, 55, 85
Totet, Matthew, 58
Tourangeau, R., 333, 337, 342, 344
Trolley problem, 83
Twitter, 58

United States
  California Consumer Privacy Act (CCPA), 65
  Literary Digest presidential election poll (1936), 9
  representativeness of the population, 18, 52

validity of measures
  challenges of measure validation, 225–228
  context effects, 226–228
  desirable properties of valid measures, 215–216
  error minimization techniques
    calibration, 222–223
    collection of multiple measurements, 223
    control of potentially contaminating variables, 223
    gathering validity evidence, 224–225
    training, 223
  example of invalid methods, 212
  overview, 211–212, 214
  potential sources of measurement tool invalidity, 216–218
  properties to consider, 218–221
  psychometrics data, validation with physiological measures, 465
  reasons for emphasis on good management practice, 228
  recommendations, 221–222
validity, scale length and, 357
Verma, Inder, 63
Visser, L., 168, 172, 178, 179

"white coat effect", 457
Winfrey, Oprah, 573
within-subject differences, 13
Wu, S. J., 100, 103, 125
Wundt, W., 140, 375
Wylie, Christopher, 62

Yan, T., 341–342
Yarow, Rosalyn, 437
Yin, R. K., 617, 668

Zuell, C., 553, 554

www.ingramcontent.com/pod-product-compliance
Ingram Content Group UK Ltd.
Pitfield, Milton Keynes, MK11 3LW, UK
UKHW050701171224
452676UK00008B/114